Question Help

MyLab Economics homework and practice questions are correlated to the textbook, and many generate algorithmically to give students unlimited opportunity for mastery of concepts. If students get stuck, Learning Aids including Help Me Solve This and eText Pages walk them through the problem and identify helpful information in the text, giving them assistance when they need it most.

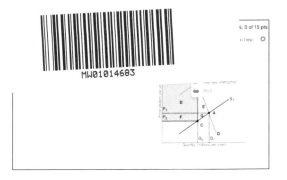

"[MyLab Economics] provides ample practice and explanation of the concepts at hand."
— Heather Burkett, University of Nebraska at Omaha

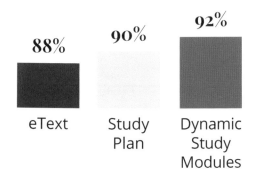

88% eText

90% Study Plan

92% Dynamic Study Modules

% of students who found learning tool helpful

Dynamic Study Modules help students study chapter topics effectively on their own by continuously assessing their **knowledge application** and performance in real time. These are available as prebuilt Prepare assignments, and are accessible on smartphones, tablets, and computers.

Pearson eText enhances student learning—both in and outside the classroom. Worked examples, videos, and interactive tutorials bring learning to life, while algorithmic practice and self-assessment opportunities test students' understanding of the material. Accessible anytime, anywhere via MyLab or the app.

The **MyLab Gradebook** offers an easy way for students and instructors to view course performance. Item Analysis allows instructors to quickly see trends by analyzing details like the number of students who answered correctly/incorrectly, time on task, and median time spend on a question by question basis. And because it's correlated with the AACSB Standards, instructors can track students' progress toward outcomes that the organization has deemed important in preparing students to be **leaders.**

87% of students would tell their instructor to keep using MyLab Economics

For additional details visit: www.pearson.com/mylab/economics

THE ECONOMICS OF
MANAGERIAL DECISIONS

The Pearson Series in Economics

Abel/Bernanke/Croushore
*Macroeconomics**

Acemoglu/Laibson/List
*Economics**

Bade/Parkin
*Foundations of Economics**

Berck/Helfand
The Economics of the Environment

Bierman/Fernandez
Game Theory with Economic Applications

Blair/Rush
*The Economics of Managerial Decisions**

Blanchard
*Macroeconomics**

Boyer
Principles of Transportation Economics

Branson
Macroeconomic Theory and Policy

Bruce
Public Finance and the American Economy

Carlton/Perloff
Modern Industrial Organization

Case/Fair/Oster
*Principles of Economics**

Chapman
Environmental Economics: Theory, Application, and Policy

Daniels/VanHoose
International Monetary & Financial Economics

Downs
An Economic Theory of Democracy

Farnham
Economics for Managers

Froyen
Macroeconomics: Theories and Policies

Fusfeld
The Age of the Economist

Gerber
*International Economics**

Gordon
*Macroeconomics**

Greene
Econometric Analysis

Gregory/Stuart
Russian and Soviet Economic Performance and Structure

Hartwick/Olewiler
The Economics of Natural Resource Use

Heilbroner/Milberg
The Making of the Economic Society

Heyne/Boettke/Prychitko
The Economic Way of Thinking

Hubbard/O'Brien
*Economics**
InEcon
*Money, Banking, and the Financial System**

Hubbard/O'Brien/Rafferty
*Macroeconomics**

Hughes/Cain
American Economic History

Husted/Melvin
International Economics

Jehle/Reny
Advanced Microeconomic Theory

Keat/Young/Erfle
Managerial Economics

Klein
Mathematical Methods for Economics

Krugman/Obstfeld/Melitz
*International Economics: Theory & Policy**

Laidler
The Demand for Money

Lynn
Economic Development: Theory and Practice for a Divided World

Miller
*Economics Today**

Miller/Benjamin
The Economics of Macro Issues

Miller/Benjamin/North
The Economics of Public Issues

Mishkin
*The Economics of Money, Banking, and Financial Markets**
*The Economics of Money, Banking, and Financial Markets, Business
   School Edition**
*Macroeconomics: Policy and Practice**

Murray
Econometrics: A Modern Introduction

O'Sullivan/Sheffrin/Perez
*Economics: Principles, Applications and Tools**

Parkin
*Economics**

Perloff
*Microeconomics**
*Microeconomics: Theory and Applications with Calculus**

Perloff/Brander
*Managerial Economics and Strategy**

Pindyck/Rubinfeld
*Microeconomics**

Riddell/Shackelford/Stamos/Schneider
Economics: A Tool for Critically Understanding Society

Roberts
The Choice: A Fable of Free Trade and Protection

Scherer
Industry Structure, Strategy, and Public Policy

Schiller
The Economics of Poverty and Discrimination

Sherman
Market Regulation

Stock/Watson
Introduction to Econometrics

Studenmund
Using Econometrics: A Practical Guide

Todaro/Smith
Economic Development

Walters/Walters/Appel/Callahan/Centanni/Maex/O'Neill
Econversations: Today's Students Discuss Today's Issues

Williamson
Macroeconomics

*denotes **MyLab™ Economics** titles. Visit www.pearson.com/mylab/economics to learn more.

ROGER D. BLAIR
University of Florida

MARK RUSH
University of Florida

THE ECONOMICS OF MANAGERIAL DECISIONS

 Pearson

New York, NY

Vice President, Business, Economics, and UK Courseware:
 Donna Battista
Director of Portfolio Management: Adrienne D'Ambrosio
Senior Portfolio Manager: Christina Masturzo
Development Editor: Lena Buonnano, Karen Trost
Editorial Assistant: Courtney Paganelli
Vice President, Product Marketing: Roxanne McCarley
Senior Product Marketer: Tricia Murphy
Product Marketing Assistant: Marianela Silvestri
Manager of Field Marketing, Business Publishing:
 Adam Goldstein
Senior Field Marketing Manager: Carlie Marvel
Vice President, Production and Digital Studio, Arts and
 Business: Etain O'Dea
Director of Production, Business: Jeff Holcomb
Managing Producer, Business: Alison Kalil
Content Producer: Carolyn Philips

Operations Specialist: Carol Melville
Design Lead: Kathryn Foot
Manager, Learning Tools: Brian Surette
Content Developer, Learning Tools: Sarah Peterson
Managing Producer, Digital Studio and GLP, Media Production
 and Development: Ashley Santora
Managing Producer, Digital Studio: Diane Lombardo
Digital Studio Producer: Melissa Honig
Digital Studio Producer: Alana Coles
Digital Content Team Lead: Noel Lotz
Digital Content Project Lead: Noel Lotz
Project Manager: Susan McNally, Cenveo® Publisher Services
Interior Design: Cenveo® Publisher Services
Cover Design: Carie Keller, Cenveo® Publisher Services
Printer/Binder: LSC Communications, Inc.
Cover Printer: LSC Communications, Inc.

Microsoft and/or its respective suppliers make no representations about the suitability of the information contained in the documents and related graphics published as part of the services for any purpose. All such documents and related graphics are provided "as is" without warranty of any kind. Microsoft and/or its respective suppliers hereby disclaim all warranties and conditions with regard to this information, including all warranties and conditions of merchantability, whether express, implied or statutory, fitness for a particular purpose, title and non-infringement. In no event shall Microsoft and/or its respective suppliers be liable for any special, indirect or consequential damages or any damages whatsoever resulting from loss of use, data or profits, whether in an action of contract, negligence or other tortious action, arising out of or in connection with the use or performance of information available from the services.

The documents and related graphics contained herein could include technical inaccuracies or typographical errors. Changes are periodically added to the information herein. Microsoft and/or its respective suppliers may make improvements and/or changes in the product(s) and/or the program(s) described herein at any time. Partial screen shots may be viewed in full within the software version specified.

Microsoft® and Windows® are registered trademarks of the Microsoft Corporation in the U.S.A. and other countries. This book is not sponsored or endorsed by or affiliated with the Microsoft Corporation.

Library of Congress Cataloging-in-Publication Data is on file at the Library of Congress.

ISBN-10: 0133548236
ISBN-13: 9780133548235

For Chau, our kids and our grandkids
Roger D. Blair

For Sue's memory and our kids
Mark B. Rush

Roger D. Blair is the Walter J. Matherly Professor and chair of economics at the University of Florida. He has been a visiting professor at the University of Hawaii and the University of California–Berkeley as well as Visiting Scholar in Residence, Center for the Study of American Business, Washington University. Professor Blair's research centers on antitrust economics and policy. He has published 10 books and 200 journal articles. He has also served as an antitrust consultant to numerous corporations, including Intel, Anheuser-Busch, TracFone, Blue Cross–Blue Shield, Waste Management, Astellas Pharma, and many others.

Mark Rush is a professor of economics at the University of Florida. Prior to teaching at Florida, he was an assistant professor of economics at the University of Pittsburgh. He has spent eight months at the Kansas City Federal Reserve Bank as a Visiting Scholar. Professor Rush has taught MBA classes for many years and has won teaching awards for his classes. He has published in numerous professional journals, including the *Journal of Political Economy*; the *Journal of Monetary Economics*; the *Journal of Money, Credit, and Banking*; the *Journal of International Money and Finance*; and the *Journal of Labor Economics*.

BRIEF CONTENTS

CONTENTS

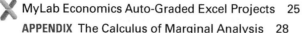

PART 2
MARKET STRUCTURE AND MANAGERIAL DECISIONS

 4 Production and Costs   138

6   Monopoly and Monopolistic Competition   227

8 Game Theory and Oligopoly   318

PART 3
MANAGERIAL DECISIONS

Contents   **xxiii**

16 Using Present Value to Make Multiperiod Managerial Decisions 677

Why Did Ziosk's Managers Give Their Tablets to Chili's for Free? 677

Introduction 677

16.1 Fundamentals of Present Value   678
Calculating Future Values   679
Calculating Present Values   680
Valuing a Stream of Future Payments   683
Future and Present Value Formulas   688

SOLVED PROBLEM Choosing a Loan Repayment Schedule   688

16.2 Evaluating Investment Options   689
Net Present Value and the Net Present Value Rule   689
Extensions to the Net Present Value Rule   692

DECISION SNAPSHOT Salvage Value at a Car Rental Firm   693

DECISION SNAPSHOT Depreciation Allowance: Should a Tax Firm Take It Now or Later?   697

Selection of the Discount Rate   698
Risk and the Net Present Value Rule   698

SOLVED PROBLEM Investment Decision for an Electric Car Maker   700

16.3 Make-or-Buy Decisions   701
Make-or-Buy Basics   701
Make-or-Buy Net Present Value Calculations   703

SOLVED PROBLEM A Make-or-Buy Decision with Learning by Doing   704

16.4 Present Value and Net Present Value   704
Valuing Financial Assets   704
Using the Net Present Value Rule in the Real World   705
The Effect of Tax Shields on Net Present Value   706

Revisiting Why Ziosk's Managers Gave Their Tablets to Chili's for Free   707

Summary: The Bottom Line   708

Key Terms and Concepts   709

Questions and Problems   709

 MyLab Economics Auto-Graded Excel Projects   712

CASE STUDY Analyzing Predatory Pricing as an Investment   715

Answer Key to Chapters   717

Answer Key to Calculus Appendices   756

Index   765

MANAGERIAL
APPLICATION

Content on the Web

The following content is available on www.pearson.com/mylab/economics

Web Appendix: The Business Plan

Web Chapter: Franchising Decisions

Solving Teaching and Learning Challenges

Students who enroll in the managerial economics course are typically not economics majors. They take the course with the goal of building skills that will help them become better managers in a variety of business settings, including small and large firms, nonprofit organizations, and public service. In teaching our classes, we often skipped theoretical, abstract coverage in existing books—such as indifference curves, isoquants, the Cobb–Douglas production function, the Rothschild Index, and the Lerner Index—because these topics are not useful to students pursuing careers in management. Based on our teaching experiences and feedback from many reviewers and class testers, we have omitted this sort of theoretical, abstract coverage from our book.

Our decision to omit these topics does not mean that we shortchange economic theory. On the contrary, our book and a wide range of media assets show students how economic theory and concepts—including opportunity cost, marginal analysis, and profit maximization—can provide important insights into real-world managerial challenges such as how to price a product, how many workers to hire, whether to expand production, and how much to spend on advertising. Applications and extensions of the core theory abound. Some of the topics include bundled pricing, vertical integration, resale price maintenance, industry-wide advertising, settlement of legal disputes, present value and investment decisions, auctions and optimal bidding, and optimal patent search. We focus on how to think critically and make decisions in real-world business situations—in other words, how to *apply* economic theory.

MyLab Economics

MyLab Economics is an online homework, tutorial, and assessment program that delivers technology-enhanced learning in tandem with printed textbooks and etexts. It improves results by helping students quickly grasp concepts and by providing educators with a robust set of tools to easily gauge and address the performance of individuals and classrooms.

The Study Plan provides personalized recommendations for each student, based on his or her ability to master the learning objectives in your course. This allows students to focus their study time by pinpointing the precise areas they need to review, and allowing them to use customized practice and learning aids—such as videos, eText, tutorials, and more—to keep them on track.

First-in-class content is delivered digitally to help every student master critical course concepts. MyLab Economics includes Mini Sims, Auto-Graded Excel Projects, and Digital Interactives to not only help students understand important economic concepts, but also help them learn how to apply these concepts in a variety of ways so they can see how they can use economics long after the last day of class.

MyLab Economics allows for easy and flexible assignment creation, so instructors can assign a variety of assignments tailored to meet their specific course needs.

Visit www.pearson.com/mylab/economics for more information on Mini Sims, Auto-Graded Excel Projects, Digital Interactives, our LMS integration options, and course management options for any course of any size.

Chapter Features

The following key features and media assets demonstrate how *The Economics of Managerial Decisions* keeps the spotlight on the student as a future manager.

Real-world chapter openers and closers: Each chapter begins with a real-world example that piques student interest and poses a managerial decision-making question. We revisit this question and apply the chapter content to provide an answer at the end. Because students pursue careers in various fields, the chapter openers present challenges faced by a number of different types of organizations, including large and small profit-seeking firms, government organizations, nongovernmental organizations, and nonprofits.

Managers at the Gates Foundation Decide to Subsidize Antimalarial Drugs

The Bill and Melinda Gates Foundation (Gates Foundation) is the world's largest philanthropic organization, with a trust endowment of nearly $40 billion. The foundation provides grants for education, medical research, and vaccinations around the world. As of 2015, the foundation had made total grants of $37 billion. The goal of the Gates Foundation is not maximizing profit. Instead, its goal is to save lives and improve health in developing countries.

In 2010, the Global Fund to Fight AIDS, Tuberculosis and Malaria presented proposals to the Gates Foundation to subsidize antimalarial drugs in Kenya and other nations of sub-Saharan Africa. Although the Gates Foundation provides nearly $4 billion in grants per year, there are more than $4 billion worth of competing uses for its resources. Consequently, before the managers accepted these proposals, they needed to determine their expected impact: How many people would these projects save compared to alternative uses of the funds? The managers realized that lives hinged on their decision, so they wanted to be certain that they were getting the most value for their money.

The proposed subsidy programs would lower the price patients pay for the drugs. As you learned in Chapter 2, according to the law of demand, a decrease in the price of a product increases the quantity demanded. Antimalarial drugs are no exception; if their price falls, more patients will buy them. To make the proper decision about the proposals, however, the foundation's managers needed a more quantitative estimate: Precisely how many additional patients would buy the drugs when their prices were lower?

This chapter explains how to answer this and other questions that require quantitative answers. At the end of the chapter, you will learn how the Gates Foundation's managers could forecast the number of patients they would help by subsidizing the drugs.

Sources: Karl Mathiesen, "What Is the Bill and Melinda Gates Foundation?" *The Guardian*, March 16, 2015; Gavin Yamey, Marco Schäferhoff, and Dominic Montagu, "Piloting the Affordable Medicines Facility-Malaria: What Will Success Look Like?" *Bulletin of the World Health Organization*, February 3, 2012, http://www.who.int/bulletin/volumes/90/6/11-091199/en; Erinstar, "Availability of Subsidized Malaria Drug" *Behavioral Foundations of Primary Health Care Policy Advocacy*, March 11, 2012, https://.com/2012/03/11/availability-of-subsidized-malaria-drugs-in-kenya-18-2.

Revisiting How Managers at the Gates Foundation Decided to Subsidize Antimalarial Drugs

As noted at the beginning of the chapter, the managers at the Bill and Melinda Gates Foundation want to use their funds in the best way possible. Because wasting their resources means that people could die unnecessarily, managers at the foundation want to fund the most cost-effective programs. To achieve that goal, they must determine the quantitative impact of the proposals presented to them.

In the case of the proposals to subsidize antimalarial drugs in Kenya and other nations, the managers were unlikely to have an estimated demand curve for the drugs in these countries because of data limitations. Instead, they probably relied on estimates of the price elasticity of demand to determine the increase in the quantity of drugs demanded.

The subsidy programs lowered the price of these drugs between 29 percent and 78 percent (the fall in price differed from nation to nation and from drug to drug). Overall, the average decrease in price was roughly 50 percent. Because there are few substitutes, the demand for pharmaceutical drugs is price inelastic. The price elasticity of demand for pharmaceutical drugs for low-income Danish consumers is estimated to be 0.31. Denmark and Kenya differ in an important respect: Low-income consumers in Kenya have much lower incomes than their counterparts in Denmark. Consequently, the expenditure on drugs in Kenya is a much larger fraction of consumers' income, which means that the price elasticity of demand for drugs in Kenya is larger than in Denmark. If the managers at the Bill and Melinda Gates Foundation estimated that the price elasticity of demand for drugs in Kenya was about twice that in Denmark—say, 0.60—they could then predict that lowering the price of the drugs by 50 percent would increase the quantity demanded by 50 percent × 0.60 = 30 percent.

The Gates Foundation funded the proposals to subsidize antimalarial drugs. The actual outcome was that the quantity of the drugs demanded in the different nations increased by 20 to 40 percent. The quantitative estimate was right in line with what occurred. Using the price elasticity of demand to estimate the impact of the drug subsidy proposals allowed the managers at the foundation to compare them to competing proposals and to make decisions that saved the maximum number of lives.

Managerial Applications: Fifteen of the sixteen chapters include a major numbered section devoted to managerial applications of the chapter content.

---

120 CHAPTER 3 Measuring and Using Demand

3.5 Regression Analysis and Elasticity

Learning Objective 3.5 Use regression analysis and the different elasticity measures to make better managerial decisions.

Regression analysis and the different elasticity measures are important to managers because they help quantify decision making. As a manager, you will face situations in which you need to know the exact amount of a change in the price of an input, the precise change in your cost when you change your production, or the actual decrease in quantity demanded when you raise the price of your product. Regression analysis and the application of the different elasti[...] you answer these and many other important questions.

Using Regression Analysis

Using the results from regression analysis is an essential tas[...] positions. Analysts can use regression analysis for much m[...] demand curve. For example, you can use it to estimate how y[...] production changes. We explain this important concept, c[...] Chapter 4 and use it in all future chapters. Large compan[...] depends significantly on a specific influence often use regress[...] changes in such factors as personal income (important to aut[...] such as General Motors and Honda) or new home sales (impo[...] ment stores such as Home Depot and Lowe's).

The ultimate goal of regression analysis is to help you ma[...] example, as a manager at the high-end steak restaurant chai[...] mated demand function to help you make both immediate de[...] to set *and* long-term decisions about whether to open a new[...] an analyst for your firm has used regression to determine th[...] for your chain's steak dinners depends on the following facto[...]

1. The price of the dinners, measured as dollars per dinner
2. The average income of residents living within the city, m[...] person
3. The unemployment rate within the city, measured as the[...] ment rate
4. The population within 30 miles of the restaurant

Suppose that Table 3.4 includes the estimated coefficients[...] rors, *t*-statistics, and *P*-values.[4] The R^2 of the regression is 0.72[...] dicts the data reasonably well. In the table, the *t*-statistics for[...] greater than 1.96, and accordingly all five *P*-values are less[...] Therefore, you are confident that all the variables included[...] the demand for steak dinners. The coefficient for the price var[...] a $1 increase in the price of a dinner decreases the quantity der[...] or 12.9 dinners per night. Similarly, the coefficient for the av[...] 0.0073, shows that a $1,000 increase in average income inc[...]

4. Often regression results are written with the standard errors in parentheses be[...]
$Q^d = 139.2 − (12.9 \times \text{PRICE}) + (0.0073 \times \text{INCOME}) − (10.0 \times \text{UNEMPLOYMEN}[...]$
$\quad\quad\ (11.9)\quad\quad (1.8)\quad\quad\quad (0.0012)\quad\quad\quad (3.2)$

3.5 Managerial Application: Regression Analysis and Elasticity 121

Table 3.4 **Estimated Demand Function for Steak Dinners**
The table shows the results of a regression of the demand for meals at an upscale steak restaurant, with the estimated coefficients for the price, average income in the city in which the restaurant is located, unemployment rate in the city, and population of the city.

	Coefficient	Standard Error	t Stat	P-value	Lower 95%	Upper 95%
Constant	139.2	11.9	11.7	0.00	117.3	163.1
Price of dinner	−12.9	1.8	7.2	0.00	−9.4	−16.4
Average income	0.0073	0.0012	6.1	0.00	4.9	9.7
Unemployment rate	−10.0	3.1	3.1	0.00	−3.9	−16.5
Population	0.0005	0.0002	2.5	0.02	0.0001	0.0009

0.0073 × 1,000, or 7.3 dinners per night. The coefficient for the unemployment rate variable, −10.0, shows that a one percentage point increase in the unemployment rate decreases the demand by −10.0 × 1, or 10 dinners per night. And the coefficient for the population variable, 0.0005, shows that a 1,000-person increase in population increases the demand by 0.0005 × 1,000, or 0.5 dinners per night.

Short-Run Decisions Using Regression Analysis

Although a more detailed explanation of how managers determine price must wait until Chapter 6, intuitively it is clear that demand must play a role. The estimated demand function can help determine what price to charge in different cities because you can use it to estimate the nightly quantity of dinners your customers will demand in those cities. Suppose that one of the restaurants is located in a city of 900,000 people, in which average income is $66,300 and the unemployment rate is 5.9 percent. If you set a price of $60 per dinner, you can predict that the nightly demand for steak dinners equals

$$Q^d = 139.2 − (12.9 \times \$60) + (0.0073 \times \$66,300) − (10.0 \times 5.9) + (0.0005 \times 900,000)$$

or 240 dinners per night. You can now calculate consumer response to a change in the price. For example, if you raise the price by $1, then the quantity of dinners demanded decreases by 12.9 per night, to approximately 227 dinners.

Long-Run Decisions Using Regression Analysis

You can also use the estimated demand function to forecast the demand for your product. Such forecasts can help you make better decisions. For example, you and the other executives at your steak chain might be deciding whether to open a restaurant in a city of 750,000 residents, with average income of $60,000 and an unemployment rate of 6.0 percent. Using the estimated demand function in Table 3.4 and a price of $60 per dinner, you predict demand of about 118 meals per night. Suppose this quantity of sales is too small to be profitable, but you expect rapid growth for the city: In three years, you forecast the city's population will rise to 950,000, average income will increase to $70,000, and the unemployment rate will fall to 5.8 percent. Three years from now, if you set a price of $60 per dinner, you forecast the demand will be 293 dinners per night. This quantity of dinners provides support for a plan to open a restaurant in three years. You might start looking for a good location!

Other companies can use an estimated demand function to forecast their future input needs. General Motors, for example, can use an estimated demand function for their automobiles to forecast the quantity of steel it expects to need for next year's production. This information can help its managers make better decisions about the contracts they will negotiate with their suppliers.

NEW! Mini Sims: The Managerial Applications are accompanied by Mini Sims that are located in MyLab Economics. Written by David Switzer of St. Cloud State University and Casey DiRienzo of Elon University, these Mini Sims are designed to build students' critical-thinking and decision-making skills through an engaging, active learning experience. Each Mini Sim requires students to make a series of decisions based on a business scenario, which helps them move from memorization to understanding and application. These also allow students to experience how different functional areas of a business interact and how each employee's decisions affect the organization.

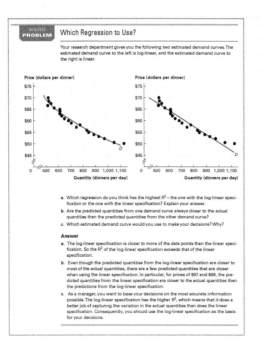

Solved Problems: This section-ending feature guides students step by step in solving a managerial problem, set in the context of a situation managers may encounter.

DECISION SNAPSHOT

Advertising and the Price Elasticity of Demand

Your marketing department estimates that at the current price and quantity, your firm's product has a price elasticity of demand of 1.1. You run an advertising campaign that changes the demand, so that at the current price and quantity the elasticity falls to 0.8. In response to this change, would you raise the price, lower it, or keep it the same? Explain your answer.

Answer

You should raise your price. Before the advertising campaign, the demand for your product was elastic, so according to the total revenue test, a price hike would lower your firm's total revenue. After the campaign, the demand became inelastic. You now will be able to increase your firm's profit by raising the price. Because the demand is inelastic, a price hike raises your firm's total revenue. A price hike also decreases the quantity demanded, so your firm produces less, which decreases your costs. Raising revenue and lowering cost unambiguously boost your firm's profit!

Decision Snapshots: This feature places readers in the role of managers facing a decision in a range of industries, including large and small for-profit firms, public service organizations, and nonprofits. An answer is included so students can confirm the decision they have made.

Integrated examples: We consistently present economic concepts in the context of business scenarios from a range of industries. For example:

- Chapter 4, "Production and Costs," uses dinners at a restaurant to present the concepts of production and costs.
- Chapter 13, "Marketing Decisions: Advertising and Promotion," includes examples of advertising by a private company as well as by an entire industry.
- Chapter 14, "Business Decisions Under Uncertainty," discusses the effect of uncertainty on business decisions using examples including Starbucks and Samsung.

Case studies: Four chapters end with case studies that illustrate how managers used the topics in the chapter to approach or solve a business challenge. The case studies conclude with open-ended questions about a similar situation that instructors can use for class discussion or assign as homework. Here are the four cases:

- Chapter 3 Case Study: Decision Making Using Regression
- Chapter 9 Case Study: Student Athletes and the NCAA
- Chapter 14 Case Study: Decision Making with Final Offer Arbitration
- Chapter 16 Case Study: Analyzing Predatory Pricing as an Investment

Assessment: End-of-chapter Questions and Problems are grouped by the titles of the major numbered sections and the accompanying learning objectives so that instructors can easily assign problems based on those objectives, and students can efficiently review material that they find difficult. Students can complete these problems and questions on MyLab Economics, where they receive tutorial help, instant feedback, and assistance with incorrect responses.

NEW! MyLab Economics Auto-Graded Excel Projects: Excel is a software application that managers in all industries and all functional areas, such as marketing, sales, and finance, use to analyze data and make decisions such as what to produce, how much to produce, and how to price products. Mandie Weinandt of the University of South Dakota created Excel projects for each chapter based on the content of the chapter. Kathryn Nantz of Fairfield University accuracy checked the projects and solutions. The projects are accessible in MyLab Economics, where instructors can seamlessly integrate Excel content into their courses without having to manually grade spreadsheets. Students simply download a spreadsheet, work live on a problem in Excel, and then upload that file back into MyLab Economics, where they receive personalized, detailed feedback in the form of reports that pinpoint where they went wrong on any step of the problem.

Optional calculus appendices: The mathematics we use in the chapters is algebra and geometry because this level is appropriate for managers. For those who want to delve more deeply into the math, appendices showing calculus derivations of the important results accompany 9 of the 16 chapters (Chapters 1, 3, 4, 5, 6, 7, 10, 12, and 13). Each appendix includes five homework problems that use calculus.

Developing Career Skills

Students who want to succeed in a rapidly changing job market should be aware of their career options and how to go about developing a variety of skills. As featured on the previous pages, the text focuses on developing these skills in various features:

- *Real-world chapter openers and closers* show how managers from a variety of business organizations apply economic concepts to make decisions.
- *Solved Problems* and *Decision Snapshots* help students build their analytical and critical-thinking skills.
- *Mini Sims* related to the Managerial Application at the end of each chapter, except Chapter 1, help build students' critical-thinking and decision-making skills through an engaging, active learning experience. The screen on the left shows one decision-point step in the Mini Sim that accompanies Chapter 2, "Demand and Supply."
- *Auto-Graded Excel Projects* at the end of each chapter help students build their skill using Excel, a software application that they will need to use as managers regardless of the industry or functional area in which they choose to work.

Table of Contents Overview

Chapters 1 through 6 are core chapters. An instructor can cover these chapters in order and then proceed either to Chapters 7 and 8 or to Chapter 10. The chapters in Part 3 (Chapters 10–16) can be covered in any order. For those who want to delve more deeply into the mathematics, appendices showing calculus derivations of the important results accompany 9 of the 16 chapters (Chapters 1, 3, 4, 5, 6, 7, 10, 12, and 13). An appendix on how to write a business plan and an additional chapter on franchising decisions are located at www.pearson.com/mylab/economics.

The following content is posted on www.pearson.com/mylab/economics:
Web Appendix: The Business Plan
Web Chapter: Franchising Decisions

Instructor Teaching Resources

The following supplements are available to instructors for download at www.pearsonhighered.com.

The **Instructor's Manual** was prepared by David Switzer of St. Cloud State University and includes the following features:

- Solutions to all end-of-chapter and appendix questions and problems, which the authors prepared and then revised based on an accuracy review by two other professors.
- Chapter summaries
- Lists of learning objectives
- Chapter outlines, section summaries, and key term definitions
- Extra examples
- Teaching tips

The **Test Bank** was prepared by Casey DiRienzo of Elon University and includes over 2,400 questions, with approximately 125 multiple-choice questions and 25 true/false questions *per chapter*. Between 5 and 10 questions per chapter include a graph and ask students to analyze that graph. The questions are organized by learning objective, and each question has the following annotations:

- Topic
- Skill
- AACSB learning standard (Written and Oral Communication; Ethical Understanding and Reasoning; Analytical Thinking; Information Technology; Interpersonal Relations and Teamwork; Diverse and Multicultural Work; Reflective Thinking; Application of Knowledge)

The **PowerPoint Presentation** was prepared by Julia Frankland of Malone University and includes the following features:

- All the graphs, tables, and equations in each chapter
- Section summaries for all chapters
- Lecture notes

Acknowledgments

We are grateful for the guidance and recommendations of our many reviews, class testers, and accuracy checkers. Their constructive feedback and support was indispensable in the development of the chapters, media assets, and supplements.

Eric Abrams, *McKendree University*
Basil Al Hashimi, *Mesa Community College*
Jasmin Ansar, *Mills College*
Elena Antiniadou, *Emory University*
Sisay Asefa, *Western Michigan University*
Joseph Bailey, *University of Maryland*
Lila Balla, *St. Louis University*
Sourav Batabyal, *Loyola University Maryland*
Jason Beck, *Armstrong State University*
Ariel Belasan, *Southern Illinois University at Edwardsville*
Jeanne Boeh, *Augsburg College*
David Bouras, *Lincoln University*
Terry Brownschidle, *Rider University*
Donald Bumpass, *Sam Houston State University*
Louis P. Cain, *Northwestern University*
Hugh Cassidy, *Kansas State University*
Hector Chade, *Arizona State University*
Kalyan Chakraborty, *Emporia State University*
Keith W. Chauvin, *University of Kansas*
Jihui Chen, *Illinois State University*
Abdur Chowdhury, *Marquette University*
Jan Christopher, *Delaware State University*
Kalock Chu, *Loyola University at Chicago*
Christopher Colburn, *Old Dominion University*
Kristen Collett-Schmitt, *University of Notre Dame*
Benjamin Compton, *University of Tennessee*
Cristanna Cook, *Husson University* and the *University of Maine*
Akash Dania, *Alcorn State University*
Tina Das, *Elon University*
Dennis Debrecht, *Carroll University*
Lisa Dickson, *University of Maryland–Baltimore County*
Cassandra DiRienzo, *Elon University*
Carol Doe, *Jacksonville University*

Juan Du, *Old Dominion University*
Nazif Durmaz, *University of Texas–Victoria*
Maxwell Eseonu, *Virginia State University*
Xin Fang, *Hawaii Pacific University*
Jose Fernandez, *University of Louisville*
Darren Filson, *Claremont McKenna College*
John Fizel, *Pennsylvania State University*
John Flanders, *Central Methodist University*
Julia Frankland, *Malone University*
Yoshi Fukasawa, *Midwestern State University*
Chris Gingrich, *Eastern Mennonite University*
Tuncer Gocmen, *Shepherd University*
Rajeev Goel, *Illinois State University*
Natallia Gray, *Southeast Missouri State University*
Anthony Greco, *University of Louisiana at Lafayette*
Gauri S. Guha, *Arkansas State University*
John Hayfron, *Western Washington University*
Martin D. Heintzelman, *Clarkson University*
J. Scott Holladay, *University of Tennessee*
Adora Holstein, *Robert Morris University*
John Horowitz, *Ball State University*
Jack Hou, *California State University at Long Beach*
Syed Jafri, *Tarleton State University*
Andres Jauregui, *Columbus State University*
Russ Kashian, *University of Wisconsin at Whitewater*
Mark Keightley, *George Mason University*
David Kelly, *University of Miami*
Abdullah Khan, *Claflin University*
Felix Kwan, *Maryville University*
Jacob LaRiviere, *University of Tennessee*
Marc Law, *University of Vermont*

Robert Lawson, *Southern Methodist University*
Mahdi Majbouri, *Babson College*
Michael Maloney, *Clemson University*
Russ McCullough, *Ottawa University*
Eric McDermott, *University of Illinois*
Hannah Mead, *George Mason University*
Douglas Meador, *University of St. Francis at Fort Wayne*
Saul Mekies, *University of Iowa/Kirkwood Community College*
Evelina Mengova, *Governors State University*
Matt Metzgar, *University of North Carolina at Charlotte*
Phillip Mixon, *Troy University*
Masoud Moallem, *Rockford University*
Francis Mummery, *California State University at Fullerton*
Kathryn Nantz, *Fairfield University*
Michael Newsome, *Marshall University*
Dmitri Nizovtsev, *Washburn University*
Christian Nsiah, *Baldwin Wallace University*
Tunay Oguz, *Lenoir Rhyne University*
Charles Parker, *Wayne State College*
Robert Pennington, *University of Central Florida*
Paul Pieper, *University of Illinois at Chicago*
Chung Ping, *University of North Florida*
Harvey Poniachek, *Rutgers University*
John Reardon, *Hamline University*
Jean Ricot, *Valencia Community College*
Katy Rouse, *Elon University*
Stefan Ruediger, *Arizona State University*
Charles R. Sebuharara, *Binghamton University SUNY*

Stephanie Shayne, *Husson University*
Dongsoo Shin, *Santa Clara University*
Steven Shwiff, *Texas A&M University at Commerce*
Kusum Singh, *LeMoyne Owen College*
Ken Slaysman, *York College of Pennsylvania*
John Spytek, *Webster University*
Denise Stanley, *California State University at Fullerton*
Paul Stock, *University of Mary Hardin–Baylor University*
Brock Stoddard, *University of South Dakota*
David Switzer, *St. Cloud State University*
Michael Tasto, *Southern New Hampshire University*
Bill Taylor, *New Mexico Highlands University*
Kasaundra Tomlin, *Oakland University*
Suzanne Toney, *Savannah State University*
Dosse Toulaboe, *Fort Hays State University*
Julianne Treme, *University of North Carolina at Wilmington*
Jennifer VanGilder, *Ursinus College*
Elizabeth Wark, *Worcester State University*
Mandie Weinandt, *University of South Dakota*
Keith Willet, *Oklahoma State University*
Mark Wilson, *West Virginia University Tech*
Shishu Zhang, *University of the Incarnate Word*
Ting Zhang, *University of Baltimore*

A Note of Thanks…

When we first started work on this book, we never realized how many people would be so heavily involved, helping us, assisting us, and frequently prodding us along the way. In truth, it is impossible to convey an adequate measure of thanks for their input. But we shall try:

- Christina Masturzo, Senior Portfolio Manager with Pearson, was our guiding light. We owe her a huge debt for her belief in our vision and for her tireless work helping us achieve this vision. The team she assembled was first class, as were her comments and inputs. Simply put, without her this book would not exist.

- Lena Buonanno, Content Development Specialist with Pearson, helped keep us on track and our noses to the grindstone. Lena was with us every step of the way, literally from the first day to the last. We believe we would still be working on the project were it not for her incredibly cheerful emails (most of which reminded us about missed deadlines).
- Karen Trost, Freelance Development Editor, together with Lena, helped convert our writing into something that has at least a passing resemblance to English. We cannot believe the number of hours Karen put in making grammatical improvements that sharpened and clarified the text. Because she will not have a chance to edit this preface, all wee kan say is thanx.
- Carolyn Philips, Content Producer with Pearson, played a crucial role in helping our thoughts progress from a manuscript to a finished product. We shudder to think what the book would look like without her help.
- Courtney Paganelli, Editorial Assistant with Pearson, truly kept us organized—at least as much as possible. We cannot imagine how Courtney was able to keep all the details about all the aspects of the project straight and especially how she was able to do so when working with us, disorganized as we are. We would doff our hats to her if we could find them.
- Susan McNally, Production Manager with Cenveo, had what is probably the most thankless task of all. Susan had to work with us when we had *no* idea how to edit pages for publication. Her explanations about what could be (and what could not be) done were invaluable. Time after time she patiently answered our neophyte questions, making us eternally grateful and forever in her debt.

CHAPTER 1

Managerial Economics and Decision Making

Learning Objectives

After studying this chapter, you will be able to:

1.1 Describe managerial economics and explain how it can help advance your career.

1.2 Define what a firm is and describe the legal structures of for-profit firms.

1.3 Compare opportunity cost and accounting cost and explain why using opportunity cost leads to better decisions.

1.4 Explain how managers can use marginal analysis to make better decisions.

Managers at Sears Holdings Use Opportunity Cost to Make Tough Decisions

Ask people in your parents' generation about Sears, and their answers will be the same: Yes, they shopped at Sears. Who didn't? For decades, Sears was the dominant retailer in the United States, selling homes (and home insurance to protect them), blouses (and washing machines to clean them), and nails (and hammers to drive them). Today, Sears no longer sells homes or home insurance at all, and it sells far fewer blouses, washing machines, nails, and hammers.

In 2005, Kmart purchased the original company and now runs it as a subsidiary of the new parent company, Sears Holdings. When Kmart purchased the company, Sears had over 1,600 stores. Sales and profit at Sears had been declining slowly over three decades but accelerated in more recent years as customers embraced online shopping. As sales rapidly declined, Sears Holdings' top executives knew they had to close some stores and faced two difficult decisions: how many stores to close and which ones. Profitability was the key: The executives needed to close unprofitable stores and retain profitable ones. They consulted their accountants about each store's profit. Should they use the numbers the accountants provided? Or should they use another definition of profit?

This chapter introduces some of the fundamental concepts of managerial economics that will help you answer these questions. At the end of this chapter, you will see how Sears Holdings' managers used the concepts of opportunity cost and marginal analysis to make their decisions.

Sources: Krystina Gustafson, "Sears to Accelerate Closings, Shutter 235 Stores," CNBC, December 4, 2014 http://www.cnbc.com/2014/12/04/sears-to-accelerate-closings-shutter-235-stores.html; Phil Wahba, "Sears CEO Lampert Explains Why He Closed 200 Stores," *Fortune*, December 15, 2014; Suzanne Kapner, "Department Stores Need to Cull Hundreds of Sites, Study Says," *Wall Street Journal*, April 24, 2016; http://money.cnn.com/2017/01/05/investing/sears-kmart-closing-stores/; https://blog.searsholdings.com/eddie-lampert/moving-forward/.

Introduction

Decision making is the most important task you will face as a manager. Companies pay most managers quite well to make decisions. In some cases, the decisions are small: Which custodial service should your company hire? On other occasions, the decisions are large: Should your company build another plant to expand into China? Your decisions will help determine the success of your company—and your career.

The quality of your decisions as a manager can help or hurt every functional area within the firm. Unfortunately, there is no cut-and-dried formula that will always lead to the correct decision, but basic economic principles can help you make better decisions. Although these principles obviously apply to economic decisions such as pricing, they apply equally well in virtually every business division, including marketing, finance, and human resources.

We base many examples in this text on for-profit firms, and for simplicity, we frequently refer to "firms." But keep in mind that the lessons and economic principles you will learn apply equally well to making decisions and achieving goals in all types of organizations, ranging from nonprofit organizations to government agencies to nongovernment organizations (NGOs). Once you understand the basic economic principles, you will be well prepared for success as a manager of any type of organization.

To begin your study of the economic principles involved in managerial decision making, Chapter 1 includes four sections:

- **Section 1.1** defines managerial economics, describes economic models, and explains why using them can help your career.
- **Section 1.2** explains how economists define a firm and provides an overview of the common legal categories of for-profit firms.
- **Section 1.3** focuses on opportunity cost, which should guide the decision-making process for managers of all types of organizations, and compares it to accounting cost.
- **Section 1.4** defines and then applies the key decision-making tool of marginal analysis.

1.1 Managerial Economics and Your Career

Learning Objective 1.1 Describe managerial economics and explain how it can help advance your career.

When you realized your program of study required a course in managerial economics, you may have asked yourself a question or two:

1. "Why do I need this class? I've already taken an economics course."
2. "How will a course in managerial economics help my career?"

These are excellent questions. Let's start with the first one: Your previous economics courses helped you understand how the economy functions. In contrast, this course explains how microeconomic concepts can help you manage a firm more effectively. **Managerial economics** is the application of microeconomic principles and tools to business problems faced by decision makers.

Whenever you must make a business decision on behalf of your firm, microeconomic principles can assist you in making the best decision possible. That brings us to the answer to the second question: Applying the microeconomic principles we discuss in this text can help you make better decisions and, as a result, have a successful career as a manager. Understanding how to use economics to make better decisions is the driving goal of this class and text.

As we guide your study of managerial economics, we present and illustrate microeconomic principles and tools using economic models. An **economic model** is an abstract, simplified representation of the real world and real-world situations. In the real world, there are an infinite number of complications. Models strip away those complications to focus on what is important. For example, suppose

Managerial economics The application of microeconomic principles and tools to business problems faced by decision makers.

Economic model An abstract, simplified representation of the real world and real-world situations.

that you want to use Google Maps to plot a quick driving tour of Napa Valley's highlights, including its many wineries. The satellite photos in the "Earth" view reveal an immense amount of detail—including buildings, parked cars, pedestrians, and traffic signals. You don't need this level of detail to plan your trip. It is far easier to use the "Map" view, which focuses on the roads. Economic models are similar: They strip away the inessential minor details that clutter the issue and focus directly on the key factors important to your managerial decisions—and to your career.

Because they are abstract and simplified, economic models are not recipes that tell you exactly how to make a business decision. You will often find that getting to an optimal outcome is a repetitive trial-and-error process. Fortunately, following economic principles and models can help you identify both the optimal solution *and* the steps you need to take to reach it.

Before we examine some of the tools of economic analysis, let's review basic information about firms and their organization.

1.2 Firms and Their Organizational Structure

Learning Objective 1.2 Define what a firm is and describe the legal structures of for-profit firms.

Understanding two concepts—the exact definition of a firm and the different legal methods of organizing for-profit firms—is an essential first step in your study of managerial economics.

Definition of a Firm

A **firm** is an organization that converts inputs (such as labor) into outputs (goods and services) that it can sell or distribute. This definition applies to *all* firms. It is as true for Intel, which purchases silicon to produce computer chips, as it is for Frito-Lay, which purchases potatoes to produce a different kind of chip. It is easy to see that the definition applies to for-profit firms, such as Intel and Frito-Lay. But it also applies to nonprofits, such as the American Red Cross; to government agencies, such as the U.S. Justice Department; and to NGOs, such as Amnesty International. These groups all use various inputs to produce an output, such as housing people made homeless because of a tornado, enforcing the nation's antitrust laws, or increasing justice worldwide. Managers in all of these different types of firms can use the principles of managerial economics to make better decisions that further the goal of their organization.

Firm An organization that converts inputs (such as labor) into outputs (goods and services) that it can sell or distribute.

The Legal Organization of Firms

Let's focus for the moment on privately owned, profit-seeking firms. For-profit firms include giants, such as Microsoft in the United States, Total S.A. in the European Union, and Industrial Bank Company, Limited, in China, as well as small, local firms, such as the thousands of local laundries and restaurants that we find in all the cities of the world. For-profit firms are pervasive in the economies of virtually all nations. These firms come in a vast array of sizes and produce a nearly infinite variety of goods and services, so their owners use different methods to legally organize them. Let's review the four major categories of legal organization of firms used in the United States: sole proprietorships, partnerships, limited liability companies, and corporations.

Sole Proprietorship

The simplest form of business organization is a *sole proprietorship*, a firm owned by one person. Examples of sole proprietorships include an owner–operator of a taxi, a farmer, a solo-practitioner lawyer, and an owner of a small laundry or restaurant. In some of these firms, the owner has minimal supervisory duties: The owner–operators of taxis must organize their own labor services, but they have few, if any, supervisory duties. In other firms, the owners have more responsibilities: Owners of small retail stores have employees to supervise, which complicates their business operations and requires increased decision making.

As a form of business organization, a sole proprietorship offers several advantages. First, legal formation is easy, since the owner does not need to prepare any paperwork. Another advantage is that the government taxes a sole proprietorship's profits only once. The owner of a sole proprietorship adds all of the firm's profit to any other income and then pays personal income tax on the sum of the profit plus other income. Of course, a sole proprietorship also has disadvantages. When the owner dies, the sole proprietorship also dies, which makes it difficult for sole proprietorships to raise large sums of money to invest in the business. Another disadvantage is that the owner of a sole proprietorship faces unlimited liability. If the sole proprietorship fails, the owner can be liable for *all* of the company's debts, such as payments to creditors or back rent on office space.

Partnership

Partnerships are businesses owned by two or more people. Although the laws that govern partnership formation vary from state to state, partners must register their partnership with the state, and at the very least, they must carefully spell out each partner's responsibilities and rights in the registration papers. Types of partnerships differ depending on the rights and responsibilities accorded to the partners,[1] but most partnerships share a few characteristics. Let's start with the advantages of partnerships:

1. The government taxes a partnership's profits only once. Each of the owners reports his or her share of the profit, along with any other income, on his or her personal income tax form and pays the required tax. In this sense, partnerships are like proprietorships.
2. Many partnerships, such as law firms and accounting firms, motivate their employees by offering them the chance to become a partner, an opportunity that can often be lucrative.

Most partnerships, however, have a significant disadvantage: Partners face unlimited joint and individual liability for the decisions made by all of the partners and for all the debts of the partnership. If a partnership goes bankrupt, each partner is personally responsible for *all* of the partnership's debts. Exceptions to the rule of unlimited liability are limited partnerships and limited liability partnerships. The latter form of organization is available only to a few types of professional services.

Limited Liability Company

A relatively new form of business organization, the *limited liability company* (LLC), is a firm owned by one or more members who have limited liability for its debt. In three respects, LLCs are similar to partnerships:

---

1 For instance, *general partnerships* typically divide management rights and profit shares equally among partners. In contrast, *limited partnerships* have two types of partners: general partners, who run the company and have unlimited liability, and limited partners, who have limited management rights and enjoy limited liability.

1. The LLC members may create an operating agreement that carefully describes each member's rights and responsibilities. If they do not, the state laws from the state in which the LLC is formed will govern many of these issues.
2. The LLC members must file paperwork with the state in which the LLC is formed; regulations determining what information must be filed differ from one state to the next.
3. All of the LLC's profit is allocated to the members, who pay personal income tax on their share of the profit.

As suggested by their name, however, LLCs differ in one important way from partnerships (and sole proprietorships): The members of an LLC have limited liability for the company's debt. If the LLC goes bankrupt, its members are not personally liable for the company's debt.

Corporation

A more complicated form of business organization is the *corporation*, a firm owned by one or more shareholders. Professional managers often run corporations on a day-to-day basis. In the United States, a board of directors usually serves as the interface between the shareholders and the management team. The shareholders, who generally have one vote for each share owned, elect the board members. Typically, the top executives of the company are board members, but in the United States, in aggregate approximately two-thirds of board members are independent, with no direct connection to the management of the firm. Board members are responsible for ensuring that the executives run the company for the benefit of the shareholders and must approve significant actions of the firm, such as purchasing another large company or entering into a major new product line. The board also decides the amounts of any dividends. A *dividend* is a dollar amount per share the company pays to the shareholders, who are the owners of the firm. For example, the pharmaceutical firm Pfizer Inc. might pay an annual dividend of $1.08 per share.

Compared to the other organizational forms, corporations have more legal requirements, such as setting up a double-entry bookkeeping system to record business transactions and filing an annual report to the state in which they are incorporated. One important disadvantage is that the government taxes a corporation's profits twice, once at the corporate level via a corporate income tax and again at the personal level when the owners pay their personal income taxes on any dividends they receive and on any gain they make when they sell shares. Corporations, however, have at least two major advantages:

1. Because a corporation has perpetual life, its managers can raise funds more easily. Lenders know that a corporation with many shareholders will survive the death of any one shareholder, so they are more willing to lend money to corporations than to sole proprietorships or partnerships.
2. Shareholders have limited liability for the debts and actions of their company. Consequently, if a corporation fails, owing millions or perhaps even billions of dollars, the shareholders are *not* responsible for repaying any of the debt.

Table 1.1 summarizes the key characteristics of the four forms of legal organization.

Now that you understand the definition of a firm and the different ways of organizing for-profit firms, it is time to focus on the goal of many business owners: profit. This discussion leads naturally to an examination of your first economic tool, opportunity cost, and how it differs from accounting cost.

Table 1.1 Legal Organization of Firms

Type of Firm	Characteristics	Advantages	Disadvantages	Examples
Sole proprietorship	• A firm owned by one person	• Easy to organize • Profits taxed only once	• Exists only for the life of the owner • Unlimited liability	• Taxi owner–operator • Solo-practitioner lawyer • Restaurant owner
Partnership	• A firm owned by two or more people	• Profits taxed only once • Employees motivated to become partner	• Registration required • Unlimited liability (except for limited partnerships and limited liability partnerships)	• Law firm • Medical practice
Limited liability company	• A firm owned by one or more members	• Limited liability • Profits taxed only once	• Registration required	• Edgeworth Management, LLC • Mack Construction, LLC
Corporation	• A firm owned by one or more shareholders • Typically run on a day-to-day basis by professional managers and overseen by a board of directors	• Perpetual life • Limited liability	• Registration required • Additional legal requirements • Profits taxed twice (corporate income tax on profits and personal income tax on shareholder income)	• Pfizer • Microsoft • Ford Motor Company

1.3 Profit, Accounting Cost, and Opportunity Cost

Learning Objective 1.3 Compare opportunity cost and accounting cost and explain why using opportunity cost leads to better decisions.

Profit The difference between total revenue and total cost.

Total revenue The firm's total receipts from the sale of its goods and services.

A key factor motivating owners and managers of profit-seeking firms is the firm's **profit**, the difference between total revenue and total cost. In order to better understand profit, you need to understand total revenue and total cost in more detail. Defining **total revenue** is easy: It is the firm's total receipts from the sale of its goods and services. Identifying *total cost* is more difficult because *cost* means different things to different people. Let's begin by discussing the role played by profit and then turn to total revenue and total cost.

Goal: Profit Maximization

Although many goals might motivate the owners of profit-seeking firms, generally the prime motivator is profit maximization. Owners who put profits first have the most income to spend on the goods and services they want to consume.

If an owner puts other considerations, such as staff maximization, revenue maximization, or even the appearance of the employees, ahead of profits when making business decisions, the firm's profit will decrease, along with the owner's personal consumption of goods and services. In addition, competition from profit-maximizing firms will drive firms that do *not* maximize profit out of business. Most empirical evidence suggests that profit maximization is the goal pursued by owners, so assume that all owners of for-profit firms seek to maximize their firms' profits.

The owners of a profit-seeking firm may have a primary goal of profit, but the professional managers who run that firm on a day-to-day basis may have different goals. Managers are interested in enhancing their own well-being, an objective not always consistent with the goals of the owners, so some conflict of interest can easily arise when managers are not owners of the firm. Managers who believe that their prestige depends on the number of people reporting to them may hire too many staff members. Others may put family concerns ahead of business concerns and hire their own children. These actions could decrease profits. Owners often respond to this challenge by making it costly for managers *not* to maximize profit. For example, owners can use executive stock options, bonuses, and raises as incentives for the managers to put the firm first and maximize its profit. Chapter 15 examines the ways in which owners can motivate managers to maximize profit in more detail. Because the evidence suggests that managers as well as owners are rewarded for profit maximization, assume that successful managers also make decisions that maximize their firms' profits.

In general, because firms have a stream of profits and losses over time, owners and managers strive to maximize the value of the stream of profits. Often, however, the decisions that maximize profit in a given year are the same ones that maximize profit over time. For this reason, and to simplify the analysis, most of the discussion throughout the text focuses on maximizing profit for a shorter time period. You can then apply the lessons you learn from this shorter-term analysis to the more complex situation of maximizing profit over time after you study Chapter 16, which focuses on multiperiod decision making.

Profit does not motivate managers of nonprofits, government agencies, or NGOs. Instead, achievement of the organization's goal serves as a motivator. These managers, however, still need to use their resources as effectively as possible. Opportunity cost remains crucial for managers in these sectors because it will show them the true cost of their resources and help them efficiently allocate these resources. Although the examples in this section use for-profit firms, the lessons about cost are important for managers of *any* type of firm.

Total Revenue

Total revenue generally means the same thing to accountants, economists, and managers: the firm's total receipts from the sale of its goods and services. At its most basic level, a firm's total revenue (*TR*) is the price of the good or service (*P*) multiplied by the quantity sold (*Q*):

$$TR = P \times Q$$

For example, Gannett Company publishes *USA Today*, a newspaper that covers nationwide news, and sells it nationally. If Rogermark, a company like Gannett, sells 1.8 million issues of its newspaper, *America Today*, per day to its distributors at a wholesale price of 40¢, then the firm's total revenue is 40¢ × 1.8 million or $720,000 per day.

Of course, total revenue is not always this straightforward. Some complications can occur, but fortunately they are not overly complex. Discounts, rebates, returns, and allowances—all called *contra revenue* by accountants—can affect a firm's total revenue:

1. **Discounts and rebates.** Producers offer buyers discounts for various reasons. For example, Gannett sells *USA Today* to distributors such as Hudson Group, which in turn sells the newspapers to consumers at its Hudson News stores. Suppose that Rogermark sells its newspapers to another distributor, Realnews. Rogermark's contract with Realnews might set a price of 40¢ per paper but might also offer Realnews a discount if Realnews pays its bill promptly. A "1/10 net 30" discount is common. If the distributor pays the bill within 10 days, the distributor can take a 1 percent discount. If the distributor does not pay during that period, the bill is due in full after 30 days. If Realnews purchases 1,000 newspapers at a price of 40¢ for its store in Boston's Logan Airport and pays within 10 days, it receives a discount of 0.4¢ × 1,000 = $4. In this case, Rogermark's total revenue is (40¢ × 1,000) − $4 = $396. Effectively, Rogermark receives a price of $396/1,000 = 39.6¢ per paper.

2. **Returns.** Producers often allow retailers to return unsold product at the end of the selling season. For example, Rogermark's contract might specify that Realnews pays 40¢ per paper but can return all unsold copies for credit. If Rogermark sells 2,500 issues of *America Today* to Realnews for distribution at LaGuardia Airport and the Realnews stores sell only 1,500 papers, Realnews will return 1,000 papers for credit. In this case, Realnews will claim a credit of 40¢ × 1,000 = $400. With the returns, Rogermark's total revenue is (40¢ × 2,500) − $400 = $600. With the return credit, Rogermark receives an effective price of $600/2,500 = 24¢ per paper for the 2,500 papers.

3. **Allowances.** Producers frequently enter into agreements with retailers about allowances for various factors, such as advertising, retail display, or spoilage. Rogermark might offer Realnews a contract including a 5 percent retail display allowance for placing the *America Today* issues at eye level. If Rogermark sells 1,200 issues of *America Today* to Realnews to sell in Penn Station, before the discount Rogermark would receive 40¢ × 1,200 = $480. Realnews will claim an allowance of 5 percent, or 0.05 × $480 = $24, leaving Rogermark with total revenue of $480 − $24 = $456, for an effective price of $456/1,200 = 38¢ per paper for the 1,200 sold to Realnews.

To calculate total revenue, it is easier to adjust the price than to take these sorts of factors explicitly into account. The equation $TR = P \times Q$ is still used, but P is now the adjusted price. For example, if Rogermark offers a 5 percent advertising allowance, reduce the price by 5 percent (from 40¢ to 38¢) to capture the effect of the discount. With this change, the total revenue from 1,200 issues of *America Today* equals 38¢ × 1,200 = $456. Although the economic models you will study in this text do not specifically discuss adjustments for discounts, rebates, returns, or allowances, in *your* calculations as a manager you might need to make some modifications depending on the contractual arrangement.

Accounting Cost and Opportunity Cost

Cost is more complicated than revenue. Accountants use a measure of cost called accounting cost, while economists and successful managers use a different measure, called opportunity cost. Why do accountants use one measure and economists use another, and which should you use in making decisions? Let's compare the two and see why opportunity cost is the preferred measure for managers to use.

Accounting Cost

When keeping a firm's financial records, accountants generally record what are called **accounting costs**. For the most part, accounting costs are **explicit costs**, costs incurred by running a business that involve cash outflows. Examples of explicit costs include wages paid to employees and rent paid on a lease. Sometimes accountants also include **implicit costs**, costs incurred by running a business that do not involve cash outflows. Depreciation creates a noncash expense, that is, an implicit cost. In general, *depreciation* refers to the wear and tear on buildings or machinery that lowers its value. For example, newspaper publishers, such as Gannett (and Rogermark), use huge web presses (printing presses that use paper fed from rolls) to print each issue of their newspapers. As operators use these presses, the wear and tear lowers their value. The fall in the presses' value is a cost of producing the newspapers. No cash leaves the firm to pay for the machines' depreciation, so the fall in value is an implicit cost for the publisher.

Accounting costs The costs accountants use to keep a firm's financial records.

Explicit cost A cost incurred by running a business that involves cash outflows.

Implicit cost A cost incurred by running a business that does not involve cash outflows.

Opportunity Cost

When economists use the term *cost*, they mean **opportunity cost**, the return from the best alternative use of a resource. Of all of the possible ways to use a resource, the best alternative use is the one that, if selected, would yield the highest return. Because opportunity cost measures what a firm gives up when a resource is used, it is the best decision-making tool for managers. For a profit-seeking firm, the return is often the profit that the alternative use would have provided. For example, if Rogermark uses a web press to print its *America Today* newspaper, it cannot use the same press to print its *Dallas Sun* newspaper. If printing the *Dallas Sun* is the only other option for the press and it has a profit of $2,000, then the opportunity cost of using the press to print *America Today* is the profit lost from not printing the *Dallas Sun*, $2,000.

Opportunity cost The return from the best alternative use of a resource.

Like accounting cost, opportunity cost includes both explicit and implicit costs. There is often no difference in how accountants and economists measure explicit costs. If Rogermark pays a press operator a salary, including all benefits and taxes, of $44,000 per year, then both accountants and economists agree that the explicit cost to Rogermark of employing the press operator is $44,000. Accountants and economists, however, treat implicit costs in substantially different ways. These differences can be particularly large when considering the cost of inventory, capital assets, competitive return on investment, and owner's time. We consider each of these topics in turn in the following sections.

Cost of Inventory   Manufacturing, construction, retail, and many other businesses hold inventories of raw materials, works-in-progress, and/or finished goods. These goods either are ready to be sold (finished goods) or, after some additional work, will be finished and then available for sale (raw materials, works-in-progress). Managers need to determine the cost of items held in inventory. Accountants and economists value the cost of inventory differently. Accountants must use one of the inventory valuation methods approved by the Internal Revenue Service (IRS), and these methods depend on the historical acquisition cost. In contrast, economists use the opportunity cost, the best alternative use for the goods, in the valuation of inventory. These two measures are rarely equal.

To see the difference between accounting and opportunity costs, suppose that Christina Corporation, a jewelry manufacturer and retailer like Zale Corporation, bought 1,000 ounces of gold at a price of $1,300 per ounce and then purchased an additional 1,000 ounces at a price of $1,400 per ounce. Christina now has 2,000 ounces of gold in its inventory. When the firm uses 500 ounces of gold to manufacture necklaces to sell in its jewelry stores, what is the cost of the gold? An accountant answers this question by using one of the following three IRS-approved inventory valuation methods:

1. *Last in, first out (LIFO)* assumes that the last units added to the inventory are used first. Using this method, the accounting cost of the gold is $1,400 per ounce.
2. *First in, first out (FIFO)* assumes that the first units added to the inventory are used first. This method yields an accounting cost of the gold of $1,300 per ounce.
3. A *weighted average valuation* uses the weighted average of the costs, making the accounting cost of the gold $1,350.[2]

The managers' selection of an inventory valuation method is important because it affects the taxes the firm must pay. However, none of these methods determines the opportunity cost to the firm of using the gold. To determine the opportunity cost of using the gold to make necklaces, you must ask the following question: "Other than using the gold to make necklaces, what else can Christina do with it?" The answer that gives the largest profit is the opportunity cost of using the gold. Because the company owns the gold, often its most profitable alternative action is to sell the gold at the current market price. For example, if the current market price of an ounce of gold has risen to $1,600, then the opportunity cost of using the gold to make necklaces is $1,600 per ounce. By using the gold to make necklaces, Christina loses the opportunity of selling it at $1,600 per ounce. Regardless of what price the firm paid for the gold, its opportunity cost of using the gold to make necklaces is the current market price of gold.

The jewelry company example generalizes easily: The opportunity cost to *any* firm of *any* good or product in inventory is the current market price of the item. If there is a well-established market, as is the case with gold, the market price is easy to discover. Many items, however, have no market price. In the case of half-finished air conditioners or six-month-old red wine being held to age for three years, a market price is more difficult to establish, and a manager must come up with an estimated price to determine the opportunity cost.

The Christina Corporation example made a very important point: The price initially paid for the gold has no bearing on the opportunity cost of using it to make necklaces. The price paid for the gold is an example of a **sunk cost**, a cost that cannot be recovered because it was paid or incurred in the past.

Sunk cost A cost that cannot be recovered because it was paid or incurred in the past.

For Christina, the initial price paid for the gold is a sunk cost. For Intel, last month's cost of research and development is a sunk cost. Profit-maximizing managers realize that sunk costs have no bearing on current decisions. Why? Managers make decisions to minimize costs; because they cannot change sunk costs, effective managers ignore them when making business decisions.

Cost of Using a Capital Asset   Virtually every firm owns some *capital assets*, assets that managers cannot quickly sell and that the firm must have to produce its goods or services. Capital assets include machinery (such as the web presses owned by Gannett), buildings (such as the building occupied by the Walgreens drugstore at 7600 Debarr Road in Anchorage), and land (such as the 6,800 acres

---

2 The weighted average is calculated according to $\left(\dfrac{1,000 \text{ ounces}}{2,000 \text{ ounces}}\right) \times \$1,300 + \left(\dfrac{1,000 \text{ ounces}}{2,000 \text{ ounces}}\right) \times \$1,400$, where the weights, $\left(\dfrac{1,000 \text{ ounces}}{2,000 \text{ ounces}}\right)$, are the fractions of the gold purchased at the different prices.

Sunk Costs in the Stock Market

Suppose that you are a manager of a mutual fund specializing in biotech companies that spent $4.5 million to purchase 100,000 shares of Dendreon Corporation for $45 per share. Dendreon made a treatment for prostate cancer, but the treatment did not prove profitable, and the price of a share fell to $3. As a fund manager, should you hold (not sell) the stock because you paid $4.5 million for shares of stock that are now worth only $300,000? Explain your answer.

Answer

The $4.5 million spent for the shares is a sunk cost because you have already incurred it and you cannot change it. Consequently, you should ignore it in making your decision. As a manager, you should compare the profit you expect from holding the 100,000 shares of Dendreon to the profit you expect from the most profitable alternative use of the funds and then select whichever is the larger. You can sell the stock and invest the $300,000, or you can hold onto the stock hoping that the price increases. As it happens, Dendreon eventually went bankrupt, and its stock became worthless. If you had decided you could not sell because of your initial $4.2 million loss, you would eventually have lost the entire $4.5 million!

of fertile farmland in Michigan owned by Zwerk & Sons Farm). These capital assets are quite different from inventory because they are not immediately used up in the production process.

What is the cost of using a capital asset? Both accountants and economists measure this cost, but they calculate it differently. Accountants use the *depreciation allowance* as the cost of using a capital asset, but as usual, economists use the opportunity cost of using the capital asset.

Depreciation. Some capital assets, such as Gannett's presses and Walgreens' building, have finite lives: They eventually wear out. For these assets, accountants must use one of the IRS-approved methods to calculate the depreciation allowance of using the asset. Land, on the other hand, is a capital asset that does not wear out—it lasts forever—so there is no depreciation allowance.

One IRS-approved depreciation formula is *straight-line depreciation*, which distributes the depreciation allowance evenly over the expected useful life of the asset. For example, Rogermark has purchased a $20 million web press with an expected useful life of 10 years. After 10 years, the press is valueless. If Rogermark's accountants use straight-line depreciation for the 10 years, then each year they record 1/10 of the initial expenditure on the press as that year's depreciation allowance: $1/10 \times \$20$ million $= \$2$ million per year. These accountants then record a cost of $2 million on Rogermark's books.

The accounting depreciation allowance is essentially an arbitrary number created by an arbitrary depreciation formula that the IRS has approved for tax purposes, so it rarely equals the true depreciation cost of the asset. The true cost of depreciation is the change in the market value of the asset. **Economic depreciation** is the change in the market value of a capital asset such as land, equipment, or a

Economic depreciation
The change in the market value of a capital asset such as land, equipment, or a building.

building.[3] Notably, the accounting depreciation allowance for land is zero because it does not wear out. Its economic depreciation, however, is not necessarily zero because the market value of land can change.

Suppose that during a particular year the market value of a press Rogermark owns falls from $20 million to $17 million. In this year, the economic depreciation of the press equals $20 million − $17 million, or $3 million. By owning the press, Rogermark has incurred an opportunity cost equal to its economic depreciation of $3 million. Rogermark's true depreciation cost of using the press is not the $2 million depreciation allowance accountants must use but rather the loss of $3 million in value. Managers should use economic depreciation rather than the accounting depreciation allowance when making their decisions because economic depreciation accurately measures the firm's opportunity cost of the depreciation from using the asset.

The Opportunity Cost of the Capital Asset. Because accountants must adhere to IRS-approved depreciation schedules, they record the accounting depreciation allowance as the cost of using a capital asset. Economists realize that a firm has options for the capital asset other than using it, so the firm incurs an opportunity cost in addition to the economic depreciation when it uses the asset. To determine this opportunity cost, you must ask yourself the following question: "Other than using the asset itself, what else can a firm do with it?" The best alternative use—the one that generates the largest profit—is the opportunity cost of using the asset.

Take Rogermark's $20 million web press, for example. Suppose that if Rogermark uses the press, the firm's only option is to use it to print *America Today* newspapers. Other than using the press to print that paper, what else can Rogermark do with it? There are two possible answers to this question: Rogermark can either rent the press (presuming there is a rental market for presses) or sell it. Comparing renting and selling is difficult because it involves comparing a stream of payments over time (from renting the press) to a single payment (from selling the press). Chapter 16 explains how you can make this comparison if the company rents the asset for more than one year. For now, to simplify the analysis, assume that Rogermark is interested in the opportunity cost of using the press for a single year, so the relevant comparison becomes rental of the press for one year versus its sale.

In general, the profit from renting a capital asset is the rental payment minus any related costs incurred by the owner. These costs can depend on the rental contract. For example, a building owner can rent a building using a *triple net lease*, in which case the owner receives the rent and the renter is responsible for the maintenance costs, property insurance, and property taxes. For our Rogermark example, let's suppose that some other printer rents the press for $3.6 million per year under a triple net lease, so the renter covers the maintenance and insurance costs. There is, however, also the cost of the economic depreciation. At the end of the year, Rogermark still owns the press, so the firm has incurred the opportunity cost of the economic depreciation. Suppose, as above, that the economic depreciation is $3 million. Subtracting this cost from the rental payment gives Rogermark a net profit of $0.6 million.[4]

Compare this amount to the return from the other alternative, selling the press. If Rogermark sells the press, how do you determine its return for one year? Suppose

---

3 Sometimes a capital asset, such as land, rises in value; that is, it appreciates. Regardless of whether the asset rises or falls in value, the change in the market value is still called economic depreciation.

4 If the capital asset (such as land) appreciates in value, you must add the gain to the rental revenue to calculate the profit from renting the asset.

that the firm sells the press for its market value, $20 million. This price buys ownership of the press. It is *not* the one-year return. To determine the one-year return, you need to analyze Rogermark's investment opportunities. Assuming that the most profitable investment opportunity for the year yields a profit of 12 percent, Rogermark can use the $20 million gained from the sale of the press to fund this opportunity, for a profit at the end of the year of $20 million × 0.12 = $2.4 million. More generally, the one-year profit from selling an asset is equal to

$$P \times r$$

where P is the price of the asset and r is the highest one-year profit rate available to the seller. Economic depreciation does not affect the firm's return from selling the asset because the firm no longer owns it.

Now that you have calculated the values of the alternative uses of the press, you can determine Rogermark's opportunity cost of using it. The opportunity cost equals the higher of the two returns. The return for renting the press is $0.6 million, and the return for selling the press is $2.4 million. The most profitable alternative is obviously selling the press, so the opportunity cost to Rogermark of using the press to print *America Today* is $2.4 million per year.

The example demonstrates a critical difference between accounting cost and opportunity cost: The accounting depreciation allowance ($2 million per year) is *not*

DECISION SNAPSHOT

Opportunity Cost at Singing the Blues Blueberry Farm

You belong to a group of local entrepreneurs that owns a 10-acre blueberry farm called Singing the Blues. You could farm the land yourselves or rent it out for $7,000 per year. Another option is to sell the land this year at its current market price of $80,000. The price of the land next year will be $78,000. If you sell it, your group has an investment opportunity from which you expect to make a return of 6 percent per year. What is the opportunity cost of using the land this year to grow blueberries?

Answer

To decide how to use the land, your group needs to know its opportunity cost, its best alternative use. The alternative uses are to rent the land or to sell it. If you rent the land, your return is the rent ($7,000) adjusted by any economic depreciation (change in the market value). In this case, the economic depreciation is $2,000 because the market price of the land falls from $80,000 to $78,000. Accordingly, the total return from renting the land is the rental payment minus the economic depreciation:

$$7,000 - \$2,000 = \$5,000$$

The one-year return from selling the land is

$$\$80,000 \times 0.06 = \$4,800$$

The opportunity cost to the owners of using the land is the greater of these two numbers, or $5,000. Consequently, when calculating the profit from using the land to grow blueberries, your group should include $5,000 as the cost of using the land.

the same as the opportunity cost of using the press ($2.4 million per year). In this particular case, if Rogermark's managers use the accounting allowance, they will underestimate the actual cost of using the press. This error might lead the managers to make bad decisions. For example, underestimating the cost of using the press will encourage the managers to use the press even if the firm's profit would be greater if they sell it.

Cost of Competitive Return on Invested Funds   Accountants often ignore the opportunity cost of the funds the owners have invested in the firm. In order to start a business, the founders almost always use some of their own funds, perhaps to purchase machinery, a building, or inventory. By investing their funds in the firm, the owners lose the opportunity to use the funds elsewhere. The opportunity cost of the funds tied up in the firm is the return the owners could have made by using the funds in the next best endeavor. The return the owners can make is determined in competitive markets, so this opportunity cost is called the **competitive return**. For example, if the owners invest $600,000 in their business when they could make an alternative rate of return of 9 percent on these funds, the owners' competitive return is equal to $600,000 × 0.09 = $54,000. In other words, the owners have lost the opportunity to make $54,000 by committing their funds to the business instead of the alternative opportunity.

Competitive return The opportunity cost of the owners' funds invested in a company.

Cost of Owner's Time   Owners of firms who also work in the business typically pay themselves a salary, which constitutes an explicit opportunity cost. This salary, however, does not necessarily reflect the true opportunity cost of the owners' time because owners frequently have other options that affect their opportunity costs. You must take account of the return from these other options to calculate the owners' opportunity cost of working for their own company.

For example, suppose that after graduation, you receive an offer from Compton Consulting, a firm similar to Deloitte Consulting, for a position that pays a salary, including all benefits, of $105,000 per year. Instead of taking the offer, you opt to create a marketing firm. You pay yourself a salary, again including all benefits, of $65,000 per year. Your salary is definitely part of the opportunity cost of running the firm, but it is not the total opportunity cost of your time. If you were not running the firm, you would be working at Compton Consulting, making $105,000 per year. Because working at that firm is your best alternative, the total opportunity cost for your time is $105,000. Your marketing firm incurs an opportunity cost of $105,000 for each year you spend in the company. Of the $105,000 opportunity cost, $65,000 is an explicit opportunity cost and $40,000 is an implicit opportunity cost.

Suppose that you decide to pay yourself $120,000 rather than $65,000. In this case, the opportunity cost to your firm for your time is *still* $105,000, your best alternative foregone—that is, the best alternative use of your time. Of your $120,000 salary, $105,000 is the opportunity cost of your time, and the remainder, $15,000, is a payment to you of some of the competitive return on the funds you have invested in your company.[5]

---

5 The IRS limits the amount of salary that owners of a corporation can pay themselves. If owners distribute the corporation's profit to themselves as dividends, the IRS collects both the corporate income tax on the profit and the personal income tax on the dividend income. The IRS's concern is that by "overpaying" themselves, owners transfer the corporation's profit to themselves as salary, thereby avoiding the corporate income tax and paying only the personal income tax.

Comparing Accounting Cost and Opportunity Cost

As you have already learned, there are definite differences between accounting cost and opportunity cost. The following example compares the accounting cost and the opportunity cost for a hairdressing shop. Often these salons are franchised. Regis Corporation, for example, offers franchise opportunities for many different hair salon concepts. Suppose that two friends form a partnership and decide to buy a franchise from Swift Cuts Hair Salon. You will see how accounting cost can give a misleading picture of their firm's health.

To acquire the right to run the Swift Cuts franchise from the parent company, the two partners must pay a franchise fee and a fee based on their sales. They already own the building and all of the equipment they need, but they will have to hire employees and pay various costs of operating the business. The cost and revenue data are as follows:

- **Building and equipment.** Currently at the beginning of the year, the building and equipment are worth $800,000; at the end of the year, they are worth $780,000. The owners purchased the building and equipment five years ago for $1,000,000. Their accountants use straight-line depreciation for the 20-year life of the building and equipment, so one year's depreciation allowance is $50,000. Currently, the owners can sell the building and equipment for $800,000 or rent them for $60,000 per year. If they rent the building and equipment, they will do so with a triple net lease, so that the renter pays all maintenance costs, property insurance, and property taxes.
- **Salaries.** The owners employ eight hair stylists, an office manager, and themselves. Each of the eight hair stylists is paid $40,000, the office manager is paid $50,000, and the two owners pay themselves $60,000 each. If the owners did not own the business, each would work for a competitor for $80,000.
- **Other costs.** The costs of the electricity, hair coloring, property taxes, and everything else required to run the business are $200,000.
- **Franchise fee.** To purchase the right to operate a Swift Cuts franchise, the owners paid a franchise fee of $1,250,000.
- **Alternative investment.** The owners can invest any funds they possess and make a profit of 4 percent.
- **Revenue.** The franchise sells 27,000 hair stylings per year at a price of $31.25 each. From this revenue, the franchise must pay the parent company a fee of 4 percent.

Table 1.2 shows the total revenue, accounting cost, and opportunity cost. Computing the total revenue is straightforward. Adjusting the $31.25 price per hairstyling downward by 4 percent because of the franchise fee gives an adjusted price of $30.00, making the total revenue after the fee $30.00 per styling × 27,000 stylings = $810,000. This total revenue is the same in the accounting cost and opportunity cost columns of Table 1.2.

Now compare the costs of doing business:

- The costs for the salaries of the hair stylists ($40,000 × 8 = $320,000) and the office manager ($50,000) are explicit costs and are the same in both the accounting cost and the opportunity cost columns of Table 1.2.
- The cost of the owners' efforts differs. The accounting costs column records the explicit cost of the owners' *salaries* ($60,000 + $60,000 = $120,000). Because each owner's next best opportunity is to work for a competitor at a salary of

Table 1.2 Comparing Accounting Cost and Opportunity Cost

Profit Using Accounting Cost			Profit Using Opportunity Cost		
Total revenue		$810,000	Total revenue		$810,000
Cost			Costs		
Hair stylists	$320,000		Hair stylists	$320,000	
Office manager	50,000		Office manager	50,000	
Owners' salary	120,000		Owners' time	160,000	
Other costs	200,000		Other costs	200,000	
Depreciation allowance	50,000		Cost of using building and equipment (opportunity cost)	40,000	
			Competitive return	50,000	
Total cost		$740,000	Total cost		$820,000
Total profit		$ 70,000	Total profit		$−10,000

$80,000, the owners' opportunity cost of working for their business is $80,000 + $80,000 = $160,000, the opportunity cost of the owners' *time*.

- "Other costs" are the miscellaneous other (explicit) costs of operating the business, such as the cost of the hair colorings used. These amounts are the same ($200,000) in both the accounting cost and the opportunity cost columns in Table 1.2.
- The accounting cost column records the depreciation allowance, calculated using straight-line depreciation, for a charge of $50,000. The opportunity cost column includes the opportunity cost of using the building and equipment, which depends on the return from selling the building and equipment versus the return from renting them. If the owners sell the building and equipment, they receive $800,000, which they can invest for a profit of 4 percent or $800,000 × 0.04 = $32,000. Or the owners can rent them out for $60,000. Over the year, the building and equipment fall in value from $800,000 to $780,000 for an economic depreciation of $20,000. The net profit from renting the building and equipment equals $60,000 minus the cost of the economic depreciation ($20,000) for a profit of $40,000. The profit from renting exceeds that from selling, so the opportunity cost of using the building and equipment is $40,000.
- The opportunity cost column includes one additional cost, the competitive return on the invested funds. This entry represents the opportunity cost to the owners for the franchise fee of $1,250,000. Because their alternative use for these funds yields a 4 percent return, the competitive return on these funds is $1,250,000 × 0.04, or $50,000.

As shown in Table 1.2, the owners have an accounting profit of $70,000 when using accounting cost but a *loss* of $10,000 when considering opportunity cost. As you will learn in Chapter 5, this loss, called an *economic loss*, indicates that the owners' income from running the business is not enough to compensate them for all of their opportunity costs. In other words, the owners' total income from operating the business is $10,000 less than it would be if they closed the business and used their resources (their time, the building and equipment, and the funds they invested in the business) in their best alternative endeavors (working for the competitor, renting the building and equipment to someone else, and investing the funds at a competitive return).

Using Opportunity Cost to Make Decisions

Opportunity cost is a better estimate of the true costs faced by a business than accounting cost and is therefore crucial to managerial decision making. If you accept for a moment the reasonable idea that more accurate cost estimates lead to better decisions, you will understand the value of using opportunity cost. In the Swift Cuts example, the total revenue from the franchise is less than the opportunity cost of running the business. The accounting cost gives the appearance of a highly profitable operation that is likely to remain in business indefinitely. Yet because the owners are not covering their opportunity cost, they would be better off if they closed the business and invested their resources in other endeavors. Similarly, the managers at Christina Corporation who use the opportunity cost approach to value their gold inventory will better understand whether selling the gold or using it to make jewelry is more profitable. In both cases, opportunity cost leads to the best decision.

Managers who rely on accounting cost as the basis for their decisions will make poorer decisions than managers who use opportunity cost. For example, the managers at state transportation departments have a goal of reducing traffic deaths. Suppose that one state's transportation department analysts predict that spending $10 million on a program to increase the number of bicyclists who wear helmets will save 5 lives. The accounting cost of this program is $10 million. The accounting cost might make this program seem worthwhile. But suppose that the alternative use for this funding is a program to decrease aggressive driving that the same analysts forecast will save 10 lives. The opportunity cost of the program to increase helmet wearing is the aggressive driving program. Once the managers consider the opportunity cost, they are likely to reject the program to increase helmet wearing in favor of the program to decrease aggressive driving. As this example shows, it is safe to conclude that managers who base their decisions on opportunity cost will have more successful careers.

Opportunity cost is one tool economists use to make decisions. The next section introduces marginal analysis, another decision-making tool that you will find useful throughout both your study of managerial economics and your career.

Resting Energy's Opportunity Cost

SOLVED
PROBLEM

The managers at Resting Energy, a major producer of solar cells, buy a solar wafer inspection system from Adjunct Materials for $5 million. Resting Energy's managers expect to use the inspection machine for two years, after which it will be obsolete and worthless. They believe that the machine's resale price is $5 million at the start of the first year, $3 million at the start of the second year, and $0 at the start of the third year. Resting Energy's managers have investment opportunities that enable them to make a one-year return of 10 percent. Alternatively, they can lease the machine with a triple net lease for $3 million for the first year and $2 million for the second year. What is the opportunity cost of using the machine for each of the two years?

Answer

The opportunity cost is the profit from the best alternative use of the machine. Resting Energy's managers have two alternative uses: They can sell the machine, or they can lease it.

(Continues)

SOLVED PROBLEM (*continued*)

If they sell the machine at the start of the first year, they make

$$\$5 \text{ million} \times 0.10 = \$0.5 \text{ million}$$

If they sell it at the start of the second year, they make

$$\$3 \text{ million} \times 0.10 = \$0.3 \text{ million}$$

If they lease the machine, they receive the rental payment but must subtract the economic depreciation, the fall in the market price of the machine—$2 million the first year and $3 million the second year. So if they lease it for the first year, they make

$$\$3 \text{ million} - \$2 \text{ million} = \$1 \text{ million}$$

If they lease it for the second year, they make

$$\$2 \text{ million} - \$3 \text{ million} = -\$1 \text{ million}$$

Whichever action has the highest profit is the opportunity cost. For the first year, the opportunity cost (from leasing the machine) is $1 million, and for the second year, the opportunity cost (from selling the machine) is $0.3 million.

1.4 Marginal Analysis

Learning Objective 1.4 Explain how managers can use marginal analysis to make better decisions.

As a manager, you know that the decisions you make will have different effects on your firm's goal and your career, some small and some large. You always want to make the decision that most strongly advances your firm's goal, whether it is profit for Intel, justice for the Justice Department, or lives saved for the Bill and Melinda Gates Foundation.

Marginal analysis The comparison of the marginal benefit from an action to its marginal cost in order to decide whether to take the action.

Any action you take gains benefit and incurs cost. Perhaps the most important decision-making device in an economist's toolkit is **marginal analysis**, the comparison of the marginal benefit from an action to its marginal cost in order to decide whether to take the action. The word *marginal* means "additional." So marginal analysis focuses on the additional benefit from an action (*not* the total benefit from all of the actions taken), as well as the additional cost of an action (*not* the total cost from all of the actions taken). You can use marginal analysis in many different circumstances to help make your decisions. We introduce marginal analysis in this chapter but revisit it in Chapter 4 and succeeding chapters throughout the text to illustrate how managers can use it to achieve their firm's goals, whether they are maximizing profit or saving lives.

The Marginal Analysis Rule

As a manager, you should use marginal analysis in making decisions about a multitude of issues, including the quantity of a product to produce, the amount of advertising to buy, the extent of auditing to undertake, and which life-saving projects to fund. Although these decisions differ dramatically, in each case you must compare the marginal benefit from a unit of the activity to its marginal cost. If the marginal benefit of the action exceeds its marginal cost, then the action should be performed. If the marginal benefit of the action is less than its marginal cost, then the action should not be performed. These conclusions are referred to collectively as the *marginal analysis rule*.

MARGINAL ANALYSIS RULE

- If the marginal benefit of an action exceeds the marginal cost of the action, then the action should be performed.
- If the marginal benefit of an action is less than the marginal cost of the action, then the action should not be performed.

The intuition behind the marginal analysis rule is powerful. If the marginal benefit of the action exceeds its marginal cost, then undertaking the action results in a net gain. Conversely, if the marginal benefit of the action is less than its marginal cost, then undertaking the action creates a net loss. No manager wants to incur a loss, so in this case you definitely do not want to undertake the action.

Using Marginal Analysis

As a manager, decisions you make may include how much flour to produce, whether to purchase boosted Facebook posts, how many auditors to hire, or which antimalaria project to fund. In this introductory chapter, you do not yet have the foundation to examine a specific business decision, so we look at the marginal benefit and marginal cost of an action without identifying the specific action.

Figure 1.1 includes two curves to help illustrate marginal analysis. The marginal benefit curve (*MB*) is linear, and the marginal cost curve (*MC*) is curved, but that is not always the case. Both might be linear or curved, or *MC* might be linear and *MB* curved. The shape of the curves is not important. However, the vertical distance between the two curves is crucial for marginal analysis because it measures the difference between the marginal benefit and the marginal cost. In Figure 1.1, the 10th unit of the action has a marginal benefit of $50, labeled as point *A*, and a

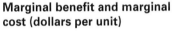

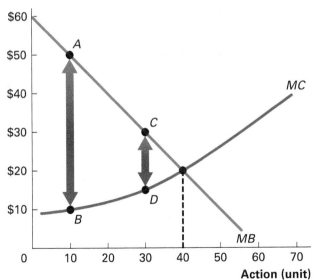

Figure 1.1 Marginal Analysis

The marginal benefit curve (*MB*) shows the marginal benefit from each unit of the action. The marginal cost curve (*MC*) shows the marginal cost of each unit of the action. For the 10th unit of the action, the marginal benefit is $50 (point *A*), and the marginal cost is $10 (point *B*), so undertaking this unit yields a surplus of benefit over cost (or profit) of $50 − $10 = $40. Similarly, the 30th unit, with points *C* and *D*, has a surplus of $15. *All* units of the action up to the 40th unit have a surplus and should be undertaken. All units beyond the 40th unit have a loss and should not be undertaken. Forty units of the action provides the maximum gain.

marginal cost of $10, labeled as point *B*. The vertical distance between these two points indicates that if the managers undertake this unit of the action, they will receive a surplus of benefit over cost of $50 − $10, or $40. This amount is equal to the length of the arrow between points *A* and *B*. Similarly, the arrow between points *C* and *D* shows that the 30th unit has a surplus of benefit over cost of $15. For a profit-seeking firm, the surplus of benefit over cost equals the profit. For a charity or other nonprofit organization, it might be the additional number of people helped.

Figure 1.1 shows that the marginal benefit exceeds the marginal cost up to the 40th unit of action, so each of these units has a surplus of benefit over cost and thereby increases the *total* surplus. Some units of the action increase the total surplus by more than others (compare the surplus of benefit over cost of the 10th unit and that of the 30th unit), but managers want to undertake all of the units up to the 40th because they all increase the total surplus. The marginal benefit is less than the marginal cost for all units of the action beyond the 40th, so each of these units has a loss. Needless to say, managers do not want to undertake any of these units.

In short, to maximize total surplus (or total profit), managers want to undertake all of the profitable units of the action and none of the unprofitable ones. As you can see from Figure 1.1, at 40 units the marginal benefit of the action equals its marginal cost, or $MB = MC$. By performing 40 units, the managers have maximized their total surplus because they have undertaken *all* of the profitable units and *none* of the unprofitable ones. This conclusion generalizes: To maximize total surplus (profit), managers want to undertake the quantity at which $MB = MC$.[6] You will return to this important conclusion throughout future chapters.

In your career as a manager, it is highly unlikely that you will possess a figure, such as Figure 1.1, that shows the marginal benefit curve and marginal cost curve. Instead, you must apply marginal analysis to informed estimates of marginal benefits and marginal costs. The goal remains the same, however: Undertake all the actions until you reach the point where $MB = MC$.

SOLVED PROBLEM

How to Respond Profitably to Changes in Marginal Cost

Suppose that the marginal cost of the action illustrated in Figure 1.1 increases by $15 for each unit of the action. For a profit-maximizing firm, what quantity of the action maximizes the firm's profit?

Answer

The increase in marginal cost shifts the marginal cost curve in Figure 1.1 upward, as shown in the figure here. The new marginal cost curve is labeled MC_1. For each unit of the action, the arrows show that the new MC_1 curve lies $15 above the initial MC curve. With the higher cost, only the units up to the 30th are profitable. To maximize the profit from this activity, the manager should undertake 30 units of the action, the quantity at which $MB = MC_1$.

---

6 The appendix to this chapter uses calculus to demonstrate that undertaking the quantity that sets $MB = MC$ maximizes the total surplus.

If the marginal cost of the activity increases, keeping the action level at 40 units means that for some units the marginal benefit now falls short of the higher marginal cost. The amount of the action must be reduced until the marginal benefit equals the marginal cost, in this case from 40 to 30.

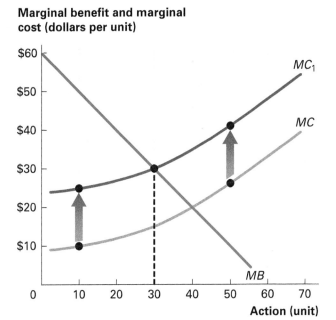

The marginal analysis rule indicates that *anytime* the marginal cost increases, less of the action should be undertaken because fewer units have a marginal benefit that exceeds its marginal cost. Of course, the converse is also true: *Anytime* the marginal cost decreases, more of the action should be undertaken.

Revisiting How Managers at Sears Holdings Used Opportunity Cost to Make Tough Decisions

At the beginning of the chapter, you learned how Sears' falling sales forced Sears Holdings' executives to make decisions about closing stores. These executives used marginal analysis to make their decisions. Because Sears is a for-profit business, you can identify the stores with a marginal benefit (*MB*) that exceeds marginal cost (*MC*) as profitable and the stores with a marginal. benefit that falls short of marginal cost as unprofitable. Sears' executives determined that the optimal number of stores for Sears Holdings was 630 because, ranking their stores by profitability, all the stores up to the 630th were profitable and additional stores were unprofitable. When Kmart purchased Sears, Sears operated over 1,600 stores, so the executives needed to close over 900 unprofitable stores.

Sears' executives had accounting data on which stores were profitable. This information can be helpful when making decisions about which stores should close and which should remain open, but the accounting data should not be definitive. As you have learned, accountants do not consider opportunity cost when calculating cost and profit. Effective and successful managers always use opportunity cost in making managerial decisions. Edward Lampert, the chief executive officer and a major shareholder of Sears Holdings, definitely used opportunity cost when making his decision about which stores to close.

Sears' accountants used the rent charged the stores as the cost of their location, but as Mr. Lampert knew, sometimes the rental payment does not equal the *opportunity* cost. Many of the Sears stores had long-term leases, and other companies had offered Sears Holdings substantial payments to use these spaces. When another retailer offers to pay to take over a space, the opportunity cost of keeping the store open at that location includes the foregone payment. If the payment is large enough, it can increase the store's opportunity cost so much that its accounting profit masks an economic loss. Marginal analysis then shows that Sears Holdings could increase its profit if it took the action to close the store to eliminate the economic loss.

Mr. Lampert explained his decision to close some stores by writing the following: "In some places mall owners and developers have approached us with the opportunity to reposition our stores for other uses and are willing to compensate us. When they've offered us more money to take over a location than our store there could earn over many, many years, we've accepted offers." Although he did not use economic jargon in his answer, Mr. Lampert clearly understood how to use the concepts presented in this chapter when making profit-maximizing decisions. He correctly decided to close stores that Sears' accountants might have concluded were making a profit because he knew that the *opportunity* cost of keeping some of these stores open was so high that closing them was the profit-maximizing decision.

Summary: The Bottom Line

1.1 Managerial Economics and Your Career

- The goal of this text is to show you how to make better decisions by using managerial economics, the application of microeconomic principles to business problems faced by decision makers.
- Microeconomic principles are frequently illustrated using economic models, which are abstract, simplified representations of the real world and real-world situations. These principles can improve the decision-making process.

1.2 Firms and Their Organizational Structure

- A firm is any organization that converts inputs into outputs that it can sell or distribute. Firms can be for-profit or nonprofit, as well as government or nongovernment organizations.
- Sole proprietorships businesses owned by one person, are easy to organize, and their profits are taxed only once. The owners of sole proprietorships face unlimited liability.
- The profits of partnerships, businesses owned by two or more people, are taxed only once. Generally, partners face unlimited liability—they are jointly and individually liable for all debts of the partnership.
- The profits of a limited liability company, a company owned by one or more members who have limited liability for its debt, are taxed only once.
- The profits of corporations, businesses owned by one or more shareholders, are taxed twice. Corporate shareholders have limited liability.

1.3 Profit, Accounting Cost, and Opportunity Cost

- The primary objective of for-profit business owners is maximizing their firm's profit.
- Accounting cost is based on accounting rules and guidelines. Opportunity cost is the value of the best alternative use of a resource. The two cost measures differ most frequently for implicit costs, including the use of capital assets and the competitive return on invested funds.
- The opportunity cost of a capital asset is its best alternative use, the use that generates the largest profit. Economic depreciation, the change in the market value of a capital asset, is part of the opportunity cost if the firm retains ownership of the asset.
- The opportunity cost of the funds invested in the business is the competitive return the owners could make by using the funds in another endeavor.
- Managers of all types of organizations make better decisions if they consider opportunity cost rather than accounting cost.

1.4 Marginal Analysis

- Marginal analysis compares the marginal benefit from an action to its marginal cost in order to decide whether to take action.
- According to the marginal analysis rule, if the marginal benefit from an action exceeds its marginal cost, the decision maker should take the action, but if the marginal benefit is less than its marginal cost, the decision maker should not take the action.

Key Terms and Concepts

Accounting costs

Competitive return

Economic depreciation

Economic model

Explicit cost

Firm

Implicit cost

Managerial economics

Marginal analysis

Opportunity cost

Profit

Sunk cost

Total revenue

Questions and Problems

All exercises are available on MyEconLab; solutions to even-numbered Questions and Problems appear in the back of this book.

1.1 Managerial Economics and Your Career

Learning Objective 1.1 Describe managerial economics and explain how it can help advance your career.

1.1 How do you think your course in managerial economics will help you advance your career?

1.2 Consider the following statement: "Economic models are useless because they are so abstract and so simple." Is this statement true or false? Explain your answer.

1.2 Firms and Their Organizational Structure

Learning Objective 1.2 Define what a firm is and describe the legal structures of for-profit firms.

2.1 How do the advantages and disadvantages of sole proprietorships and partnerships compare to those of corporations?

2.2 Why are nearly all large firms organized as corporations?

1.3 Profit, Accounting Cost, and Opportunity Cost

Learning Objective 1.3 Compare opportunity cost and accounting cost and explain why using opportunity cost leads to better decisions.

3.1 Rob Kalin founded Etsy, an online marketplace where crafters sell unique products. Etsy competes with eBay and Amazon.com. Six years after its founding, Mr. Kalin said that maximizing shareholders' value, which is effectively the same as maximizing profit, was "ridiculous." The major investors financing the company removed Mr. Kalin from his position as the head of the company within a few months. Explain why they favored his removal.

3.2 Pete Kendall, an offensive lineman with the New York Jets, was extremely cooperative when the team needed help. At the club's request, he switched positions, helped two promising rookies, and restructured his contract to help the Jets squeeze under the salary cap. The following year, when the Jets had more room under the salary cap, Mr. Kendall was disappointed that the Jets did not reciprocate and adjust his contract higher. He said, "You never can expect a team to do the right thing out of the goodness of their hearts." Explain why the actions of the Jets' managers should not have surprised Mr. Kendall.

3.3 Several decades ago, the British and French governments agreed to jointly produce the Concorde, a supersonic plane. After British taxpayers had spent £300 million (over $2 billion in terms of money today) to help develop the plane, the British government concluded that because this vast sum of money had been spent, any decision to cancel the plane was nonsensical and, consequently, the only reasonable decision was to finish the project. Does this reasoning make economic sense? Why or why not? (Incidentally, the plane was finished and flew for 27 years before it was retired in 2003.)

3.4 Why should managers use opportunity cost rather than accounting cost when making managerial decisions?

3.5 Ace Alexia plays professional tennis for a living, but in spite of her big first serve, she is not very successful. During the last year, Ace could have earned $75,000 as a tennis instructor at the Atlanta Tennis Club. She would have spent $7,000 on meals, paid rent on a condo in Atlanta at $800 per month, and made car payments of $300 per month. Instead, she remained a pro and won $100,000 in prize money in various tournaments around the country. In doing so, she spent $20,000 on transportation and lodging and paid her coach/trainer $15,000 for the year. She also spent $7,000 on meals, paid rent on her condo in Atlanta at $800 per month, and made the payments on her car of $300 per month.

   a. Would Ace's total income minus her costs (her net income) be larger if she became a tennis instructor than if she played professional tennis? Provide calculations to support your answer.

   b. What was Ace's opportunity cost of playing tennis last year?

3.6 In addition to its namesake cupcake, Hostess Brands produces Twinkies. Huge mixing-baking-cooling-wrapping machines produce both these products in Hostess Brands' factory in Emporia, Kansas. These machines mix the batter for each of the products, pour the batter into pans, and move the pans into long, winding ovens where they are baked and then into equally long, winding tunnels where they are cooled. Before wrapping them, the machines finish the tasty treats by injecting filling into them and applying any necessary topping. The machines even automatically clean the baking pans! Which of the following are explicit costs for Hostess Brands, which are implicit costs, and which are not costs at all? Explain each of your answers.

   a. The cost of the electricity used to run the production machines

   b. The salary paid to the night-shift manager

   c. The wear on the machines as they are used

   d. The price paid for the paper used to wrap the products

   e. The fixed lease payments made on the factory

3.7 Henry Hacker, a professional golfer who was having some trouble with his driver, decided to skip the next two tournaments on the PGA tour to work with his swing coach. He paid his coach $1,000 and used $1,000 worth of golf balls. As a result, his driving must have improved considerably because he now hits his tee shots longer and straighter. What explicit and implicit opportunity costs did Henry incur during the time spent with his swing coach?

3.8 The owners of a local retailer once remarked, "We can always beat the price that Kohl's charges for identical merchandise." When questioned, the owners revealed that this was possible because "Kohl's must pay rent on its store while we own our building and have no rent to pay." Do these owners have a problem with their economic logic? Explain your answer.

3.9 During its telecast of the Olympics, NBC ran an ad promoting its new "Fall Shows." Because the advertisement aired when there was a lull in the action, an analyst said that the promotion was free. Is the analyst correct? Explain your answer.

3.10 Grocery stores must allocate shelf space to different brands. What is the opportunity cost to Safeway, a large grocery store chain, of allocating more space to Post cereals?

3.11 Harvey owns both a hardware business and the building that he uses to run the business. What information would you need to calculate the total opportunity cost of operating Harvey's hardware business?

3.12 You are the manager of a medium-sized farm with 100 acres of workable land. You can farm the land yourself, rent the land using a triple net lease to another farmer for $2,000 per acre, or sell the land to a developer for $40,000 per acre. You have an investment opportunity that pays a return of 6 percent a year. What is your opportunity cost for a year if you decide to farm the land yourself?

3.13 You are a manager of a firm like Oasis Petroleum, an explorer and developer of shale oil in the Williston Basin. You own a drilling rig that you purchased for $10 million. The life of a drilling rig is 10 years, and your accountants use straight-line depreciation. It's the start of the year, and the current market value of the rig is $6 million, so you can sell it to another driller for $6 million. If you sell the rig, you can use the funds in an investment that returns a profit of 9 percent. Alternatively, you can rent the rig using a triple net lease to another developer for this year for $1.1 million. At the end of the year, the rig will be worth $5.5 million.

   a. What is the depreciation allowance?

   b. What is your opportunity cost if your firm uses the rig?

   c. What is the true cost to your firm of using the rig? Explain your answer.

3.14 You are employed by a firm like Adams Land and Cattle Company, a huge cattle feedlot in Nebraska with a capacity of 85,000 to 90,000 head of cattle. Cattle on feedlots are fed diets that are heavy in barley; one steer eats more than 8 pounds of barley per day. Suppose that your firm feeds your cattle 200 tons of barley per day and has a stockpile of 4,000 tons of barley for which it paid $250 per ton.
  a. If the current price of barley is $300 per ton, what is your company's opportunity cost per day of feeding all its cattle?
  b. If the current price of barley is $200 per ton, what is the opportunity cost per day of feeding all the cattle?
  c. Are your answers to parts a and b the same, or are they different? Explain why.

3.15 Christina Corporation, a firm like Kay Jewelers, purchased a supply of gold at $1,400 per ounce. Christina Corporation makes and sells pendants made with one ounce of gold. When gold is $1,400 per ounce, the firm sells a pendant for $1,600 at its Christina Jewelry stores. If the price of gold falls to $800 per ounce and Christina Corporation's FIFO method of valuing inventory leads the manager to continue pricing the pendants at $1,600, what is likely to happen to the firm's business, and why?

1.4 Marginal Analysis

Learning Objective 1.4 Explain how managers can use marginal analysis to make better decisions.

4.1 Say that you are a manager with the Transportation Security Administration (TSA). The table shows fictional estimates of the marginal benefit and marginal cost of additional TSA security lines at Mahlon Sweet Field, the airport in Eugene, Oregon.

Number of Security Lines	Marginal Benefit	Marginal Cost
1	$10,000	$ 2,000
2	9,000	3,000
3	7,000	4,000
4	5,000	5,000
5	4,000	8,000
6	3,000	12,000

  a. What is the surplus of benefit over cost for the second security line? For the third security line? If your goal is to maximize the total surplus, would you want to operate the third security line? Explain your answer.
  b. What is the optimal number of TSA security lines? Relate this answer to your answer to part a.

4.2 Suppose that you are a marketing manager for the Keebler Company, the largest cookie and cracker manufacturer in the United States. You determine that the marginal benefit from advertising has increased. Using marginal analysis, explain how you will change Keebler's marketing budget.

4.3 As an executive for the Elizabeth Glaser Pediatric AIDS Foundation, you have hired the number of auditors that sets the marginal benefit of auditing your firm equal to its marginal cost.
  a. Explain why this number of auditors maximizes your organization's surplus of benefit over cost. Draw a figure similar to Figure 1.1 to support your answer.
  b. Explain why it is important for you to maximize the surplus of benefit over cost.

MyLab Economics Auto-Graded Excel Projects

1.1 Kristen Larson just graduated at the top of her massage class from the Aveda Institute in Des Moines, IA. Her plan is to move to Sioux City, IA, for at least five years so she can spend time with her elderly grandparents and gain experience before branching out into a top salon in a large city.

    Upon graduation, Kristen received a job offer from Belle Touché, an Aveda Salon and Spa in Sioux City, for $60,000 dollars (including salary and health insurance). Kristen would have to work Tuesday through Saturday from 9 A.M. to 6 P.M. for 50 weeks out of the year. The salon would pay for all of Kristen's supplies and equipment, but she would need to put 20 percent of her tips each day into tipshare for the front desk and clean-up employees. Tips are estimated at $10,000 per year.

Kristen also is considering using her $7,500 savings to be her own boss so she can work fewer and more flexible hours. For $125 per week ($6,500 per year), she can rent a room at Salon Volume, but she would have to provide her own supplies, equipment, and health insurance. She plans to schedule massages for 25 hours per week at an average rate of $60 per hour and spend 5 hours per week on other business duties (scheduling, bookkeeping, cleaning, purchasing, etc.) for 50 weeks of the year. Tips average 15 percent of the cost of services, and the cancellation rate (when a client makes an appointment but ultimately cancels, leaving the time slot unfilled) is 5 percent. Kristen's estimated costs are detailed below.

- Massage table: $1,500 (one-time expense)
- Lotions, oils, linens, candles, and other supplies: $150 per month
- Remaining on her parents' health insurance (she is only 20): $100 per month
- Advertising: $60 per month
- Liability insurance: $50 per month

If Kristen takes the job at Belle Touché, she will be able to earn 2 percent interest on the money in her savings account. If she decides to work for herself, she will have 10 more hours of leisure each week, which she values at $20 per hour.

Calculate Kristen's annual economic profit for each alternative using the template provided. (Please note that each cell may not have an entry for both options.) Which option should she choose based on her economic profit?

Are there aspects of this situation that might change Kristen's decision that haven't been discussed?

1.2 Cakes by Monica (a bakery under the umbrella of the Café Brulé restaurant) in Vermillion, SD, makes cupcakes for purchase from three different kinds of customers:

- Type 1: Customers who purchase cupcakes at their individual price in the store
- Type 2: Customers who order cupcakes at least 3 days in advance in increments of 1 dozen of each flavor; discount from the individual cupcake price: $0.25 per cupcake
- Type 3: Customers who order cupcakes at least 2 weeks in advance but order at least 4 dozen of each flavor; discount from the individual cupcake price: $0.50 per cupcake

Cakes by Monica charges customers ordering more cupcakes of the same kind less per cupcake because there is less waste and less expense for larger orders placed further in advance, since she can order ingredients in bulk from a less expensive supplier.

Using the information provided, calculate the total revenue Cakes by Monica will receive from each type of customer and in total from the sale of cupcakes at each price. What do you notice about sales of cupcakes and total revenue as cupcake prices decline?

Accompanies problem 1.1.

	A	B	C
1		Belle Touché	Salon Volume
2	Salary/Total Revenue		
3	Tips		
4	Interest Received		
5	Value of Leisure Time		
6	TOTAL ECONOMIC BENEFIT		
7	One-Time Expenses		
8	Rental Expenses		
9	Monthly Expenses		
10	Cancellation Expenses		
11	TOTAL ECONOMIC COST		
12	TOTAL ECONOMIC PROFIT		
13			

If Cakes by Monica wants to make as much revenue as possible but keep its current discount structure, how much should the bakery charge for its cupcakes? How much total revenue does the bakery make?

Is there another pricing and discount structure that would increase total revenue for Cakes by Monica? If so, what is the total revenue Cakes by Monica will receive?

	A	B	C	D	E	F	G	H
1				Weekly Sales/Revenue Estimates				
2	Individual Cupcake Price	Type 1 Sales (individual)	Type 2 Sales (in dozens)	Type 3 Sales (in dozens)	Type 1 TR	Type 2 TR	Type 3 TR	Total Revenue
3	$4.00	30	3	4				
4	$3.75	35	5	8				
5	$3.50	40	7	12				
6	$3.25	45	9	16				
7	$3.00	50	11	20				
8	$2.75	55	13	24				
9	$2.50	60	15	28				
10	$2.25	65	17	32				
11	$2.00	70	19	36				
12	$1.75	75	21	40				
13	$1.50	80	23	44				
14								

The Calculus of Marginal Analysis

Section 1.4 introduced *marginal analysis*, the comparison of the marginal benefit from an action to its marginal cost, as a way to decide whether to take action. Marginal analysis will emerge as a crucial managerial decision-making tool. In future chapters, you will learn how managers can use it in a variety of different circumstances.

The objective of marginal analysis is to maximize the total surplus, the difference between the total benefit and the total cost of an action. The total surplus for a profit-seeking firm is usually its total profit. Section 1.4 used a graph (Figure 1.1) to show that the total surplus is maximized when the quantity of the action taken is such that the marginal benefit (*MB*) of the action equals the marginal cost (*MC*), or *MB* = *MC*. Deriving this result more formally using calculus is straightforward. But before we start with the mathematical definitions of marginal benefit and marginal cost and the derivation of the maximization rule, we will review a few mathematical results that occur with some frequency in these appendices.

A. Review of Mathematical Results

In economics, the most commonly used calculus concept is the derivative. Derivatives measure how one variable changes in response to a change in another variable.

Power Rule

Frequently, we will take the derivative of a power function, such as a cubic function. Equation A1.1 shows a general cubic function:

$$y = a + bx + cx^2 + dx^3 \qquad \textbf{A1.1}$$

where a, b, c, and d are coefficients, y is the dependent variable, and x the independent variable. In Equation A1.1, to take the derivative of y with respect x, or dy/dx, use the power rule. The power rule for differentiation of a general power function, such as $y = ax^n$, is

$$\frac{dy}{dx} = (n \times a)x^{(n-1)}$$

Using this result, the derivative of y with respect to x in Equation A1.1 is

$$\frac{dy}{dx} = b + (2c)x + (3d)x^2$$

For example, if the cubic formula is $y = 10 + 5x + 4x^2 - 6x^3$, then the derivative, dy/dx, is

$$\frac{dy}{dx} = 5 + (2 \times 4)x - (3 \times 6)x^2 = 5 + 8x - 18x^2$$

Quotient Rule

Another differentiation rule that is often used in economics is the quotient rule. For example, suppose we need the derivative dy/dx of the equation $y = h(x)/g(x)$. Then the quotient rule shows that:

$$\frac{dy}{dx} = \frac{h(x) \times g'(x) - g(x) \times h'(x)}{[g(x)]^2}$$

in which $h'(x)$ is the derivative of $h(x)$ with respect to x and $g'(x)$ is the derivative of g with respect to x.

Quadratic Formula

Another mathematical tool that we use with frequency is the quadratic formula, the formula used to solve a quadratic equation. Equation A1.2 shows a general quadratic equation:

$$ax^2 + bx + c = 0 \qquad \text{A1.2}$$

Two values of x solve this quadratic equation. The quadratic formula to solve for the two values of x is Equation A1.3:

$$x = \frac{-b \pm \sqrt{b^2 - 4 \times a \times c}}{2 \times a} \qquad \text{A1.3}$$

Although you can use the quadratic formula in Equation A1.3 to solve any quadratic equation, multiple Internet websites have this formula preprogrammed. On these websites, you insert the values for the coefficients—a, b, c—and the xs that solve the specific quadratic equation are immediately presented.

Maximization of a Function

To maximize a function with only one independent variable, take the derivative of the function with respect to the independent variable, then set the resulting equation equal to zero. This equation is the first-order condition. Solving the first-order condition gives the independent variable that maximizes the function.[1] Call the independent variable that maximizes the function x^*. Using x^* in the function gives the maximum value of the function.

If the function has more than one independent variable, take partial derivatives with respect to all the independent variables, and then set the resulting equations equal to zero. Solving these first-order conditions gives the independent variables that maximize the function. Using the maximizing x^*s in the function gives the maximum value of the function.

B. Marginal Benefit and Marginal Cost

The marginal benefit of an action is the change in the total benefit (TB) that results from a change in the amount or quantity (q) of the action. Using calculus, marginal benefit is

$$MB = \frac{\mathrm{d}TB}{\mathrm{d}q}$$

The marginal cost of an action is defined similarly. It is the change in the total cost (TC) that results from a change in the quantity (q):

$$MC = \frac{\mathrm{d}TC}{\mathrm{d}q}$$

C. Maximizing Total Surplus

The total surplus from an action is equal to the total benefit minus the total cost, where both are functions of q, or

$$\text{Surplus}(q) = TB(q) - TC(q)$$

---

1 Taking the derivative of a function and setting it equal to zero gives either an extreme point—that is, either a maximum or a minimum point—or an inflection point. Technically, to be certain that the point is a maximum, minimum, or an inflection point, you must determine that the second derivative of the function is negative, positive, or zero (respectively). The functions we use in this book, however, are such that when we maximize a function, the resulting extreme point gives the maximum and when we minimize a function, the resulting extreme point gives the minimum.

The goal of marginal analysis is to find the quantity of the action that maximizes the total surplus. To maximize total surplus, take the derivative of Surplus(q) with respect to q and set it equal to zero:

$$\frac{\text{dSurplus}}{\text{d}q} = \frac{\text{d}TB}{\text{d}q} - \frac{\text{d}TC}{\text{d}q} = 0 \qquad \textbf{A1.4}$$

Equation A1.4 is the first-order condition to maximize the total surplus. In it, $\dfrac{\text{d}TB}{\text{d}q}$ is MB and $\dfrac{\text{d}TC}{\text{d}q}$ is MC. Consequently, the surplus-maximizing condition in Equation A1.4 can be rewritten as

$$MB - MC = 0 \Rightarrow MB = MC \qquad \textbf{A1.5}$$

which is precisely the result presented in the chapter.

D. Maximizing Total Surplus: Example

When marginal analysis is used in future chapters, the total benefit and total cost functions will be specified. Often the surplus will be the firm's profit. For a nongovernment organization (NGO), however, the surplus could be the number of vaccines delivered. For a charity, the surplus could be the net amount of money raised from a funding campaign.

Maximizing Using Total Benefit and Total Cost

For the purposes of this discussion, simply suppose that the total benefit function is $TB = -0.5q^2 + 60q$ and the total cost function is $TC = 0.00194q^3 + 0.0208q^2 + 9q + 10$. These are the total benefit and total cost functions that lead to the marginal benefit and marginal cost curves graphed in Figure 1.1.

To determine the q^* that maximizes the total surplus, start by using the definition of total surplus (TS) as $TB - TC$, or

$$TS = (-0.5q^2 + 60q) - (0.00194q^3 + 0.0208q^2 + 9q + 10) \qquad \textbf{A1.6}$$

Following Equation A1.4, use the power rule to take the derivative of the total surplus with respect to q and then set it equal to zero:

$$\frac{\text{d}TS}{\text{d}q} = (-1.0q + 60) - (0.00582q^2 + 0.0416q + 9) = 0 \qquad \textbf{A1.7}$$

Simplifying the first-order condition in Equation A1.7 gives

$$-0.00582q^2 - 1.0416q + 51 = 0 \qquad \textbf{A1.8}$$

Use the quadratic formula to solve Equation A1.8. The result is that the surplus-maximizing quantity of actions, q^*, is 40, which is the same answer as in Figure 1.1.[2] Next, use the profit-maximizing quantity of actions, 40, in Equation A1.6 to determine the maximum total surplus from this action:

$$TS = (-0.5 \times 40^2 + 60 \times 40) - (0.00194 \times 40^3 + 0.0208 \times 40^2 + 9 \times 40 + 10)$$

or

$$TS = 1{,}072.56$$

The maximum total surplus from this action is 1,072.56, which is achieved by undertaking 40 units of the action.

Maximizing Using Marginal Benefit and Marginal Cost

Marginal benefit and marginal cost also can be used to find the surplus-maximizing quantity, q^*. Let's use the same total benefit and total cost functions as before, $TB = -0.5q^2 + 60q$ and

---

2 The other root of Equation A1.7 is −219, which is meaningless because the quantity of actions must be positive.

$TC = 0.00194q^3 + 0.0208q^2 + 9q + 10$. Using the power rule to differentiate the total benefit function with respect to q gives the marginal benefit function:

$$MB = -1.0q + 60 \qquad\qquad \textbf{A1.9}$$

Similarly, differentiating the total cost function with respect to q gives the marginal cost function:

$$MC = 0.00582q^2 + 0.0416q + 9 \qquad\qquad \textbf{A1.10}$$

You can now use the marginal benefit function, Equation A1.9, and the marginal cost function, Equation A1.10, in the surplus-maximizing equation, Equation A1.5, where $MB = MC$:

$$(-1.0q + 60) = (0.00582q^2 + 0.0416q + 9) \Rightarrow -0.00582q^2 - 1.0416q + 51 = 0 \quad \textbf{A1.11}$$

The quadratic equation in the second part of Equation A1.11 is the same quadratic equation as in Equation A1.8 when we directly maximized the total surplus using the total benefit and total cost functions. Consequently, the surplus-maximizing quantity, q^*, of actions in Equation A1.11 is 40, just as before. Whether calculating the surplus-maximizing quantity using the total benefit and total cost or using the marginal benefit and marginal cost, the answer is the same.

Calculus Questions and Problems

All exercises are available on MyEconLab; solutions to even-numbered Questions and Problems appear in the back of this book.

A1.1 Suppose that an NGO provides medical treatments to prevent the spread of an epidemic. It can prevent $72q^{1/2}$ infections by providing q medical treatments. Each treatment costs $3. The NGO aims to maximize its surplus, which is defined as

$$\text{Surplus}(q) = (72q^{1/2}) - (3q)$$

   a. Determine the surplus-maximizing number of treatments, q^*, that the NGO should provide.

   b. How many infections do the NGO's efforts prevent when it provides q^* treatments?

A1.2 You are a manager of Moose's Munchies, a hamburger restaurant. The price of hamburgers is $5 per hamburger, and Moose's Munchies incurs a total cost of

$$TC(Q) = 0.01Q^2 - 25$$

when it produces Q hamburgers.

   a. Moose's Munchies' total benefit is its total revenue, which equals the price multiplied by the quantity of hamburgers, $P \times Q$. What is Moose's Munchies' marginal benefit of producing and selling each additional hamburger?

   b. What is Moose's Munchies' marginal cost of producing and selling each additional hamburger?

   c. Determine the profit-maximizing number of hamburgers, Q^*, that Moose's Munchies should produce and sell.

A1.3 Belinda's Berries is a berry farm located just outside of town. All the locals know Belinda's farm produces some of the best berries around. Belinda uses costly fertilizer on her land to increase its yield. Belinda's berry production is $q = 27f^{1/2}$, where f is the bags of fertilizer she uses and q is the pounds of berries she produces. Each pound of berries sells for $2, and each bag of fertilizer costs $3. Belinda aims to maximize her farm's surplus, which is equal to

$$\text{Surplus}(f) = (54f^{1/2}) - (3f)$$

   a. What is the surplus-maximizing number of bags of fertilizer, f^*, that Belinda should apply?

   b. How many pounds of berries, q^*, does Belinda's Berries produce when Belinda uses f^* bags of fertilizer?

   c. Belinda's total revenue equals the price multiplied by the quantity of berries, $P \times q$. When Belinda's Berries applies the quantity of bags of fertilizer that maximizes its surplus, f^*, and sells the resulting quantity of berries, q^*, how much total revenue does Belinda receive?

A1.4 Security at sporting events is very important, but it is also costly. Scott's Security has the contract to provide security at a high school football game this Friday. Scott must determine how many security personnel he should schedule for that night. He is attempting to maximize his surplus, which equals the level of security, measured on a 1-to-100 scale, minus his cost of scheduling security personnel. The security level, SEC, is equal to

$$SEC(x) = \frac{(100x^2 - 20)}{(x^2 + 4)}$$

where x is the number of security personnel. Scott pays each of his employees \$8.40 per game that they work, so Scott's total cost is 8.40x. Scott's total surplus equals the level of security minus his total cost, or

$$\text{Surplus}(x) = \frac{(100x^2 - 20)}{(x^2 + 4)} - 8.40x$$

a.   What is the surplus-maximizing number of security personnel, x^*, that Scott should hire for this Friday's game?
b.   When Scott hires the surplus-maximizing number of security personnel, x^*, what level of security does Scott provide, measured on the 1-to-100 scale?

A1.5   You are a manager of Kelly's Koffie, a local coffee shop that produces the best iced lattes around. The price of an iced latte is \$4, so Kelly's Koffie's total revenue is

$$TR(Q) = 4Q$$

when it produces Q iced lattes. Kelly's Koffie incurs a total cost of

$$TC(Q) = 0.01Q^2 + 2Q$$

Kelly's Koffie's total profit equals total revenue minus total cost.

a.   What is Kelly's Koffie's marginal benefit of producing and selling each additional iced latte?
b.   What is Kelly's Koffie's marginal cost of producing and selling each additional iced latte?
c.   What is the profit-maximizing number of iced lattes, Q^*, that Kelly's Koffie should produce and sell?

Demand and Supply

Learning Objectives

After studying this chapter, you will be able to:

2.1 Describe the factors that affect the demand for goods and services.

2.2 Describe the factors that affect the supply of goods and services.

2.3 Determine the market equilibrium price and quantity using the demand and supply model.

2.4 Explain why perfectly competitive markets are socially optimal.

2.5 Use the demand and supply model to predict how changes in the market affect the price and quantity of a good or service.

2.6 Explain the effects of price ceilings and price floors.

2.7 Apply the demand and supply model to make better managerial decisions.

Managers at Red Lobster Cope with Early Mortality Syndrome

Red Lobster is one of the world's largest casual dining companies, operating over 700 restaurant locations worldwide that specialize in seafood. From 2009 to 2013, Red Lobster's managers faced a significant problem: Shrimp in Asia suffered from a bacterial infection called early mortality syndrome (EMS). EMS poses no health risk to humans, but it is deadly to shrimp, killing them before they mature and reproduce. Shrimp is one of Red Lobster's major ingredients, and the company sources the majority of its shrimp from Asia. How could the company's managers predict what would happen to the price they paid their suppliers for the shrimp and the quantity they would be able to buy?

Successful managers are aware of how markets respond to changes, and they react in ways that help their organization reach its goal. Red Lobster's issue with EMS is one dramatic example. This chapter will demonstrate how you can use the demand and supply model to predict changes in the price and quantity of goods and services that affect your firm. At the end of this chapter, we'll apply this model to evaluate how Red Lobster's managers dealt with the EMS challenge and how their actions boosted Red Lobster's profit.

Sources: John McDuling, "Shrimp Inflation Is Killing Red Lobster," Quartz, February 10, 2014; Kristen Reed and Sharon Royales, "Shrimp Disease in Asia Resulting in High U.S Import Prices," Bureau of Labor Statistics, June 2014 https://qz.com/175438/shrimp-inflation-is-killing-red-lobster/; Nopparat Chaichalearmmongkol and Julie Jargon, "Disease Kills Shrimp Output, Pushes U.S. Prices Higher," *Wall Street Journal*, July 12, 2013 https://www.bls.gov/opub/btn/volume-3/shrimp-disease-in-asia-resulting-in-high-us-import-prices.htm.

Introduction

Like all other consumers, you use markets to purchase goods such as coffee, smartphones, and jeans and services such as those provided by attorneys, accountants, and hairdressers. Economists define a **market** as any arrangement that allows buyers and sellers to transact their business. Markets can range from competitive to concentrated. *Competitive markets*, such as the market for cotton, have so many buyers and sellers that no one buyer or seller can affect the price charged for a

Market Any arrangement that allows buyers and sellers to transact their business.

product. *Concentrated markets,* such as the market for soda dominated by The Coca-Cola Company and PepsiCo, have so few sellers that these sellers have significant influence on price. This chapter covers the factors that determine the price and quantity in competitive markets. Later chapters deal with firm-level managerial decisions in competitive markets (Chapter 5) and in concentrated markets (Chapters 6, 7, 8, and 10).

In a competitive market, the interactions between the buyers (the *demanders*) and the sellers (the *suppliers*) determine the price and quantity of the good or service. The demand and supply model is the most powerful tool economists have developed for understanding how changes within a competitive market affect price and quantity. The model provides insight into market responses to changes in factors such as income, technology, and costs. Understanding the demand and supply model will help you make better, more profitable decisions.

To appreciate how demand and supply determine the price and quantity of a good or service, you must understand the factors that motivate buyers and sellers. Countless idiosyncratic reasons motivate individuals to buy or sell. For instance, you might decide to buy a pizza tonight because you worked late and would rather spend your time studying managerial economics than cooking dinner. Managers, however, are not interested in factors that influence only a few people because they have no discernible effect on price and quantity. Managers need to understand the factors that affect the vast majority of demanders or suppliers because they cause changes in price and quantity. To help you understand and use the demand and supply model, Chapter 2 includes seven sections:

- **Section 2.1** explores the key factors that affect the demand for a good or service.
- **Section 2.2** explains the key factors that affect the supply of a good or service.
- **Section 2.3** combines the separate analyses of demand and supply to explain how they jointly determine the equilibrium price and equilibrium quantity of a good or service.
- **Section 2.4** describes how perfectly competitive markets can be optimal for society.
- **Section 2.5** shows how to determine the effect of changes in demand and supply on the price and quantity of goods and services.
- **Section 2.6** explains the consequences of government price controls that limit the maximum or minimum price within a market.
- **Section 2.7** applies the demand and supply model to show you how to make better managerial decisions.

2.1 Demand

Learning Objective 2.1 Describe the factors that affect the demand for goods and services.

Millions of different goods and services, including food, clothing, physical therapy, legal services, and haircuts, are bought and sold in markets. Individual consumers are the demanders in these markets, so you need to consider the factors that affect their demands for a good or service.

Law of Demand

Price is an important factor that influences the quantity of a good or service demanders are willing and able to buy during a given time period. The law of demand summarizes how the price of the good or service affects the quantity that buyers will purchase: All other things remaining the same, the higher the price of the good or service, the smaller the quantity demanded; the lower the price of the good or service, the larger the quantity demanded.

LAW OF DEMAND

- All other things remaining the same, the higher the price of the good or service, the smaller the quantity demanded; the lower the price of the good or service, the larger the quantity demanded.

A change in the price of a good or service changes the quantity demanded through two distinct channels: the substitution effect and the income effect. The **substitution effect** refers to the fact that when the price of a good or service changes, its price compared to the prices of other substitute goods or services changes. So, when the price of jeans rises, some consumers will decide to switch to cargo pants or denim skirts instead of buying the now-more-expensive jeans. As consumers make these substitutions, the quantity of jeans demanded decreases. Alternatively, when the price of jeans falls, some consumers will switch from denim skirts or cargo pants to the now-less-expensive jeans, increasing the quantity of jeans demanded.

Substitution effect When the price of a good or service changes, its price compared to the prices of other substitute goods or services changes.

The **income effect** refers to the fact that when the price of a good or service changes, consumers' purchasing power changes. Continuing the jeans example, a rise in the price of jeans means that consumers have less income left over after they buy them. With less income, consumers must decrease their purchases. Some of that decrease is likely to be decreased purchases of additional jeans.[1] If the price of jeans falls, on the other hand, consumers' purchasing power increases. With more income left over after buying jeans, consumers purchase more products, probably including more jeans.

Income effect When the price of a good or service changes, buyers' purchasing power changes.

The income effect and the substitution effect combine to create the law of demand, which, as noted above, states that, other things remaining the same, a higher price decreases the quantity demanded and a lower price increases the quantity demanded.

Demand Curve

A demand curve shows how consumers respond to a change in the price of the product. More formally, a **demand curve** is a curve that shows the relationship between the price of a good or service and the quantity demanded.

Demand curve A curve that shows the relationship between the price of a good or service and the quantity demanded.

Figure 2.1 illustrates a hypothetical demand curve, D, for jeans. This demand curve shows the quantity of jeans consumers will buy at different prices.

The demand curve shown in Figure 2.1 is linear, but demand curves do not have to be straight lines. The important feature of a demand curve is its negative slope, which shows how consumers respond to a change in the price of the product. If the price of a pair of jeans rises from $60 to $80, there is a movement along the demand curve from point A to point B. The quantity of jeans demanded decreases from 300 million to 200 million pairs per year. When the price changes so there is a movement along the demand curve, there is a *change in the quantity demanded*. If the price

---

1 For a few products, a fall in income from the rise in the price increases the amount purchased. Intercity bus travel is an example. For these goods, in theory the income effect might be large enough that a rise in price increases the quantity demanded. In the real world, however, the income effect is never this large, so invariably a higher price decreases the quantity demanded.

Figure 2.1 A Demand Curve

The demand curve for jeans, *D*, shows the quantity of jeans demanded at all different prices. The slope of the demand curve reflects the law of demand: As the price rises, the quantity of jeans demanded decreases. When the price rises from $60 to $80, there is a movement up along the demand curve from point *A* to point *B*. The quantity demanded decreases from 300 million to 200 million pairs of jeans.

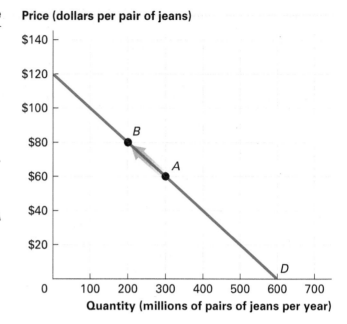

Price (dollars per pair of jeans)

Quantity (millions of pairs of jeans per year)

rises, so the movement is upward along the demand curve, the quantity demanded decreases. If the price falls, so the movement is downward along the demand curve, the quantity demanded increases. These changes are consistent with the law of demand: When the price rises, the quantity demanded decreases, and when the price falls, the quantity demanded increases.

Demand curves have two interpretations. For example, point *A* shows the following:

1. If a pair of jeans sells for a price of $60, consumers will buy 300 million pairs. This interpretation is useful in this chapter because it enables you to determine how the quantity consumers buy changes as different factors influencing the demand change.
2. The highest price consumers are willing to pay for the 300 millionth pair of jeans is $60. This interpretation can prove powerful for managers who are trying to set the highest prices their customers are willing to pay, a topic covered in Chapter 10.

The Demand Function

It is also possible to represent demand algebraically using a demand function. A **demand function** is an algebraic expression showing how the quantity demanded depends on relevant variables.

Demand function An algebraic expression showing how the quantity demanded depends on relevant variables.

Assuming that the only factor affecting the quantity demanded is the price of the product, the general demand function is

$$Q^d = f(P) \qquad\qquad 2.1$$

where Q^d is the quantity demanded of the product, f is the demand function, and *P* is the price of the product. Equation 2.1 shows a general function. If the demand curve is linear, the demand function is

$$Q^d = a - (b \times P)$$

As before, Q^d is the quantity demanded, and P is the price. Both a and b are coefficients. The value of a is the quantity of the product demanded when the price is $0, and the value of b is the change in the quantity of the product demanded when the price changes by $1. The negative sign in the equation reflects the law of demand, showing that an increase in the price decreases the quantity demanded.

Analysts frequently use regression analysis, a statistical tool explained in Chapter 3, to estimate the values of a and b. You can determine the coefficients of the linear demand curve illustrated in Figure 2.1 more simply. The value of a is the quantity of jeans demanded if the price is $0, so a equals 600 million pairs of jeans per year. The value of b is the change in the quantity of jeans demanded when the price changes by $1, so b equals 5 million pairs of jeans per dollar.[2] This value for b means that if the price of a pair of jeans rises by $1, the quantity of jeans demanded decreases by 5 million pairs. Accordingly, the demand function for the demand curve in Figure 2.1 is

$$Q^d = 600 \text{ million} - (5 \text{ million} \times P)$$

In any mathematical function, the variable on the left of the equation is the *dependent variable*, and the one or more variables on the right are the *independent variables*. The dependent variable responds to changes in the independent variables. In a demand equation, the quantity demanded responds to changes in price, making quantity the dependent variable and price the independent variable. Typically, mathematicians plot equations with the dependent variable on the vertical axis and the independent variable on the horizontal axis. For historical reasons, economists flout that convention by plotting the dependent variable, Q^d, on the horizontal axis and the independent variable, P, on the vertical axis.

Price is not the only factor that affects consumers' demand for a good or service. For example, consumers' income plays a role in determining the quantity of jeans they will buy. The next section presents the effect of income and other factors that influence demand.

Factors That Change Demand

You have seen how consumers' responses to a change in the price of a product affect the quantity they buy and lead to a movement along the product's demand curve. Of course, other factors also affect consumers' demand for the good or service. These include consumers' income, the price of related goods and services, consumers' preferences and advertising, financial market conditions, the expected future price of the product, and the number of demanders. A change in any of these factors changes the demand for the product and, as you will see, causes the demand curve to shift.

Consumers' Income

Changes in Income One very important factor that affects consumers' demand for almost all goods and services is income.[3] If consumers' incomes increase, they

---

2 Because the demand curve is linear, the value of b is the same at all points along it, so you can calculate the value of b between any two points on the demand curve. Consequently, between points A and B on the demand curve, the price rises by $20 per pair of jeans (from $60 to $80), and the quantity demanded decreases by 100 million pairs (from 300 million to 200 million pairs). Between these points, b equals (100 million pairs of jeans)/($20 per pair of jeans,) or 5 million pairs of jeans per dollar.

3 This factor is different from the *income effect*, covered earlier, because the income effect results from a change in the product's price, not a change in consumers' income.

Figure 2.2 A Shift of the Demand Curve

The figure shows a change in the demand for jeans. The entire demand curve has shifted to the right, from D_0 to D_1. A rightward shift of the demand curve represents an increase in demand. At *all* prices, the quantity of jeans demanded has increased.

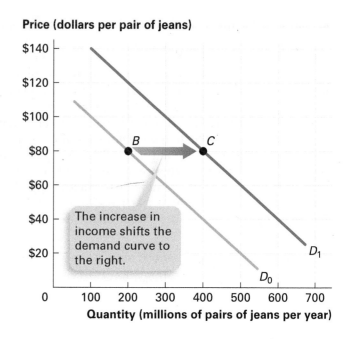

Price (dollars per pair of jeans)

The increase in income shifts the demand curve to the right.

Quantity (millions of pairs of jeans per year)

can and will want to buy more of many products, including jeans. In this case, the quantity of jeans demanded at every price increases. Figure 2.2 illustrates how a change in income affects the demand curve. Demand curve D_0 is the initial demand curve when people's incomes are lower, and demand curve D_1 is the demand curve when people's incomes are higher, perhaps as a result of strong economic growth. Before the change in income, point B shows that consumers demanded 200 million pairs of jeans at the price of $80 per pair. After the increase in income, at the price of $80, point C shows that consumers have increased the quantity of jeans they demand from 200 million to 400 million pairs per year. Figure 2.2 illustrates that the quantity demanded increases at *all* prices, not just at the price of $80 per pair of jeans. This fact causes the entire demand curve to shift to the right. The shift is called a *change in demand*. In the case of jeans and income, the increase in income leads to an increase in demand.

Similarly, a decrease in the quantity demanded at all prices causes a leftward shift of the demand curve. In our example, a decrease in income leads to a decrease in demand for jeans.

Shift of the Demand Curve Versus a Movement Along the Demand Curve As you have just learned, a change in income affects the demand curve differently than does a change in price. Figure 2.1 shows that a change in price results in a *movement along* the demand curve, and Figure 2.2 shows that a change in income results in a *shift* of the demand curve. The change in price illustrated in Figure 2.1 leads to a *change in the quantity demanded*, and the change in income illustrated in Figure 2.2 leads to a *change in demand*. This distinction is important. The only factor that creates a movement along the demand curve and changes the quantity demanded is the price of the product itself. All of the other factors that affect demand, including income, shift the demand curve and change the demand.

Although income is not the only factor that can change the demand and shift the demand curve for a good or service, it is an important one. Before examining the other factors, let's take a closer look at the effects of a change in income.

Normal and Inferior Goods and Services   Returning to the jeans example, you have seen that an increase in income increases the demand for jeans and shifts the demand curve to the right. For some other goods and services, an increase in income *decreases* the demand and shifts the demand curve to the left. For example, an increase in income decreases the demand for intercity bus travel because people with more income can afford to rent or buy a car or even fly to their destinations.

These two different relationships between income and demand mean that goods and services fall into two categories: normal and inferior. When an increase in income increases the demand for a good or service and a decrease in income decreases that demand, the good or service is a **normal good or service**. As described earlier, a pair of jeans is an example of a normal good. So, too, is dining at Red Lobster. The majority of goods and services are normal. In contrast, when an increase in income decreases the demand for a good or service and a decrease in income increases that demand, the good or service is an **inferior good or service**. Used clothing and boxed mac and cheese are examples of inferior goods. It is important to note that the term *inferior* does not imply low quality. It refers only to the relationship between income and demand. In fact, depending on the income range, some goods can be both normal and inferior. For example, in lower income ranges, ground beef is a normal good—when the incomes of lower-income consumers rise, they demand more ground beef and fewer hot dogs or noodles. In higher income ranges, however, ground beef is an inferior good—when the incomes of middle-income consumers rise, they demand less ground beef and more roasts and steaks.

Normal good or service A good or service for which an increase in income increases demand and a decrease in income decreases demand.

Inferior good or service A good or service for which an increase in income decreases demand and a decrease in income increases demand.

Price of Related Goods and Services: Substitutes and Complements

Another factor that changes the demand and shifts the demand curve is the relationship some goods and services have with other products. These relationships are of two types: substitutes and complements. **Substitutes** are alternative goods and services—a consumer buys one *or* the other. For example, if you are looking to buy a smartphone, you might choose an Apple iPhone *or* a Samsung Galaxy. **Complements** are separate goods and services that a consumer buys to use together—a consumer buys one *and* the other. For example, when purchased in a grocery store, hot dogs *and* hot dog buns are complements.

Substitutes Alternative goods and services; a consumer buys one *or* the other.

Complements Separate goods and services purchased for use together; a consumer buys one *and* the other.

If the price of a substitute rises, the demand for the good in question increases, shifting its demand curve to the right. The reverse is also true: If the price of a substitute falls, the demand for the good in question decreases, and its demand curve shifts to the left. For example, chicken and beef are substitutes. You might have one or the other for dinner. Consider the demand for chicken. If the price of beef rises, consumers substitute chicken, increasing the demand for chicken and shifting the demand curve for chicken to the right. If the price of beef falls, consumers will buy more beef and less chicken, so the demand for chicken decreases, shifting its demand curve to the left. Keep in mind that in both cases the change in the price of beef creates a *movement along* the demand curve for beef but *shifts* the demand curve for the substitute, chicken.

If the price of a complement rises, the demand for the good in question decreases, and its demand curve shifts to the left. Of course, the reverse also is true: If the price of a complement falls, the demand for the good in question increases, and its demand curve shifts to the right. Think of the demand for bicycle helmets. Bicycles and bicycle helmets are complements. If the price of a bicycle rises, fewer people buy bicycles, decreasing the demand for bicycle helmets and shifting the demand curve for bicycle helmets to the left. Alternatively, if the price of a bicycle falls, then the demand for bicycle helmets increases, and the demand curve for bicycle helmets shifts to the right. Once again, remember that the change in the price of a bicycle creates a *movement along* the demand curve for bicycles but *shifts* the demand curve for the complement, bicycle helmets.

Consumers' Preferences and Advertising

Economists refer to people's likes or dislikes for products as their preferences. Changes in preferences change demand. If preferences change and consumers like a good more than before, then demand increases, and the demand curve shifts to the right. Conversely, if preferences change and consumers like a good less, then demand decreases, and the demand curve shifts to the left.

What factors can lead to changes in preferences? The most relevant for managers is advertising. The goal of most advertising campaigns is to increase people's preferences for a product, thereby increasing demand. Watch an evening of network television or spend a few hours on the Internet and you will see almost too many advertisements to count. Not only individual firms but also some industries advertise. The National Milk Processor Education Program's slogan "Got milk?" tried to change consumers' preferences in favor of drinking milk to increase the demand for milk. (Chapter 13 examines such industry-wide promotions in more detail.) Of course, not all advertising tries to increase demand. For example, many states use funds from the 1998 Tobacco Master Settlement Agreement to run advertisements designed to discourage smoking and decrease the demand for cigarettes.[4] Nonprofits also advertise, though often to promote donations rather than increase demand for a product.

New information can lead to changes in preferences. Sometimes this information might come from advertisements, as when Apple advertised its then-innovative new product, the iPad. Other times the information might come from news reports, as when they spread the information over the past couple of decades that salmon contains oils that are heart healthy. Regardless of the source, as the information becomes more widespread, consumers' preferences may change, thereby changing the demand for the product and shifting its demand curve.

Financial Market Conditions

The ability of individuals and firms to obtain loans in financial markets, such as the market for bank loans or the bond market, affects the demand for some goods. Most people need to obtain a loan to purchase big ticket items such as cars and homes. Similarly, most firms need to borrow to help finance their purchase of capital goods, as when Brinker International Restaurants purchased new kitchens for all of its Chili's restaurants. Financial market conditions affect the demand for these types of products. With good financial market conditions—when the interest rates on loans are low and financial institutions' lending standards are easy to meet—the demand for the goods purchased with the help of these loans is high. With bad financial market conditions—when it is difficult to obtain even a high-interest-rate loan—the demand for these goods is low.

Of course, financial market conditions have little to no effect on the demand for many goods. No one thinks about taking out a loan to buy a slice of pizza. But for the expensive goods that typically require a loan, financial market conditions can play a crucial role in demand. In the recession of 2007–2009, home mortgage loans became significantly more difficult to obtain. The demand for homes decreased so much that the number of homes purchased was about 25 percent lower in 2008 than in 2005.

Expected Future Price

Changes in the expected future price of a good or service can change its *current* demand. For example, managers of refineries demand oil to refine into gasoline, fuel oil, and other products. If they think that turmoil in the Middle East will lead to higher crude oil

---

4 The Tobacco Master Settlement Agreement is a legal settlement agreement between the four major tobacco companies and 46 states that sued the companies to recover tobacco-related health-care costs.

DECISION
SNAPSHOT   Demand for the Cadillac Escalade

Suppose that you are a manager at General Motors. The Cadillac Escalade is a full-size, luxury SUV produced by your firm that gets fewer miles per gallon of gasoline than other cars. During the recession of 2007–2009, people's incomes plunged, it became very difficult to obtain loans, and the price of gasoline soared. What was the effect of these changes on the demand for the Escalade?

Answer
Three factors changed: (1) Income fell, (2) loans became difficult to obtain, and (3) the price of gasoline soared. Start by looking at each effect separately. The Escalade is a normal good, so the fall in income decreased the demand for Escalades. The Escalade is also an expensive car, so the difficulty in obtaining loans decreased the demand. Finally, gasoline and automobiles are complements, so the higher price of gasoline decreased the demand for the Escalade. Individually, each factor decreased the demand for Escalades, so combining them means that the demand for Escalades definitely decreased.

prices in the future, the current demand for crude oil increases as these demanders try to buy before the price rises. Conversely, if the refinery managers expect the future price of crude oil to fall, the current demand for crude oil decreases as these demanders delay buying crude oil until they can take advantage of the lower price. Of course, this factor does not affect the demand for all goods and services equally. It is stronger for durable goods, such as oil, than for nondurable goods, such as fresh fish, because demanders can more easily accelerate or delay their purchases of durable goods.

Number of Demanders

A change in the number of demanders—the number of consumers or companies purchasing a good or service—changes demand and shifts the demand curve. An increase in the number of demanders increases demand and shifts the demand curve to the right. A decrease in the number of demanders decreases demand and shifts the demand curve to the left.

Demographic changes can lead to changes in the number of demanders. For example, older people use more pharmaceutical drugs than do younger people. As the average age in the population increases, the demand for pharmaceutical drugs increases, and the demand curve for pharmaceutical drugs shifts to the right.

Seasonal changes can also trigger changes in the number of demanders. The approach of fall and winter decreases the number of people who want to barbecue outdoors. So at the end of summer, the demand for barbecue grills decreases, and the demand curve for barbecue grills shifts to the left.

Changes in Demand: Demand Function

The basic demand function you saw earlier in the chapter assumed that demand depends only on the price. Including the other factors just presented makes the demand function more complex and more realistic. For now, let's focus on including just two additional factors, but know that you can incorporate other factors using a similar process. Assume that the demand for jeans depends on their price, on the price of denim skirts (a substitute good), and on consumers' average income. The equation for this more elaborate demand function is

$$Q^d = f(P, P_{SKIRTS}, INCOME) \qquad 2.2$$

where Q^d is the quantity demanded, f is the demand function, P is the price of jeans, P_{SKIRTS} is the price of the substitute good, and INCOME is consumers' average income. The function in Equation 2.2 could literally be almost anything. However, if it is linear, it can be written as

$$Q^d = a - (b \times P) + (c \times P_{SKIRTS}) + (d \times INCOME) \qquad 2.3$$

In Equation 2.3, a, b, c, and d are coefficients. The meanings of the coefficients a and b are similar to before. For example, b is the change in the quantity of jeans demanded when the price changes by \$1. The value of c is the change in the quantity of jeans demanded when the price of the substitute (denim skirts) changes by \$1. Because skirts are a substitute for jeans, there is a positive sign preceding the $(c \times P_{SKIRTS})$ term, showing that a \$1 rise in the price of a denim skirt increases the demand for jeans. The value of d is the change in the quantity of jeans demanded when average income changes by \$1. Because jeans are a normal good, an increase in average income increases the demand for jeans, so the sign preceding the $(d \times INCOME)$ term is positive.

Figure 2.3 Changes in Demand

(a) An Increase in Demand

Demand increases and the demand curve shifts to the right when

- Income increases (for a normal good).
- Income decreases (for an inferior good).
- The price of a substitute rises.
- The price of a complement falls.
- Preferences change toward the good.
- Financial market conditions are good.
- The expected future price rises.
- The number of demanders increases.

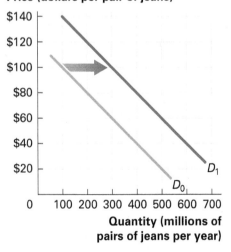

Price (dollars per pair of jeans)

(b) A Decrease in Demand

Demand decreases and the demand curve shifts to the left when

- Income decreases (for a normal good).
- Income increases (for an inferior good).
- The price of a substitute falls.
- The price of a complement rises.
- Preferences change away from the good.
- Financial market conditions are bad.
- The expected future price falls.
- The number of demanders decreases.

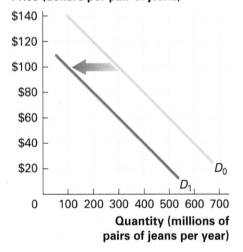

Price (dollars per pair of jeans)

The coefficients c and d affect the amount by which the demand curve shifts when the price of denim skirts and average income change, respectively. For example, if the coefficient d is equal to 200,000 pairs of jeans per dollar of income, then a $1,000 increase in average income shifts the demand curve to the right by 200,000 pairs × 1,000, or 200 million pairs, precisely the shift illustrated in Figure 2.2. Of course, in reality, no one simply hands you the values for the coefficients; analysts must estimate the values, often using regression analysis, which is explained in Chapter 3.

Figure 2.3 summarizes how the six factors discussed in this section—consumers' income, the price of related goods and services, consumers' preferences and advertising, financial market conditions, the expected future price of the product, and the number of demanders—change the demand and shift the demand curve. The following section explores the other side of the market—supply.

Demand for Lobster Dinners

SOLVED
PROBLEM

You are a manager at Lobster Brisk, a seafood restaurant chain similar to Red Lobster. Your supervisor asks you to determine the quantity of lobster to buy for the chain's Brisk Feast, an annual month-long promotion when Lobster Brisk features a variety of lobster dinners, including its signature lobster bisque soup. Your research department reports that the demand for lobster dinners is

$$Q^d = 1{,}300{,}000 \text{ dinners} - (100{,}000 \text{ dinners} \times P) + (32 \text{ dinners} \times \text{INCOME})$$

where Q^d is the quantity of lobster dinners demanded per week, P is the price of a lobster dinner, and INCOME is the average family income of Lobster Brisk customers.

a. If the average family income of Lobster Brisk customers is $40,000 and you set the price of a lobster dinner at $18 per dinner, what is the quantity of dinners demanded?

b. If you raise the price of a lobster dinner from $18 to $20 and the average family income remains equal to $40,000, what is the change in the quantity of dinners demanded? Is there a movement along the demand curve or a shift of the curve?

c. With the price of a lobster dinner set at $20, what is the change in the quantity of dinners demanded if your advertising brings in families with an average income of $42,000 rather than $40,000? Is there a movement along the demand curve, or does the curve shift?

Answer

a. The demand function shows that the quantity of lobster dinners demanded equals 1,300,000 dinners − (100,000 dinners × $18) + (32 dinners × $40,000) = 780,000 dinners.

b. The coefficient for the price variable, 100,000 dinners per dollar, shows that a $2 increase in the price of a lobster dinner decreases the quantity demanded by 100,000 dinners × 2, or 200,000 dinners per week. The increase in price leads to an upward movement along the demand curve.

c. The coefficient for the income variable, 32 dinners per dollar, shows that a $2,000 increase in the customers' average income increases the quantity demanded by 32 dinners × $2,000, or 64,000 dinners per week. The increase in income leads to a rightward shift of the demand curve equal to 64,000 dinners.

2.2 Supply

Learning Objective 2.2 Describe the factors that affect the supply of goods and services.

In markets for goods and services, firms are the suppliers. The primary factor influencing supply decisions is profit. Chapter 5 provides more detail about the effect of the pursuit of profit on firms' behavior. In this chapter, assume that the larger the profit from producing a good or service, the more of the good or service the firms will produce. Conversely, the smaller the profit from producing a good or service, the less of the good or service the firms will produce.

Law of Supply

The price of a good or service is a very important factor affecting firms' profits. If the price rises and nothing else changes, the profit from producing the good or service will be larger, so firms will produce more in a given time period. Alternatively, the lower the price, the smaller the profit and the less firms will produce. The law of supply summarizes these insights: All other things remaining the same, the higher the price of the good or service, the larger the quantity supplied; the lower the price of the good or service, the smaller the quantity supplied.

LAW OF SUPPLY

- All other things remaining the same, the higher the price of the good or service, the larger the quantity supplied; the lower the price of the good or service, the smaller the quantity supplied.

Supply Curve

Supply curve A curve illustrating the relationship between the price of a good or service and the quantity supplied.

A **supply curve** illustrates the relationship between the price of a good or service and the quantity supplied.

Figure 2.4 illustrates a supply curve for jeans that shows the quantity of jeans suppliers will produce at different prices. At a price of $60 per pair, point A on the supply curve shows that the quantity of jeans produced is 300 million pairs per year. If the price rises to $80 per pair, point B on the supply curve shows that the quantity of jeans supplied increases to 400 million pairs per year. The supply curve in Figure 2.4 is linear, but like demand curves, supply curves are not necessarily straight lines. What is crucial is the positive slope of the supply curve, which reflects the law of supply: When the price rises, the quantity supplied increases, and when the price falls, the quantity supplied decreases.

A change in the price of the product causes a movement along the supply curve, which is called a *change in the quantity supplied*.[5] If the price rises, the quantity supplied increases, leading to the movement upward along the supply curve illustrated by the arrow in Figure 2.4 between points A and B. If the price falls, the quantity supplied decreases, resulting in a movement downward along the supply curve.

---

5 These results are analogous to what you saw for the demand curve: A change in the price of the product creates a movement along the demand curve, called a change in the quantity demanded.

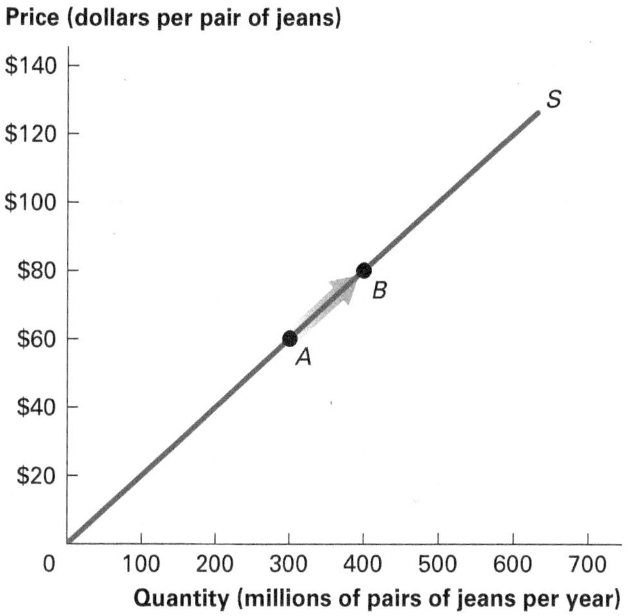

Price (dollars per pair of jeans)

Figure 2.4 A Supply Curve

The supply curve for jeans, S, shows the quantity supplied at all different prices. The slope of the supply curve reflects the law of supply: As the price of jeans rises, the quantity supplied increases. When the price rises from $60 to $80 per pair, the arrow shows there is a movement upward along the supply curve from point A to point B, and the quantity of jeans supplied increases from 300 million to 400 million pairs per year.

The Supply Function

Supply can be represented using an algebraic function called the supply function just as demand was represented using the demand function. Suppose that the only factor affecting supply is the price of the product. In this case, the general supply function is

$$Q^s = g(P) \qquad\qquad 2.4$$

where Q^s is the quantity supplied, g is the supply function, and P is the price of the product. Equation 2.4 shows a general function. If the supply curve is linear, the supply function is

$$Q^s = r + (s \times P) \qquad\qquad 2.5$$

where Q^s is the quantity supplied, P is the price of the product, and r and s are coefficients. The value of r is the quantity supplied if the price is $0, and the value of s is the change in the quantity supplied when the price changes by $1. The positive sign in the equation before the $(s \times P)$ term reflects the law of supply: An increase in the price increases the quantity supplied.

You can use Equation 2.5 to determine the coefficients of the supply function for the linear supply curve illustrated in Figure 2.4. As Figure 2.4 shows, when the price is $0, the quantity of jeans supplied is 0, so r equals 0. The value of s is the change in the quantity of jeans supplied when the price changes by $1, so s equals 5 million pairs of jeans per dollar.[6] This value for s means that if the price of jeans rises by $1, the quantity supplied increases by 5 million pairs. Therefore, the supply function for the supply curve shown in Figure 2.4 is

$$Q^s = 0 + (5 \text{ million} \times P)$$

---

6 As with the value of the coefficient b on a linear demand curve, the value of s is the same at every point on a linear supply curve. Between points A and B on the supply curve in Figure 2.4, as the price of jeans rises by $20 (from $60 to $80), the quantity of jeans supplied increases by 100 million pairs (from 300 million to 400 million pairs). So between these two points, s equals (100 million pairs)/($20 per pair), or 5 million pairs per dollar.

As you may already have guessed, price is not the only thing that affects the supply of a product. The next section examines the other factors that affect supply and the supply curve.

Factors That Change Supply

A change in price creates a movement along the supply curve, but other factors that affect supply shift the supply curve. These factors include cost, the price of related goods and services, technology, the state of nature, the expected future price of the product, and the number of suppliers. Of these six factors, the first five reflect firms' profit-seeking behavior, while the last directly affects the amount of the product available at each price.

Cost

One factor that affects the supply of all goods and services is the cost of producing them. Cost and price differ. *Cost* is what the producers pay to produce the product, and *price* is the amount the producers receive when they sell the product. When the cost of producing a good or service rises and nothing else changes, the profit from producing that good or service decreases. Firms respond to the fall in profit by decreasing their production. For example, suppose that the cost of producing jeans rises because of an increase in the price of the denim used in their manufacture. For any given price, this increase in cost decreases the profit from jeans, so firms respond by decreasing their production. In Figure 2.5, supply curve S_0 is the initial supply curve before the change in cost, and supply curve S_1 is the supply curve after the cost has increased. At the price of $80 per pair of jeans, before the rise in cost, firms supply 400 million pairs of jeans per year, point B on the initial supply curve, S_0. After the rise in cost, the quantity supplied at the price of $80 decreases to 200 million pairs of jeans per year, point C on the new supply curve, S_1. As Figure 2.5 shows, the quantity supplied decreases at not only the price of $80 per pair of jeans but also at *all* prices, so that the entire supply curve shifts to the left. The increase in cost leads to a decrease in supply.

Similarly, if the cost of production falls, the profit from producing the good or service rises. Firms respond to the higher profit by increasing their production of the good or service, so the supply increases and the supply curve shifts to the right.

Shift of the Supply Curve Versus a Movement Along the Supply Curve   As was the case with the demand curve, the effect on the supply curve of a change in the price of the product is significantly different from the effect of a change in any other relevant factor, such as cost. Figure 2.4 illustrates that a change in price results in a *movement along* the supply curve, while Figure 2.5 shows that a change in cost results in a *shift* of the supply curve. The change in price illustrated in Figure 2.4 leads to a *change in the quantity supplied*, and the change in cost illustrated in Figure 2.5 leads to a *change in supply*. The only factor that creates a movement along the supply curve (and a change in the quantity supplied) is the product's price. Changes in any of the other relevant factors shift the supply curve (and change the supply).

Price of Related Goods: Substitutes in Production and Complements in Production

Changes in the prices of related goods in production change the supply of a product and shift its supply curve. There are two possible relationships between goods. Some

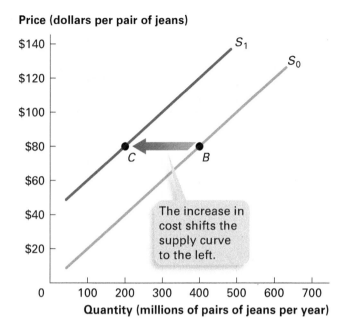

Price (dollars per pair of jeans)

Figure 2.5 A Shift in the Supply Curve

The figure shows a decrease in the supply of jeans. The supply curve shifts to the left, from S_0 to S_1. A leftward shift of the supply curve represents a decrease in supply because the quantity of jeans supplied decreases at all prices.

products, called **substitutes in production**, are alternatives in production—a firm can produce one *or* the other. For example, bakeries such as the Great Harvest Bread Company can use their ovens to produce either white bread or wheat bread. For Great Harvest Bread, these two goods are substitutes in production. Other products, called **complements in production**, are produced simultaneously—a firm produces one *and* the other. For example, when refineries such as those operated by Shell Oil Company refine a barrel of oil, the refining process simultaneously produces gasoline, kerosene, and diesel fuel. For Shell Oil, gasoline, kerosene, and diesel fuel are complements in production.[7]

For both substitutes in production and complements in production, the price of the second product affects the supply of the first.

- **Substitutes in production.** If the price of a substitute in production rises, firms switch production toward the substitute and away from the first product because the substitute has become more profitable. The supply of the first product decreases, and its supply curve shifts to the left. For example, if the price of wheat bread rises, how does this change affect the supply of white bread? Great Harvest Bread's managers and managers of all bakeries use their ovens to produce more wheat bread and less white bread, decreasing the supply of white bread and shifting the supply curve of white bread to the left. The reverse is also true: If the price of a substitute in production falls, the supply of the first good increases, and its supply curve shifts to the right.
- **Complements in production.** If the price of a complement in production rises, firms produce more of the complement because it has become more profitable.

Substitutes in production Products that are alternatives in production; a firm can produce one *or* the other.

Complements in production Products that are produced simultaneously; a firm produces one *and* the other.

7 Traditionally, economists call products that are substitutes or complements *for consumers* simply *substitutes* or *complements* but refer to goods that are substitutes or complements *for firms* as *substitutes in production* or *complements in production*.

When firms produce more of the complement, they also automatically produce more of the first product. The supply of the first product increases, and its supply curve shifts to the right. For example, if the price of gasoline rises, how does this change affect the supply of diesel fuel? The managers of Shell Oil's refineries and the managers of all refineries produce more gasoline by refining more oil. Because more oil is refined, the production of diesel fuel automatically increases. The supply of diesel fuel increases, and the supply curve of diesel fuel shifts to the right. Of course, if the price of a complement in production falls, the supply of the first product also decreases, and its supply curve shifts to the left.

Technology

Changes in technology affect the supply in many markets. Economists take a broad view of *technology* by thinking of it as information that provides a recipe (or instructions) describing how to combine various inputs in order to produce the output. It is common to view technology in terms of *technological advances*, the discovery of improved methods of production of existing goods or services or even methods of production of entirely new products or services. The automobile industry provides examples of both types of technological advances:

- The installation of industrial robots to produce cars illustrates a new and improved method of production.
- The introduction of hybrids or driverless automobiles illustrates the production of new products.

In both cases, a technological advance increases the supply of a good or service and shifts the supply curve to the right.

State of Nature

Although you might first think that the state of nature affects only the supply of agricultural products, the concept is actually much broader. As a factor affecting supply, the state of nature includes both the wide-scale flooding in China's Yangtze River basin in the summer of 2016 that destroyed nearly 4 million acres of crops and caused a total of $28 billion in damages, and the earthquake and resulting tsunami that devastated northern Japan in March 2011, severely damaging many of Japan's automobile factories. Floods, tsunamis, earthquakes, hurricanes, and bad growing seasons are all examples of bad states of nature. Because these events either increase the cost of producing the affected goods and services or directly reduce the amount firms can produce, they decrease the supply of affected goods and services and shift their supply curves to the left. Conversely, a good state of nature—no flooding, an absence of tsunamis, fewer hurricanes than normal, a good growing season—increases the supply of the affected products and shifts their supply curves to the right.

Expected Future Price

Changes in a good's expected future price can change its *current* supply. For example, Marathon Pipe Line owns six massive underground storage caverns for propane. If the future price of propane is expected to rise, Marathon and other propane suppliers will delay selling propane today in order to take advantage of the higher price (and larger profit) expected in the future. Consequently, the current supply of propane decreases, and the supply curve shifts to the left. Conversely, if the future price of propane is expected to fall, the current supply of propane increases as Marathon and the other suppliers rush to sell now before the price and profit fall in the future. Of course, this factor does not affect the supply for all goods and services equally. Goods that can be stored or that have production processes that can easily be accelerated or delayed will have the strongest reaction to changes in the expected future price.

Number of Suppliers

Of the factors that shift the supply curve, only a change in the number of suppliers is *not* motivated by profit. A change in the number of suppliers directly changes the amount of the product available at each price. When more firms enter a market, the number of suppliers increases, which increases the supply and shifts the supply curve to the right. When firms close or otherwise exit a market, the number of suppliers decreases, which decreases the supply and shifts the supply curve to the left.

Changes in Supply: Supply Function

The supply function presented in Equation 2.4 assumes that supply relies only on the price of the product. Including other relevant factors from among the six just presented makes the supply function more realistic. For now, this discussion focuses on just two additional factors, but as you will see shortly, you can add any of the others using a similar process. So assume that the supply of jeans depends on their price, the cost of producing each pair, and the number of firms producing jeans. In this case, a general equation for the supply function is

$$Q^s = g(P, \text{COST}, \text{NUMBER})$$

where Q^s is quantity of jeans produced, g is the supply function, P is the price of jeans, COST is the cost of producing the jeans, and NUMBER is the number of suppliers. You can extend the linear supply function shown in Equation 2.5 to include the effects of the cost and number of firms:

$$Q^s = r + (s \times P) - (t \times \text{COST}) + (u \times \text{NUMBER})$$

The coefficients in the linear supply equation are $r, s, t,$ and u. The meanings of the r and s coefficients are the analogous to those in Equation 2.5. For example, the value of s is the change in the quantity of jeans supplied when the price changes by \$1. The new coefficients are t and u. The value of t is the change in the quantity supplied when the cost of producing jeans changes by \$1. The negative sign in the equation for the $(t \times \text{COST})$ term indicates that an increase in cost decreases the supply of jeans. The value of u is the change in the quantity of jeans supplied when the number of firms changes by one. The $(u \times \text{NUMBER})$ term has a positive sign because an increase in the number of firms leads to an increase in the supply.

These new coefficients determine how much the supply changes and how much the supply curve shifts if there is a change in the cost or number of firms. For example, if the coefficient t is equal to 100 million pairs of jeans per dollar of cost, then a \$2 increase in cost changes the supply by -100 million $\times$ 2, or -200 million pairs. In this case, the supply curve shifts to the left by 200 million pairs, precisely the shift illustrated in Figure 2.5.

Figure 2.6 summarizes the effects that the factors just discussed have on supply and the supply curve. Now that you have learned about the concepts of demand and supply separately, it's time to discover how they interact to determine the quantity and price of a good or service.

Figure 2.6 Changes in Supply

(a) An Increase in Supply
Supply increases and the supply curve shifts to the right when

- Cost decreases.
- The price of a substitute in production falls.
- The price of a complement in production rises.
- Technology advances.
- The state of nature is good.
- The expected future price falls.
- The number of suppliers increases.

Price (dollars per pair of jeans)

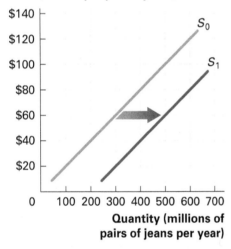

(b) A Decrease in Supply
Supply decreases and the supply curve shifts to the left when:

- Cost increases.
- The price of a substitute in production rises.
- The price of a complement in production falls.
- The state of nature is bad.
- The expected future price rises.
- The number of suppliers decreases.

Price (dollars per pair of jeans)

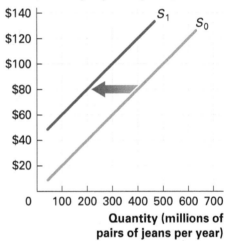

SOLVED PROBLEM

The Supply of Gasoline-Powered Cars and the Price of Hybrid Cars

Suppose that the supply function for gasoline-powered cars is

$$Q^S = 7{,}800{,}000 \text{ cars} + (300 \text{ cars} \times P) - (200 \text{ cars} \times P_{HYBRID})$$

where Q^S is the quantity of gasoline cars supplied, P is the price of a gasoline-powered car, and P_{HYBRID} is the price of a hybrid car. Suppose the price of a hybrid car is $39,000.

a. Are hybrids a complement in production or a substitute in production for gasoline-powered cars?

b. Suppose the price of a gasoline-powered car is $30,000 and the price of a hybrid car rises by $2,000. What is the effect on the supply curve of gasoline-powered cars? Draw a figure showing the initial supply curve and the new supply curve after the increase in the price of the hybrid.

Answer

a. The term showing how the price of a hybrid car affects the supply of gasoline-powered cars, $(200 \text{ cars} \times P_{HYBRID})$, is preceded by a negative sign, so an increase in the price of a hybrid decreases the supply of gasoline-powered cars. A hybrid is a substitute in production for gasoline-powered cars.

b. The $2,000 increase in the price of the hybrid car decreases the supply of gasoline-powered cars by 200 cars × $2,000 = 400,000 cars, so the supply curve of gasoline-powered cars shifts to the left by 400,000 cars. In the figure, the initial supply curve is S_0. The increase in the price of a hybrid shifts the supply curve left to S_1, a shift equal to 400,000 cars at every price.

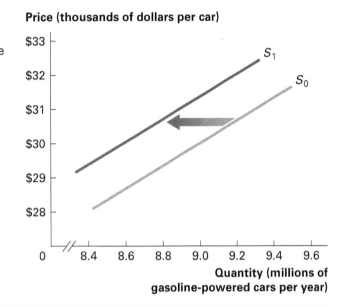

2.3 Market Equilibrium

Learning Objective 2.3 Determine the market equilibrium price and quantity using the demand and supply model.

In competitive markets, the actions of buyers and sellers jointly determine the price and quantity of a given good or service. As you have learned, the demand curve reflects the behavior of buyers, and the supply curve reflects the behavior of sellers. Combining the two curves allows managers to determine the price and quantity of the product.

Equilibrium Price and Equilibrium Quantity

Figure 2.7 combines the demand curve, D, shown in Figure 2.1 and the supply curve, S, shown in Figure 2.4. The curves cross at a price of $60 per pair of jeans. This price, called the **equilibrium price**, is the *only* price at which the quantity demanded equals the quantity supplied.

If the price does not equal the equilibrium price, it will change so that it does. At any price higher than the equilibrium price, there is a *surplus* of jeans—sellers offer more jeans for sale than demanders want to buy. For example, at a price of $100 per pair, the supply curve shows that the quantity of jeans supplied is 500 million pairs, but the demand curve shows that the quantity of jeans demanded is only 100 million pairs. At this price, there is a surplus of 400 million pairs (500 million minus 100 million), resulting in undesired inventories of unsold jeans. The inventories, piling up

Equilibrium price The price at which the quantity demanded equals the quantity supplied.

Figure 2.7 Equilibrium Price and Equilibrium Quantity

The intersection of the demand curve, *D*, and supply curve, *S*, determines the equilibrium price and equilibrium quantity. As shown, the equilibrium price is $60 per pair of jeans, and the equilibrium quantity is 300 million pairs. At any price higher than the equilibrium price, there is a surplus, which forces the price lower until it falls to the equilibrium price. At any price lower than the equilibrium price, there is a shortage, which forces the price higher until it rises to the equilibrium price. *Only* at the equilibrium price is there neither a surplus nor a shortage of jeans.

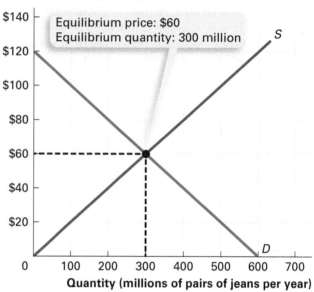

ever higher, lead the firms' managers to lower the price. As the price falls, suppliers cut their production plans, so the quantity supplied decreases and the quantity demanded increases. Both of these changes help decrease the surplus, but as long as there is a surplus, the unwanted inventories continue to accumulate, and the price continues to fall. Eventually, the price falls to the equilibrium price. At this price, there is no longer a surplus of jeans: The quantity of jeans supplied equals the quantity of jeans demanded: 300 million pairs. Because there is no surplus, the price stops falling once it equals the equilibrium price.

Similarly, at any price lower than the equilibrium price, there is a *shortage* of jeans—the quantity of jeans offered for sale is less than the quantity demanders want to buy. Suppose that the price is $20 per pair; at this price, the quantity of jeans demanded is 500 million pairs, but the quantity supplied is only 100 million pairs. The shortage is 500 million minus 100 million, or 400 million pairs of jeans. The shortage means that producers cannot keep jeans in inventory; every pair they place on the racks is gone almost immediately. So the managers raise the price of jeans. As the price rises, the quantity demanded decreases, and producers increase their production plans, so the quantity supplied increases. Although both changes reduce the shortage, the price rises as long as a shortage exists. Eventually, the price rises to $60 per pair. At this equilibrium price, there is no longer a shortage of jeans: The quantity of jeans demanded equals the quantity supplied: 300 million pairs. Once the price equals the equilibrium price, it stops rising because the shortage has been eliminated.

Because the only price that can persist and not change is the equilibrium price, it is reasonable to assume that the market price equals the equilibrium price. Now that you know the price, you need to determine the quantity. At the equilibrium price, the quantity demanded equals the quantity supplied. The **equilibrium quantity** is the quantity bought and sold at the equilibrium price, which equals both the quantity demanded and the quantity supplied. In Figure 2.7, the equilibrium quantity is 300 million pairs of jeans per year, the quantity bought and sold at the $60 equilibrium price.

Equilibrium quantity The quantity bought and sold at the equilibrium price.

The equilibrium price and equilibrium quantity are examples of the general concept of **equilibrium**: a situation in which no automatic forces lead to change. Once at the equilibrium, the situation will persist until some factor changes. You will explore the idea of equilibrium further in future chapters, such as Chapters 5, 6, 7, and 8, when you learn how firms determine the price to charge and the quantity to produce.

Equilibrium A situation in which no automatic forces lead to change; once at the equilibrium, the situation will persist until some factor changes.

Demand and Supply Functions: Equilibrium

In Figure 2.7, the equilibrium price is $60 per pair of jeans, and the equilibrium quantity is 300 million pairs of jeans. You can use the demand function that corresponds to the demand curve in Figure 2.7, $Q^d = 600 \text{ million} - (5 \text{ million} \times P)$, and the supply function that corresponds to the supply curve, $Q^s = 5 \text{ million} \times P$, to check that you get the same equilibrium price and quantity algebraically that you did graphically. At the equilibrium price, the quantity demanded, Q^d, equals the quantity supplied, Q^s, or $Q^d = Q^s$. Equating the demand function and the supply function gives

$$600 \text{ million} - (5 \text{ million} \times P) = 5 \text{ million} \times P$$

To solve for the equilibrium price, first add $(5 \text{ million} \times P)$ to both sides:

$$600 \text{ million} = (5 \text{ million} \times P) + (5 \text{ million} \times P)$$

Next, add the terms on the right side of the equality:

$$600 \text{ million} = 10 \text{ million} \times P$$

Finally, divide by 10 million to solve for the equilibrium price:

$$P = \frac{600 \text{ million}}{10 \text{ million}} = \$60$$

precisely the same equilibrium price shown in Figure 2.7. Using the $60 equilibrium price in *either* the demand or the supply function yields the equilibrium quantity. For example, using the equilibrium price of $60 per pair of jeans in the supply function shows that $Q = 5 \text{ million} \times 60$, or 300 million pairs per year, which also corresponds to the equilibrium quantity shown in Figure 2.7.

More generally, if the demand function is linear and depends only on the price of the product, it can be written as $Q^d = a - (b \times P)$. If the supply function is also linear and also depends only on the price, it can be written as $Q^s = r + (s \times P)$. Then equating the demand function and the supply function gives

$$a - (b \times P) = r + (s \times P)$$

This equation can be solved for the equilibrium price as

$$P = \frac{a - r}{s + b}$$

Use this value for the price in either the demand or the supply function and some algebra to solve for the equilibrium quantity:

$$Q = \frac{(a \times s) + (b \times r)}{s + b}$$

Now that you have learned how to determine the equilibrium price and quantity in a competitive market, you are ready for a related topic: discovering why economists have a strong preference for competitive markets and, as a result, use them as the standard of comparison for all other types of markets.

SOLVED PROBLEM

Equilibrium Price and Quantity of Plush Toys

You are a manager at Content Colleague, a company similar to Happy Worker, a Canadian company that manufactures vinyl, plush, and resin toys and collectibles. Your research specialist has given you demand and supply functions for one of your product lines, plush toys. The demand function for plush toys is $Q^d = 30$ million $- (2$ million $\times P)$. The supply function for plush toys is $Q^s = 3$ million $\times P$. Your supervisor asks you to determine the equilibrium price and equilibrium quantity of plush toys.

Answer
To determine the equilibrium price and quantity, you need to set the demand function equal to the supply function:

$$30 \text{ million} - (2 \text{ million} \times P) = 3 \text{ million} \times P$$

Now solve for the equilibrium price, P:

$$30 \text{ million} = (3 \text{ million} \times P) + (2 \text{ million} \times P)$$

$$30 \text{ million} = 5 \text{ million} \times P$$

$$P = (30 \text{ million})/(5 \text{ million}) = \$6 \text{ per stuffed toy animal}$$

Use this equilibrium price in either the demand or the supply function to determine the equilibrium quantity. Using it in the supply function gives $Q = 3$ million $\times \$6 = 18$ million plush toys.

2.4 Competition and Society

Learning Objective 2.4 Explain why perfectly competitive markets are socially optimal.

Society has a limited amount of resources, such as labor and capital. This limitation makes it impossible to produce unlimited amounts of a good or service, so it is important for society to obtain the greatest benefit from its resources. This section describes how competitive markets foster the optimal allocation of society's scarce resources.

Total Surplus

Figure 2.8 shows the demand and supply curves for jeans. You can use these to determine what quantity of jeans is the socially best quantity to produce.

As we described earlier, the market demand curve, D, shows the maximum price consumers are willing and able to pay for any particular pair of jeans. For example, point A shows that some consumer is willing to pay a maximum price of $100

Price (dollars per pair of jeans)

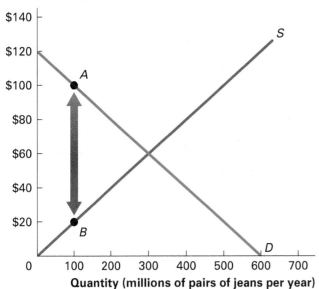

Quantity (millions of pairs of jeans per year)

Figure 2.8 Marginal Benefit and Marginal Cost

The market demand curve, D, shows the highest price a consumer is willing to pay for any particular pair of jeans. This amount equals the marginal benefit to the consumer of that particular pair. Point A shows that the marginal benefit of the 100 millionth pair is $100. The supply curve, S, shows the lowest price a supplier is willing to accept for any pair of jeans. This amount equals the marginal cost of that particular pair of jeans. Point B shows that the marginal cost of the 100 millionth pair is $20. For this pair of jeans, society gains a surplus of marginal benefit over marginal cost of $80. For *all* of the jeans up to 300 million pairs, society enjoys a surplus of marginal benefit over marginal cost.

for the 100 millionth pair. The maximum price the consumer will pay for a pair of jeans equals the consumer's marginal benefit from that pair, so the consumer's marginal benefit from *this* pair is $100. Why is the maximum price equal to the marginal benefit?

- If the marginal benefit exceeded $100, the consumer would be willing to pay more than $100. But the consumer is *not* willing to pay more than $100.
- If the marginal benefit was less than $100, the consumer would not be willing to pay $100. But the consumer *is* willing to pay $100.

Since the consumer's marginal benefit from the pair of jeans cannot be greater than $100 nor can it be less than $100, the marginal benefit must be equal to $100. Because the consumer of this pair of jeans is the recipient of the benefit and is a member of society, the marginal benefit to society is equal to the consumer's marginal benefit. So, society's marginal benefit from the 100 millionth pair of jeans is $100.

The producer's marginal cost of producing any particular pair of jeans can be determined from the supply curve. For example, in Figure 2.8, point B on the supply curve shows that the minimum price some firm is willing to accept to produce the 100 millionth pair of jeans is $20. The minimum price equals the producer's marginal cost of producing *this* pair. Why does the minimum price equal the marginal cost of producing the pair of jeans?

- If the marginal cost exceeded $20, the producer would not be willing to accept $20 for the jeans because that price would inflict a loss on the producer. But the producer *is* willing to accept $20.
- If the marginal cost was less than $20, then the producer would be willing (but not eager!) to accept a lower price because at a lower price the producer still would not incur a loss. But the producer is *not* willing to accept less than $20.

Since the producer's marginal cost of producing the pair of jeans cannot be more than $20 nor can it be less than $20, the marginal cost must be equal to $20. Because the producer pays the marginal cost, the marginal cost to society is equal to the producer's marginal cost. In other words, society's marginal cost of the 100 millionth pair of jeans is $20.

The marginal benefit to society ($100) is greater than the marginal cost ($20). Therefore, producing and consuming this pair of jeans gives society a surplus of marginal benefit over marginal cost of $80. In Figure 2.8, the surplus is equal to the length of the double-headed arrow. The figure also shows that *all* jeans up to the 300 millionth pair (the equilibrium quantity) have a surplus of marginal benefit over marginal cost. If you apply the marginal analysis rule (produce each unit for which the marginal benefit exceeds the marginal cost), you will see that each of the 300 million pairs of jeans should be produced. The *total surplus of benefit over cost* to society from production of the 300 million pairs is the sum of the surpluses of all the pairs of jeans produced. When all 300 million surpluses are added, their sum is equal to the area of the green triangle in Figure 2.9.

The quantity of output that yields the largest total surplus for society is called the **efficient quantity**. In a competitive market, the equilibrium quantity equals the efficient quantity,[8] so in Figure 2.9 the efficient quantity is 300 million pairs of jeans.

Efficient quantity The quantity of output that yields the largest total surplus of marginal benefit over marginal cost for society.

Figure 2.9 Total Surplus

When the equilibrium quantity (300 million pairs of jeans) is produced, the total surplus of benefit over cost to society is equal to the area of the green triangle. The quantity that creates the largest total surplus is the efficient quantity.

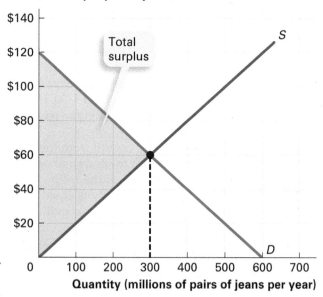

8 There are exceptions to this rule. In particular, the rule fails if the producer does not pay some of the costs of production. For example, if the production creates pollution, then part of the cost of production is the cost of pollution, but the victims of the pollution rather than the producer pay this cost. The rule also fails if the consumer does not receive some of the benefits of consumption. For example, a person who has a flu shot benefits, but so, too, does everyone else who comes in contact with that person. In such cases, the equilibrium quantity does not have the largest total surplus. These topics are beyond the scope of this text, however, and are best left to courses covering microeconomic theory.

Underproduction and Overproduction

What happens to society's total surplus if the quantity produced is not the efficient quantity? Setting aside for a moment the question of why more or less might be produced, marginal analysis can help answer this question. Let's begin by considering the situation in which less than the efficient quantity of 300 million pairs of jeans is produced (underproduction) and then move to the situation in which more than efficient quantity of 300 million pairs is produced (overproduction).

- **Underproduction.** If production is less than 300 million pairs of jeans, some pairs that would have a surplus of marginal benefit over marginal cost are not produced. But according to marginal analysis, these units should be produced. Because these units have a surplus, failure to produce them lowers the total surplus, resulting in a smaller total surplus for society.
- **Overproduction.** If production is more than 300 million pairs of jeans, all of the pairs beyond 300 million have a marginal benefit that is less than their marginal cost. According to marginal analysis, from society's perspective these units should not be produced. The production of any of these units subtracts from the total surplus, again resulting in a smaller total surplus for society.

Figure 2.10 shows the decrease in total surplus. The loss in total surplus from producing less or more than the efficient quantity is called the **deadweight loss**. A deadweight loss is a loss to society. No one gains from a deadweight loss.

At the most fundamental level, manufacturing jeans means that society is putting resources to use. When the quantity of jeans produced is the efficient quantity, resources are allocated optimally, with no deadweight loss and with the largest total surplus. In contrast, when less than the efficient quantity of jeans is produced, a deadweight loss occurs because the marginal benefit of the last pair of jeans exceeds its marginal cost, which means resources are misallocated: More

Deadweight loss The loss in total surplus from producing less or more than the efficient quantity.

Price (dollars per pair of jeans)

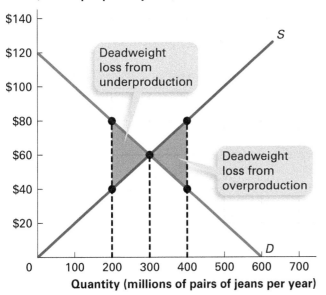

Figure 2.10 Deadweight Loss

A deadweight loss is the loss in total surplus from producing less (underproduction) or more (overproduction) than the efficient quantity, 300 million pairs of jeans. Producing less (say, 200 million pairs) or more (say, 400 million pairs) results in a deadweight loss.

resources should be directed to producing jeans and fewer to producing other goods and services. When more than the efficient quantity of jeans is produced, a deadweight loss occurs because the marginal benefit of the last pair of jeans is less than its marginal cost, which again means resources are misallocated: Fewer resources should be directed to producing jeans and more to producing other goods and services.

Because the equilibrium quantity in a competitive market leads to the largest total surplus for society, economists use competitive markets as the standard of comparison for other market structures. Although this conclusion has no direct implication for you as a manager, it is the basis for the nation's antitrust laws, which certainly do have important consequences for managerial decision making, as you will learn in Chapter 9.

Consumer Surplus

Total surplus can be divided into consumer surplus and producer surplus. Keep in mind that the equilibrium price is the actual price that consumers pay (and suppliers receive). Some consumers are willing to pay more than this price, but the market does not require them to do so. For example, point A in Figure 2.11 shows what you saw in Figure 2.8—that some consumer is willing to pay $100 for the 100 millionth pair of jeans. But that consumer actually pays only $60 (the equilibrium price). The **consumer surplus** is the difference between the maximum price consumers are willing and able to pay for each unit of a product and the price actually paid, summed over the quantity of units purchased. For example, the consumer of the 100 millionth pair of jeans has a consumer surplus equal to $100 − $60 = $40 for that pair. The consumer surplus in the entire market is the total of all of these surpluses on all of the pairs of jeans purchased.

The demand curve in Figure 2.11 shows the maximum price consumers are willing to pay for each pair of jeans. The equilibrium price is the price consumers

Consumer surplus The difference between the maximum price consumers are willing and able to pay for each unit of a product and the price actually paid, summed over the quantity of units purchased.

Figure 2.11 Consumer Surplus

The consumer surplus is the difference between the maximum price consumers are willing to pay for each pair of jeans and the price actually paid, summed over the total number of pairs of jeans purchased. The consumer surplus in the market is equal to the green triangular area under the demand curve (which shows the maximum price the consumer is willing to pay for any pair) and above the equilibrium price (which is the price actually paid).

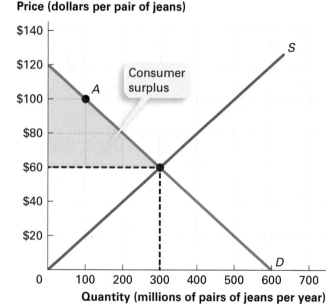

Price (dollars per pair of jeans)

actually pay, so the consumer surplus in the market equals the green triangular area under the demand curve and above the equilibrium price in Figure 2.11.

Consumer surplus presents an intriguing concept for managers. It reveals that consumers are willing to pay more than the amount they actually pay. Future chapters will explore pricing schemes that share the basic goal of transferring consumer surplus from consumers to suppliers as increased profit.

Producer Surplus

The consumer surplus in Figure 2.11 is only part of the total surplus shown in Figure 2.9. The remaining piece goes to producers as producer surplus. The **producer surplus** is the difference between the actual price producers receive for each unit and the minimum price they are willing to accept to produce that unit, summed over the quantity of units produced. In Figure 2.12, as in Figure 2.8, point *B* shows that some producer is willing to produce and sell the 100 millionth pair of jeans for $20 (its marginal cost). But that producer actually receives $60 (the equilibrium price). The producer surplus on this pair is $60 − $20 = $40.[9] The producer surplus in the entire market is the total of the producer surpluses for all the units produced. In Figure 2.12, the producer surplus is the green triangular area under the equilibrium price and above the supply curve.

If you compare Figures 2.11 and 2.12, you will see that the consumer surplus is equal to the producer surplus. This result is a fluke; it occurs only by chance. However, if you compare Figures 2.9, 2.11, and 2.12, you will see that the total surplus shown in Figure 2.9 equals the sum of the consumer surplus in Figure 2.11

Producer surplus The difference between the actual price producers receive for each unit and the minimum price they are willing to accept to produce that unit, summed over the quantity of units produced.

Price (dollars per pair of jeans)

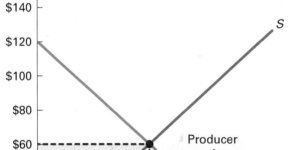

Quantity (millions of pairs of jeans per year)

Figure 2.12 Producer Surplus

Producer surplus is the difference between the actual price suppliers receive for each unit and the minimum price they would be willing to accept to produce that unit (their marginal cost), summed over the quantity of units produced. The producer surplus in the market is equal to the green triangular area under the equilibrium price (which is the actual price the suppliers receive for each pair of jeans) and above the supply curve (which shows the minimum price the suppliers are willing to accept to produce any pair).

---

9 Producer surplus and economic profit are related. In particular, the economic profit for all of the firms in the market equals the total producer surplus minus all of the firms' fixed costs. But the details of this relationship are best covered in a microeconomic theory course.

and the producer surplus in Figure 2.12. This result is *not* a fluke; it is always the case because the total surplus can always be divided into the part that goes to consumers (the consumer surplus) and the part that goes to producers (the producer surplus).

You have seen how to use the demand and supply model to determine the equilibrium price and quantity and why producing the equilibrium quantity is socially optimal because it maximizes the total surplus. The real power of the model, however, comes from its ability to predict what happens to price and quantity if something in the market changes, which is the topic of the next section.

SOLVED PROBLEM

Total Surplus, Consumer Surplus, and Producer Surplus in the Webcam Market

When a market is producing the efficient quantity, must the consumer surplus always equal the producer surplus? Use the market for webcams, and suppose that the equilibrium price is $30 and the equilibrium quantity is 3 million. Then draw two graphs to support your answer.

Answer

Your graphs should look similar to those below. When the market produces the efficient quantity, 3 million webcams per year, the consumer surplus does *not* necessarily equal the producer surplus. In Figure a, the consumer surplus exceeds the producer surplus, while in Figure b, the producer surplus exceeds the consumer surplus. The amounts of the consumer surplus and producer surplus depend on the slopes and shapes of the demand and supply curves.

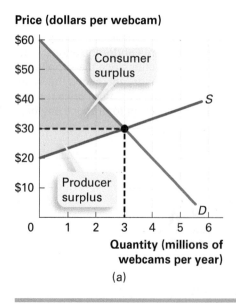

(a)

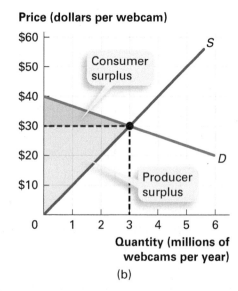

(b)

2.5 Changes in Market Equilibrium

Learning Objective 2.5 Use the demand and supply model to predict how changes in the market affect the price and quantity of a good or service.

The demand and supply model is a powerful tool that can predict what happens to price and quantity if something in the market changes. Making these predictions is an important managerial skill. Once you become familiar enough with figures using demand and supply curves, determining the impact of changes in demand or supply will become second nature—you will know the answer *immediately* without needing a figure. Reaching that stage takes practice, however. This section begins by outlining a four-step procedure that shows how to use a demand and supply figure to predict the effect of a change. We then use this process to explore two scenarios: (1) changes in demand with no change in supply and (2) changes in supply with no change in demand. As a manager, however, you will often deal with situations in which more than one factor changes. The section concludes by presenting and then using a modified four-step procedure to deal with the more complex scenario of simultaneous changes in demand and supply.

Let's start with the four-step procedure that you can use when one factor that affects the market changes:

1. Draw a demand and supply figure like the one shown in Figure 2.7, and label everything—the curves, the axes, and the initial equilibrium price and quantity.
2. Determine which curve, the demand curve or the supply curve, is affected by the factor that changes.
3. Determine whether the change shifts the curve to the right or to the left.
4. Add the new curve to your original diagram to determine the new equilibrium price and quantity.

Now let's apply this procedure, starting first with a change in demand.

Use of the Demand and Supply Model When One Curve Shifts: Demand

What happens to the price and quantity of a good or service if demand increases or decreases? Let's begin by examining the effect of an increase in demand. Recall that the factors that change demand and shift the demand curve include consumers' income, the price of related goods and services, consumers' preferences and advertising, financial market conditions, the expected future price of the product, and the number of demanders. The effect of the change in demand on the price and quantity of a good or service is the same regardless of the factor involved, so let's return to our jeans example and presume that jeans are a normal good so that an increase in consumers' income will increase the demand for jeans.

Increase in Demand

Suppose that the economy enters a strong economic expansion, so people's incomes increase. As a manager at a company that produces jeans, you are interested in how this change will affect the price in the market because that will affect the price you can charge for your jeans. Start with step 1 of the four-step procedure by drawing a demand and supply figure like that in Figure 2.13, with demand curve D_0 and supply

Figure 2.13 An Increase in Demand for Jeans

When the demand for jeans increases, the demand curve shifts to the right, from D_0 to D_1. This shift increases the price of jeans, from $60 to $80 per pair, and increases the quantity, from 300 million to 400 million pairs per year.

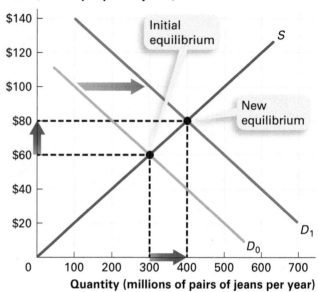

Price (dollars per pair of jeans)

curve S. The initial equilibrium price is $60 per pair, and the initial equilibrium quantity is 300 million pairs of jeans. From Section 2.1, you know that an increase in income for a normal good increases its demand (step 2) and shifts its demand curve to the right (step 3). Finally, draw the new demand curve, D_1, in your figure (step 4). Figure 2.13 shows this as a shift of the demand curve to the right, from D_0 to D_1. The increase in demand raises the equilibrium price of a pair of jeans from $60 to $80 and increases the equilibrium quantity from 300 million to 400 million pairs per year.

Notice that the change in income shifts only the demand curve. There is a *movement along* the supply curve rather than a shift because a change in income is not one of the factors that shifts the supply curve. Regardless of the reason for an increase in demand, the demand curve shifts to the right, there is a movement along the supply curve, and the effects on the price and quantity are identical to what Figure 2.13 illustrates: The price rises and the quantity increases.

Decrease in Demand

A decrease in demand has the opposite effect of the scenario illustrated in Figure 2.13. For example, suppose that people's preferences change: They come to prefer yoga pants more and jeans less. Now start the four-step process once again by drawing your demand and supply diagram (step 1). From Section 2.1, you know that such a change in preferences decreases the demand for jeans (step 2) and shifts the demand curve for jeans to the left (step 3). Draw this new demand curve in your diagram, and determine the effect on the price and quantity (step 4).

Figure 2.14 illustrates this process. The initial demand curve is D_0, and the initial supply curve is S. The change in preferences away from jeans decreases the demand for jeans and shifts the demand curve left to D_1. After the change in preferences decreases the demand, the new equilibrium is where the new demand curve, D_1, and the supply curve, S, intersect. The new equilibrium price is $40 per pair, and the new equilibrium quantity is 200 million pairs per year. As in the previous example,

Price (dollars per pair of jeans)

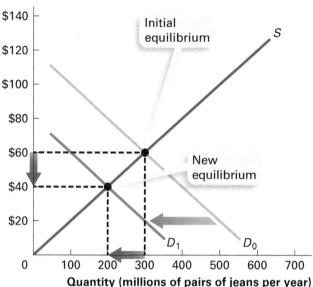

Figure 2.14 A Decrease in Demand for Jeans

When the demand for jeans decreases, the demand curve shifts to the left, from D_0 to D_1. This shift decreases the price of jeans, from $60 to $40 per pair, and decreases the quantity, from 300 million to 200 million pairs per year.

Quantity (millions of pairs of jeans per year)

only the demand curve shifts because a change in preferences is not among the factors that shift the supply curve. Regardless of the reason for a decrease in demand, the effects on the price and quantity are identical to what Figure 2.14 illustrates: The price falls and the quantity decreases.

Use of the Demand and Supply Model When One Curve Shifts: Supply

You have seen how to tackle changes that affect demand. Now you will learn how to handle changes that affect supply using the same four-step procedure. Recall that the factors that change supply and shift the supply curve include changes in cost, the price of related goods and services, technology, the state of nature, the expected future price of the product, and the number of suppliers. The effect on the price and quantity is the same regardless of the factor involved.

Increase in Supply

Suppose that the producers of jeans develop new, more highly automated methods of manufacturing jeans. To determine the effect on the price and quantity of jeans, start by drawing a demand and supply diagram like that in Figure 2.15, with demand curve D and supply curve S_0 (step 1). The intersection of supply curve S_0 and demand curve D determines the initial equilibrium price ($60 per pair) and the initial equilibrium quantity (300 million pairs). The new methods of automation are a technological advance, which affects the supply (step 2) by increasing it and causes a rightward shift in the supply curve (step 3). As shown in Figure 2.15, the supply curve shifts to the right, from S_0 to S_1 (step 4). The new equilibrium is where the new supply curve, S_1, and the demand curve, D, intersect. The equilibrium price falls from $60 to $40 per pair, and the equilibrium quantity increases from 300 million to 400 million pairs per year.

Notice how the technological advance changes only the supply and shifts only the supply curve. The demand curve does not shift because technology is not one of

Figure 2.15 An Increase in Supply of Jeans

When the supply of jeans increases, the supply curve shifts to the right, from S_0 to S_1. This shift lowers the price of jeans, from $60 to $40 per pair, and increases the quantity, from 300 million to 400 million pairs of jeans per year.

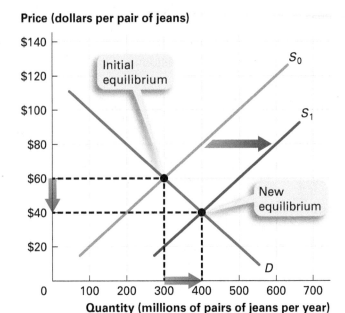

the factors that affect demand. Instead, there is a movement along the demand curve. Regardless of the reason for an increase in the supply, the effects on the price and quantity are identical to what Figure 2.15 illustrates: The price falls and the quantity increases.

Decrease in Supply

Finally, suppose that the price of denim rises. This price hike increases the cost of producing jeans. How will the increase in cost affect the price and quantity of jeans? Again, use the four-step procedure to find the answer. Draw the initial supply curve, S_0, and the demand curve, D, as shown in Figure 2.16 (step 1). The initial equilibrium is where the demand curve, D, intersects the original supply curve, S_0. Now you must determine which curve is affected by the increase in cost. Only the supply curve shifts because a change in cost is not a factor that affects demand (step 2). The increase in cost decreases the supply and shifts the supply curve to the left, from S_0 to S_1 in Figure 2.16 (step 3). After the supply decreases, the new equilibrium is where the demand curve, D, intersects the new supply curve, S_1 (step 4). Figure 2.16 shows that the increase in cost raises the price from $60 to $80 per pair of jeans and decreases the quantity from 300 million to 200 million pairs per year. The demand curve does not shift because cost is not one of the factors that affect demand. Instead, there is a movement along the demand curve. Regardless of the reason for a decrease in the supply of a good or service, the effects on the price and quantity are identical to what Figure 2.16 illustrates: The price rises and the quantity decreases.

Use of the Demand and Supply Model When Both Curves Shift

So far you have learned about the effects of a shift in *either* the supply curve *or* the demand curve. In real-world markets, two or more factors can change at the same time, however, causing both curves to shift simultaneously. The ability to use the demand and supply model to determine the effect on the price and quantity when there is a change in *both* demand and supply is another important managerial skill. Although this situation is slightly more complicated than the one in which only the demand *or* only

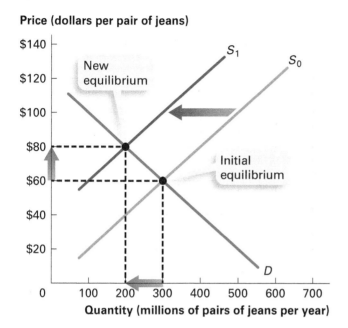

Price (dollars per pair of jeans)

Figure 2.16 A Decrease in Supply of Jeans

When the supply of jeans decreases, the supply curve shifts to the left, from S_0 to S_1. This shift raises the price, from $60 to $80 per pair, and decreases the quantity, from 300 million to 200 million pairs of jeans per year.

the supply changes, if you practice solving problems when both change using the demand and supply model, once again eventually you'll be able to quickly determine the answers without the model. Until that time, however, practice using figures and the following modified version of the four-step procedure described earlier:

1. Draw *two* demand and supply figures, and label everything—the curves, the axes, and the initial equilibrium price and quantity.
2. For the first factor that changes, determine (a) whether it is the demand curve or the supply curve that is affected and (b) the direction of the change.
3. Repeat step 2 for the second factor that changes.
4. In one of your demand and supply figures, draw the new demand curve with a large shift and the new supply curve with a small shift. In the other figure, draw the new demand curve with a small shift and the new supply curve with a large shift. This step might appear odd, but it is necessary because the effect on the price or the quantity depends on which shift is larger. Then you must compare the answers to see if the effect on the price or quantity is certain or ambiguous.

To see how this modified procedure works, we will begin with situations in which demand and supply change in the same way: Both increase or both decrease. Then we will move to situations in which demand and supply change in opposite directions: One increases and the other decreases.

Similar Changes in Demand and Supply

Suppose that both the demand and the supply of a particular product increase. Consider the following scenario: Jeans and denim skirts are substitutes for consumers and the price of denim skirts rises at the same time that more firms start to produce jeans. What will be the impact of these changes on the price and quantity of jeans?

Figure 2.17 demonstrates how to conduct the analysis of this scenario. Begin with step 1 by drawing two demand and supply figures (in parts a and b), with initial demand curve D_0 and initial supply curve S_0. The initial equilibrium price is $60 per pair

Figure 2.17 Increase in Demand for Jeans and Increase in Supply of Jeans

The quantity definitely increases. But without knowing which effect is larger, the price might rise (if the change in demand is larger, as in part a), fall (if the change in supply is larger, as in part b), or not change (not illustrated but occurs if the two changes are of the same magnitude).

(a) **Large Increase in Demand, Small Increase in Supply**
If the increase in demand exceeds the increase in supply, the price rises and the quantity increases.

(b) **Small Increase in Demand, Large Increase in Supply**
If the increase in supply exceeds the increase in demand, the price falls and the quantity increases.

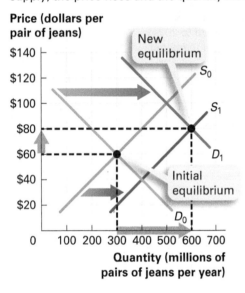

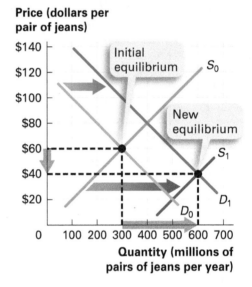

Quantity (millions of pairs of jeans per year)

of jeans, and the initial equilibrium quantity is 300 million pairs of jeans. Next, move to step 2: The increase in the price of denim skirts increases the demand for jeans and shifts the demand curve for jeans to the right. Follow with step 3: The increase in the number of firms increases the supply of jeans and shifts the supply curve to the right. Finally, step 4 is drawing the shifts with different sizes. In both parts of Figure 2.17, the demand curve shifts rightward from D_0 to D_1 and the supply curve shifts rightward from S_0 to S_1. In Figure 2.17(a), however, the demand curve has shifted by more than the supply curve. In this case, the price rises, from $60 to $80 per pair, and the quantity increases, from 300 million to 600 million pairs per year. Compare these results with those in Figure 2.17(b), in which the supply curve has shifted by more than the demand curve. In this case, the price falls, from $60 to $40 per pair, but the quantity still increases, from 300 million to 600 million pairs per year. (The result that the increase in quantity is the same in both situations is a coincidence.)

When both curves shift to the right, the quantity always increases. But unless you know which shift is larger, the impact on the price is ambiguous. If demand increases by more than supply, the price rises. If supply increases by more than demand, the price falls. In fact, in a third scenario, not illustrated in Figure 2.17, if demand increases by the same amount as supply, the price does not change. Knowing the size of each effect—perhaps because your company's research department has determined the relative sizes of the changes—will allow you to determine which result is appropriate so then you can predict the change in *both* price and quantity.

If both the demand and the supply decrease, the situation is the reverse of what you just learned: Both curves shift to the left. The effect on the quantity is certain: Quantity decreases. The effect on the price is uncertain. If demand decreases by more than supply, the price falls. If supply decreases by more than demand, the price rises. If demand and supply decrease by the same amount, the price does not change. In all cases, the quantity decreases, but until you know which effect is larger, the impact on the price is ambiguous.

Opposite Changes in Demand and Supply

You have just learned what happens if both the demand and the supply change in the same direction. Let's now examine what happens if one increases and the other decreases. Consider this scenario: Jeans are a normal good, and people's incomes increase at the same time that significant flooding occurs in the regions where the jean factories are located, damaging many of the factories. What will be the impact of these two changes on the price and quantity of jeans?

Draw two demand and supply diagrams, such as those shown in parts a and b in Figure 2.18 (step 1). The increase in income increases the demand for jeans and shifts the demand curve to the right (step 2). The flooding, a bad state of nature, decreases the supply of jeans and shifts the supply curve to the left (step 2). As in the previous example, for step 4 you need to include the new demand and supply curves in your diagrams, but, following step 3, in one, you make the demand shift larger, and in the other, you make the supply shift larger. Figure 2.18 illustrates this. In both parts of the figure, the demand curve shifts rightward, from D_0 to D_1, and the supply curve shifts leftward, from S_0 to S_1. In Figure 2.18(a), the demand curve has shifted by more than the supply curve. In this case, the price of jeans rises, from $60 to $120 per pair, and the quantity increases, from 300 million to 400 million pairs per year. In Figure 2.18(b), however, the supply curve has shifted by more than the demand curve. The price of jeans still rises, coincidentally again from $60 to $120 per pair, but now the quantity decreases, from 300 million to 200 million pairs per year.

Figure 2.18 Increase in Demand for Jeans and Decrease in Supply of Jeans

The price definitely rises. But without knowing which effect is larger, the quantity might increase (if the change in demand is larger, as in part a), decrease (if the change in supply is larger, as in part b), or not change (not illustrated but occurs if the two changes are of the same magnitude).

(a) **Large Increase in Demand, Small Decrease in Supply**

If the increase in demand exceeds the decrease in supply, the price rises and the quantity increases.

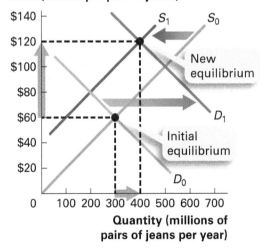

(b) **Small Increase in Demand, Large Decrease in Supply**

If the decrease in supply exceeds the increase in demand, the price rises and the quantity decreases.

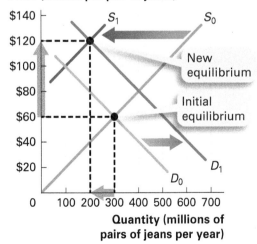

When the demand increases and the supply decreases, the price always rises, but the impact on the quantity is ambiguous. If demand increases by more than supply decreases, the quantity increases. If, on the other hand, supply decreases by more than demand increases, the quantity decreases. In a third scenario, not illustrated in Figure 2.18, the quantity does not change if demand increases by the same amount that supply decreases. Until you know the relative magnitudes of the shifts, the effect on the quantity is uncertain. Of course, if you are working for a large company, your research department might be able to provide you with estimates of the sizes of the changes.

You have probably already guessed that the result of a decrease in demand and an increase in supply will be the opposite of what you just learned. With a decrease in demand and an increase in supply, the demand curve shifts to the left, and the supply curve shifts to the right. Regardless of the magnitude of the shifts, the effect on the price is certain: The price falls. The effect on the quantity is ambiguous. If demand decreases by more than supply increases, the quantity decreases. If supply increases by more than demand decreases, the quantity increases. If the decrease in demand is the same size as the increase in supply, the quantity does not change. You must determine the relative sizes of the shifts in order to determine the impact on the quantity.

Demand and Supply Functions: Changes in Market Equilibrium

As a manager, it is unlikely that you will use algebraic demand and supply functions to determine how the price and quantity of a good or service change when some relevant factor changes. But understanding how to solve for changes in price and quantity helps reinforce the graphical analysis just presented. To keep the algebra straightforward, let's explore the effect of a single change—namely, how an increase in income affects the price and quantity of jeans.

The demand function that depends on the price and income is

$$Q^d = a - (b \times P) + (d \times \text{INCOME})$$

and a simple supply function that depends only on the price is

$$Q^s = r + (s \times P)$$

At the equilibrium price, the quantity demanded, Q^d, equals the quantity supplied, Q^s. Equating the quantity demanded and the quantity supplied gives

$$a - (b \times P) + (d \times \text{INCOME}) = r + (s \times P) \qquad \textbf{2.6}$$

Solving this equation for the equilibrium price[10] gives

$$P = \frac{a + (d \times \text{INCOME}) - r}{s + b} \qquad \textbf{2.7}$$

Use this price in *either* the demand or the supply function to solve for the equilibrium quantity. Using it in the supply function gives

$$Q = r + \left[s \times \frac{a + (d \times \text{INCOME}) - r}{(s + b)} \right] \qquad \textbf{2.8}$$

---

10 To solve for the price, first add $(b \times P)$ to both sides of Equation 2.6 to get $a + (d \times \text{INCOME}) = r + (s \times P) + (b \times P)$. Then subtract r from both sides to get $a + (d \times \text{INCOME}) - r = (s \times P) + (b \times P)$. Next, collect the terms on the right side to give $a + (d \times \text{INCOME}) - r = (s + b) \times P$. Finally, divide both sides by $(s + b)$ to get the expression for the price, $P = \frac{(a + (d \times \text{INCOME}) - r)}{(s + b)}$.

After some algebra, Equation 2.8 can be written as

$$Q = \frac{(r \times b) + (s \times a) + (s \times d \times \text{INCOME})}{s + b} \qquad \text{2.9}$$

The equilibrium price and quantity can now be determined using the values of the coefficients, a, b, d, r, and s, and the level of income. For example, suppose that $a = 200$ million pairs of jeans, $b = 5$ million pairs per dollar, $d = 10,000$ pairs per dollar of income, $r = 0$, $s = 5$ million pairs per dollar, and INCOME $= \$40,000$. Using the values for the coefficients and income in the equations for the equilibrium price, Equation 2.7, and equilibrium quantity, Equation 2.9, gives $P = \$60$ per pair and $Q = 300$ million pairs per year.

These equations for the equilibrium price and quantity show the effect of a change in income on the price and the quantity. If income falls to $20,000, you can plug this new value into the equations for the equilibrium price and quantity to show that the decrease in income changes the price, P, to $40 per pair and the quantity, Q, to 200 million pairs per year. Just as illustrated in Figure 2.14, a decrease in income decreases both the price and the quantity of a normal good.

Table 2.1 summarizes the results when both demand and supply change, so that both curves shift.

So now you know how the equilibrium price and quantity are determined in competitive markets and how they change with a change in a factor that influences those markets. In some markets, however, the government imposes price controls that place restrictions on the price so that it cannot reach its equilibrium. Price controls are covered in the next section.

Table 2.1 Summary of the Effects of Changes in Both Demand and Supply

	DEMAND INCREASES, SUPPLY INCREASES				DEMAND DECREASES, SUPPLY DECREASES			
	Demand Increase > Supply Increase	Demand Increase = Supply Increase	Demand Increase < Supply Increase	Unknown if Demand Increase >, =, or < Supply Increase	Demand Decrease > Supply Decrease	Demand Decrease = Supply Decrease	Demand Decrease < Supply Decrease	Unknown if Demand Decrease >, =, or < Supply Decrease
Price	↑	No change	↓	Ambiguous	↓	No change	↑	Ambiguous
Quantity	↑	↑	↑	↑	↓	↓	↓	↓
	DEMAND INCREASES, SUPPLY DECREASES				DEMAND DECREASES, SUPPLY INCREASES			
	Demand Increase > Supply Decrease	Demand Increase = Supply Decrease	Demand Increase < Supply Decrease	Unknown if Demand Increase >, =, or < Supply Decrease	Demand Decrease > Supply Increase	Demand Decrease = Supply Increase	Demand Decrease < Supply Increase	Unknown if Demand Decrease >, =, or < Supply Increase
Price	↑	↑	↑	↑	↓	↓	↓	↓
Quantity	↑	No change	↓	Ambiguous	↓	No change	↑	Ambiguous

Demand and Supply for Tablets Both Change

The demand function for tablets is

$$Q^d = 240 \text{ million} - (0.5 \text{ million} \times P) + (1,000 \times INCOME)$$

where P is the price of a tablet and INCOME is average income. The supply function for tablets is

$$Q^s = (400,000 \times P) - (200,000 \times COST)$$

where COST is the cost of producing a tablet. Without calculating the values of the equilibrium price and quantity, if the cost of producing a tablet rises by $1 and average income rises by $1, what is the effect on the equilibrium price and equilibrium quantity of tablets?

Answer

The increase in cost decreases the supply, which raises the price and decreases the quantity; the increase in income increases the demand, which also raises the price but increases the quantity. Clearly, the price rises. The effect on the quantity depends on which change is larger. The $1 increase in cost decreases the supply by $-200,000 \times \$1$, or $-200,000$ tablets, so the supply curve shifts to the left by 200,000 tablets. The $1 increase in income increases the demand by $1,000 \times \$1$, or 1,000 tablets, so the demand curve shifts to the right by 1,000 tablets. The decrease in supply is larger than the increase in demand, so the quantity of tablets decreases.

2.6 Price Controls

Learning Objective 2.6 Explain the effects of price ceilings and price floors.

You have learned how to determine the equilibrium price and quantity using the demand and supply model. Sometimes, however, laws prevent the market price from reaching its equilibrium. For example, in Takoma Park, Maryland, the local government has passed an ordinance that limits the maximum rent landlords can charge. This is an example of a **price ceiling**, which is a government regulation that sets the maximum legal price. The federal government has also passed laws establishing minimum prices. In 2017, the minimum price for runner peanuts is $354 per ton throughout the United States. Such laws are examples of a **price floor**, which is a government regulation that sets the minimum legal price. These types of government regulations can affect the market by making the equilibrium price illegal. As a manager, you need to know how they affect your firm. Let's begin by examining the effects from a price ceiling and then move to those from a price floor.

Price ceiling A government regulation that sets the maximum legal price.

Price floor A government regulation that sets the minimum legal price.

Price Ceiling

Figure 2.19 shows the market for apartments in a city like Takoma Park. The price measured along the vertical axis is the rent per month, and the quantity measured along the horizontal axis is the number of apartments rented per month. With no price ceiling, the equilibrium rent is $800 per month, and the equilibrium quantity is 1,200 apartments rented per month.

Suppose, however, that the city government sets a price ceiling of $600 per month. Because the price ceiling is below the equilibrium rent, the price ceiling

Price (rent per month)

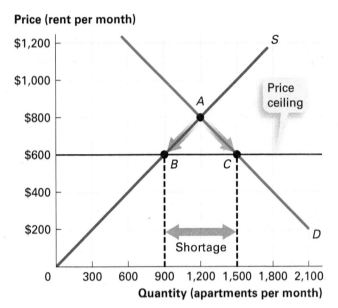

Figure 2.19 A Price Ceiling

Without a price ceiling, the equilibrium rent is $800 per month, and the equilibrium quantity is 1,200 apartments rented per month. If the government imposes a price ceiling of $600 per month, the quantity of apartments demanded is 1,500 (point *C*), and the quantity supplied is only 900 (point *B*). There is a shortage equal to the length of the light red double-headed arrow, which is 1,500 apartments minus 900 apartments, or 600 apartments per month.

makes the equilibrium rent illegal.[11] The law forces the rent down, from $800 to $600. As the rent falls, there is a movement along the demand curve from point *A* to point *C*, so that the quantity demanded increases from 1,200 to 1,500 apartments. Simultaneously, there is a movement along the supply curve from point *A* to point *B*, representing a decrease in the quantity supplied to 900 apartments. With the lower rent, some landlords will convert their buildings from apartments to condominiums; others may elect to stop renting their basements as apartments because they decide that with the lower rent, it is simply not worth the hassle. With the rent control, although tenants want to rent 1,500 apartments, only 900 are rented because that is the quantity supplied. There is a shortage of 600 apartments, or 1,500 demanded minus 900 supplied. If there is no price control, a shortage pushes the price higher. With a price ceiling, the price cannot rise, however, so the shortage persists indefinitely.

A shortage has two effects:

- **Search.** Because many buyers are frustrated in their attempt to buy the product, they search to find it. **Search**, the activity of finding a seller who has the good or service available for sale, is costly in terms of both the time and effort spent and the direct costs, including gasoline and other transportation costs.
- **Black markets.** As a result of a persistent shortage and the frustration of buyers who cannot find the product to buy, **black markets**—markets in which buyers and sellers illegally purchase and sell goods or services at unlawful prices—frequently arise.

Search The activity of finding a seller who has the product available for sale.

Black market A market in which buyers and sellers illegally purchase and sell goods or services at unlawful prices.

Price ceilings harm the affected suppliers because they receive a lower price for their product. Demanders who buy the product at the lower ceiling price and do not have to undertake much search benefit from a price ceiling. Demanders who either cannot find the product at all or wind up paying substantial search costs before buying it are harmed. As you learned in Section 2.4, society is worse off because the rent control forces the quantity away from the efficient amount, thereby creating a deadweight loss.

---

11 If the price ceiling is set above the equilibrium price, it has no effect: Because the equilibrium price remains legal, the price remains at its equilibrium.

Price Floor

The government has imposed price floors in the markets for some agricultural products. The minimum wage in the labor market is another example of a price floor. In this section, we examine the effects of both of these price floors.

Price Floor in an Agricultural Market

Figure 2.20 shows the market for peanuts. Suppose that in the absence of government intervention, the equilibrium price is $520 per ton of peanuts, and the equilibrium quantity is 1.6 million tons per year. Further suppose that the government imposes a price floor of $535 per ton. This price floor is above the equilibrium price of $520 and makes the equilibrium price illegal.[12] The price must rise from the equilibrium price to the floor price of $535. As Figure 2.20 shows, the price rise creates a movement along the supply curve from point A to point C and increases the quantity supplied to 2.2 million tons per year. The price rise also creates a movement along the demand curve from point A to point B and decreases the quantity demanded to 1.0 million tons per year. With the price floor, peanut consumers buy only 1.0 million tons of peanuts. There is a surplus of peanuts equal to 2.2 million tons supplied minus 1.0 million tons demanded, or 1.2 million tons. If there was no price floor, a surplus would push the price lower. With a price floor, the price cannot fall, so the surplus persists indefinitely.

To maintain the price floor in agricultural markets, the government must somehow take the surplus off the market. At times, it has done so by paying farmers not to grow the crop, which decreases the supply and eliminates the surplus before it occurs. At other times, it has purchased the surplus and either stored it or used it as food aid abroad. Because the government removes the surplus, all producers gain from a price floor because they *receive* a higher price. All demanders lose from a price floor because they *pay* a higher price.

Figure 2.20 A Price Floor

Without a price floor, the equilibrium price is $520 per ton of peanuts, and the equilibrium quantity is 1.6 million tons of peanuts per year. If the government imposes a price floor of $535 per ton, the quantity of peanuts supplied is 2.2 million tons (point C), and the quantity demanded is only 1.0 million tons (point B). There is a persistent surplus of peanuts equal to the length of the green doubled-headed arrow, 1.2 million tons of peanuts per year.

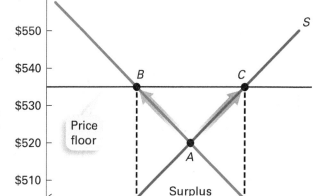

12 If the price floor is set below the equilibrium price, it has no effect: Because the equilibrium price remains legal, the price remains at its equilibrium.

Minimum Wage in the Labor Market

To this point, the discussion has dealt exclusively with markets for the products firms produce. But there also are markets for the inputs firms use, such as labor. These markets are often highly competitive, especially for low-skilled labor. There is a significant difference between product markets and input markets: In a product market, households demand the product, and firms supply it. In an input market, such as the labor market, households supply labor, and firms demand it. Even with this difference, the law of demand and the law of supply still apply in labor markets:

- **The law of demand in the labor market.** When the wage rate rises and nothing else changes, workers become more expensive to employ. Managers respond to the increased cost by decreasing the quantity of labor they demand. Similarly, when the wage rate falls and nothing else changes, managers increase the quantity of labor they demand. The downward slope of the labor demand curve, LD, in Figure 2.21 shows this inverse relationship between wage rate and quantity of labor demanded.
- **The law of supply in the labor market.** When the wage rate rises and nothing else changes, some people respond by increasing the hours they will work. In addition, people who were not working at the lower wage rate decide that the higher wage rate will make it worthwhile to take a job. As a result, workers increase the quantity of labor supplied when the wage rate rises. Conversely, when the wage rate falls and nothing else changes, workers decrease the quantity of labor they supply. This direct relationship between wage rate and quantity of labor supplied is illustrated by the upward slope of the labor supply curve, LS, in Figure 2.21.

The minimum wage can have an effect in the market for low-skilled labor. In the absence of government intervention, in Figure 2.21 the equilibrium wage rate and employment are determined at point A, where the labor demand and labor supply curves intersect. In this case, the equilibrium wage rate is $10 an hour, and the equilibrium quantity is 40 million hours of labor per year.

Wage rate (dollars per hour)

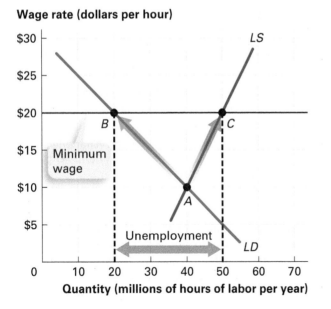

Figure 2.21 A Minimum Wage

Without a minimum wage, the equilibrium wage rate is $10 per hour, and the equilibrium quantity is 40 million hours of labor per year. If the government sets a minimum wage of $20 per hour, the quantity of labor supplied is 50 million hours (point C), and the quantity demanded is only 20 million hours (point B)— that is, 20 million hours of labor are employed. There is a surplus, or unemployment, of 30 million hours per year, equal to the length of the light red double-headed arrow.

Minimum wage The lowest legal wage rate an employer can pay a worker.

The federal government and many state and local governments have established minimum wage laws for the labor market. A **minimum wage** is the lowest legal wage rate an employer can pay a worker. It is effectively a price floor in the labor market. Proponents of minimum wages sometimes call them "living wages."

Suppose that the government imposes a minimum wage of $20 per hour in the labor market, as illustrated in Figure 2.21. Because the minimum wage is set above the equilibrium wage rate, it makes the equilibrium wage rate illegal and therefore changes the outcome in the labor market.[13] The lowest wage rate that can be paid (or received) is $20 per hour, so the wage rate must rise from its equilibrium value of $10 per hour. The rise in the wage rate creates a movement along the labor supply curve from point A to point C and increases the quantity of labor supplied to 50 million hours per year. The rise in the wage rate also creates a movement along the labor demand curve from point A to point B and decreases the quantity of labor demanded to 20 million hours per year. The quantity of labor employed with the $20 minimum wage is 20 million hours per year, the quantity that firms demand. At the minimum wage, there is a surplus of 30 million hours of labor, equal to 50 million hours of labor supplied minus 20 million hours of labor employed. This surplus of hours represents unemployment: Workers are searching for work but are unable to find it because of the lower demand.

Unlike the situation in agricultural markets, the government does not employ the surplus of labor. The workers remain unemployed. Consequently, not all low-skilled workers gain from the minimum wage. Workers who retain their jobs receive a higher wage rate, so they gain. Workers who lose their job and cannot find another or find one only after a long and costly search lose. Of course, all employers who hire low-skilled workers lose because they must pay a higher wage rate.

---

13 Similar to the situation with a price floor, if the minimum wage is set below the equilibrium wage rate, the minimum wage has no effect: Because the equilibrium wage rate remains legal, the wage rate remains at its equilibrium.

SOLVED PROBLEM

The Effectiveness of a Minimum Wage

In Figure 2.21, the initial equilibrium wage is $10 per hour, and employment is 40 million hours per year.

a. Suppose that the government sets a minimum wage of $5 per hour. What effect does this minimum wage have on the wage rate and quantity of employment? Draw a graph to support your answer.

b. Suppose that the government sets a minimum wage at $15 per hour. What effect does this minimum wage have on the wage rate and quantity of employment? Draw a graph to support your answer.

Answer

a. The minimum wage has been set *below* the equilibrium wage so it will have no effect. In particular, your figure should look similar to Figure a. It shows that at the minimum wage of $5 per hour, the quantity of labor demanded, 50 million hours, exceeds the quantity supplied, 35 million. At this wage rate, there is a shortage. Nothing prevents the wage rate from rising, so the shortage pushes the wage rate

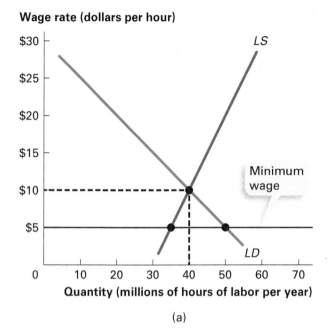

Wage rate (dollars per hour)

(a)

Wage rate (dollars per hour)

(b)

back to its initial equilibrium level, $10 per hour. Once at the equilibrium wage, employment remains equal to 40 million hours per year.

b. The minimum wage has been set *above* the equilibrium wage, so it will have an effect. Your figure should look similar to Figure b. The wage becomes $15 per hour, the minimum wage. At this wage rate, the quantity of labor supplied, 45 million hours, exceeds the quantity demanded, 30 million. So employment is 30 million hours per year, the quantity of labor firms will hire, and unemployment (a surplus) is 15 million hours per year, shown in Figure b by the double-headed arrow. Unemployment persists because the wage rate cannot fall, since $15 per hour is the minimum legal wage.

2.7 Using the Demand and Supply Model

MANAGERIAL APPLICATION

Learning Objective 2.7 Apply the demand and supply model to make better managerial decisions.

As a manager, you can use the demand and supply model to predict how the costs or the price of your product might change. Let's begin by exploring how the model can help you predict your costs and thereby increase your profit.

Predicting Your Costs

Kellogg Company, a major cereal and cookie manufacturer based in Battle Creek, Michigan, buys tons of corn annually. Because corn is a significant expense for the firm, its purchasing managers carefully monitor corn prices. Although Kellogg is a major corn buyer, the market for corn is so huge that the firm has no influence on its price. Suppose that a similar company employs you in its purchasing department. Your company also has no influence on the price of corn, but just like Kellogg's purchasing managers, you, too, will carefully monitor the market for corn.

Figure 2.22 The Market for Corn

When the government passed laws requiring that refineries add ethanol to gasoline, the demand for corn increased, and the demand curve for corn shifted to the right, from D_0 to D_1. This shift raised the price of corn, which has the potential to raise your company's costs dramatically.

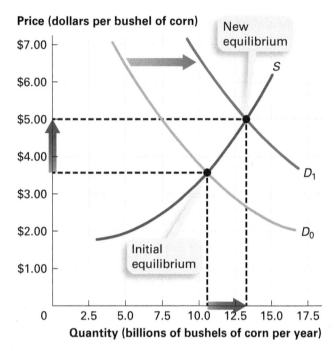

Between 2004 and 2008, oil prices rose from $40 per barrel to near $90. In response, the U.S. Congress passed the Energy Policy Act of 2005 and the much more ambitious Energy Independence and Security Act of 2007. These laws required refineries to add renewable fuels, largely ethanol, to the gasoline they refined. Within four years, this legal requirement nearly tripled the amount of ethanol produced, from 3.5 billion gallons in 2004 to 9.3 billion gallons in 2008. In the United States, corn is the primary input used to produce ethanol. The demand and supply model provides a straightforward way to determine how passage of these laws affected the price (and quantity) of corn.

As ethanol producers stepped up their purchases of corn to make more ethanol, there was a vast increase in the number of buyers of corn. You have learned that an increase in the number of buyers increases the demand and shifts the demand curve to the right. As illustrated in Figure 2.22, from 2006 to 2007 the increase in demand raised the price of corn from an average of about $3.50 per bushel to $5.00 per bushel. This change also increased the quantity, but the key for you as a purchaser is the higher price you will be forced to pay. Knowing that the price of corn will rise in response to the passage of these laws gives you a potential edge: If you can buy corn using a long-term contract before the price rises, you can save your company a substantial sum of money. Of course, people in the purchasing departments of other companies and major growers of corn will also be alert to the possibility of a higher price, so you will need to act quickly to scoop up any savings. But it's clear how using the demand and supply model gives you an opportunity to reduce your costs.

Predicting Your Price

In addition to providing information about the inputs you buy, the demand and supply model can give you key insights into changes in the price of the products and services you sell. Suppose that you are an executive working for a company like Toyota. You are overseeing the pricing and production of hybrid cars like Toyota's Prius. Your firm, of course, is one of many automakers producing and selling hybrids. A crucial selling point of hybrids is their notable fuel economy. For example, many

Price (thousands of dollars per hybrid car)

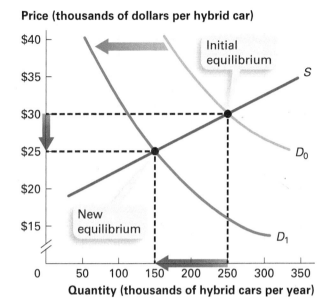

Quantity (thousands of hybrid cars per year)

Figure 2.23 The Market for Hybrid Cars

When the price of gasoline falls, the demand for hybrid cars decreases, so the demand curve shifts to the left, from D_0 to D_1. This shift lowers both the price and the quantity of hybrid cars.

hybrid models have EPA fuel economy ratings over 50 mpg. Consumers view hybrids as substitutes for gasoline-powered cars—they buy hybrids to avoid buying as much gasoline as they would if they purchased a gasoline-powered car. So the demand for hybrids depends on the price of gasoline. Since it reached its peak of near $4.00 per gallon in 2012, the price of gasoline has fallen substantially. This remarkable decrease in price has reduced the cost of operating a gasoline-powered car. Suppose that government analysts forecast that gasoline prices will remain low for the next several years and your research department agrees with this prediction. How can you use the demand and supply model to increase your profit?

Because hybrids are a substitute for gasoline-powered cars, the lower price of gasoline decreases the demand for hybrids. In Figure 2.23, the demand curve for hybrids shifts left, from D_0 to D_1. The decrease in demand lowers the price and quantity of hybrid cars. Knowing that the price and quantity will decrease in the future allows you to make better, more informed decisions. You can take several approaches in order to produce fewer hybrids:

- You might begin planning to run one shift a day on the assembly lines producing hybrids rather than two.
- You could explore converting assembly lines away from producing hybrids and toward producing more popular vehicles.
- You might try to make deals with your suppliers to decrease purchases of hybrid components, such as batteries, so they will not pile up in inventory, where they could depreciate due to technological obsolescence or simply aging.
- The federal government has imposed Corporate Average Fuel Economy regulations that automakers must meet. These standards set average-miles-per-gallon requirements for the automakers' fleets of small cars, small trucks, large cars, and large trucks. Knowing that the demand for high-mpg hybrid cars will decrease means you must take other actions to meet these targets.

Using the demand and supply model can allow you to make decisions such as these that can help increase your firm's profit.

Revisiting How Managers at Red Lobster Coped with Early Mortality Syndrome

At the start of the chapter, you learned that early mortality syndrome (EMS) in Asia affected the supply of shrimp. Using what you have learned in this chapter, you can classify EMS as a bad state of nature. A bad state of nature decreases supply, so you know that the supply curve for shrimp shifts to the left. Thailand is the world's largest shrimp exporter. EMS caused the price of Thai shrimp to rise about 40 percent, from $4,500 to $6,000 per ton of shrimp, as shown in Figure 2.24. It also decreased the quantity of shrimp from 600 thousand tons to 300 thousand tons per year.

Using this sort of analysis, Red Lobster's managers realized that EMS was a potentially severe problem even before it spread from its initial location in China. Using demand and supply analysis, the managers knew that the price of shrimp might soar. They quickly arranged to buy shrimp under long-term contracts at a fixed price, locking in the price before other buyers and sellers of shrimp realized that the price was soon to skyrocket. Once other buyers and sellers learned that the price of shrimp was heading up, its price under new long-term contracts also rose. As EMS spread, the price of shrimp rose, as analyzed above. But the long-term contracts temporarily insulated Red Lobster from the higher price. The managers' use of the demand and supply model significantly increased profit for Red Lobster.

Figure 2.24 A Decrease in the Supply of Shrimp

When the supply of shrimp decreases, the supply curve shifts to the left, from S_0 to S_1. This shift raises the price of shrimp, from $4,500 per ton to $6,000 per ton, and decreases the quantity of shrimp, from 600 thousand tons to 300 thousand tons per year.

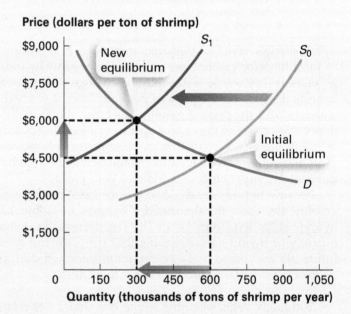

Summary: The Bottom Line

2.1 Demand

- The law of demand states that, everything else remaining the same, a higher price decreases the quantity demanded and a lower price increases the quantity demanded. This law explains the downward slope of the demand curve.
- A change in the price of a product results in a change in the quantity demanded and a movement along the demand curve. Changes in other relevant factors— including consumers' income, the price of related goods and services, consumers' preferences and advertising, financial market conditions, the expected future price of the product, and the number of demanders—change the demand and shift the demand curve. If demand increases, the demand curve shifts to the right. If demand decreases, the demand curve shifts to the left.

2.2 Supply

- The law of supply states that, every else remaining the same, a higher price increases the quantity supplied and a lower price decreases the quantity supplied. This law explains the upward slope of the supply curve.
- A change in the price of a product results in a change in the quantity supplied and a movement along the supply curve. Changes in other relevant factors—including cost, the price of related goods or services, technology, the state of nature, the expected future price of the product, and the number of suppliers—change the supply and shift the supply curve. If supply increases, the supply curve shifts to the right. If supply decreases, the supply curve shifts to the left.

2.3 Market Equilibrium

- In the demand and supply model, the intersection of the demand and supply curves determines the equilibrium price and quantity. The equilibrium price sets the quantity demanded equal to the quantity supplied. The equilibrium quantity is the quantity bought and sold at the equilibrium price.
- The market price is the equilibrium price, and the market quantity transacted is the equilibrium quantity.

2.4 Competition and Society

- Perfectly competitive markets are socially optimal because the equilibrium quantity maximizes society's total surplus of benefit over cost from the product. Producing more or less than the equilibrium quantity decreases the total surplus by creating a deadweight loss.
- Consumer surplus is the difference between the maximum price consumers are willing to pay and the price they actually pay, summed over the quantity consumed. Producer surplus is the difference between the price the firm actually receives and the lowest price it would be willing to accept to produce the product, summed over the quantity produced. The total surplus is the sum of the consumer surplus and the producer surplus.

2.5 Changes in Market Equilibrium

- To use the demand and supply model to predict how changes in relevant factors affect the price and quantity of a product, determine whether the factor changes demand and/or supply and whether it causes an increase or a decrease.
- If only demand *or* only supply changes, the demand and supply model shows how *both* the price and the quantity change. If both the demand *and* the supply change, the demand and supply model unambiguously predicts changes in *either* price *or* quantity. Without information about the relative size of the changes, the change in the other variable is ambiguous.

2.6 Price Controls

- Price ceilings set the maximum legal price. If a price ceiling is set below the equilibrium price, the new price in the market becomes the ceiling price, and a shortage results. The shortage leads to increased search and the creation of black markets.
- Price floors set the minimum legal price. Price floors are often set in agricultural markets and in the labor market. If a price floor is set above the equilibrium price, the new price in the market becomes the floor price, and a surplus of the product results. In agricultural markets, the government buys the surplus to maintain the price floor. In the labor market, the labor surplus is unemployment.

2.7 Managerial Application: Using the Demand and Supply Model

- The demand and supply model can help guide purchasing and production decisions.
- The demand and supply model can help you predict when the price of inputs will rise or fall, thereby leading you toward profitable decisions about when to buy them. The model can also help you predict the future price of a product, enabling you to make profitable decisions about whether to expand or contract your business or when to increase or decrease your production.

Key Terms and Concepts

Black market	Equilibrium	Price ceiling
Complements	Equilibrium price	Price floor
Complements in production	Equilibrium quantity	Producer surplus
Consumer surplus	Income effect	Search
Deadweight loss	Inferior good or service	Substitutes
Demand curve	Market	Substitutes in production
Demand function	Minimum wage	Substitution effect
Efficient quantity	Normal good or service	Supply curve

Questions and Problems

All exercises are available on MyEconLab; solutions to even-numbered Questions and Problems appear in the back of this book.

• 2.1 Demand

Learning Objective 2.1 Describe the factors that affect the demand for goods and services.

1.1 Which represents the law of demand: a shift of the demand curve or a movement along the demand curve? Explain your answer.

1.2 "Romaine lettuce is far more nutritious than iceberg lettuce. Therefore, iceberg lettuce is an inferior good." Is this description of iceberg lettuce as an inferior good correct in economic terms? Explain your answer.

1.3 Suppose that banks increase the amount of information they require from potential borrowers before approving car loans. How would this change affect the demand curve for automobiles?

1.4 What effect does each of the following have on the demand curve for jeans?
   a. A decrease in income if jeans are a normal good
   b. A fall in the price of jeans
   c. A rise in the price of cargo pants, a substitute for jeans
   d. A widespread perception that wearing jeans is not as fashionable as it once was

1.5 Your firm, Content Colleague, is similar to Happy Worker, a Canadian company that designs and manufactures toys and collectibles. Your research analyst has estimated the demand function for your stuffed toy animals is

$$Q^d = 30 \text{ million} - (2 \text{ million} \times P)$$

   a. If you set the price of a plush toy at $5, how many will consumers buy?
   b. If you increase the price of a plush toy by $1, how will this change the quantity that your customers buy?

2.2 Supply

Learning Objective 2.2 Describe the factors that affect the supply of goods and services.

2.1 What is the difference between cost and price? If the cost of producing a good or service rises, what is the effect on the supply curve? What is the effect on the supply curve of an increase in the price of the good or service?

2.2 How does an increase in the price of the cheese used to produce pizza affect the supply curve of pizza?

2.3 Toyota's factory in Georgetown, Kentucky, can use its assembly lines to produce either the Toyota Camry or the Camry Hybrid.
   a. For this Toyota factory, are the Camry and Camry Hybrid substitutes in production or complements in production?
   b. How will the supply of the Camry respond to an increase in the price of the Camry Hybrid?

2.4 What effect does each of the following have on the supply curve of jeans?
   a. A rise in the price of transporting the jeans from Thailand, where they are made, to the United States, where they are sold
   b. A fall in the wages paid the workers who sew jeans
   c. A rise in the price of jeans
   d. An increase in the number of companies manufacturing jeans

2.3 Market Equilibrium

Learning Objective 2.3 Determine the market equilibrium price and quantity using the demand and supply model.

3.1 Among all possible prices, what makes the equilibrium price unique?

3.2 If the price in a market is less than the equilibrium price, what happens to restore the equilibrium price?

3.3 The figure shows a hypothetical market for NFL-caliber punters.
   a. How many punters will the NFL hire? Explain your answer.
   b. What salary will these punters receive? Explain your answer.

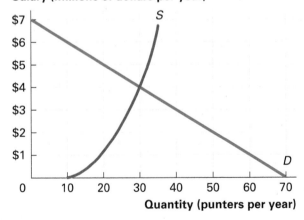

Salary (millions of dollars per year)

3.4 The demand function for a product is $Q^d = 1,000 - 10P$, and its supply function is $Q^s = 100 + 2P$. Calculate the equilibrium price and equilibrium quantity of the good. Check your answer by drawing the demand and supply curves in a figure.

2.4 Competition and Society

Learning Objective 2.4 Explain why perfectly competitive markets are socially optimal.

4.1 Carefully explain how economists
  a. Use the demand curve to measure the marginal social benefit of a good or service.
  b. Use the supply curve to measure the marginal social cost of a good or service.
  c. Measure the total surplus of a unit of a good or service.

4.2 Describe the social gains from competitive markets.

4.3 Explain how producing less than the equilibrium quantity decreases society's total surplus and how producing more than the equilibrium quantity also decreases society's total surplus.

2.5 Changes in Market Equilibrium

Learning Objective 2.5 Use the demand and supply model to predict how changes in the market affect the price and quantity of a good or service.

5.1 Does an increase in the price of jet fuel shift the demand curve for airline travel, the supply curve of airline travel, or both? Explain your answer.

5.2 How does a change in people's preferences in favor of wearing jeans shift the demand curve for jeans? The supply curve? How does a decrease in the number of producers of jeans shift the demand curve for jeans? The supply curve?

5.3 High-quality pasta products are made from 100 percent semolina, which is made from durum wheat. Suppose that a drought decreases the quantity of durum wheat. Answer each of the following questions. Draw demand and supply diagrams to illustrate each answer.
  a. How will the drought affect the equilibrium price and quantity of high-quality spaghetti?
  b. How will the drought affect the equilibrium price and quantity of spaghetti sauces?
  c. For consumers, pasta and rice are substitutes. How will the drought affect the equilibrium price and quantity of rice?

5.4 Peanut butter and jelly are complements for consumers. What happens to the equilibrium price and quantity of jelly if the peanut harvest is especially bountiful? Explain your answer, and illustrate it with a demand and supply figure.

5.5 The figure shows the market for televisions. The initial supply curve is S_0. After a change occurs, the supply curve becomes S_1.

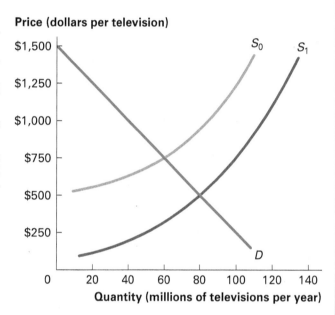

  a. Before the change occurs, what were the initial equilibrium price and quantity? After the change occurs, what are the new equilibrium price and quantity?
  b. Give an example of a change that could lead to the shift illustrated in the figure.
  c. Based on your answer to part b, if you are an executive at a firm like LG Corporation, a Korean manufacturer of televisions, what managerial decisions will you make?

5.6 Baseball gloves are made from cowhide. Suppose that reports of bovine spongiform encephalopathy (mad cow disease) have decreased the demand for beef. Using a demand and supply diagram, explain the impact of mad cow disease on the equilibrium price and quantity of baseball gloves.

5.7 Suppose that you own Lauderdale Aerial Spraying, a large Texas crop-dusting company. Drones are able to spray crops at lower cost than manned planes. Currently, Federal Aviation Administration (FAA) regulations prohibit the use of drones for crop dusting or other precision agricultural use.

a. If the FAA eliminates these regulations, what will happen to the price and quantity of crop spraying? Explain your answer using a demand and supply figure.

b. If the FAA eliminates these regulations, what will happen to the price and quantity of soybeans, which require regular spraying? Explain your answer using a demand and supply figure.

5.8 As an executive with KB Home, a large home builder, you know that new homes are a normal good and that incomes are growing. Builders use plywood in the construction of new homes, and the price of plywood has soared because of environmental restrictions on logging. What do you expect will happen to the equilibrium price and quantity of new homes? Use demand and supply figures to help explain your answer.

5.9 The demand function for pork is $Q^d = 300 - 100P + 0.01\text{INCOME}$, where Q^d is the tons of pork demanded in your city per week, P is the price of a pound of pork, and INCOME is the average household income in the city. The supply function for pork is $Q^s = 200 + 150P - 30\text{COST}$, where Q^s is the tons of pork supplied in your city per week, P is the price of a pound of pork, and COST is the cost of pig food.

a. If INCOME is $50,000 and COST is $5, what are the equilibrium price and quantity of pork?

b. If INCOME falls to $40,000 and COST does not change, what are the new equilibrium price and quantity of pork?

c. If INCOME is $50,000 and COST rises to $10, what are the new equilibrium price and quantity of pork?

d. If INCOME is $40,000 and COST is $10, what are the new equilibrium price and quantity of pork?

5.10 Suppose that a competitive market is in equilibrium and the firms in this industry employ many workers who are paid the minimum wage.

a. If Congress raises the minimum wage that the firms must pay their workers, what happens to the equilibrium price and output?

b. What happens to the consumer surplus?

2.6 Price Controls

Learning Objective 2.6 Explain the effects of price ceilings and price floors.

6.1 Why does a price ceiling set above the equilibrium price have no effect on the market?

6.2 Why is an increase in the minimum wage apt to affect teenagers more than other age groups?

6.3 Suppose that you are a manager working for Yum in the Taco Bell division. Taco Bell employs many employees at the minimum wage. If the minimum wage is already set above the equilibrium wage rate and then the government raises it still higher, what are the effects in the labor market? How do the changes in the labor market affect Taco Bell?

2.7 Managerial Application: Using The Demand and Supply Model

Learning Objective 2.7 Apply the demand and supply model to make better managerial decisions.

7.1 You are a manager at a firm like Whirlpool in a market with other manufacturers of refrigerators. The figure shows the initial market demand and supply curves for refrigerators. You know that refrigerators are a normal good and income is increasing, so the demand for refrigerators will change by 100,000 at every price.

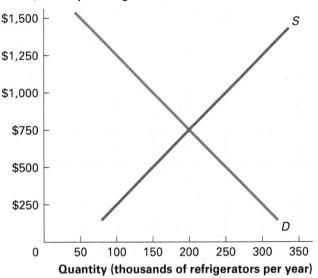

Price (dollars per refrigerator)

Quantity (thousands of refrigerators per year)

a. What are the initial equilibrium price and quantity of refrigerators? After the change in income, what are the new equilibrium price and quantity?

b. Based on your answer to part a, what managerial decisions might you make?

7.2 In Section 2.7, you learned how to analyze the effect on cereal producers of laws that required the addition of significant amounts of ethanol to gasoline. Suppose that at the same time these laws were passed, consumers' incomes increased. If name-brand cereal, such as that produced by Kellogg, is a normal good, what will be the impact on the price and quantity? Use a demand and supply figure as part of your answer.

7.3 Ethanol producers persistently lobby the government to issue regulations increasing the amount of ethanol that oil refiners must add to gasoline. Using the demand and supply model, explain why ethanol producers lobby the government for these regulations.

7.4 Young adult males drink more beer than other age and gender groups. Why do executives at breweries track the demographics of the various nations in which they operate?

7.5 Say that you are a manager working for a casual dining chain similar to Brinker International Restaurants' chain of Chili's restaurants. Just like Chili's, baby back ribs are one of your major sale items. Baby back ribs come from pigs. Answer each of the following questions independently; that is, when answering part b, assume that the situation in part a is not occurring. Use demand and supply figures to explain your answers.
   a. You read that droughts are raising the price of corn and soy, both major foodstuffs for pigs. What action(s) should your firm take?

b. Dining out at casual restaurants such as Chili's or your restaurant is a normal good. You read predictions that the economy will soon sink into a recession, with people's incomes falling. What do you expect will happen to the price and quantity of dining at casual restaurants?

c. Upper management has asked you to prepare recommendations for the next one to two years. You read that droughts are raising the price of corn and soy *and* that the economy will soon enter a recession. Based on what you have discovered, what will happen to the price and quantity of casual dining? What managerial recommendation(s) will you make to your superiors?

7.6 Increased consumption of natural foods by pet owners has led to increased demand for natural foods for their pets. The Colgate-Palmolive Company produces and sells Hill's Science Diet cat food. Suppose that you work for a similar company, also producing "scientific" cat food. Your marketing team presents research showing that consumers do not consider so-called scientific cat food natural. Based on the trend toward natural cat foods, what do you expect will happen to the equilibrium price and quantity of scientific cat food? Based on this result, what recommendation(s) would you make to top management?

MyLab Economics Auto-Graded Excel Projects

2.1 Saxum Vineyard, in Paso Robles, CA, is one of the more than 8,000 wineries in the United States. While Saxum produces a number of different kinds of wine, it focuses its production on Syrah (also known as Shiraz). Saxum sells its wines all over the United States. Suppose the market demand function for Syrah is as follows.

$$Q^d = 200 - 38.18P + 8.35P_S - 2P_C + 10INC + 0.8TS + 0.5M21$$

where Q^d is the monthly demand for bottles of Syrah (in millions), P is the price of Syrah, P_S is the average price of substitute bottles of wine (other varieties), P_C is the average price of a pound of cheese and is used to gauge the price of complementary goods, INC is average U.S. income (in thousands of dollars), TS is the number of wine trade shows and competitions each year that firms can attend to market their wines, and M21 is the number (in millions) of millenni-

als over the age of 21. This last variable captures a change in consumer preferences; millennials are drinking wine at a much higher rate than previous generations.

The market for Syrah also has supply, produced by Saxum Vineyard and other wineries, which can be stated as follows:

$$Q^s = -100 + 22.93P - 5PPI - 10P_S + 8TEMP + 1SUP$$

where Q^s is the monthly supply of bottles of Syrah (in millions), P is the price of Syrah, PPI is the Producer Price Index (an index used to gauge changes in the costs of production in the United States), P_S is the price of substitute wines that could easily be produced instead of Syrah, TEMP is the expected temperature during the harvest season for grapes, and SUP is the number of wineries that supply Syrah in the market (in thousands).

	A	B	C	D	E	F	G
1		MARKET DEMAND				MARKET SUPPLY	
2		Coefficients	Values			Coefficients	Values
3	Intercept				Intercept		
4	Price of Syrah				Price of Syrah		
5	Price of Substitutes				PPI		
6	Price of Cheese				Price of Substitutes		
7	Income				Temperature		
8	Trade Shows				Suppliers		
9	Millennials					$Q^s=$	
10			$Q^d=$				
11							

Using the market supply and demand functions for Syrah, fill in the template provided with the coefficient for each function. Using the information below, fill in the value for each of the variables except Price of Syrah. Then set up your Q^d and Q^s to automatically calculate as you adjust the values for each variable.

Demand:

- Price of substitutes: $18
- Price of cheese: $15
- Income: $53,000
- Trade shows: $3
- Millennials = 43 million

Supply:

- PPI: 111
- Price of substitutes: $18
- Temperature: 60
- Number of suppliers: 8,000

Now that you have set up your demand and supply functions, answer the following questions:
1. When the price of Syrah increases by $1, what is the effect on quantity demanded and quantity supplied?
2. How much does a $1 decrease in the price of substitute bottles of wine shift the demand and supply curves?
3. Suppose that the price of Syrah is currently $22 per bottle. How many bottles will be demanded and supplied monthly? Is there a shortage or surplus and of how much?
4. If the market price of Syrah falls to $16 per bottle, how many bottles will be demanded and supplied monthly? Is there a shortage or surplus and of how much?
5. Trying prices in $1 increments between $16 and $22, at what price and quantity does the market equilibrium occur?

6. Suppose that the PPI increases to 123.222. If the price of wine stays at $20 per bottle, what quantity will be supplied in the market, and will the increase in the PPI create a shortage?
7. With the increase in PPI to 123.222, at what price will the market be in equilibrium? What quantity will be demanded and supplied at this price?

2.2 We are going to use Excel to examine changes in the consumer and producer surpluses in a competitive market when the market is not in equilibrium. Consider the market for corn in the United States. Suppose the demand and supply functions for corn are as follows:

$$Q^d = 100 - 14.5P$$
$$Q^s = 0 + 5.5P$$

where Q is bushels of corn (in billions) and P is the market price per bushel.

Using the template provided, enter the coefficients for demand and supply, and set up your Q^d and Q^s to automatically calculate as you adjust the value for price. When the market is not at its equilibrium, the amount sold in the market will be the minimum of the quantity demanded and the quantity supplied. So to determine the quantity sold, use Excel's MIN function, and set the cell reference to Q^d and Q^s.

Set up Excel to calculate consumer surplus (CS), producer surplus (PS), and total surplus (TS) for you using the following formulas:

CS = .5*(Demand Intercept − Price)*Total Sold in Market
PS = .5*Price*Total Sold in Market
TS = CS + PS

	A	B	C	D	E	F
1	MARKET DEMAND				MARKET SUPPLY	
2		Coefficient	Value		Coefficient	Values
3	Intercept			Intercept		
4	Price			Price		
5		$Q^d=$			$Q^s=$	
6		TOTAL SOLD IN MARKET				
7	Consumer Surplus			Producer Surplus		
8		TOTAL SURPLUS				
9						

Once you have this set up, answer the following questions:

1. Start at a price of $3 per bushel, and increase the price in $0.50 increments until you reach market equilibrium. What are the equilibrium price and quantity?

2. What happens to the consumer, producer, and total surpluses as you increase the price from $3 to the equilibrium?

3. Now increase the price from the equilibrium by $0.25 two times. What happens to the market quantity and the consumer, producer, and total surpluses as you increase the price to a level higher than the equilibrium?

4. Do these results support the discussion in the text about overproduction, underproduction, and the efficient market quantity? Explain why or why not.

Measuring and Using Demand

Learning Objectives

After studying this chapter, you will be able to

3.1 Explain the basics of regression analysis.

3.2 Interpret the results from a regression.

3.3 Describe the limitations of regression analysis and how they affect its use by managers.

3.4 Discuss different elasticity measures and their use.

3.5 Use regression analysis and the different elasticity measures to make better managerial decisions.

Managers at the Gates Foundation Decide to Subsidize Antimalarial Drugs

The Bill and Melinda Gates Foundation (Gates Foundation) is the world's largest philanthropic organization, with a trust endowment of nearly $40 billion. The foundation provides grants for education, medical research, and vaccinations around the world. As of 2015, the foundation had made total grants of $37 billion. The goal of the Gates Foundation is not maximizing profit. Instead, its goal is to save lives and improve health in developing countries.

In 2010, the Global Fund to Fight AIDS, Tuberculosis and Malaria presented proposals to the Gates Foundation to subsidize antimalarial drugs in Kenya and other nations of sub-Saharan Africa. Although the Gates Foundation provides nearly $4 billion in grants per year, there are more than $4 billion worth of competing uses for its resources. Consequently, before the managers accepted these proposals, they needed to determine their expected impact: How many people would these projects save compared to alternative uses of the funds? The managers

realized that lives hinged on their decision, so they wanted to be certain that they were getting the most value for their money.

The proposed subsidy programs would lower the price patients pay for the drugs. As you learned in Chapter 2, according to the law of demand, a decrease in the price of a product increases the quantity demanded. Antimalarial drugs are no exception; if their price falls, more patients will buy them. To make the proper decision about the proposals, however, the foundation's managers needed a more quantitative estimate: Precisely how many additional patients would buy the drugs when their prices were lower?

This chapter explains how to answer this and other questions that require quantitative answers. At the end of the chapter, you will learn how the Gates Foundation's managers could forecast the number of patients they would help by subsidizing the drugs.

Sources: Karl Mathiesen, "What Is the Bill and Melinda Gates Foundation?" *The Guardian*. March 16, 2015; Gavin Yamey, Marco Schaferhoff, and Dominic Montagu, "Piloting the Affordable Medicines Facility-Malaria: What Will Success Look Like?" *Bulletin of the World Health Organization*, February 3, 2012, http://www.who .int/bulletin/volumes/90/6/11-091199/en; Erinstar, "Availability of Subsidized Malaria Drugs in Kenya," *Social and Behavioral Foundations of Primary Health Care Policy Advocacy*, March 11, 2012, https://sbfphc.wordpress .com/2012/03/11/availability-of-subsidized-malaria-drugs-in-kenya-18-2.

Introduction

According to the law of demand, when you raise the price of your product, the quantity your customers buy decreases. In some cases, this qualitative information is all you need to know, but in other cases, you need a more precise estimate. Your decision to raise the price of your product by 10 percent might depend on its impact on the quantity demanded: Will it decrease by 5 percent or by 20 percent? To make the best decision, you need more precise information about the demand for your product. Understanding how to obtain this information and what it means is important, but as a manager, knowing how to use it is even more important.

Chapter 3 features two important quantitative concepts: regression analysis and elasticity. **Regression analysis** (or, more simply, regression) is a statistical method used to estimate the relationship between two or more variables. Regression analysis can be used to estimate the coefficients of the demand function, the a and b in the equation $Q^d = a - (b \times P)$, or the coefficients of any other relationship. As a manager, you will probably not conduct the actual regression analysis, but you will quite likely rely on demand estimates from your marketing research department. This chapter will help you understand how to interpret those estimates and use the results of the regression to make predictions and forecasts that can be important for your business.

Regression analysis A statistical method used to estimate the relationship between two or more variables.

Sometimes you will not have the data necessary to use regression analysis. In those cases, you may be able to use **elasticity** to help predict consumer response to a change in your price. For instance, the price elasticity of demand will help you determine whether your 10 percent price hike will decrease your sales by 5 percent or by 20 percent.

Elasticity A measure of the responsiveness of the demand for a product to a change in a factor affecting the demand.

Regression and elasticity build on the concepts presented in Chapter 2 by allowing you as a manager to gain a more quantitative understanding of demand as well as other important relationships between key variables, such as cost and total production. To achieve these important goals, Chapter 3 includes five sections:

- **Section 3.1** explains regression analysis, the most common technique for estimating relationships such as those represented by a demand curve.
- **Section 3.2** demonstrates how to interpret regression results, including how to calculate the range of values within which a regression coefficient is likely to fall, test the hypothesis that the value of a coefficient equals zero, and measure the fit of the regression.
- **Section 3.3** describes weaknesses of regression analysis and how they affect its use.
- **Section 3.4** introduces the price elasticity of demand, income elasticity of demand, and cross-price elasticity of demand, which deal with how strongly consumers respond to changes in the price of the product, income, and the price of a related good, respectively.
- **Section 3.5** demonstrates how you can use regression analysis, price elasticity of demand, income elasticity of demand, and cross-price elasticity of demand to make better managerial decisions.

3.1 Regression: Estimating Demand

Learning Objective 3.1 Explain the basics of regression analysis.

Chapter 2 illustrated a demand curve for jeans, described algebraically as

$$Q^d = a - (b \times P)$$

In Figure 2.1 in Chapter 2, the linear demand curve was used to calculate that the coefficient a was equal to 600 million pairs of jeans and that the coefficient b was equal to 5 million pairs of jeans per dollar. The negative sign in the equation reflects the law of demand: A higher price reduces the quantity demanded. As a manager, however, you will never be given a figure with a linear demand curve for use to compute these values. Instead, you must use data on the quantity sold and the price charged to calculate the best estimates for the coefficients. The method used to make these estimates is regression analysis. Regression is used to estimate the coefficients of a demand function as well as many important economic relationships, such as the relationship between a firm's quantity and its cost. Studying the details of regression will help you understand the strengths and weaknesses of reports submitted to you and thereby help you make better decisions.

The Basics of Regression Analysis

The Capital Grille is a chain of upscale steak restaurants. Suppose that you are an upper-level executive working for a similar chain. To make better decisions, you want to know the demand for your company's dinners. Assume that the demand function for steak dinners at your restaurants can be written as

$$Q^d = a - (b \times P)$$

where Q^d is the *dependent variable* we are predicting and P is the *independent variable*, also called the *explanatory variable*. This is a *univariate equation* because there is only one independent variable. Adding other independent variables that affect customer demand, such as income or the price of a related good, transforms a *univariate equation* into a *multivariate equation* because it includes more than one independent variable. We use the simpler univariate case to explain regression analysis because the more complicated—and probably more realistic—multivariate case is similar. The goal of regression analysis is to estimate the coefficients of the demand function, a and b in the equation we are using, so that we can find how the dependent variable, Q^d, changes when the independent variable(s) change(s).

The demand equation in this example has only one independent variable, the price of a dinner (P). Even if you included many other independent variables, however, you would not be able to precisely replicate the quantities demanded. There always will be some error because there are inevitably random elements in demand that you cannot capture. For example, a particularly severe snowstorm might lead some consumers to eat at home rather than drive to the restaurant. Alternatively, the popularity of dining at this restaurant chain might skyrocket after a popular rap artist mentions it in an interview. Because these factors occur randomly, you will never be able to accurately capture their impact on the demand for dinners. So you add a random error term to the demand equation to account for the randomness and get

$$Q^d = a - (b \times P) + \eta$$

where η is the random error term. You will never know for sure what η equals. But assume that η is random, has a mean (average) of zero, and is *normally distributed*, which means it has the usual bell-shaped distribution that you have undoubtedly seen for variables such as weight or height.

Your goal of obtaining the best estimates for the coefficients a and b now must take into account the random error term. If you knew that the error term was *always* zero, so that $a - (b \times P)$ *always* equaled Q^d, the restaurant chain's managers could set different prices at a few of its locations and collect data on the quantity of dinners

Price (dollars per dinner)

Quantity (dinners per day)

Figure 3.1 Price and Quantity Data for Dinners

The figure plots the price of dinners and the quantity demanded per day at different restaurants in the chain. Because there is a random element to demand, the points on this scatter diagram do not fall precisely on a straight line; however, the data do cluster around a negatively sloped straight-line demand curve.

sold. They could then plot quantities and prices in a standard demand and supply graph and determine the a and b coefficients from the straight line plotted—a would equal the horizontal intercept, and b would equal the inverse of the slope, as shown in Figure 2.1 in Chapter 2.

The presence of the random error term complicates your task. For example, Figure 3.1 shows 21 hypothetical data points for the price and quantity of steak dinners demanded at your restaurants. You can obtain these types of data by setting different prices at different locations and then collecting data over several months on the average quantity of dinners sold each day.

The random element of demand makes it impossible to draw a straight line connecting the scattered points. Even so, Figure 3.1 shows that the points lie around a negatively sloped straight line, which would be the demand curve. However, it is possible to draw many lines through this cluster of points. Each line would give slightly different estimates of the a and b coefficients and therefore different estimates of the demand function, $Q^d = a - (b \times P)$. Using only Figure 3.1, we cannot determine which of these lines best approximates the actual demand curve.

Regression Analysis

Regression analysis gives estimates for the a and b coefficients—say, $\hat{a}$ and $\hat{b}$—thereby choosing one of the many lines through the data points. But which line should it select? Intuitively, the line that is closest to the data points seems desirable—that is, the line that makes the difference between the actual quantities, Q^d, and the predicted quantities—say, $\widehat{Q^d}$—as small as possible. Using the actual prices and the estimated $\hat{a}$ and $\hat{b}$ coefficients in the demand function will give the predicted quantities, $\widehat{Q^d} = \hat{a} - (\hat{b} \times P)$. The differences between the actual quantities and the predicted quantities, $Q^d - \widehat{Q^d}$, are called the *residuals*. The goal of regression is to make the residuals as small as possible.

There are various ways of minimizing the residuals. The most common regression technique is *ordinary least squares (OLS) regression*. OLS regression locates the line through the scatter of data points that minimizes the sum of the squared residuals between the actual quantities and the predicted quantities. We called the actual random term η, so let's call the estimated residual for the first quantity $\hat{\eta}_1$, for the second quantity $\hat{\eta}_2$, and so forth. OLS regression minimizes the sum of the squared residuals. Figure 3.1 includes 21 data points, so the sum of the squared residuals OLS minimizes is

$$\hat{\eta}_1^2 + \hat{\eta}_2^2 + \hat{\eta}_3^2 + \cdots + \hat{\eta}_{21}^2$$

You can use one of many statistical programs to calculate the regression coefficients, $\hat{a}$ and $\hat{b}$. Microsoft Excel can perform OLS regressions. Other statistical software programs go further, allowing calculation of even more sophisticated regressions. We'll restrict ourselves to OLS regression because that is by far the most commonly used technique in business. Let's use Microsoft Excel 2013 to demonstrate how to calculate the OLS regression line for the 21 data points in Figure 3.1, so that you can see and interpret the reported results.

The first step in using Microsoft Excel is to click the "Data" tab. Then make sure the "Data Analysis" icon is present (see the arrow in Figure 3.2). If the icon is not present, follow the instructions in Figure 3.2 to install it.

To conduct the regression, start by entering the data. Use two columns in your spreadsheet. Label the first "Quantity" and the second "Price." Next, enter the data. First, enter the dependent variable, quantity. Then enter the independent variable, price. Figure 3.3 illustrates this process for the data in Figure 3.1 about the price and quantity of steak dinners at your restaurant chain. Once you have entered all the data,

1. Click the "Data" tab and then the "Data Analysis" icon.
2. When the "Data Analysis" box pops up, highlight the "Regression" entry, and click "OK."

Figure 3.2   Microsoft Excel: The Data Analysis Icon

The "Data Analysis" icon (see the arrow) is necessary to conduct regression analysis using Microsoft Excel. If the icon is missing, you must install the Analysis ToolPak, an add-in included in Excel. To install the Analysis ToolPak:
- Click on the "File" tab.
- Click on "Options."
- When the "Excel Options" window opens, click on "Add-ins."
- At the bottom of the "Add-ins" screen, click "Go."
- Find the "Analysis ToolPak" box, check it, and click "OK."

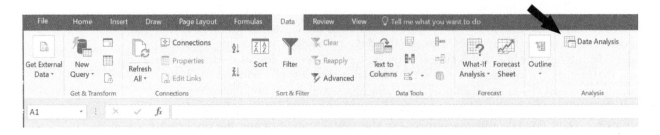

Figure 3.3 Microsoft Excel: Entering Data

The dependent variable is entered in column A under the heading "Quantity."
The independent variable is entered in column B under the heading "Price."

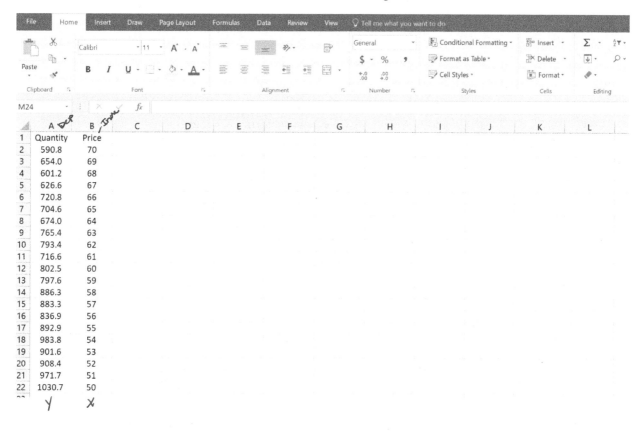

3. The "Regression" box, which enables you to specify the range of data you want to use and where you want to display the results, will pop up. For the data you are using, complete the "Regression" box as illustrated and explained in Figure 3.4.
4. In the "Regression" box, click "OK," and Excel will estimate the regression.

The procedure just outlined estimates a univariate regression. Frequently, however, you will want to estimate a multivariate regression. For example, instead of price alone, you might want to explore whether the demand for dinners at your chain also depends on the price charged by Sea's Harvest, a competitive upscale fish restaurant. So suppose that you also have data on the prices for a dinner at Sea's Harvest for each of the 21 quantity/price observations given in Figure 3.3. In this case, you would enter the heading "Competitor Price" in cell C1 and the data on these prices directly below it. You now have two independent,

Figure 3.4 Microsoft Excel: The "Regression" Box

The "Input Y Range" refers to the dependent variable, the quantity. The "Input X Range" refers to the independent variable, the price. For this example and these data, use the ranges shown. Be certain to include the cell with the title of the variable as part of the range. Also, check the "Labels" box as shown.

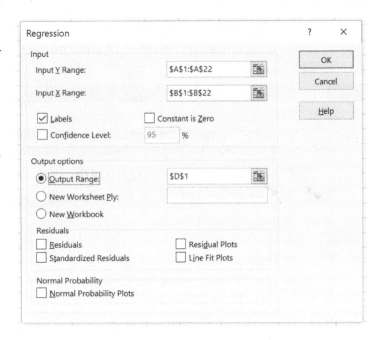

or *X*, variables. Consequently, in the "Regression" box, you would specify the "Input X Range" as $B$1:$C$22, which is the new range for the independent variables. Click "OK," and Excel now estimates your multivariate regression.

Regression Results: Estimated Coefficients and Estimated Demand Curve

Figure 3.5 shows the results from the univariate regression analysis of the data on price and quantity of steak dinners. Excel also includes a section of results entitled "Analysis of Variance (ANOVA)." Because we do not need this section for our regression analysis, it is not displayed in Figure 3.5. The results shown have been limited to two decimal places. Often analysts report the results with many more decimal places, but that is false precision.

Figure 3.5 Microsoft Excel: Results of Regression

These are the results of the Excel regression using the data in Figure 3.1.

D	E	F	G	H	I	J
SUMMARY OUTPUT						
Regression Statistics						
Multiple R	0.96					
R Square	0.92					
Adjusted R Square	0.91					
Standard Error	38.12					
Observations	21.00					
	Coefficients	Standard Error	t Stat	P-value	Lower 95%	Upper 95%
Intercept	1999.82	82.84	24.14	0.00	1826.43	2173.22
Price	-20.04	1.37	-14.59	0.00	-22.92	-17.17

The first result to note is the "Coefficients" column. The coefficient labeled "Intercept" is our $\hat{a}$ (recall that $\hat{a}$ is the horizontal intercept of the demand equation). The estimate from the regression is that $\hat{a}$ equals 1,999.82. This value for $\hat{a}$ means that the estimated demand curve crosses the horizontal axis at a quantity of 1,999.82 dinners per day. The coefficient labeled "Price" is our $\hat{b}$ (recall that $\hat{b}$ is the coefficient that multiplies the price variable). Excel estimates that $\hat{b}$ equals –20.04, which means that for every dollar increase in the price, consumers decrease the quantity of steak dinners they demand at your restaurant chain by 20.04 dinners per day. So, using these estimated coefficients, we find that the estimated demand curve is

$$Q^d = 1,999.82 - (20.04 \times P)$$

Figure 3.6 uses these coefficients to plot the estimated demand curve, labeled D, and shows its relationship to the actual data points. Although the estimated demand curve is closer to some data points than to others, this demand curve minimizes the sum of the squared residuals between the actual quantities and the predicted quantities.

As a manager, you can use the estimated demand curve for dinners at your restaurant chain to forecast the quantity of steak dinners demanded at different prices. For example, if you set a price of $62 per dinner, the estimated demand curve predicts that the quantity of dinners demanded is $1,999.82 - (20.04 \times \$62)$, or 757.3 dinners per day. This prediction represents a point on the estimated demand curve—specifically, the white point in Figure 3.6. The actual quantity for the price of $62 (from the data in Figure 3.3) is 793.4 dinners per day. The difference between the actual quantity and the predicted quantity, 793.4 dinners – 757.3 dinners = 36.1 dinners, is the estimated residual. This difference results from the effect of the random factors on the actual quantity.

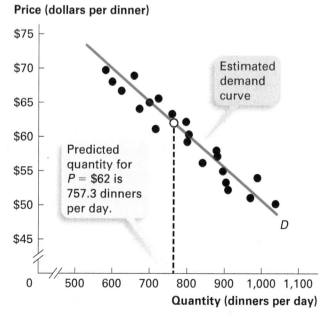

Price (dollars per dinner)

Figure 3.6 An Estimated Demand Curve for Steak Dinners

The demand curve estimated using ordinary least squares regression is labeled D. The white dot shows that at the price of $62 per dinner, the predicted quantity of dinners demanded is 757.3.

As a manager, you need to know how to interpret the results from a regression. For example, you need to know how close the estimated coefficients are to the true coefficients. This topic is covered in the next section.

Regression Analysis at Your Steak Chain

You are an upper-level executive at an upscale steak restaurant chain. Suppose that you have the same data shown in Figure 3.3 but only for prices from $70 to $55 per dinner. Using those 17 data points of price/quantity, estimate a univariate regression, and use it to answer the following questions:

a. What are the estimated coefficients? What is the new estimated demand function?

b. Did the omission of the data points with prices from $54 to $50 per dinner make a large change in the estimated demand function?

Answer

a. The estimate from the regression is that $\hat{a}$ equals 1,990.48 and $\hat{b}$ equals −19.90. The new estimated demand function is $Q^d = 1990.48 - (19.90 \times P)$.

b. Omitting the five data points did not lead to a large change in the estimated coefficients. The estimated $\hat{a}$ changes from 1,999.82 to 1,990.48, a change of 0.5 percent, and the estimated $\hat{b}$ changes from −20.04 to −19.90, a change of 0.7 percent. These changes are very small.

3.2 Interpreting the Results of Regression Analysis

Learning Objective 3.2 Interpret the results from a regression.

The *estimated* demand curve shown in Figure 3.6 might not be the same as the *actual* demand curve. In other words, the estimated coefficients from the univariate regression, $\hat{a} = 1,999.82$ and $\hat{b} = -20.04$, might not be identical to the actual coefficients. Of course, the same is true when your analysts estimate a multivariate regression. Consequently, before you use the estimated demand curve, you need to know how confident you are that the estimated coefficients are close to the true coefficients. Measuring that confidence is the first step in interpreting the results from a regression. Fortunately, the procedure used is the same for the coefficients from both multivariate and univariate regressions.

Estimated Coefficients

The estimated coefficients from any regression depend on the data, which in turn depend in part on the random element of the demand. Consequently, reestimating the regression with new data means the estimated coefficients will change randomly because the new data will contain new values of the random element. For example, if your analysts ran the same pricing experiment reported in Figure 3.3 a second time, setting the same 21 different prices at the same locations they used before, they would gather 21 new quantity data points which would differ from the original quantities due to the random fluctuations in demand. Your analysts could use these new data points to estimate a new regression. This new regression would have new estimates for $\hat{a}$ and $\hat{b}$ that would differ from the initial estimates because of the random element. Indeed, if your chain ran this experiment a large number of times, you would wind up with a large number of estimates for $\hat{a}$ and $\hat{b}$. The large number of estimates would create a distribution that would allow you to use statistics to make inferences about the true values of a and b. But as a manager, you know it is simply not feasible to run this pricing experiment more than once, much less a "large number" of times!

Fortunately, such replication is unnecessary. If you look again at the regression results in Figure 3.5, you will see that next to the column for "Coefficients" is a column labeled "Standard Error." The standard error reflects the fact that the estimated coefficients have a random element. The standard error of a coefficient is a measure of how much the estimated coefficient is likely to change if another set of data is collected and another regression estimated. For example, the estimated coefficient for price, $\hat{b}$, is −20.04, with a standard error of 1.37. Compared to the coefficient estimate, this standard error is relatively small. A small standard error means that the change from reestimation of the regression probably will be small, which, in turn, means that the estimated coefficient is likely close to the true value. A large standard error, however, means that the change may be large, which suggests that the estimated coefficient might not be particularly close to the true value. You can go beyond this qualitative description of the effect of the size of the standard error to construct a range that for repeated samples has a pre-selected probability of containing the true value of the coefficient. For example, you can construct a range that will contain the true value of the coefficient 95 percent of the time. Such a range is called a **confidence interval**.

Confidence interval
A range that for repeated samples has a pre-selected probability of containing the true value of the coefficient.

Confidence Intervals

In randomized pricing experiments like the one we suppose that your restaurant chain conducted, OLS regression has a very nice statistical property: The estimated coefficients are *unbiased*, meaning that they are systematically neither greater than nor less than the actual true values. Moreover, the statistical properties of OLS regression mean that if you gather many data samples and reestimate the regression many times, all the new estimated coefficients you obtain will create a range that is centered around the true value of the coefficients. These facts provide a starting point for the confidence interval. Because the estimated coefficients from your regression are unbiased, they are your best estimate of the true value of the coefficients. Consequently, the range of the confidence interval will be centered around the estimated coefficients. For instance, if you are calculating a confidence interval for the b coefficient, the range of the confidence interval will be centered around −20.04, the estimated value $\hat{b}$ from the regression.

The range for a confidence interval depends on two factors:

1. **The size of the standard error**. Because the standard error measures how much the estimated coefficient is likely to change with reestimation of the regression using a new data sample, the larger the standard error, the larger the possible change of the coefficient. It follows that the larger the standard error, the larger the confidence interval.

2. **How confident the manager wants to be that the range contains the true value of the coefficient.** The more confident the manager wants to be, the larger the confidence interval. Conventionally, 95 percent or 99 percent is used as the desired level of confidence, though nothing prevents managers from using other levels. A 95 percent confidence level means that if the pricing experiment is run over and over, each time estimating the demand function regression, 95 percent of the time the confidence interval from any regression will contain the true value of the coefficient.

Analysts can use a statistical formula to calculate a confidence interval. Happily, however, most statistical software automatically calculates and reports the endpoints of the confidence interval. Excel automatically reports the two ends of the 95 percent confidence interval for the estimated coefficients, called "Lower 95%" and "Upper 95%." For example, in Figure 3.5, the 95 percent confidence interval for $\hat{b}$ runs from −22.92 to −17.17. This result means that you can be 95 percent confident that this range contains the true value of b. This range has an important managerial implication: You are 95 percent confident that in response to a dollar increase in price, your customers will decrease the quantity of dinners they demand by an amount that lies between 22.92 and 17.17 dinners per day.

Figure 3.5 also reports the two ends of the 95 percent confidence interval for the estimated intercept, $\hat{a}$. In a multivariate regression with more than one independent variable, the statistical software will usually present the lower and upper ends of a confidence interval for each coefficient *separately*. Calculating a confidence region for two or more coefficients *jointly* requires a more sophisticated test, which is best covered in a class devoted to business statistics.

Hypothesis Testing

Often you will be interested in the impact of a particular variable on your prediction. For example, we mentioned earlier that as a manager of a steak restaurant chain, you might be interested in determining whether the demand for steak dinners depends not only on the price you set but also on the price charged by Sea's Harvest, the competing fish restaurant. Let's suppose that a multivariate regression results in the estimated coefficient for the price of meals at Sea's Harvest presented in Table 3.1.

The estimated coefficient, 8.04, is positive and indicates that a $1 increase in the price of a dinner at Sea's Harvest increases the demand at your restaurant chain by 8.04 dinners per day. But the standard error of this coefficient is large compared to the coefficient, so the 95 percent confidence interval ranges all the way from −4.83 dinners per day up to 20.91 dinners per day. Given this broad range, you might wonder if the price charged at Sea's Harvest actually affects the demand for your steak dinners. In particular, if the true

Table 3.1 Results for an Estimated Coefficient for Meals at Sea's Harvest

	Coefficient	**Standard Error**	**t Stat**	**P-value**	**Lower 95%**	**Upper 95%**
Competitor Price	8.04	6.12	1.31	0.21	−4.83	20.91

coefficient turns out to be zero (which *is* among the values included in the confidence interval), then the price charged at Sea's Harvest has no effect on the demand for your steak dinners. In this case, as a manager you can ignore the price charged at Sea's Harvest. So you want to know if the estimated coefficient—which is your best estimate of the true coefficient—is different from zero. Fortunately, there is a statistical test to determine whether an estimated coefficient is significantly different from zero. This test, like all statistical tests, begins with two fundamental steps:

1. The test starts by posing the *null hypothesis*, which in this case is that "the true coefficient equals zero." For example, as a manager at the steak chain, your null hypothesis is that in the demand for your meals, the true coefficient for Sea's Harvest's price is zero, in which case the price of fish dinners does not affect the demand for your steak dinners. If you reject (or "nullify") the hypothesis that the true coefficient equals zero, then you have rejected the null hypothesis in favor of the *alternative hypothesis*, that the true coefficient is not equal to zero, so that the price of fish dinners affects the demand for your steak dinners.

2. You can never know for sure what the true coefficient equals, so there is some probability that you might draw the wrong conclusion. Accordingly, you must select how confident you want to be that rejecting (nullifying) the null hypothesis is the correct decision. The most common confidence levels are the same as those you saw before for confidence intervals, 95 percent and 99 percent. When you reject the null hypothesis at a confidence level of, say, 95 percent, you know that 95 percent of the time rejecting the null hypothesis is the correct decision. Of course, that means that 5 percent of the time you are making the incorrect decision—5 percent of the time the null hypothesis is correct, but you are rejecting it. The **significance level** of a test is the probability that you are making the *wrong* decision. For example, the 95 percent confidence level has a significance level of $1 - 0.95 = 0.05$, or 5 percent.

Significance level The probability of making the wrong decision, which is equal to 1 minus the confidence level.

In our restaurant example, you want to test the null hypothesis that the true value of the coefficient for the price of meals at Sea's Harvest is zero. To do this, you use what is called a *t* test by calculating a measure called a *t*-statistic. The **t-statistic** equals the estimated coefficient divided by its estimated standard error.

Regression software, such as Excel, reports the *t*-statistic for each coefficient. In Table 3.1, the competitive price coefficient for meals at Sea's Harvest has a *t*-statistic of 1.31, calculated from $8.04/6.12$. The *t*-statistic is positive if the estimated coefficient is positive, and it is negative if the estimated coefficient is negative. The sign of the *t*-statistic is unimportant; what is important is its magnitude (absolute value). If the magnitude of the *t*-statistic is large, then the definition of the *t*-statistic shows that the estimated coefficient is large compared to its estimated standard error. In this case, the confidence interval is unlikely to include zero, so it is unlikely that the true coefficient equals zero.[1]

t-statistic The estimated coefficient divided by its estimated standard error.

---

1 The *t* test is closely related to the confidence interval. If the 95 (99) percent confidence interval includes zero, the *t* test will not reject the null hypothesis that the true coefficient equals zero at the 95 (99) percent confidence level.

So a large t-statistic leads you to reject the null hypothesis (that the true coefficient equals zero) in favor of the alternative hypothesis (that the true coefficient is not zero).

How large must the t-statistic be to reject the null hypothesis? Statisticians have calculated the probability of each value of the t-statistic when the null hypothesis is true. This distribution provides the **critical value** of the t-statistic—that is, the value of the t-statistic above which the null hypothesis is rejected.

Critical value The value of the t-statistic above which the null hypothesis is rejected.

The critical value depends on the confidence level, with a higher confidence level (a lower significance level—that is, a lower probability of error) leading to a larger critical value. The critical value also depends on the number of observations, but it does not change much once there are more than 40 or 50 observations. For a large number of observations, the 95 percent confidence level (the 5 percent significance level) has a critical value of 1.96. (For the 99 percent confidence level, the critical value is 2.58.) If the computed value of the t-statistic exceeds 1.96, you can reject the null hypothesis, knowing that you are making the correct decision at least 95 percent of the time.

In Table 3.1, the computed value of the t-statistic is 1.31, which is below the 95 percent confidence level critical value, so you cannot reject the null hypothesis. Instead, you retain the null hypothesis that the true coefficient is zero, which means that the price of meals at Sea's Harvest has no effect on the demand for steak dinners at your restaurant chain. Contrast this result with the t-statistic for the price coefficient (the $\hat{b}$), reported in Figure 3.5 as −14.59. The absolute value of the t-statistic, 14.59, is well above the 95 percent confidence level critical value of 1.96, so you can easily reject the null hypothesis in favor of the alternative hypothesis that the true coefficient is not zero.

P-value Assuming the null hypothesis is true, the probability in repeated samples of obtaining a value of the t-statistic equal to or larger than the computed t-statistic.

Table 3.1 (along with Figure 3.5) reports one other result: the P-value. Assuming that the null hypothesis is correct (the true coefficient equals zero), the **P-value** is the probability in repeated samples of obtaining a value of the t-statistic equal to or larger than the computed t-statistic reported in the results. Table 3.1 shows that when the t-statistic is 1.31, the P-value is 0.21, or 21 percent. So even when the true coefficient equals zero, if you repeatedly re-estimated the regression each time using new data you gather, 21 percent of the time the computed t-statistic would be 1.31 or larger. If you rejected the null hypothesis that the true coefficient is zero based on a t-statistic equal to 1.31 or larger, you would be making an error 21 percent of the time. So, the P-value is equal to the significance level of testing the null hypothesis; that is, it is equal to the probability of erroneously rejecting the null hypothesis. Conventionally, users reject a null hypothesis when the significance level is 0.05 (5 percent) or less, which makes the confidence level 0.95 (95 percent) or more. Only when the P-value is 0.05 or less should you reject the null hypothesis in favor of the alternative hypothesis that the coefficient is not zero.

The P-value is useful because it gives you finer detail than the t-statistic about how strongly you reject (or do not reject) a hypothesis. The results of a t-statistic are usually reported simply as "reject" or "do not reject" and that is it. Returning to Figure 3.5 dealing with the univariate demand function for steak dinners, you see that the estimated coefficient for the price of a steak dinner has a P-value so small that it is rounded to 0.00 (0 percent). In other words, there is virtually a 0 percent chance you are making a mistake by rejecting the null hypothesis that the true coefficient is zero. In this case, you can *very* confidently reject the null hypothesis, which means you can be *very* confident that the price of a steak dinner affects the quantity of steak dinners demanded.

The following box summarizes guidelines for interpreting regression coefficients.

TESTING REGRESSION COEFFICIENTS

t test

If the magnitude of the *t*-statistic is larger than the critical value:

- Reject the null hypothesis that the true value of the coefficient equals zero.
- Accept the alternative hypothesis that the true value of the coefficient is nonzero.

If the magnitude of the *t*-statistic is less than the critical value:

- Fail to reject (accept) the null hypothesis that the true value of the coefficient equals zero.

P-value

If the *P*-value is less than the significance level (typically 0.05 or 0.01):

- Reject the null hypothesis that the true value of the coefficient equals zero.
- Accept the alternative hypothesis that the true value of the coefficient is nonzero.

If the *P*-value is larger than the significance level (typically 0.05 or 0.01):

- Fail to reject (accept) the null hypothesis that the true value of the coefficient equals zero.

Fit of the Regression

In addition to establishing your confidence in the values of the regression coefficient, you may want to know how accurate the regression is overall—that is, how close the predicted values are to the actual data points. For the estimated demand curve shown in Figure 3.7(a), you can see that the predicted values (the points on the estimated demand curve) are close to the actual data points. The estimated demand curve shown in Figure 3.7(b) is not particularly close to the data points, so the predicted values are not close to the actual values. Is it possible to *measure* how well the regression fits the data? The answer is yes: One of the results reported by Excel in Figure 3.5 provides a measure of the fit between the regression and the data. The **R^2 statistic** (R-squared statistic), more commonly called simply R^2 (R squared), is a measure of how much of the variation in the observed values of the dependent variable is captured by the predicted values of the regression. Specifically, R^2 is the fraction of the data points' variation accounted for by the regression's predicted values. It ranges from 1.00 (100 percent) to 0.00 (0 percent). The closer R^2 is to 100 percent, the more closely the predicted values fit the actual data.

R^2 statistic A measure of how much of the variation in the observed values of the dependent variable is captured by the predicted values of the regression.

The R^2 statistic for the demand curve in Figure 3.7(a) is 0.92. The predicted values from the regression account for 92 percent of the variation in the observed values of the dependent variable, which indicates a very good fit. The R^2 statistic for the demand curve in Figure 3.7(b) is 0.52. The predicted values from this regression account for only 52 percent of the variation in the observed values of the dependent variable, which indicates a poorer fit.

Figure 3.7 **Fit of Estimated Demand Curves**

(a) Demand Curve with a High R^2
The estimated demand curve, D, is close to the data points, so it has a higher R^2 statistic.

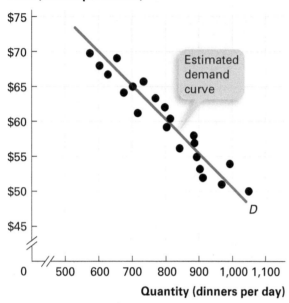

(b) Demand Curve with a Low R^2
The estimated demand curve, D, is not close to the data points, so it has a lower R^2 statistic.

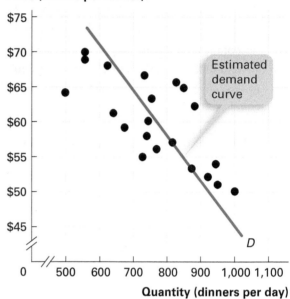

When you receive a report based on regression analysis, you must be concerned with R^2. If it is small—say, 0.12 (12 percent)—you need to be aware that the predicted values do not capture much of the variation in the actual values of the dependent variable. In other words, the predicted values are not particularly close to the observed, actual values. If R^2 is large—say, 0.88 (88 percent)—you can be more confident in the results because the predicted values are close to the observed, actual values.

SOLVED PROBLEM

Confidence Intervals and Predictions for the Demand for Doors

You are a manager of a company similar to Pella Corporation, a producer of high-quality doors and windows. The members of your marketing group give you the results of their research into the demand for your company's doors. They report that the estimated coefficient for the effect of price on the demand for doors is −700 doors per dollar, with a standard error of 200 doors per dollar and a 95 percent confidence range of −1,092 doors per dollar to −308 doors per dollar.

a. Is the estimated coefficient significantly different from zero at the 95 percent confidence level? Explain your answer.

b. If you raise the price of a door by $10, what decrease in quantity do you expect? Using the 95 percent confidence interval, what would be the largest decrease in quantity? The smallest?

Answer

a. The estimated coefficient is significantly different from zero because the magnitude of its t-statistic, which equals $700/200 = 3.5$, easily exceeds the critical value of 1.96.

b. Using the estimated coefficient, you expect the increase in price to change the quantity demanded by -700 doors $\times$ \$10 $= -7{,}000$ doors. Using the range of the 95 percent confidence interval, the largest decrease would occur if the coefficient equaled $-1{,}092$ doors, in which case the decrease in quantity demanded would be 1,092 doors $\times$ \$10 $= 10{,}920$ doors. The smallest decrease in the quantity demanded would occur if the coefficient equaled -308 doors, in which case the decrease in quantity demanded would be 308 doors $\times$ \$10 $= 3{,}080$ doors.

3.3 Limitations of Regression Analysis

Learning Objective 3.3 Describe the limitations of regression analysis and how they affect its use by managers.

When you receive a report including analysis based on a regression equation, you need to know the potential limitations of the regression. We will discuss two possible weaknesses: (1) the specification of the regression—that is, which variables are included; and (2) its functional form—that is, how the variables are entered in the function the analyst estimated.

Specification of the Regression Equation

Whenever you examine regressions you must always consider whether they include all of the relevant factors. If not, you should view the results and analysis with at least a touch of skepticism. For example, as a manager at your high-end steak restaurant chain, you might receive a regression analysis from your market research team, using data accumulated over 21 years, that shows how the price of a steak dinner affects the quantity of steak dinners demanded. Price is the only independent variable, so the regression equation is similar to what you have already seen, $Q^d = a - (b \times P)$. In the last section, the research department collected the data at several locations at a single point in time. In the current case, the data have been accumulated over more than two decades. Because the data cover 21 years, a long period of time, another relevant variable that affects consumer demand is surely missing: their incomes. As you learned in Chapter 2, income is a factor that affects demand, and income has definitely changed over the last 21 years. Omitting this important variable could result in a low R^2, which means predictions using the equation might not be very accurate. Its omission might also bias the estimated price coefficient because, if both price and income have been trending higher over the past 21 years, then the price coefficient could be capturing both the effect of changes in price and also the effect of changes in income. Because analysts may be able to obtain income data, you should probably return the report to the market research team with a request to include income as an additional independent variable in the regression.

Unlike income, some potentially relevant variables are simply not measurable. For example, there may have been a couple of years during the 21-year period when there was a substantial scare about mad cow disease, an untreatable and fatal disease that attacks the brain. If enough consumers believed that they might catch mad cow disease by eating steaks, their preferences would have changed, decreasing the demand for steak dinners. Perfectly measuring this type of change in preferences is impossible. In the short run, the only course of action is to omit this variable and hope that its omission does not have a large effect on the results. In the long run, it might be possible to accumulate more data for years not affected by this factor and ultimately omit from the regression analysis those years that could be anomalous.

Functional Form of the Regression Equation

So far, all of the figures showing price and quantity data points for steak dinners have strongly suggested a straight-line demand curve. But what if the price and quantity data points looked like those in Figure 3.8? In this case, you might suspect that the true demand curve is not a straight line because the data points seem to lie around a convex (bowed inward) curve. Analysts can use various transformations of the data to account for the nonlinearity of a demand curve. One of the most common is to take the natural logarithms of both the price and the quantity data and then assume that the true demand curve is linear in the natural logarithms, a specification called *log-linear*:

$$\ln Q^d = a - (b \times \ln P) + \eta$$

where $\ln Q^d$ is the natural logarithm of the quantity, $\ln P$ is the natural logarithm of the price, a and b are coefficients, and η is the random error term. This functional form results in a demand curve with an inward bow, as illustrated in Figure 3.8. For a log-linear demand curve, the regression is estimated using the transformed data series $\ln Q^d$ for the dependent variable and the transformed data series $\ln P$ for the independent variable. Figure 3.9 illustrates the estimated demand curve that results from this regression.

Figure 3.9 shows that a log-linear specification yields a demand curve that can fit the convex shape of the data points. The log-linear specification has an additional advantage: When the data are in logarithms, the estimated $\hat{b}$ coefficient is equal to the price elasticity of demand, a concept you will learn about in the next section. For now, you just need to know that this result can be useful.

The predictions from the log-linear regression are for $\ln \widehat{Q^d}$. However, the result usually desired is $\widehat{Q^d}$; that is, you want to know the predicted quantity, not

Figure 3.8 Alternative Data for Steak Dinners

The data points in this scatter diagram of an alternative data set for the price of dinners and the quantity demanded per day do *not* seem to cluster around a negatively sloped *straight-line* demand curve.

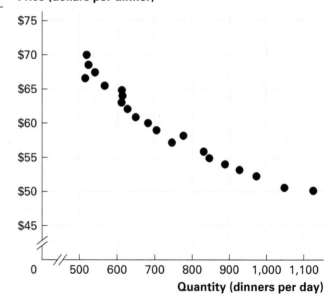

Price (dollars per dinner)

Price (dollars per dinner)

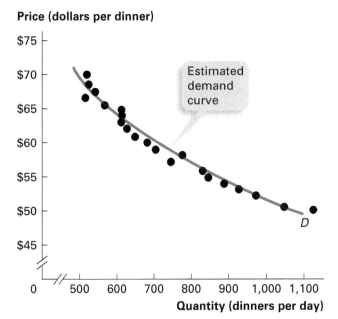

Figure 3.9 Estimated Nonlinear Demand Curve

A nonlinear (log-linear) demand curve best fits the data points in Figure 3.8.

its logarithm. Mathematically, you can change the logarithm of a number to the number itself by raising e to the logarithm of the number. So to obtain $\widehat{Q}^d$ itself, it is common to use $e^{\ln\widehat{Q}d}$. For reasons dealing with the statistics of the error term, this procedure is an approximation, but any error is usually small and therefore is typically ignored.

The examples of regression we have used all focus on estimating the demand function. But regression is used for much more than simply estimating demand functions. For example:

- Every 5 to 10 minutes, at the front of each popular attraction, The Walt Disney Company posts estimated wait times for the attraction. Regression is used to help forecast these wait times.
- The Portland Trailblazers have used a sophisticated type of regression to help forecast the probability that college basketball players will have successful NBA careers.
- Schneider Logistics, a part of the large transportation company Schneider National, uses regression models to help predict the profitability of different freight flows.

Clearly, regression analysis plays an important role in many aspects of many different businesses.

Using regression to estimate the coefficients of the demand for your product results in precise estimates of how much consumers respond to changes, enabling you to make better decisions about pricing and production. There will be times, however, when you do not have enough data to use regression analysis to estimate the demand for your product. In other situations, you might want precise estimates of, say, the effect of a change in supply on the price you must pay for an input, and again you may not have enough data to estimate a regression. In these and other cases, another tool, called elasticity, sometimes can provide the valuable information you need.

Which Regression to Use?

Your research department gives you the following two estimated demand curves. The estimated demand curve to the left is log-linear, and the estimated demand curve to the right is linear.

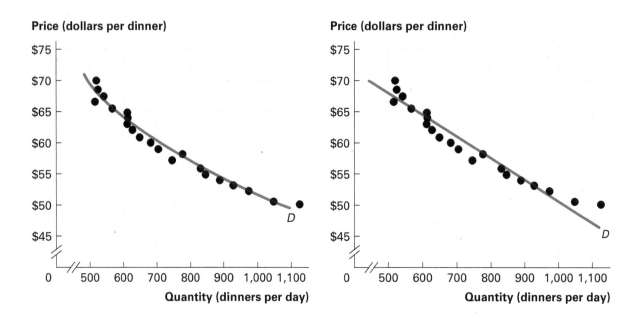

a. Which regression do you think has the highest R^2—the one with the log-linear specification or the one with the linear specification? Explain your answer.

b. Are the predicted quantities from one demand curve *always* closer to the actual quantities than the predicted quantities from the other demand curve?

c. Which estimated demand curve would you use to make your decisions? Why?

Answer

a. The log-linear specification is closer to more of the data points than the linear specification. So the R^2 of the log-linear specification exceeds that of the linear specification.

b. Even though the predicted quantities from the log-linear specification are closer to most of the actual quantities, there are a few predicted quantities that are closer when using the linear specification. In particular, for prices of $67 and $64, the predicted quantities from the linear specification are closer to the actual quantities than the predictions from the log-linear specification.

c. As a manager, you want to base your decisions on the most accurate information possible. The log-linear specification has the higher R^2, which means that it does a better job of capturing the variation in the actual quantities than does the linear specification. Consequently, you should use the log-linear specification as the basis for your decisions.

3.4 Elasticity

Learning Objective 3.4 Discuss different elasticity measures and their use.

At its most basic level, *elasticity* measures responsiveness: How strongly does the quantity demanded of a product respond to a change in one of the factors affecting demand? This section describes elasticity for three of these factors: the price of the product, income, and the price of a related good. Elasticity gives a quantitative measure of the strength of the demand response to all three factors.

The Price Elasticity of Demand

The most fundamental elasticity is the price elasticity of demand. The **price elasticity of demand** measures how strongly the quantity demanded changes when the price of the product changes—it measures the movement along a demand curve resulting from a change in the price. More specifically, the price elasticity of demand (ε) is the absolute value of the percentage change in the quantity demanded divided by the percentage change in the price:

$$\varepsilon = \left| \frac{\text{Percentage change in quantity demanded}}{\text{Percentage change in price}} \right| \qquad 3.1$$

> **Price elasticity of demand** A measure of how strongly the quantity demanded changes when the price changes, equal to the absolute value of the percentage change in the quantity demanded divided by the percentage change in the price.

Recall that, according to the law of demand, whenever the price of a product rises, the quantity demanded falls, and whenever the price falls, the quantity demanded rises. So in the formula the sign of one of the changes is always positive and that of the other is always negative. Because the resulting elasticity would always be negative, it is common to take the absolute value to eliminate the negative sign.[2]

The percentage change in the quantity demanded is $(\Delta Q^d / Q^d) \times 100$, where the Δ means "change in." The percentage change in price is $(\Delta P / P) \times 100$. Combining these shows that the price elasticity of demand equals

$$\varepsilon = \left| \frac{(\Delta Q^d / Q^d) \times 100}{(\Delta P / P) \times 100} \right| = \left| \frac{(\Delta Q^d / Q^d)}{(\Delta P / P)} \right| \qquad 3.2$$

Why does the price elasticity of demand use percentages? For a linear demand curve, such as $Q^d = a - (b \times P)$, it might seem more logical to use the estimated value of b as the measure of elasticity because, as you learned in Chapter 2, b tells you how much the quantity demanded changes in response to a \$1 change in the price. For example, the estimated demand function for steak dinners at your restaurant chain had an estimated value for $\hat{b}$ of −20.04, which meant that a \$1 increase in the price of a steak dinner decreased the quantity demanded by approximately 20 dinners per night. But suppose that you were interested in the decrease per week rather than the decrease per day. In that case, you would estimate the demand function using quantity data accumulated for seven days rather than for a single day. With this change, a \$1 increase in the price decreases the quantity of steak dinners demanded (for the week) by approximately 140 dinners per week. The estimated value of $\hat{b}$ would increase sevenfold, to 7×-20.04, or −140.28. If you used $\hat{b}$ as your measure of elasticity, you would see that it changed by merely switching the quantity from daily demand to weekly demand. Indeed, *any* change in the units of quantity or price affects the estimated value of $\hat{b}$. If your chain of steak restaurants had locations in

---

2 Some sources, however, retain the negative sign. In those cases, you can convert the elasticities you find there to the elasticity we discuss by dropping the negative sign.

England, the estimated value of $\hat{b}$ for the U.K. demand function would be different from that of the U.S. demand function simply because the price in the United Kingdom is measured in pounds and the price in the United States is measured in dollars *even if the response to a $1 change in the price is identical* for the two demand functions.

To avoid the problems of using a measure of elasticity that changes with the units, economists have defined the price elasticity of demand using percentages because percentages do not change when the units change.

Using the Price Elasticity of Demand

Equation 3.1 enables you to calculate the price elasticity of demand using information on the percentage change in the quantity demanded and the percentage change in the price. For instance, if a 10 percent increase in the price of a good leads to a 5 percent decrease in the quantity demanded, the price elasticity of demand for the good equals

$$\left| \frac{-5 \text{ percent}}{10 \text{ percent}} \right| = 0.5$$

Equation 3.1 can also be rearranged to calculate (or predict) the percentage change in the quantity demanded that results from a percentage change in the price or the percentage change in the price that results from a percentage change in the quantity. For example, suppose that at your steak restaurants you determine the price elasticity of demand for steak dinners is 1.3 and the price of a dinner rises by 6 percent. What does the decrease in the quantity of dinners demanded equal? To answer this question, rearrange the formula for price elasticity of demand to isolate the percentage change in the quantity demanded:

$$\varepsilon \times (\text{Percentage change in price}) = (\text{Percentage change in quantity demanded}) \quad \textbf{3.3}$$

Using the value for the price elasticity of demand and the percentage change in the price in Equation 3.3, the percentage change in the quantity demanded will be $1.3 \times 6 \text{ percent} = 7.8 \text{ percent}$. With the knowledge that you will sell 7.8 percent fewer dinners, you can now make better managerial decisions.

In addition to your steak dinners, suppose that your restaurants also serve chicken. Because of lower food costs for chicken, suppose that analysts predict the quantity of chicken will increase by 10 percent. The price elasticity of demand for chicken is approximately 0.4. Managers at your restaurant chain will be interested in how much the price of chicken will fall with the increase in quantity. Once again, you can use the equation for price elasticity of demand to forecast the fall in the price. This time you rearrange the equation to isolate the percentage change in price:

$$(\text{Percentage change in price}) = \frac{(\text{Percentage change in quantity})}{\varepsilon}$$

In the rearranged equation, two changes have been made:

- The calculation uses the percentage change in the quantity rather than the percentage change in the quantity demanded. This change reflects the fact that at equilibrium the percentage change in the quantity demanded must equal the percentage change in the quantity.
- Because you already know that an increase in the quantity lowers the price, there is no negative sign in the percentage change in price term.

You can combine the rearranged equation with the elasticity and the predicted change in quantity to predict that the percentage fall in the price will be 10 percent/0.4 = 25 percent. This information is valuable to managers of the chain because it helps them make better decisions about potential menu specials—featuring more dishes with chicken might increase profit!

Elasticity Along a Linear Demand Curve

Rearranging the formula for the price elasticity of demand from Equation 3.2, $\varepsilon = |(\Delta Q^d/Q^d)/(\Delta P/P)|$, helps demonstrate a possibly unforeseen result in the behavior of the price elasticity of demand at different points along a linear, downward-sloping demand curve:

$$\varepsilon = \left|\frac{\frac{\Delta Q^d}{Q^d}}{\frac{\Delta P}{P}}\right| = \left|\frac{\Delta Q^d}{Q^d} \times \frac{P}{\Delta P}\right| = \left|\frac{\Delta Q^d \times P}{Q^d \times \Delta P}\right| = \left|\frac{\Delta Q^d \times P}{\Delta P \times Q^d}\right| = \left|\frac{\Delta Q^d}{\Delta P} \times \frac{P}{Q^d}\right|$$

In this string of equalities, the second equality reflects the division of $\Delta Q^d/Q^d$ by $\Delta P/P$; the third equality is the result of multiplying the two fractions; the fourth equality switched the terms in the denominator; and the last equality breaks the fraction into two components. In the last expression, $|(\Delta Q^d/\Delta P) \times (P/Q^d)|$, the term $(\Delta Q^d/\Delta P)$ is the change in the quantity demanded brought about by a \$1 change in the price. Sound familiar? In the algebraic equation for the linear demand function you have been using, $Q^d = a - (b \times P)$, the coefficient b is the change in the quantity demanded brought about by a \$1 change in the price. So in the last expression, substitute the coefficient b for the $(\Delta Q^d/\Delta P)$ term to show that for a linear demand curve[3]

$$\varepsilon = |b \times (P/Q^d)| \qquad\qquad 3.4$$

You can use Equation 3.4 to calculate the price elasticity of demand at any *one* point on a linear, downward-sloping demand curve, so Equation 3.4 is called the *point elasticity* formula. In Figure 3.10, a linear demand curve showing the price and quantity of

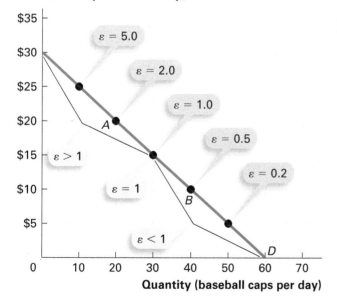

Price (dollars per baseball cap)

Quantity (baseball caps per day)

Figure 3.10 Price Elasticity of Demand Along a Linear Demand Curve

The point elasticity formula, $\varepsilon = |b \times (P/Q^d)|$, can be used to calculate the price elasticity of demand at each of the points on a linear demand curve. On a linear, downward-sloping demand curve, the price elasticity of demand falls in value moving down the curve.

---

3 Section 3.A of the Appendix at the end of this chapter uses calculus to derive a general version of Equation 3.4 for any demand function.

baseball caps, the price elasticity of demand can be calculated at any of the points on the demand curve. The value of b for the demand curve illustrated in the figure is –2 baseball caps per dollar. Using the point elasticity formula, you find that at point A on the demand curve, the elasticity equals $|-2 \times (\$20/20)| = 2.0$. And at point B, the elasticity is $|-2 \times (\$10/40)| = 0.5$. Equation 3.4 and Figure 3.10 show a remarkable result: The price elasticity of demand changes with movements along the linear demand curve. In particular, moving downward along the demand curve, the price elasticity of demand falls in value. At the midpoint of the demand curve, the price elasticity of demand equals 1.0. At points above the midpoint, it exceeds 1.0, and at points below the midpoint, it is less than 1.0. As a manager, keep in mind that the price elasticity of demand will be different at each point on a linear demand curve. If your decision revolves around a certain price, you must be certain that you use the elasticity at *that* price.

You can also use Equation 3.4 to calculate the elasticity at points on an estimated demand curve. Assuming that the demand curve is linear, the regression analysis gives $\widehat{Q}^{\mathrm{d}} = \hat{a} - (\hat{b} \times P)$, where $\hat{b}$ is the estimated value of the b coefficient and $\widehat{Q}^{\mathrm{d}}$ is the predicted quantity demanded. Then for any price (P), you can use the estimated value of $\hat{b}$ and the predicted quantity demanded, $\widehat{Q}^{\mathrm{d}}$, in Equation 3.4 to calculate the estimated value of the price elasticity of demand at that point on the demand curve:

$$\hat{\varepsilon} = |\hat{b} \times (P/\widehat{Q}^{\mathrm{d}})| \qquad\qquad \textbf{3.5}$$

Elasticity Along a Log-Linear Demand Curve

Calculating the price elasticity of demand for a log-linear demand curve, $\ln Q^{\mathrm{d}} = a - (b \times \ln P)$, is immediate: The elasticity equals the value of the b coefficient. Refer to the Appendix at the end of this chapter to see a proof of this result using calculus. In Figure 3.11, the b coefficient for the illustrated demand curve for baseball caps is –1.00, so the price elasticity of demand equals 1.00 at points A and B. In fact, at *all* points on this demand curve, the price elasticity of demand is equal to 1.00. Demand curves for which the price elasticity of demand is the same at all points are called *constant elasticity of demand* curves.

Figure 3.11 Price Elasticity of Demand Along a Log-Linear Demand Curve

The price elasticity of demand is constant at all points along a log-linear demand curve.

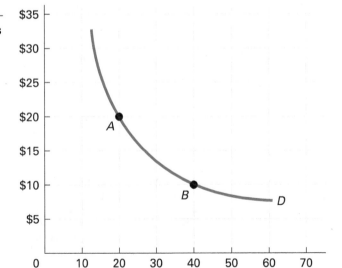

If a log-linear demand curve has been estimated, such as $\ln \widehat{Q^d} = \hat{a} - (\hat{b} \times \ln P)$, the estimated price elasticity of demand is $\hat{b}$ and is the same at all points on the estimated demand curve.

Elastic, Unit-Elastic, and Inelastic Demand

The price elasticity of demand measures how strongly demanders respond to a change in the price of the good. For example, economists have estimated the price elasticity of demand for coffee to be 0.25. Rearranging the formula for the price elasticity of demand,

$$\varepsilon = \left| \frac{\text{Percentage change in quantity demanded}}{\text{Percentage change in price}} \right|$$

shows that

$\varepsilon \times$ (Percentage change in price) = (Percentage change in quantity demanded)

Using the rearranged formula, if the price of coffee rises by 10 percent, you can calculate that the percentage change in the quantity of coffee demanded is 0.25×10 percent = 2.5 percent. In other words, a 10 percent increase in the price of coffee leads to a 2.5 percent decrease in the quantity of coffee demanded. In contrast, economists have estimated the price elasticity of demand for Pepsi to be 1.55. If the price of Pepsi rises by 10 percent, then the quantity of Pepsi demanded decreases by 1.55×10 percent = 15.5 percent. There is a significant difference between the strength of the consumer response to a change in the price of coffee and the consumer response to a change in the price of Pepsi. The definitions of elastic demand, unit-elastic demand, and inelastic demand formalize this difference.

Elastic demand means that consumers respond strongly to a change in price. For a product with elastic demand, the percentage change in the quantity demanded exceeds the percentage change in the price, so the definition of the price elasticity of demand shows that it is greater than 1.00. Using this definition, we see that the demand for Pepsi is elastic.

Unit-elastic demand means that consumer response to a change in price is one-to-one; that is, a 10 percent increase in the price creates a 10 percent decrease in the quantity demanded. In this case, the definition of elasticity shows that the price elasticity of demand is equal to 1.00.

Inelastic demand means that consumers respond weakly to a change in price. The percentage change in the quantity demanded is less than the percentage change in the price, so the price elasticity of demand is less than 1.00 for a product with inelastic demand. Using this definition, we see that the demand for coffee is inelastic.

When two demands have different elasticities, how is the difference reflected in their demand curves? Figure 3.12 answers this question for the case in which two demand curves cross. Starting from point A, the figure shows that in response to a $5 increase in the price of baseball caps, the decrease in the quantity demanded along demand curve D_2 (20 caps) exceeds the decrease in the quantity demanded along demand curve D_1 (5 caps). This difference in response means that the elasticity on demand curve D_2 at point A is larger than the elasticity on demand curve D_1 at point A. This result is precisely in line with the intuitive meaning of elasticity as responsiveness: At the point where the demand curves cross, the percentage change in price from $15 to $20 is exactly the same for both demand curves, but along the (flatter) demand curve, D_2, the percentage response from consumers is stronger than along the (steeper) demand curve, D_1.

Elastic demand Demand is elastic when the percentage change in the quantity demanded exceeds the percentage change in the price; the price elasticity of demand is greater than 1.00.

Unit-elastic demand Demand is unit elastic when the percentage change in the quantity demanded equals the percentage change in the price; the price elasticity of demand is equal to 1.00.

Inelastic demand Demand is inelastic when the percentage change in the quantity demanded is less than the percentage change in the price; the price elasticity of demand is less than 1.00.

Figure 3.12 **Elastic Demand and Inelastic Demand**

At point *A*, where the demand curves cross, the difference in the lengths of the arrows shows that the quantity demanded along demand curve D_2 responds more strongly to the price hike from $15 to $20 than the quantity demanded along demand curve D_1. So, the price elasticity of demand at point *A* is larger on demand curve D_2 than on demand curve D_1.

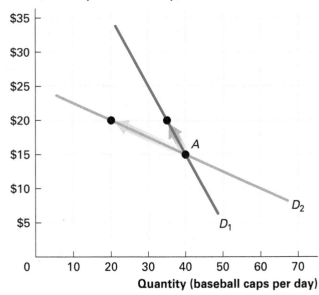

Price (dollars per baseball cap)

Perfectly Elastic Demand and Perfectly Inelastic Demand

At the point where two demand curves cross, the flatter demand curve has a larger elasticity. This observation leads to the definitions of two extreme elasticities: perfectly elastic demand and perfectly inelastic demand. **Perfectly elastic demand** means consumer response to a change in the price is the largest possible response in the quantity demanded: A rise in the price decreases the quantity demanded to zero, and a fall in the price increases the quantity demanded to infinity. The demand for milk from a particular dairy is very close to perfectly elastic. If the dairy's managers raise its price, no one buys from the dairy because they can buy from hundreds of thousands of other dairies, so the quantity demanded falls to zero. If the dairy's managers lower its price, everyone in the world will want to buy from it. When demand is perfectly elastic, the elasticity is defined to equal infinity (∞). A horizontal demand curve is the flattest possible demand curve, showing the largest possible response. As illustrated in Figure 3.13(a), all points on a horizontal demand curve are perfectly elastic.

Perfectly elastic demand
Demand is perfectly elastic when a change in the price creates the largest possible response in the quantity demanded: A rise in the price decreases the quantity demanded to zero, and a fall in the price increases the quantity demanded to infinity.

Perfectly inelastic demand means consumer response to a change in the price is the smallest possible response: *no* change in the quantity demanded. The demand for a lifesaving drug can be perfectly inelastic: Whether managers raise the price or lower the price, consumers will buy the same quantity. When demand is perfectly inelastic, the price elasticity of demand equals 0. A vertical demand curve is the steepest possible demand curve, showing the smallest possible response. As Figure 3.13(b) shows, all points on a vertical demand curve are perfectly inelastic.

Perfectly inelastic demand
Demand is perfectly inelastic when a change in the price creates the smallest possible response: There is *no* change in the quantity demanded.

Factors Affecting the Size of the Price Elasticity of Demand

Skilled managers often try to change the price elasticity of demand for their product to increase their firm's profit. But to be able to affect the price elasticity of demand, you must understand the factors involved.

Figure 3.13 Perfectly Elastic Demand and Perfectly Inelastic Demand

(a) Perfectly Elastic Demand
At any point on the horizontal demand curve for the milk from a particular dairy demand is perfectly elastic, so the elasticity equals ∞ at all points on the demand curve.

(b) Perfectly Inelastic Demand
At any point on the vertical demand curve for a lifesaving drug demand is perfectly inelastic, so the elasticity equals 0 at all points on the demand curve.

Price (dollars per gallon of milk)

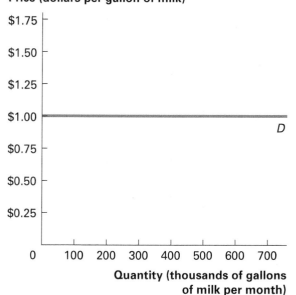

Price (dollars per dose)

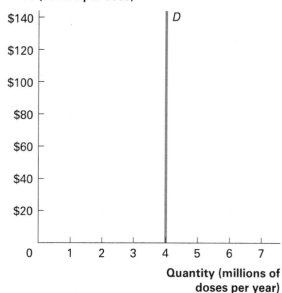

Two general factors influence the size of the price elasticity of demand: the number of close substitutes and the fraction of the budget spent on the product. There is no formula into which you can plug these factors to calculate a precise value. Nonetheless, these factors provide valuable insights into the size of the price elasticity of demand for a product and how you might be able to change it to your advantage.

The Number of Close Substitutes The larger the number of close substitutes for a product, the larger its price elasticity of demand. You probably already understand intuitively that the existence of a large number of close substitutes means that consumers will respond strongly to a price change. For example, New Balance athletic shoes have many substitutes, including Nike, Converse, and Puma. When the price of New Balance shoes rises, the quantity demanded will decrease substantially because consumers can switch to one of the many other substitute shoes. Alternatively, when the price falls, the quantity demanded will increase as consumers switch away from the many other brands of shoes they had been buying to the now-cheaper New Balance shoes.

Of course, the reverse also applies: The smaller the number of close substitutes, the smaller the price elasticity of demand. The same intuition applies: When the price rises, consumers cannot decrease the quantity they demand by much because of a lack of alternatives. And when the price falls, there is not much switching away from other substitutes precisely because there are not many substitutes. This result is why the price elasticity of demand for gasoline, a product with few substitutes, is much smaller than the price elasticity of demand for New Balance shoes, a product with many substitutes.

The general principle that the availability of more substitutes leads to a larger price elasticity of demand has three implications:

1. **The more broadly defined the product, the smaller the price elasticity of demand**. For instance, soda is a broadly defined product that includes *all* types of carbonated beverages, including Pepsi-Cola, Coca-Cola, and Mountain Dew. In contrast, Pepsi-Cola is narrowly defined to only that drink. Economists have estimated that the price elasticity of demand for soda is 0.80, while that for Pepsi is 1.55. Why is the price elasticity of demand for soda so much smaller than the price elasticity of demand for Pepsi? The answer is that soda has fewer substitutes than Pepsi. Fruit drinks, energy drinks, coffee, and other liquids serve as substitutes for soda. All of these other products can substitute for Pepsi, *plus* all other types of soda also can substitute for Pepsi. So a narrowly defined, specific product such as Pepsi has many more substitutes and hence a larger price elasticity of demand than a broadly defined, general product such as soda.

   This distinction can save you from making erroneous decisions. For example, suppose that you are the brand manager for the Ford Focus and are considering raising the price by 2 percent. To help with the decision, you want to forecast how the change in price will affect sales. Suppose that you do not have an estimate of either the demand curve or the price elasticity of demand for the Focus. Analysts have estimated the price elasticity of demand for the broader category of automobiles to be 0.9. You might be tempted to use this elasticity as your estimate of the price elasticity of demand for the Focus. If you use this number, your forecast is that sales of the Focus will decrease by 0.9×2 percent $= 1.8$ percent. But you want the elasticity for the Ford Focus, *not* the elasticity for automobiles in general. The Focus is a more specific product, so its price elasticity of demand is larger than the price elasticity of demand for automobiles. Indeed, the price elasticity of demand for a Ford compact car, such as the Focus, has been estimated to be 6.0, changing the forecasted decrease in sales to 6.0×2 percent $= 12.0$ percent. Using the price elasticity of demand for a general product category such as cars rather than the specific product under consideration (the Focus) could lead you to a bad decision!

2. **A luxury good has a larger price elasticity of demand than does a necessity**. Luxury goods have more substitutes than necessities. For instance, compare a cruise vacation to toothpaste. A cruise easily qualifies as a luxury. Most people (hopefully) classify toothpaste as a necessity. There are many more substitutes for cruises than for toothpaste. Instead of going on a cruise, people can tour Europe by rail, go on a safari in Africa, trek through Alaska, spend time at a beach house, or enjoy any number of alternatives. There are not nearly as many substitutes for toothpaste. Baking soda might qualify, but it is not a close substitute for toothpaste (and it does not taste as good!). The fact that there are more substitutes for luxuries than necessities helps explain why the price elasticity of demand for luxuries is larger than that for necessities.

3. **The more time that has elapsed since a price change, the larger the price elasticity of demand**. This result again hinges on the number of substitutes. Consider a price hike. The quantity demanded immediately decreases a little, but many consumers who are buying the good will not immediately know of substitutes. As time passes, consumers will search for, find, and buy substitutes. This additional switch away from the now-higher-priced good makes the decrease in its quantity demanded larger. Consequently, the price elasticity of demand increases in size as time passes. The effect of a price cut is analogous: Immediately after the price of an item falls, few consumers are aware of the price drop, so the increase in the quantity demanded is small. As time passes, more consumers learn of the lower price and switch from other alternatives to the good with the lower price, so its quantity demanded and its price elasticity of demand both increase. The managerial implication is clear: Advertise price reductions so that more consumers know of them immediately, thereby increasing the price elasticity of demand for your product. On the flip side, conceal price hikes so that fewer consumers are immediately aware of them, thereby delaying the inevitable increase in the price elasticity of demand.

   The effect on the demand and the price elasticity of demand for existing products is not immediate when a firm introduces a *new* substitute product to the marketplace for the same reason that the effect of a price change is spread out over time: It takes consumers time to learn of the new product and its properties. For example, in 2011, Bayer AG, a large German pharmaceutical company, received approval to market a first-in-its-class drug, Xarelto, to combat deep vein thrombosis (DVT). (A deep vein thrombosis occurs when a blood clot in a vein deep in the body forms. If part of the clot breaks free, it may travel to the lungs with fatal consequences.) Although other drugs existed to fight DVT, because of its unique attributes, Xarelto had no close substitutes and, consequently, a relatively small price elasticity of demand. In 2014, Pfizer and Bristol-Meyers Squibb received approval to combat DVT with their similar drug, Eliquis. Because the presence of Eliquis gave Xarelto a close substitute, analysts believed that Xarelto's market share would quickly fall and its price elasticity of demand would quickly rise. This forecast turned out to be incorrect. Xarelto's three-year lead over Eliquis meant that physicians were familiar with Xarelto and its effects. It took physicians some time to become as familiar with the new substitute, Eliquis. As time passed and physicians learned about Eliquis's effects, Xarelto's market-share growth slowly fell, and due to the increased knowledge and use of the new substitute, presumably its price elasticity of demand slowly rose.

As a manager, you can attempt to alter elasticity to your benefit. For example, if you are planning to boost your price, you definitely want consumers to believe that your product has no close substitutes because a lack of substitutes will lower the price elasticity of demand for your product and limit the decrease in sales from the price hike. To create this view, you want your advertisements to stress the unique properties of your product and make consumers believe that it is irreplaceable. Alternatively, you want consumers to think that your product will readily take the place of many other products if you are planning to cut your price. If consumers believe that your product can serve as a substitute for many alternatives, the price elasticity of demand for your product will be larger, which in turn means your sales increase will be larger after the price cut. If you are planning to introduce a new product, you need to get information out to potential consumers rapidly so that they can see how your product will substitute for products already on the market.

The Fraction of the Budget Spent on the Product The second general factor affecting the size of the price elasticity of demand is the fraction of buyers' budgets spent on the product. The larger the fraction, the larger the price elasticity of demand. Intuitively, if a product accounts for only a small fraction of consumers' budgets, they are less likely to react to a price change. The change in the quantity demanded and the price elasticity of demand will be small. However, if the product accounts for a large fraction of consumers' budgets, they notice and respond to the price change, which makes the price elasticity of demand larger. This effect goes a long way toward understanding the difference in the price elasticity of demand for housing (1.2) and that for salt (0.1). Of course, you need to keep in mind that salt is a larger fraction of the budget for some consumers than for others. For instance, the City of Rochester, New York, spends a bit more than 1 percent of its total budget, or near $7 million per year, on snow and ice removal; a substantial part of that amount goes toward the purchase of salt to help remove snow and ice. Salt accounts for a larger part of Rochester's budget than for most consumers, so Rochester's price elasticity of demand for salt is probably larger than that of most consumers.

Price Elasticity of Demand and Total Revenue

Managers who know whether the demand for their product is elastic or inelastic find it easier to make good decisions. Sometimes these decisions revolve around the total revenue of their product. As you learned in Chapter 1, the total revenue of a product (TR) is the total amount collected from sales of the product; it equals the price of the product (P) multiplied by the quantity sold (Q). In equilibrium, the quantity sold equals the quantity consumers demand (Q^d), so $TR = P \times Q^d$. Total revenue is *not* the same as total profit. To get the total profit, you must subtract the total opportunity cost from the total revenue. In some cases, however, the total revenue rather than total profit can be relevant to your decisions. Here are some examples:

- Authors and musicians receive royalties based on a percentage of the total revenue from their creation.
- Universities and professional sports teams often negotiate royalties based on the total revenue from sales of paraphernalia or clothing adorned with their logo.
- Small biotech companies frequently license their drugs to large pharmaceutical companies in exchange for a percentage of the total revenue from sales of the drug.

In all of these cases, understanding the relationship among total revenue, changes in price, and price elasticity of demand enhances decision making. Consider an increase in the price of a product. What will be the effect on the total revenue? Using the definition of total revenue, $TR = P \times Q^d$, the answer might seem clear: The increase in price boosts the total revenue. But that quick answer is too simple because it neglects the fact that an increase in price decreases the quantity demanded, which offsets the effect of the higher price. The net effect of a price hike on total revenue depends on whether the increase in price or the decrease in quantity is larger. In turn, that depends on how strongly consumers respond to the increase in price: Do they respond strongly (with a substantial decrease in the quantity demanded), or do they respond weakly (with only a minor decrease in the quantity demanded)?

Because the price elasticity of demand measures the strength of the response, it plays a key role in determining the effect of a price change on the total revenue. Take the case of a price increase:

- **Elastic demand.** If the demand for the good is elastic, then the response to a price hike will be a large decrease in the quantity demanded, so that the total revenue decreases.
- **Inelastic demand.** If the demand for the good is inelastic, then the response to a price hike will be a small decrease in the quantity demanded, so that the total revenue increases.
- **Unit-elastic demand.** If the demand for the good is unit-elastic, then the response to a price hike will be a decrease in the quantity demanded by a proportionally equal amount, so that the total revenue does not change.

Clearly, the effect of a change in the price on total revenue depends on the price elasticity of demand. The following box summarizes this relationship in what is called the *total revenue test*.

TOTAL REVENUE TEST

If $\varepsilon > 1 \Rightarrow$ Demand is elastic (consumers respond strongly to a price change).
- Price hike $\Rightarrow$ Larger percentage decrease in quantity $\Rightarrow$ Total revenue decreases: $P\uparrow, Q^d\downarrow \Rightarrow TR\downarrow$
- Price cut $\Rightarrow$ Larger percentage increase in quantity $\Rightarrow$ Total revenue increases: $P\downarrow, Q^d\uparrow \Rightarrow TR\uparrow$

If $\varepsilon = 1 \Rightarrow$ Demand is unit-elastic (consumers respond one-to-one to a price change).
- Price hike $\Rightarrow$ Equal percentage decrease in quantity $\Rightarrow$ Total revenue does not change: $P\uparrow, Q^d\downarrow \Rightarrow TR\rightarrow$
- Price cut $\Rightarrow$ Equal percentage increase in quantity $\Rightarrow$ Total revenue does not change: $P\downarrow, Q^d\uparrow \Rightarrow TR\rightarrow$

If $\varepsilon < 1 \Rightarrow$ Demand is inelastic (consumers respond weakly to a price change).
- Price hike $\Rightarrow$ Smaller percentage decrease in quantity $\Rightarrow$ Total revenue increases: $P\uparrow, Q^d\downarrow \Rightarrow TR\uparrow$
- Price cut $\Rightarrow$ Smaller percentage increase in quantity $\Rightarrow$ Total revenue decreases: $P\downarrow, Q^d\uparrow \Rightarrow TR\downarrow$

Although the total revenue test can be proven mathematically, the intuition behind the test is extremely strong. (If you're interested in the proof, see Section 3.B of the Appendix at the end of this chapter.) The test is divided into three parts:

1. **Elastic demand.** An increase in the price ($P\uparrow$) leads to a decrease in the quantity demanded ($Q^d\downarrow$). Because the demand is elastic, the percentage decrease in the quantity demanded exceeds the percentage increase in the price, so the $\downarrow$ quantity arrow is larger than the $\uparrow$ price arrow. Consequently, total revenue, $P \times Q^d$, decreases ($TR\downarrow$) because the percentage decrease in the quantity exceeds the percentage increase in the price.

2. **Unit-elastic demand.** The percentage increase in the price equals the percentage decrease in the quantity demanded, which makes the arrows next to P and Q^d the same size. In this case, the effect on total revenue from the decrease in the quantity demanded exactly offsets the effect from the higher price, so the total revenue does not change ($TR \rightarrow$).

3. **Inelastic demand.** An increase in the price ($P\uparrow$) leads to a decrease in the quantity demanded ($Q^d\downarrow$), but the percentage decrease in the quantity demanded is less than the percentage increase in the price, so the $\uparrow$ price arrow is larger than the $\downarrow$ quantity arrow. The total revenue increases ($TR\uparrow$).

Figure 3.14(a) uses the linear demand curve from Figure 3.10 to show the relationship of the changes in total revenue and elasticity along a linear, downward-sloping demand curve. When demand is elastic, the range from $30 to $15 per baseball cap, lowering the price and increasing the quantity demanded increase the total revenue. When demand is inelastic, the range from $15 to $0 per cap, lowering the price and increasing the quantity demanded decrease the total revenue. As the figure illustrates, along a linear demand curve, the total revenue equals its maximum when the price elasticity of demand equals 1.0.

Suppose that you are an executive in a biotech company that has licensed a drug to Pfizer and will receive a royalty of 10 percent of the total revenue Pfizer collects from the sale of the drug. Your goal is to have Pfizer set the price that

Figure 3.14 Relationship Between Total Revenue and Elasticity Along a Linear, Downward-Sloping Demand Curve

(a) Linear Demand Curve
Moving down along a downward-sloping linear demand curve by lowering the price, the price elasticity of demand falls in value.

(b) Total Revenue
When demand is elastic, moving down along the demand curve by lowering the price increases the total revenue. When demand is inelastic, however, moving down along the demand curve by lowering the price decreases the total revenue. The total revenue reaches its maximum when the price elasticity of demand equals 1.0.

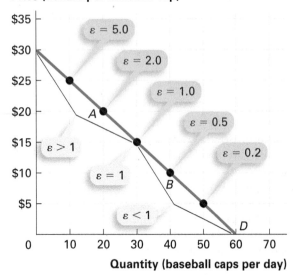

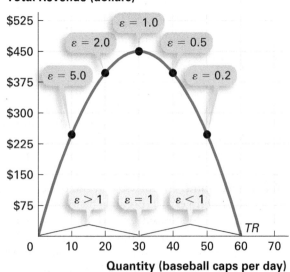

maximizes Pfizer's total revenue because that will maximize your royalty and profit. Knowing the price elasticity of demand for your drug is important to you. For example, if your drug is the only one to treat an illness, Pfizer has a monopoly. In other words, it is the only seller in the market. You will learn in Chapter 6 that because Pfizer has a monopoly, its profit-maximizing price for the product will fall in the elastic range of the demand. Accepting this result, you can see that when you license your drug to Pfizer, you need to push Pfizer to cut the price from what it wants to set because the total revenue test shows that when demand is elastic, a decrease in the price increases total revenue. If Pfizer's total revenue increases, the royalty revenue your company receives will get a boost as well. Of course, Pfizer will resist lowering the price, but because you know that the demand for the drug is elastic, your biotech company will keep pressuring Pfizer.

DECISION SNAPSHOT

Advertising and the Price Elasticity of Demand

Your marketing department estimates that at the current price and quantity, your firm's product has a price elasticity of demand of 1.1. You run an advertising campaign that changes the demand, so that at the current price and quantity the elasticity falls to 0.8. In response to this change, would you raise the price, lower it, or keep it the same? Explain your answer.

Answer
You should raise your price. Before the advertising campaign, the demand for your product was elastic, so according to the total revenue test, a price hike would lower your firm's total revenue. After the campaign, the demand became inelastic. You now will be able to increase your firm's profit by raising the price. Because the demand is inelastic, a price hike raises your firm's total revenue. A price hike also decreases the quantity demanded, so your firm produces less, which decreases your costs. Raising revenue and lowering cost unambiguously boost your firm's profit!

Income Elasticity and Cross-Price Elasticity of Demand

So far, you have learned about only one type of elasticity, the price elasticity of demand. Although this is the most important elasticity, there are two others to keep in mind: the income elasticity of demand and the cross-price elasticity of demand. You are unlikely to use either of these two measures often, but understanding the different types of elasticity will help you avoid confusing them. In addition, learning about income elasticity and cross-price elasticity will help reinforce your understanding of the price elasticity of demand because *all* elasticities have four points in common: (1) changes are expressed as percentages, (2) fractions are used, (3) the factor driving the change is in the denominator, and (4) the factor responding to the change is in the numerator. (The Appendix at the end of this chapter presents a calculus treatment of these elasticities.)

Income Elasticity of Demand

Income elasticity of demand A measure of how strongly the quantity demanded responds to a change in consumers' income; it equals the percentage change in the quantity demanded divided by the percentage change in income.

The **income elasticity of demand** measures how strongly the quantity demanded responds to a change in consumers' income. The income elasticity of demand (ε_{INC}) is defined as the percentage change in the quantity demanded divided by the percentage change in income:

$$\varepsilon_{INC} = \frac{(\text{Percentage change in the quantity demanded})}{(\text{Percentage change in income})}$$

The definition differs from that of the price elasticity of demand in one important respect: The price elasticity of demand uses the absolute value, but the income elasticity of demand does not. The reason for this difference is straightforward. The price elasticity of demand is always negative, so its sign is inconsequential. In contrast, the income elasticity of demand is positive for a normal good and negative for an inferior good. Recall that an increase in income (a positive change in income) leads to an increase in demand for a normal good (which, for a given price, means a positive change in the quantity demanded). Therefore, the income elasticity of demand for a normal good equals one positive number divided by another, so the resulting elasticity is positive. In contrast, an increase in income leads to a *decrease* in demand for an inferior good. Therefore, the income elasticity of demand for an inferior good equals a negative number divided by a positive number, and the resulting elasticity is negative. Because the sign of the income elasticity of demand indicates whether the good is normal or inferior, the absolute value is not used.

Goods with income elasticities that exceed 1.0 are called *luxury goods*. Air travel, Caribbean cruises, and fine dining are examples of luxury goods. If you are a manager of a company producing a luxury good, such as steak dinners, you must keep an eye on forecasts of how income is changing. Any change in income will affect the demand for your product, and the change in demand will be larger than the change in income. So the effect on your business will be very important.

Goods with income elasticities between zero and 1.0 are called *necessities*. Groceries, gasoline, and shampoo are examples of necessities. If you are a manager of a company producing a necessity, changes in consumers' income are not as important to you. Any change in income will affect the demand for your product, but the change will be smaller than the change in income. It will affect your business, but the effect will be minor.

Table 3.2 summarizes the key points about the income elasticity of demand, including its formula and the meaning of a positive or negative sign.

Table 3.2 Income Elasticity of Demand

- $\varepsilon_{INC} = \dfrac{(\text{Percentage change in the quantity demanded})}{(\text{Percentage change in income})}$
- ε_{INC} is positive for a normal good.
- ε_{INC} is negative for an inferior good.

Cross-Price Elasticity of Demand

Cross-price elasticity of demand A measure of how strongly the quantity demanded changes when the price of a related product changes; it equals the percentage change in the quantity demanded divided by the percentage change in the price of the related product.

The **cross-price elasticity of demand** measures how strongly the quantity demanded responds to a change in the price of a related product. The cross-price elasticity of demand (ε_{CROSS}) is equal to the percentage change in the quantity demanded divided by the percentage change in the price of the related good:

$$\varepsilon_{CROSS} = \frac{(\text{Percentage change in the quantity demanded})}{(\text{Percentage change in the price of the related good})}$$

The cross-price elasticity of demand is similar to the income elasticity of demand—and different from the price elasticity of demand—with regard to absolute value. The cross-price elasticity of demand does not use the absolute value because the sign of the elasticity again provides information about the relationship of the products. Consider substitutes. Nike athletic shoes are a substitute for New Balance athletic shoes. A rise in the price of the substitute good, Nike athletic shoes, leads to an increase in demand (and, for any price, an increase the quantity demanded) for New Balance athletic shoes. For substitutes, the cross-price elasticity of demand equals one positive number divided by another, so the resulting elasticity is positive. For complementary goods, such as hot dogs and hot dog buns at a grocery store, an increase in the price of a complement leads to a *decrease* in the quantity demanded of the first good. For complements, the cross-price elasticity of demand equals a negative number divided by a positive number, so the cross-price elasticity of demand is negative for complements.

Table 3.3 summarizes the key points about the cross-price elasticity of demand, including its formula and the meaning of a positive or negative sign.

Table 3.3 **Cross-Price Elasticity of Demand**

- $\varepsilon_{CROSS} = \dfrac{(\text{Percentage change in the quantity demanded})}{(\text{Percentage change in the price of the related good})}$
- ε_{CROSS} is positive for substitute goods.
- ε_{CROSS} is negative for complementary goods.

The Price Elasticity of Demand for a Touch-Screen Smartphone

SOLVED **PROBLEM**

When Apple introduced the iPhone in 2007, it was one of the first smartphones to have a touch screen. You are a manager at a smartphone company similar to Apple and your company has quickly introduced its own smartphone with a touch screen.

a. Suppose your marketing department tells you that the demand curve for your smartphone is $Q^d = 9{,}900{,}000 - (9{,}000 \times P)$. The price is $650, and the predicted quantity demanded is 4,050,000. At that price and estimated quantity, what is the price elasticity of demand for your smartphone?

b. At a sales meeting, some of the participants ask you what would happen to total revenue if you raised the price by 2 percent. Do not calculate the change in revenue; instead, just indicate whether your total revenue would rise, fall, or not change.

c. It's now a few years later, and other companies, like HTC and Samsung, have introduced smartphones with touch screens. How did introduction of these new phones affect the price elasticity of demand for your touch-screen smartphone? Explain your answer.

Answer

a. The price elasticity of demand can be calculated using the estimated demand function and Equation 3.5. Using this equation, the price elasticity of demand equals

$$|-9{,}000 \times (\$650/4{,}050{,}000)| = 1.44$$

b. At this point on the demand curve, the demand is elastic. The total revenue test shows that when the demand is elastic, an increase in price decreases total revenue. So if you raised the price of your smartphone by 2 percent, your total revenue would decrease.

c. The new smartphones with touch screens are substitutes for your smartphone. The presence of more substitutes increases the price elasticity of demand, so as time passed after the new phones were introduced, the price elasticity of demand for your smartphone increased.

3.5 Regression Analysis and Elasticity

Learning Objective 3.5 Use regression analysis and the different elasticity measures to make better managerial decisions.

Regression analysis and the different elasticity measures are important to managers because they help quantify decision making. As a manager, you will face situations in which you need to know the exact amount of a change in the price of an input, the precise change in your cost when you change your production, or the actual decrease in quantity demanded when you raise the price of your product. Regression analysis and the application of the different elasticity measures can help you answer these and many other important questions.

Using Regression Analysis

Using the results from regression analysis is an essential task in many managerial positions. Analysts can use regression analysis for much more than estimating a demand curve. For example, you can use it to estimate how your costs change when production changes. We explain this important concept, called *marginal cost*, in Chapter 4 and use it in all future chapters. Large companies with demand that depends significantly on a specific influence often use regression analysis to forecast changes in such factors as personal income (important to automobile manufacturers such as General Motors and Honda) or new home sales (important to home improvement stores such as Home Depot and Lowe's).

The ultimate goal of regression analysis is to help you make better decisions. For example, as a manager at the high-end steak restaurant chain, you can use an estimated demand function to help you make both immediate decisions about the price to set *and* long-term decisions about whether to open a new location. Suppose that an analyst for your firm has used regression to determine that the nightly demand for your chain's steak dinners depends on the following factors:

1. The price of the dinners, measured as dollars per dinner
2. The average income of residents living within the city, measured as dollars per person
3. The unemployment rate within the city, measured as the percentage unemployment rate
4. The population within 30 miles of the restaurant

Suppose that Table 3.4 includes the estimated coefficients and their standard errors, t-statistics, and P-values.[4] The R^2 of the regression is 0.72, so the regression predicts the data reasonably well. In the table, the t-statistics for all five coefficients are greater than 1.96, and accordingly all five P-values are less than 5 percent (0.05). Therefore, you are confident that all the variables included in the regression affect the demand for steak dinners. The coefficient for the price variable, −12.9, shows that a $1 increase in the price of a dinner decreases the quantity demanded by −12.9 × $1, or 12.9 dinners per night. Similarly, the coefficient for the average income variable, 0.0073, shows that a $1,000 increase in average income increases the demand by 0.0073 × 1,000, or 7.3 dinners per night. The coefficient for the unemployment rate

---

4 Often regression results are written with the standard errors in parentheses below the estimated coefficients:
$Q^d = 139.2 - (12.9 \times \text{PRICE}) + (0.0073 \times \text{INCOME}) - (10.0 \times \text{UNEMPLOYMENT}) + (0.0005 \times \text{POPULATION})$
    (11.9)   (1.8)   (0.0012)   (3.2)   (0.0002)

Table 3.4 Estimated Demand Function for Steak Dinners

The table shows the results of a regression of the demand for meals at an upscale steak restaurant, with the estimated coefficients for the price, average income in the city in which the restaurant is located, unemployment rate in the city, and population of the city.

	Coefficient	Standard Error	t Stat	P-value	Lower 95%	Upper 95%
Constant	139.2	11.9	11.7	0.00	117.3	163.1
Price of dinner	−12.9	1.8	7.2	0.00	−9.4	−16.4
Average income	0.0073	0.0012	6.1	0.00	4.9	9.7
Unemployment rate	−10.0	3.1	3.1	0.00	−3.9	−16.5
Population	0.0005	0.0002	2.5	0.02	0.0001	0.0009

variable, −10.0, shows that a one percentage point increase in the unemployment rate decreases the demand by −10.0 × 1, or 10 dinners per night. And the coefficient for the population variable, 0.0005, shows that a 1,000-person increase in population increases the demand by 0.0005 × 1,000, or 0.5 dinners per night.

Short-Run Decisions Using Regression Analysis

Although a more detailed explanation of how managers determine price must wait until Chapter 6, intuitively it is clear that demand must play a role. The estimated demand function can help determine what price to charge in different cities because you can use it to estimate the nightly quantity of dinners your customers will demand in those cities. Suppose that one of the restaurants is located in a city of 900,000 people, in which average income is $66,300 and the unemployment rate is 5.9 percent. If you set a price of $60 per dinner, you can predict that the nightly demand for steak dinners equals

$$Q^d = 139.2 - (12.9 \times \$60) + (0.0073 \times \$66{,}300) - (10.0 \times 5.9) + (0.0005 \times 900{,}000)$$

or 240 dinners per night. You can now calculate consumer response to a change in the price. For example, if you raise the price by $1, then the quantity of dinners demanded decreases by 12.9 per night, to approximately 227 dinners.

Long-Run Decisions Using Regression Analysis

You can also use the estimated demand function to forecast the demand for your product. Such forecasts can help you make better decisions. For example, you and the other executives at your steak chain might be deciding whether to open a restaurant in a city of 750,000 residents, with average income of $60,000 and an unemployment rate of 6.0 percent. Using the estimated demand function in Table 3.4 and a price of $60 per dinner, you predict demand of about 118 meals per night. Suppose this quantity of sales is too small to be profitable, but you expect rapid growth for the city: In three years, you forecast the city's population will rise to 950,000, average income will increase to $70,000, and the unemployment rate will fall to 5.8 percent. Three years from now, if you set a price of $60 per dinner, you forecast the demand will be 293 dinners per night. This quantity of dinners provides support for a plan to open a restaurant in three years. You might start looking for a good location!

Other companies can use an estimated demand function to forecast their future input needs. General Motors, for example, can use an estimated demand function for their automobiles to forecast the quantity of steel it expects to need for next year's production. This information can help its managers make better decisions about the contracts they will negotiate with their suppliers.

Using the Price Elasticity of Demand

There might be situations in which you need information about a demand but cannot obtain what you need from regression analysis, perhaps because you lack the necessary data. In such cases, you might be able to take advantage of preexisting estimates of the price elasticity of demand, based on either your previous experience or one of the many available estimates in print or on the Internet.

Suppose that your career leads you to an executive position with a company similar to Pacific Ethanol, an ethanol producer with plants located in the western United States. Because your company uses field corn to make ethanol, corn is a significant expense. (Field corn—also called cow corn—is less sweet than the corn people eat.) You read a report predicting that bad weather during the growing season will decrease the supply of field corn by 3 percent. As you learned in Chapter 2, a decrease in supply will raise the price; with this information, you can immediately forecast that the price of corn will rise. For planning purposes, however, you need a more precise forecast: By *how much* will the price of corn rise? You lack the data needed to estimate a demand curve for corn, but estimates of the price elasticity of demand for corn are easy to obtain. According to one such estimate, the price elasticity of demand for field corn is 0.2.[5] Using this estimate, you can forecast that the percentage rise in the price of corn will equal (3 percent decrease in quantity)/(0.2) = 15 percent. You now know that you must either prepare for a large increase in your costs or try to moderate the increase, perhaps by signing contracts to lock in the price of corn at a lower level.

In later chapters, you will learn that you also can use the price elasticity of demand to help you make pricing decisions (see Sections 6.2, 6.3, and 10.1). In the meantime, it should be obvious that the price elasticity of demand is useful to managers because they can use it to determine the change in the quantity demanded with a change in price.

Using the Income Elasticity of Demand Through the Business Cycle

The income elasticity of demand is similarly useful in making better managerial decisions. For example, suppose that the income elasticity of demand for new automobiles is 1.9. Because it is a positive number, new automobiles are a normal good—demand increases when the economy is expanding and people's incomes are growing, and demand decreases when the economy is in a business cycle recession and people's incomes are falling. Because the value exceeds 1, the swings in demand for automobiles are larger than the changes in income. If you are a manager at Kia Motors Corporation (the South Korean automotive company), when you make decisions about your future production plans, you must keep in mind that rapid growth in demand for automobiles in a growing economy might be followed by an equally rapid decrease in demand in response to a recession.

For a contrasting example, say that you are a manager at FirstGroup plc (the British-based owner of Greyhound Lines, which offers inter-city bus travel). The income elasticity of demand for intercity bus travel is negative because it is an inferior good. Your planning must take into account the decrease in demand for your product in a growing economy and the increase in demand during a recession. The magnitude of the income elasticity of demand will provide information about the sizes of the changes in demand, and you can use that information to improve your decisions.

5 This estimate is from Lihong McPhail and Bruce Babcock, "Impact of US Biofuel Policy on US Corn and Gasoline Price Variability," *Energy*, January 2012, p. 509.

Revisiting How Managers at the Gates Foundation Decided to Subsidize Antimalarial Drugs

As noted at the beginning of the chapter, the managers at the Bill and Melinda Gates Foundation want to use their funds in the best way possible. Because wasting their resources means that people could die unnecessarily, managers at the foundation want to fund the most cost-effective programs. To achieve that goal, they must determine the quantitative impact of the proposals presented to them.

In the case of the proposals to subsidize antimalarial drugs in Kenya and other nations, the managers were unlikely to have an estimated demand curve for the drugs in these countries because of data limitations. Instead, they probably relied on estimates of the price elasticity of demand to determine the increase in the quantity of drugs demanded.

The subsidy programs lowered the price of these drugs between 29 percent and 78 percent (the fall in price differed from nation to nation and from drug to drug). Overall, the average decrease in price was roughly 50 percent. Because there are few substitutes, the demand for pharmaceutical drugs is price inelastic. The price elasticity of demand for pharmaceutical drugs for low-income Danish consumers is estimated to be 0.31. Denmark and Kenya differ in an important respect: Low-income consumers in Kenya have much lower incomes than their counterparts in Denmark. Consequently, the expenditure on drugs in Kenya is a much larger fraction of consumers' income, which means that the price elasticity of demand for drugs in Kenya is larger than in Denmark. If the managers at the Bill and Melinda Gates Foundation estimated that the price elasticity of demand for drugs in Kenya was about twice that in Denmark—say, 0.60—they could then predict that lowering the price of the drugs by 50 percent would increase the quantity demanded by 50 percent $\times$ 0.60 = 30 percent.

The Gates Foundation funded the proposals to subsidize antimalarial drugs. The actual outcome was that the quantity of the drugs demanded in the different nations increased by 20 to 40 percent. The quantitative estimate was right in line with what occurred. Using the price elasticity of demand to estimate the impact of the drug subsidy proposals allowed the managers at the foundation to compare them to competing proposals and to make decisions that saved the maximum number of lives.

Summary: The Bottom Line

3.1 Regression: Estimating Demand

- Regression analysis is a statistical tool used to estimate the relationships between two or more variables.
- Regression analysis assumes that the function to be estimated has a random element. The estimated coefficients minimize the sum of the squared residuals between the actual values of the dependent variable and the values predicted by the regression.

3.2 Interpreting the Results of Regression Analysis

- The coefficients estimated by a regression change when the data change. The statistical programs used in regression analysis calculate confidence intervals for each estimated coefficient. For the 95 percent confidence interval, the value of the true coefficient falls within the interval 95 percent of the time.
- The P-value indicates whether an estimated coefficient is statistically significantly different from zero. If the P-value is 5 percent (0.05) or less, then you can be 95 percent confident that the true coefficient is not equal to zero.

- The R^2 statistic, which measures the overall fit of the regression, varies between 100 percent (the predicted values capture *all* the variation in the actual dependent variable) and 0 (the predicted values capture none of the variation in the actual dependent variable).

3.3 Limitations of Regression Analysis

- Managers should examine regressions reported to them to be certain that all the relevant variables are included.
- Managers should determine whether a regression's functional form (curve or straight line) is the best fit for the data.

3.4 Elasticity

- The price elasticity of demand measures how strongly the quantity demanded responds to a change in the price of a product. It equals the absolute value of the percentage change in the quantity demanded divided by the percentage change in the price.

- If the price elasticity of demand exceeds 1.0, consumers respond strongly to a change in price, and demand is elastic. If the price elasticity of demand equals 1.0, demand is unit elastic. If the price elasticity of demand is less than 1.0, consumers respond weakly to a change in price, and demand is inelastic.
- The more substitutes available for the product and the larger the fraction of the consumer's budget spent on the product, the larger the price elasticity of demand.
- The income elasticity of demand equals the percentage change in the quantity demanded divided by the percentage change in income. It is positive for normal goods and negative for inferior goods.
- The cross-price elasticity of demand equals the percentage change in the quantity demanded of one good

divided by the percentage change in the price of a related good. It is positive for products that are substitutes and negative for those that are complements.

3.5 Managerial Application: Regression Analysis and Elasticity

- Regression analysis can estimate a firm's demand function and other important relationships. You can use the estimated functions to make forecasts and predictions that improve your decisions.
- When there are not enough data to estimate a demand function, you can use the price elasticity of demand, the income elasticity of demand, and/or the cross-price elasticity of demand to estimate or forecast the effect of changes in market factors.

Key Terms and Concepts

Confidence interval	Inelastic demand	R^2 statistic
Critical value	Perfectly elastic demand	Significance level
Cross-price elasticity of demand	Perfectly inelastic demand	t-statistic
Elastic demand	Price elasticity of demand	Unit-elastic demand
Elasticity	P-value	
Income elasticity of demand	Regression analysis	

Questions and Problems

All exercises are available on MyEconLab; solutions to even-numbered Questions and Problems appear in the back of this book.

3.1 Regression: Estimating Demand

Learning Objective 3.1 Explain the basics of regression analysis.

1.1 In the context of regression analysis, explain the meaning of the terms *dependent variable, independent variable, explanatory variable, univariate equation,* and *multivariate equation.*

1.2 Why does regression analysis presume the presence of a random error term?

1.3 Explain why minimizing the sum of the squared residuals is a reasonable objective for regression analysis.

3.2 Interpreting the Results of Regression Analysis

Learning Objective 3.2 Interpret the results from a regression.

2.1 Your marketing research department provides the following estimated demand function for your

product: $Q^d = 500.6 - 11.4P + 0.5INCOME$, where P is the price of your product and INCOME is average income.

a. Is your product a normal good or an inferior good? Explain your answer.

b. The standard error for the price coefficient is 2.0. What is its t-statistic? What can you conclude about the coefficient's statistical significance?

c. The standard error for the income coefficient is 0.3. What is its t-statistic? What can you conclude about the coefficient's statistical significance?

2.2 What does the R^2 statistic measure? Why is it important?

2.3 The estimated coefficient for a variable in a regression is 3.5, with a P-value of 0.12. Given these two values, what conclusions can you make about the estimated coefficient?

3.3 Limitations of Regression Analysis

Learning Objective 3.3 Describe the limitations of regression analysis and how they affect its use by managers.

3.1 You are a manager at a company similar to KB Home, one of the largest home builders in the United States. You hired a consulting firm to estimate the demand for your homes. The consultants' report used regression analysis to estimate the demand. They assumed that the demand for your homes depended on the mortgage interest rate and disposable income. The R^2 of the regression they report is 0.24 (24 percent). What suggestions do you have for the consultants?

3.2 Your research analyst informs you that "I *always* estimate log-linear regressions." Do you think the analyst's procedure is correct? What would you say to the analyst?

3.3 You are an executive manager for HatsforAll, a major producer of hats. You are studying a preliminary report submitted by a research firm you hired. The report includes a regression that estimates the demand for your hats. The research firm used 20 years of data on sales of your hats and included two independent variables: the annual average price of your hats and the annual average winter temperature in your marketing areas. (The theory behind the temperature variable is that consumers are more likely to buy hats when the temperature is colder.) The estimated coefficient for the price variable is −5.8, with a standard error of 0.8, and the estimated coefficient for the temperature variable is −20.8, with a standard error of 15.6. Based on the results of survey cards included with the hats, you are confident that higher-income people buy more hats. You are writing a memo to the research firm regarding the report. What additional information will you request from the research firm, and what changes will you recommend it make?

3.4 Elasticity

Learning Objective 3.4 Discuss different elasticity measures and their use.

4.1 The short-run price elasticity of demand for oil is 0.3. If new discoveries of oil increase the quantity of oil by 6 percent, what will be the resulting change in the price of oil?

4.2 Complete the following table.

Elasticity		Percentage Change in Price	Percentage Change in Quantity Demanded
a.	——	8 percent	12 percent
b.	1.4	6 percent	————
c.	0.6	6 percent	————
d.	1.2	————	6 percent
e.	0.4	————	6 percent

4.3 The slope of a linear demand curve is −$2 per unit.
  a. What is the price elasticity of demand when the price is $300 and the quantity is 100 units?
  b. What is the price elasticity of demand when the price is $250 and the quantity is 125 units?
  c. What is the price elasticity of demand when the price is $100 and the quantity is 200 units?
  d. As the price falls (causing a downward movement along the demand curve), how does the price elasticity of demand change?

4.4 Your marketing research department estimates that the demand function for your product is equal to $Q^d = 2{,}000 - 20P$. What is the price elasticity of demand when $P = \$60$?

4.5 Your marketing research department estimates that the demand function for your product is equal to $Q^d = 2{,}000 - 20P$. What is the price elasticity of demand when $P = \$40$?

4.6 Your marketing research department estimates that the demand function for your product is equal to $\ln Q^d = 7.5 - 2.0\ln P$. What is the price elasticity of demand when $P = \$60$?

4.7 As a brand manager for Honey Bunches of Oats cereal, you propose lowering the price by 4 percent. What will you tell your supervisor about what you expect will be the impact on sales in the short run and in the long run? Explain your answer.

4.8 You own a small business and want to increase the total revenue you collect from sales of your product.
  a. If the demand for your product is inelastic, what can you do to increase total revenue?
  b. If the demand for your product is elastic, what can you do to increase total revenue?
  c. If the demand for your product is unit elastic, what can you do to increase total revenue?

4.9 You are a literary agent for an author who writes very popular mystery novels. As the agent, you receive 0.5 percent of the total revenue from sales of the books. You are currently in negotiations with Amazon about the price Amazon will charge for your author's e-books. You believe that your author's books are unique—no one else writes similar stories. What implication does this belief have for your estimate of the price elasticity of demand for your author's books and for your negotiations with Amazon?

4.10 As a manager for the fresh chicken division of a firm like Tyson Foods, Inc., you know that the price elasticity of the total market demand for broiler chickens is 0.5. When one of your assistants suggests raising the price of your chicken by 10 percent, asserting that such a move would increase revenue, how do you respond, and why?

4.11 Only the price elasticity of demand uses the absolute value. Why don't the other elasticities (income elasticity of demand and cross-price elasticity of demand) also use the absolute value?

4.12 Economists estimate that the income elasticity of demand for clothing and footwear is 0.96. As incomes grow, what happens to the fraction of income spent on clothing and footwear? Explain your answer.

4.13 Say that as a manager at a company supplying processed chicken, you are aware that a rise in the cost of feeding steers is predicted to lead to a 15 percent rise in the price of beef. Your analysts have estimated the cross-price elasticity between the demand for chicken and the price of beef is 0.12. You and a customer are negotiating the price at which you will sell them chicken for the next year. What do you predict will be the impact on the demand for chicken from the rise in the price of beef, and how does this estimate affect your negotiating position?

3.5 Managerial Application: Regression Analysis and Elasticity

Learning Objective 3.5 Use regression analysis and the different elasticity measures to make better managerial decisions.

5.1 You are managing a division of a large company. The marketing department submits a report to you about the demand for the product you manage. The report includes the following estimated demand function:

$$Q^d = 2{,}910.0 - 11.3P + 0.050\text{INCOME} - 3.0P_{\text{other}}$$
$$(100.4) \quad (3.2) \quad (0.012) \quad (1.0)$$

where P is the price of your product, INCOME is average income, P_{other} is the price of a related product, and the numbers in parentheses are the standard errors of the estimated coefficients directly above them. The R^2 statistic for the regression is 0.84 (84 percent).

a. What are your general comments about the regression, such as its fit and the significance of the coefficients? As a manager, would you use this estimated demand function to help you make decisions? Explain your answer.

b. Is the product a normal good? Explain your answer.

c. Is the related product a complement or a substitute for your product? Explain your answer.

d. The current price of your product is $200, average income is $50,000, and the price of the related product is $300. What is the quantity demanded of your product?

e. Based on the prices and income in part d, what is the price elasticity of demand for your product? Round your answer to one decimal point.

f. If you raise the price of your product, what do you predict will happen to the total revenue?

5.2 Using disposable personal income (people's income after paying taxes) as their measure of income, General Motors' economists estimate that the income elasticity of demand for its cars is 1.9. The economists forecast that disposable personal income will grow 3.8 percent next year. What will be the effect on the demand for General Motors' cars?

5.3 Your marketing research department estimates that the log-linear demand function for your product is $\ln Q^d = 9.3 - 1.6\ln P$. The standard error of the coefficient for $\ln P$ is 0.3, and the 95 percent confidence interval runs from -2.2 to -1.0.

a. At a price of $50, what is the predicted price elasticity of demand? Calculate the 95 percent confidence interval for the elasticity using the 95 percent confidence interval for the estimated coefficient.

b. At a price of $30, what is the predicted price elasticity of demand? Calculate the 95 percent confidence interval for the elasticity using the 95 percent confidence interval for the estimated coefficient.

5.4 Say that you work for U.S. Steel Corporation. Energy accounts for a significant fraction of U.S. Steel's costs. One of its sources of energy is natural gas. Because of new methods of production, such as hydraulic fracking, the quantity of natural gas is increasing. Suppose that forecasters predict the quantity of natural gas will increase by 10 percent and you know the price elasticity of demand for natural gas is 0.4. U.S. Steel will be very interested in how much the price of natural gas will change. What is your prediction for the change in the price of natural gas?

5.5 You are a midlevel manager for a seafood restaurant. You and your supervisor discuss new regulations that decrease the quantity of cod caught on Georges Bank by 55 percent. Your restaurant features Georges Bank cod, so your supervisor asks you for a quick estimate of the impact of the new regulations on its price. You know that the price elasticity of demand for Georges Bank cod is 2.0.
   a. Will the new regulations shift the demand curve for cod? Will they shift the supply curve? Explain your answers.
   b. What will you report to your supervisor? What managerial suggestions will you make?

5.6 The table below has data for the price of pizzas and the quantity demanded at each price.
   a. Use these data to estimate the demand curve for pizza. You want to report and discuss the estimated coefficients. Are they what you expected? How well does your estimated regression fit the data? Provide a figure if you think it would be useful.
   b. Your manager knows that the elasticity of demand can help you make good decisions. So once you have your demand curve, calculate the elasticity at a price of $10, $15, $20, $25, and $30. Carefully describe how you calculated the elasticity. How does the elasticity change along the demand curve? Using the estimated demand curve, over what price range is the demand elastic? At what price is the demand unit elastic? Over what price range is the demand inelastic?

5.7 The St. Louis Cardinals' website has data on players' batting averages, and the Deadspin website has data on the players' salaries. (For example, the 2015 batting salaries are at http://deadspin.com/nl-central-chicago-cubs-jon-lester-20-000-000-edwin-ja-1695058450.) Excluding pitchers, presumably a higher batting average leads to a higher salary.
   a. Using regression, determine whether this hypothesis is correct for players on the opening day payroll for the St. Louis Cardinals in 2015. Explain your regression results.
   b. It may be that a player's salary depends on his batting average and the number of his home runs. Using regression, determine whether this hypothesis is correct for the players on the opening day payroll for the St. Louis Cardinals in 2015. Explain your regression results.

Accompanies problem 5.6.

Quantity (pizzas per evening)	Price (dollars)	Quantity (pizzas per evening)	Price (dollars)	Quantity (pizzas per evening)	Price (dollars)
69	$30	92	$18	141	$12
42	29	125	17	141	12
66	28	140	16	163	11
57	28	106	16	154	11
78	27	115	15	141	11
72	25	104	15	151	10
81	24	148	14	151	10
83	23	143	14	147	10
70	22	124	14	135	9
101	21	138	13	160	9
93	20	129	13	163	8
100	19	131	13	163	8
107	18	138	12	172	7

MyLab Economics Auto-Graded Excel Projects

3.1 Bret's Accounting & Tax Services is a small but locally well-known accounting firm in Sioux City, IA, that completes taxes for individuals. Every year firms like Bret's decide how much they will charge to complete and file an individual tax return. This price determines how many tax returns firms complete each year.

Suppose that you are an office manager for a firm like Bret's Accounting & Tax Services and you are trying to determine what your firm should charge next year for tax returns. Use the data provided to complete the following:

a. Graph the data using a scatter plot. Using the Insert Trendline function in Excel, determine whether you should use linear or log-linear regression. (Place the graph beneath the data; be sure to label both axes.)

b. Using Excel's Regression Analysis function, run a regression, and answer the following questions about your output. (Place your regression results beneath the graph from part a.)

c. What is your estimated demand function? (Round the estimated coefficients to two decimal places.)

d. What is the R^2? (Report this as a percentage; round to two decimal places.)

e. Based on the R^2, do you think this regression can be used for analysis?

f. How many returns do you expect to be completed if the firm charges $85 per return?

g. What is the elasticity at this point on the demand curve?

h. At this price, are you on the elastic, inelastic, or unit-elastic portion of your demand curve?

i. Do you recommend an increase, a decrease, or no change in the price with this information?

3.2 Hawaiian Shaved Ice, in Newton Grove, NC, sells shaved ice and snow cone equipment and supplies for individual and commercial use. Suppose that you purchased a commercial-grade machine and supplies from a company similar to Hawaiian Shaved Ice to open a shaved ice stand on a beach busy with tourists. Because this is a new business, you've tried a number of prices and run a few specials to try to attract customers. As such, you have 20 days' worth of data to analyze and help you set a more permanent price.

	A	B
1	Smoothie Price	Smoothie Quantity
2	4.08	56
3	3.61	67
4	3.5	69
5	2.46	84
6	1.69	108
7	5.33	45
8	2.33	91
9	3.14	76
10	4.33	51
11	4.72	49
12	2.57	86
13	2.58	88
14	3.62	70
15	4.78	53
16	4.24	60
17	2.19	97
18	3.86	67
19	3.38	70
20	2.91	79
21	4.58	57
22		

a. Graph the data provided using a scatter plot. Using the Insert Trendline function in Excel, determine whether you should use linear or log-linear regression. (Place the graph beneath the data; be sure to label both axes.)

b. Using Excel's Regression Analysis function, run a regression, and answer the following questions about your output. (Place your regression results beneath the graph from part a.)

c. What is your estimated demand function?

d. Discuss the fit and significance of the regression.

	A	B
1	Return Price	Returns Completed
2	70	932
3	70	932
4	75	910
5	75	920
6	80	876
7	80	852
8	85	811
9	80	857
10	80	847
11	80	865
12	90	785
13	90	802
14	95	789
15	95	731
16	100	663
17	100	709
18	90	771
19	90	792
20	85	831
21	80	834
22		

3.3 Ben and Jerry's is a popular brand of ice cream based in South Burlington, VT. The company is known for its delicious and cleverly named flavors and its commitment to social responsibility. Suppose that the marketing department for a firm like Ben and Jerry's estimates monthly demand for a pint of ice cream to be $Q = 1000 - 150P$.

a. Using the table provided and Excel functions, calculate quantity demanded for each of the prices given.

b. Using the prices provided and quantities demanded that you calculated in part a, calculate the elasticity of demand for each of the prices in the table.

c. Comment on how elasticity changes as you move along the demand curve.

d. Are there prices between $3 and $6 that you are certain the company should not charge based on the elasticities you observe? Why or why not?

e. If the goal of this firm is to maximize revenue, what price do you recommend it charge for a pint of ice cream?

	A	B	C
1		a.	b.
2	Price	Quantity	Elasticity
3	6		
4	5.75		
5	5.5		
6	5.25		
7	5		
8	4.75		
9	4.5		
10	4.25		
11	4		
12	3.75		
13	3.5		
14	3.25		
15	3		
16			

Introduction

Upper-level managers frequently make important long-run strategic decisions about acquisitions, mergers, plant or store locations, pricing, financing, and marketing. Indeed, a major focus of this book is to explain how managers can use economic principles as a guide to making these types of decisions. But even the best guidance can fail without adequate information and data analysis.

Company analysts often use regression analysis to help them provide quantitative information to managerial decision makers. In this chapter, you learned how regression analysis can help managers estimate demand functions. But regression can be used to help managers answer other questions, such as these: How many more units of a product will we sell if our store stays open an extra hour each day? Is San Diego a good location to open a new store? How will consumers react if we change the packaging of our product? In this case study, we explore how regression analysis can help provide invaluable information about another important managerial issue, whether to remodel the company's stores and/or change how the company prices its products.

Regression Example

Regression can help managers make the decisions faced by companies that are debating whether to remodel their stores and/or their operations. Companies such as restaurant chains continually struggle to retain their market share by remaining fresh and relevant for consumers. Most restaurant chains undertake constant innovation, moving specials on and off their menus as well as tweaking and refining their more permanent offerings. Occasionally, however, upper-level managers decide that some of their restaurants need renovation. Take, for example, Olive Garden, a division of Darden with more than 800 restaurant locations. In 2013, the new president of Olive Garden, Dave George, announced that Olive Garden would remodel and modernize its interiors.

Suppose that you work in the research department for a similar restaurant chain. Your chain has a new president, and your president also is considering a new style of remodeling for your restaurants. Remodeling is expensive, so the new president asks your research team to determine if the expense is justified by the projected increased in the chain's profit.

To obtain the information needed to make this type of decision, a firm often remodels a few stores and then uses regression analysis to compare the profitability of the remodeled stores to that of stores that are not remodeled. Suppose, however, that your chain faces a more complicated situation: Under the previous president, the chain had already remodeled some locations but in a way that differs from your new president's vision.[1] So you have two types of restaurants—already remodeled and not previously remodeled. The regression analysis needs to consider this factor.

To use regression, your chain needs to remodel several restaurants according to the new president's vision. Which restaurants are remodeled is unimportant because your regression should be able to predict the profitability regardless of location. After the remodeling, your group must collect data over several months to measure the profitability of all your restaurants. Ideally, you would collect the *economic* profits of the restaurants. In practice, however, their economic profit is impossible to measure, so you will need to use their *accounting* profits as a proxy for their economic profits. Your research group will use these data as the dependent variable in the regression.

Your team of analysts needs to determine how the new remodeling scheme affects profitability. But other factors also affect profitability. A restaurant's profit equals its total revenue minus its total cost, so you and the other analysts need to determine what variables affect total revenue and total cost:

- **Total revenue.** The higher the demand for meals at your restaurants, the greater the total revenue. So the regression should include independent variables that affect the demand for dining at your restaurants. For example, your group might decide to include two independent variables that affect demand and thereby total revenue: (1) the population of the county or locality in which the restaurant is located and (2) income in that county or locality. When these variables are included in the regression, the estimated coefficients for both these variables are expected to be positive—higher population and higher income both increase demand and thereby increase the restaurant's total revenue and raise its profit.

---

1 This situation is similar to what Darden's analysts faced in 2013 because Olive Garden had started remodeling its stores' exteriors and some of the interiors to present a different view of Italy. That approach, however, was not what the incoming president, Mr. George, envisioned. His goal was modernization, not changing the geographic region the stores presented.

- **Total cost.** The higher the total cost, the lower the profit. So your team should include independent variables in the regression that affect a restaurant's cost. For example, your group might settle upon two variables: (1) the rent paid for the restaurant, which will vary among locations, and (2) the legal minimum wage employees receive, which will also vary among locations. When these variables are included in the regression, the estimated coefficients for both of them are expected to be negative—a higher rent and a higher minimum wage both increase the restaurant's cost and thereby reduce its profit.

In addition to the factors that affect total revenue and total cost, the regression needs to take account of whether the restaurant was remodeled according to the past president's scheme, remodeled according to the new president's ideas, or not remodeled at all. To do so, your team needs to include indicator variables (colloquially called "dummy variables") as additional independent variables. Indicator variables equal 1 when a condition is met and equal 0 otherwise. For example, one indicator variable should equal 1 if the restaurant had previously been remodeled and 0 if it had not been remodeled. Call this variable OLDREMODEL. For the purposes of determining the profitability of the new style of remodeling, the crucial indicator variable measures whether the location has been remodeled according to the new scheme. This variable equals 1 for restaurants that are newly remodeled and 0 for the other restaurants. Call this variable NEWREMODEL. The estimated coefficient of each indicator variable measures the effect of whatever condition is being met.[2] That means that the coefficient for the variable NEWREMODEL is key because when the variable equals 1, the restaurant has been newly remodeled along the lines suggested by the new president. The change in profit for a restaurant going from no remodeling at all to the new remodeling equals the estimated coefficient of NEWREMODEL—call it $\hat{g}$—multiplied by the value of the

variable when the location is newly remodeled, which is 1, or $\hat{g} \times 1 = \hat{g}$.[3]

There are other factors you and your group could include that affect the total revenue and total cost, but let's limit the discussion to what we have discussed. Using these variables, to predict the profitability of a restaurant in your chain, your team would estimate the regression as

$$\text{PROFIT} = a + (b \times \text{POPULATION}) + (c \times \text{INCOME})$$
$$- (d \times \text{RENT}) - (e \times \text{MINIMUMWAGE})$$
$$+ (f \times \text{OLDREMODEL}) + (g \times \text{NEWREMODEL})$$

in which a, b, c, d, e, f, and g are the coefficients the regression will estimate.

Once your team has estimated the regression, you can use what you have learned in Chapter 3 to judge the adequacy of the regression: Are the estimated coefficients statistically different from zero? Is the fit of the regression high? Or do you and your group need to either add or remove some variables? Once you are satisfied with the regression, you can use it to determine the profitability of the proposed new remodeling. In particular, the estimated $\hat{g}$ coefficient measures the change in profit from the new remodeling. If this estimated coefficient is positive and significantly different from zero, you can present it to your new president as an estimate of the profit from remodeling a previously unremodeled store according to the new style and allow the president to use it when deciding whether to proceed with the new remodeling.

Your Decisions

Regression analysis can be used in any industry, not just the restaurant industry. Take, for example, the retail industry. In November 2011, Ron Johnson was hired to be the new CEO of JCPenney. Less than two months later, Mr. Johnson announced the following sweeping changes:

1. JCPenney's pricing had relied on heavy discounting and extensive use of coupons; Mr. Johnson immediately changed the pricing policy to adopt "full-but-fair prices" with no discounts or coupons.
2. JCPenney had offered a large selection of middle-of-the-road store brands; Mr. Johnson discontinued the store brands in favor of selling more "trendy," high-fashion brands.

2 For technical reasons, when a set of conditions taken together equals the entire set of observations, it is not possible to use an indicator variable for each type of condition; one type must not have an indicator variable. For example, in the analysis discussed above, you cannot use an indicator variable that equals 1 if the location had been previously remodeled, another indicator variable that equals 1 if the location is newly remodeled, and yet a third indicator variable that equals 1 if the location has not been remodeled. You cannot use all three of these indicator variables because taken together these three conditions equal the entire set of observations. Consequently, in the regression discussed in the example, there is no indicator variable for the stores that have not been remodeled.

3 More specifically, the NEWREMODEL indicator variable's coefficient, $\hat{g}$, measures the profit from the new remodeling relative to whichever condition has not been given an indicator variable. In the example at hand, $\hat{g}$ measures the restaurant's change in profit from being newly remodeled *compared to* not being remodeled at all.

3. JCPenney's customer base was generally older and middle to lower income; Mr. Johnson moved to establish smaller "stores within a store" with more expensive merchandise to target younger, higher-income customers.

Mr. Johnson immediately started to implement his new policies without any testing. Unfortunately for both him and the company, customers rejected his changes: JCPenney's sales dropped about 30 percent, its profit turned to billions of dollars of losses, and in April 2013, the board of directors fired Mr. Johnson as CEO.

Suppose you work in the research department of a retail department store chain that is considering three similar changes—ending discounts, offering trendy brands, and creating stores within the store. Your chain, however, decides to test these ideas before rolling them out chain-wide. So your supervisor asks you to write a proposal that will allow your company's executives to determine the profitability of these possible changes. You will use regression analysis to decide on the profitability of the changes.

Prepare a proposal that answers the following questions:

1. The changes can be implemented separately, all together, or in combinations of two, so how do you want to test the three changes? Be sure to explain why you made your decision.

2. If you want to compare the profitability of stores in different locations, explain what variables you expect to use. Be certain to mention variables other than those discussed above in the restaurant example that might affect the stores' profitability. Carefully explain what effect you expect from each variable you include. For each variable, do you expect that the estimated coefficient will be positive or negative? Mention the source from which you plan to obtain the data you will use.

3. Will you use any indicator variables? If so, what will they be?

4. Is there any feature (or features) about the specification or functional form of the regression that needs additional explanation?

5. After you estimate the regression, how do you plan to decide whether the estimated regression is adequate? How might the regression results be inadequate? What do you plan to do if the results are inadequate?

6. Once you have an acceptable regression, explain how you plan to use the results to determine the profitability of the changes.

Sources: Steve Denning, "J.C. Penney: Was Ron Johnson Wrong?" Forbes.com, April 9, 2013, http://www.forbes.com/sites/stevedenning/2013/04/09/j-c-penney-was-ron-johnsons-strategy-wrong/#32427add283c; James Surowiecki, "The Turnaround Trap," *New Yorker*, March 25, 2013.

The Calculus of Elasticity

Many of the elasticity results discussed in this chapter, including the elasticity formulas for linear and log-linear demand functions and the total revenue test, can be derived using calculus. Indeed, we can start by giving the definition of the price elasticity of demand (ε) from Equation 3.2 (Section 3.4),

$$\varepsilon = \left| \frac{\left(\frac{\Delta Q^{\mathrm{d}}}{Q^{\mathrm{d}}} \right)}{\left(\frac{\Delta P}{P} \right)} \right|$$

a precise calculus interpretation:

$$\varepsilon = \left| \frac{\left(\frac{\mathrm{d}Q^{\mathrm{d}}}{Q^{\mathrm{d}}} \right)}{\left(\frac{\mathrm{d}P}{P} \right)} \right| \qquad \textbf{A3.1}$$

where the discrete Δ changes are now differential d changes.

A. Price Elasticity of Demand for a Linear and a Log-Linear Demand Function

Some algebra using the definition of the price elasticity of demand in Equation A3.1 gives another measure of elasticity:

$$\varepsilon = \left| \frac{\frac{\mathrm{d}Q^{\mathrm{d}}}{Q^{\mathrm{d}}}}{\frac{\mathrm{d}P}{P}} \right| = \left| \left(\frac{\mathrm{d}Q^{\mathrm{d}}}{Q^{\mathrm{d}}} \right) \times \left(\frac{P}{\mathrm{d}P} \right) \right| = \left| \frac{\mathrm{d}Q^{\mathrm{d}} \times P}{Q^{\mathrm{d}} \times \mathrm{d}P} \right| = \left| \frac{\mathrm{d}Q^{\mathrm{d}} \times P}{\mathrm{d}P \times Q^{\mathrm{d}}} \right| = \left| \left(\frac{\mathrm{d}Q^{\mathrm{d}}}{\mathrm{d}P} \right) \times \left(\frac{P}{Q^{\mathrm{d}}} \right) \right| \qquad \textbf{A3.2}$$

If you use a general specification of the demand function, $Q^{\mathrm{d}} = \mathrm{f}(P)$, then $\dfrac{\mathrm{d}Q^{\mathrm{d}}}{\mathrm{d}P} = \mathrm{f}'(P)$, where $\mathrm{f}'(P)$ is the derivative of the demand function with respect to the price. Substituting $\mathrm{f}'(P)$ into Equation A3.2 shows that the price elasticity of demand equals

$$\varepsilon = \left| \left(\frac{\mathrm{d}Q^{\mathrm{d}}}{\mathrm{d}P} \right) \times \left(\frac{P}{Q^{\mathrm{d}}} \right) \right| = \left| \mathrm{f}'(P) \times \left(\frac{P}{Q^{\mathrm{d}}} \right) \right| \qquad \textbf{A3.3}$$

Equation A3.3 has the following interpretation: At any price and for any demand function, the price elasticity of demand equals the derivative of the demand function at that price multiplied by the price divided by the quantity demanded at that price.

We can use Equation A3.3 to determine the equations for the price elasticity of demand for two common demand functions, a linear demand function and a log-linear demand function. For a linear demand function—say, $Q^{\mathrm{d}} = a - (b \times P)$, where a and b are coefficients— the derivative of the quantity with respect to the price is $\frac{\mathrm{d}Q^{\mathrm{d}}}{\mathrm{d}P} = -b$. Using Equation A3.3, for a linear demand function the price elasticity of demand equals

$$\varepsilon = \left| b \times \left(\frac{P}{Q^{\mathrm{d}}} \right) \right|$$

which is shown as Equation 3.4 in the chapter (see Section 3.4). For a log-linear demand function—say,

$$\ln Q^d = a - (b \times \ln P) \qquad \textbf{A3.4}$$

where ln represents the natural logarithm—the derivative of the quantity with respect to the price is[1]

$$\frac{dQ^d}{dP} = -b \times \left(\frac{Q^d}{P}\right)$$

Accordingly, using Equation A3.3 once again shows that, for a log-linear demand function, the price elasticity of demand equals

$$\varepsilon = \left| \left(-b \times \left(\frac{Q^d}{P}\right)\right) \times \left(\frac{P}{Q^d}\right)\right| = b$$

precisely as stated in the chapter. In other words, for a log-linear demand function, the price elasticity of demand is the same for all prices and equals b, the coefficient multiplying the logarithm of the price in Equation A3.4.

B. Total Revenue Test

Calculus also helps prove the total revenue test presented in the chapter (see Section 3.4). Recall that the total revenue test shows how the total revenue changes when the price changes; that is, it measures dTR/dP. The total revenue test includes three assertions: Demand is elastic when ε is greater than 1, unit-elastic when ε equals 1, and inelastic when ε is less than one.

1. **Elastic demand ($\varepsilon > 1$):**
   - If the price rises, the total revenue decreases, which means that dTR/dP is negative.
   - Conversely, if the price falls, the total revenue increases, which (again) means that dTR/dP is negative.

2. **Unit-elastic demand ($\varepsilon = 1$):**
   - If the price rises or falls, the total revenue does not change, which means that dTR/dP is equal to zero.

3. **Inelastic demand ($\varepsilon < 1$):**
   - If the price rises, the total revenue increases, which means that dTR/dP is positive.
   - Conversely, if the price falls, the total revenue decreases, which (again) means that dTR/dP is positive.

Total revenue equals the price of the product (P) multiplied by the quantity sold (Q), and the quantity sold equals the quantity demanded by consumers (Q^d):

$$TR = P \times Q^d$$

The quantity demanded is given by $Q^d = f(P)$, so total revenue equals

$$TR = P \times f(P) \qquad \textbf{A3.5}$$

Taking the derivative of total revenue in Equation A3.5 with respect to the price by using the product rule gives

$$\frac{dTR}{dP} = [P \times f'(P)] + f(P) \qquad \textbf{A3.6}$$

---

1 Taking the total derivative of $\ln Q^d = a - (b \times \ln P)$ gives $(1/Q^d) \times dQ^d = -b \times (1/P) \times dP$. Multiplying both sides of the equality by Q^d and dividing both sides by dP yields $dQ^d/dP = -b \times (Q^d/P)$.

In Equation A3.6, $f(P) = Q^d$. Using this equality and rearranging the terms in the right side of Equation A3.6 yields

$$\frac{dTR}{dP} = Q^d + [f'(P) \times P] \qquad \textbf{A3.7}$$

Next, multiply the second term (the term in Equation 3.7 in the brackets) on the right side of Equation 3.7 by 1 in the form of $\left(\dfrac{Q^d}{Q^d}\right)$:

$$\frac{dTR}{dP} = [Q^d] + \left[\left(\frac{Q^d}{Q^d}\right) \times (f'(P) \times P)\right]$$

Finally, factor Q^d out of both terms, and then rearrange the terms to give

$$\frac{dTR}{dP} = Q^d \times \left\{[1] + \left[\left(\frac{1}{Q^d}\right) \times (f'(P) \times P)\right]\right\} = Q^d \times \left\{[1] + \left[\left(f'(P) \times \frac{P}{Q^d}\right)\right]\right\} \quad \textbf{A3.8}$$

The term $\left[f'(P) \times \dfrac{P}{Q^d}\right]$ is the same as the price elasticity of demand in Equation A3.3 *except* that there is no absolute value sign. Recall that we use the absolute value sign because otherwise the price elasticity of demand would be negative, since the law of demand means that $f'(P)$, which equals $\dfrac{dQ^d}{dP}$, is negative. Consequently, the $\left[f'(P) \times \dfrac{P}{Q^d}\right]$ term in Equation A3.8 has the same numeric value as the price elasticity of demand but is negative, so $\left[f'(P) \times \dfrac{P}{Q^d}\right] = -\varepsilon$. Using this equality, we can rewrite Equation A3.8 as

$$\frac{dTR}{dP} = Q^d \times [1 - \varepsilon] \qquad \textbf{A3.9}$$

Equation A3.9 shows how the total revenue changes when the price changes. In it, the quantity demanded, Q^d, is always positive, so the sign of $\dfrac{dTR}{dP}$ depends on the $[1 - \varepsilon]$ term. Using this result, we can now prove the total revenue test:

1. **Elastic demand ($\varepsilon > 1$):**
   - If $\varepsilon > 1$, then $1 - \varepsilon$ is negative, so from Equation A3.9, dTR/dP is negative.
2. **Unit-elastic demand ($\varepsilon = 1$):**
   - If $\varepsilon = 1$, then $1 - \varepsilon$ equals 0, so from Equation A3.9, dTR/dP is equal to zero.
3. **Inelastic demand ($\varepsilon < 1$):**
   - If $\varepsilon < 1$, then $1 - \varepsilon$ is positive, so from Equation A3.9, dTR/dP is positive.

C. Income Elasticity of Demand and Cross-Price Elasticity of Demand

It is probably no surprise that both the income and the cross-price elasticities of demand can be defined using calculus. If the demand function is $Q^d = f(P, INCOME, P_j)$, where P is the price of the good, INCOME is consumers' average income, and P_j is the price of a substitute or complement, then the income and cross-price elasticities of demand are

$$\varepsilon_{\text{INC}} = \frac{\left(\dfrac{\partial Q^d}{Q^d}\right)}{\left(\dfrac{\partial \text{INCOME}}{\text{INCOME}}\right)} = \left(\frac{\partial Q^d}{\partial \text{INCOME}}\right) \times \left(\frac{\text{INCOME}}{Q^d}\right)$$

$$\varepsilon_{\text{CROSS}} = \frac{\left(\dfrac{\partial Q^d}{Q^d}\right)}{\left(\dfrac{\partial P_j}{P_j}\right)} = \left(\frac{\partial Q^d}{\partial P_j}\right) \times \left(\frac{P_j}{Q^d}\right)$$

In both of the definitions, we take a partial derivative because the demand function is multivariate; that is, the demand function has more than one independent variable. Even so, as Table A3.1 shows, the meanings of the signs of the income and cross-price elasticities do not change from what was explained in the chapter.

Table A3.1 Signs of Income Elasticity and Cross-Price Elasticity of Demand

Income elasticity of demand	
• If $\partial Q^d/\partial \text{INCOME}$ is positive	then ε_{INC} is positive, and the product is a normal good.
• If $\partial Q^d/\partial \text{INCOME}$ is negative	then ε_{INC} is negative, and the product is an inferior good.
Cross-price elasticity of demand	
• If $\partial Q^d/\partial P_j$ is positive	then $\varepsilon_{\text{CROSS}}$ is positive, and the products are substitutes.
• If $\partial Q^d/\partial P_j$ is negative	then $\varepsilon_{\text{CROSS}}$ is negative, and the products are complements.

Calculus Questions and Problems

All exercises are available on MyEconLab; solutions to even-numbered Questions and Problems appear in the back of this book.

A3.1 The hourly demand for music downloads is given by

$$Q^d = 500 - 100P$$

where Q^d is the number of songs demanded per hour and P is the price of downloading a song.
a. Suppose that $P = \$3$. At this price, what does the price elasticity of demand equal? What is the total revenue?
b. At what price does $\varepsilon = 1$? What is the total revenue when the price is $2.50?
c. Explain whether your results to parts a and b are consistent with the total revenue test.

A3.2 The weekly demand for sandwiches at a local sandwich shop is given by

$$Q^d = 2{,}000 - 5P + 2P_j - 0.01\text{INCOME}$$

where Q^d is the number of sandwiches demanded per week, P is the price of a sandwich, P_j is the price of a related product, and INCOME is the average monthly income of consumers.

a. Suppose that $P = \$10$, $P_j = \$50$, and INCOME = $5,000. What is the value of the cross-price elasticity of demand? Is the related product a substitute or a complement?
b. Suppose that $P = \$10$, $P_j = \$50$, and INCOME = $5,000. What is the value of the income elasticity of demand? Are sandwiches a normal good or an inferior good?

A3.3 The hourly demand for corndogs at the local state fair is estimated to be

$$Q^d = 360P^{-2}$$

where Q^d is the number of corndogs demanded per hour and P is the price of a corndog.
a. Using the estimated demand function for corndogs, calculate the price elasticity of demand as a function of the price of a corndog.
b. Using the demand function for corndogs, the quantity demanded is 90 corndogs when the

price is \$2 per corndog, and the quantity demanded is 40 corndogs when the price is \$3 per corndog. Does the total revenue from selling corndogs rise or fall as the number of corndogs sold increases?

c. Is your answer to part b consistent with the total revenue test? Explain.

A3.4 The monthly demand for bus rides in Miami, Florida, depends on the price of a train ride, the price of a bus ride, and the average monthly income of riders. Some consumers might choose to ride the train instead of the bus, while other riders might use both forms of transportation to get to their final destination. The demand function for bus rides is

$$Q^d = 9{,}750 - 500P + 250P_j + 5INCOME$$

where Q^d is the number of bus rides demanded per month, P is the price of a bus ride, P_j is the price of a train ride, and INCOME is the average monthly income of riders.

a. Suppose that $P = \$1.50$, $P_j = \$4.00$, and INCOME $= \$3{,}000$. What is the monthly quantity of bus rides demanded?

b. Suppose that $P = \$1.50$, $P_j = \$4.00$, and INCOME $= \$3{,}000$. What is the value of the cross-price elasticity of demand? Based on your answer, are train rides and bus rides substitutes or complements?

c. Suppose that $P = \$1.50$, $P_j = \$4.00$, and INCOME $= \$3{,}000$. What is the value of the income elasticity of demand? Based on your answer, are train rides an inferior or a normal good?

A3.5 The monthly demand for personal pizzas depends on the price of a personal pizza and the price of a separate related good. The demand function for personal pizzas is

$$Q^d = 480 - 5P + 10P_j$$

where Q^d is the number of personal pizzas demanded per month, P is the price of a personal pizza, and P_j is the price of the related good.

a. Suppose that $P = \$6$ and $P_j = \$9$. What does the cross-price elasticity of demand equal?

b. Based on the answer to part a, is the related good a substitute or a complement to pizza?

Production and Costs

Learning Objectives

After studying this chapter, you will be able to:

4.1 Explain the relationship between a firm's inputs and its output as well as calculate the marginal product of an input.

4.2 Use the cost-minimization rule to choose the combination of inputs that produces a given quantity of output at the lowest cost.

4.3 Distinguish between fixed cost and variable cost and calculate average total cost, average variable cost, average fixed cost, and marginal cost.

4.4 Derive the long-run average cost curve and explain its shape.

4.5 Apply production and cost theory to make better managerial decisions.

Pizza Hut Managers Learn That Size Matters

In 2014, Pizza Hut had about 6,300 restaurants in the United States. Although this number is impressive, executive managers at Pizza Hut realized that they had a problem. Most of the existing locations featured both delivery and dine-in services, so they were large restaurants with correspondingly high costs. Potential franchisees became unwilling to open new restaurants because their high costs made them unprofitable. From 2001 to 2014, the number of Pizza Hut restaurants in the United States actually decreased from 7,700 to 6,300 because franchisees closed more restaurants than they opened.

After crunching some data, Pizza Hut's research department calculated that the fraction of their pizza sales involving home delivery had fallen. Delivery is the most popular way for consumers to buy pizza, so Pizza Hut's executive managers needed to boost delivery sales. They also recognized a cost problem: Conventional Pizza Hut restaurants were too large to make focusing primarily on home delivery profitable. What could Pizza Hut's managers do to increase the number of their stores, and thereby their profit, in the face of these challenges?

This chapter explains the relationship between the costs of inputs, such as labor and capital, and the amount of output. At the end of the chapter, you will learn how Pizza Hut's executives could have evaluated these factors in creating a plan to improve their company's operation.

Sources: Annie Gasparro, "Pizza Hut Scales Down to Boost Delivery," *Wall Street Journal,* October 2, 2012; Annie Gasparro, "Yum Pizza Hut Pares Outlet size; Delivery Is Focus," Marketwatch, October 3, 2012; Rick Hynum, "The 2015 Pizza Power Report," *PMQ Pizza Magazine,* December 2014; *A World of Yum!* (2005 YUM Annual Report).

Introduction

Successful businesses must respond to consumers' demands for goods and services. The amount of a good or service a firm produces depends on the demand for that good or service and the opportunity costs of producing it.[1] The costs depend on four factors:

1. The quantity of inputs, such as labor and capital, utilized
2. The cost of each input

---

1 For the sake of brevity, we usually drop the modifier *opportunity* in front of the word *cost*, but keep in mind that as a manager you must always be concerned with opportunity cost rather than accounting cost.

3. The production technology utilized
4. The managers' efforts to minimize the cost of production

The chapter begins with an analysis of the firm's production function, which is the relationship between the firm's inputs and its output. For simplicity, the discussion assumes that managers know their firm's production function. Unfortunately, managers often begin with only a vague idea. Discovering the best way to organize inputs to produce a good or service can be a challenging trial-and-error process. This chapter can help you develop a strategy to work through this trial-and-error process and make the managerial decisions that lead to the most efficient production.

Next, you will learn about costs by deriving and illustrating a firm's cost curves. Because the firm incurs costs for its use of inputs, the cost curves are closely related to the firm's production technology and the productivity of the inputs. The cost curves are the foundation for the next several chapters, which provide valuable insights into managers' profit-maximizing decisions about the amount of output to produce and the price to charge.

To help you understand the important concepts of production and costs, Chapter 4 includes five sections:

- **Section 4.1** explores the production function, the difference between the short run and the long run, and the definitions of the marginal product of labor and capital.
- **Section 4.2** describes how to determine the combination of inputs that produces the desired quantity of output at the minimum cost.
- **Section 4.3** explains how costs change in the short run when production changes.
- **Section 4.4** examines how costs change in the long run when production changes.
- **Section 4.5** discusses how you can apply production and cost theory to make better managerial decisions.

4.1 Production

Learning Objective 4.1 Explain the relationship between a firm's inputs and its output as well as calculate the marginal product of an input.

Suppose that you are a general manager of an Italian restaurant, like Olive Garden, and you report to a district manager. One of your goals is to produce your output (Italian dinners) as efficiently as possible, which generally means producing the dinners at the lowest possible cost. If you minimize the cost of producing the output, you will be well on your way to maximizing the profit of your restaurant. To make the best decisions about costs, you must understand some basic elements of production.

Production Function

When a firm produces a good or service, it combines inputs, called *factors of production*, according to a precise procedure or "recipe," called a production function. At your Italian restaurant, inputs consist of

- The workers you hire, such as chefs and servers
- Raw materials, such as lettuce and chicken
- Capital equipment, such as grills and ovens
- Intermediate goods, such as olive oil and flour

Production function The relationship between different amounts of a firm's inputs and the maximum quantity of output it can produce with those inputs.

The **production function** is the relationship between different amounts of a firm's inputs and the maximum quantity of output it can produce with those inputs. Mathematically, the production function is written as $Q = f(X_1, X_2, \ldots, X_n)$, where

- Q is the quantity of output
- Xs are the inputs
- f is the function, or "recipe," that converts the inputs into output

The function, f, incorporates the current state of technology. Changes in technology change the production function and generally enable firms to produce more output using the same or even smaller quantities of inputs.

A production function that uses many inputs can be complex. For simplicity, let's focus on a simple firm that uses only two inputs, labor and capital equipment. This firm's two-input production function can be written as $Q = f(L, K)$, where Q is the quantity of output, f is the production function, L is the quantity of the labor input, and K is the quantity of the capital input. This simplified two-input production function will provide lessons and insights that you can apply to real-world production decisions involving many more than two inputs.

Short Run and Long Run

Short run The period of time during which at least one input is fixed, so that a firm cannot vary the quantity of that input.

Long run A period of time long enough that no input is fixed, allowing a firm to vary the quantity of *all* the inputs it uses.

Within a given period of time, it is more difficult for a firm to obtain and use additional units of some inputs than others. For instance, at your Italian restaurant, it would be very expensive, if not impossible, to increase the size of the dining area by 20 percent in the space of a week. During that same week, however, you could easily hire an additional server. On the other hand, if you had a year to make changes, it would be easy to both increase the size of your dining area and hire another server. Economists define two periods of time that reflect these differences: the short run and the long run. The **short run** is the period of time during which at least one input is fixed, so that a firm cannot vary the quantity of that input. Using the two-input production function with capital and labor as the only inputs, in the short run capital is the *fixed input* and labor is the *variable input*. For a restaurant, the size of the dining room (capital) is a fixed input in the short run. The **long run** is a period of time long enough that no input is fixed, allowing a firm to vary the quantity of *all* the inputs it uses. Because managers can change the amounts used, in the long run both capital (expansion of the dining area) and labor (the addition of a server) are variable inputs.

The long run varies widely among firms. It might take a firm like Darden, the parent company of Olive Garden, two years to obtain the permits and construct a new Olive Garden restaurant. By comparison, it might take as long as six years for a computer chip–producing company like Intel to obtain permits, construct a new manufacturing facility, and then certify it.

Long-run decisions are often more difficult or more costly to reverse—the cost of building an unnecessary factory dwarfs the cost of hiring an unnecessary worker. So decisions about the long run are more strategic in nature. Generally, upper-level management or executives make long-run decisions. Short-run decisions are often more tactical, however, and can be made by midlevel managers.

With more than two inputs, the complexity of the production function increases because it takes different amounts of time for different inputs to become variable. For example, at your restaurant, it is possible to change the number of servers within a week, but it could take two months to hire a new skilled chef, three months to add a new oven, and two years to remodel the entire restaurant. As this example shows, you can make more profound changes as time passes, which is reflected in differences in the short-run production function and the long-run production function.

Short-Run Production Function

The previous section pointed out that firms can vary the quantity of labor (number of servers) more quickly than capital (expansion of the dining area), which for the short run makes capital a fixed input and labor a variable input. So the *short-run production function*, when there is at least one fixed input, is

$$Q = f(L, \overline{K})$$

where the bar over K signifies that the quantity of capital is fixed.

You can get a feeling for this short-run production function for your Italian restaurant by examining the hypothetical data and graph in Figure 4.1. Figure 4.1(a) assumes that the restaurant's capital—the size of the dining room, number of ovens, and number of booths—is fixed and equal to 5 units of capital. The curve labeled *PF* in Figure 4.1(b) is the short-run production function for 5 units of capital, plotted from the data in Figure 4.1(a). The *PF* curve illustrates the relationship between the quantity of labor (the number of workers) on the horizontal axis and quantity of output (the number of dinners per day) on the vertical axis.

To derive the data and then the graph in Figure 4.1, you need to determine the relationship between the number of dinners produced and the number of employees. Conceptually, you could experiment by starting with one employee per shift and then adding extra workers, while keeping track of the quantity of dinners served. The production data in Figure 4.1 represent these hypothetical findings. As you can

Figure 4.1 The Short-Run Production Function

(a) **Production Data**
The data represent the short-run production function for 5 units of capital.

Capital, *K* (units of capital)	Labor, *L* (workers)	Output, *Q* (dinners per day)
5	0	0
5	1	10
5	2	30
5	3	60
5	4	110
5	5	170
5	6	220
5	7	260
5	8	290
5	9	310
5	10	320
5	11	310

(b) **Short-Run Production Function**
The figure graphs the data from part a and shows the short-run production function, *PF*.

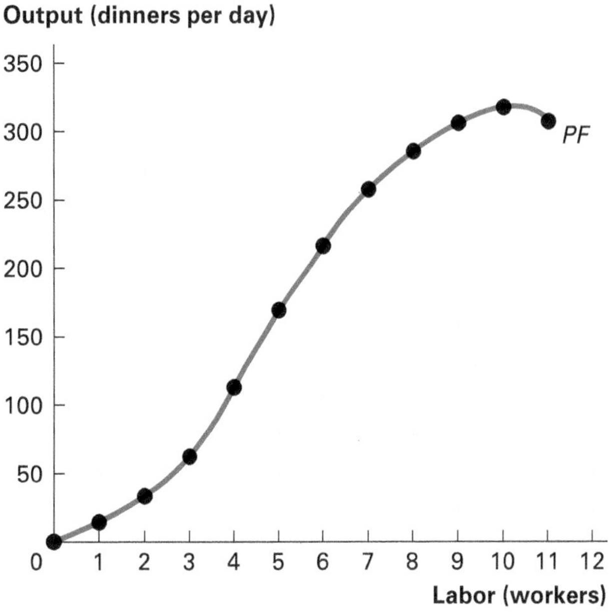

see from the data and curve in Figure 4.1, the output begins to decrease with the 11th worker. No manager would add more workers when doing so decreases output, so there is no need to include data beyond 11 workers.

For small quantities of labor, output responds dramatically to changes in labor. Why? Suppose you start with a single worker. This worker would need to seat the customers, take the orders, cook the food, serve the food, collect the payment, and bus the tables. As you add more workers, they waste less time scurrying around from one place to another, allowing them to be more efficient and produce more output (dinners) and thereby serve more customers. In addition, greater specialization of labor is possible. Some workers specialize in cooking, others in serving the customers, and still others in busing the tables. Specialization also increases the output (the dinners). Both the more efficient use of labor and the increase in specialization mean that as the managers hire more labor, each additional worker increases the firm's output by more than the previous worker. As more labor is used, however, eventually output increases more slowly in response to increases in the number of workers because the opportunity for additional gains diminishes. Finally, as the managers add more and more workers, the congestion of workers becomes so severe that the restaurant reaches its maximum output. In Figure 4.1, the maximum output is 320 dinners per day. Any further additions to the workforce—say, going from 10 to 11 workers per shift—actually decrease the quantity of output.

Marginal Product

Marginal product The change in total output that results from changing an input by one unit while keeping the other inputs constant.

Marginal product of labor The change in total output that results from changing labor by one unit while keeping the other inputs constant.

The production function highlights a crucial decision for managers: determining the optimal quantity of an input to employ. This decision depends on the input's productivity and its cost compared to other inputs' productivities and costs. The relevant measure of productivity is the input's **marginal product**, which is the change in total output that results from changing the input by one unit while keeping the other inputs constant.

Using this definition, the **marginal product of labor** (MP_L) is the change in total output that results from changing labor by one unit while keeping the other inputs constant. It equals

$$MP_L = \frac{(\text{Change in output})}{(\text{Change in labor})} = \frac{(\Delta Q)}{(\Delta L)}$$

In this equation, the delta symbol (Δ) means "change in," Q is output, and L is labor.

Figure 4.2(a) shows the marginal product of labor from the same data included in Figure 4.1(a). To calculate the marginal product of labor, divide the change in the number of dinners by the change in the number of workers. For example, the marginal product of labor of increasing the number of workers from 6 to 7 equals

$$\frac{(260 \text{ dinners} - 220 \text{ dinners})}{(7 \text{ workers} - 6 \text{ workers})} = 40 \text{ dinners per worker}$$

which means that increasing the number of workers from 6 to 7 enables your Italian restaurant to produce an additional 40 dinners per day. In Figure 4.2(a), this marginal product is located between 6 and 7 workers. The remaining results in the third column of Figure 4.2(a) are calculated in the same way.

Figure 4.2(b) shows the behavior of the MP_L curve. As the number of workers increases, the marginal product of labor starts small, rises, hits a maximum, and then decreases. This is a graphic example of the economics of the situation. When only a

Figure 4.2 **The Marginal Product of Labor**

(a) **Marginal Product of Labor Data**

The marginal product of labor equals $\frac{(\text{Change in } Q)}{(\text{Change in } L)}$.

The third column shows the marginal product of labor obtained by dividing the change in output (column 2) by the change in labor (column 1). For example, the marginal product of labor of increasing employment from 4 to 5 workers equals $\frac{(170 \text{ dinners} - 110 \text{ dinners})}{(5 \text{ workers} - 4 \text{ workers})} = 60$ dinners per worker.

(b) **Marginal Product of Labor Curve**

The figure plots the marginal product of labor (MP_L) for each worker using the data from part a.

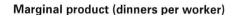

Labor, L (workers)	Output, Q (dinners per day)	Marginal Product of Labor (dinners per worker)
0	0	
		10
1	10	
		20
2	30	
		30
3	60	
		50
4	110	
		60
5	170	
		50
6	220	
		40
7	260	
		30
8	290	
		20
9	310	
		10
10	320	
		-10
11	310	

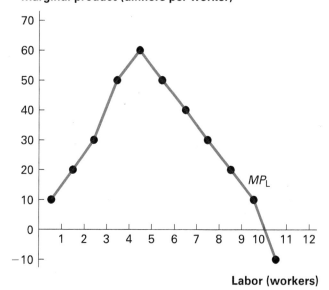

Marginal product (dinners per worker)

Labor (workers)

few workers are employed, hiring another worker results in increased specialization and increases the efficiency of all of the workers, leading to a large increase in output—that is, a large MP_L. Eventually, the marginal product of labor hits its maximum, which occurs at 4½ workers in Figure 4.2(b). Then as managers hire more workers, congestion sets in, and there is a smaller increase in output from hiring another worker. Of course, the number of workers and the numerical value of the maximum marginal product of labor differ from company to company, but the general appearance of the curve is similar to the one shown in Figure 4.2(b).

Figure 4.3 shows the relationship between the production function and the marginal product of labor curve by illustrating both in the same diagram. As labor increases from 1 worker to 4½ workers, the production function rises and becomes steeper—each additional worker increases output by more than the previous worker—so the marginal product of labor increases in this range. The range over which the marginal product of labor increases is defined as the range with **increasing marginal returns to labor.**

For the range of workers between 4½ and 10, the production function still rises, but it becomes less steep—each additional worker increases output by less than the previous worker—so the marginal product of labor decreases in this range. The range over which the marginal product of labor decreases but remains positive is defined as the range with **decreasing marginal returns to labor.**

Increasing marginal returns to labor The range of labor input over which the marginal product of labor increases.

Decreasing marginal returns to labor The range of labor input over which the marginal product of labor decreases but remains positive.

Figure 4.3 Increasing, Decreasing, and Negative Marginal Returns to Labor

The range over which the marginal product of labor increases, from 0 to 4½ workers in the figure, has increasing marginal returns to labor. The range over which the marginal product of labor decreases but is positive, 4½ to 10 workers in the figure, has decreasing marginal returns to labor. The range over which the marginal product of labor decreases and is negative, more than 10 workers in the figure, has negative marginal returns to labor.

Output and marginal product

Increasing marginal returns to labor

Decreasing marginal returns to labor

Negative marginal returns to labor

PF

MP_L

Labor (workers)

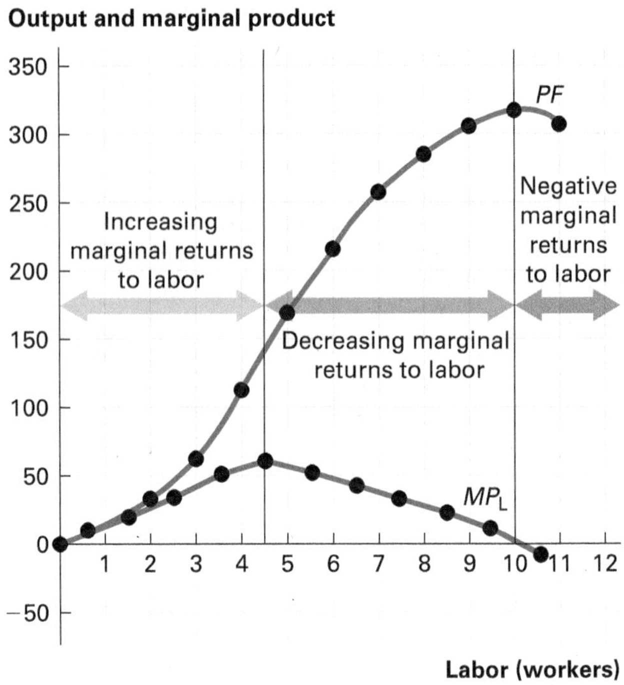

Finally, for all workers beyond 10, the production function falls—each additional worker *decreases* output. Consequently, the marginal product of labor is negative in this range. The range over which the marginal product of labor is negative is defined as the range with **negative marginal returns to labor**.

Negative marginal returns to labor The range of labor input over which the marginal product of labor is negative.

The concept of marginal product applies to other inputs besides labor. Each input has its own marginal product, equal to the change in output that results from changing that input by one unit while keeping all the other inputs constant. For example, in the long run, managers can change the quantity of capital, so at that point the *marginal product of capital (MP_K)* is equal to

$$MP_K = \frac{\Delta Q}{\Delta K}$$

More realistic production functions include more than two inputs, but the marginal products for all other inputs are calculated in the same way. The inputs will have the same three ranges described above: initially increasing marginal returns followed by decreasing marginal returns and ending with negative marginal returns.

The marginal product for each input is important knowledge for managers because it helps determine the cost-minimizing combination of inputs. Unfortunately, as a manager, you will never know the precise production function or the precise marginal product of your inputs. You can estimate approximate values using records of changes in output resulting from changes in the use of an input, perhaps by using regression analysis as explained in Chapter 3 (see Section 3.1). Alternatively, you might use your best managerial judgment to estimate the marginal product. Regardless of how you obtain your estimate, as you will learn in Section 4.2, knowing the marginal product is essential to accomplishing the goal of minimizing your firm's costs.

Figure 4.4 The Effects of a Technological Advance

(a) **The Effect of a Technological Advance on the Production Function**

An improvement to technology shifts the production function upward, from PF_0 to PF_1.

(b) **The Effect of a Technological Advance on the Marginal Product of Labor Curve**

An improvement to technology shifts the marginal product of labor curve upward, in the figure from MP_0 to MP_1, though in general the unit of labor with the maximum marginal product will change.

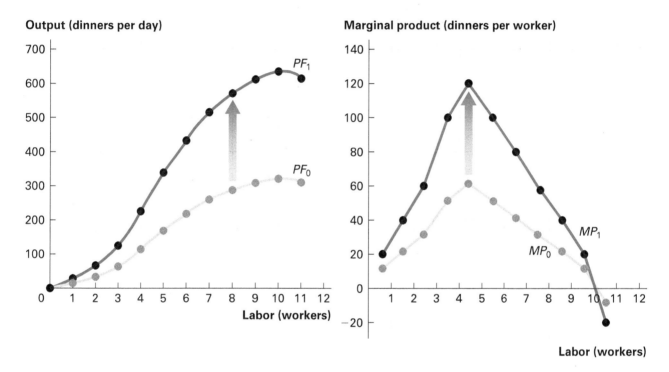

The Impact of Changes in Technology

A change in technology shifts the production function. Typically, advances in technology allow the firm to produce more output from the same quantity of inputs. For example, suppose that a new convection oven technology doubles the number of dinners your Italian restaurant can produce at each quantity of workers. As illustrated in Figure 4.4(a), the technological advance shifts the production function upward. Technological advances also generally increase the marginal product of labor. The technological advance that doubles the number of dinners shifts the marginal product of labor curve upward, as shown in Figure 4.4(b).

2 input

Long-Run Production Function

In the long run, all inputs are variable, so managers can change the quantity of *all* of the inputs. For a two-input production process, you can write the *long-run production function*, when all inputs are variable, as $Q = f(L, K)$, where both labor, L, and capital, K, can be changed. The long-run production function is more difficult to illustrate in a figure because even with just two inputs the figure needs to be three-dimensional to take account of the two inputs and one output. Instead of trying to illustrate a long-run production function, Table 4.1 presents a portion of the long-run production function using data from the Italian restaurant example.

Table 4.1 **The Long-Run Production Function**

These data represent the long-run production function.

Production Data								
Capital, K (units of capital)	Labor, L (workers)	Output, Q (dinners per day)	Capital, K (units of capital)	Labor, L (workers)	Output, Q (dinners per day)	Capital, K (units of capital)	Labor, L (workers)	Output, Q (dinners per day)
4	0	0	5	0	0	6	0	0
4	1	8	5	1	10	6	1	12
4	2	26	5	2	30	6	2	34
4	3	50	5	3	60	6	3	72
4	4	85	5	4	110	6	4	140
4	5	130	5	5	170	6	5	230
4	6	170	5	6	220	6	6	300
4	7	205	5	7	260	6	7	350
4	8	235	5	8	290	6	8	390
4	9	250	5	9	310	6	9	420
4	10	240	5	10	320	6	10	440
4	11	230	5	11	310	6	11	450

For any given amount of capital, such as the 4 units shown in Table 4.1, the marginal product of labor follows the same pattern described earlier: It rises to a maximum during a range with increasing marginal returns and then falls during a range with decreasing marginal returns. Although there are not enough data in the table to show its entire pattern, the marginal product of capital follows the same behavior: It rises to a maximum during a range with increasing marginal returns and then falls during a range with decreasing marginal returns. For example, holding employment constant at 5 workers, the marginal product of capital when capital is increased from 4 to 5 units is

$$\frac{(170 \text{ dinners} - 130 \text{ dinners})}{(5 \text{ units of capital} - 4 \text{ units of capital})} = 40 \text{ dinners per unit of capital}$$

Then the marginal product of capital when capital is increased from 5 to 6 units is

$$\frac{(230 \text{ dinners} - 170 \text{ dinners})}{(6 \text{ units of capital} - 5 \text{ units of capital})} = 60 \text{ dinners per unit of capital}$$

These two marginal products of capital fall within the increasing marginal returns range, but if you continued to calculate the marginal product of capital for larger and larger amounts of capital, eventually it would hit a maximum and then begin to decrease.

Using the marginal product along with the prices of the different inputs enables you to make decisions that minimize the cost of producing your firm's product. The next section explains how to make these decisions.

Marginal Product of Labor at a Bicycle Courier Service

You are a manager at a firm like Snap Delivery, a bicycle courier service in New York City. You estimate that if you hire 10 couriers, you can deliver 180 packages a day and if you hire 11 couriers, you can deliver 198 packages a day. You also estimate that the price you can charge for the delivery of each package will be $25. What is the marginal product of labor for the 11th courier? What is the effect of the price on the marginal product of labor?

Answer

The marginal product of labor is equal to the change in the output divided by the change in labor, or

$$MP_L = \frac{\Delta Q}{\Delta L}$$

The total output using 11 couriers is 198 packages, and the total output using 10 couriers is 180 packages. So the change in output, ΔQ, that occurs by adding the 11th courier is 198 packages − 180 packages, or 18 packages. The change in employment, ΔL, is 1 worker, so the marginal product of the 11th courier is (18 packages)/(1 worker), or 18 packages. The price of the delivery plays *no* role in determining the marginal product because the marginal product is based solely on the change in output and the change in input.

4.2 Cost Minimization

Learning Objective 4.2 Use the cost-minimization rule to choose the combination of inputs that produces a given quantity of output at the lowest cost.

When a firm uses an input, it incurs a cost. Regardless of whether you are managing a for-profit firm, a not-for-profit organization, a government agency, or an NGO, your goal should be to use the mix of inputs that minimizes the cost of producing the desired quantity of the good or service. You will constantly face decisions about the amount of each input to use when producing your product. For instance, if you are a general manager at a restaurant, should you hire another server and let a table busser go, or should you purchase another dish-washing machine and fire a dishwasher? If you are a manager at a nonprofit like the American Red Cross, should you buy another emergency response vehicle and fire five disaster workers and two CPR trainers? As the choices faced by these managers demonstrate, all the different types of organizations use multiple inputs. For simplicity, however, the text discussion continues to use the two-input production function, $Q = f(L, K)$. Learning how to minimize cost with only two inputs will help you understand the process for the real-world case of many inputs.

As you have already learned, some inputs are fixed in the short run. You cannot change the quantity of fixed inputs, so you must focus on minimizing the cost of the variable inputs to optimize production and minimize the total cost. To demonstrate how to choose the quantities of variable inputs to minimize costs, assume that you are dealing with the long run so that both inputs (labor and capital) are variable. Although the demonstration uses labor and capital, the results apply to any combination of variable inputs.

The decision to use an additional unit of an input—say, hire a worker—has two immediate effects:

1. **The firm's output increases.** Recall that the marginal product of labor is the amount by which production increases, so hiring another worker increases the firm's output by MP_L units.
2. **The firm's total cost increases.** Assume that the cost of hiring a worker is the wage rate (W), the amount that the worker must be paid. In reality, firms must also pay taxes, unemployment insurance, and possibly fringe benefits. Moreover, merely employing another worker usually does not increase production on its own because additional raw materials must often be purchased. For example, when you hire another cook for your restaurant, you might also need to purchase more flour to enable that worker to boost production of pasta and bread. For simplicity, consider *all* of these costs (taxes, fringe benefits, unemployment insurance, and price of other necessary materials) as part of the wage rate, W.

Cost-Minimization Rule

To derive the cost-minimization rule, start by combining the marginal product of labor and the wage rate into one term, $\frac{MP_L}{W}$. This term measures the change in output that results from a $1 change in the quantity of labor employed. For example, if the wage of a restaurant worker is $100 and the marginal product of the worker is 20 dinners, then

$$\frac{MP_L}{W} = \frac{20 \text{ dinners}}{\$100} = 0.2 \text{ dinners per dollar}$$

In other words, as the restaurant's general manager, for each additional dollar spent on labor you gain 0.2 dinners. Alternatively, for each decrease of a dollar spent on labor you lose 0.2 dinners.

Similar calculations hold for any input. For example, if R is the cost of using an additional unit of capital equipment,[2] then $\frac{MP_K}{R}$ is the change in production from a $1 change in the quantity of capital used.

Using both of these fractions, you arrive at the cost-minimization rule: To minimize cost, a firm should use the combination of labor and capital that produces the desired amount of output and is such that $\frac{MP_L}{W} = \frac{MP_K}{R}$.

COST-MINIMIZATION RULE

To minimize cost, a firm should use the combination of labor and capital that produces the desired amount of output and is such that $\frac{MP_L}{W} = \frac{MP_K}{R}$.

Why does this equality minimize cost? It minimizes cost because if the two terms are not equal, a manager can adjust the quantity of inputs used and lower the cost without changing the total quantity produced. Let's see how these adjustments work:

---

2 Both the services from and the expenditures for a piece of capital equipment typically accrue for many periods. This fact complicates the proper measurement of the cost of capital. Chapter 16 covers these issues in detail. This chapter sidesteps this difficulty by assuming that both MP_K and R are measured correctly.

- If $\frac{MP_L}{W} > \frac{MP_K}{R}$, the quantity of inputs can be changed to lower the firm's cost. For example, suppose that $\frac{MP_L}{W} = 6$ units per dollar and $\frac{MP_K}{R} = 2$ units per dollar. At these values, reducing the amount spent on capital by \$3 decreases production by 6 units (2 units $\times$ \$3), and increasing the amount spent on labor by \$1 increases production by 6 units. Combining these changes leaves the quantity produced unchanged but lowers the cost by \$2 (\$3 − \$1). More generally, whenever $\frac{MP_L}{W} > \frac{MP_K}{R}$, you can lower the total cost by increasing the amount of labor used and decreasing the amount of capital used. As you make these changes, the increase in the quantity of labor decreases the marginal product of labor, and the decrease in the quantity of capital increases the marginal product of capital, thereby driving the inequality $\frac{MP_L}{W} > \frac{MP_K}{R}$ toward the cost-minimizing equality, $\frac{MP_L}{W} = \frac{MP_K}{R}$. But as long as $\frac{MP_L}{W}$ exceeds $\frac{MP_K}{R}$, increasing the amount of labor used and decreasing the amount of capital used lowers the total cost.

- If $\frac{MP_K}{R} > \frac{MP_L}{W}$, the cost can once again be reduced by adjusting the quantity of inputs employed. In this case, however, you would increase the quantity of capital and decrease the quantity of labor. Suppose that $\frac{MP_K}{R} = 8$ units per dollar and $\frac{MP_L}{W} = 1$ unit per dollar. At these values, reducing the amount spent on labor by \$8 decreases production by 8 units (1 unit $\times$ \$8), and increasing the amount spent on capital by \$1 increases production by 8 units. Combining these changes again leaves the quantity produced unchanged but lowers the cost, this time by \$7 (\$8 − \$1). As you make this change, the increase in the quantity of capital decreases the marginal product of capital, and the decrease in the quantity of labor increases the marginal product of labor, driving the inequality $\frac{MP_K}{R} > \frac{MP_L}{W}$ toward the cost-minimizing equality, $\frac{MP_L}{W} = \frac{MP_K}{R}$. As long as $\frac{MP_K}{R}$ exceeds $\frac{MP_L}{W}$, increasing the amount of capital used and decreasing the amount of labor used lowers the total cost.

The cost-minimizing lesson from these examples is straightforward: Increase spending on the input with the larger output per dollar, and reduce spending on the input with the lower output per dollar.

Generalizing the Cost-Minimization Rule

The cost-minimization rule generalizes beyond the example of two inputs. To minimize the cost of producing the desired quantity of output with more than two inputs requires that

$$\frac{MP_1}{P_1} = \frac{MP_2}{P_2} = \frac{MP_3}{P_3} = \cdots = \frac{MP_n}{P_n} \qquad \textbf{4.1}$$

In Equation 4.1, MP_1 is the marginal product of the first input and P_1 is the price of the first input, MP_2 is the marginal product of the second input and P_2 is the price of the second input, and so on. For example, if the first input is labor, then MP_1 is the marginal product of labor, MP_L, and P_1 is the wage rate, W.

The intuition behind Equation 4.1 and that behind the two-input cost-minimization rule are identical. When MP_i is the marginal product of input i and P_i is its price, then the term $\frac{MP_i}{P_i}$ equals the change in output from changing spending on input i by \$1. According to the cost-minimization rule, these terms must be equal for all inputs, so the change in output from changing spending by \$1 on any input must be equal for all inputs. If these quantities are not equal, the manager can lower costs by buying more of the inputs that give the manager more output (those with high $\frac{MP}{P}$) and buying fewer of the inputs that give the manager less output (those with low $\frac{MP}{P}$). No matter how many inputs managers use in the production process, whenever the change in output from spending \$1 on one input differs from that for another input, managers can lower the total cost by using more of the input with the larger change in output and less of the input with the smaller change.

Successful managers make decisions that minimize the cost of producing a given quantity of output. They also know how costs change when the quantity of output changes. You will begin to learn about this important topic in the next section on short-run changes in cost.

Cost Minimization at a Construction Firm

As a construction manager for a firm like KB Home, you employ carpenters and carpenter assistants. You pay your carpenters \$800 per week and your carpenter assistants \$500 per week. The marginal product of a carpenter is construction of 2 rooms per week, and the marginal product of a carpenter assistant is construction of 1 room per week. Are you minimizing your costs? Explain your answer.

Answer

Cost minimization requires that

$$\frac{MP_{\text{CARPENTER}}}{W_{\text{CARPENTER}}} = \frac{MP_{\text{ASS'T CARPENTER}}}{W_{\text{ASS'T CARPENTER}}}$$

But using the data in the problem shows that

$$\frac{2 \text{ rooms per week}}{\$800 \text{ per week}} \neq \frac{1 \text{ room per week}}{\$500 \text{ per week}}$$

so you are not minimizing your costs. Spending an additional dollar on a carpenter increases your construction of rooms by more than spending that dollar on a carpenter assistant, so increasing the number of carpenters and decreasing the number of carpenter assistants will decrease your cost. You can verify this conclusion by noticing that hiring an additional carpenter for ½ of a week enables you to construct 1 room at a cost of \$400, while laying off a carpenter assistant for a week decreases your construction by 1 room but saves you \$500 in cost. Combining these changes leaves the number of rooms you construct the same, but your costs fall by \$100. As long as the $\frac{MP_{\text{CARPENTER}}}{W_{\text{CARPENTER}}}$ and $\frac{MP_{\text{ASS'T CARPENTER}}}{W_{\text{ASS'T CARPENTER}}}$ terms are not equal, you can decrease your cost by using more of the input with the larger change in production per dollar and less of the input with the smaller change in production per dollar.

4.3 Short-Run Cost

Learning Objective 4.3 Distinguish between fixed cost and variable cost and calculate average total cost, average variable cost, average fixed cost, and marginal cost.

Effective managers make decisions based on understanding how their firm's costs change when the production of output changes. This section begins by examining short-run costs. As you learned in Section 4.1, the short run is the time period during which at least one input is fixed. To capture this difference between inputs, again use the two-input short-run production function, $Q = f(L, \overline{K})$. Recall that the bar over K signifies that the quantity of capital is fixed. This two-input short-run production function means that managers can change the quantity produced *only* by changing the quantity of the variable input, labor. In reality, managers can change the quantity produced by adjusting the amount(s) of any of a larger number of variable inputs. But as usual, once you understand the two-input production function, you can apply this simplified approach to more realistic situations.

Fixed Cost, Variable Cost, and Total Cost

Regardless of the number of inputs, all the inputs can be sorted into one of two categories: fixed or variable. The sum of the costs paid for all fixed inputs is called the **fixed cost** (*FC*). Fixed cost does not change with changes in output because the quantity of fixed inputs cannot be changed. The sum of the costs paid for all variable inputs is called the **variable cost** (*VC*). Variable cost changes with changes in output because managers must change the quantity of variable inputs in order to change output. Since every input falls into one of the two groups (fixed inputs or variable inputs), the **total cost** (*TC*) of the inputs equals the sum of the fixed costs (for the fixed inputs) and the variable costs (for the variable inputs), or

$$TC = FC + VC$$

Fixed cost The sum of the costs paid for all fixed inputs; fixed cost does not change when output changes.

Variable cost The sum of the costs paid for all variable inputs; variable cost changes when output changes.

Total cost The sum of the fixed cost and the variable cost; $TC = FC + VC$.

Table 4.2 relates a firm's production function to its costs. The first three columns of Table 4.2 are from the production function shown in Table 4.1 when your Italian restaurant uses 6 units of capital (*K*). The fixed input is capital, so the cost of the capital is the fixed cost. Suppose that the cost of each unit of capital, which might represent rental payments on the building, interest payments due on the capital equipment, or the economic depreciation of the capital, is $83.33. The fixed cost (*FC*) for all 6 units is $500, 6 units of capital multiplied by $83.33 per unit of capital. The variable input is labor, so the cost of the labor is the variable cost. Suppose that the cost of each unit of labor (the sum of the wage rate plus other costs of hiring a worker) is $100. In the first row of Table 4.2, when no workers are hired, the variable cost is $0. In the second row, when one worker is hired, the variable cost is $100. In the third row, when two workers are hired, the variable cost is $200.

Table 4.2 illustrates a fundamental difference between fixed cost and variable cost: The fixed cost remains constant when output changes, but the variable cost changes with a change in output. This difference reflects the distinction between a fixed input and a variable input. In the short run, a firm cannot change the amount of its fixed input(s), so the fixed cost remains constant—fixed—when output changes. But to change its output, the firm must change the amount of its variable input(s), so when output changes, so does the variable cost.

Table 4.2 shows two other significant aspects of total cost:

1. Even when output is zero—that is, even when the firm is closed—the firm still incurs a cost. In particular, the firm still must pay its fixed costs. Although the variable costs are zero when the firm is closed, the total cost is not zero.
2. When output changes, the total cost changes. When output increases, the total cost increases. When output decreases, the total cost decreases. This relationship is due entirely to the changes in the variable costs when output changes.

Table 4.2 Short-Run Production Function and Cost Data

The table presents a short-run production function and the resulting costs. The cost of a unit of labor is $100, and the cost of a unit of capital is $83.33. Because marginal cost is calculated for a change in output, each *MC* is placed midway between two rows, indicating that it applies to the change in output between the rows.

Capital, K	Labor, L	Output, Q	Fixed Cost, FC	Variable Cost, VC	Total Cost, TC	Average Fixed Cost, AFC	Average Variable Cost, AVC	Average Total Cost, ATC	Marginal Cost, MC
6	0	0	$500	$0	$500	X	X	X	
									$8.33
6	1	12	500	100	600	$41.67	$8.33	$50.00	
									4.55
6	2	34	500	200	700	14.71	5.88	20.59	
									2.63
6	3	72	500	300	800	6.94	4.17	11.11	
									1.47
6	4	140	500	400	900	3.57	2.86	6.43	
									1.11
6	5	230	500	500	1,000	2.17	2.17	4.35	
									1.43
6	6	300	500	600	1,100	1.67	2.00	3.67	
									2.00
6	7	350	500	700	1,200	1.43	2.00	3.43	
									2.50
6	8	390	500	800	1,300	1.28	2.05	3.33	
									3.33
6	9	420	500	900	1,400	1.19	2.14	3.33	
									5.00
6	10	440	500	1,000	1,500	1.14	2.27	3.41	
									10.00
6	11	450	500	1,100	1,600	1.11	2.44	3.56	

Sunk Cost Versus Fixed Cost

In Chapter 1 you learned about *sunk costs*, costs that you cannot recover because they have been paid or incurred in the past. Costs that have already been paid do not change when output changes. Consequently, all sunk costs are fixed costs, but not all fixed costs are sunk costs. For example, your restaurant might have a month-to-month rental agreement that specifies rent on the site of $200 per day. The rent is a fixed cost because it pays for a fixed input and does not change with the number of dinners produced. But the rent is not a sunk cost because the restaurant pays it month by month.

Average Fixed Cost, Average Variable Cost, and Average Total Cost

Average fixed cost Fixed cost divided by the amount of output; $AFC = \frac{FC}{Q}$.

Average variable cost Variable cost divided by the amount of output; $AVC = \frac{VC}{Q}$.

Average total cost Total cost divided by the amount of output; $ATC = \frac{TC}{Q}$.

The next three columns of Table 4.2 have data related to three more cost concepts: average fixed cost, average variable cost, and average total cost. The definitions of these three cost concepts are similar. **Average fixed cost** (*AFC*) is the fixed cost (*FC*) divided by the amount of output (*Q*), or, in algebraic terms, $AFC = \frac{FC}{Q}$. The **average variable cost** (*AVC*) is the variable cost (*VC*) divided by the amount of output, or $AVC = \frac{VC}{Q}$. Finally, the **average total cost** (*ATC*) is the total cost (*TC*) divided by the amount of output, or $ATC = \frac{TC}{Q}$.

Average total cost also equals the sum of the average fixed cost and the average variable cost: $ATC = AFC + AVC$. This alternative expression is derived from the definition of total cost: $TC = FC + VC$. Divide both sides of the total cost definition by the quantity (*Q*), and the result is

$$\frac{TC}{Q} = \frac{FC}{Q} + \frac{VC}{Q} \Rightarrow ATC = AFC + AVC$$

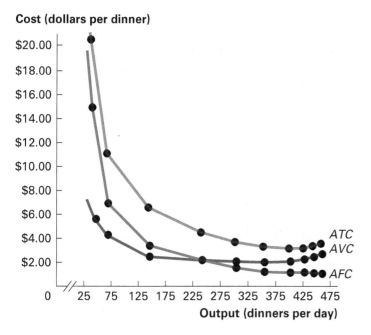

Cost (dollars per dinner)

Figure 4.5 *AFC, AVC,* and *ATC* Curves

The three cost curves are derived from the data in Table 4.4. Both the *AVC* and the *ATC* curves are U-shaped. The vertical distance between the *AVC* and *ATC* curves becomes smaller as the quantity increases.

Figure 4.5 shows how the average fixed cost, average variable cost, and average total cost change when quantity increases or decreases. The behavior of the *AFC* curve is unique: The average fixed cost constantly falls as the quantity increases.[3] In Figure 4.5, the average fixed cost (the blue curve) falls from $14.71 when 34 dinners are produced to $1.11 when 450 dinners are produced. As additional dinners beyond 450 are produced, the average fixed cost continues to fall.

The shapes of the *AVC* curve and the *ATC* curve are more complicated. As Table 4.2 and Figure 4.5 show, both of these costs start out large, decrease until they hit a minimum, and then increase. The U shape is typical of the *AVC* curve (in red) and the *ATC* curve (in green) for any type of firm, not just a restaurant. Of course, different firms reach the minimum points on the curves at different amounts of production.

The explanation of the U shape must wait until the next section, which covers marginal cost. For now, note that in Figure 4.5 the vertical distance between the two curves becomes smaller as output increases. The equation $ATC = AFC + AVC$ shows why. Rearranging it to $ATC - AVC = AFC$ shows that the difference between the average total cost and the average variable cost is the average fixed cost. As you just learned, the average fixed cost becomes smaller as output increases. With average fixed cost becoming smaller, the difference between the average total cost and average variable cost becomes smaller, which means that the *AVC* curve approaches the *ATC* curve.

Marginal Cost

As a manager, knowing your average total cost and average variable cost can be helpful in making decisions, but knowing yet another cost, the marginal cost, is significantly more important. Like all marginal concepts, the marginal cost focuses on changes. The **marginal cost (*MC*)** is the change in the total cost brought about by a

Marginal cost (*MC*) The change in total cost (*TC*) divided by the change in output (*Q*); $MC = \frac{\Delta TC}{\Delta Q}$.

---

3 As output increases, fixed cost does not change. Consequently, for the average fixed cost, as output increases the numerator does not change and the denominator increases, so the fraction falls in value.

change in output and is defined as $MC = \frac{\Delta TC}{\Delta Q}$, where, as usual, the symbol delta (Δ) means "change in." Marginal cost is most meaningful when calculated for small changes in output. When output increases by a single unit, the marginal cost is the additional cost incurred to produce the additional unit. Conversely, when output decreases by a single unit, the marginal cost is the decrease in cost from *not* producing the unit. You will see throughout this text that the marginal cost plays a vital role in decision making.

DECISION SNAPSHOT

Input Price Changes and Changes in the Marginal Cost of an Eiffel Tower Tour

Fat Tire Tours is a Paris-based company selling "skip-the-line" tours to the Eiffel Tower and other Paris landmarks. Suppose that you manage a similar company and each year your company sells tours to 60,000 sightseers, with a marginal cost of $47 per tour. In addition, suppose that last year the monthly insurance premium you paid to insure against accidents was $6,000. This year the insurance company increases the premium to $9,000. How would this change affect your company's marginal cost?

Answer

It may surprise you that the change in the insurance premium has no effect on the marginal cost. In other words, the marginal cost does not change. The marginal cost measures how the total cost changes when output changes (when the number of tours changes). The insurance premium is a fixed cost. The premium does not change when your company sells more or fewer tours. Accordingly, the (fixed) insurance premium has no effect on the marginal cost.

The marginal cost shows the change in total cost when output changes. Because the fixed cost does not change when output changes, it has no effect on the marginal cost.

The last column in Table 4.2 shows the marginal cost for your Italian restaurant. Because marginal cost is calculated for a change in output, each MC listing in the table is placed midway between two rows, indicating that it applies to the change in output between the rows. For example, when output increases from 300 to 350 units, the total cost increases from $1,100 to $1,200, so the marginal cost equals $\frac{\$100}{50} = \$2.00$ per dinner.

Figure 4.6 shows the MC curve calculated from the data in Table 4.2, along with the AVC curve and the ATC curve. In Figure 4.6, the marginal cost values are plotted midway between the relevant quantities, indicating that the marginal cost applies to the change in output between these quantities. For example, the marginal cost of increasing production from 34 to 72 dinners, $2.63, is plotted at 53 dinners, midway between 34 and 72 dinners.

Figure 4.6 shows that the marginal cost initially falls and then rises as the quantity increases. The general U shape of the MC curve is common to all firms. In fact, the U shape of the MC curve is the consequence of how the marginal product of the variable inputs changes as output changes.

Suppose that labor is the only variable input. The cost of hiring an additional worker is W, and the increase in output is MP_L. Consequently, the cost of producing one more unit of output—the marginal cost—by hiring an additional worker is equal to $\frac{W}{MP_L}$. For example, using the data in Table 4.2, hiring the first restaurant worker increases the production of dinners from 0 dinners to 12 dinners, so the marginal product of this worker is 12 dinners. At a wage rate of $100, the marginal cost of

Cost (dollars per dinner)

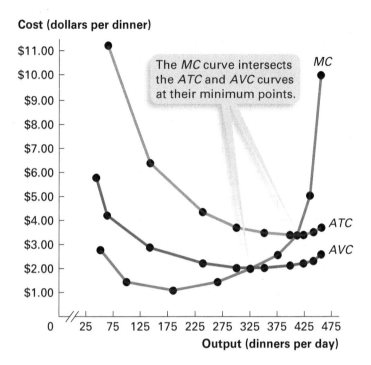

The *MC* curve intersects the *ATC* and *AVC* curves at their minimum points.

Output (dinners per day)

Figure 4.6 *MC, ATC,* and *AVC* Curves

The figure shows three cost curves from Table 4.2. The values for the *MC* curve are plotted midway between the relevant quantities. The *MC* curve intersects the *AVC* curve and the *ATC* curve at their minimums.

producing one more dinner between 0 and 12 dinners is $\frac{\$100}{12\,\text{dinners}} = \$8.33$ per dinner. The marginal product of the second worker is 22 dinners, so the marginal cost of producing one more dinner between 12 and 34 dinners is $\frac{\$100}{22\,\text{dinners}} = \$4.55$ per dinner. The larger the marginal product, the smaller the marginal cost. Over the range of output with increasing marginal returns to labor, the marginal product increases, so the marginal cost decreases and the *MC* curve slopes downward. Eventually, as more workers are hired, the range with decreasing marginal returns to labor is reached, and the marginal product starts to decrease. For example, the 11th worker has a marginal product of only 10 dinners, so the marginal cost of producing one more dinner here is $\frac{\$100}{10\,\text{dinners}} = \$10.00$ per dinner, much larger than the marginal cost when hiring the first or second worker. Once the marginal product starts to decrease, the marginal cost of an additional dinner increases, so over this range of output the *MC* curve slopes upward.

The following box summarizes the general relationship between the marginal product of labor and marginal cost.

RELATIONSHIP BETWEEN THE MARGINAL PRODUCT OF LABOR AND MARGINAL COST

- Over the range of output where the marginal product of labor increases, the marginal cost decreases.
- At the level of output where the marginal product of labor is at its maximum, the marginal cost is at its minimum.
- Over the range of output where the marginal product of labor decreases, the marginal cost increases.

Marginal/Average Relationship

Figure 4.6 illustrates another notable result: The *MC* curve intersects the *AVC* curve and the *ATC* curve at their minimum points, an example of a more general relationship called the *marginal/average relationship*. The marginal/average relationship has two parts:

- If the marginal _____ is greater than the average _____, then the average _____ increases.
- If the marginal _____ is less than the average _____, then the average _____ decreases.

As the blanks imply, this relationship applies anytime a marginal and an average are involved. For example, every student is familiar with this general relationship: If the grade you receive in an additional class (a marginal class) exceeds your grade point average (GPA), then your GPA will rise. Conversely, if the grade you receive in an additional class is less than your GPA, then your GPA will fall. What is true for grades is also true for costs: If the marginal cost of another unit is greater than the average cost, then the average cost will rise. If the marginal cost of another unit is less than the average cost, then the average cost will fall.

These results mean that the *MC* curve must intersect the *AVC* curve and the *ATC* curve at their minimums. In Figure 4.6, examine the relationship between average variable cost and marginal cost when your Italian restaurant produces less than 325 dinners. Over this range of production, the marginal cost of another dinner is less than the average variable cost, so producing an additional dinner means a decrease in the average variable cost. As the figure shows, the *AVC* curve slopes downward.

Now look at this same relationship when the production exceeds 325 dinners. Over this range of output, the marginal cost of another dinner is greater than the average variable cost, so producing another dinner increases the average variable cost. As Figure 4.6 shows, the *AVC* curve slopes upward. Combining these two results demonstrates that the *AVC* curve slopes downward until it reaches 325 dinners, after which it slopes upward. Therefore, average variable cost must equal its minimum at 325 dinners, the quantity where it intersects the *MC* curve. The same reasoning leads to the conclusion that the *MC* curve intersects the *ATC* curve at its minimum.[4]

In Figure 4.6, the *AVC* curve is flat at its minimum value, between 300 and 350 dinners. If Table 4.2 had a finer division for the labor input—for instance, increasing the numbers of workers fractionally by hiring part-time labor—then the curves might not have long, straight sections. Even with hiring fractional numbers of workers, however, some firms' production techniques are such that their average cost curves still have long flat sections at their minimums.

Competitive Return

This section has developed cost theory with the assumption that a firm uses only two inputs. Realistically, of course, any firm will use many more inputs. When considering costs such as the average total cost or marginal cost, it is essential that you include the opportunity costs of *all* of the inputs. As you learned in Chapter 1, one key input is the assets made available by the firm's owners, such

---

4 We formally prove this result using calculus in Section 4.C of the Appendix at the end of this chapter.

as the funds supplied to a large corporation by its investors. The opportunity cost of the owners' resources is the return these resources would earn if invested in the next best alternative use (the competitive return). As an opportunity cost of the business, the competitive return is included among all the other costs, such as wages and rent, when calculating the average total cost, average variable cost, and marginal cost.

Shifts in Cost Curves

Understanding how cost changes when output changes will help you make optimal managerial decisions. The cost curves just presented provide a good framework for organizing your thoughts. But you must also understand the factors that change costs and shift the cost curves because shifts in cost curves can change business decisions. Three factors shift the cost curves: (1) changes in the prices of the inputs, (2) changes in technology that alter the production function, and (3) economies and diseconomies of scope.

The Effect of Changes in Input Prices on the Cost Curves

Costs change and cost curves shift if the price of an input changes. The curves that shift depend on the type of input that changes in price. For example:

- If the price of a fixed input (such as the rent on a firm's store or factory) rises, then the fixed cost increases, and the FC curve shifts upward. Because the fixed cost is part of the total cost, the average total cost increases, and the ATC curve also shifts upward. Neither the AVC nor the MC curve shifts, because the fixed cost does not affect the variable or marginal costs. Figure 4.7 shows the effect an increase in the fixed cost has on the ATC, AVC, and MC curves for your Italian restaurant.

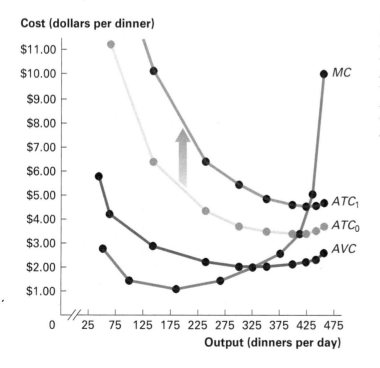

Figure 4.7 Effect of an Increase in Fixed Cost

An increase in the fixed cost shifts the ATC curve upward. It does not shift the AVC and MC curves.

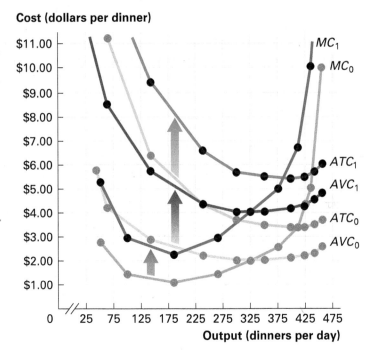

Figure 4.8 Effect of an Increase in Variable Cost

An increase in the variable cost shifts the *ATC*, *AVC*, and *MC* curves upward.

- If the price of a variable input (such as the wage rate) rises, then the variable cost increases, and the *AVC* and *ATC* curves both shift upward. The *MC* curve also shifts upward. Figure 4.8 shows the effect of an increase in the variable cost for your restaurant.

The Effect of Changes in Technology on the Cost Curves

Changes in technology shift both the production function and the cost curves. Sometimes technological change means that fewer inputs are necessary to produce the same quantity of output. For example, Toyota has redesigned its assembly lines from a straight line to a U shape. The U shape allows the workers to accomplish more work in the same time on each vehicle, decreasing the number of workers that Toyota must use to produce a car. Airbus provides another example: The company used to install overhead bins directly part-by-part in the plane. It now assembles the bins outside of the plane and then installs them in one piece. This change has decreased the time and labor spent installing bins. These types of technological changes reduce the cost for each unit of output produced and shift the *AVC*, *ATC*, and *MC* curves downward.

Learning-by-doing is an important source of technological change. *Learning-by-doing* refers to the idea that as a firm produces more of a particular product, its workers become better at the production process, thereby lowering costs. Computer chips are a prime example. Computer chip–manufacturing firms like Intel produce computer chips on large wafers, approximately 12 inches in diameter. Each wafer has many chips etched into it, but minuscule errors result in some of the chips malfunctioning. As a firm produces the same wafer week after week and month after month, its technicians learn how to increase the yield of good chips. The knowledge gained from learning-by-doing is a technological change that shifts the cost curves downward.

DECISION
SNAPSHOT

Changes in Input Prices and Cost Changes at *Shagang Group*

Suppose that you are an executive at a steel mill owned by Shagang Group, one of China's top five steel producers. Heating iron and other ores to high temperatures is one of the first steps in steel making. The heat to melt the ores often comes from burning coal. How does an increase in the price of iron affect your average total cost and marginal cost? How does an increase in the price of coal affect your average total cost and marginal cost? Finally, how does an increase in the wage paid your employees affect your average total cost and marginal cost?

Answer

Increases in the prices of all three inputs increase your average total cost. All three inputs—iron, coal, and workers—are variable inputs. More iron, more coal, and more workers are necessary to produce more steel. Increases in any of these three prices increase your marginal cost.

A firm like Intel can use its *learning curve*, a curve that shows how the average total cost of a chip falls as the firm produces more wafers, to help predict its average total cost of a particular chip. Figure 4.9 shows such a learning curve. After the firm has produced 100,000 wafers, the average total cost of this chip is $70, but the average total cost falls to $50 and then $30 after 200,000 and then 500,000 wafers have been produced.

The flip side of learning-by-doing is forgetting-by-not-doing. *Forgetting-by-not-doing* refers to a situation in which workers forget the most efficient way of

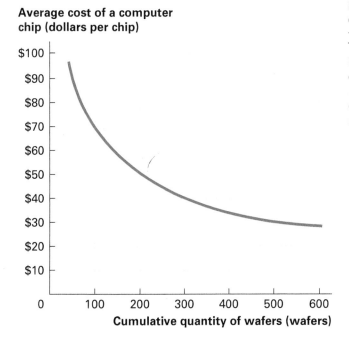

Average cost of a computer chip (dollars per chip)

Cumulative quantity of wafers (wafers)

Figure 4.9 A Learning Curve for a Computer Chip

The learning curve shows how the average total cost of a chip falls as the firm reaps learning-by-doing economies from producing more wafers.

doing an activity because of a decrease in production, causing the company's cost curves to shift upward. There is evidence that learning-by-doing can be important in many industries and for many firms. There is less evidence supporting the perils of forgetting-by-not-doing, though in recent years NASA had to spend significant sums of money to rediscover how to produce huge rockets, such as the Saturn V rocket (the rocket that sent astronauts to the moon). Because no one had made such huge rockets for decades, NASA engineers had effectively forgotten how to produce them.

Often technological changes are embedded in capital. In other words, new capital is required to implement technological change. For example, JCPenney, a mid-level U.S. retailer, and Burberry, a high-end U.K. retailer, have recently changed the procedure by which customers use credit and debit cards to purchase their products. Previously, customers lined up at fixed cash registers, but these companies decided to equip their associates with mobile iPod and iPad checkout devices. This technological change altered the type and the quantity of capital required at their stores.

The Effect of Economies and Diseconomies of Scope on the Cost Curves

Firms that produce more than one good are called multiproduct firms. Producing multiple goods can have varied effects on a firm's costs. We discuss two: economies of scope and diseconomies of scope. The first lowers the firm's costs and shifts its cost curves downward, and the second raises the firm's costs and shifts its cost curves upward.

Economies of scope The total cost of producing two goods is lower if they are produced within one firm than if they are produced separately by two different firms.

1. **Economies of scope** occur when the total cost of producing two or more goods is lower if they are produced within one firm than if they are produced separately by two different firms. For example, Intel and other chip-manufacturing firms produce computer chips and spend billions of dollars researching methods of shrinking the transistors used on each chip. When Intel started to produce chips for wireless communication, it used the same research to shrink the transistors on these chips. Spreading the cost of the research across the different types of chips means Intel's total cost is lower when compared to the total costs of two independent firms, each one specializing in the production of one type of chip and separately performing the research to shrink transistors.

   Cost complementarities are a special case of economies of scope. Cost complementarities occur when the production of one good makes the marginal cost of producing another good at the same firm lower compared to the marginal cost of a firm that produces only the second good. For example, refineries produce kerosene by heating petroleum until it evaporates and then allowing it to cool. They collect the kerosene as it condenses from the petroleum vapor at temperatures between 600°F and 350°F. Refineries also produce gasoline, in this case by simply letting the vapor cool some more and collecting the gasoline when *it* condenses at temperatures between 210°F and 140°F. By producing kerosene *and* gasoline, the petroleum is heated only once to a very high temperature to collect the kerosene, so there is no need to incur a separate cost of heating the petroleum to collect gasoline, thereby making the marginal cost of producing gasoline lower than it would be at a firm that refined petroleum and produced only gasoline.

Diseconomies of scope The total cost of producing two goods is higher if they are produced within one firm than if they are produced separately by two different firms.

2. **Diseconomies of scope** occur when the total cost of producing two goods is higher if they are produced within one firm than if they are produced separately by two different firms. In this case, the total cost of producing any of the goods increases as the firm produces more types of goods. For example,

McDonald's executive managers apparently determined that McDonald's was suffering from diseconomies of scope because the firm had allowed its menu to get too large. The managers decided to simplify the menu by reducing the number of different items McDonald's sells. The reduction in the number of menu items decreased McDonald's total cost of producing the products they continued to sell.

So far, you have learned how short-run costs change when output changes. As a manager, you must also be concerned with the impact of your decisions in the long run. As you learned earlier in this chapter, you can make more profound changes in the operation of your business in the long run, such as remodeling to increase the size of the dining area or the kitchen in your Italian restaurant. Such changes are costly and not easily reversed, both of which are excellent reasons to learn about long-run cost curves, the topic of the next section.

Calculating Different Costs at a Caribbean Restaurant

The following table includes the various costs involved in operating a restaurant like Bahama Breeze, an American restaurant chain that serves Caribbean-inspired dishes. Supposing all the workers are paid the same wage, fill in the missing numbers.

Capital, K	Labor, L	Output, Q	Fixed Cost, FC	Variable Cost, VC	Total Cost, TC	Average Fixed Cost, AFC	Average Variable Cost, AVC	Average Total Cost, ATC	Marginal Cost, MC
2	0	0				X	X	X	
2	1	10		200		$35.00			$20.00
2	2	40						18.75	
2	3	90							
2	4	150					5.33		
2	5	220							
2	6	300				1.17			
2	7	350						5.00	
2	8	390							5.00
2	9	420							
2	10	440					4.54		
2	11	450	350						20.00

Answer

The completed table is on the next page. The fixed cost is the same for all quantities, so it is $350 for all the rows. The second row in the table shows that the variable cost is $200 per worker, so the variable cost equals $200 per worker multiplied by the number of workers. The total cost is equal to the sum of the fixed cost and the variable cost. The average fixed cost equals the fixed cost divided by the output, the average variable cost equals the variable cost divided by the output, and the average total cost equals the total cost divided by the output. Finally, the marginal cost equals the change in the total cost divided by the change in the output.

(Continues)

SOLVED PROBLEM (*continued*)

Capital, K	Labor, L	Output, Q	Fixed Cost, FC	Variable Cost, VC	Total Cost, TC	Average Fixed Cost, AFC	Average Variable Cost, AVC	Average Total Cost, ATC	Marginal Cost, MC
2	0	0	$350	$0	$350	X	X	X	
									$20.00
2	1	10	350	200	550	$35.00	$20.00	$55.00	
									6.67
2	2	40	350	400	750	8.75	10.00	18.75	
									4.00
2	3	90	350	600	950	3.89	6.67	10.56	
									3.33
2	4	150	350	800	1,150	2.33	5.33	7.66	
									2.86
2	5	220	350	1,000	1,350	1.59	4.55	6.14	
									2.50
2	6	300	350	1,200	1,550	1.17	4.00	5.17	
									4.00
2	7	350	350	1,400	1,750	1.00	4.00	5.00	
									5.00
2	8	390	350	1,600	1,950	0.90	4.10	5.00	
									6.67
2	9	420	350	1,800	2,150	0.83	4.29	5.12	
									10.00
2	10	440	350	2,000	2,350	0.80	4.54	5.34	
									20.00
2	11	450	350	2,200	2,550	0.78	4.89	5.67	

4.4 Long-Run Cost

Learning Objective 4.4 Derive the long-run average cost curve and explain its shape.

The long run is important for planning purposes because in the long run managers can adjust the scale of the firm's operations by changing not only the amount of labor employed but also the amount of capital (and all other inputs). Managers' long-run decisions about the scale of their operations are very important. For example, if Darden's regional managers were to approve a remodeling plan that makes some Olive Garden restaurants too large for the most profitable operation, the firm would need to live with this mistake for years.

Long-Run Average Cost

In the long run, managers can adjust the scale of production by changing some or all inputs. For simplicity, assume once again that the firm uses only two inputs, capital (K) and labor (L), to produce its output (Q). With this assumption, the long-run production function is $Q = f(L, K)$. In the long run, managers can change the quantities of *both* inputs. Efficient managers select the amounts of capital and labor that minimize the average cost of its output.

Table 4.3 presents some more production data for your Italian restaurant. In this long-run case, all inputs are variable. So unlike Table 4.1(a), which examined the short run and therefore had only one quantity of capital, included in Table 4.3 are three different quantities of capital. From these data, you can calculate three sets of average total costs—one for 4 units of capital, one for 6 units of capital, and one for 8 units of capital. Assuming again that one unit of capital costs $83.33 and one unit of labor costs $100, Table 4.4 shows the average total costs in the short run for the three different amounts of capital. The columns in the tables are shaded to help you to see the linkage between the tables.

The Long-Run Average Cost Curve

Part of a manager's job is to determine the combination of inputs that minimizes the average total cost of its output. As a manager, you will make day-to-day decisions that minimize your short-run average cost, but the long-run decision about

Table 4.3 The Long-Run Production Function

All inputs are variable in the long-run production function.

Capital, K (units of capital)	Labor, L (workers)	Output, Q (dinners per day)	Capital, K (units of capital)	Labor, L (workers)	Output, Q (dinners per day)	Capital, K (units of capital)	Labor, L (workers)	Output, Q (dinners per day)
4	0	0	6	0	0	8	0	0
4	1	8	6	1	12	8	1	14
4	2	26	6	2	34	8	2	40
4	3	50	6	3	72	8	3	90
4	4	85	6	4	140	8	4	170
4	5	130	6	5	230	8	5	290
4	6	170	6	6	300	8	6	370
4	7	205	6	7	350	8	7	440
4	8	235	6	8	390	8	8	500
4	9	250	6	9	420	8	9	550
4	10	240	6	10	440	8	10	580
4	11	230	6	11	450	8	11	600

the quantity of capital to use determines what choices are available on any given day. Figure 4.10 illustrates the three sets of short-run average total cost data from Table 4.4. The figure shows that the amount of capital that minimizes the average cost depends on the scale of output—that is, quantity of dinners produced. For example, if you project that your Italian restaurant will serve 80 dinners per day, using 4 units of capital will have the lowest average total cost, approximately $9 per

Table 4.4 Short-Run Average Total Costs

The table shows the average total costs for different amounts of capital.

4 Units of Capital		6 Units of Capital		8 Units of Capital	
Output, Q	Average Total Cost, ATC	Output, Q	Average Total Cost, ATC	Output, Q	Average Total Cost, ATC
0	X	0	X	0	X
8	$54.17	12	$50.00	14	47.62
26	20.51	34	20.59	40	21.67
50	12.67	72	11.11	90	10.74
90	8.63	140	6.43	170	6.27
130	6.41	230	4.35	290	4.02
170	5.49	300	3.67	370	3.42
210	5.04	350	3.43	440	3.11
240	4.82	390	3.33	500	2.93
250	4.93	420	3.33	550	2.85
240	5.56	440	3.41	580	2.87
230	6.23	450	3.56	600	2.94

Figure 4.10 Using Short-Run Average Total Cost Curves to Create a Long-Run Average Cost Curve

The three short-run average total cost curves have been created using data from Table 4.4. The subscript of each curve denotes the amount of capital used. The *LAC* curve will run along the ATC_4 curve until point *A*, then along the ATC_6 curve until point *B*, and then along the ATC_8 curve.

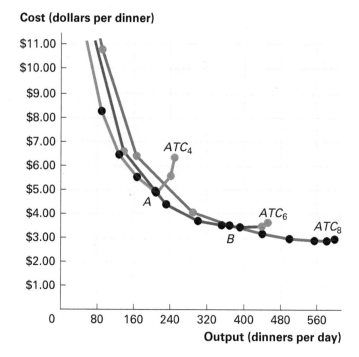

Long-run average cost
The minimum average total cost of producing any given quantity of output when all inputs can be changed.

dinner. If instead you forecast that the restaurant will serve 240 dinners per day, 6 units of capital minimizes the average total cost, and 8 units of capital is optimal at 440 dinners per day.

You can use this type of analysis to determine the minimum average total cost of producing any quantity of output. The **long-run average cost** is defined as the minimum average total cost of producing any given quantity of output when all inputs can be changed.

The long-run average cost (*LAC*) curve shows how the long-run average cost depends on the level of output. In Figure 4.10, if the only quantities of capital that can be used are 4, 6, and 8 units, the *LAC* curve runs along the ATC_4 curve to point *A*, then along the ATC_6 curve to point *B*, and finally along the ATC_8 curve.

Figure 4.10 shows the long-run average cost with only three possible amounts of capital for your Italian restaurant. In contrast, Figure 4.11 shows a more general case, in which the managers can use many possible amounts of capital (and other fixed inputs), thereby creating many *short*-run *ATC* curves. Only a few of the many possible curves are illustrated in the figure. The point on each short-run *ATC* curve that is the minimum average total cost of producing an amount of output becomes a point on the *LAC* curve. In other words, in Figure 4.11 the short-run blue *ATC* curves are combined to trace the red *LAC* curve.

Note that it is only on the horizontal section of the *LAC* curve that the actual minimum points of the individual (short-run) *ATC* curves fall on the *LAC* curve. For example, take point *B* on ATC_1. To produce 200 units, the managers could produce at point *B*, which is the minimum-cost point on ATC_1. If they do so, the average cost is $12.00. However, the managers could use more capital and produce at point *C* on ATC_2, for an average cost of $9.00. Even though the firm is *not* producing at the minimum point on ATC_2, its average cost is still lower than at the minimum point on ATC_1, which is why point *C* is on the *LAC* curve and point *B* is not.

The quantity at which the long-run average cost first reaches its minimum is called the *minimum efficient scale*. In Figure 4.11, the minimum efficient scale is 300 units per day.

Cost (dollars per unit)

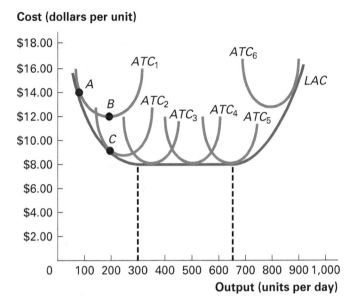

Figure 4.11 Long-Run Average Cost Curve

The long-run average cost curve, the red curve labeled *LAC*, shows the minimum average total cost to produce different quantities of output. The *LAC* curve is comprised of the points on the short-run *ATC* curves that are the minimum average total cost for each different amount of output.

Figure 4.11 illustrates the importance of your decision about the quantity of capital (and other fixed inputs) to utilize. If you use too much capital (for your restaurant, increasing your dining area too much) or too little capital (not expanding your kitchen when you increase the size of the dining area), your firm faces higher costs for an extended period of time until you can correct your mistake. Because the stakes are high, long-run decisions about the quantity of capital are usually made by higher-level executives.

The *LAC* curve also contains some insight about your optimal response to a permanent change in the quantity produced. Suppose that your firm initially produces 75 units and you had made short-run decisions that minimized costs, so production occurred at minimum cost at point *A* on the long-run average cost curve in Figure 4.11. If the firm's sales expand to 200 units, in the short run you can increase the quantity of the variable inputs so the firm moves down along short-run average total cost curve ATC_1 to point *B*, decreasing the firm's average cost to $12.00. In the long run, you can lower the average cost still more by changing inputs that are fixed in the short run. You can increase the firm's capital, move along the *LAC* curve to point C (which is on short-run average total cost curve ATC_2), and lower the firm's average cost from $12.00 to $9.00.

This same result—increasing the quantity of capital in the long run—can be obtained using the cost-minimization analysis presented in Section 4.2. At point *A* in Figure 4.11, the managers are minimizing the firm's costs by producing 75 units of output, so at this point $\frac{MP_L}{W} = \frac{MP_K}{R}$. Moving from point *A* to point *B* requires the firm to hire more variable inputs, such as labor. Using more labor decreases the marginal product of labor, MP_L. The fall in the marginal product of labor means that at point *B* the cost-minimization equality has changed to an inequality, $\frac{MP_L}{W} < \frac{MP_K}{R}$. As you learned in Section 4.2, this inequality indicates that you can lower the total cost by increasing the quantity of capital and moving to average total cost curve ATC_2, though, of course, this change cannot be made until the long run.

Long-Run Marginal Cost

To determine the cost of each additional unit of output in the long run, you must use the long-run marginal cost. The **long-run marginal cost** (LMC) is the cost of producing an additional unit of output when all inputs are variable. The long-run marginal cost corresponds to the least costly of all the possible ways to increase output.

Long-run marginal cost
The cost of producing an additional unit of output when all inputs are variable.

Figure 4.12 Long-Run Average Cost and Long-Run Marginal Cost Curves

The *LMC* curve shows the marginal cost of producing an additional unit of output when all inputs are variable. When the *LMC* curve lies below the *LAC* curve, the *LAC* curve slopes downward; when it lies on top of the *LAC* curve, the *LAC* curve is horizontal; and when it lies above the *LAC* curve, the *LAC* curve slopes upward.

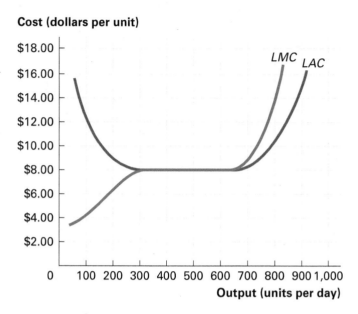

The relationship between the long-run marginal cost and the long-run average cost is the same as the relationship between the short-run marginal cost and the short-run average total cost. As Figure 4.12 shows, when the long-run marginal cost is less than the long-run average cost, the *LAC* curve slopes downward. When the long-run marginal cost is greater than the long-run average cost, the *LAC* curve slopes upward. When the long-run marginal cost equals the long-run average cost, the long-run average cost is at its minimum. In Figure 4.12, along the horizontal section of the *LAC* curve, the range where the long-run average cost is at its minimum, the long-range marginal cost lies directly on the *LAC* curve. Indeed, whenever the *LAC* curve is horizontal—which occurs if the long-range average cost is constant when changing production—it is always equal to the long-range marginal cost.

Economies of Scale, Constant Returns to Scale, and Diseconomies of Scale

A firm's *LAC* curve typically has three segments: one with economies of scale, one with constant returns to scale, and one with diseconomies of scale. Figure 4.13 identifies the segments for a bakery like Texas Star Bakery, which manufactures delicious loaves of bread. These different returns to scale reflect features of the firm's technology.

Economies of scale The long-run average cost falls when output increases; the downward-sloping segment of the long-run average cost curve.

The region with **economies of scale** is one in which the long-run average cost falls when output increases, so the *LAC* curve is downward sloping. In this range, when a firm increases all of its inputs by the same percentage, the firm's production process is such that its output increases by an even larger percentage. Economists say the firm has *increasing returns to scale*. Increasing returns to scale lead to economies of scale. For example, if a firm increases its use of all inputs by 10 percent at the same time, its cost rises by 10 percent. If the firm's output increases by more than 10 percent, however, then the average cost falls.

Constant returns to scale The long-run average cost does not change when output increases; the horizontal segment of the long-run average cost curve.

The range with **constant returns to scale** is one in which the long-run average cost does not change when output increases, so the *LAC* curve is horizontal. In this case, when a firm increases all of its inputs by the same percentage, the technology is such that its output increases by the same percentage. Therefore, a 10 percent

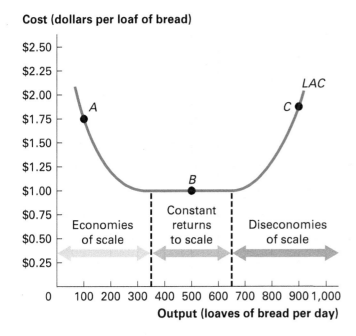

Cost (dollars per loaf of bread)

LAC

- A
- C
- B

$2.50
$2.25
$2.00
$1.75
$1.50
$1.25
$1.00
$0.75
$0.50
$0.25

Economies of scale   Constant returns to scale   Diseconomies of scale

0   100 200 300 400 500 600 700 800 900 1,000

Output (loaves of bread per day)

Figure 4.13 Regions of the Long-Run Average Cost Curve

The three segments of the *LAC* curve are
- Economies of scale: The long-run average cost falls when output increases
- Constant returns to scale: The long-run average cost does not change when output increases
- Diseconomies of scale: The long-run average cost rises when output increases

increase in all inputs results in a 10 percent increase in the firm's cost *and* in its output, so the firm's average cost does not change.

Finally, the segment with **diseconomies of scale** is one in which the long-run average cost rises when output increases, so the *LAC* curve is upward sloping. Over this range of the *LAC* curve, when a firm increases all of its inputs by the same percentage, its output increases by a smaller percentage. The firm has *decreasing returns to scale*. Decreasing returns to scale lead to diseconomies of scale: If the firm increases all of its inputs by 10 percent, again raising its cost by 10 percent, its output increases by less than 10 percent, so the average cost rises.

Diseconomies of scale The long-run average cost rises when output increases; the upward-sloping segment of the long-run average cost curve.

The Challenges of Economies of Scale

Economies of scale are often the result of increased specialization. As a firm's production expands, it buys more specialized equipment. For instance, consider again the humble loaf of bread. A bakery starting out with a small scale of production, such as at point *A* in Figure 4.13, makes the loaves by hand. A chef measures and combines all ingredients, kneads the dough, lets it rise, shapes it into a loaf, bakes the loaf in the oven, wraps it, and moves it to the front of the store, where a clerk sells it. The average cost of producing a loaf is high. In the long run, as the bakery expands in size and increases the scale of its production, ultimately the bread is made almost exclusively by machine. Workers pour flour, water, yeast, and other ingredients into enormous vats, where large mixers combine the ingredients and knead the dough. Workers then wheel the vats of dough to huge machines that do the rest: proof the dough (let it rise), shape it into loaves, bake the loaves, slice them, wrap them, and then deliver them to workers who place the loaves in boxes ready to be shipped nationwide. The scale of production is immensely larger than that of the small bakery, and with the increased capital in the form of specialized machinery, the firm has moved along its *LAC* curve and gained economies of scale.

Executives managing firms in which economies of scale are important must always be alert to the growth of competitors. If competitors increase their scale of operations, they gain the advantage of lower costs. If your firm lags behind the competition and your rivals use their cost advantage to lower their prices, your outlook can quickly become dire. In addition, if the source of economies of scale lies in the utilization of specialized equipment, as a manager you must make certain that your firm is using the specialized equipment appropriate to its scale of production.

Constant Returns to Scale

Eventually, economies of scale taper off and reach a region of the *LAC* curve with constant returns to scale, such as at point *B* in Figure 4.13. For firms in many industries, the region with constant returns to scale is quite large. Some firms' *LAC* curves are effectively L-shaped: One segment has economies of scale and a second has persisting constant returns to scale. Regression results for firms in a large variety of industries show that their *LAC* curves have constant returns to scale. Paper mills, insurance companies, and producers of glass containers, construction equipment, and men's footwear seem to have little in common, but their *LAC* curves all display extended regions with constant returns to scale.

Managers of firms in industries producing in the region of constant returns to scale need not fear that competitors will gain a cost advantage by increasing the scale of their operations. They cannot relax completely, however, because they must constantly be on the alert in order to minimize cost.

The Challenges of Diseconomies of Scale

With increases in scale come increases in complexity, bureaucracy, and the size of a firm's labor force. All of these factors may eventually cause the average cost to increase when a firm increases production. As the firm becomes large and complex, decision making suffers because information must be filtered through layers of management before a decision can be made and then communicated back through the same channels before any action can be taken. As the bureaucracy builds and the labor force increases in size, managers and workers have increasing opportunities to focus on their own self-interest and office politics, rather than spending their time advancing the firm's interest. In the largest organizations, wasteful duplication of effort can easily occur, with one group of managers and/or workers hard at work, blissfully unaware that another group elsewhere in the firm is diligently working on the same task. The slowdown and loss of quality in decisions, the pursuit of advancement by engaging in office politics, and the growing likelihood of duplication of effort *all* mean that as the firm increases its scale of production, its average cost rises.

Executives managing a firm that suffers from diseconomies of scale, such as a firm at point *C* in Figure 4.13, face difficult decisions. To lower the firm's costs, the managers must decrease the scale of operations, creating a movement down along its *LAC* curve to a scale of production with lower average cost. Decreasing production means decreasing the amount of inputs. In the popular vernacular, the managers must downsize the firm. Downsizing is never easy because of the human cost inflicted on the downsized workers, but at times, these decisions are necessary. In some cases, the only way to assure the firm's survival is to reduce its costs. Of course, when decreasing inputs, the managers must be careful to follow the rules you have learned about cost minimization.

Changes in the Long-Run Average Costs

In Section 4.3, you learned that a fall in the price of an input, a technological change, and learning-by-doing lower a firm's average total costs and thereby shift its short-run *ATC* curve downward. Anything that shifts the short-run *ATC* curve also shifts the *LAC* curve. For example, a fall in the price of an input decreases the short-run average total cost and shifts the short-run *ATC* curves downward. It also decreases the long-run average cost and shifts the *LAC* curve downward.

Changes in the price of inputs and changes in technology are likely to affect all competitors' costs more or less equally. Learning-by-doing, however, may result in an important competitive advantage. As a manager, you must realize that accepting an apparently unprofitable contract might actually wind up being profitable if it enables your workers to learn by doing. Such a contract could lower your long-run production costs below those of your competitors.

Long-Run Average Cost

SOLVED
PROBLEM

In the table below, identify points on the firm's *LAC* curve. Then graph the *LAC* curve. Over what ranges of output are there economies of scale? Constant returns to scale? Diseconomies of scale?

2 Units of Capital		4 Units of Capital		6 Units of Capital		8 Units of Capital	
Output, Q	Average Total Cost, ATC	Output, Q	Average Total Cost, ATC	Output, Q	Average Total Cost, ATC	Output, Q	Average Total Cost, ATC
5	$40	5	$60	5	$80	5	$100
10	20	10	30	10	50	10	70
15	15	15	10	15	25	15	50
20	20	20	15	20	9	20	30
25	40	25	35	25	5	25	15
30	70	30	60	30	20	30	5
35	110	35	90	35	40	35	15
40	160	40	130	40	80	40	30

Answer

2 Units of Capital		4 Units of Capital		6 Units of Capital		8 Units of Capital	
Output, Q	Average Total Cost, ATC	Output, Q	Average Total Cost, ATC	Output, Q	Average Total Cost, ATC	Output, Q	Average Total Cost, ATC
5	*$40*	5	$60	5	$80	5	$100
10	*20*	10	30	10	50	10	70
15	15	*15*	*10*	15	25	15	50
20	20	20	15	*20*	*9*	20	30
25	40	25	35	*25*	*5*	25	15
30	70	30	60	30	20	*30*	*5*
35	110	35	90	35	40	*35*	*15*
40	160	40	130	40	80	*40*	*30*

(*Continues*)

SOLVED PROBLEM (*continued*)

The points on the *LAC* curve are in red in the table and are graphed in the figure, which shows the *LAC* curve. For each quantity, these points have the lowest average total cost. From 5 units to 25 units, there are economies of scale because the long-run average cost falls between these levels of output. There are constant returns to scale between 25 units and 30 units because the long-run average cost is constant between these levels of output. There are decreasing returns to scale after 30 units because the long-run average cost rises after this quantity.

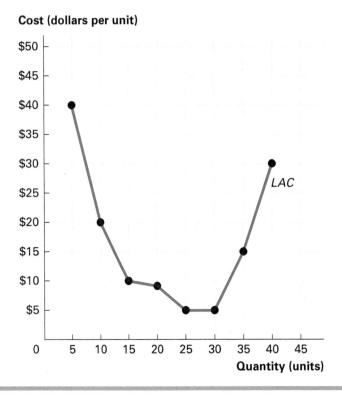

4.5 Using Production and Cost Theory

Learning Objective 4.5 Apply production and cost theory to make better managerial decisions.

Costs serve as a fundamental factor in virtually every business decision you will encounter in your career. Consequently, the material in this chapter serves as the foundation for the economic models presented in many of the later chapters. Even before you proceed to those chapters, some noteworthy lessons emerge that can be extremely helpful in making decisions.

Effects of a Change in the Price of an Input

Suppose that you are a manager at a firm like Sticky's Finger Joint, a fast-food restaurant in New York specializing in unique, delicious chicken fingers. As an alert manager, one of your goals is to minimize the impact of a change in input price on the cost of producing a given output. Recall the cost-minimization equation for two inputs: $\frac{MP_L}{W} = \frac{MP_K}{R}$. The City of New York has passed regulations that will require the minimum wage you pay your workers to rise, eventually reaching $15 per hour on July 1, 2021. Suppose that the wage rate will rise from its current level—say, W—to a higher level—say, $\widetilde{W}$. The increase in the wage rate changes the equality to $\frac{MP_L}{\widetilde{W}} < \frac{MP_K}{R}$. Section 4.2 showed that with this inequality your restaurant can lower costs by using less labor and more capital. More generally, according to the cost-minimization equation, the marginal products of *all* inputs divided by their costs should be equal, not just capital and labor. So when the cost of any variable input rises, cost-minimizing managers decrease the quantity of that input and increase the quantities of the other variable inputs to maintain the equality.

Of course, in the short run, it might be impossible for you to change the quantity of capital, but in the long run, you can do so. Accordingly, you might decide to decrease your order staff by creating self-order kiosks, where customers can use tablets to order and pay for their items. Or you might cut back on the number of cooks by purchasing fryers that automate more of the cooking process.

This general conclusion—that managers should decrease use of an input that rises in cost and increase use of other inputs—probably does not come as a surprise. The issue is determining the magnitude of the changes. Unfortunately, there is no easy, cut-and-dried method to determine precisely how much to change the inputs, but keep in mind the intuition behind the cost-minimization rule. In particular, you learned in Section 4.2 that cost minimization requires that the change in output from spending one more dollar on one input must equal the changes in output from spending one more dollar on the other inputs. When the price of an input changes, ask yourself, "How much more output would I obtain if I spent one more dollar on that input?" Then ask yourself the same question for another input. Comparing the two answers will guide you to lower the total cost by using less of the input that produces less output and more of the other input. If you continue to make changes until your answers are all the same, you will have responded correctly to the change in the price of an input. Of course, the difficult part of this procedure is determining the marginal products of the inputs. As a manager, you may be forced to come up with educated estimates of the marginal products. Thinking about how output changes when spending an additional dollar on an input can help you refine your estimates. If you are working for a company with research analysts, you may be able to call on them to use regression analysis (explained in Section 3.1) to provide you with estimates of the marginal products.

Economies and Diseconomies of Scale

Suppose that you are an executive at a firm like Groupon, an online deal company that offers to sell consumers discount coupons for different products if enough consumers sign up for the deal. There is no simple, instantaneous way to determine where on its *LAC* curve your firm is producing. However, you can infer whether it is operating on the *LAC* curve where there are economies of scale or diseconomies of scale by thinking about the short-run average total cost:

- **Economies of scale.** If your firm is producing at a point such as point *A* in Figure 4.14, where the firm can lower the short-run average total cost by increasing the scale of production—say, from 50,000 deals per year to 100,000—then you can infer that it is producing at a point on the *LAC* curve with economies of scale.

Figure 4.14 Determining the Returns to Scale

A manager can determine if the firm is producing at a point on its *LAC* curve with economies of scale, constant returns to scale, or diseconomies of scale by considering the effect of a change in production on the short-run average total cost.

- If increasing production lowers the short-run average total cost (point *A*), then the firm is producing at a point with economies of scale.
- If decreasing production lowers the short-run average total cost (point *C*), then the firm is producing at a point with diseconomies of scale.
- If increasing or decreasing production does not change the short-run average total cost (point *B*), then the firm is producing at a point with constant returns to scale.

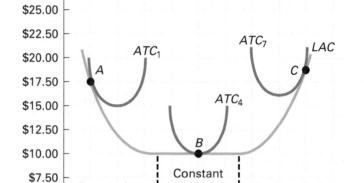

Cost (dollars per deal offered)

- **Diseconomies of scale.** If your firm is producing at a point such as point *C* in Figure 4.14, where the short-run average total cost can be lowered by decreasing the scale of production—say, from 450,000 deals per year to 400,000—you can conclude that it is producing at a point on the *LAC* curve with diseconomies of scale.
- **Constant returns to scale.** If your firm is producing at a point such as point *B* in Figure 4.14, where you cannot decrease your short-run average total cost by either increasing or decreasing the scale of production, you can deduce that the firm is producing at a point with constant returns to scale.

Once you know the segment of the *LAC* curve on which your firm is operating—economies of scale, constant returns to scale, or diseconomies of scale—you can make much better decisions than managers who either lack this information or choose to ignore it. For example, if your firm is producing 450,000 deals per year at point *C* on its *LAC* curve, you know that decisions designed to expand output might fail. Because your firm is producing at a point with diseconomies of scale, the expansion will raise its long-run average costs. Indeed, you may want to contract your scale of business in order to lower your long-run average costs. If instead your firm is producing 50,000 deals per year at point *A*, you should be more inclined to make decisions that increase the scale of output. Because the firm is producing at a point with economies of scale, the increase in production will lower its long-run average costs. As it happens, initially Groupon was producing at a point such as *A* because it expanded rapidly. But apparently its managers expanded too much. Groupon wound up offering approximately 450,000 deals per year, but Groupon's executives then announced that they planned to reduce its scale of operations and would cease operating in 12 countries, offering deals in 15 countries instead of 27.

Revisiting How Pizza Hut Managers Learned That Size Matters

At the beginning of the chapter, you read about a challenge facing managers at Pizza Hut: How could they increase the number of stores and thereby boost their profit? You can now apply the concepts of this chapter to explain how those managers answered that question.

The hypothetical data in Figure 4.15 show Pizza Hut's problem. Pizza Hut's standard restaurants were large and designed to feature both dine-in and delivery services. In Figure 4.15, the average total cost curve of these large stores is ATC_0. For simplicity, assume that ATC_0 means Pizza Hut is operating where it has constant returns to scale, but note that the results would be the same if Pizza Hut was operating where it had economies or diseconomies of scale. In Figure 4.15, the lowest average total cost ($3 per pizza) occurs at production of 700 pizzas per day on ATC_0. A delivery-only restaurant, however, sells fewer pizzas—say, 350 per day. As the black dot on ATC_0 at the quantity of 350 pizzas shows, the average total cost for a large restaurant that sells only 350 pizzas per day is $8 per pizza, which is much too high to be profitable.

Pizza Hut's executive managers realized that they needed to develop a new concept: a restaurant that would have lower average total cost when producing 350 pizzas per day and would concentrate on home delivery. Pizza Hut's managers designed a smaller store for delivery only, with no dine-in services. The smaller store used less capital, less land, and fewer other inputs. The new design was appropriate for a smaller scale of production because the designers planned a restaurant that would have lower average total costs when producing fewer pizzas per day. The smaller restaurant's average total cost curve is ATC_1 in Figure 4.15. Its average total cost when producing 350 pizzas per day is only $3 per pizza, a cost that would enable franchisees to make a profit selling

350 pizzas. After Pizza Hut began offering this new concept, the franchisees gobbled them up: The number of Pizza Hut restaurants stopped decreasing and started to increase, thereby increasing Pizza Hut's profit.

Figure 4.15 Determining the Returns to Scale for Pizza Hut

Pizza Hut designs its large restaurants to support both home delivery and dine-in services, which requires producing and selling 700 pizzas per day. The average total cost curve for a large restaurant is ATC_0, so the average total cost of 700 pizzas is $3.00. A restaurant that provides delivery only sells a smaller number of pizzas—say, 350 per day. Along ATC_0, the average total cost of producing 350 pizzas per day is $8.00. Pizza Hut's managers designed a smaller restaurant optimized to sell only 350 pizzas. The smaller restaurant has average total cost curve ATC_1 and an average total cost of only $3.00 for 350 pizzas.

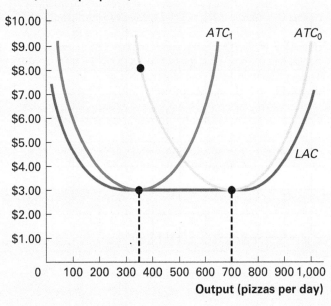

Summary: The Bottom Line

4.1 Production

- The production function is the relationship between different amounts of a firm's inputs and the maximum quantity of output it can produce with those inputs.
- The short run is the period of time during which at least one input is fixed, so that a firm cannot vary the amount of that input. The long run is a period of time long enough that no input is fixed, allowing a firm to vary the amounts of *all* the inputs it uses.
- The marginal product of an input is the change in output that results from changing the input by one unit while keeping other inputs constant.

4.2 Cost Minimization

- The cost-minimization rule shows that costs are minimized when managers use the combination of inputs that produces the desired quantity of output and for which $\frac{MP_1}{P_1} = \frac{MP_2}{P_2} = \frac{MP_3}{P_3} = \ldots$.

4.3 Short-Run Cost

- The total cost (TC) is equal to the fixed cost (FC) plus the variable cost (VC): $TC = FC + VC$.
- The average fixed cost (AFC) equals the fixed cost divided by the output (Q): $AFC = FC/Q$. The average variable cost (AVC) equals the variable cost divided by the output: $AVC = VC/Q$. The average total cost (ATC) equals the total cost divided by the output: $ATC = TC/Q$.
- The marginal cost (MC) equals the change in total cost divided by the change in output: $MC = \Delta TC/\Delta Q$.
- Both the ATC curve and the AVC curve are U-shaped. The MC curve intersects the minimum points on the AVC and ATC curves.
- Changes in the prices of inputs and changes in technology alter the costs and shift the cost curves.

4.4 Long-Run Cost

- The long-run average cost (LAC) is the minimum average cost of producing any given quantity of output when all inputs can be changed. The LAC curve is U-shaped.
- If increasing output lowers a firm's LAC, the firm has economies of scale, and the LAC curve is downward sloping. If the firm's long-run average cost does not change as output increases, the firm has constant returns to scale, and its LAC curve is horizontal. If increasing output raises a firm's LAC, the firm has diseconomies of scale, and the LAC curve is upward sloping.

4.5 Managerial Application: Using Production and Cost Theory

- If the price of an input changes, you can use the cost-minimization rule to adjust the quantity of inputs and lower your costs.
- If you are producing at a point on the LAC and an increase in output lowers short-run average total cost, your firm is operating in a region with economies of scale. If you are producing at a point on the LAC and a decrease in output lowers short-run average total cost, your firm is operating in a region with diseconomies of scale. If you are producing at a point on your LAC and your firm cannot lower its average total cost by either increasing or decreasing its production, it is operating in a region with constant returns to scale.
- If your firm is operating on its LAC curve in a region with increasing returns to scale, you can decrease its average cost by increasing production.
- If your firm is operating on its LAC curve in a region with decreasing returns to scale, you can decrease its average cost by decreasing production.

Key Terms and Concepts

Average fixed cost	Economies of scope	Marginal product of labor
Average total cost	Fixed cost	Negative marginal returns to labor
Average variable cost	Increasing marginal returns to labor	Production function
Constant returns to scale	Long run	Short run
Decreasing marginal returns to labor	Long-run average cost	Total cost
Diseconomies of scale	Long-run marginal cost	Variable cost
Diseconomies of scope	Marginal cost	
Economies of scale	Marginal product	

Questions and Problems

4.1 Production

Learning Objective 4.1 Explain the relationship between a firm's inputs and its output as well as calculate the marginal product of an input.

1.1 What is the difference between the short run and the long run? As a manager producing 3,000 units of output, if you can lower your cost, will you be able to lower it more in the short run or the long run? Explain your answer.

1.2 As a manager, how would you expect the marginal product of labor to change as you hire more workers?

1.3 "A firm will never find it optimal to employ so much of an input that its marginal product is negative." Is this statement true or false? Explain your answer.

1.4 A technological change increases the amount of output that a firm can produce from a given quantity of inputs. It increases the marginal product of labor for each quantity of labor and shifts the marginal product of labor curve upward. How does this technological change affect the marginal product of capital?

4.2 Cost Minimization

Learning Objective 4.2 Use the cost-minimization rule to choose the combination of inputs that produces a given quantity of output at the lowest cost.

2.1 The production of ABC, Inc.'s output requires only two inputs. Its manager says, "Because the two input prices are equal, to minimize cost I employ equal quantities of the two inputs." Is the manager correct? Explain your answer.

2.2 The wage rate of high-skilled labor is $40 per hour, and the wage rate of low-skilled labor is $15 per hour. The marginal product of high-skilled labor is 60 units per hour, and the marginal product of low-skilled labor is 15 units per day. Is a firm operating under these conditions minimizing its cost? If not, what should the firm do? Explain your answers.

2.3 As a production manager, your job depends on your ability to minimize the cost of production. You hire a consulting firm, and its report suggests that you have plenty to worry about: The cost of capital is $200 per hour, the wage paid to your workers is $16 per hour, the marginal product of capital is 10 units per hour, and the marginal product of labor is 32 units per hour. What is the consulting firm going to recommend, and why?

2.4 You are an executive for a firm like VCA Antech, which operates over 600 animal hospitals in the United States. Each hospital is treating the desired number of cases per day. At each hospital, you estimate that hiring another veterinarian enables the location to treat 20 additional cases per day and firing one decreases the number of cases treated by 20 per day. Hiring another veterinary assistant enables the location to treat 10 more cases per day, and firing one decreases the number of cases treated by 10 per day. Finally, hiring another veterinary technician enables the location to treat 15 more cases per day, and firing one decreases the number of cases treated by 15 per day. A veterinarian is paid $300 per day, a veterinary assistant is paid $100 per day, and a veterinary technician is paid $150 per day. Are your hospitals minimizing the cost of treatment? If so, explain why. If not, identify the change(s) that you should make.

2.5 As a manager for a nonprofit like Doctors Without Borders, you are charged with determining what supplies to send to South Sudan. You can send different boxes of medicine. The marginal product is the number of lives saved. Suppose that the cost of a box of medicine to treat cerebral malaria is $40 and will save 10 lives. The cost of a box of medicine to treat diarrhea is $60 and will save 20 lives. Which box will you ship first? Explain your answer.

2.6 Suppose that your manufacturing firm has the following production function with three inputs:

$$Q = F(X_1, X_2, X_3)$$

where X_1, X_2, and X_3 are the three inputs. As a manager, how will you determine the cost-minimizing quantities of X_1 and X_2 if the quantity of X_3 is fixed?

4.3 Short-Run Cost

Learning Objective 4.3 Distinguish between fixed cost and variable cost and calculate average total cost, average variable cost, average fixed cost, and marginal cost.

3.1 Assuming that all units of labor are paid the same wage rate, complete the table below.

Capital, K	Labor, L	Output, Q	Fixed Cost, FC	Variable Cost, VC	Total Cost, TC	Average Fixed Cost, AFC	Average Variable Cost, AVC	Average total cost, ATC	Marginal Cost, MC
2	0	0	$400			X	X	X	
2	1	100		$400					
2	2	800							
2	3	1,200							
2	4	1,500							
2	5	1,700							
2	6	1,800							

3.2 Why is a firm's short-run average total cost curve typically U-shaped?

3.3 How does marginal cost differ from average total cost?

3.4 As a manager, you know that as your firm uses more of a variable input, the marginal product of the input decreases. What conclusion can you draw about the behavior of the marginal cost curve?

3.5 What is the competitive return for the resources the owners provide? Why is it included as part of a firm's costs?

3.6 Quick-service restaurants like Burger King (also called fast-food restaurants) typically employ many minimum wage workers. If the government raises the minimum wage, what happens to a Burger King's cost curves?

3.7 Clerical workers form a union that successfully raises its members' wages. What happens to the short-run average total cost curve and long-run average cost curve of a firm that hires clerical workers? What happens to the firm's marginal costs?

3.8 Energizer Holdings initially produced only its namesake batteries. Over the years, it acquired other divisions that produced personal care products such as razors (Schick) and sunscreen (Hawaiian Tropic and Banana Boat). The executives at Energizer Holdings decided that they would split the company into two independent firms, one producing batteries and the other the personal care products, because they thought the split would lower the two firms' costs. Using the concepts presented in this chapter, explain the executives' reasoning.

3.9 Apple Inc.'s research and development for its iPhone eventually helped the firm develop its first iPad. How did Apple's production of iPads affect its costs?

4.4 Long-Run Cost

Learning Objective 4.4 Derive the long-run average cost curve and explain its shape.

4.1 Explain the relationship between the short-run average total cost and the long-run average cost. Include a figure in your answer.

4.2 The table shows production data for three quantities of capital. Suppose that each unit of capital costs $1,000 and each unit of labor costs $200.

Labor, L	Capital, K	Output, Q	Average Total Cost, ATC	Capital, K	Output, Q	Average Total Cost ATC,	Capital, K	Output, Q	Average Total Cost, ATC
0	2	0	X	3	0	X	4	0	X
1	2	100		3	160		4	210	
2	2	800		3	1,200		4	1,350	
3	2	1,300		3	1,800		4	2,200	
4	2	1,475		3	2,100		4	2,600	
5	2	1,500		3	2,200		4	2,700	
6	2	1,510		3	2,220		4	2,710	

a. Complete the table.
b. If you estimate that your production will be 1,300 units, how much capital do you want to use?
c. If you estimate that your production will be 2,100 units, how much capital do you want to use?
d. Over what approximate range of production would you use 2 units of capital? Explain your answer.

4.3 If doubling all inputs increases output by 70 percent, what can you conclude about the shape of the long-run average cost curve?

4.4 Your company has a long-run average cost curve that has a range of output with economies of scale, followed by a range with constant returns to scale, and then followed by a range with diseconomies of scale. You know that you are producing at a point where you have constant returns to scale. You want to lower your average cost. Can you do so by increasing your output by using more labor? By using more capital? By using more labor *and* more capital? Explain your answers.

4.5 Suppose that the only inputs your company uses are labor and capital.
a. Explain how it is possible to simultaneously have negative marginal returns to labor and increasing returns to scale.
b. As a manager in this situation, what changes would you make to minimize your average total cost in the short run?
c. What changes would you make to minimize your average total cost in the long run?

4.5 Managerial Application: Using Production and Cost Theory

Learning Objective 4.5 Apply production and cost theory to make better managerial decisions.

5.1 A firm uses only labor (L) and capital (K) as inputs and is minimizing the cost of producing Q_1 units of output by using L_1 worth of labor and K_1 worth of capital. How should the firm respond to an increase in the price of capital? Be sure to explain your answers for both the short run and the long run.

5.2 A large architectural firm has just landed a contract to build a hospital. Eight architects currently work 40 hours per week in this firm, and all are available to work full-time on this project. The managers estimate that they need 400 architect-hours per week for 20 weeks to complete this project. Architects earn $500 per 40-hour week. Suppose that there is a fixed cost of hiring an architect of $2,000. (This cost reflects the advertising costs, interviewing costs, and so forth.)
a. The firm's current architects are willing to work overtime to complete this project if they receive 1.5 times their usual wage rate for any hours in excess of 40 hours per week. How much would the managers pay in overtime wages for the project?
b. Alternatively, the firm can handle this project by hiring new workers (for 20 weeks only) and having all architects work 40 hours per week. How many new architects would the firm need to hire?
c. Should the managers hire new architects or ask the firm's current architects to work overtime? Explain your answer.

5.3 Suppose that the government offers to pay a firm that hires low-skilled labor a subsidy. In particular, for each low-skilled worker hired, the government will pay a part of the wage rate. How would this program affect the firm's hiring decisions?

5.4 The Monroe County Public Defender's Office in New York has a budget of approximately $8 million and employs nearly 70 attorneys and 25 staff people. The courts have imposed new requirements for representation: Indigent people must now be represented at their first hearing. The Public Defender has given you the task of determining how many new attorneys to hire while simultaneously minimizing the cost. Suppose that you can hire Special Assistant Public Defenders at a salary of $12,000 per month, Senior Assistant Public Defenders at a salary of $10,000 per month, and Assistant Public Defenders at a salary of $6,000 per month. You know that you will need to provide representation for 700 new cases per month. The precceding table shows how many cases each class of attorney can

Accompanies problem 5.4.

Special Assistant Public Defender	Additional Cases Handled (per month)	Senior Assistant Public Defender	Additional Cases Handled (per month)	Assistant Public Defender	Additional Cases Handled (per month)
1	240	1	200	1	140
2	200	2	160	2	120
3	160	3	110	3	60

handle. How many Special Assistant, Senior Assistant, and Assistant Public Defenders will you hire? Explain your answer.

5.5 Your company is producing at a point on its long-run average cost curve with economies of scale. As a manager, you have the opportunity to sign a long-term, fixed-price contract for your product that would significantly increase the size of your firm. If you sign the contract and do not expect the prices of your inputs to change, do you think your profit will be larger in the short run or the long run?

MyLab Economics Auto-Graded Excel Projects

4.1 Cakes by Monica (a bakery under the umbrella of the Café Brulé restaurant) in Vermillion, SD, makes cupcakes for customers to purchase both in the store and in bulk orders for birthday parties and weddings.

Suppose that in the short run Cakes by Monica has a fixed amount of capital but can easily hire college students from the University of South Dakota to increase production as needed. A production schedule is provided for you where Q is dozens of cupcakes.

a. Using the schedule provided, calculate the marginal product of labor when $K = 3$.

b. Using your calculations, for which workers are there increasing, decreasing, and negative marginal returns to labor?

c. Suppose Cakes by Monica decides to add another unit of capital in the long run. Find the marginal product of the 4th unit of capital and the marginal product of labor when $K = 4$.

d. Create a graph of the marginal product of labor for $K = 3$ and $K = 4$.

e. Using your graph and the data, how does the addition of another unit of capital affect the productivity of labor?

4.2 Sugar Plum Oak is a company based in Norfolk, NE, that produces handmade Amish furniture. One of its signature items is handmade rocking chairs. The table provides weekly cost data for handmade rocking chairs.

a. Using the total cost schedule provided, calculate total and average fixed cost and variable cost, average total cost, and marginal cost.

b. Use Excel to graph the ATC, AVC, and MC curves. What does the distance between the ATC and AVC curves represent?

c. Using the same graph, where does the MC curve intersect the ATC curve? What does this point mean to the firm from a cost perspective?

	A	B	C	D	E	F	G	H
1	Q	Total Cost	TFC	TVC	ATC	AFC	AVC	MC
2	0	525						
3	1	552.5						
4	2	585						
5	3	622.5						
6	4	665						
7	5	712.5						
8	6	765						
9	7	822.5						
10	8	885						
11	9	952.5						
12	10	1025						
13	11	1102.5						
14	12	1185						
15	13	1272.5						
16	14	1365						
17	15	1462.5						
18	16	1565						
19	17	1672.5						
20	18	1785						
21	19	1902.5						
22	20	2025						

Accompanies problem 4.1.

	A	B	C	D	E	F	G	H
1		Production Schedule for $K = 3$				Production Schedule for $K = 4$		
2	$K = 3$	L	Output (Q)	$MP_L (K = 3)$	$K = 4$	Output (Q)	$MP_L (K = 4)$	MP_K
3	3	0	0		4	0		
4	3	1	10		4	15		
5	3	2	25		4	35		
6	3	3	45		4	60		
7	3	4	60		4	80		
8	3	5	70		4	95		
9	3	6	75		4	105		
10	3	7	75		4	110		
11	3	8	70		4	110		
12	3	9	60		4	105		

The Calculus of Cost

Demonstrating some of the production and cost results discussed in the chapter using calculus can help reinforce your understanding. We start with the definition of marginal product.

A. Marginal Product

You have learned that the marginal product of an input is the change in total output that results from changing the input by one unit while keeping other inputs constant. As you will see in many of these appendices, all "marginal" concepts have calculus interpretations that revolve around "changes," and marginal product is no exception. If a firm's production function is $Q = f(L, K)$, where Q is the quantity produced, L is labor input, K is capital input, and f is the function that relates the inputs to the output, then the marginal product of labor is equal to

$$MP_L = \frac{\partial f(L, K)}{\partial L} \qquad \textbf{A4.1}$$

and the marginal product of capital is equal to

$$MP_K = \frac{\partial f(L, K)}{\partial K} \qquad \textbf{A4.2}$$

In both cases, we take the partial derivative because the production function depends on more than one variable and the concept of marginal product studies the change in output that results from changing one input while keeping the others constant. In this case, the variables are the inputs labor and capital.

Equations A4.1 and A4.2 use a general specification for the production function. Often economists use a specific production function—in, particular, $Q = AL^\alpha K^\beta$. This production function is called a Cobb–Douglas production function after the first two researchers to use it. In it, A, α, and β are parameters that determine some of the properties of the production function. A is a scale parameter because it has a direct effect on the quantity produced. α and β are both less than one and influence the relative importance of labor and capital in production. Using the power rule to take the partial derivative of the Cobb–Douglas production function with respect to labor, the marginal product of labor equals

$$MP_L = \alpha AL^{\alpha-1} K^\beta$$

and taking the partial derivative with respect to capital, the marginal product of capital is equal to

$$MP_K = \beta AL^\alpha K^{\beta-1}$$

To explore the Cobb–Douglas production function in more detail, we can specify some values for the A, α, and β parameters and then observe how the marginal product of labor changes when labor changes and when capital changes. Figure A4.1 shows two MP_L curves for $A = 50$, $\alpha = 0.7$, and $\beta = 0.3$ for two levels of capital: $K = 4$ and $K = 6$. These curves show that the Cobb–Douglas production function misses the region with increasing marginal returns to labor because the MP_L curves always slope downward. They also, however, demonstrate that when the quantity of capital increases, the MP_L curve shifts upward, which means that for any quantity of labor, the marginal product of labor is larger with more capital.

Figure A4.1 The Marginal Product of Labor for a Cobb–Douglas Production Function

The marginal products of labor are from the Cobb–Douglas production function, $Q = 50L^{0.7}K^{0.3}$. The first column of marginal products has $K = 4$, and the second has $K = 6$. As labor increases, the marginal product of labor decreases. And as capital increases, the MP_L curve shifts upward.

Labor, L (workers)	MP_L, for $K = 4$	MP_L, for $K = 6$
1	53	60
2	43	49
3	38	43
4	35	40
5	33	37

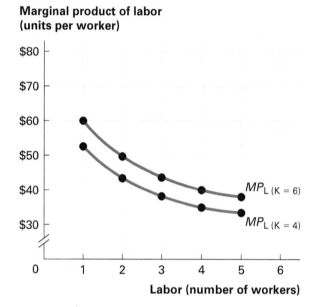

You can check that the MP_K curves are similar: They always slope downward as capital increases, and they shift up when labor increases.

B. Cost Minimization

The marginal products of labor and capital play an important role in minimizing the total cost of producing a given quantity of output. Suppose that the firm produces a fixed amount of output, $\overline{Q}$. The production function, $\overline{Q} = f(L, K)$, shows that any number of combinations of labor and capital can be used to produce this quantity of output. The firm's managers, of course, want to use the combination of labor and capital that minimizes the firm's cost. Suppose that the cost of employing a worker is W and the cost of using a unit of capital is R. Then the firm's total cost is $TC = (W \times L) + (R \times K)$. Formally, the firm's managers face this problem:

$$\text{Min } TC = (W \times L) + (R \times K) \text{ subject to } \overline{Q} = f(L, K)$$

This constrained minimization problem can be solved using calculus and a Lagrange multiplier. Alternatively, we can also solve the problem using a figure. To use a figure, let's start by determining the different combinations of labor and capital that produce $\overline{Q}$—that is, the different combinations of L and K such that $f(L, K) = \overline{Q}$. For production to stay at $\overline{Q}$, an increase in one input must be offset by a decrease in the other. For example, using the Cobb–Douglas production function with the parameters featured in Figure A4.1, when $L = 2$ workers and $K = 4$ units, output is 123.[1] Then if labor increases to 3 workers, to keep output equal to 123 capital must decrease to 1.55 units. Economists call the curve showing the combinations of inputs, labor and capital, that keep output at a fixed amount an *isoquant*.

---

1 The output rounds to 123; more precisely, it is 123.11.

Capital (units)

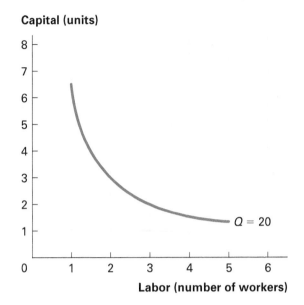

Labor (number of workers)

Figure A4.2 An Isoquant

The isoquant in the figure shows the different combinations of capital and labor that produce 20 units of output. The magnitude of the slope of the isoquant equals the marginal product of labor divided by the marginal product of capital, or MP_L/MP_K.

Figure A4.2 illustrates an isoquant for a general production function, not necessarily Cobb–Douglas. This isoquant shows the combinations of labor, L, and capital, K, that produce 20 units of output, $f(L, K) = 20$. Though the figure shows only the isoquant for producing 20 units of output, there are isoquants for each possible level of production.

We can calculate the slope of an isoquant, dK/dL, by taking the total differential of $f(L, K) = 20$:

$$\left(\frac{\partial f}{\partial L} \times dL\right) + \left(\frac{\partial f}{\partial K} \times dK\right) = 0 \qquad \textbf{A4.3}$$

In Equation A4.3, $\frac{\partial f}{\partial L}$ is the marginal product of labor, MP_L, and $\frac{\partial f}{\partial K}$ is the marginal product of capital, MP_K. Using these definitions in Equation A4.3 gives

$$(MP_L \times dL) + (MP_K \times dK) = 0 \qquad \textbf{A4.4}$$

We can rearrange Equation A4.4 to give

$$\frac{dK}{dL} = -\frac{MP_L}{MP_K} \qquad \textbf{A4.5}$$

Equation A4.5 shows that the magnitude of the slope of the isoquant equals the marginal product of labor divided by the marginal product of capital. This result explains the convex shape of the isoquant in Figure A4.2. Moving down the isoquant, the quantity of labor increases and the quantity of capital decreases, so that the marginal product of labor decreases and the marginal product of capital increases. Equation A4.5 shows that these changes in the marginal products decrease the magnitude of the isoquant's slope, so that the isoquant becomes flatter as labor increases and capital decreases.

The isoquant in Figure A4.2 shows the combinations of labor and capital that produce 20 units of output. To find the least costly combination, we need to introduce the cost function, $TC = (W \times L) + (R \times K)$. Economists call the line showing the combinations of labor and capital that keep the cost at a fixed amount an *isocost*. For example, if $W = \$30$, $R = \$20$, and $TC = \$90$, then $L = 1$ worker and $K = 3$ units and also $L = 2$ workers and $K = 1.5$ units both have a total cost of $90. Consequently, these two combinations of labor and capital fall on the isocost line for $W = \$30$, $R = \$20$, and $TC = \$90$. Figure A4.3 illustrates this isocost line and two others for the same labor and capital cost but total costs of $120 and $150.

Figure A4.3 Isocost Lines

Isocost$_{\$90}$ shows the different combinations of capital and labor that have a total cost of $90 when the wage rate is $30 and the cost of a unit of capital is $20. Isocost$_{\$120}$ shows the different combinations of capital and labor that have a total cost of $120 with the same costs per unit as before for labor and capital. The magnitude of the slope of the isocost equals the wage rate divided by the cost of capital, or *W/R*.

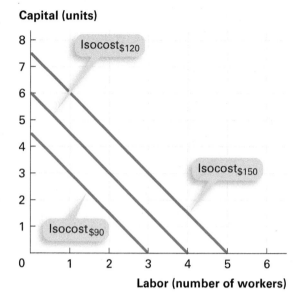

The isocosts in the figure are straight lines. We can check this result by calculating the slope of an isocost, dK/dL. Take the total differential of $TC = (W \times L) + (R \times K)$:

$$\mathrm{d}TC = (W \times \mathrm{d}L) + (R \times \mathrm{d}K)$$

Because the total cost is constant, d$TC = 0$. So, solving for the slope of the isocost, dK/dL, gives

$$\frac{\mathrm{d}K}{\mathrm{d}L} = -\frac{W}{R}$$

This equation shows that the magnitude of the slope of an isocost line is equal to the wage rate divided by the cost of a unit of capital. Because the slope equals $-W/R$, it is the same at every point on the isocost line, which means that the isocost is a straight line. This value for the slope also shows that the isocost line will rotate and change its slope if the wage rate or cost of capital changes. If the total cost rises—say, from $90 to $120 to $150—then, as illustrated in Figure A4.3, the isocost line shifts outward, and its slope does not change.

Suppose that the managers' goal is to produce 20 units of output using the minimum-cost combination of labor and capital. Further assume that the isoquant in Figure A4.2 is the relevant isoquant and that $W = \$30$ and $R = \$20$, so the isocost lines in Figure A4.3 are relevant. Then Figure A4.4 shows that the cost-minimizing combination of labor and capital is 2 workers and 3 units of capital. This combination of labor and capital is on the isoquant for 20 units of output *and* is on the lowest isocost line that touches the isoquant. Isocost lines with lower total costs, such as Isocost$_{\$90}$, do not touch the isoquant because they do not buy enough inputs to produce the 20 units of output. Isocost lines with higher total costs, such as Isocost$_{\$120}$, cross the isoquant at two points and so buy enough inputs to produce 20 units of output, but because the goal is to minimize total costs, they are not optimal.

Figure A4.4 shows that at the cost-minimizing combination of inputs, the isoquant is tangent to the isocost, so their slopes are equal. In terms of an equation, this result means that at the cost-minimizing combination of inputs

$$-\frac{MP_\mathrm{L}}{MP_\mathrm{K}} = -\frac{W}{R} \qquad\qquad \textbf{A4.6}$$

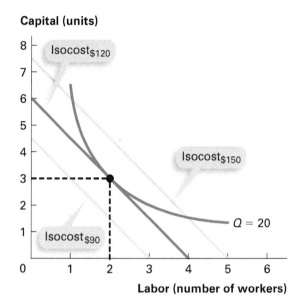

Capital (units)

Figure A4.4 Cost-Minimizing Combination of Inputs

To produce 20 units of output, the cost-minimizing combination of labor and capital is 2 workers and 3 units of capital because this combination is on the lowest isocost that touches the isoquant for 20 units of output.

In Equation 4.6, multiply both sides by −1 (to remove the annoying negative sign from the equality), and then divide both sides by W and multiply by MP_K. So doing gives the cost-minimizing condition as

$$\frac{MP_L}{W} = \frac{MP_K}{R}$$

which is exactly the same result as the cost-minimization rule presented in the chapter. More generally, just as demonstrated in Equation 4.1 in the chapter, to minimize the cost of production managers must employ the quantity of inputs such that

$$\frac{MP_1}{P_1} = \frac{MP_2}{P_2} = \frac{MP_3}{P_3} = \cdots \frac{MP_n}{P_n}$$

where MP_1 is the marginal product of the first input and P_1 is the price of the first input, MP_2 is the marginal product of the second input and P_2 is the price of the second input, and so on.

Because the cost-minimization conditions are the same in the chapter and here, so, too, are the implications. For example, as the price of an input rises, to minimize costs managers should decrease their use of the higher-cost input and use more of the relatively lower-cost input(s).

C. Marginal Cost and the Marginal/Average Relationship

Chapter 4 has one last, very important marginal concept: marginal cost. Once managers have selected the cost-minimizing combination of inputs, the firm's total cost then becomes a function of the quantity produced–that is, $TC(Q)$. The firm's marginal cost then equals the derivative with respect to the quantity, or

$$MC = \frac{dTC}{dQ} \qquad\qquad \textbf{A4.7}$$

We can use the definition of the marginal cost to demonstrate that when the average total cost is at its minimum, the marginal cost equals the average total cost. Start with the definition $ATC = \frac{TC}{Q}$. Then average total cost is at its minimum when $\frac{dATC}{dQ}$ equals zero. Accordingly, applying the quotient rule for differentiation,

$$\frac{dATC}{dQ} = \frac{d\left(\frac{TC}{Q}\right)}{dQ} = \frac{\left(Q \times \frac{dTC}{dQ}\right) - (TC)}{Q^2} = 0 \qquad \textbf{A4.8}$$

The term after the second equal sign follows by taking the derivative of the fraction $\frac{TC}{Q}$. When taking this derivative, recall that total cost is a function of the quantity, $TC(Q)$.

For Equation A4.8 to equal zero, the numerator of the fraction, $(Q \times \frac{dTC}{dQ}) - (TC)$, must equal zero, which means

$$\left(Q \times \frac{dTC}{dQ}\right) - (TC) = 0 \qquad \textbf{A4.9}$$

In Equation A4.9, divide both terms by Q and recall that $\frac{dTC}{dQ} = MC$ to obtain

$$MC - \left(\frac{TC}{Q}\right) = 0 \qquad \textbf{A4.10}$$

Finally, use the definition of ATC as TC/Q to get

$$MC - ATC = 0 \Rightarrow MC = ATC$$

This last equation shows the desired result: When the derivative of the average total cost equals zero, so that the average total cost is at its minimum, the marginal cost equals the average total cost; that is, $MC = ATC$.

Calculus Questions and Problems

A4.1 Suppose that blueberries are produced using land and labor according to the following production function:

$$Q = L_1 + 0.5L_2^{0.5}$$

where Q is the number of tons of blueberries harvested, L_1 is the number of acres of blueberry fields, and L_2 is the number of labor-hours hired.
a. What is the marginal product of land, MP_1? What is the marginal product of labor, MP_2?
b. What is the slope of the isoquant curve, dL_2/dL_1?
c. Suppose that the price of using an acre of land is $W_1 = \$144$ and the price of an hour of labor is $W_2 = \$9$. What is the slope of the isocost line, dL_2/dL_1?
d. If the price of using an acre of land is $W_1 = \$144$ and the price of an hour of labor is $W_2 = \$9$, what is the cheapest combination of land and labor that a firm could employ to produce 5 tons of blueberries?
e. Suppose that the price of land changes so that the price of using an acre of land is $W_1 = \$216$ and the price of an hour of labor is $W_2 = \$9$. What is the slope of the isocost line?
f. If the new price of land is $W_1 = \$216$ and the price of an hour of labor is $W_2 = \$9$, what is the cheapest combination of land and labor that a firm could employ to produce 5 tons of blueberries?

A4.2 Suppose that the total cost of producing a business law handbook is

$$TC(Q) = 10{,}000 + 25Q^2 - 10Q$$

where Q is the total number of handbooks produced.
a. What is the equation for the average total cost of producing handbooks as a function of the quantity of handbooks produced?
b. At what quantity, Q^*, is the average total cost of producing a handbook minimized? What is the value of the average total cost at Q^*?
c. At the quantity Q^* that you identified in part b, what is the marginal cost of an additional handbook?

A4.3 Train locomotives are produced using labor and capital. The quantities of these inputs that a firm employs determine the number of locomotives that the firm can produce. Thomas's Trains produces locomotives according to the following production function:

$$Q = \ln(L) + 2\ln(K)$$

where ln is the natural logarithm, Q is the quantity of locomotives produced, and L and K are the quantities of labor and capital employed, respectively. The price of one unit of labor is $w_L = \$10$, and the price of one unit of capital is $r_K = \$60$.
a. Using the production function given above, what is the slope of the isoquant curve, dK/dL?

b. What is the slope of the isocost line, dK/dL?

c. The specific production function above means that Thomas's Trains will always use a specific capital-to-labor ratio, K/L. Based on your answers to parts a and b, what is the value of this capital-to-labor ratio?

A4.4 Rose's Roses is a local flower shop specializing in rose bouquets for weddings. Rose can produce her magnificent bouquets using roses imported from Colombia or roses imported from Ecuador. Due to altitude and Ecuador's location on the equator, the Ecuadorean roses are slightly larger, meaning Rose needs fewer of them to produce each bouquet. Rose produces her bouquets according to the following production function:

$$Q = 0.1R_C + 0.125R_E$$

where Q is the quantity of bouquets produced and R_C and R_E are the quantities of Colombian roses and Ecuadorian roses used, respectively. The price of a Colombian rose is $P_C = \$0.45$, and the price of an Ecuadorian rose is $P_E = \$0.45$.

a. Referring to the production function given above, what is the slope of the isoquant line, dR_E/dR_C?

b. What is the slope of the isocost line, dR_E/dR_C?

c. Based on your answers to parts a and b, how many Colombian roses and how many Ecuadorian roses will Rose use in each of her magnificent bouquets?

A4.5 Victoria Vineyards is an American wine producer, specializing in premium red blends (red wines that use multiple different varieties of grapes). Victoria Vineyards' total cost of producing its famous red blend is

$$TC(Q) = 200{,}000 + 5Q^2 - 100Q$$

where Q is the quantity of cases Victoria Vineyards produces.

a. What is Victoria Vineyards' marginal cost equation, MC, of producing one case of its premium red blend?

b. What is Victoria Vineyards' average total cost equation, ATC, of producing one case of its premium red blend?

c. Identify the range of quantities over which $MC < ATC$.

d. Identify the quantity range over which the slope of ATC is negative; that is, $\frac{dATC}{dQ} < 0$.

CHAPTER 5

Perfect Competition

Learning Objectives

After studying this chapter, you will be able to:

5.1 Summarize the conditions that make a market perfectly competitive.

5.2 Use marginal analysis to determine the profit-maximizing quantity that a perfectly competitive firm produces in the short run.

5.3 Describe the long-run adjustments that managers in perfectly competitive markets make to maximize profit.

5.4 Apply the theory of perfectly competitive firms and markets to help make better managerial decisions.

Burger King Managers Decide to Let Chickens Have It Their Way

Executives at the nation's major restaurants realize that American consumers are clamoring for more natural food, such as cage-free eggs. Caged chickens live in small spaces that prevent them from standing or stretching their wings. Cage-free chickens, on the other hand, are free to roam the barn and engage in roosting, foraging, and nesting. However, only about 10 percent of hens raised in the United States are cage-free.

Farmers who raise cage-free chickens are part of a perfectly competitive industry. One farmer's cage-free egg is a perfect substitute for any other farmer's cage-free egg, and entry into the industry is cheap. The increased consumer demand for cage-free eggs, however, is a relatively recent change. Consequently, the farms producing cage-free eggs are small compared to the farms producing eggs from caged hens. Eggs produced by cage-free chickens are more expensive than eggs produced by caged chickens due to differences in costs. For example, raising cage-free chickens requires farmers to employ more labor, and the mortality of cage-free chickens is approximately twice that of caged birds.

The executives at Restaurant Brands International's Burger King division have been paying attention to consumers' changing preferences. In 2016, these executives announced that Burger King would immediately start using some cage-free eggs and would switch to 100 percent cage-free by 2025. Why did Burger King's managers decide to give themselves nine years to make this switch? Why didn't they announce a more rapid changeover? This chapter explains how the adjustments that occur in perfectly competitive markets shaped the decision made by Burger King's managers.

Sources: Gregory Barber, "Are Cage-Free Eggs All They're Cracked Up to Be?" *Mother Jones*, February 10, 2016, http://www.motherjones.com/blue-marble/2016/02/corporations-are-going-cage-free-whats-next-hens; Jennifer Chaussee, "The Insanely Complicated Logistics of Cage-Free Eggs for All," *Wired*, January 25, 2016, http://www.wired.com/2016/01/the-insanely-complicated-logistics-of-cage-free-eggs-for-all/.

Introduction

In Chapter 4, you learned how managers minimize costs when producing the desired quantity of output. The profit-maximizing quantity of a good or service depends on the extent of competition the firm faces. The amount of competition varies in different markets. Happy Jack's Maple Syrup is one of several thousand maple syrup producers in North America. In contrast, PepsiCo is one of only two dominant soda producers in the world. This chapter and the next three describe five market structures that differ in the extent of competition. Table 5.1 outlines defining characteristics of each.

Table 5.1 **Different Market Structures**

| | Level of Competition | | | | |
| | High ← | | | | → Low |
	Perfect Competition (Chapter 5)	**Monopolistic Competition (Chapter 6)**	**Oligopoly (Chapters 7 and 8)**	**Dominant Firm (Chapter 6)**	**Monopoly (Chapter 6)**
Number of firms in the industry	Many	Many	A few	Few or many	One
Barriers to entry by new firms	None	None	High to medium	Medium	High
Type of product	Identical	Differentiated	Identical or differentiated	Identical	Unique
Control over price	None; price taker	Some; price setter	Some; price setter	Some; price setter	Price setter
Long-run economic profit	Zero	Zero	Possible	Possible	Possible
Strategic behavior	No	No	Yes	No	No
Example	Maple syrup producer	Apple	PepsiCo	Frito-Lay	Roche Holding's drug Avastin

This chapter tackles perfect competition by extending the analysis of competitive markets (first introduced in Chapter 2) to study the profit-maximizing decisions of managers of *individual* firms in this market. Managers of firms in competitive markets make fewer pricing decisions than managers of firms that face few or no competitors. Nonetheless, the decisions they do make affect their firms' profitability.

The amount of competition a firm faces and the specific product it produces influence managerial decisions. Common threads will emerge, however, that can help you manage any firm producing any product. To assist your optimal decision making, Chapter 5 includes four sections:

- **Section 5.1** explains the conditions that define perfectly competitive markets.
- **Section 5.2** examines how managers of a perfectly competitive firm can use marginal analysis to determine the quantity that maximizes profit. The section also examines decisions about when to close a company and how to respond to a change in price.
- **Section 5.3** discusses long-run adjustments to the scale of production.
- **Section 5.4** applies the concepts of the chapter to managerial decisions in a perfectly competitive market and includes a cautionary tale for managers of competitive firms.

5.1 Characteristics of Competitive Markets

Learning Objective 5.1 Summarize the conditions that make a market perfectly competitive.

In economics, the term *competition* refers to a market structure and the behavior of buyers and sellers in that market. Popular usage of the word generally conjures up images of intense personal rivalry, such as that among players on the football field, opponents on the tennis court, or contestants on reality television shows. In contrast, economic competition is highly impersonal. There is no active rivalry among individual market participants. In fact, competitors might even be friends: Two neighboring dairy farmers might be best friends and help each other out even as they are competing in the dairy market.

Defining Characteristics of Perfect Competition

Perfectly competitive market A market with the following five characteristics: many buyers and sellers, no barriers to entry, a homogeneous product, perfect information, and no transaction costs.

Five characteristics define a **perfectly competitive market**:

1. There are many buyers and sellers
2. There are no barriers to entry.
3. Products are homogeneous.
4. Buyers and sellers have perfect information about the price and product characteristics.
5. There are no transaction costs.

Let's examine each of these characteristics in turn.

Many Buyers and Sellers

Price takers Market participants (buyers and sellers) who individually have no ability to change the price of the good or service being bought and sold.

There are many buyers and many sellers in a competitive market. How many? The number of buyers must be large enough that no one buyer can influence the price. Similarly, the number of sellers must be large enough that no single seller can influence the price. In most markets, the number of buyers is so large that an individual consumer's purchases are minuscule relative to the total market sales. For example, no matter how many soft drinks, tomatoes, shares of Microsoft, or legal pads you buy, you know that your purchases are a minute fraction of the total number purchased and have no impact on the price. Similarly, if a firm accounts for a very small share of the total market output, its managers know they cannot affect the price of the product. Each seller has *no* market power—that is, no control over the price that is set. More formally, the sellers are **price takers**, with no ability to change the price of the good or service being bought and sold. Firms in an industry with a large number of sellers of similar size are more likely to be price takers than firms in an industry with only a few sellers.

No Barriers to Entry

Barrier to entry Any factor that makes it difficult for new firms to enter a market.

Why are there many firms in the market? There are many firms because a perfectly competitive market has *no* barriers to entry. A **barrier to entry** is any factor that makes it difficult for new firms to enter a market. Some barriers to entry are legal barriers, such as a patent or copyright. Others are cost based, as when an existing firm has a substantial cost advantage over a new entrant into the market.

Perfectly competitive markets have *free entry*, which means that new firms are free to enter the market. Free entry is the reason that a perfectly competitive market includes many firms. Free entry, however, does not mean that entry is costless. For example, to enter the restaurant business, an entrepreneur needs enough capital to buy or rent a building as well as the necessary equipment, which might cost several hundred thousand or even millions of dollars. Entry into this market is still said to be free because there are no artificial barriers to surmount: The entrepreneur is not legally prevented from opening, and once the business has opened, it is not at a cost disadvantage relative to the previously existing restaurants.

Homogeneous Products

The products sold in perfectly competitive markets are *homogeneous*, or essentially identical. For example, all Yukon gold potatoes are virtually the same, so potato buyers do not care from which farmer they buy. Similarly, manufacturers who want sheet metal of a particular specification are indifferent to its source because all producers provide the same product. One seller's product is a perfect substitute for any other seller's product.

Perfect Information

The economic model of perfect competition assumes that all buyers and sellers have perfect information about all prices and product characteristics. In reality, no one can have *perfect* information. But frequently buyers and sellers have *enough* information that their market functions as if it were perfectly competitive. For example, even if the managers of an egg producer in Georgia do not know the price of eggs in Oregon, they will still operate their company as if it was in a perfectly competitive market because they know the prices of all relevant competitors.

No Transaction Costs

Transaction costs are the costs of using a market, *not* the price of the good or service itself. For example, the cost of driving to the local farmers' market and then the time and effort you spend examining the produce before you buy it are examples of transaction costs. If transaction costs are too high, then goods that otherwise would be identical are not: Egg consumers in Georgia don't think eggs in Oregon are identical to eggs in Georgia. For simplicity, the theoretical model of perfect competition assumes that there are no transaction costs. Reality, of course, is different. But as long as transaction costs are not so large as to create many small, separate markets for the product, transaction costs are low enough for the market to be perfectly competitive.

Transaction costs The costs of using a market.

Perfectly Competitive Markets

When all of the conditions just described are satisfied, the market is perfectly competitive, and the firms within the market are perfectly competitive firms. Many markets approximate the theoretical model closely enough that it is fair to analyze them as perfectly competitive. For example:

- There are over 2,500 textile mills in the United States, and one mill's product is very close to being a perfect substitute for any other mill's product.
- Lumber (and sawdust!) produced by any one of the 2,729 sawmills in the United States is a virtually perfect substitute for that produced by any of the others.
- Financial markets, such as stock markets, are often close to perfectly competitive, as is the market for banking services.

The classic examples of perfectly competitive markets, however, are agricultural, such as the markets for eggs, wheat, cotton, and maple syrup. Consider the market for maple syrup. The product is homogeneous because one company's Grade A, light amber maple syrup is identical to any other company's similarly graded syrup. Clearly, there are a large number of buyers and, with 8,000 producers in the United States, a large number of sellers. There are no barriers to entry—if entrepreneurs want to enter the market, all they must do is buy a stand of sugar maple trees.

Information is close to perfect because it is easy to learn the prices different firms charge. Transaction costs are low—discovering different producers is simple, and it is not difficult to buy or sell maple syrup.

Buyers and sellers in the maple syrup market are price takers. A buyer's purchase of an additional bottle or even a case of maple syrup does not change its price, which demonstrates the effect of competition on the buying side: The price per unit is unaffected by the quantity purchased. There is also competition on the selling side: The managers of a single producer—say, once again, Happy Jack's Maple Syrup—know that producing an extra 100 gallons has no discernible effect on the price of maple syrup.

As you learned in Chapter 2, market demand and supply determine the price in perfectly competitive markets. Although managers within such firms cannot control the price of their products, they must accomplish many other tasks. As a manager, you must pay close attention to details such as productive efficiency and maintenance of product and service quality. More importantly, however, you must determine the amount to produce that will maximize the firm's profit. We turn to this decision in the next section.

SOLVED PROBLEM

The Markets for Fencing and Cell Phones

The Affordable Fence Company is one of approximately 50 fencing companies in Pittsburgh, Pennsylvania. U.S. Cellular is one of four cell phone companies in Bangor, Maine.

a. Is the Affordable Fence Company competing in a perfectly competitive market? Is it a price taker? Explain your answers.

b. Is U.S. Cellular competing in a perfectly competitive market? Is it a price taker? Explain your answers.

Answer
To determine if these companies compete in perfectly competitive markets, you need to decide how closely the market meets the five criteria of a perfectly competitive market.

a. A fence built by the Affordable Fence Company is virtually identical to a fence of the same style built by any other company, so the products are close to homogeneous. There are a large number of buyers and sellers. Because any entrepreneur can open a fencing company and not face a cost disadvantage compared to the existing companies, there are no barriers to entry into this market. Buyers and sellers can easily determine the prices different fencing companies charge, so information is nearly perfect. Additionally, the transaction costs of buying a fence are not large, so there is effectively only one market for fences in Pittsburgh. Consequently, the Affordable Fence Company operates in a market that is very close to perfectly competitive. Because the company competes in a perfectly competitive market, it is a price taker.

b. U.S. Cellular does *not* compete in a perfectly competitive market. One of the characteristics of perfectly competitive markets is a large number of buyers and sellers. While there are a large number of buyers in this market, with only four sellers the market is not perfectly competitive. So U.S. Cellular is not a price taker.

5.2 Short-Run Profit Maximization in Competitive Markets

Learning Objective 5.2 Use marginal analysis to determine the profit-maximizing quantity that a perfectly competitive firm produces in the short run.

Continue to assume that the objective of all managers, including managers of perfectly competitive firms, is profit maximization. Total profit is equal to the difference between the total revenue (TR) and the total opportunity cost (TC) of producing and selling the product:

$$\text{Total profit} = TR - TC$$

To maximize profit, a manager must select the quantity of output that maximizes the difference between total revenue and total cost.

Marginal Analysis

As you learned in Chapter 1, *marginal analysis* compares the marginal benefit of an action to its marginal cost (see Section 1.4). In this and other chapters, you will see more specifically how managers can use marginal analysis as an extremely important decision-making tool in many different circumstances. In this chapter, it helps determine the profit-maximizing quantity to produce.

How does the marginal analysis rule help you determine how much output to produce? First, recall that the word *marginal* means "additional." Marginal analysis focuses on the *additional* benefit and *additional* cost from an action, *not* the total benefit or total cost from all of the actions. In this case, the *action* is to produce another unit of output. The marginal benefit is the change in total revenue from selling the additional unit because that is the additional benefit. The change in the total revenue from selling an additional unit is the marginal revenue. The marginal cost is the change in total cost from producing the additional unit because that is the additional cost of the unit. The first step in applying marginal analysis to profit maximization is to determine the demand for the firm's product because demand dictates the change in total revenue from an additional unit.

Market Demand and Firm Demand in a Competitive Market

When analyzing a perfectly competitive market, you must distinguish between market demand and an individual firm's demand. Figure 5.1 illustrates the difference between the market demand curve and an individual firm's demand curve in the competitive market for maple syrup. Figure 5.1(a) shows the market demand curve (D) and the market supply curve (S) for maple syrup. Figure 5.1(b) shows the demand curve (d) for one individual firm—say, Happy Tree Maple Syrup, which is one of thousands of firms producing maple syrup. The equilibrium price and the equilibrium quantity are determined in the market as a whole from the intersection of the market supply curve and the market demand curve, so in Figure 5.1(a) the equilibrium price and quantity are $30 per gallon and 12 million gallons. As the arrow extending from Figure 5.1(a) to Figure 5.1(b) indicates, Happy Tree has no control over the price and takes the equilibrium price as given. It can sell whatever quantity of maple syrup it produces at the equilibrium price. Its demand is perfectly elastic at the equilibrium price, as demonstrated by the horizontal demand curve (d) at the price of $30 per gallon, because all other firms' maple syrup is a perfect substitute for Happy Tree's syrup. With perfectly elastic demand, Happy Tree's managers effectively have no control over the price they set. If they set a price above the equilibrium price, their sales collapse to zero—no one will buy from them because there

Figure 5.1 Market Demand Curve and Individual Firm Demand Curve in a Competitive Market

(a) Market Demand Curve
The market demand curve for maple syrup (*D*) and the market supply curve for maple syrup (*S*) determine the equilibrium price of maple syrup, $30 per gallon.

(b) Individual Firm Demand Curve
Happy Tree Maple Syrup is one of thousands of firms producing maple syrup. As the arrow extending between parts (a) and (b) indicates, Happy Tree takes the equilibrium price of $30 as given. At this price, Happy Tree is able to sell as much maple syrup as it produces, so its demand curve (*d*) is horizontal.

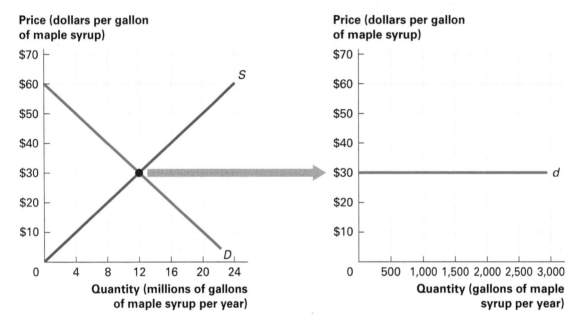

are other, perfect substitutes available at a lower price. There is no need for them to set a price lower than the equilibrium price because they can sell whatever quantity they want at the (higher) equilibrium price.

Marginal Revenue

To use marginal analysis, the managers at Happy Tree Maple Syrup must understand how changes in output change the firm's total revenue. The first two columns of Table 5.2 show details of part of Happy Tree's demand curve shown in Figure 5.1(b). In the table, the quantity ranges from 1,494 gallons to 1,505 gallons of maple syrup. (Because the firm is a small part of the market, we use "*q*" to indicate a firm's quantity and "*Q*" to indicate the market's quantity.) Of course, Happy Tree can sell *any* quantity it produces, from 1 gallon to whatever quantity its trees can produce, for $30 per gallon. Happy Tree's total revenue (*TR*), price (*P*) multiplied by quantity (*q*), is included in the third column of Table 5.2.

To make their production decision, the managers at Happy Tree need to know the marginal revenue. Marginal revenue shows how total revenue changes when the firm sells another unit, so, more formally, **marginal revenue** (*MR*) is the change in total revenue (*TR*) divided by the change in quantity (*q*): $MR = \frac{\Delta TR}{\Delta q}$, where the delta symbol (Δ) means "change in." Typically, marginal revenue is calculated using a small change in output—say, one unit.

Marginal revenue The change in the total revenue divided by the change in quantity: $MR = \frac{\Delta TR}{\Delta q}$.

Using this definition, the marginal revenue from increasing production of Happy Tree's maple syrup by one unit, from 1,494 gallons to 1,495 gallons, equals $\frac{\$44,850 - \$44,820}{1,495 - 1,494} = \$30$.

Table 5.2 **Demand, Total Revenue, and Marginal Revenue for Happy Tree Maple Syrup**

The first two columns show part of the demand facing Happy Tree Maple Syrup. Total revenue (*TR*) equals $P \times q$. Marginal revenue (*MR*) is the change in total revenue caused by a change in sales. For a perfectly competitive firm, marginal revenue equals the price: $MR = P$.

Price, *P*	Quantity Demanded, *q*	Total Revenue, *TR*	Marginal Revenue, *MR*
$30.00	1,494	$44,820	$30.00
30.00	1,495	44,850	30.00
30.00	1,496	44,880	30.00
30.00	1,497	44,910	30.00
30.00	1,498	44,940	30.00
30.00	1,499	44,970	30.00
30.00	1,500	45,000	30.00
30.00	1,501	45,030	30.00
30.00	1,502	45,060	30.00
30.00	1,503	45,090	30.00
30.00	1,504	45,120	30.00
30.00	1,505	45,150	

Column 4 of Table 5.2 shows the marginal revenue for the rest of the quantities in the range, and Figure 5.2 illustrates the results. Notice anything striking? The marginal revenue (*MR*) is always the same ($30) and is always equal to the price (*P*). As an equation,

$$P = MR \qquad\qquad 5.1$$

This equality is true for *all* perfectly competitive firms. Because the price equals the marginal revenue for all quantities, the marginal revenue curve (*MR*) is horizontal and is identical to the firm's demand curve (*d*) shown in Figure 5.2.

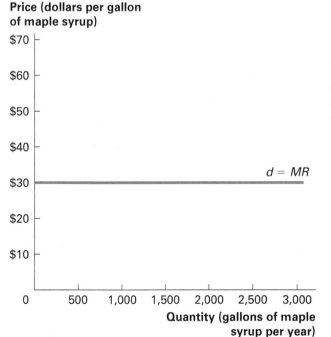

Figure 5.2 A Perfectly Competitive Firm's Demand and Marginal Revenue Curves

For a perfectly competitive firm, the marginal revenue curve (*MR*) is identical to the firm's demand curve (*d*). Both are horizontal at the market's equilibrium price.

Figure 5.3 Marginal Cost Curve

The marginal cost curve (*MC*) is a U-shaped curve that reaches a minimum at 750 gallons and then rises.

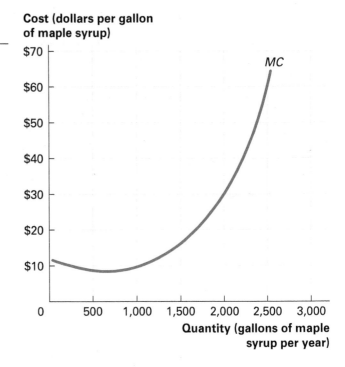

Cost (dollars per gallon of maple syrup)

Marginal Cost

To use marginal analysis, managers need not only the marginal revenue but also the other half of the comparison, the marginal cost. As you learned in Chapter 4, *marginal cost (MC)* is the change in total cost (*TC*) divided by the change in output (*q*):

$$MC = \frac{\Delta TC}{\Delta q}$$

Figure 5.3 shows Happy Tree's marginal cost curve (*MC*). This U-shaped curve should be familiar because it is similar to those you saw in Chapter 4. As the quantity produced increases, the marginal cost curve in Figure 5.3 falls to its minimum (at 750 gallons) and then rises.

Using Marginal Analysis to Maximize Profit

Figure 5.4 combines the marginal revenue curve in Figure 5.2 and the marginal cost curve in Figure 5.3. Marginal analysis shows that Happy Tree Maple Syrup maximizes its profit by producing the quantity (*q*) at which marginal revenue equals marginal cost (*MR* = *MC*), 2,000 gallons of maple syrup per year. You can use Figure 5.4 to illustrate how marginal analysis leads to this conclusion. Consider two quantity ranges:

- **Quantity less than 2,000 gallons.** Take a quantity less than 2,000 gallons—say, 1,000 gallons. Producing the 1,000th gallon increases total revenue by $30 (the *MR*) but increases total cost by only $10 (the *MC*). If this gallon is produced, profit increases by $20 ($30 − $10), which is equal to the length of the double-headed arrow at this quantity. Because the 1,000th gallon increases Happy Tree's profit, it should be produced. This conclusion is confirmed by application of the marginal analysis rule: If the marginal benefit of producing the unit—in this case, the marginal revenue (*MR*)—exceeds the marginal cost (*MC*) of producing the unit, the unit should be produced. Applying this reasoning to Figure 5.4, you will see that *all* of the gallons of maple syrup up to 2,000 gallons should be produced because for each gallon in this range *MR* > *MC*, so each gallon is profitable.

- **Quantity greater than 2,000 gallons.** Now take a quantity greater than 2,000 gallons—say, 2,500 gallons. At this quantity, the revenue from the 2,500th gallon is $30 (the *MR*), and the cost of producing it is $60 (the *MC*). Producing this gallon imposes a loss of $30 ($60 − $30), which is equal to the length of the double-headed arrow at this quantity. So Happy Tree's profit increases if it does *not* produce the 2,500th gallon. Again, the marginal analysis rule confirms this conclusion: If the marginal benefit of producing the unit—the marginal revenue (*MR*)—is less than the marginal cost (*MC*) of producing the unit, the unit should not be produced. *None* of the gallons of maple syrup beyond 2,000 gallons should be produced. Each gallon in this range has *MR* < *MC*, so each gallon imposes a loss on Happy Tree.

By producing where *MR* = *MC*, the managers maximize Happy Tree's profit because the firm is producing *all* of the profitable units and *none* of the unprofitable units.[1] Now that the managers know the profit-maximizing quantity, what price should they set for Happy Tree's maple syrup? As you have already learned, the managers have no choice: In a competitive market, the price of a gallon of maple syrup is the equilibrium price of $30. From a managerial standpoint, however, it is useful to ask "What is the highest price at which every unit produced

Price and cost (dollars per gallon of maple syrup)

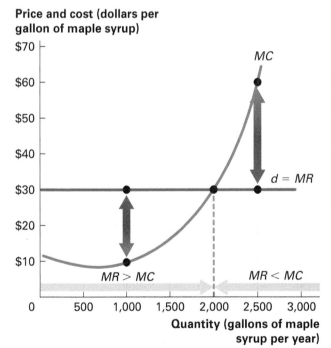

Figure 5.4 Profit Maximization

The firm maximizes its profit by producing the quantity where *MR* = *MC*, which occurs at 2,000 gallons. If the firm produces less, it loses profit because it is *not* producing some profitable units. If the firm produces more, it loses profit because it is producing some unprofitable units.

---

1 Section 5.B of the Appendix at the end of this chapter demonstrates how to use calculus to solve for the profit-maximizing quantity.

Marginal Analysis at the American Cancer Society

Say that you are a manager at the American Cancer Society, a nonprofit organization, and are considering a mass mailing to ask people for donations. You know that each letter will cost $1.00 + $0.00001Q$, where Q is the number of letters mailed. You also estimate that each recipient will donate $21. How many letters should you mail?

Answer

Although the goal of the American Cancer Society is to raise funds to fight cancer rather than to maximize profit, you still need to use marginal analysis to determine how many letters to mail. You want to mail all the letters for which the donation exceeds the cost, so the optimal number is the one at which $MR = MC$, where MR is the donation from the recipient, $21, and MC is the cost of mailing the letter, $1.00 + $0.00001Q$. You will therefore use the equation $21 = $1.00 + 0.00001Q$ to determine the number of letters to mail. Solving this equation shows that $Q = 2$ million letters. By mailing 2 million, you will mail *all* the letters that result in a donation above the cost of the letter and *none* of the letters with a cost exceeding the amount of the resulting donation.

can be sold?" because that price will maximize the firm's profit. The firm's demand curve answers this question. The demand curve shows that when Happy Tree produces 2,000 gallons of syrup, the highest price consumers are willing to pay for this quantity is $30 per gallon. If the managers set a higher price—say, $31 per gallon—then consumers buy 0 gallons from Happy Tree because in a competitive market they can buy maple syrup elsewhere for $30. In this unhappy case, Happy Tree earns no revenue and incurs a loss. The managers could instead set a lower price and sell all 2,000 gallons produced, but setting a lower price lowers profit. The profit-maximizing price is $30.

This analysis can be summarized with the profit-maximization rule: Produce the quantity for which $MR = MC$, and then set the highest price that sells the quantity produced.

PROFIT-MAXIMIZATION RULE

- Produce the quantity for which $MR = MC$.
- Set the highest price for which every unit produced can be sold.

Changes in Costs

If the marginal cost of production changes, you must change the quantity produced to maximize profit. Suppose that the price of one of the variable inputs needed to produce Happy Tree's maple syrup rises, perhaps the price of the fuel

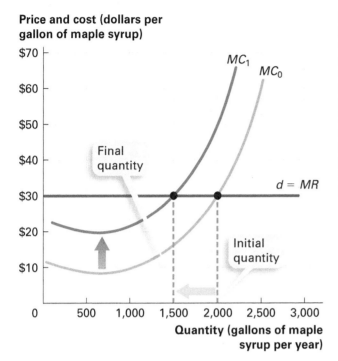

Price and cost (dollars per gallon of maple syrup)

Figure 5.5 A Change in Marginal Cost

An increase in Happy Tree's variable cost increases its marginal cost, shifting the marginal cost curve upward from MC_0 to MC_1. Profit-maximizing managers respond to the increase in marginal cost by decreasing the firm's production from 2,000 to 1,500 gallons.

used to boil the tree sap to produce the maple syrup. You learned in Section 4.3 that an increase in variable cost increases the marginal cost. Figure 5.5 shows that when a variable input rises in price, the marginal cost curve shifts upward from MC_0 to MC_1. The increase in the marginal cost changes the profit-maximizing quantity. Assuming that the price of maple syrup does not change, Figure 5.5 demonstrates that the profit-maximizing quantity of syrup decreases from 2,000 to 1,500 gallons per year. The increase in marginal cost means that the gallons between 1,500 and 2,000 are no longer profitable—their marginal revenue is less than their marginal cost. If you apply marginal analysis, you see that Happy Tree should *not* produce these gallons of syrup because they would decrease profit.

As a perfectly competitive firm, there is nothing Happy Tree can do to offset the higher costs. Happy Tree's managers are at the mercy of the market. As long as the firm stays open, the best the managers can do is respond to the increase in their cost by decreasing the quantity they produce.

Amount of Profit

Once you have discovered the profit-maximizing quantity, your work is done, right? Wrong—in addition to monitoring production to continue to minimize costs and/or take account of changes in costs, you must be vigilant about changes in the price. In contrast to the simplified maple syrup example, in some markets prices change frequently—from day to day or even minute to minute. As a manager, in most industries you will not be able to respond to minute-by-minute price changes. But when a price change lasts long enough, you will want to respond by changing your production. Indeed, the price may even fall low enough that you want to close the firm, either temporarily or permanently. To understand when this decision is necessary, you must first determine the firm's profit.

Economic Profit

You know that producing the quantity at which marginal revenue equals marginal cost ($MR = MC$) maximizes profit, but to this point, the discussion has not included the amount of that profit. Economists measure the firm's total profit as its total revenue minus its total *opportunity* cost. Recall from Chapter 1 (Section 1.4) and Chapter 4 (Section 4.3) that the owners' competitive return (the return the owners could have made by using their funds in another endeavor) is one part of the firm's opportunity cost.

Figure 5.6, which shows the average total cost curve (ATC), the marginal cost curve (MC), and marginal revenue curve (MR), can help you calculate total profit. The total revenue is the price of the product (P) multiplied by the quantity (q), or $P \times q$, and the total cost is the average total cost (ATC) multiplied by the quantity (q), or $ATC \times q.$[2] Therefore, the total profit is equal to

$$(P \times q) - (ATC \times q) \qquad \text{5.3}$$

Note that both terms in Equation 5.3 have the same factor, q. Taking that factor out and rewriting the equation, total profit is equal to

$$(P - ATC) \times q \qquad \text{5.4}$$

Equation 5.4 has an immediate intuitive interpretation: The price minus the average total cost ($P - ATC$) is the profit per unit. Equation 5.4 shows that the total profit equals the profit per unit multiplied by the previously determined profit-maximizing number of units, q.

In Figure 5.6, this profit is equal to the area of the green rectangle. The area of a rectangle equals the height multiplied by the base. The height of the

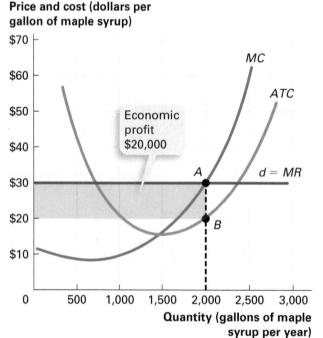

Price and cost (dollars per gallon of maple syrup)

Quantity (gallons of maple syrup per year)

Figure 5.6 Economic Profit for a Perfectly Competitive Firm

The firm's economic profit equals its total revenue, $P \times q$, minus its total cost, $ATC \times q$. The area of the green rectangle equals the firm's economic profit, $20,000. A firm makes an economic profit if $P > ATC$.

2 The result stems from the definition of average total cost, $ATC = \frac{\text{Total cost}}{q}$. Multiplying both sides of this equality by Q gives $ATC \times q = $ Total cost.

rectangle in Figure 5.6 is the distance between points A and B. Point A is the price ($30), and point B is the average total cost of producing 2,000 gallons of syrup ($20), so the height is $P - ATC$, the profit per unit, or $30 - $20 = $10. The base of the rectangle in the figure equals 2,000 gallons, the profit-maximizing quantity (q). So the area of the rectangle is equal to the total profit, or ($30 - $20) $\times$ 2,000 gallons = $20,000.

The profit just calculated is the firm's total revenue minus its total *opportunity* cost. Because the owners' competitive return is already part of the opportunity cost, the $20,000 profit calculated using Equation 5.4 and illustrated in Figure 5.6 is a profit over and above the normal competitive return. This profit is an **economic profit**, the firm's profit over and above the competitive return. Figure 5.6 and Equation 5.4 show that a business makes an economic profit whenever the price per unit is greater than the average total cost: $P > ATC$.

Economic profit A firm's profit over and above the competitive return.

Competitive Return

Although managers (and owners) definitely prefer making an economic profit, sometimes the best they can achieve is a competitive return. Figure 5.7 illustrates a situation in which the market price of maple syrup has fallen to $15 per gallon. The managers at Happy Tree continue to maximize profit by producing the quantity for which $MR = MC$. Figure 5.7 shows that the best managers can do is produce 1,500 gallons of syrup because this quantity is the profit-maximizing amount when the price is $15 per gallon.

Figure 5.7 also shows that when Happy Tree produces 1,500 gallons of maple syrup, the average total cost equals the price ($15 per gallon). Total revenue *and* total cost both equal $15 $\times$ 1,500 gallons, or $22,500. Because the total revenue and

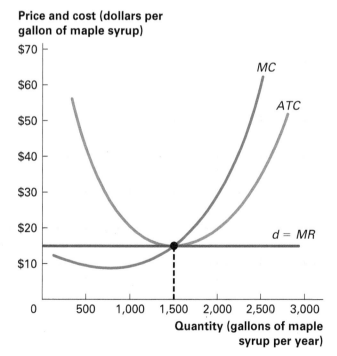

Price and cost (dollars per gallon of maple syrup)

Figure 5.7 Competitive Return for a Perfectly Competitive Firm

The firm's economic profit equals its total revenue, $P \times q$, minus its total cost, $ATC \times q$. If $P = ATC$, the firm makes zero economic profit; that is, its owners make a competitive return on the funds they have invested in the business.

the total cost are equal, the owners of Happy Tree make no economic profit. You can calculate this same result using Equation 5.4: Economic profit is $(P - ATC) \times q$, or $(\$15 - \$15) \times 1{,}500 \text{ gallons} = \$0$. Zero economic profit does not mean that Happy Tree is making no profit at all. Instead, the owners are making a competitive return, the same profit they expect they would make if they used their resources in some other competitive venture. A firm makes zero economic profit whenever $P = ATC$ because at that point the total revenue equals the total opportunity cost, which includes the owners' competitive return.

Economic Loss

Despite managers' best efforts, a firm sometimes cannot make even a competitive return. In this case, the best the managers can do is to minimize the firm's loss. Figure 5.8 illustrates this outcome for Happy Tree. Note that the equilibrium price in the market has fallen still lower, to $13 per gallon. The managers continue to maximize profit, which in this case means minimizing loss, by producing the quantity that sets $MR = MC$, 1,300 gallons of syrup at $13 per gallon.

When Happy Tree produces 1,300 gallons of syrup, average total cost is $16 per gallon. Total revenue is $13 \times 1{,}300$ gallons, or $16,900, and total cost is $16 \times 1{,}300$ gallons, or $20,800. The "profit" is $16,900 − $20,800, or a loss of $3,900. Happy Tree incurs an **economic loss**, the amount by which the firm's total opportunity cost exceeds its total revenue. Happy Tree's owners are not happy because they are making $3,900 less than a competitive return. A firm incurs an economic loss whenever $P < ATC$ because the firm's total opportunity cost is greater than its total revenue. The economic loss is equal to $(P - ATC) \times q$, which is the area of the light red rectangle in Figure 5.8.

Economic loss The amount by which the firm's total opportunity cost exceeds its total revenue.

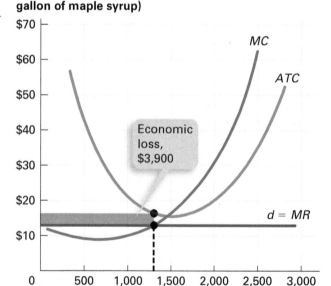

Figure 5.8 Economic Loss for a Perfectly Competitive Firm

The firm's economic profit equals its total revenue, $P \times q$, minus its total cost, $ATC \times q$. If the average total cost exceeds the price, $P < ATC$, the total cost exceeds the total revenue. The area of the light red rectangle, $3,900, equals the firm's economic loss.

In summary, a perfectly competitive firm makes an economic profit if $P > ATC$, makes a competitive return if $P = ATC$, and incurs an economic loss if $P < ATC$. The following box summarizes these results.

RULES FOR DETERMINING THE AMOUNT OF PROFIT

- *Economic profit*: For *any* firm, if $P > ATC$, the firm makes an economic profit—that is, more than a competitive return.
- *Competitive return*: For *any* firm, if $P = ATC$, the firm makes a competitive return—that is, zero economic profit.
- *Economic loss*: For *any* firm, if $P < ATC$, the firm incurs an economic loss—that is, less than a competitive return.

Shutting Down

The managers of a business that is incurring an economic loss face a very important decision: Should their firm stay open, or should it close? If they believe that conditions will improve in the future, so the economic loss will not persist, their initial response might be to keep the firm open. Indeed, that is a reasonable option. Another option is to close temporarily and then reopen. The managers must decide which option is more profitable.

Suppose, however, that the managers believe that conditions will not change in the future, so the economic loss will persist indefinitely. Even in this dismal situation, they might decide to keep the firm open temporarily because the loss might be lower than if they close it. Managers should choose the option that minimizes the amount of loss. So, let's take a closer look at the losses in these two situations:

- **Firm closes.** A closed firm has no sales, so its total revenue is zero. Because the closed firm does not employ any variable inputs, its variable cost (*VC*) is also zero. Fixed costs (*FC*), however, are unavoidable in the short run, so the firm must continue to pay them. Therefore, the closed firm's loss is *FC*.
- **Firm remains open.** The firm's loss is its total revenue minus its total cost, $TR - TC$. It is useful to separate the total cost into fixed cost and variable cost, in which case you can see that the loss when the firm remains open is $TR - (FC + VC)$.

Now suppose that total revenue is greater than variable cost: $TR > VC$. In this case, if the firm remains open, its revenue pays all of its variable cost with some revenue left over to pay some of its fixed cost. The key observation is that if the business is open, the loss is less than the fixed cost. In this case, the firm should remain open.

Next, suppose that $TR < VC$. In this case, the revenue the firm collects if it is open *cannot* pay all of its variable cost. The total loss if open equals the fixed cost *plus* whatever part of the variable cost cannot be paid. In this unfortunate situation, the loss if the business is open is greater than the fixed cost, so to minimize the loss, the managers must close the firm.

Shut-Down Rule

The analysis of the loss when open and closed shows that the decision to stay open or to close hinges on the comparison of total revenue and variable cost. The decision to keep a firm open if $TR > VC$ and close if $TR < VC$ is generally called the *shut-down rule*.

This rule can be transformed into an alternative formulation that is useful. To transform the rule, use price (P) multiplied by quantity (q) in place of total revenue (because $TR = P \times q$) and average variable cost (AVC) multiplied by quantity (q) in place of variable cost (because $VC = AVC \times q$).[3] The shut-down rule can then be rewritten as "stay open if $P \times q > AVC \times q$ and close if $P \times q < AVC \times q$." There's one more step: Divide both sides of the inequalities by q, so the rule finally becomes to "stay open if $P > AVC$ and close if $P < AVC$."

SHUT-DOWN RULE

- *Stay open*: The firm stays open if $TR > VC$ or, equivalently, if $P > AVC$. The firm's loss is less if it stays open than if it closes.

- *Close*: The firm closes if $TR < VC$ or, equivalently, if $P < AVC$. The firm's loss is less if it closes than if it stays open.

Figure 5.9 illustrates the modified version of the shut-down rule by adding the average variable cost curve (AVC) to the marginal cost and average total cost curves presented in Figure 5.8. As shown, the minimum average variable cost is $10 per gallon of maple syrup. Consequently, at *any* price less than $10 per gallon, the price is less than the average variable cost, so if you apply the shut-down rule, Happy Tree

Figure 5.9 Shutting Down

The minimum average variable cost is $10 per gallon of maple syrup. At any price less than $10, Happy Tree closes.

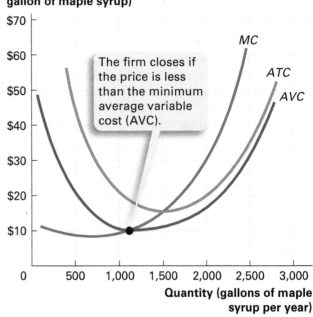

Price and cost (dollars per gallon of maple syrup)

The firm closes if the price is less than the minimum average variable cost (AVC).

---

3 The second equality comes from the definition of $AVC = \dfrac{\text{Variable cost}}{q}$. Multiplying both sides of the equality by q yields $AVC \times q = $ Variable cost.

closes whenever the price is less than $10 per gallon. At any price higher than $10 per gallon, the firm remains open.

What should Happy Tree's managers do if the price is exactly the minimum average variable cost, $10 per gallon? Unfortunately, there is no clear-cut answer to this question. At $10 per gallon, the loss will be the same whether Happy Tree remains open or closes its doors. If there is a cost associated with closing and then reopening, the firm might stay open. After taking into account all revenues and all costs, if the loss is the same in both cases, it just might be time for a coin flip.

Long-Run Exit

In the short run, a firm that incurs an economic loss stays open as long as the total revenue exceeds the variable cost. But what happens in the long run? As you learned in Chapter 4, fixed costs become variable costs with the passage of time. For example, when a lease comes up for renewal, the rent changes from a fixed cost to a variable cost. Ultimately, as time passes, the variable cost increases enough that it

Lundberg Family Farms Responds to a Fall in the Price of Rice

The market for rice is a perfectly competitive, worldwide market. Between 2013 and 2014, the price of rice fell approximately 18 percent, from $519 per ton to $426 per ton. Lundberg Family Farms is a large rice grower located in Richvale, California. This company has many different fields in which it can grow rice. Assume that when the price of rice was $519 per ton, the company was making zero economic profit, so that the owners were making a competitive return on the funds they had invested in the company. As a manager at Lundberg Family Farms, what decisions should you make in response to the fall in the price of rice?

Answer

As a manager of a perfectly competitive firm, you must first decide how much rice to produce. By applying marginal analysis, you conclude that the fall in the price of rice (which is a fall in the marginal revenue) means that the profit-maximizing quantity of rice decreases. Selecting which fields you will plant determines how much rice Lundberg Family Farms will produce. You must determine which of your rice fields are still profitable: For which fields does the marginal revenue from the field exceed the marginal cost of using the field? Fields that are less fertile or require additional transportation after harvesting the rice might not be profitable with the lower price of rice and accordingly should be left fallow.

After determining which fields you will plant, you face an additional decision: Because the firm was making only a competitive return (zero economic profit) with the higher price of rice of $519 per ton, when the price falls to $426 per ton, the firm incurs an economic loss. You must determine whether the economic loss is less if Lundberg Family Farms remains open or if it closes. This decision requires you to compare the total revenue and the variable cost. Once you have determined which fields to plant, if the total revenue exceeds the variable cost, you minimize the loss by staying open. If the total revenue is less than the variable cost, however, you minimize the loss by closing.

ultimately becomes greater than the total revenue $(TR < VC)$. When this happens, the managers' decision switches from keeping the business open to closing it. If the loss will recur when the business reopens, the business stays closed permanently, or as an economist would put it, the business *exits* the market.

The managerial lesson is straightforward: A business incurring a persistent economic loss might continue to operate for a while, but eventually it closes and exits the market. In other words, no business will sustain a long-run economic loss. As a manager, your responsibility is clear: When the passage of time converts fixed costs to variable costs, you must determine whether the loss incurred by remaining open is less than the loss incurred by exiting.

The Firm's Short-Run Supply Curve

Suppose that the price of maple syrup is above the minimum average variable cost, so that the firm is open. As a Happy Tree manager, how do you respond to a change in the price? How much should you produce at different prices? Figure 5.10 helps answer both of these questions.

Figure 5.10 shows the demand curves (d) for three prices: $15 per gallon, $30 per gallon, and $45 per gallon. Managers maximize profit by producing the quantity for which $MR = MC$, so when the price is $15 per gallon, Happy Tree produces 1,500 gallons; when it is $30 per gallon, Happy Tree produces 2,000 gallons; and when it is $45 per gallon, Happy Tree produces 2,250 gallons.

Short-run firm supply curve The curve that shows the quantity the firm produces at different prices; the short-run firm supply curve is the portion of the marginal cost curve above the minimum average variable cost.

These three price/quantity combinations are three points on Happy Tree's supply curve, the curve that shows the quantity the firm produces at different prices. All three points fall on the marginal cost curve. In general, a **short-run firm supply curve** shows the quantity the firm produces at different prices; it is the portion of the marginal cost curve above the minimum of the average variable cost. In Figure 5.10, Happy Tree's short-run supply curve is the wide blue part of the marginal cost curve.

Figure 5.10 The Firm's Short-Run Supply Curve

At a price of $15 per gallon of syrup, Happy Tree maximizes its profit by producing 1,500 gallons. If the price is $30 per gallon, Happy Tree's profit-maximizing quantity increases to 2,000 gallons. And if the price is $45 per gallon, Happy Tree produces 2,250 gallons. Because Happy Tree maximizes its profit by producing the quantity for which $MR = MC$, Happy Tree's supply curve is the wide blue portion of the marginal cost curve above the minimum point on the average variable cost curve.

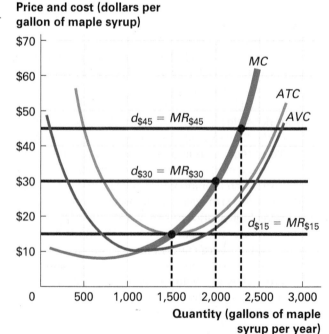

Price and cost (dollars per gallon of maple syrup)

If the price is lower than the minimum average variable cost, the managers close the firm, so that the quantity produced is zero.

The fact that the firm's short-run supply curve is the same as its marginal cost curve is no accident: Managers are producing the quantity that sets the price (which equals the marginal revenue) equal to the marginal cost. At any price for which Happy Tree remains open (at any price above the minimum average variable cost), the quantity produced is a point on its marginal cost curve. In other words, a firm's short-run supply curve is equal to its marginal cost curve at all points above its average variable cost curve. For all prices *below* the minimum point on the average variable cost curve, the managers maximize the firm's profit (minimize its loss) by producing zero output and just closing its doors.

**DECISION
SNAPSHOT**

A Particleboard Firm Responds to a Fall in the Price of an Input

Particleboard is made, in part, from sawdust. The market for particleboard is worldwide and is perfectly competitive. Suppose that you are a manager of a firm like Collins Products, located in Klamath Falls, Oregon, when the price of sawdust falls from $75 per ton to $50 per ton. In the short run, how will you respond to this fall in price? What do you expect will happen to the price of particleboard? In the short run, what do you expect will happen to your company's profit? Draw a graph to support your answer.

Answer
Sawdust is a variable input because the more particleboard you produce, the more sawdust you use. The fall in the price of sawdust means that your marginal cost of producing particleboard falls, shifting the marginal cost curve downward. For example, in the figure, the marginal cost curve shifts downward, from MC_0 to MC_1. At the original quantity you produced—30 million square feet, as shown in the figure—the marginal revenue now exceeds the marginal cost. To maximize your profit, you should apply marginal analysis and respond to the fall in cost by increasing the quantity of particleboard that you produce to 40 million square feet. Because all particleboard suppliers will be increasing the quantity they produce, the market supply curve shifts to the right, so the price of particleboard falls. In the short run, however, you can expect to make an economic profit.

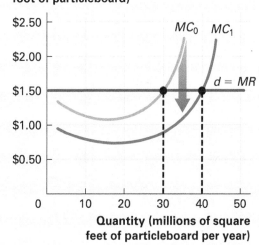

Price and cost (dollars per square foot of particleboard)

The Short-Run Market Supply Curve

As you have already learned, in a perfectly competitive market the production deci-sion of any single firm does not affect the equilibrium price. Instead, market demand and the collective supply produced by *all* firms in the market determine the equilib-rium price. The short-run market supply curve represents the quantity supplied by *all* of the firms in the market at various prices in the short run.

To construct the short-run market supply curve, add the quantities produced by the individual firms at any given price. For simplicity, assume that the market has only two firms in it. Of course, a perfectly competitive market contains many more than sim-ply two firms, but once you understand how the market supply curve is created for two firms, understanding its creation for any number of firms is immediate. Figure 5.11 illustrates the quantities of maple syrup produced by the two firms. Firm 1's supply curve is s_1, and firm 2's supply curve is s_2. At a price of $20 per gallon, firm 1 supplies 1,000 gallons, and firm 2 supplies 2,000 gallons. The quantity supplied in the market is 1,000 gallons plus 2,000 gallons, for a total market quantity of 3,000 gallons, at point A on the short-run market supply curve (S). When the price is $30 per gallon, firm 1 sup-plies 1,500 gallons, and firm 2 supplies 2,500 gallons, for a total market supply of 4,000 gallons (point B). At a price of $60 per gallon, the quantity supplied in the market is 2,000 gallons plus 3,000 gallons, or 5,000 gallons (point C). These are three points on the short-run market supply curve. All the other points are calculated similarly: At any price, add the quantity produced by firm 1 to that produced by firm 2.

Recall from Chapter 2 that an increase in the number of firms in the market shifts the market supply curve to the right (see Section 2.2). Now you can see why in more detail: At each price, the market quantity supplied equals the quantities supplied by the firms already in the market plus the quantities supplied by the new entrants. So, for example, if a third firm entered the market illustrated in Figure 5.11, to create the market supply curve you would add the quantity supplied by the third firm at the price of $20, at the price of $30, at the price of $60, and at all other prices to the quantities supplied by the first two firms already in the market. Conversely, a decrease in the number of firms in the market shifts the supply curve to the left: At each price, the market quantity supplied is less because the quantities supplied by the firms that exit are no longer included.

Figure 5.11 The Short-Run Market Supply Curve

At a price of $20 per gallon, firm 1 produces 1,000 gallons and firm 2 produces 2,000 gallons, for a total market supply of 3,000 gallons (point *A*). At a price of $30 per gallon, firm 1 produces 1,500 gallons and firm 2 produces 2,500 gallons so the market supply is 4,000 gallons (point *B*). At any price, the market supply equals the sum of the quantities supplied by all of the firms in the market.

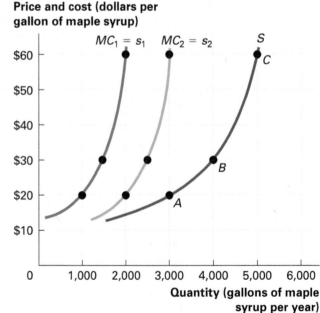

Amount of Profit and Shutting Down at a Plywood Producer

Suppose that you are a manager at a perfectly competitive producer of plywood similar to Nashville Plywood, a plywood producer located in Nashville, Tennessee. The following figure shows your marginal cost curve (*MC*), average total cost curve (*ATC*), and average variable cost curve (*AVC*).

a. At what price or prices do you make an economic profit?

b. At what price or prices do you make a competitive return?

c. At what price or prices do you incur an economic loss?

d. Below what price do you shut down the company?

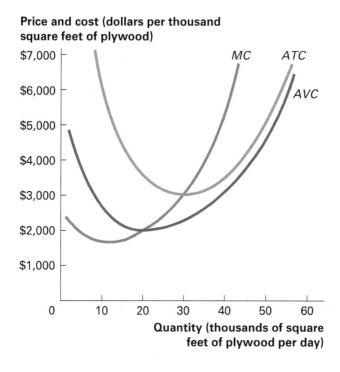

Answer

a. At any price greater than $3,000 per thousand square feet of plywood, you make an economic profit because $P > ATC$.

b. At the price of $3,000 per thousand square feet of plywood, you make a competitive return because $P = ATC$.

c. At any price less than $3,000 per thousand square feet of plywood, you incur an economic loss because $P < ATC$.

d. At any price less than $2,000 per thousand square feet of plywood, you shut down the company because $P < AVC$.

5.3 Long-Run Profit Maximization in Competitive Markets

Learning Objective 5.3 Describe the long-run adjustments that managers in perfectly competitive markets make to maximize profit.

In the short run, managers maximize their firm's profit, but they are limited because at least one input is fixed. In the long run, however, all of a firm's inputs are variable, which provides managers with additional options. Even managers who have maximized short-run profit might have an incentive to alter the quantity they use of a newly variable input to further increase their firm's profit.

Long-Run Effects of an Increase in Market Demand

The market as a whole and the managers of the individual firms within it all respond to a change in market demand. As you will see, the long-run market adjustments following a change in demand force individual managers to make further responses in order to continue to maximize profit.

The Firm's Adjustment to an Increase in Market Demand

Figure 5.12 helps illustrate the adjustments managers make in response to an increase in market demand. Initially, the market demand curve is D_0, and the market supply curve is S; Happy Tree's short-run marginal cost curve is MC_0, its short-run average total cost curve is ATC_0, its long-run marginal cost curve is LMC, and its long-run average cost curve is LAC. Recall from Chapter 4 that these long-run curves reflect the marginal cost and average cost in the long run after the managers have made adjustments to *all* inputs (see Section 4.4). For clarity in illustrating the long-run marginal cost curve, assume that the LAC is U-shaped, with a single minimum point. The LMC intersects the minimum point on the LAC.

With demand curve D_0, the price of maple syrup is $15 per gallon. This price means Happy Tree's demand and marginal revenue curve is $d_0 = MR_0$, so Happy Tree's managers maximize profit by producing 1,500 gallons of maple syrup. For reasons that will become clear shortly, assume that Happy Tree is initially producing at the minimum point on the LAC.

Suppose that the market demand for maple syrup permanently increases to D_1, so that the price of maple syrup rises to $30 per gallon. Happy Tree's demand and marginal revenue curve shifts upward to $d_1 = MR_1$. The managers' short-run response is to boost production to 2,000 gallons by employing more variable inputs and moving upward along the short-run marginal cost curve. At 2,000 gallons, the short-run marginal cost (MC_0) is $30, which equals the new marginal revenue (MR_1). Because the short-run marginal cost equals the marginal revenue, marginal analysis shows that Happy Tree's managers have maximized their short-run profit. Indeed, Happy Tree is now making an economic profit.

In the short run, the managers cannot change the quantity of fixed inputs they use, so the short-run marginal cost curve remains MC_0, and the short-run profit-maximizing quantity is 2,000. The profit-maximizing *long-run* quantity is the amount at which the long-run marginal cost equals the marginal revenue. Figure 5.13 shows that Happy Tree's LMC equals marginal revenue when it produces 2,500 gallons,

Figure 5.12 A Firm's Short-Run Adjustment to an Increase in Demand

(a) Before the Increase in Market Demand
Initially, the demand curve is D_0, and the equilibrium price is $15 per gallon. At this price, in part (b) Happy Tree's demand and marginal revenue curve is $d_0 = MR_0$, and Happy Tree produces 1,500 gallons. The firm's owners make a competitive return because $P = ATC$.

(b) A Firm's Short-Run Response to an Increase in Market Demand
When the demand increases to D_1, part (a) shows that the price rises to $30 per gallon. Happy Tree's demand and marginal revenue curve shifts upward to $d_1 = MR_1$. The managers maximize profit by producing 2,000 gallons, where the short-run marginal cost curve, MC_0, intersects the new marginal revenue curve, MR_1. Happy Tree now makes an economic profit because $P > ATC$.

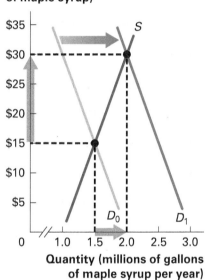

Price (dollars per gallon of maple syrup)

Quantity (millions of gallons of maple syrup per year)

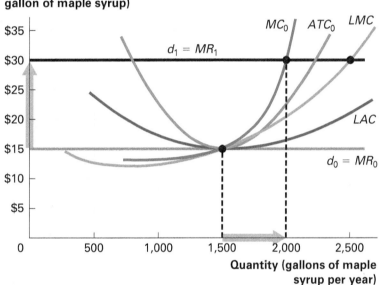

Price and cost (dollars per gallon of maple syrup)

Quantity (gallons of maple syrup per year)

which means that if Happy Tree's managers expect the price to remain at $30 per gallon for a sufficient period of time, they can increase the firm's profit by increasing the scale of its operations. In the long run, the managers can buy more of the inputs that are fixed in the short run, perhaps by buying more sugar maple trees and increasing the size of the sugar house (the plant in which the sap is boiled) to move along the *LAC* and minimize the average cost of producing its 2,500 gallons. With the increase in the scale of operations, Figure 5.13 shows that the new short-run average total cost curve (ATC_1) allows production of 2,500 gallons at the minimum long-run average cost for this quantity, $21 per gallon. Corresponding to the new average total cost curve is the new short-run marginal cost curve (MC_1). By producing 2,500 gallons, as long as the price remains equal to $30, the newly expanded Happy Tree maximizes its short-run profit (because $MR_1 = MC_1$) *and* its long-run profit (because $MR_1 = LMC$). In other words, Happy Tree is not only making an economic profit (because $P > ATC$) but also making the *largest* possible economic profit when the price is $30 per gallon.

Figure 5.13 A Firm's Long-Run Adjustments

If the managers believe the price will remain $30 for an extended period of time, they increase the scale of production to reduce costs. The short-run average total cost curve and short-run marginal cost curve become ATC_1 and MC_1, respectively. The firm now maximizes its profit by producing 2,500 gallons, where its new MC_1 curve crosses the MR_1 curve. The firm has maximized its short-run and long-run economic profit because it is producing 2,500 gallons, the quantity that sets its short-run marginal cost, MC_1, and its long-run marginal cost, LMC, equal to its marginal revenue MR_1. It is producing this quantity at the lowest possible average cost since it is producing at a point on the long-run average cost curve.

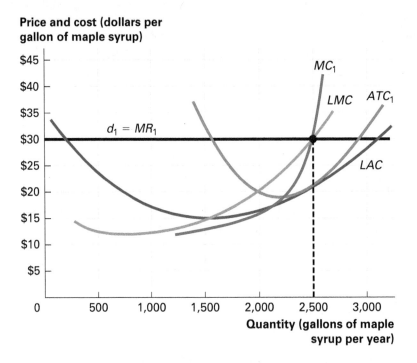

The Market's Adjustment to an Increase in Market Demand

After Happy Tree Maple Syrup has adjusted the scale of operations so its average total cost curve is ATC_1, its managers are satisfied. The firm is maximizing its profit, and unless something else changes, the managers foresee making no further changes. Unfortunately for them, in a competitive market further change outside their control can and does occur.

In Figure 5.13, Happy Tree is making an economic profit. Presumably all other firms in the market are making an economic profit as well. The economic profit in the market for maple syrup attracts entrepreneurs who are always seeking new markets with the potential for an economic profit. As you learned in Section 5.1, a perfectly competitive market has no barriers to entry, so entrepreneurs flock to the syrup market. As new firms enter, the market supply curve shifts to the right, lowering the price. How low the price goes depends on whether the entry of the new firms affects the other firms' costs.

Entry That Does Not Affect Firms' Costs To start, assume that the entry of new firms has no effect on other firms' costs and that the firms have identical costs. The question remains: How low will the price go? As long as there is an economic profit

Figure 5.14 **The Long-Run Outcome**

(a) Increase in Market Supply

In the long run, entry of new firms increases the supply and lowers the price. If entry by new firms does not affect the existing firms' costs, new firms continue to enter the market until the price equals the initial price, $15 per gallon, which occurs when the supply curve is S_1.

(b) A Firm's Response to an Increase in Market Supply

In the long run the price is the same as the initial price, so the "new" demand and marginal revenue curve is $d_0 = MR_0$, exactly the same as the initial demand and marginal revenue curve. Happy Tree again adjusts the scale of production, so its average total cost curve is ATC_0 and its marginal cost curve is MC_0. The company maximizes profit by producing 1,500 gallons, the quantity at which MC_0 intersects MR_0. The firm is making a competitive return because $P = ATC$. Once Happy Tree and the other firms in the market make only a competitive return, entry of new firms into the market stops.

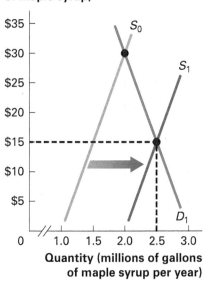

Price (dollars per gallon of maple syrup)

Quantity (millions of gallons of maple syrup per year)

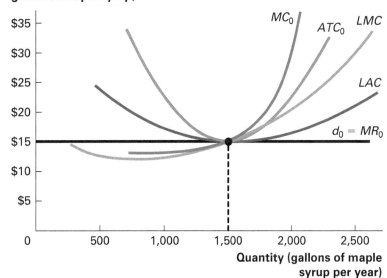

Price and cost (dollars per gallon of maple syrup)

Quantity (gallons of maple syrup per year)

to be made, new firms continue to enter the market. Entry stops when the economic profit is eliminated, which occurs when the firms in the market are making zero economic profit. Figure 5.14 shows that this outcome occurs only when the price of maple syrup is forced all the way back down to the initial price, $15 per gallon. At this price, and after the firms have again adjusted the scale of their operations, you see that the price equals the average total cost, which is the condition required for zero economic profit.

Other than again changing the scale of their production, the existing firms, such as Happy Tree, play no active role in this series of adjustments. Instead, profit-seeking entrepreneurs cause these changes. Because there are no barriers to entry, the managers of the firms already in the market are, as always, at the mercy of the market and can do nothing but sit back and watch both their price and their profit fall.

Entry That Does Affect Firms' Costs Suppose that as entrepreneurs start up new maple syrup enterprises, the demand for land with sugar maple trees increases, thereby increasing its price and hence its cost for maple syrup firms. In this case, entry raises the costs for *all* firms. What is the long-run outcome in this case?

If the entry of new firms raises the costs for all firms, the path leading to the long-run outcome is similar to what you just learned: Firms continue to enter until the economic profit is gone, at which point entry ceases. The difference is this: In addition to lowering the price, entry raises all the firms' average costs. The lower price *and* the higher cost both squeeze the economic profit. Because of the rise in average total cost, the price will not fall all the way back to the original level. It will fall only until it equals the new, *higher* average total cost. Once the price equals the higher average total cost, the economic profit is eliminated, which stops entry by new firms.

Decrease in Market Demand

If the market demand for maple syrup decreases, the reverse scenario plays out. In the short run, the equilibrium price falls, each firm's demand and marginal revenue curve shifts downward, and the managers decrease production as their firms incur economic losses. As time passes, the economic loss causes some managers to close their businesses. As firms close, the market supply decreases, which raises the price. The higher price decreases the surviving firms' economic losses. However, as long as firms incur an economic loss, from time to time some exit the industry by closing. As those firms close, they further decrease the supply, raising the price still higher. Ultimately, the price rises enough to eliminate the economic losses. In the long run, there are fewer firms in the market, but each firm makes at least a competitive return. The market equilibrium quantity decreases, but the effect on the price depends on how the costs of the surviving firms are affected by the exit of the firms that close. If the costs of the remaining firms are unaffected, then in the long run the price will return to its original level, the price before the decrease in market demand.

Change in Technology

In many industries, technological change is practically a day-to-day occurrence. But even in industries in which it is less frequent, technological change can be critical to managers. For example, managers and owners of strawberry farms are paying attention to entrepreneurs who are developing robots (such as the Agrobot with 14 arms) to harvest the fruit. Many maple syrup producers have switched from the traditional method of collecting sap (hanging a bucket on the tree under the tap and then sending workers out to the trees to collect the buckets) to using long blue tubes extending from the tree's tap to a vacuum pump that extracts a larger amount of sap from the tree and delivers it to a central collection station. These sorts of technological changes affect the market as a whole as well as the managerial decisions at individual firms.

The costs of a sap-sucking vacuum pump and a strawberry picking robot are fixed costs. Both technologies decrease the use of workers, which decreases the producers' variable cost. The increase in fixed cost raises a firm's short-run average total cost (ATC) at low levels of production, but the decrease in variable cost lowers the short-run average total cost and long-run average cost (LAC) at larger levels of production. The larger levels of production are more relevant because managers will adopt new technology if it lowers the cost of producing their equilibrium output. Accordingly, Figure 5.15 shows that when the managers at Happy Tree adopt the new sap extraction technology, the firm's cost curves shift downward from the initial cost curves labeled with a "0" to the cost curves labeled with a "1."

Before the advance in technology, Happy Tree's demand and marginal revenue curve, $d_0 = MR_0$, was horizontal at the market equilibrium price of $25 per gallon of syrup. Happy Tree was maximizing profit at point A, where $MR_0 = MC_0$,

Figure 5.15 The Effect of New Technology

Initially, Happy Tree's cost curves are those labeled with a "0" (MC_0, ATC_0, and LAC_0), and its demand and marginal revenue curve is $d_0 = MR_0$. Happy Tree maximizes its profit at point A, producing 1,500 gallons of syrup at a price of $25 per gallon. Happy Tree makes zero economic profit. The new technology shifts the cost curves downward to those labeled with a "1" (MC_1, ATC_1, and LAC_1). If Happy Tree is one of the early adopters of the new technology, so that the price has not yet changed from $25 per gallon, Happy Tree initially maximizes its profit at point B, producing 2,250 gallons of syrup. Happy Tree makes an economic profit. As more firms adopt the new technology and as new firms enter the market, the market supply of syrup increases, driving the equilibrium price lower. Eventually, the price falls to $10 per gallon. At this price, Happy Tree's demand and marginal revenue curve is $d_1 = MR_1$. Happy Tree's managers now maximize profit at point C, producing 2,000 gallons of syrup at a price of $10 per gallon. Happy Tree makes zero economic profit. Those firms that did not adopt the new technology have cost curves that remain MC_0, ATC_0, and LAC_0, incur an economic loss, and eventually close.

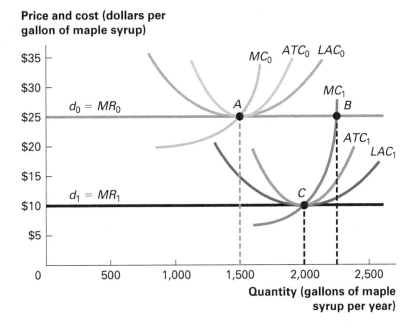

producing 1,500 gallons of syrup at a price of $25 per gallon and making zero economic profit. After Happy Tree's managers adopt the new technology, they initially maximize profit at point B, where $MR_0 = MC_1$, producing 2,250 gallons of syrup at a price of $25 per gallon and make an economic profit.

But the good times won't last! As more syrup producers use the new technology, the market supply of maple syrup increases, which drives the price down. Eventually, enough incumbent firms have adopted the technology and new firms, also using the new technology, have entered so that the market supply increases, lowering the price to $10 per gallon. In the long run, Happy Tree's demand and marginal revenue curve becomes $d_1 = MR_1$, and the managers maximize profit by producing at point C, where $MR_1 = MC_1$. The long-run outcome is sadly familiar for managers of competitive firms: In the long run, the firms make zero economic profit, so the owners make only a competitive return. But firms that opt not to adopt the new technology face an even bleaker fate. Because they do not gain the advantage of lower costs, they incur economic losses and eventually close.

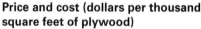

The Long Run at a Plywood Producer

You are still a manager at a firm similar to Nashville Plywood. The following figure illustrates your marginal cost, average total cost, long-run marginal cost, and long-run average cost curves.

Price and cost (dollars per thousand square feet of plywood)

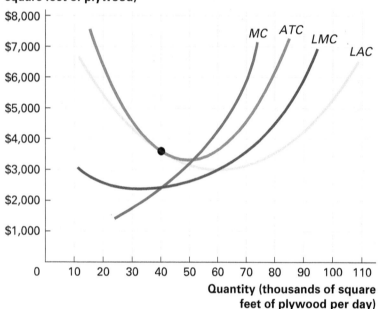

Quantity (thousands of square feet of plywood per day)

a. In the short run, if the price of plywood is $6,000 per thousand square feet of plywood, what quantity of plywood will your firm produce? Does your firm make an economic profit at this quantity?

b. If all other plywood producers have the same cost curves as yours, what will be the price of a thousand square feet of plywood in the long run? If you stay open, will you increase or decrease the scale of operations?

c. What quantity of plywood will you produce in the long run? Does your firm make an economic profit at this price?

Answer

a. As a manager, to maximize your profit you will produce the quantity of plywood that sets the marginal revenue equal to the marginal cost. For a perfectly competitive firm, the price equals the marginal revenue, so your marginal revenue equals $6,000 per thousand square feet. Using the figure, the profit-maximizing quantity is 70,000 square feet of plywood because at this quantity the marginal cost, *MC*, equals the marginal revenue. Since at this quantity $P > ATC$, your firm makes an economic profit.

b. In a perfectly competitive market, in the long run the price equals the minimum of the long-run average cost curve, $3,000 per thousand square feet of plywood. Your firm's current scale of production has the average total cost curve (*ATC*) shown in the figure. You will increase the scale of production and move to a new short-run *ATC* with its minimum equal to $3,000 per thousand square feet of plywood.

c. In the long run, in a perfectly competitive market the price equals the minimum of the long-run average cost (*LAC*), and the firms' owners make only a competitive return. Accordingly, in the long run, your company will produce 60,000 square feet of plywood and will make zero economic profit.

5.4 Perfect Competition

Learning Objective 5.4 Apply the theory of perfectly competitive firms and markets to help make better managerial decisions.

Managers can use marginal analysis—which involves comparing the additional benefit of an action to its additional cost—to determine the profit-maximizing quantity to produce. Marginal analysis is an important tool in the arsenal of managers of firms in perfectly competitive markets because they can use it to make a wide variety of decisions.

Applying Marginal Analysis

To maximize profit, a firm produces the quantity that sets $MR = MC$. Unfortunately, as a manager, no one will give you graphs or equations showing the marginal revenue and marginal cost. Instead, your discovery of the profit-maximizing amount of output is often a trial-and-error process, in which you use your judgment and are guided by marginal analysis. Apply the lessons you have learned: If you believe that the marginal revenue from an additional unit exceeds its marginal cost, marginal analysis indicates that you want to produce that unit because it will increase your firm's total profit. Conversely, if you estimate that the marginal revenue from the unit is less than its marginal cost, you do *not* want to produce that unit because doing so will decrease the total profit.

The profit-maximization rule, $MR = MC$, can be rewritten as $MR - MC = 0$. Although the change is small, the managerial interpretation of this modified version can be large when it comes to using your judgment about whether to produce additional units. The amount $MR - MC$ is the additional profit or loss on each unit of production. The profit-maximization rule means that you, as a manager, should continue to produce additional units of output as long as they are profitable, which will be the case as long as $MR - MC$ is positive. You should stop producing additional units when you hit the unit for which $MR - MC = 0$. If you continue beyond that point, you will produce units for which $MR - MC$ is negative, which creates losses for your firm. Consequently, reworking the profit-maximization rule in the form of $MR - MC = 0$ causes you to ask whether producing a unit is profitable—in which case it should be produced—or unprofitable—in which case it should not be produced. Sometimes simply deciding whether a unit will be profitable is significantly easier than separately estimating the unit's marginal revenue and marginal cost.

Optimal Long-Run Adjustments

You can learn a critical managerial lesson from the analysis of long-run profit maximization: Use caution. If you are managing a competitive firm and economic times are good (demand, price, and profit are all high), do not expect the good times to last forever. Even if an increase in demand is permanent, the initial increase in price and resulting economic profit are temporary. With no barriers to entry, new firms will enter your market, force the price lower, and compete away your economic profit.

It is extremely easy for managers to believe that the price of their product will remain high for much longer than it actually does. Optimistic managers who make this mistake and elect to expand the scale of their firm may certainly later regret their decision. For example, if the managers at Happy Tree think the price of maple syrup will be $30 per gallon indefinitely, they might expand the firm's scale of production, shifting the average cost curve to *ATC* in Figure 5.16. With this

Figure 5.16 Overexpansion

If the managers believe the price will remain $30 for an extended period of time, they increase the scale of production so that their (short-run) average total cost curve is *ATC*, with short-run marginal cost curve *MC*. As long as the price remains equal to $30, the firm produces 2,500 gallons and makes an economic profit because $P > ATC$. But if the price rapidly falls to $15 per gallon and if the firm cannot quickly decrease the scale of its production, the firm incurs an economic loss. It produces 2,000 gallons, the quantity where *MC* is equal to the lower *MR* of $15. But the firm incurs an economic loss because $P < ATC$. To eliminate the firm's economic loss, the managers must decrease the scale of production, thereby moving down the long-run average cost curve. Eventually, with the revised, smaller scale of production, the firm eliminates its loss and makes zero economic profit, so the owners make a competitive return.

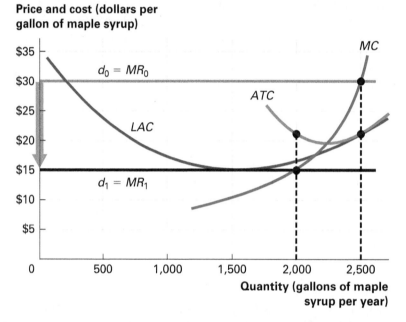

expansion, when the price is $30 per gallon Happy Tree produces 2,500 gallons and makes an economic profit because $P > ATC$. Once the entry of new firms drives the price down to $15 per gallon, Happy Tree's managers are in a less happy place. In that case, the firm produces 2,000 gallons (the quantity where *MC* equals the lower *MR* of $15 per gallon) and incurs an economic loss because $P < ATC$. Indeed, Happy Tree will incur economic losses until it can decrease the scale of its operations and move down its long-run average cost curve. If the firm cannot make this change quickly enough, it faces the decision of whether to remain open or close its doors.

This cautionary tale is not a mere theoretical curiosity. You have probably seen industries and firms that expanded like rapidly growing weeds, only to regret the expansion shortly thereafter. For example, in the face of high demand for ethanol, in the mid-2000s ethanol producers expanded rapidly to take advantage of what they expected would be a long-lasting high price. Additionally, there are virtually no barriers to entry into this market, so new producers streamed in. By the time the price collapsed in 2008, scores of producers had overexpanded and ultimately about half of them declared bankruptcy. The same cycle—increased demand, expanded scale and entry, and then a fall in price and numerous bankruptcies—occurred again in 2012.

Revisiting How Burger King Managers Decided to Let Chickens Have It Their Way

As you learned at the beginning of the chapter, in 2016 Burger King executives announced that the company would switch to 100 percent cage-free eggs by 2025. The executives made the announcement nine years in advance because they wanted to give time for the market for cage-free eggs to adjust and evolve. In particular, they want enough time (1) to enable more farmers to enter the cage-free egg market, (2) to give farmers already producing cage-free eggs time to increase their scale of operation, and (3) to allow technological innovations to occur. All of these changes will lower the price of cage-free eggs.

Figure 5.17 shows the effect of these changes by illustrating the situation at a (hypothetical) typical cage-free egg producer. Suppose that in 2016 the price was $3.50 for a dozen cage-free eggs. In this case, the demand and marginal revenue curve was $d_{2016} = MR_{2016}$. Farmers maximized their profit by producing at point A. These farmers made an economic profit because the price exceeded the average total cost. Now let's consider each change that Burger King's managers anticipate:

- **Entry.** Economic profit attracts entry by new producers. As time passes, entry increases the supply, decreasing the price. Assuming that the farmers do not change the scale of their production, eventually the price falls to $3.00 per dozen, so that the farmers wind up producing at point B, where the price equals the minimum average total cost.
- **Increase in scale.** From point B, however, with the passing of more time the farmers make further adjustments by increasing the scale of their production and moving down the long-run average cost curve (LAC_{2016}) to point C. Once farmers are producing at point C, competition forces the price of a dozen eggs to $2.50.

Figure 5.17 Costs at a Cage-Free Egg Producer

When Burger King's executives announced they would switch to cage-free eggs, the price of cage-free eggs was $3.50 per dozen, and farmers were producing at point A. Because the farmers were making an economic profit, entry occurs, lowering the price to $3.00 per dozen and leading the farmers to produce at point B. From point B, as more time passes the farmers increase the scale of their production, moving down the LAC curve to point C and lowering the price still more to $2.50 per dozen. Burger King's managers also hope that over the period of time during which they are switching to cage-free eggs, technological progress occurs, so that the long-run average cost curve shifts downward to LAC_{2025}. In this happy state of affairs, the farmers eventually produce at point D on the new LAC curve, at which the price of a dozen cage-free eggs will be only $1.00.

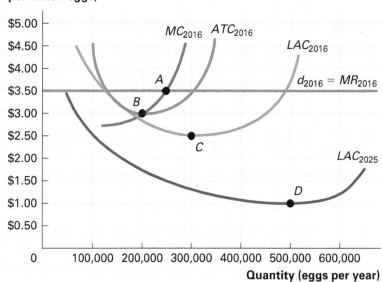

- **New technology.** Perhaps the largest change Burger King's managers are anticipating is new technology to produce cage-free eggs. This technology—perhaps the discovery of ways to reduce hen mortality or the development of robots to monitor the chickens—will change the farmers' long-run average cost, shifting the LAC curve downward, as shown in Figure 5.17, to LAC_{2025}. In this case, competition pushes the farmers to produce at point D, the minimum point on LAC_{2025}, and the price of a dozen cage-free eggs is only $1.00.

(Continues)

Revisiting How Burger King Managers Decided to Let Chickens Have It Their Way (*continued*)

Using insights from the analysis of perfectly competitive markets, Burger King's managers decided that rather than switch immediately to cage-free eggs, they would slowly switch over nine years. Burger King's managers know that during this extended period of time, changes in the competitive market will lower the price of cage-free eggs. The decision made by these executives increased Burger King's profit.

Summary: The Bottom Line

5.1 Characteristics of Competitive Markets

- Perfectly competitive markets have five characteristics: (1) The market includes a large number of buyers and sellers, (2) the market has no barriers to entry, (3) each firm produces a homogeneous product, (4) buyers and sellers have perfect information about the price and product characteristics, and (5) there are no transaction costs.
- Firms in perfectly competitive markets are price takers.

5.2 Short-Run Profit Maximization in Competitive Markets

- A perfectly competitive firm's demand is perfectly elastic at the market price, so its demand curve is horizontal at that price. Marginal revenue is the change in total revenue divided by the change in quantity. A perfectly competitive firm's marginal revenue equals the market price, so the marginal revenue curve is horizontal and is the same as the firm's demand curve.
- A firm maximizes profit by producing the quantity that sets marginal revenue equal to marginal cost ($MR = MC$). If $MR > MC$, managers can increase their firm's profit by increasing production. If $MR < MC$, managers can increase profit by decreasing production. The profit-maximizing price is the highest price the firm can set and sell the quantity it produces. For a firm in a perfectly competitive market, the profit-maximizing price equals the market price.
- The firm (1) makes an economic profit if the price exceeds the average total cost ($P > ATC$), (2) makes zero economic profit (its owners make a competitive return) if the price equals the average total cost ($P = ATC$), and (3) incurs an economic loss if the price is less than the average total cost ($P < ATC$).

- Managers will keep their firm open—even if it is incurring an economic loss—if the price exceeds the average variable cost ($P > AVC$), but they will close it if the price is less than the average variable cost ($P < AVC$).
- The firm's short-run supply curve is the portion of its marginal cost curve above the shut-down point, the minimum of the average variable cost.

5.3 Long-Run Profit Maximization in Competitive Markets

- In the long run, managers can adjust all inputs.
- If a firm in a perfectly competitive market is making an economic profit, new firms enter the market, increase the supply, lower the price, and compete away the economic profit. In the long run, firms in a perfectly competitive market are limited to making a competitive return—that is, zero economic profit.

5.4 Managerial Application: Perfect Competition

- Marginal analysis shows that you, as the manager of a perfectly competitive firm, maximize profit by producing the units of output for which $MR - MC$ is positive and stopping when you reach the unit for which $MR - MC$ equals zero.
- If a price change is expected to last for a more extended period, you might adjust the scale of your firm's production by changing your fixed inputs. Any change in price will not be permanent, however, so your scale of production should not be changed so much that your firm incurs large economic losses after the entry of firms moderates the price change.

Key Terms and Concepts

Barrier to entry	Marginal revenue	Short-run firm supply curve
Economic loss	Perfectly competitive market	Transaction costs
Economic profit	Price takers	

Questions and Problems

5.1 Characteristics of Competitive Markets

Learning Objective 5.1 Summarize the conditions that make a market perfectly competitive.

1.1 Which of the following firms compete in a perfectly competitive market or a market that closely approximates perfect competition?
a. Verizon Wireless
b. Swaz Potato Farms
c. Alcoa Aluminum
d. Gucci Perfumes

1.2 Why does it make no sense for the managers of a perfectly competitive firm to spend money on advertising?

1.3 No matter how many soft drinks you buy, you have no effect on the price of soft drinks. The soft drink industry includes two very large producers and several smaller ones. Is this industry perfectly competitive? Explain your answer.

1.4 Give three examples of products or firms protected by barriers to entry. Describe the barrier to entry for each example.

1.5 In a perfectly competitive market, no individual producer can affect the price of the product. How, then, is the price of the product determined?

5.2 Short-Run Profit Maximization in Competitive Markets

Learning Objective 5.2 Use marginal analysis to determine the profit-maximizing quantity that a perfectly competitive firm produces in the short run.

2.1 In your own words, explain the concept of marginal analysis, making sure to include the *marginal* aspect of this rule.

2.2 What is the difference between a market demand curve and a perfectly competitive firm's demand curve?

2.3 How does a perfectly competitive firm's price compare to its marginal revenue? How does its demand curve compare to its marginal revenue curve?

2.4 What is the relationship between marginal cost and total cost?

2.5 A perfectly competitive firm is producing the quantity that sets its marginal revenue equal to its marginal cost. Explain to this firm's managers why producing more output or less output would decrease the firm's profit.

2.6 You are managing a perfectly competitive landscaping firm. You have carefully calculated that the cost of mowing and tending one additional yard is $25 and the price of that work is $40. To increase your profit, what decision should you make? Explain your answer.

2.7 In the figure, if the price is $500 per unit, what is the firm's profit-maximizing price and quantity? What is the amount of the firm's economic profit or loss?

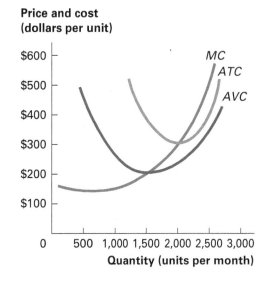

Price and cost
(dollars per unit)

2.8 Suppose that you are a manager of a firm like Sproule Farms, a perfectly competitive grower of sugar beets. The market price of sugar beets is $50 per ton. The table has your total cost. What is the profit-maximizing quantity of sugar beets? What is the amount of your economic profit or loss?

Quantity (tons)	Total Cost (dollars)
5,000	$235,510
5,001	235,550
5,002	235,600
5,003	235,651
5,004	235,703
5,005	235,756

2.9 Suppose that you are a manager at a firm like Yulong Machine Company, a perfectly competitive producer of pellets used in biomass plants to generate electricity. The price of a ton of pellets is $120. In the figure, producing 30,000 tons of pellets per year minimizes the average total cost of producing the pellets. Does producing 30,000 tons maximize your firm's profit? Explain your answer.

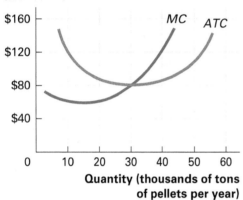

2.10 In a perfectly competitive market, the equilibrium market price for a good is $60 per unit, and a firm has a marginal cost curve given by

$$MC = 10 + 0.25q$$

What is the firm's profit-maximizing quantity and price?

2.11 Your company just spent $5.0 million on a state-of-the-art production facility. As a result, the marginal cost of producing the product is

$$MC = 10 + 0.0001q$$

If the market is perfectly competitive and the price is $50 per unit, how many units will you produce? If the price falls to $25, how many units will you produce?

2.12 A perfectly competitive firm's marginal cost curve is upward sloping but not vertical. If the price of the product increases, in the short run is it possible for the firm's economic profit to decrease (or for its economic loss to increase)? Explain your answer.

2.13 In the figure, in the short run what is the lowest price at which the firm will remain open? At this price, what does the firm's economic loss per day equal?

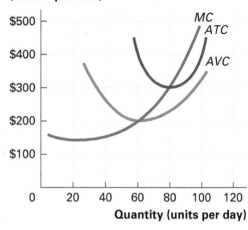

2.14 You are managing a perfectly competitive dairy farm, and sadly you have determined that your firm is incurring an economic loss. You do not foresee any future changes in your costs or the price of milk. Discuss all factors that influence your decision about whether to close or remain open.

2.15 "A manager of any firm that is paying out more in costs than it is making in revenue should shut down operations at once." Is this advice sound? Explain your answer.

2.16 You are the manager of a large, perfectly competitive wheat farm. The price of wheat is $6 per bushel. The table gives your total costs for different quantities. What is the profit-maximizing quantity of wheat? Carefully explain your answer.

Quantity (bushels of wheat)	Total Cost (dollars)
100,000	$555,000
100,001	555,002
100,002	555,005
100,003	555,009
100,004	555,014
100,005	555,020

5.3 Long-Run Profit Maximization in Competitive Markets

Learning Objective 5.3 Describe the long-run adjustments that managers in perfectly competitive markets make to maximize profit.

3.1 In the long run, why does a firm in a perfectly competitive market produce the quantity that minimizes its long-run average cost?

3.2 What sort of profit does a perfectly competitive firm make in the long run?

3.3 Peach growing is perfectly competitive. For simplicity, suppose that all peach growers have the same cost curves. In the figure, each grower's initial average total cost curve is ATC, its initial marginal cost curve is MC, and its long-run average cost curve is LAC.

Price and cost (dollars per bushel of peaches)

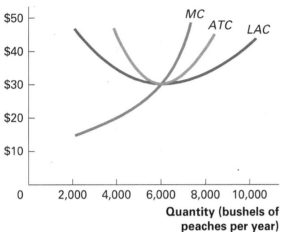

a. If the price is $20 per bushel and the firm stays open, in the short run what is the firm's profit-maximizing price and quantity? Explain whether the firm makes an economic profit or loss.

b. Will firms enter or exit the market? In the long run, will the price rise, fall, or not change? If there are no technological changes, what will be the price in the long run? Explain your answers.

3.4 The market for paper is perfectly competitive. Draw a demand and supply figure showing the entire paper market and another figure for a typical paper manufacturing firm with the long-run average cost (LAC), average total cost (ATC), marginal cost (MC), demand (d), and marginal revenue (MR) curves showing the long-run outcome. Presuming that an increase in the number of firms does not affect the firms' cost curves, describe the short-run and long-run effects of an increase in the market demand for paper.

3.5 The plywood market is perfectly competitive. The demand for home construction increases, increasing the demand for plywood. If the increase in demand for plywood is permanent, should the managers of a plywood firm increase their firm's capacity? Why or why not?

3.6 You are the manager of a bagel producer that is in a perfectly competitive industry comprised of identical firms. The cost of flour used to produce bagels decreases from $25 to $20 per hundred pounds.

a. In the short run, how do you respond to the fall in the price of flour?

b. Describe the long-run adjustments that take place in the market.

c. What long-run decisions will you make as the manager of your firm?

3.7 Describe the long-run outcome for a competitive wild rice producer and the competitive wild rice industry. Now suppose that the demand for wild rice increases.

a. Discuss the adjustments by the firm and the industry.

b. What happens to the firm's long-run economic profit?

Now suppose that demand increases again but that the government forbids entry by new wild rice producers.

c. Discuss the adjustments by the firm and the industry.

d. What happens to the firm's long-run economic profit?

e. Is the firm's long-run economic profit higher when entry is forbidden or when entry is allowed?

f. What is the managerial lesson illustrated in your answer to part e?

5.4 Managerial Application: Perfect Competition

Learning Objective 5.4 Apply the theory of perfectly competitive firms and markets to help make better managerial decisions.

4.1 As a manager of a house painting firm like the Queen Anne Painting Company, a perfectly competitive firm in Seattle, Washington, you are maximizing your profit and are currently making an economic profit. For simplicity, assume that you use only capital and labor. You determine that at your current production, your long-run average cost curve is downward sloping; that is, if you increased both your capital and your labor by the same proportion, your long-run average cost would fall.

a. Draw a figure to illustrate your situation. In your figure include short-run average total cost (ATC) and marginal cost (MC) curves, a long-run average cost (LAC) curve, and a demand and marginal revenue ($d = MR$) curve.

b. Using your figure, do you want to increase the scale of your production? Explain your answer.

4.2 Managers of perfectly competitive firms must be cautious when deciding to permanently expand (or contract) the scale of production. What factors should go into the decision to expand the scale of production? Which factors make it necessary to proceed with caution?

MyLab Economics Auto-Graded Excel Projects

5.1 The Weinandt Family Farm in Wynot, NE raises livestock and grows crops. Commonly grown crops in Nebraska are corn and soybeans. Suppose you are helping a farm similar to the Weinandt Farm make decisions about how much corn to grow this year. As an agricultural product, the market for corn meets the requirements of a perfectly competitive market.

a. Using the market data provided, create a market supply and demand graph.

b. What are the market equilibrium price and quantity?

c. Using the firm cost and quantity data, find FC, VC, ATC, AFC, AVC, and MC. Graph ATC, AFC, AVC, and MC.

d. Based on your answers in part c, between which quantities is ATC minimized?

e. Based on your answers in part c, between which quantities should the farm aim to produce?

f. Using the lower of these two quantities, caculate TR, TC, and the firm's economic profit or loss.

g. Will the farm decide to grow corn or leave the fields bare? Explain your answer.

h. Will farms enter this market, leave the market, or remain constant? Explain your answer.

5.2 The Weinandt Family Farm in Wynot, NE raises livestock and grows crops. Commonly grown crops in Nebraska are corn and soybeans. Suppose you are helping a farm similar to the Weinandt Farm make decisions about how much corn to grow this year. As an agricultural product, the market for corn meets the requirements of a perfectly competitive market.

The original market demand (Q^{d1}) and market supply (Q^s) are given. Suppose the market demand shifts to Q^{d2} because, in addition to being used as a food product, corn is now used for ethanol production.

a. Using the market data provided, create a market supply and demand graph which includes both Q^{d1} and Q^{d2}.

b. What are the market equilibrium price and quantity before and after the demand shift?

Accompanies problem 5.1.

	A	B	C	D	E	F	G	H	I	J	K	L
1	Q^d (millions of bu)	Q^s (millions of bu)	Price/bu		Firm q (thousands of bu)	TC	FC	VC	ATC	AFC	AVC	MC
2	0	6000	10		0	10000						
3	200	5700	9.5		0.5	10128						
4	400	5400	9		1	10505						
5	600	5100	8.5		1.5	11133						
6	800	4800	8		2	12010						
7	1000	4500	7.5		2.5	13138						
8	1200	4200	7		3	14515						
9	1400	3900	6.5		3.5	16143						
10	1600	3600	6		4	18020						
11	1800	3300	5.5		4.5	20148						
12	2000	3000	5		5	22525						
13	2200	2700	4.5		5.5	25153						
14	2400	2400	4		6	28030						
15	2600	2100	3.5		6.5	31158						
16	2800	1800	3		7	34535						
17	3000	1500	2.5		7.5	38163						
18	3200	1200	2		8	42040						
19	3400	900	1.5		8.5	46168						
20	3600	600	1		9	50545						
21	3800	300	0.5		9.5	55173						
22	4000	0	0		10	60050						
23												

c. Using the firm cost and quantity data, find FC, VC, ATC, AFC, AVC, and MC.

d. Based on your answers in part c and b, between which quantities should the farm aim to produce before and after the demand shift?

e. Using the lower of these two quantities, calculate TR, TC, and the firm's economic profit or loss before and after the change in demand.

f. Will farms enter this market, leave the market, or remain constant after the demand shift? Explain your answer.

	A	B	C	D	E	F	G	H	I	J	K	L	M
1	Qd¹ (millions of bu)	Qd² (millions of bu)	Qs (millions of bu)	Price/bu		Firm q (thousands of bu)	TC	FC	VC	ATC	AFC	AVC	MC
2	0	400	6000	10		0	10000						
3	200	800	5700	9.5		0.5	10128						
4	400	1200	5400	9		1	10505						
5	600	1600	5100	8.5		1.5	11133						
6	800	2000	4800	8		2	12010						
7	1000	2400	4500	7.5		2.5	13138						
8	1200	2800	4200	7		3	14515						
9	1400	3200	3900	6.5		3.5	16143						
10	1600	3600	3600	6		4	18020						
11	1800	4000	3300	5.5		4.5	20148						
12	2000	4400	3000	5		5	22525						
13	2200	4800	2700	4.5		5.5	25153						
14	2400	5200	2400	4		6	28030						
15	2600	5600	2100	3.5		6.5	31158						
16	2800	6000	1800	3		7	34535						
17	3000	6400	1500	2.5		7.5	38163						
18	3200	6800	1200	2		8	42040						
19	3400	7200	900	1.5		8.5	46168						
20	3600	7600	600	1		9	50545						
21	3800	8000	300	0.5		9.5	55173						

The Calculus of Profit Maximization for Perfectly Competitive Firms

The most important result in Chapter 5 is the profit-maximization rule, $MR = MC$. Deriving this rule using calculus is straightforward. We can start with the definition of marginal revenue.

A. Marginal Revenue

Marginal revenue is the change in total revenue (TR) that results from a change in quantity (q), or using calculus, marginal revenue (MR) is defined as

$$MR = \frac{dTR}{dq} \qquad \text{A5.1}$$

Total revenue equals price multiplied by quantity, $P \times q$. For a perfectly competitive firm, the price is the same no matter the quantity the firm produces. Consequently, for a perfectly competitive firm,

$$\frac{dTR}{dq} = \frac{d(P \times q)}{dq} = P \qquad \text{A5.2}$$

Combining Equations A5.1 and A5.2 shows that for a perfectly competitive firm $MR = P$.

B. Maximizing Profit

Managers want to determine the amount of output that maximizes the firm's profit. The profit equals total revenue minus total cost, or

$$\text{Profit}(q) = TR(q) - TC(q)$$

To maximize profit, take the derivative of Profit(q) with respect to q, and set it equal to zero:

$$\frac{dProfit}{dq} = \frac{dTR}{dq} - \frac{dTC}{dq} = 0 \qquad \text{A5.3}$$

Recall from Chapter 4 that the marginal cost (MC) equals the derivative of total cost (TC) with respect to quantity, or $MC = dTC/dq$. Accordingly, in Equation A5.3, dTR/dq is MR and dTC/dq is MC, so the equation can be rewritten as

$$MR - MC = 0 \Rightarrow MR = MC$$

which is precisely the same result presented in the profit-maximization rule in Section 5.2 of the chapter.

C. Maximizing Profit: Example

Suppose that you are a manager of a company like B.W. Recycling, a perfectly competitive gold scrap recycler near Fort Lauderdale, Florida. Your company has daily fixed cost of $18,000 and variable cost given by $VC = 0.05q^3 - 4.5q^2 + 600q$. The total cost is equal to the sum of the variable cost plus the fixed cost, or $TC = 0.05q^3 - 4.5q^2 + 600q + 18{,}000$. Using the power rule to differentiate the total cost with respect to q gives your marginal cost function:

$$MC = 0.15q^2 - 9.0q + 600 \qquad \text{A5.4}$$

The average total cost (ATC) equals TC/q, so the average total cost function is

$$ATC = 0.05q^2 - 4.5q + 600 + \frac{18,000}{q} \qquad \textbf{A5.5}$$

If the market price for the recycled gold is \$1,005 per ounce, then $P = MR = \$1,005$. To maximize profit, you must produce the quantity at which $MR = MC$, or using Equation A5.4

$$1,005 = 0.15q^2 - 9.0q + 600 \Rightarrow 0 = 0.15q^2 - 9.0q - 405 \qquad \textbf{A5.6}$$

Using the quadratic formula to solve the second part of Equation A5.6, the profit-maximizing quantity is 90 ounces of gold.[1] Of course, the profit-maximizing price equals the market price, \$1,005 per ounce.

To determine the economic profit or loss, using Equation A5.5 and the price we can first calculate the economic profit per ounce as $P - ATC$, or

$$1,005 - \left[(0.05 \times 90^2) - (4.5 \times 90) + 600 + \frac{18,000}{90} \right] = 1,005 - 800 = 205$$

The total economic profit equals the profit per ounce multiplied by the quantity of ounces, or

$$\$205 \times 90 = \$18,450$$

Figure A5.1 illustrates these calculations. The MC curve is based on Equation A5.4, and the ATC curve is based on Equation A5.5. The demand and marginal revenue curve is horizontal at \$1,005 per ounce. The profit-maximizing quantity is 90 ounces per day because this is the quantity at which $MR = MC$. The price is \$1,005 per ounce. Figure A5.1 shows that at the profit-maximizing quantity, the firm's average total cost is \$800 per ounce. The firm's economic profit is therefore the area of the green rectangle, which is equal to \$18,450.

Price and cost (dollars per ounce of gold)

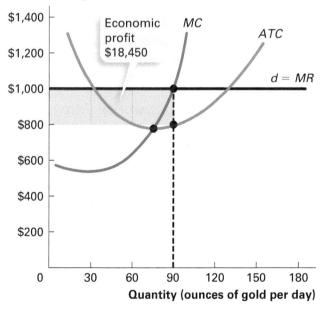

Figure A5.1 Profit-Maximizing Quantity, Price, and Economic Profit

The profit-maximizing quantity is the quantity at which $MR = MC$, which is 90 ounces of gold per day. The profit-maximizing price is equal to the market price, \$1,005 per ounce. The economic profit per ounce equals the price per ounce minus the average total cost of producing an ounce, or $P - ATC$. At the profit-maximizing quantity, the average total cost is \$800 per ounce, so the firm's economic profit per ounce is \$1,005 − \$800, or \$205 per ounce. The firm's total economic profit equals the economic profit per ounce multiplied by the number of ounces, \$205 per ounce × 90 ounces, which equals the area of the green rectangle in the figure, \$18,450.

---

1 The other root of Equation A5.6 is −30, which is meaningless because the quantity must be positive.

Calculus Questions and Problems

A5.1 Suppose that Nuñez Consulting offers management consulting services in a perfectly competitive market and that the total cost the firm incurs when providing consulting services is

$$TC(q) = 4{,}500 + 5q^2$$

where q is the number of hours of consulting services provided by Nuñez Consulting.

a. What is the average total cost of providing consulting services as a function of the number of hours of consulting services provided?
b. The price of consulting services is $500 per hour. At what quantity is Nuñez Consulting's profit maximized? What is the maximum amount of economic profit that Nuñez Consulting can earn in this market?
c. Suppose that the price of a consulting services rises to $600 per hour. At what quantity is Nuñez Consulting's profit maximized after this price change? What is the maximum amount of economic profit that Nuñez Consulting can earn?

A5.2 Suppose that Laylita sells empanadas at a perfectly competitive local farmers' market and that her total cost of producing an empanada is

$$TC(q) = 40 + 0.1q^2 - 0.2q$$

where q is the total number of empanadas that she produces.

a. What is the average total cost of producing empanadas as a function of the quantity of empanadas produced?
b. At what quantity, q^*, is the average total cost of producing an empanada minimized? What is the value of the average total cost at q^*?
c. The price of an empanada is $4.20. What quantity of empanadas should Laylita produce to maximize her profit? If she remains open, what is her economic profit or loss?
d. Suppose that the price of an empanada falls to $3. What quantity of empanadas should Laylita produce to maximize her profit? If she remains open, what is her economic profit or loss?

A5.3 Gerardo's Geraniums is a flower farm, specializing in the production of cut geraniums. The cut geranium market is a perfectly competitive market. Gerardo has hired an economist to determine his total cost function, which the economist reports as

$$TC(q) = 30{,}000 + 0.0025q^2$$

where q is the number of cut flowers Gerardo's Geraniums produces.

a. What is Gerardo's Geraniums' marginal cost of supplying an additional cut geranium?
b. Suppose that the price of a cut geranium is $2.50. How many cut geraniums will Gerardo's Geraniums supply?
c. Suppose that the price of a cut geranium rises to $3.00. How many cut geraniums will Gerardo's Geraniums supply?

A5.4 Jessica is a 10-year-old entrepreneur. She produces lemonade in her family's kitchen and sells that lemonade at a stand that she sets up in front of her family's house each Saturday afternoon. Jessica lives in a neighborhood with many other entrepreneurial children, all selling identical lemonade. Therefore, along Jessica's street, the lemonade market is perfectly competitive. The price of a cup of lemonade on Jessica's street is $2. Jessica's total cost of setting up her lemonade stand and producing lemonade is

$$TC(q) = 10 + 0.025q^2$$

where q is the number of cups of lemonade Jessica produces.

a. What is Jessica's marginal cost of producing an additional cup of lemonade?
b. What is Jessica's marginal revenue of producing an additional cup of lemonade?
c. What is the profit-maximizing number of cups of lemonade? What is Jessica's economic profit at this quantity?

A5.5 Larry's Lasers is a laser hair-removal firm that operates in the perfectly competitive laser hair-removal market. Dr. Larry specializes in removing women's facial hair, and his total cost of performing these procedures is

$$TC(q) = 200{,}000 + 5q^2 - 100q$$

where q is the number of facial hair removal procedures he performs.

a. What is Larry's Lasers' marginal cost of performing an additional facial hair removal procedure?
b. Suppose that the price of a facial hair removal procedure is $2,300. How many facial hair removal procedures does Larry perform?
c. If the price of a facial hair removal procedure is $2,300, does Larry make an economic profit? If so, how much?
d. What is the long-run price of a facial hair removal procedure?

CHAPTER 6

Monopoly and Monopolistic Competition

Learning Objectives

After studying this chapter, you will be able to:

6.1 Explain the relationship between a monopoly's demand curve and its marginal revenue curve.

6.2 Discuss how managers of a monopoly can determine the quantity and price that maximize profit and how they compare to those of a perfectly competitive firm.

6.3 Describe how managers of a dominant firm determine the quantity and price that maximize profit.

6.4 Explain how managers of a monopolistically competitive firm determine the quantity and price that maximize profit.

6.5 Apply what you have learned about monopolies, dominant firms, and monopolistically competitive firms to make better managerial decisions.

Premature Rejoicing by the Managers at KV Pharmaceutical

A pharmaceutical company typically spends approximately 10 years and over $1 billion to research, develop, and test a potential drug in order to prove its safety and effectiveness to the federal Food and Drug Administration (FDA). The company can apply for a government patent for exclusive rights to sell the drug for 20 years from the date of filing, though sometimes the company can gain extra time if the FDA is slow to approve the drug.

An exception to this general policy is the orphan drug policy. Orphan drugs are legally defined as drugs developed for diseases that affect 200,000 or fewer individuals in the United States. Under this policy, a pharmaceutical company that receives FDA approval has a seven-year period of marketing exclusivity even if the company does not have a patent on the drug.

In 1956, the FDA approved hydroxyprogesterone caproate to treat various issues during pregnancy, including premature birth. After the patent expired, the market evolved. From 2000 until 2011, a number of different compounding pharmacies (smaller companies that manufacture drugs for specific individuals) made the drug under the name 17P. In this competitive market, the price for a shot of 17P was approximately $15. To prevent premature birth, typically doctors prescribe weekly shots for the last 20 weeks of the pregnancy.

Studies conducted after 2000 indicated that 17P helped prevent subsequent premature births in women with a history of premature births. KV Pharmaceutical used these studies to gain orphan drug designation and then conducted its own test with 463 women, which confirmed the findings. KV Pharmaceutical submitted these studies to the FDA. The March of Dimes, a charity group concerned with preventing premature births, lobbied the FDA for quick approval of KV's submission. Based on KV's study, the FDA granted the firm the standard seven-year period of orphan-drug marketing exclusivity for its drug, which the firm called Makena. The FDA's decision effectively made the firm a monopoly. Believing that the FDA ruling gave KV Pharmaceutical a seven-year monopoly, its managers celebrated, and its stock price doubled. Managers set the price at $1,500 per dose, up approximately 100 times from the $15 competitive price for 17P.

How did the managers at KV Pharmaceutical determine the price of their drug? How can they ensure that it is the profit-maximizing price? This chapter will show you how to answer these key questions about KV Pharmaceutical and other monopolies. At the end of the chapter, we revisit the situation faced by KV Pharmaceutical's managers and show how they made a fundamental error in their pricing process.

Sources: Courtney Hutchison and ABC News Medical Unit, "KV Pharma Cuts Price of Costly Premature Birth Prevention Drug," ABC News. April 1, 2011; Yesha Patel and Martha M. Rumore, "Hydroxprogesterone Caproate Injection (Makena) One Year Later," *Pharmacy and Therapeutics*, July 2012, pp. 404–411; Tom Schoenberg, "K-V Pharmaceutical Loses FDA Lawsuit over Makena Drug," Bloomberg, September 6, 2012.

Introduction

In Chapter 5, you learned that the price-taking behavior of a firm in a perfectly competitive market severely limited its managers' pricing responsibilities. In this chapter, you will see that a manager's pricing responsibilities increase when a firm has *market power*, the ability to determine the price of its good or service. Later chapters will examine different pricing schemes that managers of firms with market power can use. First, however, you need to understand the economic fundamentals of managerial decisions in these firms. To explain these fundamentals, Chapter 6 includes five sections:

- **Section 6.1** explains the conditions that define a monopoly market and compares a monopoly's demand curve and marginal revenue curve to those of a perfectly competitive firm.
- **Section 6.2** explains how managers of monopolies can use marginal analysis to determine the profit-maximizing quantity and price and compares these results to those in a perfectly competitive market.
- **Section 6.3** explains why managers of dominant firms face the same decisions as those of monopolies—but with an added wrinkle: They must take into account the actions of all of the competitive firms in the market.
- **Section 6.4** examines how monopolistically competitive firms compete with a large number of other firms, all producing similar but somewhat differentiated products. Because of a limited degree of market power, managers of these firms make profit-maximizing decisions similar to those of monopolies, but the amount of economic profit differs.
- **Section 6.5** applies what you have learned about monopolies, dominant firms, and monopolistically competitive firms to help you make better managerial decisions.

6.1 A Monopoly Market

Learning Objective 6.1 Explain the relationship between a monopoly's demand curve and its marginal revenue curve.

Chapter 5 covered perfectly competitive markets and perfectly competitive firms. Now it is time to turn your attention to monopoly markets and monopoly firms to explain how they determine their profit-maximizing price and quantity. The first step is understanding the definition of a monopoly. Then you will learn how a firm's monopoly position affects its demand and marginal revenue.

Defining Characteristics of a Monopoly Market

It is tempting to define a monopoly market as a market with a single seller. Although this aspect is the most prominent characteristic, it is not the only one. A more complete definition of a monopoly market includes three parts:

Market power The ability of a firm to determine the price of its good or service.

1. **Single seller.** There is only one firm in the market, which gives it immense market power. As noted in the introduction, **market power** is the ability of a firm to determine the price of its good or service. By definition, perfectly competitive firms have no market power, but monopoly firms do—they are free to decide the price of their product. Essentially, the managers of a monopoly firm set the price in a monopoly market, while the market sets the price in a perfectly competitive market.
2. **No close substitute.** The good or service a monopoly produces has no close substitutes. This characteristic is necessary to adequately define the market. For

instance, you cannot assert that McDonald's is a monopoly at a particular inter-section if there is a Burger King one block away. Both McDonald's and Burger King sell their own unique versions of a hamburger, but most consumers find them very close substitutes. McDonald's and Burger King are examples of firms in monopolistic competition, a market structure you will learn more about in Section 6.4. On the other hand, Roche Holdings' drug Herceptin is a monoclonal antibody used to treat certain breast and gastric cancers, and there is no other drug that has a similar genetic target. The market for Herceptin meets this part of the definition of a monopoly market.

3. **Insurmountable barriers to entry.** As you learned in Chapter 5, a *barrier to entry* is any factor that makes it difficult for new firms to enter a market. In a monopoly, the barriers to entry are insurmountable, which is why there is only one firm in the market. Patents, trademarks, copyrights, and significant cost advantages for a firm already in the market can serve as barriers to entry. For example, the market for Herceptin is a monopoly because Roche Holdings has a patent that prevents other pharmaceutical or biotech companies from producing the drug. As long as the patent remains in force, it is an insurmountable barrier to entry. Barriers to entry ensure there is only one firm in the market. They play a crucial role in the firm's long-run outcome. You will learn more about their long-run role in Section 6.2.

So a complete definition of a **monopoly market** is a market with only a single seller, which is producing a product that has no close substitute and is protected by an insurmountable barrier to entry.

Monopoly market A market with only a single seller, which is producing a product that has no close substitute and is protected by an insurmountable barrier to entry.

Demand and Marginal Revenue for a Monopoly

Although a monopoly and a perfectly competitive firm differ in important character-istics, the managers' ultimate goal in both firms is the same: to maximize profit. Man-agers of a perfectly competitive firm control only the quantity they produce because the price is determined by the market. As you learned in Chapter 5, marginal analysis helps guide these managers to the profit-maximizing quantity. Managers of a monop-oly might appear to have a more difficult task because they must determine *both* the

DECISION SNAPSHOT   ## Is Delta Airlines a Monopoly?

You are a government official responsible for monitoring the behavior of monop-olies to discover violations of antitrust laws. For a small fee, airlines can fly in and out of the airport in Rochester, New York. Say that Delta Airlines is the only carrier flying from Rochester to LaGuardia Airport in New York City, but JetBlue Airways flies from Rochester to JFK International, also in New York City. Do you decide that Delta Airlines is a monopoly? Explain your answer.

Answer
Delta Airlines is *not* a monopoly for two reasons. First, flying to JFK International Airport is a close substitute for flying to LaGuardia Airport. Second, there is no insurmountable barrier to entry: If another airline wants to fly from Rochester to LaGuardia Airport, it can do so at only a small expense.

quantity to produce and the price to charge. It turns out, however, that marginal analysis is a powerful tool for monopoly managers as well. Of course, to use marginal analysis, the monopoly's managers must know the firm's marginal revenue and marginal cost. Let's begin by examining marginal revenue.

Monopoly's Demand and Marginal Revenue Curves

In your study of a perfectly competitive firm, you had to distinguish between the firm's demand curve and the market demand curve (see Section 5.2). You do not need to make this distinction for a monopoly. Because the monopoly is the only firm in the market, the monopoly's demand curve is the same as the market demand curve. For example, Roche Holdings' patent on Herceptin makes it the only company allowed to sell Herceptin, so the market demand curve for Herceptin is also Roche Holdings' demand curve for it.

Suppose that you are a manager for a pharmaceutical company that also has a patent on a drug. Similar to Roche Holdings, your company is the only one allowed to sell that drug. Figure 6.1 shows the (hypothetical) market demand curve for this drug. Because you are the only seller, the *market* demand curve is also your *firm's* demand curve.

Even with the difference in demand, marginal revenue is calculated for a monopoly firm in the same way as for a perfectly competitive firm: the change in total revenue resulting from a change in quantity sold, or

$$MR = \frac{\Delta TR}{\Delta Q}$$

Although the definition of marginal revenue is the same for a perfectly competitive firm and a monopoly, a monopoly's marginal revenue curve differs from that of a perfectly competitive firm because of the differences in their demand curves. Table 6.1 shows some data from points on the demand curve for your drug from Figure 6.1.

Figure 6.1 The Market Demand Curve and Monopoly Firm Demand Curve

Because your firm is the only company allowed to sell your drug, the market demand curve, *D*, is also your demand curve for the drug.

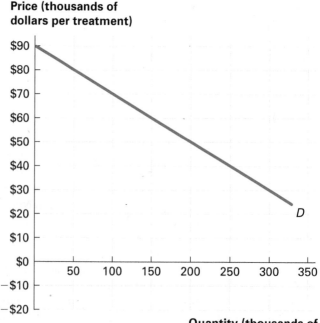

Price (thousands of dollars per treatment)

Quantity (thousands of treatments per year)

Table 6.1 Demand, Total Revenue, and Marginal Revenue

The first two columns are (part of) the demand facing your firm. Total revenue equals $P \times Q$. Marginal revenue is the change in total revenue caused by a change in quantity, or $\frac{\Delta TR}{\Delta Q}$. For a monopoly, price is greater than marginal revenue, $P > MR$.

Price, P	Quantity Demanded, Q	Total Revenue, TR	Marginal Revenue, MR
50,000.40	199,998	$9,999,979,999.20	
			$10,000.60
50,000.20	199,999	9,999,989,999.80	
			10,000.20
50,000.00	200,000	10,000,000,000.00	
			9,999.80
49,999.80	200,001	10,000,009,999.80	
			9,999.40
49,999.60	200,002	10,000,019,999.20	

Figure 6.2 illustrates your demand curve and the resulting marginal revenue curve. Both curves show that for any quantity, the price, measured from the demand curve, is greater than the marginal revenue, measured from the marginal revenue curve. Why is $P > MR$? In Table 6.1, you can see that your pharmaceutical company can sell 199,999 units at a price of $50,000.20 for each unit. Because the demand curve is downward sloping, the managers can sell an *additional* unit, the 200,000th unit, only if they lower the price for *all* the units. Table 6.1 shows that the price of a treatment must fall to $50,000.00 in order to sell the 200,000th unit. The extra unit directly adds $50,000.00 to your firm's total revenue, but to sell that unit, you had to lower the price of a treatment from $50,000.20 to $50,000.00, a loss of $0.20 in revenue on each of the initial 199,999 treatments you had been selling at the higher price. The price reduction means that your firm *loses* a total of $0.20 × 199,999 or $39,999.80 in revenue on the quantity that it had been selling. So the total change in revenue from selling the 200,000th unit equals $50,000.00 − $39,999.80 or $10,000.20, making the marginal revenue from the 200,000th unit $10,000.20.

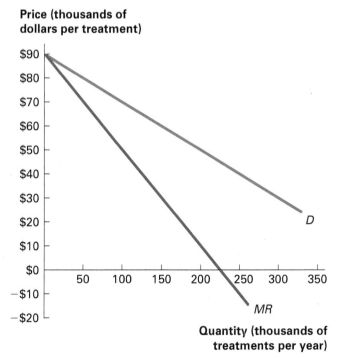

Price (thousands of dollars per treatment)

Quantity (thousands of treatments per year)

Figure 6.2 A Monopoly's Demand and Marginal Revenue Curves

The graph shows the market demand curve (*D*) and the resulting marginal revenue curve (*MR*) for your drug. For any quantity, $P > MR$. Because the demand curve is linear, the marginal revenue is also linear, with the same intercept on the price axis and a slope that is twice the slope of the demand curve.

This reasoning applies to all units produced and makes clear why $P > MR$ for a monopoly: To sell an additional unit, you must lower the price, thereby losing some revenue on the initial units already sold. Recall that for a perfectly competitive firm, $P = MR$ because the competitive firm's demand curve is horizontal—the managers do *not* need to lower the price to sell additional units. When a perfectly competitive firm sells another unit, there is no need to subtract a loss in revenue from the initial units because the constant price means there is no loss in revenue.

Figure 6.2 shows that there are quantities where the marginal revenue (MR) is negative. This occurs when there are so many units sold before the price change that the revenue lost on these initial units is larger than the revenue gained on the newly sold unit. In this case, the change in total revenue is negative, which makes the marginal revenue negative.

Marginal Revenue Curve for a Linear Demand Curve

Figure 6.2 also shows that when the demand curve is linear, the marginal revenue curve also is linear. In addition, while both curves have the same intercept on the price axis, the marginal revenue curve is twice as steep as the demand curve.[1] This mathematical result is correct *only* for linear demand curves. For these sorts of curves, it is a *very* handy result because it allows you to quickly determine the marginal revenue curve. The result that for a monopoly $P > MR$ is more general. Indeed, as long as the demand curve is downward sloping, $P > MR$ no matter if the demand curve is linear or not.

Elasticity, Price, and Marginal Revenue

Closer analysis of the definition of marginal revenue reveals an important relationship among the elasticity of demand, the price, and the marginal revenue. Some mathematics relegated to a footnote[2] shows that the marginal revenue from a one-unit change in Q is equal to

$$MR = \left(\frac{\Delta P}{\Delta Q} \times Q \right) + P \qquad\qquad 6.1$$

Equation 6.1 reflects the two effects of a change in the quantity on the total revenue: (1) the effect of the change in the price on the initial quantity, the first term (in parentheses), and (2) the effect of the change in quantity itself. With an increase in the quantity, Equation 6.1 divides the marginal revenue from the increase in Q into the following:

1. $\left(\frac{\Delta P}{\Delta Q} \times Q \right)$ **term.** An increase in the quantity sold requires a decrease in price. In other words, there must be a downward movement along the demand curve. The amount of the decrease in price depends on the slope of the demand curve, $\frac{\Delta P}{\Delta Q}$. Because the slope of the demand curve is negative, the term $\left(\frac{\Delta P}{\Delta Q} \times Q \right)$ is negative. This term captures the effect of the lower price decreasing the revenue collected from *all* the initial units previously sold—that is, from Q units.
2. P **term.** An increase in the quantity directly increases the total revenue. This increase in the total revenue equals $P \times \Delta Q$, so a one-unit increase in the quantity raises the total revenue by P. The second term, P, captures this effect.

---

1 We prove this result in Section 6.A of the Appendix at the end of this chapter.

2 Using the definition of total revenue ($P \times Q$) in the equation for marginal revenue gives $MR = \frac{\Delta TR}{\Delta Q} = \frac{\Delta(P \times Q)}{\Delta Q} = \frac{(\Delta P \times Q) + (P \times \Delta Q)}{\Delta Q} = \left(\frac{\Delta P}{\Delta Q} \times Q \right) + P.$

You can rearrange Equation 6.1 into a form that is more valuable for managers and managerial decision making[3]:

$$MR = P \times \left(1 - \frac{1}{\varepsilon}\right) = P \times \left(\frac{\varepsilon - 1}{\varepsilon}\right) \qquad \textbf{6.2}$$

Equation 6.2 shows important relationships among the firm's marginal revenue, price, and price elasticity of demand for its product that hold for *any* demand curve[4]. As a manager, you can use these relationships to help make decisions. For example, if you know or have an estimate of your firm's price elasticity of demand (recall that this can change at different points on a demand curve), you can use it along with the price of the product to calculate the marginal revenue of a unit. In addition to its managerial use, Equation 6.2 has two significant implications for your study of monopoly:

1. The equality $MR = P \times (1 - \frac{1}{\varepsilon})$ shows that unless $\frac{1}{\varepsilon}$ equals zero, marginal revenue is less than the price, in which case the marginal revenue curve lies below the demand curve. The amount by which the marginal revenue is less than the price depends on ε, the price elasticity of demand—the larger ε, the larger $(1 - \frac{1}{\varepsilon})$ and therefore the closer MR to P.
2. The equality $MR = P \times (\frac{\varepsilon - 1}{\varepsilon})$ demonstrates that the marginal revenue is

   - Positive when the price elasticity of demand exceeds 1 because $(\frac{\varepsilon - 1}{\varepsilon})$ is positive.
   - Zero when the price elasticity of demand equals 1 because $(\frac{\varepsilon - 1}{\varepsilon})$ is zero.
   - Negative when the price elasticity of demand is less than 1 because $(\frac{\varepsilon - 1}{\varepsilon})$ is negative.

Using the definitions of elastic, unit-elastic, and inelastic demand from Chapter 3 (see Section 3.4), these results mean that for *any* demand curve, the marginal revenue is positive when demand is elastic, zero when demand is unit elastic, and negative when demand is inelastic.

The Relationship Among the Price Elasticity of Demand, Marginal Revenue, and Price

SOLVED PROBLEM

Use the relationship among the price elasticity of demand, marginal revenue, and price to answer the following questions.

a. If the price elasticity of demand is 3 and the price is $100, what is the marginal revenue?

b. If the price elasticity of demand is 1 and the price is $100, what is the marginal revenue?

c. If the price elasticity of demand is 0.4 and the price is $100, what is the marginal revenue?

d. If the price elasticity of demand is 1.1 and the marginal revenue is $100, what is the price?

(Continues)

---

3 In Section 6.B in the Appendix at the end of this chapter, we prove Equation 6.2 using calculus.

4 The price elasticity of demand equals the percentage change in the quantity demanded caused by a one-percentage-point change in the price. The more substitutes for a product, the stronger the response to a change in the price, which means the larger the elasticity. Chapter 3 defines and discusses elasticity in more detail.

SOLVED PROBLEM (*continued*)

Answer

All of the answers require using the equation $MR = P \times \left(\frac{\varepsilon - 1}{\varepsilon}\right)$ to quantify the relationship among the marginal revenue, price, and price elasticity of demand.

a. $MR = \$100 \times \left(\frac{3 - 1}{3}\right) = \$66.67$. When $\varepsilon > 1$, the marginal revenue is positive.

b. $MR = \$100 \times \left(\frac{1 - 1}{1}\right) = \$0$. When $\varepsilon = 1$, the marginal revenue equals zero.

c. $MR = \$100 \times \left(\frac{0.4 - 1}{0.4}\right) = -\$150$. When $\varepsilon < 1$, the marginal revenue is negative.

d. Rearrange the equation $MR = P \times \left(\frac{\varepsilon - 1}{\varepsilon}\right)$ to $MR \times \left(\frac{\varepsilon}{\varepsilon - 1}\right) = P$, so

$P = \$100 \times \left(\frac{1.1}{1.1 - 1}\right) = \$1,100$.

6.2 Monopoly Profit Maximization

Learning Objective 6.2 Discuss how managers of a monopoly can determine the quantity and price that maximize profit and how they compare to those of a perfectly competitive firm.

Now that you understand the basics of a monopoly market, you are ready to investigate how managers of a monopoly can maximize their profit. Then you will learn how the profit-maximizing price and quantity compare for monopoly markets and perfectly competitive markets.

Profit Maximization for a Monopoly

In Chapter 5, marginal analysis demonstrated that managers of a perfectly competitive firm maximize profit by producing the amount of output that sets the marginal revenue (*MR*) equal to the marginal cost (*MC*). Marginal analysis and the profit-maximization rule can help managers of a monopoly maximize their firm's profit as well.

Profit Maximization for a Monopoly: Marginal Analysis

The key to maximizing profit in any firm, whether it is a monopoly or one of thve many firms in a perfectly competitive market, is to produce all of the profitable units and none of the unprofitable units. Using this fundamental insight, in Chapter 5 you learned that marginal analysis led to the *profit-maximization rule*: Produce the quantity for which $MR = MC$, and then set the highest price that sells the quantity produced. Managers of monopolies can use the same profit-maximization rule to maximize their firm's profit.

To use marginal analysis and the profit-maximization rule, you compare the marginal revenue of a unit to its marginal cost. Continuing the example with you as a manager of a pharmaceutical company, Figure 6.3 includes the marginal cost curve for your firm's drug along with the demand and marginal revenue curves that appear in Figure 6.2. As Figure 6.3 shows, the marginal revenue of all quantities up to 150,000 exceeds their marginal cost. Following the profit-maximization rule, you produce all of these units. The figure also shows that the marginal revenue of all quantities beyond 150,000 is less than their marginal cost. So you produce none of these units. The conclusion from this analysis is identical to that for a perfectly competitive firm: To maximize profit, your firm produces the quantity of output for which the marginal revenue equals the marginal cost ($MR = MC$ or $MR - MC = 0$).

You must now set a price. Monopolies, and other firms with market power, have control over the price they set. In this chapter, assume that the same price is set for all units sold and for all buyers. In Chapter 10, you will learn about other pricing strategies that can lead to increased profit.

Price and cost (thousands of dollars per treatment)

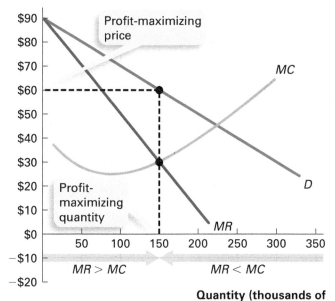

Figure 6.3 Profit Maximization for a Monopoly

The quantity that sets $MR = MC$ (150,000 treatments) maximizes your company's profit. This quantity produces all of the profitable units (those for which $MR > MC$) and none of the unprofitable units (those for which $MR < MC$). The demand curve shows that the profit-maximizing price is $60,000 per treatment, the highest price demanders will pay for 150,000 treatments.

According to the profit-maximization rule, the price is determined from the demand curve as the highest price that sells the quantity produced. In Figure 6.3, the demand curve shows that the highest price buyers are willing to pay for 150,000 treatments is $60,000 per treatment, so $60,000 is the profit-maximizing price.

Markup Equation

In Figure 6.3, the price of a treatment, $60,000, is twice the marginal cost of $30,000. The factor by which the price is higher than the marginal cost, $\frac{P}{MC}$, or 2.0 in this case, is the *markup*. You can use the relationship among the price elasticity of demand, price, and marginal revenue shown in Equation 6.2, $MR = P \times \left(\frac{\varepsilon - 1}{\varepsilon}\right)$, to determine the role the price elasticity of demand plays in determining the profit-maximizing price and markup. When the managers maximize profit, $MR = MC$. Accordingly, substituting MC for MR, Equation 6.2 becomes

$$MC = P \times \left(\frac{\varepsilon - 1}{\varepsilon}\right) \qquad \text{6.3}$$

Rearranging Equation 6.3 illustrates two key results. First, dividing both sides of Equation 6.3 by $\frac{\varepsilon - 1}{\varepsilon}$ shows the role the price elasticity of demand plays in setting the profit-maximizing price:

$$P = MC \times \left(\frac{\varepsilon}{\varepsilon - 1}\right) \qquad \text{6.4}$$

Second, dividing both sides of Equation 6.4 by MC gives the **markup equation**, the equation showing the markup of the price over marginal cost:

$$\frac{P}{MC} = \left(\frac{\varepsilon}{\varepsilon - 1}\right) = 1 + \left(\frac{1}{\varepsilon - 1}\right) \qquad \text{6.5}$$

Markup equation The equation showing the markup of the price over marginal cost: $\frac{P}{MC} = \frac{\varepsilon}{\varepsilon - 1}$.

Equation 6.4 shows how to use your estimates of the marginal cost and price elasticity of demand to set the profit-maximizing price, and Equation 6.5 shows how the markup depends on the price elasticity of demand. The equations also show a key qualitative result: The smaller the price elasticity of demand, the higher the price and the larger the markup. Figure 6.4 illustrates these general results. In Figure 6.4(a), at the profit-maximizing quantity on the demand curve (point A), the price elasticity of demand is 3.0.[5] When the price elasticity of demand equals 3, the markup is $\frac{3}{3-1}$, or 1.5, so the price is 1.5 times the marginal cost, $30. In Figure 6.4(b), however, the price elasticity of demand at the profit-maximizing point (point B) is smaller, 1.67. Consequently, the markup, $\frac{1.67}{1.67-1}$, or 2.5, is larger, so that the price, $50, is higher.

The intuition that a smaller price elasticity of demand leads to a higher price is as important as the actual formula. Recall from Chapter 3 that the fewer substitutes for a good, the smaller its price elasticity of demand. That observation combined with the markup equation means that the fewer the substitutes for a good, the higher the price a monopoly can charge. This intuition (and the quantitative result in Equation 6.4) explains why pharmaceutical companies that produce unique, lifesaving drugs are free to set sky-high prices for those drugs.

Figure 6.4 Markup and Elasticity

(a) Markup with Larger Elasticity

To maximize profit, managers produce 400 units per day. The profit-maximizing markup of price over marginal cost is $\frac{\varepsilon}{\varepsilon-1}$. At point A on the demand curve, the price elasticity of demand (ε) is 3.0, so the markup is $\frac{3}{3-1} = 1.5$. Consequently, the profit-maximizing price equals $20 × 1.5 = $30 per unit.

(b) Markup with Smaller Elasticity

To maximize profit, managers produce 400 units per day. The profit-maximizing markup of price over marginal cost is $\frac{\varepsilon}{\varepsilon-1}$. At point B on the demand curve, the price elasticity of demand (ε) is 1.67, so the markup is $\frac{1.67}{1.67-1} = 2.5$. Consequently, the profit-maximizing price equals $20 × 2.5 = $50 per unit.

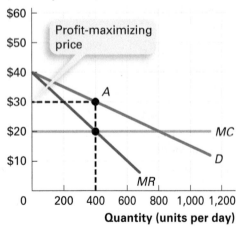

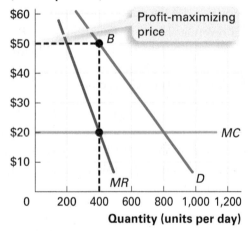

---

[5] From Chapter 3, the price elasticity of demand along a linear demand curve is $\varepsilon = |b × (P/Q^d)|$, where b is the change in the quantity demanded from a $1 change in price. In Figure 6.4(a), b equals 40 units per dollar, so at point A the price elasticity of demand is $|40 × ($30/400)| = 3.0$. In Figure 6.4(b), b equals 13.33 units per dollar, so at point B the price elasticity of demand is $|13.33 × ($50/400)| = 1.67$.

DECISION SNAPSHOT	Profit-Maximizing Range of Prices for Tires

Suppose that you are a manager in the pricing department of a tire-producing company like Michelin US. Your research department reports that the best esti- mate of the price elasticity of demand for your tires is 1.6 but that the elasticity might be as large as 1.8 or as small as 1.4. Your marginal cost is $100 per tire. What is the range of the profit-maximizing price for your product? What might you ask your research department to do next?

Answer

Equation 6.4 shows that the profit-maximizing price equals $MC \times \frac{\varepsilon}{\varepsilon - 1}$. If the price elasticity of demand is 1.8, then the price equals $100 \times \frac{1.8}{1.8 - 1}$, or $225 per tire. If the price elasticity of demand is 1.4, then the price equals $100 \times \frac{1.4}{1.4 - 1}$, or $350 per tire. Consequently, your profit-maximizing price per tire ranges from $350 to only $225, a rather wide range. You might return to your research department and ask the analysts to try to tighten the range for the price elasticity of demand.

Amount of Profit

In Chapter 5, you learned that a perfectly competitive firm makes an economic profit if $P > ATC$, makes a competitive return if $P = ATC$, and incurs an economic loss if $P < ATC$. Thankfully, you do not need to memorize yet another rule because the same set of results holds true for monopoly firms. In fact, these relationships apply to *any* firm.

Figure 6.5 includes the average total cost curve (ATC) for your firm's drug, assum- ing that it makes an economic profit. In the figure, the price ($60,000 per treatment) exceeds the average total cost ($40,000), which shows that your company is making an economic profit. The area of the green rectangle in Figure 6.5 is $(P - ATC) \times Q$. As you learned in Chapter 5, this area equals the amount of the firm's economic profit because it is the economic profit per unit $(P - ATC)$ multiplied by the quantity sold (Q). In Figure 6.5, the economic profit is ($60,000 - $40,000) × 150,000 treat- ments, which comes out to $3 billion.

Figure 6.5 shows the monopoly is making an economic profit, so it would be easy to suppose that all monopolies make an economic profit. However, the fact that there is only one firm in the industry is no guarantee that a monopoly will make an economic profit, much less an exorbitant one. If production costs are high relative to demand, profits will be low, and economic losses may even occur. For instance, take the classic online failure, Pets.com. This pet-food delivery company was founded in 1998 and used a sock puppet dog in its advertising. Pets.com faced no competition in the market for home delivery of pet supplies, so it was effectively a monopoly. The company had both high costs—it offered free shipping for heavy products, such as dog food and cat litter, which were expensive to ship—and low demand—consumers tend to buy pet food and litter when they run out and therefore did not want to wait for delivery from Pets.com. Observers suggested that $P < ATC$ for each item Pets.com shipped; that is, each bag of dog food and cat litter shipped increased Pets.com's loss. Pets.com incurred a large economic loss and survived for approximately two years before it declared bankruptcy. What happened to the sock puppet dog remains a mystery.

Figure 6.5 Economic Profit for a Monopoly

Your firm is making an economic profit because its price, $60,000 per treatment, exceeds its average total cost, $40,000 per treatment. The amount of the economic profit equals the area of the green rectangle.

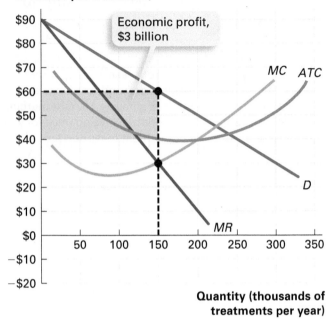

Shut-Down Rule for a Monopoly

Pets.com ultimately closed. In Chapter 5, you learned the shut-down rule for a firm in a perfectly competitive market: The firm closes if total revenue is less than total variable cost and remains open if total revenue is greater than total variable cost. Equivalently, the firm closes if price is less than average variable cost $(P < AVC)$ and remains open if price is greater than average variable cost $(P > AVC)$. When does a monopoly close? It turns out that the same shut-down rule applies. If *any* firm cannot make enough revenue to cover its variable costs, which means $P < AVC$, the firm minimizes its loss by closing.

Long-Run Profit Maximization for a Monopoly

Because there is only one firm in a monopoly market, when the firm is in long-run equilibrium, the market is also in long-run equilibrium. Recall from Chapter 5 that when firms in a perfectly competitive market are making an economic profit, entry occurs, and in the long run, the entry drives the firms' economic profit to zero. In a monopoly, however, the presence of insurmountable barriers to entry prevents entry by new firms, so the firm can continue to make an economic profit. Even so, the managers may still need to adjust the scale of production to minimize the firm's long-run average cost and increase its economic profit even more.

Figure 6.6 shows the long-run outcome for your pharmaceutical firm after you have changed the scale of production of your firm's drug by adjusting the firm's inputs. The managers are maximizing long-run profit by producing so that marginal revenue equals *long-run* marginal cost, or $MR = LMC$. In the figure, the firm maximizes its long-run profit by producing 175,000 treatments and setting a price of $55,000 per treatment. The company is producing its profit-maximizing quantity, 175,000, at the lowest possible average cost, $15,000, and is making the largest possible economic profit, $7 billion. As long as no other firm can enter the market, the economic profit can persist.

Price and cost (thousands of dollars per treatment)

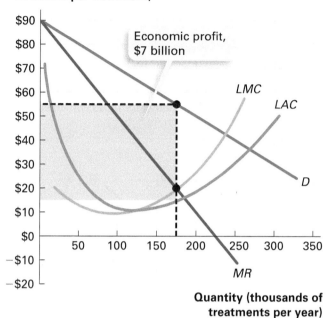

Figure 6.6 **Long-Run Profit Maximization**

Your firm is maximizing its long-run economic profit because its marginal revenue equals its long-run marginal cost, $MR = LMC$. You are producing the profit-maximizing quantity, 175,000 treatments, at the lowest average cost for this quantity, $15,000 per treatment. The price is $55,000 per treatment so the economic profit equals the area of the green rectangle, $7 billion.

Quantity (thousands of treatments per year)

Comparing Perfect Competition and Monopoly

You have learned that the profit-maximization rule and the shut-down rule apply to both monopoly firms and firms in perfectly competitive markets. How does the equilibrium in a perfectly competitive *market* compare to the equilibrium in a monopoly *market*? Understanding the differences is essential for the formulation of public policy, such as antitrust policy (presented in Chapter 9).

Comparing a Perfectly Competitive Market and a Monopoly Market

Although the goal of managers of both monopolies and firms in perfectly competitive markets is to maximize profit, their impact on society differs dramatically. As you learned in Section 2.4, perfectly competitive markets maximize society's total surplus of benefit over cost. Figure 6.7(a) illustrates the maple syrup market first presented in Chapter 5. In a perfectly competitive market for maple syrup, the equilibrium quantity is 12 million gallons, and the price is $30 per gallon. In this perfectly competitive market, the total surplus of benefit over cost to society is equal to the area of the green triangle.[6] The area equals the largest possible amount of total surplus, which is why economists generally favor perfectly competitive markets.

Suppose that one firm becomes a monopoly by buying all of the others and somehow manages to create a barrier to entry that keeps any other firm from entering the market. Instead of having many separate firms under independent ownership and control, there is now a single firm with many separate plants or production

---

6 Applied to the maple syrup market, Chapter 2 explained that for any gallon of maple syrup, the maximum price a consumer is willing to pay, measured by the demand curve, is the marginal benefit from that gallon. The supply curve measures the marginal cost of any gallon. So the difference between the demand curve and the supply curve equals society's surplus of marginal benefit over marginal cost for each gallon of syrup. The total surplus is the sum of the surpluses of all gallons produced, 12 million gallons in Figure 6.7(a).

Figure 6.7 Comparing the Total Surplus to Society in a Competitive Market and a Monopoly Market

(a) **Total Surplus in a Competitive Market**
The equilibrium quantity is 12 million gallons, and the equilibrium price is $30 per gallon. Society's total surplus of benefit over cost is equal to the area between the demand and supply curves (the area of the green triangle). This is the maximum possible amount of surplus.

(b) **Total Surplus in a Monopoly Market**
The managers of the monopoly maximize profit by producing the quantity that sets *MR* equal to *MC*, 8 million gallons, and setting a price of $40 per gallon. With this price and quantity, society's total surplus equals the area of the green trapezoid. This surplus is less than that shown in Figure 6.7(a) for a competitive market because of the deadweight loss, which is equal to the area of the red triangle.

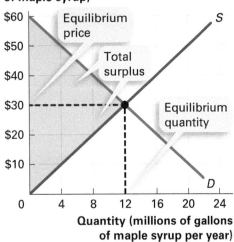

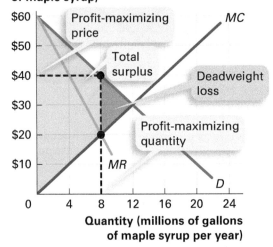

facilities. Figure 6.7(b) shows this situation in the monopoly market. The market demand curve (*D*) is the monopoly firm's demand curve. Associated with this demand curve is the monopoly's marginal revenue curve (*MR*). This marginal revenue curve was present when the market was competitive, but because it was irrelevant, it was omitted from Figure 6.7(a). Now, however, the *MR* curve matters. Because the monopolist's managers equate marginal revenue and marginal cost to determine the profit-maximizing output, you also need the marginal cost curve. As you learned in Chapter 5, the competitive supply curve is the sum of the individual competitive firms' supply curves, and each individual firm's supply curve is that firm's marginal cost curve. Once these firms are brought under single ownership as a monopoly, the sum of the individual firms' marginal cost curves becomes the monopoly's marginal cost curve, *MC* in Figure 6.7(b). The monopoly's managers now use marginal analysis to maximize their profit by producing 8 million gallons and setting a price of $40 per gallon.

You can see that, when compared to a perfectly competitive market, the monopoly sets a higher price—$40 per gallon versus $30—and produces a smaller quantity—8 million gallons versus 12 million. The higher price means that the firm's owners are better off at the expense of the consumers. Economists have traditionally had little to say about such reallocations between groups because both producers and consumers are members of society and everyone counts. Rather, economists' main objection to monopoly stems from the resulting misallocation of resources, which can be seen by considering the total surplus to society. In Figure 6.7(b), all of the 8 million gallons of syrup the monopoly produces have a surplus to society because their marginal benefit exceeds their marginal cost. The total surplus for these 8 million gallons is the sum of all the individual surpluses, which equals the area of the green trapezoid in Figure 6.7(b).

Comparing the green triangle in Figure 6.7(a) to the green trapezoid in Figure 6.7(b), you can see that society's total surplus is less with the monopoly. The difference in total surplus to society is the deadweight loss. The **deadweight loss** is society's loss of total surplus from producing less than or more than the efficient quantity, 12 million gallons. In Figure 6.7(b), where the monopoly produces less than the efficient quantity, the deadweight loss from the monopoly is equal to the area of the red triangle, $40 million per year. The deadweight loss is the fundamental economic social harm created by monopoly. The damage a monopoly causes is the production of too little output and the decrease in the number of employees and other resources involved in producing the product. Neither the economic profit nor the high monopoly price is the social problem. Instead, these are symptoms of the real problem, which from the *social* perspective is the misallocation of resources and the resulting deadweight loss. The deadweight loss from monopoly is the basis for the nation's antitrust laws, but aside from this rationale, it has no direct relevance to managers.

Deadweight loss The loss in total surplus from producing less than or more than the efficient quantity.

Comparing a Perfectly Competitive Firm and a Monopoly Firm

You know that managers of both perfectly competitive firms and monopoly firms follow the same profit-maximization rule: Produce the quantity that sets marginal revenue equal to marginal cost ($MR = MC$), and charge the highest price possible that still allows the firm to sell the quantity produced. This similarity, however, masks the differences between monopolies and perfectly competitive firms summarized in Table 6.2.

Barriers to entry are significant to a firm and its managers because they enable a monopoly to make a long-run economic profit. Let's turn to a more detailed examination of this important concept.

Barriers to Entry

As you learned in Chapter 5, a *barrier to entry* is any factor that makes it difficult for new firms to enter a market. Examples include legal barriers (such as patents, trade secrets, copyrights, and trademarks), control of an essential raw material, the existence of overwhelming economies of scale, government control of entry, sunk costs, and—possibly—advertising.

Table 6.2 Comparing a Perfectly Competitive Firm to a Monopoly

	Perfectly Competitive Firm	**Monopoly**
Amount of markup?	Zero; the price equals marginal cost	Positive; the amount of the markup of the price over marginal cost depends on the price elasticity of demand
Can make a short-run economic profit?	Yes	Yes
Can make a long-run economic profit?	No	Yes; some type of barrier to entry protects the economic profit from entry by new firms
Always produces at the minimum average total cost in the long run?	Yes	No; the firm might produce at the minimum average total cost but does not necessarily do so

Patents, Trade Secrets, Copyrights, and Trademarks

Chapter 15 presents a more complete discussion of patents, trade secrets, copyrights, and trademarks. This chapter focuses on how they serve as legal barriers to entry, how they provide their owners some legal protection from infringement, and the different types of products they protect.

- **Patents.** Patents protect products or specific production processes by giving the owner the exclusive right to produce a certain commodity or to use a specific production process for a 20-year period that begins at the time the patent application is filed. Granting a patent ensures that no competitor can legally copy the inventor's creation during the life of the patent. Although it affords legal protection against blatant copying, a patent does not provide absolute protection. The market power from a patent is limited because patents are often narrowly defined, which may allow other firms to approximate closely the process or product without infringing. For example, Merck patented the first statin (a cholesterol-lowering drug), Mevacor, and began marketing it in the United States in 1987. Ultimately, however, other companies began selling six other, closely related statins. After Mevacor enjoyed a U.S. market share of 100 percent for the first three years, other companies started selling their statins, and its market share fell to less than 15 percent within seven years.
- **Trade secrets.** The fact that patents are often narrowly defined may leave managers concerned that a patent on a product or production process will not prevent competitors from selling or using a closely related product. For this reason, some managers opt to keep their production process a trade secret. KFC's "secret recipe of eleven herbs and spices" is a trade secret. Less tasty examples include Google's search algorithms and the ingredients of the WD-40 Company's namesake product, WD-40.
- **Copyrights.** Copyright law gives legal protection to works of authorship, such as movies, songs, and books. This book is copyrighted, as is the film *Avatar*, which to date has grossed $2.7 billion. The length of copyright protection varies. For works produced after January 1, 1978, the copyright protection lasts for the life of the creator plus an additional 70 years, but the copyright for a work-for-hire (such as a pamphlet) is typically 95 years from the first publication.
- **Trademarks.** Trademarks protect brand names, symbols, or designs that identify the source of the product. For example, The Walt Disney Company has trademarked Mickey Mouse, and Nike, Inc., has trademarked its "Swoosh" logo. No one else can use Mickey Mouse or the "Swoosh" design without permission from Disney or Nike, respectively. In the United States, trademark owners are protected for 10 years, but they can renew their trademarks indefinitely.

The economic value of patent, trade secret, copyright, or trademark protection depends on the value of the protected item in the marketplace. For example, a patent on a solar-powered mousetrap would not be worth much because few people want to buy them. Similarly, copyright protection on a film about famous economists that no one wants to see is worthless. In contrast, a patent on a cure for cancer would be worth a fortune. Patents, trade secrets, copyrights, and trademarks offer legal protection to a monopoly and protect its economic profit by preventing the entry of copycat producers into the market.

Control of an Essential Raw Material

It should be obvious that if one firm controls the supply of an essential input, other firms will be unable to compete. The classic example of this situation is the alleged control of bauxite reserves in the 1930s and 1940s by the Aluminum Company of America (Alcoa). Through purchases and long-term contracts, Alcoa was purported to have preempted control of the available supplies of bauxite ore, the ore used to produce aluminum. Through that control, Alcoa allegedly prevented the entry of other firms into the U.S. aluminum market. More recently, in 1987, De Beers had approximately a 90 percent share of the gem diamond market because it controlled virtually all of the world's raw gem diamonds.

In some cases, it may be possible to restrict the *availability* of the raw material. For example, New York's ban on hydraulic fracturing (fracking) has limited the supply of natural gas from the Marcellus Shale. Although this ban does not create a monopoly producer of natural gas, it does protect natural gas firms from entry by competitors located in New York.

Ultimately, it is difficult for managers to preserve their grasp on an essential raw material. For example, Alcoa lost its alleged death grip on bauxite after the U.S. government financed a vast expansion of U.S. aluminum capacity during World War II and then sold its interests to competing firms after the war. De Beers also failed to protect its positions and fell prey to competition from new sources of raw diamonds that were not under the firm's control: Today, De Beers' market share is under 40 percent.

Economies of Scale

Sometimes new firms do not enter the industry because they would be at a substantial cost disadvantage to the larger established firm. Natural monopolies, such as water, sewage, electricity, and natural gas utilities, are extreme examples. **Natural monopolies** have massive economies of scale, so that as their production increases, their long-run average cost constantly falls throughout the range of demand. Recall from Chapter 4 that *economies of scale* refers to the region of the long-run average cost curve where the long-run average cost falls as production increases; it is the downward-sloping segment of the curve. A natural monopoly's economies of scale are so extensive that the firm's *minimum efficient scale*—the quantity at which the long-run average cost first reaches its minimum—exceeds the quantity customers demand. Figure 6.8 illustrates this situation. Suppose that a firm like Georgia Power, an electric utility operating out of Atlanta, reaches its minimum efficient scale of 60 billion kilowatt hours per year at a cost of 6¢, while at the price of 6¢, customers demand only 47 billion kilowatt hours per year.

The interaction between the demand for the product and the technological conditions that require large scale for efficient, low-cost production limits the number of firms in the market. For example, Figure 6.8 shows that this electric utility company's managers maximize profit by producing 20 billion kilowatt hours per year—the quantity that sets the marginal revenue (*MR*) equal to the long-run marginal cost (*LMC*)—and setting a price of 14¢ per kilowatt hour—the highest price consumers will pay for 20 billion kilowatt hours per year. The firm's average cost of producing 20 billion kilowatts is 10¢ per kilowatt hour. If another firm enters the market, it will be unable to immediately attain the economies of scale that this firm enjoys. Suppose that the new firm has the same long-run average cost as this one but produces only one-half of the output, or 10 billion kilowatt hours. Even though the new firm's scale of production is remarkably large, the

Natural monopoly A firm with economies of scale so large that as its production increases, its long-run average cost constantly falls throughout the range of demand.

Figure 6.8 A Natural Monopoly

This electric utility company has such extensive economies of scale that its minimum efficient scale of 60 billion kilowatt hours, with a long-run average cost of 6¢, exceeds the quantity demanded of 47 billion kilowatt hours at a price of 6¢.

To maximize profit, managers produce 20 billion kilowatt hours because that is the quantity at which the marginal revenue equals the long-run marginal cost. The profit-maximizing price is 14¢ per kilowatt hour and its average cost is 10¢ per kilowatt hour. If another firm entered the market, the new firm's scale of production would be less than 20 billion kilowatt hours. The smaller scale of production places the new firm at a severe competitive disadvantage because its average cost would be much higher than this firm's average cost.

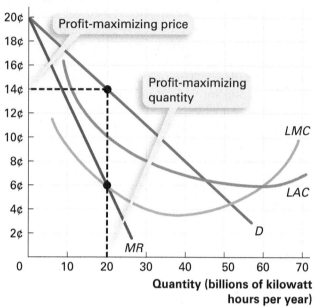

new entrant still has higher costs. The new firm's lowest possible average cost of producing 10 billion kilowatt hours is 15¢ per kilowatt hour, much higher than the existing firm's average cost of 10¢ per kilowatt hour. Indeed, the 15¢-per-kilowatt-hour *cost* is above the existing firm's monopoly *price* of 14¢ per kilowatt hour. If the new firm tried to match this price, it would incur a significant economic loss. The prospect of such an economic loss will deter many—likely all—other firms from entering the market. The profound economies of scale operate as a barrier to entry and create a natural monopoly.

As Figure 6.8 shows, because the minimum efficient scale is larger than the quantity demanded, the long-run average cost curve (*LAC*) continues to decrease even after it crosses the demand curve (*D*). This result poses a problem for society because it means that one firm can produce the quantity demanded in the market at a lower total cost than could two or more firms. For example, with one firm in the market, the electric utility can produce 20 billion kilowatt hours at an average cost of 10¢ per kilowatt hour, for a total cost of 10¢ × 20 billion or $2.0 billion. If two equal-sized firms produced the 20 billion kilowatt hours, each would produce 10 billion kilowatt hours at an average cost of 15¢ per kilowatt hour. Each firm's total cost would be 15¢ × 10 billion = $1.5 billion. The total cost of producing 20 billion kilowatt hours in a market with two firms is $3.0 billion ($1.5 billion + $1.5 billion), higher than the total cost of the single firm. Why is the total cost lower with only one firm? With only one firm distributing electricity in a city, only one set of poles and wires must be erected, but if two (or more) companies distribute power, two (or more) sets of poles and wires are necessary which drastically increases the total cost of distributing power.

The lower total cost with one firm makes it socially desirable to have a single firm supply the entire market. As a monopoly, however, the firm produces less than a competitive market would, thereby creating a deadweight loss. Because of this social tension—lower costs versus deadweight loss—state governments generally regulate natural monopolies. While all firms face some government regulation, the magnitude of the regulation imposed on natural monopolies, such as utilities, is considerably higher. In particular, the regulators (state public utility commissions) effectively determine what price the firm can charge and require production of the quantity consumers demand. In exchange, the government grants the firm a legal franchise that prevents other firms from entering the market. The regulatory goal is to preserve the social benefits of the lower costs while avoiding the social drawback of the deadweight loss. The type of regulation used and the question of whether the regulators achieve their admirable goals are best described in courses dealing exclusively with government regulation of business.

The overwhelming economies of scale relative to demand enjoyed by a natural monopoly make for a highly effective barrier to entry. To serve as a barrier to entry, however, economies of scale do not need to be so extreme. The presence of economies of scale that are merely substantial also creates an entry barrier. In Figure 6.9, the managers of a monopoly producer of eyeglasses maximize profit by producing 300 million pairs of eyeglasses per year and setting a price of $250 per pair. The firm makes an economic profit because the price ($250) exceeds the long-run average cost ($150). If another firm enters the market and immediately also produces 300 million pairs of eyeglasses, the total quantity produced by the two firms is 600 million. The demand curve shows that in this case the price falls to $100 per pair. Both firms would incur an economic loss. More generally, an entrant that produces a substantial quantity in order to gain economies of scale so it can successfully compete causes a large decrease in price and creates the possibility of an economic loss. The risk of an economic loss deters entry into the market even though the firm already in the market is making an economic profit. On the other hand, an entrant that produces only a small quantity does not lower the price significantly but has

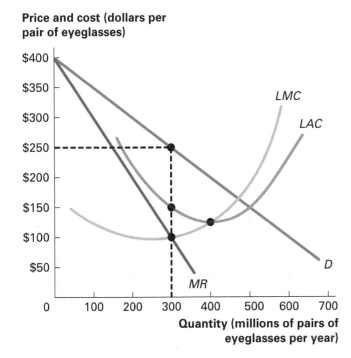

Price and cost (dollars per pair of eyeglasses)

Quantity (millions of pairs of eyeglasses per year)

Figure 6.9 Economies of Scale as a Barrier to Entry

The firm maximizes its profit by producing 300 million pairs of eyeglasses per year and setting a price of $250 per pair. If a new firm enters the market and, in order to gain economies of scale, also produces 300 million pairs, the total market quantity becomes 600 million pairs. The demand curve shows that at this quantity the price falls to $100 per pair so that both firms incur economic losses.

higher costs because it does not gain any economies of scale. So the new entrant (again) faces the possibility of an economic loss. Once again, the risk of an economic loss may be enough to prevent entry.

Government Control of Entry

The government controls market entry in a variety of industries. The agency that exercises jurisdiction can confer market power on a firm, at least locally, simply by restricting or prohibiting the entry of competing firms, as in the electric utility example. Industries in which the government regulates entry include banking, television and radio broadcasting, and hospitals. In other markets, such as that for sugar, government tariff and quota restrictions mean that firms need government approval to import sugar. None of these markets is strictly a monopoly because the firms in them face at least some competition, but the government limitations often create substantial barriers to entry.

In other circumstances, government regulations do not prohibit entry but instead impose requirements that must be met before entry is allowed. Certification and licensing are examples. At the individual level, physicians, nurses, and lawyers must pass qualifying exams before they are allowed to practice. So, too, must hair stylists, interior designers, and greenhouse managers. Many people will agree that requiring physicians, nurses, and lawyers to pass qualifying exams is reasonable but will doubt the validity of the similar requirements imposed on people who cut hair, design home interiors, and oversee plant greenhouses. Clearly, these professions are not monopolies, but the licensing requirements serve as barriers to entry and boost the salaries earned by those in these professions.

Sunk Costs

Over the years, the economics literature has pointed to the existence of substantial sunk costs from entering a market as a barrier to entry. As you learned in Chapter 1, sunk costs are costs that cannot be recovered because they were paid or incurred in the past. Many of the costs necessary to enter a market become sunk because they cannot be recouped upon exit. For example, when the managers at Alamo Drafthouse Cinema open a new theater, they must purchase specialized digital projectors. Say that these cost $100,000 per screen, so opening an 8-plex theater requires spending $800,000 on projectors. In addition, the owners must spend a sizable amount on advertising to alert potential customers to the theater's opening. If the theater fails, the resale price of the projectors is substantially less than $800,000, and all of the funds spent on advertising are irretrievable. Because sunk costs are lost if the entering firm later exits the industry, the presence of large sunk costs increases the financial risk of entering the market, thereby creating a barrier to entry. Clearly, the greater the sunk costs of entry, the higher the barrier to entry.

Advertising

As noted above, advertising can increase the sunk cost of entering a market, but economists have debated its other effects on market entry. On the one hand, advertising by the incumbent producers can create brand loyalty that new entrants must overcome. On the other hand, advertising by the new entrant can make consumers aware of the new product's attributes and price, facilitating profitable entry into the market. So, in addition to creating a sunk cost, advertising can both discourage and encourage market entry. Because its net effect varies from one industry to another, the status of advertising as a barrier to entry is unclear.

6.3 Dominant Firm   **247**

Merck's Profit-Maximizing Price, Quantity, and Economic Profit

SOLVED
PROBLEM

The following figure shows hypothetical demand, marginal revenue, marginal cost, and average total cost curves for Januvia, a patented medicine made by Merck & Company to help treat diabetes. Januvia has a very large market share in its market (that for DPP-4 inhibitors) because of its safety profile, so for simplicity we assume it is a monopoly. Use the figure to answer the following questions.

a. What is the profit-maximizing quantity and price? What is the average total cost of the profit-maximizing quantity?

b. Is Merck & Company making an economic profit or incurring an economic loss? How much is the economic profit or loss?

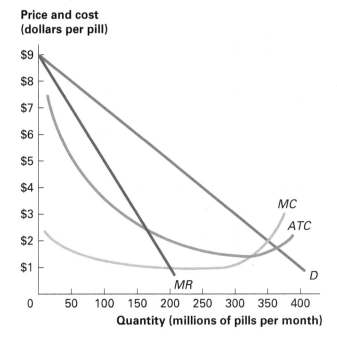

Answer

a. The profit-maximizing quantity is the quantity that sets $MR = MC$, which is 200 million pills per month. The profit-maximizing price is the highest price the managers can set and sell 200 million pills, which from the demand curve in the figure is $5 per pill. The average total cost at the quantity of 200 million is $2 per pill.

b. Merck & Company is making an economic profit because $P > ATC$. The economic profit equals $(P - ATC) \times Q$, or ($5 - $2) \times 200$ million $= 600 million.

6.3 Dominant Firm

Learning Objective 6.3 Describe how managers of a dominant firm determine the quantity and price that maximize profit.

Outside the economics classroom, a single-firm monopoly is a relatively rare sight. There are, however, many markets containing multiple firms in which one firm is substantially larger than the others. Take the corn chip market. Frito-Lay, a division of PepsiCo, controls about 76 percent of the corn chip market in the United States. General Mills is the next largest company. It produces Bugles, which has about a 12 percent market share. The market also includes a number of small, regional producers, each with market shares smaller than 3 percent. In this market structure, Frito-Lay is considered a dominant firm, and the other producers are the competitive fringe. A **dominant firm**, the one large firm in a market that includes many other, smaller competing firms, has the lion's share of the market. The **competitive fringe** is a collective term for the many smaller firms in the market competing with the one large, dominant firm.

Dominant firm The one large firm in a market that includes many other, smaller competing firms.

Competitive fringe The many smaller firms in a market that includes a dominant firm.

The dominant firm model assumes that the dominant firm acts as a monopoly, using its demand curve to maximize its profit, while the firms in the competitive fringe act as perfectly competitive firms, maximizing their profit by taking the market price—the dominant firm's price—as given.

Dominant Firm's Profit Maximization

Figure 6.10 is a hypothetical depiction of the corn chip market. Start by supposing that Frito-Lay has a monopoly in this market. Using the profit-maximization rule, Frito-Lay's managers produce 140,000 tons of corn chips and set a price of $2.05 per pound.

In reality, Frito-Lay is a dominant firm rather than a monopoly, so its managers face the challenge of taking the collective supply response of the competitive fringe into account when making their production and pricing decisions.

Figure 6.10 A Monopoly and the Market Demand Curve

The graph shows the hypothetical market demand curve (*D*), the marginal revenue curve (*MR*), and marginal cost curve (*MC*) for Frito-Lay. If Frito-Lay was a monopoly, its managers would maximize profit by producing 140,000 tons of corn chips and setting a price of $2.05 per pound.

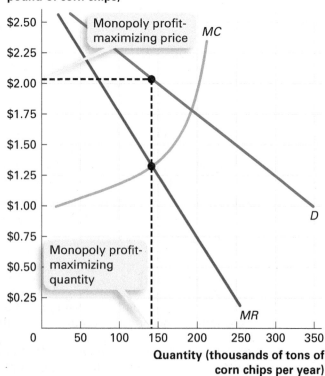

Residual Demand

In the more realistic case of Frito-Lay as a dominant firm, the competitive fringe affects the demand for Frito-Lay's corn chips. Figure 6.11 is a hypothetical depiction of this effect. The graph shows the market demand curve (D) and the supply curve of the competitive fringe (S_{CF}). The demand that Frito-Lay faces does not equal the market demand. Instead, it is the market demand minus the quantity supplied by the competitive fringe, referred to as the **residual demand**. In Figure 6.11, the residual demand is RD. To see how the residual demand is constructed, take the price of $2.00 per pound. At this price, the market demand curve (D) shows that the total quantity demanded is 150,000 tons of chips, and the competitive fringe supply curve (S_{CF}) shows that the fringe firms produce 100,000 tons. Frito-Lay's residual demand is the quantity left over for consumers to demand from Frito-Lay and equals 150,000 − 100,000, or 50,000 tons. Consequently, at a price of $2.00 per pound, Frito-Lay's residual demand is 50,000 tons. The rest of the residual demand is determined similarly. Therefore, the dominant firm's demand curve (D) has two parts: It is the residual demand curve (RD) until it reaches the price at which it intersects the market demand curve (D). After it reaches this point, the dominant firm's demand curve is identical to the market demand curve because after this point the competitive fringe's supply curve shows that its production is zero. Figure 6.12 illustrates the residual demand curve more clearly (without the irrelevant upper part of the market demand curve).

> **Residual demand** The market demand minus the quantity produced by the competitive fringe.

The marginal revenue curve for the dominant firm also has two separate parts. The top part is the marginal revenue curve that corresponds to the residual demand curve—the light green line labeled RMR in Figure 6.12. At the quantity where the

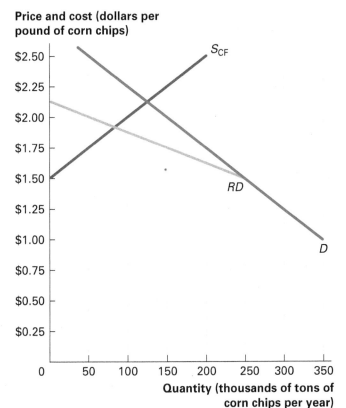

Price and cost (dollars per pound of corn chips)

Quantity (thousands of tons of corn chips per year)

Figure 6.11 Residual Demand Curve

The graph shows the hypothetical market demand curve (D) for corn chips. The dominant firm, Frito-Lay, faces the residual demand curve, which is the market demand minus the quantity supplied by the small, competitive fringe firms. For example, at the price of $1.75 per pound of corn chips, the supply curve of the competitive fringe (S_{CF}) shows that these firms produce 50,000 tons of chips. At this price, the total quantity demanded is 200,000 tons of chips, so Frito-Lay's residual demand is 200,000 minus 50,000, or 150,000 tons of chips. The remainder of Frito-Lay's residual demand is derived similarly. Frito-Lay's demand curve is the light blue residual demand curve (RD) until it intersects the market demand curve (D), after which Frito-Lay's demand curve becomes the same as the dark blue market demand curve.

Figure 6.12 A Dominant Firm's Profit Maximization

The dominant firm faces the light blue residual demand curve, *RD*, until it intersects the market demand curve at 250,000 tons of chips, after which its demand curve becomes the dark blue market demand curve, *D*. The marginal revenue curve for the residual demand curve is the light green residual marginal revenue curve, *RMR*, until the quantity at which the residual demand curve merges with the market demand curve, 250,000 tons of chips. After that, the marginal revenue curve drops down and becomes the dark green market marginal revenue curve, *MR*. The dominant firm produces the quantity that sets its marginal cost equal to its residual marginal revenue, *MC* = *RMR*, and sets the price using the residual demand curve. In the figure, the dominant firm produces 150,000 tons of corn chips and sets a price of $1.75 per pound. The competitive fringe supply curve, S_{CF}, shows that at this price the fringe firms produce 50,000 tons of corn chips.

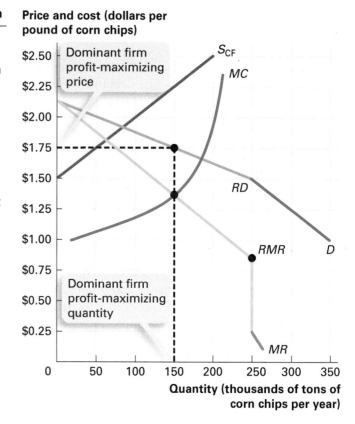

residual demand curve merges into the market demand curve, 250,000 tons, the dominant firm's marginal revenue curve drops downward and becomes the same as the market marginal revenue curve, the dark green line labeled *MR*.

To maximize profit, Frito-Lay's managers use the residual demand curve (*RD*) and residual marginal revenue curve (*RMR*) because they represent the demand and the marginal revenue for their chips, respectively. Frito-Lay produces the quantity that sets its residual marginal revenue equal to its marginal cost (*RMR* = *MC*), so Frito-Lay produces 150,000 tons of corn chips. The managers set the price using the residual demand, resulting in a price of $1.75 per pound. The competitive fringe firms are price takers, so they take the price of $1.75 as given and as their supply curve shows, produce a total of 50,000 tons of corn chips at this price. The total quantity of chips produced in the market is 200,000 tons—150,000 tons by the dominant firm and 50,000 tons by the competitive fringe firms. The price is $1.75 per pound. This price and *total* quantity reflect a point on the market demand curve (*D*) shown in Figure 6.11.

Effect on the Dominant Firm of the Competitive Fringe

You can see the effect of competition on the choices the dominant firm's managers make. Faced with competition from the fringe firms, the managers increase production from their monopoly amount of 140,000 tons of chips to 150,000 tons and lower the price from the monopoly price of $2.05 per pound to $1.75 per pound. You can understand why the managers lower the price by using the markup equation, Equation 6.5:

$$\frac{P}{MC} = \left(\frac{\varepsilon}{\varepsilon - 1}\right)$$

The markup depends on the price elasticity of demand (ε): The larger the price elasticity of demand, the smaller the markup. At any quantity, the price elasticity of demand is larger on the residual demand curve than on the market demand curve. Why? Because a given change in the price leads to a larger change in the quantity demanded along the residual demand curve than along the market demand curve. Suppose that the price falls. Then the quantity demanded along the market demand curve increases. The quantity demanded along the residual demand curve also increases, but for *two* reasons: (1) The quantity demanded in the market as a whole increases (the same effect just noted), and (2) the fringe firms decrease the amount they sell. Because the change in the quantity demanded is larger along the residual demand curve than the market demand curve, the elasticity of demand for Frito-Lay's chips is larger when it faces competition. Consequently, the presence of the competitive fringe decreases Frito-Lay's price markup. This result is analogous to that illustrated in Figure 6.4, in which a monopoly's markup falls as the price elasticity of demand for its product increases.

A dominant firm's profit is less with the presence of the competitive fringe than if it were a monopoly. As illustrated in Figure 6.12, even with an increase in production (which conceivably could increase profit), the price falls substantially (which substantially *decreases* the firm's profit). From the perspective of Frito-Lay's managers, the presence of the other firms decreases Frito-Lay's profit. Indeed, the larger the number of other firms, the greater the supply of the fringe firms, and the larger the decrease in Frito-Lay's profit. The managerial lesson is easy to state but difficult to accomplish: Managers of dominant firms must strive to decrease the number of competitive fringe firms.

How a Technology Firm Responds to Changes in the Competitive Fringe

Data centers and local area networks use Ethernet switches to join computers together. Suppose that you are a manager at a firm like Cisco Systems, and yours is the dominant firm in this market. Your market share exceeds 60 percent. Suppose also that the next largest market shares are much smaller: Hewlett-Packard has 9 percent, Alcatel-Lucent has 3 percent, Dell has 2 percent, and a number of still smaller firms share the remaining 26 percent. Several of the competitive fringe firms close. How should you adjust your firm's quantity and price in response to their exit from the market?

Answer
When several fringe firms exit, the supply of the competitive fringe decreases, so your residual demand and marginal revenue increase. You should respond to the increase in demand and marginal revenue by raising the quantity and price of your Ethernet switches, increasing your firm's economic profit.

SOLVED PROBLEM

The Demand for Shoes at a Dominant Firm

The following table shows the hypothetical demand and competitive fringe supply for the market for athletic shoes. Your firm has a market share of approximately 45 percent and dominates this market. The next largest firm has a market share of less than 10 percent. The table shows the market demand and competitive supply at different prices. Use the table to solve the following problems.

a. Complete the table by calculating the residual demand at each price.

b. Use the formula from Chapter 3 for the price elasticity of demand, $\varepsilon = |b \times (P/Q^d)|$, where b is the change in the quantity from a $1 change in price (calculated for any two points on the demand curve as the change in quantity divided by the change in price), to calculate the price elasticity of demand on the market demand curve and on the residual demand curve at prices of $90, $85, $80, and $75 per pair of shoes. How do the price elasticities of demand on the two demand curves compare?

Price (dollars per pair of shoes)	Market Demand (millions of shoes)	Competitive Supply (millions of shoes)	Residual Demand (millions of shoes)
$90	100	40	
85	120	30	
80	140	20	
75	160	10	
70	180	0	
65	200	0	

Answer

a. The residual demand equals the market demand minus the competitive supply, so at the price of $90, the residual demand equals 100 million shoes − 40 million shoes = 60 million shoes. Moving down the column, in millions of shoes, the rest of the residual demands are 90, 120, 150, 180, and 200.

b. On the market demand curve, $b = 4,000,000$, and on the residual demand curve, $b = 6,000,000$. At the price of $90 on the market demand curve, the price elasticity of demand is 3.6, and on the residual demand curve, the price elasticity of demand is 9.0; at the price of $85, they are 2.8 and 5.7; at the price of $80, they are 2.3 and 4.0; and at the price of $75, they are 1.9 and 3.0. At each price, the price elasticity of demand is larger on the residual demand curve than on the market demand curve.

6.4 Monopolistic Competition

Learning Objective 6.4 Explain how managers of a monopolistically competitive firm determine the quantity and price that maximize profit.

To this point in the chapter, you have learned about firms that are either alone in the market or large relative to the competition. Not all firms with market power are alone or dominant, however. For example, Apple has some control over the price it sets for its iPhone, but it faces numerous similar-sized competitors, including Samsung, Google, LG, Microsoft, Huawei, Xiaomi, and HTC. Although Apple has a large market share—about 15 percent worldwide—effectively it is only one firm among many selling smartphones. The smartphone market is a monopolistically competitive market, and Apple is a monopolistically competitive firm. Let's begin our study of monopolistic competition by discussing the characteristics that define this market structure and the firms that compete within it.

Defining Characteristics of Monopolistic Competition

As its name implies, monopolistic competition combines elements of perfect competition and monopoly. **Monopolistic competition** is a market with many firms, with no barriers to entry, and in which each firm produces a differentiated product. Let's begin with the two characteristics that monopolistic competition shares with perfect competition and conclude with the one it shares with monopoly:

> **Monopolistic competition** A market with many firms, with no barriers to entry, and in which each firm produces a differentiated product.

1. **Many sellers.** Both monopolistically competitive markets and perfectly competitive markets include many firms, which limits each firm's market power over its price. Unlike the situation in a perfectly competitive market, however, a monopolistically competitive firm's market power is not totally eliminated (see item 3).
2. **No barriers to entry.** Both perfectly competitive and monopolistically competitive markets have many firms for the same reason: There are no barriers to entry. This characteristic is a key difference between monopolistically competitive firms and monopolies.
3. **Differentiated products.** Each product produced by a monopolistically competitive firm is slightly different from the ones produced by other firms. Smartphones are an example of a differentiated product. All of the producers listed above produce smartphones, but each smartphone is different—differentiated—from the others. Although Apple's smartphone is a substitute for those produced by its competitors, it is not a perfect substitute, which gives Apple some market power to set its price.

Short-Run Profit Maximization for a Monopolistically Competitive Firm

Assume that the managers of a monopolistically competitive firm want to maximize profit. Like the managers of the other types of firms presented, these managers can use marginal analysis and the profit-maximization rule to achieve their goal. They need to determine their firm's marginal revenue and combine it with their marginal cost to determine the profit-maximizing quantity.

Demand, Marginal Revenue, and Marginal Cost for a Monopolistically Competitive Firm

What does a monopolistically competitive firm's demand curve look like? Consider Apple and the iPhone. Because Apple's smartphone differs from those of its competitors, if Apple raises its price, some consumers will still buy it because they prefer the iPhone. Likewise, if Apple lowers its price, not all consumers will switch to an Apple smartphone because some still prefer their Android phones. So the demand curve for an Apple smartphone is downward sloping, illustrated in Figure 6.13 by hypothetical demand curve D. As you saw with the downward-sloping

Figure 6.13 Demand, Marginal Revenue, and Marginal Cost Curves for a Monopolistically Competitive Firm

The downward-sloping demand curve (*D*) for a monopolistically competitive firm makes the marginal revenue curve (*MR*) lie below the demand curve. The marginal cost curve (*MC*) is the same as the marginal cost curves for monopolies and perfectly competitive firms.

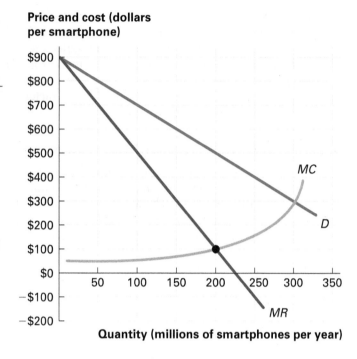

monopoly and dominant firm demand curves, the downward-sloping monopolistically competitive firm's demand curve makes its marginal revenue curve (*MR*) lie beneath the demand curve so that $P > MR$. The marginal cost curve (*MC*) shown in Figure 6.13 is the same as the marginal cost curves used for monopolies and perfectly competitive firms.

Figure 6.13 looks very similar to Figure 6.3, which shows the same curves for a monopoly. This similarity, however, conceals a key difference: Figure 6.3 shows demand and marginal revenue curves for the *market*, while Figure 6.13 shows the demand and marginal revenue curves for the firm's *specific product*.

Short-Run Profit Maximization for a Monopolistically Competitive Firm: Marginal Analysis

The managers at a monopolistically competitive firm like Apple face the same profit-maximization problem as the managers at a monopoly or dominant firm: They must produce the quantity for which marginal revenue equals marginal cost and use the demand to set their price. Figure 6.14 shows that short-run profit maximization is the same for a monopolistically competitive firm as for a monopoly or dominant firm. The figure shows that managers produce 200 million smartphones per year, the quantity that sets the firm's marginal revenue equal to its marginal cost, $MR = MC$, or, equivalently, $MR - MC = 0$. All of the phones up to 200 million are profitable because for each of them $MR > MC$. None of the phones beyond 200 million is profitable because for each of them $MR < MC$. The firm then uses the demand for its smartphones to set the highest price that consumers will pay for the 200 million smartphones produced, $500.

As Figure 6.14 shows, the firm is making an economic profit because its price exceeds its average total cost ($P > ATC$). The amount of the economic profit equals the area of the green rectangle, ($500 per phone − $300 per phone) × 200 million phones, or $40 billion. But can the firm's economic profit last? Answering that important question is the topic of the next section.

Price and cost (dollars per smartphone)

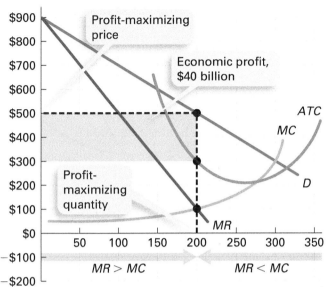

The managers maximize profit by producing 200 million smartphones, the quantity that sets $MR = MC$. The price of $500 is set using the demand: It is the highest price that consumers will pay for the 200 million smartphones produced. The firm is making an economic profit because its price exceeds its average total cost. The amount of the economic profit equals the area of the green rectangle, $40 billion.

Long-Run Equilibrium for a Monopolistically Competitive Firm

To this point, the analysis of a monopolistically competitive firm has been identical to that of a monopoly. There is a key difference, however: A barrier to entry does not protect the economic profit. Other firms can produce differentiated products similar to those produced by the original firm. Once again, take Apple as an example. After Apple released the first iPhone, many companies started to produce similar smartphones, such as the Samsung Galaxy and HTC One. As new products appear on the market, some consumers prefer them, so the initial firm's demand decreases, and its demand and marginal revenue curves shift leftward. As long as the firms in the market make an economic profit, new firms continue to enter. Entry stops only when the firms are making zero economic profit, so that the owners are making only a competitive return.

Figure 6.15 illustrates the long-run equilibrium for a monopolistically competitive firm. As you can see, its managers maximize profit by producing 100 million smartphones, the quantity for which $MR = MC$. Because of the new competition it faces, the firm no longer makes an economic profit, since the price equals the average total cost, $P = ATC$. In Figure 6.15, the price and average total cost are $400 per smartphone. The long-run, zero economic profit result means that the firm produces where its ATC curve is tangent to (just touches at one point) its demand curve.

This conclusion reinforces what you learned in Chapter 5 about perfectly competitive firms. If a monopolistically competitive firm is making a short-run economic profit, the absence of a barrier to entry leads to increased competition in the long run, which in turn forces the firm to produce at a point where it makes no economic profit. This result clearly highlights the managerial importance of a barrier to entry!

Figure 6.15 Long-Run Equilibrium for a Monopolistically Competitive Firm

The managers maximize profit by producing 100 million smartphones, the quantity that sets $MR = MC$. The price, $400 per smartphone, is determined using the demand curve (D). In the long run, competition from new producers decreases the demand for smartphones sufficiently that the firm no longer makes an economic profit. The price equals the firm's average total cost.

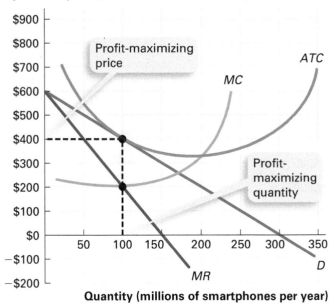

Price and cost (dollars per smartphone)

Quantity (millions of smartphones per year)

SOLVED PROBLEM

J-Phone's Camera Phone

In 2000, the Japanese cell phone company J-Phone introduced the first widely successful cell phone camera. It caught on quickly because it had a new feature not included in any of the competitors' phones: Customers were able to snap pictures and then immediately share them with friends. J-Phone was a monopolistically competitive firm because it competed with several other cell phone producers, each producing their own unique cell phone.

a. As a manager of J-Phone, how would you expect the price of your phone to change over the next five years? How would you expect your sales to change over the same period of time?

b. How do your answers to part a affect your decision about whether to expand your manufacturing facilities?

Answer

a. Because J-Phone competes in a monopolistically competitive market, you must expect that your wildly popular phone will soon face new competition from other cell phone companies, causing the price of a cell phone with a camera to fall. (In fact, prices fell quickly from $500 in 2000 to less than $300 in 2005.) You also must expect that J-Phone's market share will decrease when other companies market their new phones. (Indeed, that is precisely what occurred: J-Phone's market share initially rose from 16.4 percent in 2001 to 18.5 percent in 2003 before falling back to approximately 15.5 percent in 2005.)

b. Your answers to part a must give you pause when it comes to expanding your manufacturing plant. You should worry that once your demand and price fall with the arrival of new competition, you will be stuck with an uneconomically large production facility if you expand.

6.5 The Monopoly, Dominant Firm, and Monopolistic Competition Models

Learning Objective 6.5 Apply what you have learned about monopolies, dominant firms, and monopolistically competitive firms to make better managerial decisions.

The most crucial managerial lesson about monopolies, dominant firms, and monopolistically competitive firms has been presented repeatedly throughout this chapter: Use marginal analysis to determine the profit-maximizing quantity of production. Managers in virtually all types of firms can reach the profit-maximizing quantity by comparing the estimated marginal revenue to the estimated marginal cost and then increasing production if marginal revenue exceeds marginal cost or decreasing production if marginal revenue falls short of marginal cost.

A second, almost equally significant lesson is the importance of barriers to entry, which enable you to maintain your firm's economic profit indefinitely. If your barriers to entry disappear, so, too, will your economic profit. Successful managers search for ways to strengthen existing barriers or erect new ones, such as lobbying the government to impose regulations or requirements for new suppliers to fulfill.

Using the Models in Managerial Decision Making

As a manager, it is unlikely that you will have a figure showing marginal revenue, marginal cost, and demand. But you still need to make decisions about the quantity to produce and the price to charge. Section 5.4 pointed out that for perfectly competitive firms, the profit-maximization rule, can be restated as "Produce all the units for which $MR - MC > 0$, and stop when you hit the unit with $MR - MC = 0$." This same result applies to firms with market power. In other words, managers of monopolies, dominant firms, and monopolistically competitive firms can all use the profit-maximization rule to determine their profit-maximizing quantity.

Determining the Profit-Maximizing Price

The second part of the profit-maximization rule, "Set the highest price that sells the quantity produced," is immediately applicable if you have an estimate of your demand. You can use your profit-maximizing quantity in your estimated demand function and solve for the price. If you do not have an estimate of demand, you have additional tools at your disposal: the relationships among price, marginal cost, and elasticity of demand shown in Equation 6.4 and 6.5 and summarized in the following box.

You can use estimates of your marginal cost and price elasticity of demand to set the profit-maximizing price or, perhaps more realistically, to set a range of prices for your product. Suppose that you again work for a pharmaceutical firm and your

RELATIONSHIPS AMONG PRICE, MARGINAL COST, AND ELASTICITY OF DEMAND

- *Price and marginal cost:* The profit-maximizing relationship between price and marginal cost is $(P = MC \times \frac{\varepsilon}{\varepsilon - 1})$.
- *Markup equation:* The profit-maximizing markup of price over marginal cost is $\frac{P}{MC} = \frac{\varepsilon}{\varepsilon - 1}$.

company has another, newly developed drug with a marginal cost of $1,000 per dose. As a manager, you believe that the price elasticity of demand for this drug is likely to lie between 1.5 and 1.1. You can use the first equation to set a range for the price you will charge. If the price elasticity of demand is 1.5, the price should be

$$\$1{,}000 \times \left(\frac{1.5}{1.5 - 1}\right) = \$3{,}000$$

If the price elasticity of demand is 1.1, the price should be

$$\$1{,}000 \times \frac{1.1}{1.1 - 1} = \$11{,}000 \qquad \textbf{6.6}$$

In other words, if you are confident that your estimates are correct, your profit-maximizing price will be between $3,000 and $11,000 per dose.

If you have already set a price for the product, you also can determine if you are maximizing your profit. Suppose that after you set a price of $8,000 per dose, you refine your estimate of the price elasticity of demand to 1.1. Equation 6.6 shows that you have not set the profit-maximizing price. In this case, you must think carefully about whether your estimates are correct. If you are confident that the price elasticity of demand is 1.1 and the marginal cost is $1,000 per dose, you know that the price of $8,000 is too low. To maximize profit, you should raise the price to $11,000 per dose.

The second relationship in the box shows how the profit-maximizing markup of price over marginal cost depends on the price elasticity of demand. This equation shows that the smaller the value of ε, the larger the markup. If you know that there are only a few substitutes for your product, you know that its price elasticity of demand is small, which gives you greater ability to mark up your price over the marginal cost. Consequently, managers often focus their marketing efforts on convincing consumers that their firm's product is unique and has no substitutes. If this approach succeeds, the managers can increase the markup and the firm's profit.

Erecting Barriers to Entry

Barriers to entry allow a firm already in the market to protect its economic profit. You must be alert to opportunities to erect such a barrier to protect your firm. Some are outside of a manager's control: You cannot affect the presence of economies of scale or gain immediate control over a vital input. On the other hand, patents, copyrights, and trademarks are relatively easy to obtain and can serve as important barriers to entry.

Lobbying the government to make entry of new firms difficult can also help preserve some of your firm's market power. Although the government is unlikely to create a monopoly, it may require new firms to present some sort of difficult-to-obtain certification or costly permit, which helps create a barrier to entry. For example, when Internet sales of contact lenses first became possible, lobbyists descended on some state regulatory boards, suggesting that online sellers should be required to obtain a state-issued optician's license. Requiring these licenses would have served as a barrier to entry but those efforts generally failed. A more recent example involves Uber, an app-based ride-sharing service that competes with taxi companies. Taxi drivers in both the United States and other countries have lobbied local authorities to require Uber to obtain government licenses or certifications for its drivers. These requirements are an attempt to make it difficult for the new competitor, Uber, to enter the market for rides. Indeed, in 2015 and 2016, France jailed and fined Uber's two highest-ranking French executives for violating licensing laws passed in response to successful lobbying by French cab companies!

Keep in mind that as a matter of social policy, economists generally oppose firms' efforts to erect barriers to entry because they can give a firm market power, which leads to a deadweight loss. From your perspective, however, that same barrier to entry also increases your firm's economic profit.

Applying the Monopolistic Competition Model

The most basic lesson from monopolistic competition is familiar: Barriers to entry protect economic profit. The absence of barriers to entry means that in the long run your firm will make only a competitive return. In the smartphone market, Apple's managers tried to erect barriers to entry by applying for patents and then suing HTC, Samsung, and other manufacturers for patent infringement in the United States, the European Union, China, Japan, and many other countries.

Without barriers to entry, managers of monopolistically competitive firms can try to increase the demand for their product and/or increase the difference between their product and those of their competitors. Any increase in demand or differentiation will be temporary, since rivals will soon step in to produce their version of the product, but the firm can temporarily make an economic profit.

Innovation

Managers of monopolistically competitive firms often strive for *innovation*, creation of a novel product that meets consumers' needs. As long as your firm's product stays one step ahead of those of its competitors, you have the opportunity to make an economic profit. Apple's innovative iPad tablet, first sold in 2007, serves as a good example. The initial introduction of the iPad was a huge success. Nothing similar existed in the marketplace, and the demand was strong—Apple sold 300,000 iPads on their first day of availability. Continuing its success, in 2014, Apple sold three recently designed, different full-size iPads. By 2016, the number of different full-size iPads was down to two, and only one (the iPad Pro) had been designed within the previous two years. Apple faced tremendous competition from other companies, each producing its own variation of a tablet. The first generations of the iPad were widely acclaimed as bringing something new, fresh, and exciting to the market. As product innovations became more costly, it became more difficult for Apple to fend off the competition. Samsung, Asus, Lenovo, and others entered the market, making similar tablets. Apple's share of the tablet market fell from approximately 60 percent in early 2012 to 30 percent in early 2014 to 25 percent in early 2016. The demand for Apple's iPads decreased, and Apple's total revenue from these products fell, from approximately $70 billion in 2013 to $46 billion in 2016.

Marketing

The tale of Apple's iPad demonstrates how difficult it is to consistently increase the demand for your products by innovation alone. So managers also extensively market their products to keep the demand for the products robust. For example, Apple's annual Worldwide Developers Conference (WWDC), during which Apple executives highlight new technologies, receives extensive publicity on all Internet technology websites, as do Apple's widely publicized new product introductions. These marketing events increase the demand for Apple's products. During such events, Apple's managers strive to differentiate their products, making the case that they are different from and superior to those of their competitors. (Chapter 13 is devoted to a more detailed examination of marketing and advertising decisions.)

Apple's efforts show that marketing is crucial for any type of firm with market power. Marketing generally has two related objectives: (1) increase the demand for the product; and (2) convince consumers that the product is unique, with no close substitutes, thereby reducing its price elasticity of demand. Successful marketing accomplishes both goals. Increasing the demand and/or decreasing the price elasticity of demand allows the producer to increase the markup and, consequently, increase the profit.

Green marketing is becoming more prevalent (as is the similarly named—but very different—concept of *greenwashing*, falsely claiming green attributes for a product—see Section 13.3). *Green marketing* refers to marketing that emphasizes the positive environmental aspects of a product. Ben & Jerry's, an ice cream, frozen yogurt, and sorbet company that is now a division of Unilever, has consistently marketed itself as following green values. Unilever's executives determined that such advertising boosts the demand for Ben & Jerry's products, particularly among consumers who are concerned about the environment, so Ben & Jerry's advertises the use of non-GMO ingredients (those without genetically modified organisms) and cage-free eggs. Ben & Jerry's, however, also runs marketing campaigns stressing other product attributes, such as its Instagram campaign for its Scotchy Scotch Scotch ice cream and its stop-motion television advertisements for various flavors. Clearly, Ben & Jerry's uses a diverse mixture of themes in its marketing because the firm's managers want to appeal to a wider customer base beyond "green consumers."

Green marketing is similar to other types because its goal is to increase demand and differentiate the product. It differs from other marketing efforts because of the major role played by certification. For example, Ben & Jerry's uses Fairtrade-certified sugar, coffee, bananas, and other inputs. Fairtrade International is an organization that creates fair trade standards, designed to ensure that producers get a "fair" price for their product, and certifies that products used by different companies meet these fair trade standards. Other green certifications are provided by government programs, such as the USDA Organic label for food and Energy Star standards for appliances, as well as by nongovernment organizations, such as the U.S. Green Building Council's LEED (Leadership in Energy & Environmental Design) certification for buildings.

Overexpansion

You learned in Section 5.4 that as a manager of a perfectly competitive firm, you must be careful about increasing your capacity simply because your profit has increased. The same advice holds true for managers of monopolistically competitive firms. If you successfully introduce a new product or create a marketing campaign that yields an economic profit, keep in mind that economic profit in a monopolistically competitive market is not permanent. If you overexpand your production capacity, you might wind up with an economic loss in the long run as the entry of new firms decreases the demand and price for your product. Starbucks initially started growing rapidly in the early 1990s and by 2007 had grown to over 7,000 U.S. stores. It had grown too rapidly, however, and was facing new competition from McDonald's, Dunkin Donuts, and smaller, regional competitors that had all entered the premium coffee market. So in 2008, with its profit falling, Starbucks retrenched and closed over 8 percent of its U.S. stores. The executives at Starbucks, however, did not let this negative experience shape their company's future. Instead, they innovated new ways to sell coffee. In particular, Starbucks partnered with Target and Safeway to open smaller stores within large Target and Safeway locations. These innovative smaller stores have lower costs than stand-alone locations and have allowed Starbucks to resume growing.

Additionally, if you are a supplier of an input to a monopolistically competitive firm with a hot new product, you, too, must be alert to overexpansion. When competitors for your customer arrive on the scene, your customer will decrease production and reduce purchase of inputs. Unless you think you can pick up business by providing your input to the new rivals, hesitate before increasing the scale of your operation.

Revisiting Premature Rejoicing by the Managers at KV Pharmaceutical

Recall that the managers at KV Pharmaceutical celebrated after the FDA gave them a seven-year period of marketing exclusivity for the drug 17P because they thought it made them a monopoly for the next seven years. They knew that the price elasticity of demand for Makena, their name for 17P, was small because of the absence of substitutes. Suppose that the managers believed that the price elasticity of demand was 1.01 and the marginal cost was $15 per dose (the same as the competitive price). Using the equation $P = MC \times \left(\frac{\varepsilon}{\varepsilon - 1}\right)$, the profit-maximizing price would be $15 \times \left(\frac{1.01}{1.01 - 1}\right) = \$1,515$. KV Pharmaceutical's actual price was $1,500 per dose, which was approximately 100 times the competitive price.

Unfortunately for the managers, setting such a high price immediately alienated groups that had previously supported their efforts to create a standardized version of 17P. Many believed that the managers' actions were immoral. Within just a few days of KV Pharmaceutical's price announcement, the March of Dimes, which had lobbied the FDA to approve Makena, abandoned its support and called for a lower price. More importantly, the FDA turned against KV Pharmaceutical by announcing that it would not take action against compounding pharmacies that continued to make 17P. The FDA's action—or, perhaps more accurately, *inaction*—changed KV Pharmaceutical from a monopoly to, at best, a dominant firm. As you have learned by reading this chapter, a dominant firm's price is lower than that of a pure monopoly. Within a week after the FDA's response to the pricing announcement, the managers at KV Pharmaceutical lowered the price from $1,500 to $690 per dose.

If you use the equation relating price, marginal cost, and price elasticity of demand, $P = MC \times \left(\frac{\varepsilon}{\varepsilon - 1}\right)$, you will see that KV Pharmaceutical's managers believed that with the competition from compounding pharmacies, the price elasticity of demand had risen to 1.02. Their estimate was, however, surely wrong. The initially high price alienated so many potential demanders who deemed it highly unethical—from the doctors who would prescribe the drug to the insurance companies that would help pay for it—that the demand was lower than they thought it would be and the price elasticity of demand was larger than they expected. Even at $690 per dose, few patients purchased Makena. Within a year and a half of receiving FDA approval to exclusively market the drug, KV Pharmaceutical declared bankruptcy.

The managers at KV Pharmaceutical made an important miscalculation when they set their initial price: When they calculated the profit-maximizing price, they did not consider the furiously negative response to the 100-fold price hike or the FDA's decision to allow compounding pharmacies to produce the drug. Both of these reactions drastically decreased the demand and increased the elasticity of demand for Makena, and they led to a bad outcome for KV Pharmaceutical. The managers should have considered the possibility that demanders and regulators would consider their extremely large price hike both immoral and unjustified and that these views would lead radically decrease the demand for Makena. The managerial lesson from KV Pharmaceutical's experience is clear: When setting a price, managers must determine whether the price will cause other factors to change and thereby affect demand.

Summary: The Bottom Line

6.1 A Monopoly Market

- A monopoly market has three characteristics: a single seller, a product with no close substitutes, and insurmountable barriers to entry.
- A monopoly firm's demand curve is the same as the market demand curve, so it is downward sloping. Due to the downward-sloping demand curve, the marginal revenue curve lies below the demand curve.
- The firm's marginal revenue (MR), price (P), and price elasticity of demand (ε) are related to one another using the equation $MR = P \times \left(1 - \frac{1}{\varepsilon}\right)$.

6.2 Monopoly Profit Maximization

- Monopoly managers maximize profit via the profit-maximization rule: Produce the quantity that sets the marginal revenue equal to the marginal cost, and charge the highest price that sells the quantity produced.
- The profit-maximizing price (P), marginal cost (MC), and price elasticity of demand (ε) are related according to $P = MC \times \left(\frac{\varepsilon}{\varepsilon - 1}\right)$, which can be rearranged to show that the markup of price over marginal cost equals $\frac{P}{MC} = \frac{\varepsilon}{\varepsilon - 1}$.

- A monopoly makes an economic profit if $P > ATC$, makes a competitive return if $P = ATC$, and incurs an economic loss if $P < ATC$.
- Because barriers to entry protect a monopoly by preventing other firms from entering the market, the monopoly can make an economic profit indefinitely. Barriers to entry include legal barriers, control of an essential raw material, large economies of scale, and substantial sunk costs.
- Competitive markets are better for society because monopolized markets create a deadweight loss and give society a smaller total surplus of benefit over cost.

6.3 Dominant Firm

- A dominant firm market has one large firm competing with a number of smaller firms, collectively called the competitive fringe.
- The dominant firm's demand is the residual demand, the market demand minus the quantity produced by the competitive fringe. Managers of dominant firms maximize profit by producing the quantity that sets residual marginal revenue equal to marginal cost and setting the price from the residual demand curve.
- The presence of the competitive fringe decreases the dominant firm's profit.

6.4 Monopolistic Competition

- Monopolistic competition is a market with many firms, with no barriers to entry, and in which each firm produces a differentiated product.
- Monopolistically competitive firms use the same profit-maximization rule as firms in other market structures:

Produce the quantity that sets the marginal revenue equal to the marginal cost, and charge the highest price that sells the quantity produced.

- Because there are no barriers to entry, monopolistically competitive firms making an economic profit in the short run can make only a competitive return in the long run, since new firms enter the market and compete away the short-run economic profit.

6.5 Managerial Application: The Monopoly, Dominant Firm, and Monopolistic Competition Models

- Two results are key for managerial decision making: (1) Regardless of market structure, apply the profit-maximization rule, and (2) the presence of barriers to entry is necessary for your firm to continue to make an economic profit, so you should look for ways to sustain barriers to entry or create new ones.
- You can use the relationship among the profit-maximizing price, marginal cost, and price elasticity of demand, $P = MC \times (\frac{\varepsilon}{\varepsilon - 1})$, along with estimates of the marginal cost and elasticity of demand, to determine your profit-maximizing price.
- As a manager of a monopolistically competitive firm, successful innovation and/or marketing can allow you to make a short-run economic profit. But the economic profit is only temporary, so you must be careful to not overexpand your scale of operations.

Key Terms and Concepts

Competitive fringe	Market power	Monopoly market
Deadweight loss	Markup equation	Natural monopoly
Dominant firm	Monopolistic competition	Residual demand

Questions and Problems

6.1 A Monopoly Market

Learning Objective 6.1 Explain the relationship between a monopoly's demand curve and its marginal revenue curve.

1.1 As a manager, do you want to possess market power? Why or why not?

1.2 "Only one firm produces Kellogg's Corn Flakes, so Kellogg's is a monopolist." Is this assertion correct? Explain your answer.

1.3 What role do barriers to entry play in determining whether or not a firm is a monopoly?

1.4 The table shows part of a monopoly's demand. Complete the table, and then plot the demand curve and marginal revenue curve in a diagram with price on the vertical axis and quantity on the horizontal axis. Assuming that both curves are linear, extend the demand and marginal revenue curves to the vertical axis. What is the vertical intercept of the demand curve? Of the marginal revenue curve? What is the slope of the demand curve? Of the marginal revenue curve?

Accompanies problem 1.4.

Price, P	Quantity, Q	Marginal Revenue, MR
$30	12	
29	13	
28	14	
27	15	
26	16	
25	17	
24	18	
23	19	
22	20	
21	21	
20	22	
19	23	

1.5 For a monopoly, $P > MR$. For a perfectly competitive firm, $P = MR$. What accounts for this difference?

1.6 Use the definition of marginal revenue to explain why marginal revenue is negative over some range of the demand curve for a monopoly.

1.7 You are a manager of a pharmaceutical firm that has a monopoly for a particular drug. Your staff has estimated the price elasticity of demand for the drug. When the price of the drug is $1,000 per dose, the price elasticity of demand is 3.0, and when the price is $400 per dose, the price elasticity of demand is 2.0.
  a. What is the marginal revenue when the price is $1,000 per dose?
  b. What is the marginal revenue when the price is $400 per dose?

6.2 Monopoly Profit Maximization

Learning Objective 6.2 Discuss how managers of a monopoly can determine the quantity and price that maximize profit and how they compare to those of a perfectly competitive firm.

2.1 Why do the managers of a monopoly produce the quantity that sets marginal revenue equal to marginal cost?

2.2 "If a monopolist maximizes its profits, at the profit-maximizing quantity the demand for its product must be elastic." Do you agree with this statement? Why or why not?

2.3 You are managing a pharmaceutical company that makes a patent-protected drug. According to your calculations, at the current level of production the marginal revenue of one unit of the drug is less than the marginal cost of producing

that unit. To maximize your profit, should you increase, decrease, or maintain the current level of production? Explain your answer.

2.4 The first two columns of the table show a monopoly's marginal revenue, and the last two columns show its marginal cost.

Marginal Revenue, MR	Quantity, Q	Marginal Cost, TC	Quantity, Q
$11.00	10	$5.00	10
10.00	11	5.50	11
9.00	12	6.00	12
8.00	13	6.50	13
7.00	14	7.00	14
6.00	15	7.50	15
5.00	16	8.00	16

  a. What is the firm's profit-maximizing quantity?
  b. Assume that the marginal revenue and marginal cost curves are linear. Draw them in a diagram. Draw the firm's demand curve in the diagram. (Hint: Recall that the demand curve and the marginal revenue curve have the same vertical intercept and the slope of the marginal revenue curve is twice that of the demand curve.) What is the firm's profit-maximizing price?

2.5 The figure illustrates the demand for soybean seeds, which your firm's scientists genetically modified to be resistant to herbicide sprays. The figure shows the demand curve (D), the marginal revenue curve (MR), the average total cost curve (ATC), and

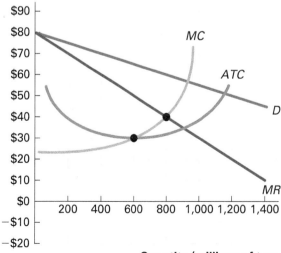

Price and cost (dollars per ton of soybean seeds)

Quantity (millions of tons of soybean seeds)

the marginal cost curve (*MC*). Your supervisor wants to produce 600 million tons of seeds, the quantity that minimizes the average total cost.

   a. Explain why your supervisor's approach is incorrect.

   b. How can you determine the profit-maximizing quantity?

   c. According to the figure, what is the profit-maximizing price and quantity?

2.6 The following figure illustrates the demand for a new, patented memory chip.

   a. To maximize profit, what price do you set, and what quantity do you produce?

   b. What is your economic profit or economic loss?

   c. Do you expect your current economic profit or economic loss to continue? Explain your answer.

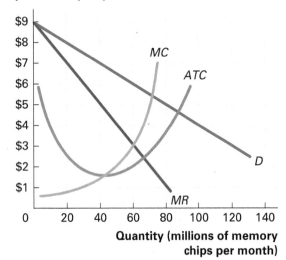

Price and cost (dollars per memory chip)

Quantity (millions of memory chips per month)

2.7 Your marketing research department has estimated the demand for your firm's product to be

$$Q = 10,000 - 100P$$

and the marginal revenue to be

$$MR = 100 - 0.02Q$$

If marginal cost and average total cost are constant at $40,

   a. How much would you produce?

   b. What price would you charge?

   c. How much economic profit would your firm earn?

   d. Illustrate your answers to parts a through c in a diagram.

2.8 Suppose that the market demand curve for your product is given by

$$Q = \$25 - 0.5P$$

In a figure, plot this demand curve, and label it *D*. Then plot the corresponding marginal revenue curve and label it *MR*. (Recall that that the marginal revenue curve has the same vertical intercept as the demand curve and has a slope twice that of the demand curve.) Assume that the marginal cost and average total cost equal $2 for all levels of production. Draw the marginal cost curve and the average total cost curve. What is the profit-maximizing price and quantity? How much economic profit will you earn?

2.9 Suppose that the demand for a monopoly firm's product is given by

$$Q = 80 - P$$

   a. If the firm's marginal cost is constant at $10, what is the profit-maximizing price and output?

   b. Suppose that the demand changes to $Q = 100 - P$. After this change, what is the new profit-maximizing price and quantity?

   c. If the demand changes to $Q = 160 - 2P$, what is the new profit-maximizing price and quantity?

2.10 Biotech companies employ many highly skilled workers.

   a. Suppose the wage rate paid these workers falls, perhaps because more students graduate from college with the necessary skills. In the short run, how does a fall in the wage rate affect the firm's marginal revenue and marginal cost curves?

   b. If each of the biotech companies produces a unique drug so each is a monopoly in its market, how does the fall in wages change the managers' decisions about the profit-maximizing quantity and price?

2.11 The demand for a monopoly's product increases. In a diagram, show how the increase in demand changes the monopoly's price and quantity.

2.12 "When the managers of a monopoly maximize its profit, the price always exceeds the marginal cost." Is this assertion true or false? Explain your answer.

2.13 You are the manager of a monopoly.

  ✓ a. If the marginal cost of your product is $100 and the price elasticity of demand for your product is 2, what markup of price over marginal cost do you set?

  ✓ b. If the price elasticity of demand is 3 rather than 2, what markup do you set?

   c. Use your knowledge of factors that affect the magnitude of the price elasticity of demand to your answers to parts a and b.

2.14 A monopolist's profit-maximizing price is $10, and its profit-maximizing output is 300 units.
   a. If the average total cost of production is $7.50 per unit, what is the firm's economic profit?
   b. What happens to economic profit if managers change price and output?

2.15 Would you expect a profit-maximizing monopolist to produce the quantity of output that is socially efficient? Explain your answer.

2.16 It is possible for chemists to determine the chemical composition of many pharmaceutical drugs. With this fact in mind, why do you think that pharmaceutical companies patent their drugs rather than keep their formulations as trade secrets?

2.17 Biotech drugs are those produced within living biological systems. Making these drugs is quite complicated and can be very sensitive to small manufacturing changes. The Food and Drug Administration (FDA), which must approve any drug before it is marketed, is trying to determine the procedures it will require to allow the production and sale of generic copies of biotech drugs that can be labeled as interchangeable with the original brands (called *biosimilar interchangeability*).
   a. As a manager of a biotech company that manufactures an approved biotech drug with an expired patent, what arguments would you make to the FDA regarding approval of interchangeable biosimilar drugs?
   b. If you are a manager of a generic drug company, what arguments would you make to the FDA?

2.18 You are a manager of a natural monopoly with the costs and demand illustrated in the figure.

Price and cost (cents per kilowatt hour)

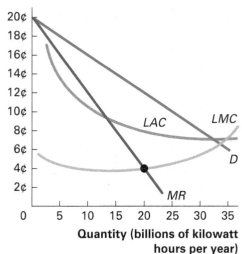

Quantity (billions of kilowatt hours per year)

   a. What is the minimum efficient scale of production?
   b. If you are free to maximize profit, what price do you set, and what quantity do you produce? What is your economic profit or loss?
   c. Suppose that a new firm enters the market and produces one-fourth of your production. What is the firm's average cost? If you do not change your price, is the new firm likely to make an economic profit or incur an economic loss? Explain your answers.

2.19 In a small city, you are the owner of the only plumbing company offering in-home service. You run your operation from a small hole-in-the-wall office, with your plumbers arriving at their job sites in their own, unmarked vehicles. You catch wind that another rival might enter the market, so you schedule a presentation with the city commissioners. During this presentation, you can make one of two arguments: (1) Plumbers offering in-home service should be required to purchase a plush office (in case consumers wish to complain about the service), or (2) plumbers must pass a costly certification test given at the local community college (so that consumers are assured of quality service). Of course, as a long-time, proven business, you would be exempt from either regulation. You believe that if you argue for both policies, the commission will see it for what it is—an attempt to erect barriers to entry—so you must argue for only one. Suppose that both would increase your rival's costs by $100,000. Does one of these proposals have a significant advantage over the other? Carefully explain your answer.

6.3 Dominant Firm

Learning Objective 6.3 Describe how managers of a dominant firm determine the quantity and price that maximize profit.

3.1 In 1911, American Tobacco produced over 90 percent of the cigarettes sold in the United States. Small, competitive firms produced the remaining 10 percent.
   a. How did American Tobacco's managers determine the profit-maximizing quantity?
   b. How would the decisions change if the company eliminated the competitive fringe?

3.2 In 1936, Alcoa sold 90 percent of the aluminum ingot sold in the United States. The rest was imported.
   a. As a manager at Alcoa, how would you determine the price to charge?
   b. How would your decision change if the government barred all imports?

3.3 The table shows the market demand and competitive fringe supply for a market with a dominant firm. Complete the residual demand column of the table.

Price (dollars per unit)	Market Demand (units)	Competitive Fringe Supply (units)	Residual Demand (units)
$50	40	30	
45	50	25	
40	60	20	
35	70	15	
30	80	10	
25	90	5	

3.4 The following table shows the market demand and competitive fringe supply for a market with a dominant firm.

  a. From Chapter 3, an equation for the price elasticity of demand is $\varepsilon = |b \times (P/Q^d)|$, where b is the change in the quantity demanded from a $1 change in price. (For any two points on the demand curve, b is equal to the change in quantity demanded divided by the change in price.) Use this formula to calculate the price elasticity of demand at the three different prices on the market demand curve and on the residual demand curve. Record your answers in the table.

  b. How does the price elasticity of demand on the market demand curve compare to the price elasticity of demand on the residual demand curve?

3.5 The figure shows the market demand curve (D), the competitive fringe's supply curve (S_{CF}), and the dominant firm's marginal cost curve (MC).

  a. Use the figure to draw the residual demand curve, the market marginal revenue curve, and the residual marginal revenue curve.

  b. If the firm is a monopoly, so that the competitive fringe does not exist, what price and quantity will its managers select?

Accompanies problem 3.5.

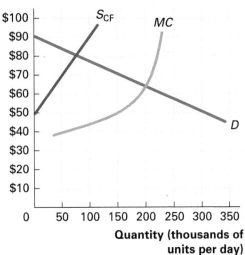

Price and cost (dollars per unit)

  c. If the firm is a dominant firm, what price and quantity will its managers select?

  d. Is the firm's markup higher when it is a monopoly or a dominant firm? Explain your answer.

  e. Is the firm's profit larger when it is a monopoly or a dominant firm? Explain your answer.

3.6 How does the presence of a competitive fringe affect the profit of the dominant firm? Why does the competitive fringe have this effect?

3.7 In India, Cisco's market share of the Ethernet switch and router market is approximately 67 percent. Juniper and HP each have market shares of about 6.5 percent, and several other firms have somewhat smaller market shares. Draw a diagram showing the equilibrium in this dominant firm market. Identify the equilibrium price and the equilibrium quantity produced by the dominant firm and the competitive fringe firms. Illustrate what happens to the equilibrium price and the equilibrium quantity produced by the dominant firm and the competitive fringe firms if additional fringe firms enter the market.

Accompanies problem 3.4.

Price (dollars per unit)	Market Demand (units)	Price Elasticity of Demand for Market Demand	Competitive Fringe Supply (units)	Residual Demand (units)	Price Elasticity of Demand for Residual Demand
$50	70		50	20	
45	80		30	50	
40	90		10	80	

6.4 Monopolistic Competition

Learning Objective 6.4 Explain how managers of a monopolistically competitive firm determine the quantity and price that maximize profit.

4.1 How is a monopolistically competitive firm similar to a perfectly competitive firm? How is it similar to a monopoly?

4.2 Suppose that you are a manager in Whirlpool's appliance division. Your accountants provide you with a report on costs and revenues. You determine that the cost to produce another top-loading washing machine is $200 and its marginal revenue is $250. Presuming Whirlpool is competing in a monopolistically competitive market, how do you change the quantity and the price of the washing machines?

4.3 The figure shows the demand curve (D), marginal revenue curve (MR), and marginal cost curve (MC) for a monopolistically competitive hamburger restaurant. What is the profit-maximizing quantity and price of hamburgers?

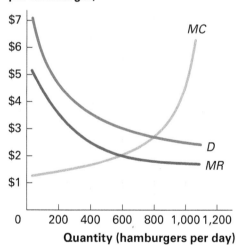

4.4 You are a manager of a firm like J.P. Licks, a monopolistically competitive ice cream store in Boston. You are determining the price and quantity of your Cookies 'n' Cream Pie. Economists you have hired report that the marginal cost of an ice cream pie is constant and is equal to $10 per pie. They also report that the demand is given by $Q = 300 - 10P$, where Q is the quantity of ice cream pies demanded per day and P is their price. What is the profit-maximizing price and quantity of Cookies 'n' Cream Pies?

4.5 Australian yogurt is a new product that is not strained and is made from whole milk, so it is creamier than regular or Greek yogurt. Suppose that you are a manager for Publix supermarkets and some colleagues suggest that the company produce a Publix-brand Australian yogurt. They explain that producing Australian yogurt is currently very profitable, and they predict this trend will continue. How do you respond to your colleagues, and why?

6.5 Managerial Application: The Monopoly, Dominant Firm, and Monopolistic Competition Models

Learning Objective 6.5 Apply what you have learned about monopolies, dominant firms, and monopolistically competitive firms to make better managerial decisions.

- **5.1** Explain how marginal analysis can help determine the profit-maximizing quantity for managers of monopolies, dominant firms, and monopolistically competitive firms.

5.2 The price elasticity of demand for your product is 2.0, and your marginal cost is $30. What is your profit-maximizing price? Suppose that you can run a new advertising campaign and differentiate your product by emphasizing its unique features, thereby decreasing the price elasticity of demand to 1.8. What is your new profit-maximizing price?

5.3 You are managing a firm with market power, and you think the price elasticity of demand for your product is between 1.3 and 1.5. You estimate that your marginal cost is between $50 and $70. In what range should you set your price? If you refine your estimate of the marginal cost to $60, in what range should you set your price?

5.4 As a manager of a monopolistically competitive firm like Starbucks, you are pleased that your green advertising, which proclaims your coffee is ethically and sustainably grown, has convinced consumers that your coffee is vastly superior to anything else sold by your competitors. The demand for your coffee has increased, and at every price, the price elasticity of demand has decreased. Presuming that your marginal cost is the same for every cup of coffee— say $2 per cup—and has not changed, illustrate these changes in a diagram, showing how they affect your profit-maximizing price and quantity of coffee.

MyLab Economics Auto-Graded Excel Projects

6.1 1880 Town is a tourist attraction in Midland, SD. Its owners have collected buildings built between 1880 and 1920, filled them with antique furniture and collectables, and charge admission for tourists to experience history. Because of its exclusivity and location, this tourist attraction enjoys some market power power.

	A	B	C	D	E	F
1	QD	P	TC	TR	MR	MC
2	0	70	1000			
3	25	65	1275			
4	50	60	1525			
5	75	55	1750			
6	100	50	1950			
7	125	45	2125			
8	150	40	2275			
9	175	35	2400			
10	200	30	2550			
11	225	25	2725			
12	250	20	2925			
13	275	15	3150			
14	300	10	3400			
15	325	5	3675			
16	350	0	3975			
17						

Suppose you run a tourist attraction similar to 1880 Town. After running some tests with pricing, you have determined the daily demand schedule for admission as given. In addition to tracking demand at various prices, you also monitor costs closely.

a. Using the demand schedule provided, find total revenue and marginal revenue at each point.

b. Using total costs, find the marginal cost at each point. (Just as marginal revenue is the change in total revenue divided by the change in Q, remember that marginal cost is the change in total cost divided by the change in Q.)

c. How much should you charge for entrance to the tourist attraction and how many visitors do you expect to have?

d. What is the economic profit when you maximize profit?

6.2 Casey's General Stores, Inc. is a convenience store chain based in Ankey, IA and has convenience marts all over the midwest. In small towns, there may only be one or two gas stations; however, in larger towns many gas stations compete with each other. One signature of gas stations is that the prices per gallon are displayed on large signs making it easy for customers to compare prices and select the cheapest station. Many chains, like Casey's, have very loyal customers so when they have slightly higher prices, they don't lose all business.

Suppose you are in charge of pricing products at a convenience store similar to Casey's in a larger town with a number of gas stations and convenience marts. You are provided with the elasticity and marginal cost information in the Excel file in the figure.

a. Using the markup rule, determine the price you should charge for each product.

b. Why is the price elasticity of gasoline so high?

c. With the high price elasticity of gas, why do other products have lower price elasticities?

d. What is the relationship between elasticity and the amount of the markup on a product.

	A	B	C	D
1	Product	Price Elasticity	MC	P
2	Gasoline	4	2.1	
3	Quarts of Oil	1.1	0.5	
4	Bottled Water	1.2	0.25	
5	Bottled Soda	1.5	0.75	
6	Ice Cream Bar	2	1	
7	Chips	2.25	1.25	
8	Cheeseburgers	2.75	2	
9	Pizza	3	1.5	
10				

The Calculus of Profit Maximization for Firms with Market Power

The profit-maximization rule, $MR = MC$, is the same for all firms. It applies equally well to the firms with no market power that you learned about in the last chapter (perfectly competitive firms) and to the firms with market power, including monopoly, monopolistically competitive, and dominant firms.

A. Marginal Revenue Curve

The chapter stated that for a linear demand curve, the marginal revenue curve has the same vertical intercept and a slope equal to twice the slope of the demand curve. Using calculus, we can prove this claim. Start by using the definitions of total revenue as the price multiplied by the quantity, $P \times Q$, and marginal revenue as the change in total revenue (TR) that results from a change in quantity (Q), $MR = \frac{dTR}{dQ}$. Of course, the quantity must equal the quantity consumers demand, so total revenue equals $P \times Q^d$ and marginal revenue equals $\frac{dTR}{dQ^d}$. Demand is typically written as a function of the price, $Q^d = a - (b \times P)$, but it can be inverted to express P as a function of Q^d, which is called the *inverse demand* function:

$$P = \frac{a}{b} - \left(\frac{1}{b} \times Q^d\right) = c - (d \times Q^d) \qquad \text{A6.1}$$

For simplicity, the term after the second equal sign uses $c = \frac{a}{b}$ and $d = \frac{1}{b}$ to eliminate the fractions. In the demand function in Equation A6.1, c is the vertical intercept of the demand curve and d is its slope.

Because total revenue equals $P \times Q^d$, multiplying Equation A6.1 by Q^d gives

$$TR = P \times Q^d = [c - (d \times Q^d)] \times Q^d = c \times Q^d - [d \times (Q^d)^2] \qquad \text{A6.2}$$

Marginal revenue equals the derivative of total revenue with respect to quantity. Use the power rule to take the derivative of total revenue in Equation A6.2:

$$\frac{dTR}{dQ^d} = MR = c - (2 \times d \times Q^d) \qquad \text{A6.3}$$

Equation A6.3 is the equation for the MR line. It is a straight line with its vertical intercept equal to c, which is the same as the vertical intercept for the demand curve, and its slope equal to $2 \times d$, which is twice the slope of the demand curve.

One important point to keep in mind: These results hold *only if* the demand curve is a straight line, which, of course, is not always the case.

B. Elasticity, Price, and Marginal Revenue

The definition of marginal revenue is the same for both perfectly competitive firms and firms with market power. However, the relationship between the demand and marginal revenue is quite different. For perfectly competitive firms, $MR = P$. But for firms with market power, the equation in the chapter (Equation 6.2) shows that the relationship between the marginal revenue and price is more complicated:

$$MR = P \times \left(1 - \frac{1}{\varepsilon}\right) = P \times \left(\frac{\varepsilon - 1}{\varepsilon}\right) \qquad \text{A6.4}$$

Calculus makes deriving this equality straightforward. Total revenue again equals price multiplied by quantity, $P \times Q^d$, so using the product rule to differentiate total revenue with respect to quantity, the marginal revenue is

$$MR = \frac{dTR}{dQ^d} = \frac{d(P \times Q^d)}{dQ^d} = \left(\frac{dP}{dQ^d} \times Q^d\right) + \left(P \times \frac{dQ^d}{dQ^d}\right) = \left(\frac{dP}{dQ^d} \times Q^d\right) + P \quad \textbf{A6.5}$$

In Equation A6.5, $\frac{dP}{dQ^d}$ is the slope of the demand curve. This slope is negative, so $\left(\frac{dP}{dQ^d} \times Q^d\right)$ is negative. If you take the absolute value of this term, you must add a minus sign to account for the negative sign; that is, $\left(\frac{dP}{dQ^d} \times Q^d\right) = -\left|\left(\frac{dP}{dQ^d} \times Q^d\right)\right|$. You can now use this term in Equation A6.5 to yield

$$MR = -\left|\left(\frac{dP}{dQ^d} \times Q^d\right)\right| + P = P - \left|\left(\frac{dP}{dQ^d} \times Q^d\right)\right|$$

Next, multiply the absolute value term by 1 in the form $\frac{P}{P}$. Then distribute the P term in the denominator of this fraction into the denominator of the term in the absolute value. That leaves a P multiplying both terms, which can be moved outside the parentheses. Equation A6.6 shows these changes step-by-step:

$$MR = P - \left|\left(\frac{dP}{dQ^d} \times Q^d\right)\right| \times \frac{P}{P} = P - \left|\left(\frac{dP \times Q^d}{dQ^d \times P}\right)\right| \times P = P \times \left[1 - \left|\left(\frac{dP \times Q^d}{dQ^d \times P}\right)\right|\right] \quad \textbf{A6.6}$$

Finally, recall the equation for the price elasticity of demand from the appendix to Chapter 3, $\varepsilon = \left|\frac{dQ^d \times P}{Q^d \times dP}\right|$. In Equation A6.5, however, the term in the absolute value, $\left|\left(\frac{dP \times Q^d}{dQ^d \times P}\right)\right|$, is not the price elasticity of demand, ε, but rather its reciprocal, $1/\varepsilon$. Use this result in Equation A6.6 to arrive at Equation A6.4:

$$MR = P \times \left(1 - \frac{1}{\varepsilon}\right) = P \times \left(\frac{\varepsilon - 1}{\varepsilon}\right)$$

C. Maximizing Profit

The profit-maximization rule from Chapter 5—produce so that $MR = MC$—remains true in this chapter even though the firms in this chapter possess market power. Profit equals total revenue minus total cost, or

$$\text{Profit}(Q) = TR(Q) - TC(Q)$$

As in the previous chapter, to maximize profit take the derivative of Profit(Q) with respect to Q, and set it equal to zero:

$$\frac{d\text{Profit}}{dQ} = \frac{dTR}{dQ} - \frac{dTC}{dQ} = 0 \quad \textbf{A6.7}$$

In Equation A6.7, $\frac{dTR}{dQ}$ is MR and $\frac{dTC}{dQ}$ is MC, so Equation A6.7 can be rewritten as

$$MR - MC = 0 \Rightarrow MR = MC \quad \textbf{A6.8}$$

which is, of course, the same result presented in this chapter as well as in Chapter 5. This derivation shows that producing so that $MR = MC$ maximizes profit for *any* type of firm with market power—a monopoly, a dominant firm, or a monopolistically competitive firm—even though their demand curves differ. For example, a dominant firm faces the residual demand, while a monopoly faces the market demand. Although these demands differ, producing where $MR = MC$ maximizes profit for both types of firms.

For perfectly competitive firms as well as firms with market power, the profit-maximizing price is the highest price that allows the firm to sell the quantity produced. For perfectly competitive firms, that price is determined by the market. Firms with market power, however, must determine what price to set. The method you can use depends on the information you possess. If you have an estimate of the demand for your product, you can use the profit-maximizing quantity in the demand to determine the price to set. Alternatively, if you know your price elasticity of demand and marginal cost, you can use the results in Equations A6.4 and A6.8 to determine your price. In particular, using the profit-maximization condition in A6.8, $MR = MC$, as a substitute for MR in Equation A6.4 gives

$$MC = P \times \left(\frac{\varepsilon - 1}{\varepsilon} \right)$$

Then, as in the chapter, divide both sides by $\frac{\varepsilon - 1}{\varepsilon}$:

$$P = MC \times \frac{\varepsilon}{\varepsilon - 1} \qquad\qquad \textbf{A6.9}$$

Equation A6.9 shows you that the profit-maximizing markup of price over marginal cost is $\frac{\varepsilon}{\varepsilon - 1}$.

D. Maximizing Profit: Example

Vertex is a medium-sized pharmaceutical company. One of Vertex's major products is Kalydeco, the first drug to treat a genetic cause of cystic fibrosis rather than just its symptoms. For the patients with the specific genetic flaw treated by Kalydeco, no other drug is a close substitute. The patents protecting Kalydeco have over a decade before they expire, so Vertex has a monopoly in the production of Kalydeco. Suppose that you are working for a company similar to Vertex with a monopoly in the production of a lifesaving drug. You are in the department charged with setting the price and quantity for your company's drug.

The profit-maximizing quantity sets $MR = MC$, so you need to determine the marginal revenue and the marginal cost. Your research analysts estimate that the demand for your drug is equal to

$$Q = 2{,}050 - 0.002778P \qquad\qquad \textbf{A6.10}$$

where Q is the quantity of prescriptions demanded per year and P is the price. The analysts also estimate that the total cost of producing your drug is equal to

$$TC = 0.086Q^3 - 124Q^2 + 8{,}000Q + 50{,}000{,}000 \qquad\qquad \textbf{A6.11}$$

To calculate the marginal revenue, $\frac{dTR}{dQ}$, start by solving Equation A6.10 for P. Subtract 2,050 from both sides of the equation and then divide by -0.002778 to obtain

$$P = 737{,}941 - 360Q \qquad\qquad \textbf{A6.12}$$

The inverse demand function in Equation A6.12 shows the price, P, as a function of the quantity, Q. Total revenue equals $P \times Q$, so multiply the expression for P in Equation A6.12 by Q to get total revenue:

$$TR = (737{,}941 - 360Q) \times Q = 737{,}941Q - 360Q^2 \qquad\qquad \textbf{A6.13}$$

Finally, use the power rule to take the derivative of total revenue in Equation A6.13 with respect to quantity to find the marginal revenue function:

$$MR = 737{,}941 - 720Q \qquad\qquad \textbf{A6.14}$$

Next, use Equation A6.11 to calculate the marginal cost, $\frac{dTC}{dQ}$, by differentiating the total cost in Equation A6.11 with respect to Q. Once again, using the power rule for derivatives gives the marginal cost function:

$$MC = 0.258Q^2 - 248Q + 8{,}000 \qquad\qquad \textbf{A6.15}$$

To maximize profit, you must produce the quantity that sets $MR = MC$; using Equations A6.14 and A6.15,

$$737{,}941 - 720Q = 0.258Q^2 - 248Q + 8{,}000 \qquad \textbf{A6.16}$$

Rearrange Equation A6.16 by moving the terms on the left side to the right side:

$$0 = 0.258Q^2 + 472Q - 729{,}941 \qquad \textbf{A6.17}$$

Finally, use the quadratic formula to solve Equation A6.17 for the profit-maximizing quantity, Q. This shows that Q equals 1,000 prescriptions per year.[1] You also need to determine the profit-maximizing price. You do not have an estimate of the price elasticity of demand, but you do have the inverse demand function in Equation A6.12. Given $Q = 1{,}000$, you can use the inverse demand function to determine the profit-maximizing price: $P = 737{,}941 - (360 \times 1{,}000) = \$377{,}941$. Consequently, the profit-maximizing price is $377,941 for a yearly prescription for your company's drug.

---

1 The other root of Equation A6.17 is –2,820, which is meaningless because the quantity must be positive.

Calculus Questions and Problems

A6.1 Suppose that GNV Pool owns the only community pool in Gainesville, Florida. The market demand for annual passes to this pool is

$$Q^d = 600 - 2P$$

where Q^d is the quantity of annual passes demanded and P is the per-pass price. GNV Pool knows that its total cost of providing annual passes is

$$TC(Q) = 25{,}000 + 0.25Q^2$$

   a. What is the profit-maximizing price and quantity?
   b. What is the amount of economic profit or loss?

A6.2 You are a manager for PetCarry, a manufacturer of high-quality pet carriers. Your research department has given you the demand function for your pet carriers as

$$Q^d = 10{,}000 - 100P$$

where Q^d is the quantity of carriers demanded and P is the price. You know that your total cost of producing carriers is

$$TC(Q) = 30{,}400 + 4Q$$

   a. What is the profit-maximizing price and quantity?
   b. What is the amount of economic profit or loss?

A6.3 Walter is an antitrust consultant. He currently works in a large European city with many other antitrust consultants. Walter is considering moving to Tampa, Florida, where there are currently several other antitrust consulting firms. If Walter makes this move, he will be competing in a monopolistically competitive market. Walter knows that the demand for his antitrust consulting services in Tampa is

$$Q^d = 1{,}700 - 5P$$

where Q^d is the number of hours of antitrust consulting services demanded and P is the hourly price of antitrust consulting services. Walter's total cost of setting up an antitrust consulting firm in Tampa and producing consulting services is

$$TC(Q) = 20{,}000 + 160Q$$

where Q is the number of hours of antitrust consulting services that Walter supplies.

   a. If Walter were to open an antitrust consulting firm in Tampa, what would be his marginal revenue from an additional hour of antitrust consulting services?
   b. If Walter were to open an antitrust consulting firm in Tampa, what would be his marginal cost of an additional hour of antitrust consulting services?
   c. What is Walter's profit-maximizing number of antitrust consulting hours if he opens an antitrust consulting firm in Tampa?
   d. What is Walter's profit-maximizing price for an hour of consulting services?

A6.4 Jessica is a 10-year-old entrepreneur. She produces lemonade in her family's kitchen and sells that lemonade at a stand that she sets up in front of her family's house each Saturday afternoon. Jessica has successfully differentiated her lemonade by using Meyer lemons, so she is a monopolistically competitive firm. The demand function for her lemonade is

$$Q^d = 38.5 - 10P$$

where P is the per-cup price of lemonade and Q^d is the quantity of cups of lemonade demanded. Jessica's total cost of setting up her lemonade stand and producing lemonade is

$$TC(Q) = 30 + 0.25Q$$

where Q is the number of cups of lemonade Jessica produces.

a. What is Jessica's marginal revenue from producing an additional cup of lemonade?
b. What is Jessica's marginal cost of producing an additional cup of lemonade?

c. What is Jessica's profit-maximizing number of cups of lemonade?
d. What price for a cup of lemonade will Jessica charge?

A6.5 Smaller Swimmers is the only supplier of children's swimming lessons in town. Smaller Swimmers has a constant marginal cost of producing swimming lessons, and the demand for children's swimming lessons is

$$Q^d = 475 - 5P$$

where P is the price of a swimming lesson and Q^d is the quantity of lessons demanded.

Suppose that Smaller Swimmers maximizes its profit by supplying 200 children's swimming lessons. What is Smaller Swimmers' marginal cost of producing a children's swimming lesson?

7

Cartels and Oligopoly

Learning Objectives

After studying this chapter, you will be able to:

7.1 Explain why cartels are potentially profitable but unstable and difficult to sustain.

7.2 Describe how managers can engage in and sustain tacit collusion to boost their prices and economic profit.

7.3 Compare the assumptions and equilibrium outcomes of Cournot, Chamberlin, Stackelberg, and Bertrand oligopolies.

7.4 Apply the economic theory of cartels and the different types of oligopolies to help make more profitable managerial decisions.

Managers at Major Publishers Read the e-Writing on the e-Wall

In 2010, executives at publishing companies faced a problem: Amazon.com was selling their newly released and popular e-books for $9.99. Amazon's managers wanted to keep the price of e-books low so that they could sell more of its e-reader, the Kindle. The managers of five major publishers, including Simon & Schuster, HarperCollins, and Macmillan, worried that Amazon's pricing strategy would cap the price they could charge for their e-books in other retail markets, such as that for Barnes & Noble's e-reader, the Nook. The managers of each publishing company knew that if they tried to renegotiate the price independently, Amazon could refuse to sell their e-books. That threat was real because Amazon's share of the e-book market was large, estimated at 66 percent. In order to raise the price of their books, all

five publishing companies needed to cooperate, but such open collaboration is illegal. The managers were in quite a predicament.

Apple then arrived on the scene. Apple's managers wanted to sell e-books in its iBookstore for its iPad and iPhone, but they wanted more profit than the company would make if the price was $9.99. What type of deal could Apple's managers suggest that would appeal to the managers of all five book publishers? This chapter will help you understand the structure of Apple's proposal and why the managers of all five major publishers agreed to it. This chapter will also provide insight into government opposition to the proposal. At the end of the chapter, you will learn how Apple structured its contacts with the publishers and how the government responded.

Sources: Julianne Pepitone, "DOJ Targets Apple and Publishers for E-Book Price Fixing," CNN Money, March 9, 2012 http://money.cnn.com/2012/03/08/technology/apple-ebook-price/; Samuel Gibbs, "Apple Agrees to Pay $450m Settlement in EBook Price Fixing Case," *Guardian*, July 16, 2014; Jacob Gershman, "Apple Loses Bid for Supreme Court Review of E-Books Price-Fixing Case," *Wall Street Journal*, March 7, 2016.

Introduction

So far, you have learned about managerial decision making for firms in four market structures: perfectly competitive, monopoly, dominant firm, and monopolistically competitive (the first covered in Chapter 5 and the remaining three in Chapter 6). In this chapter, we examine another type of market. An **oligopoly** is a market structure in which a small number of mutually interdependent firms compete. Unfortunately, the exact number of firms is fuzzy, but it must be small enough that the firms

Oligopoly A market structure in which a small number of mutually interdependent firms compete.

recognize their *mutual interdependence.* That is, the actions of each firm have a large impact on the profits of its competitors. Each oligopoly's managers must therefore be concerned about the price, output, and other market-related decisions made by rival firms because these actions affect their own firm's profit. Mutual interdependence makes management of an oligopolistic firm challenging because each firm's profit depends not only on the decisions of its own managers but also on those of the managers at competing companies.

Oligopolistic markets have high to medium barriers to entry, but the fact that there is more than one firm in the market demonstrates that those barriers are not insurmountable. Because there are only a small number of firms, each has at least some *market power*, the ability to determine the price of its product or service (see Chapter 6).

Firms in an oligopolistic market might produce products that are virtually identical or merely similar. For example, the five major U.S. iron ore miners produce virtually identical products; the two major soft drink producers, Coca-Cola and PepsiCo, produce very similar beverages; and the two major producers of large passenger planes, Boeing and Airbus, produce similar planes. The major factor in oligopolistic markets is not the degree of product similarity but the firms' mutual interdependence. Of course, the extent of interdependence depends, in part, on the degree of similarity of the products or services. If the products are extremely similar, then a change in the price of one has a very large effect on the demand for the others. If, instead, the products are "just" similar, a price change will have a smaller impact.

This text devotes two chapters to oligopoly. In Chapter 8, you will study *game theory*, which can help you understand how managers in oligopoly markets make strategic decisions. This chapter, then, covers the basic foundations of oligopoly in four sections:

- **Section 7.1** examines price-fixing cartels to show that managers in an oligopoly can increase their firms' profit if they form a cartel to boost their prices. Such activity, however, is illegal.
- **Section 7.2** shows how managers can legally achieve the same economic results as a cartel through tacit collusion, which is an unstated agreement to boost prices. Tacit collusion is legal.
- **Section 7.3** applies economic models of oligopoly to firm behavior and explains choices managers make when they do not form a cartel or tacitly collude.
- **Section 7.4** explores how you can apply the economic models of cartels and oligopolies to make better managerial decisions.

7.1 Cartels

Learning Objective 7.1 Explain why cartels are potentially profitable but unstable and difficult to sustain.

As you learned in Chapters 5 and 6, the market structure in which a firm competes affects the amount of economic profit it can make. Monopolies, such as a pharmaceutical firm with a patent on a cancer-fighting drug, can make an economic profit as long as a barrier to entry protects them. Competitive firms, such as corn producers, can make an economic profit only in the short run because they have no barriers to entry. Competition is best for society, but managers try to avoid it in order to increase profit. Because an oligopoly includes only a small number of firms, there is the possibility of cooperation rather than competition. Managers from various firms might meet and determine that together they will set the same price and produce the same quantity that a monopoly would. The managers' agreement boosts the price and decreases overall production but it increases profits for all of them. This sort of price-fixing agreement creates a **cartel**, a group of producers who agree not to compete on price, quantity, quality, and promotional activity.[1]

Cartel A group of producers who agree not to compete on price, quantity, quality, and promotional activity.

Two factors make forming a cartel easier. First, the smaller the number of sellers in the market, the easier it is to reach and monitor the agreement. Second, the more similar the products produced by the firms, the easier it is for the managers to agree on price. For example, it would be virtually impossible for fast-food restaurants (also called quick-service restaurants) to form a cartel because there are literally thousands of restaurants producing a huge variety of food.

Although easy to form, they are also unstable as one manager or another tries to seize an advantage. Perhaps more importantly, cartels are illegal because of their negative impact on society. On average, cartels set the price of their products 20 to 30 percent higher than the competitive price. By driving up the price, cartels harm consumers and, as described in Chapter 2, create a deadweight loss. Because of this harm, governments of most countries have passed antitrust laws (called competition laws outside of the United States) designed to prevent cartels (see Chapter 9). Although cartels are illegal, some producers must find the potential for increased profit irresistible because government officials discover (and prosecute) cartels virtually every month. To avoid being victimized by them, you need to understand the economics of cartels, why they are unstable, and what actions cartel members need to take to sustain them.

Cartel Profit Maximization

Figure 7.1 illustrates managers' incentive to form a price-fixing cartel. Suppose that there are six taxi cab companies in a city, all with identical costs. If the firms operate as competitors, Figure 7.1(a) shows that the competitive price is $3 per mile and the competitive quantity of miles driven in the entire market is 45,000 miles per day. Figure 7.1(b) shows that the managers of each firm maximize their profit by having their cabs drive the quantity of miles that sets the marginal revenue (MR_{COM}), $3 per mile, equal to the marginal cost (MC). The figure also shows that at the competitive price the managers of each firm have their cabs drive a total of 7,500 miles per day. Unfortunately for the managers, however, their firms make only a competitive return because the price equals their average total cost. Unquestionably, the managers want to do better.

Suppose that managers from each of the firms "just happen to run into one another" at a local coffee shop. Although they know what they are doing is illegal, in pursuit of economic profit the managers form a cartel: They agree to boost their prices and decrease the quantity of miles their companies drive. If the managers agree to set the price and quantity that maximize their joint profit, they will choose the monopoly price and quantity. Figure 7.1(a) shows that the price and quantity the cartel will select are $4 per mile and 30,000 miles per day. If the managers agree to split the market equally, they divide the total quantity—the miles driven—among the six firms, so that each firm's taxis drive 5,000 miles per day and each firm charges the cartel price, $4 per mile. Figure 7.1(b) shows that the higher cartel price, labelled P_{CARTEL}, allows each firm to make an economic profit.

---

1 The economic concept of a cartel is very different than the popular conception of a cartel embodied in the phrase "drug cartel." A drug cartel is group of (generally very violent) people who work for one boss in (often very fierce) competition with groups who work for other bosses. Drug cartels are interested in reducing competition by eliminating their competitors rather than reaching agreement with them.

Figure 7.1 A Cartel Agreement

(a) The Monopoly/Cartel Price and Quantity

If the managers of the six taxi companies compete with one another, the market is competitive. The equilibrium price is $3 per mile, and the equilibrium quantity of miles driven in the total market is 45,000 per day, or 7,500 miles per day for each firm. If the managers agree to form a cartel, they set the same price and quantity that a monopoly would: The price is $4 per mile, and the total quantity of miles driven in the market is 30,000 miles per day, or 5,000 miles per day for each firm.

(b) The Economic Profit from a Cartel Agreement

If the managers of the six taxi companies compete, the price is $3 per mile, so each firm's demand and marginal revenue curve is $d_{COM} = MR_{COM}$. Each of the firms maximizes its profit by driving 7,500 miles per day, the quantity that sets $MC = MR_{COM}$. The owners make a competitive return because the price equals the average cost. If the managers agree to form a cartel and set the profit-maximizing price and quantity, $4 per mile and 5,000 miles per day for each firm, each firm makes an economic profit equal to the area of the green rectangle.

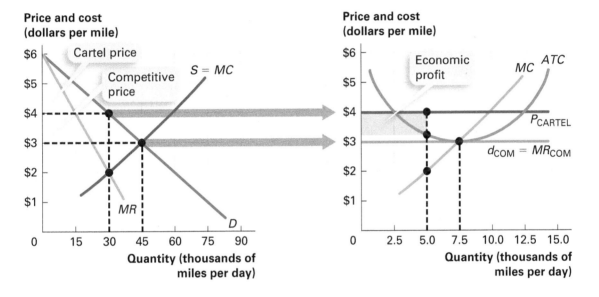

Instability of a Cartel

Causes of Instability

Although cartels can lead to a positive economic profit for their members, they are inherently unstable for three reasons:

1. The bargaining necessary to form a cartel
2. The self-interest of each member
3. Entry by new firms

Each of these factors is discussed next.

Bargaining   When initially forming a cartel, the potential members must determine each firm's price and quantity produced. The managers of each firm seek an advantage by bargaining for a price and quantity that enable their own firm to increase its market share and economic profit. Bargaining can be especially contentious and difficult when the cartel members make similar but not identical products. The more disparate the products, the harder it is to reach a consensus about the price to be charged for each. The same issues arise when member firms introduce new products: The bargaining must resume, and with it comes the chance for the cartel to break down.

Self-Interest   Even when the bargaining is successful, there still is no guarantee that a cartel will persist because each firm's managers have an incentive to cheat on the agreement by increasing the quantity beyond the bargained amount. A closer look at Figure 7.1(b) illustrates this point. With the taxi cab cartel agreement in place, each company sets the same price, P_{CARTEL}, which is $4 per mile for each mile driven. Accordingly, each firm's marginal revenue from an additional mile is $4. Once a company's cabs drive the allotted 5,000 miles called for in the agreement, the figure shows that the marginal cost of another mile is only $2. So if any firm's taxis drive some extra miles, *that* firm's profit increases because $MR > MC$ for these miles. *Each* firm's managers recognize that if they violate the agreement by driving additional miles, their firm's profit increases. Of course, driving extra miles causes the price to fall but each set of managers know that if they and they alone drive a few extra miles, the price won't fall by much. The managers also realize that *all* of the miles for which their marginal revenue exceeds their marginal cost add to their firm's profit, giving them a reason to have their taxis drive more miles than the cartel agreement specifies. Each set of managers has the incentive to cheat on the agreement by driving more miles than the amount allocated. This incentive to cheat on the agreement is a reason why cartels are inherently unstable: They can break up when one (or more) of the firms violates the arrangement by following its self-interest to produce more than the agreed-upon quantity.

Self-interest plays another role in making cartels unstable because government policy uses it to help uncover and eliminate cartels. Firms convicted of participating in a cartel face substantial fines, and their managers face potential jail time. But the laws provide immunity for the first firm to report and confess its behavior to government authorities. Because the whistle-blowing firm faces no penalties or threat of imprisonment, *each* cartel member has the self-interested incentive to be the first to report the illegal activity. Self-interest once again boosts the likelihood of a cartel collapsing.

Entry   A cartel may also crumble if its members cannot prevent entry by new firms. Entry is a real possibility. If a cartel is successful, its members make an economic profit, which attracts the interest of entrepreneurial managers. If new producers enter the market, the cartel must either incorporate them into the agreement or exclude them. Both outcomes decrease the probability of the cartel's survival. If the new firms join the cartel, the number of firms in the cartel increases. The more members in a cartel, the more difficult it becomes to reach agreement and to police members to limit cheating. If, on the other hand, the new entrants are left out of the cartel, the new firms will compete with the cartel. The cartel becomes a smaller part of the market, thereby shrinking its ability to control the price. If too many new firms enter and compete, eventually the cartel loses all ability to influence the price.

For example, the Organization of Petroleum Exporting Countries (OPEC) is a cartel of 13 oil-producing nations, including Saudi Arabia, Iran, and Venezuela, that fixes the price for its members' oil. It can operate as a cartel because its members are sovereign nations, making them immune to the laws of other nations. In 2005, OPEC produced about 43 percent of the world's crude oil, but by 2016, that share had fallen to slightly more than 30 percent. The increase in the supply of non-OPEC oil, largely due to hydraulic fracturing (fracking) in the United States, greatly concerned OPEC's executives. They feared that if the supply of non-OPEC oil continued to increase, OPEC's market power to determine the price of its oil would decrease and the economic profit from the cartel would diminish, which might ultimately cause the cartel to collapse. OPEC's managers also knew that the new producers could not join OPEC because they were private firms, such as ExxonMobil and Royal Dutch Shell, and subject to laws forbidding cartels. So in late 2016 OPEC's executives made the only decision they could: Faced with the decrease in demand and marginal revenue, the executives maximized OPEC's profit by decreasing their production and lowering their price.

Methods Used to Sustain a Cartel

If the cartel is illegal (which is generally the case), it is impossible to write a binding contract to prevent cheating or new entry because there is no legal recourse. Managers must look for other means to maintain it. Frequent meetings and information sharing help a cartel survive because of the reassurance that no member is cheating on the agreement. For example:

- In a cartel fixing the price of lysine—an essential amino acid often added to animal feed—representatives of five companies, including Archer Daniels Midland and four foreign firms, met in hotels worldwide over the three-year period of the cartel.
- In a cartel fixing the price of citric acid—a preservative and flavoring used in sodas—members, including once again Archer Daniels Midland and another four foreign firms, exchanged monthly sales figures for the four years the cartel lasted.

Trade associations, sometimes called *trade groups*, can help sustain cartels. They provide meetings during which managers from all companies can mingle, talk, and perhaps even conspire. Take laundry detergent. In 2002, the managers of three major producers of laundry detergent in Europe—Henkel, Procter & Gamble, and Unilever—met under the auspices of their trade association, the Association for Soaps and Detergents, ostensibly to set environmental standards for their detergents. In reality, the managers discussed the prices they would set and the size of the containers for their products. This illegal price-fixing cartel operated for several years until the managers of one of the members—Henkel—contacted the authorities about the agreements. Procter & Gamble and Unilever each paid fines of about $500 million. Because Henkel alerted the authorities, that company was not fined.

Another common method used to preserve a cartel is enlisting government assistance to support a cartel-like outcome. In some markets, government agencies determine who can produce the product and at what price. Suppose the city council regulates the taxi market in the city with the six cab companies depicted in Figure 7.1. Uber is a smartphone app service that enables customers to summon rides. After Uber enters the market, the existing taxi companies might succeed in convincing the city council to pass ordinances that raise Uber's cost of doing business in the city by, for example, requiring background checks for drivers, signage for vehicles, and commercial insurance. If Uber responds by exiting the market, the taxi managers have effectively used the city council to help them maintain their cartel. This scenario is not mere fiction. In many cities and counties that Uber (and Lyft, a similar ride-hailing app) have entered, the government has imposed new regulations. It is not yet clear if the new regulations will keep Uber (and Lyft) out of the market permanently.

There is another way for oligopolists to raise their profits above the competitive level without engaging in the illegal overt collusion of a cartel. The next section discusses tacit collusion, a "meeting of the minds" that does not involve overt communication or agreement.

Potential Profit from a Cellular Telephone Cartel

Suppose that a small nation has three cellular telephone providers with a linear monthly market demand for cell phone service:

$$Q = 900{,}000 - 900P$$

The demand can be rewritten as

$$P = 1{,}000 - 0.0011Q$$

The rewritten demand curve has as a vertical intercept of 1,000 and a slope of -0.0011. Because the demand curve is linear, as Chapter 6 pointed out, the marginal revenue curve has the same vertical intercept and a slope twice that of the demand curve:

$$MR = 1{,}000 - 0.0022Q$$

Suppose that each firm's marginal cost (MC) and average total cost (ATC) curves are horizontal at $20 per month, so the market's competitive supply curve is also horizontal at a price of $20.

a. If the firms compete, what are the price, quantity, and total economic profit made by all of the firms combined?

b. If the firms' managers form a price-fixing cartel that maximizes the firms' total profit, what are the quantity, price, and total economic profit made by all of the firms combined?

Answer

a. Because the market supply curve is horizontal at the price of $20 per month, the equilibrium competitive price is $20. Using this price in the market demand function shows that the equilibrium quantity is $900{,}000 - (900 \times 20)$, or service for 882,000 cell phones. Because $P = ATC$ (both equal $20), the total economic profit is $0.

b. The cartel maximizes its profit by producing the quantity that sets $MR = MC$. Using $MC = 20$ together with the MR function, profit maximization means

$$20 = 1{,}000 - 0.0022Q$$

Solving for Q gives $Q = 445{,}455$. Next, to solve for the profit-maximizing price, use this quantity in the rewritten demand function:

$$P = 1{,}000 - (0.0011 \times 445{,}455)$$

Solving for P gives $P = $510 per month. Finally, the total economic profit is $(P - ATC) \times Q$, or

$$(\$510 - \$20) \times 445{,}455 = \$218{,}272{,}950$$

7.2 Tacit Collusion

Learning Objective 7.2 Describe how managers can engage in and sustain tacit collusion to boost their prices and economic profit.

Tacit collusion An informal, unstated agreement on price and quantity among the managers of different firms.

In an oligopolistic market, managers have an incentive to agree to fix their price and quantity at the monopoly price and quantity, but as you have learned, any formal price-fixing cartel agreement is illegal. **Tacit collusion**, an informal, unstated agreement on price and quantity among the managers of different firms, however, is *not* illegal. Tacit collusion can be as profitable as the explicit collusion involved in an illegal cartel. Of course, that also means that tacit collusion harms buyers. If you are on the buying side of an oligopoly market, you need to be aware of the possibility of tacit collusion and attempt to avoid it, just as you would avoid cartels.

Four conditions make tacit collusion more likely to occur:

1. **There are few firms in the market.** It is easier to reach a tacit agreement if only a few sets of managers are involved. Accordingly, the more firms in the market, the less likely any tacit agreement will occur. This condition means that tacit collusion will be more common in oligopolistic markets than in other types.
2. **Barriers to entry are high.** If the collusion is successful, the firms make an economic profit, which attracts interest from other entrepreneurs. High barriers to entry prevent these entrepreneurs from entering, thereby limiting the number of firms in the market.
3. **Firms' costs are closely related, and their products are close substitutes.** Although this might appear to be two conditions, it is really only one. It requires firms' products and their cost of production to be so similar that any change which affects one firm's demand or costs is likely to have comparable effects on the rivals' demands or costs.
4. **The price elasticity of demand is small.** If one firm wants to cheat by lowering its price to increase sales (and profit), a small price elasticity of demand means that the increase in sales (and hence profit) will be small. Clearly, cheating is less likely if the potential increase in profit is small.

Managers can adopt four business practices that make tacit collusion more likely and easier to sustain:

1. Price visibility
2. Preannouncements
3. Precommitments
4. Price leadership

Price Visibility

Markets differ in the degree of price visibility. For example, Boeing and Airbus do not advertise the prices they charge, but Intel and AMD make their CPU prices widely known. Price visibility plays a dual role in markets that are susceptible to tacit collusion. On the one hand, the more visible the prices, the more difficult it is for managers to successfully cheat on an unstated agreement about prices. Rivals can quickly see and just as quickly act on any attempt by one firm's managers to secretly cut the price to capture more of the market. One firm's price cut can lead to an outbreak of price competition among all of the firms in the market, resulting in a loss of profit for everyone. Highly visible prices increase the cost of cheating, so visible prices effectively support tacit collusion.

On the other hand, the more visible the price are to consumers, the more informed their choices will be. Each firm's demand will be more elastic, so if the managers of one firm cut prices even slightly, they stand to gain more sales than otherwise and, accordingly, more economic profit than otherwise. The potential to make a large economic profit (even temporarily) increases managers' temptation to cheat on the agreement.

Price visibility can work either to support or to collapse tacit collusion. Most evidence, however, suggests that price visibility enhances the likelihood of tacit collusion. For example, when Germany required all gas stations to make their prices available for use in price comparison apps, researchers suggested that the price of gasoline rose between 5 to 13 cents per gallon. Managers can make their prices more visible by selling standardized products, rather than uniquely customized products. Take pool supplies. Competitive local pool supply stores generally sell a gallon of muriatic acid (hydrochloric acid) at the conventional industry-wide strength of 31.45 percent, rather than offering a uniquely customized strength. Selling a standardized product makes it easier for managers to detect if one store is violating a tacit agreement about price.

In addition, a *meet-the-competition clause* can help make prices more visible. A meet-the-competition clause, either in a contract or in an advertisement, states that the firm will meet any competitor's price on any impending sale. For example, both Lowe's and Home Depot will meet and then beat any competitor's advertised price. A variation of the meet-the-competition clause is a *meet-or-release clause* in a contract. If the buyer can find another seller with a lower price, the contracting seller agrees to either meet the lower price or else release the buyer from the contract, allowing the buyer to purchase the product from the supplier with the lower price.

A primary function of meet-the-competition clauses and meet-or-release clauses is to provide information about competitors' prices. Should some managers violate a tacit price-fixing agreement by offering reduced prices, customers with meet-the-competition clauses in their contracts will quickly notify the company with whom they deal of the lower prices. These provisions inform managers of any price-cutting behavior by their rivals and allow them to match the lower price if they so choose. Such clauses help maintain the higher, tacitly collusive price in two ways. First, the

---

DECISION SNAPSHOT

A Contract in the Market for Propane

Suppose that you are a manager at a firm like AmeriGas, the largest propane marketer in the United States. Your legal department has prepared the following clause to be included in your retail contracts:

> Company has the right to revise the price(s) charged to Customer. If within thirty (30) days after the revision, the Customer furnishes Company with a copy of a bona fide firm written offer from an established propane supplier to sell propane at the designated location in the same quantity under similar terms and conditions at a lower price than Company's revised price, Company may within ten (10) days either meet the lower price or rescind the price change.

Would you approve the inclusion of such a clause in the company's contracts? Why or why not?

Answer

This typical meet-the-competition clause enables you to keep track of the prices your competitors charge. If there is a tacit agreement among propane marketers to raise their price, managers of rival companies know that if they lower their prices in an attempt to steal some market share, you will quickly learn of their tactic and meet their price. Rival managers are more likely to boost their prices in accord with the tacit collusion, keeping propane prices higher than the competitive level. You should therefore decide to include this clause. If there is tacit collusion, the clause will help sustain it, and if there is not, the clause does you no harm because it is your decision whether to meet the competitor's price.

clauses discourage price cheating by increasing price visibility. Second, they eliminate the benefit from price cheating because the original supplier will probably match the rival's lower price in order to retain the customer. As a result, firms are more likely to abide by the joint profit-maximizing price.

Preannouncements

Preannouncing intended price changes can help promote collusion. Early price announcements facilitate any necessary price adjustments by reducing uncertainty among the managers at different firms. The preannouncements provide information to the other managers and signal agreement or disagreement about price changes.

Suppose that all of the firms in the market are operating at the joint profit-maximizing (monopoly) price and output. For example, say the six taxi companies in a city have been able to form and sustain the profit-maximizing tacit collusion illustrated in Figure 7.1. Then changes in cost, perhaps in the cost of gasoline, and/or changes in demand require some adjustment in the price. But price changes are risky: How can the managers of one taxi company know by how much its rivals will change their price? One way to avoid this problem is through early price announcements. The managers of one firm announce to its customers that a new price will become effective in 30 days or 60 days. The other managers can signal either agreement by matching the new price or disagreement by announcing a different price. In effect, the managers can collude with one another without direct communication.

Precommitments

A problem with maintaining a collusive agreement, whether explicit or tacit, is credibility: The assurances of managers that they will refrain from price cutting lack credibility. As you saw in Figure 7.1(b), if the managers of the other taxi companies are charging the monopoly price, the best strategy for the managers of any one firm is to increase the firm's output and, if necessary, reduce its price in order to make additional economic profit. So assurances by managers that they will maintain the monopoly price are not necessarily trustworthy or credible for markets in which prices are not immediately visible.

One way a firm can enhance credibility is to use a **precommitment strategy**, which involves managers voluntarily taking actions that increase the cost of an action that they have not yet taken, thereby making that action nonoptimal. By engaging in precommitment strategies, the managers eliminate various options so that charging the collusive price becomes optimal—and therefore credible.

Precommitment strategy A strategy in which managers voluntarily take actions that increase the cost of an action they have not yet taken, thereby making that action nonoptimal.

A common contractual precommitment strategy is a *most-favored-customer clause,* a clause guaranteeing a firm's customers that they will never pay more than any other customer. Such clauses are quite common. For example, Best Buy offers a 15-day low-price guarantee on televisions for everyone. If Best Buy lowers its price within 15 days after the buyer receives the television, Best Buy will refund the difference to the buyer. Although the common reaction of buyers to such announcements is favorable, offering most-favored-customer clauses can help support tacit collusion. By precommitting to refund to *previous* purchasers the amount of any subsequent price cut, a firm's managers (voluntarily) raise the cost of cheating on any tacitly collusive agreement that might be in place. If the managers of a company cheat on a collusive price-fixing agreement by lowering the price, that company will lose revenue from customers who have *already* previously purchased the product, thereby making price-cutting less profitable. The most-favored-customer clause implicitly signals to other managers in the industry the company's commitment to stand by the tacitly collusive price.

Price Leadership

Price leadership A pattern of pricing in which the managers of one oligopoly firm understood to be the price leader consistently change price before their rivals, after which the rivals make similar price changes.

A final industry practice that helps support tacit collusion is **price leadership**, a pattern of pricing in which the managers of one oligopoly firm understood to be the price leader consistently change price before their rivals, after which the rivals make similar price changes. Price leadership may also occur in dominant firm markets (see Section 6.3), which can display price leadership by the dominant firm.

In theory, the identity of the price leader is not clear. It might be the largest firm in the market or the firm with the lowest cost of production. In both of these situations, the price leader can "threaten" its rivals with a price war if they do not make similar price changes. Alternatively, the price leader might be the firm with managers who are consistently more accurate in setting prices that reflect market conditions. In this case, the other firms' managers use the leader's price as a guide.

To this point in the chapter, you have learned why managers in an oligopoly might be tempted to form a cartel and how in some instances tacit collusion can have the same effect as an overt cartel. Cartels and tacit collusion are difficult to maintain. If oligopoly managers are unable to form a cartel or even to engage in tacit collusion, how do they behave? The next section provides an answer to this question.

SOLVED PROBLEM

Price Leadership in the Market for Insulin

The market for insulin shows price leadership in action. Sanofi and Novo Nordisk are the two producers of long-acting, injectable insulin. In May 2014, Sanofi raised the price of its drug 16.1 percent. The next day Novo Nordisk raised the price of *its* drug by an equal amount, 16.1 percent. This pattern is not unique. Between 2009 and 2014, both companies raised the price of their drugs 13 times, usually within days of each other.

Sanofi's drug was launched in the United States in 2001 and Novo Nordisk's in 2005. Sanofi's drug is slightly more convenient—most patients need to inject it only once a day, while Novo Nordisk's drug often requires two injections. The patent on Sanofi's drug has expired, and at least one generic version was scheduled to be introduced near the start of 2017.

a. What factors might have lead Sanofi's managers to be the price leader?

b. How might the existence of more generic competition affect Sanofi's role as the price leader?

Answer

a. Sanofi's drug was introduced first and is more convenient. As a result of these two factors, in 2014 sales of Sanofi's drug were more than three times those of Novo Nordisk's. Probably because Sanofi is the larger producer in the market, its managers have become the price leader.

b. Sanofi's sales and market power are likely to decrease, especially among new patients as doctors become more familiar with the generic versions and as existing patients become more comfortable with leaving a drug that is working for them. The presence of increased competition might make it more difficult or even impossible for Sanofi to continue as the price leader.

7.3 Four Types of Oligopolies

Learning Objective 7.3 Compare the assumptions and equilibrium outcomes of Cournot, Chamberlin, Stackelberg, and Bertrand oligopolies.

Unlike monopoly and competition, there is no central theory to explain the basis of decisions by oligopoly managers when they cannot sustain a cartel or tacit collusion. Instead, there are several models with almost countless variations. This section examines four of them: Cournot, Chamberlin, Stackelberg, and Bertrand oligopolies. These types of oligopolies differ according to their assumptions about managers' behavior. Cournot and Stackelberg assume that managers compete on quantity, Bertrand assumes that they compete on price, and Chamberlin assumes that they do not compete at all. Clearly, oligopoly managers compete on many dimensions other than quantity and price. The next chapter examines some other forms of competition, including advertising and entry into the market, but this one focuses on quantity and price competition.

Cournot Oligopoly

The **Cournot oligopoly** is named after the French mathematician Augustin Cournot, who developed the model in 1838. The simplest Cournot oligopoly has three assumptions:

Cournot oligopoly A market with two firms in which the managers do not collude and believe that once the rival managers have chosen their quantity, they will not change it.

1. There are two firms in the market (a *duopoly*), and barriers to entry keep other firms from entering.
2. Managers determine quantities with no collusion.
3. The managers at each firm believe that once rival managers choose their quantity, they will not change it.

For simplicity, assume for now that the firms make identical products and that the firms' average total cost and marginal cost are equal and constant. Later you will explore the effects if one firm's costs increase.

Best-Response Function

Suppose that the market for large commercial jets is a Cournot oligopoly with two firms in it: Firm A and Firm B. Although the market has two firms, start by assuming that Firm B is the only firm in the market. In Figure 7.2, the market demand curve is D_{MARKET}, and the marginal revenue curve is MR_{MARKET}. When Firm B is a monopoly, the market demand and marginal revenue are Firm B's demand and marginal revenue. Firm B's marginal cost and average total cost are constant at $10 million per plane and are shown by the line labeled $MC = ATC$. Using marginal analysis and the profit-maximizing rule, Firm B's managers maximize profit by producing 300 planes per year because this is the quantity at which their marginal revenue (MR_{MARKET}) equals their marginal cost (MC). The demand curve shows that at this quantity the profit-maximizing price is $40 million per plane. The usual formula for economic profit, $(P - ATC) \times Q$, shows that Firm B's economic profit as a monopoly equals ($40 million per plane − $10 million per plane) × 300 planes, or $9 billion.

Let's phrase Firm B's production decision a little differently: If Firm A produces 0 planes (so that Firm B is the monopoly producer in the market), Firm B produces 300 planes. Now you need to determine how Firm B's managers adjust their production when Firm A enters the market. To determine Firm B's adjustment, start by supposing that when Firm A enters the market, it produces and sells 100 planes. In

Figure 7.2 An Aircraft Manufacturer as a Monopoly

When Firm B is a monopoly, its demand curve is the market demand curve (D_{MARKET}), and its marginal revenue curve is the market marginal revenue curve (MR_{MARKET}). Firm B's managers maximize profit by producing 300 planes, the quantity that sets the marginal revenue (MR_{MARKET}) equal to the marginal cost (MC).

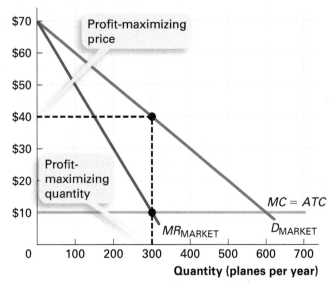

Price and cost (millions of dollars per plane)

accordance with assumption 3 of the Cournot oligopoly model, Firm B's managers believe that Firm A will not change its production from 100 planes. As Table 7.1 shows, when Firm A produces 100 planes, Firm B's demand equals the market demand minus 100 planes. Compared to Firm B's initial demand curve, the market demand curve, its new demand curve shifts to the left by 100 planes. Figure 7.3(a) shows this change: Firm B's new demand curve is D_{100}, and its new marginal revenue curve is MR_{100}. Firm B's managers now maximize profit by producing (only) 250 planes, the quantity that sets MR_{100} equal to MC. Using its new demand, Firm B's price falls to $35 million per plane. The crucial point to remember is that when Firm A produces 100 planes, Firm B responds by producing 250 planes.

Next, suppose that Firm A produces 200 planes when it enters the market and that (again) Firm B's managers assume that Firm A will not change its quantity. Firm A's production of 200 planes decreases Firm B's demand by 200, thereby shifting Firm B's demand curve to the left by 200 planes. In Figure 7.3(b), Firm B's new demand curve is D_{200}, and its new marginal revenue curve is MR_{200}. Firm B's managers now maximize profit by producing 200 planes. So when Firm A produces 200 planes, Firm B responds by producing 200 planes.

Table 7.1 Firm B's Demand

Firm B's demand equals the market demand minus Firm A's quantity.

Price (millions of dollars per plane)	Market Demand (planes)	Firm A's Quantity (planes)	Firm B's Demand (planes)
$60	100	100	0
$50	200	100	100
$40	300	100	200
$30	400	100	300
$20	500	100	400
$10	600	100	500

Figure 7.3 Effect of Firm A's Entry into the Market

(a) Effect on Firm B If Firm A Produces 100 Planes
If Firm A enters the market by producing 100 planes, Firm B's demand decreases. Its demand curve shifts left to D_{100} with the marginal revenue curve MR_{100}. To maximize profit, Firm B's managers produce 250 planes and set a price of $30 million per plane. So Firm A's production of 100 planes causes Firm B to produce 250 planes.

(b) Effect on Firm B If Firm A Produces 200 Planes
If Firm A enters the market by producing 200 planes, Firm B's demand decreases. Its demand curve shifts left to D_{200} with the marginal revenue curve MR_{200}. To maximize profit, Firm B's managers produce 200 planes and set a price of $30 million per plane. So Firm A's production of 200 planes causes Firm B to produce 200 planes.

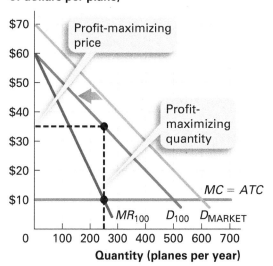

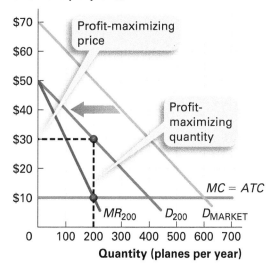

Table 7.2 summarizes the results described above. You can see that for every 100 planes Firm A produces, Firm B decreases its production by 50 planes. Although we have examined only three possible production quantities for Firm A (0, 100, and 200 planes), you can generalize these results. When Firm B's managers expect no further change in production by Firm A, for every 1 plane Firm A produces, Firm B's managers maximize their profit by decreasing their plane production by 0.5 planes.

Figure 7.4 illustrates the relationship between Firm A's production and the best responses by Firm B's managers. For example, if Firm A produces 100 planes, point A shows that Firm B's most profitable response is to produce 250 planes, just as derived above. Similarly, point B shows that if Firm A produces 400 planes, Firm B's best response is to produce 100 planes. The relationship in the figure is

Table 7.2 Firm B's Best-Response Function

For every 100 planes produced by Firm A, Firm B decreases its production by 50 planes. So for every plane produced by Firm A, Firm B responds by decreasing its production by 0.5 planes.

Firm A's Quantity (planes)	Firm B's Quantity (Planes)
0	300
100	250
200	200

Figure 7.4 Firm B's Best-Response Curve

Firm B's best-response curve shows that when Firm B's managers maximize their profit, a 1-plane increase in production by Firm A leads Firm B to decrease its production by 0.5 planes.

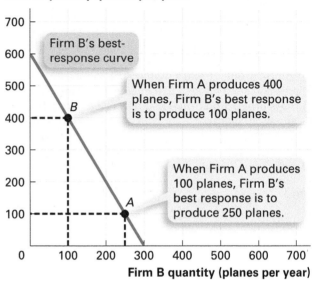

Best-response curve A curve that shows how a firm's profit-maximizing output depends on its competitor's output.

Firm B's **best-response curve** for the Cournot oligopoly, the curve that shows how a firm's profit-maximizing output depends on its competitor's output. Specifically, Figure 7.4 shows how Firm B's most profitable quantity of planes depends on the number of planes produced by Firm A.

Firm A is in the same situation as Firm B: Its most profitable level of output depends on Firm B's output. Firm A therefore also has a best-response curve. Assuming that Firms A and B have identical costs, Firm A's best-response curve, illustrated in Figure 7.5, is similar to Firm B's best-response curve. In particular, Firm A produces 300 planes when Firm B produces 0, Firm A produces 250 planes when Firm B produces 100, and Firm A produces 200 planes when Firm B produces 200. So, just as was the case for Firm B, Firm A cuts its production by 0.5 planes for every 1 plane that Firm B produces.

Figure 7.5 Firm A's Best-Response Curve

Firm A's best-response curve is similar to Firm B's best-response curve: When Firm A's managers maximize profit, a 1-plane increase in production by Firm B leads Firm A to decrease its production by 0.5 planes.

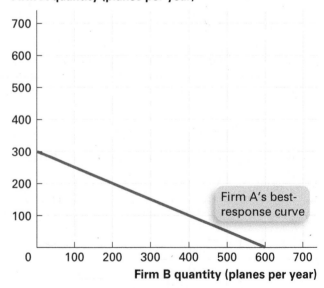

The best-response curves shown in Figures 7.4 and 7.5 illustrate the most profitable responses by the managers of Firms A and B to the other firm's production decisions. In the Cournot oligopoly model, these curves capture the firms' mutual interdependence, illustrating how the decisions of one set of profit-maximizing managers depend on the decisions of the other set.

Cournot Equilibrium

We are now almost ready to answer the key question: What is the market equilibrium? Or more specifically how many planes will the managers at Firms A and B choose to produce, what price will they set, and what will be their profit? The necessary first step to answering these questions is to define what a market equilibrium is in the Cournot model. A **Cournot equilibrium** is a situation in which each set of managers maximizes its firm's profit, taking as given the other firm's production and assuming that the other firm's production will not change. At a Cournot equilibrium, both firms are maximizing their profit, so neither firm's managers have an incentive to change the quantity produced. Of course, the firms are mutually interdependent because each firm's demand and hence its production depend on the other firm's production.

The best-response curves capture the mutual interdependence and show each firm's profit-maximizing response to the other firm's production. The Cournot equilibrium is located at the point where the two best-response curves cross. In Figure 7.6, at this point Firm A produces 200 planes and Firm B produces 200 planes. From Firm B's best-response curve, you can see that its managers maximize its profit by producing 200 planes when Firm A produces 200 planes. Similarly, Firm A's best-response curve shows that its managers maximize its profit by producing 200 planes when Firm B produces 200 planes. *Both* sets of managers are maximizing their firm's profit, taking as given the other firm's production and assuming that the other firm's production will not change, so the point where the two curves cross is the Cournot equilibrium. Because both sets of managers are maximizing their profit, once at the Cournot equilibrium, neither firm's managers will change their firm's production.

Cournot equilibrium The situation in which each set of managers maximizes its firm's profit, taking as given the other firm's production and assuming that the other firm's production will not change.

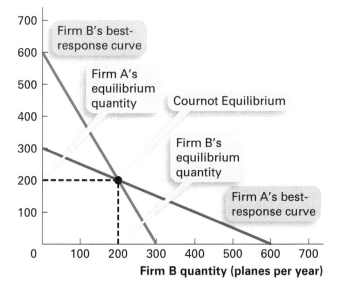

Figure 7.6 Cournot Equilibrium

The intersection of the two best-response curves determines the equilibrium quantities for Firms A and B: Both Firm A and Firm B produce 200 planes.

Figure 7.7 Reaching the Cournot Equilibrium

Starting at point 1, where Firm B is a monopoly, Firm A enters the market and produces at point 2 on its best-response curve. From point 2, Firm B reduces its production to move to point 3 on its best-response curve. From point 3, Firm A increases its production and moves to point 4 on its best-response curve. The process continues until the firms reach the equilibrium point at which both Firm A and Firm B produce 200 planes.

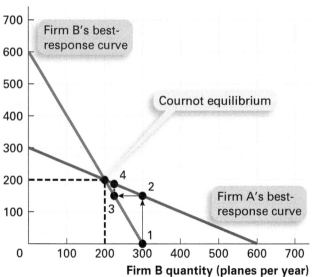

To see how this equilibrium is reached, assume that Firm B is a monopoly and Firm A is not (yet) in the market. This situation is point 1 in Figure 7.7: Firm B is producing 300 planes, and Firm A is producing 0 planes. Now Firm A enters the market. Firm A's best-response curve shows that when Firm B is producing 300 planes, Firm A's managers maximize their profit by producing 150 planes, so that the market moves from point 1 to point 2. At point 2, Firm A's managers have no reason to change, but Firm B's managers are not satisfied. In particular, when Firm A is producing 150 planes, Firm B's best response is *not* 300 planes but instead 225 planes (point 3 on Firm B's best-response curve). Firm B's managers therefore slash their production to 225 planes, and the market moves to point 3. Of course, this process continues because point 3 is not on Firm A's best-response curve. Firm A's managers boost their production, so the market moves to point 4. Eventually this process converges at the equilibrium point, where both firms produce 200 planes.

Incentive to Form a Cartel

At the Cournot equilibrium, each firm produces 200 planes, for a total of 400 planes produced. When 400 planes are produced, the demand curve in Figure 7.2 shows that the price is $30 million per plane. Therefore, Firm B's economic profit, $(P - ATC) \times Q$, equals ($30 million per plane − $10 million per plane) × 200 planes, or $4 billion. Because Firm A's costs are identical to Firm B's, Firm A's economic profit is also $4 billion. The *total* economic profit shared by the two firms is $8 billion—$4 billion each.

At the beginning of the example, when Firm B was the monopoly firm in the market (see Figure 7.2), you saw that it produced 300 planes and made an economic profit of $9 billion. If Firm A was a monopoly, it, too, would produce 300 planes and make an economic profit of $9 billion.

The *total* profit is less when two firms are competing in the market ($8 billion) than when there is only one firm in the market ($9 billion). This difference gives the managers an incentive to form an illegal cartel or a legal tacit collusion. If the managers can cooperate in such a way that production decreases to 300 planes and the price increases, they can split an extra $1 billion in profit. Of course, as you learned in Sections 7.1 and 7.2, such cooperation may be unstable, so the sustainability of cooperation between the two firms is uncertain.

Change in Costs

To this point, you have studied the behavior of two firms with identical costs. Now suppose that the government imposes a tax on only Firm B, perhaps because Firm B is in a different country than Firm A, increasing its costs. For simplicity, assume that the tax is $10 million per plane, so Firm B's marginal cost and average cost each increase by $10 million to $20 million per plane. As illustrated in Figure 7.8, if Firm B is the only firm in the market, after the cost hike its managers maximize profit by producing 250 planes, the quantity that sets the firm's marginal revenue, MR_{MARKET}, equal to its marginal cost, MC. If Firm A now enters the market by producing 100 planes, Firm B's demand and marginal revenue curves become D_{100} and MR_{100}, so the best response by Firm B's managers is to decrease their production by 50 planes, to 200.

You can see that Firm B's managers have the same reaction to Firm A's entry into the market as described earlier: For every 1 plane that Firm A produces, Firm B decreases production by 0.5 planes. After the increase in cost, Firm B's best-response curve is the same as before, with one exception: When Firm A produces 0 planes (that is, when Firm B is a monopoly), B produces 250 planes rather than the 300 it produced when its costs were lower. This difference causes Firm B's best-response curve to shift to the left, so that it crosses the horizontal axis at 250 planes rather than 300 planes. Because Firm A's costs do not change, its best-response curve does not change.

Figure 7.9 shows the two best-response curves, with the new curve for Firm B reflecting its higher costs. The Cournot equilibrium occurs where the two curves cross, which means that Firm B now produces 133 planes and Firm A now produces

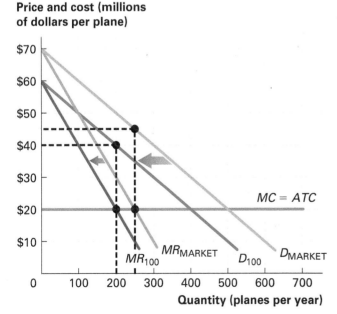

Price and cost (millions of dollars per plane)

Figure 7.8 **Effect on Firm B of an Increase in Its Costs**

When Firm B's marginal and average total costs rise so they now equal $20 million per plane, its managers maximize their profit by producing 250 planes before Firm A enters the market. If Firm A enters the market by producing 100 planes, Firm B's demand curve shifts left to D_{100}, and its marginal revenue curve also shifts left to MR_{100}. After Firm A enters, to maximize profit, Firm B's managers produce 200 planes. The production by Firm A of 100 planes causes Firm B's managers to reduce their production by 50 planes.

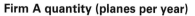

Figure 7.9 The New Cournot Equilibrium

The intersection of the two best-response curves determines the equilibrium quantities for Firm A and Firm B. Firm B produces 133 planes, and Firm A produces 233 planes.

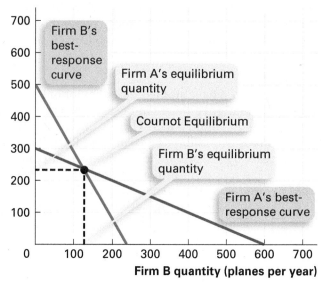

233 planes, for a total of 366. You can see mutual interdependence at work once again: Firm B's higher costs cause its managers to decrease production, which gives Firm A the chance to fill some of the gap by increasing production. The price of the planes can be determined using the demand curve in Figure 7.2, which shows that when 366 planes are produced, the price is $33.3 million per plane.

It probably comes as no surprise that the higher cost causes Firm B's managers to decrease production. More important to the managers, however, is the fact that Firm B's economic profit decreases and Firm A's economic profit increases. After the cost increase, the usual equation for economic profit, $(P - ATC) \times Q$, shows that Firm B's economic profit *falls* from $4 billion to $1.77 billion ($[\$33.3 \text{ million} - \$20 \text{ million}] \times$ 133 planes) and Firm A's economic profit *rises* from $4 billion to $5.43 billion ($[\$33.3 \text{ million} - \$10 \text{ million}] \times$ 233 planes).

Calculating the economic profits of these two companies is straightforward in this simplified example. In more realistic cases, calculating the economic profit becomes difficult. The general result continues to hold true, however: If a firm's costs increase, its economic profit decreases, and its competitor's economic profit increases. Consequently, managers in an oligopoly can increase *their* profit if they can raise their *rival's* costs. For example, suppose that Firm A is located in Europe and Firm B in the United States. Say the U.S. government lowers Firm B's costs by various subsidies, while the governments of France and the United Kingdom use similar policies to lower Firm A's costs. Consequently, to raise Firm A's costs, the top executives of Firm B lobby the U.S. government to protest Firm A's subsidies, while the top executives of Firm A lobby the French and British governments to protest Firm B's subsidies. Both sets of managers know that elimination of their rival's subsidies will increases that rival's costs. So if Firm B's lobbying efforts are successful and Firm A loses its subsidy, then Firm A's costs increase, increasing Firm B's economic profit and decreasing Firm A's economic profit. Of course, *any* action that increases a competitor's costs can benefit the firm whose cost does not increase.

South Africa's Impala Platinum as a Cournot Oligopolist

Platinum is an expensive, gray-white element used primarily in automotive cata-lytic converters and jewelry. Three of the four largest producers—Angelo Platinum, Impala Platinum, and Lonmin—are South African firms and together account for about 60 percent of worldwide sales of platinum. When one develops a new mine, its production adds to the world production. Suppose that each company's marginal cost of production is equal to that of its rivals and further assume that the platinum producers are Cournot oligopolists. Say that the managers of Angelo Platinum open a new mine and increase production. As a manager at Impala Platinum, how should you respond? What effect will Angelo Platinum's new mine have on Impala Platinum's economic profit?

Answer
As a Cournot oligopolist, your best response when a rival increases production is to decrease your production. The extent of your reduction depends on precisely how your demand and marginal cost change when output changes, information that is not given here. You do know, however, that your economic profit will decrease because the price of platinum will fall, as will your production.

Extensions of the Cournot Oligopoly

We have explored the most basic Cournot oligopoly by assuming that there are only two firms in the market with constant average and marginal costs. Relaxing these assumptions makes the model more complicated and more realistic, but the results are qualitatively similar:

- **Number of firms.** The larger the number of firms in the market is, the closer the market comes to perfect competition. In a perfectly competitive market, the quantity is determined at the equilibrium of the market demand and market supply. As you learned in Chapter 5, in a perfectly competitive market, the market supply curve is the sum of the firms' marginal cost curves, which means that in Figure 7.2 the curve labeled $MC = ATC$ is the market supply curve. Consequently, in a per-fectly competitive market, the equilibrium quantity is 600 planes. In a market with a single firm (a monopoly), you saw in Figure 7.3(a) that the equilibrium quantity is 300 planes.

  The Cournot oligopoly lies between these two extremes. If there are two firms in the market, the total quantity is 400 planes. Intuitively, it seems reasonable that the more firms in the market, the larger the quantity. This presumption is correct: The market quantity is equal to $\left(\frac{n}{n+1}\right) \times Q_{\text{COMPETITIVE}}$, where n is the number of firms and $Q_{\text{COMPETITIVE}}$ is the competitive quantity of output.[2] If the airplane market is a duopoly with two firms, the quantity equals $\left(\frac{2}{2+1}\right) \times 600$ planes, or 400 planes. If the market has three firms, the quantity

---

2 We prove this result in Section 7.A of the Appendix at the end of this chapter.

equals $\left(\frac{3}{3+1}\right) \times 600$ planes, or 450 planes. The crucial point to remember is this: The more firms in the market, the larger the quantity and the lower the price. The lower price decreases each firm's profit, which gives the managers an incentive to erect barriers to entry to keep the number of firms in the market as small as possible.

- **Constant costs.** The assumptions that the firms' marginal costs are constant and that the demand curve is linear make the best-response curves shown in Figures 7.4, 7.5, and 7.6 linear. If the marginal cost curve is not linear and/or the demand curve is not linear, then the best-response curves, while downward sloping, will not be linear.[3] Although the best-response curves are more complicated, the essential result is unaffected: The duopolists have a smaller total economic profit than a monopoly, which gives the managers the incentive to create a price-fixing cartel or a tacit collusion.

Chamberlin Oligopoly

Edward Chamberlin, a prominent American economist of the mid-20th century, argued that the managers in a Cournot oligopoly do not really behave in a profit-maximizing way. In particular, Chamberlin rejected one assumption of the Cournot model: that each firm's managers believe that after its competitors' managers choose their quantity, they will not change it. The Cournot oligopoly's best-response curves show that except at the equilibrium, managers *always* react by changing their production in response to their competitors' change. It is hard to believe that actual managers will continue to behave according to the assumption that they expect no change in their rivals' choice. Even the dullest set of managers must eventually learn that its rivals respond to its changes in output! So Chamberlin developed the **Chamberlin oligopoly**, a model of a market with two firms that produce identical products, have identical and constant average total costs and marginal costs, and in which rivals respond to one another's actions. This model is similar to the Cournot oligopoly except for the assumption that the managers expect their rivals to respond to their actions. Intuitively, the managers "look" around the market and are attracted by the outcome that maximizes their joint profit. Effectively, this model provides a foundation for tacit collusion.

The most straightforward way to determine the outcome in a Chamberlin oligopoly is to start by assuming that the market is a monopoly into which a new firm enters. Returning to our airplane example, suppose that Firm A and Firm B have the same costs—that is, an average total cost and a marginal cost of $10 million per plane. The new equilibrium can be determined by using Figure 7.10, which has the same best-response curves as Figure 7.7. Suppose once again that Firm B has the (initial) monopoly, so the market starts at point 1: Firm B produces 300 planes at a price of $40 million each and Firm A produces 0 planes. When Firm A enters the market, its best-response curve takes it to point 2, so that its output, 150 planes, is one-half of the monopoly output of 300 planes, just as before. Also as in the previous example, the issue becomes how Firm B's managers respond to Firm A's entry into the airplane market. The Cournot oligopoly model assumed that Firm B's managers respond by cutting their production to 225 planes, thereby moving to point 3 on Firm B's best-response curve. But the Chamberlin model

Chamberlin oligopoly A market with two firms that produce identical products, have identical and constant average total costs and marginal costs, and in which rivals respond to one another's actions.

3 See Section 7.A of the Appendix at the end of this chapter for an example of a nonlinear best-response curve.

Firm A quantity (planes per year)

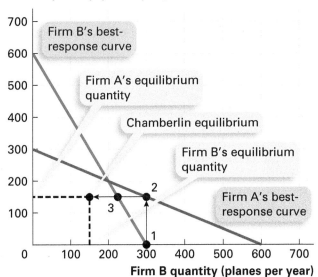

Figure 7.10 Reaching the Chamberlin Equilibrium

Firm A enters the market by going from point 1 to 2 on its best-response curve. The managers of Firm B realize that if they now decrease their production to 150 planes, they and Firm A can split the monopoly economic profit, with each firm producing 150 planes. The outcome in which the firms split the monopoly economic profit is the Chamberlin equilibrium.

makes the more realistic assumption that if Firm B's managers cut their production to 225 planes—point 3 on Firm B's best-response curve—they know that Firm A will then increase its production. According to Chamberlin's reasoning, Firm B's actual best response is to ignore its Cournot best-response curve and instead slash its production to 150 planes. In turn, Firm A will respond by maintaining its production at 150 planes. With this outcome, the two firms combined produce the monopoly quantity (300 planes), and the price is the monopoly price, $40 million per plane. The two firms can then split the monopoly economic profit of $9 billion, or $4.5 billion each.

This is the best outcome for the firms because one-half of the monopoly economic profit is more than one-half of the profit from any other output. Firm A's managers realize that if they change their production, then Firm B's managers will respond and the ultimate outcome will be worse for Firm A than sharing half of the monopoly economic profit. Consequently, once Firm B (and Firm A) each produce 150 planes, neither firm's managers have an incentive to change. The market is at its *Chamberlin equilibrium*.

In contrast to a Cournot oligopoly, which does not have an actual cartel or tacit collusion, the Chamberlin oligopoly includes at least an unspoken agreement. After Firm A's entry, Firm B's managers made a show of "good faith" or acquiescence by substantially reducing their previous output. Instead of trying to take advantage of Firm B's reduction in output, Firm A's managers reciprocated by holding their output at one-half of the monopoly output. Presumably, the two sets of managers will live happily ever after. There is a problem with this outcome, however. There is no reason for either set of managers to restrain their greed. The rationale for restraint is based on profit maximization only if you assume that the managers take into account their rival's future actions. The model effectively *assumes* that the firms will share the monopoly level of production. A more sophisticated approach examines whether the assumed outcome is reasonable using game theory, which you will learn about in Chapter 8. For now, let's turn to the Stackelberg approach, which takes a different approach to the Cournot model's problematic assumption that managers expect their rivals not to respond to their actions.

Stackelberg Oligopoly

Stackelberg oligopoly A
market in which one firm
(the leader) makes its
production decision first,
knowing that the second
firm (the follower) will
make its production
decision taking the leader's
production as given.

In 1934, Heinrich Stackelberg, a German economist, developed the **Stackelberg oligopoly**, which makes three assumptions that differ from the Cournot model:

1. One firm, called the *leader* (or the first mover) makes its production decision before the other firm, called the *follower* (or the second mover).
2. The leader will not change its initial production.
3. The leader knows that the follower will take the leader's production as given when determining its profit-maximizing production.

Effectively, the follower firm behaves as a Cournot oligopolist: The follower assumes that the leader will not respond to its production decision. Consequently, the follower will determine its production from its Cournot best-response function. Importantly, the leader knows how the follower will react.

Because the leader knows how the follower will respond, the leader can take the follower's reaction into account when deciding on its initial level of production. You might expect that the first-mover advantage should enable the leader to increase its profit. This presumption is correct. To see this result, let's return to our airplane example, in which Firm A and Firm B are a duopoly with the same average total costs and marginal costs of $10 million per plane and with the same market demand curve, illustrated in Figure 7.11. Suppose that Firm B is the leader and makes the first production decision. Firm B must choose the quantity that will maximize its profit, knowing that Firm A will respond according to its best-response function. The result of the mathematics necessary to determine Firm B's quantity is that Firm B will produce 300 planes.[4] Firm A's best-response curve in Figure 7.5 demonstrates that Firm A will respond to B's production by producing 150 planes. Together, Firms A and B produce 450 planes, so the market demand curve shows that the price is $25 million per plane. This outcome—300 planes from Firm B and 150 planes from Firm A at a price of $25 million per plane—is the Stackelberg equilibrium.

Figure 7.11 The Market Demand and the Firms' Cost Curves

The figure shows the market demand (D_{MARKET}) curve and the marginal cost (MC) and average total cost (ATC) curve for Firms A and B.

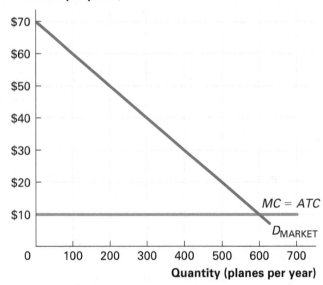

Price and cost (millions of dollars per plane)

4 Section 7.B of the Appendix at the end of this chapter formally verifies that Firm B produces 300 planes.

In both the Cournot oligopoly and the Chamberlin oligopoly, the firms split the profit equally. In the Stackelberg oligopoly, however, the leader makes off with the lion's share of the profit. In the example, Firm B's economic profit is ($25 million − $10 million) × 300 planes, or $4.5 billion, and Firm A's economic profit is only ($25 million − $10 million) × 150 planes, or $2.25 billion. The additional economic profit made by the leader reflects the first-mover advantage. By making its decision first *and* by having knowledge of how its rival will respond, the leader's managers can increase their profit.

In this example, firm B's production is the same as a monopoly's production, and it makes half of the monopoly economic profit. These results are not general; if the demand curve is not linear and/or the marginal cost curve is not linear, then the leader's production is not necessarily the same as that of a monopoly, and its economic profit is not necessarily one-half of the monopoly economic profit.

Bertrand Oligopoly

The Bertrand oligopoly is named after a French mathematician, Joseph Bertrand, who developed the model in 1883. Bertrand took issue with a different key assumption of the Cournot model than Chamberlin or Stackelberg—namely, that the firms select the quantity they will produce. Bertrand suggested that some oligopolists select the price rather than the quantity. So the simplest version of the **Bertrand oligopoly** is identical to the Cournot oligopoly except that managers choose their price rather than their quantity: a market with two firms, each producing an identical product, and in which the managers determine their price and believe that once the rival managers have chosen their price, they will not change it. The distinction between setting the quantity and setting the price might appear to have a negligible effect on the equilibrium outcome, but it actually has an unexpectedly large impact.

Returning to the commercial jet example, assume once again that the marginal and average total costs are equal and constant and that Firm B is the only firm in the market when Firm A enters. Figure 7.12 illustrates the situation confronting the managers of Firm A: Firm B is producing 300 planes at a price of $40 million each. Firm A's managers must now determine the price they will set, knowing that their planes are identical to those of Firm B. Firm A's managers know that if they set a price of

Bertrand oligopoly A market with two firms, each producing an identical product, and in which the managers do not collude and believe that once the rival managers have chosen their price, they will not change it.

Price and cost (millions of dollars per plane)

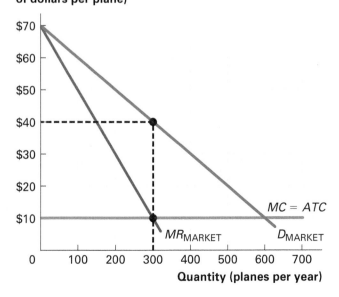

Figure 7.12 The Bertrand Oligopoly

In a Bertrand oligopoly, if Firm B is the only firm in the market, its managers set a price of $40 million per plane. When Firm A enters, its managers set a price of $39,999,999, and all of the airlines switch to buy their planes from them. But Firm B's managers respond by setting a price of $39,999,998, so all the airlines again switch to now buy from Firm B. The price continues to fall until it equals $10 million. Neither firm will set a price lower than $10 million because doing so would create an economic loss. The equilibrium has both firms setting a price of $10 million and making zero economic profit.

$39,999,999, *all* airlines will purchase their planes because they are identical to Firm B's planes and are $1 cheaper. Firm A, of course, makes a hefty economic profit because the price exceeds the average total cost ($10 million) by a healthy amount. Firm B, on the other hand, now produces 0 planes because everyone is buying from Firm A.

This is not the end of the story, however. Firm B's managers will hardly rest if they have no sales. What is their best response? Firm B's managers can reason as well as Firm A's managers. The managers at Firm B realize that if they set a price of $39,999,998, they will steal all the sales from Firm A because then every airline will buy the now-cheaper Firm B planes.

Managers at the two firms continue to respond to each other's prices until the price reaches $10 million. Neither firm's managers will decrease their price below $10 million because any lower price—say, $9,999,999—inflicts an economic loss on the firm. Therefore, at the Bertrand equilibrium, both firms set a price of $10 million for their planes and together produce 600 planes. Because the price equals the average total cost, both firms make only a competitive return, essentially the same result as they were operating in a competitive market.

This result stands in stark contrast to the Cournot equilibrium, in which both firms make an economic profit. The extreme equilibrium in a Bertrand oligopoly results from the assumption that the firms' products are identical. If you make the more realistic assumption that Firm A's and Firm B's planes are not identical, then the price competition will not force the price so low that both firms make only a competitive return. If the firms make products that are substitutes (but not perfect substitutes), the price will exceed the average total cost, and both firms will make some economic profit.

Comparing Oligopoly Models

In this section, you learned about four different oligopoly models that provide insight into how differences in market operations can affect managerial decisions. Table 7.3 summarizes those models as well as the other market structures you have studied and compares the results from applying them to the plane example.

Table 7.3 Outcomes Under Different Market Structures

Market Structure	Characteristics	Equilibrium Price and Quantity	Economic Profit
Competitive	• Many firms • No barriers to entry	• $10 million per plane • 600 planes in total	• $0 per firm • $0 in total
Monopoly	• Single firm • Insurmountable barriers to entry	• $40 million per plane • 300 planes in total	• $9 billion
Cournot oligopoly	• Two firms • Managers select quantity assuming rival will not react	• $30 million per plane • 200 planes per firm • 400 planes in total	• $4 billion per firm • $8 billion in total
Chamberlin oligopoly	• Two firms • Managers of each firm select one-half the monopoly quantity	• $40 million per plane • 150 planes per firm • 300 planes in total	• $4.5 billion per firm • $9 billion in total
Stackelberg oligopoly	• Two firms • Leader selects quantity, knowing follower chooses quantity assuming leader will not react to the choice	• $25 million per plane • Leader: 300 planes • Follower: 150 planes • 450 planes in total	• Leader: $4.5 billion • Follower: $2.25 billion • $6.75 billion in total
Bertrand oligopoly	• Two firms • Managers select price assuming rival will not react	• $10 million per plane • 300 planes per firm • 600 planes in total	• $0 per firm • $0 in total

The prices, quantities, and economic profits in Table 7.3 are specific to the airplane example with Firms A and B, but the qualitative results are more general. For example, only in a Chamberlin oligopoly, in which the managers of the firms tacitly collude, are both firms able to make one-half of the economic profit a monopoly would make. And only in the Stackelberg oligopoly is the leader able to make more profit than the follower. In all other types of oligopolies, each firm makes less than one-half of a monopoly's economic profit. Indeed, in the case of a Bertrand oligopoly, firms that make identical products wind up with zero economic profit.

Coca-Cola Reacts to PepsiCo

SOLVED
PROBLEM

The Coca-Cola Company (Coca-Cola) and PepsiCo have a combined market share of approximately 70 percent of the soda market, but for the purposes of this example, assume that they are a Cournot duopoly. The figure shows the hypothetical market demand curve and marginal revenue curve for 12-packs of soda. For both companies, suppose that the marginal costs and average total costs are constant at $2 per 12-pack of soda.

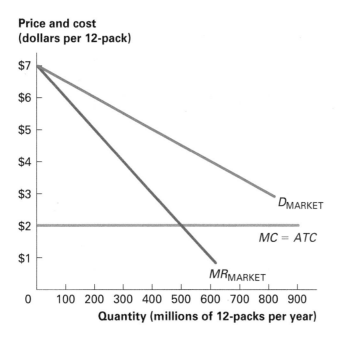

a. If Coca-Cola is the only firm in the market, draw a figure showing the equilibrium quantity and price of a 12-pack of soda.

b. Suppose that PepsiCo enters the market and produces 400 million 12-packs of soda. In the figure you drew for part a, show how Coca-Cola's managers respond.

c. If PepsiCo produces 800 million 12-packs of soda, in the figure you used for parts a and b, show how Coca-Cola's managers will respond.

d. Identify three points on Coca-Cola's best-response curve.

(Continues)

SOLVED PROBLEM (*continued*)

Answer

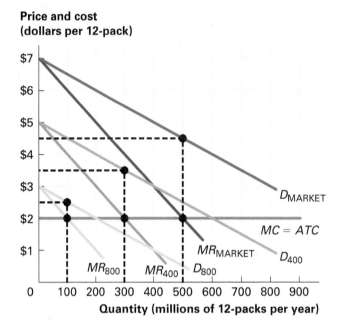

a. If Coca-Cola is a monopoly, the figure shows that its profit-maximizing quantity is 500 million 12-packs per year and its profit-maximizing price is $4.50 per 12-pack.

b. When PepsiCo produces 400 million 12-packs of soda, both the demand curve and the marginal revenue curve faced by Coca-Cola shift to the left by 400 million, in the figure to D_{400} and MR_{400}, respectively. Coca-Cola's managers maximize their profit by producing 300 million 12-packs and setting a price of $3.50 per 12-pack.

c. When PepsiCo produces 800 million 12-packs of soda, both the demand curve and the marginal revenue curve faced by Coca-Cola shift to the left by 800 million, to D_{800} and MR_{800}, respectively. Coca-Cola's managers maximize their profit by producing 100 million 12-packs and setting a price of $2.50 per 12-pack.

d. Three points on Coca-Cola's best-response curve are as follows: (1) Coca-Cola produces 500 million 12-packs/PepsiCo produces zero 12-packs; (2) Coca-Cola produces 300 million 12-packs/PepsiCo produces 400 million 12-packs; and (3) Coca-Cola produces 100 million 12-packs/PepsiCo produces 800 million 12-packs.

MANAGERIAL APPLICATION

7.4 Cartels and Oligopoly

Learning Objective 7.4 Apply the economic theory of cartels and the different types of oligopolies to help make more profitable managerial decisions.

As you have learned in previous chapters, economic analysis is not a cookbook of specific recipes that give you exact measurements and directions for managing your business. Instead, using the models and guidelines can help you analyze the situation and make more profitable managerial decisions.

Many of the guidelines from previous chapters apply to oligopolies and cartels as well as other types of market structures. For example, the most basic lesson learned from marginal analysis is to continue to produce until the marginal revenue from additional production equals the marginal cost. This lesson applies equally to decision making in competitive markets, monopoly markets, and cartels. To make the maximum economic profit, firms in a cartel or engaged in tacit collusion follow the same profit-maximizing rule: Produce the quantity that sets the marginal revenue equal to the marginal cost. Because a cartel or tacit collusion sets the price and quantity for the market, it guides its production by using the *market* marginal revenue rather than using the marginal revenue that each member firm faces.

Using Cartel Theory and Tacit Collusion for Managerial Decision Making

Although potentially quite profitable, cartels are illegal, and as a manager, you are responsible for avoiding them. Tacit collusion, on the other hand, is *not* illegal. So if you compete in an oligopolistic market, the most important takeaway from our examination of tacit collusion is that you need to observe and interpret your competitors' actions in the following three categories:

- **Price visibility.** If the managers of one of your rivals change the firm's standard contract with its buyers to include a new meet-the-competition clause, those managers might be tacitly suggesting that they are willing to raise their price because, with the new clause, they will immediately know if you set a lower price. Accordingly, they know that if you agree with their implicit suggestion to raise price, you will be more likely to keep your price high, thereby making the tacit agreement more profitable.
- **Preannouncements.** Has a rival started to preannounce price changes? If so, the rival's managers may be signaling their intent to engage in tacit collusion. For example, if one of the three major theme parks in Orlando preannounces price changes, those managers might be trying to create a tacit collusion featuring higher prices.
- **Price leadership.** If one firm in your market is consistently the first to change price, it might be a signal that those managers are offering to be the price leader. For example, in a small town with just two or three nearby gas stations, if one station is always a day or two ahead of the others when changing price, the managers of this station might be volunteering to be the price leader in a tacit collusion.

Of course, if you are *buying* from an oligopolistic market, these same practices can help warn you that your suppliers might be tacitly colluding to boost the price of your purchases. For example, has your supplier changed the specifications of the product to match those of its rivals and started to publicize the product's price? You might want to worry because both changes help sustain a tacit collusion. If you believe that your supplier is engaged in cartel activity, in the United States you can involve government antitrust authorities, such as the Department of Justice, as well as file a private lawsuit seeking damages. Under U.S. law, a winning plaintiff can claim three times the amount of damages it suffered, called treble damages, which is a nice reward if you have been the victim of an illegal cartel. Chapter 9 covers U.S. antitrust law and international competition laws in more detail.

Using Types of Oligopolies for Managerial Decision Making

As shown in Table 7.3, the difference between the firms' economic profit in a Cournot oligopoly and in a Bertrand oligopoly is striking. In the simplest versions of these models, the Bertrand model's price competition eliminates all possible economic profit. This extreme result of zero economic profit hinges on two assumptions: that the firms' products are identical and that the firms compete using price. If the products are not identical, Bertrand price competition will force the price down, but the firms may still make some economic profit. And if the firms compete using quantity, as in the Cournot model, they can make an economic profit. Two managerial implications are clear: First, earning an economic profit is difficult when producing identical products. Differentiating your product so it is no longer identical to your rival's product can help you make economic profit. Second, competing on price in a market where firms produce identical or, more generally, very similar products is a bad idea. Competing on other attributes might prove more profitable. According to the Cournot oligopoly model, the only other attribute is quantity, but in the real world, other features such as product safety and delivery time also come into play.

The key general lesson you can learn from the various types of oligopolies is straightforward: As a manager in an oligopolistic market, you must take into account your rivals' best responses to your decisions and consider *your* best response to *their* actions. As a manager, you will never calculate a best-response curve (as we did for the Cournot oligopoly in Section 7.3), but this exercise demonstrates the importance of placing yourself in the shoes of the rival managers and thinking about how they will respond to your decisions. In the discussion of the Chamberlin oligopoly, you saw that the decision by the existing firm's managers to slash production after the new firm enters the market helped create tacit collusion that allowed both firms to split the largest possible economic profit. In the discussion of the Stackelberg oligopoly, you learned that the leader (or first mover) who knows the follower's response was able to grab a larger portion of the potential economic profit. More generally, an understanding of these models and of your rivals' positions and motivations helps you make the managerial decision that leads to your preferred outcome.

The idea that managers of oligopolistic firms have a best response to their rivals' actions is fundamental to competing in any situation with mutual interdependence. Chapter 8 continues examining this idea using a different approach, called game theory, which focuses more directly on managerial strategies. As you will learn, game theory has immediate applications to oligopoly and many other business decisions.

Revisiting How Managers at Major Publishers Read the e-Writing on the e-Wall

You saw at the beginning of this chapter that publishing company executives wanted to raise the $9.99 price Amazon.com was charging for their newly published e-books. The executives knew that they could not individually force Amazon to raise the price and that any explicit joint action, such as forming a cartel, is illegal. The managers were therefore eager to listen as Apple's managers presented their ideas for selling e-books in Apple's iBookstore. The most appealing aspect of the arrangement with Apple was "agency pricing," in which the publishers, not the retailers, set the price of the books. Importantly, Apple's contracts also included one of the precommitment strategies that was described in this chapter—a most-favored-customer clause. If any other retailer sold an e-book at a lower price, the publisher would be required to match the price in Apple's iBookstore. Apple was willing to list the e-books for a higher price in its iBookstore—say, $15.99—but if the publishing company allowed Amazon to set a lower price, the publisher was then obligated to set the same lower price in Apple's iBookstore.

When publishing executives signed Apple's contracts with its most-favored-customer clause, they forced themselves to lower their price in the iBookstore if they allowed Amazon to sell their e-books at $9.99. In terms of lost profit, this clause raised the cost to those publishers who agreed to Amazon's price. Because all five publishers signed similar contracts, they were able to present a united front when threatening to cease wholesaling e-books to Amazon. The contract with Apple effectively allowed the publishers to establish a cartel and boost the price set by Amazon.

The U.S. Department of Justice entered the fray, alleging that Apple's contract violated U.S. antitrust laws. The Justice Department took Apple and the five publishing companies to court, seeking to overturn the contracts. The executives of all five publishing companies settled before the case was heard. Apple refused to settle but lost in court. The publishing executives agreed to let Amazon and other retailers set whatever price they wanted for e-books for two years and to forego any most-favored-customer clauses in their contracts for five years.

Summary: The Bottom Line

7.1 Cartels

- An oligopoly is a market structure in which a small number of mutually interdependent firms compete. A duopoly is a market structure with two firms.
- A cartel is an illegal arrangement in which a group of producers agrees to not compete on price, quantity, quality, and promotional activity.
- Cartels are unstable because each firm's self-interest often conflicts with the common interest of the cartel. Cartels are easier to form and maintain if the products are similar and there are only a small number of firms in the market.

7.2 Tacit Collusion

- Tacit collusion is an informal, unstated agreement on price and quantity among the managers of different firms. In contrast to cartels, tacit collusion is legal.
- Business practices that increase the possibility of tacit collusion include heightened price visibility, preannouncements of price changes, precommitment strategies such as most-favored-customer clauses and meet-the-competition clauses, and price leadership by one firm.

7.3 Four Types of Oligopolies

- In a Cournot oligopoly, the managers determine their quantities with no collusion and believe that once rival managers choose their quantity, they will not change it. At a Cournot equilibrium, both firms are on their best-response curves, and both make an economic profit.
- In a Chamberlin oligopoly, the managers take account of the fact that their rivals will respond to one another's actions. Both firms in a Chamberlin duopoly split the profit-maximizing monopoly economic profit.
- In a Stackelberg oligopoly, one firm (the leader) makes its production decision, knowing that the second firm (the follower) will make its production decision taking the leader's production as given. The leader makes a larger economic profit than the follower.
- In a Bertrand oligopoly, the managers determine their prices with no collusion and believe that once rival managers choose their price, they will not change it. If the products produced by the firms are identical, the firms set their price equal to the competitive price and make zero economic profit. If the products are not identical, the firms can make an economic profit.

7.4 Managerial Application: Cartels and Oligopolies

- Managers must be alert to the actions of market rivals to determine whether they are attempting to engage in tacit collusion and be prepared to respond.
- When thinking about changing price or quantity, put yourself in your rivals' shoes to try to determine their best response to your change and how their response will affect you.

Key Terms and Concepts

Bertrand oligopoly	Cournot equilibrium	Price leadership
Best-response curve	Cournot oligopoly	Stackelberg oligopoly
Cartel	Oligopoly	Tacit collusion
Chamberlin oligopoly	Precommitment strategy	

Questions and Problems

7.1 Cartels

Learning Objective 7.1 Explain why cartels are potentially profitable but unstable and difficult to sustain.

1.1 The figure shows the market for central processing unit (CPU) chips. If the firms' managers compete with each other, what are the price and quantity of CPU chips? Now suppose that the producers form a cartel that maximizes the firms' total profit. What now are the price and quantity of CPU chips? In which scenario do the firms make a larger economic profit?

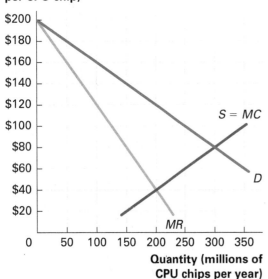

Price and cost (dollars per CPU chip)

1.2 The market demand for a month's supply of a generic medicine is $Q^d = 400 - 0.5P$. The demand can be rewritten as $P = 800 - 2Q$, so that the marginal revenue is $MR = 800 - 4Q$. The marginal cost (MC) and average total cost (ATC) are constant, and both equal $40. Consequently, the supply curve is $P = MC = \$40$.

   a. If the firms' managers compete, what quantity is produced, what is the price, and what is the total economic profit made by all of the firms combined?

   b. If the firms' managers form a price-fixing cartel that maximizes the firms' total profit, what total combined quantity do the firms

produce, what price do they set, and what is the total combined economic profit made by the firms?

   c. Suppose that the managers have formed the price-fixing cartel described in part b. If one firm increases its production by one unit and the price does not change, what is the change in that firm's economic profit?

1.3 Suppose that all five of the producers of ready-mix cement in the Denver area have entered into a cartel agreement, so that they are producing and pricing at the profit-maximizing monopoly level.

   a. How would a firm's managers "cheat" on this agreement?

   b. Given that the four other competitors' reactions are *not* instantaneous, can cheating be profitable?

1.4 It is illegal for a trade association to report the prices charged by each of its members. Why?

1.5 Successful cartels raise the participants' profit. Why, then, do nations have laws making cartels illegal?

7.2 Tacit Collusion

Learning Objective 7.2 Describe how managers can engage in and sustain tacit collusion to boost their prices and economic profit.

2.1 How does tacit collusion differ from a cartel, and why is the difference important for managers?

2.2 In the cement industry, producers generally announce their prices by sending price lists to customers 60 to 90 days in advance of the effective date. Inevitably, the managers of other cement producers find out the rivals' prices. What might the managers of the cement producers be attempting to achieve with these price announcements?

2.3 In a small town, the managers of the three janitorial service firms have tacitly agreed to charge $150 per week for cleaning a standard-sized office. Each firm services 200 offices. The marginal cost and average total cost of cleaning an office are both $130.

   a. What is each firm's economic profit?

   b. Suppose that a new office opens. Its owners tell the managers of one of the janitorial service firms that they will hire the janitorial service—but only if the price is $140 per week. Is this new contract profitable for this firm? If the janitorial service managers sign the contract, how would it affect the tacit collusion among the firms?

c. Suppose that the janitorial service's contracts with its 200 existing customers all have most-favored-customer clauses. Now if the owners of the new office offer to sign a contract only if the price is $140 per week, is it profitable for the janitorial service firm to sign the contract? Why or why not? How does this clause affect the tacit agreement? If the company agrees to the new contract, what will be the effect on the tacit agreement?

2.4 Of the 13 nations in OPEC, Saudi Arabia has the second-largest oil reserves and the lowest cost of production. How do these facts support the idea that Saudi Arabia is the price leader in OPEC?

7.3 Four Types of Oligopolies

Learning Objective 7.3 Compare the assumptions and equilibrium outcomes of Cournot, Chamberlin, Stackelberg, and Bertrand oligopolies.

3.1 Two airlines, Global Air and World Air, fly out of an airport in a medium-sized city. The airlines' costs are the same and are illustrated in the figure. The figure also shows the market

demand curve (*D*) and marginal revenue curve (*MR*). Suppose that the two firms act as Cournot duopolists.

a. If there is only one airline in the market, what are the price and quantity of tickets? What is the firm's economic profit?

b. Draw the best-response curves for Global Air and World Air.

c. What is the Cournot equilibrium? How does the total economic profit compare to the total economic profit when the market had only one firm in it?

d. What is the Chamberlin equilibrium? What is each firm's price and quantity of tickets? What is each firm's economic profit?

e. What is the Bertrand equilibrium? What is each firm's price and quantity of tickets? What is each firm's economic profit?

f. Do the firms have an incentive to form a price-fixing cartel? Why or why not?

3.2 Suppose that there are only two companies producing video-game consoles, Gamer Great and Player. Say that the companies' costs, illustrated in the figure, are the same. The figure also shows the market demand curve (*D*) and marginal revenue curve (*MR*) for game consoles. The market demand curve is given by $Q^d = 21{,}000{,}000 - 30{,}000P$. Suppose that Gamer Great initially was the only firm producing a game console.

Price and cost (dollars per seat)

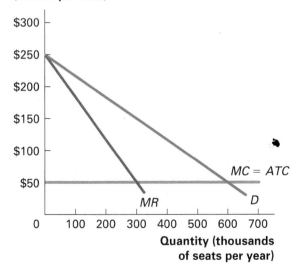

Price and cost (dollars per game console)

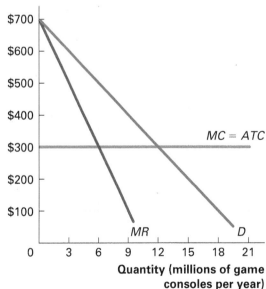

a. When Gamer Great is the monopoly producer of game consoles, what are the price and quantity of consoles? What is Gamer Great's economic profit?

b. Supposing that Gamer Great and Player compete as Cournot duopolists, draw their best-response curves.

c. If Gamer Great is a monopoly and then Player enters the market, how many game consoles will Player produce?

d. After Player has entered the market and produces the number of consoles in the answer to part c, how will Gamer Great react? How many consoles will Gamer Great now produce?

e. What is the Cournot equilibrium? What is each firm's price and quantity of consoles? What is each firm's economic profit?

3.3 Two dry cleaners in a small city have reached a Cournot equilibrium. What occurs in the long run, when other firms enter the market?

3.4 You are a manager of one of two firms competing in a Bertrand oligopoly. You and your competitor have reached the Bertrand equilibrium.

a. If your products and those of your rival are identical (they are perfect substitutes), what happens to the quantity demanded of your product if you raise the price $1 above the equilibrium price? What happens to your profit?

b. If your products and those of your rival are not identical (they are imperfect substitutes), what happens to the quantity demanded of your product if you raise the price $1 above the equilibrium price?

3.5 In the Stackelberg oligopoly example in Section 7.3, Firm B produces 300 planes and Firm A, using its best-response curve, responds by producing 150 planes. Once Firm A produces 150 planes, suppose that Firm B can change its production. In this case, is 300 planes Firm B's best response to Firm A's production of 150 planes? If Firm A can next change *its* production, what is the likely outcome? How important is it for Firm B to commit to *not* changing the initial quantity of planes?

3.6 Suppose that the market demand for expensive steak dinners is given by $Q = 1,000 - 10P$, so that the marginal revenue is $MR = 100 - 0.2Q$, where Q is the number of steak dinners per day

and P is the price of a dinner. The marginal cost and average total cost are both constant and equal to $40 per dinner.

a. If there is only one firm in the market, what quantity will the firm produce, what price will the firm set, and what is the firm's economic profit?

b. If a second firm that produces identical steaks and has identical costs enters the market and acts according to the Cournot oligopoly model, what are the equilibrium price, the equilibrium quantity, and each firm's economic profit?

c. If the second firm instead acts according to the Bertrand oligopoly model, what are the equilibrium price, the equilibrium quantity, and each firm's economic profit?

7.4 Managerial Application: Cartels and Oligopolies

Learning Objective 7.4 Apply the economic theory of cartels and the different types of oligopolies to help make more profitable managerial decisions.

4.1 Suppose that you are a manager for PepsiCo, working on the pricing of its sodas. PepsiCo's major rival, The Coca-Cola Company, just announced a 3 percent increase in price. What actions could you take? Explain what you hope to accomplish with each.

4.2 You are the owner of the only concrete producer in your vicinity. You are able to charge $110 per cubic yard and produce 60,000 cubic yards per year, thereby making an economic profit of $300,000 per year. A new company opens in your area and begins by producing 30,000 cubic yards per month and selling at your price, $110 per cubic yard. What actions could you take, and why?

4.3 As the chapter-opening story explained, Apple's contract with book publishers gave them a unified front to approach Amazon to demand higher prices for their e-books. The Department of Justice leaped into the fray and ultimately forced the publishers to back down. Suppose that the Department of Justice had not been so quick to act. What actions could Amazon's managers have taken to preserve their bargains with the publishers?

MyLab Economics Auto-Graded Excel Projects

7.1 The Sioux Gateway Airport (SUX) is a small airport located in Sioux City, IA. Currently, American Airlines is the only airline that flies out of SUX; flights go from SUX to Chicago's O'Hare Airport (ORD). Other airlines, such as Frontier, have considered offering flights from SUX to Denver International Airport (DEN).

Suppose that an airport similar to SUX, say TUX, has a single, dominant carrier (DC) that makes four round trips per day between TUX and ORD. As the only carrier, DC can charge the monopoly price and make the same economic profit as would a monopoly. DC's demand function is $D^{DC} = 285 - 0.75P^{DC}$. DC has $15,000 per day in fixed cost and the marginal cost per passenger is $40.

a. Using the template provided and Excel's Solver function, find the profit-maximizing price for DC. How many tickets does it sell each day (round to the nearest passenger)? What is DC's daily profit?

Suppose that another, secondary carrier (SC) decides to offer a round-trip flight each day between TUX and DEN; this monopoly market has become a two-firm oligopoly with a dominant firm. SC's demand

function is $D^{SC} = 120 - 0.5P^{SC} + 0.2P^{DC}$. SC has $5,000 per day in fixed costs, and the marginal cost per passenger is $60.

Additionally, DC's demand function changes to $D^{DC} = 225 - 0.75P^{DC} - 0.25P^{SC}$.

Using the template provided, update DC's demand information. Add SC's demand and cost information. Also add a formula to calculate DC and SC's joint profit. Be sure to connect DC's price to the SC template and SC's price to the DC template.

b. Assuming that DC continues to charge the price you found in part a, how does DC's quantity and profit change? (Use Solver to find this; round to the nearest passenger where necessary.)

c. Assuming that DC continues to charge the price you found in part a, what price should SC charge? How many tickets does it sell? What is its profit?

d. Suppose that DC and SC can find a way to collude and maximize their joint profits. What price will each charge, and how many tickets will each sell (round tickets to the nearest passenger)? What are DC's and SC's profits?

	A	B	C	D	E	F	G
1	Dominant Carrier Demand				Secondary Carrier Demand		
2	Variables	Coefficients	Values		Variables	Coefficients	Values
3	Constant				Constant		
4	DC Price				SC Price		
5	SC Price				DC Price		
6		$Q^{DC} =$				$Q^{SC} =$	
7		$TR =$				$TR =$	
8	Dominant Carrier Costs				Secondary Carrier Costs		
9	Variables	Coefficients	Values		Variables	Coefficients	Values
10	Fixed Costs				Fixed Costs		
11	Marginal Cost				Marginal Cost		
12		$TC =$				$TC =$	
13		Profit =				Profit =	
14				Joint Profit			
15							
16							

e. Should SC keep the agreement with DC and maintain a higher price? Why or why not? Use Solver to find the price SC should charge assuming that DC keeps the agreement. How many tickets will SC sell, and what will its profit be?

f. Should DC respond to SC's price change? Why or why not? Use Solver again to figure out what DC should do in response to SC's price change. At what price does DC maximize profits with SC's new price? How many tickets does DC sell, and what will its profit be?

The Calculus of Oligopoly

In this appendix, we focus on the Cournot and Stackelberg oligopoly models. Determining the equilibrium in these models using only graphs can be difficult in many cases. Calculus, however, makes their derivation easier and has the added advantage of bringing some additional insights.

A. Cournot Oligopoly

The discussion of the Cournot oligopoly in the chapter (Section 7.3) uses a model with a linear market demand curve and with two firms that produce an identical good and have constant marginal and average total costs. These demand and cost assumptions are very specific; they make it straightforward to solve for the equilibrium price and quantity. We follow a different path in this appendix: We start with very general demand and cost functions, but then we apply the results to the specific demand and cost functions used in the chapter to demonstrate that the solutions given in the chapter are correct.

To begin, assume that the market demand for planes is given by

$$Q = f(P) \qquad\qquad \textbf{A7.1}$$

where Q is the market quantity demanded and P is the price. We can rearrange Equation A7.1 to solve for the price as a function of the quantity demanded. The resulting equation is called the *inverse demand* function:

$$P = p(Q) \qquad\qquad \textbf{A7.2}$$

Because the market has two firms, Firms A and B, producing identical goods, the market quantity demanded, Q, equals the quantity demanded from Firm A, q_A, plus the quantity demanded from Firm B, q_B, or

$$Q = q_A + q_B$$

We can use this equality in Equation A7.2 to obtain the market price as a function of each firm's quantity demanded:

$$P = p(q_A + q_B) \qquad\qquad \textbf{A7.3}$$

Best-Response Functions

Firm B's profit is equal to total revenue minus total cost. Total revenue for Firm B equals $P \times q_B$. Total cost is a function of Firm B's quantity and is given by Total cost $= TC(q_B)$. Using these in the definition of profit gives Firm B's profit function

$$\text{PROFIT} = (P \times q_B) - TC(q_B)$$

The inverse demand function, Equation A7.3, shows that price, P, is a function of q_B, so the profit function can be rewritten as

$$\text{PROFIT} = [p(q_A + q_B) \times q_B] - TC(q_B) \qquad\qquad \textbf{A7.4}$$

Firm B's managers must choose the quantity, q_B, that maximizes their profit, which means the quantity that sets $\frac{d\text{PROFIT}}{dq_B} = 0$. Consequently, using the product rule to differentiate Equation A7.4 gives

$$p(q_A + q_B) + \frac{dp(q_A + q_B)}{dq_B} \times q_B - \frac{dTC(q_B)}{dq_B} = 0 \qquad\qquad \textbf{A7.5}$$

The first two terms in Equation A7.5 are Firm B's marginal revenue, and the last term is Firm B's marginal cost, which means the equation is the familiar profit-maximizing rule of producing so that $MR - MC = 0$, or, equivalently, $MR = MC$. Equation A7.5 shows how Firm B's profit-maximizing quantity, q_B, depends on Firm A's output, q_A. Therefore, it is Firm B's best-response function.

An analogous analysis gives Firm A's best-response function:

$$p(q_A + q_B) + \frac{dp(q_A + q_B)}{dq_A} \times q_A - \frac{dTC(q_A)}{dq_A} = 0 \qquad \textbf{A7.6}$$

Simultaneously solving the best-response functions, Equations A7.5 and A7.6, for q_A and q_B yields the Cournot equilibrium; that is, it gives Firm A's quantity, q_A, and Firm B's quantity, q_B.

Cournot Equilibrium: The Linear Case

The best-response functions we just derived are very general in nature. We can make them more specific by using the model in the chapter to check that the Cournot equilibrium we present there is correct. In that model, we assume that the marginal cost is constant and equal to $10, so $\frac{dTC(q_B)}{dq_B} = 10$. Next, the market demand is given by $Q = 700 - 10P$. We can use this demand to solve for the price as a function of the market quantity (the inverse demand function) and then use the fact that the market quantity is the sum of the quantities produced by Firms A and B, $q_A + q_B$. The inverse demand function for the price, Equation A7.3, therefore becomes

$$P = 70 - 0.1Q = 70 - 0.1(q_A + q_B) \qquad \textbf{A7.7}$$

Equation A7.7 shows that $\frac{dP}{dq_B} = -0.1$. Using (1) this result for $\frac{dP}{dq_B}$, (2) the result that the marginal cost $\frac{dTC(q_B)}{dq_B}$ equals $10, and (3) Equation A7.7 for P all in Firm B's best-response function, Equation A7.5, gives

$$[70 - 0.1(q_A + q_B)] - 0.1q_B - 10 = 0$$

Rearranging the equation by moving the terms with q_A and q_B to the right side of the equality and then solving for q_B, we have

$$60 = 0.1q_A + 0.2q_B \Rightarrow q_B = 300 - 0.5q_A \qquad \textbf{A7.8}$$

Equation A7.8 is Firm B's best-response function for the model in the chapter. Figure 7.4 in the chapter shows the graph of this function. Firm A's best-response function is derived similarly and is

$$q_A = 300 - 0.5q_B \qquad \textbf{A7.9}$$

Solving Equations A7.8 and A7.9 simultaneously yields the Cournot equilibrium quantities, $q_A = 200$ and $q_B = 200$. In other words, in the Cournot equilibrium both Firm A and Firm B produce 200 planes, which is the same equilibrium outcome given in Figure 7.6 in the chapter.

Cournot Equilibrium: The Nonlinear-Cost Case

We can explore the effect of a more realistic marginal cost function by assuming Firm A and Firm B both have quadratic marginal cost functions. For simplicity, suppose that the firms' marginal cost functions are the same and are

$$MC = 0.0049q^2 + 0.0001q + 0.9$$

where q is the quantity the particular firm produces. Accordingly, Firm B's marginal cost function is

$$MC_B = 0.0049q_B^2 + 0.0001q_B + 0.9 \qquad \textbf{A7.10}$$

Price and cost (millions of dollars per plane)

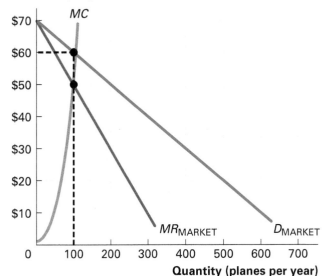

Figure A7.1 One Firm as a Monopoly

If Firm B is a monopoly, its managers maximize profit by producing 100 planes, the quantity that sets $MR = MC$, and setting a price of $60 million per plane.

To easily compare this case, with nonlinear costs, to the linear-cost case we just solved, suppose that the market demand is still given by $Q = 700 - 10P$.

To start, we can determine the profit-maximizing price and quantity if Firm B is a monopoly. In that case, B's demand is the same as the market demand, $q_B = 700 - 10P$. Figure A7.1 graphs these demand, marginal revenue, and marginal cost curves. As the figure shows, Firm B's profit-maximizing quantity of planes is 100, and its profit-maximizing price is $60 million per plane.

We can use the marginal cost and marginal revenue functions to check the results from the figure. Equation A7.10 is the marginal cost function. The following three steps help us derive the marginal revenue function:

1. Invert the market demand to give P as a function of q_B: $P = 70 - 0.1q_B$.
2. Multiply P by q_B to get total revenue: $P \times q_B = 70q_B - 0.1q_B^2$.
3. Take the derivative of the total revenue with respect to the quantity to get the marginal revenue: $\frac{d(P \times q_B)}{dq_B} = MR = 70 - 0.2q_B$.

Then equating marginal revenue to marginal cost gives

$$70 - 0.2q_B = 0.0049q_B^2 + 0.0001q_B + 0.9$$

which can be rearranged to

$$0.0049q_B^2 + 0.2001q_B - 69.1 = 0 \qquad\qquad \textbf{A7.11}$$

Solving the quadratic equation in Equation A7.11, using either the quadratic formula from Chapter 1's appendix or one of the websites on the Internet that preprograms this formula, gives $q_B = 100$, the same result as in Figure A7.1.[1] Using this value for q_B in the equation for the price, $P = 70 - 0.1q_B$, gives $P = \$60$, once again the same result as in the figure.

Now let's determine Firm B's and Firm A's best-response functions and the Cournot equilibrium. Equation A7.5 gives Firm B's best-response function. Because the demand is the same as in the linear-cost case, the first two terms in the best-response function, Equation A7.5,

---

1 The other root to Equation A7.11 is -141, which we can discard because the quantity can never be negative.

which involve the demand, are the same as before. Consequently, using Equation A7.10 for the marginal cost, Firm B's best-response function is

$$[70 - 0.1(q_A + q_B) - 0.1q_B] - (0.0049q_B^2 + 0.001q_B + 0.9) = 0$$

which, by collecting like terms, becomes

$$-0.0049q_B^2 - 0.2001q_B - 0.1q_A + 69.1 = 0 \qquad \textbf{A7.12}$$

Equation A7.12 is Firm B's best-response function. Firm A's best-response function is analogous to this equation, so it is

$$-0.0049q_A^2 - 0.2001q_A - 0.1q_B + 69.1 = 0 \qquad \textbf{A7.13}$$

Figure A7.2 shows both firms' best-response curves. These curves are nonlinear because the marginal cost functions are nonlinear. Nonetheless, the Cournot equilibrium remains the quantities where the best-response curves intersect, which in Figure A7.2 shows that both Firm A and Firm B produce 91 planes; that is, $q_A = 91$ and $q_B = 91$. The total quantity of planes is 182, so the inverse demand function, Equation A7.7, shows that the price is $51.8 million per plane.

Rather than use Figure A7.2 to determine the Cournot equilibrium, the best-response functions in Equations A7.12 and A7.13 can be solved simultaneously for q_B and q_A. Because these equations are quadratics, there are actually four possible solutions. Three of the solutions, however, have at least one negative quantity, and we can discard those solutions because negative quantities are meaningless. The only solution in which both quantities are positive is the same one as in Figure A7.2; that is, $q_B = 91$ and $q_A = 91$.

The significant point to note about this analysis is that even though the firms' marginal cost functions are more complicated than those used in the chapter, we still get the same qualitative result as in the chapter: As Cournot duopolists, Firm A and Firm B produce more planes and set a lower price than would a monopoly. So their incentive to form a cartel or a tacit collusion remains intact because it would allow them to raise their price, decrease their production, and increase their profit.

Figure A7.2 The Cournot Equilibrium

Firm A's and Firm B's best-response curves are nonlinear. The Cournot equilibrium has both Firm A and Firm B producing 91 planes.

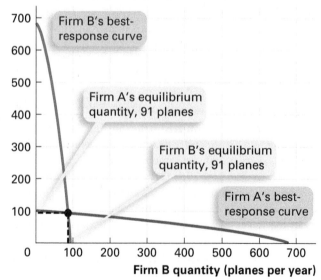

Firm A quantity (planes per year)

Firm B's best-response curve

Firm A's equilibrium quantity, 91 planes

Firm B's equilibrium quantity, 91 planes

Firm A's best-response curve

Firm B quantity (planes per year)

Cournot Equilibrium with More Than Two Firms

To this point, we have calculated the Cournot equilibrium with only two firms in the market. This assumption is restrictive, but we can relax it by assuming there are n firms in the market, Firm A, Firm B, Firm C, and so on to Firm N. The goal now is to find the Cournot equilibrium with this number of firms.

Start by noting that the total quantity in the market is the sum of the quantities produced by each of the n firms:

$$Q = q_A + q_B + q_C + \ldots + q_N$$

The price is a function of the quantity, so similar to Equation A7.3

$$P = p(Q) = p(q_A + q_B + q_C + \ldots + q_N) \qquad \textbf{A7.14}$$

Each firm's managers will select their profit-maximizing quantity assuming that none of the other $n - 1$ competitors will change their quantity. Take Firm A, for example. This firm's total revenue equals $P \times q_A$. Its total cost depends on its level of production and can be written as total cost $= TC(q_A)$. The firm's profit is its total revenue minus its total cost so its profit function is

$$\text{PROFIT} = (P \times q_A) - TC(q_A) \qquad \textbf{A7.15}$$

The firm's managers choose the quantity, q_A, that maximizes their profit, which means the quantity that sets $\frac{d\text{PROFIT}}{dq_A} = 0$. Keeping in mind that the price, P, is a function of the quantity, q_A, and using the product rule to differentiate Equation A7.15, we have:

$$P + \left(\frac{dP}{dq_A} \times q_A \right) - \frac{dTC(q_A)}{dq_A} = 0$$

This equation is Firm A's profit-maximization condition. We can use the result that the price depends on the combined sum of the firms' productions, Equation A7.14, to rewrite the profit-maximization condition as

$$p(q_A + q_B + q_C + \ldots + q_N) + \frac{dp(q_A + q_B + q_C + \ldots + q_N)}{dq_A} \times q_A - \frac{dTC(q_A)}{dq_A} = 0 \quad \textbf{A7.16}$$

Equation A7.16 is Firm A's best-response function because it shows how Firm A's profit-maximizing quantity depends on the other $n - 1$ firms' quantities. Each of the other $n - 1$ firms has its own similar best-response function, so there are n best-response functions. These n best-response functions are solved simultaneously to determine the n Cournot equilibrium quantities.

Simultaneously solving n in very general equations is daunting. To proceed, we need to simplify the analysis. So return to the case in which the demand function is linear and each firm's marginal cost and average total cost are constant and equal. We can use the same demand we used in the chapter, $Q = 700 - 10P$, and make the same assumption that each firm's marginal and average total costs equal \$10. Now, proceeding as we did to derive the two-firm best-response functions, Equations A7.8 and A7.9, the analogous n-firm best-response function for Firm A is

$$60 = [0.1(q_B + q_C + \ldots + q_N)] + 0.2q_A$$

and for Firm B, the n-firm best-response function is

$$60 = [0.1(q_A + q_C + \ldots + q_N)] + 0.2q_B$$

The rest of the n best-response functions follow the same pattern. Simultaneously solving these n best-response functions gives the n Cournot quantities. But there is an easier solution method. Each of the n firms has identical costs and faces the same price. Consequently, each of the n sets of managers will choose to produce the same profit-maximizing quantity; that is, $q_A = q_B = q_C = \ldots = q_N$. Call this quantity q. In the parentheses within the square brackets in the best-firm response functions above, there are $(n - 1)$ of the q_i terms, so with each q_i equal to q, the sum of these terms equals $(n - 1) \times q$. Use this result and the quantity q in any of the best-response function to get

$$60 = [0.1 \times (n - 1) \times q] + 0.2q$$
$$60 = [(n - 1) \times 0.1q] + 0.2q$$
$$60 = (n + 1) \times 0.1q$$

The second equality follows by multiplying the q term by 0.1. The third equality arrow follows from noting that $0.2q = 0.1q + 0.1q$ and then adding these two additional "$0.1q$" terms to the initial $n - 1$ "$0.1q$" terms. Simplifying further by first multiplying both sides of the third equation by 10 and then solving for q gives

$$600 = (n + 1) \times q \Rightarrow \frac{600}{n + 1} = q \qquad \textbf{A7.17}$$

Equation A7.17 shows how the quantity produced by a firm depends on the number of firms in the market. For example, if there are two firms, so that $n = 2$, then Equation A7.17 shows that each firm produces $\frac{600}{2 + 1} = \frac{600}{3} = 200$ planes, precisely the result we obtained in the chapter (Section 7.3) and in this appendix. Equation A7.17 also shows that as n increases, the quantity produced by each firm, q, decreases.

While Equation A7.17 shows the quantity each firm produces, what is the quantity produced by all the firms? That is, what is the market quantity? Because there are n firms in the market, each producing the quantity given by Equation A7.17, to calculate the market quantity we multiply that quantity by n:

$$Q = \left(\frac{n}{n + 1}\right) \times 600 \qquad \textbf{A7.18}$$

We can make the result in Equation A7.18 more insightful by noting that

1. In a perfectly competitive market, firms produce the quantity that sets $MR = MC$, so because $MR = P$ and in our case $MC = \$10$, we can conclude that $P = \$10$.

2. Using this price of \$10 in the market demand function, $Q = 700 - 10P$, we can determine the competitive quantity, 600.

Therefore, calling the competitive quantity (600) $Q_{competitive}$, rewrite Equation A7.18 as

$$Q = \left(\frac{n}{n + 1}\right) \times Q_{competitive} \qquad \textbf{A7.19}$$

Equation A7.19 shows the result asserted in Section 7.3 of the chapter, namely that

- As the number of firms in a Cournot oligopoly increases, the market quantity increases. As n becomes infinity large, the market quantity equals the quantity produced in a competitive market.

The increase in the market quantity as more firms are in the market means that the price falls, which decreases the firms' economic profits. This result reinforces the chapter's conclusion that restricting entry of new firms is crucial to maintaining an economic profit.

B. Stackelberg Oligopoly

The Stackelberg model of oligopoly differs from the Cournot model by its assumption that one firm—the leader, also called the first mover—makes its quantity decision first, knowing that the second firm—the follower, or second mover—will respond using its Cournot best-response function to determine its quantity. The leader does not have a best-reaction function because the leader chooses its output first and then the follower must react to the leader's choice.

Stackelberg Equilibrium: The Linear Case

We can determine the Stackelberg equilibrium—that is, the quantities produced by the leader and the follower—using three steps:

1. Determine the follower's best-response function.
2. Use the follower's best-response function in the leader's profit function and its profit-maximization calculation to determine the leader's quantity.
3. Use the leader's quantity in the follower's best-response function to determine the follower's quantity.

We will demonstrate how to solve for the Stackelberg equilibrium by using the specific model presented in the chapter: The linear market demand is $Q = 700 - 10P$, and both firms have the same constant marginal and average total costs, equal to $10 million. As in Section 7.3, we assume that Firm B is the leader and Firm A is the follower. Now, we work through the three steps:

1. We already know Firm A's best-response function from Equation A7.9, $q_A = 300 - 0.5q_B$. This equation shows explicitly how Firm A reacts to any amount of Firm B's production.
2. The novelty in the Stackelberg case revolves around Firm B's profit maximization. As before, the market quantity equals the quantity produced by Firm A plus the quantity produced by Firm B, or $Q = q_A + q_B$. So using the market demand equation to obtain the inverse demand function, which expresses the price as a function of the quantity, gives

$$P = 70 - 0.1Q = 70 - 0.1(q_A + q_B)$$

We have seen this result before—it's Equation A7.7. But now we can use Firm A's best-response function for q_A from step 1 in it to give the price as a function of q_B only:

$$P = 70 - 0.1(300 - 0.5q_B + q_B) = 70 - 0.1(300 + 0.5q_B) = 40 - 0.05q_B$$

Firm B's total revenue equals $P \times q_B$, or, using the expression we just calculated for the price,

$$\text{Total revenue} = (40 - 0.05q_B) \times q_B = 40q_B - 0.05q_B^2 \qquad \textbf{A7.20}$$

Firm B's total revenue in Equation A7.20 is different from anything we have seen before in this appendix because it incorporates Firm A's best-response function. So Firm B's profit-maximizing choice of output takes account of how Firm A will respond. Firm B's total cost is $TC(q_B)$. Therefore, Firm B's profit function is:

$$\text{PROFIT} = \text{Total revenue} - \text{Total cost} = 40q_B - 0.05q_B^2 - TC(q_B)$$

Recall that $\frac{dTC(q_B)}{dq_B} = \$10$. Maximizing profit by taking the derivative of the profit function with respect to q_B and setting it equal to zero therefore gives

$$40 - 0.10q_B - 10 = 0$$

Finally, we can solve for q_B:

$$40 - 0.10q_B - 10 = 0 \Rightarrow 30 - 0.10q_B = 0 \Rightarrow 30 = 0.10q_B \Rightarrow 300 = q_B \qquad \textbf{A7.21}$$

We can conclude from Equation A7.21 that Firm B's profit-maximizing quantity is 300 planes.

3. We can now use Firm A's best-response function from the first step, $q_A = 300 - 0.5q_B$, and Firm B's quantity, 300, to solve for Firm A's quantity: $q_A = 300 - (0.5 \times 300) = 150$ planes.

Summarizing, the Stackelberg equilibrium has Firm B, the leader, producing 300 planes and Firm A, the follower, producing 150 planes.

Although we demonstrated how to solve for the Stackelberg equilibrium in the context of a specific example, the general procedure follows precisely the three steps we outlined above: (1) Determine the follower's Cournot best-response function, (2) use it in the leader's profit-maximization problem to calculate the leader's quantity, and (3) return to the follower's best-response function to calculate the follower's quantity.

Calculus Questions and Problems

A7.1 Suppose that you are the manager of Matt's Prime Steakhouse, one of only two premium steakhouses in Gainesville, Georgia. The nightly demand for steak dinners in town is given by

$$Q^d = 80 - 2P$$

where Q^d is the market quantity of steak dinners demanded and P is the price of a steak dinner. Matt's Prime Steakhouse produces q_M dinners, and Matt's only competitor in the premium steak market, Emberwood Grill, produces q_E dinners. Each firm's total cost of producing and selling q dinners is

$$TC(q) = 400 + 10q$$

a. What is Matt's best-response function to the quantity produced by Emberwood?
b. How many steak dinners does each firm produce?
c. What is the price of a dinner when each restaurant sells its equilibrium quantity of steaks?

A7.2 The market for management consulting services is a Stackelberg duopoly. Alvarez Inc. acts as the Stackelberg leader and The Beaulieu Group as the Stackelberg follower. An independent research firm has estimated that the daily demand for consulting services is

$$Q = 25 - 0.25P$$

where Q is the quantity of consulting hours and P is the hourly price of consulting services. The total quantity, Q, of consulting hours is equal to

$$Q = q_A + q_B$$

where q_A is the quantity of consulting hours sold by Alvarez Inc. and q_B is the quantity of consulting hours sold by The Beaulieu Group. The demand function can be solved for the price as a function of the quantity, which is the inverse demand:

$$P = 100 - 4(q_A + q_B)$$

Each firm's marginal and average total cost of supplying an hour of consulting services is $36.
a. How many hours of consulting services does each consulting firm provide?
b. How much economic profit does each consulting firm make?

A7.3 You are the manager of Billy's Burritos, one of only two suppliers of tasty fish tacos in town. Billy's Burritos and its competitor, Ellen's Enchiladas, compete in a Cournot duopoly. The weekly demand for fish tacos is

$$Q = 187.5 - 12.5P$$

where Q is the quantity of fish tacos and P is the price of a fish taco. The total quantity, Q, of fish tacos is equal to

$$Q = q_B + q_E$$

where q_B is the quantity of fish tacos produced by Billy's Burritos and q_E is the quantity of fish tacos produced by Ellen's Enchiladas. The demand function can be solved for the price as a function of the quantity, which is the inverse demand:

$$P = 15 - 0.08Q$$

Each firm incurs a total cost of producing and selling q_i fish tacos of

$$TC(q_i) = 120 + 3q_i$$

a. Determine the Cournot quantity of fish tacos that each firm produces each week.
b. When each firm produces its Cournot quantity, what is the resulting market price of a fish taco?

A7.4 You are the top student in your economics class, and you decide that you will make some extra money by tutoring college freshmen in the Introduction to Economics course. Your only competitor is your classmate Bernardo. You and Bernardo engage in Cournot competition, and you both know that the monthly demand for economics tutoring services is

$$Q = 160 - 2P$$

where Q is the total monthly number of hours of economics tutoring services demanded and P is the hourly price of economics tutoring services. Solving for P from the market demand gives the inverse market demand:

$$P = 80 - 0.5Q$$

You supply q_A hours of economics tutoring services, and Bernardo supplies q_B hours of economics tutoring services. Each of you incurs a total cost of supplying q_i hours of economics tutoring services equal to

$$TC(q_i) = 240 + 0.25q_i^2$$

a. Determine the number of economics tutoring hours that each tutor supplies.
b. When Bernardo and you supply your equilibrium quantities, what is the resulting market price of an hour of economics tutoring services?

A7.5 The market for knitted scarves at a local, weekend farmers' market is a Stackelberg duopoly. Sammy's Scarves acts as the Stackelberg leader and Knitting Nancy as the Stackelberg follower. Both Sammy and Nancy know that the market demand for knitted scarves at the farmers' market is

$$Q = 160 - 4P$$

where Q is the quantity of knitted scarves demanded and P is the price of a knitted scarf. Solving the market demand for P as a function of Q gives the inverse market demand:

$$P = 40 - 0.25Q$$

Sammy produces q_S knitted scarves, and Nancy produces q_N knitted scarves. Each incurs a total cost of producing q_i knitted scarves of

$$TC(q_i) = 20 + 10q_i$$

a. How many scarves does each supplier sell at the local, weekend farmers' market?
b. How much economic profit does each supplier earn?

Game Theory and Oligopoly

Learning Objectives

After studying this chapter, you will be able to:

8.1 Identify the elements of game theory and explain the Nash equilibrium, a prisoners' dilemma game, a dominated strategy, and the advantages of a repeated game.

8.2 Describe how to determine the equilibrium in games with more than one Nash equilibrium and in games with no pure-strategy Nash equilibrium.

8.3 Explain the importance of backward induction and credible commitments in sequential games.

8.4 Apply game theory to help make better managerial decisions.

Managers at Pfizer Welcome a Competitor in the Market for Lipitor

Pfizer Pharmaceutical Company (Pfizer) had a patent on Lipitor, a cholesterol-lowering drug. From 2004 to 2011, Lipitor was the world's best-selling drug, with sales that peaked at approximately $12 billion per year. All of the sales and all of the economic profit belonged to Pfizer. November 30, 2011, was not a day of celebration at the company, however, because its patent-protected monopoly on Lipitor expired and a generic drug company was set to enter the market.

In the market for prescription drugs, companies that make generic drugs race to file an abbreviated new drug application (ANDA) with the Food and Drug Administration (FDA) and challenge the patent(s) protecting a drug. The

FDA grants the first company to file an ANDA and win the patent challenge a 180-day exclusivity period, during which other makers of generic drugs generally cannot enter the market. After this time period, all drugmakers who have received FDA approval for their generic version of the drug are free to enter the market.

Pfizer's managers did not want to lose their profit, so they needed to develop a strategy for maintaining the largest possible profit. What actions could they take to maintain their sales and their profit? What tools could they use to deal with the competition from a new rival in the market? At the end of this chapter, you will learn how Pfizer's managers answered these questions and handled this challenge.

Sources: Linda Johnson, "Against Odds, Lipitor Became World's Top Seller," *Seattle Times*, December 28, 2011; Josh Sanburn, "Lipitor Already Cheaper After Patent Expiration," *Time*, December 1, 2011; James DeGuilio, "Pfizer's Lipitor: A New Model for Delaying the Effects of Patent Expiration," Patent Docs, December 1, 2011 http://www.patentdocs.org/2011/12/pfizers-lipitor-a-new-model-for-delaying-the-effects-of-patent-expiration.html; Duff Wilson, "Facing Generic Lipitor Rivals, Pfizer Battles to Protect Its Cash Cow," *New York Times*, November 29, 2011; Leigh Purvis and Stephen Schondelmeyer, *Rx Price Watch Case Study: Efforts to Reduce the Impact of Generic Competition for Lipitor* (Washington, DC: AARP Public Policy Institute, June 2013).

Introduction

This chapter presents a new, important approach to the study of oligopoly. Because oligopolistic competitors are mutually interdependent, their managers must make strategic decisions about how to compete with, interact with, and react to the actions of rival companies. For example, if PepsiCo cuts the price of Pepsi by 20 percent, will sales of Pepsi soar? Probably not, because the managers at The Coca-Cola Company

(Coca-Cola) most likely will respond to PepsiCo's action by lowering the price of Coke. The probable outcome for PepsiCo is a small increase in Pepsi sales. Alternatively, say that managers at PepsiCo decide to cut their advertising by $100 million per year, expecting to add the cost savings to their bottom line as increased profit. If the executives at Coca-Cola decide to continue to advertise at the old rate, however, the outcome may not be favorable for PepsiCo: Coke may gain market share and profit, and Pepsi may lose market share and profit. Indeed, at one point, PepsiCo slashed its advertising budget for its sodas, but the result was so bleak that outside analysts called for the firing of Indra Nooyi, PepsiCo's chief executive officer. Ms. Nooyi eventually restored PepsiCo's advertising budget for its sodas and kept her job.

These examples demonstrate mutual interdependence: The decisions made by the managers and executives at one company (PepsiCo) interacted with the responses from the managers and executives at another company (Coca-Cola). This relationship affects managerial strategy: What actions do you pursue, knowing that your competitors will respond? How do you react to a competitor's actions? How do managers of one company decide on strategies when rival managers are making the same decisions? Such strategic issues require analysis unlike any we have considered to this point in the text. **Game theory** is a mode of analysis used to study decision making in situations with mutual interdependence and strategic behavior.

Game theory A mode of analysis used to study decision making in situations with mutual interdependence and strategic behavior.

As you learned in earlier chapters, economic theory and models can help guide the managerial decision-making process. The real world, however, is unpredictable, and events rarely coincide exactly with models or predictions. Game theory helps you make decisions whenever there is mutual interdependence and strategic behavior, but it rarely, if ever, specifies the exact action to take or the precise decision to make. It does, however, provide guidance and insights that will assist you when you are making your strategic business decisions. This chapter includes four sections that show you how to use game theory:

* **Section 8.1** describes the basic elements of a game and game theory, using a pricing game to illustrate the concepts of Nash equilibrium, repeated games, and dominated strategies.
* **Section 8.2** explains how the Pareto criterion, focal points, and cheap talk can possibly help determine which of multiple Nash equilibria are selected and shows how to calculate a mixed-strategy equilibrium for games that have no pure-strategy Nash equilibria.
* **Section 8.3** introduces sequential games and explains how to use a technique called backward induction to solve them.
* **Section 8.4** shows how to apply game theory's basic games, advanced games, and sequential games to help you make better managerial decisions.

8.1 Basic Game Theory and Games

Learning Objective 8.1 Identify the elements of game theory and explain the Nash equilibrium, a prisoners' dilemma game, a dominated strategy, and the advantages of a repeated game.

John von Neumann, the brilliant mathematician, statistician, physicist, and economist, devised game theory in an article published in the late 1920s. In 1944, he and Oskar Morgenstern coauthored an important and influential book, *Theory of Games and Economic Behavior*. Von Neumann's groundbreaking work paved the way for new insights into strategic behavior.

This section begins by defining the elements of a game and then uses a sample game to illustrate how managers determine their strategy and how equilibrium is reached. The equilibrium in some games, however, creates a dilemma: When each firm uses the strategy that maximizes its profit, the resulting equilibrium is the worst possible joint equilibrium for all firms combined. So the section then examines whether the managers can avoid the dilemma if they repeat the game. It concludes by examining strategies that managers should never use.

Elements of a Game

Game An interaction between players in which the players follow rules, use strategies, and receive a payoff at the end.

In the 1920s, Von Neumann identified and analyzed what he called a game. He pointed out that games such as chess, football, and competition between companies have three factors in common: rules, strategies, and payoffs. A **game** is an interaction between players—who might be individuals, teams, firms, or countries—who follow rules, use strategies, and receive a payoff at the end.

1. **Rules.** Every game has rules, some of which are arbitrary. For example, the rules of Canadian football specify that teams of 12 play the game on a field 110 yards long and the offense has three downs to advance 10 yards. The rules of American football differ: Teams of 11 play the game on a field 100 yards long, and the offense has four downs to advance 10 yards. Other rules are not arbitrary but rather are determined by nature: For example, it is a "rule" of nature that American steel producers like Nucor Corporation must have iron to make steel. Some rules are specific to the game at hand, such as the timing of each player's move, the number of rounds of the game, and the information each player possesses.

Strategy A complete contingency plan consisting of the actions a player may take, which might depend on the other players' actions.

2. **Strategies.** The players in the game use strategies, which are plans that indicate what the players will do. More formally, a **strategy** is a complete contingency plan consisting of the actions a player may take, which might depend on the other players' actions. For example, depending on an opponent's opening move, a chess grandmaster responds in different ways. On the other hand, an American football team faced with a fourth down and 23 yards to go on its own 17-yard line will almost surely punt regardless of what the other team does.

3. **Payoffs.** A game has payoffs. For chess and football, the payoff is the thrill of victory or the agony of defeat. For soft drink companies like PepsiCo and Coca-Cola, the payoff is profits or losses. The payoff depends not only on the player's own strategy but also on the strategies used by all of the other players in the game. As in previous chapters, assume that players in a business context strive to maximize profit.

A Sample Game

For simplicity, suppose that Boca-Cola and TragoCo are the only two producers of sodas in South America, so the market is a *duopoly*. A stylized interaction between these two firms can serve as an example of a game. The two firms are the game's players. Each firm must set the price of its soda. Three assumptions simplify the analysis: The managers of both firms (1) have only two strategies—set a low price or set a high price, (2) make their decisions simultaneously, and (3) know the profits of their firm and the rival firm no matter what prices the firms choose. Each choice—set a low price or set a high price—is a strategy. The two choices are referred to collectively as the managers' *strategy set*, the list of the strategies available to a player.

Because the managers of each firm make their choice simultaneously, neither knows what the other will do. Each set of managers has two strategies—set a low price or set a high price—so there are four possible outcomes:

1. Both TragoCo and Bola-Cola set high prices.
2. TragoCo sets a high price, and Boca-Cola sets a low price.
3. TragoCo sets a low price, and Boca-Cola sets a high price.
4. Both TragoCo and Boca-Cola set low prices.

The payoffs to TragoCo and Boca-Cola are their profits. Presume that, if their managers both choose a high price, the firms can effectively operate as a giant monopoly so that their combined economic profit is at its maximum. In this case, assume that TragoCo's economic profit is $7 billion and Boca-Cola's economic profit is $8 billion. If TragoCo's managers set a high price and Boca-Cola's managers set a low price, Boca-Cola steals customers and market share from TragoCo. Assume that TragoCo's economic profit falls to $3 billion and Boca-Cola's economic profit rises to $10 billion. Conversely, if TragoCo's managers set a low price and Boca-Cola's managers set a high price, assume that TragoCo gains market share and its economic profit rises to $9 billion, while Boca-Cola loses market share and its profit falls to $4 billion. Finally, if both sets of managers set a low price, both pick up a few more sales but at a lower price, so assume that TragoCo's economic profit is $4 billion and Boca-Cola's economic profit is $5 billion. Table 8.1 displays these profits in a payoff matrix showing each firm's hypothetical profit in all four possible cases. A **payoff matrix** is a table showing how each player's profit depends on the combination of the player's decision and the rival's decision. In the payoff matrix, the columns show the effects from TragoCo's strategy, and the rows show the effects from Boca-Cola's strategy. The four cells in the matrix show the four possible outcomes.

The payoff matrix illustrates the reality of mutual interdependence in this market: Each firm's profit depends on the choices of its managers *and* those of competing managers. For instance, TragoCo's profit is *not* determined solely by

Payoff matrix A table showing how each player's profit depends on the combination of the player's strategy and the rival's strategy.

Table 8.1 A Payoff Matrix for a Duopoly

In a duopoly, the firms' economic profits depend on their joint choices about what price to set. The columns present TragoCo's managers' possible choices, and the rows present Boca-Cola's managers' possible choices. The four cells are the four possible outcomes. Each cell contains TragoCo's profit (in blue) and Boca-Cola's profit (in red). The payoff matrix shows the interdependence between TragoCo and Boca-Cola: Each firm's profit depends on the decisions by its own managers *and* by the competing managers.

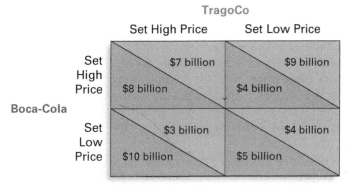

the decisions of its own managers: If TragoCo's managers set a high price, they make an economic profit of $7 billion if Boca-Cola's managers also set a high price, but they make an economic profit of only $3 billion if Boca-Cola's managers set a low price.

Nash Equilibrium

Nash equilibrium The outcome in which each player's strategy is best for that player, taking as given the other player's strategy; at a Nash equilibrium, no one player can unilaterally improve his or her payoff by playing another strategy.

In order to determine the likely outcome of this duopoly game, you need to understand what an equilibrium is in the context of game theory. The most basic and widely used equilibrium concept is the Nash equilibrium, named after Nobel Prize winner John Nash.[1] A **Nash equilibrium** occurs when each player's strategy is best for that player, taking as given the other player's strategy; at a Nash equilibrium, no one player can unilaterally improve his or her payoff by playing another strategy. In this sense, a Nash equilibrium is self-enforcing because once at a Nash equilibrium, no player can unilaterally change and be better off.

Finding the Nash equilibrium for the game in Table 8.1 takes two steps: (1) Determine the optimal strategy for TragoCo's managers, and (2) do the same for Boca-Cola's managers. Let's start with TragoCo's optimal strategy. TragoCo's managers realize that Boca-Cola's managers can set a high price or a low price. TragoCo's managers need to determine how they will react to Boca-Cola's choice. Let's examine their response to each of Boca-Cola's choices:

- **Boca-Cola sets a high price.** The first *row* in the payoff matrix in Table 8.1 applies in this case. This row shows that TragoCo's managers maximize their profit by setting a low price, thereby making an economic profit of $9 billion. If they respond by setting a high price, their profit is only $7 billion.
- **Boca-Cola sets a low price.** Now the second *row* in the payoff matrix applies. It shows that TragoCo's managers maximize their profit by setting a low price, thereby making an economic profit of $4 billion. If they opt to set a high price, their economic profit is only $3 billion.

The conclusion from the analysis is clear: Regardless of the strategy the managers at Boca-Cola use, the best strategy for TragoCo's managers to use is to set a low price. A strategy that is *always* better for the player than any alternative strategy, regardless of the opponent's actions, is a **dominant strategy**. A dominant strategy is also a **pure strategy**—a strategy that identifies the specific action the player will select in every possible circumstance.

Dominant strategy A strategy that is *always* better for the player than any alternative strategy regardless of the opponent's actions.

Pure strategy A strategy that identifies the specific action the player will select in every possible circumstance.

Next, you need to determine the optimal strategy for Boca-Cola's managers—that is, how they will respond to TragoCo's choice. So let's consider each of TragoCo's choices:

- **TragoCo sets a high price.** The first *column* in the payoff matrix in Table 8.1 applies. It shows that Boca-Cola's managers maximize their profit by setting a low price, thereby making an economic profit of $10 billion. If they respond by setting a high price, their economic profit is only $8 billion.
- **TragoCo sets a low price.** Now the second *column* in the payoff matrix applies. It shows that Boca-Cola's managers maximize their profit by setting a low price, thereby making an economic profit of $5 billion. If they opt to set a high price, their economic profit is only $4 billion.

1 John Nash first devised the concept of a Nash equilibrium in his 1950 Ph.D. dissertation. The 2001 Academy Award-winning film *A Beautiful Mind* dramatized Nash's life.

Regardless of the strategy TragoCo managers select, the best strategy for Boca-Cola's managers is to set a low price. In other words, given the profits in the payoff matrix, Boca-Cola's managers also have a dominant strategy: set a low price.

The Nash equilibrium in this game is clear: Managers at both TragoCo and Boca-Cola play their best strategy—their dominant strategy—which for each is to set a low price, so the Nash equilibrium is for both sets of managers to set a low price. In the equilibrium, TragoCo makes an economic profit of $4 billion, and Boca-Cola makes an economic profit of $5 billion.

You can also check that the Set Low Price/Set Low Price outcome is the Nash equilibrium by using Table 8.1 to see if either firm can unilaterally change its strategy and increase its payoff. At the Set Low Price/Set Low Price outcome, if TragoCo's managers' change their strategy to set a high price, TragoCo's profit falls from $4 billion to $3 billion. Similarly, at the Set Low Price/Set Low Price outcome, if Boca-Cola's managers change their strategy to set a high price, Boca-Cola's profit falls from $5 billion to $4 billion. Because neither set of managers can gain by unilaterally changing its strategy, the Set Low Price/Set Low Price outcome is indeed a Nash equilibrium.

At any outcome other than a Nash equilibrium, the managers of at least one of the firms can increase their firm's profit by changing their strategy. For example, examine the outcome in the top right cell in Table 8.1, in which TragoCo's managers set a low price and Boca-Cola's managers set a high price. At this outcome, Boca-Cola is making an economic profit of $4 billion. But Boca-Cola's managers can increase their profit to $5 billion by changing their strategy to instead set a low price. The top right cell cannot be a Nash equilibrium because one player—Boca-Cola's managers—can unilaterally change its strategy and increase its profit. Similar reasoning rules out all the other outcomes except the Set Low Price/Set Low Price cell, which therefore is the unique Nash equilibrium.

Because the players are using a pure strategy, the equilibrium is also a pure-strategy Nash equilibrium. A *pure-strategy Nash equilibrium* is an equilibrium in which each player uses a strategy that identifies what specific action the player will select in every possible circumstance. In addition, because both players have a dominant strategy, the equilibrium in this game is also a *dominant strategy equilibrium*. Each dominant strategy equilibrium is a Nash equilibrium, but as you will learn in Section 8.2, not every Nash equilibrium is a dominant strategy equilibrium.

A Dilemma

From the perspective of TragoCo and Boca-Cola, the Nash equilibrium (in which both firms set a low price) is distinctly inferior to the situation in which both firms set a high price. In that case, *both* TragoCo and Boca-Cola would make a larger economic profit: $7 billion (versus $4 billion) for TragoCo and $8 billion (versus $5 billion) for Boca-Cola. In other words, if both firms cooperated by setting a high price, both firms' economic profit would be higher.

The TragoCo and Boca-Cola game is an example of a prisoners' dilemma game because both companies (players) gain if they cooperate but each has an incentive to defect from cooperation, so in the Nash equilibrium both defect. The game is named after the situation faced by two prisoners being interrogated separately by police. Both prisoners gain if neither confesses, but each gains from confessing if the other does *not* confess because each is offered a plea bargain if he or she alone confesses, whereas that bargain is voided if both prisoners confess. The Nash equilibrium of the prisoner game is for both prisoners to confess, so that each serves a longer prison sentence than if neither confesses. The outcome of the game between TragoCo and Boca-Cola is similar: Both companies would be better off if they cooperated by setting a high price, but instead both set a low price, to the ultimate harm of each. Pursuit of their self-interest by both players leads to an inferior outcome, which is a real dilemma for the players!

An obvious answer to the soft drink firms' dilemma is for the firms to sign a contract that commits them to set a high price. Unfortunately for the managers, any price-fixing agreement—such as the suggested contract—is illegal. Chapter 9, which examines antitrust law, points out that if the courts find firms guilty of price fixing, the firms face hefty fines, and the managers who made the agreement face prison time. Consequently, the managers can rule out a contract because it is illegal. However, tacit collusion, a "meeting of the minds" that does not involve explicit communication or agreement, *is* legal for the firms and can potentially offer an escape from the managers' dilemma.

DECISION SNAPSHOT — An Advertising Game

In 2009 and 2010, PepsiCo's executives slashed the advertising for their namesake soda, Pepsi-Cola, by about $100 million. Suppose in our South American context that TragoCo's managers do the same—they cut their advertising by $100 million. The payoff matrix shows the game that TragoCo's managers are playing with Boca-Cola's managers. The numbers in the payoff matrix are the firms' profits. How did TragoCo's managers hope that Boca-Cola's managers would respond? What response did they fear? If you were a manager at Boca-Cola, what decision would you make?

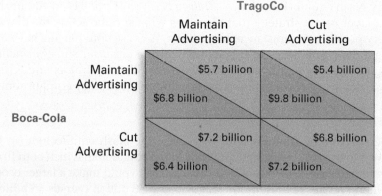

Answer
TragoCo's managers hoped that Boca-Cola's managers would likewise cut their advertising. If both companies cut their advertising, both would make a larger profit than if they both maintained their advertising. TragoCo's managers feared that Boca-Cola's managers would maintain their advertising at its usual amount. In this case, TragoCo's profit falls to the lowest amount, while Boca-Cola's profit soars to the highest amount. In this game, Boca-Cola's most likely choice is to maintain its advertising because that is a dominant strategy. When PepsiCo reduced its advertising, Coca-Cola's managers maintained their advertising. PepsiCo's profit fell, and, ultimately, after two years, PepsiCo's executives returned their advertising back to its higher level. The Nash equilibrium with both firms advertising at a high level was restored.

One potential avenue for tacit collusion is for each firm to announce independently that it will set a high price. While legal, however, such announcements are hardly credible. For example, suppose that TragoCo's managers announce that they will set a high price. This sort of announcement is called cheap talk. *Cheap talk* is an announcement that has no direct effect on the announcer's payoff. As you will see in Section 8.2, cheap talk can sometimes alter the outcome of a game—but not in this case. The managers at Boca-Cola realize that TragoCo's announcement has no credibility. Instead, the announcement just causes Boca-Cola's managers to fear that TragoCo's managers have set a trap. Boca-Cola's managers worry that TragoCo's managers are lying in wait for Boca-Cola to set a high price so they can ambush Boca-Cola by turning around and setting a low price.

Repeated Games

Cheap talk certainly does not work as a solution to the managers' dilemma in the soft drink example. How else might the firms achieve a **cooperative equilibrium**, an outcome in which the players coordinate their actions in order to increase their payoffs? The Nash equilibrium just explored assumed that the firms interacted only once—a scenario called a *one-shot game*—but this assumption is often unrealistic because businesses interact time after time after time. Taking the repeated interactions between the managers of TragoCo and Boca-Cola into account creates a potential opportunity for the firms to avoid the dilemma outcome and reach the cooperative equilibrium.

A **repeated game**—a game played more than once—offers managers many more strategies than one-shot games. In repeated games, the managers can base their strategies on their opponent's past actions and "punish" that opponent in the future if it defected from the cooperative high-price strategy and cheated by setting a low price sometime in the past. The possibility of punishment enhances the likelihood that the managers wind up cooperating with each other. A **trigger strategy** occurs in a repeated game when a player starts by cooperating until a rival fails to cooperate, which "triggers" a punishment by a switch to noncooperation. In one type of trigger strategy, the *grim trigger strategy*, a player cooperates in the first round (by setting a high price) and continues to cooperate until the opponent cheats, which causes the player using the grim trigger strategy to punish the rival by setting a low price until the end of time. A much less grim strategy is a tit-for-tat strategy. In a **tit-for-tat strategy**, players start by cooperating in the first round and then copy the rival's previous period strategy.[2] In a tit-for-tat strategy, when a firm cheats by setting a low price, the action triggers punishment by the other firm in the form of a similar low price the next period and every period thereafter until the first firm once again sets a high price.

A tit-for-tat strategy makes it more likely that the firms will reach the cooperative equilibrium: If a firm cheats, it gains profit from cheating but then loses profit in the future period(s) during which it is punished. In a one-shot game, there is no chance for future punishment. This distinction is why the cooperative equilibrium is more likely in a repeated game than in a one-shot game.

To demonstrate how the potential for punishment changes firms' incentives, consider the game outlined in Table 8.1, in which Boca-Cola's profits are $8 billion if both companies set a high price, $10 billion if Boca-Cola sets a low price while TragoCo sets a high price, and $5 billion if both companies set a low price. Suppose that both TragoCo's and Boca-Cola's managers have been setting high prices and using a tit-for-tat strategy. As Table 8.2 shows, by using this strategy Boca-Cola's profit in periods 1 and 2 is $8 billion, for a total profit of $16 billion. Suppose,

Cooperative equilibrium An outcome in which the players coordinate their actions in order to increase their payoffs.

Repeated game A game played more than once.

Trigger strategy A strategy in a repeated game in which a player starts by cooperating and continues until the rival fails to cooperate, which "triggers" punishment by switching to noncooperation.

Tit-for-tat strategy A strategy in a repeated game in which the players start by cooperating in the first round and then copy the rival's previous period strategy.

---

2 Both the tit-for-tat strategy and the more general grim trigger strategy are pure strategies because they state the player's specific action in every situation.

Table 8.2 Profit from Using a Tit-for-Tat Strategy and from Defecting from a Tit-for-Tat Strategy

	Profit from Using a Tit-for-Tat Strategy	Profit from Defecting from a Tit-for-Tat Strategy
Period 1	$8 billion	$10 billion
Period 2	$8 billion	$5 billion
Total Profit	$16 billion	$15 billion

however, that Boca-Cola's managers decide to defect from their cooperative tit-for-tat strategy by setting a low price in Period 1. Table 8.2 shows that Boca-Cola's profit in that period is $10 billion. In the next period, however, TragoCo's managers punish Boca-Cola's managers by setting a low price, so the largest profit Boca-Cola can then make is $5 billion. By defecting, Boca-Cola's profit over these two periods, $15 billion, is smaller than its profit from remaining at the cooperative equilibrium.

A tit-for-tat strategy makes the cooperative equilibrium possible but does not guarantee that the firms will be able to maintain it. In particular, the defecting firm makes a higher profit in the period during which it cheats and a lower profit during future periods. Funds received in the future, such as future profits, are worth less than the same amount of money received today because the money received today can be saved and gain interest income. Consequently, the profits lost in the future must be adjusted to make them equivalent to the profit gained in the present from cheating. Chapter 16 explains in more detail the relationship between the interest rate and the value today of profits received in the future. For now, just note that the higher the interest rate, the lower the value today of future profits and therefore the lower the value of lost future profits. As a result, to make cheating on a tit-for-tat strategy profitable, the interest rate must be high enough that the gain in profit from current-period cheating is greater than the loss from the lower future-period profits.

A tit-for-tat strategy can also fail if managers make mistakes that lead to a breakdown in cooperation. In particular, errors in perception can lead managers to believe that a competitor has defected from the cooperative strategy. For example, over the last decade, the demand for carbonated sodas has dropped due in part to people's changing tastes and concern about obesity. Consequently, suppose profits at TragoCo and Boca-Cola have declined. The fall in profits could lead to a breakdown in a cooperative equilibrium if one firm's managers mistakenly attribute their lower profit to cheating by their rival. For example, if the managers at TragoCo erroneously believe that their lower profits are the result of Boca-Cola cheating on a cooperative agreement, they may punish Boca-Cola by defecting from the tit-for-tat strategy. Once Boca-Cola's managers discover that TragoCo's managers have abandoned the tit-for-tat high-price strategy, Boca-Cola's managers will respond by also setting a low price, and the cooperative equilibrium is nothing but a (fond) memory.

End-Period Problem

Reaching and then maintaining the cooperative equilibrium faces another challenge if both players know that the repeated game ultimately ends. If the game ends, in the last period there is no chance for future punishment, which eliminates the incentive to cooperate in the last period of a repeated game. This absence of any incentive to

DECISION
SNAPSHOT

TragoCo and Boca-Cola Play a Repeated Game

Suppose that Boca-Cola and TragoCo are engaged in an advertising game. If the game is played only once, the Nash equilibrium is for both firms to maintain their advertising. But in reality, Boca-Cola and TragoCo advertise year after year, so they actually repeatedly play their advertising game. If TragoCo's managers cut their advertising budget, what strategy might they be pursuing? As a Boca-Cola manager, what choices do you face? Suppose that Boca-Cola's managers maintain their advertising. Explain why they might make this choice.

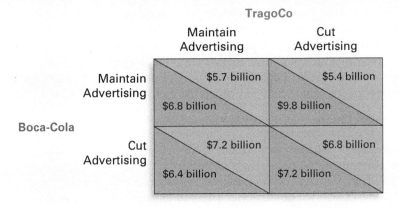

Answer

The cooperative equilibrium in the game is for the managers of both firms to cut their advertising. By reducing their advertising expenditure, TragoCo's managers might be starting to play a tit-for-tat strategy and trying to reach the cooperative equilibrium. Boca-Cola's managers might play a tit-for-tat strategy by following TragoCo's lead but suppose that they do not. Why? Starting from Boca-Cola's profit in the Nash equilibrium (in which both firms maintain advertising, so Boca-Cola's profit is $6.8 billion), the added profit from cutting its advertising to reach the cooperative equilibrium is only $0.4 billion ($7.2 billion − $6.8 billion), while the added profit from maintaining its advertising when TrageCo cuts its advertising is $3.0 billion ($9.8 billion − $6.8 billion). Although the $3.0 billion in added profit from maintaining their advertising is only temporary and the $0.4 billion added profit from the cooperative equilibrium might persist forever, that one-time $3.0 billion profit may be sufficiently large that Boca-Cola's managers decide to shun the cooperative tit-for-tat strategy in favor of maintaining their advertising budget.

cooperate in the last period of a repeated game because there is no possibility of punishment in the future creates the **end-period problem.**

For an example of how the end-period problem can make reaching the cooperative equilibrium difficult or impossible, suppose that TragoCo and Boca-Cola are playing their repeated price-setting game in Venezuela when the government announces it will nationalize the local production and distribution facilities of both companies a few periods in the future. Consequently, the managers at both companies know when the last period of their game will occur.

End-period problem The problem created by the absence of any incentive to cooperate in the last period of a repeated game because there is no possibility of punishment in the future.

Let's analyze TragoCo's and Boca-Cola's decisions in the last period of the game (the period right before nationalization) and then roll the game back to their decisions in the second-to-last period and to their decisions in the third-to-last period. Once you see how the last period affects decisions in the second-to-last and third-to-last periods, you will be able to see the impact in any period.

Last Period   Table 8.3 shows the one-period payoff matrix for TragoCo and Boca-Cola. In the last period—the period before nationalization—TragoCo's managers reason that if they cooperate by setting a high price but Boca-Cola's managers no longer cooperate and instead set a low price, Boca-Cola's profit soars to $10 billion but TragoCo's profit is only $3 billion *and* they are unable to punish Boca-Cola in the next period *because there is no next period*. TragoCo's managers next reason that if they set a low price, their profit is at least $4 billion and might be $9 million plus Boca-Cola's managers will be unable to punish them. This analysis means that TragoCo's managers will set a low price. The reasoning by Boca-Cola managers is similar, so they also set a low price. In other words, knowing that they are in the last period, both sets of managers are playing the one-period prisoners' dilemma game. Consequently, in the last period, both sets of managers defect from the tit-for-tat Set High Price/Set High Price strategy by setting a low price regardless of what the other managers did in the previous period.

Second-to-Last Period   Now let's roll the game back to the second-to-last period. At this time, the managers of both companies can look ahead to the last period and arrive at the same conclusion we just did: In the last period, both companies are going to set a low price no matter what the other company does in the second-to-last period. With this result in mind, let's examine how TragoCo's managers analyze Boca-Cola's response to TragoCo's two possible decisions in the second-to-last period:

- **TragoCo sets a high price.** TragoCo's managers start by asking what they can expect from the managers at Boca-Cola if TragoCo continues the cooperative strategy by setting a high price. If Boca-Cola's managers also continue to cooperate by setting a high price, Boca-Cola's profit is $8 billion, but if they cheat on the cooperative strategy by setting a low price, Boca-Cola's profit is $10 billion, an increase of $2 billion. Boca-Cola's managers do not fear punishment for cheating in the next period (the last period) because they already know that TragoCo is going to set a low price in that last period. So if TragoCo continues to play the cooperative tit-for-tat strategy by setting a high price, TragoCo's managers expect that Boca-Cola's managers are going to defect by setting a low price.

Table 8.3 One-Period Payoff Matrix

This payoff matrix duplicates the payoff matrix from Table 8.1.

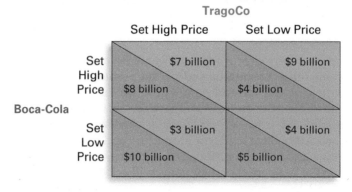

- **TragoCo sets a low price.** TragoCo's managers then ask what they can expect if they defect from the cooperative tit-for-tat strategy by setting a low price. First TragoCo's managers realize that by setting a low price they will make a profit of at least $4 billion and maybe even $9 billion (if Boca-Cola continues to set a high price). And they also know that Boca-Cola will set a low price in the final period, so they already know they will be "punished" in the next period. TragoCo's managers reason that setting a low price gives them more profit than setting a high price (at least $4 billion versus only $3 billion) and they will not suffer any extra punishment from this action. So TragoCo's managers set a low price.

TragoCo's managers have determined that setting a low price is their optimal strategy. Boca-Cola's managers employ similar reasoning. They conclude that their profit will be larger by setting a low price, so Boca-Cola also sets a low price. Consequently, in the second-to-last period, both firms (again) depart from the cooperative tit-for-tat strategy by (again) setting a low price.

Third-to-Last Period   The analysis in the third-to-last period is identical to that in the second-to-last period. Consequently, in the third-to-last period, both sets of managers once again set a low price and defect from the cooperative tit-for-tat strategy.

The end-period problem might now be apparent: If the players know a final period is coming, the cooperative tit-for-tat strategy unravels period by period as the managers play their optimal strategy. The reason for the unraveling is straightforward. For the tit-for-tat strategy to work, managers must be able to impose future punishment on their competitor for departing from it, but the presence of a final period eliminates that potential. There is no possibility of future punishment in the last period, so both firms can freely defect from the cooperative tit-for-tat strategy in the last period. In turn, that defection eliminates the possibility of future punishment from the second-to-last period because both sets of managers are already going to set a low price in the last period. In the second-to-last period, the managers of both firms once again defect from the cooperative strategy. That means there is no possibility of future punishment in the third-to-last period, so both groups of managers again defect in that period. Clearly, the process continues to roll back to the present period, the one in which the Venezuelan government announced the impending nationalization of the production facilities that ends the game. In other words, the cooperative equilibrium immediately falls apart.

Solution to the End-Period Problem

The end-period problem occurs because both players know there is a period that is definitely the last. Suppose, however, that there is some uncertainty about whether the game will end. For example, in the TragoCo/Boca-Cola game, it is unlikely that the managers know with certainty that at a given time the government will nationalize their companies. More realistically, there might be a probability—say, 20 percent—that the game will end in a certain period because of nationalization. But that means there is a probability of 80 percent that the game will continue without nationalization. In this situation, the managers now must worry about the possibility of punishment in future periods if they defect. Because of the uncertainty, the managers adjust the future penalty by the probability of its occurrence: The greater the probability that the game will continue, the greater the likelihood of being penalized for defecting from the cooperative strategy. As long as the probability that the game might continue is sufficiently high, the managers might fear the future penalty enough that they continue to play the cooperative strategy. In particular, as long as the gain in profit from defecting in the current period is less than the sum of the expected future penalties, the managers cooperate. So the larger the probability that the game continues and the larger the penalties that might be incurred in the future, the more likely that the managers will use the cooperative strategy, maintaining the cooperative equilibrium. Returning to the soft drink example, if the managers at TragoCo and Boca-Cola both believe that the probability of nationalization is low, they might play the cooperative tit-for-tat strategy and sustain the high price.

Another possible solution to the end-period problem is to create an alternative game that has an additional period (or periods) beyond the "last" period. For example, in the TragoCo/Boca-Cola scenario, the Venezuelan government nationalizes the assets of both companies only in Venezuela. But because the companies compete throughout South America, the "last" period in Venezuela is not the last period in the wider game, which includes other countries. So if TragoCo defects from the cooperative strategy in Venezuela, Boca-Cola can punish it in future periods in, say, Colombia.

Dominated Strategies

For the initial, one-time price-setting game, you saw that setting a low price was a dominant strategy for both TragoCo and Boca-Cola. Table 8.4 is a hypothetical payoff matrix for a more complicated version of the same game, in which both sets of managers are able to set *three* prices: a high price, a medium price, and a low price. Once again you are looking for the likely outcome, the Nash equilibrium. Continue to assume that the managers at both TragoCo and Boca-Cola are aware of each other's profits and potential actions.

Table 8.4 A Payoff Matrix with Three Strategies

The payoff matrix summarizes how the economic profits of TragoCo and Boca-Cola depend on the prices they set. The columns represent TragoCo's choices, and the rows represent Boca-Cola's choices. For TragoCo's managers, the strategies of setting a high price and setting a low price are dominated by the strategy of setting a medium price: No matter the strategy Boca-Cola employs, setting a medium price *always* gives TragoCo a larger profit than setting either a high price or a low price. A rational player never plays a dominated strategy, which means TragoCo's managers rule out the high-price and low-price strategies. Boca-Cola's managers do not initially have a dominant strategy, so they cannot rule out any of their strategies at the start. But Boca-Cola's managers know that TragoCo's managers will not use a dominated strategy, so they know that TragoCo's managers will set a medium price. Consequently, Boca-Cola's managers set a medium price because that strategy is now their profit-maximizing dominant strategy once they have eliminated TragoCo's high-price and low-price strategies.

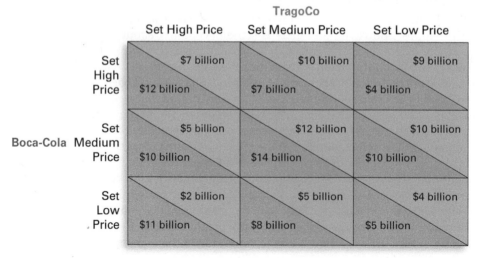

		TragoCo	
	Set High Price	Set Medium Price	Set Low Price
Boca-Cola Set High Price	$7 billion / $12 billion	$10 billion / $7 billion	$9 billion / $4 billion
Set Medium Price	$5 billion / $10 billion	$12 billion / $14 billion	$10 billion / $10 billion
Set Low Price	$2 billion / $11 billion	$5 billion / $8 billion	$4 billion / $5 billion

Start by examining the situation faced by TragoCo's managers. Regardless of Boca-Cola's strategy, TragoCo's profit from setting a high price is *always* less than their profit from setting a medium price. If Boca-Cola's managers set a high price, TragoCo's profit is $7 billion from a high price and $10 billion from a medium price. If Boca-Cola's managers set a medium price, TragoCo's profit is $5 billion from a high price and $12 billion from a medium price. Finally, if Boca-Cola's managers set a low price, TragoCo's profit is $2 billion from a high price and $5 billion from a medium price. Because TragoCo's high-price strategy *always* creates less profit than its medium-price strategy, its high-price strategy is a **dominated strategy**, a strategy with outcomes that are always inferior to those of another strategy. In other words, TragoCo's medium-price strategy dominates its high-price strategy, so the high-price strategy is a dominated strategy. Similarly, regardless of the decision by Boca-Cola's managers, TragoCo's profit from setting a low price is *always* less than that from setting a medium price. Consequently, TragoCo's low-price strategy also is a dominated strategy. TragoCo's medium-price strategy is better than *both* the low-price strategy and the high-price strategy, so it is the dominant strategy.

Dominated strategy A strategy with outcomes that are *always* inferior to those of another strategy.

Unlike TragoCo, Boca-Cola initially has no dominated strategies. For example, if you compare Boca-Cola's profits from its high-price strategy and its medium-price strategy, you will see that its high-price strategy has a higher profit if TragoCo sets a high price but a lower profit if TragoCo sets a medium price. Initially, no strategy dominates another.

Eliminating Dominated Strategies

Unless they are cooperating with their rival(s), rational, profit-maximizing managers never use a dominated strategy because its outcome is worse in *all* situations than that of another strategy. In our soft drink case, the managers at TragoCo know that their medium-price strategy dominates their low-price and high-price strategies. Accordingly, TragoCo's managers never set a low price or a high price—they always set a medium price.

When Boca-Cola's managers duplicate the reasoning just outlined, they realize that TragoCo's managers definitely will set a medium price. Eliminating TragoCo's two dominated strategies—setting a low price and setting a high price—leaves Boca-Cola's managers facing the payoff matrix in Table 8.5. Once TragoCo's two

Table 8.5 A Payoff Matrix That Eliminates Dominated Strategies

After eliminating TragoCo's dominated strategies, the new payoff matrix contains only one strategy for TragoCo: Set a medium price.

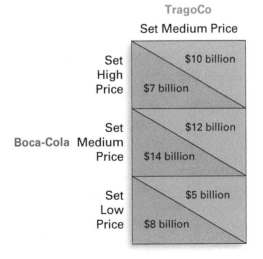

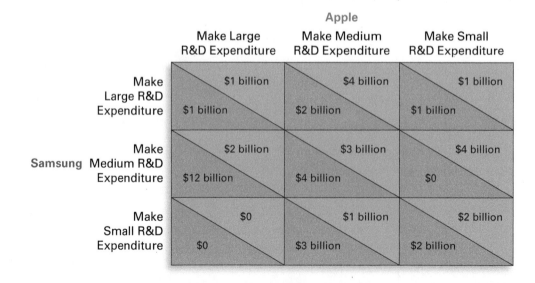

		Apple		
		Make Large R&D Expenditure	Make Medium R&D Expenditure	Make Small R&D Expenditure
Samsung	Make Large R&D Expenditure	$1 billion / $1 billion	$4 billion / $2 billion	$1 billion / $1 billion
	Make Medium R&D Expenditure	$2 billion / $12 billion	$3 billion / $4 billion	$4 billion / $0
	Make Small R&D Expenditure	$0 / $0	$1 billion / $3 billion	$2 billion / $2 billion

a. Identify and eliminate one dominated strategy for Apple and one for Samsung.

b. Using the payoff matrix from the answer to part a, if Apple and Samsung play the game only once, what is the Nash equilibrium?

c. Using the payoff matrix from the answer to part a, if Apple and Samsung play the game repeatedly, what is the cooperative equilibrium?

Answer

a. Initially, Samsung does not have a dominated strategy. But Apple's medium-expenditure strategy dominates its large-expenditure strategy. In particular, if Samsung makes a large expenditure on R&D, Apple's profit from a medium expenditure ($4 billion) exceeds its profit from a large expenditure ($1 billion); if Samsung makes a medium expenditure, Apple's profit from a medium expenditure ($3 billion) exceeds its profit from a large expenditure ($2 billion); and if Samsung makes a small expenditure, Apple's profit from a medium expenditure ($1 billion) exceeds its profit from a large expenditure ($0 billion).

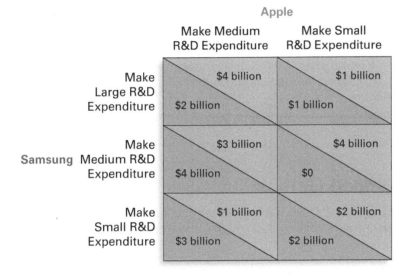

Once Apple's dominated strategy is eliminated, the new payoff matrix shows that Samsung's large-expenditure strategy is dominated by its small-expenditure strategy. If Apple makes a medium expenditure, Samsung's profit from a small expenditure ($3 billion) exceeds its profit from a large expenditure ($2 billion), and if Apple makes a small expenditure, Samsung's profit from a small expenditure ($2 billion) exceeds its profit from a large expenditure ($1 billion). Eliminating this dominated strategy results in the 2 × 2 payoff matrix.

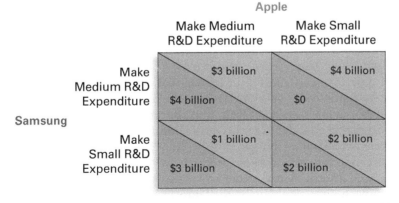

(*Continues*)

SOLVED PROBLEM (*continued*)

b. With the 2 × 2 payoff matrix from part a, if Apple and Samsung play the game once, the Nash equilibrium is for both firms to make a small R&D expenditure.
Apple's strategy of making a "medium R&D expenditure" is dominated by its strategy of making a "small R&D expenditure," so making a small R&D expenditure is a dominant strategy:

- If Samsung makes a medium R&D expenditure, Apple's profit from making a small R&D expenditure ($4 billion) exceeds its profit from making a medium R&D expenditure ($3 billion).
- If Samsung makes a small R&D expenditure, Apple's profit from making a small R&D expenditure ($2 billion) exceeds its profit from making a medium R&D expenditure ($1 billion).

With Apple's dominant small-expenditure strategy, Samsung's small-expenditure strategy becomes its dominant strategy: When Apple makes a small R&D expenditure, Samsung's profit from making a small R&D expenditure ($2 billion) exceeds its profit from making a medium R&D expenditure ($0 billion). Consequently, the Nash equilibrium is for both firms to make a small R&D expenditure.

c. With the 2 × 2 payoff matrix from part a, if Apple and Samsung play the game repeatedly, the cooperative equilibrium is for both firms to make a medium R&D expenditure.

8.2 Advanced Games

Learning Objective 8.2 Describe how to determine the equilibrium in games with more than one Nash equilibrium and in games with no pure-strategy Nash equilibrium.

All of the games explored in this chapter so far have had a single Nash equilibrium. Some games, however, have more than one. In such games, determining which Nash equilibrium occurs is important because it helps managers know what to expect. Other games have no pure-strategy Nash equilibrium. In those games, managers can use a *mixed strategy*, a strategy that randomly adopts different pure strategies according to predetermined probabilities. This sort of game is the last topic in this section.

Multiple Nash Equilibria

In games with more than one Nash equilibrium, selecting the Nash equilibrium that actually occurs is not always straightforward. Economists have suggested various ways that may lead to a single equilibrium. To explore these suggestions and understand how they can affect your managerial decisions, we need a game with multiple Nash equilibria. For a purely hypothetical game, suppose that in India managers at two major fast-food restaurants, Burger Best and McBurger's, are considering introducing a lamb burger because Hindus do not eat beef. Each firm's set of managers expects its lamb burger to be profitable. Before their upper-level executives allow them to roll out their new product, however, both sets of managers need to provide more information in order to persuade the executives of the potential profitability. Each firm could gain this information by test-marketing its lamb burger in one or two Indian states. Alternatively, one of the firms could wait until the other firm initially test-markets and then introduce its lamb burger nationwide, using the competing firm's results as the evidence the managers need to convince their upper management of the product's profitability. Finally, if neither firm test-markets its lamb burger, neither firm's upper management will sign off on introduction of the product.

Suppose that McBurger's managers expect its economic profit to be (1) $26 million if only McBurger's engages in test-marketing, (2) $25 million if only Burger Best test-markets the lamb burger and McBurger's managers use those results, and (3) $24 million if McBurger's and Burger Best both engage in test-marketing. Say that Burger Best has fewer stores in India, so its managers expect a smaller gain in market share and profit from its lamb burger: (1) $11 million if only Burger Best test-markets the lamb burgers, (2) $13 million if only McBurger's engages in test-marketing and Burger Best's managers use those results, and (3) $7 million if Burger Best and McBurger's both engage in test-marketing. If neither firm test-markets its lamb burger, upper-level management does not give permission to roll out the burger, so both firms' economic profit is $0. Table 8.6 collects these payoffs from the game.

In this game, there are two possible Nash equilibria:

- McBurger's managers test-market, and Burger Best's managers do not test-market (the top right cell in Table 8.6).
- McBurger's managers do not test-market, and Burger Best's managers test-market (the bottom left cell in Table 8.6).

You can readily check that both outcomes are Nash equilibria by determining if either firm can unilaterally increase its profit by changing its strategy. In the top right cell, McBurger's is test-marketing, and Burger Best is not. If McBurger's managers choose their other strategy (not to test-market), McBurger's profit decreases from $26 million to $0. If Burger Best's managers choose their other strategy (to test market), Burger Best's profit falls from $13 million to $7 million. Accordingly, the top right

Table 8.6 A Payoff Matrix for Test-Marketing Lamb Burgers

The payoff matrix summarizes how the two firms' economic profits depend on their choices about whether or not to test-market their lamb burger. This game has two Nash equilibria: (1) McBurger's test-markets its lamb burger, and Burger Best does not, and (2) Burger Best test-markets its lamb burger, and McBurger's does not.

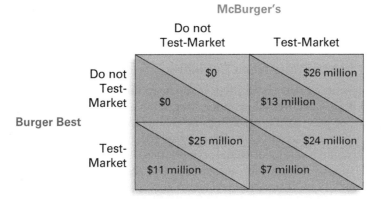

cell is a Nash equilibrium because no player can unilaterally change its strategy and increase its profit. You can use similar reasoning to demonstrate that the bottom left cell also is a Nash equilibrium.

You can also determine that the other two outcomes shown in Table 8.6 are not Nash equilibria. In the bottom right cell, McBurger's and Burger Best both test market. From this cell, *both* McBurger's and Burger Best can unilaterally change their strategy and increase their profit. If McBurger's managers change their strategy to not test marketing, their profit will rise from $24 million to $25 million. If Burger Best's managers change their strategy to not test marketing, their profit will rise from $7 million to $13 million. Consequently, the bottom right cell is not a Nash equilibrium because either firm can unilaterally change its strategy and increase its profit. You can use similar reasoning to demonstrate that the top left cell also is not a Nash equilibrium.

Refinements

Unfortunately, there is no certain way to determine which of the two Nash equilibria occurs—that is, which company does the test marketing and which does not. Economists have suggested various methods called *refinements* to determine which one of multiple Nash equilibria to select as the equilibrium. Here are two refinements:

- **Pareto criterion.** The Pareto criterion, named after the Italian economist Vilfredo Pareto, suggests that the most likely pure-strategy Nash equilibrium is one for which any change to another equilibrium that makes one firm better off makes the other firm worse off, that is, it is impossible to change to another equilibrium that makes *both* firms better off. For example, if Burger Best test-markets the lamb burger and McBurger's does not, it is possible to increase both firms' profits by switching to the equilibrium in which McBurger's test-markets and Burger Best does not. Consequently, the equilibrium in which Burger Best test-markets and McBurger's does not is *not* selected by the Pareto criterion. The equilibrium in which McBurger's test-markets and Burger Best does not *is* selected by the Pareto criterion because a change from this equilibrium to the other decreases both firms' profit.
- **Focal point.** The focal point is an outcome on which the players naturally focus. For example, as the larger firm, McBurger's might be the one that "always" does marketing research. If this belief is the focal point, then the equilibrium again is the one in which McBurger's does the test-marketing and Burger Best does not.

Unfortunately, there is no refinement that is universally applicable to all scenarios. Some games, but not all, have a Nash equilibrium that the Pareto criterion selects, and other games may or may not have a focal point. Consequently, there is no technique that always determines which equilibrium occurs in a game with two (or more) Nash equilibria.

Cheap Talk and Multiple Nash Equilibria

In Section 8.1, you learned about the role of cheap talk in the pricing game between TragoCo and Boca-Cola. In that instance, TragoCo's managers made the (cheap) pronouncement that they would set a high price, but this had no effect on the game's equilibrium. Boca-Cola's managers disregarded the announcement and continued to play their dominant strategy of setting a low price. Let's see whether cheap talk can affect the players in the current game. Suppose that before making their choice, McBurger's managers announce a plan to test-market their lamb burger. Their announcement is, of course, nonbinding because they may not follow through. It is also cheap talk because the announcement costs McBurger's nothing. But sometimes cheap talk can have an effect. For example, if McBurger's and Burger Best are playing a repeated game and previous announcements made by McBurger's managers have been truthful, their current announcement might be credible, causing Burger Best's managers to focus on the Nash equilibrium in which McBurger's does test-marketing and Burger Best does not.

Setting aside the reputation gained from past truthful announcements, there is another reason why the cheap talk by TragoCo's managers had no effect but the similarly cheap talk by McBurger's managers might have an effect. The reason hinges on the alignment of the players' interests. In the TragoCo/Boca-Cola game, the players' interests collide. If Boca-Cola's managers set a high price because they believe TragoCo's announcement of a high price for its soda, TragoCo's managers will immediately take advantage of Boca-Cola's high-price response by setting a low price to boost TragoCo's profit. Whenever the players' interests conflict, a firm should immediately disregard an announcement by its rival. The McBurger's/Burger Best game is different because the players' interests align. For example, once McBurger's announces it will test-market, Burger Best's profit is higher if it does not test-market. If McBurger's reneges on its announcement, then *McBurger's* profit falls from $26 million to $0. Clearly, McBurger's will not renege. Indeed, in the McBurger's/Burger Best game, the interests correspond perfectly. As Table 8.6 shows, if McBurger's reneges on any announced choice that Burger Best had believed, the profits of both companies fall. Indeed, if Burger Best reneges on an announcement that McBurger's had believed, the profits of both companies also fall. Because the firms' interests align, managers should believe their rival's announcements. More generally, however, interests will not align perfectly. The likelihood of the announcement being truthful depends on the degree to which the competitors' interests align or conflict.

Mixed-Strategy Nash Equilibrium

Although some games have multiple pure-strategy Nash equilibria, other games have none. The payoff matrix in Table 8.7 is an example. It shows a hypothetical interaction between the managers of Kingster and PureFood, two large grocery store chains. The managers of both chains must put either beef or chicken on sale. The payoff matrix assumes that if the same product is on sale at both chains, more customers prefer to shop at PureFood. So when both chains put beef on sale, PureFood's profit is larger and Kingster's profit is smaller. And when both chains put chicken on sale, PureFood's profit is larger and Kingster's profit is smaller. If one chain puts beef on sale and the other puts chicken on sale, Kingster gains customers who want whichever protein it has on sale, so Kingster's profit is larger (and PureFood's profit is smaller) compared to the situation when *both* firms have that particular protein on sale.

There is no pure-strategy Nash equilibrium for this game. No matter what cell you consider, the managers of one of the firms can unilaterally change their strategy and increase their company's profit. For example, the top left cell, in which both sets of managers put beef on sale, is not a Nash equilibrium because Kingster's managers can change their choice and put chicken on sale, thereby moving to the top right cell and boosting their profit from $4 million to $6 million. The top right cell is not a Nash equilibrium either because PureFood's managers can change their strategy and put chicken on sale, thereby moving from the top right cell to the bottom right cell and increasing PureFood's profit from $8 million to $12 million. Similar reasoning eliminates the remaining two cells as potential Nash equilibria.

Table 8.7 A Payoff Matrix with a Mixed-Strategy Nash Equilibrium

The payoff matrix summarizes how Kingster's and PureFood's economic profits depend on their choices about whether to put chicken or beef on sale. This payoff matrix has no pure-strategy Nash equilibrium. From any cell, one firm can unilaterally change its strategy and increase its profit. For example, if managers at both chains put beef on sale, the top left cell, Kingster's managers can change their strategy to put chicken on sale, thereby boosting their profit from $4 million to $6 million. Similar reasoning shows that in the other three cells one of the firms can increase its profit by changing its strategy.

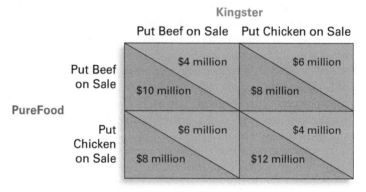

Kingster

	Put Beef on Sale	Put Chicken on Sale
Put Beef on Sale	$4 million / $10 million	$6 million / $8 million
Put Chicken on Sale	$6 million / $8 million	$4 million / $12 million

PureFood

Mixed strategy A strategy in which a player randomly chooses among different pure strategies according to predetermined probabilities.

Although there is no pure-strategy Nash equilibrium in this example, there is an alternative Nash equilibrium, in which the players use a mixed strategy. A **mixed strategy** is a strategy in which a player randomly chooses among different pure strategies according to predetermined probabilities. Unlike the nonrandom pure strategies you have seen before, mixed strategies are inherently random. Each period the players use a strategy randomly selected from the set of strategies available to them. For instance, PureFood's managers might determine that they will put beef on sale 50 percent of the time and put chicken on sale the other 50 percent of the time. Given these probabilities, the managers could effectively flip a coin each period to determine which product they will put on sale.

Mixed-strategy Nash equilibrium The outcome in which each player's *mixed* strategy is the best strategy for that player, taking as given the other player's *mixed* strategy.

A pure-strategy Nash equilibrium requires each player's strategy to be the best for that player, taking as given the other player's strategy. The **mixed-strategy Nash equilibrium** is similar: Each player's *mixed* strategy is the best for that player, taking as given the other player's *mixed* strategy.[3] When using mixed strategies, the probabilities each player uses are the best for that player, taking as given the other player's probabilities.

Why should PureFood's managers use a mixed strategy? If they use a nonrandom pure strategy, Kingster's managers can develop a strategy that boosts their profit and reduces PureFood's profit. For example, if PureFood's managers alternated, first putting beef on sale for a week and then putting chicken on sale for the next week in a regular, nonrandom pattern, Kingster's managers would also alternate. But they would first put *chicken* on sale and then put beef on sale, thereby increasing Kingster's profit and decreasing PureFood's profit. Any nonrandom

---

3 As a technical issue, if there are multiple pure-strategy equilibria, there is also a mixed-strategy equilibrium. In this situation, however, each player prefers at least one of the pure-strategy equilibria to the mixed-strategy equilibrium. Consequently, we consider mixed-strategy equilibria only in games that have no pure-strategy equilibria.

strategy opens PureFood to exploitation by Kingster. PureFood's managers are safe from consistent exploitation by Kingster's managers only if they randomly select a choice each period. Of course, the same conclusion applies to Kingster's managers: They also must use a mixed strategy to avoid exploitation by PureFood's managers.

Calculating Mixed Strategies

The mixed strategy adopted by PureFood's managers means that each period they must randomly put either beef or chicken on sale. If you are a manager for Pure-Food, you need to determine how frequently to put beef on sale and how frequently to put chicken on sale. In other words, you need to determine the probability of putting beef on sale and the probability of putting chicken on sale. Section 14.1 includes a more complete discussion of the basics of probability, but for now, you need to understand only two of its characteristics:

1. The probability of putting an item on sale can be written as a decimal (such as 0.60) or a percentage (such as 60 percent). For example, if p is the probability of PureFood putting beef on sale and PureFood puts beef on sale 20 percent of the time, then $p = 20$ percent, or 0.20.
2. If beef is on sale 20 percent, or 0.20, of the time, then chicken is on sale the remaining 80 percent, or 0.80, of the time. So, using decimals to write the probabilities, if the probability of putting beef on sale is equal to p, then the probability of putting chicken on sale is $(1 - p)$.

As a manager for PureFood, your goal is to select the probability of putting beef on sale that maximizes your expected profit.[4] Your expected profit equals your profit in each of the four cells in the payoff matrix shown in Table 8.7 weighted by the probability of occurrence of that cell, so it is your weighted average profit. For example, if each cell in Table 8.7 has a probability of occurrence of 0.25 (25 percent), then PureFood's expected profit equals

$$(0.25 \times \$10\,M) + (0.25 \times \$8\,M) + (0.25 \times \$8\,M) + (0.25 \times \$12\,M) = \$9.5\,M$$

where M = million. You must focus on the expected profit because in any period what turns out to be the *actual* profit depends on both your decision and the decision by Kingster's managers about what to put on sale. Because the choices are random and unknown in advance, in any given period the actual profit will also be random and unknown in advance.

Choosing the probabilities relates directly to game theory: When you are determining the probability of putting beef on sale, you must take into account the response from Kingster's managers. You want to choose probabilities in such a way that rival managers cannot take advantage of you to boost their expected profit and lower your expected profit. In particular, you want to set probabilities that make Kingster's expected profit from putting beef on sale equal to Kingster's expected profit from putting chicken on sale. Why? Suppose that the probabilities you use mean that Kingster's expected profit from putting beef on sale exceeds that from putting chicken on sale. In this situation, Kingster could increase its expected profit—and thereby *decrease* your expected profit—by always putting beef on sale.

---

4 Once you have determined that the probability of putting one item on sale is p, the probability of putting the other item on sale is $(1 - p)$. Accordingly, determining the probability of putting one item on sale automatically determines the probability of putting the other item on sale.

In general, whenever the expected profit from one pure strategy exceeds the expected profit from the other, the rival managers can use their more profitable pure strategy to increase their expected profit and decrease your expected profit. To rule out the possibility that Kingster's managers can decrease your expected profit, Kingster's expected profit from its two pure strategies must be the same.

As a PureFood manager, suppose that you will put beef on sale p percent of the time. To determine the optimal p, you must think about *Kingster's* expected profit. Look at the situation from the perspective of Kingster's managers: When Kingster's managers put beef on sale, p percent of the time PureFood has beef on sale, so Table 8.7 shows that Kingster's profit is \$4 million. The other $(1 - p)$ percent of the time PureFood has chicken on sale, so Kingster's profit, also from Table 8.7, is \$6 million. With these probabilities, Kingster's expected profit from putting beef on sale is

$$\text{PROFIT}^K_{\text{Beef}} = (p \times \$4 \text{ million}) + [(1 - p) \times \$6 \text{ million}] \qquad \textbf{8.1}$$

Similarly, if the managers at Kingster put chicken on sale, p percent of the time Pure-Food has beef on sale, so Kingster's profit (from Table 8.7) is \$6 million, and $(1 - p)$ percent of the time PureFood has chicken on sale, so Kingster's profit (also taken from Table 8.7) is \$4 million. Therefore, Kingster's expected profit from putting chicken on sale is

$$\text{PROFIT}^K_{\text{Chicken}} = (p \times \$6 \text{ million}) + [(1 - p) \times \$4 \text{ million}] \qquad \textbf{8.2}$$

You, as a PureFood manager, choose the probability, p, of putting beef on sale. Your goal is to set this probability in such a way that *Kingster's* expected profit from putting beef on sale is equal to its expected profit from putting chicken on sale—in other words, $\text{PROFIT}^K_{\text{Beef}} = \text{PROFIT}^K_{\text{Chicken}}$, or

$$(p \times \$4 \text{ M}) + [(1 - p) \times \$6 \text{ M}] = (p \times \$6 \text{ M}) + [(1 - p) \times \$4 \text{ M}]$$

where M = million. Solving this equality yields $p = 0.50$, which means that you put beef on sale 50 percent of the time. Chicken is on sale $(1 - p)$ of the time, so you put chicken on sale $1 - 0.50 = 0.50$, or 50 percent, of the time.

Now that you have determined the probability that you put beef or chicken on sale, you can also determine Kingster's expected profit from putting beef or putting chicken on sale. Using the formula for $\text{PROFIT}^K_{\text{Beef}}$ in Equation 8.1, when Kingster's managers put beef on sale, their expected profit is $(0.50 \times \$4 \text{ million}) + (0.50 \times \$6 \text{ million}) = \$5 \text{ million}$. Using the formula for $\text{PROFIT}^K_{\text{Chicken}}$ in Equation 8.2, when Kingster's managers put chicken on sale, their expected profit is $(0.50 \times \$6 \text{ million}) + (0.50 \times \$4 \text{ million}) = \$5 \text{ million}$. When $p = 0.50$, Kingster's expected profit is the same *no matter what* its managers put on sale. So Kingster's managers cannot choose a strategy that boosts their profit and decreases your profit.

You have just determined PureFood's optimal mixed strategy: randomly put beef on sale 50 percent of the time and chicken on sale the remaining 50 percent of the time. To finish determining the mixed-strategy Nash equilibrium, you must determine the strategy that Kingster's managers use—that is, their probabilities of putting beef on sale and putting chicken on sale. The analysis is similar to the analysis for PureFood. In particular, Kingster's managers want to select their probabilities for putting beef and chicken on sale in such a way that your choices as a PureFood manager cannot decrease their expected profit. In other words, comparable to the previous calculation, Kingster's managers want PureFood's expected profit from putting beef on sale to equal its expected profit from putting chicken on sale.

Suppose that the probability that Kingster's managers put beef on sale is k, so that the probability that Kingster puts chicken on sale is $(1 - k)$. Now it is Kingster's managers who need to use the most important managerial lesson from game theory: They must analyze the situation from your perspective as a PureFood manager. If you put beef on sale, k percent of the time they have Kingster putting beef on sale, so Table 8.7 shows that your profit is $10 million. The other $(1 - k)$ percent of the time they have Kingster putting chicken on sale, so Table 8.7 shows your profit is $8 million. With these probabilities, PureFood's expected profit from putting beef on sale is

$$\text{PROFIT}^P_{\text{Beef}} = (k \times \$10\text{ million}) + [(1 - k) \times \$8\text{ million}] \qquad 8.3$$

Finally, if you, as a PureFood manager, put chicken on sale, then k percent of the time Kingster has beef on sale, so that your profit is $8 million, and $(1 - k)$ percent of the time Kingster has chicken on sale, so that your profit is $12 million. Therefore, PureFood's expected profit from putting chicken on sale is

$$\text{PROFIT}^P_{\text{Chicken}} = (k \times \$8\text{ million}) + [(1 - k) \times \$12\text{ million}] \qquad 8.4$$

The goal of Kingster's managers is to select the probability, k, of putting beef on sale in such a way that *PureFood's* expected profit from putting beef on sale is equal to its expected profit from putting chicken on sale—that is, $\text{PROFIT}^P_{\text{Beef}} = \text{PROFIT}^P_{\text{Chicken}}$, or

$$(k \times \$10\text{ M}) + [(1 - k) \times \$8\text{ M}] = (k \times \$8\text{ M}) + [(1 - k) \times \$12\text{ M}]$$

where M = million. Solving this equation for k gives $k = 0.67$, which means that Kingster's managers put beef on sale 67 percent of the time and put chicken on sale the remaining 33 percent of the time. Using these probabilities in Equations 8.3 and 8.4, PureFood's expected profit is $9.3 million *regardless* of whether PureFood puts beef on sale or chicken on sale. Because PureFood's expected profit is the same no matter what you, as its manager, put on sale, you cannot choose a strategy that boosts your profit and decreases Kingster's profit.

You have just calculated the mixed-strategy Nash equilibrium: PureFood's managers randomly put beef on sale 50 percent of the time and chicken on sale the other 50 percent of the time, and Kingster's managers randomly put beef on sale 67 percent of the time and chicken on sale the remaining 33 percent of the time. In this example, Kingster's expected profit is $5 million per period, and PureFood's expected profit is $9.3 million per period. If either firm deviates from its optimal mixed strategy by changing the frequency with which it puts beef and chicken on sale, its expected profit falls and its rival's expected profit rises.

The Role Played by the Competitor's Best Response

When making a decision about your strategy, you must think about your competitor's best response. For example, the payoff matrix in Table 8.7 shows that when Kingster has beef on sale, PureFood's profit from putting chicken on sale ($8 million) is less than PureFood's profit from putting beef on sale ($10 million). This result might suggest that PureFood's managers should put beef on sale more frequently than chicken. However, you saw from the formal analysis above that putting beef on sale more frequently than chicken would be a mistake. The optimal strategy for PureFood's managers is to put beef and chicken on sale with equal probability, so that each goes on sale 50 percent of the time. The difference between the naïve suggestion and the optimal strategy is focus. If PureFood's managers focus only on their own profit, they are making a mistake—they must also consider the response of Kingster's managers. If the managers at PureFood put beef on sale more often than chicken, Kingster's managers react by increasing the frequency with which they put chicken on sale. The net outcome of a change depends on both the action *and* the reaction. If PureFood's managers switch to putting beef on sale more frequently, the action of PureFood putting beef on sale and the *reaction* of Kingster putting chicken on sale more frequently, lowers PureFood's expected profit.

An extreme case can help reinforce the need to consider your rival's payoff as well as your company's profit. Suppose that your rival has a dominant strategy— that is, a strategy it always plays. Once you know the strategy your rival will use, you can easily determine the strategy you must use to maximize your profit. If, however, you concentrate *only* on your own profit and ignore your opponent's strategies, you will miss the fact that your rival always plays one strategy, and you will maximize your profit only by chance.

In short, you must think about your opponent's response when you are considering a strategy. In the PureFood/Kingster game, you followed this insight by calculating the profit-maximizing probabilities for each strategy. In more complicated real-world interactions, implementing this insight can be very difficult, but considering it carefully leads you to better managerial decisions.

Randomness

In our example, each period the managers at PureFood can flip a coin to determine what to put on sale because at their mixed-strategy Nash equilibrium the probability of putting beef or chicken on sale is 50 percent. The managers at Kingster can roll a die: A 1, 2, 3, or 4 (67 percent of the possible outcomes) means that they put beef on sale, and a 5 or 6 (33 percent of the possible outcomes) means that they put chicken on sale. In reality, of course, not many managers are willing to flip a coin—or roll a die—to decide what to put on sale. However, the factors that go into a manager's decisions are often so complicated and so particular to the firm that from the outside the choice about what to put on sale appears random. Regardless of whether the strategy is actually random, as a manager you must be careful to avoid giving competitor(s) a chance to exploit your choice by using a strategy that boosts their profit and lowers yours.

There are occasions, however, when actual randomness can be desirable. One duty of the U.S. Bureau of Customs and Border Protection (Customs) is to inspect cut flowers imported into the United States to ensure that the boxes of flowers do not contain harmful pests. Some types of flowers are at a higher risk for infestation than others. Roses, for example, have a very low risk of infestation. Customs inspectors examine boxes of each particular type of low-risk flower only three days a month. Inspecting the flowers takes additional time, which decreases the importers' profit from that flower on that day. If inspectors find pests, the shipper's entire shipment is lost because the flowers must be fumigated, which essentially destroys them. Each day Customs officials select a "flower of the day," the particular low-risk flower they will inspect. The inspectors want their selection to be random to prevent shrewd importers from shipping each type of low-risk flowers only on days when the importers know that Customs will not inspect that type of flower.

Custom's Flower of the Day

Say that you are a manager at one of the firms that import flowers from Ecuador through the Miami airport. Flowers differ according to their risk of pest infestation. Suppose that your firm imports two types of flowers, one with a high risk of pest infestation and the other with a low risk. Further suppose that each day Customs inspects flowers from only one of these risk types. If Customs officials inspect the particular type of flower being imported that day, the importer incurs a loss rather than a profit, but the inspection budget increases. In the payoff matrix, the importer's payoff is profits (or losses), and Custom's payoff is its budget.

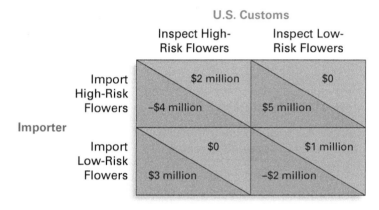

a. Is there a pure-strategy Nash equilibrium? If so, what is it?

b. Is there a mixed-strategy Nash equilibrium? If so, what is it?

c. At the Nash equilibrium, what is the importer's expected profit from importing high-risk flowers? From importing low-risk flowers?

Answer

a. There is no pure-strategy Nash equilibrium because with each possible outcome, one player is always able to increase its return by changing its strategy. For example, in the top left cell, the importer can increase its profit by switching to low-risk flowers, since that change would increases its profit from −$4 million to $3 million. In each of the other outcomes, one player can increase its return by switching.

b. There is a mixed-strategy Nash equilibrium: The inspectors check high-risk flowers 1/2 of the time and low-risk flowers 1/2 of the time, and the importer imports high-risk flowers 1/3 of the time and low-risk flowers 2/3 of the time. To determine its strategy, Customs must set the probabilities of its inspections in such a way that the importer's expected profit from importing high-risk flowers equals its expected profit from importing low-risk flowers. Call the probability of inspecting high-risk flowers p, so the probability of inspecting low-risk flowers is $(1 - p)$. If the importer imports high-risk flowers, p percent of the time the flowers are inspected, so the importer has a loss (−$4 million), and $(1 - p)$ percent of the time the flowers are not inspected, so the importer has a profit ($5 million). The importer's expected profit from high-risk flowers is

$$\text{Profit}_{\text{High-Risk}}^{\text{Importer}} = (p \times -\$4 \text{ million}) + [(1 - p) \times \$5 \text{ million}]$$

(*Continues*)

SOLVED PROBLEM (*continued*)

Similar reasoning shows that the expected profit from importing low-risk flowers is

$$\text{Profit}_{\text{Low-Risk}}^{\text{Importer}} = (p \times \$3 \text{ million}) + [(1 - p) \times -\$2 \text{ million}]$$

Setting the two expected profits equal gives

$$(p \times -\$4 \text{ million}) + [(1 - p) \times \$5 \text{ million}] = (p \times \$3 \text{ million}) + [(1 - p) \times -\$2 \text{ million}]$$

Solving this equation for p gives $p = 1/2$, so Customs officials inspect high-risk flowers $1/2$ of the time and low-risk flowers the other $1/2$ of the time. Analogous reasoning shows that the importer imports high-risk flowers $1/3$ of the time and low-risk flowers the other $2/3$ of the time.

c. The expected profit from importing high-risk flowers is $(1/2 \times -\$4 \text{ million}) + (1/2 \times \$5 \text{ million}) = \$0.5 \text{ million}$. The expected profit from importing low-risk flowers is $(1/2 \times \$3 \text{ million}) + (1/2 \times -\$2 \text{ million}) = \$0.5 \text{ million}$.

8.3 Sequential Games

Learning Objective 8.3 Explain the importance of backward induction and credible commitments in sequential games.

Sequential game A game in which the players make decisions one after the other.

To this point, we have presented games in which the managers must make simultaneous decisions. At times, however, the nature of the interaction requires that the managers of competing firms make their decisions sequentially. One set of managers makes a decision that is known to the rival set of managers when they make their decision. The second decision is known by the first set of managers, who then make another decision, and so forth. This series (or sequence) of events is a **sequential game**, a game in which the players make decisions one after the other. Sequential games involve strategy because each set of managers realizes that its decisions will influence its competitor's actions in the future. The roles played by credibility and commitment are often crucial to the outcomes of these games.

An Entry Game

Entry game A game in which one player decides whether to enter the market and the second player responds to the first player's entry decision.

A classic example of a sequential game is the entry game. In an **entry game**, one player decides whether to enter the market, and the other player responds to the first player's entry decision. For example, look at fast-food giants McDonald's and Burger King. In 2016, McDonald's had 100 outlets in Ukraine, and Burger King had none. Perhaps Burger King is contemplating entry into this market. What might McDonald's do to keep Burger King from entering the Ukrainian market? To explore this question, let's return to McBurger's and Burger Best. Suppose that they are in a similar situation with respect to, say, the French market: McBurger's is already in the market, and Burger Best is considering entry. If Burger Best enters, McBurger's managers must decide how to respond: Do they slash their prices and decrease their profit in order to "welcome" Burger Best by inflicting an economic loss on Burger Best's restaurants, or do McBurger's managers maintain their high prices even if it means that Burger Best also makes an economic profit? The decision making here is sequential and strategic. The managers at Burger Best make the first decision, whether to enter the market. When making that decision, they must take into account how McBurger's managers will react. The managers at McBurger's go second, realizing that their reaction will influence the entry decision by Burger Best's managers.

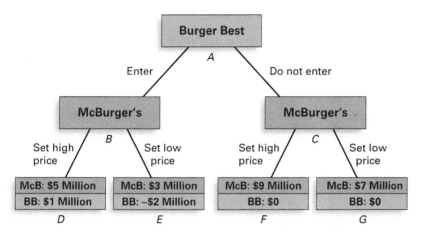

Figure 8.1 An Entry Game

The box at the top of the game tree is a decision node for Burger Best's managers, where they make the decision to enter or not to enter the French market. The boxes in the next level are decision nodes for McBurger's managers, where they decide whether to set a high price or a low price. At the bottom are terminal nodes, where the game ends, with the firms' payoffs at that particular end (McB = McBurger's; BB = Burger Best).

Once again, the payoffs in this game are economic profits. It is possible to record the profits of both companies in a payoff matrix similar to those you have already seen in this chapter. However, because the decisions are sequential, it is easier and more revealing to illustrate the profits in a game tree. A **game tree** is a diagram illustrating the players' sequential choices and the ultimate payoffs that result from the choices. Figure 8.1 shows a game tree for our sequential game, including profits for Burger Best and McBurger's. A **decision node** is a point in a game tree at which a player makes a decision. For example, the first decision node in Figure 8.1 is the blue box at the top of the tree labeled *A*. At this node, Burger Best's managers make the decision to enter or not to enter the French market. The second decision nodes, labeled *B* and *C*, are the red boxes below *A*. At these nodes, McBurger's managers make their decision about pricing. For simplicity, assume that McBurger's managers have only two strategies: set a high price and set a low price. At the bottom of the tree are the terminal nodes labeled *D*, *E*, *F*, and *G*. A *terminal node* is a point in a game tree at which the game terminates. Each terminal node includes the players' payoffs for the outcome at that node. For example, at terminal node *D*, Burger Best's managers have decided to enter the market, and McBurger's managers have decided to set a high price. With these decisions, Figure 8.1 shows that McBurger's profit (*McB*) is $5 million and Burger Best's profit (*BB*) is $1 million. You can interpret the other terminal nodes similarly.

Game tree A diagram illustrating the players' sequential choices and the ultimate payoffs that result from the choices.

Decision node A point in a game tree at which a player makes a decision.

Backward Induction

In sequential games, players make their choices when their decision node is reached. For example, if Burger Best enters the market, McBurger's must decide how to respond. Use the realistic assumption that players will make their profit-maximizing choices. Because players anticipate the future profit-maximizing choices of their rivals and take these choices as given, you are finding a Nash equilibrium.[5]

The game tree is an especially handy tool to determine the Nash equilibrium. Start by assuming that you are one of Burger Best's managers, who must make the first decision. To choose your strategy, you use a technique called *backward induction*:

---

5 When the players always make the choices that maximize their profit, the Nash equilibrium in the game is called a *subgame perfect equilibrium* because each player makes the best choice at each node. The solution method we use, backward induction, always gives a subgame perfect equilibrium. Some sequential games (but not the one we use) have other terminal nodes that are Nash equilibria, but these equilibria require that the players make suboptimal—non-profit-maximizing—choices at some decision node(s) so we ignore them.

Figure 8.2 Backward Induction Using a Decision Tree

To use backward induction, Burger Best's managers first determine McBurger's decisions at decision nodes *B* and *C*. At decision node *B*, McBurger's managers will set a high price because that choice gives McBurger's the higher profit, $5 million (terminal node *D*), rather than only $3 million from setting a low price (terminal node *E*). This decision gives Burger Best a profit of $1 million, which is entered next to decision node *B*. At decision node *C*, McBurger's managers will set a high price because that choice gives McBurger's the higher profit $9 million, at terminal node *F*. This decision gives Burger Best a profit of $0, which is entered next to decision node *C*. Finally, from decision node *A*, Burger Best's managers choose to enter because that strategy moves them to node *B* and gives them a profit of $1 million versus $0 if the managers choose not to enter, moving them to node *C*.

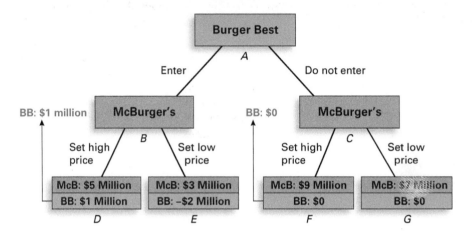

You begin at the last row of decision nodes (*B* and *C*) and determine the optimal strategy for McBurger's managers at each of these nodes. You then move back up the tree to determine your optimal strategy at decision node *A* based on your predictions of McBurger's strategies at *B* and *C*.

Begin the backward induction at decision node *B*. At that node, you reason that the managers at McBurger's will use the high-price strategy because that option moves them to terminal node *D*, which gives them a larger profit of $5 million than the low-price strategy, which moves them to terminal node *E* and a profit of only $3 million. At node *D*, Burger Best's profit is $1 million. Consequently, you know that if the game reaches node *B*, Burger Best's profit will be $1 million, labeled "BB: $1 million" next to node *B* in Figure 8.2.

Now switch focus to decision node *C*. As a Burger Best manager, you realize that if this node is reached, McBurger's managers (again) use the high-price strategy because that choice moves them to terminal node *F* and gives them more profit ($9 million) than the low-price strategy, which moves them to terminal node *G* and gives them a lower profit ($7 million). When McBurger's managers use the high-price strategy at decision node *C*, Burger Best's profit is $0, as shown in Figure 8.2 next to node *C* and labeled "BB: $0 million."

Now you need to make the decision about *your own* strategy at decision node *A*. At this point, you know that if you choose to enter, the game goes to decision node *B* and your profit is $1 million, and if you choose not to enter, the game goes to decision node *C* and your profit is $0. To maximize your profit, you decide to enter. This choice moves the game to decision node *B*, where the managers at McBurger's choose to keep their price high to maximize their profit.

The Nash equilibrium to this game has Burger Best entering the market and McBurger's managers setting a high price. The game ends at terminal node *D*, where Burger Best makes a profit of $1 million and McBurger's makes a profit of $5 million.

A key managerial lesson from studying the entry game should sound familiar to you by now: As a manager, you must put yourself in your competitor's shoes and examine their decisions from their perspective. The difference in a sequential game is that you need to look into the future and work backward. Although you are unlikely to be able to create a complete game tree like the one shown in Figure 8.2, you must still think about the payoff period, the potential outcomes, and how to reach those outcomes. Then you can work backward to choose how to proceed. Determining your own choices will probably be straightforward, but determining your competitor's choices requires some assumptions about their objectives and values. Although profit maximization is often the main objective, in some cases your competitors might have concerns other than profits. For example, rival managers may be interested in market share and sales growth because those serve as the basis for the managers' compensation. Consequently, you must think carefully about your rival's objectives as you formulate your strategy. You probably will not need to make precise numeric assumptions about the payoffs (such as dollar amounts of profit), but you may need to make assumptions about how the payoffs rank. In other words, you may need to decide which outcome results in your rival's largest payoff, the second-largest payoff, and so on.

DECISION SNAPSHOT

Game Tree Between Disney and Warner Brothers

Movie studio executives realize that movies must open in certain time periods to be successful. Summer is one of those time periods. Suppose that you are a manager at Warner Brothers (WB), which is hoping for a blockbuster with the sequel to the 2014 hit *The Lego Movie*. Say that in February 2014, your company announced that the film would open on May 18, 2018, but two years later, in February 2016, the executives at Disney (Dis) announced that they planned to open a Star Wars movie (featuring Han Solo before he joined the rebellion) on May 25, 2018. You and the other Warner Brothers managers realized that your Lego movie would probably not compete well against a new Star Wars film. In particular, you think that if you open the same weekend as the Star Wars movie your profit will be less than if you open in another weekend. So you changed the opening date of the Lego movie to February 8, 2019. Assume that the Star Wars film could also open on that date.

a. What game are you and the managers at Disney playing?

b. Explain why Disney's managers decided to open their movie in May 2018 and your studio decided to postpone the *Lego Movie* sequel's opening until February 2019. Draw a game tree with hypothetical profits as part of your answer.

Answer

a. The managers are playing a sequential game. Disney's managers have the choice of opening their movie in May or February. After they announce their choice, you and the other managers at Warner Brothers face a decision about when to open your movie. The figure illustrates this sequential game using a decision tree with some hypothetical profits.

(Continues)

(*continued*)

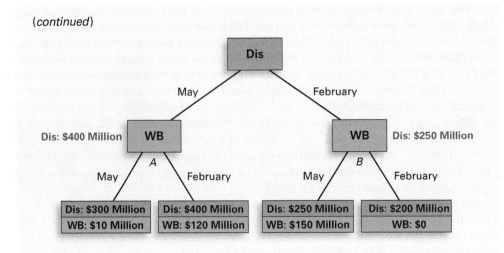

b. Using backward induction, Disney's managers determine that if you are at
decision node *A*, you and the other Warner Brothers managers will switch
the *Lego Movie* sequel to February because that decision maximizes Warner
Brothers' profit. Accordingly, Disney's managers project that at decision node
A, *their* economic profit will be $400 million, as indicated in the figure by
"Dis: $400 million" next to node *A*. Additionally, Disney's managers project
that at decision node *B*, you will open the *Lego Movie* sequel in May, giving
Disney an economic profit of $250 million. This profit is indicated in the figure
by "Dis: $250 million" next to node *B*. Disney's managers decided to open
their movie in May and move to node *A* because that choice yields the higher
economic profit for them, $400 million. After reaching node *A*, Warner Brothers'
managers moved their *Lego Movie* sequel's opening to February because
from node *A* that decision maximizes their profit, $120 million.

Commitment and Credibility

If you were a McBurger's manager, you surely would not consider the Nash equilibrium you just derived to be the most preferred outcome because Burger Best
entered the market. From McBurger's perspective, keeping Burger Best from entering the market is definitely preferable because, regardless of McBurger's price,
McBurger's profit is larger if Burger Best does not enter than if Burger Best enters.
An obvious question arises: What can McBurger's do to keep Burger Best from
entering? McBurger's might try announcing in the financial press that it will
immediately lower its price if Burger Best enters the market. In terms of the game,
if Burger Best's managers choose to enter the market, McBurger's managers will
supposedly choose the low-price strategy, thereby moving the game in Figure 8.2
to terminal node *E* and inflicting an economic loss of $2 million on Burger Best.
The problem with this commitment is that it is cheap talk and it is not a credible
threat. The managers at Burger Best know that if they choose to enter the market,
once they arrive at decision node *B*, the managers at McBurger's will disregard
their threat because the high-price strategy gives them a higher profit than the
announced low-price strategy.

As the game currently stands, McBurger's will not carry out its commitment to set a low price if Burger Best enters. The issue McBurger's managers face is credibility: How can they make their threat to inflict an economic loss on Burger Best believable? In other situations, rather than a threat the issue of credibility might revolve around a promise: How can one firm make its promise or threat to another firm credible?

Advertising and Credibility

In the McBurger's/Burger Best interaction, one method that McBurger's might employ effectively changes the game by allowing McBurger's managers the first move. McBurger's managers can do more than just engage in cheap talk. One strategy is to promise the public that they will *always* set low prices by advertising that all of their food items will always be value priced. McBurger's advertisements mean that the firm will set a low price regardless of whether Burger Best enters the market.

Advertising has two direct effects on McBurger's profit: (1) It is expensive, which decreases McBurger's profit, and (2) it increases the demand for McBurger's food, which increases McBurger's profit. For simplicity, assume that the net effect of advertising reduces McBurger's total profit by $1 million.

The value-price advertising also has a crucial indirect effect on McBurger's. If the firm's managers raise prices following this advertising campaign, McBurger's could face a backlash. Consumers who feel deceived will respond by substantially decreasing their demand for McBurger's food. Suppose that if McBurger's managers set a high price, the decrease in demand lowers McBurger's profit by an additional $3 million.

McBurger's advertising changes the game. Figure 8.3 shows the new game tree, with a new decision node: At the very top, McBurger's managers face the strategic

Figure 8.3 Changing the Game

McBurger's managers can enhance their credibility by widely advertising their low-price policy. The advertising lowers their relative profit from setting a high price. The Nash equilibrium for this game is for Burger Best not to enter the market and McBurger's to set a low price, so that the game winds up at terminal node *G'*. (The profits and losses are in millions of dollars: M = million.)

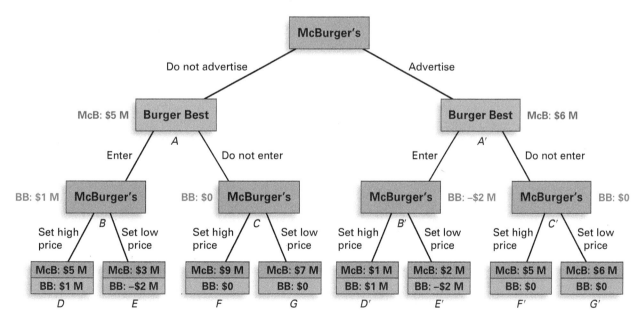

choice of whether to advertise. If they decide not to advertise, the left side of the extended game tree (with nodes labeled *A*, *B*, *C* and so on) is the same game previously analyzed. If they decide to advertise, the game tree includes new branches with nodes labeled *A'*, *B'*, *C'*, and so on. The terminal nodes in the new branches show that Burger Best's hypothetical profits have not changed, but McBurger's have. If McBurger's managers renege on their advertising by setting a high price, McBurger's profit at nodes *D'* and *F'* are $4 million less than their profit at nodes *D* and *F*. This difference represents the loss of $3 million of profit from the decrease in demand because of the price hike plus the loss of $1 million of profit from the cost of advertising. McBurger's profits at nodes *E'* and *G'* are $1 million less than those at nodes *E* and *G* because here they lose only $1 million of profit from the cost of advertising.

You can again use backward induction to find the Nash equilibrium. Since McBurger's managers make the first decision, you analyze their situation. Begin in the last row of decisions (decision nodes *B*, *C*, *B'*, and *C'*). If decision node *B* is reached, McBurger's managers will decide to set a high price and move to terminal node *D* because setting a high price gives them a larger profit than setting a low price. McBurger's managers note that at node *D*, Burger Best's profit is $1 million (recorded next to node *B* as $1 M). McBurger's managers then determine their choices at the other three decision nodes (*C*, *B'*, and *C'*) and record Burger Best's profit from these choices next to the relevant nodes *C*, *B'*, and *C'*.

McBurger's managers are interested in Burger Best's profit because they need to determine what Burger Best's managers will do at decision nodes *A* and *A'*. So McBurger's managers next look at the situation at node *A* from the point of view of Burger Best's managers. At that node, if Burger Best enters (and moves to node *B*), its profit is $1 million. If Burger Best does not enter (and moves to node *C*), its profit is $0. McBurger's managers easily predict that Burger Best will enter and move to node *B*. Then, based on McBurger's managers' decision to set a high price at node *B*, the outcome will be node *D*, where McBurger's profit is $5 million. Consequently, if Burger Best reaches node *A*, McBurger's managers know that their profit ultimately will be the amount recorded at node *A*: "McB: $5 M." Looking now at Burger Best's decision at node *A'*, McBurger's managers can see that Burger Best's optimal decision is not to enter, so it moves to node *C'*, with a profit of $0, rather than entering and moving to node *B'*, with a loss of $2 million. From node *C'*, McBurger's will move to node *G'* by setting a low price that results in a profit of $6 million, which is entered at node *A'*: "McB: $6 M." In other words, if node *A'* is reached, ultimately McBurger's profit is $6 million.

Finally, McBurger's managers are ready to decide whether to advertise. If they decide not to advertise, they move to node *A*, with a profit of $5 million. If they decide instead to advertise, they move to node *A'*, with a profit of $6 million. McBurger's managers immediately determine that their profit is greater if they advertise. Consequently, moving along the nodes, the Nash equilibrium for the game has McBurger's advertising (node *A'*), Burger Best not entering (node *C'*), and McBurger's setting a low price (node *G'*). McBurger's profit is $6 million, and Burger Best's is $0.

When you compare the outcome in this game with the outcome of the earlier McBurger's/Burger Best entry game, you see that the advertising by McBurger's has boosted its profit and reduced Burger Best's profit. Advertising raised McBurger's profit because it made credible the firm's commitment to set a low price if Burger Best entered. The credibility of McBurger's threat made Burger Best's managers change their decision about entering the market. When the threat *is not* credible, Burger Best enters. When the threat *is* credible, Burger Best does not enter.

Increasing Capacity and Credibility

Advertising is not the only way McBurger's managers can increase the credibility of their commitment. Another technique they might employ to deter Burger Best's entry is expansion of capacity. McBurger's managers can adopt new technology and other changes that enable their restaurants to serve more customers. For example, McBurger's executives could decide to expand the use of touchscreen kiosks for ordering and paying for meals; double the number of "McDrives" (a name for drive-throughs in France), which allow restaurants to sell to twice as many customers; increase the speed of transferring customers' orders to the cook staff; or invest in new cooking methods and/or modernize their kitchen areas to serve customers faster. These changes are expensive, but they all lower the marginal cost of serving customers.

The lower marginal cost has two effects that can help McBurger's managers prevent Burger Best's entry:

1. **Direct effect.** The lower marginal cost increases McBurger's profit-maximizing quantity and lowers its profit-maximizing price. By itself, McBurger's lower price might cause Burger Best to incur an economic loss if it enters, which, of course, effectively prevents Burger Best from entering the market.
2. **Strategic effect.** If Burger Best enters the market and thereby decreases the demand McBurger's faces, McBurger's lower marginal cost from its investment means that McBurger's profit-maximizing price is lower. Effectively, the investment can change McBurger's profits in a way similar to the effect from advertising, illustrated in Figure 8.3. In particular, McBurger's investment can increase its post-entry profit from setting a low price so much that McBurger's managers *will* set a low price if Burger Best enters. In turn, McBurger's low price ideally—at least from the perspective of its managers—decreases Burger Best's profit enough that Burger Best incurs an economic loss if it enters. The prospect of an economic loss removes Burger Best's incentive to enter the market.

Cost of Commitment

In the advertising example, McBurger's managers decided to undertake the entry-prevention measure, but this will not always be the outcome. The previous discussion assumed that advertising by itself decreased McBurger's profit by $1 million. Now, however, suppose that advertising is more expensive. Specifically, assume that advertising decreases McBurger's profit by $3 million. Figure 8.4 shows a new game tree that includes the higher cost of advertising. It differs from the game tree in Figure 8.3 because McBurger's profits under terminal nodes D', E', F', and G' are each $2 million less than before because of the additional cost of the advertising. The analysis for the left branches of the game tree remains exactly the same: If McBurger's managers choose not to advertise, the game winds up at terminal node D, with Burger Best choosing to enter and McBurger's managers setting a high price. The analysis for the right branches of the tree is similar but not identical to before. The difference is at decision node A': At this node, Burger Best's managers decide not to enter, and McBurger's managers decide (at node C') to set a low price, but McBurger's profit is now only $4 million in contrast to $6 million in the previous scenario with the less expensive advertising. In this case, at McBurger's very first decision node, McBurger's profit is $4 million (at node A') if its managers decide to advertise, but it is $5 million (at node A) if its managers decide not to

Figure 8.4 An Advertising Decision with Expensive Advertising

If the cost of advertising rises, McBurger's managers decide not to advertise. So the Nash equilibrium for this game is for Burger Best to enter the market and McBurger's to set a high price. The game ends at terminal node *D*. (The profits and losses are in millions of dollars: M = million.)

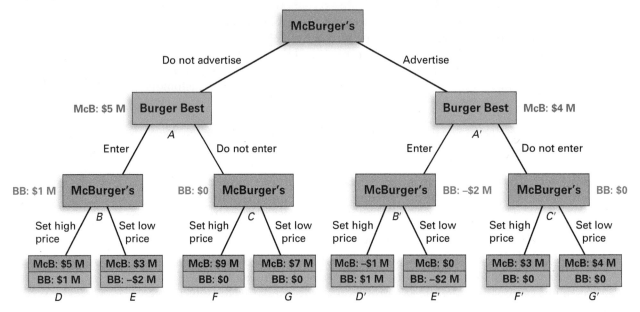

advertise. Consequently, McBurger's managers choose not to advertise, which means that Burger Best enters the market.

Even though McBurger's could advertise and thereby keep Burger Best from entering, McBurger's managers choose not to do so. Why? Keeping Burger Best from entering is too expensive. McBurger's profit is higher if Burger Best enters than if it advertises to keep Burger Best from entering. The general lesson from this analysis is that sometimes it is simply too costly to keep a competitor at bay by making a commitment credible. Even though it is possible to prevent entry, the profit after preventing entry is less than the profit if entry occurs.

SOLVED PROBLEM

A Pharmaceutical Company Uses Game Theory to Make an Offer

Suppose that you are a manager at a giant pharmaceutical company like Pfizer. Your firm is competing with another giant to purchase a small, cutting-edge biotechnology company. You and other executives at your firm are tasked with determining whether to make an offer. You can make a high offer or a low offer, but you realize that after you make your offer, your competitor's managers must decide whether to top that offer. You create the game tree at the top of the next page with estimates of economic profit for both firms. In the payoff rows, *Y* is your firm's economic profit, and *C* is your competitor's economic profit. Should you make an offer? If so, should it be a high offer or a low offer?

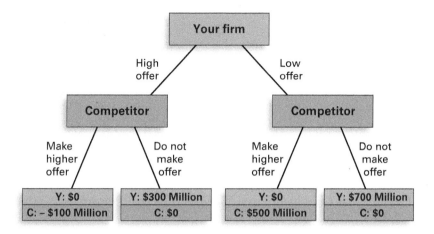

Answer

Backward induction shows that your firm should make a high offer for the company. Use the game tree below, and start at node *B*.

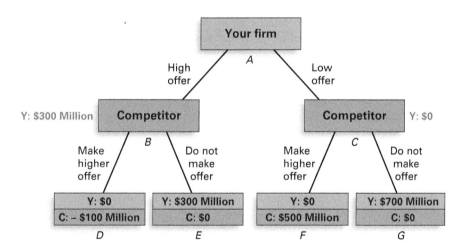

- At node *B*, the competitor will choose not to make an offer and will move to node *E* because that action has a higher profit for it than the strategy of making a higher offer and moving to node *D* ($0 versus −$100 million). At node *E*, your profit is $300 million, so at node *B*, as noted in the figure, your profit is $300 million.

- At node *C*, the competitor will choose to make a higher offer and will move to node *F* because that action has a higher profit for it than the strategy of not making an offer and moving to node *G* ($500 million versus $0). At node *F*, your profit is $0, so at node *C*, as noted in the figure, your profit is $0 million.

- Finally, from node *A*, you can make a high offer and move to node *B*, where your profit is $300 million, or you can make a low offer and move to node *C*, where your profit is $0. Clearly, you will make a high offer, move to node *B*, and then ultimately wind up at node *E*, where you buy the biotech company and make a profit of $300 million.

8.4 Game Theory

Learning Objective 8.4 Apply game theory to help make better managerial decisions.

Similar to most other economic models, such as demand and supply, game theory is a valuable tool that provides insights and advice but not precise recommendations for making managerial decisions. The most fundamental managerial advice from game theory is straightforward to present but difficult to accomplish: When a manager is engaged in a strategic situation, his or her decisions must take into account the responses of the competing managers. As a manager, you must think about business situations not only from your perspective but also from the perspective of your rivals. This advice is valid in all types of games, whether they are basic, advanced, or sequential.

Using Basic Games for Managerial Decision Making

As you may already have noticed, actually creating a complete payoff matrix for a business decision is challenging because you need perfect knowledge of your rival's strategies and potential profits. One useful managerial lesson does not depend on the creation of an entire payoff matrix, however: If you know that a particular strategy is dominated, eliminate it from consideration immediately. For example, say that Intel's managers have several potential research paths to follow with the goal of improving their graphics processing units. If Intel's profit from the different research opportunities depends on the research path that managers at a competitor like Advanced Micro Devices (AMD) pursue, Intel's managers should immediately discard any of their research avenues that are dominated—that is, any research opportunities that *always* have a lower profit than another choice regardless of AMD's strategy.

Most games that managers face are repeated games. In these games, managers must be alert to cooperative play. For example, at one point in time, ENI, the market leader in the Italian gasoline market, announced that it would change from a policy of frequent and small price changes in response to cost changes to a policy of infrequent but large price changes. Other firms soon followed suit. ENI emerged as the price leader, and research indicates that this cooperative play caused the price of gasoline to rise in Italy relative to other EU countries. The managers of these firms may have reached the cooperative equilibrium via tacit collusion. They carefully observed each other's actions and decided not to violate the implicit cooperative strategy they were playing.

In a repeated game, managers can engage in tacit collusion and reach the cooperative outcome by using strategies that (tacitly) threaten to punish the other players if they defect from the cooperative strategy. In a repeated game with a last period, the players have an incentive to defect from cooperative strategies in the final period because they know that defection cannot be punished at the end of the game. Although the incentive to defect from the cooperative strategy can roll backward to the start, managers can increase the likelihood that the other players will use a cooperative strategy by looking to a broader alternative game with periods past the first game's last period. In other words, to avoid the defection from the cooperative equilibrium that results from a conclusive end to the game, create a probability that the game will continue. Let's see what happens when you follow this advice in two games dealing with employees and employers and another dealing with a supplier and a manufacturer.

Executive/Employer Game

Consider the relationship between the president of a union and the union itself. We can analyze this situation as a repeated game between two players, the president and the union, with a period being a term in office. The union has established a mandatory retirement age of 65 for its president. This mandatory retirement age creates a last period—that is, a last term. If the president simply retires after the last term and has no possible further interaction with the union, the union members might well fear malfeasance during that term. But if the union can make the retired President an "elder statesperson" who retains some power and respect if his or her behavior in the last term is careful and responsible, the union has effectively created another game with future periods beyond the retirement period. This extended game decreases the likelihood of malfeasance in the last term. Of course, a similar problem and solution also applies to executives with other organizations such as NGOs or for-profit firms.

Employee/Employer Game

It is not just executives who create an end-period problem for employers. Consider the relationship between a worker and an employer. Once again, you can analyze this relationship as a two-player (employee and employer), repeated game. Many workers would rather take it easy than work diligently, but employers much prefer that their employees work hard. To help motivate the worker, the employer can threaten punishment by firing the worker in the next period (say, next week) if the worker is caught shirking in the present period (this week). (We discuss other mechanisms that can align the employee's effort with the employer's goal in Chapter 15.) But what if the worker plans to quit? The decision to quit sets a last period. After the last period, no future punishment is possible, which gives the worker a greater tendency to dodge work in the last period. This incentive is captured by the common expression "short-timer's attitude." The employer can avoid this outcome by firing the worker in the last period, but that action simply moves the end-period problem backward a period. The worker realizes that the second-to-last period is now his or her last period, so short-timer's attitude strikes in this period. Of course, the employer can fire the worker in *this* period. But then the third-to-last period is the new last period, and it's obvious that the process of shirking/firing continues to roll on. So what can the employer do?

The employer's goal is to create a future beyond the last period. As long as the worker is not permanently leaving the workforce, creating a game with future periods is straightforward: Workers typically want letters of recommendation. Letting the worker know that the letter will be written *after* the worker leaves creates a new future period—the period in which the employer writes the letter. Clearly if the worker behaves poorly in the last period, the recommendation letter will be less glowing.

Year-end bonuses also can be used to create a future period beyond the last period. If the employer makes the bonus conditional on good performance in all periods the worker is present, the bonus creates another game with a period beyond the first game's final period. These "new" future periods decrease the worker's incentive to shirk in the "old" last period, exactly the outcome desired by the employer.

Supplier/Manufacturer Game

The expiration of a supply contract can easily lead to a significant end-period problem. For example, take a contract between a potato grower and Frito-Lay, a large producer of potato chips. In all periods *except* the final one, if the supplier provides low-quality potatoes, the supplier faces punishment if Frito-Lay can cancel the contract. In the last period of the contract, however, cancellation in the next period is no longer possible, so the supplier has much less incentive to provide high-quality potatoes. Of course, even in the last period Frito-Lay's managers want high-quality potatoes.

The solution to this end-period problem is similar to those used in the previous examples: The producer must create a new game with the possibility of a period beyond the last one. Frito-Lay's managers can create a "new" game by dangling the possibility of a new contract in front of the grower. Frito-Lay's managers might put the new supply contract out to bid and not declare a winner until after the last delivery of potatoes under the old contract. In this situation, the grower is motivated to continue to supply high-quality potatoes to enhance the chances of winning the new contract, exactly the outcome desired by Frito-Lay.

Using Advanced Games for Managerial Decision Making

When you are engaged in a strategic interaction with more than one possible equilibrium, you need to determine if you and your opponent can easily reach one particular equilibrium. A focal point, for example, can help you predict which equilibrium is likely to occur, allowing you to plan accordingly. Take Samsung and Sony: Both offer warranties for their televisions. The firms could offer a long warranty—say, for five years—or a shorter warranty—say, for one year. Of course, the long warranty is more expensive for the manufacturers. Historically, when televisions were more prone to failure, warranties were commonly offered for one year. Consequently, a focal point in this interaction is probably one year. In fact, Samsung and Sony (as well as virtually all manufacturers of televisions) have reached and maintained the cooperative equilibrium with the shorter, less expensive one-year parts and labor warranty.

Alternatively, if you know your profit and have some idea of your opponent's profit for the different outcomes, it is worth pondering the existence of a cooperative equilibrium that supports the Pareto criterion. Recall from Section 8.2 that the Pareto criterion suggests that the most likely pure-strategy Nash equilibrium is the one from which any change to another Nash equilibrium that increases one firm's profit must decrease the other firm's profit. Once at a cooperative outcome suggested by the Pareto criterion, if a change makes you better off but your rival worse off, signaling your intention to remain at the particular cooperative equilibrium, perhaps by some sort of announcement, could help you maintain that outcome and avoid a movement to a dilemma equilibrium.

Announcements, of course, are not always a solution to a problem because they are not always credible. If the managers at a competing firm have announced their intentions, you must determine the likelihood that they are being truthful. You need to examine how closely your interests align with those of your competitor: The more closely they align, the more likely the other managers are being truthful and the more credible their announcement is. The more your interests diverge, the less likely their announcement is credible. For example, two top-notch skiing destinations located near Jackson Hole, Wyoming, are the Jackson Hole Ski Resort and Grand Targhee Resort. Their interests align in publicizing the Jackson Hole region. If the Jackson Hole Ski Resort announces that it will conduct an extensive advertising campaign in the East, publicizing the great skiing conditions at Jackson Hole, managers at the Grand Targhee Resort have little reason to doubt that the campaign will be carried out. Their interests diverge, however, in pricing. If the Jackson Hole Ski Resort announces a 20 percent boost in price in the next season, managers at the Grand Targhee Resort might be skeptical that Jackson Hole Ski Resort actually will follow through on the price hike.

Predictability

Whenever you are engaged in a strategic interaction, you must determine whether you want to use or avoid an easily predictable strategy. On the one hand, ensuring that your competitor knows that you are using a tit-for-tat strategy is important in a repeated game, such as the one between TragoCo and Boca-Cola in which the managers had to determine whether to set a low price or a high price. That knowledge can help you and your rival maintain the cooperative equilibrium. On the other hand, in the PureFood and Kingster example in Section 8.2, any strategy that allows your competitor to predict your choice is inferior to a strategy that makes your choice difficult or nearly impossible to predict. The PureFood/Kingster example included calculations of the optimal probabilities for each firm's strategy. Although you will *never* be able to make these calculations as a manager, the lesson they teach is essential: To be a successful manager, avoid giving your competitor(s) in any strategic interaction the chance to exploit you by making their gain your loss. In these situations, do *not* make predictable choices, such as putting a product on sale in a consistent pattern.

In the PureFood/Kingster example, PureFood's managers determined their optimal probabilities by focusing on Kingster's payoffs. You can generalize this lesson: It is an error to ignore your rival's payoffs to focus only on your own. You must ensure that your competitors cannot systematically increase their profits—and decrease your profit—by using one of their pure strategies.

Using Sequential Games for Managerial Decision Making

In Section 8.3, you learned how to analyze entry into a market as a sequential game. But sequential games have insights that you can use in other circumstances because most business decisions that involve bargaining can be analyzed as a sequential game.

Bargaining

At its core, any type of bargaining is a sequential game: One party makes an offer (or threat), after which the other party responds. The process of offer/counteroffer continues until ultimately the bargaining concludes.

Negotiations between a union and a firm are an example of one type of bargaining. In these negotiations, both sides want to reach a consensus about wages, employment, and other job conditions. Because both parties want to reach an agreement, often the credibility of threats made during the negotiations is important. For example, the union might threaten to strike if the firm does not agree to its demands. The firm's managers know that a strike is expensive to the workers because the firm is not paying them while they strike. This expense makes a strike threat less credible. A union, however, can make the strike less costly to the workers if it has a strike fund from which it pays its members. For example, the union representing workers at Verizon has such a strike fund and would use it to pay the workers during the strike. The fund reduced the workers' cost of striking and enhanced the union's strike threat *if* Verizon negotiators were aware of the strike fund. But if the Verizon negotiators were unaware of the strike fund, the negotiators might erroneously conclude that the threat was not credible and take negotiation stances that would lead to the strike. The union negotiators should be careful to widely publicize the union's willingness to pay striking members from the strike fund to ensure that their threat of a strike was more credible.

Firm-to-firm contractual negotiations are another sequential game. For example, GlobalFoundaries makes computer chips for STMicroelectronics. Say that, during the contract negotiations, the managers at STMicroelectronics both promise large orders and threaten to take the firm's business elsewhere if its terms are not met. Of course, the negotiators at GlobalFoundaries can also make promises and/or threats. In order to strike the best deal possible, both sets of managers should think of all possible outcomes and the stream of decisions that can get them there before determining which strategy will be best for them. Carefully consider your rival's goals and how the choice made at each decision node affects reaching these goals. This process forces you to put yourself in your rival's position and take into account its interests and responses when making your decisions. Additionally, ensuring the credibility of any threats—such as a threat to break off negotiations—or promises—such as a promise to deliver chips by a certain date—is an important component of *any* threat or promise.

Commitment and Credibility

Because sequential games work out over time, players can make commitments, including threats or promises, about future actions. As you have already learned, the credibility of the commitment is important because that will help you determine how seriously to consider it. The credibility of a rival's threat or promise often hinges on determining whether carrying out the action is in your rival's best interest. If the future action is not in your competitor's best interest, then you have sound reason to doubt whether your competitor will carry through with its commitment. If, however, a threat is in your competitor's best interest, then you might try changing the game—perhaps by offering a different type of contract, or modifying your product, or opening talks with some of your rival's competitors. Select the action that is most appropriate in the specific context of your negotiating game. If a promise is in your competitor's best interest, you can bask in the knowledge that your rival likely will keep it.

Of course, the same credibility lesson applies to your own actions. If you try to influence your competitor by threatening or promising action, your threat or promise must be credible. If you make a threat, you must think about what actions you can take to enhance its credibility. One option is precommitting yourself to specific responses to your rivals' actions. For example, selling your product with a meet-the-competition clause in the contract precommits you to offer a lower price if your rivals lower their price. Chapter 7 (see Section 7.2) described such clauses, which enhance the credibility of your threat to lower your price if your competitors lower their price.

In other cases, enhancing your credibility involves changing the payoffs in the game in a way that makes your threatened or promised action relatively more profitable and, consequently, more credible. For example, say that a competitor is considering whether to enter your market. You can enhance the credibility of an implicit threat to lower your price through an investment that increases your firm's capacity or lowers your costs, making it more profitable for you to follow through. In 2011, Intel, for example, started building a $5.2 billion chip factory in Chandler, Arizona, which in 2014 it then decided not to open. Although this decision likely represents a miscalculation by Intel's managers about needed capacity, the empty plant also represents increased capacity that Intel could bring online to increase the supply of chips if it wanted to "punish" a rival who entered the chip fabrication market.[6]

---

6 In 2017, Intel announced it would make additional investments in the plant and then open it.

Like the publicity surrounding the initial construction of the Intel plant, your credibility-enhancing action must be visible so your rivals understand that your pay-offs have changed. Although there are times when it is optimal to keep your competitors in the dark about your plans, you should not do so when trying to enhance your credibility. If your competitors are unaware of your actions, they can mistakenly distrust your commitment and make a decision that can cost them profit. More crucially, their decision can cost *you* profit. Your competitors will believe your commitment only if they know of your actions.

Finally, regardless of the specific credibility-enhancing action you are considering, be alert to the possibility that the action might be too expensive. For example, your profit might be lower if you prevent market entry by a rival than if you allow it.

Is a Threat Credible?

Nvidia and Gigabyte Technology depend on each other: Nvidia designs and manufactures graphics chips that Gigabyte Technology then uses to produce and market graphics cards. We can view this relationship as a sequential game. Nvidia can expend a large or small amount of funds in research and development (R&D), and Gigabyte Technology can have a large, medium, or small marketing budget for the cards it manufactures. Their joint profits depend on the decisions of both firm's managers.

Suppose there are similar firms—say, Nchip (*N*) and Gcard (*G*)—that engage in a similar game. The figure illustrates this game, in which the payoffs are the firms' economic profits. Nchip's and Gcard's managers are negotiating a contract that specifies the amount of Nchip's R&D expenditure and Gcard's marketing budget. In the course of the negotiations, Nchip's managers threaten to provide only a small level of funding for R&D unless Gcard commits to a large marketing budget. Is this threat credible? Explain your answer.

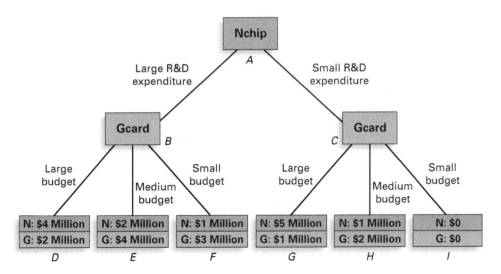

(*Continues*)

SOLVED PROBLEM (*continued*)

Answer

Gcard's managers can use backward induction to determine whether the threat is credible. They reason that if node *B* is reached, they will certainly choose to spend a medium budget on marketing and move to node *E* because that decision maximizes their profit ($4 million versus $2 million if they spend a large budget or $3 million if they spend a small budget). Nchip's profit at node *E* is $2 million, so if the game reaches node *B*, Nchip makes $2 million. Similarly, if node *C* is reached, Gcard's managers will (again) maximize their profit by spending a medium budget on marketing and moving to node *H*. At this node, Nchip's profit is $1 million, so if the game reaches node *C*, Nchip makes $1 million. Finally, Gcard's managers realize that from node *A*, Nchip will make more profit by making a large expenditure on R&D ($2 million profit) than by making a small expenditure ($1 million profit). Nchip's threat to make only a small expenditure on R&D is empty–that is, not credible.

Revisiting How Managers at Pfizer Welcomed a Competitor in the Market for Lipitor

At the start of the chapter, you read about a challenge facing Pfizer's managers—they were losing their monopoly on the world's best-selling drug, Lipitor, because their patent was expiring. Applying the concepts from this chapter can show you how those managers met that challenge.

Ranbaxy Laboratories was the first company to file an abbreviated new drug application and successfully challenge some of Pfizer's patents, so FDA regulations allowed it to be the first independent generic company to enter the market. Pfizer's managers knew that the potential economic profit from producing atorvastatin (the generic chemical name for Lipitor) was large enough that Ranbaxy would enter the market the moment it was allowed to do so. Consequently, Pfizer's managers faced a sequential game in which the prices and profits of Lipitor and generic atorvastatin would be determined.

Pfizer's managers realized that price was the first decision Ranbaxy's managers faced: When they enter the market, what price should they set? Simplify the analysis by assuming that the managers had two options: set a low price and set a high price. Pfizer's managers also faced a choice: They could do nothing (not change their price), or they could adopt policies that would influence Ranbaxy's managers to set a high price. The possible policies included the following:

• **Make a credible threat to lower the price.** Perhaps by mentioning it in an interview or in advertising, Pfizer's

executives could signal a threat to lower the price of Lipitor if Ranbaxy's managers set a low price for their generic drug. This threat should be credible: Because Pfizer had years of experience producing large quantities of the drug, its costs likely were lower than Ranbaxy's costs. Pfizer could lower the price to privately insured patients by offering them a card that let them purchase Lipitor for only a $4 copayment. Pfizer could pay up to $50 of the difference between the insurance plan's actual copayment and $4, so as long as the plan's actual copayment was less than $54, the patient paid only $4.

• **Offer a meet-the-competition clause.** If the generic producer offers to sell atorvastatin for a lower price than Lipitor, Pfizer could offer rebates to large insurance plans and pharmacy benefit managers in order to lower Lipitor's price. This strategy would decrease Ranbaxy's incentive to set a low price because it makes any attempt to undercut Pfizer's price futile.

• **Create a competitor for Ranbaxy.** Pfizer could take advantage of an infrequently used quirk in the patent laws to license another generic drugmaker, such as Watson Pharmaceuticals (now Allergan, PLC), to produce an "authorized generic." Pfizer could manufacture and sell the drug to Watson and receive the lion's share of Watson's profit. Giving Ranbaxy competition in the market for generic atorvastatin eliminates its ability to market its drug as *the* low-price generic alternative to Lipitor and encourages Ranbaxy to maintain a higher price.

Figure 8.5 illustrates the sequential game, including hypothetical economic profits. Pfizer's managers can solve the game using backward induction. They start by analyzing Ranbaxy's decisions at nodes *B* and *C*:

- If node *B* is reached, Pfizer's managers know that Ranbaxy will maximize its profit by setting a high price. So *Pfizer's* profit from reaching node *B* is $3.0 billion.

- If node *C* is reached, Pfizer's managers know that Ranbaxy will maximize its profit by setting a low price. So *Pfizer's* profit from reaching node *C* is $0.5 billion.

Based on the calculations Pfizer's managers just made, at node *A* Pfizer's profit-maximizing decision is to adopt policies, such as the three outlined above, aimed at influencing Ranbaxy to set a high price. Pfizer's decision moves the game to node *B*, from which Ranbaxy decides to set a high price, leading to the Nash equilibrium with Pfizer taking the actions to influence Ranbaxy and Ranbaxy setting a high price.

Figure 8.5 Pfizer's Decision

Pfizer (P) can adopt various policies that make Ranbaxy's (R) profit from setting a high price for its generic atorvastatin more than its profit from setting a low price.

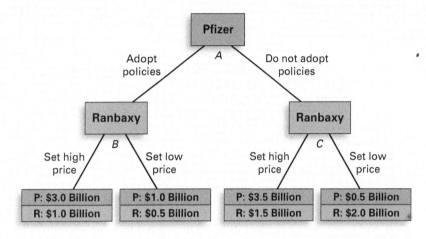

What happened in reality when Pfizer's patent expired? In fact, when Pfizer lost the patent protection on Lipitor, its managers implemented all three of the policies outlined above and made a significantly larger economic profit than if it had not taken action.

Summary: The Bottom Line

8.1 Basic Game Theory and Games

- A game is an interaction between players in which the players face rules, use strategies, and receive a payoff at the end.
- A Nash equilibrium occurs when each player's strategy is best for that player, taking as given the other players' strategies. At the Nash equilibrium, no one player can unilaterally improve his or her payoff by playing another strategy.
- A prisoners' dilemma is a game in which the players can both gain if they cooperate with each other but each has an incentive to defect from cooperation, so at the Nash equilibrium both defect.
- In a repeated game—a game played more than once—players can use trigger strategies, such as a tit-for-tat strategy, to make attaining the higher-profit, cooperative equilibrium more likely.

- If a repeated game ends, the end-period problem makes the cooperative equilibrium less likely, since there is no possibility of punishment in a future period. Uncertainty can keep the threat of potential future period punishment alive and prevent the players from defecting from the cooperative strategy.
- Rational players never use a dominated strategy—a strategy that is *always* inferior to another—so managers can eliminate dominated strategies when evaluating a rival's strategy set.

8.2 Advanced Games

- Some games have multiple Nash equilibria. Refinements, such as the Pareto criterion and a focal point, suggest which Nash equilibrium will be reached. If rival players' interests align, then cheap talk can be credible and help determine which Nash equilibrium is selected.

- In games with no pure-strategy Nash equilibria, players can use a mixed strategy, which is a strategy that randomly adopts different pure strategies according to predetermined probabilities. The mixed-strategy Nash equilibrium occurs when each player's mixed strategy is the best strategy available, taking as given the other players' mixed strategy.

8.3 Sequential Games

- In a sequential game, the players make decisions one after the other. A classic example is an entry game, a game in which one player decides whether to enter the market and the other player, already in the market, responds to the first player's entry decision.
- A sequential game is illustrated using a game tree, a diagram illustrating the players' sequential choices and the ultimate payoffs that result from the choices. Game trees include decision nodes and terminal nodes.

- Sequential games are solved using backward induction: Start at the end of the process (the last row of decision nodes in the game tree), and determine the optimal strategies working to the first decision node.

8.4 Managerial Application: Game Theory

- When engaged in a game with a rival, to make your best decision determine your competitor's goal, and then assume that the competitor makes decisions to reach this goal.
- In repeated games, such as an employee contract or a supply contract, be alert for ways you can create a broader game with additional periods past the end of the initial game to avoid the end-period problem.
- Credibility is important when making a threat or promise. You must determine the credibility of a competitor's threat or promise and consider the cost of enhancing the credibility of your own threats or promises.

Key Terms and Concepts

Cooperative equilibrium	Game theory	Repeated game
Decision node	Game tree	Sequential game
Dominant strategy	Mixed strategy	Strategy
Dominated strategy	Mixed-strategy Nash equilibrium	Tit-for-tat strategy
End-period problem	Nash equilibrium	Trigger strategy
Entry game	Payoff matrix	
Game	Pure strategy	

Questions and Problems

8.1 Basic Game Theory and Games

Learning Objective 8.1 Identify the elements of game theory and explain the Nash equilibrium, a prisoners' dilemma game, a dominated strategy, and the advantages of a repeated game.

1.1 John von Neumann defined a game as containing three elements. Explain each of the three elements using basketball as your example.

1.2 In the market for video game consoles, Microsoft and Sony are essentially a duopoly, with Nintendo a distant third. Consider a purely hypothetical game in which the executives of the two companies are deciding how much they will spend on advertising. To simplify, assume that they can either spend a lot or spend a little. If both firms spend a lot, Sony's hypothetical profit will be $3 billion, and Microsoft's hypothetical profit will be $2 billion. If they both spend a little, Sony's profit will be $8 billion, and Microsoft's profit will be $6 billion. If Sony spends a lot and Microsoft spends a little, Sony's profit will be $9 billion, and Microsoft's profit will be $1 billion. Finally, if Sony spends a little and Microsoft spends a lot, Sony's profit will be $2 billion, and Microsoft's profit will be $7 billion. Assume that Sony and Microsoft play this advertising game only once.

a. Create the payoff matrix for this game.
b. Does Sony have a dominant strategy? If so, what is it? Does Microsoft have a dominant strategy? If so, what is it?
c. What is the Nash equilibrium of the game?

1.3 Firms A and B form a cartel. Once the cartel is formed, each firm has the option of either complying with its cartel agreement by keeping its price high and its production low or cheating on the agreement by lowering its price and increasing its production. The payoff matrix shows the firms' economic profits. If the game is played only once, what is the Nash equilibrium? Is the game a prisoners' dilemma game? Is this equilibrium the best outcome for Firm A? For Firm B? Explain your answers.

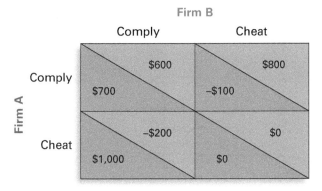

Firm B

	Comply	Cheat
Comply	$600 / $700	$800 / -$100
Cheat	-$200 / $1,000	$0 / $0

Firm A

1.4 UPS and FedEx are the two largest small-package shipping companies. Their managers can either set a high price or set a low price. The payoff matrix shows the hypothetical economic profits of the two companies when they set high and low prices.

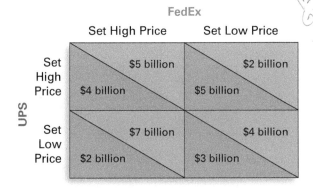

FedEx

	Set High Price	Set Low Price
Set High Price	$5 billion / $4 billion	$2 billion / $5 billion
Set Low Price	$7 billion / $2 billion	$4 billion / $3 billion

UPS

a. What is the Nash equilibrium of the game?
b. Is the game a prisoners' dilemma game? Explain your answer.
c. Are the managers likely to be satisfied with the Nash equilibrium? Why or why not?

◐1.5 The market for landfills is essentially a duopoly: Waste Management owns the largest number of landfills, and Republic Services owns the second-largest number. When municipalities put their trash-collecting contracts out to bid, Waste Management and Republic Services can submit either high bids or low bids. The payoff matrix shows how each company's hypothetical economic profit depends on its own bid and its competitor's bid. It is, of course, illegal for the two companies to enter into a price-fixing cartel to submit high bids, so rule out that possibility.

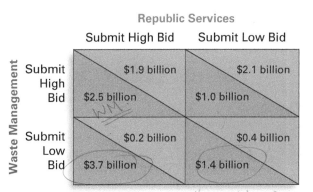

Republic Services

	Submit High Bid	Submit Low Bid
Submit High Bid	$1.9 billion / $2.5 billion	$2.1 billion / $1.0 billion
Submit Low Bid	$0.2 billion / $3.7 billion	$0.4 billion / $1.4 billion

Waste Management

a. If the companies bid on only one contract, what is the Nash equilibrium? What do the firms' managers think of this equilibrium?
b. What is the cooperative equilibrium? If the companies bid repeatedly on different contracts, what can the managers do to reach the cooperative equilibrium?

1.6 You are playing a repeated game with one rival and no end-period problem. The game is a prisoners' dilemma. Would you rather play a tit-for-tat strategy or a grim trigger strategy? Carefully explain your answer, making certain to discuss your rival's incentive to depart from the cooperative strategy.

1.7 Discuss the role played by punishment in both creating and solving the end-period problem.

1.8 Why will profit-maximizing managers never use a dominated strategy?

◑1.9 Intel and Applied Micro Devices are the two major producers of CPU chips used in personal computers. They can each research and enhance their chips' computational speed, reduce their power consumption, or enhance their graphics ability. The economic profit depends on each company's choice of which

Accompanies problem 1.9.

[handwritten: Pick Columns Intel= H⊖1|20]
[handwritten: AMD Vertical]
[handwritten: AMD picks row]
[handwritten: Intel Highest]
[handwritten: Nash eq]

		Intel		
		Enhance Speed	Reduce Power Consumption	Enhance Graphics
Applied Micro Devices	Enhance Speed	$12 billion / $2 billion	$7 billion / $4 billion	$8 billion / $7 billion
	Reduce Power Consumption	$17 billion / $5 billion	$14 billion / $6 billion	$9 billion / $4 billion
	Enhance Graphics	$16 billion / $4 billion	$8 billion / $6 billion	$6 billion / $5 billion

attribute to research. The payoff matrix shows each firm's hypothetical economic profit for all possible choices. What is the Nash equilibrium of this game? Explain your answer.

8.2 Advanced Games

Learning Objective 8.2 Describe how to determine the equilibrium in games with more than one Nash equilibrium and in games with no pure-strategy Nash equilibrium.

2.1 When does cheap talk have an effect? When is it ineffective? Which of the following examples of cheap talk will most likely have an effect? Explain your answers.

a. Boeing and Airbus, the two dominant producers of large passenger planes, realize that both their profits would increase if they both submitted high-price offers to airline companies looking to purchase planes. Boeing's managers announce that going forward they will submit only high-price offers that allow Boeing to make a large profit.

b. You are the manager of an oil exploration company. You have won an auction for a potential oil field that is immediately adjacent to a field owned by a competitor. You are considering whether to test drill on your field when your competitor's managers announce plans to test drill on their field very near your property.

c. You are an executive for a local home builder. You and another competitor own

land on which you could build either a few high-end homes or many affordable homes. You believe that if you both build high-end homes or both build affordable homes, the profits of both firms will be lower because the two of you will glut the market. Your rival's managers announce that they will build affordable homes on their property.

2.2 In Australia, supermarket chains Woolworths and Coles have about a 70 percent combined market share. Suppose that both companies are considering an expansion in South Australia. The hypothetical payoff matrix shows how the firms' economic profits depend on their joint decisions.

		Coles	
		Expand	Do Not Expand
Woolworths	Expand	$0.8 billion / $1.9 billion	$1.5 billion / $2.0 billion
	Do Not Expand	$1.6 billion / $3.0 billion	$1.1 billion / $1.9 billion

a. List all the Nash equilibria. Carefully explain why each is a Nash equilibrium.

b. If Coles announces expansion in South Australia, is this announcement likely to affect which Nash equilibrium occurs?

2.3 In Uganda, consumers are likely to buy cell phones from either MTN Rwanda Ltd or Tigo Rwanda Ltd because the two firms have a combined market share that approaches 90 percent. These companies can either set a high price or set a low price. The payoff matrix shows how each company's hypothetical economic profit depends on its price and its rival's price. The hypothetical profits are in Ugandan shillings, and price-fixing cartels are illegal in Uganda.

MTN Rwanda

	Set High Price	Set Low Price
Tigo Rwanda — Set High Price	USH 50 billion / USH 20 billion	USH 20 billion / USH 30 billion
Tigo Rwanda — Set Low Price	USH 30 billion / USH 25 billion	USH 40 billion / USH 10 billion

a. Is there a pure-strategy Nash equilibrium? If so, what is it? Explain your answer.
b. Is there a mixed-strategy Nash equilibrium? If so, what is it? Explain your answer.

2.4 Express Scripts and CVS/Caremark are the two largest pharmacy benefits managers (PBMs). Companies hire a PBM to handle the prescription drug component of their health plans. Express Scripts and CVS/Caremark bid on these contracts. They can either submit a high bid or submit a low bid. The payoff matrix shows how each company's hypothetical economic profit depends on its own bid and the bid by its competitor. A price-fixing cartel to submit only high bids is illegal.

Express Scripts

	Submit High Bid	Submit Low Bid
CVS/Caremark — Submit High Bid	$4 billion / $2 billion	$5 billion / $0
CVS/Caremark — Submit Low Bid	$3 billion / $1 billion	$2 billion / $2 billion

a. Is there a pure-strategy Nash equilibrium? If so, what is it? Explain your answer.
b. Is there a mixed-strategy Nash equilibrium? If so, what is it? Explain your answer.

2.5 Visa and MasterCard are the two largest credit and debit card companies, with a combined market share exceeding 80 percent of the cards in circulation. Whenever a consumer buys a product using one of their cards, Visa or MasterCard charges the selling company a fee. The firms can either charge a high fee or charge a low fee. The payoff matrix shows each company's hypothetical economic profits.

MasterCard

	Charge High Fee	Charge Low Fee
Visa — Charge High Fee	$3 billion / $6 billion	$2 billion / $5 billion
Visa — Charge Low Fee	$2 billion / $5 billion	$3 billion / $4 billion

a. Looking at only MasterCard's profits, does MasterCard have a dominant strategy?
b. Explain what the Nash equilibrium is.
c. In the Nash equilibrium, do MasterCard's managers use a mixed strategy or a pure strategy? Explain your answer.

8.3 Sequential Games

Learning Objective 8.3 Explain the importance of backward induction and credible commitments in sequential games.

3.1 Would backward induction be useful in determining the optimal decision in the following situations? If so, describe the decisions in each game being played.
a. You and a rival are introducing very similar products at the same time and must determine what price to set.
b. You are an executive at an oil-drilling and oil-producing company that is considering drilling in a new field. You are negotiating with a pipeline company that would build a pipeline from the field to the market.
c. You are an executive at the American Cancer Society. You are setting a single date for a fund-raising walk-a-thon to be held in cities throughout the nation. You learn that the American Diabetes Association is considering the same sort of fund-raiser. The funds raised for each charity will be larger if the walk-a-thons do not conflict with each other.

3.2 In a sequential game, what makes a threat credible?

Accompanies problem 3.3.

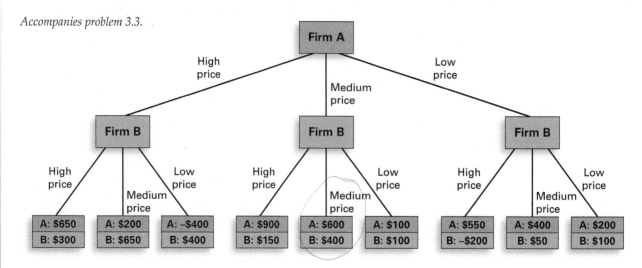

3.3 Firm A and Firm B are competitors. Each firm can set a high price, a medium price, or a low price. These prices must be set independently, and Firm A must set its price first. The game tree shows their profits from different prices. What will be the outcome? Explain your answer.

3.4 Microsoft and Electronic Arts are separate companies. Microsoft produces the Xbox One game console, and Electronic Arts creates games for the Xbox One. The two firms must independently decide on the amount to invest in two separate but complementary projects: Electronic Arts must decide how much to invest in the development of games for the next generation of the Xbox, and Microsoft must decide how much to invest in the development of the next generation of the Xbox game console. Each firm can invest a high amount, a medium amount, or a low amount. The game tree shows hypothetical profits of the two firms from different scenarios.

a. Suppose that the amount of Microsoft's investment must be set first. What will the outcome be? Explain your answer.

b. Now suppose that Microsoft and Electronic Arts can sign a contract specifying the amount of each firm's investment. Will the outcome differ from part a? If so, what will it be? Explain your answers.

Accompanies problem 3.4.

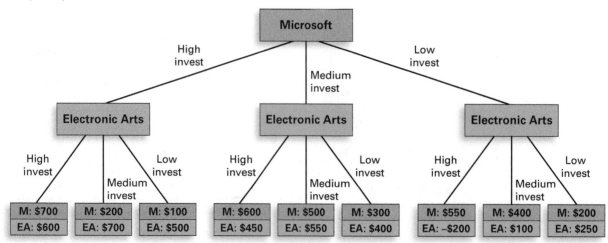

3.5 You are a manager of Firm A, which has a rival, Firm B. You are deciding whether to introduce a new product. If you do not introduce it, Firm B will introduce it. If you do introduce it, Firm B must decide whether to introduce it. If both firms introduce the product, each firm's economic profit is $2 million. If only one firm introduces the product, that firm's economic profit is $3 million, and the other firm's economic profit is $0. If neither introduces it, both have $0 economic profit.

  a. Draw the game tree for this game.
  b. What is the Nash equilibrium of the game?

8.4 Managerial Application: Game Theory

Learning Objective 8.4 Apply game theory to help make better managerial decisions.

4.1 You are negotiating with another firm to become one of its suppliers. What types of promises might you make to the other negotiating team? Discuss how you could enhance the credibility of your promises.

4.2 You own a sushi restaurant in Kansas City. Your annual contract with one of Kansas City's many tuna suppliers expires in a month. What problem do you foresee in this situation? How can you overcome it?

4.3 The market for add-in graphics cards is a duopoly: Nvidia has the largest share, and Advanced Micro Devices (AMD) has the remainder. The companies can set one of the

three prices: high, medium, and low. The payoff matrix shows the firms' hypothetical economic profits in billions of dollars. If Nvidia and AMD play the game only once, what is the Nash equilibrium?

4.4 You and a competitor own two stores in the same town that sell musical instruments. The two of you can either set high prices or set low prices. You know your profits but can only estimate your rival's profits. If you both set high prices, your economic profit will be $2 million, and you think your rival will make a large profit. If you both set low prices, your economic profit will be zero, and you think your rival also will make no economic profit. If you set high prices and your rival sets low prices, you will have an economic loss of $1 million, and you forecast that your rival will have a very large profit. Finally, if you set low prices and your rival sets high prices, you will have a profit of $3 million, and you believe your rival will have an economic loss.

  a. What is the payoff matrix for this game?
  b. If the game is played only once, do you have a dominant strategy? If so, what is it? Does your rival have a dominant strategy? If so, what is it? What is the Nash equilibrium of the game?
  c. If the game is played repeatedly, what is the cooperative equilibrium? What strategy (or strategies) could you adopt?

4.5 In football, the offensive coach may call a running play or a passing play. Of course, the defense can either defend against a run or

Accompanies problem 4.3.

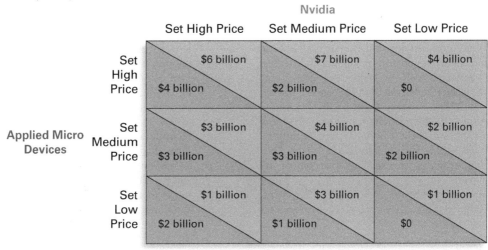

	Nvidia		
	Set High Price	Set Medium Price	Set Low Price
Applied Micro Devices — Set High Price	$6 billion / $4 billion	$7 billion / $2 billion	$4 billion / $0
Set Medium Price	$3 billion / $3 billion	$4 billion / $3 billion	$2 billion / $2 billion
Set Low Price	$1 billion / $2 billion	$3 billion / $1 billion	$1 billion / $0

defend against a pass. The defense "wins" if it defends against the correct type of play, and the offense "wins" if the defense is not defending against the play that it runs. Offensive coaches are always told to mix up their plays. Interpret this advice in terms of a mixed strategy, and explain why using any sort of nonrandom strategy is a bad idea.

4.6 You and your competitor are close to identical: You both own one undeveloped lot in each of two towns that are eager for the lots to be developed. The first town, Gainesville, offers tax concessions to the owner of the first lot developed in Gainesville, so that the owner makes a $10 million economic profit. The second town, Ocala, offers a smaller tax incentive package, so that the owner of the first lot developed in Ocala makes a $5 million economic profit. Both towns structure the tax rebates so that they apply only when one lot is developed in their town; if the second lot in their town is developed, all tax concessions are lost, and the owners of both lots will make a $1 million economic profit. You and your rival each have enough financing to develop only one lot and developing a lot is the only option for both you and your rival. Before you can start the project, both you and your rival need to have your building plans approved. Suppose that your rival is first in line in both cities to submit a building plan.

a. What is the game tree for this game? What is the Nash equilibrium?

b. Before your rival submits a building plan, you announce that you will develop your lot in Gainesville. Is this announcement credible? What is the Nash equilibrium of this game?

c. Before your rival submits a building plan, you (truthfully) announce that you have sold your lot in Ocala to someone who has no immediate plans to develop it. What is the Nash equilibrium of this game?

d. Compare your answers to parts b and c. Are they similar or different? Why?

4.7 Another firm is threatening to enter your industry. You announce that if the other firm enters, you will slash your prices to the bone rather than keep them high.

a. If the other firm enters and you cut your prices, your profit will be $30 million. If you keep your prices high after the other firm's entry, your profit will be $40 million. Is your threat credible? Explain your answer.

b. Before the other firm makes its decision, you quickly arrange an increase in your capacity. Now if the other firm enters and you cut your prices, your profit will be $70 million, while if your keep them high, your profit will be $50 million. Is your threat to cut your prices credible? Explain your answer.

MyLab Economics Auto-Graded Excel Projects

8.1 TOMS, a shoe retailer founded in 2006 by Blake Mycoskie, was founded on the One to One principle. For each pair purchased of TOMS shoes, the TOMS company would donate a pair to a child in need; over 60 million pairs of shoes have been donated worldwide so far. Sketchers, another shoe retailer, decided to release a line of shoes in 2010 and name them BOBS. For every purchase of BOBS, Sketchers will also donate a pair of shoes to a child in need; over 14 million pairs of shoes have been donated to date. This scenario provides an excellent example of an entry game.

Suppose you are making decisions for firms like Toms (Firm A) or Sketchers (Firm B). Suppose

Firm A currently enjoys $20 million in profit each year. If Firm B enters the market with a similar product and Firm A does nothing, Firm A will lose $5 million in profit and Firm B will gain enough market share to earn $6 million in profit. Firm A could try to combat the entry of Firm B by lowering prices, increasing advertising, or moving to a Two for One principle though this policy would lower their profit an additional $5 million; but, if Firm A combats Firm B's entry, Firm B's estimated profits will be lower by $7 million if they enter. Firm A could also take the same actions to combat entry if Firm B decided not to join the market; the effect on their profit is the same.

a. Using the template provided, create a tree modeling this game. Use Enter, Do Not Enter, Combat Entry, and Allow Entry as your decision options for each mode and enter payoffs in millions of dollars.

b. What will Firm A and B each decide to do?

c. How much profit will each firm make based on this decision?

d. Is a threat from Firm A to combat entry credible? Why or why not?

8.2 Taco Bell and Taco John's are two competing fast-food restaurant chains which serve Mexican inspired food items and low prices. Many restaurants have holiday inspired menu items such as the Nachos Navidad at Taco John's.

Suppose two restaurants similar to Taco Bell and Taco Johns are considering the addition of a holiday menu item. Restaurant 1 is considering a holiday inspired burrito while Restaurant 2 is considering a holiday inspired quesadilla. If neither company releases its product, Restaurant 1 will earn their typical $10 million in quarterly profit while Restaurant 2 will earn $9 million. If Restaurant 1 decides to release their burrito, they will spend an additional $3 million introducing the new product but gain $4 million in additional revenue while Restaurant 2's profit will be lower by $1 million. If Restaurant 2 decides to release their quesadilla, they will spend $3 million introducing the new product but gain $4 million in revenue while Restaurant 1's profit will be lower by $1 million. If both firms release a holiday product, they will each spend $3 million but will each only gain $1 million in revenue.

a. Using the above information, create a payoff matrix using the template provided. Enter the profits in millions of dollars.

b. If Restaurant 1 decides to release their burrito, what will Restaurant 2 decide to do?

c. If Restaurant 1 decides not to release their burrito, what will Restaurant 2 decide to do?

d.   Suppose Restaurant 1 and Restaurant 2 make this decision each year around the holidays. Restaurant 1 is a little more innovative and likes releasing limited time products; they tend to release a holiday menu item 75% of the time. Restaurant 2, on the other hand, is more conservative and only releases holiday menu items 40% of the time. Using this additional information and the profits calculated in the payoff table, what is the expected profit for each firm under each decision?

CHAPTER 9

A Manager's Guide to Antitrust Policy

Learning Objectives

After studying this chapter, you will be able to:

9.1 Explain the goals of the major U.S. antitrust laws and policies that promote competition.

9.2 Provide examples of the restraints of trade and types of monopolization prohibited by the Sherman Act.

9.3 Describe the business practices prohibited by the Clayton Act.

9.4 Explain how U.S. antitrust agencies determine whether to challenge a proposed merger.

9.5 Compare U.S. antitrust laws to competition laws in the European Union and China.

9.6 Relate guidelines managers should use to avoid antitrust violations.

The Managers of Sea Star Line Walk the Plank

The Merchant Marine Act of 1920, also known as the Jones Act, requires that goods transported by water between U.S. ports be carried on U.S.-flagged ships constructed in the United States, owned by U.S. citizens, and crewed by U.S. citizens. A ship that does not meet these requirements must stop at a foreign port between its U.S. departure port and its U.S. destination port. Ships that qualify under the Jones Act spend less time at sea and less money on fuel because they steam directly from the U.S. departure port to the U.S. destination port.

Shipping between the ports of Jacksonville, Florida, and San Juan, Puerto Rico, falls under the Jones Act. Prior to 2002, three shipping firms serviced the Jacksonville–to–San Juan run. The competition was intense, and all three firms had incurred a series of annual economic losses. Early in 2002, one of the firms gave up and closed. The owners of the two surviving firms, Sea Star Line and Horizon Lines, celebrated the potential increase in profit but also realized that it was not guaranteed. No one likes uncertainty, so the top executives from Sea Star Line and Horizon Lines met in April 2002 to discuss how to divide the market and boost their prices. The executives decided to divide the market evenly so that each shipping firm would get 50 percent.

They also discussed how to raise their prices by at least 10 percent. The executives agreed that when bidding on contracts, they would determine in advance the winner and winning bid. Over the years, the executives of the two firms met at golf courses in Washington, Puerto Rico, and elsewhere to discuss how the agreement was working.

Sea Star Line's vice president of marketing, Peter Baci, was responsible for communicating with his counterpart at Horizon Lines to ensure maintenance of the unwritten agreement. The two executives spoke on the telephone three or four times per week and even set up personal e-mail accounts so that they could more privately exchange pricing and bidding information. Sea Star Line's president, Frank Peake, presumably received reports of Mr. Baci's work.

In 2008, the U.S. Justice Department accused the firms of violating the Sherman Act, one of two major U.S. antitrust laws. What actions by Sea Star Line and Horizon Lines led to the indictment? How did these actions place Mr. Baci and Mr. Peake in jeopardy of substantial fines and imprisonment? This chapter explains what antitrust policies are, why they exist, and why managers need to follow them. At the end of the chapter, the information you learn is applied to answer these questions about Sea Star Line and Horizon Lines.

Sources: Michelle Kantrow, "Horizon Lines Agrees to Pay $45M to Settle Antitrust Case," News Is My Business, February 24, 2011 http://newsismybusiness.com/horizon-lines-agrees-to-pay-45m-to-settle-antitrust-case/; "Crowley Liner Services Offers Statement In Collusion Scandal," 2 Know About Blog, August 4, 2012 http://2knowabout .blogspot.com/2012/08/crowley-liner-services-offers-statement.html; "Former Sea Star Line President Sentenced to Serve Five Years in Prison for Role in Price-Fixing Conspiracy Involving Coastal Freight Services Between the Continental United States and Puerto Rico," U.S. Department of Justice, Office of Public Affairs, December 6, 2013.

Introduction

Antitrust laws Laws that promote competition.

It is a manager's responsibility to make decisions that improve profits. Some profit-making strategies, however, are unlawful because they violate **antitrust laws**, laws that promote competition. For example, the major producers of LCD screens—including Hitachi, Sharp, Samsung, Toshiba, LG, and AU Optronics—became mired in legal trouble in 2006. According to the U.S. Department of Justice (DOJ), between 1999 and 2006 the producers of the LCD screens used in products such as TV sets, computer monitors, cell phones, and tablets conspired to raise prices. They cooperated, rather than competed, in the market. This collusion resulted in huge corporate fines, as high as $500 million for a single company. Collectively, the fines totaled $1.39 *billion* in the United States alone. In addition, the defendants settled numerous private antitrust damage suits, which, taken together, may have cost them even more than the fines. The fines paid by the individual managers were relatively modest, but many of them received prison sentences ranging from six months to three years.

Around the world, antitrust and competition laws govern competition in the marketplace. To identify which business behaviors are permissible by law, this chapter includes six sections:

- **Section 9.1** explains the history of U.S. antitrust policy and provides brief descriptions of the three most important U.S. antitrust laws: the Sherman Act, the Clayton Act, and the Federal Trade Commission Act.
- **Section 9.2** explores the Sherman Act in more detail and covers the important distinction between per se illegality and rule-of-reason illegality.
- **Section 9.3** examines the Clayton Act, which prohibits certain business practices if they substantially lessen competition or tend to create monopolies.
- **Section 9.4** explains why not all mergers are permissible under antitrust laws and how government agencies determine which mergers to challenge.
- **Section 9.5** compares U.S. antitrust laws to competition laws in the European Union and China.
- **Section 9.6** shows how antitrust laws shape your interactions with competitors and affect your managerial decisions.

9.1 Overview of U.S. Antitrust Policy

Learning Objective 9.1 Explain the goals of the major U.S. antitrust laws and policies that promote competition.

Following the Civil War, a variety of socioeconomic factors caused considerable unrest among members of the American public. Industrialization proceeded rapidly, replacing small local firms with large, anonymous mass-market manufacturers. There were burgeoning monopolies in the petroleum and cigarette industries. Even when there was no actual monopoly, manufacturers often gained significant market power by creating *cartels*, groups of producers who agree not to compete on price, quantity, quality, and other promotional activity (see Section 7.1). Although many of the offending firms were not strictly monopolies, reporters nonetheless characterized this state of economic affairs as the *monopoly problem*.

The Monopoly Problem

In 1890, Congress passed the Sherman Act to deal with the monopoly problem. Before providing an overview of the law, let's review what you learned in Chapter 6.2 about the economic inefficiency of a monopoly.

Price and cost (dollars per LCD screen)

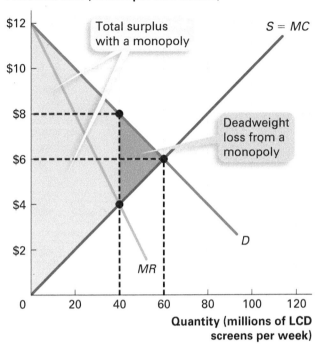

**Figure 9.1 Inefficiency of a
Monopoly**

In a competitive market, the
intersection of the demand
curve (*D*) and the supply
curve (*S*) determines the
price and the quantity
produced: here $6 per screen
and 60 million screens. In a
monopoly market, the
intersection of the marginal
revenue curve (*MR*) and the
marginal cost curve (*MC*)
determines the quantity
produced, 40 million
screens, and the demand
curve determines the price,
$8 per screen. The decrease
in society's total surplus is
the deadweight loss, which
equals the area of the red
triangle.

Inefficiency of Monopoly

Figure 9.1 shows the inefficiency of a monopoly in the market for LCD panels. In a
competitive market, the price is $6 per screen, and the quantity produced is 60 million
screens each week. In a monopoly, the price rises to $8 per screen and the quantity
falls to 40 million screens per week. Remember that a monopoly decreases society's
total surplus. The loss in total surplus from producing less (or more) than the efficient
quantity is the *deadweight loss*. (Section 2.4 introduces the concept of deadweight loss.)
In Figure 9.1, the area of the green trapezoid is the total surplus with the monopoly,
and the area of the red triangle is the amount of the deadweight loss. The deadweight
loss is the cost imposed on society by a monopoly or, more generally, by a firm with
substantial market power. One of your goals as a manager is to increase your firm's
market power because that can increase its economic profit, but in doing so, you must
be careful to not violate the law.

    Vertical and horizontal agreements are often the source of market power. A **vertical
agreement** is an agreement between a supplier and a customer. A **horizontal
agreement** is an agreement between competitors. Figure 9.2 illustrates the distinction between these agreements using as an example a small part of the supply chains
for Apple's iPhone and Samsung's Galaxy. Both phones offer Bluetooth support,
which allows the phones to pair with a variety of devices. The iPhone uses a Broadcom chip for its Bluetooth support, and the Galaxy uses a chip from Skyworks. As
illustrated in Figure 9.2, an agreement between the managers at Apple and Broadcom is a vertical agreement (depicted in the figure with a vertical arrow), and an
agreement between the managers at Apple and Samsung is a horizontal agreement
(depicted with a horizontal arrow).

    The United States and other developed countries have laws intended to limit the
harm created by firms with substantial market power. In part, these laws focus on
vertical and horizontal agreements and behavior between firms.

Vertical agreement An
agreement between a
supplier and a customer.

Horizontal agreement An
agreement between
competitors.

Figure 9.2 Vertical and Horizontal Agreements

The flowchart shows parts of the supply chains for Apple's iPhone and Samsung's Galaxy. A vertical agreement is an agreement between a supplier and a customer, such as an agreement between Apple and Broadcom. A horizontal agreement is an agreement between competitors, such as Apple and Samsung.

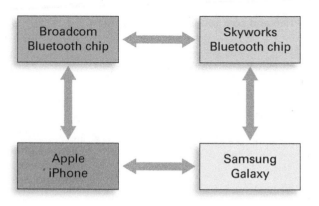

The Sherman Act, 1890

In 1890, Congress passed the Sherman Act to deal with monopolies and cartels. Two substantive provisions of this law deal with the monopoly problem. Section 1 prohibits collaborative efforts by firms to act collectively as a monopoly:

> Section 1. Every contract, combination in the form of trust or otherwise, or conspiracy, in restraint of trade or commerce among the several States, or with foreign nations, is hereby declared to be illegal. Every person who shall make any such contract or engage in any such combination or conspiracy shall be deemed guilty of a felony. . . . (15 U.S.C. §1)

Because all contracts restrain trade to some extent, Section 1 cannot be read literally. The general language of Section 1 requires judicial interpretation, which will be examined further in Section 9.2. As you will see, this interpretation has resulted in distinctions between reasonable and unreasonable restraints of trade.

Section 2 of the Sherman Act addresses single-firm conduct that results in monopoly or is likely to do so. The language of Section 2 does not outlaw the structural condition of monopoly. Instead, it condemns the act of becoming or trying to become a monopoly:

> Section 2. Every person who shall monopolize, or attempt to monopolize, or combine or conspire with any other person or persons, to monopolize any part of the trade or commerce among the several States, or with foreign nations, shall be deemed guilty of a felony. (15 U.S.C. §2)

This general language also requires judicial interpretation to distinguish those monopolies that warrant prosecution from those that do not, which is also covered in Section 9.2.

The Clayton Act, 1914

The vague and general language of the Sherman Act was disconcerting to both the business community and Congress. Congress became concerned that the courts would not enforce the Sherman Act as it desired, so in 1914 it passed the Clayton Act—the second major piece of antitrust legislation. The Clayton Act provided clearer direction by outlawing specific anticompetitive business practices if they "substantially lessen competition or tend to create a monopoly." If the activity in question does not substantially lessen competition and does not tend to create a monopoly, it remains legal. The prohibited acts fall into three main categories of business practices:

- Price discrimination
- Conditional sales
- Mergers

The Clayton Act, price discrimination, and conditional sales are described in more detail in Section 9.3. Merger policies are covered in Section 9.4.

The Federal Trade Commission Act, 1914

Congress kept busy in 1914 passing antitrust legislation. In addition to the Clayton Act, Congress passed the Federal Trade Commission Act (FTC Act), which established the Federal Trade Commission (FTC), an agency responsible for prohibiting unfair or deceptive practices affecting consumers and unfair competition among businesses. For managers, the most relevant part of the FTC Act is Section 5(a):

> Section 5. (a) Unfair methods of competition in or affecting commerce, and unfair or deceptive acts or practices in or affecting commerce, are hereby declared unlawful. (15 U.S.C. §45)

The FTC does not have the authority to unilaterally fine violators, but it can issue cease-and-desist orders. If the business ignores the cease-and-desist order, the FTC can seek civil penalties in court.

Sanctions for Antitrust Violations

Understanding that antitrust laws alone would not prevent managers from engaging in activities that might increase their economic profit, Congress put the FTC and the Antitrust Division of the Department of Justice in charge of overseeing and enforcing laws governing competition among businesses. The Antitrust Division enforces antitrust laws through both civil suits and criminal suits. A criminal suit can result in a prison sentence for managers convicted of breaking the law. The FTC, however, cannot file criminal suits. In addition to the sanctions that the government can impose, if the antitrust violation directly harms individuals or other companies, they can file private damage suits, seeking payment for the harm inflicted on them.

Government-Imposed Sanctions

The consequences for violating the Sherman Act are substantial. For the business itself, the maximum fine for violating either Section 1 or Section 2 is $100 million, but DOJ attorneys can and do use other provisions of the U.S. Code to impose fines up to twice the gross gain from the illegal act. So actions that violate the Sherman Act can result in penalties that total substantially more than $100 million. For example, in 2014, the courts fined Bridgestone Corporation $425 million for its role in a conspiracy fixing the prices of rubber anti-vibration car parts.

For individuals, the maximum fine for a Sherman Act violation is $1.0 million, and the maximum prison sentence is 10 years. Some penalties imposed on individuals have exceeded $800,000, but most are less than $100,000. To date, the longest prison sentence for violating the Sherman Act has been five years, and some managers receive no prison time at all. Imprisonment, however, is becoming an increasingly common punishment. In recent years, almost 75 percent of convicted managers have gone to prison, with an average sentence of two years.

Private Damage Suits

Section 4 of the Clayton Act provides the following guidelines for filing private damage suits:

> Section 4. Any person who shall be injured in his business or property by reason of anything forbidden in the antitrust laws may sue therefore in any district court of the United States in the district in which the defendant resides or is found or has an agent, without respect to the amount in controversy, and shall recover threefold the damages by him sustained, and the cost of suit, including a reasonable attorney's fee. (15 U.S.C. §15)

Figure 9.3 shows the amount of damages that can be tripled (or, as the attorneys would say, trebled). Suppose that the LCD screen producers have agreed to operate together as would a monopoly. This agreement is illegal. You saw in Figure 9.1 that the competitive price for an LCD screen is $6 per screen and the competitive quantity is 60 million screens, while the monopoly price is $8 per screen and the monopoly quantity is 40 million screens. The overcharge is the difference between the price actually paid and the competitive price. In the example, this amount is $8 per screen − $6 per screen = $2 per screen. The total damages are the total overcharges paid by everyone who purchased the product. Because the monopoly quantity is 40 million LCD screens, the total damages in the example are $2 per screen × 40 million screens, or $80 million dollars, which equals the area of the red rectangle in Figure 9.3. Since the Clayton Act allows these damages to be trebled, the producers portrayed in Figure 9.3 could face a total damage payment of $240 million.

The trebling provision of Section 4 of the Clayton Act provides a powerful economic incentive to file private antitrust suits. Worldwide, however, trebling damages is uncommon. For example, a winning plaintiff in the European Union may collect

Figure 9.3 Private Damages

If the market is a monopoly, consumers purchase 40 million screens at a price of $8 per screen. If the market is competitive, the price is $6 per screen. There is an overcharge of $2 per screen on 40 million screens. The total damages (overpayment) equal $2 per screen multiplied by 40 million screens, or $80 million, which equals the area of the red rectangle. If a private party prevails in an antitrust lawsuit, the Clayton Act allows the trebling of these damages.

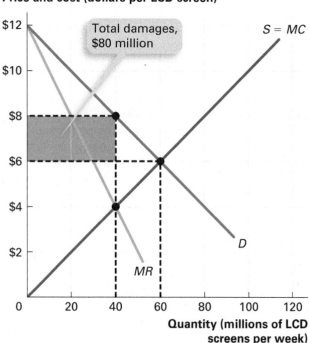

only the amount of the damages, not trebled damages. The more generous provision in the Clayton Act may lead to *nuisance lawsuits*, in which a plaintiff files an unjustified suit in the hopes of being paid in a settlement to drop the suit. (The economics behind settling lawsuits is discussed in Section 14.5.) This more liberal legislation also leads to jurisdiction shopping, as plaintiffs look for ways to tie their antitrust action to the United States rather than a foreign country.

Recent Antitrust Cases

Companies that violate the nation's antitrust laws face both government fines and damages awarded in lawsuits filed by injured individuals and companies. Even though all managers know that antitrust laws prohibit some types of behavior and agreements, government antitrust authorities need not fear unemployment. Table 9.1 shows a sampling of recent antitrust cases from around the world.

Now that you have had a brief overview of U.S. antitrust laws, let's examine each of them in more detail. We start with the Sherman Act.

Table 9.1 Recent Antitrust Cases

Industry	Country	Offense	Companies	Sanctions
LCD flat screens	United States	Price fixing of LCD screens	Samsung Electronics, Sharp, LG Display, AU Optronics, Chunghwa Picture Tubes, and others	More than $1 billion in penalties (AU Optronics fined $500 million in the United States); some top executives fined and imprisoned
Auto parts	United States	Price fixing of auto parts; bid rigging	Bridgestone, Mitsubishi Electric, Hitachi Automotive Systems, Yamashita Rubber, and others	More than $2 billion in penalties (Bridgestone fined $425 million); some top executives fined and imprisoned
Real estate foreclosure auctions	United States	Bid rigging	Various individuals	Fines, payment of restitution, imprisonment
Milk	England	Price fixing of milk and cheese	Tesco PLC, Asda Stores, Sainsbury's	Approximately £116 million
Cement	Brazil	Price fixing and creating barriers to entry	Votorantim Group, Intercement, Holcim, and others	R$3.1 billion (approximately US$1.4 billion)
Automotive shipping	Japan	Price fixing	Nippon Yusen Kabushiki Kaisha and three others	¥22.7 billion (approximately US$223 million)

Sources: LCD flat screens: http://money.cnn.com/2012/07/16/technology/lcd-class-action-settlement/; https://www.justice.gov/opa/pr/au-optronics-corporation-executive-sentenced-role-lcd-price-fixing-conspiracy; https://www.ft.com/content/e49c787e-039b-11e2-bad2-00144feabdc0; https://www.cnet.com/news/lg-sharp-chunghwa-admit-to-lcd-price-fixing/
Auto parts: https://www.justice.gov/opa/pr/nine-automobile-parts-manufacturers-and-two-executives-agree-plead-guilty-fixing-prices; https://www.justice.gov/opa/pr/bridgestone-corp-agrees-plead-guilty-price-fixing-automobile-parts-installed-us-cars
Real estate foreclosure auctions: http://business.cch.com/ald/DOJCalifRealEstateInvestorsBidRiggingPressRelease9132016.pdf
Milk: https://www.theguardian.com/business/2007/dec/08/supermarkets.asda; http://www.telegraph.co.uk/finance/newsbysector/retailandconsumer/9895895/Tesco-to-pay-6.5m-fine-in-dairy-price-fixing-settlement.html
Cement: http://www.reuters.com/article/brazil-cement-antitrust-idUSL1N0OE2IF20140529
Automotive shipping: http://www.jftc.go.jp/en/pressreleases/yearly-2014/March/140318.html; https://www.law360.com/articles/519608/japan-fines-car-shippers-223m-for-price-fixing

SOLVED
PROBLEM

A Perfectly Competitive Market Versus a Monopoly Market

In a perfectly competitive market, the market demand curve is $Q^d = 100 - P$, and the market supply curve is $Q^s = 20 + P$. Suppose that one firm buys all of the other firms and ultimately becomes a monopoly. Draw a diagram, and use it to determine the following:

a. The competitive price and quantity

b. The monopoly price and quantity

c. The deadweight loss

(Hints: For a reminder about how to draw the market demand and marginal revenue curves, see Section 6.1; for a reminder about how monopolies determine their profit-maximizing price and quantity, see Section 6.2.)

Answer

a. The figure shows the market demand curve (D) and competitive market supply curve ($S = MC$). The competitive price is $40 per unit, and the competitive quantity is 60 units.

Price and cost (dollars per unit)

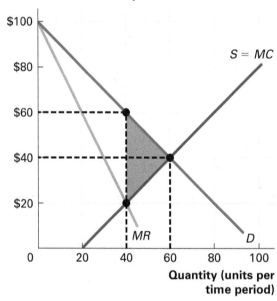

b. The marginal revenue curve (MR) lies below the demand curve with a slope twice as steep as the demand curve. The marginal cost curve is the same as the competitive supply curve. The profit-maximizing quantity for a monopoly is 40 units, with the profit-maximizing price of $60 per unit.

c. The deadweight loss is equal to the area of the red triangle. The area of a triangle equals $\frac{1}{2} \times$ Base $\times$ Height. The base equals 60 units minus 40 units, or 20 units. The height equals $60 per unit minus $20 per unit, or $40 per unit. Accordingly, the deadweight loss equals $\frac{1}{2} \times 20$ units $\times$ $40 per unit, or $400.

9.2 The Sherman Act

Learning Objective 9.2 Provide examples of the restraints of trade and types of monopolization prohibited by the Sherman Act.

In his book *The Wealth of Nations*, published in 1776, Scottish philosopher and political economist Adam Smith observed, "People of the same trade seldom meet together, even for merriment and diversion, but the conversation ends in a conspiracy against the public, or in some contrivance to raise prices." You can witness the truth of Smith's now-famous statement in many industries. Antitrust agencies use the Sherman Act to address some of Smith's concerns with horizontal agreements among competitors. This legislation has two sections: The first deals with restraint of trade, and the second deals with monopolization and the attempt to monopolize.

Sherman Act Section 1: Restraint of Trade

Section 1 of the Sherman Act prohibits contracts or conspiracies that restrain trade. The classic restraint of trade is **price fixing**, an agreement among competing managers to raise the prices of products they are selling or lower the prices of inputs they are buying. Other methods of restraining trade include bid rigging, output restrictions, market division, and resale price maintenance.

Price fixing: An agreement among competing managers to raise the prices of products they are selling or lower the prices of inputs they are buying.

Price-Fixing Agreements

To appreciate the objection to price-fixing agreements, let's begin with the competitive equilibrium and then introduce an industry-wide price-fixing agreement. Figure 9.4 returns to the market for LCD screens. For simplicity, assume that the LCD screen market includes 10 firms of equal size. Suppose that one of them is AG Screens, a firm like AU Optronics, a Taiwanese major producer of LCD screens. Figure 9.4(a) depicts the market, and Figure 9.4(b) illustrates the situation facing the managers at AG Screens. In a competitive market, the firms produce a total of 60 million LCD screens at a price of $6 per screen. Figure 9.4(b) shows that in a competitive market the managers at AG Screens maximize their profit by producing the quantity that sets the marginal revenue, MR_{COM}, equal to the marginal cost, MC. Accordingly, they produce 6 million LCD screens (1/10 of the total market quantity). AG Screens makes only a competitive return because the price equals the average total cost.

Imagine that at a trade association meeting for LCD screen producers the participants complain about the lack of economic profit. In a closed-door meeting among the competing managers, someone suggests raising the price in order to generate an economic profit. This suggestion finds immediate, universal agreement. In a flash, the firms form a price-fixing cartel. The managers agree to maximize the industry's total profit by setting a price equal to the monopoly price, $8 per LCD screen, as shown in Figure 9.4(a). At the higher price, customers decrease the quantity of LCD screens they demand, so the managers must also agree to decrease production to make the price stick. In actual cartels, the extent to which each firm must cut its production is subject to a great deal of negotiation and intense bargaining. To simplify the analysis, suppose that each manager agrees to reduce production by an equal amount. As Figure 9.4(b) shows, AG Screens decreases production to 4 million screens per week.

Figure 9.4(b) shows why the cartel agreement is appealing to the managers at AG Screens. In particular, the agreement's higher price and lower quantity create an economic profit equal to the area of the green rectangle. The managers of the other nine firms find the cartel agreement attractive as well because it allows all of them to sell their output at a higher price and make an economic profit. From the

Figure 9.4 A Price-Fixing Agreement

(a) The Market
In a competitive market, the price is $6 per screen, and the quantity produced is 60 million LCD screens per week. If the managers agree to fix their price at $8 per LCD screen (the monopoly price), consumers purchase only 40 million LCD screens per week.

(b) An Individual Firm
In a competitive market, each of the 10 firms produces the quantity that sets marginal cost equal to marginal revenue, $MC = MR_{COM}$, 6 million LCD screens per firm per week. The owners make only a competitive return. If the managers of each firm agree to fix the price at $8 per LCD screen and to produce only 4 million LCD screens per week, the owners of each firm make an economic profit equal to the area of the green rectangle.

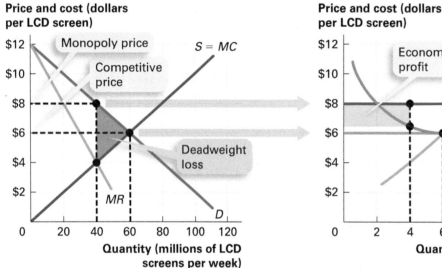

perspectives of the managers and owners of the member firms, everyone benefits. But a comparison of Figure 9.4(a) with Figure 9.1 reveals that the price-fixing cartel is the collusive equivalent of monopoly. Unlike the firms' managers and owners, society loses because there is a deadweight loss. As you can see, the economic harm shown in Figure 9.4(a) is identical to that illustrated in Figure 9.1. So how does antitrust policy deal with such price-fixing agreements?

In the late 1800s, the Supreme Court declared that price-fixing agreements among competing railroads violate Section 1 of the Sherman Act because they are unreasonable restraints of trade. Since then, the Supreme Court and the lower courts have made price fixing among competitors illegal per se. The phrase *per se* is Latin, meaning "by itself." **Illegal per se** is a legal doctrine stating that once a particular act is proven to have occurred, guilt is established with no defense possible; the act itself is illegal. The conduct is presumed to be harmful and inherently unreasonable.

Certain business practices are illegal per se because they always harm society. Although price fixing-agreements have long been illegal per se, there are many modern examples (see Table 9.1). The largest in recent years was the worldwide agreement among managers of LCD screen producers to fix prices. For six years, managers of AU Optronics and other producers held "Crystal Meetings" once a month in hotel conference rooms and karaoke bars around the world in order to agree on the prices they would charge. In 2006, after some buyers started to suspect that there was a price-fixing scheme in operation, Samsung executives took advantage of the DOJ leniency program, under which the first company to confess to a conspiracy will not face criminal prosecution. After the Samsung managers confessed, the FBI raided the

Illegal per se A legal doctrine stating that once a particular act is proven to have occurred, guilt is established with no defense possible; the act is innately illegal.

Houston office of AU Optronics, and the conspiracy was cracked. The DOJ penalized the participating companies (except for Samsung) with substantial fines totaling $1.39 billion in the United States alone. It also fined at least 13 executives and sent them to jail for terms ranging from six months to three years. AU Optronics refused to settle the case and went to trial, but it lost the case and paid a $500 million fine. In addition, three managers of AU Optronics were convicted of violating the Sherman Act. They were all fined (two were fined $200,000) and sentenced to jail terms of between two and three years. Even though AU Optronics is a Taiwanese company and the imprisoned executives are citizens of Taiwan, the DOJ did not treat the company or the managers any differently because they were foreigners. This case shows that being a foreign firm or citizen is not a defense against the enforcement of U.S. antitrust laws.

Price-fixing agreements are the most prominent illegal per se practice. Other agreements—to rig bidding, restrict output, and divide markets—receive similar per se treatment.

Bid Rigging

When transactions involve large dollar amounts—for example, road construction contracts and large supply contracts for manufacturers—a buyer may select a supplier on the basis of bids submitted in an auction. (For more on auctions, see Section 15.3.) Bidders, never fans of competition, may "rig" or cheat in preparing their bids. When **bid rigging** occurs, bidders agree prior to an auction on which bidder will submit the winning bid and all others will submit losing bids. Bid rigging is equivalent to price fixing because the bidders jointly determine the price (the winning bid). Managers who are engaged in bid rigging often agree that the designated winner will give the chosen losers lucrative subprojects.

Bid rigging Bidders agree prior to an auction on which bidder will submit the winning bid and all others will submit losing bids.

Because bid rigging is analogous to price fixing, it has been illegal per se in the United States for well over 100 years. Although its legal status is well known, again numerous recent examples are easy to find. Recently, one of the largest involved companies, such as Bridgestone and Mitsubishi Electric, in the market for rubber anti-vibration car parts sold to Toyota Motor, Nissan Motor, and Suzuki Motor. From 2001 through 2008, executives from the companies supplying the anti-vibration parts met and colluded on the bids they would submit to the auto producers. The conspiring managers instructed the losers to submit very high offers, allowing the prearranged winner to grab the contract at a higher-than-competitive price. After the FBI and the DOJ uncovered the conspiracy, they charged 28 managers with violations of the Sherman Act, and the auto parts suppliers paid approximately $2 billion in penalties.

Some industries are more subject to bid rigging than others. For example, bid rigging can occur easily in the construction industry because sealed bid auctions are frequently used to award projects to the low bidder.

Bid suppression is a form of bid rigging. In *a bid suppression* scheme, some competitors agree to refrain from bidding so that a predesignated rival can win. For example, during the recession of 2007–2009, thousands of homeowners lost their homes to foreclosure. The foreclosing banks usually auctioned the homes to recoup some of their losses. But from 2008 to 2011, in Northern California a group of approximately 50 participants in these auctions engaged in bid suppression, thereby keeping prices lower than they would have been in truly competitive auctions. Ironically, after the group members successfully purchased homes at below-market prices, they held secondary auctions among themselves to determine which participants would actually wind up with the houses. The members then divided the difference between the higher prices in the secondary auctions and the lower prices in the original auctions among themselves as profit from their scheme.

Output Restrictions

Decreasing production is the most straightforward output restriction agreement managers can make to increase their profit. Like price-fixing agreements, output restrictions raise the participating firms' prices and are illegal per se. For example, in 2009, six farmers filed suit against the major potash producers, claiming that the producers had engaged in illegal output restrictions. (Farmers use potash to fertilize fields.) The suit alleged that when one major Russian firm, Silvinet, had to cease production because of a sinkhole, four others cut the supply of their product instead of aggressively boosting production to take advantage of Silvinet's bad luck. The lawsuit noted other instances of simultaneous decreases in production as well, indicating that potash producers reduced production in order to raise the price of potash from $150 per ton in 2003 to $1,000 per ton in 2008. Although they continued to deny they had done anything illegal, executives of three of the largest potash producers agreed to settle the suit in 2013 by paying the farmers almost $100 million.

Market Division

In other instances, firms attempt to reduce competition by dividing markets rather than decreasing production over the entire market. Market division can be based on geographic areas—"you take Florida, and I'll take Georgia"—or on customer type— "you sell to pharmacy chains, and I'll sell to independent pharmacies." Either scenario denies buyers the benefits of competition. To see how profitable such a strategy can be, consider the market division scheme two publishing companies used in Georgia. Prior to the agreement, Harcourt Brace Jovanovich (HBJ) and BRG of Georgia had been competing in the market for study guides that law students purchase to prepare for the bar exam. The two publishers agreed that HBJ would withdraw from Georgia and BRG would confine its sales efforts to Georgia. After the market division, the study guide price in Georgia promptly rose from $150 to $400. As it had with other horizontal agreements that limit competition, the Supreme Court took a dim view of this market division and ruled it illegal per se.

Resale Price Maintenance

Resale price maintenance
A business practice in which manufacturers sell products to retailers with the explicit condition that the retailers may not resell the products below a specified price.

Resale price maintenance is a business practice in which manufacturers sell products to retailers with the explicit condition that the retailers may not resell the products below a specified price. Chapter 13 includes a complete analysis of resale price maintenance. For the purposes of this discussion, note that manufacturers use resale price maintenance to prevent distributors from competing with one another by lowering the price of the product.

It might seem strange that the managers of the manufacturer want to prevent distributors from lowering the price. After all, doesn't a lower price increase the quantity demanded? Presumably, the manufacturer makes a profit on each unit sold, which suggests that the more sales the distributors make, the larger the manufacturer's profit is. There are, however, two reasons the manufacturer might want to limit reductions in price:

1. **Reputation.** The product's reputation might depend on its price. For example, it is unlikely that the executives at Hermès want one of their authorized retailers to slash the price of a Hermès Birkin bag to use it as a loss leader to attract customers to its store. If customers saw Hermès bags on sale for prices significantly lower than usual, undoubtedly the low prices would tarnish the Hermès brand. Customers might come to see it as just another bag. Consequently, Hermès

managers use a resale price maintenance agreement that prevents their authorized retailers from discounting the bags to protect their brand's image of high-quality luxury.

2. **Visibility.** The manufacturer's managers might worry that distributors do not properly display or promote their products. For example, as those who stream Netflix on their TV know, televisions are becoming more and more complicated to use. Say that you are a manager at a firm like Sony and you want retailers to demonstrate your televisions because you believe that will increase sales. It is, however, expensive for distributors such as Best Buy to train salespeople to demonstrate products. You worry that customers will "showroom" your brick-and-mortar distributors: They will visit to see the television demonstrated but buy it from another source, such as an online retailer like Amazon.com. Because online retailers do not incur any training expense, their costs are lower, so they can undercut your distributors' prices. To compete, the distributors' managers will lower their costs by eliminating training programs and not demonstrating the televisions, thereby defeating your firm's goal. You can prevent showrooming by using resale price maintenance. Setting the minimum price for the television that both the online and also the brick-and-mortar distributors must charge eliminates online retailers' ability to undercut your distributors. The distributors' managers now find it worthwhile to train their salespeople to demonstrate the televisions, satisfied that online retailers will not be able set a lower price. Consumers gain from the resale price maintenance because they are able to make a more educated purchase.

The Supreme Court has never wavered in the view that certain horizontal agreements among competitors—including price fixing, bid rigging, output restrictions, and market division—are always harmful to society, so they are illegal per se. But the Court's thinking about resale price maintenance has evolved substantially over time. Initially, the Supreme Court viewed resale price maintenance as simply another price-fixing agreement, albeit a vertical restraint. In a 1911 case involving the Dr. Miles Medical Company, the Court ruled that resale price maintenance was illegal per se. But 96 years later, the Supreme Court acknowledged the economic rationales for resale price maintenance outlined above and overturned the *Dr. Miles* decision in a 2007 case involving Leegin Creative Leather Products. In that case, the Court acknowledged that resale price maintenance is sometimes harmful and sometimes helpful, so determining its effects requires a complete economic analysis. As you will learn, the courts also view other types of business practices as sometimes helpful and sometimes harmful. For these situations, the courts use a rule-of-reason analysis. The **rule of reason** is a legal concept that makes a particular business activity illegal only if the activity *unreasonably* restrains trade or is *unreasonably* exclusionary or predatory. Consequently, as long as its use is "reasonable," managers in the United States can legally use resale price maintenance as a pricing strategy.

Rule of reason A legal concept that makes a particular business activity illegal only if the activity unreasonably restrains trade or is unreasonably exclusionary or predatory.

Table 9.2 summarizes the legal status of different restraints of trade in the United States.

Sherman Act Section 2: Monopolization and Attempt to Monopolize

Section 2 of the Sherman Act makes it illegal to monopolize. As described in Chapter 6, one of the defining characteristics of a monopoly is that it is the only firm in the market, which means it has a 100 percent market share. For antitrust purposes,

Table 9.2 **Legality of Different Restraints of Trade Under U.S. Antitrust Law**

Horizontal Restraints	Legality
• Price fixing	Illegal per se
• Bid rigging	Illegal per se
• Output restrictions	Illegal per se
• Market division	Illegal per se
Vertical Restraints	**Legality**
• Resale price maintenance	Determined using rule-of-reason analysis

however, lawyers often describe firms with less than 100 percent of the market as monopolies. For example, United Shoe Machinery was characterized as a monopoly with only a 75 percent market share. As a general rule, antitrust authorities refer to any firm with a market share above 75 percent as a monopoly even though it is technically a dominant firm (see Section 6.3).

Section 2 of the Sherman Act condemns "[e]very person who shall monopolize, or attempt to monopolize, or combine or conspire with any other persons to monopolize." This language does not prohibit monopoly as such. Instead, it focuses the law on business conduct that either results in a monopoly or maintains a monopoly. The law effectively forbids the process of *attempting to become* or *maintaining* a monopoly, rather than merely *being* a monopoly. But what exactly does attempting to become a monopoly mean? In the 1946 *American Tobacco* decision, the Supreme Court defined "attempt to monopolize" as "the employment of methods, means, and practices which would, if successful, accomplish monopolization, and which, though falling short, nevertheless approach so close as to create a dangerous probability of it. . . ."

To illegally monopolize a market, a firm's managers must have acquired or maintained their monopoly power in the relevant market through the use of unreasonably exclusionary or predatory conduct. The fact that the actions must be unreasonable signals that the courts use the rule-of-reason approach in these cases.

There are good reasons for this approach to monopoly. For example, some markets are *natural monopolies*, monopolies that exist because technology allows one firm to produce whatever quantity is demanded in the market at a lower average cost than could two or more firms (see Section 6.2). In this case, economies of scale are so large that one firm "naturally" emerges from the competitive process as a monopoly, so competition cannot exist in the long run. Natural monopolies, however, are uncommon.

Other times a firm comes to dominate an industry through its managers' superior skill, foresight, and/or hard work. It does not make sense to prosecute a firm just for being successful. Prosecution of a company that acquired its dominance by, say, being more efficient in meeting consumers' needs would have unfortunate effects on other managers' incentives. Managers of all firms, faced with the prospect of an antitrust suit, would be inclined to avoid future prosecution by dialing back their efforts to efficiently produce goods and services that consumers want. These firms would produce less desirable products at higher costs, thereby harming society.

Illegal Attempts to Monopolize

The behavior of the managers of a single firm constitutes an illegal attempt to monopolize under the Sherman Act when (1) the firm is dangerously close to monopoly and (2) the managers have employed unreasonably exclusionary conduct. To prevail in a Section 2 case, a plaintiff (which could be an antitrust agency or a private firm) must satisfy three requirements:

1. **Market definition.** The plaintiff must appropriately define the defendant's product and geographic market. Products and geographic locations that are reasonable substitutes must be distinguished from those that are not. For example, if the defendant is a milk producer, reasonable substitutes include soy milk and rice milk but surely do not include brandy, so milk and brandy do not compete in the same market. Regarding geographic market, a consumer might travel from Atlanta to St. Louis to get a good deal on a BMW, so those locations are in the same geographic market for expensive cars. Consumers would not make the same trip to buy an ice cream cone, so Atlanta and St. Louis are not in the same ice cream cone market.
2. **Monopoly power.** The plaintiff must establish that the defendant holds a large market share. As noted above, if a defendant's market share exceeds 75 percent, most courts will conclude that the firm is a monopoly. If the market share exceeds 50 percent, the courts are likely to conclude that the firm is coming "dangerously close" to being a monopoly.
3. **Exclusionary, predatory, or other anticompetitive practices.** The plaintiff must demonstrate that the monopolist's success is due to unreasonable exclusionary, predatory, or other unreasonable anticompetitive conduct.

You will learn about market definition in more detail in Section 9.4. For the purposes of this discussion, let's examine the third requirement. As a manager, it is important to understand how to avoid unreasonable exclusionary and predatory practices.

Exclusionary Practices   A dominant firm must be careful about aggressive conduct that the courts might deem an unreasonably exclusionary practice, but this is a slippery concept. Two examples show the range of conduct that has been challenged:

- One key legal precedent involves Aspen Highlands Skiing Corporation's case against Aspen Skiing Company. In 1978, Aspen Skiing Company owned three of the four ski slopes in Aspen, Colorado, thereby making it the dominant firm. In previous years, its managers had offered an "all Aspen" ticket, which allowed skiers to ski their slopes as well as an additional slope owned by Aspen Highlands Skiing, but in 1978, Aspen Skiing Company discontinued this offer. Managers at Aspen Skiing Company also refused Aspen Highlands Skiing's request to buy tickets to Aspen Skiing Company's slopes, thereby preventing Aspen Highlands Skiing from presenting its own "all Aspen" offer. Aspen Highlands Skiing took Aspen Skiing Company to court, charging that Aspen Skiing Company's decision was unreasonably exclusionary. Aspen Highlands Skiing won and collected treble damages.
- More recently, in 2009, the managers at Intel, the dominant producer of microprocessors, ran afoul of the FTC. The FTC challenged contracts that gave computer manufacturers lower prices if they purchased only Intel microprocessors, thereby excluding competitors. Intel's managers settled the suit by agreeing to no longer offer manufacturers lower prices in exchange for exclusively purchasing Intel processers.

Some competitive practices, however, are almost universally legal. For example, every firm can compete on the basis of product desirability. The drugs Sovaldi, Harvoni, and Epclusa, all produced by Gilead Sciences, treat hepatitis C. Compared to previous treatments, they cure a much higher percentage of patients, have far fewer and milder side effects, and are taken as a pill for no more than 12 weeks, rather than being administered as a shot over 12 months. If Gilead were to become dominant—if its drugs displaced all of the other treatments aimed at hepatitis C—because of superior benefits, such exclusion raises no antitrust concerns. Managers are also free to compete on quality. Depending on the product in question, factors such as superior fit and finish, color fastness, shrinkage control, durability, taste, visual appeal, texture, on-time arrival, or service might lead to a single firm's dominance in the market. If a dominant firm is supplying products with superior attributes that its rivals have failed to supply, consumers benefit. In spite of the fact that its rivals are falling by the wayside, the dominant firm cannot be faulted on antitrust grounds.

Predatory Pricing   Behavior that can get managers and their firms in trouble with authorities is *predatory conduct*, conduct intentionally designed to punish or injure competitors in an effort to drive them from the market. A prime example of predatory conduct is **predatory pricing**, which occurs when a firm sets the price of a product below its cost with the goal of driving competitors out of the market and then raising the price to make an economic profit. Predatory pricing has been unlawful for more than a century. In 1911, the courts found Standard Oil (now ExxonMobil) guilty of monopolizing the petroleum industry through exclusionary conduct that included predatory pricing.[1] The image conjured up by this case is a large, financially powerful firm with managers who slash their price below their cost in markets with smaller rivals. The dominant firm finances these local skirmishes with profits earned in other markets. The rivals try valiantly to compete, but setting price below cost eventually forces them from the industry. After driving their competitors from the market, the managers of the now-monopoly firm reward themselves with a hefty price hike.

As a manager, it is important for you to distinguish competitive pricing from predatory pricing and to know what the courts look for in predatory pricing cases. *Brooke Group Limited v. Brown & Williamson Tobacco Corporation* is the most recent important Supreme Court case to address the issue of predatory pricing. In 1993, Brooke Group Limited (Brooke Group) accused Brown & Williamson (B&W) of selling generic (non-brand-name) cigarettes below cost. Brooke Group presented the following scenario in court: Brooke Group introduced low-priced generic cigarettes, which lured customers away from B&W's regular, higher-priced cigarettes. After a few years, B&W introduced its own generic cigarettes, which it priced aggressively low. Brooke Group alleged that B&W was engaging in predatory pricing to force Brooke Group to abandon the generic cigarette market. B&W would then raise the price of its own generic cigarettes, easing the pressure on B&W's standard, full-priced brands. Eventually, this case made its way to the Supreme Court, which ruled against Brooke Group. The Court indicated that to win a predatory pricing case, the plaintiff must prove two elements:

Predatory pricing When a firm sets the price of a product below its cost with the goal of driving competitors out of the market and then raising the price to make an economic profit.

---

1 The conventional wisdom behind the 1911 Standard Oil case is that by systematically using predatory pricing, Standard Oil's monopoly spread geographically until it blanketed the country. Whenever a firm dared to enter the industry, Standard Oil would reduce its price below cost in the entrant's market and eventually bankrupt the smaller firm. This explanation of Standard Oil's ascendancy in the petroleum industry was widely accepted until researchers subjected it to closer scrutiny, which suggested that the orthodox story regarding Standard Oil's conduct is incorrect. Whether the conventional wisdom is correct or not is unresolved. Predatory pricing, however, remains illegal.

1. **Price below cost.** The price must be below the cost. Unfortunately, the Court did not specify which cost: average total cost, average variable cost, or marginal cost. Consequently, there is no single standard for distinguishing true predation from aggressive competition.

2. **Recoupment.** The defendant had to have a reasonable expectation that it would subsequently be able to recoup its investment in those below-cost prices, a concept introduced by the Court that it called *recoupment*. Recoupment can occur only if today's low prices lead to a significant increase in future prices that result from a substantial lessening of competition. Justice Kennedy wrote: "The plaintiff must demonstrate that there is a likelihood that the predatory scheme alleged would cause a rise in prices above a competitive level that would be sufficient to compensate for the amounts expended on the predation."

The recoupment requirement means that predatory pricing *must* reduce competition because it is only when competition is reduced that the predator can raise the price. Therefore, the plaintiff must show that, ultimately, a reduction in competition is likely to take place. Demonstrating this result is difficult unless it has already occurred, which means that winning a predatory pricing case is difficult.

Going, Going, Gone: Price Fixing in the Market for Fine Art

SOLVED
PROBLEM

Sotheby's and Christie's are two leading auction houses that together control over 90 percent of the auction market for expensive fine art. Auctioneers earn revenue by charging buyer's and seller's fees. In 1995, both Sotheby's and Christie's charged a seller's fee of 9 percent on sales between $100,000 and $249,999. The percentage fee decreased as the dollar amount of the sales increased. The fee schedules of the two companies were identical up to sales of $10,000,000 because the CEOs of the two companies met to discuss and set their fees.

a. Did the companies violate the Sherman Act? Explain your answer.

b. If the companies violated the Sherman Act, what penalties might they face?

c. If the CEOs violated the Sherman Act, what penalties might they face?

Answer

a. The companies were definitely guilty of violating the Sherman Act. Fixing prices is a per se violation of the Sherman Act.

b. The companies faced penalties from two sources: the U.S. government and the buyers and sellers harmed by the price fixing. In fact, antitrust authorities fined Sotheby's $45 million. (The government did not fine Christie's because it provided evidence to the DOJ.) Additionally, the buyers and sellers that sued Sotheby's and Christie's received a total of $256 million in damages.

c. The CEOs faced both imprisonment and fines. The CEO of Sotheby's was convicted of price fixing, fined $7.5 million, and sentenced to a year in jail. The CEO of Christie's was an English citizen. Though the laws are now different, at the time English law did not allow extradition for price fixing, so Christie's CEO was neither fined nor imprisoned.

9.3 The Clayton Act

Learning Objective 9.3 Describe the business practices prohibited by the Clayton Act.

The Clayton Act was enacted in 1914 in response to Congress's desire for greater specificity regarding prohibited business practices. Business practices affected by the Clayton Act fall into three general categories: (1) price discrimination, (2) conditional sales, and (3) mergers. The Clayton Act prohibits these practices only if their effect is to "substantially lessen competition or tend to create a monopoly." If they do not substantially lessen competition and do not tend to create monopoly, they remain legal.

Clayton Act Section 2: Price Discrimination

Section 2 of the Clayton Act deals with price discrimination. As amended by the Robinson–Patman Act in 1936, Section 2 states:

> Section 2. (a) . . . It shall be unlawful for any person engaged in commerce, . . . either directly or indirectly, to discriminate in price between different purchasers of commodities of like grade and quality . . . where the effect of such discrimination may be substantially to lessen competition or tend to create a monopoly. . . . (15 U.S.C. §13)

Price discrimination The practice of charging customers different prices that are not based on differences in marginal costs.

Chapter 10 covers price discrimination in detail. For the purposes of this discussion, you need to know that **price discrimination** is the practice of charging customers different prices that are not based on differences in marginal costs. One type of price discrimination sells different units of the same product to the same consumer at different markups between the marginal cost and price. Another type sells the same product to different customers at different markups between the marginal cost and the price. A pizza chain's quantity discount, which makes the price of a second pizza less than the price of a first pizza ordered at the same time, is an example of the first type of price discrimination. A movie theater's sale of discounted tickets to senior citizens or students is an example of the second type of price discrimination.

Neither of the two price discrimination examples described above substantially lessens competition or tends to create monopoly, so both are perfectly legal, which explains the presence of price discrimination in many markets. In addition, Section 2(b) of the Clayton Act provides a good-faith meeting competition defense: If managers cut their firm's price to meet—but not beat—the lower price offered by a rival to a particular customer, then the resulting price discrimination is legal.

In creating this legislation, Congress was aware that managers are clever and might try to devise methods of offering lower prices through more indirect means such as hiding discounts, providing promotional allowances and services, and gaining concessions from suppliers. If any of these practices substantially lessens competition or tends to create monopoly, Sections 2(c), 2(d), and 2(e), respectively, prohibit it.

Clayton Act Section 3: Conditional Sales

Section 3 of the Clayton Act prohibits making sales with conditions that exclude competitors and thereby might have an adverse effect on competition:

> Section 3. That it shall be unlawful for any person engaged in commerce . . . to lease or make a sale of goods, wares, merchandise, machinery, supplies, or other commodities, whether patented or unpatented, . . . on the condition, agreement, or understanding that the lessee or purchaser thereof shall not

use or deal in the goods, wares, merchandise, machinery, supplies, or other commodities of a competitor or competitors of the lessor or seller, where the effect . . . may be to substantially lessen competition or tend to create a monopoly in any line of commerce. (15 U.S.C. §14)

These contractual clauses, referred to as conditional sales, all involve the vertical relationship between a seller and a buyer. To be illegal under the Clayton Act, conditional sales must either substantially lessen competition or tend to create a monopoly. This section of the Clayton Act has been used to forbid various contractual clauses, including territorial confinement, tying arrangements, and exclusive dealing and requirements contracts. We take each of these up in turn.

Territorial Confinement

Territorial confinement is a vertical contractual requirement in which the seller prohibits a buyer from reselling its product outside a prespecified geographic territory. For example, Anheuser-Busch designates the territory in which a particular beer wholesale distributor can make sales.

If the seller has little or no market power, territorial confinement restrictions are almost always legal. If the seller has significant market power, the restrictions might be illegal.

Territorial confinement A vertical contractual requirement in which the seller prohibits the buyer from reselling its product outside a prespecified geographic territory.

Tying Arrangement

A **tying arrangement**, also called a tying sale or tying contract, is an agreement in which the seller conditions the sale of one product on the buyers' agreement to buy a second product. For example, in 1996, a group of retailers filed suit charging Visa and Master-Card with illegal tying because they required merchants who wanted to accept their credit cards to also accept Visa or MasterCard debit cards. The debit cards had higher costs for the merchants, so they were less profitable for the merchants than credit cards.

A tying arrangement raises two antitrust concerns. First, the tie appears to coerce buyers into buying the tied product. As a result, there is some concern that the buyers will be overcharged for the tied good. Second, because the buyers of the first product must also buy the tied product, the tie excludes rival suppliers from selling their version of the tied good.

As a manager, you need to know if your own tying contract is legal as well as be able to determine if a competitor is engaged in an illegal tying contract. Four elements make tying arrangements vulnerable to antitrust prosecution:

Tying arrangement An agreement in which the seller conditions the sale of one product on the buyers' agreement to buy a second product.

1. **Two products.** There must be (at least) two products, a tying product and a separate tied product.
2. **Actual conditioning.** There must be proof of an actual tie between the products. That is, the seller must condition the sale of one good on the purchase of another.
3. **Market power in the tying product's market.** In order to coerce customers or to foreclose rivals from making the sale, the supplier must have substantial market power in the market for the tying product.
4. **Not insubstantial volume of commerce in the tied product.** Finally, there must be some nontrivial amount of commerce affected by the tying contract. Using convoluted grammar, the Court has referred to this volume threshold as "not insubstantial," a standard that obviously varies from market to market.

If all four elements are present, the tying arrangement is illegal per se, while if less than four are present, the courts judge the arrangement using a rule-of-reason approach. If the arrangement is illegal per se, the defendant cannot offer any assertion that it increases competition. This outcome is unfortunate because some tying arrangements are promotional and therefore promote competition. The key takeaway for you, as a manager, is to exercise caution when using a tying arrangement.

Exclusive Dealing and Requirements Contracts

Exclusive dealing contract A vertical contractual requirement that forbids the retailer from handling or selling products that compete with the supplier's product or forbids the supplier from selling its product through another retailer.

An **exclusive dealing contract** is a vertical contractual requirement that forbids the retailer from handling or selling products that compete with the supplier's product or forbids the supplier from selling its product through another retailer. For example, the only sodas that passengers riding on Amtrak can purchase are Pepsi products. This point suggests that the managers of the supplier, PepsiCo, and the managers of the buyer, Amtrak, have signed an exclusive dealing contract that allows Amtrak to sell *only* Pepsi products. The PepsiCo and Amtrak deal is legal because it does not "substantially lessen competition or tend to create a monopoly."

A close cousin of an exclusive deal is the requirements contract. Under a requirements contract, the supplier does not forbid the buyer to deal with rival firms. Instead, the supplier agrees to sell its product on the condition that the buyer purchases 100 percent of that product that it needs from the supplier. More formally, a **requirements contract** is a contractual clause in which a seller requires a buyer to purchase all of a particular product that it needs from the seller. For example, if Intel sells its microprocessors to Dell on the condition that Dell buys all of the microprocessors that it needs from Intel, then Intel and Dell have entered into a requirements contract.

Requirements contract A contractual clause in which the seller requires a buyer to purchase all of a particular product that it needs from the seller.

Exclusive dealing contracts and requirements contracts can have both procompetitive and anticompetitive motivations:

- **Procompetitive.** In some cases, the producer attracts business for the distributor by promoting its brand. For example, SVP Worldwide's Husqvarna Viking produces high-tech, computerized Husqvarna sewing machines that it sells through authorized distributors. Say that the only computerized sewing machines that Husqvarna Viking allows the distributors to sell are Husqvarna products; that is, the distributors have entered into an exclusive dealing (or requirements) contract with Husqvarna Viking. Husqvarna Viking extensively advertises the features of its machines, increasing the demand for its machines and causing potential customers to go to the distributors' stores. If Husqvarna Viking allowed the distributors to carry other brands, a distributor's managers would have the incentive to switch customers to different brands if they had higher profit margins. In this case, Husqvarna Viking would lose the benefit of its investment in promotion and, consequently, would decrease its advertising. Because the advertising gives consumers valuable information about sewing machine features, reducing it decreases competition and efficiency. An exclusive dealing contract prevents this outcome because the distributors have no rival to offer customers.

  Some exclusive dealing contracts and requirements contracts also give the *distributors* greater incentive to advertise and promote the product. For example, if Anheuser-Busch InBev has an exclusive deal with a distributor who is the only distributor serving a particular locale, the distributor has the incentive to promote Anheuser-Busch's products. If the distributor's promotional activities succeed, its managers realize they will capture 100 percent of the increase in sales. Advertising and other forms of promotion can inform consumers, so once again the contract enhances efficiency and is procompetitive.

- **Anticompetitive.** If an exclusive dealing contract or requirements contract raises a rival's costs, it will reduce the profits of the rival and might lead to its demise. For this ill effect to materialize, however, three conditions must be present:

(1) The producer must have substantial market power, (2) there must be few alternative distributors, and (3) the time period the deal covers must be long enough that the rival only infrequently gets the chance to bid on a new contract with the distributors. For example, if Husqvarna Viking were to sign long-lasting exclusive dealing contracts with most of the nation's sewing machine dealers, its competitor, Bernina, would be unable to find many dealers. Husqvarna Viking's contracts would force Bernina to deal with less efficient dealers at a greater distance from each other, increasing Bernina's costs.

As you can see, exclusive dealing contracts and requirements contracts can be procompetitive at some times and anticompetitive at other times. Consequently, using the rule of reason to determine the legality of exclusive dealing and requirements contracts is the appropriate approach. In fact, under modern case law, a rule-of-reason approach *is* required. The burden of proof required for a plaintiff to win an exclusive dealing contract or requirements contract case is high, and the outcomes of recent cases reflect that burden.

Clayton Act Section 7: Mergers

The Sherman Act deals in a remedial way with problems of existing monopolies—both structural and collusive. In contrast, Section 7 of the Clayton Act provides some preventive measures. More specifically, Section 7 forbids a merger that might result in a substantial lessening of competition or tendency toward monopoly:

> Section 7. That no corporation engaged in commerce shall acquire, directly or indirectly, the whole or any part of the stock or other share capital and no corporation subject to the jurisdiction of the Federal Trade Commission shall acquire the whole or any part of the assets of another corporation engaged also in commerce, where in any line of commerce in any section of the country, the effect of such acquisition may be substantially to lessen competition, or tend to create a monopoly. (15 U.S.C. §18)

Section 7 of the Clayton Act applies to both **horizontal mergers**—the combination of competing firms—and **vertical mergers**—the combination of a firm with a customer or a supplier. The merger AT&T proposed between itself and one of its cellular competitors, T-Mobile, is an example of a horizontal merger. The merger proposed by Live Nation, the nation's largest concert promotion company, with Ticketmaster, the nation's largest ticketing company, is an example of a vertical merger.

Horizontal merger
Combination of competing firms.

Vertical merger
Combination of a firm with a customer or a supplier.

Section 8 of the Clayton Act prohibits an individual from serving on the boards of directors of competing companies if a merger of the companies would be illegal. For example, Dr. Eric Schmidt is the executive chair of Alphabet, Inc. the company that owns Google, so he serves on Alphabet's board of directors. In 2006, Dr. Schmidt was elected to the board of directors of Apple. At that time, Apple was primarily a computer hardware producer, and Google's main business was Internet search. They were not competitors because they operated in different markets. But by 2009, Google and Apple were competitors in the smartphone and tablet markets, Google with its Android operating system and Apple with its iOS. In 2009, Dr. Schmidt resigned from the board of directors of Apple to avoid violating the Clayton Act.

Both the Clayton Act and the Sherman Act address mergers. As a manager, a merger is an important business decision. The decision by antitrust agencies to approve a merger (as between Ticketmaster and Live Nation) or oppose it (as in the case of AT&T and T-Mobile) could have a major impact on your business. Consequently, the next section covers U.S. merger policy in more detail.

The Business Practices Covered in the Clayton Act

Identify the contracts or contractual clauses described in each of the following examples.

a. A wireless company offers to sell you a smartphone only if you also buy a bluetooth headset.

b. A car manufacturer limits the area in which a dealership can sell to 20 miles beyond the city boundary.

c. A printer company sells its printers to a customer at a very low price, with the contract specifying that the customer must purchase only its printers.

d. A state university signs a 10-year, $32 million contract with a soft drink company specifying that only the company's products may be sold on the campus.

Which of these examples, if any, would be illegal under the Clayton Act and should therefore be avoided?

Answer

a. This offer is a tying arrangement.

b. This limitation is a territorial confinement.

c. The contract is a requirements contract.

d. The contract is an exclusive dealing contract.

It is likely that none of the examples is illegal under the Clayton Act because none "substantially lessens competition or tend[s] to create monopoly."

9.4 U.S. Merger Policy

Learning Objective 9.4 Explain how U.S. antitrust agencies determine whether to challenge a proposed merger.

Managers take mergers very seriously because they can have important consequences for their firms' futures. Preparation for a merger can be quite extensive and costly, so the managers in charge of the merger must consider its antitrust implications very carefully. Because merger challenges by the antitrust agencies are typically resolved administratively rather than by going to court, managers must understand the administrative procedures used by the antitrust agencies, the Antitrust Division of the DOJ and the Federal Trade Commission.[2]

Firms must report mergers involving assets that exceed a certain value. The FTC adjusts the threshold annually—in 2017, the FTC increased it to $80.8 million from the 2016 level of $78.2 million. Along with the notification, the firms must supply the agencies with industry information and some firm-specific information. When the merging firms submit their data to the FTC and to the Antitrust Division of the DOJ, they often include an economic analysis designed to demonstrate that the proposed merger is not anticompetitive. The managers' goal is to head off a potential challenge by whichever antitrust agency handles their merger. The DOJ and the FTC consult with each other to determine which agency will examine a proposed merger.

---

2 The FTC does not directly enforce the Sherman Act or the Clayton Act. But actions that violate the Sherman Act or Section 7 of the Clayton Act are considered to be unfair methods of competition, so they also violate the FTC Act, which brings the FTC into the fray.

The chosen agency has 30 days to review the submission and evaluate the likely competitive consequences. If the firms have not heard back within 30 days, they are free to pursue the merger, but they run a risk because the agency can decide to challenge the merger even after the firms have merged. At any time within the 30 days, the agency can request additional data. If the agency requests more data, then it has up to an additional six months to make a decision, though the amount of extra time is subject to negotiation between the agency and the companies' managers. Typically, the antitrust agencies closely examine horizontal mergers. Vertical mergers receive much less scrutiny. Therefore, this discussion focuses on horizontal mergers.

Economic Effects of Horizontal Mergers

The antitrust authorities are aware that horizontal mergers can lead to increased market power and potentially even to monopoly. Figure 9.1 showed the consequences of a competitive market becoming a monopoly: The monopoly decreased the total surplus and created a deadweight loss. In Figure 9.1, the mergers that led to the monopoly did not affect the firms' costs. There are times, however, when mergers create production efficiencies that lower the cost of production, which can lead to complications. Suppose that there are 100 competitive hotels on the "Big Island" of Hawaii. For simplicity, also suppose that their marginal costs are all equal and constant at $300 per guest stay, so the supply curve is horizontal at a price of $300 per stay. Figure 9.5(a) illustrates the demand curve (D) and supply curve ($S_{PRE} = MC_{PRE}$) before any mergers take place. The equilibrium price of a stay in one of the hotels is $300 per night, and over the year, there are 3 million stays. The total surplus, which is all consumer surplus (see Figure 2.4 and Figure 2.11), equals the area of the lighter red triangle and is $450 million. Now suppose that the firms merge. For simplicity, assume that the firms *all* merge, resulting in a single monopoly firm. The crucial difference from the case outlined in Figure 9.1 is that as a result of merging, the merged firms can reduce their costs. For example, once there is only a single firm, there is no longer a need for 100 separate marketing departments or 100 courtesy cars and drivers. These and other economies reduce costs, so suppose that the post-merger marginal cost falls to $200 per visit. If the firm continues to behave as if it is in a competitive market the price and quantity are determined by supply and demand. Figure 9.5(a) shows that the new supply curve is $S_{POST} = MC_{POST}$. The price falls to $200 per stay, and the quantity increases to 4 million stays. The total surplus, again all consumer surplus, increases by the area of the darker red trapezoid, $350 million, to $800 million.

Once the firms have merged, however, it is unlikely that the resulting monopoly will continue to act as if it is competitive. Instead, as Figure 9.5(b) shows, the firm maximizes its profit by producing the quantity that sets marginal revenue equal to marginal cost, $MR = MC_{POST}$ and using the demand curve to set the price. Consequently, the managers reduce the quantity to 2 million stays per year and raise the price to $400 per stay. Compared to the surplus that would result if the firm acts as if it is competitive, the total surplus decreases by the area of the deadweight loss shown in Figure 9.5(b), $200 million. Even with that decrease, however, the total surplus equals $600 million. Compared to the situation before the merger, the total surplus in the market *increases* from $450 million to $600 million *even though* the firm sets the monopoly price and produces the monopoly quantity. The efficiencies from the merger have swamped the deadweight loss because society's total surplus is larger with the merger. The distribution of the surpluses differs: Before the merger, the entire $450 million of surplus was consumer surplus. After the merger, the consumer surplus is only $200 million. The remaining $400 million of total surplus is producer surplus. Consequently, the antitrust authorities face a dilemma: Should they approve the merger because it increases society's total surplus or challenge it because it decreases the consumer surplus and thereby harms consumers?

Figure 9.5 The Effect of a Merger with Production Efficiencies

(a) Production Efficiencies, Firm Behaves Competitively

If a merger creates production efficiencies that lower costs, from MC_{PRE} to MC_{POST} in the figure, *and* the resulting monopoly still behaves as if it is in a competitive market (so that the price and quantity are determined by demand and supply), the price falls from $300 per visit to $200, and the quantity increases from 3 million visits per year to 4 million. Society's total surplus increases by an amount equal to the area of the darker red trapezoid. Before the merger, the total surplus was $450 million; after the merger, it is $800 million.

(b) Production Efficiencies, Firm Behaves as a Monopoly

If a merger creates production efficiencies that lower costs, from MC_{PRE} to MC_{POST} in the figure, *and* the resulting monopoly behaves as a monopoly (so that it maximizes its profit by producing where $MR = MC$ and sets the price using its demand), the price rises from $300 per visit to $400, and the quantity decreases from 3 million visits per year to 2 million. There is a deadweight loss, but compared to the initial situation before the mergers, society's total surplus increases. Before the merger, the total surplus was $450 million; after the merger, it is $600 million.

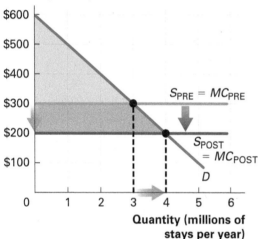

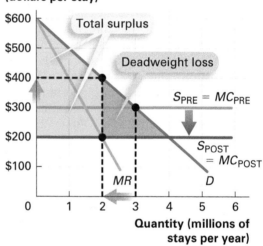

As a practical matter, it is highly unlikely the firms would merge to become a monopoly. In the real world, a horizontal merger reduces but does not eliminate competition within the market. The reduction in competition may cause the price to rise even though costs fall, so that consumer surplus decreases while total surplus increases, leaving the antitrust authorities facing the same dilemma: Should they focus on consumer surplus or total surplus? U.S. antitrust agencies seem to emphasize primarily consumer surplus. They compare the price before the merger to the (predicted) price afterward and generally challenge the merger if the antitrust authorities think the price will rise. They will challenge the merger even if the total surplus increases because the rise in price reduces consumer surplus. Consequently, production efficiencies seem to matter only if they are large enough and if enough competition remains after the merger that the price falls and the consumer surplus increases. If not, the merger usually will be challenged.

Antitrust Merger Policy

Aside from the effect of any efficiencies from a merger, the antitrust agency faces many additional issues. For example, the antitrust agency must identify both the geographic and the product markets affected by the merger. Identifying the product market is not as simple as it sounds. The antitrust agencies use many tools, both qualitative and quantitative, to determine the market. The basic goal is to determine products that consumers (or sometimes suppliers) consider close substitutes. If the products are close substitutes, then they compete in the same market.

Qualitatively, the agencies might examine the similarity of the products. If they determine that products have similar uses, are of similar quality, have a similar distribution network, and sell for similar prices, then the agencies often conclude that these products compete in the same market.

One quantitative factor the agencies can consider is the *cross-price elasticity of demand*, a measure of how strongly the quantity demanded changes when the price of a related good changes. This concept was defined and explained in Chapter 3 (see Section 3.4). If two products have a large cross-price elasticity of demand, then the antitrust agencies can conclude that the products compete in the same market because they are close substitutes for each other.

Another semi-quantitative/semi-qualitative measure used to help define the market is the SSNIP test. SSNIP is an acronym for Small but Significant Nontransitory Increase in Price. The **SSNIP test** determines the smallest set of products that a monopolist needs to control in order to profitably increase the price by a small but significant amount above the competitive price for a non-transitory period of time. Usually, the "small" price increase means 5 percent, and the "nontransitory" period of time is one year. If a monopolist controls a set of products that allows the monopolist to profitably boost their price by at least 5 percent for at least a year, then the products compete in the same market.

To see how the SSNIP test works, suppose that Nike, Inc., proposes a merger with Adidas AG. Both Nike and Adidas produce sports shoes. But do "sports shoes" constitute a market? To help make this determination, economists at the antitrust agency pose the following: Suppose that *all* the makers of sports shoes—Nike and Adidas along with New Balance, Altra, Mizuno, Under Armour, and the others—became a single monopoly firm. Would this company be able to profitably raise the price of sports shoes by 5 percent for a year? If the answer is yes, then sports shoes constitute a market because consumers are not easily able to find a substitute for this product. But if the answer is no, then consumers are able to substitute another product so easily that sports shoes cannot be considered a market. Suppose that the agency economists conclude that the answer is no. In this case, the next step is to add another product—say, boat shoes. The economists then pose this: Suppose that all the makers of sports shoes *and* boat shoes become a monopoly. Is *this* monopoly able to profitably raise the price of these shoes by 5 percent for one year? If the answer is yes, then this combination is a market. If the answer is no, then this combination is not a market, and another product is included—say, sandals. The economists repeat this procedure until finally the answer is yes. At that point, they have defined the relevant market.

After determining the product and geographic markets, the agencies next examine the industry structure, attempting to determine the amount of competition. If sales are concentrated among just a few firms, the market is less competitive than if sales are distributed more widely. One tool the agencies use to determine the extent of competition in the market is the **Herfindahl–Hirschman Index** (HHI). The HHI is the sum of the squared market shares of the firms in the market, or, supposing there are N firms in the market,

$$HHI = \sum_{i=1}^{N} S_i^2$$

where S_i is the percentage market share of the *i*th firm. To avoid decimals, in the formula a 20 percent market share (or 0.20) is entered as 20. The larger the HHI is, the more sales are concentrated among a few firms and the less competitive the market is. Of course, the reverse is also true: The smaller the HHI is, the less sales are concentrated

SSNIP test Small but Significant Nontransitory Increase in Price; the test determines the smallest set of products that a monopolist needs to control in order to profitably increase the price by a small but significant amount above the competitive price for a nontransitory period of time.

Herfindahl–Hirschman Index: A measure of market concentration; it equals the sum of the squared market share percentages of firms in the market, $HHI = \sum_{i=1}^{N} S_i^2$.

<table>
<tr><td>DECISION
SNAPSHOT</td><td>The XM/Sirius Satellite Radio Merger</td></tr>
</table>

Suppose that it is the year 2007 and you are a manager at Sirius Satellite Radio, at that time one of the nation's two satellite radio providers. XM Satellite Radio and Sirius Satellite Radio announce that they intend to merge. In examining the merger, the crucial issue the DOJ must resolve is the definition of the market: Does the market in which XM and Sirius compete consist of just the satellite radio market, or is the market comprised of satellite radio, terrestrial radio, online streaming, smartphones, and tablets? What actions can you and your counterparts at XM take to increase the likelihood of the merger?

Answer

The DOJ will definitely challenge the merger if the market is defined to include only satellite radio because the merged firms will constitute a monopoly and therefore be in violation of the Sherman Act. If the market is determined to be larger, the merger will not result in a market with a single firm. While the government is debating the market definition, you and the managers of XM can (and should) provide analysis supporting a broader view of the market. For example, can your analysts determine that the cross-price elasticity of demand between satellite radio and terrestrial radio is positive and large?

Ultimately, the DOJ decided that the market in which XM and Sirius competed was the broader market comprised of satellite radio, terrestrial radio, online streaming, smartphones, and tablets, so it approved the merger.

among a few firms and the more competitive the market is.[3] For example, if the market is a monopoly, one firm has a market share of 100 percent, so the HHI equals $100^2 = 10,000$. If the market is competitive, sales are widely dispersed. In this case, suppose there are 100 firms in a market and each has a market share of 1 percent. In this case the HHI equals $1^2 + 1^2 + 1^2 + \ldots = 100$.

The antitrust agencies have issued guidelines based on the pre-merger HHI and the post-merger HHI. Although they occasionally change the guidelines, currently if the pre-merger HHI is less than 1,500, the market is considered competitive (unconcentrated), and a merger is unlikely to be challenged. If the pre-merger HHI is between 1,500 and 2,500, the market is considered moderately competitive (moderately concentrated). If a merger in this market raises the HHI by more than 100, the agencies worry about potential loss of competition. Finally, if the pre-merger HHI is greater than 2,500, the market is considered not competitive (highly concentrated), and mergers receive heightened scrutiny. In this case, the antitrust agencies will thoroughly scrutinize a merger that raises the HHI by between 100 and 200 points and are very likely to challenge a merger that raises the HHI by more than 200.

Antitrust agencies also use other information in assessing competitive effects, such as the ease of entry by totally new firms and those in related industries, possible merger

---

3 An alternative measure of competition is the 4-firm concentration ratio. The 4-firm concentration ratio equals the sum of the market shares of the four largest firms. This concentration ratio ranges from 100—in the case of a monopoly or an industry with four or fewer firms—to near 0—in the case of a perfectly competitive market.

efficiencies, and any more relevant factors. The antitrust agencies challenge the merger if they conclude that the merger likely will lead to less competition, increased prices, and reduced output.

Following a challenge to a merger, in most cases the would-be merger partners try to resolve the antitrust agency's concern. One approach is to spin off some assets to avoid reducing competition. For example, in 2012, when Anheuser-Busch InBev (ABI), the world's largest beer brewer, proposed merging with Grupo Modelo, Mexico's largest beer brewer, the Antitrust Division of the DOJ challenged the merger by filing an anti-trust lawsuit. The DOJ alleged that the merger would substantially decrease competition in the U.S. beer market. To salvage the merger, in 2013 ABI and Grupo Modelo agreed to sell to Constellation Brands all of Grupo Modelo's U.S. business. They also agreed to sell to that company the exclusive right to import Modelo's beers into the United States. With these sales and divestitures, the DOJ agreed to drop its opposition to the merger, believ-ing that these sales and divestitures would maintain competition in the beer market.

In other instances, a settlement may be quite difficult. For example, suppose that two acute care hospitals want to merge, but the merger appears to be anticompeti-tive. If each hospital operates on its own campus within a single facility, it would be difficult to overcome any antitrust objections because there is no obvious way to spin off a portion of the facility to a third party.

When antitrust agencies challenge a merger and a settlement cannot be reached, some managers attempt to proceed anyway. The appropriate agency then must go to court to block the merger by getting an injunction and initiating litigation. Because such litigation is expensive, risky, and very time consuming, the firms' managers very often abandon their merger plans.

Mergers in the Office-Supply Market

In 2013, Staples was the largest office-supply company, followed by Office Depot and OfficeMax. Then Office Depot proposed a merger with OfficeMax. After a seven-month investigation, the FTC approved the merger, and Office Depot purchased OfficeMax. Two years later, in 2015, Staples proposed to merge with Office Depot. This time, after a 15-month investigation, the FTC blocked the merger. Why did the FTC's decisions differ in the two cases?

Answer

The decisions differed because the FTC's view of the impact the mergers would have on market competition differed. The 2013 case involved the second- and third-largest firms, and even after the merger, the resulting firm was still smaller than Staples. The FTC also considered online retailers such as Amazon.com to be additional competitors. Consequently, the FTC's analysis concluded that after the merger, enough firms remained to ensure that the market continued to be competitive. The proposed 2015 merger, however, would have joined the two largest firms in the market, resulting in a firm that dwarfed its competitors. The FTC determined that such a large firm would have sufficient market power to raise the prices paid by large nationwide companies that need to acquire supplies at locations spread throughout the country. The FTC went to court to ask a judge to issue an injunction forbidding the merger until a trial could be held. When the judge announced that he would issue the injunction, the executives at Staples and Office Depot abandoned their attempted merger.

9.5 International Competition Laws

Learning Objective 9.5 Compare U.S. antitrust laws to competition laws in the European Union and China.

As a manager, you may work for a firm that conducts business abroad. Effective managers know how to operate and deal with the antitrust laws of different countries. In this section, you will learn some of the basics about antitrust laws in the European Union and China, two of the world's most important markets.

European Union Laws

The European Union (EU) consists of 28 nations in Europe, ranging as far east as Cyprus, as far south as Greece, as far north as Finland and Sweden, and as far west as Portugal. Most of the major economies of Europe, including Italy, France, and Germany, are members of the EU. Each member nation has its own national antitrust laws, called *competition laws*. However, the EU competition laws are the most significant such laws in Europe. The European Commission, comprised of one person from each member country, enforces EU competition laws.

EU competition laws are similar to U.S. antitrust laws, but there are some significant differences. In the United States, antitrust law focuses primarily on efficiency, consumer welfare, and the means used to monopolize a market. In the EU, the law concentrates more on considerations absent from U.S. law, including fairness, ethics, and the leveling of the competitive playing field. Additionally, EU competition laws impose special limitations on what the EU calls dominant firms.

The history of EU competition laws starts with the 1957 Treaty of Rome, signed by the six nations that founded the European Economic Community. As the group grew over the years to become the European Union, the treaty and related laws were amended. The most recent treaty is informally known as the Lisbon Treaty, but formally it is the Treaty on the Functioning of the European Union (TFEU).

Articles 101 and 102 of the TFEU contain the most important EU competition laws. Article 101 concerns the behavior of cartels and other groups of firms. Article 102 limits the actions of dominant firms. We begin by examining the EU laws concerning cartels and then move to the laws for dominant firms. We conclude by examining the EU policy toward mergers.

EU Policy on Cartels

Article 101 targets cartels and other groups of firms. Section 1 prohibits agreements among firms that prevent, restrict, or distort competition by any of the following:

a. Fixing prices
b. Limiting or controlling production or markets
c. Applying "dissimilar conditions to equivalent transactions with other trading partners"
d. Making contracts subject to obligations that have no connection with the original contract

Point c above refers to price discrimination, and point d pertains to tying or exclusive dealing contracts.

The Sherman Act makes price fixing and market division among competitors illegal per se in the United States; provisions a and b of Article 101 makes price fixing and market division effectively illegal per se in the European Union. Provision a is also interpreted to make resale price maintenance generally illegal if the selling firm has more than a 30 percent market share of the product being sold or the buying firm has more than a 30 percent market share of product purchases. The EU stance on resale price maintenance is definitely different from the U.S. view. As you learned earlier in the chapter, U.S. courts use a rule-of-reason approach when judging resale price maintenance. In the European Union, resale price maintenance is a "hardcore violation" of competition laws. As such, when challenged by legal authorities, firms using resale price maintenance must prove that the agreement creates substantial gains in efficiency in order for the agreement to be legal. Proving substantial gains in efficiency, however, is difficult.

Similar to U.S. law, EU competition law considers price discrimination, tying, and exclusive dealing contracts permissible as long as they do not restrict competition. For example, EU law allows small firms to price discriminate, enter into tying contracts, and create exclusive deals because EU law presumes their actions will have a negligible effect on competition. Additionally, Section 3 of Article 101 allows larger firms to engage in these practices if they increase economic efficiency and if consumers receive "a fair share of the resulting benefit."

The only sanctions for violating Article 101, or for violating *any* part of the EU competition laws, are fines imposed on the guilty firms. The courts cannot sentence managers or other individuals who violate the laws to jail. This difference may be the reason that the fines levied in the EU are often significantly larger than those imposed in the United States. Indeed, the EU can impose fines of up to 10 percent of a guilty firm's *worldwide* total revenue!

EU Policy on Dominant Firms

Article 102 applies to dominant firms and imposes special limitations on their behavior. The EU concept of a dominant firm is not the same as the textbook definition of monopoly. For example, EU policy almost automatically presumes that a single firm with a market share that exceeds 50 percent is dominant. In fact, EU law can consider a firm dominant with a market share as low as 35 to 40 percent if its competitors are numerous and small. Article 102 of the TFEU prohibits a dominant firm from doing any of the following:

a. Charging an unfair price or imposing other unfair trading conditions
b. Applying "dissimilar conditions to equivalent transactions with other trading partners, thereby placing them at a competitive disadvantage"
c. Making contracts subject to obligations that have no connection with the original contract

As noted above, point b refers to price discrimination, and point c pertains to tying contracts or exclusive deals. A dominant firm violates point b only if it places a trading partner at a competitive disadvantage.

In 2017 Google ran afoul of point a. Google, with a 92 percent share of global Internet searches, was deemed a dominant firm and fined $2.7 billion by the EU for unfairly favoring its shopping services over competitors when a potential customer searched for a product. Point a also forbids a dominant firm from selling its product at a price that is "unfairly" too high or buying at a price that is "unfairly" too low. This provision has no direct counterpart in U.S. antitrust law. In the United States, it is generally acceptable for a firm to charge a high price or buy at a low price regardless of market structure. Indeed, in a 2004 decision the U.S. Supreme Court said, "The mere possession of monopoly power, and the concomitant charging of monopoly prices, is not only not unlawful; it is an important element of the free-market system." The EU firmly rejects this view and prosecutes dominant firms for setting prices deemed unfairly high or buying at prices deemed unfairly low.

Provisions b and c also limit the behavior of dominant firms. Price discrimination, tying, and exclusive deals by a dominant firm are examined closely. For instance, tying by a producer that has more than a 30 percent share in the market for either the original product or the tied product is almost always challenged. One major goal of EU competition laws is to help integrate all national markets into a single community-wide market. Therefore, the authorities treat price discrimination by a dominant firm that involves selling products at different prices in different countries especially harshly.

EU Policy on Mergers

EU and U.S. competition laws both prohibit mergers that, using the words of the TFEU, "would significantly impede effective competition . . . in particular as a result of the creation or strengthening of a dominant position." In addition, EU and U.S. authorities typically reach similar conclusions about mergers, but when they disagree, more often than not it is the EU that prohibits the merger. Part of the EU philosophy is to protect competitors rather than competition, which reflects the greater emphasis of EU competition law on level playing fields and fairness.

EU competition authorities examine mergers between firms if they are incorporated in the EU, if they have subsidiaries or branches in the EU, or if their sales within the EU are large enough even if neither firm has subsidiaries or branches in Europe.[4] For example, the EU examined the proposed merger between General Electric (GE) and Honeywell even though both firms were incorporated in the United States. GE had a dominant market share in large jet engines, and Honeywell had a dominant market share in avionics, so there was not significant overlap in any one market. Remarkably, even though the United States approved the merger, the European Union blocked the merger because it was afraid the merged company would tie the sales of jet engines and avionics. The two companies did not merge.

Chinese Laws

China's most recent Anti-monopoly Law was adopted in 2008. The Chinese Ministry of Commerce has primary responsibility for enforcing the Anti-monopoly Law. China's laws are generally similar to EU competition laws. For example, like the EU, China outlaws price fixing and generally prohibits resale price maintenance. Firms that are convicted of violating the Chinese Anti-monopoly Law can face significant fines. One significant difference, however, is that China, like the United States, can imprison executives convicted of violating the Anti-monopoly Law.

As with EU law, Chinese law singles out dominant firms for special treatment. According to Chinese law, to be a dominant firm, an individual firm must have a market share of more than 50 percent, or be one of two firms that together have a market share of more than 66.6 percent, or be one of three firms that together have a market share of more than 75 percent. This definition means that a firm with, say, a 10 percent market share is a dominant firm if another firm in the market has a 56.6 percent share. A dominant firm (or firms) can face prosecution under the Anti-monopoly Law if it

- Sells at unfairly high prices.
- Uses predatory pricing.
- Creates tying arrangements.
- Engages in exclusive deals.

---

4 The EU sales requirement is complicated, but roughly speaking, the EU will claim jurisdiction if the combined sales of the merging firms exceed €250 million.

Dominant firms that violate these provisions run the risk of substantial fines. For example, China deemed Qualcomm a dominant firm and fined it $975 million for setting prices (royalty rates for its patents) that were considered "excessively high."

China's Anti-monopoly Law, however, has certain unique characteristics. For example, the Ministry of Commerce can declare a particular instance of resale price maintenance legal if it does not substantially restrict competition and consumers share in the benefits or if the actions further the social interest. Neither the United States nor the European Union considers furthering the social interest when examining alleged violations of policy.

Many of the large firms in the Chinese economy are state-owned enterprises. In theory, the Anti-monopoly Law applies to both state-owned and privately owned businesses. In practice, however, state-owned enterprises are often able to avoid prosecution or challenge under the Anti-monopoly Law, perhaps because the authorities believe the actions of state-owned enterprises further the social interest.

China also examines mergers for their effect on concentration within the Chinese market. The law does not specify the level of concentration that will be challenged, however, and too few merger decisions have been announced to determine whether there is a sharp cutoff. The law allows the Ministry of Commerce to consider, in addition to concentration, noneconomic effects, such as development of the national economy and any other relevant factors as determined by the State Council Anti-monopoly Enforcement Authority (a branch of the Chinese government).

China's Anti-monopoly Law applies to any behavior that affects markets within China. So China fines offending firms even if their behavior takes place outside China. For example, China fined six makers of LCD panels for fixing prices in China even though the price-fixing agreement was reached outside of China and none of the firms was incorporated in China. China also examines mergers of firms domiciled outside of China if they have more than $63 million in sales within China. The Chinese Ministry of Commerce examined the purchase of Motorola Mobility by Google even though both firms are incorporated in the United States. To approve the merger, the ministry forced Google to pledge to keep its Android operating system free to Chinese cell-phone producers for at least five years after the merger.

Worldwide Competition Laws

Competition laws and antitrust policies are not confined to the United States, the European Union, and China. Canada, Japan, South Korea, South Africa, India, Brazil, and about 90 other countries have competition laws. The specific prohibitions vary from country to country, but there are some fundamental similarities:

1. **Suspicion among regulators toward monopoly and dominance.** This fear of bigness is not always warranted, but everyone is concerned that very large firms can act unilaterally to raise prices, thereby harming consumers and decreasing economic welfare.
2. **Universal condemnation of cartels.** Almost by its definition, the purpose of a cartel is to reduce output and elevate price. Put differently, cartels want to emulate monopoly to the detriment of consumers and the economy. Other forms of collaborative conduct, such as resale price maintenance, are treated differently from one country to another, but actions that help create cartels do not fare well.

SOLVED
PROBLEM

Gazprom Gas Prices Create Indigestion in the European Union

The Russian government controls Gazprom, one of the world's largest firms. Gazprom exports natural gas from Siberia throughout Europe. It has a 30 percent share of the European market, but its market share in many countries is much higher: 100 percent in Finland, 78 percent in the Czech Republic, 60 percent in Hungary, 50 percent in Austria, and 36 percent in Germany. In 2012, the European Commission, the competition authority of the European Union, started to investigate whether Gazprom had set prices that were too high. Would antitrust authorities in the United States have decided to pursue a similar antitrust inquiry? Explain your answer.

Answer

Gazprom would almost surely *not* have faced a similar inquiry in the United States. The European Commission can prosecute dominant firms for abuse of their dominance, including setting prices deemed "too high." Gazprom meets the EU's definition of dominance in many countries. There is nothing similar to this dominance clause in U.S. antitrust law. In the United States, dominant firms can set whatever price they want.

9.6 Antitrust Policy

Learning Objective 9.6 Relate guidelines managers should use to avoid antitrust violations.

Understanding the basics of antitrust law is important to you, as a manager, on two fronts. First, you do not want to inadvertently violate the law. Such violation can harm both your company and your career. Generally, a prison sentence is not a positive on your resume. Second, you want to avoid being the victim of an antitrust violation. Remember that if another firm's antitrust violation harms your company, in the United States you have the possibility of collecting treble damages.

Using the Sherman Act and the Clayton Act

In nearly all circumstances, horizontal agreements among managers of rival firms are suspect and quite possibly illegal. If it reduces competition, a horizontal agreement exposes your firm to criminal fines and civil penalties and exposes you to fines and possible imprisonment.

From a profit-maximizing managerial perspective, however, a key question remains: Can price fixing, output restrictions, and other illegal acts be profitable? Let's return to the LCD screen price-fixing conspiracy discussed in Section 9.2 to explore this possibility. For simplicity, let's restrict our analysis to the U.S. market. The price-fixing agreement lasted about six years. Analysts estimated that total sales of LCD screens in the United States during the last year of the conspiracy were $23 billion. Because sales were increasing over time, you can approximate the total U.S. sales over the life of the conspiracy at $100 billion. If the scheme increased the firms' profits by 10 percent of their revenue, price fixing increased the firms' collective profit by approximately $10 billion. The firms have paid about $1.4 billion in government fines. They also face other, ongoing private suits asking for treble damages. If these damages amount to three times the government fines, the firms will pay a total of $5.6 billion in fines and damages, leaving them with an aggregate net profit of $4.4 billion. Most private suits, however, settle without going to trial, and the defendants pay less than treble damages. If the firms settle and pay an amount equal to the government-imposed fines ($1.4 billion), the total fines and damages will be $2.8 billion, leaving them with an aggregate net profit of $7.2 billion.

We hasten to add that we do *not* recommend that you engage in price fixing, output restrictions, or any of the other illegal acts discussed in this chapter. Illegal activities are unethical and subject *you* to the possibility of imprisonment and substantial personal fines. In fact, many of the managers of the LCD conspiracy were imprisoned. In addition, it should be obvious that not all price-fixing agreements or other illegal schemes will be profitable once the fines and damages are paid.

Using International Competition Laws

Managers within the United States are generally aware of U.S. antitrust law. As the brief overview in Section 9.5 demonstrated, knowledge of only U.S. antitrust laws is insufficient if your company operates abroad, is thinking of operating abroad, or is merging with another company that operates abroad. You need to be aware of the laws in each of the countries in which your company does business.

Many countries treat dominant firms differently than firms considered non-dominant, so you must be aware of whether your company is a dominant firm. This determination is not always as straightforward as it might seem. As you learned in Section 9.5, in some countries like China, *your* company might have a small market share, but if there is another company in the market with a large market share, the law can consider your company dominant because the two firms combined exceed the dominant-firm threshold. In this situation, the actions of your (smaller) firm are constrained by the laws limiting the behavior of dominant firms.

You must also avoid actions that are legal in the United States but that might violate competition laws in other countries. As described in Section 9.5, many instances of resale price maintenance that are legal in the United States are illegal in the European Union. As a manager, you must be careful that all of your actions within a market comply with the competition laws of the nation in which the market is located.

Antitrust Advice for Managers

Antitrust laws are complex. Unless you are an attorney specializing in antitrust or competition law, it is unreasonable to expect you to be aware of every legal wrinkle. But it is possible to provide some general advice about avoiding antitrust violations. Table 9.3 briefly summarizes actions you should avoid.

404 **CHAPTER 9** A Manager's Guide to Antitrust Policy

Table 9.3 Guidelines for Managers to Avoid Antitrust Violations

Avoid these topics when speaking with managers of competing firms.	Never agree with a competitor to undertake any of the following actions.	Avoid rule-of-reason violations with customers by asking an attorney to review these contractual areas.
• Your firm's prices, pricing policy, or other conditions of sale • Any competitor's prices, pricing policy, or other conditions of sale • Forthcoming changes in your firm's prices • Forthcoming changes in any competitor's prices • Your bids or your intent to bid or not to bid on a contract • Any competitor's bids or their intent to bid or not to bid on a contract • Your planned production amounts • Any competitor's planned production amounts	• Fix your prices or the conditions of sale such as credit terms, discounts, or freight allowances • Rig the amount you are bidding on contracts • Agree to bid or not to bid on a contract • Divide the market or sales territories • Sell or not sell to a particular customer or buy or not buy from a certain supplier • Adjust the amount you produce	• An agreement with a customer about the resale price the customer will charge for your product • An agreement with a customer about the markets in which the customer is allowed to resell your product • A tying sale with a customer • A requirements contract or an exclusive dealing contract with a customer • Any differences in the prices, terms of payment, or other conditions of sale for competing businesses

Revisiting How the Managers of Sea Star Line Walked the Plank

At the start of the chapter, you learned about the legal situation that managers at Sea Star Line and Horizon Lines faced. Let's apply the concepts of the chapter to explore what antitrust laws the companies violated and what penalties the courts imposed on the companies and managers.

The alleged actions by Sea Star Line and Horizon Lines that led to the indictment included a price-fixing agreement, bid rigging, and market division. All of these were designed to limit competition, violated Section 1 of the Sherman Act, and are considered illegal per se. When the DOJ suspected antitrust violations, its first move was to authorize an FBI raid of the companies' offices. The FBI then began interviewing managers to learn what they knew about the alleged conspiracy. Some of these individuals confessed immediately in order to lessen any punishment they faced. For example, Mr. Baci, by then the senior vice president of marketing, cooperated with the investigators and pled guilty at his first court appearance in October 2008.

Because the government had many cooperating witnesses, it was close to a foregone conclusion that the court would find Sea Star Line and Horizon Lines guilty of

Sherman Act violations, and indeed it did. Sea Star Line was fined $14.2 million and Horizon Lines $15.0 million.

The courts also found Mr. Baci and Mr. Peake guilty of Sherman Act violations. In 2009, Mr. Baci was fined $20,000 and sentenced to four years in prison. At the time, his prison sentence was the longest on record for an antitrust violation. That record, however, did not last. Following a two-week jury trial in early 2013, the jury found Mr. Peake guilty, and in December of that year, he was sentenced to the longest criminal sentence ever imposed in an antitrust case: a five-year term of imprisonment. The court also fined Mr. Peake $25,000.

For *your* career as a manager, the moral is straightforward: Violating antitrust laws can be detrimental to your business and put you in personal jeopardy. From the perspective of the two shipping firms, the story is not yet finished. The profit from the conspiracy probably exceeded Sea Star Line's $14.2 million and Horizon Lines' $15.0 million in fines. The companies, however, continue to battle their customers in court. The damages sought by the customers might be sufficient to bankrupt the firms. This outcome is not yet determined.

Summary: The Bottom Line

9.1 Overview of U.S. Antitrust Policy

- Antitrust laws are laws that promote competition.
- A monopoly harms society by raising the price above the competitive level and decreasing production below the competitive level, which creates a deadweight loss.
- In 1890, Congress passed the first federal U.S. antitrust law, the Sherman Act. In 1914, Congress passed the Clayton Act and the Federal Trade Commission Act (FTC Act).
- The FTC Act created the Federal Trade Commission (FTC), an agency that prohibits unfair or deceptive practices affecting consumers and unfair methods of competition among businesses.
- Companies that violate U.S. antitrust laws face criminal prosecution, including the risk of significant fines. Managers convicted of violating antitrust laws face fines and imprisonment.

9.2 The Sherman Act

- The first section of the Sherman Act prohibits "[e]very contract, combination in the form of trust or otherwise, or conspiracy, in restraint of trade." The Supreme Court has ruled that price-fixing agreements among competitors, bid rigging, output restrictions, and market division are per se illegal restraints of trade. However, U.S. courts judge resale price maintenance under the rule of reason.
- The second section of the Sherman Act makes the attempt to monopolize a felony. This section of the act applies to managers who use unreasonable exclusionary and predatory practices.

9.3 The Clayton Act

- The Clayton Act prohibits specific business practices that "substantially lessen competition or tend to create monopoly," including price discrimination, conditional sales, and certain mergers.
- Price discrimination is the practice of selling different units of the same product to the same consumer at different markups between the marginal cost and price or selling the same product to different customers at different markups between the marginal cost and the price.
- Conditional sales include territorial confinement, tying arrangements, exclusive dealing contracts, and requirements contracts.

9.4 U.S. Merger Policy

- When two large firms propose a merger, they must notify the Antitrust Division of the DOJ and the FTC, one of which will investigate to determine if the merger violates antitrust law.
- The agency must determine the market in which the firms compete and the impact on competition within that market if the merger is approved. A merger is disallowed if it is determined to have a substantially negative effect on competition.
- If the firms decide to proceed with a disallowed merger, the firms and the agency can litigate the case, but more commonly the firms try to resolve the agency's objections by spinning off or selling enough parts of the businesses to avoid the negative effect on competition.

9.5 International Competition Laws

- Nations and regions outside the United States also have antitrust laws, called competition laws.
- These laws are generally similar to those in the United States, but there can be some significant differences, such as the EU and Chinese legal restrictions on the behavior of dominant firms.

9.6 Managerial Application: Antitrust Policy

- To avoid antitrust violations, *never* discuss with a competitor your own or another competitor's current or forthcoming prices, terms of sale, plans to bid on contracts, or planned amount of production.
- To avoid antitrust violations, *never* agree with a competitor to fix your prices or other terms of sale, divide the market, or change the amount you produce.

Key Terms and Concepts

Antitrust laws	Illegal per se	Rule of reason
Bid rigging	Predatory pricing	SSNIP test
Exclusive dealing contract	Price discrimination	Territorial confinement
Herfindahl–Hirschman index	Price fixing	Tying arrangement
Horizontal agreement	Requirements contract	Vertical agreement
Horizontal merger	Resale price maintenance	Vertical merger

Questions and Problems

9.1 Overview of U.S. Antitrust Policy

Learning Objective 9.1 Explain the goals of the major U.S. antitrust laws and policies that promote competition.

1.1 Apple and Samsung are the two major producers of smartphones. If Apple agrees to acquire Samsung's Galaxy line, would that agreement be a horizontal agreement or a vertical agreement? Explain your answer.

1.2 In 1883, the Lightning Bolt train provided the only rail transportation between Cedar Rapids, Iowa, and Chicago. Farmers had no choice but to ship their corn to Chicago on the Lightning Bolt. At the time, some farmers claimed that the railroad charged "all that the traffic would bear." If you had been the manager of the Lighting Bolt, what rate would you have charged, and why? Is your rate "all that the traffic will bear"?

1.3 Figure (a) shows the market demand and supply curves for a product, and Figure (b) shows the marginal and average total cost curves for one of the 10 firms in the market. For simplicity, assume that all 10 firms have the same costs as shown in Figure (b).

　　a. What is the competitive equilibrium price and output for the market? For the firm?

What is each firm's economic profit? Explain how you determined your answers.

　　b. If the 10 firms form a cartel that operates as if it was a monopoly, what is the equilibrium price and output for the market? For the firm? Explain how you determined your answers.

　　c. If the firms' managers form a cartel that operates as if it was a monopoly and split the economic profit equally among the 10 firms, what is each firm's economic profit? Explain how you determined your answer.

　　d. Explain the incentive for the managers to form the cartel.

　　e. In the United States, if the firms are found guilty of forming a profit-maximizing cartel, what are the industry-wide damages?

9.2 The Sherman Act

Learning Objective 9.2 Provide examples of the restraints of trade and types of monopolization prohibited by the Sherman Act.

2.1 An industry is composed of eight firms. The CEOs of these firms realize that their industry creates air pollution and contributes to climate change. Dismayed at this thought, they meet

Accompanies problem 1.3.

Price (dollars per unit)

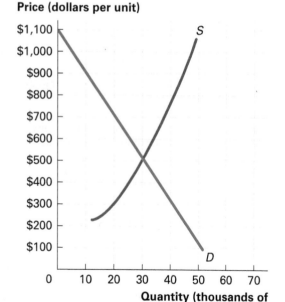

(a)

Price and cost (dollars per unit)

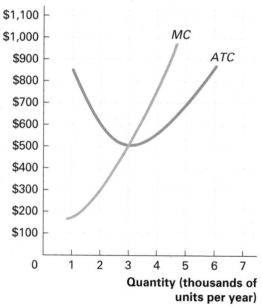

(b)

and decide to do something about it. But reducing pollution is expensive, so the CEOs agree to boost their prices by 2 percent and use the extra revenue to combat their pollution. All of the CEOs abide by this agreement and significantly decrease their contributions to air pollution. Would this agreement violate the Sherman Act? Why or why not?

2.2 The traditional Hawaiian art of weaving lauhala hats is nearly lost because so few people know how to do it. In a gesture of cultural support, the Chinese Restaurant Association pledges financial support to keep this art alive. Because the restaurant industry is fiercely competitive and no economic profits exist, each member of the association agrees to raise the price of its meals by 5 percent to provide the funds necessary to support the weavers. Will the Antitrust Division of the DOJ file an antitrust suit? If it does file a suit, what will be the result? Explain your answers.

2.3 Following the bursting of the housing bubble in 2007, there were many real estate foreclosures. Lenders accumulated a large inventory of foreclosed houses and decided to sell them at real estate auctions. In some places, bidder cartels were formed.
  a. How would such a cartel work to the advantage of the conspirators?
  b. Suppose that the cartel is uncovered and the courts convict the bidders of violating the Sherman Act. As a manager of one of the lenders, how would you calculate the damage that your firm suffered at the hands of the cartel?

2.4 When interest rates soared in the early 1980s, beer wholesalers began to worry about the cost of providing 30–45 days of interest-free credit to their retailer customers. As a group, the wholesalers decided to stop this practice. The retailers filed suit, claiming that the wholesalers had violated Section 1 of the Sherman Act. What do you think was the outcome of this case? Explain your answer.

2.5 Suppose that only Regal Entertainment Group had movie theaters in Gainesville but then Cinemark Theaters entered by opening a theater downtown. As a result of Cinemark's entry into the Gainesville market, competition for the exhibition rights to first-run films increased substantially. This competition caused the license fees, the revenue guarantees, and the advances paid to the distribution companies to escalate dramatically. The owners of the theaters found that competitive bidding caused their costs to rise and their profits to fall, as they had to pay

unreasonable prices to the distributors. They decided to solve this problem by splitting the films and not bidding competitively.
  a. Is this agreement an illegal restraint of trade? Why or why not?
  b. Who suffers if the theaters reduce their costs in this way?

2.6 "The managers of the two largest soft drink firms agree that one will stay out of Georgia and the other will stay out of Florida. Because this is not a price-fixing agreement, it does not violate the Sherman Act." Is this assertion correct? Why or why not?

2.7. Scott Crane is the CEO of Smashburger, a chain of burger restaurants. The superior quality of Smashburger's burger has caused it to be one of the most rapidly growing burger concepts. The firm's announced intention is to dominate the fast-food burger field. Smashburger is a fast-casual restaurant "designed to be every city's favorite place for burgers." Is Mr. Crane guilty of a Section 2 Sherman Act violation? Why or why not?

2.8 Your firm has entered the shampoo market. In order to get consumers to try your wonderful new product, you have decided to give away samples in 3-ounce bottles. Is this promotion illegal predatory pricing? Explain your answer.

2.9. In the figure, the firm's managers have set the firm's price, $400 per unit, below its average total cost, $600 per unit. Is this price predatory? Why or why not?

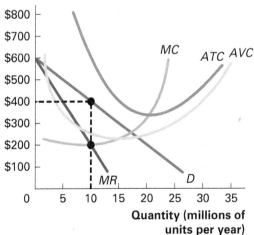

2.10 Under the *Brooke Group* ruling, to prevail in a predatory pricing case, a plaintiff must demonstrate the feasibility of recoupment. Why is proof of recoupment a sensible requirement?

9.3 The Clayton Act

Learning Objective 9.3 Describe the business practices prohibited by the Clayton Act.

3.1 If the marginal cost of serving different customers is the same but a company charges the customers different prices, the company is engaging in price discrimination. If a company charges different customers the same price even though the marginal cost of serving them is different, the company is also price discriminating. Provide two examples of each type of price discrimination, and indicate why each example is legal or illegal.

3.2 A gasoline station has a car wash that charges $8.95 for a wash. The station offers a free car wash with every fill-up. Is this offer a tying arrangement? If so, is it illegal under the Clayton Act? Explain your answers.

3.3 You are a newly hired manager of a biotech company with a patented drug that is administered intravenously. Your company sells the drug only if the purchaser also buys a needle to administer the drug. Your sales and economic profit are both substantial. Are there any circumstances under which you would suggest a change to any aspect of your new firm's policy? Any circumstances under which you would suggest no changes? Explain your answers.

3.4 Ford dealerships are franchises, owned by the dealers. The contract they have with Ford Motor Company generally obligates them to sell only cars produced by Ford. What type of contract have the dealers signed? Why are these contracts legal?

3.5 You are a manager of a paper producer. You buy the wood pulp necessary to produce paper from a number of local lumber mills. One day a couple of the managers of one of the mills come to you and offer to sell you all the wood pulp you need at a lower price than what you currently pay—but only if you agree to buy all of your wood pulp from them. What type of agreement are the managers proposing? Is the proposed contract definitely legal, definitely illegal, or somewhere in between? Explain your answer.

3.6 Why is the phrase "substantially lessen competition or tend to create a monopoly" important in interpreting the Clayton Act?

9.4 U.S. Merger Policy

Learning Objective 9.4 Explain how U.S. antitrust agencies determine whether to challenge a proposed merger.

4.1 Which of the following pairs of products are in the same market?
a. Pepsi-Cola and Coca-Cola
b. Pork and chicken
c. Beef and tofu
d. Rice and potatoes

Describe how the antitrust agencies make this determination.

4.2 When two firms propose a merger, the antitrust agencies must determine the market in which the firms compete. Explain how the antitrust agencies define the market and determine the market structure.

4.3 Calculate the Herfindahl–Hirschman Index (HHI) for each of the following markets. Using your results, arrange the markets from most competitive to least competitive.
a. The market has two firms, each with a market share of 50 percent.
b. The market has two firms, one with a market share of 90 percent and the other with a market share of 10 percent.
c. The market has 10 firms, 5 with a market share of 18 percent each and 5 with a market share of 2 percent each.
d. The market has 10 firms, 2 with a market share of 30 percent each and 8 with a market share of 5 percent each.

9.5 International Competition Laws

Learning Objective 9.5 Compare U.S. antitrust laws to competition laws in the European Union and China.

5.1 How does the antitrust treatment of price discrimination, tying contracts, and exclusive dealing contracts in the European Union compare with their treatment in the United States?

5.2 How does the antitrust treatment of resale price maintenance in the European Union compare with its treatment in the United States?

5.3 Observers frequently assert that EU competition authorities consider it important to preserve competitors rather than competition. How would this philosophy affect their decisions in merger cases?

5.4 In China, is it possible for a firm with a market share of 10 percent to be a dominant firm? Why or why not?

9.6 Managerial Application: Antitrust Policy

Learning Objective 9.6 Relate guidelines managers should use to avoid antitrust violations.

6.1 You are a top executive for Archer Western, a large road builder located in Atlanta. The CEO of one of your major competitors calls you. In the course of the conversation, the CEO suggests that the two of you stop bidding against each other in auctions for various construction projects. How should you respond to this suggestion? Explain your answer.

6.2 Google has hired you to consult on pricing strategies in Europe and the United States. The firm's Internet search market share is approximately 90 percent in Europe and approximately 70 percent in the United States.

    a. Do you advise Google's managers to be careful about how high they set the prices they charge their customers for advertising in the European market? In the U.S. market? Explain your answers, and discuss any consequences Google and its managers might face.

    b. Suppose that Google's research has determined that in Europe Italians are more likely to click on advertisements for local restaurants than Germans are. Further suppose that in the United States, Pennsylvanians are more likely to click than Floridians are. The more likely consumers are to click, the more valuable the advertisements are. Google's managers are considering setting a higher price for restaurant advertisements in Italy and Pennsylvania than in Germany and Florida. What do you advise about these pricing strategies, and why?

6.3 You are a manager at a sugar producer that is a dominant firm. Your firm sells sugar to both wholesalers and retailers. You charge a wholesaler a price so high that after it pays for packaging and distributing the sugar to retailers, the wholesaler's cost is too high to compete with you. Are you in violation of Article 102 of the TFEU, which sets out the European Union's competition laws? Explain your answer.

6.4 In the Chinese Internet search market, Baidu is the largest firm, with a market share of over 55 percent. Qihoo 360 is the second largest, with a 28 percent share, and Sogou is the third largest, with a 13 percent share. The Chinese competition authorities have accused Sogou of setting unfairly high prices. They have not, however, made similar charges against either Baidu or Qihoo 360. Presuming Sogou's prices are "unfairly high," do the managers of Sogou face a legal problem even though their market share is less than 15 percent? Explain your answer.

MyLab Economics Auto-Graded Excel Projects

9.1. There are a number of industries which have high levels of market concentration in the United States. Wholesalers and Supercenters, Department Stores, and Cigarette and Tobacco Production are three such industries. The data provided are market shares from firms in these industries, reported by IBIS World Database; hypothetical firms are added in cases where 100 percent of the market is not reported.

Use these data to complete the following steps and answer the following questions. Place your answers in the cells provided.

a. For each industry, find the 4-firm concentration ratio. Recall from Chapter 9 that this concentration ratio equals the sum of the market shares of the four largest firms in the market. Which industry appears most concentrated based on this measure?

b. For each industry, find the Herfindahl-Hirschman Index (HHI). Recall from Chapter 9 that this index is sum of the squared market shares for every firm in the market. Which industry appears most concentrated based on this measure?

c. In which industry would the Department of Justice (DOJ) be most likely to allow a merger?

d. Suppose Nordstrom and Husdon's Bay decide to merge. What would the new 4-firm concentration ratio and HHI for Department Stores equal if the merger goes through? Would antitrust agencies be likely to challenge this merger? Explain your answer.

e. Return to the original data and repeat part d for Macy's and Sears. Would antitrust agencies be likely to challenge this merger? Explain your answer.

9.1 AG. There are a number of industries that have high levels of market concentration in the United States. Wholesalers and supercenters, department stores, and cigarette and tobacco production are three such industries. The data provided are market shares from firms in these industries, reported by IBIS World Database; hypothetical firms are added in cases where 100 percent of the market is not reported.

Use these data to complete the following steps and answer the following questions. Place your answers in the cells provided.

a. For each industry, find the four-firm concentration ratio (CR_4). Recall from Chapter 9 that this concentration ratio equals the sum of the market shares of the four largest firms in the market. Which industry appears most concentrated based on this measure?

b. For each industry, find the Herfindahl–Hirschman Index (HHI). Recall from Chapter 9 that this index is the sum of the squared market shares for every firm in the market. Which industry appears most concentrated based on this measure?

c. In which industry would the Department of Justice be most likely to allow a merger?

d. Suppose that Nordstrom and Hudson's Bay decide to merge. What would the new CR_4

Accompanies problem 9.1.

	A	B	C	D	E	F	G	H
1	Wholesalers and Supercenters	Mkt Share		Department Stores	Mkt Share		Cigarettes and Tobacco	Mkt Share
2	Walmart	69.80%		Neiman Marcus	3.00%		Altria Group	49.10%
3	Costco Wholesale	17.40%		Hudson's Bay	4.60%		Reynolds American	32.90%
4	Meijer Inc.	3.50%		JCPenney	7.60%		Imperial Brands	7%
5	Target Corp.	2.90%		Nordstrom	8.80%		Vector Holding	2.60%
6	BJ's Wholesale Club	2.50%		Walmart	11.60%		Other Firm 1	2.40%
7	Other Firm 1	2.10%		Sears	13.20%		Other Firm 2	2.10%
8	Other Firm 2	1.80%		Macy's	15.70%		Other Firm 3	1.90%
9				Target	36.20%		Other Firm 4	1.50%
10							Other Firm 5	0.50%
11								

	A	B
14	a. Wholesalers	
15	Department	
16	Cigarettes	
17	Most Concentrated	
18	b. Wholesalers	
19	Department	
20	Cigarettes	
21	Most Concentrated	
22	c.	
23	d. CR_4	
24	HHI	
25	Challenge?	
26	e. CR_4	
27	HHI	
28	Challenge?	
29		

and HHI for department stores be if the merger goes through? Would antitrust agencies be likely to challenge this merger? Explain your answer.

e. Return to the original data, and repeat part d for Macy's and Sears. Would antitrust agencies be likely to challenge this merger? Explain your answer.

Introduction

The Sherman Act prohibits managers of different companies from colluding to fix the prices of a good or service. Violators are subject to fines and other sanctions. But suppose that the managers themselves do not directly fix the prices; suppose that instead they use other means to limit price competition and collude indirectly. Do such alternative mechanisms stand up to Supreme Court scrutiny? Can profit-maximizing managers create alternative, third-party groups that allow them to fix prices? An actual case will help answer these questions. It is followed by another case for you to consider.

Limiting Price Competition Using a Third Party

Government agencies decide when a city or state needs a bridge. When a government agency makes this determination, it needs to hire civil engineers to help prepare design plans and construct the bridge. The agency usually determines which engineering firms are qualified to provide the requisite services. Then, in an effort to minimize the cost of bridge construction, the agency generally solicits competitive bids from these rival engineering firms. But at one point in time, the National Society of Professional Engineers (NSPE) thwarted the attempt to obtain competitive bids. At that time, the NSPE Code of Ethics required each engineering firm to market its services on the basis of quality and past performance, but an ethical canon prohibited engineering firms from competitive bidding. In particular, the Code of Ethics said, "The Engineer will not compete unfairly with another engineer by attempting to obtain employment or . . . professional engagements by competitive bidding." In addition, the Code of Ethics required the government agency to select the engineering firm it would hire before the firm's managers could even discuss the fees it would charge. So when agencies attempted to solicit bids, each engineering firm dutifully informed them that the NSPE Code of Ethics prevented them from participating. As you might expect, the absence of competitive bidding and the inability of government officials to discuss fees with the firms until after the agency had selected the firm resulted in higher fees.

When the U.S. Department of Justice (DOJ) challenged these practices, the NSPE explained that competitive bidding was undesirable, arguing that it could lead to reduced fees that would encourage firms to produce low-quality designs or even faulty designs, which could

endanger the public, or to spend less time optimizing designs, which could lead to overengineered bridges that were too expensive. According to the NSPE, preventing the engineering firms from competing in the auction arena was for the public good. The DOJ disagreed, arguing that requiring the agency to select the engineering firm before starting price negotiations effectively gave the chosen firm significant market power to set a high price. The DOJ also said that prohibiting auctions allowed the firms to limit price competition. According to the DOJ, both effects meant that the Code of Ethics violated the Sherman Act.

The Supreme Court agreed with the DOJ. In its decision on April 25, 1978, the Court explained that the agreement violated the basic premise of the Sherman Act that competition among firms is good for society. The Court concluded that relief from the obligation to compete must come from new laws passed by Congress because existing laws made no exception for "professional ethics."

From a managerial perspective, this Supreme Court ruling prevents managers from making an end-run around the Sherman Act's prohibition against price fixing by using a third party—in this case, the NSPE.

Your Case

The National Collegiate Athletic Association (NCAA) is a nonprofit association that regulates many aspects of its members' collegiate sports behavior. Although there are other collegiate athletic organizations, the NCAA is by far the dominant one; nearly 1,300 colleges and universities in the United States and Canada are members. Member schools must abide by the NCAA rules or face financial and/or eligibility sanctions. In extreme cases, the NCAA can ban a school from participating in a particular sport (called the "Death Penalty"). It can also fine schools, as when Pennsylvania State University was fined $60 million for its part in a child molestation case centered around a former football coach.

Many of the NCAA rules and regulations have the effect of increasing the member schools' "profit" by raising the schools' revenue or lowering their costs. Rules that lower costs include the following:

- The NCAA has a sport-by-sport limit on the number of scholarships a school may award—for example, fencing is allowed a maximum of 4.5 scholarships and ice hockey 18.
- The NCAA limits what a school may spend on a recruit and his or her parents during recruiting visits.

A rule that raises revenue is as follows:

- The NCAA sponsors annual basketball tournaments for men and women attending Division 1 schools (346 colleges and universities that generally have the largest sports programs). Teams that are selected for the tournament are required to play and cannot play in any alternative tournament. The NCAA then distributes most of the (monopoly) profit from the tournaments (and its other sporting endeavors) to the Division 1 schools, over $500 million in 2014.

In the past, the NCAA also has had rules designed to increase revenue or lower costs that have been determined to violate antitrust laws. For example:

- When television was initially becoming widely available, the NCAA required member schools to give it the sole right to determine which college football games would be televised. The NCAA severely limited the number of televised games and, for the most part, did not allow individual colleges to sell the broadcast rights to their games. The television networks were forced to bid for the NCAA's contract to televise games. The NCAA's monopoly position lasted until the University of Georgia and the University of Oklahoma filed suit, alleging that the NCAA's rule violated the Sherman Act's prohibitions about output restrictions and price fixing. The Supreme Court agreed with the universities and required the NCAA to allow colleges to sell broadcast rights.

  After colleges were allowed to sell rights to their games, the market for televising college football games became more competitive. As economic theory teaches, the number of games broadcast increased dramatically, and the price the television networks paid for broadcast rights fell. The immediate effect was to reduce the colleges' combined revenue from the games.
- College basketball teams hire assistant coaches to help the head coach. In 1992, the NCAA imposed a rule that reduced the maximum number of assistant coaches a school could hire from five to four and limited the maximum salary a school could pay to the fourth coach to $12,000. This rule was aimed at controlling the colleges' costs. A group of coaches filed suit, alleging that the NCAA policy violated Section 1

of the Sherman Act by fixing the salaries that colleges and universities could pay. The NCAA defended its policy by asserting that it merely lowered the school's costs and did not restrain trade or commerce. The courts rejected the NCAA's position and overturned the limits on assistant coaches' salaries.

One of the foundational beliefs of the NCAA is amateurism. So NCAA rules prohibit its members from paying student athletes to play. While ensuring amateurism, this policy also reduces the schools' costs. Colleges, however, do give scholarships to student athletes that fully pay the cost of attending the college for which they play. And, of course, a student athlete can graduate with his or her degree.

NCAA rules also forbid student athletes from signing with an agent to market a student athlete's ability until after the completion of that athlete's last intercollegiate contest. In addition to helping guarantee amateurism, this regulation raises the schools' revenue by making it more difficult for star student athletes to leave college to turn pro. This increases the demand to see the college games.

Your Decisions

1. Do you think either of the NCAA's amateurism policies noted above violates antitrust laws? Explain your answer.
2. As an executive working for a sports agency, what would you assert about the NCAA's amateurism rules? If you filed suit against the NCAA, what antitrust law(s) would you claim the NCAA violates?
3. As an executive working for the NCAA, what would you assert about the NCAA's amateurism rules? If a sports agency files a suit alleging that one or both of the NCAA regulations explained above violate an antitrust law, what points would you use to defend the organization?

Sources: Jason Kersey, "Exploring the History of College Football Media Rights," *Oklahoman*, August 28, 2013, http://www.forbes.com/sites/marcedelman/2012/12/19/why-a-salary-cap-on-ncaa-coaches-is-illegal/#23e862641b8a; Kirk Johnson, "Assistant Coaches Win N.C.A.A. Suit; $66 Million Award," *New York Times*, May 5, 1998; Taylor Branch, "The Shame of College Sports," *Atlantic*, October 2011; Steve Berkowitz, "NCAA Nearly Topped $1 Billion in Revenue in 2014," *USA TODAY Sports*, March 11, 2015.

CHAPTER 10

Advanced Pricing Decisions

Learning Objectives

After studying this chapter, you will be able to:

10.1 Explain how the different types of price discrimination can boost a firm's profit.

10.2 Analyze how peak-load pricing can increase profit for a firm that faces predictable changes in demand.

10.3 Explain how two-part pricing, all-or-nothing offers, and commodity bundling can raise a firm's profit.

10.4 Apply the different advanced pricing techniques to increase economic profit.

Managers at the Turtle Bay Resort Think Kama'aina Pricing Is Par for the Course

Turtle Bay Resort is a luxury resort in Hawaii with a golf course designed by Arnold Palmer. Recently the resort underwent an extensive renovation. Suppose you are one of the managers who must determine the new price to charge for a round of golf.

In Hawaii, local residents, known as *Kama'aina* or "children of the land," often pay far less than visitors for a wide array of products. Charging Hawaiian residents less for the same product is called Kama'aina pricing. For example, Hard Rock Cafe offers a 15 percent Kama'aina discount, and Five Palms Beach Grill offers a 20 percent discount. Some hotels, such as Marriott, also offer residents substantial discounts.

As a Turtle Bay Resort manager, do you want to use Kama'aina pricing? If so, why do you want to give local residents a price break? At the end of this chapter, you will be able to answer these questions and explain why charging locals a lower price can increase a firm's profits.

Sources: http://www.turtlebayresort.com/; Loretta Winters and Herman DuBose, *New Faces in a Changing America: Multiracial Identity in the 21st Century* (Thousand Oaks, CA: Sage, 2002), 239; *Maui Time* 19, no. 12 (September 3, 2015): 10; http://www.marriotthawaii.com/kamaaina-deals/.

Introduction

To this point in the text, you have read about relatively uncomplicated pricing schemes in order to understand the basics of profit maximization. For example, consider Figure 10.1, which shows the situation faced by managers at an ice cream store like Häagen-Dazs. The fact that the demand curve is downward sloping indicates this firm has some market power. The managers maximize profit by producing the quantity where $MR = MC$ and by setting the highest price that allows them to sell that quantity. In the figure, the managers maximize profit by producing 200,000 scoops of ice cream per year and setting the price as $2.50 per scoop. The firm makes an economic profit equal to the area of the green rectangle.

In Chapter 2, you learned that consumer surplus equals the difference between the maximum price customers are willing to pay for each unit of a product (such as each scoop of ice cream) and the price they actually pay, summed over the quantity of

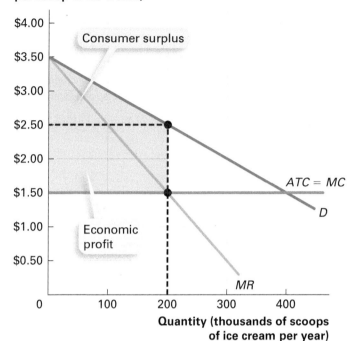

Price and cost (dollars per scoop of ice cream)

Figure 10.1 Consumer Surplus = Potential Profit

The managers at an ice cream store maximize profit by producing the quantity where $MR = MC$ (200,000 scoops per year) and then using the demand curve to set the price ($2.50 per scoop). Although the firm makes an economic profit equal to the area of the green rectangle, the chosen price and quantity leave the customers with consumer surplus equal to the area of the blue triangle. More sophisticated pricing schemes can transfer some of the consumer surplus to the firm, thereby increasing its economic profit.

units purchased. In Figure 10.1, the consumer surplus equals the area of the blue triangle. The existence of any consumer surplus in the market means that there is the potential for the firm to increase its profit because it means that customers are willing to pay a higher price than what they are currently charged. Take the consumer surplus on the 100,000th scoop. For this particular scoop, the consumer surplus equals $3.00 (the maximum price a customer is willing to pay for that scoop) minus $2.50 (the price he or she actually pays), or $0.50. Suppose that the managers at the store can somehow set the price of the 100,000th scoop (and only the 100,000th scoop) equal to $3.00, rather than $2.50. The demand curve shows that at this higher price, the customer will still buy the 100,000th scoop even though there is no consumer surplus on that scoop. The higher price has changed $0.50 of consumer surplus into $0.50 more revenue for the firm with no change in cost. The result? The firm makes $0.50 more profit. The lesson is clear: The straightforward pricing scheme used so far leaves untouched a source of potential profit. The prospect of losing profit dismays profit-maximizing managers, who want to change as much consumer surplus as possible into additional profit.

The five advanced pricing methods covered in this chapter—price discrimination, peak-load pricing, two-part pricing, all-or-nothing offers, and commodity bundling—all have the same general goal: converting consumer surplus into additional economic profit. Unfortunately, however, managers cannot use these five techniques in just any market because all require some specific market conditions. One condition is immediate and common to all advanced pricing methods: The firm must possess market power. In other words, the firm must be able to determine what price to charge for its product. But all the methods have additional requirements beyond possessing market power.

To explain these advanced pricing methods, Chapter 10 includes four sections:

- **Section 10.1** explains the different forms of the most common advanced pricing method, price discrimination.
- **Section 10.2** presents peak-load pricing, an advanced pricing method that managers can use if their firms face predictable sequential changes in demand.
- **Section 10.3** deals with three nonlinear pricing strategies, all of which include some restrictions on buying the product: two-part pricing, all-or-nothing offers, and commodity bundling.
- **Section 10.4** demonstrates how using these advanced pricing methods can help you make better, more profitable managerial decisions.

10.1 Price Discrimination

Learning Objective 10.1 Explain how the different types of price discrimination can boost a firm's profit.

Price discrimination The practice of charging different customers different prices that are not based on differences in marginal costs.

In many cases, firms sell their output in a single market and charge all customers the same price for all of the units purchased. As Figure 10.1 shows, however, this pricing method leaves customers with a consumer surplus that managers would like to convert into economic profit. Managers often can use price discrimination to obtain at least some of the consumer surplus. **Price discrimination** occurs when a firm charges different customers different prices that are not based on differences in marginal costs.

Price discrimination is a common business practice. It occurs when Häagen-Dazs ice cream stores charge one price for a single scoop of ice cream, a lower price for a second scoop, and a still lower price for a third scoop or when Yankee Candle runs specials in which a customer can buy one candle and get a second one for 50 percent off. Price discrimination is also at work in the Magic Kingdom: Walt Disney World, in Orlando, Florida, sells a one-day regular ticket to non-Florida residents for $107 and a similar ticket to Florida residents for $99. Managers engage in price discrimination for a very simple reason: It can increase profit. Economists differentiate among three types of price discrimination: first-degree, second-degree, and third-degree price discrimination.

First-Degree Price Discrimination

First-degree price discrimination The practice of charging every customer the maximum price that customer is willing to pay for every unit purchased.

First-degree price discrimination occurs when a firm charges every customer the highest price that customer is willing to pay for every unit purchased. In this case, the customers receive no consumer surplus. In reality, of course, this level of price discrimination is impossible. New-car dealerships perhaps come closer to first-degree price discrimination than any other business because they train their salespeople to evaluate each customer to try to determine the highest price that particular customer will pay. Although successful salespeople are good at this, in reality the dealership can never actually achieve perfect first-degree price discrimination. Nonetheless, understanding first-degree price discrimination is useful because it shows the maximum profit a firm could gain from its customers. In this sense, first-degree price discrimination sets a goal for managers.

Figure 10.2 compares the profit made by a company when it charges everyone the same price for every unit purchased (Figure 10.2[a]) to the profit made by the company when it uses first-degree price discrimination (Figure 10.2[b]). In Figure 10.2(a), the managers at the ice cream store sell all 200,000 scoops of ice cream at the same

Figure 10.2 How First-Degree Price Discrimination Increases Economic Profit

(a) **Single Price**
If the managers of the ice cream store can set only one price, to maximize profit they produce 200,000 scoops of ice cream and set a price of $2.50 per scoop. In this benchmark case, the consumer surplus is equal to the area of the blue triangle, $100,000, and the economic profit is equal to the area of the green rectangle, $200,000.

(b) **First-Degree Price Discrimination**
If the managers at the ice cream store can use first-degree price discrimination, they maximize profit by producing the quantity where $MR = MC$ (400,000 scoops per year) and setting the highest price a customer is willing to pay for each scoop produced, which ranges from $3.50 to $1.50. Customers receive no consumer surplus. The use of first-degree price discrimination transfers the *entire* potential consumer surplus to the firm, increasing its total economic profit to $400,000.

Price and cost (dollars
per scoop of ice cream)

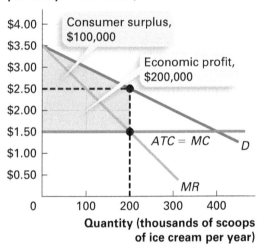

Price and cost (dollars
per scoop of ice cream)

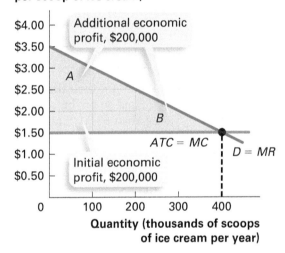

price of $2.50 per scoop and make an economic profit of $200,000. Figure 10.2(b) shows what happens when the managers use first-degree price discrimination. The first step in the analysis behind Figure 10.2(b) is to determine the profit-maximizing quantity when using first-degree price discrimination. To answer that question, notice that when a firm using first-degree price discrimination sells an additional unit of output, it does not change the prices charged for previous units sold. Consequently, the additional revenue the store gains when it sells another scoop of ice cream (its marginal revenue) equals the price of the newly sold unit, so $MR = P$. For any quantity, the demand curve shows the price, so the demand curve is the same as the firm's marginal revenue curve. Accordingly, Figure 10.2(b) labels the demand curve as $D = MR$. Now, as usual, the managers maximize profit by producing the quantity that sets $MR = MC$, which in the figure is 400,000 scoops per year. The next step is to determine the price the company sets. In this case, however, the company will not set just one price. For each scoop they sell, they charge the highest price a customer is willing to pay for *that* scoop, so the price ranges from $3.50 for the first scoop down to $1.50 for the 400,000th scoop.

Because the price is the highest each customer is willing to pay for each scoop, customers receive *no* consumer surplus. Instead, first-degree price discrimination transfers the *entire* amount of (potential) consumer surplus to the firm as additional economic profit, increasing its total economic profit to $400,000. Comparing the firm's profit from setting a single price (Figure 10.2[a]) to that from using first-degree price discrimination (Figure 10.2[b]) shows that first-degree price discrimination increases the firm's economic profit by an amount equal to areas A plus B. Because the firm absorbs all of the consumer surplus, first-degree price discrimination gives the firm the maximum possible economic profit.

Second-Degree Price Discrimination

Second-degree price discrimination The practice of charging the same customer different prices for different units of the product.

Although first-degree price discrimination is ideal from the firm's standpoint, in reality it is impossible to attain because it is impossible to determine the precise maximum price every customer is willing to pay. More realistic is second-degree price discrimination. A firm using **second-degree price discrimination** charges the same customer different prices for different units of the product. The "buy-one, get-one at a reduced price" signs you notice at stores are examples. Second-degree price discrimination is similar to first-degree price discrimination because customers pay higher prices for the first units they buy. It differs because the price(s) customers pay may not be the highest that they are willing to pay.

Let's continue the ice cream store example by specifying a bit more about the demand. Suppose that the store has 100,000 customers who each visit once a year. For simplicity, assume that these 100,000 customers are willing to pay between $3.50 and $3.00 for their first scoop. In other words, some are willing to pay $3.40, others $3.15, and so on, but all are willing to pay at least $3.00, and none is willing to pay more than $3.50. Similarly, assume that the customers are willing to pay between (just under) $3.00 and $2.50 for their second scoop and between (just under) $2.50 and $2.00 for their third scoop. The demand curve shown in Figure 10.3 reflects this demand from the 100,000 customers. Further suppose that the store will sell single-scoop, double-scoop, and triple-scoop cones.

Figure 10.3(a) repeats the case shown in Figure 10.2(a), in which the managers set a single, profit-maximizing price of $2.50 per scoop. At that price, the customers buy a two-scoop cone for $5.00, and the store makes an economic profit of $200,000. In Figure 10.3(b), the demand curve shows that the store can sell the 100,000 customers three scoops of ice cream if the managers use second-degree price discrimination by setting a price of $3.00 for the first scoop, $2.50 for the second scoop, and $2.00 for the third scoop. The store sells 100,000 first scoops at $3.00 per scoop, 100,000 second scoops at $2.50 per scoop, and 100,000 third scoops at $2.00 per scoop. With these prices, each customer buys a triple-dip cone and pays $7.50.

In Figure 10.3(b), the consumer surplus is the sum of the areas of the three small blue triangles above the price, labeled a for the first scoop, b for the second scoop, and c for the third scoop. The total consumer surplus is less with second-degree price discrimination ($75,000 in Figure 10.3[b]) than with a single price ($100,000 in Figure 10.3[a]). While customers lose, the ice cream store gains additional economic profit. For the first 100,000 scoops, the store now receives $3.00 per scoop instead of the $2.50 it received when it charged a single price. The firm's profit for the first scoop increases by $0.50 per scoop × 100,000 scoops = $50,000, the area of the light green rectangle labeled A. For the second 100,000 scoops, the price and profit have not changed from the single-price scenario. Finally, by engaging in second-degree price discrimination, the store sells an additional 100,000 scoops that it did not sell in the single-price scenario. Each of the third scoops sold gives the store an additional $2.00 in revenue (the marginal revenue) at an additional cost of $1.50 (the marginal cost), yielding $0.50 in profit. The increase in profit from these 100,000 scoops is $0.50 × 100,000 scoops = $50,000, equal to the area of the light green rectangle labeled B. By using second-degree price discrimination, the managers increase their total economic profit by the sum of areas $A + B$, or $100,000, for a total economic profit of $300,000.

Figure 10.3 How Second-Degree Price Discrimination Increases Economic Profit

(a) **Single Price**

If the ice cream store's managers can set only one price, to maximize profit they sell 200,000 scoops of ice cream at a price of $2.50 per scoop. In this benchmark case, the consumer surplus is equal to the area of the blue triangle, $100,000, and the economic profit is equal to the area of the green rectangle, $200,000.

(b) **Second-Degree Price Discrimination**

If the ice cream store's managers engage in second-degree price discrimination, they set a price of $3.00 for the first scoop of ice cream, $2.50 for the second scoop of ice cream, and $2.00 for the third scoop of ice cream. The consumer surplus is the sum of the areas of the three blue triangles, $a + b + c$, $75,000. The consumer surplus with second-degree price discrimination is less than the consumer surplus when the firm sets a single price. The firm's economic profit increases by the sum of the areas of the two light green rectangles, $A + B$, for a total economic profit of $300,000.

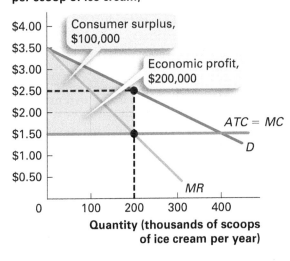

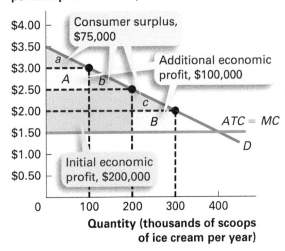

Similar to first-degree price discrimination, second-degree price discrimination converts consumer surplus into additional economic profit. However, second-degree price discrimination has left customers with some consumer surplus. Because second-degree price discrimination changes less of the consumer surplus into economic profit, the increase in economic profit is less than with first-degree price discrimination. Of course, in reality, second-degree price discrimination is feasible, while first-degree price discrimination is not.

Third-Degree Price Discrimination

The last type of price discrimination is third-degree price discrimination. **Third-degree price discrimination** occurs when a firm sells the same unit of a product to different groups of customers at different prices. For example, movie theaters often give senior citizens a break by selling tickets to them at a lower price than they charge younger adults. For an example of this "generosity," consider the town of Starke, the county seat of Bradford County in Florida. Starke has one movie theater, the Florida Twin Theatre. The closest alternative movie theater is about 40 miles away, so it is reasonable to assume that the Florida Twin Theatre has some market power. The price of a movie ticket is $7.00 for younger adults

Third-degree price discrimination The practice of charging different groups of customers different prices for the same product.

and $6.00 for senior citizens. Why do Florida Twin's managers decide to offer seniors a lower price? To explore this question, let's suppose that you are a manager of a similar theater.

You can understand your firm's generosity by extending the basic model of a monopoly presented in Chapter 6. That model has a firm with a single-production facility selling its output in a single market. Although your theater has a single production facility, the theater, it is actually selling its output in two separate markets with different demands—one market for younger adults (the adult market) and another for senior citizens (the senior market). These markets differ because their demands differ. Movie studios aim few movies at the senior market, and senior citizens have lower average incomes than younger adults, so the price of a movie is a greater fraction of a senior citizen's income than that of an adult. These factors make the senior demand more elastic than the adult demand. While the demands differ, it is not this factor that most complicates the analysis, however. The complicating factor is the link between the markets: the firm's production. Changing the production in one market affects the marginal cost of producing for the other market. So as a manager, you must answer two questions, the first about the combined markets and the second about the individual markets:

1. How much *total* output should the firm produce?
2. How much of the total output should the firm sell in each market?

Once these two questions are answered, you can set the prices in the two markets according to relevant demand.

Let's begin by examining the second question. Suppose that the marginal revenue from selling a unit in the adult market (MR_A) is greater than the marginal revenue from selling a unit in the senior market (MR_S): $MR_A > MR_S$. Now use marginal analysis, and consider switching a unit from the senior market to the adult market. Losing a sale in the senior market loses MR_S of revenue, but gaining a sale in the adult market gains MR_A of revenue. This switch increases your firm's total revenue because the gain in revenue exceeds the loss. Production has not changed, so the firm's cost remains the same. Therefore, transferring the unit from one market to the other increases the firm's profit. *Anytime* a firm is selling its product in more than one market and the marginal revenue from selling in one market exceeds that in another market, moving a unit from the low-return market to the high-return market increases the firm's profit. Allocating production so that the marginal revenues are the same in every market maximizes profit because only then is it impossible to increase profit by switching a unit from one to the other. So, in the case of your theater, you must divide the total quantity of tickets sold so that $MR_A = MR_S$.

You can now use Figure 10.4 to answer the first question: How much total output should the firm produce to maximize profit? The answer, as always, is the quantity that sets MR equal to MC. With two sources of demand for movies (the demand from adults and the demand from seniors), there are two sources of marginal revenue. Figure 10.4(a) shows the demand curve (D_A) and corresponding marginal revenue curve (MR_A) for adults, and Figure 10.4(b) shows the demand curve (D_S) and corresponding marginal revenue curve (MR_S) for seniors. To determine the profit-maximizing *total* quantity, the managers must use the *overall* marginal revenue curve for adults and seniors. At any value of marginal revenue, the overall quantity equals the quantity of tickets with that marginal revenue from adults (MR_A) plus the quantity of tickets with that same marginal revenue from seniors (MR_S). For example, when the marginal revenue equals $3 per ticket, the total quantity of tickets is 300 tickets per day from adults (shown by the gray arrow in Figure 10.4[a]) plus

Figure 10.4 Sources of Demand and the Resulting Marginal Revenue Curve

(a) Adult Demand
The adult demand curve is D_A, and the adult marginal revenue curve is MR_A.

(b) Senior Demand
The senior demand curve is D_S, and the senior marginal revenue curve is MR_S.

(c) Overall Marginal Revenue
The overall marginal revenue curve, $MR = MR_A + MR_S$, is the marginal revenue curve for the total market. The curve equals the sum of the adult marginal revenue curve and the senior marginal revenue curve. The marginal cost curve is MC. The firm's profit-maximizing quantity is 250 tickets per day because this quantity sets $MR = MC$.

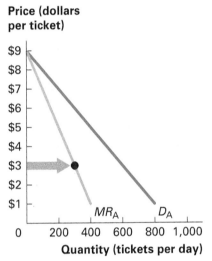

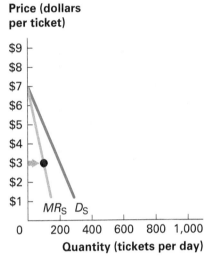

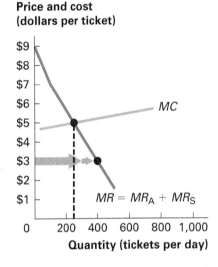

100 tickets per day from seniors (shown by the gray arrow in Figure 10.4[b]), for a total of 400 tickets per day (recorded as the sum of the two gray arrows in Figure 10.4[c]). In Figure 10.4(c), the curve labeled $MR = MR_A + MR_S$ is the overall marginal revenue curve. The overall marginal revenue curve shows how the firm's total marginal revenue changes when the firm changes its production.

Figure 10.4(c) also includes the marginal cost curve for your theater. You can now apply the basic principle of profit maximization: The quantity produced should be the amount that sets the marginal revenue of an additional unit equal to the marginal cost of that unit. In Figure 10.4(c), this quantity is 250 tickets. This is the answer to the first question: To maximize profit, your theater should sell 250 tickets each day.

Now that you have the total quantity, you need to determine the allocation of these tickets across the two markets. At the profit-maximizing quantity, the marginal revenue is $5 per ticket. From Figure 10.4(a), you can see that in the adult market the marginal revenue is $5 per ticket when selling 200 adult tickets and the demand curve shows you can sell these tickets for a price of $7. Figure 10.4(b) shows that in the senior market the marginal revenue is $5 per ticket when selling 50 senior tickets and these tickets can be sold for a price of $6. So to maximize its profit, each day your theater should sell 200 tickets to adults at $7 and 50 tickets to seniors at $6.

By maximizing its profit in the adult market and the senior market, the theater has maximized its *total* profit. Any other combination of quantities and prices in the two markets will give it a smaller total profit.

Price Markup in Each Market

In Figure 10.4, the price adults pay exceeds the price seniors pay. In Section 6.2, you learned that the markup of price above marginal cost (and marginal revenue) depends on the price elasticity of demand. To determine the price elasticity of demand for adults and seniors, you can use Equation 3.4 from Chapter 3. For a linear demand curve, this equation shows that $\varepsilon = |b \times (P/Q^d)|$, where b is the change in the quantity demanded brought about by a \$1 change in the price (which is 100 tickets for adults and 50 tickets for seniors). Because the demand curves are linear, the price elasticity of demand is different at different points on the curves. Use the price of \$3 as an example. At that price, the price elasticity of demand for adults is equal to $|100 \times (\$3/600)| = 0.5$, and the price elasticity of demand for seniors is $|50 \times (\$3/200)| = 0.75$. Indeed, at *any* price you select, $\varepsilon_A < \varepsilon_S$. In general, as a manager, you should charge a higher price in the market that is less responsive to price changes (the market with the smaller price elasticity of demand) and a lower price in the market that is more responsive to price changes (the market with the larger price elasticity of demand). Since $\varepsilon_A < \varepsilon_S$, the profit-maximizing price is higher for adults than for seniors; that is, $P_A > P_S$.

There is a more formal way of demonstrating this result. In Section 6.1, you learned that $MR = P \times [1 - (1/\varepsilon)]$. For the senior market this equation gives $MR_S = P_S \times [1 - (1/\varepsilon_S)]$ and for the adult $MR_A = P_A \times [1 - 1/\varepsilon_A)]$. Because these marginal revenues must be equal, equating the two gives $P_S \times [1 - (1/\varepsilon_S)] = P_A \times [1 - (1/\varepsilon_A)]$. Rewrite this last equation as

$$P_S = \left[\frac{1 - (1/\varepsilon_A)}{1 - (1/\varepsilon_S)}\right] \times P_A$$

Because $\varepsilon_A < \varepsilon_S$, the term in brackets

$$\left[\frac{1 - (1/\varepsilon_A)}{1 - (1/\varepsilon_S)}\right]$$

is less than 1.0. Therefore, the price the theater charges seniors (P_S) is less than the price it charges adults (P_A).

More generally, in order to make more profit, managers need to charge a lower price in the markets with the more elastic demand and a higher price in the markets with the less elastic demand. This pricing strategy will make the markup from marginal cost to price greater in the markets with the smaller price elasticity of demand. If managers set the same price in each market, the marginal revenues will differ, so they are *not* maximizing their firm's profit.

Conditions for Successful Third-Degree Price Discrimination

Although firms engage in third-degree price discrimination to make higher profits, many products, such as groceries, purses, beer at the local pub, and everything in Walmart, are sold at the same price to all groups of customers. If selling to different groups at different prices is profitable, why don't all managers practice price discrimination? The answer lies in four market conditions that must be satisfied in order to use third-degree price discrimination:

1. **Market power.** The firm must have some degree of market power, or it will not be able to raise its price above its marginal cost to any customer in any of its markets. Although some market power is a necessary condition, the Florida

Twin Theatre shows that price discrimination does not require significant amounts of market power. Managers can price discriminate even in markets that are widely perceived to be effectively competitive. For example, movie theaters in locations with many competitors still price discriminate among adults and seniors (and often children and students as well).

2. **Different groups of customers.** The firm must sell its product to at least two different groups of customers with different price elasticities of demand. In other words, there must be one group with a relatively small price elasticity of demand (a high willingness to pay) and another group with a larger price elasticity of demand (a lower willingness to pay).

3. **Distinct groups.** The managers must be able to determine in which group a particular customer belongs. In some cases, this identification is straightforward, such as adults versus children or in-state versus out-of-state college students. In other cases, however, the identification process is considerably more difficult. For example, how can a firm producing tennis rackets distinguish between those customers who are willing to pay a higher price for its products and those who are not? While some customers will certainly pay more for tennis rackets than others, there may be no feasible way to sort these customers into different customer groups. In such situations, the inability to divide customers into different groups forces managers to charge all of them the same price.

4. **No arbitrage.** The managers must be able to prevent arbitrage between customer groups. *Arbitrage*, the practice of buying a product in a low-price market and immediately reselling it at a higher price with little or no risk, can frustrate managers' attempts to sell at different prices: Those customers who otherwise would buy the product from the producer at a high price might instead buy it from other customers who acquired it at the low price.

If all four of these conditions are met, managers can increase profit by using third-degree price discrimination. All four conditions are present at the Florida Twin Theatre. Distance from competitive theaters gives the Florida Twin Theatre some measure of market power. Adults and seniors are different types of customers because they have different demands and different price elasticities of demand for movies. By requiring some sort of identification whenever a customer claims a senior discount, the theater can easily sort customers into distinct groups. Finally, social conventions preclude seniors from engaging in arbitrage by selling their tickets to adults for prices less than the $7.00 adult ticket price.

Self-Selection and Third-Degree Price Discrimination

Sometimes managers do not need to know whether a particular customer is a high-demand, small-elasticity customer or a low-demand, large-elasticity customer because they can create conditions that force customers to *self-select*—to reveal the group into which they fall.

For example, higher-income customers are often less price sensitive—have a smaller price elasticity of demand—than lower-income customers. Consequently, managers might use *versioning*—segmenting the market for their product into a higher-priced "premium" version of the product and a lower-priced "regular" version. For example, the price of a bag of Starbucks espresso roast ground coffee, sold in a strikingly designed black bag, is about twice that of Starbucks dark espresso roast ground coffee, sold in a more common-looking white bag. The cost to Starbucks of producing a (black) bag of espresso roast ground coffee may be higher than the cost of producing a (white) bag of dark espresso roast ground coffee, but it is probably not twice as much—Starbucks probably marks up the price of its espresso roast more than its dark espresso roast. Nestlé does the same thing in England, selling the premium Alta Rica version of its Nescafé coffee for about twice the price of its Fine Blend version. Managers at Starbucks and Nestlé are price discriminating by segmenting the market for coffee into demand from high-income customers and demand from lower-income customers. Of course, it is not necessary to limit the versions produced to just two. Honda Motor Company set suggested retail prices for its 2017 LX, EX, and EX-L Sedan Accords of $22,455, $25,830, and $28,920, respectively. These cars differ in their standard equipment— among other features, the lower-priced LX model lacks heated side mirrors and fog lights—but the markup reflects more than just the difference in cost. Honda Motor Company is segmenting the market for its cars by selling premium cars for a premium price.

Coupons are another common method of segmenting the market to allow for third-degree price discrimination. Customers who are unusually price sensitive—that is, who have a large price elasticity of demand—are willing to clip coupons from fliers or search for them on the Internet in order to pay a lower price. Consequently, use (or nonuse) of a coupon reveals whether the customer is a high-elasticity, price-sensitive customer or a low-elasticity, price-insensitive customer.

Today's tech-savvy managers are going well beyond coupons, whether in paper or electronic form. Increasingly, managers are using mobile apps and loyalty cards to create databases that keep track of individual customers' purchases in order to offer personalized coupons or lower prices. For example, if a database at grocery chain Safeway shows that a customer at a particular store buys Tide detergent regardless of whether it is on sale, that customer has a low elasticity of demand and is unlikely to receive a coupon for Tide. If the database shows that another customer buys Tide *only* if it is on sale, that customer has a higher elasticity of demand and will probably receive a Tide coupon, either via smartphone or in the mail. As such practices become more common, managers will get closer to their ideal—that is, first-degree price discrimination.

Sometimes managers can use the timing of product purchases as their self-selection method because the first adopters of a product are usually the customers with the smallest elasticity/highest demand. When Apple introduced its first iPhone in 2007, it set a price of $599 for the first two months and then dropped it to $399.[1] Apple used time to segment its market into high-demand and not-quite-so-high-demand customers. Publishers use the timing of book purchases to segment their market. For example, Berkeley Books publishes the popular "alphabet" series of mysteries by Ms. Sue Grafton. Berkeley's managers know that some readers are true fans of the series and cannot wait to read the latest book. So Berkeley initially publishes the book only in hardcover for a price of about $20. After several months, Berkeley issues the book in paperback for about $10. Hardcover books are more costly to produce than paperback books, but the cost difference is less than the price difference. Berkeley's managers use the two versions of

---

1 Apple received some pushback from its early adopters, so it ultimately offered them a $100 credit for use in Apple stores.

DECISION
SNAPSHOT

American Airlines Identifies a Customer Type

In July 2016, American Airlines charged $634 for a round-trip, one-stop flight from Atlanta to San Francisco that departed on a Monday and returned on a Friday. If the traveler returned a week after departure, on the next Monday rather than on Friday, the air fare was only $508. Why did the managers of American Airlines decide to give a $126 discount for the second flight?

Answer

American Airlines' managers are engaging in third-degree price discrimination. Business travelers and vacation travelers have different price elasticities of demand. Business travelers generally have a low price elasticity of demand for air travel to a particular city because they *must* get to their meeting or venture in that city on a particular date. Vacation travelers generally have a higher price elasticity of demand for air travel to a specific city because they have many options when considering where and when to fly. American Airlines' managers know that business travelers do not want to spend the weekend away from their homes because they will need to return to work on Monday. Vacation travelers, on the other hand, are happy to prolong their vacations by spending the weekend at their destinations. By requiring the weekend stay, American Airlines' managers are letting their customers self-select into a low-elasticity group and a high-elasticity group. Travelers who leave on Monday but are unwilling to spend the weekend are more likely to be business travelers and pay a high price because of their low price elasticity of demand. Travelers who leave on Monday and are willing to spend the weekend are more likely to be vacation travelers and pay a lower price because of their high price elasticity of demand. The managers maximize American Airlines' profit by charging different prices to these different groups.

the book to segment the market into early buyers—low-elasticity, high-demand customers—and later buyers—high-elasticity, low-demand customers—and then price discriminate: The early buyers pay a higher price, and the later buyers pay a lower price.

You have just learned how third-degree price discrimination can increase a firm's economic profit. In cases such as the Florida Twin Theatre, the high-demand and low-demand customers watch the movie at the same time. In other cases, such as the alphabet series of mysteries, the high-demand customers enjoy the book before the low-demand customers. But some firms face a situation in which the demand for their product is sequential and repetitive, that is, high demand is followed by low demand is followed by high demand and so on. The sequential nature of demand makes for a different set of issues than you have seen so far, such as determining the firm's capacity. These issues will be taken up in Section 10.2.

SOLVED
PROBLEM

Price Discrimination at Warner Brothers: That's All, Folks!

Managers at movie studies, such as Warner Brothers, must decide on the price they set for their DVDs. In May 2017, the Looney Tunes Golden Collection with 24 DVDs sold for $139 in the United States and the equivalent of $45 in the United Kingdom. The managers at Warner Brothers were price discriminating between the two regions. The demands of the markets were different, and resales of DVDs between the two markets are nearly impossible because DVDs use region encoding, which allows use only within a specified geographic area.

Suppose that you are a manager in charge of pricing DVDs for another studio. The following table gives hypothetical data on the marginal cost of producing DVDs and the demand and marginal revenue for the United States and Europe.

Marginal Cost		Demand and Marginal Revenue					
Quantity	MC	Q_{US}	P_{US}	MR_{US}	Q_{EU}	P_{EU}	MR_{EU}
2	$6.00	1	$11.50	$10.00	1	$8.50	$8.00
3	7.00	2	11.00	9.00	2	8.00	7.00
4	8.00	3	10.50	8.00	3	7.50	6.00
5	9.00	4	10.00	7.00	4	7.00	5.00
6	10.00	5	9.50	6.00	5	6.50	4.00

All quantities are in millions, and all costs and revenues are in U.S. dollars. To maximize profit,

a. What quantity of DVDs should you produce?

b. What quantity of DVDs should you sell in the United States? In Europe?

c. What price should you set in the United States? In Europe?

Answer

Because the demands in the United States and Europe are different, you can use price discrimination to increase your profit.

a. The profit-maximizing quantity of DVDs is the quantity that sets $MR = MC$. Derive the total marginal revenue schedule by adding the quantity in the United States to the quantity in Europe for each value of the marginal revenue:

- When $MR = \$8.00$, $Q_{US} + Q_{EU} = 3 + 1 = 4$.
- When $MR = \$7.00$, $Q_{US} + Q_{EU} = 4 + 2 = 6$.
- When $MR = \$6.00$, $Q_{US} + Q_{EU} = 5 + 3 = 8$.

Therefore, the profit-maximizing quantity of DVDs is $Q = 4$ (million) because at this quantity $MR = \$8$ and $MC = \$8$, so $MR = MC$.

b. To maximize profit, the marginal revenue in the United States must equal that in Europe. This condition means that 3 (million) DVDs are sold in the United States and 1 (million) DVDs are sold in Europe. With these quantities, the marginal revenue is $8 in each region.

c. The profit-maximizing price in the United States is $10.50, the price from the U.S. demand data for the quantity of 3 million DVDs. The profit-maximizing price in Europe is $8.50, the price from the European demand data for the quantity of 1 million DVDs.

10.2 Peak-Load Pricing

Learning Objective 10.2 Analyze how peak-load pricing can increase profit for a firm that faces predictable changes in demand.

The Wequassett Resort on Cape Cod in Massachusetts is a lovely vacation getaway with many different bungalows and cottages. The demand for rooms at this resort is much higher in the summer than in the winter. In fact, the resort closes completely during the depths of winter. Suppose that you help manage a similar resort. Figure 10.5 illustrates your resort's peak demand curve (D_{PEAK}) and off-peak demand curve (D_{OFF}) and their associated marginal revenue curves. Clearly, the peak demand is much greater than the off-peak demand.

In the Florida Twin Theatre case presented in Section 10.1, the firm faced two different demand functions simultaneously. The situation at the Wequassett Resort and your resort is different: Both face a high-demand period (*peak period*) followed by a low-demand period (*off-peak period*). There are many examples of products that exhibit such sequential demands, including restaurants, urban transportation, and electricity. The peak and off-peak periods can occur on a seasonal basis, as is the case for the resorts, or they can be part of a daily cycle, as happens for restaurants. The period of peak demand requires a large productive capacity, and the off-peak period requires less. Because the demands are sequential, both peak-period customers and off-peak-period customers at your resort use the same capacity—that is, the same rooms—but at different times. The fact that the demands are sequential rather than simultaneous makes this case significantly different from the third-degree price discrimination examined in the previous section.

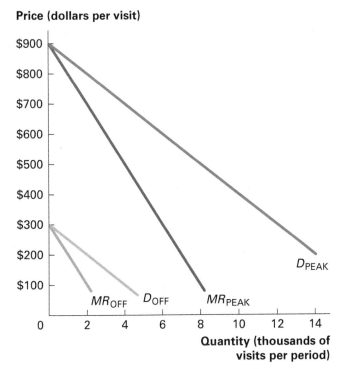

Price (dollars per visit)

Figure 10.5 Demand in Peak and Off-Peak Periods

The demand and marginal revenue curves during the peak period are D_{PEAK} and MR_{PEAK}, respectively; the demand and marginal revenue curves during the off-peak period are D_{OFF} and MR_{OFF}, respectively.

You must make two decisions:

1. **Capacity.** You must first make a long-run decision by determining the amount of capital stock (number of cottages and lodges) you need because the capital stock fixes your capacity (number of visits). This is a long-run decision because you can change the firm's capital only in the long run.
2. **Prices and quantities.** After the capacity is determined, you must make short-run decisions about the peak and off-peak prices to charge and the quantities to produce in each period.

The situation in which managers must determine capacity, price, and quantity for a firm that faces a high-demand period followed by a low-demand period is called **peak-load pricing**. Let's begin by examining your long-run choice, determining the profit-maximizing capacity.

Long-Run Capacity Decision

For simplicity, suppose that each nightly visit at your resort requires one room. The number of rooms in its capital stock—that is, its cottages and lodges—determines its capacity, so you need to make the long-run decision on the number of rooms to construct. Managers base their capacity decision on conditions *only* during the peak period because only during that time will the demand reach capacity. For example, visitors will fill all the rooms at your resort only during the peak period. During the off-peak period, some of the rooms will be empty. The off-peak-period demand therefore does not influence the capacity decision. So to maximize overall profit, you must build the capacity that maximizes peak-season profit.

Because the capacity is based only on the peak period, the long-run capacity decision depends on the peak-period marginal revenue and the long-run marginal cost. For any firm with a peak-load pricing decision, the long-run marginal cost has two parts: the marginal operating cost and the marginal cost of providing the capacity. Specifically for the resort, these costs are as follows:

- **Marginal operating cost.** The *marginal operating cost* of a visit to the resort includes factors such as the costs of cleaning the room, checking the visitor into the room, and laundering the bedding and towels. For simplicity, assume that this marginal cost is constant and equals $100 per nightly visit.
- **Marginal cost of providing the capacity.** For the resort, the *marginal cost of providing the capacity* is the marginal cost of the bungalows and cottages. As discussed in Section 1.3, the opportunity cost for the buildings is their best alternative use (renting or selling them to another firm). So the marginal cost of providing the capacity is the opportunity cost of providing another room in a lodge or bungalow. Once again for simplicity, assume that this cost is also constant at $200 per visit.

The long-run marginal cost equals the sum of the marginal operating cost and the marginal cost of providing the capacity. As Figure 10.6 shows, the long-run marginal cost (MC_{LR}) equals $300 ($100 + $200) per visit. For simplicity, suppose that the long-run average cost (LAC_{LR}) is also constant and equal to the marginal cost of $300 per visit.[2]

You can now make the capacity decision. The profit-maximizing number of peak-season visits is the quantity that sets the peak-period marginal revenue equal

---

[2] Figure 4.12 demonstrates that if the long-run average cost is constant, the marginal cost is also constant, so the (flat) long-run average cost curve and marginal cost curve coincide.

Price and cost (dollars per visit)

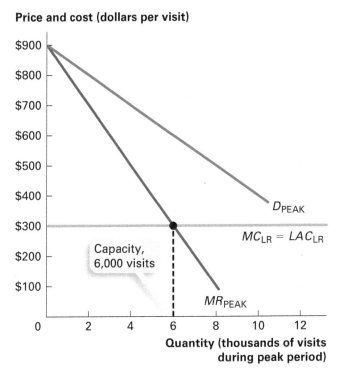

Figure 10.6 The Capacity Decision

The resort's capacity depends on its peak demand and marginal revenue curves, D_{PEAK} and MR_{PEAK}, and its long-run marginal cost curve, MC_{LR}. To maximize profit, managers build capacity that allows the profit-maximizing quantity of output, 6,000 visits, the point where $MR_{PEAK} = MC_{LR}$.

to the long-run marginal cost; that is, $MR_{PEAK} = MC_{LR}$. In Figure 10.6, the profit-maximizing quantity (number of visits) is 6,000 visits during the peak period. Therefore, you must build the number of lodges and bungalows that allows you to sell 6,000 visits during the peak season.

Short-Run Pricing and Quantity Decisions

If the resort was open only during the single peak period, then Figure 10.7 would illustrate the only demand it faces, so the profit-maximizing quantity would be 6,000 visits, with a price (from the demand curve) of $600 per visit. Because the price exceeds the long-run average cost, in this case the resort makes an economic profit of $1.8 million equal to the area of the green rectangle in Figure 10.7.

In reality, however, the resort is open during both peak and off-peak periods. So, once the managers have determined the capacity, the next step is finding the profit-maximizing prices and quantities during the peak *and* off-peak periods.

Profit-maximizing managers make these short-run decisions using the relevant demand and marginal revenue curves along with the short-run marginal cost curve. Let's begin with short-run marginal cost.

Short-Run Marginal Cost After Capacity Is Determined

Your capacity decision determines the shape and position of the short-run marginal cost curve. Once the capacity is in place, the cost of providing the capacity is a fixed cost that does not affect the marginal cost. So the short-run marginal cost is equal to the marginal operating cost of a visit up to the capacity number of visits. Figure 10.8 shows that the short-run marginal cost curve, MC_{SR}, is horizontal at the cost of $100 per visit (the marginal operating cost) up to the capacity number of visits (6,000). After reaching capacity, the short-run marginal cost curve becomes vertical because it is impossible to exceed the capacity number of visits.

Figure 10.7 Single-Period Profit Maximization

The profit-maximizing quantity is the number of visits that sets $MR_{PEAK} = MC_{LR}$, 6,000 visits. From the peak demand curve, D_{PEAK}, the profit-maximizing price is $600 per visit. The economic profit is equal to the area of the green rectangle, $1.8 million.

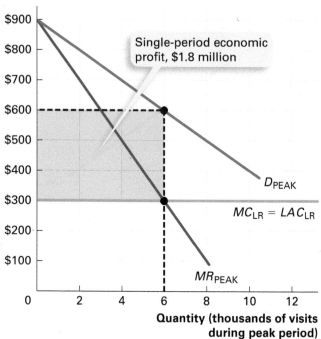

Single-period economic profit, $1.8 million

Peak-Period Profit Maximization

Using the short-run marginal cost in Figure 10.8, you can now determine the peak-period profit-maximizing quantity and price. The profit-maximizing quantity is the number of visits that sets the short-run marginal cost equal to the peak-period marginal revenue, or $MC_{SR} = MR_{PEAK}$. As Figure 10.9 illustrates, the peak-period profit-maximizing quantity

Figure 10.8 Short-Run Marginal Cost Curve After the Capacity Decision

The short-run marginal cost curve, MC_{SR}, is equal to the marginal operating cost of a visit until the resort reaches capacity. The marginal operating cost of a visit is constant and equals $100 per visit, so MC_{SR} is horizontal at $100 until reaching capacity. After capacity is reached, MC_{SR} becomes vertical because it is impossible to exceed the capacity number of visits.

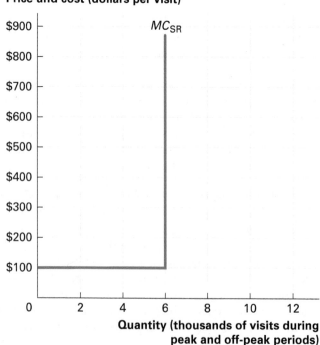

Price and cost (dollars per visit)

Figure 10.9 **Peak-Period Profit Maximization**

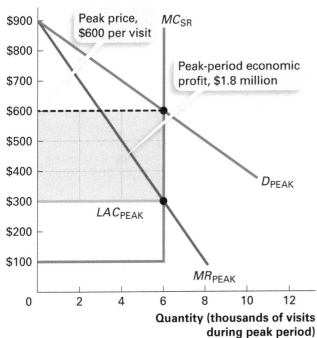

During the peak period, the profit-maximizing quantity and price are determined by producing the quantity that sets the short-run marginal cost equal to the *peak-period* marginal revenue, or $MC_{SR} = MR_{PEAK}$, and then setting the price using the peak-period demand. In the figure, the peak-period quantity is 6,000 visits, which equals the capacity number of visits. The peak-period price is $600 per visit. The firm makes an economic profit equal to the area of the green rectangle, $1.8 million.

equals 6,000 visits. The profit-maximizing price is determined using the peak-period demand curve (D_{PEAK}), and Figure 10.9 shows that this price is $600 per visit.

It is useful to note that the profit-maximizing quantity *is exactly the same as* the capacity quantity and that the profit-maximizing price *is exactly the same as* the price in Figure 10.7 that sold out the capacity quantity. Indeed, even though you have just seen the usual profit-maximization rule in action—produce the quantity that sets $MR = MC$, and then set the price using the demand—the managers' profit-maximizing decisions in the peak period can be put more succinctly and perhaps more intuitively: Maximize profit in the peak season by setting the highest price that fills the resort to capacity.

The light blue LAC_{PEAK} curve in Figure 10.9 shows the relevant part of the long-run average cost curve for the peak period. This curve includes *both* the average of the operating costs (which are the variable costs) *and* the costs of providing the capacity (which are the fixed costs). In the peak season, your resort makes an economic profit of $(P - LAC_{PEAK}) \times Q$, or $($600 - $300) \times 6,000$ visits $= $1.8 million, which is equal to the area of the green rectangle in Figure 10.9. Comparing Figures 10.9 and 10.7, you can see that the resort's economic profit in the peak period also is exactly equal to what its economic profit would be if it was open *only* during the peak period. In the peak period, the firm's total revenue is enough to pay *all* of the total cost of providing the capacity as well as all of the total operating costs incurred during the period. So when the managers maximize their profit for the off-peak period, they do not have to take into consideration the total cost of providing the capacity because *that cost has already been paid.*

Off-Peak-Period Profit Maximization

In the off-peak period, the profit-maximizing quantity is the number of visits that sets the marginal revenue equal to the marginal cost, $MR_{OFF} = MC_{SR}$. The price follows from the off-peak demand (D_{OFF}). In Figure 10.10, the profit-maximizing off-peak quantity is 2,000 visits at a price of $200 per visit.

The resort makes an economic profit during the off-peak period. In the off-peak period, the only costs are the operating costs because the peak-period price and

Figure 10.10 Off-Peak-Period Profit Maximization

During the off-peak period, the profit-maximizing quantity is the quantity that sets the short-run marginal cost equal to the off-peak marginal revenue, $MC_{SR} = MR_{OFF}$, or 2,000 visits. The price is set using the off-peak demand, $200 per visit. The firm makes an economic profit equal to the area of the green rectangle, $200,000.

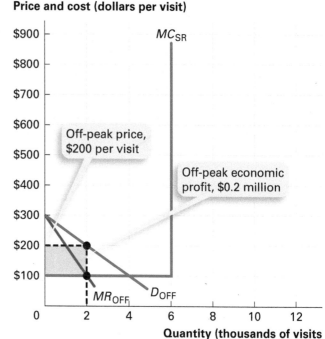

Price and cost (dollars per visit)

Off-peak price, $200 per visit

Off-peak economic profit, $0.2 million

quantity have already covered the cost of building the capacity. The operating cost is constant at $100 per visit, so the average total cost (ATC) also is constant at $100 per visit. Therefore, the economic profit during the off-peak period is $(P − ATC) \times Q$, which is the area of the green rectangle in the figure and equals ($200 − $100) × 2,000 visits = $0.2 million. By staying open for the off-peak period, you have increased your resort's economic profit by $0.2 million. Your total economic profit is $2.0 million, $1.8 million in the peak period plus $0.2 million in the off-peak period.

Even though your price in the off-peak season, $200, is less than the long-run average total cost, $300, staying open in the off-peak season *increases* your total economic profit. The reason for this seemingly paradoxical result is that the only relevant costs for the off-peak period are the operating costs. The fixed costs of providing the capacity are irrelevant because they have been paid during the peak period, when the quantity equals the capacity quantity. Consequently, your lower price in the off-peak period covers the operating costs and allows you to earn an additional $200,000 of economic profit.

You and the other managers at your resort have maximized the resort's profit in both the peak period and the off-peak period, so you have maximized its total profit. Any other price or quantity in either period will result in a lower economic profit.

DECISION
SNAPSHOT

Peak-Load Pricing by the Minneapolis–St. Paul Metropolitan Airport

The Minneapolis–St. Paul Metropolitan Airports Commission (MAC) is a government agency that owns and operates the Minneapolis–St. Paul International Airport. The vast majority of flights leave between 6:00 A.M. and 10:00 P.M., but within that range, some time periods—such as between 1:00 P.M. and 2:00 P.M.—have many more departures than others—say, between 9:00 P.M. and 10:00 P.M. The price of a departure is the same throughout the day: $2.73 per 1,000 pounds of weight. Because it is a government agency, the MAC might not run the airport to maximize profit. Suppose, however, that the MAC's Board of Commissioners decides it wants to run the airport more like a business and hires you as a consultant to maximize the MAC's *net revenue* (the term that nonprofit organizations use for their profit, their total revenue minus total cost). Assuming that the board tells you that changing the size of the airport is out of the question, what suggestions would you make to maximize net revenue?

Answer

The airport has a peak-load pricing problem. Because you cannot change the capacity, you should suggest that the airport raise its price during the peak periods and lower it during the off-peak periods. You should set the peak-period price high enough that the quantity of landing and take-off slots demanded by the airlines just equals the quantity available at the airport. Then you should aim for an off-peak price at which the marginal revenue from a flight equals the marginal cost of using the runway. These prices will maximize the MAC's net revenue.

For both price discrimination and peak-load pricing, customers pay only one price for a single unit of the good and, in the case of third-degree price discrimination and peak-load pricing, can buy as many or as few units as they desire at the going price. Other pricing methods require that buyers pay two prices—one for the right to buy the good and another for the good itself—or require buyers to purchase more than one unit of a product. These pricing methods are the topic of the next section.

Peak-Load Pricing

SOLVED
PROBLEM

You are in charge of pricing for a chain restaurant in Brazil. You have the data in the following table on the marginal costs and marginal revenues for different quantities of meals that can be served in a three-hour time block for restaurants of differing capacities (sizes). The costs and revenues include the marginal capacity cost (MC_{CAP}), the marginal operating cost (MC_{OP}); the marginal revenue at peak dining hours, 6 P.M. to 9 P.M. for dinner (MR_{PEAK}); and the marginal revenue at off-peak dining hours, 11 A.M. to 2 P.M. for lunch (MR_{OFF}). All costs and revenues are in U.S. dollars.

Quantity of Meals	MC_{CAP}	MC_{OP}	MR_{PEAK}	MR_{OFF}
200	$3	$6	$13	$7
300	3	6	11	6
400	3	6	9	5
500	3	6	7	4
600	3	6	5	3

The price elasticity of demand is 3.25 during the peak hours and 5.0 during the off-peak hours. To maximize the restaurant's profit,

a. What restaurant capacity (quantity of meals) should you select?

b. What should be the quantity and price for the meals served during the peak dinner hours?

c. What should be the quantity and price for the meals served during the off-peak lunch hours?   (*Continues*)

SOLVED PROBLEM (*continued*)

Answer

Because of the sequential demand, peak-load pricing maximizes the profit.

a. The profit-maximizing capacity is the quantity that sets $MR = MC$. The relevant marginal revenue is the peak-period marginal revenue. The marginal cost includes *both* the marginal cost of capacity *and* the marginal operating cost: $3 + $6 = $9. The capacity to serve 400 meals in a three-hour time block is the profit-maximizing capacity because at this quantity both the peak-period marginal revenue and the peak-period marginal cost equal $9.

b. The short-run marginal cost is equal to $6 (the marginal operating cost) until the capacity of 400 meals is reached, at which quantity the short-run marginal cost curve become vertical. The profit-maximizing quantity of meals in the peak period is 400 because that quantity sets the short-run marginal cost (along its vertical portion) equal to the *peak* marginal revenue of $9. It also is the capacity quantity. The profit-maximizing price is equal to

$$P = MR \times \frac{\varepsilon}{\varepsilon - 1}$$

so

$$P_{\text{PEAK}} = \$9 \times \frac{3.25}{3.25 - 1} = \$13$$

c. As before, the short-run marginal cost is equal to $6 (the marginal operating cost) until the capacity of 400 meals is reached. At this quantity, the short-run marginal cost curve become vertical. The profit-maximizing quantity of meals is 300, the quantity that sets the short-run marginal cost (along its horizontal portion) equal to the *off-peak* marginal revenue of $6. The profit-maximizing price is equal to

$$P_{\text{US}} = \$6 \times \frac{5.0}{5.0 - 1} = \$7.50$$

10.3 Nonlinear Pricing

Learning Objective 10.3 Explain how two-part pricing, all-or-nothing offers, and commodity bundling can raise a firm's profit.

When buyers can purchase as much or as little as they want and pay the same price per unit for all the units they purchase, the pricing is said to be linear. **Nonlinear pricing** is a term for different pricing methods that require buyers to either pay two prices, purchase more than one unit of product, or purchase more than one product. This section examines three related nonlinear pricing strategies: two-part pricing, all-or-nothing offers, and commodity bundling. Each of these strategies increases profit by extracting more consumer surplus than can be obtained by simple monopoly pricing.

Nonlinear pricing
Different pricing methods that require buyers to either pay two prices, purchase more than one unit of product, or purchase more than one product.

Two-Part Pricing

Two-part pricing is a method of pricing in which each customer pays a fixed fee for access to a product (the *access fee*) plus a separate per-unit price for use of the product (the *user fee*). For example, tennis and racquetball clubs often have an annual membership fee (access fee) that gets you in the door. Then as you use the facility, you pay an hourly court fee (user fee). Cell phone contracts offer another example: Often these contracts involve a fixed monthly fee and a separate fee that varies with the use of minutes or data.

Two-part pricing A method of pricing in which each customer pays a fixed fee for access to a product (the access fee) plus a separate per-unit price for use of the product (the user fee).

Table 10.1 **Two-Part Pricing and College Football**

The University Athletic Association at the University of Florida uses two-part pricing to sell season tickets for football games to nonstudents. In 2016, a donation of $15,000 (the access fee) was required for the purchase of 10 season tickets. Following the donation, the donor was eligible to purchase up to 10 season tickets at $620 each (the user fee).

Fixed Donation	Number of Season Tickets	Price of One Season Ticket	Average Price of a Season Ticket
$3,100	4	$620	$1,395
4,800	6	620	1,420
8,600	8	620	1,695
15,000	10	620	2,120

Source: http://www.gatorboosters.org/membership.html (donor benefits).

Managers of nonprofit institutions sometimes use two-part pricing as well. For example, the University of Florida sells relatively low-priced season tickets to Gator football games to fans who are not students at the university. For the privilege of buying such season tickets, however, the buyers must make a fixed donation to the University Athletic Association (UAA). Table 10.1 shows that a fan can purchase between 4 and 10 season tickets, depending on the amount of the donation. If you are a Gator fan and want to buy 10 season tickets at $620 each, you must donate at least $15,000. The $15,000 is the access fee, and the $620 per season ticket is the user fee. (The average price per season ticket rises substantially for the $8,600 and $15,000 donation levels because these include added benefits, such as parking. This difference may well reflect the UAA's use of *versioning*, selling a premium package at a higher price to fans with a lower price elasticity of demand.)

Two-Part Pricing: Identical Demands

Managers can use two-part pricing to transform consumer surplus into additional profit. Consider the managers at Arnold Palmer's Bay Hill Club and Lodge in Orlando, Florida. These managers display a remarkable talent for pricing: They have separate plans for residents (those who live within 50 miles of the club), nonresidents (those who live more than 50 miles from the club), and young executives (those under 40), among others. All of the plans use two-part pricing. Although the analysis of each plan is similar, focus on the two main features of the nonresidents' plan. As a nonresident member, to play golf at the Bay Hill Club and Lodge you must pay a one-time $14,000 membership fee (the access fee) and then a greens fee of $90 per round (the user fee). This is an example of two-part pricing.

Suppose that you are a manager at a similar golf club. Start by assuming that all of the members have identical demands for playing golf. You maximize the club's total profit by maximizing its profit for each member. Figure 10.11 shows the demand curve (D_{NR}) for a single nonresident golfer. For simplicity, assume that the marginal cost and average total cost are constant at $50 per round of golf. Figure 10.11 shows the average total cost and marginal cost line as the horizontal line labeled $MC = ATC$.

Figure 10.11(a) is the benchmark case. If you set a single price, you will sell each non-resident member 20 rounds of golf per year (the quantity at which $MR_{NR} = MC$) at a price of $400 per round (the price from the demand curve for 20 rounds). Your club makes an economic profit equal to $(P - ATC) \times Q$. So the economic profit equals the area of the green rectangle labeled B in Figure 10.11(a): $(\$400 - \$50) \times 20 = \$7,000$.

Figure 10.11 Single Price Versus Two-Part Pricing

(a) Single Price	(b) Two-Part Pricing
If your club charges a single price, you sell 20 rounds of golf per year because that is the quantity that maximizes the profit by setting $MR_{NR} = MC$. The price is $400 per round. The economic profit, equals the area of the green rectangle, $7,000, and the customer receives consumer surplus equal to the area of the blue triangle, $3,500.	If your club can use two-part pricing, you maximize profit by setting a membership fee of $14,000 and a greens fee (the price per round) of $50 (the marginal cost of a round of golf). Your club makes an economic profit of $14,000, equal to the area of the green triangle, which includes *all* the potential consumer surplus.

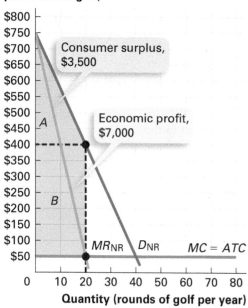

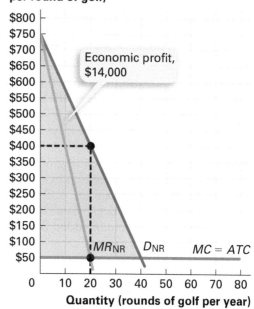

Figure 10.11(a) shows that the customer is left with a consumer surplus equal to the area of the blue triangle labeled *A*, or $3,500. In other words, the customer is willing to pay an additional $3,500 to play the 20 rounds of golf. To maximize profit, you would definitely like to convert this consumer surplus into economic profit. You can do just that with two-part pricing: Set the greens fee equal to the marginal cost, and then charge a membership fee equal to the resulting consumer surplus.

Figure 10.11(b) shows the amount of economic profit your club can make by utilizing two-part pricing. If you use a two-part pricing strategy, the greens fee (the user fee) equals the marginal cost, $P = MC$, which is $50 in this example. This price maximizes the nonresident member's consumer surplus, *all* of which you can gain through a lump-sum membership fee (the access fee). When the price is $50 per round, the nonresident member plays 40 rounds per year. At this price, and with no membership fee, the consumer surplus is the area of the green triangle in Figure 10.11(b). The base is 40 rounds, and the height is $750 - $50 = $700, so the consumer surplus equals $\frac{1}{2} \times 40$ rounds of golf $\times$ $700 per round $=$ $14,000. This amount means that the member gains additional benefit of $14,000 over the total amount paid for the 40 rounds of golf. So the member is willing (but definitely not eager) to pay up to an additional $14,000 to play 40 rounds of golf at a price of $50 per round. By setting the price of the membership fee at $14,000 and the price of the greens fee at $50 per round, you induce the customer to join the club and play 40 rounds of golf per year, but the member has *no* consumer surplus. The $50 greens fee covers your cost for each round played, so the membership fee of $14,000 is all economic profit. In other words, using two-part pricing has allowed your club to convert *all* the potential consumer surplus into economic profit. Comparing Figures 10.11(a) and 10.11(b) shows that two-part pricing has substantially increased your club's economic profit per customer, doubling it from $7,000 to $14,000 per customer. Of course, your total profit is much greater, as it is the profit per member multiplied by the number of members.

Two-Part Pricing: Nonidentical Demands

Setting two-part prices becomes more complicated when the demands of different customers are not identical. One reason the complication arises is that some customers might not have enough consumer surplus for them to justify paying a substantial lump-sum access fee. Accordingly, it might or might not be profitable to set the membership fee low enough to keep those customers in the market.

Let's return to the golf club example. Suppose that there are equal numbers of two types of potential customers: (1) the nonresidents included previously and (2) a second type of golfer we'll call young executives (YE). The demand curve from one nonresident (D_{NR}) and that from one young executive (D_{YE}) are illustrated in Figure 10.12. A young executive has a lower income than a nonresident, so at every price the young executive demand is one-half of the demand of the (wealthier) nonresident. Assume it is not possible for your club to charge different prices to the young executives and nonresidents.

If you use the prices from the previous example (a membership fee of $14,000 and a greens fee of $50), you already know that the nonresident customer is willing to join. Because of lower income, however, the young executive is not. Figure 10.12 shows that the young executive plays only 20 rounds of golf at $50 per round compared to the 40 rounds played by the nonresident. At this price and quantity, the young executive's consumer surplus is $7,000, equal to the area of the green triangle labeled A in the figure. In other words, the young executive is willing to pay a maximum of only $7,000 more to play 20 rounds of golf at a price of $50 per round. This amount is less than the

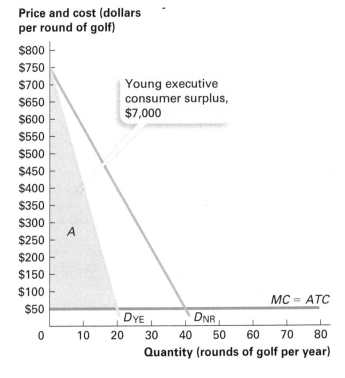

Price and cost (dollars per round of golf)

Figure 10.12 Two-Part Pricing, Nonidentical Demands

The demand from a nonresident (D_{NR}) is the same as in Figure 10.11, and the demand from a young executive (D_{YE}) is half the nonresident's demand. If the price of a round of golf is $50, the young executive plays 20 rounds per year and, with no membership fee, has a consumer surplus of $7,000, equal to area A. The nonresident plays 40 rounds and, with no membership fee, has a consumer surplus of $14,000.

membership fee of $14,000, so the young executive does not join. With a membership fee of $14,000 and a greens fee of $50, the club makes an economic profit of $14,000 per pair of customers, though only one, the nonresident, actually joins the club.

Now suppose that you set the membership fee for both groups equal to the young executive's consumer surplus of $7,000. Because the nonresident is willing to pay a maximum of $14,000, a membership fee of $7,000 is a real bargain, so the nonresident joins eagerly. The young executive also joins because $7,000 just equals his or her consumer surplus. Consequently, *both* the nonresident and the young executive join the club. The nonresident plays 40 rounds per year, and the young executive plays 20 rounds per year. The $50 greens fee covers the costs of these rounds of golf, so your club makes a total economic profit of $14,000 per pair of customers: $7,000 from the membership fee of the nonresident plus $7,000 from the membership fee of the young executive.

Your club's total economic profit ($14,000 per pair of golfers) is the same whether it sets its prices to exclude or to include the young executive. If the demand from the young executive had been more than half of the nonresident's demand, then setting the membership fee equal to the young executive's consumer surplus would have increased the firm's profit. But if the demand from the young executive had been less than half of the nonresident's demand, then setting the fee to include the young executive could *decrease* the firm's profit. The lesson is clear and important: Sometimes the demand from some potential customers is simply so low that setting a price that appeals to them lowers the total profit. In this case, profit-maximizing managers will forego selling to these customers.

If lowering the membership fee to include the extra customer (the young executive) does not change the total profit, it appears hardly worth the effort to set prices to include the young executive. The managers, however, can make another change that *will* boost their profit. In particular, the managers can raise the greens fee (the user fee or per-unit price) and lower the membership fee (the access fee). Done correctly these changes increase the total economic profit. To see why, note that raising the greens fee has two effects:

1. It decreases the customers' consumer surplus, which then decreases the membership fee the club can charge.
2. It increases the profit on each round of golf played (or, more generally, on each unit sold.)

Balancing these two effects, even with the use of marginal analysis in a case as relatively straightforward as this one, is mathematically complex.[3] This discussion skips the calculations and simply asserts that the profit-maximizing greens fee is $225, as shown in Figure 10.13. Given this user fee, the nonresident plays 30 rounds of golf per year and, with no membership fee, has a consumer surplus of $7,875 (equal to the combined areas of the light green triangle, *A*, and the green triangle, *B*). The young executive plays 15 rounds and, with no membership fee, has a consumer surplus of $3,937.50 (equal to the area of the light green triangle, *A*). Together the nonresident and the young executive play a total of 45 rounds of golf per year. It is profit maximizing to set the fixed membership fee equal to the smaller of the consumer surpluses ($3,937.50). Then, with a membership fee of $3,937.50 and a greens fee of $225, your club has three sources of economic profit:

1. The membership fee from the nonresident of $3,937.50, equal to the light green triangle, *A*

---

3 Section 10.B of the Appendix at the end of this chapter explains how to use calculus to determine the profit-maximizing prices for two-part pricing with nonidentical demands.

Price and cost (dollars per round of golf)

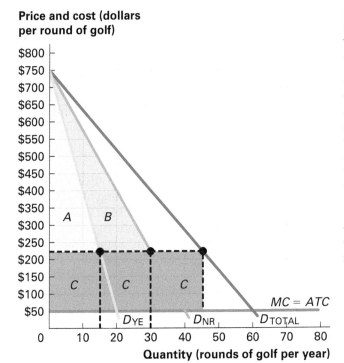

As a manager of the golf club, you maximize profit by setting a greens fee of $225 and a membership fee of $3,937.50. A nonresident plays 30 rounds per year and, with no membership fee, has a consumer surplus of $7,875 (equal to areas $A + B$). A young executive plays 15 rounds and, with no membership fee, has a consumer surplus of $3,937.50 (equal to area A). You set the membership fee equal to the young executive's consumer surplus, $3,937.50. The club's economic profit equals the sum of the two membership fees, $7,875, plus the economic profit made on all rounds of golf, $7,875 (which is equal to the area of the large dark green rectangle labeled with the three Cs), for a total economic profit of $15,750.

2. The membership fee from the young executive of $3,937.50, also equal to the light green triangle, A
3. The economic profit on the rounds of golf played, $(P - ATC) \times Q$, which in this case is $(\$225 - \$50) \times 45 = \$7,875$, equal to the three areas of the large dark green rectangle labeled with three Cs

The total economic profit from all three sources is $15,750. (The result that the sum of the two consumer surpluses equals the economic profit from the rounds of golf is a coincidence.) The significant lesson from this analysis is that you have increased your profit from $14,000 to $15,750 by: 1) boosting the user fee (the greens fee) above the marginal cost of use; and, 2) reducing the access fee (the membership fee).

In the case of the golf club, the club makes more profit if both the nonresident and the young executive are members than if just the nonresident is a member. Remember that this result is not universal. There are situations in which it is profit maximizing to set the access fee so high that some potential customers just do not buy. For example, if the demand from the lower-demand young executives is less than half that from the higher-demand nonresidents, then it may be profit maximizing to set the access fee equal to the nonresident's consumer surplus, which means that the young executive does not join. Or if the number of young executives is less than the number of nonresidents, it may again be profit maximizing to set the access fee so high that the (few) lower-demand young executives do not join.

You will never have enough information to solve a two-part pricing problem with the mathematical precision displayed in this example. Nonetheless, there are three important general managerial decision-making lessons that use the data you do have:

1. When two-part pricing is feasible, more profit is possible than with simple linear pricing. As a manager, you need to look for the opportunity to use two-part pricing to boost your profit.

2. The model with two types of customers demonstrates that, in the realistic case of customers with different demands, the profit-maximizing user fee is greater than the marginal cost of use.

3. When using two-part pricing, the access fee (membership fee) and user fee (per-unit fee) must be adjusted in an effort to keep the right number of customers in the market while extracting as much of their consumer surplus as possible. In some cases, the demand from some potential customers is just too low to make it worthwhile to adjust your prices to gain their business, so you must forego selling to them.

All-or-Nothing Offers

All-or-nothing offer A pricing method that gives customers the choice of either buying a package with a certain quantity of the product or buying nothing at all.

Another pricing strategy that managers sometimes can use to boost their profit is a close cousin of two-part pricing: all-or-nothing offers. An **all-or-nothing offer** is a pricing method that gives customers the choice of either buying a package with a certain quantity of the product or buying nothing at all. All-or-nothing pricing is common in grocery stores, as anyone can testify who has ever wanted to buy a single can of soda rather than a 12-pack or one roll of paper towels rather than four (or six or eight). The Green Bay Packers offer another example. They sell *only* season tickets for *all 10* home games, which in 2017 ranged in price from $664 (for end zone seats) to $823 (for seats between the 20-yard lines). They do not sell tickets to individual games. The Packers give their fans the option of buying tickets to 10 games or to no games. All-or-nothing offers are sometimes also called *block pricing* because the seller bundles identical products—soda, paper towels, or football tickets—into a single block (or package) about which the customer must make an all-or-nothing decision.

Under ideal circumstances, an all-or-nothing offer can convert the entire consumer surplus into economic profit. To see how, suppose that a football team allows its fans to purchase tickets to individual games and that all customers have the same demand. Figure 10.14 shows the key curves for a single customer: the demand curve (D), the marginal revenue curve (MR), the average total cost curve (ATC), and the marginal cost curve (MC). Both the average total cost and the marginal cost are assumed to be constant up to 10 games, after which the marginal cost rises vertically because there are only 10 home games per year.

The conventional single-price monopoly solution is the usual useful benchmark: Produce the quantity that sets the marginal revenue equal to the marginal cost, and then set the price using the demand. In Figure 10.14, the managers sell each fan tickets to five games and set a price of $120 per game to maximize profit. The average cost is $20 per game, and the ticket price is $120 per game, so the team makes an economic profit of ($120 − $20) × 5 games, or $500 per customer.

Profit Maximization with All-or-Nothing Offers

All-or-nothing offers alter the customer's choice in a significant way. Normally, customers observe the price and can buy as much or as little as they want. In an all-or-nothing offer, however, the seller offers to sell a package with a specific quantity of the product at a specific price. Customers either accept that offer or buy nothing at all. The key observation is that it is in a customer's best interest to accept the offer unless the consumer surplus falls below zero. If the consumer surplus becomes negative, the total value to the customer is less than the total amount paid, in which case the customer will decide not to buy the package. If the consumer surplus is positive, the customer will definitely buy the package, and if it is zero, any particular customer may or may not buy it.

For example, in the single-price case for tickets just illustrated in Figure 10.14, customers can buy any quantity of game tickets they want at the price of $120 per ticket.

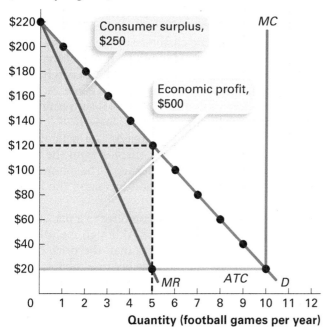

Price and cost
(dollars per game)

Consumer surplus,
$250

Economic profit,
$500

MC

MR   ATC   D

Quantity (football games per year)

Figure 10.14 Profit with a Single-Price Monopoly

The marginal cost curve, MC, of a football game ticket is constant at $20 per game up to 10 games per year, after which it becomes vertical. The average total cost, ATC, is also constant and equal to the marginal cost for the 10 games, so the ATC curve is also horizontal at $20 per game up to 10 games. The demand curve is D, and the associated marginal revenue curve is MR. The team's managers maximize profit by selling five tickets to games at a price of $120 per ticket, for an economic profit of $500 per customer (the area of the green rectangle).

The demand curve in Figure 10.14 (the same one that appears in Figure 10.15) shows that the customers buy tickets to five games and each customer has a consumer surplus. In Figure 10.15, the consumer surplus from these five games has been divided into three parts: A, B, and C. Now suppose that the managers change the deal, so customers can purchase tickets to six games—and *only* six games—at a price of $720, which works out to $120 per ticket. Will the customers accept this all-or-nothing deal?

As shown in Figure 10.15, if customers were free to buy a ticket to the sixth game *by itself* at a price of $120, they would not do so. The demand curve, which

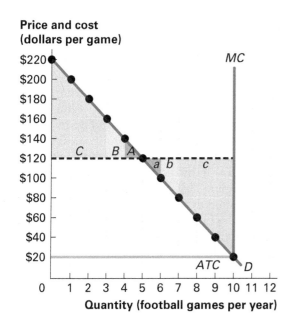

Price and cost
(dollars per game)

MC

C   B A
     a b   c

ATC   D

Quantity (football games per year)

Figure 10.15 Profit with an All-or-Nothing Offer

With a single-price offer that lets customers buy tickets to as many games as they want, they purchase tickets to five games at a price of $120 per game, with consumer surplus of areas A + B + C. If the managers instead require customers to purchase tickets to six games at a price of $720, or $120 per game, the value of the sixth game is less than the price of the ticket by an amount equal to area a. Customers still take the deal, however, because their *total* consumer surplus is positive—it is equal to areas B + C. Ultimately, the managers can maximize profit with an all-or-nothing offer of tickets to 10 games for $1,200, which leaves customers with no consumer surplus and allows the team to make a larger economic profit.

measures the value to the customer of the games, shows that the value of the sixth game is less than $120. Buying the ticket to the sixth game decreases the customer's consumer surplus by an amount equal to the area of the dark green triangle labeled *a*. However, even though the sixth game *by itself* is not worth $120, the customer will still buy the entire package because the value to the customer of the package of *all six games* exceeds the total price tag of $720 for tickets to all six games. More precisely, the loss in consumer surplus from the sixth game is equal to area *a*, which in Figure 10.15 is the same as area *A*, the consumer surplus for the fifth game. Accordingly, buying the six-game package leaves the customer with a total consumer surplus equal to the consumer surplus from the first five games (areas $C + B + A$) minus the loss in surplus from the sixth game (area a = area A), for a total consumer surplus of areas $C + B$. Because the total consumer surplus from the *entire* six-game package is positive, the customer still buys the package.[4] The all-or-nothing offer has decreased the customer's consumer surplus and increased the firm's economic profit.

Now suppose that the managers modify the all-or-nothing offer to a package of seven games at a price of $840, which again is $120 per game. Although the value of the seventh game, measured from the demand curve, is less than the price of the ticket to the seventh game, the customer will buy the package because the total surplus from all seven games is still positive. In Figure 10.15, the seventh game decreases the consumer surplus by an amount equal to area *b* (which is the same as area *B*). Therefore, purchasing the seven-game package leaves the customer with consumer surplus equal to the consumer surplus from six games (areas $C + B$) minus the loss in surplus from the seventh game (area b = area B), so that the total consumer surplus is equal to area *C*. Once again, because the consumer surplus from the entire seven-game package is positive, the customer will buy the package.

The same reasoning works for all-or-nothing packages with 8 and 9 games and prices of $960 and $1,080, respectively. All-or-nothing packages with 8 and 9 games progressively lower the consumer surplus, but the customer's total consumer surplus is still positive. An all-or-nothing offer with 10 games at a price of $1,200 leaves no consumer surplus, so customers are equally well-off buying or not buying the 10-game package. In this case, some customers will buy the 10-game package, and some will not. As long as there are enough fans to sell out the stadium, the Green Bay Packers make the maximum economic profit with the 10-game all-or-nothing offer. The economic profit per customer equals $(P - ATC) \times Q$, which from the figure equals $(\$120 - \$20) \times 10$ games $= \$1,000$.

If the demand curve is linear and the marginal cost curve is horizontal, the profit-maximizing all-or-nothing offer results in the production of the competitive market quantity (the quantity at which the marginal cost curve and demand curve intersect) and a price per unit equal to the profit-maximizing monopoly price. In Figure 10.15, the competitive market quantity is 10 games per customer, and the profit-maximizing monopoly price is $120 per game. The customers receive no consumer surplus because the all-or-nothing offer has converted all of it into economic profit.

A linear demand curve and a constant marginal cost are very special cases and unlikely to be true in the real world. The assumption that all customers have identical demands is also unlikely. Accordingly, in the real world, the profit-maximizing all-or-nothing price is not necessarily equal to the monopoly price, the profit-maximizing

---

4 If the demand curve is nonlinear, the consumer surplus lost on the sixth game may not equal the consumer surplus for the fifth game. But the key result—that the customer buys the package if the total consumer surplus for *all* the games is positive—is still valid.

Nonlinear Pricing at the 55 Bar

Say that you are a new manager at the 55 Bar in New York City, a popular jazz and blues bar. The previous manager established a pricing scheme of a $15 cover charge and a two-drink minimum per music set, at a price of $7 per beer. What nonlinear pricing techniques did your predecessor use? Should you change? Explain your answers.

Answer

The previous manager of the 55 Bar used two-part pricing combined with an all-or-nothing offer. The $15 cover charge is the fixed fee that gains access to the bar. The two-drink minimum is both the user fee and an all-or-nothing offer: Either the customer buys two (or more) drinks, or the customer is ushered from the bar. The manager used these pricing methods because they increased the bar's economic profit. Both convert consumer surplus into economic profit. Because the customers all have different demands, the fixed cover fee cannot capture the entire consumer surplus, but the use of an all-or-nothing offer gains more profit. Presumably, many of the customers are jazz or blues lovers who, at the price of $7 per beer, would otherwise buy a single drink, nurse it through the evening, and enjoy their remaining consumer surplus from the music and the single beer. The all-or-nothing offer requiring purchase of at least two drinks per music set converts some of the remaining consumer surplus into increased economic profit. It would be irresponsible (and possibly have legal consequences) to try to capture more of the remaining consumer surplus by requiring purchase of more drinks per set. However, you might change the price of a beer and/or the cover charge if the bar is so crowded that you infer your customers still have substantial consumer surplus.

all-or-nothing quantity is not necessarily equal to the competitive quantity, and the consumer surplus is not necessarily all converted into economic profit. Even so, all-or-nothing pricing converts at least *some* of the consumer surplus into economic profit, and if they set the correct price, managers using an all-or-nothing offer can make a greater economic profit than if they use a conventional monopoly price.

Commodity Bundling

For an all-or-nothing offer, the firm creates a package containing some amount of *a* product. Commodity bundling is similar. The firm creates a package, but in this case, it contains *different* products. More specifically, **commodity bundling** is a business practice in which a seller combines separate products into a package or bundle that it sells for a single price. It is not unusual to see commodity bundling in practice. For example, a McDonald's Happy Meal bundles a cheeseburger, apple slices, a drink, and a toy for a single price. Significantly more expensive, Adobe's Creative Cloud bundles Photoshop, Illustrator, InDesign, and many other software programs into a rental package available at a single price. Still more expensive is Infiniti's $2,150 Driver Assistance Package for its Q50 2.0t sedan. McDonald's Happy Meal and Adobe's Creative Cloud are examples of *mixed bundling* because in addition to the

Commodity bundling A business practice in which a seller combines separate products into a package or bundle that it sells for a single price.

bundle, McDonald's and Adobe sell the bundled products separately. Infiniti's Driver Assistance Package is an example of *pure bundling* because Infiniti does not sell the bundled products separately.

Some bundling is promotional in nature. For example, McDonald's managers created Happy Meals to meet competition from Burger King and other similar restaurants. This bundle may also increase demand for the products because it enables parents to know immediately what their child's meal will cost, which can be important for lower-income families. But bundling can also increase a firm's profit because it decreases transaction costs or because it allows a firm to take advantage of its customers' different preferences for different products. We explore these possibilities in turn.

Bundling and Transaction Costs

Bundling can decrease some production transaction costs. For example, Infiniti's Driver Assistance Package bundle includes features such as Backup Collision Intervention, Predictive Forward Collision Warning, and Front and Rear Sonar Systems. These products are available only with the bundle, so when a car travels down the assembly line with Front and Rear Sonar Systems, the assembly-line managers automatically know that they must have available the parts for the Backup Collision Intervention and Predictive Forward Collision Warning products, and the assembly-line technicians automatically know that they will need to install them. If the Backup Collision Intervention and Predictive Forward Collision Warning products were separately available, there is the real possibility of mistakes—the managers might fail to have the parts for the Backup Collision Intervention product available when they are needed, or the technicians might fail to install that product. Bundling reduces the probability of these costly errors.

Bundling and Customer Preferences

Bundling can also increase profit by transferring potential consumer surplus to the firm as additional profit. Bundling effectively forces some customers to "spend" some of their consumer surplus from a preferred item on a less preferred item. Take, for example, Adobe's Creative Cloud. Suppose that Adobe has only two computer programs, Photoshop and Illustrator. For simplicity, assume that the marginal cost of each program is $0, so that Adobe's total revenue is also its total profit. Crucial to the potential profitability of bundling is the variation in demand among customers. Say that customer A values Photoshop highly and is willing to pay up to $15 per month but finds little value from Illustrator and is willing to pay only $5 per month. Customer B has the opposite valuation and is willing to pay a maximum of $18 per month for Illustrator but only $8 per month for Photoshop. Table 10.2 contains the maximum prices each customer will pay for each product. Finally, suppose that Adobe's managers know these maximum prices but they cannot distinguish customer A from customer B, so they cannot use price discrimination.

Table 10.2 Bundling and Customer Valuation of Adobe Products

Customer A values Photoshop at $15 per month but Illustrator at only $5 per month. Customer B has the reverse preferences, valuing Photoshop at only $8 per month and Illustrator at $18 per month.

Customer	Maximum Price Willing to Pay for Photoshop (dollars per month)	Maximum Price Willing to Pay for Illustrator (dollars per month)
A	$15	$5
B	8	18

Adobe's managers now set their rental prices. First, consider the pricing of the individual products. If they do not bundle the products, the managers want to set each price equal to the maximum a customer is willing to pay. Accordingly, they can charge a monthly rental price of $15 or $8 for Photoshop and $18 or $5 for Illustrator. Let's look at the profit from each price:

- **Photoshop.** If Adobe's managers set a price of $15 for Photoshop, only customer A rents it, for a total profit of $15. If they set a price of $8, however, both customers rent it, for a total profit of $8 + $8 = $16. Clearly, the $8 rental price yields the maximum total profit, $16.
- **Illustrator.** If Adobe's managers set a price of $18 for Illustrator, only customer B rents it, for a total profit of $18, while if they set a price of $5, both customers rent it, for a total profit of $5 + $5 = $10. In this case, the $18 rental price gives the maximum total profit, $18.

Consequently, with no bundle, Adobe's profit-maximizing prices are $8 for Photoshop and $18 for Illustrator, allowing Adobe to make a total profit of $16 + $18, or $34.

Now suppose that Adobe's managers bundle the two programs. Customer A is willing to pay a maximum rental price for the bundle of $15 + $5 = $20, and customer B is willing to pay $8 + $18 = $26. If the managers set a price of $20, both customers rent the bundle, and Adobe's total profit is $20 + $20 = $40. If the managers set a price of $26, then only customer B rents it, for a total profit of $26. Clearly, of the two prices for the bundle, $20 is the profit-maximizing price. Moreover, the $20 bundle price gives Adobe more total profit ($40) than renting the programs separately ($34). By bundling the two programs, Adobe's managers increase Adobe's profit.

How has bundling allowed Adobe to increase its profit? One insight comes from seeing how the different customers fare when the products are bundled. Customer B will rent both products, regardless of whether or not they are bundled, but is better off with the bundle because its price is only $20 compared to the $26 customer B would have paid if Adobe rented the programs separately. Customer A, however, is significantly worse off. The price of the bundle equals the maximum customer A is willing to pay, so customer A receives no consumer surplus with the bundle. If Adobe rented the programs separately, customer A would have rented only Photoshop for $8, thereby receiving a consumer surplus of $7 (the $15 maximum price customer A would have been willing to pay minus the $8 price customer A actually would have paid). The $20 price for the bundle means that customer A spends $12 more than if the programs were unbundled and customer A rented only Photoshop. Of this additional $12, the value from Illustrator accounts for $5, but the other $7 is customer A's lost consumer surplus from Photoshop. By bundling, Adobe's managers have changed $7 of customer A's consumer surplus into profit for Adobe.

The distribution of the valuations also affects Adobe's profits from bundling. In the example, the customers' preferences are negatively correlated: One customer's high valuation of a product means the other customer's valuation is low. Whenever there are groups of customers whose valuations are negatively correlated, managers are able to create a bundle that leaves one of the customer groups with much less consumer surplus than it would have had if the products were sold separately (those in the same group as customer A in our example). The bundle converts these customers' foregone consumer surplus into economic profit for the firm.

Obtaining the data in Table 10.2 is difficult—and probably impossible—in reality. But once again your marketing research department might be able to help by researching your customers to determine whether easily bundled products have negatively correlated demands.

Movie Magic

Marcus Theatres is a large movie chain based in Milwaukee. Suppose that you are a manager of a similar movie chain. You are working with a candy manufacturer like Hershey to produce a signature candy bar. You have surveyed your customers about their willingness to pay for different-sized candy bars. Each customer will buy one bar. For simplicity, assume that all customers have the same demand, which is illustrated in the figure along with the marginal cost and marginal revenue. Suppose that the only cost of a bar is the price the manufacturer charges and that it offers whatever size bar you want for a cost of $0.60 per ounce.

Price and cost (dollars per ounce of bar)

a. If you operate as a single-price monopoly, what size bar will you select, what price will you charge, and what is your economic profit per bar?

b. If you use an all-or-nothing offer, what size bar will you select, what price will you charge, and what is your economic profit per bar?

Answer

a. As a single-price monopoly, you maximize profit by selling the size of candy bar that sets $MR = MC$. In this case, your chain will sell two-ounce candy bars because the marginal revenue from adding the second ounce to the bar, $0.60, is equal to the marginal cost of adding the second ounce, also $0.60. The figure shows that your theaters can sell two ounces at a price of $0.80 per ounce, so the price of the two-ounce bar will be $1.60. The cost of the bar is $0.60 per ounce, or $1.20 per bar. The economic profit per bar will be $1.60 − $1.20, or $0.40 per bar.

b. The accompanying figure will help answer the questions involving an all-or-nothing offer. With the same demand curve from the figure above (but omitting the marginal revenue curve for simplicity), the figure illustrates the all-or-nothing reasoning. If your chain offers a four-ounce candy bar at a price of $3.20 ($0.80 per ounce), customers will buy the bar. On the first two ounces of the bar, customers gain consumer surplus equal to the green triangle labeled *a*. On the last two ounces, they lose consumer surplus equal to the green triangle labeled *A*. These two areas are the same size, so purchasing a four-ounce bar for a price of $3.20 leaves customers with no consumer surplus. The economic profit, however, is equal to the price, $3.20, minus the cost, four ounces at a cost per ounce of $0.60, or $2.40, leaving your chain with an economic profit of $0.80 per bar.

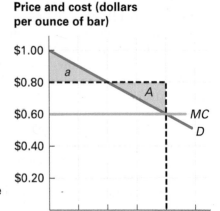

Price and cost (dollars per ounce of bar)

10.4 Using Advanced Pricing Decisions

MANAGERIAL APPLICATION

Learning Objective 10.4 Apply the different advanced pricing techniques to increase economic profit.

When your firm has some degree of market power, you may have the potential to increase your economic profit by using one or more of the advanced pricing techniques presented in this chapter. Keep in mind that the goal of these methods is to increase your profit by changing some (or all) consumer surplus into more profit.

Managerial Use of Price Discrimination

Price discrimination is a common practice because it increases a firm's profit. Indeed, as a customer, you may often see managers using price discrimination and not realize it. For example, if Walgreens offers two bags of Doritos for $5.00 and charges $3.29 for a single bag, it is using second-degree price discrimination. Effectively, Walgreens is selling the first bag of Doritos for $3.29 and the second bag for $1.71.

Using Second-Degree Price Discrimination

In the ice cream store example presented earlier in the chapter, the managers knew exactly the highest price they could charge for a scoop of ice cream. In reality, of course, obtaining this information is difficult at best and usually impossible. That said, the basic idea of second-degree price discrimination and the results from the ice cream example offer two important lessons that can help you make better managerial decisions:

1. The managers at the ice cream store engaged in price discrimination when they raised the price of the first scoop and lowered the price of the third scoop. Qualitatively, this set of changes is exactly the goal of second-degree price discrimination. As a manager, you want to charge higher prices for the first units (because customers are willing to pay more for the first units) and lower prices for later units (because customers are willing to pay less for later units).
2. You can often practice this type of price discrimination using quantity discounts, as when a firm like Yankee Candle offers to sell a second taper (a fancy name for a candle) for 50 percent off. As long as the discounted price exceeds the marginal cost of the unit being sold, selling the additional unit increases your profit.

Compared to charging a customer the same price for all units, second-degree price discrimination allows you to do two things: (1) receive a higher price for the first units sold and (2) sell more units. Both changes increase your profit.

Using Third-Degree Price Discrimination

Recall that third-degree price discrimination requires four conditions: some market power, two or more groups of customers with different demands, the ability to sort customers into their appropriate groups, and prevention of arbitrage.

Perhaps the most difficult of these conditions to meet is the ability to sort customers into the different groups. Sometimes past purchase history can help you determine a particular customer's demand. Customers who have frequently pur-chased a product in the past may be in the group with a lower price elasticity of demand than new customers. For example, customers who have used Cox Commu-nications' phone and Internet bundle continually for over a year surely have a lower price elasticity of demand than new customers who have not experienced its benefits. Accordingly, in 2017, Cox Communications charged its long-term customers $83 per month while giving new customers, with their higher price elasticity of demand, a lower price of $50 per month for the first 12 months.

Arbitrage can also be a problem because it can thwart efforts to engage in price discrimination. Managers can try to prevent arbitrage by employing vari-ous tactics to prohibit customers from reselling the product. For example, the Kraft Heinz Company sells ketchup to two markets, the retail grocery market and the restaurant market. The restaurant market has a larger price elasticity of demand for ketchup, so Kraft Heinz charges restaurants a lower price than gro-cery stores. It labels the bottles of ketchup it sells to restaurants "not for resale," which facilitates policing against arbitrage between the two markets. Company representatives who see a restaurant bottle labeled "not for resale" on the shelf in a grocery store could punish the retailer by withholding other company products.

The firm is even better off if it does not have to pay for policing against resale. Indeed, if the costs of preventing arbitrage exceed the increased profit due to price discrimination, you maximize profit by *not* engaging in price discrimination. Any manager whose firm is price discriminating must search for lower-cost methods of preventing arbitrage. Some managers accomplish this by persuading the govern-ment to make resale of the firm's product illegal. Lobbying is one way a firm may be able to enlighten politicians about the "evils" of resale. For example, the average price of prescription drugs in Canada is about 51 percent of the average price in the United States because of Canadian laws. Managers of U.S. drug companies are effec-tively price discriminating by selling their products at lower prices in Canada and higher prices in the United States. These managers rely on U.S. Food and Drug Administration regulations that prohibit the importation of prescription drugs from Canada to prevent arbitrage.

Managerial Use of Peak-Load Pricing

If your firm faces sequential changes in demand, with a peak demand followed by an off-peak demand, you can increase your firm's profit by using peak-load pric-ing. Indeed, the changes in demand do not need to be easily predictable, as Uber pricing shows. Uber, the ride-hailing smartphone app, boosts its prices when demand for rides is high, a pricing technique Uber calls *surge pricing*. Surge pricing is effectively a variation of peak-load pricing: When demand is high in the peak period, Uber's price rises. Surge pricing differs from the usual peak-load pricing, however, because Uber's capacity is not strictly fixed. Instead, the higher price for a ride also attracts some additional Uber drivers to the road, thereby increasing Uber's capacity.

Uber's surge pricing is an example of another general point. In Section 6.2, you learned that the profit-maximizing price is marked up from the marginal cost (and from the marginal revenue) according to $P = MC \times (\frac{\varepsilon}{\varepsilon - 1})$. You can use this markup rule to set the profit-maximizing price in both the peak and the off-peak periods. Note that the price elasticity of demand is unlikely to be the same in both the peak and the off-peak periods, so your markup in the two periods may differ.

In Uber's case, the marginal cost of providing a ride in the peak and off-peak periods is probably similar, so the higher price with surge pricing means that Uber's markup is higher in peak demand times and lower in off-peak times. Uber's policy of setting a higher price in the peak period indicates that the price elasticity of demand is smaller (less elastic) during the peak period than during the off-peak period.

Managerial Use of Nonlinear Pricing

If your firm is able to use nonlinear pricing, you can increase its economic profit. Two types of nonlinear pricing presented in this chapter are two-part pricing and all-or-nothing offers.

Using Two-Part Pricing

The simplest two-part pricing model with identical customers shows that the profit-maximizing user fee equals the marginal cost of the product and the profit-maximizing access fee equals the consumer surplus. In reality, however, you will never encounter a market with identical customers. The second model, with two different customers, is slightly more realistic, though it stretches the imagination to think of a real-world market with exactly two different types of customers. Regardless, one of the results from the model with two customers applies more generally: With nonidentical customers, the profit-maximizing user fee is greater than the marginal cost of the product.

Consider the possibility of combining price discrimination and two-part pricing by charging different classes of customers (such as students and nonstudents) different access fees and/or user fees. For example, Amazon allows its Amazon Prime members "free" two-day shipping for many products. In this case, the Prime membership fee is the access fee. Amazon discounts the membership fee for students because the firm has determined that a student's consumer surplus from Prime membership is less than that of a nonstudent. This difference is likely because students, with lower incomes, buy less from Amazon and so benefit less from the free shipping. Amazon's managers are charging different groups of customers different access fees based on their different consumer surpluses, enabling the firm to make more economic profit than it would by charging all groups the same access fee. Indeed, if it is possible, combining two or more of the advanced pricing methods can prove to be a powerful tool for boosting your firm's profit.

Using All-or-Nothing Offers

In some cases, you can use all-or-nothing offers to increase profit. Of course, using an all-or-nothing offer requires market power. The example presented in Section 10.3 of season tickets for a football team is a straightforward all-or-nothing offer by a firm with market power.

Some firms create all-or-nothing offers using the size of their products. As anyone who shops at Costco or Sam's Club knows, all-or-nothing offers that compel customers to buy a large quantity of a product (48 rolls of toilet paper, anybody?) or none at all are common. The goal of an all-or-nothing offer is to force customers to "spend" the consumer surplus they would otherwise receive on the early units by making them purchase the later units. Interestingly, Costco and Sam's also use two-part pricing because both clubs charge membership fees for the privilege of shopping at their stores. Clearly, both firms are combining multiple advanced pricing techniques to maximize profit.

Revisiting How the Managers at Turtle Bay Resort Came to Think Kama'aina Pricing Is Par for the Course

Kama'aina pricing is an example of third-degree price discrimination. As a manager of the Turtle Bay Resort, you know that this sort of price discrimination for a round of golf can increase your profit. You also know that four conditions must be present to enable you to use third-degree price discrimination. Fortunately, all of the conditions for successful price discrimination are present:

1. **Market power.** Turtle Bay Resort definitely has market power because many golfers look at the chance to play a course designed by Arnold Palmer as a once-in-a-lifetime opportunity.

2. **Different customers.** Turtle Bay Resort has two types of customers: local residents, with greater knowledge of their options and thus a larger price elasticity of demand, and visitors, with poorer knowledge of their options and consequently a smaller price elasticity of demand. In addition, visitors' incomes are usually higher than residents' incomes. Because the price of golf is a smaller fraction of visitors' incomes, this is a second reason why they have a smaller price elasticity of demand than residents.

3. **Distinct groups.** It is easy for the managers of the Turtle Bay Resort to divide customers into the appropriate groups because local residents who want to pay Kama'aina prices must show a valid Hawaii driver's license or a State of Hawaii identification card. Customers without the appropriate identification are classified as visitors.

4. **No arbitrage.** For the Turtle Bay Resort, arbitrage among its customers is difficult because the staff at the resort can check to ensure that the person to whom a round of golf is sold is the person actually playing the round. Additionally, social conventions preclude low-price customers from standing at the first hole, selling their rounds to customers who otherwise would pay a higher price to the Turtle Bay Resort.

The managers of every golf course in Hawaii must be aware that price discrimination boosts profits because virtually all practice Kama'aina pricing. Table 10.3 shows the prices at five of the premier Hawaiian golf courses. In each case, the managers price discriminate by setting a lower Kama'aina price.

As one of the managers of Turtle Bay Resort, you, too, will want to engage in price discrimination to increase your profit. The prices you will charge depend on the marginal

Table 10.3 Kama'aina Pricing

The table shows the prices at five premier golf courses in Hawaii.

Course	Visitor Price	Resident Kama'aina Price
Olomana	$95	$42
Coral Creek	130	50
Hawaii Kai Championship Club	100	46
Makaha Valley Country Club	65	37
Waikele Golf Club	130	50

Source: http://the.honoluluadvertiser.com/specials/golf/golf courses.

cost of playing a round of golf and the price elasticities of demand for visitors and for residents. Suppose that the marginal cost of playing a round is $20. Further, suppose that your marketing research department has estimated that the price elasticity of demand equals 1.12 for visitors and 1.44 for residents. To set the prices, you know that the profit-maximizing markup of price over marginal cost equals

$$P = MC \times \left(\frac{\varepsilon}{\varepsilon - 1} \right)$$

so the price for visitors equals

$$\$20 \times \frac{1.12}{1.12 - 1} = \$187$$

and the Kama'aina price for residents is

$$\$20 \times \frac{1.44}{1.44 - 1} = \$65$$

These prices, incidentally, are close to Turtle Bay's actual prices of $185 for visitors and $65 for residents.

Interestingly, Turtle Bay Resort uses peak-load pricing for resort stays (with higher prices during the peak period, late winter/early spring, when many potential visitors are growing weary of snow), practices price discrimination with lower per-night prices for longer stays, and offers bundles of different services (such as spa or culinary packages). Clearly, the managers of Turtle Bay Resort use a variety of advanced pricing methods to maximize profit!

Summary: The Bottom Line

10.1 Price Discrimination

- Price discrimination, the practice of charging customers different prices that are not based on differences in marginal costs, increases profit.
- Managers using first-degree price discrimination charge every customer the highest price that customer is willing to pay for every unit purchased.
- Managers using second-degree price discrimination charge customers a higher price for the first unit purchased and lower prices for later units.
- Managers using third-degree price discrimination sell the same product to different customers at different prices. Four requirements must be met: (1) some market power, (2) at least two different customer groups, (3) the ability to classify a particular customer into the appropriate group, and (4) prevention of arbitrage. To maximize profit, the firm produces the quantity that sets the marginal cost equal to the marginal revenue derived from *all* customers and then allocates the quantity among the different customer types. Customers with a smaller price elasticity of demand pay higher prices, and customers with a larger price elasticity of demand pay lower prices.
- Customers often self-select into high- and low-demand groups based on versioning, the use of coupons, and/ or the timing of product purchases.

10.2 Peak-Load Pricing

- Peak-load pricing is required when firms face sequential changes in demand, with demand high during a peak period and low during an off-peak period.
- Managers of such firms must first determine the profit-maximizing capacity, the capacity at which the long-run marginal cost equals the marginal revenue from the peak-period demand.
- The profit-maximizing quantity in the peak period sets the short-run marginal cost equal to the peak-period marginal revenue. The peak-period price is based on the peak demand.
- The profit-maximizing quantity in the off-peak period sets the short-run marginal cost equal to the off-peak period marginal revenue. The off-peak period price is based on the off-peak demand.

10.3 Nonlinear Pricing

- Managers who use two-part pricing charge their customers a fixed access fee and a separate user fee for each unit purchased. If all customers are identical, managers maximize profit by setting the user fee equal to the marginal cost and setting the access fee equal to the consumer surplus. If customers are not identical, managers maximize profit by raising the user fee above the marginal cost and lowering the access fee.
- All-or-nothing offers give customers the choice of buying a certain quantity of the product or none at all. Customers facing an all-or-nothing offer buy units with a negative consumer surplus that is offset by other units with a positive consumer surplus.
- Commodity bundling combines different products into a package that customers buy for a single price. Commodity bundling can increase profit by reducing the transaction costs of production; it can also increase profit when customers have negatively correlated valuations.

10.4 Managerial Application: Using Advanced Pricing Decisions

- All of the advanced pricing techniques described in this chapter require a firm to have some market power. All of the pricing techniques aim to convert consumer surplus into economic profit, thereby increasing total profit.
- Combining different advanced pricing methods can result in greater profit than using a single method.

Key Terms and Concepts

All-or-nothing offer	Nonlinear pricing	Second-degree price discrimination
Commodity bundling	Peak-load pricing	Third-degree price discrimination
First-degree price discrimination	Price discrimination	Two-part pricing

Questions and Problems

10.1 Price Discrimination

Learning Objective 10.1 Explain how the different types of price discrimination can boost a firm's profit.

1.1 What role does consumer surplus play in the profitability of price discrimination?

1.2 Samoa Airlines has begun setting its ticket prices based on the combined weight of the passengers and their luggage. Say that a 200-pound passenger with a 20-pound suitcase pays more than a 150-pound passenger with a 30-pound suitcase. Is this pricing method price discrimination? Explain your answer.

1.3 The price of a one-way ticket to Atlanta for a flight leaving at 6:00 A.M. is $450. The price of a 9:30 A.M. flight is $600. Is this difference price discrimination? Explain your answer.

1.4 An 18-pound bag of Cherished Cat Premium Cat Litter has a price of $8.24; a 40-pound bag has a price of $15.99. Are the managers at Cherished Cat price discriminating? Explain your answer.

1.5 The figure illustrates the demand at a pizza franchise. Suppose that there are 10,000 customers with identical demands. Each customer will visit the pizza shop once a year and buy either one, two, or three pizzas. Each customer is willing to pay some price between $14.00 and $12.00 for the first pizza (so some will pay $13.50, others will pay $12.25, and so on), between $12.00 and $10.00 for the second pizza, and between $10.00 and $8.00 for the third pizza.

Price and cost (dollars per pizza)

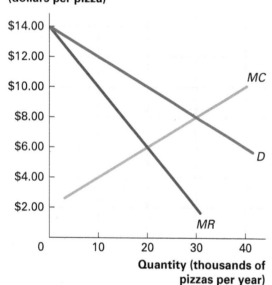

Quantity (thousands of pizzas per year)

a. If the managers do not price discriminate, what price will they charge, and what quantity will they sell? What does the consumer surplus equal?

b. If the managers price discriminate by charging one price for a customer's first pizza, a second price for a customer's second pizza, and a third price for a customer's third pizza, what will be their profit-maximizing prices? What is the amount of consumer surplus? By how much has the economic profit changed?

1.6 Sled dogs in Alaska must be fed year-round. They are generally fed USDA-inspected ground beef, identical to that sold for human consumption. Meat producers often add activated charcoal to the ground beef destined for dogs. The activated charcoal is harmless but makes the meat

significantly less appealing for humans. Activated charcoal is not free, but the price of meat for dogs is less than the price of meat for humans. Why do meat producers add charcoal to meat intended for dog food and then sell it at a lower price?

1.7 The managers of an upscale seafood restaurant have determined that adult and senior diners have different demands. The adult demand function for dinners is

$$Q^d = 200 - P$$

and the senior demand function for dinners is

$$Q^d = 180 - 2P$$

The marginal cost of a dinner is constant at $20.

a. If the managers do not price discriminate, what price will they charge? (Hint: The demand curve in this case will have a kink in it at the price at which the senior demand is first positive so that the quantity they demand needs to be added to the quantity the adults demand. The kink creates a jump in the marginal revenue curve at this quantity.)

b. If the managers do price discriminate, what price will they charge adults, and what price will they charge seniors? What quantity of dinners will they sell to adults, and what quantity will they sell to seniors?

c. If there is no fixed cost, what is the restaurant's economic profit if the managers charge one price? If the managers engage in price discrimination? Do the managers want to price discriminate?

1.8 MasterCuts is a midlevel hair salon that has some market power. Suppose that the managers of MasterCuts have set prices for a basic haircut of $22 for an adult and $12 for a child. The marginal cost of both types of haircuts are equal. The managers discover that the marginal revenue from an adult haircut is $18 and the marginal revenue from a child haircut is $10. To maximize their profit, should these managers change the prices of the adult and child haircuts? Why or why not?

1.9 The model of price discrimination assumes that customer demand is unaffected by price discrimination, but that is not always the case. In Hawaii, Kama'aina pricing at a golf course could backfire. Insulted and/or irritated by this pricing strategy, some visitors may choose not to play golf.

a. If some visitors are insulted enough to choose not to play golf, how would this influence the demand for golf? How would it affect the price charged visitors?

b. Could eliminating Kama'aina pricing increase the course's economic profit? Explain your answer.

1.10 Suppose that you are a manager for Adobe Systems, the creator of Photoshop and other software products. Adobe rents most of its products to its customers. Suppose that it has two classes of customers for its Photoshop program: students and businesspeople. Say that the demand function from students is $Q_S = 400,000$ programs $- 1,000P$ and the demand function for businesspeople is $Q_B = 900,000$ programs $- 1,000P$. In both demand functions, P is the annual rental price of the program. Because Photoshop is delivered over the Internet, the marginal cost of another program is $0. Suppose that Adobe has fixed costs of $5 million.

   a. If price discrimination is possible, what rental price will you recommend that Adobe charge students, and what quantity will it rent? What rental price will you recommend that it charge businesspeople, and what quantity will it rent? What will be Adobe's economic profit or economic loss?

   b. If price discrimination is not possible, what rental price will you recommend that Adobe charge, and what quantity will it rent? What will be Adobe's economic profit or loss?

   c. Is Adobe's economic profit larger when it price discriminates or when it sets a single rental price? Explain your answer.

   d. How might Adobe successfully engage in price discrimination?

● **1.11** Say that you are a manager for Bloomin' Brands, the restaurant company that owns Outback Steakhouse. Your research department has determined that the demand from adults is different than the demand from seniors and has estimated the demand curves shown in Figures (a) and (b). Your estimate of the marginal cost curve appears in Figure (c).

   a. To maximize your profit, how many dinners should you sell in a month?

   b. What price will you charge for adult dinners? How many dinners will you sell to adults in a month?

   c. What price will you charge for senior dinners? How many dinners will you sell to seniors in a month?

10.2 Peak-Load Pricing

Learning Objective 10.2 Analyze how peak-load pricing can increase profit for a firm that faces predictable changes in demand.

2.1 Why is the off-peak price unaffected by the marginal cost of expanding capacity?

2.2 At a popular sports bar in Bismarck, North Dakota, all drinks are half price on Wednesday from 9:30 P.M. to 11:30 P.M. Are these lower prices an example of peak-load pricing? Explain your answer.

2.3 Athens, Georgia, is the home of the University of Georgia. Its football team, the Georgia Bulldogs, is a perennial powerhouse, and home games are virtually always sold out. The Graduate Athens is a wonderfully eclectic Athens hotel. Suppose that a weekend stay in a king

Accompanies problem 1.11.

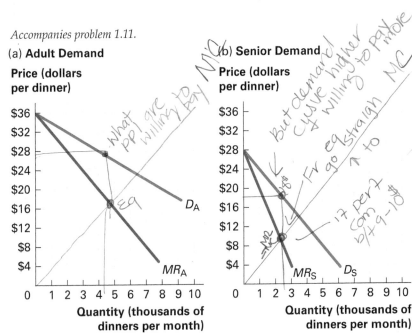

(a) Adult Demand

(b) Senior Demand

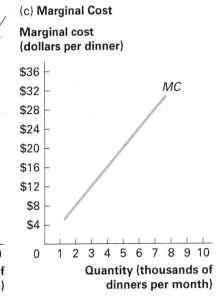

(c) Marginal Cost

suite at a similar hotel is $639, with a two-night stay required, when the Bulldogs are playing at home but is only $329, with no two-night stay required, on weekends without home football games. Is this price difference peak-load pricing? Explain your answer.

2.4 Do you need market power to practice peak-load pricing? Why or why not?

2.5 Sun Life Stadium is an 80,000-seat football stadium in Miami, Florida, where the NFL's Miami Dolphins and the University of Miami's Hurricanes both play football. Say that the demand function for Dolphins football tickets is $Q_{DOLPHINS} = 160,000$ tickets $- 2,000P_{DOLPHINS}$ and the demand function for Hurricanes football tickets is $Q_{HURRICANES} = 60,000$ tickets $- 4,000P_{HURRICANES}$. P is the price of a ticket. The demand for Dolphins games is much higher than the demand for Hurricanes games, so the weekends when the Dolphins are playing are the peak periods and the weekends when the Hurricanes play are the off-peak periods. The marginal cost of an additional spectator is $0 up to 80,000, after which it becomes infinite. What is the profit-maximizing price for tickets to Miami Dolphins games? To University of Miami Hurricanes games?

2.6 You are thinking of building a restaurant on Cape Cod. The marginal cost of building the restaurant is equal to $15 per diner, and the marginal cost of an additional meal is $20 per diner. In the peak vacation period, the weekly demand function is $Q_{PEAK} = \$4,200 - 40P_{PEAK}$. In the off-peak period, the weekly demand function is $Q_{OFF-PEAK} = \$1,800 - 20P_{OFF-PEAK}$. P is the price of a meal. What is the profit-maximizing price and quantity of a meal during the peak vacation period? What is the profit-maximizing price and quantity of a meal during the off-peak period?

10.3 Nonlinear Pricing

Learning Objective 10.3 Explain how two-part pricing, all-or-nothing offers, and commodity bundling can raise a firm's profit.

3.1 Publix is one of several major grocery store chains in the Southeast. Explain why Publix does not engage in two-part pricing.

3.2 In Honolulu, an unlimited use, one-month bus pass costs $50. Explain how this pass is an example of two-part pricing.

3.3 Assume that the demand for a round of golf at a premier club is $Q = 150 - P$, so the marginal revenue is $MR = 150 - 2Q$, where P is the price per round (the greens fee) and Q is the number of

rounds. Further, suppose that all players have this same demand. With a constant marginal cost of $10, what are the firm's price, quantity, and economic profit if the managers maximize profit by setting a single price? What are the firm's prices, quantity, and economic profit if the managers maximize profit by using two-part pricing?

3.4 Suppose that all individuals' demand for rounds of golf at a private club is given by $Q = 100 - P$, where P is the price per round (the greens fee) and Q is the number of rounds. The marginal revenue is $MR = 100 - 2Q$. The marginal cost is constant at $20, and there is no fixed cost.
  a. What single price will maximize a monopolist's profit?
  b. What will be the prices and quantity under two-part pricing?
  c. What would the terms be in an all-or-nothing offer?
  d. Calculate the economic profits for each of the options outlined in parts a through c.

3.5 There are 200 golfers with identical monthly demands equal to $Q = 25 - 0.25P$, where P is the price per round (the greens fee) and Q is the number of rounds. The marginal revenue from this demand is $MR = 100 - 8Q$. The marginal cost of an additional round of golf is constant and is equal to $20. There is no fixed cost. In answering these questions, provide both a graphical solution and a mathematical solution.
  a. What is the optimal price and quantity for a monopolist that charges a single price? What is the total economic profit?
  b. If half of the golfers are men and half are women, can the managers increase their economic profit by using third-degree price discrimination (assuming that price discrimination on the basis of gender is legal)? Why or why not?
  c. Can the managers increase their economic profit with a separate membership charge (access fee) and a per-round fee (user fee)? If so, provide the optimal membership charge, per-round fee, and total economic profit. If not, explain why.

3.6 There is only one country club in Carrollton, Georgia. Suppose that it has 400 members, each with an identical demand for golf given by $Q = 100 - P$, where P is the price per round and Q is the number of rounds per year. The club's marginal cost and average total cost per round are $10. There are no fixed costs. The club's executive managers have hired you as an economic consultant to help them maximize profit. What recommendation do you make? Include what price(s) they should charge, what quantity of rounds they will sell, and what their economic profit will be. Help convince them by drawing a figure showing the demand, marginal revenue, and marginal cost curves. In the diagram, indicate your suggested price and quantity, and illustrate the resulting economic profit.

3.7 The Chicago Bears offer what are essentially two products: preseason and regular season football games. They play two preseason and eight regular season home games. Suppose that Fred is a serious football fan. He values the preseason games at $100 each and the regular season games at $200 each. Joe is a more casual fan. He values the preseason games at $150 each and the regular season games also at $150 each. Suppose that Fred and Joe are the only fans.

    a. If the Bears sell the tickets separately, what will be the price of a ticket to a preseason game? The price of a ticket to a regular season game? What total revenue will the Bears collect?

    b. If the Bears bundle tickets for the two preseason and eight regular season games together, what price will the team set for the bundle? What total revenue will the Bears collect?

    c. Should the Bears' managers sell the tickets separately or as a bundle? Explain your answer.

3.8 You are a manager of a company that sells cable television channels. You are thinking of bundling a nature channel and a travel channel. Suppose that the marginal cost of each channel is zero. You have equal numbers of two types of customers. The table lists the maximum monthly price each type is willing to pay for each product.

Customer	Maximum Price Willing to Pay for a Nature Channel	Maximum Price Willing to Pay for a Travel Channel
A	$0.75	$2.00
B	$2.00	$3.00

    a. If you sell the channels separately, what price should you charge for each? What is your monthly profit?

    b. If you bundle the channels, what price should you charge? What is your monthly profit?

    c. To maximize your profit, should you bundle the channels? Why or why not?

Now suppose that your customers' preferences change. The revised maximum prices are shown in the second table.

Customer	Maximum Price Willing to Pay for a Nature Channel	Maximum Price Willing to Pay for a Travel Channel
A	$0.75	$3.00
B	$2.00	$2.00

    d. If you sell the channels separately, what price should you charge for each? What is your monthly profit?

    e. If you bundle the channels, what price should you charge? What is your monthly profit?

    f. To maximize your profit, should you bundle the channels? Why or why not?

10.4 Managerial Application: Using Advanced Pricing Decisions

Learning Objective 10.4 Apply the different advanced pricing techniques to increase economic profit.

4.1 Suppose that Energizer sells a package with one CR 123 battery for $11 and another package with two CR 123 batteries for $19. Can Energizer's managers increase their profit by selling these two different packages, or should they sell only a one-battery package? Explain your answer.

4.2 Many restaurants have lunches that are virtually the same size as their dinners, yet the lunches are invariably cheaper. Explain how these restaurant managers are increasing their profit by engaging in this type of pricing instead of charging the same price for lunch and dinner.

4.3 Sam's Club and Costco have membership fees. Once the fee is paid, the member can buy products from these stores at relatively low prices. What type of pricing are the managers of these stores using? How should Costco and Sam's Club managers set the prices of the products they sell?

4.4 Suppose that the annual demand by adults for playing golf at Crabgrass Country Club is

$$Q_A = 120 - P_A$$

and the annual demand by junior golfers is

$$Q_J = 80 - P_J$$

These demands can be rewritten to express the price as a function of the quantity:

$$P_A = 120 - Q_A$$

and

$$P_J = 80 - Q_J$$

If the marginal cost of a round of golf is $10 and the club can set different annual dues for adults and juniors, what should the club manager set as the annual dues and the greens fee? Explain your answer.

MyLab Economics Auto-Graded Excel Projects

10.1 Many pharmaceutical products are used to treat multiple issues. One example of this is diphenhydramine. Formerly sold under patent as Benadryl, diphenhydramine is now an over-the-counter allergy relief medicine available in generic form. One of the side effects of diphenhydramine is drowsiness. More recently, it has been sold as a nighttime sleep aid (ZzzQuil). Walmart sells two generic versions of diphenhydramine; one is pink, sold as allergy relief medication, and one is blue, sold as a nighttime sleep aid. Walmart sells each version in a bottle of 100 pills with 25 mg of diphenhydramine each. The allergy relief medication sells for $4 per bottle and the nighttime sleep aid sells for $4.98 even though these are chemically identical products.

Suppose you are developing a pricing strategy for a firm in a similar situation to Walmart. You are selling a generic version of a medication which can be used to help keep someone awake but it also acts as a diuretic. Demand for this medicine from people who need to stay awake is $Q = 10000 - 800P$ while demand for individuals who use the medicine as a diuretic is $Q = 7500 - 1000P$. The cost to your company of each bottle sold is $1.50; assume there are no fixed costs.

a. Using the information provided, fill in the template provided. Set up formulas to calculate quantity demanded, total revenue, total cost, profit from each kind of customer, and combined profit.

b. Using Solver, solve for the profit maximizing price for customers who use this medication to stay awake. Suppose you charge customers who use the medication as a diuretic the same price. How many bottles will you sell to each kind of customer? What is your combined profit?

c. Using Solver, solve for the profit maximizing price for customers who use this medication as a diuretic. Suppose you charge customers who use the medication to stay awake the same price. How much will you charge per bottle? How many bottles will you sell to each kind of customer? What is your combined profit?

d. Suppose you charged customers differently based on their use of the medication. How much will you charge per bottle to each kind of customer? How many bottles will you sell to each kind of customer? What is your combined profit?

e. Which plan would you pursue if you were making the decision?

f. How would you try to enforce this price discrimination?

10.2 Shell has over 13,000 gas stations in the United States. In addition to purchasing gasoline, customers can also purchase snacks and beverages at gas stations. Most gas stations sell fountain soda which can be purchased in various sizes.

Suppose you manage a gas station and must determine how much you will charge for fountain soda. The sizes you will make available are 8 oz (S), 16 oz (M), and 24 oz (L). For simplicity, we will assume customer demand (Q) is in 8 oz increments; for example, a customer who demands 2 is demanding a 16 oz soda. Demand for soda is $Q = 2500 - 1250P$. The marginal cost per 8 oz of soda is $.20.

	A	B	C
1	Stay Awake		
2	Coefficients	Coefficients	Values
3	Intercept		
4	Price		
5		Quantity Demanded	
6		Total Revenue	
7		Total Cost	
8		Profit	
9			
10			
11	Diuretic		
12	Coefficients	Coefficients	Values
13	Intercept		
14	Price		
15		Quantity Demanded	
16		Total Revenue	
17		Total Cost	
18		Profit	
19			
20		COMBINED PROFIT	
21			

	A	B	C
1	Coefficients	Coefficients	Values
2	Intercept		
3	Price		
4		Quantity Demanded	
5		Total Revenue	
6		Total Cost	
7		Profit	
8			

a. Using the information provided, fill in the template provided. Set up formulas to calculate quantity demanded, total revenue, total cost, and profit.

b. Using Solver, find the profit-maximizing price and quantity. What are the profit-maximizing price, quantity, and profit? How much would medium and large sodas cost under this pricing structure?

c. Suppose you wanted to engage in second-degree price discrimination. You decide to charge $1.25 for a S (the first 8 oz). How many 8 oz portions do you sell and what is your profit?

d. Suppose you charge $.50 extra to increase the size from S to M. What is the price for a medium soda? How many additional 8 oz portions do you sell? How much additional profit is made?

e. Suppose you charge $.40 extra to increase the size from M to L. How many additional 8 oz portions do you sell? How much additional profit is made?

f. What is total profit using second degree price discrimination? Will you decide to price discriminate? Why or why not?

The Calculus of Advanced Pricing Decisions

Calculus can be used to derive all the advanced pricing decisions discussed in the chapter with the exception of commodity bundling. Whether a bundle increases a firm's profit and, even more complex, whether to have a pure or a mixed bundle remain difficult questions to which calculus has no immediate application. However, deriving the profit-maximizing prices for third-degree price discrimination and for two-part pricing with nonidentical customers can help reinforce the presentation in the chapter and also provide some additional insights. So we start with third-degree price discrimination and then finish with two-part pricing with two nonidentical customers. In both cases, we use the demand and cost curves presented in the chapter in order to make the comparison between the calculus and noncalculus approaches clear.

A. Third-Degree Price Discrimination

A firm using third-degree price discrimination charges different groups of customers different prices for the same product. The factor that makes third-degree price discrimination unlike the usual profit-maximization problem is that the firm sells its output to separate groups of customers with different demands but the production of the product is *not* separate. Consequently, producing more for one group changes the cost of producing for the other group. The point that the firm is selling to two different groups of demanders means that the firm is essentially selling its product in two different markets. In fact, sometimes a firm using third-degree price discrimination will sell in two actually different markets, as, for example, when a firm sells some of its product in a domestic market and the rest of its product in a foreign market.

The chapter used the example of a twin theater, which sells to two groups of customers: senior citizens and younger adults. For reasons discussed in the chapter, the demand from adults exceeds that from seniors. For the demand curves illustrated in the chapter, the adult demand function is

$$Q_A^d = 900 - 100P_A \qquad\qquad \textbf{A10.1}$$

and the senior demand function is

$$Q_S^d = 350 - 50P_S \qquad\qquad \textbf{A10.2}$$

where P is the ticket price, the A subscript applies to the adults, and the S subscript applies to the seniors. These demand functions can be solved to express each price as a function of the quantity. For adults,

$$P_A = 9 - 0.01Q_A^d \qquad\qquad \textbf{A10.3}$$

and for seniors,

$$P_S = 7 - 0.02Q_S^d \qquad\qquad \textbf{A10.4}$$

Equations A10.3 and A10.4 are called the *inverse demand* functions. The total revenue that the twin theater receives from adults, TR_A, is the price of a ticket for adults multiplied by the quantity of tickets adults demand, $P_A \times Q_A^d$, or, using the inverse demand functions for the price,

$$TR_A = (9 - 0.01Q_A^d) \times Q_A^d = 9Q_A^d - 0.01(Q_A^d)^2 \qquad\qquad \textbf{A10.5}$$

The total revenue from seniors, TR_S, is similar:

$$TR_S = (7 - 0.02Q_S^d) \times Q_S^d = 7Q_S^d - 0.02(Q_S^d)^2 \qquad\qquad \textbf{A10.6}$$

Although the firm is selling to different groups of customers, it is producing its product in one plant or, in the case of the theater example, one theater. The linear marginal cost curve in the chapter comes from the total cost function:

$$TC(Q) = 4.6Q + 0.0008Q^2$$

where Q is the total quantity produced; that is, $Q = Q_A^d + Q_S^d$. Taking the derivative of this cost function with respect to Q gives a marginal cost function of:

$$MC(Q) = 4.6 + 0.0016Q = 4.6 + 0.0016Q_A^d + 0.0016Q_S^d$$

where the last equality uses $Q = Q_A^d + Q_S^d$.

The firm's total profit is its total revenue from both the adult and the senior markets minus the total cost, $TR_A + TR_S - TC$, or

$$[9Q_A^d - 0.01(Q_A^d)^2] + [7Q_S^d - 0.02(Q_S^d)^2] - [4.6(Q_A^d + Q_S^d) + 0.0008(Q_A^d + Q_S^d)^2] \quad \textbf{A10.7}$$

where we have substituted $Q_A^d + Q_S^d$ for Q in the total cost function. The total profit function depends on two variables, Q_A^d and Q_S^d. To maximize a function that depends on two variables, take the partial derivatives of both variables, and set them each equal to zero. These will be the two first-order conditions. Then simultaneously solve the first-order conditions for the maximizing values. Applying this general procedure to the total profit in Equation A10.7, the first steps are to take the partial derivatives with respect to Q_A^d and Q_S^d and to set them equal to zero. So Equation A10.8 is the first-order condition with respect to Q_A^d and Equation A10.9 is the first-order condition with respect to Q_S^d:

$$(9 - 0.02Q_A^d) - (4.6 + 0.0016Q_A^d + 0.0016Q_S^d) = 0 \qquad \textbf{A10.8}$$

$$(7 - 0.04Q_S^d) - (4.6 + 0.0016Q_S^d + 0.0016Q_A^d) = 0 \qquad \textbf{A10.9}$$

Simultaneously solving these two equations gives $Q_A^{Dd} = 200$ and $Q_S^d = 50$, exactly the quantities derived in the chapter. All that is left is to determine the profit-maximizing prices for the two groups of demanders. Substitute $Q_A^d = 200$ into Equation A10.3, the adult inverse demand function, to calculate $P_A = \$7$ per ticket for adults. Then substitute $Q_S^d = 50$ into Equation A10.4, the senior inverse demand function, to calculate $PS = \$6$ per ticket for seniors. These prices are exactly the same prices determined in the chapter.

The profit-maximization procedure in the chapter was not as direct as the calculus derivation you have just seen. In particular, in the chapter, we added together the adult and senior marginal revenue curves to obtain the total marginal revenue curve, which we used with the marginal cost curve to determine the total quantity. That step was necessary to ensure that the marginal revenue for adults equals the marginal revenue for seniors. The calculus derivation *automatically* imposes this equality. In the first-order conditions in Equations A10.8 and A10.9, the first terms in parentheses—$(9 - 0.02Q_A^d)$ in Equation A10.8 and $(7 - 0.04Q_S^d)$ in Equation A10.9—are the marginal revenues in the adult and senior markets, respectively. The second term in parentheses in *both* equations—$(4.6 + 0.0016Q_A^d + 0.0016Q_S^d)$— is the marginal cost. Because it is the same in both equations, both the marginal revenue for adults and the marginal revenue for seniors equal the same marginal cost, which means the two marginal revenues must be equal. And, of course, Equations A10.8 and A10.9 are the usual profit-maximization condition, marginal revenue equals marginal cost.

B. Two-Part Pricing

Two-part pricing occurs when the firm charges a fixed access fee that gives customers the right to purchase the product at a specified per-unit price (the user fee). If the customers are identical, the optimal per-unit price and access fee are straightforward: To maximize profit, the per-unit price should equal the marginal cost of the product, and then the access fee should equal what otherwise would be a customer's consumer surplus. Optimal two-part pricing with *non*identical

Figure A10.1 Demand Curves

The young executive demand curve is D_{YE} and nonresident demand curve is D_{NR}.

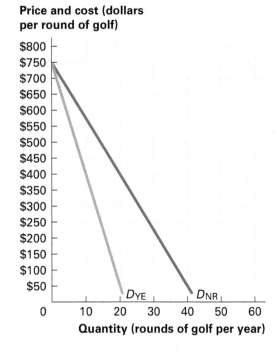

customers, however, is much harder to determine—it remains difficult even with calculus. Using the situation at a golf club similar to the Bay Hill Club and Lodge, the chapter described the trade-offs from raising the greens fee (the user fee or per-unit price) and then simply asserted what the profit-maximizing membership fee (the access fee) and greens fee were. We can use calculus to check that the prices given in the text are correct. When doing so, we will take maximum advantage of the linearity of the demand and cost functions.

Nonidentical Demands

The golf club has equal numbers of two types of members, young executives (YE) and nonresidents (NR). Figure A10.1 shows the demand curves for young executives (D_{YE}) and nonresidents (D_{NR}). The demand from young executives is given by

$$Q^d_{YE} = 21.43 - 0.0286P \qquad \textbf{A10.10}$$

and the demand from nonresidents is given by

$$Q^d_{NR} = 42.84 - 0.0571P \qquad \textbf{A10.11}$$

In both Equations A10.10 and A10.11, P is the price of a round of golf.

The managers set the per-unit price, or greens fee, equal to the value that maximizes their profit. That profit will come from two sources: the membership fee charged to the golfers that belong to the club and the greens fee charged for each round of golf played by the members. We will take each in turn:

- **Membership fee (access fee).** The membership fee is based on the members' consumer surplus. Figure A10.2(a) shows the consumer surpluses for an arbitrarily selected greens fee of $400. In it, the young executive consumer surplus is equal to area A, and the nonresident consumer surplus is equal to areas $A + B$. If the managers at the golf club set the membership fee at an amount equal to area A, both the young executives and the nonresidents join, so the *total* membership fee collected from both is $2A$. If they set it at $A + B$, then only nonresidents join, so the *total* membership fee collected is $A + B$. The managers

Figure A10.2 The Two Sources of the Golf Club's Profit

(a) **Profit from Membership Fee**
With a greens fee of $400, the young executives have a consumer surplus equal to area *A*, and the nonresidents have a consumer surplus equal to areas *A* + *B*. The club's profit from the membership fee is based on the consumer surpluses.

(b) **Profit from Greens Fee**
With a greens fee of $400, the young executives play 10 rounds of golf. On these rounds, the club makes a profit equal to area *C*. The nonresidents play 20 rounds of golf, so club makes an economic profit equal to areas *C* + *D*.

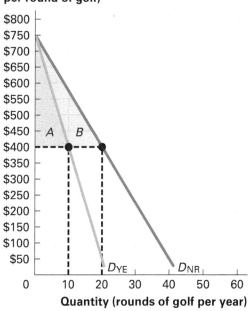

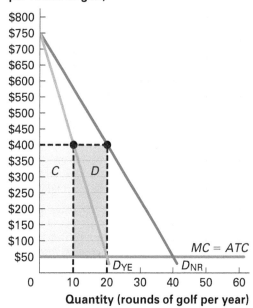

must choose which membership fee to charge based on the total profit. In this example, setting it so both groups join will ultimately yield more profit, so we assume that the managers will set it at the equivalent of *A*.

The consumer surplus for the young executives, *A*, is a triangle, so its area equals $\frac{1}{2} \times$ Base $\times$ Height. The base is the quantity demanded by the young executives at the greens fee. Call the greens fee *P*. From Equation A10.1, the quantity demanded, which equals the base, is $Q^d_{YE} = 21.43 - 0.0286P$. The height is equal to $\$750 - P$. Consequently, the young executives' consumer surplus, which will be membership fee (the access fee), equals

$$\frac{1}{2} \times (21.43 - 0.0286P) \times (\$750 - P) \qquad \textbf{A10.12}$$

Because the club will charge this membership fee to both the young executives and nonresidents, the club's profit from this fee is equal to twice the amount in Equation A10.12, so the profit equals

$$\text{Profit}_{\text{ACCESS}} = (21.43 - 0.0286P) \times (\$750 - P) = 0.0286P^2 - 42.9P + 16{,}073 \quad \textbf{A10.13}$$

- **Greens fee (user fee, or per-unit price).** The second source of profit for the club is the greens fee charged for each round of golf played by each member. As in the chapter, suppose that the marginal cost and average total cost are constant and equal to $50, so

$$MC = ATC = \$50$$

The club's economic profit from the rounds of golf equals $(P - ATC) \times Q^d$, where P is the greens fee and Q^d is the quantity of rounds played. For example, in Figure A10.2(b), with the arbitrary greens fee of $400, the profit from the young executives is equal to the area of rectangle C because that area equals the height $(P - LAC)$ multiplied by the base (Q^d). Similarly, the profit from the nonresidents is equal to rectangular area $C + D$.

In terms of a formula, for any greens fee the profit from the young executives equals the height of the rectangle—which is equal to the economic profit per round, $(P - ATC)$, or the greens fee (P) minus the ATC of $50—multiplied by the base of the rectangle—which is equal to the quantity of rounds demanded, Q^d_{YE}, or the number of rounds played. Equation A10.10 gives the quantity demanded by the young executives, so the profit is

$$\text{Profit}^{YE}_{USE} = (P - \$50) \times (21.43 - 0.0286P) = -0.0286P^2 + 22.9P - 1,072 \quad \textbf{A10.14}$$

For the nonresidents, the economic profit is the same economic profit per round, $(P - ATC)$, multiplied by the number of their rounds, Q^d_{NR}, which is obtained from Equation A10.11, so the profit is

$$\text{Profit}^{NR}_{USE} = (P - \$50) \times (42.84 - 0.0571P) = -0.0571P^2 + 45.7P - 2,142 \quad \textbf{A10.15}$$

The club's total profit equals $\text{Profit}_{ACCESS} + \text{Profit}^{YE}_{USE} + \text{Profit}^{NR}_{USE}$, or, using Equations A10.13, A10.14, and A10.15,

$$(0.0286P^2 - 42.9P + 16,073) + (-0.0286P^2 + 22.9P - 1,072) + (-0.0571P^2 + 45.7P - 2,142)$$

Simplifying the total profit equation by collecting like terms gives

$$\text{Total profit} = -0.0571P^2 + 25.7P + 12,859 \quad \textbf{A10.16}$$

To find the profit-maximizing greens fee (the per-unit price), take the derivative of the total profit function in Equation A10.16 with respect to P, and set it equal to zero:

$$-0.114P + 25.7 = 0 \Rightarrow -0.114P = -25.7 \Rightarrow P = \$225 \quad \textbf{A10.17}$$

The result in Equation A10.17 shows that the profit-maximizing greens fee is $225. Substituting this amount in Equation A10.12 results in a membership fee (access fee) of $3,936.19. Directly from the total profit function in Equation A10.16, the club's total economic profit equals $15,750: $7,875 is the sum of the access fees the young executives and nonresidents pay, and the remaining $7,875 is the economic profit from the 15 rounds of golf played by the young executives and the 30 rounds played by the nonresidents.

Marginal Analysis

The membership fee, the greens fee, the rounds played by the nonresidents and the young executives, and the total economic profit we just calculated are identical to those presented in the chapter. This calculus derivation, however, makes immediately apparent one crucial managerial point: You will never be able to precisely compute the exact profit-maximizing access fee and per-unit price in any real-world context. Nonetheless, the managers' profit-maximizing choice of the greens fee (the per-unit price) has an intuitive interpretation in terms of marginal analysis. Suppose that the managers initially set the greens fee equal to the marginal cost of a round of golf. In this case, the club makes zero economic profit from the rounds of golf. When the managers then raise the greens fee, the club gains economic profit on the rounds of golf played. But as the managers raise the greens fee, consumer surplus shrinks, which decreases the membership fee (the access fee) the club can charge, thereby losing economic profit from this source. As long as the increase in economic profit from the rounds of golf exceeds the loss in economic profit from the reduced membership fee, the managers continue to raise the greens fee because that increases their total profit. The managers stop when the gain in profit from the rounds played equals the loss in profit from the membership fee. At that value of the greens fee, marginal analysis concludes that the managers have maximized the total profit.

Calculus Questions and Problems

A10.1 BiDat is an innovative, new software product used for analyzing big data. The software package is used by both academic institutions and private business firms. Each of these groups has a distinct market demand, which allows the producers of BiDat to engage in price discrimination. The market demand functions from academic institutions and private business firms, respectively, are given by

$$q_A = 225 - 0.25P_A$$

and

$$q_B = 255 - 0.25P_B$$

where q_A is the number of software licenses purchased by academic institutions and q_B is the number of software packages purchased by private business firms. P_A is the price of a license that is charged to academic institutions, and P_B is the price of a license that is charged to private business firms. The cost of providing a BiDat license is the same for both types of customers and is

$$TC(Q) = 141Q + 0.1Q^2$$

where Q is the total quantity of BiDat licenses that are sold.
  a. What is the profit-maximizing quantity of BiDat licenses in each market? What price should each type of customer be charged for a BiDat license?
  b. What is the amount of economic profit or loss?

A10.2 ThomasAir is a new airline that operates as a club airline. Customers purchase a lifetime membership in the ThomasAir Club, after which they can purchase airline tickets to any domestic destination for a single low price. Suppose that you are hired as a pricing consultant by ThomasAir. You quickly notice that ThomasAir has business and vacation customers, each with their own distinct demand for airline travel. The number of tickets demanded by business travelers is

$$q_B = 800 - 5P$$

and the number of tickets demanded by vacation travelers is

$$q_V = 400 - 2.5P$$

where q_B is the demand of business travelers and q_V is the demand of vacation travelers. ThomasAir serves an equal number of travelers of each type. It is, however, unable to determine whether a particular traveler is a business traveler or a vacation

traveler, so it is unable to price discriminate. Call P the price of a domestic flight on ThomasAir. You know that ThomasAir's marginal cost of supplying a flight for one customer is the same for a business or a vacation traveler and is equal to $40, so ThomasAir's total cost is given by

$$TC(q) = 40 \times (q_B + q_V)$$

You advise ThomasAir to use a two-part pricing scheme. What price should ThomasAir charge per domestic flight ticket? What is the membership fee?

A10.3 Kosty Koffie is a coffee shop in Berkeley, California. The coffee market in Berkeley has two very different types of customers. There are many wealthy working professionals and a large number of considerably less wealthy college students. The demand functions for coffee from these two groups are, respectively,

$$q_P = 700 - 100P_P$$

and

$$q_S = 200 - 40P_S$$

where q_P is the number of coffee drinks demanded by professionals and q_S is the number of coffee drinks demanded by students. P_P is the price of a coffee drink for a professional, and P_S is the price of a coffee drink for a student. Solving the demand functions for the price, P, as a function of the quantity demanded, q, gives the two inverse demand functions for coffee for these two groups:

$$P_P = 7 - 0.01q_P$$

and

$$P_S = 5 - 0.025q_S$$

The cost of selling Q coffee drinks is

$$TC(Q) = 3Q + 200$$

  a. What is the profit-maximizing quantity of coffee drinks for each type of customer? What price will each type of customer be charged for a coffee drink?
  b. What is the amount of economic profit or loss that Kosty Koffie earns?

A10.4 Arnold and Associates is a strategy consulting firm based in Washington, D.C., that provides consulting services to both private companies and the federal government. Some congressionally imposed restrictions on federal government spending make the demand for consulting for private companies and that for consulting for the federal government quite different. The two demands are

$$q_P = 2{,}000 - 5P_P$$

and

$$q_G = 1{,}000 - 4P_G$$

where q_P is the number of hours of consulting services demanded by private companies and q_G is the number of number of hours of consulting services demanded by the federal government. P_P is the price per hour for consulting services paid by a private company, and P_G is the price per hour for consulting services paid by the federal government. Solving these demand functions for the price as a function of the quantity yields the inverse demand functions:

$$P_P = 400 - 0.2q_P$$

and

$$P_G = 250 - 0.25q_G$$

The total number of hours of consulting supplied is $Q = q_P + q_G$. The cost of supplying Q hours of consulting services is

$$TC(Q) = 50Q + 150{,}000$$

a. What is the profit-maximizing number of hours of consulting services that Arnold and Associates should supply to each market? What price should each type of customer be charged for an hour of consulting services?
b. What is the amount of Arnold and Associates' economic profit or loss?

A10.5 Becca's Berries is a medium-sized blueberry farm in Gainesville, Florida. The farm supplies blueberries to both not-for-profit cooperatives and for-profit grocery store chains. Becca's Berries observes that these two groups have very different demands for blueberries, so its managers decide that it will charge these two groups different prices. The demand functions for cooperatives and grocery store chains are, respectively,

$$q_C = 800 - 200P_C$$

and

$$q_G = 600 - 100P_G$$

where q_C is the number of pounds of blueberries demanded by not-for-profit cooperatives and q_G is the number of pounds of blueberries demanded by for-profit grocery store chains. P_C is the price of a pound of blueberries that Becca's Berries charges cooperatives, and P_G is the price of a pound of blueberries that Becca's Berries charges grocery store chains.

The total number of berries supplied is $Q = q_C + q_G$. The cost of selling Q pounds of blueberries is

$$TC(Q) = 2Q + 400$$

a. What is the profit-maximizing quantity of blueberries in each market? What is the profit-maximizing price Becca's Berries should charge each type of customer for a pound of blueberries?
b. What is the amount of Becca's Berries economic profit or loss?

CHAPTER 11

Decisions About Vertical Integration and Distribution

Learning Objectives

After studying this chapter, you will be able to:

11.1 Explain vertical integration, forward integration, backward integration, outsourcing, and transfer price.

11.2 Identify how transaction costs, the holdup problem, technological interdependencies, and managerial diseconomies affect vertical integration.

11.3 Analyze how the structure of the upstream and downstream markets affects the profitability of vertical integration.

11.4 Apply the economics of firm structure and distribution to make better managerial decisions about vertical integration.

Why Would Walgreens Boots Alliance Purchase Wholesaler AmerisourceBergen?

In 2014, two large drugstore chains—the U.S.-based Walgreens and the U.K.-based Boots Alliance—merged, creating a chain with over 8,000 locations in the United States and operations in more than 25 countries. Although the newly formed Walgreens Boots Alliance (Walgreens) is large, it faces substantial competition from four sources: (1) other retail drugstore chains, (2) pharmaceutical benefit managers that distribute pharmaceutical drugs through the mail, (3) pharmacy departments in large grocery stores and big-box retailers such as Walmart and Costco, and (4) pharmacies in hospitals. To simplify this discussion, assume that all the competition Walgreens faces make it a perfect competitor.

Walgreens does not buy drugs directly from pharmaceutical producers. Instead, the company buys drugs from intermediaries such as wholesale drug distributor AmerisourceBergen. The intermediaries buy the drugs from pharmaceutical producers and sell them to a number of retailers. AmerisourceBergen has market power, with approximately 25 percent of the wholesale pharmaceutical drug market.

In 2013, when they were still operating as two separate firms, Walgreens and Boots Alliance struck a deal to jointly purchase a 7 percent stake in AmerisourceBergen with the option to purchase an additional 23 percent. The resulting 30 percent ownership would give managers at the firm a controlling stake in AmerisourceBergen. Why are the managers considering this purchase? When you have completed this chapter, you will learn why a controlling interest in AmerisourceBergen offers Walgreens the opportunity to increase its economic profit.

Sources: Caroline Humer and Jessica Wohl, "Walgreens to Buy Stake in AmerisourceBergen, Cardinal Loses Out," Reuters. March 19, 2013; "AmerisourceBergen Announces Strategic, Long-Term Relationship with Walgreens and Alliance Boots," AmerisouceBergen Press Release, March 19, 2013; http://www.walgreensbootsalliance.com/.

Introduction

Products begin life as a collection of raw materials and end it as finished goods a consumer purchases. A *supply chain* consists of the many distinct production and distribution functions performed along the way: Basic raw materials are extracted, transported, and transformed into intermediate goods, which are then used as inputs in later stages of production. Some intermediate goods are used to produce other

Figure 11.1 **A Supply Chain**

Production starts at the top of the supply chain with raw materials. As the raw materials are transformed into intermediate goods, the goods move downstream until they reach the final downstream firm, which sells the finished goods to consumers.

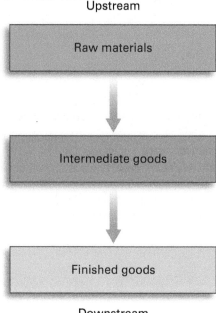

intermediate goods, and some are used to produce finished goods. Ultimately, the intermediate goods are made into finished goods, which are then distributed and sold to consumers. Companies participate in supply chains by purchasing their inputs from one set of firms and selling their output to another set of firms. These business-to-business transactions are sometimes called *B2B transactions*.

Figure 11.1 shows a simplified supply chain. The top of the supply chain, which begins with raw materials, is referred to as the *upstream* end. The bottom of the supply chain, which ends with finished goods, is called the *downstream* end. In other words, production of a good is initiated upstream and flows downstream to the consumer.

To maximize their profit, managers need to answer these questions about their supply chain:

1. **Inputs.** Should a firm that buys an input from a supplier acquire the capacity to produce the input, either by merging or by building new capacity? Or should the firm continue to buy the input from the supplier?
2. **Output.** Should a firm that sells its product to a distributor acquire the capacity to market the product, either by merging or by building new capacity? Or should the firm continue to let the distributor market the product?

Vertical integration A business strategy in which a firm acquires either downstream (closer to the consumer) or upstream (farther from the consumer) productive capacity.

As usual, profit will determine the answers to these questions. Managers must decide whether consolidating the supply chain will generate more profit for their firm. **Vertical integration** is a business strategy in which a firm acquires either downstream (closer to the consumer) or upstream (farther from the consumer) productive capacity. The firm can obtain the capacity to either market its output or produce an input through internal expansion or by merger.[1] Apple's opening of

---

1 When a firm merges with a competitor, it is engaged in *horizontal integration*. These horizontal mergers can lead to cartel behavior (covered in Chapter 7) and antitrust issues (covered in Chapter 9).

retail stores to sell its iPhones and other products is an example of vertical integration. In this case, Apple changed its supply chain so that Apple now markets its own products. Apple moved downstream, closer to the consumer.

To explore the economic factors that help determine the profitability of vertical integration, this chapter includes four sections:

- **Section 11.1** explains the basics of vertical integration, including supply chains, outsourcing, and two different types of vertical integration.
- **Section 11.2** explores the economic factors that can make vertical integration profitable, including transaction costs and transaction-specific assets.
- **Section 11.3** describes the effect of market structure type on the profitability of vertical integration.
- **Section 11.4** examines how applying the theory of firm structure and distribution can help you make better managerial decisions about vertical integration.

11.1 The Basics of Vertical Integration

Learning Objective 11.1 Explain vertical integration, forward integration, backward integration, outsourcing, and transfer price.

A product can move along its supply chain with the production performed by separate specialized firms or by different departments or divisions within a single firm. If separate firms are involved, the item moves from the upstream firm to the downstream firm using a market. If a single firm is involved, the firm transfers the product internally from its upstream division to its downstream division, often with little or no participation in a market. Managers should choose whichever method is less expensive.

Markets Versus Vertical Integration

Using a market is often the less expensive option for products or services that are standardized. For these products or services, managers might use a *spot market*, a market in which delivery of the good or service is immediate and buyers and sellers have no legal relationship to each other. For example, Lowe's stands ready to sell and immediately deliver $4' \times 8'$ sheets of PS1-09 plywood sheathing to any carpenter who needs some. In this case, the plywood moves from Lowe's, the upstream firm, to the builder, the downstream firm, using a market.

Markets are also used for products or services that are either specialized and/or needed repeatedly. But in these cases, the buyers and sellers frequently establish a legal relationship using a contract that spells out each party's responsibilities. Each Lowe's store, for example, has entered the plumbing market to contract with local plumbers to install water heaters purchased from Lowe's. Lowe's and the local plumbers have signed contracts that specify their responsibilities for two reasons: (1) Installation of water heaters is specialized because it varies from one job to the next, and (2) Lowe's sells water heaters every day. These contracts require the plumber to contact the customer within two business days, to use parts from Lowe's to install the water heater, and to collect payment from Lowe's (not the customer).

Using markets, however, usually entails a variety of transaction costs. As you learned in Chapter 5, *transaction costs* are the costs of using a market, *not* the price of the good or service. Section 11.2 details these costs as you begin to study the economics of vertical integration.

Rather than use a market, some firms produce at more than one stage of the supply chain illustrated in Figure 11.1. These firms are *vertically integrated*. Some vertically integrated firms, however, transfer only a fraction of their production internally from one department to another because they sell some in a market. For example, Energizer produces batteries. The company transfers some of these batteries to its flashlight division and sells the rest to distributors which then market them to consumers. Hyundai subsidiary Hyundai Powertech produces six-speed automatic transmissions that follow a similar path. Hyundai uses some of these transmissions in its Sonata and sells some to other automakers in the transmissions market. Other vertically integrated firms, however, do not produce enough of the intermediate product to meet their needs. For example, ExxonMobil's upstream oil extraction division produces less oil than its downstream refining division requires, so the refining division buys additional oil on the open market. Like ExxonMobil, many firms find it more profitable to produce a portion of their own inputs and purchase the rest from independent suppliers. These firms are *partially vertically integrated*.

No firm is completely vertically integrated. All firms purchase some inputs or services that they could, in principle, manufacture or provide themselves. General Motors could produce the tires on the cars it sells, but its managers have decided that it is more cost effective to use tires produced by a variety of other companies.

Types of Vertical Integration

Forward and Backward Integration

Forward integration A business strategy in which a firm acquires downstream (closer to the consumer) productive capacity.

Backward integration A business strategy in which a firm acquires upstream (farther from the consumer) productive capacity.

An upstream firm can acquire downstream productive capacity by merging with or buying a downstream firm or by adding the capacity to perform the downstream function itself. Regardless of the method, **forward integration** occurs when a firm acquires downstream (closer to the consumer) productive capacity. In this case, the firm is moving *forward* or toward the consumer in the supply chain. For example, PepsiCo engaged in forward integration when it acquired Pepsi Bottling Group, the company that bottles and distributes its product (soda) to consumers. In contrast, **backward integration** occurs when a firm acquires upstream (farther from the consumer) productive capacity. In this case, the firm is moving *backward* or away from the consumer by purchasing or merging with an input supplier or constructing its own input supply facilities. Red Lobster's construction of the world's largest lobster farm in Malaysia is an example of backward integration.

Outsourcing

Outsourcing Contracting with an outside supplier to produce an input.

The opposite of backward integration is **outsourcing**, contracting with an outside supplier to produce an input. For example, Apple's own engineers design its iPhone, and the company markets some of its phones using its own Apple stores, but Apple employees have *never* constructed the iPhone. Instead, the company outsources iPhone production to other firms, such as Samsung, Largan Precision, and Qorvo for parts and Foxconn Technology Group for assembly. Apple initially produced its Macintosh computer, but during the 1990s, its managers decided that it was more profitable to outsource Macintosh production. Today, firms outsource more than just production. TD Canada Trust Bank outsources its customer support to a call center overseas; the Blush School of Makeup in San Francisco outsources the design of its website to SDI, a software company located in India; and Walgreens outsources the production of Wal-Phed (its generic version of the antihistaminic drug Sudafed) to LNK International, a drug manufacturer located in Hauppauge, New York.

Divestiture

The opposite of integration is **divestiture**, the selling or spinning off of some lines of business. For example, at one time, ConocoPhillips was a totally integrated oil company—it had one division devoted to exploring for oil, another to pumping the oil, another to refining the oil, and still another to retailing the refined gasoline. ConocoPhillips' managers, however, decided to concentrate on finding and producing oil, so they spun off their downstream refining and distribution divisions as a new company, Phillips 66.

Not all divestiture undoes vertical integration. Harris Corporation is a major defense contractor that produces tactical radios and night vision equipment, among other products. When Harris Corporation sold its broadcasting division, which produced products such as radio on-air production consoles, it was not decreasing the extent of its integration. Instead, it was selling off a business unrelated to its main line of work.

Divestiture The selling or spinning off of some lines of business.

Transfer Prices and Taxes

Whether managers engage in either forward or backward integration, they are choosing to replace a market exchange governed by arm's-length bargaining (bargaining by two independent agents) and market prices with an internal transfer. If a vertically integrated firm combines different stages of production, managers often still assign a price to the intermediate good as it passes from the upstream division to the downstream division. A **transfer price** is an accounting entry that reflects the internal price of an input that the input-producing division charges the input-using division.

Transfer prices can affect the taxes a firm must pay. For example, the pharmaceutical company Actavis manufactures many of its drugs in Ireland. The Irish manufacturing division sells the drugs to the U.S. subsidiary, which markets them in the United States. Suppose that you work for a similar firm and that your marginal cost of manufacturing a drug in Ireland is $50 per dose and your marginal revenue when selling it in the United States is $150 per dose. From an economic standpoint, your profit on a dose of the drug is $150 − $50 = $100.

The transfer price between the manufacturing division and selling division divides this profit between the two divisions. If you set a high transfer price—say, $130 per dose—the profit at the Irish subsidiary is higher ($80), and the profit at the U.S. division is lower ($20). Your firm must pay income taxes on its profit, so the transfer price helps determine the amount of taxes it pays to Ireland and the amount it pays to the United States. Because the Irish corporate income tax rate (14.5 percent) is substantially lower than the U.S. corporate income tax rate (in 2017, 35 percent for corporate profit that exceeds $18,333,333), you have an incentive to set a high transfer price, which creates more profit in Ireland and less in the United States. Laws in many nations, however, state that a transfer price must equal the price charged to an independent customer. In other words, the transfer price should equal the price set for arm's-length bargaining. A country's government can take violators to court and impose significant financial penalties. Consequently, there are specialist firms, as well as divisions within major financial firms, devoted to selling their expertise in cross-country transfer pricing.

Transfer price An accounting entry for the within-firm price of an input that the input-producing division charges the input-using division.

Because accounting transfer prices are important in allocating accounting profit among different branches of a company, profit-maximizing managers must consider them carefully. Section 11.4 examines other issues involved in transfer pricing.

Tax Inversion

Tax inversions are a popular method of reducing the corporate taxes that a company must pay. A company is subject to the income tax laws of the country in which it is domiciled, but countries differ in the tax rates they charge and the profit they tax. The United States has a high corporate tax rate and imposes this tax rate on income a U.S. firm earns anywhere in the world. Most nations have lower tax rates and tax only profit earned domestically.

In order to lower their taxes, U.S.-domiciled firms have an incentive to create or buy a foreign parent firm so that they are then taxed at the lower foreign rate. Large U.S. firms can arrange mergers with smaller foreign firms in such a way that the foreign firm legally becomes the parent of the U.S. firm, a process called *tax inversion*. Although these mergers are often horizontal, nothing precludes a vertical tax inversion merger. Once the foreign firm "owns" the U.S.-based firm, the combined firm is subject to the corporate tax laws in the foreign nation. So a tax inversion merger can reduce the combined firm's taxes. Because these mergers reduce the amount of tax the firm pays to the U.S. government, in 2016 the U.S. government changed tax regulations to make it harder for a merging U.S. firm to qualify as being owned by the smaller foreign entity.

SOLVED PROBLEM

Vertical Integration

Are the following examples of forward integration, backward integration, or neither? Explain each of your answers.

a. General Motors (GM) purchases Delphi Automotive, a producer of automotive parts.

b. The University of Texas forms the Longhorn Network to provide 24-hour coverage of University of Texas sports.

c. T-Mobile purchases another cell phone company, MetroPCS Communications.

Answer

a. GM's purchase of Delphi Automotive is an example of backward integration because GM purchased a supplier.

b. The University of Texas's formation of the Longhorn Network is an example of forward integration because it allows the university to televise its football and basketball games for a mass audience.

c. T-Mobile's purchase of MetroPCS Communications is neither forward nor backward integration. T-Mobile purchased a competitor, which makes this a horizontal merger.

11.2 The Economics of Vertical Integration

Learning Objective 11.2 Identify how transaction costs, the holdup problem, technological interdependencies, and managerial diseconomies affect vertical integration.

At its most basic level, vertical integration replaces market transactions with intra-firm transactions. This replacement can lower firms' costs in four ways. First, vertical integration can result in cost savings from synergies such as the elimination of duplicate operations. Second, intra-firm transfers can lower the transaction costs involved in using markets. Third, vertical integration can eliminate an issue called the *holdup problem*, in which one firm behaves opportunistically to take advantage of another firm that has already made an investment designed to benefit both firms. Finally, intra-firm transactions can accommodate *technological interdependencies*—in which one stage of the production process must immediately follow another stage—more inexpensively than can use of a market. Vertical integration can also *increase* costs, however. Consequently, this section discusses the different ways that vertical integration affects a firm's costs.

Synergies

Vertical integration can result in substantial cost savings as managers eliminate duplicate operations. Prior to the merger, both companies required accounting departments, executive managers with a supporting staff, and a corporate headquarters. The merged company does not need two accounting departments or two headquarters. In addition, the merged company can trim the number of executives along with the supporting staff. These cost savings are often called *synergies* because *synergy* is the creation of a whole (the new company) that is more than just the sum of its parts (the merging companies). For example, when AT&T announced it would acquire Time Warner, AT&T's executives said they expected to achieve $1 billion in annual synergies after the first three years.

Announcements about companies merging usually focus on synergistic cost savings. The announcements almost never mention transaction cost savings, but these savings may well be more extensive than the synergies.

Costs of Using a Market: Transaction Costs, the Holdup Problem, and Technological Interdependencies

Transaction Costs

Using markets to transfer goods and services along the supply chain creates transaction costs. If the firm vertically integrates, it can save these costs. Four categories of transaction costs provide managers the incentive to vertically integrate:

1. Taxes
2. Information costs
3. Negotiation, monitoring, and enforcement costs
4. Reduced flexibility

Taxes   The government often treats market transactions differently from identical transactions within a firm. You already saw how a merger with a foreign firm (or a tax inversion) can reduce a firm's taxes. Domestically within the United States, the most obvious tax saving from vertical integration involves sales taxes. Market transactions are often subject to sales tax, so production using markets can result in substantial tax payments as the firm purchases different inputs and engages in various production activities. Integrating all activities under the umbrella of the firm means that no taxable transactions occur during production, which lowers this type of transaction cost.

Information Costs

Information costs The costs of discovering relevant information about prices or other aspects of a transaction.

Information Costs   **Information costs** include the costs of discovering relevant information about prices or other aspects of a transaction. For example, when Apple wanted to include a new accelerometer (the device that enables the display to switch to horizontal or vertical depending on how the phone is held) in its iPhone, Apple's purchasing managers had to explore the prices, capabilities, sizes, and quality of those offered by STMicroelectronics and Bosch. More generally, each time managers contemplate buying an input in a market transaction, they must search for the best price, determine the quality of the input, and investigate the supplier's delivery capabilities. Assembling all of the information is costly in terms of both expenditure of funds and use of managerial time and effort. When dealing with a new, unfamiliar supplier, these information costs can be even higher. A sizable fraction of the budgets of the purchasing and marketing departments in many corporations is attributable to the information costs involved in buying inputs and selling outputs.

Negotiation, Monitoring, and Enforcement Costs   If the transaction will involve a contract, the buyer and seller must negotiate, monitor, and, in some instances, enforce that contract using the legal system. All of these efforts are costly. These costs fall into three categories:

- Negotiation costs: costs incurred in arranging a contract for a market exchange
- Monitoring costs: costs incurred in ensuring compliance with the contract
- Enforcement costs: costs incurred in imposing compliance with the contract

Contracts must specify the price and quantity of the product to be traded. They usually stipulate other important details as well, such as product quality, warranties, delivery dates, buyback agreements, and price escalator clauses. Detailed specification is necessary to ensure that both parties live up to the terms of the agreement because the incentives to adhere to the spirit of the contract can change drastically after they sign it. As the length of the contract increases, specifying future contingencies becomes increasingly challenging. In addition, the more complex the product or trading environment is, the more difficult it becomes to predict future contingencies and the parties' contractual obligations if those contingencies should arise. Any contingencies not covered by the terms of the contract can leave one or both firms vulnerable to opportunistic behavior. Consequently, the longer the term of the contract and the more complex the product, the greater the transaction costs of negotiation, monitoring, and enforcement.

Reduced Flexibility   The reduced flexibility of contracts, particularly long-term contracts, also creates costs. For example, say that Apache Corporation, a petroleum and natural gas exploration and production company, signs a long-term contract to supply natural gas to NRG Energy, an energy company doing business in Texas and in the Northeast. If the market price of natural gas falls during the term of the contract and the contract has no contingency clause regarding price, NRG (the buyer) incurs an opportunity cost because it is unable to take advantage of the lower market price. A similar opportunity cost is borne by Apache Corporation (the seller) if the market price of natural gas increases during the term of the contract and there is no price escalator clause. Changes in other market conditions, such as new government regulations, can also impose costs. For example, if the government issues new regulations that require natural gas producers to use more expensive fracking methods, Apache

| DECISION SNAPSHOT | PepsiCo Reduces Transaction Costs |

PepsiCo produces the syrup for its sodas. Until 2009, the company sold the syrup to independent bottlers that combined it with carbonated water and distributed the finished soda to grocery stores, drugstores, convenience stores, and vending machines. In 2009, PepsiCo purchased its bottlers. As a manager at PepsiCo, why would you decide to forward integrate (purchase your bottlers)?

Answer

You would purchase PepsiCo's bottlers if you believed it would increase PepsiCo's profit by decreasing transaction costs. Here's how the CEO of Pepsi Bottling, Eric Foss, explained the purchase: "In a rapidly changing, more complicated global market, a leaner, more agile business model is pretty important." Mr. Foss was referring to the transaction costs of dealing with the market. In particular, consumers' tastes were rapidly switching away from carbonated soda toward water and other drinks. PepsiCo was continually introducing new products better aligned with consumers' tastes, which required frequent renegotiations of its contracts with bottlers and many discussions about the spirit of the contracts. Purchasing the bottlers decreased the cost of acquiring and disseminating information about market changes and reduced the negotiation and monitoring costs caused by changes in market conditions. By vertically integrating forward, the managers at PepsiCo eliminated these transaction costs, boosting their economic profit.

Corporation might incur an economic loss: Apache's costs increase, but without an appropriate contingency clause, the price it charges does not change. By entering into a contractual agreement, each party locks itself into a predetermined pattern of behavior. An unexpected change in market conditions often makes this behavior suboptimal and therefore costly ex post—that is, costly after signing the contract.

The Holdup Problem

Sometimes a firm makes an investment that has very limited use outside its intended purpose. This sort of investment is called a **transaction-specific asset**, an asset specific to one purpose that cannot be put easily to other uses. Transaction-specific assets often result from investments undertaken to support a specific set of market transactions. Examples of transaction-specific assets include the following:

Transaction-specific assets Assets specific to one purpose that cannot be easily put to other uses.

- Appalachian Power built its coal-powered Clinch River power plant close to the region's coal mines to reduce the costs of transporting coal to the plant. The plant is a transaction-specific asset because it is located to use coal from the region's mines.
- Amazon.com built small, enclosed shipment centers within large warehouses owned by Procter & Gamble to ship P&G products. The shipment centers are transaction-specific assets because Amazon can use them to ship only P&G products.

- Phoenix Technologies makes the basic input/output system (BIOS) for motherboards. (A BIOS is the program that allows a computer to boot up when started.) A BIOS program is a transaction-specific asset because its only use is to boot up a particular company's motherboard.

The returns that Appalachian Power, Amazon, and Phoenix Technologies expect from their investments depend, to a large degree, on whether the anticipated transactions take place at reasonably favorable prices. That is, the post-investment profits realized by the companies depend on the prices paid by Appalachian Power to the coal companies, by Amazon to Procter & Gamble, and by the motherboard manufacturers to Phoenix Technologies.

Holdup problem When one party to an agreement tries to increase its profit by unilaterally changing the terms of the agreement or insisting on renegotiation once the other party has invested in a transaction-specific asset.

Once transaction-specific assets are in place, the firm that owns them becomes vulnerable to the **holdup problem**. The holdup problem occurs when one party to an agreement tries to increase its profit by unilaterally changing the terms of an agreement or insisting on renegotiation after the other party has invested in a transaction-specific asset. Once a firm has invested in a transaction-specific asset, the cost of the investment is sunk. Consequently, its trading partner may be able to alter the original terms of the agreement in its favor. For example, managers at a motherboard company such as ASUS know that once Phoenix Technologies creates a BIOS program specifically for them, (1) Phoenix Technologies has already paid the costs of creating the program, and (2) the program is useless to Phoenix Technologies unless ASUS purchases it. The motherboard company's managers also know that once the program is created, the cost of providing it to them is very low. Suppose that they threaten not to buy the BIOS program at all unless Phoenix Technologies sells it to them at a much lower price than initially specified in their agreement. Because Phoenix Technologies has already paid the costs of creating the program and it would rather get something than nothing for the program, in this scenario it might agree to the reduced price.

The holdup problem can affect managers' behavior before their firm makes the investment in the transaction-specific asset. In particular, even if the investment would otherwise be highly profitable, the possibility of facing the holdup problem might deter managers from making the initial investment. The managers might decide not to make the investment at all, or they might decide to make an investment that is suboptimal but more general in nature. For example, building its Clinch River plant close to the region's coal mines would benefit Appalachian Power. But if its managers fear the holdup problem from those mines, they might instead choose to build the plant midway between this region's coal mines and a different coal field.

A contract can help mitigate the holdup problem. Envisioning all potential holdups and negotiating a solution in advance, however, is a complicated, costly task. Vertical integration can overcome the holdup problem entirely.

How Vertical Integration Reduces Transaction Costs and the Holdup Problem

By replacing market transactions with internal transfers, vertical integration can reduce transaction costs substantially and eliminate the holdup problem. Instead of buyers and sellers from different firms negotiating the purchase and sale of an intermediate product or input, managers within a single firm organize the production and transfer of the product from the upstream division to the downstream division of the integrated firm. Even setting aside the potential for tax savings, replacing market transactions with administrative decisions can reduce transaction costs and the holdup problem in four additional ways:

1. **Increased information and control.** The incentive and control options available to a firm's managers are much more extensive for intra-firm transfers than for market transactions. It is far easier for the managers of a firm to discover and, as necessary, reward or penalize the behavior of employees than it is to exercise similar controls over the behavior of another firm. In particular, vertical integration improves managers' access to relevant information about the behavior of employees or divisions and makes rewards or penalties easier to administer. In addition, if a firm produces its own inputs, its managers do not need to engage in an extensive search for a good price; they are well aware of the quality of the input; and they are equally aware of the delivery capabilities. In other words, familiarity breeds lower costs.

2. **Establishment of partnership.** Internalizing the transfer alters the relationship between the buyer and seller from largely adversarial to a partnership. Without vertical integration, one firm often stands to gain profit at the expense of the other firm. For example, if firm 1 can increase its profit by $1 through an action—say, by causing a holdup problem with its partner—it might do so even if that action reduces firm 2's profit by $100, thereby reducing the combined profits of the two firms by $99.[2] By uniting the profits of the two firms, vertical integration brings about a convergence of goals, reducing or maybe even eliminating the incentive for this sort of counterproductive holdup behavior. Such convergence reduces the costs of completing the given transaction because the parties involved no longer find it necessary to expend resources designing and negotiating contracts to protect themselves from the anticipated opportunism of the other party.

3. **Decreased incentive for litigation.** Even when the discovery of opportunistic behavior by another firm is easy, such as a demand by a motherboard manufacturer to renegotiate its agreement with Phoenix Technologies, the solution can be costly. As noted above, the potential for such opportunistic behavior and the costs of defending against it can prevent a firm from investing in transaction-specific assets even if the potential increase in the (joint) profit is large. Both renegotiation and litigation are costly options, and the latter might be the only means available for encouraging more desirable performance by the firm causing the holdup problem. Vertical integration, however, makes such actions unnecessary.

4. **Decreased search costs.** Finally, termination of a contractual relationship because of failure to elicit changes in performance brings with it the costs associated with searching for a new supplier or customer and then negotiating a new contract. Because it brings production under one roof, vertical integration makes termination of such a relationship much less likely.

If the two parties are separate divisions within the same vertically integrated firm, they can avoid all of these costs.

Technological Interdependency

The supply chains of some production processes display **technological interdependency**, which occurs when there is a technologically close relationship between two or more stages in the supply chain so that the inputs flow in a virtually continuous movement toward the final product. For example, ArcelorMittal is the world's largest steel manufacturer. It produces steel in its mill in the city of Ostrava in the Czech Republic. In this mill, a blast furnace heats the iron ore to convert it into pig iron (iron with

Technological interdependency A technologically close relationship between two or more stages in the supply chain in which the inputs flow in a virtually continuous movement toward the final product.

2 If, however, the contract is part of a repeated interaction, you learned in Chapter 8's analysis of repeated games that firm 1 might not pursue the action because it fears punishment by firm 2 in some future interaction.

relatively high carbon content). Next, the liquid pig iron is immediately poured into a converter, where oxygen is blown through the liquid. This step lowers the carbon content and changes the pig iron into steel. The technology of producing steel requires that the raw material, iron ore, flow continuously along the supply chain until it emerges as steel. On the other hand, General Motors' production of automobiles is not subject to such technological interdependencies. Managers easily stop the assembly line for as long as necessary, the different components of the car (seats, transmission, tires) can be assembled in advance and stored until needed, and the order in which the components are assembled can change.

ArcelorMittal owns both the blast furnaces and the converters at its mill. This dual ownership is common in the steel industry. Why? The vertical integration of the two successive production stages and the resulting continuous operation minimize production costs by avoiding the need to reheat the pig iron as it moves from one stage of production to the next. If one company owned the blast furnace and another owned the converter, using markets to coordinate the production would be incredibly complicated. In addition, the contractual arrangements required to achieve such coordination would be complex, and contract enforcement would contribute to increases in transaction costs. Clearly, because of the technological interdependencies in this production process, it is less expensive for a single firm to carry out the multiple production stages required to produce steel.

Costs of Using Vertical Integration

Although vertical integration reduces some costs, it increases others. Costs can increase for two reasons:

- **Increase in required areas of expertise.** A firm's managers have expertise in particular areas. Vertical integration outside of these areas requires new expertise, which can lead to significant increases in costs. For example, the managers at LongHorn Steakhouse are experts in running steak restaurants but would be at a loss if faced with raising the steers that end up on their plates. If LongHorn Steakhouse integrated backward so that it raised its own steers, its costs would rise as its managers attempted to make rational production decisions regarding the care and feeding of cattle.
- **Increase in the complexity of coordination.** Expanding a firm's operations to an additional stage of production increases the challenge of coordinating its activities. As the firm brings more and more of the supply chain within its control, efficient management of the total operation becomes increasingly costly. More managers must be hired, or existing managers must be spread thin, possibly causing them to make poorer decisions as their span of control increases. Continuing the example started above, if LongHorn Steakhouse actually integrated backward by raising its own steers, it would need to hire additional managers with different skill sets than its current managers. Executives would need to supervise managers in charge of raising steers as well as regional managers in charge of operating the restaurants. Dividing their attention over this wide span of issues might reduce the effectiveness of these executives.

Managerial diseconomies
The increased costs of managing a company that result from an increase in the scope of the firm's operations.

The increased costs of managing a company that result from an increase in the scope of the firm's operations are called **managerial diseconomies**. Regardless of their source, when considering vertical integration, you must balance the managerial diseconomies against the cost savings.

| DECISION **SNAPSHOT** | Pilgrim's Pride and the Limits of Vertical Integration |

Pilgrim's Pride is the second-largest chicken producer in the world, annually processing almost 10 billion pounds of chicken. Pilgrim's Pride owns the hens that lay the eggs hatched in their hatcheries. When the eggs hatch, the hatchlings are trucked to independently owned farms, called grow-out farms. Grow-out farmers undertake the complex task of growing and feeding the hatchlings. Their contracts with Pilgrim's Pride are straightforward: The farmers will care for the hatchlings, using food supplied by Pilgrim's Pride, for about five weeks. After five weeks, the grow-out farmers return the chickens to Pilgrim's Pride, which pays them based on the birds' weight. Pilgrim's Pride then processes the chickens and distributes them to grocers and other customers. As a manager of Pilgrim's Pride, should you complete the vertical integration by purchasing the grow-out farmers?

Answer
Pilgrim's Pride should not purchase the grow-out farmers for several reasons. The transaction costs from using the market to contract with the grow-out farmers are not large, and the contracts are relatively simple. In addition, while hatching chickens is not complicated, growing them is more so. The managers of Pilgrim's Pride have expertise in processing and distributing chickens, but they have no expertise in growing chickens, so the managerial diseconomies of taking over that stage of the production process would be large. The increase in cost from managerial diseconomies exceeds the cost savings, so vertical integration into the grow-out stage would decrease Pilgrim's Pride's profit.

Integrating forward by purchasing only one or a few customers carries with it an additional problem, the risk of alienating other customers. For example, 3dfx Interactive was the first company to design and produce graphics chips for the video cards used by gamers to play sophisticated games on their computers. 3dfx designed and produced the chips and then sold them to other companies. Those companies used the chips to create the video cards that they then sold to consumers. 3dfx's success brought competitors to the market with the same business strategy: design and produce the chips and then sell them to other companies to use in video cards. After being successful for several years, 3dfx's managers decided to buy one of their customers, STB Systems. The managers of the other video card producers did not appreciate 3dfx becoming a competitor, so they immediately stopped buying 3dfx chips, switching to chips produced by a competitor, Nvidia. Within two years, 3dfx was bankrupt. If 3dfx had been a monopoly graphics chip designer, the outcome might well have been different because then the retailers of the video cards would have had no choice but to continue to buy 3dfx's chips. As a competitive producer, however, 3dfx's forward integration strategy was a mistake.

Changes in transaction costs, technological interdependencies, and managerial diseconomies are not the only economic consequences that result from vertical integration. A firm's profit from vertical integration also depends on the market structures of the integrated markets, the topic of the next section.

SOLVED PROBLEM	**IBM Avoids a Holdup Problem**

Today, Intel and AMD compete in the market for central processing units (CPUs), the microprocessors used in PCs. At the start of the computer revolution more than 30 years ago, however, Intel had a monopoly in the market for powerful (for the time!) CPUs, and IBM was the largest company producing personal computers. IBM's executives created a strict policy against *single sourcing*, buying an input from a firm that is the only producer, so IBM forced Intel to license the right to produce compatible CPUs to AMD. Over the years, nearly 20 other companies produced compatible CPUs, but they always lagged behind the power of Intel (and AMD) CPUs. Today, AMD is Intel's only surviving competitor. AMD's survival probably resulted, in large part, from the license Intel granted.

a. Why would IBM managers decide to use the firm's market power to force Intel to license its technology to AMD?

b. How is IBM's policy against single sourcing related to the holdup problem?

Answer

a. IBM's managers were concerned that, after designing their computers to use Intel's powerful CPUs, managers at Intel might demand a higher price for their CPUs. By requiring Intel to license the right to produce this type of CPU to another company, IBM's managers created another source for its CPUs.

b. Creating another source for its CPUs allowed IBM to sidestep the holdup problem. IBM also could have avoided the holdup problem by backward integration (purchasing Intel), but it is clear that IBM's managers considered a second source for the CPUs to be the lower-cost alternative.

11.3 Vertical Integration and Market Structure

Learning Objective 11.3 Analyze how the structure of the upstream and downstream markets affects the profitability of vertical integration.

To this point, you have learned how vertical integration affects a firm's costs without considering the market structures along the supply chain. The profit from vertical integration, however, will vary depending on the structures of the involved markets. The managers of a firm with market power who are considering forward integration by merging with the distributor(s) of its product must take into account the structure of the downstream market because the profitability of the merger depends in part on whether the downstream market is competitive or monopolistic.

This section begins by assuming that the downstream market is perfectly competitive. To make the analysis more straightforward, assume that the producer buys *all* of the distributors, avoiding the problem that sank 3dfx. After analyzing these results, the section turns to a monopolistic distributor market. To focus solely on the effect market structure has on vertical integration, ignore the cost savings from reduced transaction costs and technological interdependencies as well as any cost increases from managerial diseconomies. As a result, any increase in profit from vertical integration is over and above the gains or losses discussed in Section 11.2.

Vertical Integration with Competitive Distributors

Levi Strauss & Company produces an extremely popular line of jeans that everyone knows as Levi's. Due to the style, fit, and durability of Levi's, Levi Strauss enjoys a good deal of market power. Say that you are a manager for a clothing firm like Levi Strauss and for simplicity, assume that your firm is a monopoly. Although the precise numerical results depend on this assumption, you can use the qualitative results—such as "the profit increases"—as a guide to your real-world decision making. Suppose that, as one of the managers of the firm, you must decide whether to distribute your jeans through company-owned outlets or independent retail distributors.

Derived Demand for Competitive Distributors

Begin with the case in which your firm produces its jeans and sells them to a large number of perfectly competitive independent retail distributors. Using the tools developed in Section 3.1, your marketing research department has estimated consumers' retail demand for these jeans. As a manager, you must decide how many pairs of jeans to produce and what price to charge. Because your company does not sell directly to consumers, the retailers' demand for your jeans, which is the wholesale demand for jeans, dictates your price and output decisions. The wholesale demand from retailers (distributors) for any product is a **derived demand** because it is *derived* from consumer demand.[3] Once you have determined the wholesale demand, the familiar principles of profit maximization take over.

Derived demand The wholesale demand from retailers (distributors) for any product.

For a quantity of, say, 50,000 pairs of jeans, the *wholesale* price retailers will pay your firm is P_w, and the *retail* price consumers will pay the retailers is P. The wholesale price/quantity combination is a point on the wholesale (derived) demand curve for jeans, and the retail price/quantity combination is a point on the retail demand curve.

To calculate the (wholesale) price on the wholesale demand curve, use the point that the retail market is perfectly competitive. Recall from Chapter 5 that when the firms in a perfectly competitive market maximize their profit, the *retail* price (P) equals the retailers' marginal cost, or $P = MC$. You can divide the retailers' marginal cost into two components: the wholesale price they pay your firm for the jeans (P_w) and all the other marginal costs, which we call the marginal cost of distributing the jeans (MC_D). The marginal cost of distributing the jeans includes the retailer's cost of sales personnel, rent for the retail store, and the owners' competitive return. The retailer's marginal cost is $P_w + MC_D$, so the profit-maximizing condition for the retailers is

$$P = MC = P_w + MC_D \qquad \qquad 11.1$$

If you rearrange the two end terms of Equation 11.1 to $P_w = P - MC_D$, you can determine the wholesale price that the retailers will pay. The rearranged equation shows that at each quantity of jeans the wholesale price is the retail price at that quantity (P) minus the marginal cost of distributing the jeans (MC_D). As a result, the wholesale demand curve lies below the retail demand curve by the marginal cost of distributing the jeans.

Figure 11.2 illustrates the results of these calculations for your firm's jeans. To simplify the presentation, here and throughout the chapter assume that the demand curve is linear and the marginal costs are constant. Although the specific results depend on

---

3 There are other derived demands. For example, a firm's demand for workers is a derived demand, since the firm hires workers only because the workers help produce items consumers demand.

Figure 11.2 The Wholesale Demand Curve with Competitive Distributors of Jeans

The consumer (retail) demand curve for jeans is labeled D. The wholesale demand curve (D_W) shows the wholesale price retailers will pay for any quantity of jeans. This price equals the retail price paid by consumers for a pair of jeans minus the marginal cost of distributing the jeans (MC_D). For simplicity, assume that this marginal cost is constant at $10 per pair of jeans, making MC_D horizontal. Consequently, D_W lies $10 below D.

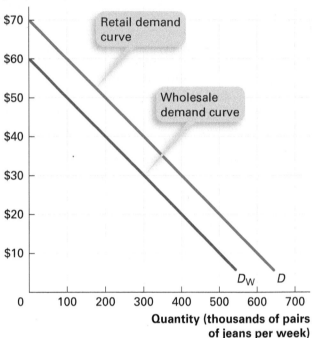

these assumptions, the general results are true for nonlinear demand and marginal cost curves. In Figure 11.2, the consumer retail demand curve for jeans is D. Assume that the marginal cost of distributing a pair of jeans is constant at $10 per pair, so for any retail price (P) the wholesale price (P_W) is $10 less. Consequently the wholesale demand curve (D_W) is parallel to and lies below the consumer retail demand curve (D) by the marginal cost of distribution, $10. As shown in Figure 11.2, the derived wholesale demand curve lies $10 below the consumer retail demand curve.

Profit Maximization Without Vertical Integration

Familiar tools now help you maximize profit. As a manager, the demand curve relevant to you is the wholesale demand curve (D_W). Recall from Section 6.1 that the marginal revenue curve from a downward-sloping straight-line demand curve lies below the demand curve and has a slope twice as steep as that of the demand curve. Figure 11.3 adds the marginal revenue curve (MR_W) for the wholesale demand curve (D_W) to the curves shown in Figure 11.2. Again for simplicity, assume that the marginal cost of producing a pair of jeans is constant at $20 per pair of jeans and equal to the average total cost, so in Figure 11.3 the curve is labeled $MC_P = ATC$.

To maximize profit, you need to produce the quantity of jeans that sets your marginal revenue (MR_W) equal to your marginal cost (MC_P). The profit-maximizing quantity shown in the figure is 200,000 pairs of jeans per week. Of course, you might not find this profit-maximizing quantity immediately, but using what you learned in Chapter 6 about determining the profit-maximizing quantity (see Section 6.2), ultimately you will manage your firm so that it produces this quantity.

Now that you have determined the profit-maximizing quantity, you need to set the price. Your profit-maximizing wholesale price is determined from the wholesale demand for the jeans. The wholesale demand curve D_W in Figure 11.3 shows that the

Price and cost (dollars per pair of jeans)

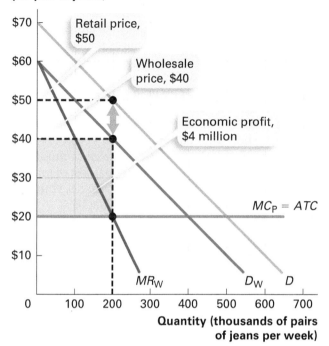

Figure 11.3 Producer's Profit Maximization Without Vertical Integration

The marginal revenue curve for the wholesale demand curve is labeled MR_W. The profit-maximizing quantity of jeans is the quantity that sets its marginal cost of production (MC_P) equal to its marginal revenue (MR_W), which is 200,000 pairs of jeans per week. The profit-maximizing wholesale price of $40 is determined from the wholesale demand curve (D_W). The retail price equals the wholesale cost of $40 plus the marginal cost of retailing the jeans ($10, equal to the length of the double-headed blue arrow), for a total of $50. (This price can also be determined from the consumer retail demand curve [D] at the quantity of 200,000 pairs of jeans per week.) The area of the green rectangle is equal to the producer's economic profit, $4 million.

profit-maximizing wholesale price is $40 per pair of jeans at the quantity of 200,000 pairs of jeans. The retail price paid by consumers can be determined from the consumers' retail demand curve. For 200,000 pairs of jeans, the light blue D curve shows that the retail price is $50 per pair of jeans. Equivalently, the $50 retail price equals the wholesale price at this quantity of jeans, $P_w = \$40$ per pair, plus the marginal cost of distributing the jeans, $MC_D = \$10$. The length of the double-headed blue arrow in the figure is $10, which, when added to the wholesale price of $40, equals the retail price, $50.

Because the retailers selling the jeans are competitive firms, they make zero economic profit (so their owners make a competitive return). With its monopoly position producing jeans, your firm can make a handsome economic profit, however. Your firm's economic profit is equal to $(P_W - ATC) \times Q$, or $(\$40 - \$20) \times 200,000 = \$4$ million, which in Figure 11.3 is equal to the area of the green rectangle.

Profit Maximization with Vertical Integration

If your firm has a monopoly producing its popular jeans, it is already making an economic profit simply by producing the jeans and letting others distribute them. Can your firm increase its profit through vertical integration? In other words, if your firm monopolizes *both* production *and* distribution, will its profits rise? Your intuition might suggest that the answer to this question is yes. Monopolizing the production sector *and* the distribution sector probably seems to be more profitable than merely monopolizing the production sector. This is not the case, however. Let's see why.

Suppose that your firm vertically integrates, both producing and distributing its own jeans. In reality, it seems unlikely that a firm like Levi Strauss would ever open its own retail stores. The goal of this discussion, however, is not to determine the optimal policy but rather to demonstrate what happens if a monopoly producer vertically integrates, which can be done using your jeans-producing firm as an example. Assuming that retail demand does not change (that is, consumers do not care if they buy from your stores or other retail distributors), it does not matter whether your firm buys all of its retail distributors or builds its own stores. Further, assume that your firm's cost of distributing the jeans is the same as that for the other retailing companies, so continue to ignore potential cost savings from a reduction in transaction costs or cost increases from managerial diseconomies.

Vertical integration affects both your firm's demand curve and its marginal cost curve. The firm is now a monopoly that both produces and sells its jeans directly to consumers. The demand relevant for your managerial decisions becomes the *retail* demand from consumers because they are now your customers. After vertical integration, your firm's costs include the costs of distributing the jeans as well as producing them, so your marginal cost of a pair of jeans is the sum of the marginal cost of production and the marginal cost of distribution: $MC_P + MC_D$. With these changes, your firm is effectively the same as the monopoly firms you learned about in Chapter 6.

Figure 11.4 illustrates the retail demand curve (D) and its marginal revenue curve (MR). As in the previous example, the marginal cost of distributing the jeans is constant at $10 per pair and the marginal cost of producing each pair is constant at $20. The vertically integrated marginal cost is the sum of these two costs, which means it is constant at $30 per pair of jeans. In Figure 11.4, this marginal cost curve is labeled $MC_{VI} = ATC$. The figure shows that the profit-maximizing quantity is 200,000 pairs of jeans, the quantity that sets the marginal revenue (MR) equal to the marginal cost (MC_{VI}). The profit-maximizing *retail* price determined by using the retail demand is $50.

Figure 11.4 illustrates a striking result: After your firm vertically integrates into the retail sector, the quantity and retail price that maximize profit are the same as before vertical integration. Has your economic profit increased? It turns out that your profit is the same as well. Your economic profit equals $(P - ATC) \times Q$, or, in the case at hand, ($50 - 30) \times 200,000 = $4 million, equal to the area of the green

Figure 11.4 Profit Maximization with Vertical Integration

If your firm vertically integrates into the retail sector so that it has a monopoly in both the production and the retail distribution of its jeans, your relevant demand curve is the *retail* demand curve (D). The marginal revenue curve for this demand curve is MR. Following vertical integration, your marginal cost now includes the marginal cost of *both* production and distribution. This marginal cost curve is labeled $MC_{VI} = ATC$. The profit-maximizing quantity is the quantity that sets the marginal cost equal to the marginal revenue (200,000 pairs of jeans per week). You determine the profit-maximizing *retail* price ($50) from the retail demand curve (D). The area of the green rectangle is equal to your economic profit, $4 million.

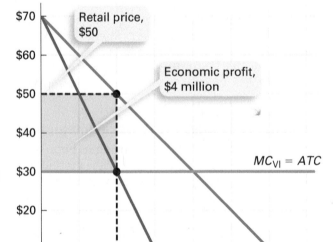

rectangle in Figure 11.4. The economic profit after vertical integration is the same as the profit before vertical integration, when your firm had a monopoly only in the production of jeans. In other words, the profit is identical whether the firm has a monopoly in *both* the production and the distribution of its jeans or a monopoly only in the production of jeans.

Recap of Vertical Integration into a Competitive Sector

The lesson from this analysis is clear: Vertical integration by a monopoly producer into a competitive downstream retailing market sector does not increase the integrated firm's profit. Our example examined forward integration, but the same conclusion holds true for backward integration: Vertical integration into a competitive production sector does not increase a monopoly distributor's profit. More generally, neither forward nor backward integration into a competitive sector increases the integrating monopoly firm's profit. The following box summarizes these results.

VERTICAL INTEGRATION INTO A COMPETITIVE SECTOR

- Forward integration by a monopoly producer into a competitive distribution sector does not increase the integrated firm's profit.
- Backward integration by a monopoly distributor into a competitive production sector does not increase the integrated firm's profit.

These results contradict the intuitive idea that extending a monopoly from one to multiple points in the supply chain will increase the firm's economic profit. Why is that intuition wrong? There is an economic profit from producing and distributing your jeans. But the competitive distribution sector has no economic profit because your firm, the monopoly producer of jeans, has absorbed all of the economic profit. With a competitive retail distribution sector, your firm's jeans are being distributed as efficiently as possible, and the distributors are making zero economic profit. If your firm takes over the distribution sector, it is not possible to wring out any cost savings or gain other efficiencies that would increase profit.[4] In other words, both before and after vertical integration, the quantity produced, the retail price, and the economic profit all remain the same.

This explanation raises another point: Suppose that the retail distributors *are* making an economic profit. Does the economic profit in the distribution sector make vertical integration into this sector by your firm profitable? This important question is answered in the next section.

Vertical Integration with a Monopoly Distributor

Suppose that in addition to your firm being the only producer of your jeans, there is only one retailer of the jeans. In particular, suppose that Marcy's, a department store like Kohl's, is the only retailer, so it is a monopoly.[5] This supply chain is an example of a **successive monopoly,** a market structure in which a monopoly producer sells its product to a monopoly distributor. As a monopoly distributor, suppose Marcy's

Successive monopoly A market structure in which a monopoly producer sells to a monopoly distributor.

---

4 Keep in mind that we are ignoring possible cost savings from any reduction in transaction costs. If there are cost savings from a reduction in transaction costs, then vertical integration will increase your firm's profit.

5 More realistically, a retail store will not be a monopoly but will have some market power, so it has a downward-sloping demand curve and likely makes some economic profit. The assumption that Marcy's is a monopoly simply makes the presentation more straightforward but has no effect on the general conclusions.

makes an economic profit. So your firm, the monopoly producer, is considering vertical integration into the monopoly distributor market in one of two ways: (1) merging with Marcy's or (2) creating its own retail stores that will be the exclusive distributors of jeans, which would prevent Marcy's from selling them.

The scenario in which firms like Levi Strauss and Kohl's are both monopolies seems highly unlikely, but it helps demonstrate the effect of vertical integration into a sector that is making an economic profit. So with no vertical integration your firm and Marcy's are independently owned and operated firms, each of which maximizes its *own* profit. As a monopoly, each firm has an incentive to reduce its total output and mark up its price above its marginal cost to make an economic profit: your firm from the production of the jeans and Marcy's from the retail distribution of them. As a manager, you must decide whether to vertically integrate to take over the distribution of your jeans or continue to allow Marcy's to be your exclusive retailer. The analysis in this section is similar to what you did before: Start by examining the situation with no vertical integration (in which your firm sells to Marcy's), and then determine if your firm can increase profit via vertical integration.

Derived Demand for a Monopoly Distributor

The key to analyzing a successive monopoly is determining the wholesale demand for the product, in this case, Marcy's wholesale demand. The wholesale demand is again a derived demand so it depends on the profit-maximizing decisions of the (now) monopoly retailer. Because the retail distributor is a monopoly, its wholesale demand differs from that of competitive retailers. In particular, the wholesale demand for competitive retailers depended on the retail *demand*, but the wholesale demand for a monopoly retailer depends on the retail *marginal revenue*. This difference occurs because Marcy's managers maximize profit by operating where their marginal revenue is equal to their marginal cost rather than where their price is equal to their marginal cost.

Marcy's marginal revenue (*MR*) is the marginal revenue from the consumers retail demand for jeans. Figure 11.5 illustrates Marcy's marginal revenue curve (*MR*) from the retail demand curve for jeans (*D*). Marcy's marginal cost includes the same two components as the marginal cost for the competitive distributors in the previous section: the wholesale price they pay your firm (P_W) and the marginal cost of distributing the jeans (MC_D), or $P_W + MC_D$. According to the profit-maximization rule ($MR = MC$),

$$MR = P_W + MC_D \qquad\qquad \textbf{11.2}$$

If you rearrange Equation 11.2, you will see that for each quantity the wholesale price (P_w) is equal to the difference between the retail marginal revenue and the marginal cost of distributing the jeans: $P_W = MR - MC_D$. These quantity/wholesale price combinations determine Marcy's wholesale demand curve. Because the wholesale price Marcy's will pay for a pair of jeans equals the marginal revenue minus the marginal cost of distribution, in Figure 11.5 Marcy's wholesale demand curve (D_W) lies below Marcy's marginal revenue curve by the amount MC_D. Assuming that the marginal cost of distributing the jeans is constant at $10 per pair, at each quantity the wholesale demand curve (D_W) lies $10 below Marcy's marginal revenue curve, as shown in the figure. The wholesale demand curve is the relevant demand curve for you as a manager at the jeans-producing firm.

Profit Maximization Without Vertical Integration

As a manager, you maximize the jeans-producing company's profit using the wholesale demand curve and its associated marginal revenue curve. In Figure 11.6, neither the retail demand curve nor the retail marginal revenue curve (*D* and *MR*) is directly

**Price and cost (dollars
per pair of jeans)**

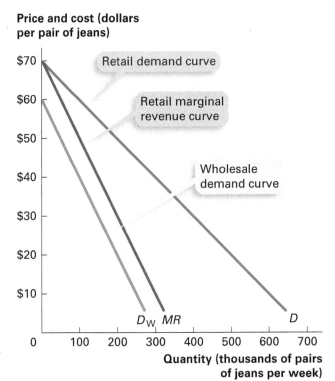

**Figure 11.5 The Wholesale
Demand Curve with a
Monopoly Distributor**

The consumers retail
demand curve for jeans is
labeled D, and Marcy's
wholesale demand curve for
jeans is labeled D_W. The
wholesale price Marcy's will
pay is equal to Marcy's
marginal revenue (MR)
minus its marginal cost of
distributing the jeans (MC_D).
Because MC_D is $10 per pair,
the wholesale demand curve
lies $10 below the marginal
revenue curve.

**Price and cost (dollars
per pair of jeans)**

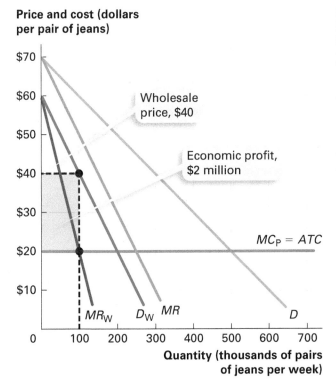

**Figure 11.6 Producer's Profit
Maximization with a
Monopoly Distributor**

The marginal revenue curve
derived from the wholesale
demand curve (D_W) is the red
MR_W curve. Your firm's profit-
maximizing quantity is
100,000 pairs of jeans per
week, the quantity that sets
your marginal cost (MC_P)
equal to your marginal
revenue (MR_W). The profit-
maximizing wholesale price
is $40, and the area of the
green rectangle equals your
firm's economic profit, $2
million.

pertinent to you. The relevant curves are the marginal revenue curve (MR_W) from the wholesale demand curve (D_W) and the marginal cost of producing the jeans curve ($MC_P = ATC$). Your firm maximizes profit by producing the quantity that sets $MR_W = MC_P$, 100,000 pairs of jeans. The wholesale price, from the wholesale demand curve, is $40. Your firm makes an economic profit equal to ($P_W - ATC$) × Q, which is ($40 − $20) × 100,000 = $2 million, the area of the green rectangle in Figure 11.6. This profit is less than that in a market with competitive distribution, where your firm made $4 million.

Next, you can determine Marcy's quantity, price, and economic profit. The marginal cost to Marcy's is the sum of the wholesale price ($40) and the marginal cost of distributing each pair of jeans ($10) so, as Figure 11.7 shows, Marcy's marginal cost curve for a pair of jeans is labeled $MC = ATC$. Marcy's marginal revenue curve (the red curve labeled MR) is the marginal revenue from the retail demand curve (D). To maximize its profit, Marcy's managers buy 100,000 pairs of jeans (the quantity that sets Marcy's marginal revenue equal to its marginal cost) and set a retail price of $60 (from the retail demand curve). Because it is a monopoly distributor, Marcy's can make an economic profit. Marcy's economic profit is equal to ($P − ATC$) × Q, which in Figure 11.7 equals ($60 − $50) × 100,000 = $1 million.

In the case of a monopoly producer and a monopoly distributor, *both* firms make economic profits. Your firm makes an economic profit of $2 million by producing the jeans and Marcy's makes an economic profit of $1 million by distributing the jeans. The two companies' combined economic profit from producing and retailing jeans is $3 million. Is it possible for your firm to increase its economic profit by vertically integrating and taking over the distribution function?

Figure 11.7 Monopoly Distributor's Profit Maximization Without Vertical Integration

Marcy's marginal revenue curve (the red *MR* curve) is derived from the retail demand curve (*D*). Marcy's marginal cost (*MC*) is the sum of the wholesale price (*P_W*) and the marginal cost of distributing each pair of jeans (*MC_D*): $40 + $10 = $50. Marcy's marginal cost curve and average total cost curve is the green line labeled *MC = ATC*. Marcy's maximizes its profit by purchasing 100,000 pairs of jeans and selling them at $60. Marcy's economic profit is equal to the area of the green rectangle, $1 million.

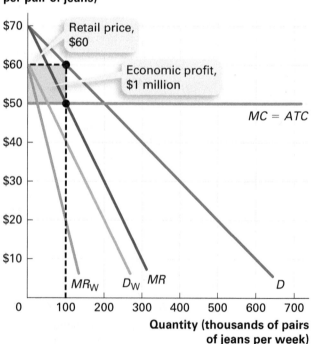

Profit Maximization with Vertical Integration

Without vertical integration and with Marcy's as its monopoly distributor, your firm has an economic profit of $2 million. You have already seen what happens if you vertically integrate and take over the distribution market: Figure 11.4 showed that as the monopoly producer and distributor, your firm made an economic profit of $4 million. If it vertically integrates, your firm's economic profit *increases* from $2 million to $4 million. Vertical integration of a successive monopoly has an important economic impact. Accordingly, vertical integration is an economically sound decision in a successive monopoly scenario.

Although this example examines only forward integration, the result is the same for backward integration. Specifically, the distributor (Marcy's) can increase *its* profit by acquiring your firm or otherwise obtaining the ability to produce a pair of jeans with the same demand. If Marcy's integrates backward, Marcy's total economic profit becomes $4 million, the same total profit as when your firm integrates forward.

Recap of Vertical Integration into a Monopoly Sector

Table 11.1 compares the profits from the various market structure combinations. This table shows the combined profits of a production sector and a distribution sector that have the same cost structures as was the case for your firm and Marcy's for four possible market structures. The profits of the first three market structures are equal and are the highest attainable. The market structure with the lowest total profit is successive monopoly (the monopoly producer/monopoly distributor structure). Although the specific profits in the table are unique to the examples presented, the qualitative results can be generalized. In particular, of these four market structures, a vertically integrated firm, a monopoly producer/competitive distribution, and a competitive production/monopoly distributor always yield the same combined profit, an amount that is greater than the combined profit of a successive monopoly.

The reason for the lower combined profit of a successive monopoly is **double marginalization**, a situation in which the upstream and downstream firms both have market power and, following typical profit-maximizing behavior, both mark up the price of their product over their marginal cost. The upstream firm (the producer) starts the ball rolling by marking up its (wholesale) price, resulting in a higher cost to the downstream firm (the retail distributor). With the markup of the wholesale price, the distributor's costs increase, so when it marks up its cost to set the retail price, the price hits retail consumers with a double whammy—that is, a double markup. Faced with a retail price boosted by markups from *both* the producer and the distributor, consumers respond by decreasing the quantity they buy. For example, in the preceding case, if your firm and Marcy's remain a successive monopoly, consumers pay a retail price $60 and buy only 100,000 pairs of jeans. If, instead, the companies vertically integrate and become a single monopoly, the retail price falls so that consumers pay $50 and buy 200,000 pairs of jeans. The firms' combined profits are more when they merge because they sell a larger quantity than when they are independent.

Double marginalization A situation in which the upstream and downstream firms both have market power and both mark up the price of their product over their marginal cost.

Table 11.1 Combined Economic Profit of Production and Distribution Sectors

Single Monopoly			Successive Monopoly
Monopoly Producer/ Competitive Distribution	Competitive Production/ Monopoly Distributor	Vertically Integrated Monopoly Firm	Monopoly Producer/ Monopoly Distributor
$4 million	$4 million	$4 million	$3 million

Price and Quantity with Competitive Distributors and a Monopoly Distributor

The figure shows the retail demand curve and marginal revenue curve for jeans produced by your firm. Assume that the marginal cost of production is constant at $20 per pair and that the marginal cost of retailing and distributing the jeans is constant at $10 per pair.

a. Draw a figure showing the wholesale price and quantity of jeans produced by your firm if the distributors are perfectly competitive. What is the profit-maximizing quantity and wholesale price?

b. Draw a figure showing the wholesale price and quantity produced if the distributor is a monopoly. What is the profit-maximizing quantity and wholesale price?

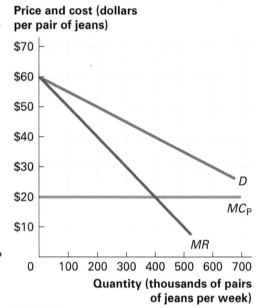

Price and cost (dollars per pair of jeans)

Answer

(a) Perfectly Competitive Market

Price and cost (dollars per pair of jeans)

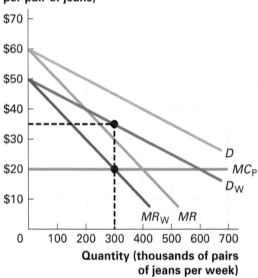

Quantity (thousands of pairs of jeans per week)

(b) Monopoly Market

Price and cost (dollars per pair of jeans)

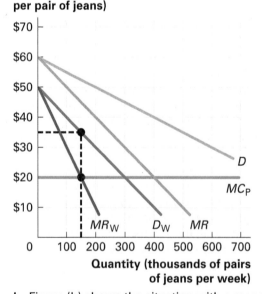

Quantity (thousands of pairs of jeans per week)

a. Figure (a) shows the situation with a competitive distribution market. The wholesale demand curve (D_W) lies below the retail demand curve (D) by the marginal cost of retailing and distributing the jeans, $10. The marginal revenue curve derived from this wholesale demand curve is MR_W. Your firm maximizes profit by producing 300,000 pairs of jeans and setting a wholesale price of $35.

b. Figure (b) shows the situation with a monopoly distribution market. The wholesale demand curve (D_W) lies below the retail marginal revenue curve (MR) by the marginal cost of retailing and distributing the jeans, $10. The marginal revenue curve derived from this wholesale demand curve is MR_W. Your firm maximizes profit by producing 150,000 pairs of jeans and setting a wholesale price of $35.

11.4 Vertical Integration and Distribution

Learning Objective 11.4 Apply the economics of firm structure and distribution to make better managerial decisions about vertical integration.

As you have already learned, economic theory generally provides a framework of analysis for decision making rather than a cut-and-dried recipe for success. The information presented here is no exception. Applying the principles you have learned about vertical integration and distribution will help guide you in making decisions about structuring or modifying your business.

Using the Economics of Vertical Integration for Managerial Decision Making

One of the main drivers of vertical integration is the elimination or reduction of the transaction costs of using a market. So as a manager you should constantly monitor these transaction costs for changes. For example, a reduction in the transaction costs of purchasing an input may reduce your incentive to integrate backward because of the reduction in potential cost savings. Managers at IC Bus, a U.S.-based manufacturer of school buses, recognized this point. The transaction costs associated with buying standardized products, such as bolts or screws, have fallen with the growth in Internet-based transactions. So IC Bus still manufactures the unique exterior panels for its buses but buys the standardized bolts and screws used to fasten the panels to the frame from other companies. IC Bus's managers have vertically integrated into some aspects of the production (the exterior panels) but not others (bolts and screws).

Of course, you also must be alert to changes in technological interdependencies and managerial diseconomies because of their impact on the profitability of vertical integration. For example, one source of managerial diseconomies from expanding the scale of operations is the inability to communicate quickly and clearly with a remote subsidiary. Today's widespread use of e-mail and Skype, however, has decreased this type of managerial diseconomy. Presumably, however, these same technological changes have also decreased the cost of negotiating and enforcing contracts, which makes using a market less expensive. So their net effect on the profitability of vertical integration is ambiguous.

Transaction costs, technological interdependencies, and managerial diseconomies are not the only considerations in determining whether to engage in vertical integration. Managers in a supply chain characterized by a successive monopoly can also increase their total profit by vertically integrating the two firms. Although the example presented used just two monopoly firms, in general, if two stages in a supply chain are making an economic profit by marking up their price, managers can eliminate the double marginalization with vertical integration and increase the total combined economic profit.

You must weigh the costs and benefits carefully when making decisions about vertical integration. If incorrect, these decisions are often costly to undo. As with other managerial decisions, you need to use marginal analysis, but in this instance, its use differs slightly. As you learned in earlier chapters, typically you use marginal analysis to decide how much of an action to do, such as how much to produce or how much to advertise. In the case of vertical integration, however, the action is a yes or no decision—integrate (merge) or not. In this scenario, you use marginal analysis to compare your profit from undertaking the action (vertically integrating) to that from maintaining (and, of course, monitoring) the current supply chain.

Using Vertical Integration and Market Structure for Managerial Decision Making Within a Firm

As an executive manager of a vertically integrated firm, you must determine how to compensate the managers of your production division and your distribution division. If your firm has a monopoly in both production and distribution, avoid compensating both sets of managers based on their ability to maximize their division's profit. Why? If you structure compensation in this way and both sets of managers maximize their division's profit, you inadvertently create a successive monopoly within the firm, with the monopoly production division "selling" to the monopoly distribution division. The managers of the production division will demand the monopoly price as the transfer price, and the managers of the distribution sector will further mark up this price when they sell to their customers, causing double marginalization to rear its ugly, profit-diminishing head. Instead of setting up the divisions as independent profit centers, instruct one set of managers to maximize profit and the other set to operate as a competitive market by fulfilling its task at the lowest average cost. This scenario emulates a monopoly production/competitive distribution supply chain or a competitive production/monopoly distribution supply chain. In a monopoly production/competitive distribution production scheme, you instruct the managers of the production division to set their transfer price equal to the monopoly price and have their compensation based on their division's profit, while the compensation of the distribution division's managers depends on their ability to distribute the product at the lowest average cost. On the flip side, in a competitive production/monopoly distribution production scheme, production managers should receive compensation based on producing at the lowest average cost, while the distribution managers receive compensation based on maximizing profit.

Revisiting Why Walgreens Boots Alliance Would Purchase Wholesaler AmerisourceBergen

At the start of the chapter, you learned about the decision of Walgreens Boots Alliance (Walgreens) to integrate backward into the wholesale drug distribution market by purchasing 7 percent of AmerisourceBergen, with the option of increasing that stake to 30 percent, which would essentially vertically integrate the two firms. Why would the managers at the then-separate companies (Walgreens and Boots Alliance) consider this purchase? The short answer is that the managers believed the purchase would increase their companies' profits, but this answer is incomplete because it does not explain the source of the additional profit.

As you have learned from studying this chapter, one source of profit from vertical integration is a reduction in transaction costs. Once Walgreens effectively controlled AmerisourceBergen, it could eliminate the transaction costs of searching for the lowest wholesale price and enforcing a contract. The arrangement would also enhance flexibility. For example, Walgreens could have AmerisourceBergen deliver to its stores every day, rather than twice a week, as was the case before vertical integration. More frequent deliveries would allow Walgreens drug stores to fill urgent orders more quickly.

Another source of profit is the elimination of the holdup problem. Any transaction-specific assets that AmerisourceBergen purchased would be less likely to fall prey to a holdup problem created by Walgreens. For example, AmerisourceBergen would be more willing to invest in a computer system that linked directly into Walgreens' inventory and sales tracking programs because Walgreens' managers would not try to renegotiate lower prices after AmerisourceBergen had made the investment.

Of course, the deal brings with it the possibility of managerial diseconomies. Although the managers at both Walgreens and AmerisourceBergen are familiar with the market for pharmaceutical drugs, they specialize in different market segments, so their business cultures might clash. For example, because AmerisourceBergen sells to only a few buyers, its salespeople may be used to wining and dining customers to establish solid, committed relationships. Walgreens, however, sells to millions of retail customers, so many that Walgreens' sales managers definitely do not wine and dine their customers. If the cultures differ enough, completely merging the two companies could be difficult and costly, which might lead Walgreens' managers to decide that the managerial diseconomies are too large to completely integrate the companies.

Following vertical integration, Walgreens' managers could tell the managers at AmerisourceBergen the price to set. Because we supposed it is a perfect competitor, Walgreens is unable to mark up its price and therefore is unable to make an economic profit.

Walgreens' managers could use AmerisourceBergen's market power to make an economic profit. Therefore, the firm's executives could instruct the managers at AmerisourceBergen to maximize their profit. This instruction would be optimal, even though Walgreens owns only 30 percent of AmerisourceBergen, because 30 percent of the maximum profit is more than 30 percent of any other lower amount of profit.

It is quite likely that the managers at Walgreens took only a small initial position (7 percent) in AmerisourceBergen to give them time to explore the net effect of a merger: They wanted to discover how the potential rise in economic profit from the decrease in transaction costs compared to the potential fall in economic profit from managerial diseconomies. If the executives at Walgreens determined that on net the economic profit increased, they would exercise their option to buy more of AmerisourceBergen. If they decided that the managerial diseconomies were too large, Walgreens would walk away from the merger by leaving the option unexercised. Walgreens' option to buy more of AmerisourceBergen gave it the right to buy at specific times in the future. In 2016, Walgreens' managers exercised their first opportunity to purchase more of AmerisourceBergen, so they apparently have concluded that a merger will be profitable.

Summary: The Bottom Line

11.1 The Basics of Vertical Integration

- A supply chain for a product starts with the upstream transformation of raw materials into intermediate goods, which move downstream for further completion until a downstream firm eventually sells the finished product to the consumer.
- A vertically integrated firm produces at two or more different stages in the supply chain. Forward integration refers to acquisition by a firm of downstream (closer to the consumer) productive capacity in the supply chain. Backward integration refers to acquisition by a firm of upstream (farther from the consumer) capacity in the supply chain.
- The opposite of both types of integration is divestiture—when a firm sells, spins off, or liquidates some line of business. The opposite of backward integration is outsourcing—when a firm's managers

decide to buy an input from another firm rather than producing it.
- When a firm transfers an input from one division to another, the transfer price is the accounting entry that is the price the input-producing division charges the input-using division. Transfer prices help allocate a firm's taxable profit to different countries (or states) with different income tax rates and policies.

11.2 The Economics of Vertical Integration

- Vertical integration can reduce or eliminate transaction costs, including information costs; reduce or eliminate negotiation, monitoring, and enforcement costs; increase flexibility; and reduce taxes and the costs associated with transaction-specific assets, including the holdup problem.

- Vertical integration also can decrease costs imposed by technological interdependencies, the technologically close relationship between two or more stages in the supply chain.
- On the other hand, vertical integration can create managerial diseconomies, which increase the costs of coordinating activities within the firm, and can force managers to make potentially poor decisions outside their area of expertise.

11.3 Vertical Integration and Market Structure

- The profitability of vertical integration is affected by the structure of the involved markets.
- A monopoly producer vertically integrating into a perfectly competitive distribution market creates a monopoly producer and distributor, but there is no change in the retail price or retail quantity or in the producer's economic profit.
- A monopoly producer/monopoly distributor market structure exhibits double marginalization because *both*

the upstream producer and the downstream distributor mark up their prices above their marginal cost. Vertical integration eliminates double marginalization, lowering the retail price and consequently increasing sales and total profit.

11.4 Managerial Application: Vertical Integration and Distribution

- Changes in transaction costs can affect the profitability of vertical integration.
- Executive managers of a vertically integrated firm with a monopoly in both production and distribution must avoid compensating the managers of both divisions based on their ability to maximize profit. This sort of compensation scheme would create double marginalization, which decreases the firm's profit. Instead, the compensation of one set of managers should be based on maximizing profit and that of the other division's managers on attaining the lowest possible average cost.

Key Terms and Concepts

Backward integration	Holdup problem	Technological interdependency
Derived demand	Information costs	Transaction-specific assets
Divestiture	Managerial diseconomies	Transfer price
Double marginalization	Outsourcing	Vertical integration
Forward integration	Successive monopoly	

Questions and Problems

11.1 The Basics of Vertical Integration

Learning Objective 11.1 Explain vertical integration, forward integration, backward integration, outsourcing, and transfer price.

1.1 Classify each of the following purchases as forward integration, backward integration, or neither.
   a. Google, the producer of the Android operating system used on smartphones, purchases Motorola Mobility, a producer of smartphones.
   b. China General Nuclear Power Group, the state-owned nuclear power corporation,

purchases Extract Resources, the Australian operator of uranium mines in Namibia.
   c. Anheuser-Busch InBev, a major worldwide producer of beers, purchases Grupo Modelo, the major producer of beers in Mexico.
   d. Kinder Morgan, the operator of two major oil fields in Texas, purchases El Paso Corporation, the owner of the pipelines that take oil from the fields to refiners.

1.2 How do managers use transfer prices to allocate profits? Why can this be important, and what constraints do managers face in setting transfer prices?

1.3 In 2014, U.S.-based Horizon Pharma purchased a smaller, Irish-based company, Vidara Therapeutics International. In 2015, the combined company had before-tax profit of approximately $40,000,000. In 2015 the U.S. corporate income tax rate was about 35 percent; the Irish corporate income tax rate was about 22 percent. If you are the CEO of Horizon Pharma, what strategy would you have pursued in making the merger, and why?

11.2 The Economics of Vertical Integration

Learning Objective 11.2 Identify how transaction costs, the holdup problem, technological interdependencies, and managerial diseconomies affect vertical integration.

2.1 You negotiate a contract with one of your suppliers specifying that for one year you will pay $120 per ton of iron for up to 50,000 tons. Unfortunately, after a few months, the market price rises to $160 per ton, and your supplier refuses to honor the contract. You must hire a law firm to go to court to force fulfillment of the contract. Ultimately, you win the case. Before the supplier refused to honor the contract, you purchased 20,000 tons of iron and paid a total of $2,400,000. After you prevailed in court, you purchased 30,000 tons for a total of $3,600,000. You paid the law firm $200,000 to litigate your case. What is the amount of the transaction costs you incurred?

2.2 When the personal computer revolution began in the 1980s and 1990s, computer parts were highly customized. For example, different computer manufacturers used different types of hard drives. As computers became increasingly common, the inputs became more standardized. By the 2000s, many of the parts used by the different computer producers were interchangeable. How does this evolution of inputs affect the transaction costs of producing computers? How does it affect the possibility of vertical integration among the companies manufacturing computers?

2.3 The Salvation Army, a religious nonprofit organization, operates charity and thrift stores called Sally's. When a donor contacts the organization, it sends a truck to pick up the goods. The Salvation Army rejects heavily used, broken, or soiled goods. The managers could hire a trucking company to pick up the donations, but instead they use their own trucks operated by their own employees. Why did the managers decide to vertically integrate rather than outsource their trucking needs?

2.4 Anheuser-Busch is the producer of Natural Light beer, perhaps better known as Natty Light. The managers decided to run a special in which cans of Natural Light contained 25 ounces of beer rather than the standard 24 ounces. The 25-ounce cans were slightly larger, which meant that new tooling and dies had to be used to produce the larger cans. Anheuser-Busch produces about 50 percent of the cans it uses and contracts with independent can producers for the rest. Because the independent producers were reluctant to produce the special cans, Anheuser-Busch's managers decided to produce them using their in-house production. Why would the managers of independent can producers be unwilling to produce the 25-ounce cans?

2.5 Starbucks has vertically integrated by purchasing a coffee farm in China. One analyst explained this purchase by asserting that increased demand for high-quality coffee would lead to a higher price for high-quality coffee beans. The analyst concluded that by purchasing this farm, Starbucks was assuring itself of a source of reasonably priced coffee beans, thereby increasing its profit at its stores. Explain why this analysis is flawed.

2.6 In the United States, Starbucks is vertically integrated and runs all its coffee shops. But as it expands to the Middle East, the company's managers plan to have their coffee shops run by local owners. What sorts of managerial diseconomies might have led Starbucks' managers to make this decision?

11.3 Vertical Integration and Market Structure

Learning Objective 11.3 Analyze how the structure of the upstream and downstream markets affects the profitability of vertical integration.

3.1 What is the difference between the derived (wholesale) demand curve for competitive distributors and the derived (wholesale) demand curve for a monopoly distributor? Why is there a difference?

3.2 Suppose that your marketing research department has found that the consumer (retail) demand for your product is

$$Q = 100 - P$$

where Q is the quantity demanded and P is the price. This demand function can be solved for the inverse demand—that is, the price as a function of the quantity demanded:

$$P = 100 - Q$$

Your marginal cost of production and average total cost of production are constant and equal to $50 per unit. The marginal cost of distribution and average total cost of distribution are also constant and equal to $10 per unit.

a. If you produce *and* distribute the product, what is your profit-maximizing price and output?

b. How much economic profit do you make?

c. If the distributors of your product are perfectly competitive, what are your profit-maximizing wholesale price and output and what will be your economic profit? What is the retail price?

3.3 Your company produces a unique style of sandals. The table shows price/quantity combinations from the retail demand curve for your sandals. This demand curve for your shoes is linear. Your marginal cost and average total cost of producing a pair of sandals are constant and equal to $20 per pair. In addition, the marginal cost of distributing and selling a pair of sandals is constant at $30 per pair and equal to the average total cost of distribution.

Price (dollars per pair of sandals)	Quantity (pairs of sandals per month)
$80	600
70	800
60	1,000
50	1,200
40	1,400
30	1,600
20	1,800

a. If you sell your sandals to retail distributors in a perfectly competitive market, what are your wholesale price

and quantity and your economic profit? What are the retail price and quantity and the total economic profit of all of the distributors?

b. If you sell your sandals to a monopoly retail distributor, what are your wholesale price and quantity and your economic profit? What are your distributor's retail price and quantity and its economic profit?

3.4 Suppose that you are a manager for a firm like Hewlett-Packard and your research department has provided the data used to construct the figure, which shows the consumer (retail) demand curve (D), marginal cost of production (MC_P), and marginal cost of distribution (MC_D) for your printers. Your firm produces the printers, which it then sells to competitive retail distributors.

a. If you do not vertically integrate, what is the wholesale price and quantity of printers? What is the retail price?

b. If you vertically integrate by taking over the distribution of the printers, what is the retail price and quantity?

Price and cost (dollars per printer)

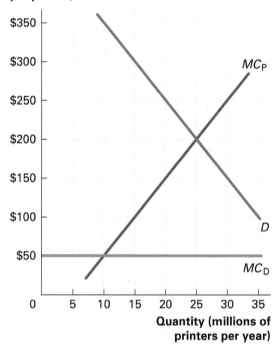

3.5 As a manager at a firm like Samsung, you are presented with the figure showing the retail demand curve (D) for your most recent smartphone. The figure also shows the marginal cost of production (MC_P) and marginal cost of distribution (MC_D) for these phones. If the retail distributors are competitive, what is your profit-maximizing wholesale price and quantity? What is the retail price of a phone?

Price and cost (dollars per smartphone)

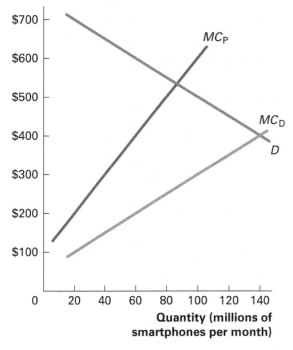

Quantity (millions of smartphones per month)

3.6 Suppose that consumer (retail) demand for a product is given by

$$Q = 100 - P$$

where Q is the quantity demanded and P is the price. The inverse demand curve (which gives the price as a function of the quantity demanded) is

$$P = 100 - Q$$

The marginal cost of production and average total cost of production are $50 per unit, and the marginal cost of distribution and average total cost of distribution are $10 per unit.
   a. If the retail distribution is monopolized by another firm, find the following:
      i. The profit-maximizing wholesale price and output
      ii. The producer's profit
      iii. The retail price and quantity
      iv. The profit of the monopoly retailer
   b. Should you vertically integrate? Explain your answer.

3.7 Suppose that your company has a patent on a particularly efficient type of nanocrystal solar cell. You sell your solar cells to other companies that manufacture solar panels and sell them to consumers. Some members of your management team have proposed forward integration, taking over the manufacture and sale of solar panels. Ignore any possible reduction in transaction costs or any managerial diseconomies in answering the following questions.
   a. If the market for solar panels is perfectly competitive, will the proposed vertical integration increase your firm's economic profit? Why or why not?
   b. If the solar panel producers are making an economic profit, will the proposed vertical integration increase your firm's economic profit? Why or why not?

3.8 PVH Corp. produces shirts and other clothing under the Tommy Hilfiger brand. Tommy Hilfiger has market power and makes an economic profit. PVH's managers source some of their Tommy Hilfiger clothing from competitive sewing companies in Bangladesh. Ignoring any transaction cost savings or managerial diseconomies, if PVH integrated backward by either purchasing some of the sewing companies or establishing its own sewing division, would the integration increase PVH's economic profit? Why or why not?

3.9 Is the economic profit from vertical integration larger when a monopoly integrates into a competitive market or when a the monopoly integrates into a monopoly market? Explain your answer.

3.10 "An upstream firm that vertically integrates forward will have a captive market. It can increase its economic profit by forcing its downstream subsidiaries to pay a higher price for the product." Is this assertion true or false? Explain your answer.

11.4 Managerial Application: Vertical Integration and Distribution

Learning Objective 11.4 Apply the economics of firm structure and distribution to make better managerial decisions about vertical integration.

4.1 Apple sells its iPhone through its online website and through Apple stores, but most sales occur through other distributors such as Walmart, Best Buy, and AT&T. Although it is not a monopoly, Apple makes an economic profit from its iPhone. Suppose that the distribution of the iPhone is perfectly competitive. Further suppose that Apple's managers decide to end their distribution contracts with other companies and become the monopoly distributor of iPhones by expanding their network of Apple stores. Ignoring any change in transaction costs, would Apple's economic profit increase? Explain your answer.

4.2 State laws require automobile manufacturers to distribute their cars through independent dealerships. An analyst asserts that as long as those dealers are efficient, the laws have no effect on the manufacturer's profit. Do you agree with the analyst? Explain your answer.

4.3 A monopoly producer merges with the monopoly distributor of its product. How does the economic profit of the merged firms compare with the combined economic profit of the independent firms? As an executive of the merged firm, should you instruct the managers of both the production division and the distribution division to maximize profit? Why or why not?

MyLab Economics Auto-Graded Excel Projects

11.1 Daktronics, located in Brookings, SD, is the world leader in design and manufacture of electronic displays. Their products include electronic scoreboards, programmable display systems, and large screen video displays. One of the most basic inputs for electronics displays are individual light emitting diodes (LED). Individual LED are grouped together to create pixels for electronic displays. The number of pixels used in production determines the brightness and clarity of the visual display. This concept is similar to how the number of pixels your cell phone camera uses relates to the quality of the photo.

Suppose a firm like Daktronics is deciding whether or not to bring production of LED in-house or renegotiating its current contract and continuing to outsource this production to another firm. Currently, the firm negotiates their outsourcing contract every 5 years; the costs of this are approximately $75,000, which includes lawyer fees, travel, and other related costs. The firm also pays lawyers approximately $5,000 per year to ensure the contract is being enacted as originally intended. The current price for outsourced LED production is $110 per thousand units while shipping and quality control costs $5 per thousand units.

If the firm were to bring production in-house, they would need to purchase, install, and train workers on new equipment. The equipment is expected to last 10 years and these initial costs are estimated at $1 million. Annual maintenance and training are expected to cost $50,000 and $10,000 each year, respectively. The benefit of bringing production in-house is the savings on production, which would cost only $70 per thousand units, and quality control, which would cost only $3 per thousand units. Because the equipment will last 10 years, this project is being considered over a 10 year timeframe.

Suppose this firm has asked you to analyze this problem and report the number of units needed over the life of the project to make bringing production in-house a viable option. Round all values to 2 decimal places.

	A	B	C	D	E	F	G	H
1		Costs for Outsourcing				Costs for Backward Integration		
2	Source	Type	Cost	Quantity for 10 years	Source	Type	Cost	Quantity for 10 years
3	Contract Negotiation	Every 5 Years			Equipment Purchase/Install/Initial Training	One-Time		
4	Contract Enforcement	Annual			Equipment Maintenance	Annual		
5	Production	Per Thousand Units			Training	Annual		
6	Shipping	Per Thousand Units			Production	Per Thousand Units		
7	Quality Control	Per Thousand Units			Quality Control	Per Thousand Units		
8		TOTAL COST					TOTAL COST	
9								
10		Quantity (thousands of units)						
11		Cost Differential						

a. Using the template provided, add cost amounts for outsourced production and backwards integration. Also, add the quantity of each cost needed over the life of this project (10 years). For cost items which are "per thousand units," set these cells as equal to the red "Quantity (thousands of units)" cell.

b. Solve for the Total Cost of each option for LED procurement. In the green "Cost Differential" cell, subtract the total cost of bringing production in-house from the total cost of outsourcing.

c. Using Solver, find the quantity of LED needed to make the costs between these two options equal. What is this quantity?

d. Suppose the company used for outsourcing decides to raise their price from $110 per thousand units to $120 per thousand units. What is the new quantity at which the costs of these two proposals are equal?

e. Returning to the original specifications, what volume of production would be required if the management of this firm would only bring production in-house if the cost of doing so saved the firm at least $500,000 over the course of the project?

f. There are likely many additional costs which would alter our calculations for this decision. What are some of these costs?

11.2 New York Process Servicers, located in New York City, is a licensed process server. This firm delivers court papers such as summons, complaints, divorce summons, subpoenas, etc. to individuals being served. Breakaway Courier Systems is a courier service in New York City that uses bike messengers to deliver documents and small packages within New York City.

Suppose you have decided to open a process server firm, similar to New York Process Servers, and are deciding how best to deliver documents from your office to their intended recipients once you have received and prepared the documents in your office. You could hire a messenger service, like Breakaway Courier, or you could hire your own bicycle messengers part time.

If you decide to hire a messenger service, you need to sign a contract with them. Costs of hiring an attorney and developing the contracts are expected to be $5,000. The rate charged by the courier service is $12 per delivery with a fee of $1.50 per mile traveled. You expect each delivery to be 3 miles.

You could also hire some part time couriers, purchase bikes and uniforms, and pay for insurance and training and keep all aspects of the deliver service internal. This choice has the added benefit of being directly involved in the serving process from start to finish and not relying on an outside firm to complete the last step of the process. Hiring your own part time workers and training them will be costly, $35,000 each year. You would also have to provide workers with bikes and uniforms at a cost of $15,000. Bikes and uniforms have to be maintained as well; this will cost $2,000 per year.

Suppose you expect to serve 1,000 papers in your first year. Follow the steps below and determine which method of delivery you should use.

a. Using the template provided, add cost amounts for outsourced delivery and foreword integration. Also, add the quantity of each cost needed for each option annually. For cost items which are "per delivery," set these cells as equal to the red "Quantity (thousands of units)" cell. Remember, each delivery will require 3 miles of travel.

b. Solve for the Total Cost of each option for document delivery. In the green "Cost Differential" cell, subtract the total cost of hiring your own delivery individuals from the total cost of using a courier service.

	A	B	C	D	E	F	G	H
1		Costs for Outsourcing				Costs for Forward Integration		
2	Source	Type	Cost	Annual Quantity	Source	Type	Cost	Annual Quantity
3	Contract Development	Annual			Start-Up Costs (bikes, uniforms, hiring, etc.)	One-Time		
4	Delivery Fee	Per Delivery			Bike and Uniform Maintenance and Insurance	Annual		
5	Mileage	Per Mile			Wages and Training	Annual		
6		TOTAL COST					TOTAL COST	
7								
8		Number of Deliveries						
9		Cost Differential						
10								

c. Based solely on cost, which option should you choose for your first year of business? What is your cost savings for this option?

d. Using Solver, find the quantity of deliveries needed to make the costs between these two options equal. What is this quantity? (Round to the nearest delivery.)

e. Suppose the courier service you hired increases their per delivery cost to $15 and per mile costs to $2 per mile. Does this change your decision in part c?

f. Suppose the new delivery costs from part e remain. Your firm expects to serve 1,500 papers in the 2nd year, 2,000 in the 3rd year, and 2,500 in the 4th year. Will your firm ever bring delivery in-house? If so, in which year will you do this?

g. In addition to the costs given in this problem, are there additional cost associated with either bringing delivery in-house or using a courier service? What are some of these costs?

Decisions About Production, Products, and Location

Learning Objectives

After studying this chapter, you will be able to:

12.1 Explain how managers maximize profit when the production of one good results in the simultaneous production of one or more other goods.

12.2 Explain how managers of multi-plant firms allocate production to maximize profit.

12.3 Describe the factors that determine the number and location of plants operated by multi-plant firms.

12.4 Use marginal analysis to determine the profit-maximizing amount of product quality.

12.5 Use the economic order quantity (EOQ) model to determine the optimal order quantity of a good stored in inventory.

12.6 Apply what you have learned about joint production, products, and location to make better managerial decisions.

Managers at Freeport-McMoRan Dig Deep to Make a Decision

Freeport-McMoRan is a large, multinational mineral and oil producer. Headquartered in Phoenix, Arizona, the company is a major world producer of copper, gold, cobalt, and molybdenum. The firm owns or has a controlling interest in mines located throughout North and South America, Africa, and Indonesia.

Freeport-McMoRan owns and operates the Morenci Mine and the Safford Mine, both located in southeast Arizona. For simplicity, our example focuses on these two Freeport-McMoRan mines and supposes that these are the only two Freeport-McMoRan mines that produce copper. Both are surface mines, also known as open pit mines. They extract copper by digging it out of a huge pit. The Morenci Mine is one of the world's largest and richest open pit mines. It produces more copper than any other mine in North America. Because its ore is richer in copper, the hypothetical figure shows that for any given quantity of copper, the marginal cost of producing a ton of copper at the Morenci Mine is less than that at the Safford Mine.

Freeport-McMoRan is one of the world's largest mining companies, and the downward-sloping demand curve in the figure shows that it has some market power; that is, the company can determine what price to charge for its products. How much copper should managers produce at the Safford Mine? At the Morenci Mine?

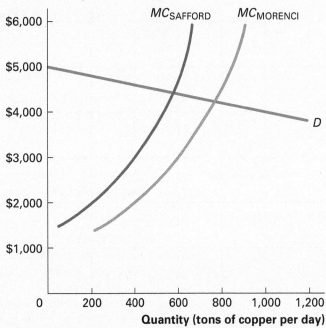

Price (dollars per ton of copper)

What price should the firm set for copper? At the end of the chapter, you will learn how Freeport-McMoRan's managers were able to answer these important questions.

Sources: http://www.fcx.com/company/who.htm; http://www.fcx.com/operations/USA_Safford.htm; http://www.fcx.com/operations/USA_Arizona_Morenci.htm.

Introduction

Managers must make a vast array of decisions about which products to produce, how to produce them, and where to produce them. Chapter 4 discussed basic aspects of production, including the production function, cost minimization, and how different costs change when production changes. This chapter builds on those fundamentals to cover a broad spectrum of production-related managerial decisions, ranging from joint production (when the production of one product simultaneously produces another) to production at multi-plant firms to inventory decisions and more. The wide range of concepts included in this chapter shares a common thread: marginal analysis. To show how marginal analysis plays a key role in making profit-maximizing decisions about production, the chapter includes six sections:

- **Section 12.1** examines how to make profit-maximizing decisions at firms with joint production.
- **Section 12.2** explains how managers of multi-plant firms can allocate production in order to maximize profit.
- **Section 12.3** describes how managers determine the number of plants to operate and where to locate them.
- **Section 12.4** explains the important role of quality in determining the profit from a product.
- **Section 12.5** presents a basic and important inventory model, the economic order quantity (EOQ) model. The EOQ model is optimal only in a very specific case, but its general decision-making lessons apply to all inventory decisions.
- **Section 12.6** demonstrates how you can apply what you have learned about joint production and the effect of transportation costs on location to make better managerial decisions.

12.1 Joint Production

Learning Objective 12.1 Explain how managers maximize profit when the production of one good results in the simultaneous production of one or more other goods.

Joint production Production that results in the simultaneous production of two or more outputs.

When production processes automatically result in the production of more than one good, it is called **joint production**. Chapter 2 introduced this topic in the discussion of how changes in the price of a complement in production affected the supply of a product. This chapter explores the managerial implications of joint production in detail.

Joint production sometimes occurs in fixed proportions, as when the production of a unit of one good invariably results in the production of a fixed amount of the other good(s). For example, when the National Beef Packing Company processes a steer, it invariably obtains one cowhide and two sides of beef. In this situation, the managers cannot alter the proportions of the products. In other cases, managers can change the proportions of the products. For example, when United Refining Company refines crude oil to make gasoline, the process also produces several other products, including kerosene, diesel, heating oil, and asphalt. Technicians can adjust the ratios of these products within certain limits, so United Refining Company's managers can increase profit by making decisions about product proportions. Let's begin with the more straightforward case of fixed proportions and then consider products produced in variable proportions.

Fixed Proportions

The case of fixed proportions is easier for managers because there is no decision to make about the relative quantities of the products. Consider the joint production of two sides of beef and one cowhide from each steer during processing. No matter how many steers are processed, each steer always produces two sides of beef and one cowhide.

The market demand for cattle consists of (1) the demand for beef, from grocery stores and restaurants, and (2) the demand for cowhides, from manufacturers of leather goods. To determine the demand for cattle, for each quantity of steers, you need to determine the price buyers will pay. Figure 12.1 shows the demand curves for sides of beef (D_B) and for cowhides (D_H) and the combined demand curve for steers (D_S). (Note that the demand curve for sides of beef represents the demand for the two sides of beef produced from each steer.) The price that buyers are willing to pay for a steer is equal to the sum of the prices that they are willing to pay for the two components. For example, at the quantity of 30 million steers per year, buyers will pay $40 for a cowhide (from demand curve D_H) and $140 for the two sides of beef (from demand curve D_B). So the total price they will pay is $40 + $140 = $180 per steer. Accordingly, for the quantity of 30 million steers the point on the demand curve for steers, D_S, is at the price of $180 per steer. The rest of demand curve D_S is calculated similarly, so the demand curve for steers is created by vertically adding together the demand curve for sides of beef and the demand curve for cowhides.

Because the cattle market is competitive, the market equilibrium occurs where the demand curve (D_S) intersects the supply curve (S). In Figure 12.2, the equilibrium quantity is 40 million steers per year, and the equilibrium price is $150 per steer.

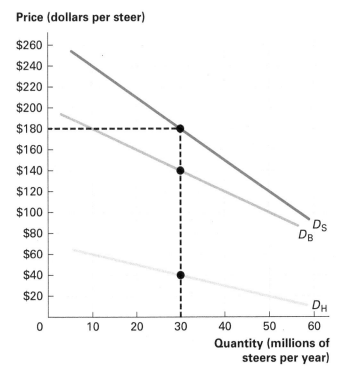

Price (dollars per steer)

Figure 12.1 The Demand Curve for Steers

The demand curve for steers (D_S) is equal to the demand curve for cowhides (D_H) plus the demand curve for sides of beef (D_B). At the quantity of 30 million steers, buyers will pay $40 for the cowhide and $140 for the two sides of beef, so they will pay $40 + $140 = $180 for the entire steer. Consequently, at the quantity of 30 million steers, the demand curve for steers goes through the price of $180.

Figure 12.2 The Market for Steers

The intersection of the demand curve for steers (D_S) and the supply curve of steers (S) determines the market equilibrium. The equilibrium quantity is 40 million steers, and the equilibrium price is $150 per steer. The demand curve for sides of beef (D_B) shows that the equilibrium price is $120 for two sides of beef. The demand curve for cowhides (D_H) shows that the equilibrium price is $30 for a cowhide.

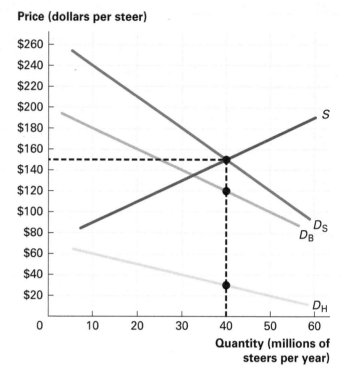

Demand curve D_B shows that buyers pay $120 for the two sides of beef, and demand curve D_H shows that buyers pay $30 per cowhide. Of course, the price of a steer ($150) is equal to the price of two sides of beef ($120) plus the price of one cowhide ($30).

As you learned in Chapter 5, managers of competitive firms take the price as given and produce the quantity of output that sets the marginal cost of production equal to the price. So managers of competitive cattle ranches produce the quantity of cattle that sets their marginal cost equal to the price of a steer, $150 in Figure 12.2. As a manager of a cattle ranch you do not need to be concerned with the separate prices of cowhides and sides of beef. All you need to know is the total price of a steer because that is the price that influences your profit-maximizing decisions.

Variable Proportions

The case of joint products produced in variable proportions is somewhat more complicated. As noted above, firms like United Refining Company refine petroleum into various products, including gasoline, diesel, and fuel oil. Suppose that you are a manager at such a firm. Because gasoline and diesel can be more profitable than fuel oil, companies often use a process called cracking—essentially heating the fuel oil, often in the presence of a catalyst—to transform fuel oil into varying proportions of gasoline and diesel.[1] Although there are chemical limitations, you can vary the proportions of gasoline and diesel produced from fuel oil,

---

1 Cracking fuel oil produces more products than just gasoline and diesel. For the purpose of this example, assume that joint production results in only two products.

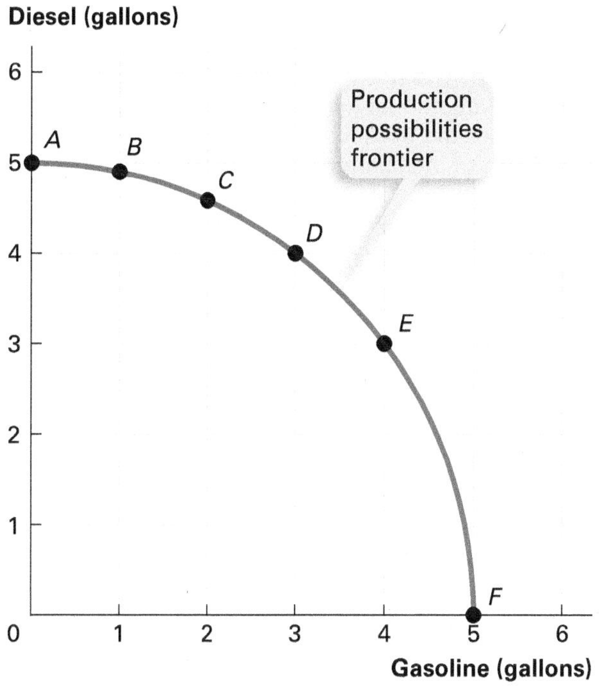

Diesel (gallons)

Figure 12.3 **The Production Possibilities Frontier for Gasoline and Diesel**

The production possibilities frontier shows the maximum combinations of diesel and gasoline that oil-refining firms can produce from a fixed amount of fuel oil. As more gasoline is produced, the foregone diesel from producing another gallon of gasoline increases. Producing the first gallon of gasoline—moving from point A to point B—decreases the production of diesel by 0.2 gallons. Producing the second gallon of gasoline—moving from point B to point C—decreases the production of diesel by 0.3 gallons. Eventually, producing the fifth gallon of gasoline—moving from point E to point F—decreases the production of diesel by 3.0 gallons.

creating a *production possibilities frontier* (PPF), a curve that shows the different quantities of diesel and gasoline your firm can produce from a given quantity of fuel oil. The hypothetical PPF illustrated in Figure 12.3 shows that as more gasoline is produced, less diesel can be produced. This reflects the trade-off managers face working with variable proportions in joint production: Producing more of one good means producing less of another. For technological reasons, as more of one good is produced, producing additional units means giving up increasing units of the other good. For example, producing the first gallon of gasoline by moving from point A to point B in Figure 12.3 means giving up 0.2 gallons of diesel. But moving from point B to point C and producing a second gallon of gasoline means giving up 0.3 gallons of diesel. Continuing the movement along the PPF and producing still more gasoline, each additional gallon of gasoline requires giving up more diesel.

Using Marginal Analysis to Determine the Profit-Maximizing Proportions

Although you can produce at any point on the PPF, your goal is to produce the combination of gasoline and diesel that maximizes profit. You can use marginal analysis to determine the profit-maximizing combination of gasoline and diesel.

Suppose that after taking account of the cost of cracking, the profit per gallon of gasoline is $0.50 and the profit per gallon of diesel is $1.00. For simplicity, assume that these profits are constant, though in reality they may change as more gasoline is produced because the cost of more extensive cracking may increase. Consider the movement along the PPF from point A to point B. This movement increases the quantity of gasoline by 1 gallon, which increases your firm's profit by $0.50, and simultaneously decreases the production of diesel by 0.2 gallons, which decreases

Table 12.1 **Marginal Benefit and Marginal Cost of a Gallon of Gasoline**

The profit from a gallon of gasoline is $0.50. The profit from a gallon of diesel is $1.00. In Figure 12.3, moving from point A to point B increases the production of gasoline by 1 gallon, thereby creating a gain of $0.50 in profit, which is the marginal benefit from the change. It also decreases the production of diesel by 0.2 gallons, thereby leading to a loss of $0.20 in profit, which is the marginal cost of the change. The remainder of the marginal benefits and marginal costs are calculated similarly.

Movement	Gasoline Gained (gallons)	Marginal Benefit (dollars of profit gained from increased gasoline)	Diesel Foregone (gallons)	Marginal Cost (dollars of profit lost from decreased diesel)
A to B	1.0	$0.50	0.2	$0.20
B to C	1.0	0.50	0.3	0.30
C to D	1.0	0.50	0.5	0.50
D to E	1.0	0.50	1.0	1.00
E to F	1.0	0.50	3.0	3.00

your firm's profit by $0.20. Table 12.1 shows the $0.50 increase in profit as the marginal benefit from the newly produced gallon of gasoline. The $0.20 loss of profit is the cost of the gallon of gasoline in the table. The table shows similar results for other changes along the PPF.

Figure 12.4 plots the marginal benefits and marginal costs from Table 12.1 midway between the relevant gallons of gasoline. According to the marginal analysis rule, the profit-maximizing quantity of gasoline is the amount that sets the marginal benefit from a gallon of gasoline equal to its marginal cost. So in Figure 12.4, the profit-maximizing

Figure 12.4 **Profit-Maximizing Quantity of Gasoline**

The marginal benefit curve shows the marginal profit gained from producing a gallon of gasoline. The marginal cost curve shows the marginal profit lost from producing less diesel. The profit-maximizing quantity of gasoline is 2.5 gallons of gasoline. The production possibilities frontier in Figure 12.3 shows that the profit-maximizing quantity of diesel is (approximately) 4.25 gallons.

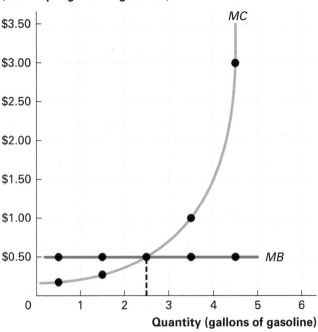

Marginal cost and marginal benefit (dollars per gallon of gasoline)

quantity is 2.5 gallons of gasoline.[2] For any quantity of gasoline up to 2.5 gallons, the increase in profit from producing more gasoline exceeds the loss of profit from producing less diesel. For any quantity of gasoline over 2.5 gallons, the loss of profit from producing less diesel exceeds the increase in profit from producing more gasoline.

Profit Maximization with Joint Production

In reality, no manager plots the marginal benefit and marginal cost curves to determine the profit-maximizing proportions of jointly produced products. There is a guideline you can use to determine the optimal proportions, however. It hinges on the fact that increasing the production of one good raises the firm's profit from that good but necessarily requires decreasing the production of the other good (or goods), which lowers the firm's profit from the other good (or goods). At the profit-maximizing combination, the increase in profit from increasing production of one good is always less than the decrease in profit from decreasing production of the other good(s) regardless of the number of joint products produced. This result is true *only* at the profit-maximizing combination. At any other combination, it is *always* possible to increase production of one good and raise the firm's profit by a greater amount than the fall in profit from decreasing production of the other good(s).

Change in Price with Joint Production

As you already know, managers of firms producing joint products with *fixed* proportions (like sides of beef and cowhides) do not need to pay attention to the separate prices of the joint goods when deciding on the amount of production. Instead, these managers determine production using the total price of the combined products. If the price of one of the joint products rises, the total price of both rises, and managers respond to the higher price by increasing their total production of the jointly produced products. The proportions of the two (or more) joint goods produced cannot change.

The situation is a more complicated for managers of firms producing joint products with *variable* proportions. If the price of one or more of the joint products changes, to maximize profit the managers must adjust *both* the total production of the jointly produced products *and* the products' proportions. Like the fixed proportions case, if the price of one of the joint products rises, the total price of the combined products rises, and the managers respond by increasing total production. In the variable proportions scenario, however, the rise in price of one of the joint goods changes the profit-maximizing proportions of the products. In particular, the managers increase production of the good that has risen in price and decrease production of the other good(s). For example, if the price of gasoline rises, your refinery will refine more oil, thereby producing more gasoline, *and also* increase the proportion of gasoline obtained by cracking fuel oil, thereby also producing more gasoline. Therefore, in the variable proportions case, the managers boost production of the product whose price rose for two reasons:

1. The higher price causes the firm to increase the production of *all* the jointly produced products, and
2. The higher price causes the firm to increase the proportion produced of the *one* product with the rise in price.

---

2 In Table 12.1, the marginal profit gained equals the marginal profit lost moving from point *C* (with 2 gallons of gasoline) to point *D* (with 3 gallons of gasoline). The profit-maximizing quantities of gasoline and diesel in Figure 12.4 lie midway between points *C* and *D*.

A Refinery Responds to an Increase in the Profit from Gasoline

In Figure 12.4, the profit from a gallon of gasoline is $0.50. Suppose that the price of a gallon of gasoline rises so much that the profit increases to $1.00 per gallon. Draw a figure similar to Figure 12.4, and use it to explain how this change affects the oil-refining company's profit-maximizing amount of gasoline and its profit-maximizing proportion of diesel.

Answer

The increase in profit from gasoline increases the firm's marginal benefit from producing gasoline. In Table 12.1, for each movement from one point to another, the marginal benefit (*MB*) rises to a $1.00 profit per gallon of gasoline. The *MB* curve shown in the figure is horizontal at the new marginal benefit of $1.00. The *MB* from producing gasoline now equals the marginal cost when 3.5 gallons of gasoline are produced. The rise in the profitability of gasoline results in an increase in the amount of gasoline produced from fuel oil. The production possibilities frontier in Figure 12.3 shows that producing more gasoline reduces the production of diesel. So the rise in the profit from gasoline causes profit-maximizing managers to increase the proportion of gasoline and decrease the proportion of diesel.

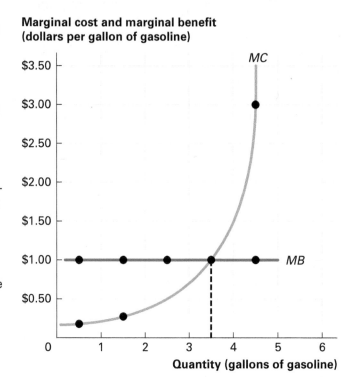

Marginal cost and marginal benefit (dollars per gallon of gasoline)

12.2 The Multi-Plant Firm

Learning Objective 12.2 Explain how managers of multi-plant firms allocate production to maximize profit.

Many firms sell their products in a single market but produce them in multiple production facilities. For example, Keebler bakes its cookies in several locations throughout the United States, and Crossroads Ag grows corn in different fields in Kansas, Colorado, and New Mexico. Firms with more than one production facility are **multi-plant firms**.

If you manage a multi-plant firm, you must decide (1) how much total output to produce and (2) how to allocate the total production across the different production facilities. These decisions hinge on profit maximization and, in particular, on the familiar profit-maximization rule from Chapter 5: Produce the quantity that sets $MR = MC$.

Multi-plant firm A firm with more than one production facility.

Table 12.2 **A Multi-Plant Firm's Marginal Cost**

At a marginal cost of $1.00 per box, plant 1 produces 10,000 boxes of Fudge Square cookies, and plant 2 produces 20,000 boxes. The overall total quantity produced at this marginal cost is the sum of these quantities, 30,000 boxes. Similarly, at a marginal cost of $1.50 per box, plant 1 produces 15,000 boxes, and plant 2 produces 25,000 boxes, so the overall total quantity produced at this marginal cost is 40,000 boxes.

Marginal Cost (dollars per box)	Quantity from Plant 1 (boxes)	Quantity from Plant 2 (boxes)	Total Quantity (boxes)
$1.00	10,000	20,000	30,000
1.50	15,000	25,000	40,000
2.00	17,000	27,000	44,000
2.50	18,000	28,000	46,000
3.00	19,000	29,000	48,000

Marginal Cost for a Multi-Plant Firm

The major difference between firms with multiple plants and those with a single plant lies in the calculation of the marginal cost. For each value of the marginal cost, you need the *overall* or total quantity produced at *all* plants. For example, suppose that you work for a firm like Keebler Company. Say your firm has two plants that make Fudge Square cookies, with different marginal costs. Table 12.2 shows the marginal costs for the two plants. When the marginal cost is $1.00 per box of Fudge Square cookies, the quantity produced in plant 1 is 10,000 boxes, and the quantity produced in plant 2 is 20,000 boxes. Therefore, the overall total quantity produced by your firm at the marginal cost of $1.00 is $10,000 + 20,000 = 30,000$ boxes of Fudge Square cookies. Similarly, when the marginal cost is $2.50 per box of cookies, the overall total quantity produced is 18,000 boxes (from plant 1) + 28,000 boxes (from plant 2) = 46,000 boxes of Fudge Square cookies.

More generally, Figure 12.5 shows that your firm's overall marginal cost curve (MC) is the horizontal sum of the individual plants' marginal cost curves. If a company has more than two plants, the overall marginal cost curve is the sum of the marginal cost curves from all of its plants.

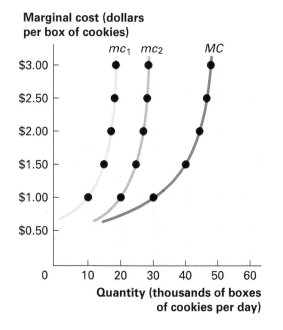

Marginal cost (dollars per box of cookies)

Quantity (thousands of boxes of cookies per day)

Figure 12.5 A Multi-Plant Firm's Marginal Cost Curve

At any marginal cost, the overall quantity produced equals the sum of the quantities produced by all of the plants.

Profit Maximization for a Multi-Plant Firm

Once the overall marginal cost is determined, managers maximize profit by using the profit-maximization rule: Produce the quantity for which $MR = MC$, and then set the highest price that sells the quantity produced. This rule maximizes profit for multi-plant firms that are perfectly competitive as well as for those with market power. The difference with a multi-plant firm, however, is that after determining the total quantity, the managers must then allocate it to the different plants.

Profit Maximization for a Perfectly Competitive Multi-Plant Firm

Suppose that your cookie-producing firm is a perfectly competitive firm. This assumption is unrealistic because firms like your firm and like Keebler definitely have some market power, but you will study that more realistic case shortly. As a manager at a perfectly competitive firm, your decisions have no discernible effect on the market price. Say that the market price is $2.50 per box of cookies. In Chapter 5, you learned that for a perfectly competitive firm, the demand and marginal revenue curves are both horizontal at the market price. Figure 12.6 shows these curves as a single horizontal line with the label $d = MR$. The figure also shows the overall marginal cost curve (MC) as well as the marginal cost curves from plant 1 (mc_1) and plant 2 (mc_2).

Your firm maximizes profit by producing 46,000 boxes of cookies per day, the quantity that sets $MR = MC$. The marginal revenue at this quantity is $2.50 per box, so at this marginal revenue Figure 12.6 shows that plant 1 produces 18,000 boxes and plant 2 produces 28,000 boxes. In other words, you allocate the total

Figure 12.6 Profit Maximization for a Two-Plant, Perfectly Competitive Firm

Use the profit-maximization rule to maximize your company's profit by producing 46,000 boxes of cookies, the quantity that sets the firm's MR equal to its MC. The marginal revenue is $2.50 per box, so at this marginal revenue the marginal cost curve mc_1 shows that plant 1 produces 18,000 boxes of cookies and marginal cost curve mc_2 shows that plant 2 produces 28,000 boxes of cookies.

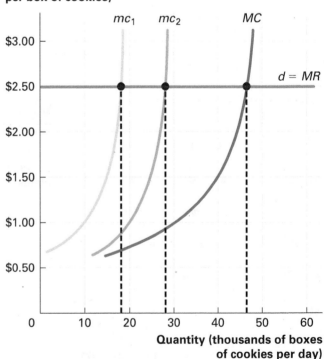

production of 46,000 boxes so that the marginal cost in each plant is equal and equals the profit-maximizing marginal revenue. If the firm has more than two plants, managers should allocate the total production so that each plant produces the quantity that sets that plant's marginal cost equal to the profit-maximizing marginal revenue.

Figure 12.6 shows that managers use *both* plants to produce the cookies. This result might seem odd because for any quantity of output, plant 1's marginal cost exceeds plant 2's marginal cost. Even so, managers use plant 1 because plant 2's marginal cost increases as more boxes are produced in that plant. So in plant 2 the marginal cost exceeds $2.50 for all boxes of cookies beyond 28,000, but in plant 1 the marginal cost is less than $2.50 for all boxes of cookies up to 18,000. Therefore, profit-maximizing managers direct plant 2 to produce 28,000 boxes of cookies and plant 1 to produce 18,000 boxes in order to produce the profit-maximizing quantity of 46,000 boxes.

Profit Maximization for a Multi-Plant Firm with Market Power

Now let's assume that your firm has some market power, so that its demand and marginal revenue curves both slope downward. Figure 12.7 illustrates the demand curve (*D*) and marginal revenue curve (*MR*). It also shows the overall marginal cost curve (*MC*) and the marginal cost curves from plant 1 (mc_1) and plant 2 (mc_2). Using the profit-maximization rule, your firm maximizes profit by producing 30,000 boxes of cookies, the quantity that sets the marginal revenue equal to the overall marginal cost. Using the demand curve shows that the profit-maximizing price is $2.50 per box. The marginal revenue at the profit-maximizing quantity is $1.00 per box. Figure 12.7 shows that at this marginal revenue, you should divide production

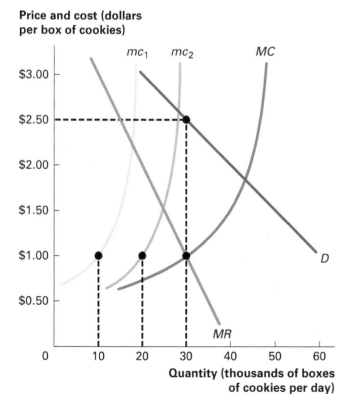

Price and cost (dollars per box of cookies)

Quantity (thousands of boxes of cookies per day)

Figure 12.7 Profit Maximization for a Two-Plant Firm with Market Power

Use the profit-maximization rule to maximize your company's profit by producing 30,000 boxes of cookies, the quantity that sets marginal revenue equal to the overall marginal cost: *MR = MC*. The profit-maximizing marginal revenue is $1 per box. At this marginal revenue, marginal cost curve mc_1 shows that plant 1 produces 10,000 boxes of cookies and marginal cost curve mc_2 shows that plant 2 produces 20,000 boxes of cookies.

so that plant 1 produces 10,000 boxes and plant 2 produces 20,000 boxes. With this allocation of production, your firm is maximizing its profit for boxes of Fudge Square cookies.

Regardless of whether a firm is perfectly competitive or has some market power, the profit-maximizing decisions about production remain the same: Produce the quantity that sets the *overall* marginal cost equal to the marginal revenue, and allocate this production among the plants so that the marginal cost in each plant equals the profit-maximizing marginal revenue.

The analysis so far has assumed a predetermined number of plants and locations. In the long run, however, managers must determine the number of plants and their locations. The next section explores these important decisions.

SOLVED PROBLEM

Can Producing Too Many Cookies Hurt Your Firm's Profit?

According to the profit-maximization rule, producing the quantity where $MR = MC$ maximizes profit. Suppose that your firm has two plants, 1 and 2. In the figure, the marginal cost of producing a box of cookies is mc_1 at plant 1 and mc_2 at plant 2. Explain why you do not maximize total profit if you instruct

- Plant 1 to maximize its profit by producing 17,500 boxes of cookies, where $mc_1 = MR$.

- Plant 2 to maximize its profit by producing 25,000 boxes of cookies, where $mc_2 = MR$.

Answer

Producing 17,500 boxes in plant 1 and 25,000 boxes in plant 2 means that your firm produces a total of 42,500 boxes of cookies.

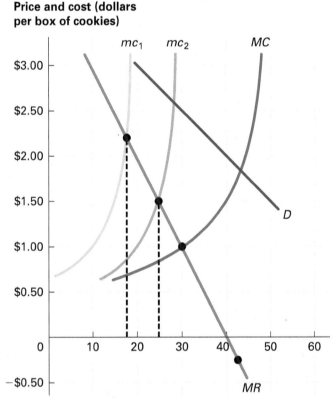

The firm is not maximizing profit by producing 42,500 boxes of cookies. The figure shows that at this quantity, marginal revenue is negative—it equals $-0.25. Because the marginal revenue at this quantity is negative, if you reduce production, (1) total revenue increases, and (2) total cost decreases. Reducing cost and increasing revenue clearly increase the firm's profit. Your firm has produced more than the profit-maximizing quantity. Only by producing the quantity where the marginal revenue equals the *overall* marginal cost (30,000 boxes in the figure) does your firm maximize profit.

12.3 Location Decisions

Learning Objective 12.3 Describe the factors that determine the number and location of plants operated by multi-plant firms.

Executives often must make decisions about how many plants to build and where to locate them. These decisions interact—for example, if only a few locations are appropriate for locating a plant, then the firm will have only a few plants. However, to most clearly illustrate the factors that answer the number-of-plants/location question(s), we examine these decisions independently. The discussion begins by presenting issues that affect the optimal number of plants and then describes factors that play a role in their location.

Changes in Costs from Adding Plants

Managers have a choice: They can operate their business using many small plants or fewer large ones. The decision revolves around cost. In particular, managers need to determine which option has the lower cost: many small plants or a few large ones. For several reasons, firms with a few large plants may have lower average costs than firms with many small plants:

- **Fewer inputs.** The number of some inputs, such as a safe and a receptionist, is the same regardless of the size of the plant. Firms with a small number of large plants need fewer of these inputs in total, so the company has lower average costs.
- **Availability of specialized capital.** Large plants can use specialized capital, which leaves smaller plants at a cost disadvantage. For example, a large farm might find it worthwhile to purchase a large John Deere R4045 sprayer, which sprays 120 feet of crops, rather than the smaller R4023 sprayer, which sprays only 60 feet of crops. The R4045 sprayer has 100 percent more crop coverage than the R4023 sprayer, but its price is only 50 percent higher.
- **Managerial diseconomies.** Managerial diseconomies can also lead a company to use fewer but larger plants. An increase in the number of plants can create *managerial diseconomies*, which, as you learned in Chapter 11, refers to the increased costs of managing a firm that result from an increase in the scope of the firm's operations, such as an increase in the number of plants. One source of managerial diseconomies from adding plants is the increase in executives' span of control, that is, an increase in the number of subordinates reporting to an executive. For example, with two plants, the operations executives at headquarters have two plant managers reporting to them. As the company adds more plants, these executives have more plant managers reporting to them. The amount of attention the executives can offer each plant manager diminishes, which can lead to delayed and poorer responses to local issues that affect a particular plant. Eventually, a new layer of (costly) bureaucracy is required.

Effect of Managerial Diseconomies

The effect of managerial diseconomies on the firm's total profit is important but can be subtle. To see this effect, suppose that you are the manager of a shrimp-farming operation with a single farm. This farm is your plant. Further assume that your firm is perfectly competitive and is making an economic profit. (If the firm had some market power, the analysis is more complicated, but the essential results are the same.) Because your farm is making an economic profit, you consider adding another.

An increase in the number of farms (or, more generally, in the number of plants) can result in managerial diseconomies that increase the cost of production at the existing farm (or plant). It will become more difficult for you to supervise the firm efficiently—your decisions will be more complicated, you will need more time to make them, and more decisions might prove to be wrong. As your difficulty increases, the cost of production in *all* of your plants increases.

To demonstrate the issues you face, use Figure 12.8 to consider the decision to add a second farm. Parts (a) and (b) illustrate the costs, revenue, and profit at the first farm. Figure 12.8(a) shows that to maximize profit with just one farm, you produce 4,000 pounds of shrimp per week and sell them for $3 per pound. You make an economic profit because the price, $3 per pound, exceeds your average total cost, $2 per pound. As you learned in Section 5.2, your economic profit equals the area of the green rectangle in the figure, or $4,000. Suppose that adding a second farm causes significant managerial diseconomies, which raise the costs at *both* locations. Figure 12.8(b) shows that the marginal cost and average total cost increase at the first farm, shifting the marginal cost curve upward from MC_1 to MC_2 and the average total cost curve upward from ATC_1 to ATC_2. As you can see

---

Figure 12.8 **Managerial Diseconomies from Adding Plants**

(a) **Costs and Economic Profit with One Plant**
With a single plant, the marginal cost curve is MC_1, and the average total cost curve is ATC_1. The managers maximize profit by producing 4,000 pounds of shrimp per week. The economic profit is $4,000, equal to the area of the green rectangle.

(b) **Costs and Economic Profit with Two Plants**
With two plants, managerial diseconomies raise the costs. At the first plant, the marginal cost curve rises to MC_2, and the average total cost curve rises to ATC_2. The managers now maximize profit by producing 3,000 pounds of shrimp per week. The economic profit falls to $900, equal to the area of the green rectangle. Adding a farm increases the firm's total economic profit only if the economic profit from the second farm exceeds the decrease in economic profit of the first farm.

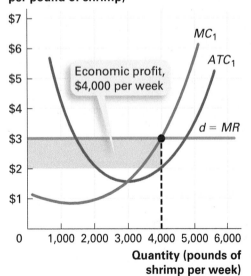

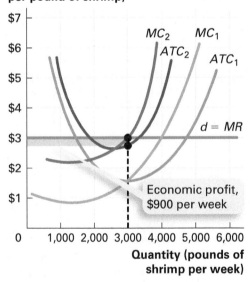

by comparing Figure 12.8(a) to Figure 12.8(b), adding the second farm creates substantial managerial diseconomies, causing the first farm's economic profit to fall from $4,000 per week to $900 per week. Adding the second farm is desirable only if its economic profit exceeds $3,100 per week. Otherwise, adding it lowers the total economic profit. Although the second location might, by itself, make an economic profit, the combined profit from the two farms could be less than the profit from a single farm.

More generally, another plant increases a firm's total economic profit only if the economic profit from the new plant is greater than any decrease in economic profit at the others. Accordingly, managers deciding whether to add another plant must determine its impact on the firm's *total* profit. The possibility of managerial diseconomies means that it is *not* sufficient to examine the profit of the new plant in isolation because the addition of a plant can reduce profit at existing plants.

The Effect of Transportation Costs on Location Decisions

Executives must not only decide how many plants to operate but also determine their locations. In some instances, firms have no choice about where to locate their operations. For example, all copper-mining companies, including Hindustan Copper, a copper-mining company owned by the government of India, *must* locate their mines where copper ore is located. At other times, the location decision is almost immediate: If an entrepreneur wants to start a company designing a new type of computer chip, Silicon Valley is close to the default location. Most firms, however, are not so constrained. In these circumstances, profit-minded managers have a single goal: minimizing the cost of producing and selling the product.

Transportation costs may cause firms to have several smaller plants rather than a few large ones. These costs play an important role in managerial decisions about the number of plants to build and where to locate them. As your focus shifts to transportation costs, assume that the cost of operating a plant does not depend on the number of plants. In other words, ignore the costs from adding plants, including any managerial diseconomies.

Firms may pay all of the transportation costs or just some of them. Let's begin by assuming that the firm directly pays the cost of shipping inputs to the plants as well as the cost of shipping the product to customers, as with the Amazon Prime program offered by Amazon.com. Next, you will learn about the situation in which consumers pay the cost of transporting the product from the store, so the firm directly pays only some of the transportation costs.

Firms Directly Pay *All* of the Transportation Costs

To maximize profit, the firm must minimize the total cost of producing a given quantity of output. Total costs include (1) the cost of transporting the inputs to the plants, (2) the cost of producing the product, and (3) the cost of transporting the product to customers. To focus on the role of transportation costs, assume that the managers have already minimized the cost of production (cost 2). That leaves the cost of transporting inputs to plants (cost 1) and the cost of transporting the product to customers (cost 3).

Many products have sizable input transportation costs. For example, the cost of transporting a ton of coal by railroad is about 40 percent of its total delivered price. A manager can reduce transportation costs to the plant by locating production closer to the source of the inputs. The new location may be farther from customers, however, which increases the cost of transporting the finished product. Moving the location of production closer to the location of the inputs has a marginal benefit—the decreased cost of transporting inputs—but also a marginal cost—the increased

DECISION
SNAPSHOT

Quaker Oats' Location Decision

Suppose that you are a manager at Quaker Oats and are determining where to locate your main plant. Quaker Oats' customers are located nationwide, but oats grow in only one region. Prime areas in the United States for farmers to grow oats include eastern North and South Dakota, the southern half of Minnesota, and all of Iowa. As befitting its name, the vast majority of Quaker Oats' products contain oats. Oats are surprisingly expensive to transport. Because their light weight per volume makes them too costly to move by rail, oats are shipped primarily by truck. Quaker's products, such as oatmeal, are less expensive to transport because they have a higher weight per volume. You decide to locate your main plant in Cedar Rapids, Iowa. Why?

Answer

By locating the plant near the heart of the oat-growing area, Quaker Oats decreases the cost of transporting oats to the plant but increases the cost of transporting its oatmeal to consumers. You determine that locating your main manufacturing plant at Cedar Rapids balances the marginal cost from moving farther away from customers against the marginal benefit from moving closer to the inputs. This location decision minimizes Quaker Oats' costs.

cost of transporting outputs. By using marginal analysis, managers can determine the profit-maximizing location, the location that minimizes costs:

- If the marginal benefit from moving closer to the inputs exceeds the marginal cost, managers move the plant location closer to the inputs to maximize profit.
- If the marginal benefit from moving closer to the inputs is less than the marginal cost, managers move the plant location closer to the customers to maximize profit.
- The plant is located at the cost-minimizing location when the marginal benefit from moving closer to the inputs is equal to the marginal cost.

So the location of plants depends on balancing the benefits and costs of locating near inputs versus locating near customers. These obviously vary from product to product. For example, in the early days of steel production, there were substantial benefits from locating steel plants next to coalfields because steel production used four tons of coal to produce each ton of steel and coal was expensive to transport. Locating next to coalfields minimized the input transportation costs. Because many coalfields were located near Pittsburgh, the owners of the major steel companies located their steel mills there, causing Pittsburgh to emerge as a national center for steel production.

The production of steel is a weight-losing process—the inputs weigh more than the finished output. In contrast, other products gain weight as inputs are combined. One such product is soft drinks. Water, a major component of soft drinks, is readily available almost anywhere. Transportation costs are minimized if water is added in a location near the customers, rather than near the source of the other inputs, such as syrup and cans. This analysis explains why soft-drink bottling plants are plentiful in most large urban areas where many consumers are located. For example, Coca-Cola Bottling Company United, one of The Coca-Cola Company's independent bottlers, has bottling locations in nine cities in the state of Georgia alone. The syrup and cans are shipped to the bottling plants, where they are combined with carbonated water and then distributed to the local customers.

Firms Directly Pay *Some* of the Transportation Costs

Retail businesses exist to distribute products to consumers. Customers arrive at the store (which is the equivalent of a retail firm's plant) and then bear the costs of transporting the products they purchase. It might appear as if these firms must minimize *only* the cost of transporting inputs to the store, but that is not the case. For example, locating all McDonald's restaurants next to meat-packing plants minimizes the cost of transporting beef patties to the restaurants, but a customer would not drive 1,200 miles from Atlantic City to a meat-packing plant in Kansas City to purchase a Big Mac!

The out-of-pocket cost of the travel to and from McDonald's and the opportunity cost of the customer's time during the trip comprise the customer's transportation costs. Although McDonald's does not directly pay the transportation cost incurred by its consumers, this cost clearly has a huge impact on the demand for its burgers. Customers are willing to pay a higher price to the producer to reduce their transportation costs. For example, if McDonald's can decrease its customers' transportation costs by $1 by locating nearer to them, these customers are willing to pay McDonald's up to $1 more when they visit McDonald's. This gives managers the incentive to minimize the sum of production and transportation costs even though

Walgreens and CVS Compete for Your Drug Prescription

Suppose that you are a manager at CVS/Caremark. For the past couple of decades, pharmacy chains such as yours and Walgreens have been rebuilding stores and moving them from strip malls to stand-alone locations. Stand-alone stores can have a drive-through, which allows customers to drop off and pick up prescriptions without getting out of their cars. Why are you and your competitors undertaking these costly renovations and moving stores out of strip malls?

Answer

By providing drive-throughs, these firms provide increased convenience to customers by reducing their shopping time. The drive-throughs decrease the time consumers spend filling their prescriptions, so the pharmacy chains have reduced consumers' transportation costs, decreasing the total price consumers pay. This allows the chains to compete with other prescription drug retailers, such as grocery stores and Walmarts, which may have lower list prices for the drugs. But because grocery stores and Walmarts are often located in strip malls, their design prevents them from providing drive-throughs, so consumers shopping there experience higher transportation costs, such as the time to park the car and walk into the store to pick up their prescriptions.

the firm is not directly paying some of the transportation costs. So their decision-making process remains the same: Managers can use marginal analysis to determine the optimal store (or plant) location, the location that minimizes the sum of input transportation costs and product transportation costs. The store (or plant) is located at the cost-minimizing location when the marginal benefit from moving closer to the inputs is equal to firm's or customers' marginal cost of transporting the products.

The Effect of Geographic Variation in Input Prices on Location Decisions

Although many inputs must be shipped to a plant (or store), some inputs are not transported. Clearly, the land on which a plant is located is not transported. Other inputs are transported but only for short distances. Workers, for example, are relatively local. A plant in Akron, Ohio, employs workers who live in Akron or the surrounding area. Very rarely would a worker live in Chicago and commute 370 miles to Akron. Managers can reduce their costs by locating a plant in an area where local inputs are less costly. Understanding the factors that help determine geographic variations in the prices of these inputs can narrow the list of potential plant locations. For example, managers can purchase utility service—electricity and water—virtually anywhere, but electricity is less expensive in areas served by hydroelectric plants, and water tends to be more expensive in arid regions. So executives of firms that are electricity intensive, such as aluminum refineries, look to locate plants in areas served by hydroelectric plants, while managers of firms that are water intensive, such as beer breweries, want to locate breweries in areas where water is plentiful.

Land Prices

Land prices vary widely depending on geographic location. Clearly, agricultural land is more expensive in locations where it is more fertile—it costs more to rent an acre in the middle of a wheat field in Kingdom, Kansas, than in Death Valley, California. The price of urban land is greater than the price of nearby rural land. Urban land prices also vary within a city. Most workers in large cities commute to their jobs, which are often near the center of the city. Few workers enjoy their commute, so the longer the commute, the lower the demand for housing and the land necessary to build it. This effect means that, other things being equal, land prices generally fall as the distance from the center of the city increases.

Land prices adjust to many other factors as well. For example, areas with higher levels of pollution have lower land prices, and areas with scenic views have higher land prices. Because drugstores such as Walgreens and CVS desire corner locations on the right side of streets heavily used for the commute home, such lots have higher prices.

Managers must determine whether higher-priced land makes sense for their businesses. Hotel and restaurant executives, for example, are more willing to pay the high price for land with stunning scenic views because they improve business. Managers of factories and dry cleaners do not receive the same benefit from the scenery. Walgreens and CVS are more willing to pay for a desirable corner lot than are supermarkets and restaurants.

Compensating wage differential The difference in wages paid to workers to offset undesirable aspects of a job.

Wages

Wages of workers in the same occupation differ by geographic location because of compensating wage differentials. A **compensating wage differential** is the difference in wages paid to workers to offset undesirable aspects of a job. For example, most workers find living in Alaska less desirable than living in Hawaii. A senior accountant makes approximately $70,000 per year in Alaska compared to $55,000 per year in Hawaii. The $15,000 difference in salary is the compensating wage differential for working in Alaska.

The concept of compensating wage differentials demonstrates that workers are willing to work for lower wages if a job sufficiently compensates them with some other reward, such as a lower cost of living, a great climate, or a shorter commute to work. It predicts that wages will be higher in areas in which it is unpleasant or more expensive to live. For example, because urban land is scarce and thus more expensive than the surrounding agricultural land, urban areas are more expensive to live in than are rural areas and have correspondingly higher wages.

Managers can take advantage of compensating wage differentials when locating their plants. In 2013, for example, Kenall Manufacturing, a firm that produces commercial lighting solutions, announced it would move its manufacturing facility from Chicago to a more rural area in Kenosha, Wisconsin, in part because its wage costs would be lower. Kenall's managers could count on lowering worker wages for two reasons: (1) the cheaper cost of living in rural areas and (2) the shorter commute for employees who could avoid the crowded Chicago transit system. The compensating wage differentials associated with these two desirable job aspects lower the wages Kenall must pay in Kenosha.

Other Factors

Of course, factors other than the cost of inputs and transportation affect location decisions. For example, the level of taxation differs considerably from area to area, while a number of regions or states offer preferential tax status to any new firm or to preferred industries in order to stimulate growth. In 2014, Nevada, California, Texas, Arizona, and New Mexico all offered more than $500 million in tax and other incentives to Tesla Motors to locate a $5 billion battery factory in their state. (Nevada won.) When making their final location decision, managers must take into account all the relevant costs (and benefits), but they can use insights from the theory of compensating wage differentials and differences in other costs to begin their search for the optimal location for a new plant.

Although the general analysis is straightforward, the details of calculating the real-world costs and benefits from an additional plant will be complicated. You need to take into account many issues, including real estate values, zoning issues, local taxes, traffic regulations involving large trucks, and any concerns unique to your firm's situation. In addition, remember that you must incorporate the effect of the rise in production costs at *all* plants, not just the plant or plants you are thinking about adding. Regardless of the details, never lose track of the general profit-maximizing approach: Compare the marginal benefit from adding a plant to its marginal cost.

So far in this chapter you have learned about production decisions—how managers should respond to changes in demand if their firm produces joint products, how to allocate production among more than one plant, and how to determine the optimal number of plants. Some production decisions affect the product itself, however. In particular, managers often must make decisions about a product's quality. Changing quality affects both the demand for a product and its cost of production. As you will see in more detail in the next section, marginal analysis plays an important role in decisions made about product quality.

<table>
<tr><td>SOLVED
PROBLEM</td><td></td></tr>
</table>

A Department Store Pays for Transportation

Suppose that you are a manager at a department store like JCPenney and are in charge of online sales of bath towels. For simplicity, assume that your firm is a perfect competitor and that consumers are willing to pay $14, including shipping, for a towel. If consumers pay for shipping, the shipping cost is $2 per towel. The table shows your marginal cost of a towel. This marginal cost does *not* include any shipping cost.

Quantity (millions)	Marginal cost (dollars per towel)
5	$11
6	12
7	13
8	14
9	15

a. If your customers must pay for the shipping cost of their towels, what price will they pay for a towel? If consumers pay for shipping, what is your profit-maximizing price (excluding shipping) and quantity of towels?

b. Suppose that your firm can ship the towels for a lower cost of $1 per towel. If you offer free shipping to consumers, what is the effect on your marginal costs?

c. If you offer free shipping to consumers, what price will they pay you for a towel? What is your profit-maximizing price and quantity of towels? How does this offer affect your profit?

Answer

a. Consumers are willing to pay your firm $14 minus the $2 cost of shipping, or $12 per towel. The marginal revenue per towel is $12, so you maximize profit by selling 6 million towels, the quantity that sets marginal revenue equal to marginal cost. You set a price of $12 per towel.

b. If your firm offers free shipping to consumers, you must pay for the shipping, which is $1 per towel. For each quantity, the marginal cost increases by $1, so that the marginal cost is $12 per towel for 5 million towels, $13 for 6 million towels, $14 for 7 million towels, $15 for 8 million towels, and $16 for 9 million towels.

c. With free shipping, consumers are willing to pay your firm $14 per towel. The marginal revenue becomes $14, so you maximize profit by selling 7 million towels, the quantity that sets marginal revenue equal to marginal cost. You set a price of $14 per towel. Your firm sells more towels at a higher price. Free shipping has increased your firm's profit.

12.4 Decisions About Product Quality

Learning Objective 12.4 Use marginal analysis to determine the profit-maximizing amount of product quality.

Product quality is a general term that acquires meaning in specific contexts. For managers at Bloomin' Brands, owner of restaurants such as Outback Steakhouse and Bonefish Grill, product quality refers to taste and service. For managers at Heritage Home Group, owner of furniture brands such as Thomasville and Drexel Heritage, product quality refers to style and finish. For other companies, quality may refer to sound, as for

Bose Corporation, or durability, as for Maytag. In fact, many different attributes are elements of *quality*. Consider the purchase of an automobile from a Honda dealership. Customers seek cars with a certain level of fuel economy, comfort, and style as well as a reputation for durability. These attributes are all elements of a car's quality. But when customers buy a car, they also consider these other components of quality: the proximity of the dealer to their residence or place of work, hours of operation, ease of financing, and knowledge and professionalism of the sales and service staff. When managers alter any of these components, they change the product's quality. Although the attributes of quality differ from one product to the next, for simplicity assume that quality can be measured in units. Reality is, of course, more difficult because in it managers must use their judgment about the amount of quality in a product.

Consumers are willing to pay a higher price for a higher-quality good because it provides them with more benefits. For example, with all other attributes the same, consumers are willing to pay more for a "higher-quality" car that gets 35 miles per gallon (mpg) than for a "lower-quality" car that gets 30 mpg. Many managers must choose between producing a lower-quality good that sells for a lower price or a higher-quality good that sells for a higher price.

As a manager, you must select the optimal production quality—that is, the level of quality that maximizes your firm's profits. Once again, you can use marginal analysis to help make this decision by comparing the marginal revenue and marginal cost of a change in quality. The marginal revenue is the additional revenue the firm collects because of the quality improvement. The marginal cost is the additional cost to the firm of making the quality improvement. If the marginal revenue exceeds the marginal cost, it is profitable to produce the higher-quality good. For example, if it costs a firm like Honda $1,000 per car to raise fuel efficiency from 30 mpg to 31 mpg and consumers will pay an additional $1,800 for the improvement, then managers will raise the fuel efficiency. The same managers will not implement the change if consumers will pay only $900 more for the added fuel efficiency.

In general, consumers' valuation of additional units of quality falls as more units of quality are included in the product, causing the marginal revenue from the quality improvement to fall. For example, consumers value an increase in gas mileage from 20 mpg to 21 mpg (a 5 percent increase) more than an increase from 50 mpg to 51 mpg (a 2 percent increase). As illustrated in Figure 12.9, the marginal revenue curve (*MR*) from additional units of quality is downward sloping.

A producer's marginal cost of additional units of quality rises as more units are included in the product. In our example, the car manufacturer's marginal cost of increasing gas mileage from 50 mpg to 51 mpg is more than its marginal cost of increasing gas mileage from 20 mpg to 21 mpg. Therefore, as illustrated in Figure 12.9 by the upward-sloping marginal cost curve (*MC*), the marginal cost for initial units of quality is less than the marginal cost for later units.

Figure 12.9 confirms the familiar result from marginal analysis: To maximize profit, increase quality until marginal revenue equals marginal cost. In the case of quality enhancements, this general result is the quality profit-maximization rule: Produce the level of quality that sets the marginal revenue from a unit of quality equal to the marginal cost of producing the unit of quality. In Figure 12.9, the profit-maximizing version of the car gets 40 mpg.

QUALITY PROFIT-MAXIMIZATION RULE

- Produce the level of quality that sets the marginal revenue from a unit of quality equal to the marginal cost of producing the unit of quality.

Figure 12.9 Marginal Revenue and Marginal Cost of Quality

One aspect of a car's quality is its miles per gallon (mpg). The marginal revenue (*MR*) from an increase in mpg equals the additional revenue the manufacturer gains from increasing the car's mileage. The marginal cost (*MC*) from an increase in mpg equals the additional cost the manufacturer incurs from increasing the car's mpg. Managers use marginal analysis to maximize profit by producing cars that get 40 mpg, the level of quality that sets *MR* = *MC*.

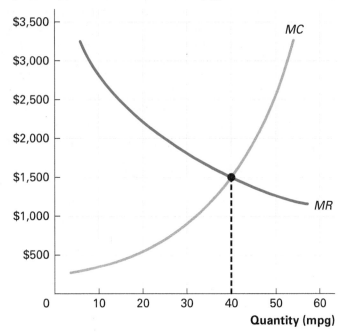

Marginal revenue and marginal cost
(dollars per one-unit increase in mpg)

The quality profit-maximization rule is most effective if you recognize that the premium consumers are willing to pay for higher quality varies by customer. For example, both gasoline and diesel have been more expensive in Europe than in the United States for decades, so consumers in Europe are willing to pay a higher price for a car with more quality—a higher mpg—than are consumers in the United States. The higher price translates into greater marginal revenue for automobile producers, so they have found it profitable to sell more-fuel-efficient cars in Europe. For example, in 2017, BMW's European 328i Gran Turismo automobile averaged 35 mpg, but the U.S. model averaged only 27 mpg.

SOLVED PROBLEM

Flower Quality

Continental Flowers is one of many companies that import cut flowers from Colombia through Miami, where wholesalers then distribute them throughout the United States. Importers can fly the flowers to the United States, which takes 4 hours, or ship them using a cargo ship, which takes 3 days. If the flowers are transported using cargo ships, their temperature can be maintained between 34° and 36°, the optimum temperature for maintaining their quality. The apparatus that cools the flowers is large, bulky, and heavy, so it is too costly to cool the flowers if they are flown. Consequently, if they are flown, their temperature will rise while they are on the plane and fall once they reach Miami and are again refrigerated. The rise and subsequent fall in temperature decreases the flowers' quality because it decreases their life span. As a manager of a flower importer like Continental Flowers, you believe you can sell a box of 24 higher-quality flowers for 50¢ more, and it costs an additional 1¢ per flower per day to transport them by cargo ship. Should you switch to delivery by cargo ship to increase the quality of your flowers? Explain your answer.

Answer
To make this decision, you must compare the marginal revenue of increasing quality to the marginal cost of that increase. The marginal revenue for a box of 24 flowers from increasing their quality is 50¢. The daily marginal cost of increasing the quality of a box of flowers is 1¢ per flower × 24 flowers per box, or 24¢ per box per day. Because it takes 3 days for the trip, the marginal cost per box is 24¢ per box × 3 days, or 72¢. The marginal cost of increasing the quality is more than the marginal revenue, so you should fly the flowers to Miami even though it decreases their quality.

12.5 Optimal Inventories

Learning Objective 12.5 Use the economic order quantity (EOQ) model to determine the optimal order quantity of a good stored in inventory.

It is impossible for the Sara Lee Corporation to set up production so that an apple pie emerges from the oven the moment a customer wants one or for Apple to arrange for a delivery truck to arrive with an iPhone precisely when a customer wants to purchase one. Fortunately, many companies can store products in inventory until needed. Managers can reduce production or delivery costs by keeping an inventory of the goods they produce or sell. Ordering and holding goods in inventory involves opportunity costs, however. So managers must determine the amount to carry in inventory that minimizes the total cost of keeping an inventory. Although the discussion focuses on inventory and ordering decisions about finished products, the results also apply to purchasing decisions about intermediate goods that are held in inventory before they are used as inputs.

Economic Order Quantity Model

For simplicity, consider the inventory problem in a situation with no uncertainty, so the managers know the exact quantity they will sell. Chapter 14 analyzes managers' inventory decisions under uncertainty, when demand fluctuates randomly. The **economic order quantity (EOQ) model** is a famous inventory model (at least among economists) that helps managers determine the cost-minimizing quantity to order to keep in inventory. The EOQ model relies on two specific assumptions: (1) Demand is known with certainty, and (2) demand is spread evenly over the time period. This model's assumptions are very specific, but you can apply its general lessons in other inventory situations.

Economic order quantity (EOQ) model A mathematical model that determines the cost-minimizing quantity managers should order to keep in their inventory.

Let's examine a hypothetical situation facing managers at an AT&T store in Santa Cruz. In order to maximize profit, they need to minimize the total cost of holding their inventory of iPhones. The total cost has two components:

1. **The carrying cost of holding an inventory.** This includes the cost of storage, the cost of securing the inventory, and the opportunity cost of keeping funds tied up financing the inventory.
2. **The ordering cost of the good held in inventory.** This includes the managerial time spent creating the order, the delivery charge for each order, and the cost of the paperwork necessary to pay for each order.

AT&T's managers must determine the optimal quantity of iPhones to order to minimize the sum of these costs.

For simplicity, assume that the phones are delivered immediately when the managers order them, so the managers will wait until they have zero iPhones in stock before placing an order. The quantity ordered and delivered is Q_{ORDER}. So the inventory starts with Q_{ORDER} units and ends with 0 units, which means the average inventory held by the store equals $\frac{Q_{ORDER}}{2}$. For example, if the managers order 70 iPhones each time, the average inventory is $(70 \text{ iPhones}/2) = 35$ iPhones. Suppose that C is the carrying cost associated with holding each unit in inventory. C includes the storage cost, the insurance cost, the opportunity cost of shelf space while the item is on display waiting to be purchased, and the opportunity cost of the funds used to finance the inventory. The total carrying cost of the inventory is equal to the carrying cost of holding each unit in inventory multiplied by the average number of units held in inventory, or

$$\text{Carrying cost} = C \times \frac{Q_{ORDER}}{2} = \frac{C \times Q_{ORDER}}{2} \qquad \textbf{12.1}$$

For example, if the annual carrying cost of an iPhone (C) is $40 per phone and the managers order 20 iPhones, the total annual carrying cost of the inventory is equal to $\frac{\$40 \times 20}{2} = \$400$ per year.

Because Q_{ORDER} is delivered in each order, the number of orders is equal to the total quantity sold during the year (Q) divided by Q_{ORDER}, or $\frac{Q}{Q_{ORDER}}$. For example, if the total number of iPhones sold is 800 and the order quantity is 40, then the managers will submit $(800 \text{ iPhones})/(40 \text{ iPhones per order}) = 20$ orders. Each order has both fixed and variable costs. The fixed cost (C_{FC}) includes the cost of submitting the order, the cost of processing the bill, and any fixed delivery charge for the order. The variable cost (C_{VAR}) includes the price of the good being delivered and any delivery cost that depends on the number of phones ordered. The total cost of one order is $C_{FC} + (C_{VAR} \times Q_{ORDER})$. Because there are $\frac{Q}{Q_{ORDER}}$ orders per year, the annual ordering cost is

$$\begin{aligned} \text{Annual Ordering Cost} &= [C_{FC} + (C_{VAR} \times Q_{ORDER})] \times \frac{Q}{Q_{ORDER}} \\ &= \left(C_{FC} \times \frac{Q}{Q_{ORDER}} \right) + (C_{VAR} \times Q_{ORDER}) \times \frac{Q}{Q_{ORDER}} \\ &= \frac{C_{FC} \times Q}{Q_{ORDER}} + (C_{VAR} \times Q) \qquad \textbf{12.2} \end{aligned}$$

For example, if the fixed cost of placing an order (C_{FC}) is $10 per order, the variable cost of placing an order (C_{VAR}) is $200 per iPhone, the total quantity sold (Q) is 800 iPhones, and the number of phones in an order is 20, then the annual ordering cost is

$$\frac{(\$10 \times 800 \text{ iPhones})}{20 \text{ iPhones}} + (\$200 \times 800 \text{ iPhones}) = \$160{,}400$$

The total annual cost equals the carrying cost (given by Equation 12.1) and the annual ordering cost (given by Equation 12.2):

$$\text{Total annual cost} = \frac{C \times Q_{ORDER}}{2} + \frac{C_{FC} \times Q}{Q_{ORDER}} + (C_{VAR} \times Q) \qquad \textbf{12.3}$$

To maximize profit, the managers must select the order quantity, Q_{ORDER}, that minimizes the total annual cost of the inventory given in Equation 12.3. If they increase the size of the order, the ordering cost falls because fewer orders are placed, but the carrying cost rises. Alternatively, if they decrease the size of the order, the ordering cost rises, but the carrying cost falls. This trade-off can be characterized in very familiar terms: marginal benefit and marginal cost. Increasing the size of the order has the marginal benefit of lowering the ordering cost but the marginal cost of increasing the carrying cost. To minimize the total annual cost, use marginal analysis to increase the order size until the marginal benefit equals the marginal cost. No matter what assumptions you make about demand or about cost, all inventory models balance the changes in these two costs by using marginal analysis, so the cost-minimizing inventory sets the marginal benefit from increasing the order size equal to its marginal cost.

The mathematics of the cost-minimizing order quantity in the EOQ model is difficult because deriving the marginal benefit requires calculus (see Section 12.B of the Appendix at the end of this chapter for that derivation). Here is the ultimate result, the cost-minimizing order quantity:

$$Q_{ORDER} = \sqrt{\frac{2 \times C_{FC} \times Q}{C}} \qquad \textbf{12.4}$$

You can use Equation 12.4 to determine the order quantity of iPhones that minimizes the AT&T store's total cost. For example, if the quantity of iPhones the store will sell in a year (Q) is 800, the annual carrying cost of holding an iPhone in inventory (C) is $40 per iPhone, and the fixed cost of an order (C_{FC}) is $10 per order, the cost-minimizing number of iPhones to order (Q_{ORDER}) is

$$\sqrt{\frac{2 \times \$10 \times 800}{\$40}} = 20 \text{ iPhones}$$

The average inventory of iPhones is $\frac{Q_{ORDER}}{2}$, which in this example is 10 iPhones.

With the cost-minimizing quantity of 20 iPhones per order, use Equation 12.2 to calculate that the total ordering cost incurred by the AT&T store is $160,400. The total carrying cost from Equation 12.1 is $\frac{C \times Q_{ORDER}}{2}$, so

$$\text{Total carrying cost} = \frac{\$40 \times 20 \text{ iPhones}}{2} = \$400$$

Therefore, the total cost of the inventory is $160,400 + $400 = $160,800. Any other order size results in a higher total cost.

General Optimal Inventory Decisions

Some of the features of the EOQ model are unique to that model. For example, the cost-minimizing quantity in Equation 12.4 takes the square root as part of the computation. This result is specific to the EOQ model. Other inventory models make different assumptions about demand and costs and reach different formulas for the cost-minimizing quantity. Four results, however, are more general and apply to both the EOQ model and other inventory models:

1. **MB = MC.** The most important result is hidden in the square root formula: The optimal order quantity sets the marginal cost of increasing the order size equal to the marginal benefit from increasing the order size. The use of marginal analysis is the key to any profit-maximizing order quantity and inventory decision.

2. **The optimal order quantity and inventory level decrease as the carrying cost increases.** The optimal order quantity and the optimal inventory level decrease as the carrying cost of holding a unit in inventory (C) rises. Bulky or expensive items cost more to hold in inventory than smaller or less expensive ones. The carrying cost of holding a unit in inventory also rises when the cost of the warehouse or store space devoted to holding inventories increases. Regardless of the reason for the increased carrying cost, profit-maximizing managers respond by holding less in inventory and ordering more frequently.

3. **Q_{ORDER} does not depend on C_{VAR}.** In most cases, the cost-minimizing order quantity does not depend on the variable cost per unit ordered (C_{VAR}). This seemingly paradoxical result reflects the fact that the variable cost per unit is the same no matter when the item is ordered or how many are ordered. It is impossible to avoid C_{VAR}—the firm must pay the variable cost for all the units ordered regardless of the number ordered at any given time—so it does not affect the optimal order quantity. If, however, the variable cost per unit varies according to the quantity ordered and/or the timing of the order, you must then include C_{VAR} in your marginal analysis. For example, if the variable cost of the first 20 iPhones in an order is $300 per phone and the variable cost of the next 20 iPhones in the order is $250 per phone, then this change in the variable cost per unit will affect your (more complicated) marginal analysis and will affect the optimal order quantity.

4. **C_{FC} has an effect on Q_{ORDER}.** The fixed cost of an order (C_{FC}) affects the optimal order quantity. A rise in the fixed cost of each order leads managers to reduce the number of orders, which increases the average inventory. For example, when the price of gasoline and diesel soared a few years ago, the fixed cost of delivering appliances also soared. In response, managers at appliance retailers such as Home Depot and Lowe's responded by increasing the size of each order from manufacturers, which increased the size of the inventory they carried in stock.

SOLVED PROBLEM

How a Decrease in Demand Affects the Economic Order Quantity

Suppose that the Samsung Galaxy smartphone suddenly becomes more popular, causing the demand for iPhones at the AT&T store in Santa Cruz to drop from 800 per year to 392 per year. If the annual carrying cost (C) of holding an iPhone in inventory remains at $40 per iPhone and the fixed cost of an order (C_{FC}) remains at $10 per order

a. How does the decrease in demand affect the economic order quantity?

b. How does the decrease in demand affect the quantity held in inventory?

Answer

a. The economic order quantity is equal to

$$\sqrt{\frac{2 \times \$10 \times 392}{\$40}} = 14 \text{ iPhones}$$

b. The average inventory of iPhones is $Q_{ORDER}/2$ or 7 iPhones. The decrease in demand for iPhones has decreased both the economic order quantity and the number carried in inventory.

12.6 Production, Products, and Location

Learning Objective 12.6 Apply what you have learned about joint production, products, and location to make better managerial decisions.

As a profit-maximizing manager, you know that anything that lowers your costs makes you better able to compete. Sometimes changes in the demand for a product can affect the cost of another product, which might be an input your firm uses. At other times, your firm may have to consider costs that are not immediately obvious because they are opportunity costs of your customers, such as transportation costs.

Joint Production of an Input

Joint production makes it a bit more complicated for managers to use the supply and demand model. For example, suppose that you are a manager of a firm like Torino Leather Company, a producer of cow-leather goods located in New Orleans. In 2014, porcine epidemic diarrhea virus (PEDv) killed about 10 percent of the nation's hogs. How does the PEDv epidemic affect your costs? You might not immediately see the link, but the supply and demand model, along with what you have learned about joint production of products, can help you better predict the changes in your cost of leather.

The decrease in the supply of hogs causes the price of pork to rise. For consumers, beef is a substitute for pork. When the price of pork rises, consumers' demand for beef increases which increases the demand for sides of beef. The increase in the demand for sides of beef increases the total demand for steers. In Figure 12.10, the demand curve for sides of beef shifts rightward from D_B to D'_B, which shifts the demand curve for steers rightward from D_S to D'_S. This increase in demand raises the price of a steer from $150 to $170. The new demand curve for sides of beef, D'_B, shows that the price of sides of beef has risen to $150. Importantly for you, as a manager at the leather company, the demand curve for cowhides, D_H, shows that the price of a cowhide has *fallen* to $20 per hide.

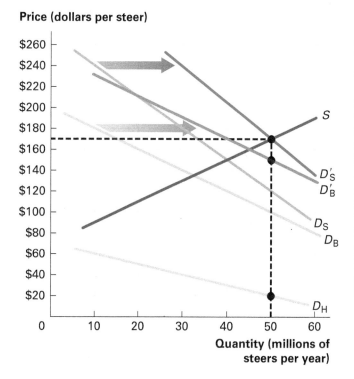

Price (dollars per steer)

Quantity (millions of steers per year)

Figure 12.10 An Increase in the Demand for Beef

The increase in the demand for cuts of beef increases the demand for sides of beef and thereby increases the total demand for steers. The demand curve for sides of beef shifts rightward from D_B to D'_B. which shifts the demand curve for steers rightward from D_S to D'_S. The price of a steer rises to $170 per steer. The price of the sides of beef rises to $150, while the price of a cowhide *falls* to $20.

The price of cowhides has fallen because of the increase in the demand for the *joint* product. So you should increase the amount of cowhides you purchase while the price is low. More generally, if you purchase an input that is jointly produced with another product, always keep an eye on the demand for the other product. Anything that increases the demand for the other product (beef) will result in a fall in the price of your input, the second product (cowhides). Taking advantage of the lower price of the input can decrease your company's costs and increase your profit. Of course, the reverse also holds true: Anything that decreases the demand for the other product will have the unfortunate effect of raising the price of the product you use as an input.

Transportation Costs, Plant Size, and Location

You know that minimizing the transportation costs of your product is important. As you have already learned, an important element of your customers' transportation costs is the opportunity cost of their time. One factor affecting this opportunity cost is income. The time customers use to transport products home could otherwise be spent at work, so consumers with higher wages have higher opportunity costs than consumers with lower wages. When managers are deciding where to locate their retail stores, placing stores closer together in areas frequented by high-income consumers maximizes profit because travel time (and the opportunity cost of the consumers' time) is lower. This is one of the reasons that there are five Starbucks in Beverly Hills, California, a city less than 6 square miles in size, and only three Starbucks in Ocala, Florida, a city of approximately 40 square miles but with a substantially lower per capita income.

Minimizing customers' transportation costs also shows how smaller stores can survive and even thrive in the face of competition from larger, lower-cost rivals. In particular, large retail stores, with lower costs, are able to sell at lower prices than small stores. How, then, can managers of smaller stores survive? For example, how can smaller drugstores like CVS compete with larger supermarkets such as Publix? After all, virtually everything sold at CVS—food, detergent, and even pharmaceuticals—is also sold at Publix, which offers many of the items at lower prices.

Transportation costs explain how CVS survives: CVS competes on location. CVS stores are local. Publix stores draw customers from a larger region. A simplified model of the competition between CVS and Publix shows the factors that affect the managerial decisions at the two companies.

The benefit to customers of traveling to Publix to purchase items at a lower price depends on the amount they buy. Consider this example: Suppose that you make two types of trips involving the purchase of provisions: you purchase 2 units of provisions on spur-of-the-moment trips and 25 units of provisions on weekly trips. You can shop at the large, regional Publix store, which charges $4 per unit of provisions, or the small, local CVS store, which charges $5 per unit of provisions. The two stores are located at different distances from your home.

For a spur-of-the-moment trip, you pay a total of $2 more for the 2 units of provisions at your local CVS store than at the regional Publix supermarket. Buying the provisions is only part of the cost of the shopping trip, however. Your total cost of making a quick trip to a small CVS is $(2 \times \$5) + T_{CVS} = \$10 + T_{CVS}$, where T_{CVS} is your total cost of transportation to CVS. Similarly, the total cost of a spur-of-the-moment trip to the large Publix supermarket is $(2 \times \$4) + T_{PUB} = \$8 + T_{PUB}$, where T_{PUB} is the cost of transportation to Publix. If you drive, the transportation costs include the cost of the wear and tear on your car and the cost of gasoline, and, regardless of how you get there, the transportation costs include the value of your time spent traveling to and from the store—CVS or Publix—as well as the value of your time spent in the store.

Like most consumers, you prefer to shop where it is cheapest, so you will shop at CVS if $10 + T_{CVS} < \$8 + T_{PUB}$. That inequality, $\$10 + T_{CVS} < \$8 + T_{PUB}$, shows that if it costs more than $2 extra in transportation costs to go to the large Publix supermarket than to the small CVS store (that is, if T_{PUB} exceeds T_{CVS} by more than $2), you and other similar consumers will shop at CVS for spur-of-the-moment trips.

Consumers are far more likely to go to a large, regional Publix store for their weekly shopping trips because they will purchase many more units of provisions. Using the same analysis with 25 units of provisions shows that the transportation costs to travel to the Publix store must be greater than $25 more than the transportation costs to go to the CVS store before you and other consumers shop at CVS for weekly trips. In conclusion, consumers will frequent the small, more expensive CVS stores for their smaller purchases when shopping at CVS is closer and/or quicker than shopping at Publix, but many consumers will find it worthwhile to travel to the larger, less expensive supermarket for their larger purchases.

The managers of the small, local CVS stores gain consumers on spur-of-the-moment trips if the additional transportation costs of visiting the large, regional Publix stores exceed the savings from the lower prices there. Anything that increases transportation costs increases the number of customers shopping at CVS and decreases the number shopping at Publix. For example, consumers with high values of time—that is, high wages—will shop more frequently at CVS than customers with low values of time. So anything that increases the value of time—such as an increase in wages—leads more consumers to shop at the more expensive, smaller (and closer) stores. Additionally, an increase in the price of gasoline or the price of bus rides sends more consumers to smaller, local stores because of the increase in transportation costs. Managers of smaller, local stores might be able to take advantage of these changes by raising prices, knowing that customers will still shop at their stores because the customers value the lower time and transportation costs.

Consider a different transportation scenario, which has a similar result. In some areas, such as Manhattan, a great deal of traveling is done on foot. Because walking is generally slow, consumers who live in these areas are not willing to travel very far to go to a large store with lower prices because of the time cost. As in the other circumstances just described, the demand increases at the small, local stores, so the managers of these stores can raise their prices. Of course, the opposite is true at the larger stores: Demand decreases, indicating that these managers need to lower their prices.

If you have stores in different locales, the value of your customers' time and the costs of transportation probably differ from one region to the next. So you must take this difference into account when determining the profit-maximizing location of your stores and the profit-maximizing prices to charge in each store.

One last lesson: If significant economies of scale exist, so that larger stores have strikingly lower prices than smaller ones and/or transportation costs are a small part of total cost, then for most consumers the total cost of shopping at large, regional stores will be less than the cost of shopping at small, local stores. So consumers will bypass expensive, small, local stores and shop at less expensive, larger, regional stores. Managers of small, local appliance stores learned this lesson the hard way as larger, regional appliance stores such as Home Depot and Lowe's drove them out of business. Unlike CVS, the small, local appliance stores were unable to survive because transportation costs are a small fraction of a consumer's total expenditure on appliances. Consequently customers were willing to drive to a Home Depot or Lowe's to take advantage of its lower prices.

Revisiting How Managers at Freeport-McMoRan Had to Dig Deep to Make a Decision

At the start of this chapter, you read about the challenge that managers at Freeport-McMoRan face when determining their levels of production at different mines. You can now apply the concepts you learned in this chapter to explain how those managers determine the profit-maximizing amounts of copper production at the company's Morenci and Safford Mines.

To maximize Freeport-McMoRan's profit, the managers use marginal analysis and the profit-maximization rule to mine the quantity of copper that sets the marginal revenue equal to the company's combined marginal cost. The managers allocate this production among their mines so that each mine produces the quantity of copper that sets its marginal cost equal to the profit-maximizing marginal revenue.

The hypothetical figure helps illustrate how the managers approach these decisions:

- To maximize profit, the managers produce where their combined marginal cost equals their marginal revenue. For each marginal cost, the combined quantity is the quantity of copper produced at the Safford Mine plus the quantity produced at the Morenci Mine. For example, at the marginal cost of $2,000 per ton, the combined quantity equals 200 tons from the Safford Mine plus 400 tons from the Morenci Mine, or 600 tons, as shown along the combined marginal cost curve (*MC*) in the figure. The figure shows that Freeport-McMoRan maximizes its profit by producing 1,000 tons of copper per day, the quantity at which $MR = MC$.
- Next, the managers use the demand curve to determine that the profit-maximizing price is $4,000 per ton of copper.
- Finally, the managers must allocate the 1,000 tons of copper produced among its mines. The profit-

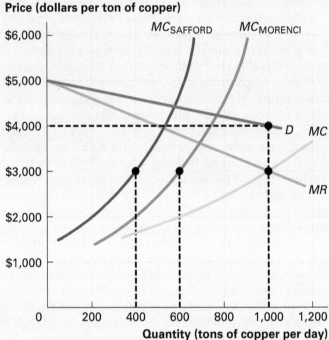

maximizing marginal revenue is $3,000 per ton. At this marginal revenue, the Safford Mine produces 400 tons, and the Morenci Mine produces 600 tons. So the managers divide the 1,000 tons of production accordingly, with the Safford Mine producing 400 tons and the Morenci Mine producing 600 tons.

By setting the company-wide combined marginal cost equal to the marginal revenue and then allocating production so that each mine produces the quantity that sets its marginal cost equal to the profit-maximizing marginal revenue, Freeport-McMoRan's managers maximize profit.

Summary: The Bottom Line

12.1 Joint Production

- Some production processes involve joint production, which can involve products produced in either fixed or variable proportions.
- An increase in the demand for one of the jointly produced products raises that product's price, which

motivates suppliers to produce more of it and, automatically, more of the other product(s) also. When the joint products are produced in variable proportions, managers use marginal analysis to increase the proportion of the higher-priced product and decrease the proportion of the other joint product(s).

12.2 The Multi-Plant Firm

- To maximize profit, a manager of a multi-plant firm must determine the total quantity to produce and allocate the production to the different plants.
- To determine the total quantity to produce, use the profit-maximization rule: Produce the quantity that sets the marginal revenue equal to the firm's combined marginal cost. Once the total quantity is determined, the manager must allocate production to the different plants so that each plant's marginal cost equals the profit-maximizing marginal revenue.

12.3 Location Decisions

- Firms with a few, large plants have lower costs because they can use fewer inputs, use specialized capital, and have fewer managerial diseconomies. Firms with more, smaller plants have lower transportation costs. In determining whether to increase the number of plants, managers must use marginal analysis to compare the increase in costs from having more plants to the decrease in transportation costs.
- The cost of plant operations differs from location to location. The theory of compensating wage differentials and knowledge of other geographic differences in costs can narrow the list of locations to consider for a new plant.

12.4 Decisions About Product Quality

- Changing a product's quality affects demand. The marginal revenue of making a quality improvement is the additional revenue that results from increasing the quality.
- Changing a product's quality also affects cost. The marginal cost of making a quality improvement is the additional cost that results from increasing the quality.

- The profit-maximizing amount of quality sets the marginal revenue from the quality change equal to the marginal cost of the quality change, or $MR = MC$.

12.5 Optimal Inventories

- The economic order quantity (EOQ) model assumes that (1) demand is known and (2) demand occurs evenly throughout the period. In the EOQ model, the cost-minimizing order quantity (Q_{ORDER}) equals $\sqrt{\frac{2 \times C_{FC} \times Q}{C}}$, where C_{FC} is the fixed cost of placing an order, Q is the demand for the product over the year, and C is the annual carrying cost of holding a unit in inventory. The average amount held in inventory is $Q_{ORDER}/2$.
- Increasing the order size decreases the fixed cost of ordering but increases the carrying cost. Marginal analysis can help determine the cost-minimizing order amount.

12.6 Managerial Application: Production, Products, and Location

- If an input your company uses is jointly produced with another product, changes in the demand for the other product affect the price of your input. An increase in the demand for the other product increases the production of your input and lowers its price.
- The value of customers' time is an important part of their transportation costs. Consumers will pay a higher price for a product that has a lower cost in terms of their time. Locating stores so as to reduce customers' transportation costs provides a competitive advantage. If the value of consumers' time varies from one locale to another, so, too, should the distance between stores and the prices within them.

Key Terms and Concepts

Compensating wage differential   Joint production
Economic order quantity (EOQ) model   Multi-plant firm

Questions and Problems

12.1 Joint Production

Learning Objective 12.1 Explain how managers maximize profit when the production of one good results in the simultaneous production of one or more other goods.

1.1 The widespread success of chains such as Buffalo Wild Wings and Wingstop indicates consumer demand for Buffalo wings is substantial and growing. Buffalo wings, of course, have nothing

to do with buffalos—they are fried chicken wings coated in various types of generally hot sauces. How does the increase in demand for Buffalo wings affect the costs of a restaurant like Chick-fil-A, which does not sell them but sells sandwiches made from chicken breasts?

1.2 Bovine spongiform encephalopathy, more commonly known as mad cow disease, causes a fatal degeneration of the brain. It can be transmitted to humans by eating food contaminated with the brain or spinal cord of infected cattle. Suppose that fears of mad cow disease decrease the demand for beef. Analyze the effect of this fear on

a. The price of steers and
b. The price of cowhides.

1.3 When Tyson Foods processes a chicken, the joint products are produced in fixed proportions: There are two wings, two thighs, two breasts, and one neck per chicken. When Chevron Corporation refines a barrel of oil, the joint products are produced in variable proportions. Compare the responses by managers at Tyson and Chevron to an increase in the price of one of the joint products.

1.4 Tesoro Corporation operates six oil refineries. Each produces a variety of products. Among its other products, the refinery in Los Angeles produces more than 50 percent of the jet fuel used at the Los Angeles airport. Suppose that the price of jet fuel falls. Identify and explain the reactions that the managers at Tesoro should have to the reduction in price.

1.5 The figure shows the production possibilities frontier for kerosene and fuel oil. If the profit per gallon of kerosene is $0.50 and the profit per gallon of fuel oil is $0.50, what is the profit-maximizing combination of kerosene and fuel oil? Explain your answer.

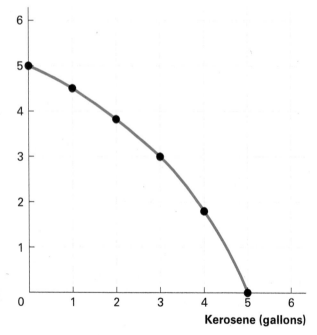

1.6 You are the manager of a firm like Hancock Lumber. When you produce boards, you also produce sawdust. Both can be sold for a profit. You can vary the proportions of boards and sawdust produced. Explain how marginal analysis helps you make the profit-maximizing decision about the production of boards and sawdust.

12.2 The Multi-Plant Firm

Learning Objective 12.2 Explain how managers of multi-plant firms allocate production to maximize profit.

2.1 Southern Copper Corporation is a perfectly competitive copper producer with two mines in southern Peru, the Cuajone and Toquepala Mines. Each mine produces only copper. Although the purity of the ore is the same, say that the managers have noticed that for the last ton of ore mined, the marginal cost at the Cuajone Mine exceeds the marginal cost at the Toquepala Mine. Are Southern Copper's managers maximizing the firm's profit? Explain your answer.

2.2 Because Newmont Mining Company is the world's second-largest gold producer, it has market power in setting the price of gold. Its mines include the Carlin and Twin Creeks Mines, both in Nevada. Although the purity of the ore is the same, say that the managers have noticed that for the last ton of ore mined, the marginal cost at the Carlin Mine exceeds the marginal cost at the Twin Creeks Mine. Are the managers of Newmont Mining Company maximizing the firm's profit? Explain your answer.

2.3 Say that you are a manager at a firm like Keebler Company. The figure shows the marginal cost curves for two of your plants that produce a certain cookie. The marginal costs differ because the workers at plant 1, with marginal cost curve mc_1, are unionized and you must pay them a higher wage than the workers at plant 2, who are not unionized.

a. What are the profit-maximizing quantities of cookies for your firm to produce in plant 1, in plant 2, and in total?
b. Suppose that a labor union organizes the workers in plant 2 and negotiates higher wages for those workers. The increase in the wages in plant 2 increases the marginal cost of producing each quantity of boxes in plant 2 by $1.00 per box. Analyze

Accompanies problem 2.3.

Marginal revenue and marginal cost (dollars per box of cookies)

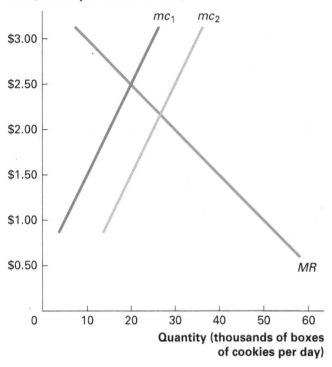

the consequences for your firm using the figure to illustrate the effect on the quantity of boxes produced in plant 1, in plant 2, and in total. Will you raise or lower the price of a box of your cookies? Explain your answer.

c. Suppose that a natural disaster destroys your firm's plant 2. Analyze the consequences for your firm by using the figure to illustrate the effect on the quantity of boxes produced in plant 1. Will you raise or lower the price of your cookies? Explain your answer.

2.4 For a multi-plant firm, profit maximization requires producing the quantity that sets the marginal revenue equal to the overall marginal cost from *all* the plants. Producing so that marginal revenue equals *each* plant's marginal cost does *not* maximize the firm's profit, however. Explain why.

2.5 Suppose that you are a manager for a firm like EBC Brakes, which manufactures brakes for automobiles and motorcycles. Your company has two plants, one in the United States and the other in the United Kingdom. The following tables include the estimated demand and marginal revenue for your brakes, along with the marginal costs at the two factories.

a. What quantity and price maximize your firm's profit?

b. What is the profit-maximizing number of brakes produced in the U.S. plant? In the U.K. plant?

Accompanies problem 2.5.

Quantity Demanded (brakes per hour)	Price (dollars per brake)	Marginal Revenue (dollars per brake)
104	$196	$92
105	195	90
106	194	88
107	193	86
108	192	84
109	191	82
110	190	80
111	189	78
112	188	76
113	187	74
114	186	72

Quantity Produced in the U.K. plant (brakes per hour)	Quantity Produced in the U.S. plant (brakes per hour)	Marginal cost (dollars per brake)
47	42	$66
48	44	68
49	46	70
50	48	72
51	50	74
52	52	76
53	54	78
54	56	80
55	58	82
56	60	84
57	62	86

2.6 Your firm operates three plants in a perfectly competitive industry. The marginal cost functions are as follows:

$$mc_1 = 10 + q_1$$
$$mc_2 = 10 + 0.5q_2$$
$$mc_3 = 10 + 0.1q_3$$

If the competitive price is $50, how much will you produce in each plant?

12.3 Location Decisions

Learning Objective 12.3 Describe the factors that determine the number and location of plants operated by multi-plant firms.

3.1 How can adding a new plant raise costs at *all* of a multi-plant firm's plants?

3.2 Between 2010 and 2012, the managers at Amazon.com more than doubled the number of warehouses to 89. Over that same period, Amazon.com's profit fell, so much so that the company recorded a loss in 2012. Explain how these two events could be related.

3.3 Managers must decide where to locate their plants between the location of their inputs and their customers. How can managers use marginal analysis to make profit-maximizing decisions about the location? In your answer, include discussion of both the marginal cost and the marginal benefit.

3.4 Bridgestone Corporation operates four tire-manufacturing plants in the United States, two in Tennessee and one each in North and South Carolina. Why don't Bridgeport's managers centralize production in a single factory?

3.5 Brunswick manufactures its Life Cycle fitness equipment at six factories in the United States. Say that you are a manager at a company like Brunswick. For simplicity, assume that your firm produces only one style of fitness equipment, an exercise bike, and that you produce it at three plants, all of which have identical costs. The table presents the costs at one of the plants. The second column includes all of the costs except the cost of transporting the bikes to the purchasers, which the table presents in the third column as the shipping costs. Suppose that your firm is a perfect competitor and the market price is $500 per bike after delivery.

a. What quantity of exercise bikes maximizes your firm's profit? At this quantity, what is the profit per plant, and what is your firm's total profit?

Accompanies problem 3.5.

Quantity (bikes per hour)	Total Cost of Production (dollars)	Shipping Cost (dollars)
100	$40,000	$8,000
101	40,380	8,080
102	40,780	8,160
103	41,200	8,240
104	41,640	8,320
105	42,100	8,400
106	42,580	8,480
107	43,080	8,560
108	43,600	8,640
109	44,140	8,720
110	44,700	8,880

b. You are deciding whether to build a fourth plant. A fourth plant has no effect on the shipping costs, and once the new plant is built, all four plants will have identical costs. Adding a fourth plant creates managerial diseconomies that raise the costs of production by $1,000 at each quantity in the table at all four plants. If your firm adds a fourth plant, what quantity of exercise bikes maximizes profit? What is the profit for each of the four plants, and what is the firm's total profit? Should you approve building the plant? Why or why not?

c. Now assume that, as in part b., building the fourth plant creates managerial diseconomies that raise the costs of production by $1,000 at each quantity in the table at all four plants. However, also suppose that the fourth plant cuts the cost of shipping in half at all four plants. What quantity of exercise bikes now maximizes your firm's profit? What is the profit per plant and your firm's total profit? With this revised scenario, should you approve building the fourth plant? Why or why not?

3.6 Reducing workers' job-related risks is costly. Even in the absence of government regulations, profit-maximizing managers frequently make expenditures to decrease these risks. How can incurring these costs increase the firm's profit?

3.7 Dollar stores like Dollar General do not pay customers' transportation costs. Nonetheless, such stores have the incentive to minimize customers' transportation costs. Why?

12.4 Decisions About Product Quality

Learning Objective 12.4 Use marginal analysis to determine the profit-maximizing amount of product quality.

4.1 In 2012, United Airlines expanded the size of the overhead bins for carry-on luggage to gain a competitive advantage over its rivals. This change increased the quality of the trip experience for fliers. Explain the factors the managers of United Airlines considered in making this decision.

4.2 Years ago, Ford Motor Company advertised the slogan "Quality Is Job 1," suggesting that the only thing its workers and managers cared about was the quality of Ford products. Explain why making quality job 1 would *not* maximize Ford's profit.

4.3 The managers of the Glenmorangie Distillery in Scotland advertise their single malt whiskey as "unnecessarily well made."
   a. What do you think this advertising slogan means?
   b. If the slogan is literally true, have the managers maximized Glenmorangie's profit? Why or why not?

4.4 Pasta makers make high-quality dry pasta from 100 percent durum wheat. Suppose that there is a crop failure and the price of durum wheat soars. As a manager at a firm like the American Italian Pasta Company, you could use a blend of durum and other, lower-quality wheat. What factors will you examine when you make your decision about adjusting product quality?

4.5 Electronic Arts (EA) is one of the world's largest producers of computer games. In 2013, EA released a new version of the very popular game SimCity, but the release was a fiasco. To prevent pirating of the game, the managers at EA made the decision to allow gamers to play only online; that is, the player had to connect to EA's servers. When EA first released the game, many players could not log in. Others, who managed to log in, could not play the game because EA's servers crashed. Ultimately the CEO of EA resigned.
   a. Define *quality* in the context of computer games.
   b. Do you think that the executives of EA made the profit-maximizing decision about quality for their game? Explain your answer.

12.5 Optimal Inventories

Learning Objective 12.5 Use the economic order quantity (EOQ) model to determine the optimal order quantity of a good stored in inventory.

5.1 One of the opportunity costs of carrying inventory is the interest rate a business must pay on the funds used to buy the products held in inventory. Suppose that the interest rate rises. Does the profit-maximizing amount of products held in inventory change? Why or why not?

5.2 Suppose the quantity of smartphones sold in a year (Q) is 800, the annual carrying cost of holding a smartphone in inventory (C) is $40 per smartphone, the variable cost of an order (C_{VAR}) is $200 per smartphone, and the fixed cost of an order (C_{FC}) is $10 per order.
   a. Use the EOQ model to determine the cost-minimizing quantity to order and the number of orders. What is the total cost when this quantity is ordered?
   b. Suppose that with each order the manager orders 80 smartphones. What are the number of orders and the total cost when this quantity is ordered?
   c. Suppose that with each order the manager orders 10 smartphones. Now what are the number of orders and the total cost?
   d. How do the total costs when 80 and 10 smartphones are ordered compare to the total cost when ordering the quantity using the EOQ model?

5.3 You are the manager in charge of stock at an office supply company in Redwood City. Suppose that each order you place for copy paper costs $10, each box costs $2, you know that you will sell 3,600 boxes per year, and each box you hold in inventory costs $20 per year. What is the economic order quantity? How many orders will you place in a year? What will be the average number of boxes you hold in inventory?

5.4 What effect does an increase in the fixed cost of placing an order have on the quantity ordered? Explain your answer using the EOQ model and marginal analysis.

5.5 How does an increase in the carrying cost of holding units in inventory affect the quantity ordered? Explain your answer using the EOQ model and marginal analysis.

5.6 How can a manager use marginal analysis to determine the profit-maximizing order quantity and the profit-maximizing quantity to carry in inventory? Carefully describe the marginal cost and marginal benefit from changing the quantity ordered.

12.6 Managerial Application: Production, Products, and Location

Learning Objective 12.6 Apply what you have learned about joint production, products, and location to make better managerial decisions.

6.1 You are a manager of a company like Torino Leather Company, a producer of cow-leather goods. Suppose that fear of bovine spongiform encephalopathy (mad cow disease) decreases the demand for beef. How does this change in demand affect the price of cowhides you must buy to make leather? Explain your answer.

6.2 Suppose that you are a manager at a firm like Walgreens Boots Alliance, a large drugstore chain with stores in Europe and the United States. Gasoline is twice as expensive in Europe as in the United States. Other things being equal, will you locate a larger number of small, local pharmacies in Europe or in the United States? Explain your answer.

MyLab Economics Auto-Graded Excel Projects

12.1 Beef Products Inc. (BPI) is a beef processing firm with production facilities in a few locations around the United States. These production facilities produce a type of ground beef additive known as lean, finely-textured beef (LFTB). BPI has production facilities in South Sioux City, NE and Holcomb, KS. The plant in Nebraska is larger and can take advantage of economies of scale; however, the plant in Kansas is in an area with a lower cost of living and can pay lower wages. This makes the costs of production of LFTB different between the two plants.

Suppose a firm like BPI is deciding how much LFTB to produce on each line at each of two plants monthly. The larger plant has fixed costs of $20,000 while the smaller plant's fixed costs are $10,000. The larger plant is in an area with higher costs of living and must pay each of its line employees $3,000 per month while the smaller plant is in an area with a lower cost of living and pays its line employees $2,500 per month. The cost of materials used as inputs are the same for both plants, $0.50 per pound.

Use the above information to complete the following tasks and answer the following questions.

a. Using the template provided, fill in the information given for fixed costs.

b. Using the information given, find the cost of materials inputs and total cost at each level of production. Keep in mind, production is in thousands of units.

c. Using the production information given and the total costs you found in part b, find the marginal cost of each pound of LFTB.

	A	B	C	D	E	F
1			Costs in Larger Plant with Higher Cost of Living			
2	Quantity of Beef (000's of lbs.)	Fixed Costs	Production Employees Needed	Cost of Materials Inputs	Total Cost	Marginal Cost
3	0		0			
4	10		2			
5	20		3			
6	30		4			
7	40		6			
8	50		9			
9	60		13			
10						
11						
12			Costs in Smaller Plant with Lower Cost of Living			
13	Quantity of Beef (000's of lbs.)	Fixed Costs	Production Employees Needed	Cost of Materials Inputs	Total Cost	Marginal Cost
14	0		0			
15	5		1			
16	10		2			
17	15		4			
18	20		6			
19	25		9			
20	30		12			

d. If ground beef producers are willing to pay $1.50 per pound of LFTB, how much will each plant produce and how much will be produced in total?

e. Suppose demand for LFTB fell, bringing the price to $1 per pound. How much would each plant produce and how much would be produced in total? What kind of market changes might cause demand to fall?

12.2 The Silver Lining Creamery is a small boutique ice cream parlor in Rapid City, SD. They produce all of their ice cream on site and, in addition to having traditional flavors like chocolate and vanilla, they create unique flavors like honey lavender and peanut butter-Oreo.

In this chapter, you learned about calculating the Economic Order Quantity (EOQ). This model is also applicable when determining how much to produce at one time or what is called the Economic Production Quantity (EPQ). In the EOQ, the order amount Q is replaced by the production amount Q and the fixed cost of placing an order is replaced by the fixed cost of a production run or batch.

Suppose you run an ice cream parlor that produces its own ice cream similar to Silver Linings. You are trying to determine how many gallons of chocolate ice cream you should make in one production batch during the summer months. Each month, your demand will be 100 gallons of chocolate ice cream. You can make up to 100 gallons of ice cream in a production batch; however, once production is stopped, the machine must

be cleaned and a few parts and inputs changed out for the next production batch. It takes one worker an hour to clean the machine and the cost of replacement parts and inputs for each batch is $5. You pay your workers $12 per hour.

You could produce 1 batch of 100 gallons each month; however, there are also some costs associated with storing larger quantities of ice cream. Each additional gallon of ice cream in inventory costs $0.50 in refrigeration costs. Your firm also has a high quality reputation due to not serving ice cream that is too far past its production date. Approximately 20 percent of ice cream in the freezer must be thrown out or given away to maintain this quality standard. Each gallon of ice cream costs $10 to produce.

Use this information and the template provided to determine the EPQ.

a. Use the given information to put the per gallon carrying costs, per batch production costs, and monthly demand in the template.

b. Start by assuming 1 batch per month (as discussed above) and use a formula to calculate the number of Q (gallons) per batch. Use this number and the formulas provided in Chapter 12 to calculate monthly carrying costs of refrigeration and spoilage in the template. Use the number of batches per month to calculate monthly costs of labor and supplies. Be sure to use cell references in your formulas. Find the total carrying and fixed production costs.

c. Is 100 gallons per production batch the EPQ for this situation? If no, should the EPQ be higher or lower?

d. Increase the number of batches to 5. How many gallons are produced in each batch? Did total costs increase or decrease by increasing the number of batches?

e. Use Solver to minimize total costs by changing the number of batches per month; be sure to add the constraint that the number of batches must be an integer. What is the EPQ? How many batches per month are needed to attain this EPQ? What are the total costs for this EPQ?

f. Suppose demand for chocolate ice cream decreases to 60 gallons per month because you introduce a number of other new flavors. Change demand and repeat part e.

	A	B	C
1	Carrying Costs		
2	Cost Type	Per Gallon	Per Production Q
3	Refrigeration Costs		
4	Spoilage Costs		
5	Total Carrying Costs		
6			
7	Fixed Costs of a Production Batch		
8	Cost Type	Per Batch	Per Number of Batches
9	Post Batch Labor		
10	Post Batch Supplies		
11	Total Proudction Costs		
12			
13	Total Carrying and Fixed Prodution Costs		
14			
15	Monthly Demand		
16	Number of Batches Per Month		
17	Production Q (Gallons) Per Batch		

The Calculus of Multi-Plant Profit-Maximization and Inventory Decisions

Chapter 12 emphasizes the role played by marginal analysis in making a variety of production decisions. Calculus can make the marginal analysis more precise. This appendix will show you how to use calculus to determine profit-maximizing production at a multi-plant firm and to derive the cost-minimizing order quantity in the economic order quantity inventory model.

A. Production Decisions at a Multi-Plant Firm

It is common for managers at medium to large firms to face the problem of making production decisions when their firm has more than one plant. These managers need to make two closely linked production decisions: the total quantity their firm should produce and the allocation of production among the plants. You will see how using calculus can help you make these decisions simultaneously.

Consider the case of a firm that has two plants, each producing the same product but with different costs. Once you understand this analysis, extending it to deal with more than two plants is straightforward. So suppose that a firm has two plants with different costs that depend on the quantity produced at the plant:

$$tc_1 = tc_1(q_1)$$

and

$$tc_2 = tc_2(q_2)$$

where tc is the total cost at a plant, q is the quantity produced at a plant, and the subscripts 1 and 2 refer to plants 1 and 2, respectively. The firm's total revenue depends on the total quantity sold. Let Q be the total quantity, so that $Q = q_1 + q_2$. Then the total revenue function (TR) is

$$TR = TR(Q)$$

Profit equals the total revenue minus the total costs from both plants, so the profit function is

$$\text{Profit}(q_1, q_2) = TR(Q) - tc_1(q_1) - tc_2(q_2)$$

To maximize profit, take the partial derivatives of the profit with respect to q_1 and q_2, and set them equal to zero. (Use the chain rule to take the derivative of $TR(Q)$ with respect to q_1 and q_2.) This gives the two first-order conditions:

$$\frac{\partial TR(Q)}{\partial Q} \times \frac{\partial Q}{\partial q_1} - \frac{\partial tc_1(q_1)}{\partial q_1} = 0 \qquad \textbf{A12.1}$$

$$\frac{\partial TR(Q)}{\partial Q} \times \frac{\partial Q}{\partial q_2} - \frac{\partial tc_2(q_1)}{\partial q_2} = 0 \qquad \textbf{A12.2}$$

To write the first-order conditions as clearly as possible, note that the equality $Q = q_1 + q_2$, means that $\partial Q/\partial q_1 = 1$ and $\partial Q/\partial q_2 = 1$. Using these results, the two first-order equations (Equations A12.1 and A12.2) can be rewritten as

$$\frac{\partial TR(Q)}{\partial Q} = \frac{\partial tc_1(q_1)}{\partial q_1} \qquad \textbf{A12.3}$$

$$\frac{\partial TR(Q)}{\partial Q} = \frac{\partial tc_2(q_2)}{\partial q_2} \qquad \textbf{A12.4}$$

The first-order conditions in Equations A12.3 and A12.4 can be solved simultaneously for the profit-maximizing quantities, q_1 and q_2. Solving for the profit-maximizing quantity produced at each of the two plants also determines the profit-maximizing total quantity to produce because the total production is equal to $q_1 + q_2$.

Marginal Analysis of Multi-Plant Firms

The first-order conditions in Equations A12.3 and A12.4 have a very intuitive interpretation. The term on the left side of each equation, $\frac{\partial TR(Q)}{\partial Q}$, is equal to the marginal revenue, or MR. The term on the right side of Equation A12.3 is the marginal cost at plant 1, which you can write as mc_1. Similarly, the term on the right side of Equation A12.4 is mc_2. So the two first-order conditions are equivalent to

$$MR = mc_1 \qquad\qquad\qquad \textbf{A12.5}$$

$$MR = mc_2 \qquad\qquad\qquad \textbf{A12.6}$$

In the chapter, the two marginal costs were added to derive the firm's overall marginal cost curve. That step was necessary to ensure that the marginal cost at each plant equaled the profit-maximizing marginal revenue (which, in turn, equaled the overall marginal cost). The first-order conditions in Equations A12.5 and A12.6 reveal why that step is not necessary when using calculus: Maximizing profit by taking the partial derivatives of the profit function with respect to the quantities produced in the different plants automatically sets the two plants' marginal costs equal to the profit-maximizing marginal revenue. In other words, because the marginal costs at the different plants are equal to the marginal revenue, the marginal costs *must* also be equal to each other. This condition is necessary to maximize profit. If the marginal cost at one plant was higher than that at another, the managers could shift production away from the high-cost plant to the low-cost plant and keep their total production and total revenue the same while lowering their costs. Consequently, managers of multi-plant firms maximize their firm's profit by ensuring that the marginal costs at *all* plants are equal to each other and are also equal to the profit-maximizing marginal revenue.

B. Economic Order Quantity Inventory Model

The chapter described the economic order quantity (EOQ) model but did not formally derive the cost-minimizing order quantity because the derivation requires calculus. So in this appendix we will use calculus to demonstrate how to derive the optimal order quantity.

The EOQ model focuses on two inventory-related costs:

1. **The carrying cost of holding an inventory.** C is the annual holding cost per unit. This cost includes factors such as interest on the funds used to finance the inventory, storage charges, and insurance costs. If the quantity ordered is Q_{ORDER}, then, just as described in the chapter, the average quantity in inventory is equal to $\frac{Q_{ORDER}}{2}$. So the carrying cost for the inventory equals

$$\text{Carrying cost} = C \times \frac{Q_{ORDER}}{2} = \frac{C \times Q_{ORDER}}{2} \qquad\qquad \textbf{A12.7}$$

2. **The ordering cost of the good held in inventory.** There are two types of ordering costs: the fixed cost of placing an order (C_{FC}) and the variable cost of placing the order (C_{VAR}). The fixed cost is the same no matter the size of the order. It includes the cost of submitting the order (which can include the cost of searching for the product and/or seller), any fixed delivery charge for the product, and the cost of processing the involved paperwork. The variable cost includes the per-unit price of the product and any delivery charge that changes when the quantity ordered changes. So the cost of an order is

$$C_{FC} + (C_{VAR} \times Q_{ORDER}) \qquad\qquad\qquad \textbf{A12.8}$$

Equation A12.8 shows the cost of *one* order. The ordering cost for *all* the orders in a year is the cost of one order multiplied by the number of orders. As in the chapter, the number of orders is equal to the total quantity sold during the year (Q) divided by the amount ordered each time, Q_{ORDER}, or $\frac{Q}{Q_{ORDER}}$. So the annual ordering cost of the inventory equals

$$\text{Ordering cost} = [C_{FC} + (C_{VAR} \times Q_{ORDER})] \times \frac{Q}{Q_{ORDER}} \qquad \textbf{A12.9}$$

Total Cost of Inventory

The total cost equals the carrying cost plus the ordering cost. The carrying cost is given by Equation A12.7 and the ordering cost by A12.9, so the total cost is

$$\text{Total cost} = \frac{C \times Q_{ORDER}}{2} + [C_{FC} + (C_{VAR} \times Q_{ORDER})] \times \frac{Q}{Q_{ORDER}} \qquad \textbf{A12.10}$$

Managers must select the order quantity, Q_{ORDER}, that minimizes the total cost of the inventory given in Equation A12.10. To minimize the total cost, it is necessary to take the derivative of Equation A12.10 with respect to Q_{ORDER}, set it equal to zero, and then solve for the cost-minimizing Q_{ORDER}. Before doing so, however, separating Equation A12.10 into three terms makes taking the derivative easier:

$$\text{Total cost} = \frac{C \times Q_{ORDER}}{2} + \frac{C_{FC} \times Q}{Q_{ORDER}} + (C_{VAR} \times Q) \qquad \textbf{A12.11}$$

Now take the derivative of Equation A12.11, using the quotient rule to take the derivative of the second term, and set the derivative equal to zero to obtain the first-order condition:

$$\frac{C}{2} - \frac{C_{FC} \times Q}{Q_{ORDER}^2} = 0$$

Add $\frac{C_{FC} \times Q}{Q_{ORDER}^2}$ to both sides of the equation:

$$\frac{C}{2} = \frac{C_{FC} \times Q}{Q_{ORDER}^2} \qquad \textbf{A12.12}$$

Then multiply both sides by Q_{ORDER}^2 to get

$$\frac{C}{2} \times Q_{ORDER}^2 = C_{FC} \times Q$$

Next, multiply both sides by $\frac{2}{C}$:

$$Q_{ORDER}^2 = \frac{2 \times C_{FC} \times Q}{C}$$

Finally, take the square root to solve for the cost-minimizing order quantity, Q_{ORDER}:

$$Q_{ORDER} = \sqrt{\frac{2 \times C_{FC} \times Q}{C}} \qquad \textbf{A12.13}$$

Of course, the cost-minimizing order quantity in Equation A12.13 is the same result given by Equation A12.4 in the chapter.

Marginal Analysis of Inventory Decisions

Using calculus helps clarify the marginal analysis involved in balancing the marginal cost of increasing the order size against the marginal benefit from increasing the order size.

- **Marginal cost of increasing order size.** Because sales occur at a constant rate, increasing the order size means more units of the product are held in inventory, so increasing the order size increases the carrying cost. Consequently, the marginal cost of increasing the order size, Q_{ORDER}, is the marginal increase in the carrying cost. Equation A12.7 shows the carrying cost, so taking the derivative of Equation A12.7 with respect to Q_{ORDER} gives the marginal increase in carrying cost as $\frac{C}{2}$. This marginal cost is on the left side of Equation A12.12.
- **Marginal benefit from increasing order size.** Because the total sales are fixed at Q, increasing the order size means that fewer orders are necessary, so increasing the order size decreases the ordering cost. Consequently, the marginal benefit from increasing the order size is the marginal decrease in the ordering cost. Equation A12.9 shows the ordering cost, so using the quotient rule to take the derivative of Equation A12.9 with respect to Q_{ORDER} gives the marginal decrease in ordering cost as $(C_{FC} \times Q)/Q_{ORDER}^2$. This marginal benefit is on the right side of Equation A12.12.

You can see that you get the usual marginal analysis result: The profit-maximizing condition (which in this case is the cost-minimizing condition) requires that the marginal cost, $\frac{C}{2}$, equal the marginal benefit, $(C_{FC} \times Q)/Q_{ORDER}^2$, which is what Equation A12.12 shows. Although Equation A12.12 applies precisely *only* to the EOQ inventory model, its general lesson holds for any inventory management problem: To minimize the cost of inventory, managers must set the marginal cost of increasing the order size equal to the marginal benefit from that increase. This equality maximizes profit (by minimizing cost) for any inventory.

Calculus Questions and Problems

A12.1 Peach Industries just released a sleek, high-powered laptop. The managers are marketing the new laptop as a business computer. Peach knows that the demand function for its laptops is

$$Q = 600 - 0.25P$$

where Q is the number of Peach laptops purchased each day and P is the price charged by Peach Industries for a laptop. Solving the demand function to express P as a function of Q gives the inverse demand function:

$$P = 2,400 - 4Q$$

The cost of producing a Peach laptop in a particular factory is

$$TC(q_i) = 4q_i^2$$

where q_i is the number of Peach laptops produced each day at factory i.
a. Suppose that Peach Industries has one factory, so that $Q = q_1$. What is the profit-maximizing quantity of laptops that Peach Industries produces and sells per day? What is the price of a laptop?
b. If Peach Industries has one factory, so that $Q = q_1$, what is Peach Industries' daily economic profit (or loss)?

c. Suppose that Peach Industries has two factories, so that $Q = q_1 + q_2$. Now what is the profit-maximizing quantity of laptops that Peach Industries produces and sells per day? What is the price of a laptop?
d. Suppose that Peach Industries has two factories, so that $Q = q_1 + q_2$. How much economic profit (or loss) does Peach Industries earn each day?

A12.2 Penny Shaving Club is an online retailer of men's razors. It purchases wholesale razors and resells them to final consumers through its website. Penny Shaving Club sells 500,000 packs of razors per year, spread evenly throughout the year. Its managers must maintain some inventory to keep their business running. The annual cost of holding a pack of razors in inventory is $6.

Penny Shaving Club can make regular orders from its wholesale provider, but it must pay a $1.50 fixed ordering fee with each order and a price of $3 per pack of razors ordered.
a. What is the marginal benefit from increasing the order size for Penny Shaving Club?
b. What is the marginal cost of increasing the order size for Penny Shaving Club?
c. What is the profit-maximizing order size?

A12.3 Jackson's Tiny Homes produces small, eco-friendly mobile homes at two factories in the Pacific Northwest. Jackson knows that the demand function for its tiny homes is

$$Q = 1,350 - 0.025P$$

where Q is the total number of tiny homes that Jackson sells and P is the price of one of its tiny eco-friendly homes. Solving this demand function for the price as a function of the quantity demanded gives the inverse demand function:

$$P = 54,000 - 40Q$$

Jackson's Tiny Homes' total cost of producing these homes is

$$TC(Q) = \$1,900,000 + 100q_1^2 + 100q_2^2$$

where q_i is the number of homes produced at factory i.
a. What is the profit-maximizing quantity of tiny homes that Jackson's Tiny Homes produces at each factory? What is the total quantity of tiny homes that Jackson produces?
b. What is the profit-maximizing price that Jackson's Tiny Homes charges for each of its tiny homes?
c. How much profit does Jackson's Tiny Homes make when it maximizes its profit?

A12.4 Jessica makes artisanal limoncello (a lemon liqueur) to sell to premium grocery stores. She produces this spirit using lemons produced in her own grove in central Florida. Jessica knows that the demand function for her limoncello is

$$Q = 36 - 0.04P$$

where Q is the number of cases she sells each day and P is the price of a case. Solving the demand function for the price as a function of the quantity gives the inverse demand function for her limoncello:

$$P = 900 - 25Q$$

The cost of producing a case of limoncello is

$$TC(q_i) = 50q_i^2$$

where q_i is the number of cases produced each day at plant i.
a. Suppose that Jessica has one production plant, so that $Q = q_1$. What is the profit-maximizing quantity of cases of limoncello that Jessica produces and sells per day? What is the price of a case of limoncello?
b. Suppose that Jessica has one production plant, so that $Q = q_1$. What is Jessica's economic profit (or loss) per day?
c. Suppose that Jessica has two production plants, so that $Q = q_1 + q_2$. What is the profit-maximizing quantity of cases of limoncello that Jessica produces at each plant and the total quantity that she sells per day? What is the price of a case of limoncello?
d. Suppose that Jessica has two production plants, so that $Q = q_1 + q_2$. What is Jessica's economic profit (or loss) per day?

A12.5 The Scarf Stop is an online retailer of premium wool scarves. The company purchases premium scarves directly from an Italian producer, holds these scarves in inventory, and then ships them to its final customers when they place an order. The Scarf Shop sells 800 scarves per month, and it must maintain inventories in order to fill orders for its scarves. The cost of holding a scarf in inventory for a month is $1.

The Scarf Shop can make regular orders from its wholesale provider, but it must pay a fixed fee of $100 per order and a per-scarf cost of $2.50.
a. What is the marginal benefit from increasing the order size for the Scarf Shop?
b. What is the marginal cost of increasing the order size for the Scarf Shop?
c. What is the profit-maximizing order size?

CHAPTER 13

Marketing Decisions: Advertising and Promotion

Learning Objectives

After studying this chapter, you will be able to:

13.1 Apply marginal analysis to determine the profit-maximizing amount of advertising.

13.2 Describe how trade association managers can determine the optimal amount of industry-wide advertising and allocate its cost.

13.3 Analyze why managers of some firms engage in false advertising despite possible sanctions by the Federal Trade Commission.

13.4 Explain the legal status of resale price maintenance and its use in product promotion.

13.5 Discuss different methods of entering foreign markets and ways to avoid violating anticorruption laws when doing business abroad.

13.6 Use the theories behind advertising and promotion to make better managerial decisions.

Heads Up for Advertising Decisions at Riddell

Football players who have repeated concussions from helmet-to-helmet collisions can experience dementia, depression, and other devastating injuries. During a typical 17-week season, approximately seven National Football League (NFL) players suffer a concussion each week. The sad and sometimes tragic stories of many former NFL players have heightened awareness of the damages from concussions.

Riddell, a division of BRG Sports, designs protective sports equipment, including football helmets. From 1989 to 2013, Riddell had a licensing agreement with the NFL. Players could—and did—use helmets produced by other companies; but only Riddell helmets were allowed to have the firm's name on the nose bumper (the front of the helmet that protects the player's forehead). Because the market for

helmets includes four companies vying for market share and profits, Riddell advertises its helmets extensively using a variety of media, including the Internet, television, radio, and sports magazines. For years, Riddell ran ads stating that its helmets decreased concussion risk by 31 percent. In 2011, then-U.S. Senator Tom Udall of New Mexico requested that the Federal Trade Commission (FTC) examine the validity of this claim.

How can Riddell's managers determine the profit-maximizing amount to spend on advertising and marketing? What if the company uses more than one method? And if FTC investigators determine that the company's advertising claim is false, what sanctions could Riddell face? This chapter will help you answer these types of questions, and at the end, you will learn how Riddell handled these challenges.

Sources: "Senator Wants FTC Investigation of Helmet Makers," *Sporting News,* January 4, 2011; Mary K. Engle, Associate Director, Federal Trade Commission, Letter Regarding Riddell Sports Group, Inc., FTC File No. 112-3065, April 24, 2013; Lisa Brown, "Rawlings Chases Growth in Football Equipment," *St. Louis Post-Dispatch,* October 27, 2013.

Introduction

Some companies spend substantial amounts of money on advertising and promotion. Executives at The Coca-Cola Company authorize annual spending of more than $4 billion on marketing. They obviously want to get the biggest bang for their 4 billion bucks! This chapter identifies the strategies that managers at both large and small companies can use to maximize their profit from advertising and promotion. It cannot, however, explain how to create successful advertising campaigns, such as the widely recognized polar bear ads that Coca-Cola uses during the holiday season, or how to avoid marketing fiascos, such as New Coke, a spectacularly unsuccessful attempt in 1985 to change the formulation of Coca-Cola's namesake drink that lasted only 77 days before the old recipe was put back on the market. Those are topics best left to marketing courses. But this chapter can help you determine how much to spend on promotional activity and how to allocate a marketing budget among different media. Your company can have the world's best advertising campaign, but if it spends too much or too little or allocates its budget unwisely, you are leaving money on the table.

To help you determine the optimal amount and best allocation of your advertising and marketing dollars as well as the roles played in marketing by resale price maintenance and anticorruption laws, Chapter 13 includes six sections:

- **Section 13.1** discusses advertising by individual firms and how marginal analysis can help you determine the optimal amount of advertising.
- **Section 13.2** covers advertising by trade associations and focuses on two major issues: the optimal amount of advertising and the allocation of advertising costs among the member firms.
- **Section 13.3** examines the types of goods that are susceptible to false or deceptive advertising and the Federal Trade Commission guidelines for and responses to such advertising.
- **Section 13.4** analyzes how manufacturers use resale price maintenance to boost their profits and explains its legal status in the United States and the European Union.
- **Section 13.5** explores different methods of entering foreign markets and how an understanding of laws such as the U.S. Foreign Corrupt Practices Act and the U.K. Bribery Act can protect your company and your career when you market products in foreign countries.
- **Section 13.6** describes how you can use what you have learned about advertising and promotion to make better managerial decisions.

13.1 Profit-Maximizing Advertising by a Firm

Learning Objective 13.1 Apply marginal analysis to determine the profit-maximizing amount of advertising.

You see advertising and other forms of promotion almost everywhere you look. Although advertising on billboards along the interstate differs substantially from sponsoring a local charity walkathon, for the sake of simplicity we refer to all types of promotional activity as *advertising*. Companies advertise for many apparent motives, such as informing new or existing customers of new or existing products or creating an aura of involvement with solving social problems. At its most basic level, however, all advertising by profit-maximizing firms has a single purpose: to increase demand for the firm's product, allowing it to increase its profit. Of course, managers at nonprofit organizations have a different goal: to spend their advertising budget in a way that maximizes the impact on their mission, possibly through increasing donations or increased public awareness of their issue.

Advertising makes sense only for firms with enough market power to raise the demand for their product and consequently raise the price they charge. Oligopolistic or monopolistically competitive firms, for example, often heavily advertise their products. Perfectly competitive firms, such as the Lussier Dairy in Alachua County,

Florida, do *not* advertise because these firms produce homogeneous (identical) products (see Section 5.1). The managers of Lussier Dairy know that distributors will never believe that their dairy's milk is superior to the milk produced by the thousands of other dairy farmers. Advertising cannot affect the demand for Lussier Dairy's milk, so advertising cannot increase Lussier's profit. Competitive *industries*, however, may advertise. This topic is discussed in Section 13.2.

Advertising and Profit Maximization

Advertising is an example of the age-old business adage that "You have to spend money to make money." For many managers, the question is not whether to spend the money but what is the profit-maximizing amount of advertising to buy. Advertising affects *both* the firm's demand and its cost. On the demand side, advertising increases demand, shifting the demand curve and the marginal revenue curve to the right. On the cost side, advertising expenditures are a fixed cost—a change in the quantity produced does not change the firm's advertising expenditure. As you learned in Chapter 4, fixed costs do not affect marginal cost, so changes in advertising do not affect the firm's marginal cost curve.

Determining the optimal amount of advertising to buy involves the use of marginal analysis. As you first learned in Chapter 1 and have seen in many other chapters, marginal analysis compares the marginal benefit from an action (which in this case is a change in advertising) to its marginal cost.

Marginal Benefit and Marginal Cost of Advertising

Suppose that you are a manager at a brewery like The Boston Beer Company (Boston Beer), with its flagship brand, Samuel Adams, commonly known as Sam Adams. You need to decide how much to spend on advertising. Your goal is to spend the amount that maximizes your firm's profit. It's useful to divide the profit into two parts, depending on whether or not you include the cost of advertising:

1. **Gross profit.** Gross profit equals a firm's profit *before* paying the cost of advertising
2. **Net profit.** Net profit equals gross profit minus the cost of advertising.

Dividing the profit this way enables you to isolate the cost of advertising. Based on this division, your goal is to buy the quantity of advertising that maximizes your *net* profit.

Figure 13.1 illustrates the situation at your firm before you advertise. Yours is a monopolistically competitive firm so, as you learned in Section 6.4, its demand curve is downward sloping and its marginal revenue curve lies below the demand curve. Before you run an advertising campaign, with zero advertising the demand curve is D_0, and the marginal revenue curve is MR_0. In order to separate the cost of advertising from the other costs, the average cost curve includes all the costs of brewing and distributing the beer *except* the cost of advertising, which is why it is labeled with the GROSS subscript. For simplicity, assume that this long-run average cost and the marginal cost are constant and equal to $164 per barrel, as shown by the curve labeled $MC = LAC_{GROSS}$. Of course, because your company is doing no advertising, the cost of advertising is zero. The profit-maximizing quantity of beer is 2.5 million barrels per year, and the profit-maximizing price is $174 per barrel. Because there is no advertising and therefore no cost of advertising, your firm's gross profit equals its net profit. Consequently, the gross and net economic profits are both equal to $(P - LAC_{GROSS}) \times Q$. The profit equals the area of the light green rectangle in the figure, which is $25 million.

Figure 13.1 Profit with No Advertising

Before your firm advertises, its demand curve is D_0 with the marginal revenue curve MR_0. The profit-maximizing price of a barrel of beer is $174 per barrel and the profit-maximizing quantity is 2.5 million barrels. Because there is no advertising, your gross profit equals your net profit. Both equal $(P - LAC_{GROSS}) \times Q$, which is the area of the light green rectangle, $25 million.

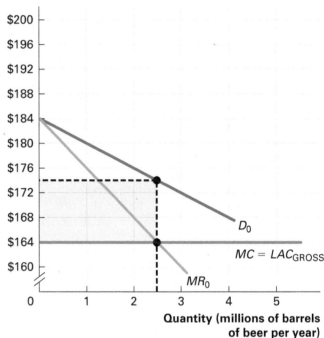

Price and cost (dollars per barrel of beer)

An advertising campaign is defined as one "unit" of advertising. Suppose that you purchase one unit of advertising. As shown in Figure 13.2, because the expenditure on advertising is a fixed cost, the marginal cost is unaffected. Since the LAC_{GROSS} curve does *not* include the cost of advertising, it also does not change. So the $MC = LAC_{GROSS}$ curve does not change. The unit of advertising, however, increases demand. As Figure 13.2 shows, this advertising shifts the demand and marginal revenue curves to the right, to D_1 and MR_1. Accordingly, following the advertising campaign, you maximize profit by producing and selling 3.5 million barrels of beer at a price of $178 per barrel. Your firm's gross profit—that is, its profit *before* paying the cost of its advertising—increases by an amount equal to the darker green area in the figure, $24 million. The gross profit increases for two reasons: First, the firm receives a higher price for the original 2.5 million barrels produced, and, second, it produces an additional 1 million barrels. The **marginal benefit from advertising** is the change in gross profit, the profit before paying the cost of advertising, from changing the amount of advertising.[1] In this case, the marginal benefit from advertising is $24 million.

As you increase your advertising, the additional units of advertising (the additional advertising campaigns) have smaller and smaller effects on demand, so the marginal benefit from the advertising decreases. The downward-sloping marginal benefit curve (MB_A) shown in Figure 13.3 reflects the decreasing marginal benefit from advertising. As Figure 13.3 shows, the marginal benefit is $24 million from the first unit of advertising, just as determined before in Figure 13.2, but the marginal benefit decreases to $16 million from the second unit, to $12 million from the third unit, and to only $10 million from the fourth unit.

Marginal benefit from advertising The change in gross profit, the profit before paying the cost of advertising, from changing the amount of advertising.

---

1 For a nonprofit seeking to raise donations, the marginal benefit from advertising is the change in gross donations, the donations before paying the cost of advertising.

Price and cost (dollars per barrel of beer)

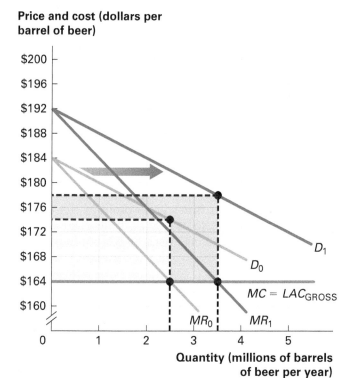

Figure 13.2 Marginal Benefit from Advertising

Advertising shifts the demand curve from D_0 to D_1 and the marginal revenue curve from MR_0 to MR_1. The profit-maximizing price rises from \$174 to \$178 per barrel, and the profit-maximizing quantity rises from 2.5 to 3.5 million barrels. Your gross profit increases by \$24 million, \$10 million of which is from the price increase of \$4 per barrel for the original 2.5 million barrels produced and \$14 million of which is from the additional 1 million barrels produced.

Marginal benefit and marginal cost (millions of dollars per unit of advertising)

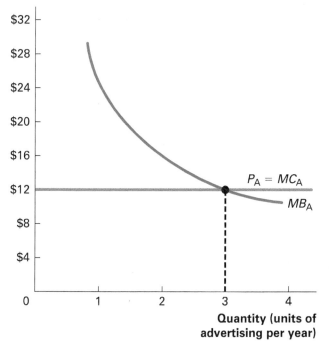

Figure 13.3 Profit-Maximizing Quantity of Advertising

The marginal benefit from advertising (MB_A) decreases as the company purchases more advertising, so the MB_A curve is downward sloping. The marginal cost of a unit of advertising (MC_A) is equal to its price (P_A), \$12 million per unit. The profit-maximizing quantity of advertising is three units, the quantity for which the marginal benefit equals the marginal cost.

Because your firm is a small buyer in the market for advertising, the price it pays for a unit of advertising (P_A) does not change regardless of the quantity you purchase. So in Figure 13.3, the marginal cost curve ($P_A = MC_A$) shows that the marginal cost of advertising is constant at $12 million per campaign.

Profit-Maximizing Quantity of Advertising

Applying marginal analysis, the profit-maximizing amount of advertising sets the marginal benefit from advertising equal to the marginal cost of advertising: $MB_A = MC_A$. Figure 13.3 shows that this quantity is three units of advertising. Why does this amount maximize your firm's net profit? All of the units up to the third unit add to the firm's net profit (because $MB_A > MC_A$), and additional units beyond the third unit subtract from the firm's net profit (because $MB_A < MC_A$). For example, the first advertising campaign increases your firm's gross profit by $24 million and increases its advertising cost by $12 million, so its net profit (its total revenue minus *all* its costs, including the cost of advertising) rises by $24 million minus $12 million, or $12 million.

Profit-Maximizing Quantity of Production

Once you and the other managers have determined the profit-maximizing quantity of advertising, you can determine the profit-maximizing quantity and price of your product. In Figure 13.4, demand curve D_3 is the demand for your beer when you purchase the profit-maximizing amount of advertising determined from Figure 13.3, three units of advertising. With this demand curve and associated marginal revenue curve (MR_3), you produce the quantity for which marginal revenue equals marginal cost (4.375 million barrels of beer) and then set the highest price that sells the quantity produced ($182.50 per barrel).

Figure 13.4 Profit-Maximizing Quantity of Production

When you purchase the profit-maximizing quantity of advertising (three units), the demand curve for beer is D_3, and the marginal revenue curve is MR_3. Your firm maximizes profit by producing 4.375 million barrels of beer, the quantity that sets $MR = MC$, and setting a price of $182.50 per barrel.

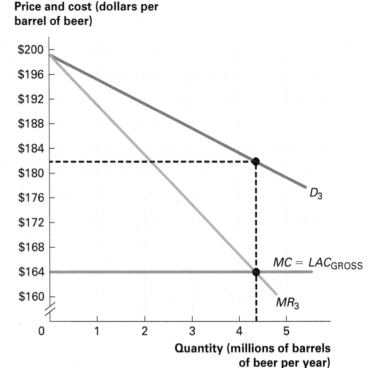

Increase in the Effectiveness of Advertising

As you have already learned, the primary goal of advertising is to increase the demand for your product. Suppose that your advertising becomes more effective—that is, for every dollar spent on advertising, the increase in demand is larger. The increase in effectiveness may be the result of better targeted online advertising on Facebook or Twitter, both of which collect data about the searching and the purchasing preferences of their users. Alternatively, an advertising campaign may create a well-known icon, such as the Energizer bunny or the AFLAC duck, which the company can use in multiple ad campaigns. Regardless of the source of the improvement, the effect on the optimal quantity of advertising is the same. The larger increase in demand from more effective advertising leads to a larger increase in gross profit. In terms of Figure 13.3, the marginal benefit curve from advertising shifts to the right, so the profit-maximizing quantity of advertising increases.

Choosing Advertising Media

To this point, the analysis has assumed a single method of advertising. In the real world, managers can spend advertising money on a variety of sources, including television, radio, the Internet, print, bulk mail (also called "junk" mail), billboards, and even blimps.

Profit Maximization with Different Advertising Media

Let's extend the analysis to two advertising media—television and the Internet. Once you understand the optimal distribution of advertising between two media, extending the analysis to three or more is straightforward.

The marginal benefit from advertising using two media is the same as that from advertising using a single medium: For each type of advertising, the marginal benefit is the increase in gross profit resulting from the increased demand the advertisement creates. If the effects on demand from one unit of television advertising and one unit of Internet advertising differ, their marginal benefits will also differ.

Supposing again that the firm is a small buyer in the markets for advertising, the marginal cost of each type of advertising is equal to the price for that type. In particular, if the price of a television advertisement is P_{TV}, then the marginal cost of a television advertisement is P_{TV}, and if the price of an Internet advertisement is P_{INT}, then the marginal cost of an Internet advertisement is P_{INT}.

With a single advertising medium, you maximize profit by advertising so that the marginal benefit from advertising equals the price of advertising ($MB_A = P_A$) and producing so that $MR = MC$. When there are two types of advertising, the profit-maximizing conditions are essentially the same:

1. Select the quantity of television advertising that sets $MB_{TV} = P_{TV}$.
2. Select the quantity of Internet advertising that sets $MB_{INT} = P_{INT}$.
3. Use the demand and marginal revenue curves, which are influenced by both forms of advertising, to produce the quantity of output at which $MR = MC$.

Items 1 and 2 maximize the profit from each type of advertising. Item 3 completes the job by maximizing profit based on the new demand.

Allocation of Advertising Expenditures

The profit-maximizing expenditure on advertising buys the amount that sets $MB_i = P_i$ for all i different types of advertising. Often you may have a fixed advertising budget, however. With a fixed budget, you face a slightly different decision: how to allocate your advertising dollars to maximize profit. Suppose that you must allocate your budget between television advertising, with marginal benefit MB_{TV} and marginal cost P_{TV}, and Internet advertising, with marginal benefit MB_{INT} and marginal cost P_{INT}. Marginal analysis shows that you have allocated your spending optimally when

$$\frac{MB_{TV}}{P_{TV}} = \frac{MB_{INT}}{P_{INT}} \qquad\qquad \textbf{13.1}$$

To see why the equality shown in Equation 13.1 maximizes profit, note that the $\frac{MB}{P}$ terms are the marginal benefit per dollar from the last unit of advertising purchased for television and Internet ads, respectively. For example, if the marginal benefit to your company from another television advertisement is $60,000 and the price of this advertisement is $10,000, then $\frac{MB_{TV}}{P_{TV}}$ is $6. In other words, $1 spent on the television advertisement returns $6 in additional gross profit. Equation 13.1 demonstrates that different advertising media are purchased in the optimal proportion only when the $\frac{MB}{P}$ terms are equal. If $\frac{MB_{TV}}{P_{TV}}$ is $6 and $\frac{MB_{INT}}{P_{INT}}$ is *not* $6, you have misallocated your advertising expenditures. For example, suppose that $\frac{MB_{INT}}{P_{INT}}$ is $8. In this case, if you decrease spending on television advertisements by a dollar, you lose $6 in (gross) profit. If you then spend that dollar on Internet advertising, you gain $8 in (gross) profit. This reallocation *increases* your profit by $2. *Any time* the marginal benefit per dollar of one type of advertising does not equal that of the other types, you can increase your profit by reallocating money away from the advertising medium with the smaller marginal benefit per dollar to the one with a higher marginal benefit per dollar. Once you have reallocated your spending so that the marginal benefits per dollar of all types of advertising are equal, you will have optimally allocated your fixed advertising budget.

DECISION SNAPSHOT

PepsiCo Allocates Its Advertising Dollars

In 2010, PepsiCo's executives announced they would switch the firm's advertising from the Super Bowl to an online web presence called the Pepsi Refresh Project. Rather than buy several Super Bowl ads, which cost more than $4 million for a 30-second ad, Pepsi would donate $20 million to social causes and projects based on the nominations and votes of visitors to the refresheverything.com website. During the two years of Internet advertising, the demand for PepsiCo's flagship soda, Pepsi-Cola, fell, so that it moved from second in sales (to Coke) to third in sales, behind both Coke and Diet Coke. As a PepsiCo manager, what should you do?

Answer

You should switch spending back to Super Bowl advertising and other traditional projects because you can infer that online advertising has a marginal benefit per dollar (MB_{INT}/P_{INT}) that is much less than the marginal benefit per dollar of television advertising (MB_{TV}/P_{TV}). With $MB_{INT}/P_{INT} < MB_{TV}/P_{TV}$, advertising has been misallocated. Indeed, PepsiCo's managers shut down the Pepsi Refresh Project and transferred their advertising dollars back to Super Bowl ads because they determined that their online advertising was too diffuse, building little or no brand equity or loyalty.

Although Equation 13.1 shows whether a given advertising budget is allocated properly among the different media, there is a larger issue. Even when your advertising purchases have set $\frac{MB_{TV}}{P_{TV}}$ equal to $\frac{MB_{INT}}{P_{INT}}$, you may still *not* be maximizing your profit. The distribution is correct, but your overall advertising budget might be wrong. You maximize profit *only* when the marginal benefit from any form of advertising equals its marginal cost, which means that $MB_{TV} = P_{TV}$ and $MB_{INT} = P_{INT}$, so that $\frac{MB_{TV}}{P_{TV}}$ and $\frac{MB_{INT}}{P_{INT}}$ both equal 1.

The Role of Economic Analysis in Advertising

The analysis of advertising demonstrates that, as usual, economics provides a guide to, rather than a recipe for, profit maximization. For example, in reality, it is not easy for a manager to determine the marginal benefit from advertising. Regression analysis (explained in Chapter 3) might help. For example, when estimating the demand for the product, you might ask your research analysts to include advertising as an additional factor affecting demand. If regression is not a viable option, you might instead use marginal analysis by asking yourself, "If the proposed advertising campaign was free, how much would my profit increase?" This amount is the gross profit. Then you should compare the answer to the cost of the campaign. If the gross profit exceeds the cost, the campaign will be profitable and should be undertaken. If the gross profit falls short of the cost, you need to investigate the possibility of negotiating a lower cost for the campaign or using a different advertising medium.

Applying marginal analysis is not easy. But its goal—accepting all advertising for which the increase in gross profit exceeds the cost of the advertising—is important. That is the outcome that maximizes profit, so it should be the ultimate objective of managers of any type of firm.

Marginal Benefit from Automobile Advertising

SOLVED **PROBLEM**

You are the general sales manager at a car dealership in Santa Fe, New Mexico. Currently, you sell 200 cars per month at a price of $25,000 per car. You are thinking of advertising on a local talk radio station—maybe KTRC. Each hour of advertising costs $10,000 per month. Not counting any advertising expenditure, the marginal cost of each car sold is constant and equals the constant average cost: $24,000. You determine that the first hour of advertising raises the price you receive for each car you sell by $100 and you sell 10 more cars; the second hour raises the price by $50 and you sell 5 more cars.

a. What is your marginal benefit from each hour of advertising?

b. What is the marginal cost of an hour of advertising?

c. What is your net profit from each hour of advertising?

Answer

a. The marginal benefit from any hour of advertising is the increase in the gross profit. That increase can be broken into two parts: the gross profit from the higher price for the cars you already sell and the gross profit from the new cars you sell. For the first hour, the price rises by $100 and you are selling 200 cars, so the gross profit from these cars increases by ($100 per car) × (200 cars) = $20,000. Additionally, you sell 10 more cars. The price is now $25,100, so the gross profit from these cars is ($25,100 − $24,000) × 10 cars = $11,000. The total gross profit for the first hour of advertising is $20,000 + $11,000 = $31,000.

(Continues)

SOLVED PROBLEM (*continued*)

For the second hour, initially you sell 210 cars. The marginal benefit from the higher price for these cars is ($50 per car) × (210 cars) = $10,500. Additionally, you sell an additional 5 cars at a price of $25,150, so these cars increase your gross profit by ($25,150 − $24,000) × 5 cars = $5,750. The total gross profit for the second hour of advertising is therefore $10,500 + $5,750 = $16,250.

b. The marginal cost of an hour of advertising is equal to the price, $10,000 per hour.

c. The net profit from advertising equals the gross profit minus the cost of the advertising. For the first hour, the net profit equals $31,000 − $10,000 = $21,000. For the second hour, the net profit equals $16,250 − $10,000 = $6,250.

13.2 Optimal Advertising by an Industry

Learning Objective 13.2 Describe how trade association managers can determine the optimal amount of industry-wide advertising and allocate its cost.

Individual firms do the most advertising, but in some industries, industry-wide advertising is undertaken by organizations on behalf of member firms. In the agricultural sector, everyone knows about "Beef. It's what's for dinner." But some still wonder if you've "Got Milk?" Sports leagues, including the National Football League, Major League Baseball, and the Women's Tennis Association, sponsor ads. These industry advertisements make no mention of any specific brands or teams. Their aim is to promote beef or milk consumption or to lead more people to watch football, baseball, or women's tennis. The idea is to increase industry demand for the product to the benefit of all producers. Franchisors, such as McDonald's, have similar advertising. McDonald's advertisements stress the enjoyment of eating at McDonald's generally, rather than the benefits of dining at a particular franchised outlet. Parallel to advertising by industry organizations, the goal of McDonald's advertising is to increase the system-wide demand to benefit all franchisees.

The obvious question elicited by these advertising campaigns is why an industry organization or franchisor would advertise on behalf of its members. The answer, of course, is that it is profitable to do so. The activities of the Cattlemen's Beef Promotion and Research Board, more typically known as the Cattlemen's Beef Board (CBB), illustrate the economic issues involved in industry-wide and franchisor advertising.

Industry-Wide Advertising as a Public Good

When the CBB advertises "Beef. It's what's for dinner," its aim is to increase the overall demand for beef consumption. All beef producers benefit from the advertising regardless of whether they paid for it or not. In addition, the benefit to one producer, such as Trinity Farms, a cattle producer in South Carolina, does *not* reduce the benefit to another producer, such as Gilbert Angus Ranch, a cattle producer in South Dakota. Consequently, industry-wide advertising is an example of a public good. A **public good** is a good or service that is nonexcludable and nonrival:

Public good A good or service that is nonexcludable (all producers in the market can use it regardless of whether they paid for it) and nonrival (one person's or one firm's use does not decrease the quantity available for everyone else).

- Nonexcludable: All producers in the market can use it regardless of whether they paid for it.
- Nonrival: One person's or one firm's use does not decrease the amount available for everyone else.

Table 13.1 **Marginal Benefit from Industry-Wide Advertising**

Because both firms simultaneously benefit from each unit of the CBB's industry-wide advertising, at each quantity of advertising the industry-wide marginal benefit equals the sum of the individual firms' marginal benefits.

Quantity of Advertising (hours per week)	Trine Farms Marginal Benefit	Gold Angus Ranch Marginal Benefit	Industry-Wide Marginal Benefit
1	$500	$600	$1,100
2	400	550	950
3	300	500	800
4	200	450	650

The problem for the CBB is deciding how much to spend on advertising. This question is not difficult to answer theoretically, but because of the public nature of the advertising, the solution may be difficult to implement.

Optimal Quantity of Industry-Wide Advertising

To simplify the problems posed by public goods, suppose that there are only two beef producers—Trine Farms and Gold Angus Ranch. The definition of the industry-wide marginal benefit from industry-wide advertising should sound familiar: it is the change in industry-wide gross profit from the change in demand. Because each producer simultaneously benefits from the same advertisement, that means that for each quantity of advertising, the industry-wide marginal benefit equals the sum of each firm's marginal benefit, that is, the sum of each firm's increase in gross profit. Table 13.1 shows how the two producers' marginal benefits depend on the quantity of advertising. The industry-wide marginal benefit for each quantity of advertising is equal to the sum of the individual firms' marginal benefits.

Figure 13.5(a) illustrates the industry-wide marginal benefit curve (MB), the marginal benefit curve for Trine Farms (MB_{TF}), and the marginal benefit curve for Gold Angus Ranch (MB_{GAR}), all based on the marginal benefit schedules in Table 13.1. Because each producer benefits from the same advertisement, the industry-wide marginal benefit curve at any quantity of advertising is derived by adding the producers' marginal benefits at that quantity of advertising, that is, as the figure shows, vertically adding the individual marginal benefit curves.

To determine the profit-maximizing quantity of industry-wide advertising, you need the marginal cost curve. The price of advertising time is $800 per hour, and the CBB is a small buyer of advertising, so its decisions do not affect the market price. Therefore, the marginal cost curve (MC) shown in Figure 13.5(b) is horizontal at the price of $800 per hour.

The optimal quantity of advertising, the amount that maximizes the industry-wide joint profit, is the quantity that sets the industry-wide marginal benefit equal to the marginal cost. In Figure 13.5(b), the optimal quantity of advertising is three hours per month, the point of intersection of the industry-wide marginal benefit and marginal cost curves. At this quantity, Gold Angus Ranch's marginal benefit is $500 per hour and Trine Farms' marginal benefit is $300 per hour.

Challenges of Industry-Wide Advertising

It is never easy for managers to determine the amount of advertising that maximizes a firm's profit. The public-goods nature of industry-wide or system-wide advertising creates additional challenges for the managers of the trade associations or franchisers. These challenges fall into three categories: knowledge of marginal benefit schedules, free riders, and cost sharing.

Figure 13.5 Industry-Wide Advertising

(a) Industry-Wide Marginal Benefit Curve
The marginal benefit for each producer from the CBB's industry-wide advertising is shown by the marginal benefit curves for Trine Farms (MB_{TF}) and Gold Angus Ranch (MB_{GAR}). The industry-wide marginal benefit curve (MB) equals the sum of the individual firms' marginal benefit curves. For example, for two hours of advertising Gold Angus Ranch's marginal benefit is $550 per hour and Trine Farms' marginal benefit is $400 per hour, so the industry-wide marginal benefit is $950 per hour.

(b) Optimal Industry-Wide Advertising
The marginal cost of advertising is constant at $800 per hour, so the marginal cost curve (MC) is horizontal at $800. The optimal quantity of industry-wide advertising, three hours per month, sets MB equal to MC. At this quantity, the marginal benefits to Gold Angus Ranch and Trine Farms are $500 per hour and $300 per hour, respectively.

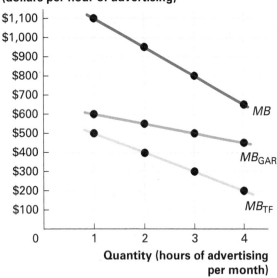

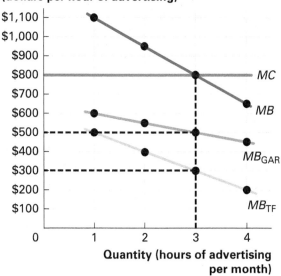

Knowledge of Marginal Benefit Schedules

Because producers in a given industry or franchise system operate in local markets and each of these markets has some unique characteristics, each producer has a different marginal benefit schedule. This fact creates a problem for the managers of the industry-wide trade associations and franchisors: For these managers to buy the optimal amount of advertising, they need to know the industry-wide marginal benefit schedule, which depends on the marginal benefit schedules of its members. If the marginal benefit schedules of the members vary dramatically, determining the industry-wide marginal benefit schedule is difficult.

In addition, in order to fund the industry-wide or system-wide advertising, managers of trade associations and franchisors often try to base each member's payment on the marginal benefit that the firm will receive from the advertising. In other words, producers who gain more pay more. However, this arrangement gives each firm's managers the incentive to understate the marginal benefit in order to pay less. For example, the managers of a cattle ranch could claim they gain nothing from the CBB's advertising and thereby should pay nothing. Each firm's incentive to understate its benefit significantly complicates the trade association's task of determining the industry-wide marginal benefit.

Free Riders

Another issue comes from the realization by each firm's managers that their individual contribution to funding the trade association's advertising is small. Each firm's managers reason that if their firm can somehow avoid paying, it will still reap all of the benefit from the advertising at no cost. In essence, each manager has an incentive to be a **free rider**, a person or firm that benefits from a good or service without paying for it. In this case, the good or service is the industry-wide advertising. If enough managers free ride, there will be too little industry-wide advertising because the funds provided to the trade association will be too low. This sub-optimal result is referred to as the *free-rider problem*.

Free rider A person or firm that benefits from a good or service without paying for it.

Franchised networks, such as McDonald's, do not have a free-rider problem because the franchisees are required to pay a percentage of their sales revenues to McDonald's Corporation (currently 4 percent), part of which the corporation uses for system-wide advertising. The managers of trade associations do not have as easy a task, however. Legally requiring the member firms to pay for the trade association's advertising is one solution to the free-rider problem. In fact, the U.S. Department of Agriculture (USDA) can establish checkoff programs that require all agricultural producers to pay their trade association to fund industry-wide advertising. For example, the USDA established a mandatory $1 per head fee that *all* sellers of beef must pay to the CBB to eliminate the possibility of free riders.

Cost Sharing

Even without free riders, prescribing a fair and practical way of sharing the cost of industry-wide advertising is a major challenge. In Figure 13.5(b), the total cost for the optimal three hours of advertising is (3 hours) × ($800 per hour), or $2,400. Figure 13.5(b) shows that at this quantity of advertising, Gold Angus Ranch has a marginal benefit of $500 per hour and Trine Farms has a marginal benefit of $300 per hour. If each producer contributes in proportion to its marginal benefit, then Gold Angus Ranch pays (3 hours) × ($500 per hour), or $1,500, and Trine Farms pays (3 hours) × ($300 per hour), or $900. This allocation of the total advertising cost is fair in terms of marginal benefit, but it might not *appear* fair because Gold Angus Ranch ends up paying a bigger share of the total cost, 62.5 percent, than Trine Farms, which pays only 37.5 percent. Even though this allocation leads each producer to want precisely three hours of advertising, you can imagine that the managers at Gold Angus Ranch will continually assert that they are unfairly shouldering the lion's share of the cost in an attempt to impose more of the cost on Trine Farms.

Splitting the cost of the advertising evenly might appear at first glance to be a fairer allocation. When each firm pays 50 percent of the cost of the advertising, each pays $1,200 to cover the total cost of $2,400. Because three hours of advertising are purchased, each firm pays $400 per hour. Unfortunately, both sets of managers will be dissatisfied with this even split—but for different reasons. The managers of Gold Angus Ranch will think that there is too little industry-wide advertising: They are paying $400 per hour, but with three hours of advertising, their marginal benefit is $500. These managers want *more* industry-wide advertising because their marginal benefit exceeds the price they pay. For Trine Farms, on the other hand, the marginal benefit with three hours of advertising is only $300. Trine Farms is paying more than its marginal benefit, so its managers want *less* industry-wide advertising. An even split is not the optimum amount for either firm. While there is no perfect solution to this problem, Section 13.6 discusses a possibility.

SOLVED
PROBLEM

The National Football League's Advertising Problem

League-wide advertising by the National Football League generally promotes the drama and excitement of professional football, rather than the entertainment value of any one of the 32 member teams. For simplicity, assume that each team's marginal benefit schedule is the same. In particular, suppose that each team's marginal benefit is given by $MB = \$10{,}000 - 100Q$, where Q is the weekly quantity of league-wide advertising minutes.

a. What is the league-wide marginal benefit from advertising?

b. If the price of an advertisement is $160,000 per minute, what is the optimal quantity of league-wide advertising?

c. At the optimal quantity, what equal amount must each team pay for the league-wide advertising?

d. At the optimal quantity of league-wide advertising, what is each team's marginal benefit for the last minute of advertising?

Answer

a. The league-wide marginal benefit from advertising is the sum of the 32 teams' marginal benefit curves. Because the teams' marginal benefits are the same, rather than adding the separate marginal benefits 32 times, the league-wide marginal benefit can be calculated by multiplying an individual team's marginal benefit by 32: $MB = 32 \times (\$10{,}000 - 100Q) = \$320{,}000 - 3{,}200Q$.

b. The optimal quantity of minutes sets $MB = MC$, where MB is the league-wide marginal benefit. Therefore, the optimal quantity is determined by $\$320{,}000 - 3{,}200Q = \$160{,}000$. Rearranging the equation to solve for Q gives $\$320{,}000 - \$160{,}000 = 3{,}200Q$, so $\$160{,}000 = 3{,}200Q$ so that $Q = 50$ minutes.

c. The *total* cost of the advertising is $(50 \text{ minutes}) \times (\$160{,}000 \text{ per minute}) = \$8{,}000{,}000$. Each team must pay $\$8{,}000{,}000/32 = \$250{,}000$.

d. Each team's marginal benefit is equal to $MB = \$10{,}000 - 100Q$. With $Q = 50$, each team's marginal benefit for the 50th (last) minute equals $\$10{,}000 - (100 \times 50)$, or $\$5{,}000$.

13.3 False Advertising

Learning Objective 13.3 Analyze why managers of some firms engage in false advertising despite possible sanctions by the Federal Trade Commission.

False advertising
Advertising that misrepresents the nature, characteristics, or qualities of goods or services.

False advertising is advertising that misrepresents the nature, characteristics, or qualities of goods or services. Typically, the goal of false advertising is to increase sales and profit. By presenting information on this topic, we do *not* suggest that you try to increase your firm's profit by engaging in false advertising. Your company can face penalties and your career can be dead-ended if you are tried for and convicted of false advertising. It is important to understand what false advertising is in order to avoid it. Moreover, at some point, you might become convinced that a competitor is falsely advertising its product. In this case, it is imperative to know what you can do. For these reasons, and more, understanding this topic is worthwhile.

The issues surrounding false advertising focus on two key questions:

1. When can false advertising be successful?
2. What are the penalties for false advertising?

When Can False Advertising Be Successful?

False advertising works for certain types of goods but not for others. To understand why, you first need to distinguish three types of goods:

- **Inspection goods.** These are products with characteristics that can be determined prior to purchase. Copier paper is an example of an inspection good because the quality of the paper can be determined before it is used.
- **Experience goods.** These are products that a consumer must use in order to assess their characteristics. A bottle of wine is a classic example of an experience good. Before consuming the wine, it is difficult to judge its quality.
- **Credence goods.** These are products with characteristics that cannot be evaluated even after the consumer has used them. For example, annual maintenance of your furnace is a credence good because even after the maintenance is performed, it is impossible for you to determine the value of the work.

Pure inspection, experience, or credence goods are rare. These definitions are best applied to particular characteristics of a product, rather than the overall product, because many products have characteristics that fit into all three categories. For example, consider a new car. The color of the automobile can be determined by examining it before purchase, so color is an inspection characteristic. The buyer can determine the quality of the ride during long trips only by experience with the car, so ride quality is an experience characteristic. The quality of the oil in the engine is impossible to determine, so engine oil is a credence good. The feature deemed most important by the consumer determines whether the car is an inspection, experience, or credence good. For example, if the consumer wants a red car—and *only* a red car—the car is an inspection good. If, however, the consumer's top priority is a smooth ride, the car is an experience good.

False Advertising for the Different Types of Goods

Advertising can inform buyers that a particular store carries a certain inspection good at a specific price. Advertising cannot successfully misinform buyers about the characteristics of an inspection good, however, because buyers can observe these features prior to purchase. For example, if the managers of an automobile dealership advertise a red car but have no red cars on the lot, customers will immediately recognize the deception. False advertising about inspection goods cannot succeed and is bound to turn off potential customers.

Advertising does have the potential to mislead first-time buyers about the characteristics of experience goods. Consumers must use an experience good before they can determine the value of its characteristics, so they cannot immediately decide if advertising about some (or all) of the characteristics is false or deceptive. The potential for misleading buyers is limited, however. Some information about quality may be available from comments by other consumers, such as those on Yelp or Amazon, or reviews by third parties, such as *Consumer Reports*.

Consumers can rent some experience goods, such as automobiles, and experience the characteristics firsthand. The potential for repeat sales also discourages the use of advertising to deceive consumers. Once consumers have experienced a particular good, they know its characteristics and will purchase it again only if they value it sufficiently. Because a seller cannot mislead purchasers of an experience good more than once, the potential for profit-increasing false advertising is greatest for seldom-purchased experience goods such as major home appliances and high-tech televisions.

Credence goods offer the largest potential for false advertising. Indeed, managers of firms selling credence goods realize that consumers are often skeptical about the value of their goods. For example, managers of some auto repair shops offer to give back to customers the damaged parts they replace. No customer truly desires damaged auto parts, but some may want the reassurance that the shop actually performed the repair and that it was necessary. Even so, judging the worth of the repair remains difficult. Unlike with experience goods, the prospect of losing repeat sales is not necessarily a deterrent to false advertising if the consumer is not in a position to judge the credence good's characteristics.

Effect of False Advertising on Reputation

Profit-maximizing managers know that a company's reputation can affect its profitability, especially if the company sells an experience good or a credence good. Consumers will be more confident about making purchases from a firm with a reputation for truthful advertising. This confidence can increase the demand for future purchases of experience or credence goods sold by the firm. However, if the firm loses its reputation, unhappy customers will cause it to lose future sales. Managers of firms selling credence goods must be especially protective of their reputations. Once consumers become dissatisfied with the product and switch to another seller, it will be very difficult to win them back. Customers can use Yelp reviews and social media to disseminate both good and bad experiences with a business, so managers *must* keep track of their firm's online reputation.

Of course, not all firms will find it profitable to avoid false advertising. From a manager's perspective, the larger the pool of buyers who can be "suckered" once, the more profitable the false advertising. As a result, false advertising is more profitable and more prevalent in communities with a large number of visitors or transient populations, such as resort towns and tourist areas, or university towns.

Greenwashing

Greenwashing False advertisements or claims that a firm is behaving in an environmentally friendly way or producing an environmentally friendly product.

Greenwashing is a particular form of false advertising. It refers to false advertisements or claims that a firm is behaving in an environmentally friendly way or producing an environmentally friendly product. Allegations of this type of false advertising have become more prominent as the "greenness" of products has become more important to customers.

As with other false advertising, credence goods are most often greenwashed. For example, Kmart advertised that its house-brand paper plates were biodegradable. The biodegradability of the plates is a credence characteristic because consumers will never know whether their plates biodegraded. The government challenged Kmart's claim because 90 percent of paper plates wind up in solid waste disposal facilities, where paper generally does not decompose. Kmart settled with the government by abandoning the biodegradability claim.

Managers of some manufacturers and/or sellers of experience and credence goods may be seduced into engaging in false advertising because of the potential for additional profit. Of course, the possibility of legal sanctions diminishes the potential profit from false advertising. The more severe the legal penalties for false advertising are, the less prevalent the practice will be.

What Are the Penalties for False Advertising?

Federal Trade Commission Act

The Federal Trade Commission (FTC), an agency of the federal government, was created by passage of the Federal Trade Commission Act in 1914. False advertising or false marketing is considered an unfair and deceptive method of competition and is therefore a violation of Section 5 of the Federal Trade Commission Act, which prohibits "unfair methods of competition and . . . deceptive acts." Ensuring truth in advertising is now one of the tasks of the FTC's Bureau of Consumer Protection.

Some false advertising can be blatant. An advertisement created decades ago for Campbell Soup Company's vegetable soup is an example. Campbell's advertisement had clear, invisible marbles at the bottom of the soup bowl, forcing vegetables to the surface where they were more visible, so consumers thought the soup contained more vegetables than it did. Other false advertising is more subtle, so the FTC has issued guidelines to help managers know what is permissible. For example, the FTC has issued Green Guides that provide guidelines for environmental marketing claims.[2]

The FTC generally relies on consumers and competitors to report false advertising. Once FTC investigators have decided that a company's advertising is illegal, the bureau generally tries to convince the company to cease or alter its advertising. If that less formal effort fails, the FTC can proceed in one or more of the following ways:

- Issue a cease-and-desist order (a legally binding order for the company to stop running the false advertisements)
- Seek a court injunction to stop the false advertising
- Force the company to run corrective advertisements, including product facts and admissions that the earlier ads were false
- Bring civil cases against the company and its managers seeking repayment to customers, financial penalties, and disgorgement of the ill-gotten profit

Lanham Act

If you determine that a competitor is engaged in false advertising, you can complain to the FTC. In addition, if the false advertising has damaged your company, you can file a civil suit under the Lanham Act. Passed in 1946, the Lanham Act prohibits trademark infringement and false advertising and allows companies to request injunctions to stop the competitor's advertisements. It also allows you to sue for *marketplace damages*, the profits lost due to the false advertising. While both the FTC and the Lanham Act can force a competitor to stop false advertising, only under the Lanham Act can you collect damages from your competitor.

---

2 Green Guides and other guidelines are available on the FTC website at www.ftc.gov.

Advertising for Skechers Shape-Ups Gets the Boot

The managers at Skechers U.S.A., Inc., thought they had a winning advertising campaign: Just walk around in Skechers Shape-Up shoes to strengthen your leg and abdominal muscles and lose weight. Kim Kardashian starred in a Super Bowl advertisement making these claims. Another television ad featured a chiropractor discussing a study that supposedly verified the claims. Although it all might have seemed too good to be true, the managers at Skechers may not have cared because sales of the $60 to $100 shoes rose to over $1 billion. The FTC wasn't so quick to buy in, however: Aside from the chiropractor's assertions, there was little to no scientific evidence supporting the claims. Further investigation revealed that Skechers paid the chiropractor for his endorsement—and he was married to a Skechers marketing executive.

a. Based on the advertised characteristics, are the Shape-Up shoes an inspection good, an experience good, or a credence good? Explain your answer.
b. Is it possible for false advertising to boost the demand for Shape-Up shoes? Why or why not?
c. If the FTC decides the advertisements are false, what sanctions can it impose?

Answer

a. Inspection alone cannot determine the validity of the advertised characteristic because merely observing the shoes cannot help the customer confirm if the claims are true. Therefore, the shoes are not an inspection good. If consumers can notice that they lose weight and/or strengthen their muscles by wearing the shoes, the shoes are an experience good, but if consumers cannot detect these changes, then the shoes are a credence good.

b. Because the shoes are either an experience good or a credence good, false advertising can increase demand, but it has the drawback of possibly decreasing future demand from unhappy customers who had previously purchased the shoes.

c. The FTC can issue a cease-and-desist order or seek an injunction to stop the advertising campaign. The FTC can also bring a civil suit seeking civil penalties, including fines imposed on the company and its managers, reimbursement for customers, and forfeiture of the profit. In the Skechers case, the FTC opted to seek an injunction, which the courts granted, and filed a civil lawsuit. Without admitting guilt, Skechers agreed to a $40 million fine, which was used to reimburse over 500,000 customers who had purchased the shoes.

13.4 Resale Price Maintenance and Product Promotion

Learning Objective 13.4 Explain the legal status of resale price maintenance and its use in product promotion.

Recall from Chapter 9 that *resale price maintenance* is a business practice in which manufacturers sell products to retailers with the explicit condition that the retailers may not resell the products below a specified price. This practice limits the pricing discretion of retailers. Typically, the manufacturer permits retailers to charge a resale price above the specified minimum, but the retailers do not do so because that would lead to lower profits. Resale price maintenance therefore acts as a constraint on a reseller's ability to reduce its resale price. Examples of products subject to resale price maintenance include pillows, blue jeans, candy, golf clubs, mattresses, women's handbags, and athletic shoes.

Manufacturers who use resale price maintenance are apprehensive that retailers who have not agreed to sell at the minimum price may acquire the product and sell it at a price lower than allowed. For example, sometimes retailers can buy the product at a much lower price in foreign countries, import it, and then sell it at a lower-than-minimum price. Manufacturers use different methods to try to quash this possibility. For example, they can attempt to distribute abroad only the quantity they predict foreign consumers will buy. They also can refuse to honor warranties on products purchased from an unauthorized retailer.

The Effect of Resale Price Maintenance

On the surface, resale price maintenance might not make sense. After all, lower retail prices should lead to the sale of larger quantities and therefore higher profits for the manufacturer as its retailers buy more of the product. This outcome is not necessarily the case, however, if the demand for a product depends on promotional efforts such as product demonstrations, warranty repairs and replacements, or free delivery. If the manufacturer cannot easily perform those promotional services, it must rely on its retailers. For example, consumers might be willing to buy a Tempur-Pedic Symphony pillow only if they can first examine it in person because these pillows have both inspection and experience characteristics. Bed Bath & Beyond stores have these pillows in stock, so consumers can go there to ask salespeople about the pillow as well as to inspect it and experience it. These promotional services increase the demand for the pillow, which is in Tempur-Pedic's best interest.

Product-Specific Services

Product-specific services are services provided by retail sellers, such as displaying the product, providing product information, demonstrating the product, and allowing consumer trials. These types of services are often valuable for complex experience goods that consumers purchase infrequently. Consumers typically desire information on the specifications, appropriate operation, and various applications of such products. For example, high-tech goods such as smartphones often require detailed explanation for optimal use because consumers buy them infrequently and they can be difficult to use. Knowledgeable salespeople can demonstrate a phone's features and allow a customer to experience it prior to purchase. For other products, such as pillows or furniture, consumers might want to actually handle or test them before they purchase them. As the point of contact with consumers, retailers play a crucial role in providing product-specific services.

Product-specific services Services provided by retail sellers, such as displaying the product, providing product information, demonstrating the product, and allowing consumer trials.

If the services create value for the consumer, they increase the retail demand. Providing these services is costly, however. For example, retailers may need to train their salespeople to demonstrate or understand the product, or they may need to construct specialized displays.

Product-Specific Services and Free Riding

Suppose that you work for a firm like Tempur-Pedic and also make a memory-foam pillow. Say that websites like Amazon.com and brick-and-mortar retailers like Bed Bath & Beyond both sell your pillow. Of course, websites have no retail locations. If consumers want to see and touch the pillow, they must go to a store. Websites like

Amazon are free riding on in-store displays—that is, gaining the benefit of the increased retail demand from the product-specific services without incurring any of the cost. Indeed, because they are not paying salespeople to demonstrate and sell the pillow, websites' costs are lower than stores' costs, so they can charge a lower price. Customers might go to a store to examine the pillow but then buy it from a website because of the lower price. Such consumer actions reduce the store's profit because it has incurred the costs of providing the display and product advice to the customers but has gained no sales.

If enough consumers follow this pattern, store managers might decide to reduce their costs by not displaying or demonstrating the pillows and by using the space to display other products that consumers are more likely to purchase. Such decisions at full-service retail outlets can result in fewer or, in the extreme, no product-specific services. If consumers are less willing to buy the pillow without examining it in person, the absence of these promotional services decreases the retail demand for the pillow, which decreases the manufacturer's profit. The end result of free riding by websites is a suboptimal amount of product-specific services, to the detriment of the manufacturer.[3]

Profit Maximization with Resale Price Maintenance

A manufacturer's managers can use resale price maintenance to ensure that competitive retailers provide the profit-maximizing amount of product-specific services. If both stores and websites must charge the same minimum price, competition breaks out on nonprice terms, such as providing the services. Of course, some retailers still might not provide these services, but because they must charge the same price as the full-service dealers, they will be less attractive to consumers. Competition forces successful retailers to provide the product-specific services that customers want.

A manufacturer's ultimate objective in specifying a minimum resale price is promotional. Its managers want to increase the quantity consumers buy so that they can increase their profit by selling more to the retailers. Offering the product-specific services increases consumer demand, shifting the market demand curve to the right. Providing product-specific services, however, also raises the retailers' cost of selling the product, decreasing supply and shifting the market supply curve to the left. For the manufacturer to achieve the goal of increasing the quantity, the increase in demand must exceed the decrease in supply.

Figure 13.6 illustrates this scenario for the memory-foam pillow example. Many retailers sell the pillows, so the market is competitive. If the retailers provide no displays or other demonstrations of the pillow, the retail demand curve is D_0, the retail supply curve is S_0, the price of a pillow is $100, and the retail quantity is 4 million pillows per year. Therefore, your firm's profit from producing the pillows is based on manufacturing and selling 4 million pillows to your retailers. If you use resale price maintenance to impose a minimum price of $130, competition will force retailers to provide valuable product-specific services (such as displaying and demonstrating the pillow), which increase consumers' demand and shift the retail demand curve to the right (to D_1). The retailers incur a cost when they provide these services, however, which decreases the supply and shifts the supply curve to the left (to S_1). The increase in demand, however, exceeds the decrease in supply, so the equilibrium quantity of pillows sold increases to 5 million per year.

3 Consumers might also lose. Although the absence of these services means they pay lower prices, they also receive less because they lose access to valuable product-specific services.

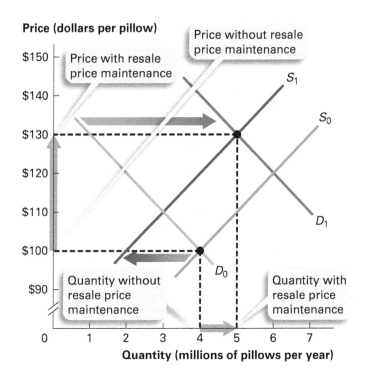

Figure 13.6 Resale Price Maintenance

Resale price maintenance gives retailers the incentive to provide the product-specific services the manufacturer wants. These services are valuable to the consumer, so they increase the demand and shift the demand curve to the right from D_0 to D_1. The product-specific services are also costly, which decreases the supply and shifts the supply curve to the left from S_0 to S_1. The increase in demand exceeds the decrease in supply, so the equilibrium quantity sold increases from 4 million to 5 million pillows per year, raising the manufacturer's profit.

The *crucial* result for your manufacturing company shown in Figure 13.6 is the increase in the equilibrium quantity because that change raises the number of pillows you sell, thereby increasing your firm's profit. Only if the product-specific services increase demand more than they decrease supply is resale price maintenance profitable for the manufacturer. So manufacturers want to set the minimum price at the level that covers retailers' costs of providing the product-specific services that increase consumers' demand more than they raise retailers' costs.

Resale Price Maintenance and Antitrust Policy

The legal treatment of resale price maintenance has changed through the years. The initial antitrust examination began in 1911, when the U.S. Supreme Court decided the case of *Dr. Miles Medical Company v. John D. Park & Sons*. The Dr. Miles Medical Company was a manufacturer of proprietary medicines and contractually required that its retailers sell these proprietary medicines at specified minimum resale prices.[4] The John D. Park & Sons Company sold Dr. Miles' medicines at prices lower than specified minimums, so the owners of the Dr. Miles Medical Company filed a lawsuit seeking to prohibit these sales. The Supreme Court found for John D. Park & Sons by ruling that resale price maintenance is price fixing and therefore illegal per se under the Sherman Act. Per se illegality means that the act, by itself, is illegal and no defense is possible (see Section 9.2).

_____

4 Rather than sign Dr. Miles' contract, the managers of the John D. Park & Sons Company, a drug retailer, convinced a few of the other retailers to sell them Dr. Miles' drugs for a lower price than the minimum resale price. John D. Park & Sons then resold the medicines to consumers at discounted prices, undercutting the other retailers. As a result, Dr. Miles sued John D. Park & Sons.

Amazon.com Markets Its Kindle

When Amazon.com introduced the Kindle in 2007, its managers believed it was important to sell the Kindle in brick-and-mortar retail stores. They signed up Target as a retailer but did *not* impose a resale price maintenance agreement. Target sold the Kindle for two years but then stopped selling it. As an Amazon manager, why did you want the Kindle sold in a retail outlet? Why didn't you require a resale price maintenance agreement? And why did Target's managers drop the product after two years?

Answer

Selling in a retail outlet allows consumers to touch and explore a Kindle before they purchase one. Target could provide these product-specific services, and Amazon.com could not. Amazon's managers did not impose a resale price maintenance agreement because, as both the manufacturer of and a retailer for the Kindle, Amazon wanted to free ride on Target's provision of the (costly) product-specific services. Amazon's managers did free ride and often undercut Target's price. After two years, Target's managers realized Amazon's free riding made it impossible for them to turn a profit on the Kindle, so Target stopped selling it.

The Supreme Court clarified its approach to resale price maintenance in 1919 with the decision in *United States v. Colgate & Company*. Colgate, a soap and toothpaste manufacturer, did not contractually require its wholesalers to sell at specified minimum prices. Instead, the managers at Colgate told their distributors that if they sold at a price lower than a specified minimum, Colgate would no longer sell them any products. Because Colgate did not require written contracts signifying agreement with the pricing scheme, the Supreme Court ruled in favor of Colgate, indicating that companies have a right to decide with whom they do business. This decision effectively made resale price *guidance* (but not resale price *maintenance*) legal.

The difference between the decisions in the *Colgate* case and the *Dr. Miles* case hinges on the existence of an agreement. The *Dr. Miles* case included a formal agreement, but the *Colgate* case did not. Between 1919 and 2006, Supreme Court decisions refined the distinction between an "agreement" and "guidance." That all changed in 2007, when the Supreme Court reversed the *Dr. Miles* decision in the case of *Leegin Creative Leather Products, Inc. v. PSKS, Inc.*[5] The Supreme Court ruled that resale price maintenance agreements are not illegal per se. Instead, the Supreme Court said that lower courts need to judge each case on its merits, using the *rule of reason* approach: The courts must examine the facts of each specific case to determine whether the procompetitive benefits of resale price maintenance outweigh its anticompetitive effects (see Section 9.2).

---

5 Leegin Creative Leather Products, Inc., makes leather products for women, such as belts and handbags. The managers at Leegin refused to sell to retailers that sold its products for less than the suggested minimum prices. Eventually, the managers at Leegin discovered that PSKS, Inc., a retailer of women's accessories, were selling its products at a 20 percent discount off the minimum price. Leegin's managers cut off sales to PSKS, so the owners of PSKS sued Leegin. The lower courts ruled for PSKS, but the Supreme Court overruled them, handing the legal victory to Leegin.

The treatment of resale price maintenance in the European Union and most other countries is quite different. Under EU law, resale price maintenance is a *hardcore restriction* on competition. Being deemed a hardcore restriction on competition probably sounds unpromising, and indeed it is. Competition authorities in the EU presume resale price maintenance is illegal. Similar to the historical situation in the United States, in the EU a manufacturer may suggest "recommended" resale prices but cannot enter into a formal agreement.

Profit-Maximizing Resale Price Maintenance for Designer Shoes   SOLVED PROBLEM

You work for a company like Nine West Group, which produces stylish shoes for women and sells them through competitive retailers. The figure shows the retail supply and demand for the shoes when retailers provide no product-specific services. Suppose that there are two services your retailers can provide. At each price, the first service increases demand by 2 million pairs per year, and the second service increases demand by 1 million pairs per year. By increasing the retailers' costs, at each price the first service decreases supply by 1 million, and the second service decreases supply by 2 million.

a. If your retailers provide no services, what are the price and quantity of shoes?

b. What is the profit-maximizing quantity of product-specific services? Explain your answer.

c. What is the profit-maximizing minimum resale price?

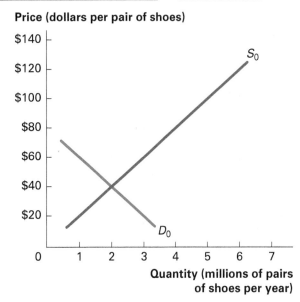

Answer

a. With no product-specific services, the demand curve is D_0, and the supply curve is S_0. The figure shows that the equilibrium price is $40 and the equilibrium quantity is 2.0 million.

b. In the figure, the first service shifts the demand curve to D_1 and the supply curve to S_1, so the equilibrium quantity is 2.5 million. The second service shifts the demand curve to D_2 and the supply curve to S_2, so the equilibrium quantity is 2.0 million. The equilibrium quantity is maximized when one product-specific service is provided, so that quantity maximizes your manufacturing firm's profit.

c. When retailers provide one service, the equilibrium price is $70 per pair of shoes. So you set the minimum retail price equal to that price. At $70, competition among retailers will drive them to provide the desired amount (one) of product-specific services.

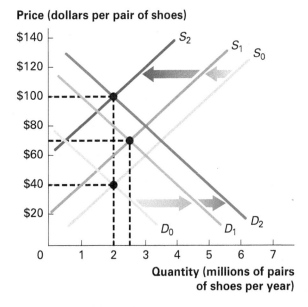

13.5 International Marketing: Entry and Corruption Laws

Learning Objective 13.5 Discuss different methods of entering foreign markets and ways to avoid violating anticorruption laws when doing business abroad.

International marketing is complex. In addition to the marketing issues already considered, such as the amount and type of advertising, you must consider the diverse political, economic, cultural, and social situations in different countries. What works in one country or region may be a miserable failure in another. A detailed discussion of all of the issues related to international marketing could fill many marketing texts, so this section focuses on two issues important to managerial economics: (1) different ways to enter a foreign market and (2) marketing behaviors to avoid when selling abroad so that you do not violate U.S. and other countries' anticorruption laws.

Entering a Foreign Market

As a manager, when you decide to enter a foreign market you face numerous choices. You could go it alone, partner with a foreign firm, establish a local office in the foreign market, engage in a joint venture with a foreign firm, acquire a foreign firm, or establish franchises in the foreign market. Because each approach has advantages and disadvantages as well as different levels of risk, the optimal entry strategy varies from one company to the next and one country to the next. Your choice depends on which market(s) you are planning to enter and your company's particular situation.

Some of the entry strategies described above involve working with a foreign firm, but all of them have one thing in common: due diligence. In addition to the due diligence you would perform when dealing intimately with a domestic firm (e.g., exploring the other firm's operations, examining its books), at a minimum you need to explore the foreign firm's reputation for ethical behavior, determine how deeply it is involved in local politics, and understand the objectives that motivate its owners. More often than not, surprises in a foreign market turn out to be bad.

Independent Entry

One entry strategy is straightforward: Your business can simply establish operations in the foreign country. Uber Technologies, the ride-hailing company, did so in 2013 by signing drivers and releasing their app in China. This type of entry means the managers retain total control over the decisions necessary to operate the business. There is no question of divided interests—the managers will make their decisions based on the interests of the firm. This type of entry also reserves all the profits (and all the losses) for the firm.

Uber's ultimate fate in China illustrates the drawbacks of this type of entry, however. Uber faced competition from Didi Chuxing Technology Company, a Chinese ride- and taxi-hailing company. Didi had a deeper knowledge of local markets, which enabled it to add localized features that Uber could not easily innovate. Didi also had deeper relationships with Chinese authorities. For example, even when app-based ride-hailing services were not totally legal, Didi partnered with Shanghai's government. Uber could not compete and in 2016 ultimately sold its business to Didi.

When entering the market with no foreign assistance, a company has little to no knowledge of local culture or business and little to no relationship with local authorities. These drawbacks can sometimes be severe, as was the case for Uber. So managers often explore other entry methods that involve some relationship with foreign individuals or companies.

Partner with a Foreign Firm

The entry strategy that involves the least commitment to a foreign firm is establishing a relationship with a foreign agent or distributor. This type of relationship instantly provides you with experienced agents who have valuable local knowledge and contacts. When using a foreign agent or distributor, a company typically does not station a representative in the country itself because the foreign agent handles all aspects of the distribution and promotion of the products.

Although this entry strategy allows you to commit a minimal amount of resources to your foreign sales, there are drawbacks. The biggest downside is your lack of control over operations. You must manage the process from a distance and decide how to incentivize your agent to work both diligently and honestly.

Local Office in a Foreign Market

Another common strategy is setting up a local office in your intended market managed by one (or more) of your employees. This commits more resources, but the advantage is greater control over the marketing and distribution of your product. In addition, your representatives provide direct contact with your customers, so they can quickly communicate any changes in the market.

One of the challenges of opening a local office in the country you want to enter is a possible lack of familiarity with the foreign market, local business laws, and/or local traditions. Your representative may not know the major local distributors or retailers. Unless your employees have previously lived in the target country, they may make social gaffes that cost you sales until they gain a greater understanding of the country's politics, culture, and social conventions.

Joint Venture with a Foreign Firm

A larger-scale entry strategy is creating a joint venture with a business already established in the foreign market. A *joint venture* results when two (or more) firms agree to develop a business unit together (jointly). The newly established joint venture might have a finite life, a designated point in time when one of the firms is entitled to buy out the other's share. Each firm contributes expertise and/or financial resources to the project and then shares in the joint venture's profits or losses. This sort of strategic alliance with an already established business may allow you to gain access to the skills and resources that are necessary for success in the new foreign market.

This approach involves risks, however, which are magnified if the objectives of the partners differ. For example, as a manager of a high-tech company, you may enter into a joint venture with a business in a developing nation. Your goal is to enter the market to make a profit. Your contribution to the joint venture is technology, and the other firm's contribution is country-based expertise in marketing and distributing the product. If, however, the objective of the foreign managers is to steal your technology for their firm's gain rather than contribute to the success of the joint venture, you are destined to fail. You must take steps to ensure achievement of the agreed-on objectives of the venture, perhaps by starting with small projects and working your way up to larger ventures as you establish trust between the firms.

Acquisition of or Merger with a Foreign Firm

If your business is large enough, you may have the option of merging with or acquiring a local business in order to enter the foreign market. Basically, this entry method provides you with all of the risks of the foreign venture as well as all of the profits.

Buying an ongoing business gives you instant access to a customer base. If you retain the local employees, you also immediately gain expertise in the market as well as knowledge of the local business climate and social mores. Buying an established firm helps you avoid some of the difficulties of entering an unfamiliar market on your own. It also allows you to sidestep the drawback of a joint venture described above: Once you own the foreign business, the acquired firm's objectives become the same as your own.

Of course, mergers or acquisitions have their own drawbacks. In addition to the significant financial investment, integrating the new foreign business into your firm can be challenging. For example, the business cultures in the two firms may be significantly different. Or on a more practical level the computer or accounting systems running the two businesses may be incompatible. In addition, you gain at least part of the reputation of the foreign firm. This can be an important benefit if the reputation is positive. On the other hand, if the foreign firm has a negative reputation, you have acquired another cost.

Franchising in a Foreign Market

Although not applicable to all business types, franchising can be an effective foreign market entry strategy. For example, Wyndham Hotels and Resorts has franchisees in over 20 countries. Franchising has the dual advantage of enlisting managers with local knowledge while expanding your worldwide presence without committing substantial financial sums.

Franchising is not a universal panacea, however. One drawback is immediately clear: Many businesses are simply not well suited to franchising. For example, it is difficult to envision how Peabody Energy, a major coal producer, could operate a coal-production franchise system.

Managers of companies that are suitable for franchising, such as Wyndham, face an important decision: Should the arrangement be direct franchising or master franchising? In *direct franchising*, the firm retains close control over their foreign franchisees. In *master franchising*, the firm deals with one local "master" franchisee that is, in turn, responsible for managing the franchise system. Direct franchising allows you to manage your franchisees as you deem best, but you sacrifice a great deal of high-level local expertise. Master franchising allows you to gain the high-level local knowledge you want at the expense of direct control over the franchisees.

Table 13.2 summarizes the advantages and disadvantages of the different methods of entering foreign markets.

U.S. Anticorruption Law: The Foreign Corrupt Practices Act

Managers marketing a product abroad must often deal with a corrupt business environment. Bribes, payoffs, and extortion are common and accepted as part of everyday life in some countries. Indeed, at one time, paying bribes to win

Table 13.2 **Comparing Entry Methods into Foreign Markets**

Entry Method	Advantages	Disadvantages
Independent	• Total control over operations • No concern that decision makers pursue their own business objectives	• No familiarity with foreign market, laws, traditions, and social customs • No relationship with local authorities • May need a significant financial commitment
Partner	• Immediately gain experienced agents • Lowest financial commitment	• No control over operations
Local office	• Control over marketing and distribution • Quick knowledge of changes in the market	• Lack of familiarity with foreign market, laws, traditions, and social customs
Joint venture	• Access to other firm's expertise, including knowledge of local markets and social customs	• Risk that the other firm may pursue objectives that interfere with the success of the joint venture
Merger or Acquisition	• Instant access to foreign customer base and knowledge of local markets and social customs • Shared profit-maximizing objective	• Significant financial commitment • Time and financial investment needed to integrate foreign business into existing company • Reputational risk
Franchising	• Typically small financial commitment • *Direct franchising:* Control over production, marketing, and distribution • *Master franchising:* Gain local expertise including knowledge of local markets and social customs	• Not applicable to some types of business • *Direct franchising:* Lack of familiarity with foreign market, laws, traditions, and social customs • *Master franchising:* Lack of control over local operations

business or favorable treatment was an accepted business practice in certain places, and these bribes were even tax deductible as a business expense. In 1977, reacting to revelations that U.S. firms had paid millions of dollars in bribes to friendly government leaders in Japan and the Netherlands, the U.S. government passed the world's first anticorruption law, the **Foreign Corrupt Practices Act (FCPA)**, which prohibits bribery of foreign officials. The FCPA applies to any company whose stock is publicly traded in the United States, is organized under the laws of the United States, and/or is principally located in the United States. For example, because its stock is publicly traded in the United States, Teva Pharmaceutical Industries falls under the FCPA even though it is an Israeli company. Indeed, in 2016, the company paid the United States $519 million to settle FCPA violations.

The aspects of the FCPA most pertinent to managing a firm in a foreign market are its positions on bribes, bookkeeping, and mergers.

Foreign Corrupt Practices Act (FCPA) A U.S. anticorruption law that prohibits bribery of foreign officials.

Bribes

The FCPA has two parts. The first part prohibits individuals and firms from "corruptly (making) . . . an offer, . . . promise, . . . payment of any money, or giving anything of value to any foreign official for the purposes of . . . securing any improper advantage . . . in obtaining or retaining business." Firms and individuals are also expected to implement policies and practices that reduce the risk that employees or agents will engage in bribery. Put more simply, this part of the FCPA prohibits employees and representatives of U.S. firms from bribing foreign officials. Two questions emerge from this brief description:

- **Who is a government official?** In some instances, the identity of a government official is clear: The official who inspects the import papers for the products you bring into the country definitely is a government official. Bribing this official is illegal. But in other cases, the answer to this question is less obvious. For example, is a doctor who works for a state-owned hospital a government official? According to judicial interpretation of the FCPA, the answer to this question is yes. Indeed, pharmaceutical companies, including Johnson & Johnson, Pfizer, and Eli Lilly, have paid millions of dollars in fines for FCPA violations in Greece, China, Poland, and elsewhere for bribing health-care providers who worked for state-owned health facilities.
- **What is a bribe?** Deciding whether an action constitutes a bribe is sometimes difficult. For example, the FCPA allows *facilitating payments*, also called *grease payments*. Facilitating payments are small payments made to government officials to expedite or secure (or grease) their routine work. For example, paying customs officials $10 each to convince them to delay their lunch hours until they have approved your team's entry papers into their country is a facilitating payment and legal under the FCPA. Paying the same officials $500 to overlook a flaw in your papers is a bribe and therefore illegal.

  Some situations are clearly illegal. For example, say that you are selling to a foreign government and invite foreign officials to a sales meeting at your headquarters. If you pay for their first-class flight to the meeting, pick up the tab for their five-star lodging and Michelin-ranked dining experience, and cover the cost of an afternoon golfing event at an exclusive private club, government authorities will consider your actions a bribe. If instead the officials pay for the flight and lodging, while your company pays for a modest dinner with sales representatives in attendance and no one plays golf, the dinner expense is probably a legal marketing expense. The amount that a firm or representative can spend on foreign officials before the expenditure is considered illegal is uncertain.

There are two final points about bribes or other illegal payments that are important for success in a foreign market:

1. The bribe need not be paid to be illegal. Simply promising a bribe or an illegal payment is an FCPA violation.
2. Even if the bribed official does not carry through on the promised action, payment or promise of the bribe remains a violation of the FCPA.

Bookkeeping

The second part of the FCPA concerns a company's bookkeeping: Companies must keep "books and records that accurately and fairly reflect the transactions" of the corporation. In other words, if a company pays a $1 million bribe to a government official, the company must record the payment as a bribe in order to avoid violating the bookkeeping provisions. Of course, recording the payment as a bribe incriminates the company under the antibribery provisions of the FCPA. It is obviously best to avoid the possibility of bribery entirely.

DECISION
SNAPSHOT

JPMorgan "Sons and Daughters" Program

For 10 years ending in 2016, JPMorgan had a policy of hiring the relatives and friends of high Chinese government officials. In 2009, JPMorgan executives issued instructions to give priority to hires that were linked to potential business transactions. The candidates employed under this program were hired as entry-level investment bankers and paid the entry-level investment banker salary even though they were often assigned tasks such as filing. If you were an enforcement official with the Department of Justice, would you pursue an FCPA case against JPMorgan?

Answer

The officials with the Department of Justice pursued and eventually won an FCPA case against JPMorgan. Although hiring relatives and friends of foreign government officials is not necessarily illegal, it becomes an FCPA bribery violation when the hiring is linked to future business. In 2016, JPMorgan paid fines and other sanctions of $264 million to settle charges of bribery and false bookkeeping as well as other charges related to its "Sons and Daughters" program.

Mergers

One last point about the FCPA is important for companies entering a foreign market. If your company purchases another company that is in violation of the FCPA, your company has purchased that company's problem. For example, Pfizer, a huge pharmaceutical company, purchased Wyeth, another large pharmaceutical company. Wyeth had violated the FCPA in China, in part by treating doctors who worked for state-owned hospitals to lunches and vacations and improperly recording the payments. Even though Pfizer cooperated with U.S. government authorities, the company had to pay a fine of nearly $20 million for the bookkeeping violations that Wyeth had made before the purchase. The lesson here should by now be clear: Before engaging in a formal business relationship with another company, due diligence is essential.

U.K. Bribery Act

After the U.S. government enacted the FCPA, many other nations promised to enact similar anticorruption laws. Only a few have actually followed through. Possibly the most significant foreign law is the **U.K. Bribery Act**, a 2010 British anticorruption law prohibiting bribery of foreign citizens and government officials. Any company doing business in the United Kingdom is subject to prosecution if it violates this law regardless of the location of the infraction. Consequently, under the U.K. Bribery Act, it would be possible for Walmart, a U.S.-based firm with operations in the U.K., to be prosecuted for bribery that took place in Mexico. Nearly all aspects of the U.K. Bribery Act are harsher than the U.S. FCPA:

U.K. Bribery Act A 2010 British anticorruption law prohibiting bribery of foreign citizens and government officials.

- The U.K. Bribery Act prohibits bribery of *both* government officials *and* private citizens.
- All facilitating payments are illegal.
- Both the receipt and the payment of a bribe are illegal.

Table 13.3 Comparing the FCPA and the U.K. Bribery Act

	FCPA	U.K. Bribery Act
Coverage	Foreign government officials	Foreign and domestic government officials; foreign and domestic private individuals
Facilitating payments	Not prohibited	Illegal
Receipt of bribe	Not prohibited	Illegal
Sanction	Fines and imprisonment	Fines and imprisonment

Under the U.K. Bribery Act, bribery is virtually illegal per se. The *only* defense is that the bribery was necessary for the functioning of the intelligence services or the armed forces. The penalties for violations can be severe. Individuals convicted under this act can face up to 10 years in prison and unlimited fines.

Table 13.3 compares the FCPA and the U.K. Bribery Act. It is clear that the U.K. Bribery Act is stricter, as it prohibits many more acts than does the FCPA.

SOLVED PROBLEM

Legal or Illegal?

Presuming the enforcing agency has jurisdiction, which of the following situations are legal under the FCPA? Under the U.K. Bribery Act?

a. In a war-torn country, military police surround your sales representatives and demand $1,000 to avoid imprisoning them. The representatives quickly hand over the money, and the police set them free.

b. Your company is trying to make a sale in France to a firm like Carrefour S.A., a privately owned French company that helped pioneer the hypermarket concept (the combination of a supermarket and a department store). Your representatives pay officials at the French company €20,000 to seal the deal.

c. In a developing country, your representative pays the local police chief $100 per month to ensure that the police patrol your local manufacturing facility.

Answer

a. This expenditure is legal under both the FCPA and the U.K. Bribery Act. Paying this ransom is not a bribe because imprisoning sales representatives is not part of the duties of the military police.

b. This expenditure is legal under the FCPA because the officials your company is bribing are not government officials. It is illegal under the U.K. Bribery Act because that law prohibits bribing government officials *and* private-sector officials.

c. Under the FCPA, the payments themselves are probably not illegal because they are facilitating payments. The U.K. Bribery Act prohibits facilitating payments, however. Although the payments are illegal, they are so small that British authorities might choose not to prosecute your firm.

13.6 Marketing and Promotional Decisions

Learning Objective 13.6 Use the theories behind advertising and promotion to make better managerial decisions.

For many organizations, marketing and promotion can make the difference between success and failure. As you have learned, marginal analysis can help guide you to making maximizing decisions. In this section, we examine two situations in which marketing and promotions decisions are particularly difficult—namely, when you must make decisions on industry-wide advertisements and when you are using resale price maintenance. Finally, we conclude with a short piece of advice on an issue that can be fraught with personal liability, decisions concerning foreign marketing and promotion.

Industry-Wide Advertising

Managers of industry-wide trade associations face some unique challenges because, as you have learned, industry-wide advertising is a public good—it's nonexcludable, so it benefits every firm even if the firm did not help pay for it, and it's nonrival, so one firm's benefit from the advertising does not decrease the other firms' benefits. The public-good issues make optimal industry-wide advertising difficult to achieve because each firm's managers have the incentive to free ride by not paying for the advertising. In addition to the problem of free riding, each participating firm also has an incentive to protest that it is paying too much for the advertising and promotion compared to its competitors. Managers of franchisors do not face these issues for their system-wide advertising because the franchisees are contractually bound to pay for the advertising. Managers of industry-wide agricultural associations are also fortunate because they can eliminate free riding using the law that makes checkoff payments mandatory. Managers of other industry trade associations are not so lucky. Although each trade association's situation is unique, some general observations apply to all.

As a manager of an industry-wide trade organization, your decisions are easier if the member firms' marginal benefits and objectives are similar. In this happy event, there will be less disagreement among the firms about the amount of the industry-wide advertising, so reaching consensus on the optimal amount is more straightforward. In addition, the greater the similarities are in the firms' marginal benefit schedules, the easier it will be for you to arrive at a payment schedule that does not create dissatisfaction. If every firm has the same marginal benefit, then requiring everyone to pay the same amount will probably not cause dissension among the managers. Identical marginal benefits of the participating firms is a pipe dream, but if you can put similar firms into groups and then charge each firm in a group the same amount, you might be able to limit some of the potential discord. For example, you could create two different groups, one for large manufacturers and the other for small manufacturers, and then set the fees so that each firm in a group pays the same amount as every other firm in that group. Creating small groups has another advantage when it comes to free riding: The smaller number of firms in a group makes it easier for the managers within that group to monitor one another's behavior, thereby making free riding less likely.

Resale Price Maintenance

For a manufacturer, increasing the equilibrium quantity sold in the retail market is the key to successful use of resale price maintenance. The product-specific services the retailers provide increase the demand for the product but also decrease the supply. To achieve the goal of increasing the quantity, the increase in demand *must* exceed the decrease in supply. To see a key economic interpretation of this result, first consider the reasons why demand and supply change:

- **Increase in demand.** The increase in demand occurs because consumers value the product-specific services. You can measure that value by the increase in the price consumers are willing to pay. Let's return to the memory-foam pillow example, illustrated in Figure 13.7. The demand curve without the product-specific services (D_0) shows that for the 4 millionth pillow the maximum price consumers will pay for that pillow *without* any services is $100. Once the retailers provide a product-specific service, such as displaying the pillows so the customers can see and touch them, the demand curve with the product-specific service (D_1) shows that for the 4 millionth pillow the maximum price consumers will pay for that pillow *with* the service is $140. The consumers value this service at $40 per pillow. This result generalizes: For each service provided, the demand curve shifts upward by an amount equal to consumers' valuation of that service.
- **Decrease in supply.** The decrease in supply occurs because of the increase in the retailers' marginal cost from providing the product-specific service. The increase in the marginal cost equals the vertical difference between the supply curve with the product-specific service (S_1) and the supply curve without the product-specific service (S_0) in Figure 13.7. For example, at a quantity of 4 million pillows, the vertical difference between the supply curves is $20, which means that the marginal cost of providing the service is $20 per pillow. This result also generalizes: For each service provided, the supply curve shifts upward by an amount equal to the marginal cost of providing of the service.

Resale price maintenance is profitable for the manufacturer only if the equilibrium quantity increases, which occurs if the increase in demand is greater than the decrease in supply. Accordingly, resale price maintenance is profitable only if the consumers' valuation of the service exceeds the retailers' marginal cost of providing it. As Figure 13.7 illustrates,

Figure 13.7 The Value and Cost of a Product-Specific Service

The vertical difference between the demand curves with and without a product-specific service is equal to consumers' valuation of the service. The vertical difference between the supply curves with and without the service is equal to retailers' marginal cost of providing the service. For the 4 millionth pillow, consumers value the service retailers provide at $40 per pillow, and retailers incur a marginal cost of $20 per pillow for providing that service.

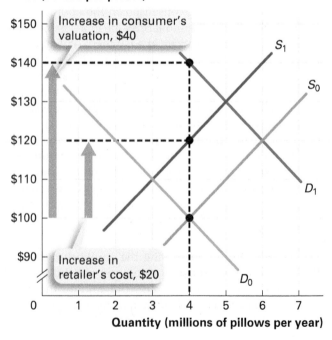

this is the case for the memory-foam pillows, so the increase in demand exceeds the decrease in supply, making this product-specific service profitable for the manufacturer.

If retail suppliers can provide a variety of product-specific services, the manufacturer's managers can increase their profit by setting the minimum resale price at a level high enough to pay for all of the services with marginal costs that are lower than consumers' valuations. Applying marginal analysis, you can conclude that the profit-maximizing amount of product-specific services is the amount that sets the marginal benefit of the service (the consumers' valuation) equal to the marginal cost (the retailers' cost of providing the service). Once you have determined the profit-maximizing quantity of services, you should set the minimum price so that it covers the retailers' costs of selling the product *plus* the cost of the quantity of product-specific services that maximizes your profit.

Foreign Marketing Issues

The managerial lessons from laws preventing corruption are difficult. If your career requires you to spend time in developing nations, undoubtedly you will face issues dealing with bribes and other forms of corruption. Clearly, paying bribes is illegal. By paying bribes, you run the risk of harming your career and even of serving jail time if the authorities discover the violation and decide to prosecute. On the other hand, by not paying bribes, you might cause both a significant loss of business for your company and a setback in your career. From the standpoint of career advancement, there is no clear-cut solution. One factor to keep in mind is that the FCPA allows you to make small facilitating payments, but the U.K. Bribery Act does *not*. Of course, there is no bright, shining line to guide you when walking the fine line between a facilitating payment and a bribe.

Here is one solid piece of advice, however: If you know that your competitors are bribing officials, there is no downside to reporting the situation to the proper U.S. or U.K. officials. If you are not paying bribes and you can force your competitors to stop their bribery, you can level the playing field and enhance your chances for success in a difficult foreign market.

Revisiting Heads Up for Advertising Decisions at Riddell

Riddell's managers maximize their profit by applying marginal analysis and purchasing the amount of advertising that sets the marginal benefit from advertising equal to its marginal cost. The marginal benefit from advertising is the increase in Riddell's gross profit—that is, its profit not counting the cost of its advertising. Because Riddell is a price taker in the market for advertising, the marginal cost is the price of advertising.

Figure 13.8 shows the effect of advertising. Initially, the demand curve for Riddell helmets is D_0, and the marginal revenue curve is MR_0. Managers maximize profit by producing 20,000 helmets and setting a price of $250 per helmet. Riddell's total (net) profit is $80,000, equal to the area of the light rectangle.

Suppose that the price of an advertising campaign is $50,000. When Riddell's managers undertake an additional campaign, demand increases, so that the demand curve shifts to D_1 and the marginal revenue curve shifts to MR_1. The marginal benefit from the additional advertising campaign is the increase in gross profit, which is the darker green area in the figure, or $160,000. Gross profit increases because (1) consumers are willing to pay a higher price for the initial 20,000 helmets sold and (2) consumers buy more helmets. The net profit from the advertising campaign equals the gross profit minus the cost of the campaign, or $160,000 − $50,000 = $110,000. Because the net profit increases, Riddell's managers will undertake the advertising. Riddell's managers continue to
(Continues)

Revisiting Heads Up for Advertising Decisions at Riddell (*continued*)

Figure 13.8 Riddell's Advertising

Before it advertises, Riddell produces 20,000 helmets a year at a price of $250 per helmet. Riddell's advertising shifts the demand curve from D_0 to D_1 and the marginal revenue curve from MR_0 to MR_1. The advertising enables Riddell to boost its price to $254 per helmet. Riddell's managers further increase their profit by raising production to 30,000 helmets. The additional gross profit (which does *not* take into account the cost of advertising) equals the additional profit from the higher price on the initial quantity of 20,000 helmets sold ($4 \times 20{,}000 = \$80{,}000$) plus the profit on the additional 10,000 helmets produced ($8 \times 10{,}000 = \$80{,}000$), or $160,000.

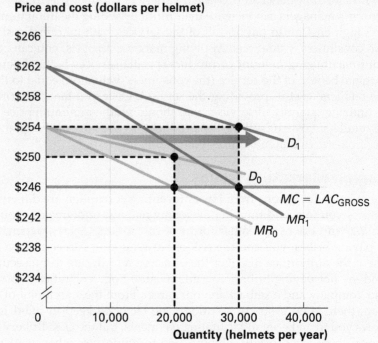

Price and cost (dollars per helmet)

buy more advertising until they reach the point where the marginal benefit from the advertising equals its marginal cost because at that point they have maximized Riddell's (net) profit.

As noted in the chapter-opening scenario, Riddell advertises in more than one medium. For simplicity, suppose that there are two: Internet and traditional retail advertising in sports-related magazines. The managers maximize their profit by purchasing the quantity of advertising that sets the marginal benefit (*MB*) from each type of advertising equal to its marginal cost. If the marginal cost is equal to the price of the advertising (*P*), then Riddell's managers maximize their profit by buying the quantity of Internet advertising that sets $MB_{INT} = P_{INT}$ and the quantity of traditional retail advertising that sets $MB_{RET} = P_{RET}$.

The helmet that Riddell advertised as reducing concussions by 31 percent has elements of all three types of goods: inspection, experience, and credence. It's an inspection good if consumers are able to check Riddell's research before buying a helmet. It's an experience good if consumers are able to confirm the *general* claim that the helmet reduces concussions by experience with the helmet. It is, however, highly unlikely that experience

alone will enable consumers to determine the validity of the precise claim of a 31 percent reduction, so, without analyzing the research that is the basis for this numerical claim, the helmet is a credence good. It is likely that this aspect of the helmet makes it an experience or a credence good, so the FTC could be concerned about the truth of Riddell's advertising claim. If FTC investigators determined that the advertised claim of fewer concussions was false or deceptive, they could secure a cease-and-desist order or seek a court injunction to stop the false advertising. The FTC could force Riddell to run corrective advertisements, to pay civil sanctions, to disgorge the ill-gotten profit, and/or otherwise penalize the company. The FTC could also pursue the managers and force them to pay civil penalties.

In the actual case mentioned in the chapter opener, the FTC did investigate Riddell's claim of reducing concussion risk by 31 percent. The investigators determined that the claim was unsubstantiated and therefore false. The FTC did not impose or seek civil sanctions for Riddell or its managers. Instead, at the FTC's insistence, Riddell's managers agreed to abandon their unsubstantiated claims that their helmets reduced the risk of concussions.

Summary: The Bottom Line

13.1 Profit-Maximizing Advertising by a Firm

- If a firm possesses market power, advertising and promoting its product can increase demand.
- The marginal benefit from advertising is the increase in gross profit (profit without taking into account the cost of the advertising) resulting from the increase in demand. The profit-maximizing amount of advertising is the quantity that sets the marginal benefit from advertising equal to the marginal cost of advertising.
- The profit-maximizing amounts of different types of advertising are the quantities that set the marginal benefit from each type of advertising equal to its marginal cost.

13.2 Optimal Advertising by an Industry

- Managers of industry-wide trade associations sometimes advertise promoting the industry rather than an individual firm.
- Industry-wide advertising is a public good—that is, a good or service that is nonexcludable (all producers in the market can use it regardless of whether they paid for it) and nonrival (one person's or one firm's use does not decrease the quantity available for everyone else).
- For each quantity of advertising, the *industry-wide* marginal benefit equals the sum of all of the *firms'* marginal benefits. The optimal quantity of industry-wide advertising is the amount that sets the industry-wide marginal benefit equal to the marginal cost of the advertising.
- The optimal quantity of industry-wide advertising is difficult to achieve for three reasons: (1) The industry-wide marginal benefit schedule requires knowledge of each firm's marginal benefit, (2) each firm's managers have the incentive to be a free rider, and (3) determining a method of allocating the cost of the advertising acceptable to all of the firms is difficult.

13.3 False Advertising

- False advertising is advertising that misrepresents the nature, characteristics, or qualities of goods or services.
- Goods can be divided into three types: inspection goods, whose characteristics consumers can assess before purchasing; experience goods, which consumers have to use before evaluating their characteristics; and credence goods, which consumers cannot evaluate even after consuming. False advertising can affect the demand for experience goods and credence goods but not inspection goods.
- Greenwashing is false advertisements or claims that a firm is behaving in an environmentally friendly way or producing an environmentally friendly product.

- Firms that engage in false advertising can harm their reputations, which decreases demand and lowers future profitability.
- The Federal Trade Commission (FTC), the government agency responsible for prosecuting false advertising, can respond to false advertising in the following ways: (1) issue a cease-and-desist order; (2) seek a court injunction to stop the advertising; (3) force the firm to run corrective advertisements; and/or (4) file civil suits against the company and its managers seeking disgorgement of the profit, repayment of customers, and other financial penalties.

13.4 Resale Price Maintenance and Product Promotion

- Resale price maintenance is a business practice in which manufacturers sell products to retailers with the explicit condition that the retailers may not resell the products below a specified price. It eliminates competition based on price, so retailers instead compete by offering product-specific services.
- In the absence of resale price maintenance, each retail firm's managers have the incentive to free ride by allowing other retailers to offer the (costly) product-specific services. Free-riding firms can sell the product at a lower price and make a higher profit. Resale price maintenance eliminates the ability of free riders to set a lower retail price.
- Manufacturers want retailers to offer those product-specific services that increase the retail demand for the product more than they decrease the retail supply because in this case the service increases the quantity manufacturers sell through retailers.

13.5 International Marketing: Entry and Corruption Laws

- Firms entering foreign markets can (1) enter independently with no foreign firm association, (2) partner with a foreign agent or distributor, (3) open an office in the foreign nation, (4) enter into a joint venture with a foreign business, (5) merge with or acquire a foreign business, or (6) establish franchisees in the foreign country.
- Companies doing business abroad should avoid violating anticorruption laws, including the U.S. Foreign Corrupt Practices Act (FCPA) and the U.K. Bribery Act.

13.6 Managerial Application: Marketing and Promotional Decisions

- Preventing disagreements among members about the advertising fees they pay and avoiding members' attempts to free ride are important challenges faced by managers

of industry-wide trade associations. Creating small groups of similar members and charging each group's members the same fee can minimize disagreement. The members of small groups can more easily monitor other members to limit attempts to free ride.
- Product-specific services increase demand because they increase the consumers' valuation of the product, but they decrease supply because they raise the retailers'

marginal cost. Manufacturers should set the minimum resale price at a level that covers the retailers' costs, including the cost of providing all the product-specific services that consumers value more than the cost of providing them.
- If you become aware that competitors are bribing foreign officials, you should report these acts to the proper authorities.

Key Terms and Concepts

False advertising	Greenwashing	Public good
Foreign Corrupt Practices Act (FCPA)	Marginal benefit from advertising	U.K. Bribery Act
Free rider	Product-specific services	

Questions and Problems

13.1 Profit-Maximizing Advertising by a Firm

Learning Objective 13.1 Apply marginal analysis to determine the profit-maximizing amount of advertising.

1.1 Successful advertising shifts the demand curve of a product. What is the relationship between the shift in the demand curve and the marginal benefit from advertising?

1.2 You are the manager of a local wood-fired pizzeria. Currently, you do not advertise. Your marginal cost and long-run average gross cost are both constant and equal to $8 per pizza. You are thinking about advertising. If you advertise, you can run one or two advertising campaigns. Each advertising campaign costs $600. The table shows three demand schedules according to the amount of advertising.

Price	Quantity Demanded (no advertising campaign)	Quantity Demanded (1 advertising campaign)	Quantity Demanded (2 advertising campaigns)
9	500	700	800
10	400	600	700
11	300	500	600
12	200	400	500
13	100	300	400
14	0	200	300
15	0	100	200
16	0	0	100
17	0	0	0

a. Draw the demand, marginal revenue, and marginal cost curves with no advertising. (Hint: The marginal revenue curve has the same vertical intercept as the demand curve, and its slope equals twice that of the demand curve.) What are the profit-maximizing price and quantity and the economic profit?

b. What is the marginal benefit from the first advertising campaign?

c. From the second campaign?

d. Is the first advertising campaign profitable? The second campaign? Explain your answers.

1.3 You are a manager at a large soft drink firm like PepsiCo. Each year you sell 6 billion servings of Mountain Delight at the price of $0.499. The long-run average gross cost of a serving is constant and is equal to $0.40 per serving. You are thinking of running an additional 30-second advertisement or an additional 60-second advertisement during the Super Bowl.

a. You determine that running the 30-second advertisement will raise the price consumers are willing to pay for the initial 6 billion servings by $0.001 (1/10 of a cent) per serving. You also determine that the advertisement will allow you to sell 1 million more servings at a new price of $0.50 per serving. The price of a 30-second Super Bowl commercial is $5 million. Should you buy the advertisement? Why or why not?

b. You determine that running the 60-second advertisement will raise the price consumers are willing to pay for the initial 6 billion servings by $0.0015 per serving. You also determine that the advertisement will allow you to sell 2 million more servings at a price of $0.5015 per serving. The price of a 60-second Super Bowl commercial is $10 million. Should you buy the advertisement? Why or why not?

1.4 As the manager of a local restaurant, you are considering various advertising campaigns. Each campaign costs $500 per week. You estimate that the first campaign raises your gross profit by $1,000, the second campaign raises it by $750, the third campaign raises it by $500, and the fourth campaign raises it by $250. What is the profit-maximizing number of advertising campaigns? Explain your answer.

1.5 Your car wash company is advertising on local radio, on local television, and via direct mail. You believe that a radio campaign raises your gross profit by $100, a television campaign raises it by $200, and a direct mail campaign raises it by $50. The cost of a radio campaign is $50, the cost of a television campaign is $75, and the cost of a direct mail campaign is $50.
   a. If you cannot change your total advertising budget, should you reallocate your spending? If yes, explain how. If no, explain why not.
   b. If you can change your advertising budget, should you change your spending on advertising? If yes, explain the changes you would make. If no, explain why not.

1.6 You are a sales manager at a firm like Orkin, a large pest control company that sells its services through annual subscriptions. You are considering a series of national advertising campaigns. Each campaign has an annual price of $4 million. You determine that the first campaign will raise your gross profit by $12 million, the second campaign will raise it by $8 million, the third campaign will raise it

by $4 million, the fourth campaign will raise it by $2 million, and the fifth campaign will raise it by $1 million.
   a. What is your marginal benefit schedule from these campaigns?
   b. What is the marginal cost of an advertising campaign?
   c. What is the profit-maximizing number of advertising campaigns to buy?

13.2 Optimal Advertising by an Industry

Learning Objective 13.2 Describe how trade association managers can determine the optimal amount of industry-wide advertising and allocate its cost.

2.1 Why is industry-wide advertising a public good? How does free riding affect industry-wide advertisements by trade associations?

2.2 According to the Cattlemen's Beef Board (CBB), each $1 from the checkoff program spent on advertising and promotion of beef raises members' gross profit by $5. Is CBB buying the profit-maximizing amount of advertising? Explain your answer.

2.3 You are a manager of a trade association. Your members have fixed your advertising budget and will not allow you to change it. You allocate your advertising in two ways: television and magazines. The price of a local television advertisement (P_{TV}) is $200, and the price of a magazine advertisement (P_{MAG}) is $4,000. The marginal benefit from a television advertisement (MB_{TV}) is $3,000, and the marginal benefit from a magazine advertisement (MB_{MAG}) is $80,000. Are you optimally allocating your advertising budget? Explain your answer.

2.4 You are the head of an industry trade association. The table shows the marginal benefit from advertising for the four firms in the industry.

Accompanies problem 2.4.

Quantity of Advertisements (units)	Firm A Marginal Benefit	Firm B Marginal Benefit	Firm C Marginal Benefit	Firm D Marginal Benefit
1	$100	$150	$200	$250
2	80	120	160	200
3	60	90	120	150
4	40	60	80	100
5	20	30	40	50

a. What is the industry-wide marginal benefit schedule from advertising?
b. Suppose that the price of an advertisement is $280. What is the profit-maximizing quantity of industry-wide advertisements?
c. What is the total cost of the profit-maximizing quantity of industry-wide advertisements?
d. What is a fair allocation of the cost of this advertising among the four firms? Explain your answer.
e. What problem do you face in trying to allocate the cost? Explain your answer.

13.3 False Advertising

Learning Objective 13.3 Analyze why managers of some firms engage in false advertising despite possible sanctions by the Federal Trade Commission.

3.1 Is it possible for a firm to make a profit by engaging in false advertising? Explain your answer.

3.2 Indicate whether each of the following is a characteristic of an inspection good, an experience good, or a credence good, and explain each answer.
a. The durability of an automobile tire
b. The *scheduled* takeoff of a flight to Atlanta
c. The organic nature of prepackaged chicken
d. The weight of a smartphone
e. The battery life of a smartphone
f. The quality of the replacement fender for an automobile involved in an accident

3.3 Why might managers of firms selling tires be more concerned about their company's reputation than managers of gas stations?

3.4 If you believe a competitor is engaging in false advertising that is reducing your profit, what can you do?

13.4 Resale Price Maintenance and Product Promotion

Learning Objective 13.4 Explain the legal status of resale price maintenance and its use in product promotion.

4.1 Provide three examples of product-specific services different from those presented in the chapter.

4.2 How can retailers free ride on the provision of product-specific services? How does free riding affect the manufacturer of the product?

4.3 How can resale price maintenance increase a manufacturer's profit?

4.4 Canon Incorporated and Nikon Corporation are both large manufacturers of cameras that they sell using a network of competitive retailers. Suppose that you are a manager at a similar company. The figure shows the retail demand and supply curves for your cameras. You and the other managers know that if your retailers display the cameras, at each price it increases the demand by 4 million cameras and decreases the supply by 1 million. And if the retailers then demonstrate the cameras, at each price it increases the demand by another 3 million and decreases the supply by another 1 million.

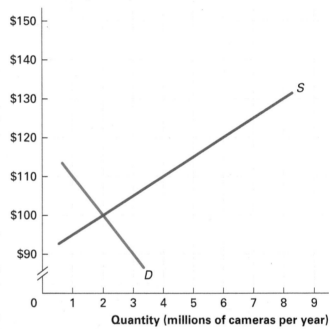

a. Which, if any, of these services (display and demonstration) should you want your retailers to perform?
b. In general, what minimum price should you set for your company's camera? Using the figure, what specific price should you set?

4.5 After you imposed resale price maintenance for your product in the southeastern part of the United States, you noticed an increase in profit. You then imposed resale price maintenance throughout the United States, and once again your profit increased. Now you are eager to require resale price maintenance in France and Germany. What issues might you face if you do so?

13.5 International Marketing: Entry and Corruption Laws

Learning Objective 13.5 Discuss different methods of entering foreign markets and ways to avoid violating anticorruption laws when doing business abroad.

5.1 Horner Sports Flooring, located in Dollar Bay, Michigan, is a long-established company producing wooden floors for basketball courts. The company makes its floors from hard maple, which is wood from sugar maple trees. Sugar maples grow in northeastern Canada and the northeastern United States. Suppose that the managers at Horner Sports Flooring want to sell their floors in Europe and have hired you as a consultant. How would you suggest the company enter the European market? Explain your recommendation.

5.2 You are involved in a joint venture with a foreign firm. The contract for the joint venture gives you the right to buy the project in three years. You worry that the foreign firm has been bribing government officials in order to win contracts. Do you have any reason to be concerned about the possible bribery if you purchase the venture? Why or why not?

5.3 You are a manager at a firm like Sanofi, a French pharmaceutical company doing business in China, the United Kingdom, and the United States. Like Sanofi, your stock is traded on the New York Stock exchange and the London Stock Exchange.
   a. Some of your sales representatives gave doctors employed in state-owned Chinese hospitals very expensive Rolex watches for prescribing your drugs. Is your firm potentially liable under the FCPA? Under the U.K. Bribery Act? Explain your answers.
   b. Other sales representatives gave doctors employed in privately owned Brazilian hospitals very expensive Rolex watches, also for prescribing your drugs. Is your firm potentially liable under the FCPA? Under the U.K. Bribery Act? Explain your answers.

5.4 Suppose that you work for a large U.S. aerospace company like Boeing. Which of the following actions is an FCPA violation? Explain each of your answers.
   a. One of your sales agents promises and then gives a Brazilian government official $50,000 to award a contract to your company. The official follows through, and your firm gets a government contract for $50 million.

   b. One of your sales agents promises but then does *not* give a Brazilian government official $50,000 to award a contract to your company. Nonetheless, the official follows through, and your firm gets a government contract for $50 million.
   c. One of your sales agents promises and then gives a Brazilian government official $50,000 to award a contract to your company. The official does not follow through, and your firm does not get the government contract.

13.6 Managerial Application: Marketing and Promotional Decisions

Learning Objective 13.6 Use the theories behind advertising and promotion to make better managerial decisions.

6.1 You are a manager of a company that produces advanced televisions sold through competitive retailers. If your retailers demonstrate the televisions, demand increases, so that consumers are willing to pay $10 more per television.
   a. The marginal cost to the retailers of demonstrating the television is $15. To maximize your profit, do you want the retailers to demonstrate your television? Why or why not?
   b. Now suppose that the marginal cost of demonstrating the television is $5. Do you want the retailers to demonstrate your television? Why or why not?

6.2 You are a sales manager for a manufacturing company that sells its product through perfectly competitive retail outlets. The table shows the market supply schedule for the retailers and the market demand schedule for the consumers.

Price (dollars per unit)	Quantity Supplied (units per week)	Quantity Demanded (units per week)
$58	10,000	12,000
59	11,000	11,000
60	12,000	10,000
61	13,000	9,000
62	14,000	8,000
63	15,000	7,000

   a. What are the equilibrium retail price and the equilibrium quantity?
   b. If the retailers offer consumers the chance to examine your product, demand increases.

At each quantity, the price consumers are willing to pay for each unit increases by $4. Offering these services increases suppliers' marginal cost by $2 per unit. What is the new equilibrium retail price and quantity? Does providing these services increase your company's profit? Why or why not?

c. You decide to use resale price maintenance to give your retailers the incentive to provide product demonstrations. What minimum price should you set? Explain your answer.

6.3 Good Burger is a chain of franchised hamburger restaurants. The franchisees are required to contribute 4 percent of their revenue to the franchisor for advertising. Suppose that the franchisor uses half of the fund for advertising that boosts the demand for the chain's burgers and the other half for advertising intended to expand the number of franchisees nationwide.

a. If the demand-enhancing advertisements are successful, how do they affect a franchisee's price and quantity of hamburgers?

b. If the advertisements intended to increase the number of franchisees wind up substantially increasing the number of Good Burger locations, how do these advertisements affect an existing franchisee's price and quantity of hamburgers?

MyLab Economics Auto-Graded Excel Projects

13.1 The Blue Line Lounge and Grill is one of the most popular martini bars in the Chicago area. While it serves food and other beverages, it is best known for its selection of 30 different martinis.

Suppose that a firm similar to the Blue Line Lounge and Grill is trying to decide how much advertising and promotion it should do and the corresponding price it should charge to maximize profit from the sale of martinis. For simplicity's sake, assume that demand for the firm's martinis is affected only by price and advertising. The firm needs to decide how many thousands of dollars to spend on advertising and promotion. Advertising and promotion for this firm include ads on local radio, social media advertising, and food and drink specials during slower times.

A template for the firm's demand and cost for martinis is completed in the illustrated spreadsheet. In it, the quantity of advertising is measured in thousands of dollars, so that advertising equal to 7 means $7,000 spent on advertising. Use this template, Solver, and the instructions to complete the table.

a. Start at an advertising level of 0, indicating no money spent on advertising. Using Solver, find the profit-maximizing price, and enter the information in the corresponding yellow cells in the table. Round all prices to the nearest penny.

b. Increase the advertising level to 1, indicating $1,000 spent on advertising. Using Solver, find the profit-maximizing price, and enter the information in the corresponding yellow cells in the table.

c. Repeat this process until you complete the table.

d. How many thousands of dollars should the firm spend on advertising? How many martinis does the firm expect to sell, and what is the expected profit from this sale?

e. Why would the firm limit its advertising to the amount you recommended in part d?

13.2 The Dakota Valley Booster Club in North Sioux City, SD, is a nonprofit organization that fundraises to support extracurricular activities at the Dakota Valley School District. The activities it supports include fine arts, athletics, and academic-related teams or groups. Each month, the club holds a tailgate or meal (depending on the season) and charges $5 a person. Food for the meals

	A	B	C
1	**DEMAND**		
2	Variables	Effect	Value
3	Intercept	500	1
4	Price	-35	0
5	Advertising	200	0
6	Advertising Squared	-15	0
7		Demand	500
8		Total Revenue	0
9	**COST**		
10	Variables	Effect	Value
11	Marginal Cost	2	500
12	Advertising Cost	1000	0
13		Total Cost	1000
14		Profit	-1000
15			

	A	B	C	D
1	Facebook Advertising			
2	Cost per Boost	$10		
3				
4	Units of Advertising	Expected Customers	Marginal Benefit in Dollars	MB/P
5	0	0		
6	1	20		
7	2	40		
8	3	55		
9	4	70		
10	5	80		
11	6	85		
12	7	90		
13	8	90		
14				
15	Newspaper Ads			
16	Cost per Week	$70		
17				
18	Units of Advertising	Expected Customers	Marginal Benefit in Dollars	MB/P
19	0	0		
20	1	45		
21	2	80		
22	3	105		
23	4	120		
24				
25	Flyers			
26	Cost per 100 (Includes Distribution)	$30		
27				
28	Units of Advertising	Expected Customers	Marginal Benefit in Dollars	MB/P
29	0	0		
30	1	30		
31	2	55		
32	3	75		
33	4	90		
34	5	100		
35	6	105		
36	7	105		
37				

is sponsored by local businesses, so all of the revenue received is "surplus" (profit) to be used for student activities. Getting the word out about the meals is important both because the amount of support the booster club can provide is related to its surplus from fund-raisers and because the businesses that agree to sponsor the food are doing so for marketing and visibility purposes. As a small nonprofit organization, advertising options and funding are limited.

Suppose that you are determining the amount of advertising to do for a small, non-profit booster club like the one at the Dakota Valley School District. You can elect to pay to boost visibility for the information placed on your Facebook group page; this means people in the area beyond those who subscribe to your posts will be able to see your event information. Another option is to place ads in the local newspaper. The local paper comes out once per week, meaning that you cannot do more than four advertisements before each meal. You can also print flyers and hire a high school student to distribute them at school functions. The cost

of each unit of advertising and the number of customers at each level of advertising are given in the tables.

a. Using the above information, calculate the marginal benefit in dollars from each unit of advertising for each type of advertising.

b. Using the marginal benefit you found in part a and the formulas from your textbook, find the marginal benefit per dollar spent on advertising for each kind of advertising at each level. This will tell you how many dollars of benefit you receive from each dollar spent.

c. Suppose that the booster club you are helping currently places an ad in the paper for each of the four weeks leading up to the meal, hands out 400 flyers, and does one boost on Facebook before the event. How much of each type of advertising would you recommend the club do?

d. If this booster club is limited to $110 of advertising for each meal, how much do you recommend it spend in each area? Why do you recommend this allocation?

The Calculus of Advertising

As a manager, you must determine how much funding to allocate to advertising your product or service. Chapter 13 uses marginal analysis to determine the profit-maximizing quantity of advertising and its allocation among different types of media. Using calculus can enhance the precision of the calculations but cannot ensure an advertising or promotion campaign's success. For example, why was one rabbit-oriented advertising campaigns (the Energizer bunny) a smash hit and another (Nesquik's National Bunny Ears Day) a total flop? A concrete answer to this question is best left to a marketing class. So to simplify our analysis we assume that the managers know the impact of their advertising in advance.

A. Profit-Maximizing Amount of Advertising with a Single Advertising Medium

All types of advertising and promotion share a single goal: to advance the agenda of the organization conducting the campaign. The focus of this section is the most common type of advertising—namely, advertising by profit-seeking firms. Determining the optimal amount of advertising by nonprofits, nongovernment organizations, and other groups is similar.

For-profit firms advertise to increase their profit, which means the goal of their advertising is to increase the demand for their product. Accordingly, we write the demand for the product as

$$Q = f(P, A)$$

where Q is the quantity demanded, f is the demand function, P is the price of the good, and A is the quantity of advertising. An increase in A increases the demand for the good or service.

The firm's total revenue equals $P \times Q$. Advertising increases the demand, which shifts the demand curve to the right and increases the profit-maximizing price and quantity. Because both the price and the quantity rise, total revenue also rises, making total revenue an increasing function of the quantity of advertising. Consequently, we can write the total revenue function as

$$\text{Total revenue} = TR(Q, A)$$

Advertising affects a firm's costs as well as product demand. It is a fixed cost because the quantity of advertising does not change when the quantity produced changes. So we can divide a firm's total cost into two parts: the variable cost of producing the good and the fixed cost of advertising:

$$\text{Total cost} = TC(Q) + (P_A \times A)$$

where $TC(Q)$ is the variable cost of producing the good, P_A is the price of a unit of advertising, and A is the quantity of advertising, so that $(P_A \times A)$ is the fixed cost of advertising.

Applying Calculus to the Profit-Maximization Rule

As you have learned, total profit equals total revenue minus total cost:

$$\text{Profit}(Q, A) = TR(Q, A) - [TC(Q) + (P_A \times A)] \qquad \textbf{A13.1}$$

To maximize profit, take the partial derivatives of the profit function in Equation A13.1 with respect to Q and A, and set them equal to zero to get the two first-order conditions:

$$\frac{\partial \text{Profit}}{\partial Q} = \frac{\partial TR}{\partial Q} - \frac{\partial TC}{\partial Q} = 0 \qquad\qquad \textbf{A13.2}$$

$$\frac{\partial \text{Profit}}{\partial A} = \frac{\partial TR}{\partial A} - P_A = 0 \qquad\qquad \textbf{A13.3}$$

In Equation A13.2, $\frac{\partial TR}{\partial Q}$ is the marginal revenue (MR), and $\frac{\partial TC}{\partial Q}$ is the marginal cost (MC), so Equation A13.2 is the familiar profit-maximization rule:

$$MR - MC = 0 \Rightarrow MR = MC \qquad\qquad \textbf{A13.4}$$

Equation A13.3 has a similar interpretation. In it, $\frac{\partial TR}{\partial A}$ is the change in revenue from changing advertising, so it is the marginal revenue from advertising. Call it MR_A. P_A is the price of a unit of advertising, so for a firm that cannot affect the price of advertising, it is the marginal cost of advertising—say, MC_A. Consequently, Equation A13.3 can be written as a version of a familiar profit-maximization rule:

$$MR_A - MC_A = 0 \Rightarrow MR_A = MC_A$$

Simultaneously solve the first-order conditions in Equations A13.2 and A13.3 to determine the profit-maximizing quantity of output, Q^*, and the profit-maximizing amount of advertising, A^*.

The procedure presented in the chapter, which does not use calculus, differs from that above. Without calculus, you solve the two first-order conditions sequentially, rather than simultaneously. So the chapter's analysis applies two steps to each possible amount of advertising:

1. For the different amounts of advertising, determine the maximum gross profit (profit excluding the cost of the advertising) by using the first-order condition to produce the quantity that sets $MR = MC$.

2. Use marginal analysis to select the amount of advertising that creates the largest profit.

Calculus allows you to solve for the profit-maximizing quantity and the profit-maximizing amount of advertising simultaneously and avoid having to determine the gross profit for each amount of advertising.

Applying Calculus to Maximize Profit from Advertising

To demonstrate how to maximize profit from a proposed advertising campaign, consider the following example. As a manager at a large soda company, you must make a decision about how many advertisements to run during the Super Bowl. These advertisements are expensive; let's assume that each costs $3.554 million. Of course, the advertisements increase the demand for your soda. Your analysts have estimated the demand function as

$$Q = 240{,}000{,}000 - 40{,}000{,}000P + 4{,}451{,}500A - 505{,}600A^2 \qquad \textbf{A13.5}$$

where Q is the quantity of 12-packs of soda, P is the price of a 12-pack, and A is the number of Super Bowl advertisements purchased. Your analysts also determine that your total cost is

$$TC = 1.22Q + 3{,}554{,}000A \qquad\qquad \textbf{A13.6}$$

where Q is (again) the number of 12-packs and A is (again) the number of advertisements. As noted above, each advertisement costs $3,554,000.

To calculate marginal revenue $\left(\frac{\partial TR}{\partial Q}\right)$, start by solving Equation A13.5 for P as a function of Q and A. The resulting equation is the *inverse demand* function:

$$P = 6 - 0.000000025Q + 0.11129A - 0.01264A^2 \qquad \textbf{A13.7}$$

Total revenue equals $P \times Q$, so multiply the expression for P in Equation A13.7 by Q to get total revenue:

Total revenue $= P \times Q = 6Q - 0.000000025Q^2 + (0.11129 \times A \times Q) - (0.01264 \times A^2 \times Q)$

A13.8

Finally, use the power rule to take the partial derivative of total revenue in Equation A13.8 with respect to quantity to determine the marginal revenue function:

$$MR = 6 - 0.00000005Q + 0.11129A - 0.01264A^2 \qquad \textbf{A13.9}$$

Next, use Equation A13.6 to calculate the marginal cost $\left(\frac{\partial TC}{\partial Q}\right)$ by partially differentiating the total cost in Equation A13.6 with respect to Q:

$$MC = 1.22 \qquad \textbf{A13.10}$$

One of the first-order conditions to maximize profit (Equation A13.4) is to produce the quantity that sets $MR = MC$. Using Equations A13.9 and A13.10, this first-order condition is

$$6 - 0.00000005Q + 0.11129A - 0.01264A^2 = 1.22 \qquad \textbf{A13.11}$$

The other first-order condition (Equation A13.3) requires setting $\frac{\partial TR}{\partial A}$ equal to P_A. To determine $\frac{\partial TR}{\partial A}$, use the power rule to take the partial derivative of total revenue (Equation A13.8) with respect to A:

$$\frac{\partial TR}{\partial A} = 0.11129Q - (0.02528 \times A \times Q) \qquad \textbf{A13.12}$$

Set Equation A13.12 $\left(\frac{\partial TR}{\partial A}\right)$ equal to P_A (\$3,554,000) to obtain the second first-order condition:

$$0.11129Q - (0.02528 \times A \times Q) = 3,554,000 \qquad \textbf{A13.13}$$

Solving the two first-order conditions (Equations A13.11 and A13.13) gives the profit-maximizing quantity of $Q = 100,000,000$ and the profit-maximizing number of advertisements of $A = 3$. In other words, your company maximizes profit by purchasing three Super Bowl advertisements and producing 100,000,000 12-packs of soda.

B. Profit-Maximizing Amount of Advertising with Two or More Advertising Media

The calculations by managers faced with a choice of more than one advertising medium are similar. Suppose that there are two different types of advertising, Internet and television. As a manager, you want to determine the profit-maximizing quantity to produce as well as the profit-maximizing amounts of both Internet and television advertising to purchase. Both types of advertising affect product demand and total revenue. In addition, both types of advertising are costly. The profit function in Equation A13.1 can be rewritten to show how the firm's total profit depends on both types of advertising:

$$\text{Profit} = TR(Q, A1, A2) - [TC(Q) + (P_{A1} \times A1) + (P_{A2} \times A2)] \qquad \textbf{A13.14}$$

where $A1$ is the quantity of Internet advertising, $A2$ is the quantity of television advertising, P_{A1} is the price of advertising $A1$, and P_{A2} is the price of advertising $A2$. To maximize profit, take the partial derivatives of profit in Equation A13.14 with respect to Q, $A1$, and $A2$ and set them equal to zero. This results in three first-order conditions:

$$\frac{\partial \text{Profit}}{\partial Q} = \frac{\partial TR}{\partial Q} - \frac{\partial TC}{\partial Q} = 0$$

$$\frac{\partial \text{Profit}}{\partial A1} = \frac{\partial TR}{\partial A1} - P_{A1} = 0$$

$$\frac{\partial \text{Profit}}{\partial A2} = \frac{\partial TR}{\partial A2} - P_{A2} = 0$$

These three first-order conditions can be solved simultaneously for the profit-maximizing quantity, Q, and the profit-maximizing amounts of both types of advertising, $A1$ and $A2$.

Extending the analysis to three or more types of advertising is straightforward: For the first-order conditions, use the $MR = MC$ rule to determine the profit-maximizing quantity, and then include an additional first-order condition for each type of advertising. Simultaneously solving these equations yields the profit-maximizing quantity and the profit-maximizing amounts of the different types of advertising.

Calculus Questions and Problems

A13.1 Roger's Lobsters serves buy-by-the-pound lobster dinners every Monday night. In order to attract customers, Roger's Lobsters can take out radio ads on local radio stations. If Roger's Lobsters buys these advertisements, the demand for its Monday night buy-by-the-pound lobster special increases. The demand function for Roger's Lobsters Monday night specials is

$$Q = 120 + 2.67A - 1.33P$$

where Q is the number of pounds of lobster that Roger's Lobsters sells each Monday night, P is the price per pound of lobster, and A is the number of radio ads that Roger's Lobsters purchases each week. Solving the demand function for P as a function of Q and A gives the inverse demand function for Roger's Lobsters' Monday night special:

$$P = 90 + 2A - 0.75Q$$

Roger's Lobsters' total cost of selling lobster, including the cost of advertising, is

$$TC(Q) = 0.25Q^2 + 26A^2 - 10A$$

a. What are the profit-maximizing quantity of pounds of lobster that Roger's Lobsters sells and the profit-maximizing number of radio advertisements that Roger's Lobsters buys each week?
b. What is Roger's Lobsters' profit-maximizing price for a pound of lobster?
c. How much economic profit (or loss) does Roger's Lobsters make each week?

A13.2 Walter Economics is a "one economist shop" economic consulting firm. Walter provides economic consulting services to multinational corporations and charges them an hourly rate for his services. In order to attract business, Walter must purchase advertisements in professional trade publications. The demand function for Walter's consulting services is

$$Q = 232.4 + 1.67A - 0.83P$$

where Q is the number of hours of consulting services Walter sells each week, A is the number of advertisements Walter buys each week, and P is the price Walter charges for his services. Solving the demand function for P as a function of Q and A gives the inverse demand function for Walter's consulting services:

$$P = 280 + 2A - 1.2Q$$

Walter's cost of selling consulting services is

$$TC(Q) = 0.8Q^2 + 25.5A^2 - 10A$$

a. What are the profit-maximizing number of consulting hours that Walter sells and the profit-maximizing number of professional trade publication advertisements that Walter takes out each week?
b. What is the profit-maximizing price for Walter's consulting services?
c. How much economic profit (or loss) does Walter earn each week?

A13.3 Esteban's Argentinian Grill is the best place to grab a steak in Sacramento, California. The restaurant uses the highest-quality meat and grills it using traditional Argentinian methods. Few customers, however, know about the restaurant. In an attempt to draw in more customers, Esteban hires an economist to determine whether taking out costly television advertisements will be profitable. His consultant determines that the demand function for a steak at Esteban's is

$$Q = 560 + 2A - 4P$$

where Q is the number of steaks that Esteban's sells, P is the price of a steak, and A is the number of advertisements. Solving the demand function for P as a function of Q and A gives the inverse demand function for Esteban's steaks:

$$P = 140 + 0.5A - 0.25Q$$

Esteban's cost of selling steak is

$$TC = 20Q + A^2$$

a. What are the profit-maximizing number of steaks that Esteban sells and the profit-maximizing number of television advertisements that he purchases?
b. What price does Esteban charge for a steak?

A13.4 A large university recently began offering an online MBA program. This program is expected to generate substantial profit that will be used to improve the overall quality of research and education in the university's business school. In order to publicize this new program, the university can purchase space on highway billboards. The demand function for the online MBA program is

$$Q = 800 + 4A - 0.04P$$

where Q is the number of students who enroll each year in the program, A is the number of billboard advertisements that the university purchases, and P is annual tuition price. Solving the demand function for P as a function of Q and A gives the inverse demand function for the MBA program:

$$P = 20,000 + 100A - 25Q$$

The university's cost of administering the online MBA program is

$$TC = 5,000Q + 200A^2$$

a. What are the profit-maximizing number of students that the university should enroll in the online MBA program each year and the profit-maximizing number of billboard advertisements that it should purchase?
b. What is the profit-maximizing tuition (P^*) that the university should charge for the online MBA program?
c. What is the online MBA program's economic profit (or loss)?

A13.5 Tina's Trophies is a small business in Miami, Florida, that sells Little League trophies. Tina has recently seen demand for her trophies fall off and is interested in advertising. She has crunched the numbers and has found that the marginal benefit from advertising is

$$MB = \frac{1,500}{A}$$

where A is the number of advertisements that Tina takes out. Tina knows that each advertisement will cost her $300.

a. What is the profit-maximizing number of advertisements that Tina should purchase?
b. How much will Tina spend on these advertisements?

CHAPTER 14

Business Decisions Under Uncertainty

Learning Objectives

After studying this chapter, you will be able to:

14.1 Apply the concepts of probability and expected values to managerial decision making.

14.2 Explain how to make profit-maximizing production decisions when demand and marginal cost randomly fluctuate.

14.3 Determine the profit-maximizing amount of inventory when demand changes randomly.

14.4 Describe how to make cost-minimizing decisions when faced with random adverse events including patent infringement, audit failure, and product failure.

14.5 Analyze when and why managers should agree to settle a lawsuit rather than litigate it.

14.6 Summarize how risk aversion affects managerial decision making.

14.7 Apply marginal analysis to make profit-maximizing managerial decisions under uncertainty.

Embezzlement Makes Managers at a Nonprofit See Red

For over four years, a financial director at a New York chapter of the American Red Cross (the Red Cross) worked diligently at her job. Over that same time, however, she also worked diligently at embezzling over $274,000 from the nonprofit organization. Deborah Leggio's scheme was straightforward. As the financial director of the chapter, Ms. Leggio instructed the bank that held the Red Cross's funds to issue her a debit card linked to several separate accounts. Then a few times a week she used the debit card at ATMs to withdraw anywhere from $800 to $2,000 per transaction. She spent the withdrawn funds on personal expenses, such as her Weight Watchers membership fees and her children's college tuition payments.

Outside auditors examined the chapter's financial books on an annual basis, but her crimes came to light only after Ms. Leggio left the Red Cross for a new position with a different nonprofit organization in California. The year after she left, an audit uncovered her frequent personal visits to ATMs and theft. Eventually, Ms. Leggio was convicted of embezzlement, and after she paid $9,500 in restitution, the judge sentenced her to between two and seven years in prison.

Were the top executives at the Red Cross asleep at the switch? Or was it in some sense "optimal" for them to fail to uncover Ms. Leggio's actions? This chapter explores these issues and others by focusing on how uncertainty affects managers' decisions. At the end of the chapter, you will learn whether the discovery of the embezzlement demonstrated negligence on the part of Red Cross executives.

Sources: "Jailed Red Cross Honcho Used Charity Cash for Nail Treatments, Weight Watchers," *New York Post*, February 27, 2013; Carl Macgowan, "DA: Ex-official Stole $274G from Red Cross," *Newsday*, February 22, 2011; Associated Press, "Former New York Red Cross Financial Director Sentenced for Stealing More Than $274,000 from the Humanitarian Organization," *New York Daily News*, February 27, 2013.

Introduction

To this point, this text has implicitly ignored an inescapable feature of the real world: uncertainty. Managers can never be certain about all aspects of the situations that confront them. It is impossible for a manager to maximize profit with every decision because of this element of randomness. Uncertainty can influence managerial decisions in many ways. To focus on those managerial decisions that are influenced most greatly by uncertainty, Chapter 14 includes seven sections:

- **Section 14.1** reviews the basic concepts of probability and expected values that are necessary for the remaining sections of the chapter.
- **Section 14.2** describes how managers can cope with random fluctuations in demand and cost when making production decisions.
- **Section 14.3** explains how managers can determine the optimal amount of inventory to hold when demand is random.
- **Section 14.4** focuses on the managerial decisions required to minimize the cost of randomly occurring adverse events such as patent infringement and audit failure.
- **Section 14.5** explores the decision whether to settle or litigate a lawsuit, including the actions a manager might take to settle on favorable terms.
- **Section 14.6** explains how risk aversion affects managerial decision making.
- **Section 14.7** shows how you can apply marginal analysis to make better business decisions under uncertainty.

14.1 Basics of Probability

Learning Objective 14.1 Apply the concepts of probability and expected values to managerial decision making.

At its most basic level, uncertainty is the result of incomplete information. Often managers have incomplete information because of random events. For example, suppose that a firm like Western Digital owns a hard-drive factory that may be subject to flooding in the upcoming year. From the managers' perspective, whether or not the flood occurs is random. In this case, the managers are uncertain what the value of the factory will be at the end of the year. To understand how successful managers handle uncertainty, you must employ some elements of probability because probability theory deals with random occurrences. This section does not replace a thorough study of probability. Instead, it provides a rudimentary coverage of the basic concepts that are essential to your understanding of business decisions under uncertainty.

Relative Frequency

Probability is the chance that an event occurs. One interpretation of probability is couched in terms of *relative frequency*, or how often a particular outcome occurs. The probability of an event is the relative frequency of its occurrence over an extended number of trials. For example, if you flipped a coin 1,000,000 times, a head would appear about 500,000 times, and the relative frequency would be very close to $\frac{500,000}{1,000,000} = 0.50$ (50 percent).

Instead of conducting long trials to obtain empirical evidence about relative frequencies, typically you count all possible outcomes and then identify those that satisfy the event in question. The ratio of the two is the probability. For example, if you want to know the probability of getting two heads on two tosses of a coin, you first identify all of the possible outcomes: HH, HT, TH, and TT. Of these four outcomes, exactly one satisfies the outcome you want—namely, two heads (HH). The probability of getting two heads on two tosses of a coin is

$$\frac{1 \text{ ``successful'' outcome}}{4 \text{ possible outcomes}} = 0.25 \text{ (25 percent)}$$

Characteristics of Probabilities

Probabilities have two important characteristics:

1. The value of a probability lies between zero and one; that is, $0 \le p \le 1$, where p is the probability of an event.
2. The probabilities of all possible outcomes add up to one. With n possible outcomes, $p_1 + p_2 + p_3 + \ldots + p_n = 1$, where p_1 is the probability of the first outcome, p_2 is the probability of the second outcome, and so on.

DECISION SNAPSHOT

Probability of Success at a New Branch

You are considering opening a new branch of your company. There are four possible outcomes: (1) The branch incurs an economic loss, (2) the branch makes zero economic profit, (3) the branch makes a small economic profit, and (4) the branch makes a large economic profit. Upon consideration, you estimate the probabilities of the first three outcomes to be $p_1 = 20$ percent, $p_2 = 10$ percent, and $p_3 = 30$ percent, respectively. You will open the branch only if the probability of success is 50 percent or greater, and you define success as "the branch makes an economic profit," no matter how large. Do you open the new branch?

Answer

The probabilities of all outcomes sum to 1.00. Therefore, the probability of a large economic profit (which would be p_4) is $1.00 - 0.20 - 0.10 - 0.30 = 0.40$ (40 percent). The probability of some economic profit is $p_3 + p_4$, or $0.40 + 0.30 = 0.70$ (70 percent). Because the probability of some economic profit is 70 percent, you open the new branch.

Probability Distributions

A **random variable** is any variable with an uncertain outcome. For example, the future value of a Western Digital hard-drive factory in Thailand is a random variable because there is a possibility that floods caused by a severe monsoon will damage the building (this actually happened a few years ago). In another example, firms like Starbucks purchase green (unroasted) coffee beans. Next year's price of green coffee beans is a random variable for these firms' managers because of unpredictable fluctuations in the weather and other growing conditions that affect the supply.

Random variable Any variable with an uncertain outcome.

The values of a random variable might not be equally likely. For this reason, we are interested in the *probability distribution* of the random variable, a listing of the possible outcomes and the associated probabilities of those outcomes. The fact that floods can do varying amounts of damage complicates the probability distribution of the value of a hard-drive factory in Thailand. To simplify the example, suppose that there are only two possible outcomes: (1) no flood, in which case the value of the factory is $30 million, and (2) a severe flood that does $20 million worth of damage to the factory, reducing its value to $10 million. If a manager uses compiled weather data to determine that floods occur 1 year out of 10, the probability of a flood is 10 percent (1 year/10 years), and the probability of no flood is 90 percent (9 years/10 years). Using these data, the manager specifies the probability distribution for the value

Table 14.1 Probability Distribution of the Value of the Factory

These data are the probability distribution of the value of a hard-drive factory.

Value of the Factory (millions of dollars)	Probability of Occurrence (percent)
$30	90
$10	10

of the Thai factory shown in Table 14.1. With no flood, there is a 90 percent chance that the factory is worth $30 million. With the flood, there is a 10 percent chance that the factory is worth $10 million.

Managers at a firm like Starbucks might review 20 years of data on coffee bean prices and see that the price of green coffee beans is $1.00 a pound for 2 years out of the 20 (10 percent of the time), $2.00 a pound for 4 years out of the 20 (20 percent of the time), and so on. Based on these data, the managers arrive at the probability distribution of the price of green coffee beans shown in Table 14.2.

The probability distributions for both the value of the factory in Table 14.1 and the price of green coffee beans in Table 14.2 satisfy the two properties of probabilities: The probabilities lie between zero and one, and the probabilities all sum to one.

Expected Value

Expected value A weighted average of the possible outcomes, where the weights are the probabilities of the outcomes.

It is impossible to know in advance the value of a random variable. For example, at the beginning of the year, Western Digital's managers have no way of knowing whether a flood will damage their Thai factory, so the factory's value at the end of the year is random. An important characteristic of a random variable is its **expected value**, a weighted average of the possible outcomes, where the weights are the probabilities of the outcome. The expected value of a random variable is computed by weighting each possible outcome with the probability of its occurrence and then adding together all of the weighted values.

For example, using the information in Table 14.1, the expected value of the hard-drive factory, $E[V]$, is equal to

$$E[V] = (\$30 \text{ million} \times 0.90) + (\$10 \text{ million} \times 0.10) = \$28 \text{ million}$$

Using the information in Table 14.2, the expected value of the price of a pound of green coffee beans, called the expected price of green coffee beans or $E[P]$, is equal to

$$E[P] = (\$1.00 \times 0.10) + (\$2.00 \times 0.20) + (\$3.00 \times 0.30) + (\$4.00 \times 0.30) + (\$5.00 \times 0.10) = \$3.10$$

Table 14.2 Probability Distribution of Green Coffee Bean Prices

These data are the probability distribution of the price of a pound of green coffee beans.

Price of a Pound of Green Coffee Beans (dollars)	Probability of Occurrence (percent)
$1.00	10
2.00	20
3.00	30
4.00	30
5.00	10

In both examples, note that the actual value will never actually equal the expected value. The hard-drive factory is either worth $30 million or $10 million; there is never a year in which it is worth $28 million. Similarly, the price of a pound of green coffee beans is never $3.10. The closest it comes is $3.00, and it hits that price only 30 percent of the time. The expected values are the average value of the hard-drive factory and the average price of a pound of green coffee beans over an extended period of time.

Expected values can be important to managers. For instance, managers at hard-drive producers might use the expected value to determine how much insurance to buy for their hard-drive plant, and the managers at the company like Starbucks might use the expected price to forecast the price of green coffee beans when they make future expansion plans.

Extent of Variation

The expected value of a random variable provides one bit of important information about the variable. The expected value, however, tells us nothing about the extent of the variable's variation. Sometimes that amount can influence decisions. In an extreme example, suppose that a company can sell its product in one of two countries but the price in each country is random. As shown in Table 14.3, in Country A, the price will be either $99 or $101, and in Country B, the price will be either $1 or $199. In Country A, the expected price is ($99 × 0.50) + ($101 × 0.50) = $100, and in Country B, the expected price is ($1 × 0.50) + ($199 × 0.50) = $100. Even though the expected price in both countries equals $100, the variation in the actual price is much larger in Country B than in Country A. Clearly, the risk of selling in Country B is larger than that of selling in Country A, which may affect managers' decisions. Section 14.6 examines in more detail the role that risk plays in decision making.

Subjective Probability

In the hard-drive factory and green coffee bean examples, the relative frequencies of the various possible outcomes determine the probabilities. Probabilities of different outcomes based on data about the relative frequencies of occurrence of the outcomes are called **objective probabilities**.

In some situations, managers cannot determine objective probabilities because they lack the repeated observations needed to determine relative frequencies. For example, a manager at Post Consumer Brands might be interested in the probability of the successful introduction of a new breakfast cereal. Because market conditions and the array of competitive products change constantly, the manager cannot repeat the introduction several times, under the same conditions, to determine relative frequencies. When repetition is impossible, managers cannot calculate objective probabilities, so they resort to **subjective probabilities**, probabilities of different outcomes based on their best estimate of the true probability of each possible outcome.

Objective probabilities
Probabilities of different outcomes based on data about the relative frequencies of occurrence of the outcomes.

Subjective probabilities
Probabilities of different outcomes based on an individual's best estimate of the true probability of each possible outcome.

Table 14.3 **Two Probability Distributions**

In both Country A and Country B, the expected price is $100, but the extent of variation in the actual price is *much* greater in Country B than in Country A.

Probability of Occurrence (percent)	Price$_A$ (dollars)	Price$_B$ (dollars)
50	$99	$1
50	101	199

Subjective probabilities obey the same two properties as objective probabilities: (1) They must lie between zero and one, and (2) they must sum to one. Managers use subjective probabilities in the same way that they would use objective probabilities if the data were available. For example, say that you are a manager for Samsung Electronics. A researcher in your department discovers a potentially new security feature for smartphones, and you are not sure whether another firm has a patent for this security feature. If you market the discovery and someone else already has a patent, Samsung will be guilty of patent infringement. The amount Samsung might have to pay for patent infringement is a random variable because you do not know if you will infringe or not nor do you know the penalty for any possible infringement. The expected value of the damages will help you decide whether to market the discovery. Objective probabilities are impossible to obtain. You could consult with technology experts and a patent attorney to give you an impression of the invention's novelty as well as a general idea of the likelihood of patent infringement. Based on your meetings and your best judgment, suppose that you wind up assigning a subjective probability of 10 percent (0.10) to the possibility that another firm has a patent for the invention. The 10 percent chance of infringing means there is a 90 percent subjective probability of no patent. Further suppose that your best estimate of the penalty for infringement is $100 million. The expected value of the damage amount, $E[D]$, is $E[D] = (\$100 \text{ million} \times 0.10) + (\$0 \times 0.90) = \$10$ million. You now face a decision with a considerable amount of uncertainty and the potential for a substantial loss—$10 million on average but $100 million if you actually infringe.

Although everyone realizes that the future is uncertain, managers must still make decisions. The next section explains how managers maximize their firms' expected profit in the face of randomly fluctuating demand and cost.

SOLVED PROBLEM

Expected Customers at a Car Dealership

Suppose that you are a manager at the only Ford dealership in Great Falls, Montana. Your service department is closed on Saturday, but you are considering whether to open. If you do, you estimate there are three possibilities: (1) You attract little business, so you have only 20 new Saturday customers each month; (2) you attract some business, so you have 40 new Saturday customers each month; or (3) your initiative is a resounding success, with 80 new Saturday customers each month.

a. If the probability of outcome 1 is 40 percent, the probability of outcome 2 is 50 percent, and the probability of outcome 3 is 10 percent, what is your expected number of customers?

b. If the probability of outcome 1 is 20 percent, the probability of outcome 2 is 50 percent, and the probability of outcome 3 is 30 percent, what is your expected number of customers?

c. If the probability of outcome 1 is 10 percent, the probability of outcome 2 is 60 percent, and the probability of outcome 3 is 30 percent, what is your expected number of customers?

Answer

Your expected number of customers equals the sum of each possible number of customers weighted by its probability of occurrence.

a. Expected number of customers $= (20 \times 0.40) + (40 \times 0.50) + (80 \times 0.10) =$ 36 customers.

b. Expected number of customers $= (20 \times 0.20) + (40 \times 0.50) + (80 \times 0.30) =$ 48 customers.

c. Expected number of customers $= (20 \times 0.10) + (40 \times 0.60) + (80 \times 0.30) =$ 50 customers.

14.2 Profit Maximization with Random Demand and Random Cost

Learning Objective 14.2 Explain how to make profit-maximizing production decisions when demand and marginal cost randomly fluctuate.

Suppose that you have a management job at a firm like Estrella River Ranch, a beautiful vineyard and one of more than 200 vineyards growing cabernet sauvignon grapes in California. At the start of each growing season, you must decide the quantity of grapes you will grow. But the demand for these grapes and the cost of growing them fluctuate unpredictably, so when you make your production decision, you do not know the price winemakers will pay you or the costs you will incur. How do you determine the quantity of grapes to produce? This section helps answer this question by first examining a scenario in which demand is random but marginal cost is not. Then it turns to random cost and predictable demand and concludes with a brief discussion of maximizing profit when both demand and cost change randomly and unpredictably.

Expected Profit Maximization with Random Demand

Because there are more than 200 vineyards in California that grow cabernet sauvignon grapes, for simplicity assume that the market is perfectly competitive. This makes the demand curve for your firm's grapes horizontal, and the price equal to the marginal revenue.[1] Assume that the demand for grapes is randomly and unpredictably high 50 percent of the time and low the other 50 percent of the time, so that the price (and the marginal revenue) of grapes is randomly high and low. Finally, you cannot instantly change production when demand changes, and grapes cannot be stored, so your firm must sell all of the grapes it grows.

Figure 14.1 illustrates the fluctuations in demand for grapes. When demand is high, the demand curve is d_H, and the price is $3,000 per ton. When demand is low, the demand curve is d_L, and the price is $1,000 per ton. Suppose you could change your production to reflect changes in demand. In this case, when the price is $3,000 per ton, you maximize profit by producing 500 tons of grapes (where $MR_H = MC$), and when the price is $1,000 per ton, you maximize profit by producing 100 tons (where $MR_L = MC$). Compared to the situation in which you can change production when demand changes, your expected profit (that is, your average profit) will be less when you must set your production in advance and cannot change it when you learn whether demand is high or low. But how much less? That depends on the amount of your production.

---

1 If the market is not perfectly competitive, the demand and marginal revenue curves are downward sloping. But the analysis of that case is analogous to the scenario for a perfectly competitive firm.

Figure 14.1

Producing 500 tons of grapes maximizes profit when demand is high (d_H). If, however, demand turns out to be low (d_L), so the price is $1,000 per ton, all of the tons between 100 and 500 create a loss. The reduction in profit is equal to the area of the dark red triangle, or $\frac{1}{2} \times (500 \text{ tons} - 100 \text{ tons}) \times (\$3,000 - \$1,000) = \$400,000$. Producing 100 tons of grapes maximizes profit when demand is low. If, however, demand turns out to be high, so the price is $5,000 per ton, then all of the profit that would have been made for the tons between 100 and 500 is lost. This reduction in profit is equal to the area of the light red triangle, or $\frac{1}{2} \times (500 \text{ tons} - 100 \text{ tons}) \times (\$3,000 - \$1,000) = \$400,000$.

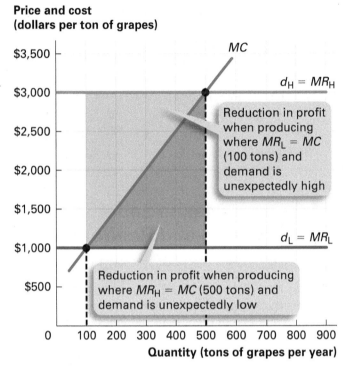

For example, suppose you base your production on the high demand so that you produce 500 tons of grapes. If demand turns out to be high, you will have maximized your profit because you are producing where the relevant marginal revenue, MR_H, equals the marginal cost. If, however, demand instead is low, so that the price is $1,000 per ton, all of the tons between 100 and 500 tons inflict a loss because the marginal cost of each of these tons exceeds their price. On these tons you incur a loss of $400,000, equal to the area of the dark red triangle in Figure 14.1. Compared to the case when you can change your production to reflect changes in demand, you make the same profit when demand is high but make $400,000 less when demand is low. Because demand is low 50 percent of the time, your expected profit when you cannot adjust demand is $400,000 \times 0.50 = $200,000 less than when you can change demand.

Alternatively, suppose you base your production on the low demand so that you produce 100 tons of grapes. If demand turns out to be low, you will have maximized your profit because you are producing where the relevant marginal revenue, MR_L, equals the marginal cost. But if demand instead is high, so that the price is $3,000 per ton, all of the tons between 100 and 500 tons would have been profitable because the marginal cost of each of these tons is less than the (high) price. The profit on these tons would have been $400,000, equal to the area of the light red triangle in Figure 14.1. Because you are not producing these tons, compared to the situation when you can change production, you make the same profit when demand is low but make $400,000 less when demand is high. Because demand is high 50 percent of the time, your expected profit when you cannot adjust demand is $400,000 \times 0.50 = $200,000 less than when you can change demand.

In both cases, you reduce your expected profit by $200,000 whether you produce 500 tons or 100 tons. (The result that the reduction in expected profit is the same in both cases is coincidental.) Can you do better?

Expected Profit

You have just seen that when demand is random, the firm's price and therefore its profit are also random. When profit is random, a reasonable managerial goal is to maximize expected profit. The **expected profit** is the weighted average profit, with the weights equal to the probabilities of the different possible profits. When demand and marginal cost are linear, then producing the quantity at which marginal cost equals expected marginal revenue maximizes the expected profit.

Expected profit The weighted average profit, with the weights equal to the probabilities of the different possible profits.

Returning to your firm's grapes, because the high marginal revenue of $3,000 occurs with a probability of 50 percent (0.50) and the low marginal revenue of $1,000 also occurs with a probability of 50 percent, the expected marginal revenue, $E[MR]$, is $(\$3,000 \times 0.50) + (\$1,000 \times 0.50) = \$2,000$. If you produce where expected marginal revenue equals marginal cost, or $E[MR] = MC$, Figure 14.2(a) shows that you produce and sell 300 tons of grapes.

Producing 300 tons of grapes means you will have a loss on each of the tons of grapes between 100 and 300 tons if the demand is randomly low because in this case the marginal cost of each of these tons exceeds the low price. The loss is equal to the area of the dark red triangle in the figure, $100,000. Consequently, compared to the

Figure 14.2 **Expected Profit with Random Demand**

(a) **Maximizing Expected Profit**
The expected marginal revenue curve is $E[MR]$. To maximize expected profit, you must produce the quantity at which $E[MR] = MC$, 300 tons of grapes.

(b) **Loss in Profit**
If demand is high (d_H), producing 300 tons makes less profit than producing 500 tons, and the reduction in profit (a foregone profit) is equal to the area of the light red triangle. If demand is low (d_L), producing 300 tons makes less profit than producing 100 tons, and the reduction in profit (a loss) is equal to the area of the dark red triangle.

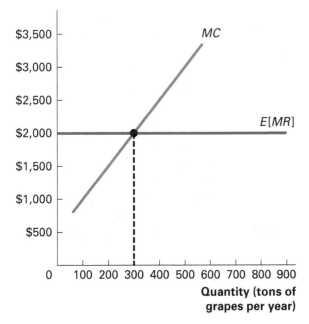

Price and cost (dollars per ton of grapes)

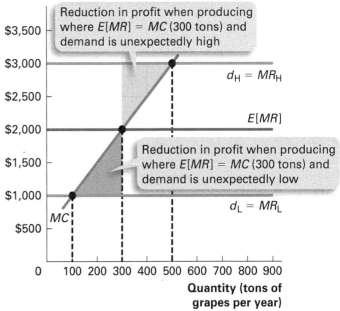

Price and cost (dollars per ton of grapes)

case in which you can change production, your profit is $100,000 less when you cannot change your production to match the demand.

Similarly, if you produce 300 tons of grapes you will have a foregone profit on each of the tons of grapes between 300 and 500 tons if the demand is randomly high because, with the high price, these tons would have been profitable to produce. The reduction in profit when the price is high equals $100,000, the area of the light red triangle in Figure 14.2(b). So, once again compared to the situation in which you can change production to reflect the demand, your profit is $100,000 less when you cannot change your production. (Once more the result that the loss in profit is the same if demand is unexpectedly low or unexpectedly high is a coincidence.)

Compared to the profit you would make if you could change your production when demand changes, the total reduction in expected profit is the loss of profit when the price is high, weighted by the probability of a high price, plus the loss of profit when the price is low, weighted by the probability of a low price, or ($100,000 × 0.50) + ($100,000 × 0.50) = $100,000. In other words, on average, you make $100,000 less profit each year by producing 300 tons than you would make if you could change production when demand changes. You have already seen that producing either 100 tons or 500 tons results in an average of $200,000 less profit per year. Indeed, producing *any* other quantity than the amount that sets $\mathrm{E}[MR] = MC$ has a larger reduction in expected profit.

Producing the quantity that sets $\mathrm{E}[MR] = MC$ minimizes your reduction in expected profit, which, in other words, maximizes your vineyard's expected profit. Although your profit is smaller when demand is random so that you cannot always produce the quantity that sets the actual marginal revenue equal to the marginal cost, your expected profit is highest when you produce the quantity that sets the expected marginal revenue equal to the marginal cost. Then, after producing this quantity, you sell the grapes for $3,000 per ton if the demand is high or $1,000 per ton if the demand is low.

Expected Profit Maximization with Random Cost

Like demand, cost can be uncertain. Input prices can vary in unanticipated, random ways: Oil prices might tumble because of new sources of energy, or drought might raise the price of water. These factors and many more can change a firm's costs. This situation poses no problem if managers can delay their output decisions until they are certain of the cost or immediately change their output decisions when cost changes. Under those conditions, profit-maximizing managers will select the output that sets the marginal revenue equal to the actual marginal cost. Managers, however, must often make production decisions before they know the actual cost. Just as with random demand, you cannot maximize your *actual* profit because actual profit is always variable in the face of random cost, but you can take steps to maximize your *expected* profit.

For simplicity, assume that demand for your firm's grapes does not change but its marginal cost varies randomly from high to low. Once again, you must make your production decision at the start of the growing season before you know your actual cost, and you must sell all of the grapes you produce because they cannot be stored. Figure 14.3(a) shows the two marginal cost curves, MC_H and MC_L. You estimate that the marginal cost is high 25 percent of the time and low 75 percent of the time. So for each quantity the expected marginal cost equals the high marginal cost weighted by 25 percent (0.25) plus the low marginal cost weighted by 75 percent (0.75). For example, at the quantity of 200 tons of grapes per year, for example, the expected marginal cost equals ($2,500 per ton × 0.25) + ($500 per ton × 0.75), or $1,000 per ton. The expected marginal cost curve is labeled $\mathrm{E}[MC]$ in Figure 14.3(a).

Figure 14.3 **Random Costs and Profit Maximization**

(a) **Random Marginal Cost**

One-quarter of the time the marginal cost curve for grapes is randomly high (MC_H), and three-quarters of the time it is randomly low (MC_L). The expected marginal cost, $E[MC]$, for each quantity equals the high marginal cost at that quantity weighted by its probability plus the low marginal cost at that quantity weighted by its probability.

(b) **Maximizing Expected Profit**

The expected marginal cost curve is $E[MC]$. To maximize expected profit, produce the quantity at which marginal revenue equals expected marginal cost—that is, $MR = E[MC]$—600 tons of grapes.

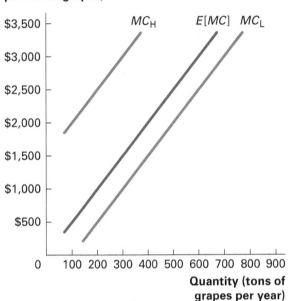

Price and cost (dollars per ton of grapes)

Quantity (tons of grapes per year)

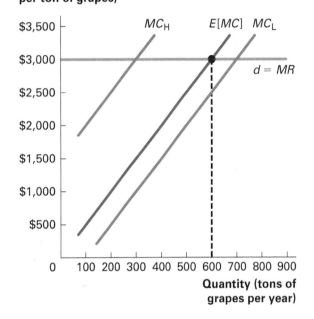

Price and cost (dollars per ton of grapes)

Quantity (tons of grapes per year)

Figure 14.3(b) adds the demand/marginal revenue curve to the marginal cost curves shown in Figure 14.3(a). You maximize the firm's expected profit by producing the quantity that sets the marginal revenue equal to the expected marginal cost, $MR = E[MC]$. As shown in Figure 14.3(b), 600 tons of grapes per year maximizes your firm's expected profit. When cost randomly changes, just as when demand randomly changes, producing the quantity that sets the marginal revenue equal to the expected marginal cost yields the highest average profit.

Figure 14.3 assumes that the high marginal cost occurs 25 percent of the time and the low marginal cost occurs 75 percent of the time. If the probability of the high marginal cost increases, perhaps from the need to treat the grapevines for Armillaria root rot, the probability of the low marginal cost decreases. In this case, the expected marginal cost increases, causing the $E[MC]$ curve in Figure 14.3 to shift upward. The expected profit-maximizing quantity decreases, which is reasonable because the profit from any given unit of output is less when the marginal cost is higher. For example, if the probability of having a high marginal cost equals 100 percent (1.00), the profit-maximizing quantity will fall to 300 tons because there is no uncertainty: The profit-maximizing quantity sets $MR = MC_H$.

Expected Profit Maximization with Random Demand and Random Cost

When *both* demand and cost are random, a manager is still tasked with maximizing expected profit. In this case, you can follow the expected-profit-maximization rule: Produce the quantity that sets the expected marginal revenue equal to the expected marginal cost—$E[MR] = E[MC]$—and then set the highest price that sells the quantity produced.

You can use Figure 14.4 to apply the expected-profit-maximization rule when both demand and cost are random. In this case, you maximize your firm's expected profit by producing the quantity where $E[MR] = E[MC]$, 400 tons of grapes. You then sell this quantity at $3,000 per ton if demand is high or $1,000 per ton if demand is low.

One of the frustrations you face as a manager is that in reality your output decision will usually be wrong after the demand and cost uncertainties are resolved. Figure 14.4 shows that when the marginal cost is low (MC_L is the actual

Figure 14.4 Random Demand and Cost

When both demand and cost are random, maximizing expected profit requires producing the quantity at which expected marginal revenue equals expected marginal cost; that is, $E[MR] = E[MC]$. In the figure, producing 400 tons of grapes maximizes expected profit.

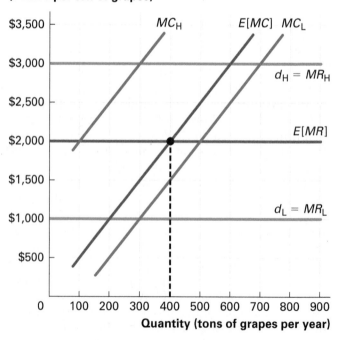

marginal cost curve) and demand is low ($d_L = MR_L$ is the actual demand curve), you will have produced too much—400 tons of grapes instead of the actual profit-maximizing quantity, 300 tons. That is the nature of decisions under uncertainty. By maximizing your expected profit, you ensure that your profit is as large as possible on average, but you cannot maximize profit with every decision you make.

Decreasing the uncertainty, however, might increase your expected profit because it shrinks the difference between the quantity you produce and the optimal quantity based on the actual marginal revenue and actual marginal cost. Managers can decrease uncertainty by more accurately forecasting their demand or their costs. Section 15.2 discusses the value of such forecasts.

Uncertain demand also affects a firm's determination of the optimal inventory to hold. Inventories of semifinished and finished goods are necessary in many businesses. Selling a unit from the inventory adds to the firm's revenue, but holding a unit in inventory adds to its cost. If demand is random, sales from inventory will also be random. The next section explains how to determine the profit-maximizing quantity to hold in inventory when sales are random.

Profit Maximization for a Vineyard

SOLVED
PROBLEM

The figure shows the two potential demand curves and the marginal cost curve for the production of grapes by your vineyard.

a. If the probability of demand being high, d_H, is 75 percent and the probability of demand being low, d_L, is 25 percent, what quantity of grapes maximizes your expected profit?

b. Suppose that the probability of high demand changes to 25 percent, so the probability of low demand is 75 percent. Now what quantity of grapes maximizes your expected profit?

c. How does a change in the expected marginal revenue affect the quantity produced?

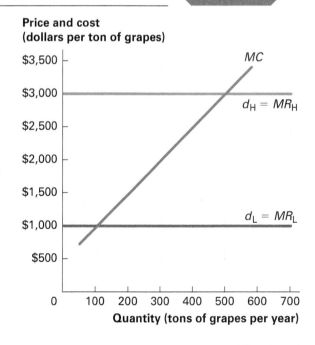

(*Continues*)

SOLVED PROBLEM (*continued*)

Answer

a. For any quantity, the probability of the high-demand marginal revenue (MR_H), $3,000 per ton, is 75 percent, and the probability of the low-demand marginal revenue (MR_L), $1,000 per ton, is 25 percent. So for any quantity the expected marginal revenue, $E[MR]$, is ($3,000 per ton $\times$ 0.75) + ($1,000 per ton $\times$ 0.25), or $2,500 per ton, as shown in the second figure. Producing 400 tons of grapes maximizes your vineyard's expected profit because this quantity sets the expected marginal revenue equal to the marginal cost.

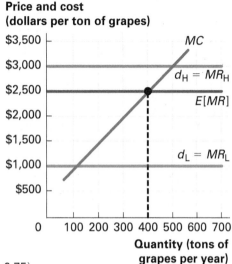

Price and cost (dollars per ton of grapes)

b. The expected marginal revenue is now ($3,000 per ton $\times$ 0.25) + ($1,000 per ton $\times$ 0.75), or $1,500 per ton. Producing 200 tons of grapes now maximizes your vineyard's expected profit because it sets $E[MR] = MC$.

c. As the expected marginal revenue falls, the profit-maximizing quantity decreases.

14.3 Optimal Inventories with Random Demand

Learning Objective 14.3 Determine the profit-maximizing amount of inventory when demand changes randomly.

An economic analysis of the optimal inventory quantity was first presented in Section 12.5. The analysis there assumed that the inventory was used at a constant rate with no randomness. That model can be useful when managers have a good idea of the level and variations in demand for a product. But in other cases, demand may fluctuate randomly, making it impossible to know how much, if any, of the inventory will be needed. Even with random demand, managers still must make decisions about how much inventory to hold. This section explains the steps you can take to determine the profit-maximizing quantity to keep in inventory when demand and sales are random.[2]

The Inventory Problem

Restaurants like Panera Bread bake fresh loaves of bread every morning and hold them in inventory for only one day. (Companies making other products hold products in inventory for more than one day, but the analysis is the same as in the case we describe.) As a manager at a firm like Panera Bread, you know the price you will charge for a loaf of whole grain bread and must determine the quantity of bread to produce for inventory. You do not know the precise quantity that will be demanded each day at that price, but you do have an idea of the probability of each possibility.

Suppose that you believe the quantity demanded will be between 50 and 57 loaves each day. Based on past sales data, the first two columns of Table 14.4 show the probabilities you assign to selling particular quantities. For example, the second column shows the probability that 53 loaves will be the quantity demanded is 0.20.

---

2 In the inventory model in Chapter 12, the fixed cost of placing an order was a factor helping determine the optimal inventory. To focus on the role played by random demand, in this chapter we ignore any fixed cost of ordering (or producing) the product for inventory.

Table 14.4 Probability Distribution of Bread Sales

These data are the probability distribution of the sale of loaves of bread.

Quantity of Loaves Demanded	Probability This Quantity Is Demanded	Probability of Selling This Quantity or More, Prob $(Q^D \geq Q)$	Probability of Selling Less Than This Quantity, Prob $(Q^D < Q)$
50	0.10	1.00	0.00
51	0.10	0.90	0.10
52	0.10	0.80	0.20
53	0.20	0.70	0.30
54	0.20	0.50	0.50
55	0.10	0.30	0.70
56	0.10	0.20	0.80
57	0.10	0.10	0.90
58	0.00	0.00	1.00

For each quantity, the third column gives the probability that you will be able to sell this number of loaves. In particular, you will sell 53 loaves if the quantity demanded is 53, 54, 55, 56, or 57 loaves, so the probability of selling 53 loaves is the probability that the quantity demanded equals or exceeds 53 loaves: Prob$(Q^D \geq 53)$. This probability is the probability of selling 53 loaves plus the probability of selling 54 loaves, and so forth up to 57 loaves: Prob$(Q^D \geq 53) = 0.20 + 0.20 + 0.10 + 0.10 + 0.10 = 0.70$. In other words, 70 percent of the time you will sell all 53 loaves. Of course, if the actual quantity demanded is, say, 54 loaves and you have baked 53 loaves, then you will be able to sell only 53 loaves, not 54 loaves.

The last column is the probability that you do not sell the given number of loaves. For example, the probability that you sell less than 53 loaves is Prob$(Q^D < 53)$. You can calculate this last probability by noting that if you sell fewer than 53 loaves, consumers must have demanded 50, 51, or 52 loaves. Add the probabilities of these three: 0.10 (for 50 loaves) + 0.10 (for 51 loaves) + 0.10 (for 52 loaves) = 0.30. This sum gives the probability of selling 50, 51, or 52 loaves, which is Prob$(Q^D < 53)$.

Suppose that the price of a loaf of whole grain bread is P. In addition, assume that the marginal cost of a loaf of bread equals its average total cost, that both are constant, and that both equal C. Therefore, the profit from selling a loaf of bread from your inventory is $P - C$. If a loaf is not sold on the day it was produced, the price must be reduced below C to a secondary price P_S, and it must be sold in the secondary market as day-old bread. In this case, you incur a loss of $C - P_S$. In reality, Panera Bread's policy is to donate unsold bread to a local food bank, so for Panera Bread $P_S = \$0$. More generally, P_S could be positive. For example, when Toyota's new model-year Prius comes out, the firm's executives typically cut the price of the old model by several thousand dollars but definitely not to zero. In this case, P_S is positive but is less than the price during the year before the introduction of the new model.

Profit-Maximizing Inventory

The optimal inventory to hold maximizes the profit of the inventory, which is the profit from the units sold minus the loss from the units that remain unsold. To determine the optimal quantity to hold in inventory, a profit-maximizing manager uses marginal analysis. Suppose that the initial quantity of loaves of bread in inventory is $Q^* - 1$ and you are considering producing one more loaf, so the inventory becomes Q^*. You must determine the expected marginal benefit and expected marginal cost of the additional loaf of bread before making your decision.

Expected Marginal Benefit and Expected Marginal Cost

The expected marginal benefit from one more loaf of bread in inventory is the expected profit from the sale of that additional loaf. On any day you sell that loaf, your profit is its price minus its cost, $P - C$. The probability that the loaf will be sold equals the probability that the actual quantity demanded, Q^D, is equal to or greater than the quantity in inventory, Q^*, or $\text{Prob}(Q^D \geq Q^*)$. The expected profit is the loaf's profit multiplied by the probability that the loaf is sold, so the expected marginal benefit is $E[MB] = (P - C) \times \text{Prob}(Q^D \geq Q^*)$. As the quantity held in inventory, Q^*, increases, the probability of selling an additional loaf, $\text{Prob}(Q^D \geq Q^*)$, decreases. So the expected marginal benefit falls as the quantity held in inventory increases.

The expected marginal cost of holding one more loaf of bread in inventory is the expected loss if the loaf remains unsold on days when demand is low. Assume for a moment that your firm sells the leftover loaf of bread on the secondary market at a loss of $C - P_S$. The probability that demand will be less than Q^* is $\text{Prob}(Q^D < Q^*)$. The expected loss is $(C - P_S) \times \text{Prob}(Q^D < Q^*)$, so the expected marginal cost of holding one more loaf in inventory is $E[MC] = (C - P_S) \times \text{Prob}(Q^D < Q^*)$. As the quantity in inventory, Q^*, increases, the probability of selling less than that quantity, $\text{Prob}(Q^D < Q^*)$, increases. So the expected marginal cost rises as the quantity held in inventory increases.

Determining the Optimal Inventory Using Marginal Analysis

Marginal analysis shows that the profit-maximizing quantity of bread to have in inventory is the amount that sets $E[MB] = E[MC]$. Suppose that the price of a loaf of bread (P) is \$4, the marginal cost (C) is \$2, and the price in the secondary market (P_S) is \$0. The probability distribution of bread sales is from Table 14.4. Using these probabilities, the expected marginal benefit for the 52nd loaf is $(P - C) \times \text{Prob}(Q^D \geq Q^*) = (\$4 - \$2) \times 0.80 = \$1.60$, and the expected marginal cost is $(C - P_S) \times \text{Prob}(Q^D < Q^*) = (\$2 - \$0) \times 0.20 = \$0.40$. The remainder of the expected marginal benefits and expected marginal costs are calculated similarly and are plotted in Figure 14.5.[3] Then, using marginal analysis, the profit-maximizing quantity sets the expected marginal benefit equal to the expected marginal cost, or

$$(P - C) \times \text{Prob}(Q^D \geq Q^*) = (C - P_s) \times \text{Prob}(Q^D < Q^*)$$

The intersection of the expected marginal benefit and expected marginal cost curves determines the optimal quantity, 54 loaves, as shown in Figure 14.5.

Although using Figure 14.5 makes short work of determining the optimal inventory, no matter how many years you work as a manager and how many companies you manage, it is unlikely that you will ever draw such a diagram to determine your profit-maximizing inventory. As usual, rather than give you a precise answer, economic theory provides valuable insight into the factors that you need to take into account when making your inventory decision. The true value of Figure 14.5 lies in demonstrating the need to compare the expected marginal benefit of having a unit in inventory to its expected marginal cost. As long as the expected marginal benefit of ordering or producing a unit to keep in inventory exceeds the expected marginal cost, you should add the unit to your inventory. And when the number of sales is random, to determine the expected marginal benefit and marginal cost, you need to take account of the probability of selling it versus of the probability of being forced to sell (or give it away or junk it) on the secondary market.

---

3 The $E[MB]$ and $E[MC]$ curves are not linear because the probabilities of selling different quantities of loaves are not constant. In particular, the probabilities of selling 53 and 54 loaves exceed the probabilities of selling the other quantities.

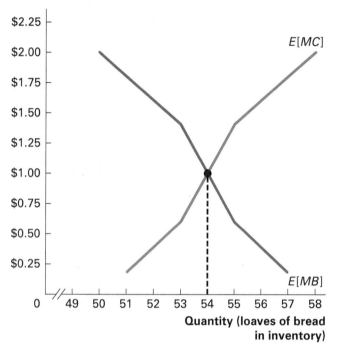

Expected marginal benefit and expected marginal cost (dollars per loaf of bread)

Quantity (loaves of bread in inventory)

Figure 14.5 Profit-Maximizing Inventory of Bread

The expected marginal benefit curve shows the expected profit for each loaf of bread held in inventory. The expected marginal cost curve shows the expected loss for each loaf held in inventory. The profit-maximizing inventory quantity sets the expected marginal benefit equal to the expected marginal cost: 54 loaves.

Profit-Maximizing Inventory of Pastry Rings

SOLVED PROBLEM

Your bakery firm sells more than loaves of bread. It also sells a delicious pastry ring for $10, and the cost of producing it is $2. If a pastry ring is not sold the day it is produced, it is donated to a local food bank. Suppose that as a manager you once again use past sales data to estimate that the probabilities of selling different quantities of the pastry ring are the same probabilities shown in Table 14.4 for loaves of bread. What is the profit-maximizing quantity of pastry rings to carry in inventory?

Answer
Your optimal inventory will be the quantity that sets $E[MB] = E[MC]$, or

$$(P - C) \times \text{Prob}(Q^D \geq Q^*) = (C - P_S) \times \text{Prob}(Q^D < Q^*)$$

The profit on each pastry ring sold is $P - C$, or $10 - 2 = 8$, and the loss on each unsold pastry ring is $C - P_S$, or $2 - 0 = 2$. If you set 56 rings as your inventory, $\text{Prob}(Q^D \geq Q^*) = 0.20$, and $\text{Prob}(Q^D < Q^*) = 0.80$. At a quantity of 56 rings, the expected marginal benefit is $8 \times 0.20 = 1.60$, and the expected marginal cost is $2 \times 0.80 = 1.60$. Because the expected marginal benefit equals the expected marginal cost, 56 pastry rings is the profit-maximizing quantity to carry in inventory.

14.4 Minimizing the Cost of Random Adverse Events

Learning Objective 14.4 Describe how to make cost-minimizing decisions when faced with random adverse events including patent infringement, audit failure, and product failure.

An *adverse event* is a bad outcome that creates damage or harm. There are situations in which the likelihood of an adverse event is random. For example, a product might infringe on some other producer's patent, an audit might fail to uncover embezzlement, or a product might fail and injure a consumer. In many cases, managers can invest some resources and reduce the probability of the adverse event. For example, a manager can reduce the expected damages from unintended patent infringement by hiring an attorney to conduct a patent search. Similarly, the probability of audit failure can be reduced by hiring more accountants to conduct a more extensive audit, and the possibility of a product failing and injuring consumers can be reduced by more extensive product testing. Of course, the actions taken to reduce the likelihood of a bad outcome are costly. In this section, you will learn how to determine the optimal amount to spend on efforts to limit the possibility of an adverse event.

Minimizing the Cost of Undesirable Outcomes

An unintended bad outcome is referred to as an *accident*. As mentioned above, an accident could be patent infringement, audit failure, or failure of a product to function safely. These three types of accidents might appear to have little in common other than the possibility of causing harm to your company. At a more basic level, however, they actually have a great deal in common. For each, the total cost is the sum of two cost components:

1. The expected cost of the accident
2. The cost of actions that decrease the expected cost of the accident

In terms of a formula, the total cost (*TC*) is given by

$$TC = \text{Expected cost of the accident} + \text{Cost of actions taken to decrease the expected cost}$$

Taking actions to lower the probability of the bad outcome decreases its expected cost, but such actions are costly. As a manager, you may be responsible for deciding how much to spend on such actions. Effective managers use marginal analysis and spend the amount that minimizes the total cost. In a nutshell, the optimal expenditure is the amount that sets the expected marginal benefit of reducing the probability of an accident equal to the marginal cost of the action(s) that reduces that probability. Now, let's elaborate on this brief summary by exploring the expected marginal benefit, the marginal cost, and the use of marginal analysis in more detail.

Expected Marginal Benefit from Avoiding Undesirable Outcomes

Managers can take actions that decrease the probability of an accident. By decreasing its probability, these actions decrease the accident's expected cost. The decrease in the expected cost is the *expected marginal benefit of reducing the probability of an accident*, or E[*MB*]. The possibility of patent infringement can be used as an example.

Expected Marginal Benefit from Avoiding Patent Infringement

Say that as a manager at a firm like Samsung Electronics, you are deciding whether to market a new smartphone security feature, which might infringe on another company's patent. If you infringe, you estimate the damage at $100 million, with a subjective probability of infringement of 10 percent. The expected cost of infringement becomes $100 million × 0.10, or $10 million. If you authorize hiring a patent attorney, you can refine your subjective probability. For example, if the attorney finds a relevant patent, your estimate of the probability of infringement becomes 100 percent, and your decision is straightforward: You will not market the product, or you will try to obtain a license from the patent holder. Now let's consider the more difficult case in which your attorney does not immediately come across a patent.

The longer your attorney searches without finding a patent, the more you can lower your estimate of the probability of infringement. For example, if your attorney searches through 100 patents and finds no relevant patents, you might lower your subjective probability of infringement to 8 percent. If your attorney searches through 400 patents, you might further reduce your subjective probability of infringement to 5 percent. A fall in the probability of infringement decreases its expected cost. For example, if your subjective probability of infringement is 8.001 percent (0.08001) after the first 99 patents are searched, the expected cost is $100 million ×0.08001 = $8,001,000. If your subjective probability of infringement falls to 8.000 percent (0.0800) after 100 patents are searched, the expected cost is $100 million ×0.0800 = $8,000,000. The expected marginal benefit from the 100th patent searched is $1,000, the decrease in expected cost from $8,001,000 (with 99 patents searched) to $8,000,000 (with 100 patents searched).

Presumably, your attorney searches the most likely patents first and the less likely patents later, so your subjective probability of infringement will fall rapidly at first and more slowly later. Consequently, the expected marginal benefit from the 100th patent searched is larger than that from the 500th patent searched. In Figure 14.6, the horizontal axis measures the quantity of patents searched, and the vertical axis measures the

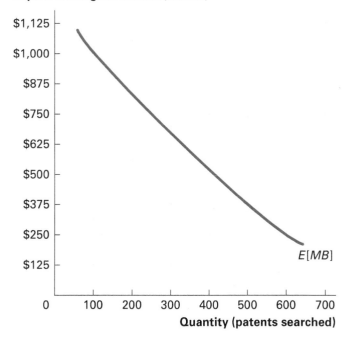

Expected marginal benefit (dollars)

Figure 14.6 Expected Marginal Benefit from Avoiding Patent Infringement

The E[MB] curve shows the expected marginal benefit from actions taken to avoid patent infringement. The expected marginal benefit is the decrease in the expected cost from infringement. The expected cost of infringement for the 100th patent searched falls by $1,000, so the expected marginal benefit for searching this patent is $1,000. The expected marginal benefit decreases as the quantity of patents searched increases.

expected marginal benefit, the decrease in the expected cost from infringement. The curve labeled E[MB] in Figure 14.6 shows the relationship between the quantity of patents searched and the expected marginal benefit of the action. The downward slope of the curve indicates that as the attorney searches more patents, the expected marginal benefit of further patent searches decreases.

Figure 14.6 shows the specific case of patent search. The illustrated relationship is more general, however: As the quantity of actions taken to reduce the probability of an accident increases, the expected marginal benefit from each additional action decreases.

Marginal Cost of Avoiding Undesirable Outcomes

As you have already learned, actions designed to decrease the expected cost of an accident are costly. If the actions are equally effective, managers should authorize the least expensive actions first, followed by the more expensive actions. This approach means that the marginal cost of additional actions increases. Again, let's use patent search as an example.

Marginal Cost of Avoiding Patent Infringement

If you hire a patent attorney and request a search of only a few patents, the law firm you hire will likely assign the job to a paralegal. If you request a larger number of searches, the law firm might run out of paralegals and need to assign associates. If you request still more searches, you ultimately will have partners conducting the searches.[4] Because the time spent by partners costs more than the time spent by associates, which in turn costs more than the time spent by paralegals, the marginal cost of avoiding patent infringement rises as more patents are searched.

Figure 14.7 illustrates the marginal cost of avoiding patent infringement. In general, the marginal cost of avoiding an accident rises as more actions are taken, and the curve labeled *MC* shows precisely this relationship.

Figure 14.7 Marginal Cost of Avoiding Patent Infringement

The *MC* curve shows the marginal cost of patent searches to avoid patent infringement. For example, the 100th patent searched, has a marginal cost of $125. The marginal cost of avoiding patent infringement increases as more patents are searched.

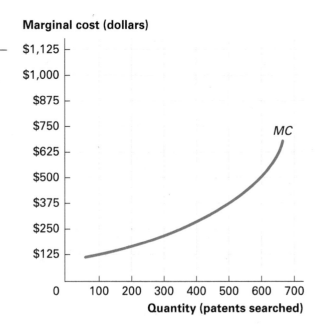

Marginal cost (dollars)

Quantity (patents searched)

4 In reality, the law firm might hire more paralegals before it assigns associates to the patent search. Hiring more paralegals, however, increases the cost of supervising them, so the marginal cost of the search still increases as described.

Optimal Accident Avoidance

Patent Infringement

To determine the optimal amount of accident avoidance, managers need to use marginal analysis and take into account both the expected marginal benefit from accident avoidance and its marginal cost. Continuing with the potential patent infringement scenario, Figure 14.8 combines the expected marginal benefit curve, E[MB], from Figure 14.6 with the marginal cost curve, MC, from Figure 14.7. Applying marginal analysis indicates that the optimal quantity of accident avoidance (patent searches in this case) occurs at the quantity that sets the expected marginal benefit equal to the marginal cost. This quantity minimizes the total cost of accidents, which is the expected cost of an accident (patent infringement) plus the cost of avoiding accidents through patent searches. In Figure 14.8, 500 patent searches is the cost-minimizing quantity. To see why the quantity that sets the expected marginal benefit equal to the marginal cost minimizes total cost, let's study two possible alternative cases: E[MB] > MC and E[MB] < MC.

- **E[MB] > MC.** Suppose that 99 patents have been searched. Figure 14.8 shows that the expected marginal benefit from searching the 100th patent is $1,000, which means that searching this patent lowers the expected cost from infringement by $1,000. The figure also shows that the marginal cost of searching the 100th patent is $125. So searching the 100th patent lowers the total cost by $875 (the $1,000 reduction in the expected cost from infringement minus the $125 cost of the search). Whenever E[MB] > MC, the total cost is decreased by undertaking more accident avoidance activities.

Expected marginal benefit and marginal cost (dollars)

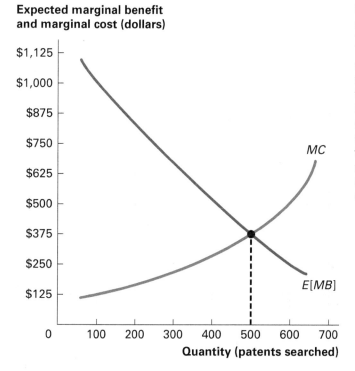

Figure 14.8 Optimal Accident Avoidance

The cost-minimizing quantity of actions taken to avoid accidents (here to avoid patent infringement) is the quantity at which E[MB] equals MC. In the figure, the cost-minimizing quantity of patent searches is 500 patents searched.

DECISION
SNAPSHOT

Patent Search at a Pharmaceutical Firm

As an executive at a pharmaceutical firm like Eli Lilly and Company, you are in charge of shepherding a potential new drug discovered in your laboratories through development and production. Your attorneys have spent 10 days conducting a patent search to determine if your drug infringes on other patents. You estimate that another day's search will decrease the likelihood of infringement by 0.01 percent (0.0001). You also estimate that if you infringe, your firm will pay damages of $10 million. Another day's search costs $2,000. Should you authorize another day's patent search? Why or why not?

Answer
The expected marginal benefit, E[MB], from another day's search equals the reduction in the expected infringement damages, $10,000,000 × 0.0001 = $1,000. Searching another day lowers your firm's expected cost only if E[MB] > MC. The most you should be willing to pay for another day's patent search is $1,000, so because the day's search would cost $2,000, you should not authorize it.

- **E[MB] < MC.** Consider searching the 600th patent. The expected marginal benefit curve in Figure 14.8 shows that searching the 600th patent lowers the expected cost from infringement by $250, but the marginal cost curve in the figure shows that the marginal cost of searching the 600th patent is $500. Searching the 600th patent raises the total cost by $250 (the $500 increase in the cost of the search minus the $250 reduction in the expected cost from infringement). Whenever E[MB] < MC, the total cost is decreased by undertaking fewer accident avoidance activities.

These scenarios show that whenever E[MB] ≠ MC, the total cost can be lowered, which means that the total cost is not minimized. When E[MB] = MC, further reductions in the total cost are impossible, so only when E[MB] = MC is the total cost minimized.

Figure 14.8 reveals a key result: It is not optimal to drive the probability of patent infringement to zero. At the optimal level of search, 500 patents, there is still some positive probability of patent infringement. The expected marginal benefit curve shows that searching the 501st patent decreases the expected cost of patent infringement, which means it decreases the probability of infringement. But an efficient manager would not pay to have the 501st patent searched because the cost saving from the decreased probability of infringement falls short of the cost of the search. In general, some probability of an accident remains because it is simply too costly to reduce the expected cost of an accident to zero.

The accident-avoidance model just developed applies to other scenarios in which a business might randomly suffer an adverse event. For example, accountants might fail to uncover theft from the company, a product produced by the company might be defective and lead to injury, burglars might break into and steal from a company's warehouse, or a company-owned mine might collapse. Your imagination can likely conjure up many more examples. We will treat the first two of these scenarios, audit failure and product failure, but the general strategy—compare the expected marginal benefit of reducing the probability of an accident to the marginal cost of the reduction—applies to all of them and should be your approach to any situation in which you face the possibility of an unintended bad outcome.

Audit Failure

In any operation you manage, typically there is some probability that an employee is stealing from the company, perhaps by embezzling funds as happened to the American Red Cross. Because of the uncertainty that someone is stealing, embezzlement is a random variable. Say that the subjective probability that embezzlement is occurring is 1 percent. If someone is stealing funds, you estimate the potential cost to the company to be $40 million. Given the probability of embezzlement and the cost if it occurs, the expected cost from embezzlement is $E[C] = \$40$ million $\times 0.01 = \$0.4$ million.

When your auditors check your operations, they search for embezzlement. Because they cannot search every entry in your books, the auditors must take a sample and might fail to discover the missing funds. *Audit failure* is the failure of auditors to uncover the theft. The expected cost of audit failure is the expected cost from embezzlement: $0.4 million. The probability of audit failure decreases as auditors increase their audit sample size. Increasing the sample size, however, increases the cost the firm must pay the auditors as well as the opportunity costs from the disruption caused by auditors rooting through accounting records and asking the staff for still more records.

As you might already have realized, the problem of audit failure is analogous to the problem of patent infringement. In both cases, there is a nonzero probability that an "accident" might occur. Managers can reduce the probability of an accident (and its expected cost) but only by incurring a cost. The cost-minimizing quantity of prevention (increased patent search or increased audit sample size) is the quantity that sets the expected marginal benefit from further prevention equal to the marginal cost of additional prevention. In neither case does the cost-minimizing amount of prevention mean that the probability of the accident (infringement or embezzlement) decreases to zero. It just means that the cost of additional prevention is greater than the expected marginal benefit.

Product Failure

In some production processes, defective products might be produced randomly and could harm consumers. For example, a particular vial of insulin might contain more or less than the expected dose. Although determining liability is a legal matter in the real world, for the purpose of this example, assume that the producer is liable for such harm. As a manager for the producer, you can reduce the probability of selling a defective product through testing. Increasing the amount of testing decreases the expected cost from defective products, but it also increases your costs. Your decision as a manager should by now be clear: The optimal amount of testing is the quantity at which the expected marginal benefit from reducing expected damage payments equals the marginal cost of further testing. As in the previous scenarios, reducing product failure to zero is not optimal.

The idea that some product failures are likely to occur might seem counterintuitive—and perhaps even unethical. The crucial point, however, is that assuring 100 percent perfection is incredibly costly, if not impossible. The testing necessary to reach this goal would drive up the price of the product so much that no one could afford it. With respect to ethics, it is important to realize that society already accepts that using some products will result in injury or even death. For example, approximately 35,000 people die each year in traffic accidents in the United States. We are in no way minimizing the impact of these tragedies, but we want to point out that society accepts these heartbreaking outcomes because designing traffic grids and vehicles to prevent 100 percent of deaths or injuries is too costly.

All-or-Nothing Decisions

The model just developed assumes that the manager can decide to take incremental actions to decrease the expected cost of an accident by authorizing searching a few more patents, checking a few more bookkeeping entries, or testing a few more product samples. In some cases, however, the decision is not a choice among incremental actions but an all-or-nothing choice. One of the most famous (or infamous) business decisions about costs and expected benefits is Ford Motor Company's decision in the 1970s to locate the gas tank outside the frame of its Pinto automobile and a few of its light trucks. In some rear-end collisions, the gas tank burst into flame, and the occupants of the car burned to death.

The business decision faced by Ford's managers was an all-or-nothing decision: whether to redesign the gas tank or leave it where it was and face product liability lawsuits. Ford's managers left the gas tank where it was, allegedly based on the expected benefit/cost reasoning shown in Table 14.5. The cost of moving the tank was $137.5 million, and the expected benefit from moving it (avoiding deaths, burn injuries, and burned vehicles) was a little less than $50 million. According to the arithmetic in the table, it was cheaper to leave the gas tank alone and pay the expected damages from the accidents than to redesign the Pinto and avoid the damages.

This business decision was rational based on the estimates shown in the table, but it turned out to be the wrong one because the managers dramatically underestimated the expected benefits from the redesign. Ford's managers thought that each death would cost Ford $200,000, but they were woefully incorrect. In fact, a single wrongful death lawsuit returned a $125 million verdict against Ford, though the courts later reduced it to $3.5 million. Ford's managers also did not take into account the tidal wave of bad publicity the company suffered over the failure to "spend $11 to move the gas tank." Avoiding the massive bad publicity should have been another line item on the expected benefit side of the equation. Indeed, the negative publicity was so

Table 14.5 All-or-Nothing Cost/Benefit Decision

	Item	Cost per Unit	Expected Benefit	
Expected benefits from redesigning the gas tank	• 180 fewer burn deaths	$200,000 per death	$36,000,000	
	• 180 fewer burn injuries	$67,000 per injury	$12,060,000	
	• 2,100 fewer burned vehicles	$700 per vehicle	$1,470,000	
	Total expected benefit			$49,530,000
	Item	Cost per Unit	Cost	
Costs of redesigning the gas tank	• 11,000,000 cars	$11 per car	$121,000,000	
	• 1,500,000 light trucks	$11 per truck	$16,500,000	
	Total cost			$137,500,000

Source: http://florinpopa.files.wordpress.com/2011/03/ford-pinto.pdf

profound that Ford stopped producing the Pinto only three years after publication of the first story revealing the alleged cost/benefit calculations. The model that Ford's managers allegedly used to make this decision was correct, but the data they used were not. The lesson for all managers is clear: Ensure that your data take into account all possibilities (including negative publicity) and are as correct as possible.

The Role of Marginal Analysis in Minimizing the Cost of Accidents

In your career as a manager, you are likely to make decisions intended to reduce the cost of a bad outcome, but you are highly unlikely to draw a figure similar to Figure 14.8, with the expected marginal benefit and marginal cost. The managerial lesson from the analysis is straightforward, however: When faced with decisions about random events (such as patent infringement, audit failure, or product failure), ask yourself the following questions before you take actions to decrease the expected cost of the bad outcome:

1. By how much will my action reduce the expected cost of the bad outcome?
2. What is the cost of my action?

If the reduction in the expected cost exceeds the cost of your action, take the action. More formally, when $E[MB] > MC$, the total cost is decreased by taking the action. Alternatively, if the reduction in the expected cost is less than the cost of your action, do not take the action. Once again more formally, when $E[MB] < MC$, the total cost is decreased by *not* taking the action. As you learned from the example of Ford's Pinto, determining the effect of your action on the expected cost of the bad outcome will not always be easy, but applying this type of analysis will lead you to minimize cost.

Uncertainty is not limited to the scenarios just explored. It is also important to litigation. Because large businesses are constantly involved in lawsuits, managers often face the decision of whether to settle or proceed with litigation. This decision is the topic of the next section.

Safety at an Energy Firm

SOLVED
PROBLEM

Coal and natural gas producers, such as CONSOL Energy, a large company headquartered in Pittsburgh, have managers in charge of safety at particular mines. Suppose that you are a safety manager for another coal firm. You estimate that if you do nothing, there is a 100 percent chance of an accident at the mine and the cost to your firm will be $64 million. You can make expenditures on safety, however. Each safety expenditure you make costs $2 million and decreases the remaining probability of an accident by one-half: The first one decreases the probability to 50 percent, the second to 25 percent, the third to 12.5 percent, and so on.

a. What are the expected marginal benefit and marginal cost of the first expenditure on safety?

b. What are the expected marginal benefit and marginal cost of the second expenditure on safety?

c. What is the cost-minimizing number of safety expenditures? Explain your answer.

(Continues)

SOLVED PROBLEM (*continued*)

Answer

a. The marginal benefit of the first expenditure is the reduction in the expected cost of an accident. The expected cost of an accident falls from $64 million × 1.00 = $64 million to $64 million × 0.50 = $32 million, a fall in cost and hence an expected marginal benefit of $64 million − $32 million, or $32 million. The marginal cost is $2 million.

b. The marginal benefit of the second expenditure is the reduction in the expected cost of an accident. The expected cost of an accident falls from $64 million × 0.50 = $32 million to $64 million × 0.25 = $16 million, a fall in cost and hence an expected marginal benefit of $16 million. The marginal cost is $2 million.

c. The cost-minimizing number of safety expenditures is five. After making four expenditures on safety, the probability of an accident is 6.25 percent, so the expected cost of an accident is $64 million × 0.0625 = $4 million. The fifth safety expenditure lowers the probability of an accident to 3.125 percent, making the expected cost of an accident $64 million × 0.03215 = $2 million. The expected marginal benefit is the decrease in the expected cost, $4 million − $2 million = $2 million. The marginal cost is $2 million. Because the expected marginal benefit equals the marginal cost, making five safety expenditures minimizes the expected cost from potential accidents.

14.5 The Business Decision to Settle Litigation

Learning Objective 14.5 Analyze when and why managers should agree to settle a lawsuit rather than litigate it.

Abraham Lincoln warned that litigation should be avoided whenever feasible:

> Discourage litigation. Persuade your neighbors to compromise whenever you can. Point out to them how the nominal winner is often a real loser—in fees, expenses, and waste of time.

As in so many other areas, Lincoln was perceptive and correct in his thoughts about litigation. To some extent, society seems to be taking his advice: Roughly 90 to 95 percent of both civil and criminal cases are settled. In many cases, defendants settle without acknowledging responsibility. For example, in recent years, Citigroup allegedly tried to fix an important financial benchmark (the ISDAFIX, now called the ICE Swap Rate) used to set some interest rates. In 2016, Citigroup settled the antitrust charges brought against it for $425 million without admitting guilt. You might ask yourself why a company would agree to pay a substantial sum to settle a case if it was blameless. As you will learn shortly, this managerial decision is often sound.

Basic Economic Model of Settlements: Parties with Similar Assessments

Suppose that Paul, Inc. (the plaintiff), sues Dana Corp. (the defendant) over a sum of money (*S*), the size of which is not in dispute. Paul alleges that Dana failed to meet her supply obligation to Paul, increasing Paul's expenses by the sum of $1.0 million. Dana disagrees, stating that she complied with the contract. With *S* equal to $1.0 million, Dana is certainly not eager to pay. To analyze the possibility of settling this dispute, the following notation is adopted:

- p is Paul's subjective probability of winning, so $1 - p$ is Paul's probability of losing.
- q is Dana's subjective probability of Paul winning, so $1 - q$ is Dana's probability of winning.
- CP and CD represent the litigation costs for Paul and Dana, respectively. These costs include legal fees, filing fees, opportunity costs, and bad publicity. The calculations presented here will use the *American rule*, in which each side must pay its litigation costs regardless of the outcome.

The actual amount Paul will win in the lawsuit is a random variable that could be either $0 or $1.0 million. Neither Paul nor Dana knows what the outcome will be, but both can calculate the expected value of the lawsuit. These expected values represent the **expected value of litigation**, the expected value of the gain from litigation for the plaintiff and the expected value of the loss from litigation for the defendant.

The expected value (the gain) of litigation to Paul is $E[L]_P$. $E[L]_P$ is equal to the probability of winning (p) multiplied by the sum Paul receives if he wins (S), plus the probability of losing ($1 - p$) multiplied by zero, minus the cost to Paul of the litigation process (CP):

> **Expected value of litigation** The expected value of the gain from litigation for the plaintiff and the expected value of the loss from litigation for the defendant.

$$E[L]_P = (p \times S) + [(1 - p) \times 0] - CP = (p \times S) - CP$$

For example, if Paul thinks he has a 60 percent chance of winning the $1.0 million and his cost of litigation is $400,000, the expected gain to Paul of the litigation is

$$E[L]_P = (0.60 \times \$1,000,000) + (0.40 \times \$0) - \$400,000 = \$200,000$$

For Dana, the expected value (the loss) of litigation is $E[L]_D$. $E[L]_D$ is equal to the probability of Paul winning (q) multiplied by the sum Dana must pay if Paul wins (S), plus the probability of Dana winning ($1 - q$) multiplied by zero, plus the cost to Dana of the litigation process (CD):

$$E[L]_D = (q \times S) + [(1 - q) \times 0] + CD = (q \times S) + CD$$

If Dana also thinks that Paul has a 60 percent chance of winning the $1.0 million and her cost of litigation is $300,000, Dana's expected loss from the litigation is

$$E[L]_D = (0.60 \times \$1,000,000) + (0.40 \times \$0) + \$300,000 = \$900,000$$

In general, Paul expects to win the value of $E[L]_P$, while Dana expects to lose the value of $E[L]_D$. Using the numerical examples above, Paul expects to gain $200,000, and Dana expects to lose $900,000. If, as in the above example, Dana expects to lose more than Paul expects to gain—that is, if $E[L]_D > E[L]_P$—it is very likely that Dana and Paul will settle without a trial. They settle because Dana is willing to pay more than Paul's expected gain and Paul is willing to accept less than Dana's expected loss. The reason the sides are likely to settle becomes clearer by rewriting the settlement condition, $E[L]_D > E[L]_P$, in terms of the expected settlements and other costs:

$$(q \times S) + CD > (p \times S) - CP \Rightarrow [S \times (q - p)] + (CD + CP) > 0 \quad \textbf{14.1}$$

The second part of Equation 14.1 shows that the difference between the plaintiff's expected gain and the defendant's expected loss is the result of differences in their subjective probabilities of winning or losing the case, $q - p$, and in the cost of the litigation itself, $(CD + CP)$. When both Paul and Dana have the same subjective probability of Paul winning the case, so that $p = q$ (both are 60 percent in the example), the difference is due only to the costs of litigation incurred by both sides. Paul pays $400,000 for his cost, and Dana pays $300,000 for her cost, so together they pay the sum of $700,000, exactly the difference between Paul's expected gain and Dana's expected loss.

It is useful to think about the settlement as the result of a transaction. Paul's lawsuit is an asset with an expected value to Paul of $E[L]_P$. The value to Dana of Paul's asset is Dana's expected loss of $E[L]_D$. If Dana's value exceeds Paul's value, then Dana will "buy" Paul's asset by settling the lawsuit. In the numerical example, Paul's lawsuit is worth $200,000 to him, but it is worth $900,000 to Dana. Dana is willing to offer any amount up to $900,000 to settle, and Paul is willing to accept any amount over $200,000 to settle. It is no wonder that Dana is able to settle the lawsuit! The settlement will fall somewhere between $200,000 and $900,000, depending on the bargaining skills of the two parties.

One point stands out: Dana is likely to settle even if she truly believes she followed the rules of the contract. From an economic standpoint, the decision—to settle or litigate—has little to do with actual guilt or innocence. From their

---

DECISION SNAPSHOT   **Actavis Versus Solvay Pharmaceuticals**

When a pharmaceutical company discovers a new drug, it invariably patents the drug. The patent gives the company the legal right to be the only producer for a number of years—typically, 20 years after the company filed the patent. Generic drug companies, however, often file lawsuits seeking to invalidate the patent so that they also can produce the drug. The generic drug company Actavis (at the time called Watson) filed suit against Solvay Pharmaceuticals, seeking to invalidate Solvay's patent on AndroGel. On average, generic drug companies win slightly less than half of the lawsuits they file. Solvay's patent still had 16 years left before it expired. Rather than litigate the suit, Actavis's managers agreed to a settlement that allowed the firm to market the drug after 9 years. As a manager at Actavis, why would you accept a settlement that provides your company with no immediate gain?

Answer

The patent had 16 more years before it expired. Although Actavis would prefer to start producing AndroGel immediately, if it lost the lawsuit, it would need to wait the entire 16-year period. Based on the probability of Actavis winning the case, the payoff if Actavis won, and the cost to Actavis of the litigation, the firm's managers decided that settling the suit was the profit-maximizing choice. By settling, Actavis's managers traded the uncertain outcome of the trial for the certainty that in 9 years the firm would be permitted to manufacture generic AndroGel. Indeed, in many of these types of lawsuits, the two sides often agree to a settlement in which the company holding the patent allows the generic drug company to produce the drug some years in the future but before the patent expires.

perspectives as managers, Dana's goal should be to minimize her costs (*not* prove her innocence), and Paul's goal should be to maximize his return (*not* win the lawsuit). Paul and Dana must set their emotions aside and make the optimal managerial choice. For defendants, that choice may be to settle even if they know they are innocent. For plaintiffs, that choice may be to settle even if they know the defendant is guilty.

Parties with Different Assessments

The previous example assumed that both the plaintiff, Paul, and the defendant, Dana, shared the same assessment of Paul's probability of winning (60 percent) and the maximum potential damages ($1.0 million). In reality, opponents may have different estimates of the probability that the plaintiff will win and different views of the maximum award. Incorporating these differences is straightforward but requires some expansion of the model. This example continues to use p as Paul's subjective probability that he will win the suit and q as Dana's subjective probability that Paul will win the suit. However, it uses S_P as Paul's estimate of the damages and S_D as Dana's estimate of the damages. With this change, Paul's expected gain from litigating the suit is

$$E[L]_P = (p \times S_P) + [(1 - p) \times 0] - CP = (p \times S_P) - CP$$

and Dana's expected loss from litigating the suit is

$$E[L]_D = (q \times S_D) + [(1 - q) \times 0] + CD = (q \times S_D) + CD$$

As in the preceding example, if $E[L]_D > E[L]_P$, then Dana and Paul should settle rather than litigate. By substituting the expected gain to the plaintiff and the expected loss to the defendant above, the inequality becomes

$$(q \times S_D) + CD > (p \times S_P) - CP \qquad \textbf{14.2}$$

According to Equation 14.2, Paul and Dana should settle the suit when Dana's expected loss from the litigation, $(q \times S_D) + CD$, exceeds Paul's expected gain, $(p \times S_P) - CP$.

Rearranging Equation 14.2 shows that the parties should settle when

$$(q \times S_D) - (p \times S_P) + (CD + CP) > 0 \qquad \textbf{14.3}$$

Differences in the assessments of probabilities and damages make drawing general conclusions from this example more complicated, but you can still use Equation 14.3 to determine the following:

- The larger the defendant's assessment of the expected payment to the plaintiff $(q \times S_D)$, the more likely the case will be settled. It does not matter why the defendant's assessment is large—whether it is a high probability of the plaintiff winning (q) or a large potential damage payment (S_D). What matters is the product of the two.
- The smaller the plaintiff's assessment of the expected payment to be received $(p \times S_P)$, the more likely the case will be settled. Again, it does not matter if the plaintiff's assessment is small because of a low probability of the plaintiff winning (p) or a small potential damage payment (S_P). What matters is the product of the two.
- The larger the total cost of litigation (the larger $CD + CP$), the more likely the parties will settle the case rather than litigate it.

SOLVED
PROBLEM

To Settle or Not To Settle, That Is the Question

You believe that one of your suppliers has violated its contract, so you file suit asking for $10 million in damages. If you win the lawsuit, you estimate the awarded damages at $10 million. You think that you have a 60 percent chance of winning the lawsuit. You must pay your attorney $2 million to try the case. The managers of the supplier estimate that you have a 40 percent chance of winning damages of $3 million. They must pay their attorney $1 million to go to trial.

a. Will you and your supplier settle the suit? Why or why not?

b. You instruct your attorney to file a flurry of motions that force the supplier's attorney to work more hours, and you raise the damages you claim to $15 million. You still think you will actually win $10 million, you estimate the probability that you will win to be 60 percent, and your attorney still charges you $2 million. The supplier's managers now believe that if they lose, they will pay you $6 million in damages and that you have a 40 percent chance of winning. They now must pay their attorney $3 million to go to trial. Should the lawsuit be settled? Why or why not?

Answer

a. You and your supplier will settle if the supplier's expected loss exceeds your expected gain. The supplier's expected loss is $(0.40 \times \$3 \text{ million}) + \$1 \text{ million} = \$2.2 \text{ million}$. Your expected gain is $(0.60 \times \$10 \text{ million}) - \$2 \text{ million} = \$4 \text{ million}$. Because the supplier's expected loss is less than your expected gain, the lawsuit will not be settled.

b. Your expected gain remains $4 million, but the supplier's expected loss has changed. It is now $(0.40 \times \$6 \text{ million}) + \$3 \text{ million} = \$5.4 \text{ million}$. Because the supplier's expected loss is greater than your expected gain, the lawsuit should be settled.

14.6 Risk Aversion

Learning Objective 14.6 Summarize how risk aversion affects managerial decision making.

The analysis to this point has focused only on expected values, including minimization of the expected cost of an adverse event and calculation of the expected value of a settlement in a court case. As you saw in Table 14.3, however, the expected value does not take into account the risk that the size of the variation around the expected value might impose. In some cases, managers might be concerned about the risk of the possible outcome in addition to its expected value. For example, say that as the owner of a small chain of auto repair shops, you face a lawsuit alleging improper repairs. The plaintiff asks for a settlement of $10 million, which you pay if you lose the suit. If the courts find you not guilty, you pay nothing to the plaintiff. You know that your company is innocent, but you still think there is a 2 percent chance you will lose the suit. In this case, your expected payment is $(0.02 \times \$10,000,000) + (0.98 \times \$0) = \$200,000$. Your company can afford to pay $200,000, but paying $10 million will bankrupt it. So you risk destroying your company by going to trial. In this case, you may be risk averse. Managers who prefer a sure prospect of paying (or receiving) a certain amount to a risky prospect with an expected value of the same amount are **risk averse**. Most people are risk averse, but some are *risk lovers*—they prefer riskier situations. Others are *risk neutral*—they care only about the expected value of a situation and are unconcerned about any risk.

Risk averse Preferring the sure prospect of paying (or receiving) a certain amount to a risky prospect with an expected value of the same amount.

Insurance

Purchasing insurance is one way for risk-averse managers to reduce risk by reducing the range of possible outcomes. For example, in 2015, the Golden State Warriors, the National Basketball Association team in Oakland, California, offered a fan chosen at random the chance to sink a half-court shot to win a BMW automobile. Suppose that the BMW costs $50,000 and the fan has a 1/10 of 1 percent (0.001) chance of making the shot, which means the fan has a 99.9 percent (0.999) chance of missing it. The promotion has an expected cost for the Warriors of $E[C] = (\$50,000 \times 0.001) + (\$0 \times 0.999) = \$50$. There is, however, a risk that the fan will make the shot, in which case the Warriors must pay $50,000 for the car. The managers of the Warriors may be risk averse and not like the risk of the possible $50,000 payout.

Companies such as Odds On Promotions sell insurance for these types of events. The insurance reduces the Warriors' risk. For example, Odds On Promotions might charge the Warriors $700 for an insurance policy that will buy the automobile if the fan makes the shot. Of course, if the fan misses, Odds On Promotion pockets the $700 and pays nothing. With this insurance, if the fan makes the shot, the cost to the Warriors is the price of the policy, $700. If the fan misses, the cost to the Warriors is the same, $700. So the expected cost to the Warriors with insurance is $E[C] = (\$700 \times 0.001) + (\$700 \times 0.999) = \$700$. Even though the expected cost with the insurance is higher than without it ($700 versus $50), the Warriors' management may prefer buying insurance because it eliminates the risk of paying $50,000. Incidentally, in 2015, the fan made the shot!

The lessons here are straightforward:

- The more risk averse people or firms are, the more likely they are to buy insurance, and the more money they are willing to pay for the insurance. The sky is not the limit, however. If Odds On Promotions tried to charge the Warriors $20,000, rather than $700, for the policy, the managers of the Warriors may well have decided that they were willing to accept the risk without insurance.
- The greater the risk is, the more likely a person or firm is to buy insurance, and the higher the price they are willing to pay for insurance. For example, vendors selling products to retail companies frequently purchase insurance to guarantee that they receive payment for their products. As sales at Sears stores have declined over the past years, the risk of nonpayment by Sears has increased. The price venders paid for insurance rose from 1.9 percent of the amount insured in 2014 to 2.7 percent in 2015.

Risk Aversion and Diversification

Suppose that different corporations are introducing new products. Even though the managers at each company might be risk averse, the shareholders may want the managers to ignore any risk from the introduction and instead focus entirely on the expected profit. The reason for the shareholders' preference is diversification, the age-old wisdom to avoid placing all of your eggs in a single basket. Risk-averse shareholders can buy shares of stock in many different companies, creating a diversified portfolio. With such a portfolio, shareholders are insuring themselves against the risk of bad outcomes because their investments in those companies with products that flop will be balanced by their investments in those companies with successful products. Diversification reduces the risk that shareholders face at little to no cost. The companies, however, cannot reduce risk for free—any risk-reducing actions they take incur costs. Because the increased costs reduce the return on investment, the shareholders may prefer that the managers focus only on the expected profit from their actions.

Risk Aversion and Litigation

To examine the role of risk aversion in litigation further, let's return to the auto repair chain example introduced at the beginning of this section. Recall that as the owner, you face the risk of losing your business if the court judgment goes against you. The risk of losing the company might be more than you are prepared to face. Your risk aversion makes you more willing to settle the lawsuit and pay a larger settlement amount. In general, the more risk averse a defendant is, the more willing the defendant is to settle, and the larger the amount the defendant will pay as a settlement.

Plaintiffs also can be risk averse. If potential financial disaster makes plaintiffs concerned about losing a lawsuit, they are willing to settle for less in order to avoid the risk of a trial. In general, the more risk averse a plaintiff is, the more willing the plaintiff is to settle and the smaller the amount the plaintiff is willing to accept as a settlement.

SOLVED PROBLEM

Merck Takes Advantage of Risk Aversion

In 2004, Merck, a large American pharmaceutical company, removed its pain-relieving drug Vioxx from the market after research demonstrated that taking the pill increased the chance of a heart attack. Almost instantly Merck faced 27,000 lawsuits from plaintiffs alleging that Vioxx had triggered their heart attacks. Merck contested the first 16 cases that came to trial, winning 11 of them. In one case it lost, the jury set the plaintiff's damages at $250 million, although a higher court quickly overturned the award. Assume that Merck's cost of litigation is $500,000 per trial and a plaintiff's cost of litigation is $1 million per trial.

a. Suppose that Merck's executives believe there is a 0.1 percent (0.001) chance of losing a trial and that if it lost, the damages awarded against Merck will be $25 million. What is Merck's expected loss from litigation, $E[L]$, for one case?

b. Suppose that the plaintiffs believe there is a 2 percent (0.02) chance of winning a trial and that if they win, the damages awarded them will be $100 million. What is the plaintiffs' expected gain from litigation for one case?

c. Based on your answers to parts a and b, would the lawsuits be settled? Explain your answer.

d. What is Merck's expected loss from litigation, $E[L]$, for *all* 27,000 cases?

e. At the time, Merck's annual profit was about $5 billion per year. Suppose that Merck's executives were risk averse. How would the risk aversion affect the likelihood of a settlement?

Answer

a. Merck's expected loss from litigation for one case would be $(0.001 \times \$25 \text{ million}) + \$500,000 = \$525,000$.

b. The plaintiffs' expected gain from litigation for one case would be $(0.02 \times \$100 \text{ million}) - \$1 \text{ million} = \$1.0 \text{ million}$.

c. No, the cases would not be settled because the expected loss to the defendant is less than the expected gain to the plaintiff.

d. Merck faces 27,000 trials, so the expected loss from all the cases would be $\$525,000 \times 27,000$, or approximately $\$14.2$ billion.

e. While Merck might have been able to handle payments totaling $14.2 billion, Merck's executives faced a real risk that trying all the cases could bankrupt the company. If they underestimated the probability of loss or the damages that juries would award, Merck might be unable to make the payments. Because the executives were risk averse, after the first 16 cases Merck ultimately negotiated a settlement of all the cases. Merck's negotiators were good (very good!) because they negotiated a total payment of approximately $5 billion, which is much less than the expected loss from trying all 27,000 cases. Merck's negotiators were helped because the plaintiffs apparently also were very risk averse. After paying their attorney fees, each plaintiff received an average of only about $100,000.

14.7 Making Business Decisions Under Uncertainty

> **MANAGERIAL APPLICATION**

Learning Objective 14.7 Apply marginal analysis to make profit-maximizing managerial decisions under uncertainty.

Making decisions when outcomes are uncertain is both common and difficult. Fortunately, as you have seen throughout this chapter, you can often use marginal analysis to guide you to the profit-maximizing decision. The models presented are simplified, but you should consider the principles they illustrate when making decisions. Approaching difficult decisions using marginal analysis ensures that you are on the right track.

The first two parts of this section illustrate the power of marginal analysis to help you maximize profit when faced with random demand and random cost and to set optimal inventories when faced with random demand for your product. The last part explores guidelines for managers involved in litigation.

Maximizing Profit with Random Demand and Random Cost

Because uncertainty and random changes in a firm's demand and/or its cost are pervasive in the real world, you will not be able to maximize your profit successfully period after period. Consequently, because it ignores uncertainty, the profit-maximization rule introduced in Chapter 5—to produce the quantity that sets $MR = MC$—is more of a target or goal rather than an operational rule. Instead, the expected-profit-maximization rule—to produce the quantity that sets your expected marginal revenue equal to your expected marginal cost, or $\text{E}[MR] = \text{E}[MC]$—is a more operational guideline. Although still difficult to achieve, it is a more realistic goal. In a sense, the expected-profit-maximization rule is the real-world counterpart of the profit-maximization rule from Chapter 5.

When you use the expected-profit-maximization rule, in some cases you may be able to use regression analysis (see Sections 3.1, 3.2, and 3.3) to predict the future demand and/or marginal cost. You can then use these predictions to calculate expected demand and/or expected marginal cost. For example, say that you work for the Seaboard Corporation, a widely diverse corporation that owns one-half of the turkey-producing company Butterball LLC. Turkeys take about seven months to grow from a hatchling (called a poult) to a full-size bird. Consequently, you must determine more than seven months in advance how many turkey hatchlings you want to purchase to have ready for Thanksgiving even though the future demand for turkeys at Thanksgiving is unknown. Market analysts at Butterball can use regression analysis to determine the firm's expected price, $E[P]$, of turkeys at Thanksgiving. Suppose that Butterball is a perfectly competitive firm, so the expected price is equal to Butterball's expected marginal revenue; that is, $E[P] = E[MR]$. Accordingly, you can maximize expected profit by purchasing and producing the quantity of hatchings that sets the marginal cost of a turkey equal to its expected price, where the expected price is the result of regression analysis.

In other instances, however, you may not have either the resources or the data to conduct a regression analysis. You can still use marginal analysis to make the decision about how much to produce, but you must think carefully when estimating marginal revenue and marginal cost. In this case, use your best estimates as the expected marginal revenue and expected marginal cost.

Regardless of the source of your estimates, remember the actions you need to take to maximize your expected profit: If the expected marginal revenue exceeds the expected marginal cost, you should increase production. In other words, if the expected profit from producing a unit of output is positive—that is, $E[MR] - E[MC] > 0$—continue to increase production as long as this condition holds. However, if the expected marginal revenue is less than the expected marginal cost, the unit has an expected loss, so you should decrease production.

Optimal Inventories with Uncertainty About Demand

Like all economic models, the inventory model developed in Section 14.3 is simplified. For example, the model assumes that the cost of production is the only cost of the product. This assumption is reasonable for firms like Panera Bread that keep their bread for only one day. Other costs play a role in alternative real-world scenarios, however:

- The interest cost of financing the inventory at an automobile dealership can be significant. Auto dealers typically borrow funds to finance their inventory of cars for sale using what is called *floor plan financing*. If the interest rate on these loans is 7 percent, then dealers pay about $5.75 in interest per day on a vehicle with a $30,000 wholesale price.
- For a computer chip manufacturer, an important factor is the cost of the chips becoming technologically obsolete the longer the company holds them. For example, in 2012, when Transcend Information first introduced its 128GB Jet-Flash 760 USB drive, the price was $199. Four years later a faster 128GB JetFlash 790 USB drive was available for $51. The value of the older, slower memory chips used to produce the initial 128GB USB drive had become virtually zero because the chips were obsolete.

Although incorporating these additional costs into the decision can be complicated, the basic insights of the model remain: Managers must estimate the expected marginal benefit and expected marginal cost of adding a unit to the inventory and then add that unit if the expected marginal benefit exceeds the expected marginal cost.

The economic model demonstrates that the profit-maximizing inventory to hold is the quantity that sets the expected marginal benefit equal to the expected marginal cost. This result shows how changes in the expected marginal benefit or the expected marginal cost affect the profit-maximizing inventory. Any change that increases the expected profit from having a unit in stock increases the expected marginal benefit, which shifts the expected marginal benefit curve upward and increases the quantity you want to hold in inventory. For example, suppose that the price of a loaf of bread at your bakery increases or the probability of selling a loaf increases. Either change increases the expected profit from a loaf held in inventory, so as Figure 14.9 illustrates, the expected marginal benefit curve shifts from $E[MB]_0$ to $E[MB]_1$. As a result, the profit-maximizing inventory increases from 54 loaves to 55 loaves. Of course, the opposite is also true: Any change that *decreases* the expected marginal benefit (a decrease in profit or probability of sale) also decreases the size of the profit-maximizing inventory.

The expected marginal cost of holding a unit in inventory equals the expected loss from the unit, so a change in the expected loss shifts the expected marginal cost curve. Any change that increases the expected loss from each unit left unsold shifts the expected marginal cost curve upward and decreases the quantity you want to hold in inventory. Similarly, any change that *decreases* the expected marginal cost increases your profit-maximizing inventory.

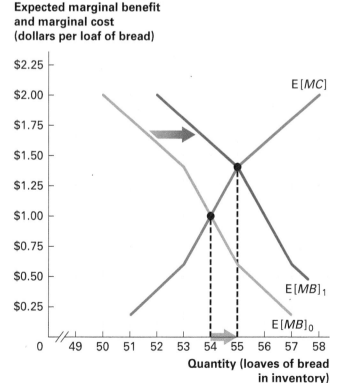

Expected marginal benefit and marginal cost (dollars per loaf of bread)

Figure 14.9 Changes in the Profit-Maximizing Inventory

An increase in the expected marginal benefit of holding a loaf of bread in inventory shifts the expected marginal benefit curve to the right. The profit-maximizing inventory quantity increases, from 54 loaves to 55 loaves.

Making Business Decisions to Settle Litigation

The implications of the economic analysis of litigation vary depending on whether you are the plaintiff or the defendant.

- **Plaintiff.** As the plaintiff, your goal is to maximize your gain. Any action that increases the defendant's expected loss from litigation increases the maximum amount the defendant is willing to pay to settle. Boosting the defendant's cost of litigation or raising the defendant's subjective probability that you will win the case increases the amount the defendant is willing to pay. So, too, will raising the defendant's estimate of the damages. Any (or all) of these three strategies makes it easier for you to negotiate a larger settlement.

  For example, in 2013, Bridgestone North America sued IBM for $600 million, alleging that a computer system IBM installed was defective and harmed Bridgestone's business. In 2016, Bridgestone issued subpoenas to seven other companies that had purchased similar computer systems from IBM. Aside from gathering information that could prove helpful to their case, Bridgestone's managers might have wanted to increase the cost of doing business with IBM in an attempt to affect the demand for IBM's systems. If IBM's managers believed that these subpoenas could harm the demand for their computer systems, then the subpoenas increased IBM's cost of litigation.

- **Defendant.** As the defendant, your goal is to minimize your loss. Any action that decreases the plaintiff's expected value of litigation decreases the minimum amount the plaintiff is willing to accept to settle. Increasing the plaintiff's cost of litigation or decreasing the plaintiff's subjective probability of winning the case decreases the amount the plaintiff will accept.

  One way to decrease the expected value is to countersue. For example, in 2016, Huawei Technologies Company, the world's third-largest smartphone manufacturer, sued Samsung Electronics, the world's largest smartphone producer, for patent infringement and asked that Samsung be required to pay royalties to Huawei. Three months later Samsung countersued Huawei and asked for $24 million in damages. This countersuit reduced Huawei's expected value of the litigation, making Huawei more likely to settle the lawsuit on terms that are more favorable to Samsung.

One last point to keep in mind is the effect of changing a risk-averse litigant's expected loss or value of the litigation. If, as a plaintiff, you can justifiably boost your claim so that it becomes significantly more threatening to the defendant, the defendant's risk aversion will increase the likelihood of a settlement offer. Of course, changing your opponent's expected value of litigation is only the first step in the settlement process, but it can make your negotiations easier.

Revisiting How Embezzlement Made Managers at a Nonprofit See Red

All managers must make decisions in the face of uncertainty. In this chapter, you have learned how managers of profit-seeking firms can make such decisions, but the same analysis applies to managers of nonprofit organizations. To further the goals of any organization, whether it is maximizing profit or maximizing the help offered to people affected by natural disasters, managers should make the decisions that minimize expected costs. For the American Red Cross, minimizing its expected costs allows it to provide more aid to more people in need.

The executives at the Red Cross—and at *any* firm—must be concerned about embezzlement or other thefts of funds, but the existence of such malfeasance is uncertain. Managers can request a more complete audit from their accountants to detect the misuse of funds, but the more extensive the audit, the greater the cost. The managers at the Red Cross must use their best judgment about the likelihood of any possible embezzlement because the probability of embezzlement affects the marginal benefit of increasing the scope of the audit: The higher the probability of embezzlement, the larger the marginal benefit from a more extensive audit. Of course, the same reasoning applies to the potential amount of an embezzlement: The larger the potential amount, the larger the marginal benefit from a more extensive audit.

Red Cross executives apparently had no reason to suspect that Ms. Leggio was misappropriating money. It is likely that managers at nonprofits such as the American Red Cross believe that their employees all share the goal of furthering the organization's good works, so they probably estimate a low probability of embezzlement. For example, suppose that the managers believe the probability

of embezzlement to be ¼ of 1 percent (0.0025). Further suppose that the managers think that if embezzlement does occur, the amount will be $300,000. In this case, the expected marginal benefit, $E[MB]$, from a more complete audit is $300,000 \times 0.0025 = 750. The managers need to compare this expected marginal benefit to the marginal cost, MC, of a more complete audit. If the marginal cost exceeds $750, then the managers should make the expected-cost-minimizing decision to limit the audit. The fact that the audits do not immediately uncover the embezzlement does not mean that the managers are negligent. The managers are simply minimizing the total expected cost of potential embezzlement, the combined cost of the audits plus the expected cost of embezzlement losses.

In *any* situation dealing with randomness, decision makers can come to regret decisions that were optimal at the time. Red Cross managers must have regretted that they did not commission more-complete audits, but based on their estimate of the probability of embezzlement, such a request would have led to a perceived unnecessary increase in costs. So their decision to limit the extent of the audit was, at the time, optimal.

Summary: The Bottom Line

14.1 Basics of Probability
- Probability measures the chance that an event occurs. Probabilities lie between zero—the event definitely will not occur—and one—the event definitely will occur. The probabilities of all possible outcomes sum to one.
- A random variable is any variable with an uncertain outcome. The expected value of a random variable is a weighted average of the possible outcomes, where the weights are the probabilities of the outcomes.
- Subjective probabilities are the probabilities of different outcomes based on the best estimate of the probability of each possible outcome.

14.2 Profit Maximization with Random Demand and Random Cost
- If demand and/or cost is random, managers can maximize expected profit.
- If demand is random, managers maximize expected profit by producing the quantity that sets the expected marginal revenue equal to the marginal cost.

- If cost is random, managers maximize expected profit by producing the quantity that sets the marginal revenue equal to the expected marginal cost.
- If *both* demand and cost are random, managers maximize expected profit by producing the quantity that sets the expected marginal revenue equal to the expected marginal cost, or $E[MR] = E[MC]$.

14.3 Optimal Inventories with Random Demand
- If demand is random, then the probability of selling a unit held in inventory is random. A manager's goal is to maximize the expected profit from the inventory.
- Managers use marginal analysis to determine the optimal inventory by comparing the expected marginal benefit of adding a unit to the inventory (the profit on the unit multiplied by the probability it is sold) to the expected marginal cost of adding the unit (the loss on the unit multiplied by the probability it remains unsold).
- The profit-maximizing inventory is the amount that sets the expected marginal benefit of a unit equal to its expected marginal cost.

14.4 Minimizing the Cost of Random Adverse Events

- All businesses face the possibility of random adverse events, also referred to as bad outcomes or accidents, such as patent infringement, audit failure, and product failure. Such events decrease profit.
- Managers can take actions to decrease the probability of a bad outcome. The expected marginal benefit from these expenditures is the reduction in the expected cost of the accident.
- Managers should use marginal analysis to balance the expected marginal benefit from the reduction in the expected cost of the accident against the marginal cost of the expenditure made to avoid the accident. The optimal amount is spent when the expected marginal benefit equals the marginal cost because that amount minimizes the total expected cost of the accident.

14.5 The Business Decision to Settle Litigation

- To maximize profit, managers must view litigation as a business decision and determine whether settling a lawsuit offers the firm a greater expected profit (or a lesser expected cost) than fighting it.
- A plaintiff's goal is to maximize the settlement, and a defendant's goal is to minimize the settlement. If the expected gain to the plaintiff of litigating a lawsuit is less than the expected loss to the defendant, it is optimal to settle the suit.

14.6 Risk Aversion

- A person who is risk averse prefers a sure prospect or paying (or receiving) a certain amount to a risky prospect with an expected value of the same amount.
- Risk aversion causes people and/or firms to buy insurance, diversify their stock portfolios, and settle lawsuits that they otherwise might litigate.

14.7 Managerial Application: Making Business Decisions Under Uncertainty

- Marginal analysis is frequently the key to making profit-maximizing decisions under uncertainty. The models presented in the chapter are simplified, but you need to consider the principles they illustrate when making real-world decisions.
- An increase in the expected marginal benefit of holding a good in inventory increases the profit-maximizing amount held in inventory, while an increase in the expected marginal cost of holding a good in inventory decreases the profit-maximizing quantity kept in inventory.
- The plaintiff in a lawsuit maximizes gain by taking actions that increase the defendant's expected loss from litigation. The defendant in a lawsuit minimizes loss by taking actions that decrease the plaintiff's expected gain from litigation.

Key Terms and Concepts

Expected profit	Objective probabilities	Subjective probabilities
Expected value	Random variable	
Expected value of litigation	Risk averse	

Questions and Problems

14.1 Basics of Probability

Learning Objective 14.1 Apply the concepts of probability and expected values to managerial decision making.

1.1 Explain why the probabilities of all the different possible events that may occur must add to one.

1.2 Lefty Larry is a relief pitcher for the Hogtown Hens. The next year of Larry's contract is an option year. His salary will be $4.0 million if the team exercises the option to keep him and $500,000 if it does not and pays a buyout. If the probability that the club will exercise the option is 0.60, what is the expected payment to Larry?

1.3 Insurance firm ABC, Inc., will earn a profit of $1.0 million this year if there are no hurricanes but only $200,000 if there is a hurricane. If only one hurricane can occur and the probability of its occurrence is 0.1, what is ABC's expected profit?

1.4 You have a base salary of $80,000 per year, with a bonus based on your company's profit. You earn no bonus if the company's profit is below $1.0 million, a bonus of $10,000 if the profit is between $1.0 million and $5.0 million, or a bonus of $25,000 if the profit exceeds $5.0 million. You believe the probability of a profit below $1.0 million is 0.30, the probability of a profit between $1.0 million and $5.0 million is 0.50, and the probability of a profit exceeding $5.0 million is 0.20. What is your expected income?

1.5 The cost of one of the inputs you must buy is uncertain: It can be $7, $10, or $12. You calculate the probability of a $7 price at 30 percent, the probability of a $10 price at 50 percent, and the probability of a $12 price at 20 percent. What is the expected cost of the input?

1.6 You are a manager for a large trucking company like J.B. Hunt Transport Services. You need to estimate the price of diesel fuel. The table has different possible prices and the probabilities of these prices. What is the expected price of diesel fuel?

Price (dollars per gallon)	Probability
$2.50	0.10
2.60	0.20
2.70	0.20
2.80	0.40
2.90	0.10

1.7 You are considering entry into a highly competitive market. The probability of failure is 0.80, and the associated losses would be $10 million. If you are moderately successful, you will make $25 million. The probability of moderate success is 0.10. If you are very successful, you will make $50 million. What is your expected profit? Will you enter the market? Explain your answers.

14.2 Profit Maximization with Random Demand and Random Cost

Learning Objective 14.2 Explain how to make profit-maximizing production decisions when demand and marginal cost randomly fluctuate.

2.1 The figure duplicates Figure 14.2(a), which shows the situation at your California vineyard. If demand is high, the price is $3,000 per ton of grapes, and if the price is low, the price is $1,000 per ton of grapes. Producing 300 tons of grapes maximizes your firm's expected profit. Suppose that there is no fixed cost.

a. If demand is high and your firm produces 300 tons of grapes, what is its economic profit on the tons of grapes between 100 and 300 tons? If demand is low and your

Accompanies problem 2.1.

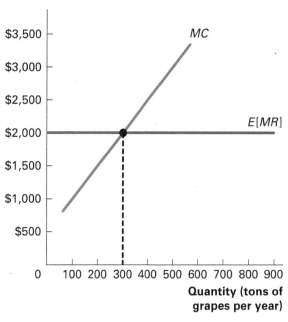

Price and cost (dollars per ton of grapes)

firm produces 300 tons of grapes, what is its economic loss on the tons of grapes between 100 and 300 tons?

b. High demand occurs 50 percent of the time, and low demand occurs 50 percent of the time. If your firm produces 300 tons of grapes, what is its expected profit on the tons of grapes between 100 and 300 tons?

c. If demand is high and your firm produces 500 tons of grapes, what is its economic profit on the tons of grapes between 300 and 500 tons? If demand is low and your firm produces 500 tons of grapes, what is its economic loss on the tons of grapes between 300 and 500 tons?

d. High demand occurs 50 percent of the time, and low demand occurs 50 percent of the time. If your firm produces 500 tons of grapes, what is the expected profit or loss on the tons of grapes between 300 and 500 tons?

2.2 You are managing a competitive corn farm that faces random demand. You must decide how much corn to produce before observing the actual price. As the figure shows, the price will be $12 or $6 per bushel. The probability the price will be $12 is 2/3, and the probability that the price will be $6 is 1/3. Your marginal cost curve is also included in the figure.

Accompanies problem 2.2.

Price and cost (dollars per bushel of corn)

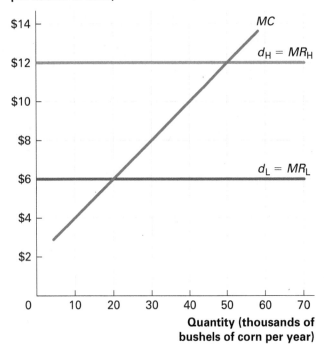

a. What quantity of corn maximizes expected profit?
b. How much would you produce if you knew the actual price before producing?
c. If you produce the quantity of corn that maximizes expected profit, compared to what you would produce if you knew the actual price before producing, how much profit is lost if the actual price is $12? If the actual price is $6?

2.3 The price in a perfectly competitive market is unknown when the manager of a firm must decide how much output to produce. The price will be $12 or $8 with equal probability. If the firm's marginal cost function is $MC = 5 + 0.01Q$, what quantity maximizes the expected profit?

2.4 You are a manager at a pizza restaurant in Scottsdale, Arizona. The demand for slices of pizza is random. The market is perfectly competitive, and on any given day, the price is either $4.40 or $4.80 with a probability of 0.50 for either possibility. The marginal cost of producing pizza is $MC = 0.02Q$.
a. What quantity maximizes your expected profit?
b. Compared to the profit if you knew the actual price in advance, if you produce the amount calculated in part a how much profit does your firm lose if the actual price turns out to be $4.80? If it turns out to be $4.40?

2.5 A monopolist's marginal revenue function is $MR = 100 - 0.2Q$. The marginal cost of production is random and is $9 or $11 with equal probabilities. What quantity maximizes the expected profit?

2.6 The demand function for a monopolist's product is $Q^D = 1{,}000 - 10P$, and its marginal revenue function is $MR = 100 - 0.2Q$. The marginal cost of production is subject to uncertainty.
a. If the firm's marginal cost is $50 with probability 0.50 or $30 with probability 0.50, what price and quantity maximize expected profit?
b. If the firm's marginal cost is $60 with probability 0.50 or $20 with probability 0.50, what price and quantity maximize expected profit?
c. Compare and explain the answers to parts a and b.

2.7 You work as a manager for the only country club in Carrollton, Georgia. The club has 400 members, each with an identical demand for golf given by $Q^D = 100 - P$, where P is the price per round and Q is the number of rounds. The marginal cost of a round of golf is random. The probability of $MC = \$15$ is one-half, while the probability of $MC = \$25$ is also one-half. The club has no fixed costs.

If you maximize expected profit, how much should the club charge for a round of golf? What is the expected number of rounds played?

14.3 Optimal Inventories with Random Demand

Learning Objective 14.3 Determine the profit-maximizing amount of inventory when demand changes randomly.

3.1 If the probability of selling a unit from inventory, $\text{Prob}(Q^D \geq Q)$, decreases, what happens to the probability of selling less than this quantity, $\text{Prob}(Q^D < Q)$? What is the effect of this change on the expected marginal benefit from keeping a unit in inventory? On the expected marginal cost? On the optimal inventory?

3.2 You are a manager at a car dealership in Mason City, Iowa. It is one month before next year's cars are distributed. You know that this month you will sell a minimum of 90 cars and a maximum of 99 cars. The table shows the probability distribution of the demand for cars between 90 and 99. The profit on each car you sell this month is $8,000. Next month you

Accompanies problem 3.2.

Probability Distribution of Car Sales

Quantity of Cars Demanded	Probability This Quantity Is Demanded	Probability of Selling This Quantity or More, $\text{Prob}(Q^D \geq Q)$	Probability of Selling Less Than This Quantity, $\text{Prob}(Q^D < Q)$
90	0.05		
91	0.05		
92	0.10		
93	0.10		
94	0.20		
95	0.20		
96	0.10		
97	0.10		
98	0.05		
99	0.05		
100	0.00		

must lower the price because of the arrival of the new models, so your loss on each car will be $2,000.

   a. Complete the table.

   b. What is the optimal quantity of cars to keep in inventory this month?

3.3 Suppose that the price of a product increases, so that the profit from selling it rises. The profit (or loss) from selling on the secondary market does not change. How does the rise in price affect the expected marginal benefit and the expected marginal cost of holding inventory? What is the impact on the optimal inventory to hold?

3.4 How does a fall in the price in the secondary market affect the expected marginal benefit and the expected marginal cost of holding inventory? What is the impact on the optimal inventory to hold?

14.4 Minimizing the Cost of Random Adverse Events

Learning Objective 14.4 Describe how to make cost-minimizing decisions when faced with random adverse events including patent infringement, audit failure, and product failure.

4.1 The BP oil spill in April 2010 caused substantial losses. BP has incurred over $61 billion in compensation costs and fines. Many critics contend that BP was at fault for the spill because of various inspection failures. Presume that the critics are correct (so that BP did

not purchase high-cost, high-quality inspections). Make an argument that in January 2010 BP's conduct was optimal.

4.2 Computerized patent searches have lowered the cost of avoiding patent infringement. Does this advance in technology shift the expected marginal benefit of avoiding an accident curve or the marginal cost of avoiding an accident curve? What happens to the profit-maximizing rate of patent infringement?

4.3 Suppose that courts begin imposing higher fines on appliance companies that manufacture products that occasionally malfunction and harm consumers. Appliance companies can make expenditures that decrease the likelihood of malfunctioning. Does the change in the court's behavior change the expected marginal benefit of avoiding an accident or the marginal cost of avoiding an accident? What happens to the rate of product malfunctions?

14.5 The Business Decision to Settle Litigation

Learning Objective 14.5 Analyze when and why managers should agree to settle a lawsuit rather than litigate it.

5.1 "As a general proposition, the higher the stakes of a lawsuit, the less likely a settlement." Is this statement true or false? Explain your answer. In your answer, assume that the plaintiff and the defendant expect the same award if the plaintiff wins the suit.

5.2 You are a defendant in a lawsuit. You know you are innocent. Should you ever consider settling the suit? Why or why not?

5.3 The plaintiffs believe that their probability of winning a $10,000 judgment at trial is 0.9. Their costs of litigation are $1,000. The defendants believe that the plaintiffs' probability of winning is 0.6, and the defendants' costs of litigation are $1,000.
   a. Is a settlement likely in this case? Why or why not?
   b. Suppose that settling is not free. Instead, the cost of settling is $300 for each party. Is a settlement more or less likely in this scenario?

5.4 A group of plaintiffs is suing your web consulting firm for alleged illegal overcharges that total $100 million. The plaintiffs believe that their probability of winning is 0.75, and their costs of litigation are $20 million. You believe that the plaintiffs' probability of winning is 0.60, and the cost of litigation to your firm is $20 million.
   a. In the United States, if the plaintiffs prevail, they can recover trebled damages plus their litigation costs, so if the plaintiffs win, they will receive $300 million plus their litigation costs. What is their expected gain from litigation? What is your firm's expected loss? Is a settlement likely in this case? Why or why not?
   b. In the European Union, plaintiffs can recover only their damages and must pay their own litigation costs. So if they win, the plaintiffs will recover their damages of $100 million. What is the expected loss to your firm? Is a settlement likely in this case? Why or why not?

5.5 GlaxoSmithKline (GSK) came under fire for its development and marketing of Avandia, a drug used by diabetics to make their cells more responsive to insulin. Critics accused the firm of concealing evidence that Avandia significantly increased a user's risk of a heart attack. GSK faced both criminal and civil actions in the United States, but in November 2011, it settled the criminal and civil actions for a total of $3.0 billion. Despite the settlement, GSK maintains that it was not guilty of any wrongdoing.
   a. Explain why GSK would settle if it was not guilty.
   b. GSK's stock price rose by about 1 percent after GSK announced the settlement. Why did GSK's stock price rise?

14.6 Risk Aversion

Learning Objective 14.6 Summarize how risk aversion affects managerial decision making.

6.1 You are the manager of a large corn farm. If you experience good weather, your profit is larger than if the weather is bad. The following table shows the probability distribution of the weather and your profit.

Weather	Probability of Occurrence	Profit
Good	80 percent	$400,000
Bad	20 percent	$50,000

   a. What is the expected profit?
   b. You can buy crop insurance for $50,000. The insurance is another cost that must be subtracted from the profits in the table. The insurance pays you nothing if the weather is good but pays you $300,000 if the weather is bad. What is your expected profit with insurance?
   c. Farmers almost always buy crop insurance. Based on your answers to parts a and b, explain why.

6.2 You are a defendant in a lawsuit. The plaintiff's expected gain from the lawsuit is $4 million. You believe there is only a 1 percent chance of losing, so that your expected loss, including the cost of litigation, is $1 million. If you do lose, however, you will be required to pay a total of $40 million.
   a. If neither you nor the plaintiff is risk averse, do you expect the suit to settle?
   b. If you become risk averse, how does this change affect the likelihood of a settlement? Explain your answer.

14.7 Managerial Application: Making Business Decisions Under Uncertainty

Learning Objective 14.7 Apply marginal analysis to make profit-maximizing managerial decisions under uncertainty.

7.1 You are a manager at a perfectly competitive firm like Scotch Plywood Company. The price of a sheet of plywood is $30. The marginal cost of producing plywood has a random element. The following table shows the data you have collected, showing the marginal cost of producing a sheet of plywood at different quantities. Estimate a regression using the marginal cost as the dependent variable and a constant and the quantity as independent variables.

Quantity (sheets)	Marginal Cost (dollars per sheet)	Quantity (sheets)	Marginal Cost (dollars per sheet)
25,000	$24.38	29,000	$30.26
26,000	25.54	30,000	31.24
26,000	26.21	30,000	31.69
27,000	27.35	30,000	30.39
27,000	26.68	30,000	30.09
27,000	26.75	30,000	29.91
28,000	28.50	31,000	31.07
28,000	28.00	31,000	31.01
28,000	27.70	31,000	33.14
29,000	31.16	31,000	32.73

(Recall that regression analysis was explained in Chapter 3, Sections 3.1, 3.2, and 3.3.) The predicted values for the dependent variable are the expected marginal costs at that quantity. What quantity of plywood maximizes your firm's expected profit?

7.2 You are a manager at a firm like Zara, one of the leaders in fast fashion. Fast-fashion companies move their designs from catwalk to stores quickly to capture current fashion trends. You are in charge of production. Amazingly, your company can design a new product and get it to your stores in seven days, so you must decide how much to produce seven days before the units are available for sale. Once a design is produced, you must sell whatever quantity has been manufactured.

The demand for your designs fluctuates unpredictably. Compared to the situation where you could adjust your production to every change in demand, your expected loss is $1.4 million. For every day by which you can reduce the lead time, your expected loss decreases by $200,000. (For example, if you can make your production decision only six days before the products appear in the stores, your expected loss becomes $1.4 million − $200,000 = $1.2 million.) Trimming the first day of lead time costs $100,000, trimming the second day costs $200,000, and so on until trimming the seventh day costs $700,000. What is the profit-maximizing reduction in your lead time?

7.3 The following table shows a bakery's probabilities of selling different quantities of bread.
   a. The price of a loaf of bread is $5, the marginal cost is $2, and the price received on the secondary market is $0. What is the profit-maximizing quantity of loaves to hold in inventory?
   b. The price of a loaf of bread rises to $10, while the marginal cost remains $2 and the price received on the secondary market remains $0. What is now the profit-maximizing quantity of loaves to hold in inventory? Explain why your answer differs from that in part a.
   c. The price of a loaf of bread returns to $5, while the marginal cost increases to $2.50 and the price received on the secondary market remains $0. What is now the profit-maximizing quantity of loaves to hold in inventory? Explain why your answer differs from that in part a.

Accompanies problem 7.3.

Quantity of Loaves Demanded	Probability This Quantity Is Demanded	Probability of Selling This Quantity or More, $\text{Prob}(Q^D \geq Q)$	Probability of Selling Less Than This Quantity, $\text{Prob}(Q^D < Q)$
50	0.10	1.00	0.00
51	0.10	0.90	0.10
52	0.10	0.80	0.20
53	0.10	0.70	0.30
54	0.10	0.60	0.40
55	0.10	0.50	0.50
56	0.10	0.40	0.60
57	0.10	0.30	0.70
58	0.10	0.20	0.80
59	0.10	0.10	0.90
60	0.10	0.00	1.00

7.4 Your small company is a defendant in a lawsuit alleging that it produced a product that failed and harmed the purchaser. Although you believe your company is innocent, you think there is a 50 percent probability you will lose the suit. If you lose, you are uncertain what you will be required to pay. The following table shows your subjective probabilities of paying different amounts. Your litigation costs are $100,000.

Probability (percent)	Loss
30	$40,000
20	$50,000
20	$70,000
10	$80,000
10	$100,000
10	$120,000

a. What is the expected value of the sum of money you might have to pay?
b. Using the expected value of what you might be required to pay, what is your expected loss from litigation?
c. Your attorney notifies you that there is only a 9 percent chance you will be required to pay $120,000 if you lose, but there is now a 1 percent chance you will be required to pay $4 million if you lose. With these changes, what is the expected value of the sum of money you might be required to pay? What is your expected loss from litigation? How has this new information changed your willingness to settle the case, and why?

 # MyLab Economics Auto-Graded Excel Projects

14.1 Many retailers and grocers, like Target and Walmart, have started using self-checkout registers instead of standard checkout registers. Retailers staff a group of self-checkout registers with a single employee to help with

problems and monitor the checkout process, rather than having a 1-to-1 ratio of employees to standard checkout registers. According to a study completed by the University of Leicester in 2016, self-checkout registers nearly double the shoplifting rate from approximately 2 percent to approximately 4 percent. As one-third of sales come from shoppers in the self-checkout lanes, this increase is substantial.

Suppose that you are helping a retailer decide whether or not to install self-checkout registers in its stores. This retailer is deciding not only whether to use self-checkout registers but also, if it decides to change, how many registers should be assigned to each employee for monitoring and assistance. Use the data reference cells provided and the concepts learned in Chapter 14 to complete the following tasks and make a decision.

a. Using the reference cells provided and formulas, fill in the known information for staffed registers. Then determine the hourly cost per lane (including wage and theft costs) of using a staffed register. Multiply this cost by the number of lanes (currently set at 1) in the Costs for Multiple Lanes cell.
b. Continuing to use the data reference cells provided, use a formula to determine hourly employee wages for managing the number of checkout registers (currently set at 1) by dividing the cost of an employee by the number of self-checkout lanes this employee will watch. Use formulas to fill in

	A	B	C	D	E
1	Data Reference Cells				
2	Employee Hourly Wages	10			
3	Standard Average Hourly Sales	2200			
4	Standard Theft Proportion	0.02			
5	Number of Checkout Registers	1			
6					
7	Staffed Register Costs			Self-Checkout Register Costs	
8	Employee Wages			Employee Wages	
9	Average Hourly Sales			Average Hourly Sales	
10	Theft Proportion			Theft Proportion	
11	Costs per Hour per Lane			Costs per Hour per Lane	
12	Costs for Multiple Lanes			Costs for Multiple Lanes	
13					
14					
15	c. Staffed				
16	Self-checkout				
17	d. Staffed 2 lanes				
18	Self-checkout 2 lanes				
19	Staffed 3 lanes				
20	Self-checkout 3 lanes				
21	Staffed 4 lanes				
22	Self-checkout 4 lanes				
23	Staffed 5 lanes				
24	Self-checkout 5 lanes				
25	Staffed 6 lanes				
26	Self-checkout 6 lanes				
27	Staffed 7 lanes				
28	Self-checkout 7 lanes				
29	e. Use self-check?				
30	How many?				
31	f. Use self-check?				
32	How many?				
33					

average hourly sales and theft proportion, assuming sales per hour at a self-checkout register are half those at a staffed register and that the theft proportion increases by 0.5 percent (or 0.005) for every additional self-checkout register added to the monitoring employee's group. Determine the hourly cost per self-checkout register, and multiply this cost by the number of checkout lanes (currently set at 1) to determine the cost for multiple checkout lanes.

c. What is the current hourly cost for staffed registers and self-checkout registers?

d. Increase the number of checkout lanes in the data reference cells to 2. What is the current hourly cost for using 2 lanes for both types of checkout? Repeat this for 3, 4, 5, 6, and 7 lanes.

e. Should this retailer use self-checkout registers? If yes, how many registers should be in a group monitored by 1 employee? If no, enter 0.

f. Suppose that a minimum wage increase to $15 per hour is passed. Change the data reference cell accordingly. Should this retailer use self-checkout registers? If yes, how many registers should be in a group monitored by 1 employee? If no, enter 0. Does this answer surprise you?

g. In addition to looking at the cost data, what are some other challenges associated with introducing self-checkout registers? Should the retailer remove all staffed registers and replace them with groups of self-checkout registers?

14.2 Macrina Bakery is a locally owned bakery started by Leslie Mackie and based in Kent, WA. This bakery has four cafés in the Seattle area and also sells its products to other restaurants and retailers in the Seattle area. One of its most popular pastry items is the Morning Glory muffin, which is baked with fruit, nuts, and coconut.

Suppose that you are helping a bakery like Macrina Bakery decide how many muffins to bake each morning for sale in a café. The bakery charges $3 for a muffin the day they are baked and $1.50 (half price) for day-old muffins; the average total cost for producing a muffin is $1 (assume the MC is the same as the ATC). Based on sales over the last year, you know that the demand for muffins is between 20 and 30 each day, with the frequencies given in the figure. (Demand in excess of 30 muffins is accompanied with an order for muffins in advance and is not part of your bakery's inventory problem.) Use the information in the table and concepts learned in Chapter 14 to complete the following tasks and answer the following questions.

a. Using the demand frequency information provided, determine the probability of each quantity demanded.

b. Using the probabilities from part a, find the probability that the bakery will sell each Q^D or more and the probability that it will sell less than each Q^D.

c. Enter the original price and cost in the cells indicated. Using this information and formulas from Chapter 14, find the expected marginal benefit of selling muffins at each Q^D.

d. Enter the day-old price in the cell indicated. Using this information and formulas from Chapter 14, find the expected marginal cost of selling muffins at each Q^D.

e. What quantity of muffins would you recommend that this bakery produce each day?

f. Suppose that a new low-carb diet fad shifts demand for the bakery's muffins. To maintain demand, the bakery must drop its price from $3 to $2. The bakery also decides to give excess muffins to their employees instead of keeping their day-old muffin policy. Update the price information based on these changes. How many muffins should the bakery now produce each day? Explain how each of the changes affected the change in daily production.

	A	B	C	D	E	F	G
1	Quantity Demanded, Q^D	Frequency of Q^D	Probability of Q^D	Probability of Selling This Q^D or More	Probability of Selling This Q^D or Less	Expected Marginal Benefit	Expected Marginal Cost
2	20	5					
3	21	14					
4	22	30					
5	23	48					
6	24	56					
7	25	73					
8	26	59					
9	27	32					
10	28	26					
11	29	15					
12	30	7					
13	TOTALS						

Introduction

When a buyer and seller are negotiating a price, at times the process hits an impasse: The seller wants a higher price, but the buyer is adamant about paying a lower one. In these cases, the buyer and seller may turn to arbitration. Sometimes each side of the dispute selects one person to serve on an arbitration panel, and the two arbitrators select a third to complete the panel. At other times, one neutral arbitrator is chosen to hear the case. Both sides of the controversy present their arguments and their offers to the arbitrator (whether an individual or a panel), who renders a decision. Often the arbitrator "splits the difference" by selecting a price between the two offers. In some arbitrations, the two sides must accept the decision; in others, the decision is advisory, and one or even both sides can reject it and resume negotiations.

In one type of arbitration, however, the arbitrator is not allowed to split the difference, and the buyer or seller must accept the judgment. In this arbitration, called *final offer arbitration*, the arbitrator selects one of the offers and cannot change it. Several states require final offer arbitration between management and public-sector unions that legally are forbidden to strike, such as police, prison guards, and firefighters. Major League Baseball (MLB), a professional baseball organization consisting of 29 teams in the United States and 1 team in Canada, also uses final offer arbitration. When an MLB player and the owners of his team cannot agree on a salary, final offer arbitration is a mechanism for resolving salary disputes.[1] The player is entitled to put the dispute before a three-person arbitration panel. The three arbitrators are neutral; that is, none of them will favor one side or the other. Both sides submit their "final" offers, along with supporting documents, to the arbitrators. The arbitrators take the midpoint between the team's offer and the player's demand. If the evidence shows that the player's market value is higher than the midpoint, the panel awards the higher salary demanded by the player. If the evidence shows that the player's market value is lower than the midpoint, the panel awards

the lower salary offered by the team to the player. The decision of the panel is binding on the two parties. If the panel chooses the team's offer, the player is obligated to sign a one-year contract for that salary. If the player wins, the team must offer the player a one-year contract with the higher salary.

These salary disputes might seem far removed from the legal disputes examined in this chapter, but the economic analysis of settlements presents a solid framework for a manager or an agent to use to make decisions in this sort of arbitration. Indeed, arbitration panels actually hear very few of the MLB cases that players and teams file because, just as is the case with lawsuits, the vast majority of these disputes are settled.

Final Offer Arbitration Example

In the 2006 baseball season, the Chicago Cubs paid pitcher Carlos Zambrano $6.6 million. He had a good year, with a record of 16 wins and 7 losses, an earned run average (ERA) of 3.41, and 210 strikeouts. When he and the Cubs could not agree on a salary for the 2007 season, Mr. Zambrano filed for arbitration. His final offer was $15.5 million, and the Cubs' final offer was $11.0 million.

Suppose that you are an executive for the Cubs. To help determine your strategy, you need to make three important decisions:

1. You must determine how much money is at stake. In other words, how much money is in dispute? At first glance, you might think the answer is $15.5 million, Mr. Zambrano's offer. This answer, however, is too easy—and it is also incorrect. If the arbitrators reject Mr. Zambrano's $15.5 million offer, they will accept your club's offer of $11.0 million. At stake is only the difference between the two offers—$4.5 million — because the player is guaranteed to receive at least $11.0 million. Call the sum of money in dispute, $4.5 million, S.

2. You must decide your subjective probability of Mr. Zambrano winning the arbitration. You think that his agent assembled a strong case, so you assess his probability of winning at 70 percent. In other words, you estimate that the arbitrators will select Mr. Zambrano's offer 70 percent of the time. His 70 percent chance of prevailing leaves you and the Cubs a 30 percent chance of winning. Call the probability that Mr. Zambrano wins q, so that the probability that the Cubs win is $1 - q$.

---

[1] Only a subset of players is eligible for final offer arbitration. Players with one or two years' experience are not entitled to final offer arbitration, and players with six years' or more experience become free agents unless they are under contract with a team. Only players in between, those who have three to five years' experience, are eligible for final offer arbitration because the rules allow them to bargain only with their current team.

3. You must decide on your estimate of the cost of going to arbitration for the Cubs. You have already incurred many of the costs necessary to assemble the supporting documents submitted to the arbitrators. These sunk costs do not factor into this calculation, but you do need to consider some other costs. In particular, if you win the arbitration, Mr. Zambrano could possibly be upset and not play to his potential. You might set this cost and all the others of going to arbitration at $1 million. Call the club's cost of going to arbitration CC.

Once you have these three numerical estimates, you can calculate the expected cost to the Cubs of going to arbitration. This cost is $E[C]_{CUBS}$, where C refers to the Cubs' cost of arbitration and the E means you are calculating the expected value. The expected cost to the Cubs is equal to the amount in dispute multiplied by the probability of losing plus the cost to the Cubs of going to arbitration. In terms of a formula, the expected cost is $E[C]_{CUBS} = (q \times S) + [(1 - q) \times \$0] + CC$. This formula is the same as the formula for the expected loss from litigation for the defendant. In this baseball example, the expected cost to the Cubs of allowing the arbitrators to decide the salary is $(0.70 \times \$4.5 \text{ million}) + \$1 \text{ million} = \$4.15 \text{ million}$.

As a Cubs executive, you know that you will pay Mr. Zambrano at least $11.0 million. If the contract goes before the arbitrators, add your expected cost of $4.15 million to the $11.0 million for the total expected cost of hiring Mr. Zambrano, $15.15 million. You can lower the Cubs' expected cost by agreeing to any contract that specifies a salary of $15.15 million or less and settling (not going before the arbitrators).

Now suppose that you are Mr. Zambrano's agent. You realize that he is guaranteed to receive at least $11.0 million, so once again the amount in dispute, S, is $4.5 million. If the contract goes to the arbitrators and they decide in favor of Mr. Zambrano's offer, he receives a contract of $15.5 million, collecting the entire $4.5 million in contention. You attach a probability, p, of 40 percent to this outcome. If the arbitrators decide in favor of the Cubs, Mr. Zambrano receives a contract of $11.0 million and collects none of the amount in dispute. The probability of this outcome is $1 - p$, or 60 percent. Finally, the cost to the player, CP, of going to arbitration is $0.5 million, perhaps because the dispute gives him a reputation of being hard to deal with, which makes other teams less likely to sign him.

Call the expected gain to Mr. Zambrano $E[G]_{ZAMBRANO}$, where G refers to his gain from arbitration. The expected gain from arbitration to Mr. Zambrano is equal to the amount in dispute multiplied by the probability that he will prevail minus the cost of going to arbitration:

$$E[G]_{ZAMBRANO} = (p \times S) + [(1 - p) \times \$0] - CP$$

Using this formula, which is precisely the same as the formula for the expected gain from litigation for the plaintiff, Mr. Zambrano's expected gain from arbitration is $(0.40 \times \$4.5 \text{ million}) - \$0.5 \text{ million} = \$1.3 \text{ million}$. Because he is guaranteed to receive at least $11.0 million, his expected contract is $11.0 million + $1.3 million = $12.3 million. As Mr. Zambrano's agent, you can increase the expected contract by agreeing to any contract specifying a salary of more than $12.3 million.

The Cubs are willing to sign any contract for less than $15.15 million; Mr. Zambrano is willing to sign any contract for more than $12.3 million. Clearly, there is room to settle the contract before the arbitrators issue their ruling. So does it surprise you that the "final offers" Mr. Zambrano and the Cubs submitted to the arbitrators are not really final offers? The two sides reached an agreement on a one-year deal for $12.4 million. The fact that the agreement was only marginally above the minimum Mr. Zambrano would accept is perhaps a testament to the bargaining prowess of the Cubs' negotiator.

The data show that approximately 90 percent of the MLB cases of final offer arbitration settle before the arbitrators issue their decision. This statistic is interesting and certainly in keeping with the analysis above, but the important general point is that you can analyze final offer arbitration in the exact same way as the litigation settlements you learned about in this chapter. The lesson from this observation is clear: Economic principles, such as how to analyze the profit or loss from a lawsuit, apply in a wide variety of situations, and they can aid you in numerous managerial decisions.

Your Decisions

In Canada, disputes between commercial shippers and railways that carry the freight can be resolved via final offer arbitration. The Canadian Transportation Act allows shippers to appeal the freight rates charged by the Canadian Pacific Railway and Canadian National Railway to the Canadian Transportation Agency (CTA). The CTA appoints an arbitrator who then uses final offer arbitration to determine what the shipper will pay the railroad. The shipper and the carrier are allowed to present a variety of information to help support their offers. For example, they can present evidence of the following:

- The presence (or absence) of alternative shipping methods and the cost of using the alternative
- The freight rate charged immediately before the dispute

- Any special cost incurred by the railroad to transport the shipper's product
- The market for the shipper's product

Suppose that you are an owner of a company that wants to ship its product on a Canadian railroad. Last year your company paid $12 million for shipping by rail. This year you and the railroad's executives have been negotiating, but the best offer they have made is $16 million. If you use a trucking company, shipping will cost you $15 million. You know that if you accept the trucking company's offer, you will make zero economic profit, so that you will receive only your competitive return. You are deciding whether to go to the CTA and ask for final offer arbitration, during which you expect the railroad will ask for $16 million. If you use final offer arbitration, you must abide by the arbitrator's decision; that is, if the arbitrator chooses the railroad's offer, you will pay the railroad $16 million for shipping for this year and cannot use the trucking company's lower-cost offer of $15 million. You are thinking of presenting one of two possible offers to the arbitrator: $12 million and $13 million. You estimate that if you offer $12 million, you have a 25 percent chance that the arbitrator will select your offer, while if you offer $13 million, you have an 80 percent chance that the arbitrator will select your offer. You also think that it will cost you $0.5 million to go to arbitration.

1. If you go to arbitration and offer $12 million, what is the expected cost of the contract?
2. If you go to arbitration and offer $13 million, what is the expected cost of the contract?
3. If you decide to go to arbitration, which of your two possible offers will you make? If you do not worry about risk and care only to minimize your expected cost, explain whether or not you will ask the CTA for arbitration.
4. If you go to arbitration, what risk do you face? Explain how this affects your decision to ask the CTA for arbitration.
5. As the owner of the business, will you ask the CTA for arbitration? Explain your decision.

CHAPTER 15

Managerial Decisions About Information

Learning Objectives

After studying this chapter, you will be able to:

15.1 Describe the reasons and methods for protecting intellectual property.

15.2 Discuss factors that affect the value of forecasting fluctuations in demand.

15.3 Explain the optimal bidding strategy for and expected revenue from different types of auctions.

15.4 Describe strategies managers can use to overcome the challenges of asymmetric information.

15.5 Apply what you have learned about information to make better managerial decisions.

Auctions Float the Navy's Boat

High-ranking officers in the U.S. Navy face a number of unique challenges. One recurring challenge is staffing a large number of positions, or duty stations, at undesirable locations. For example, many Navy sailors don't want to be stationed in Guam, perhaps because there is little to do on this warm, humid, and frequently typhoon-struck 200-square-mile island. Naval officers could simply order sailors to these duty stations, but they have determined that such unilateral action can be counterproductive. Like any workers, unhappy sailors are unlikely to give the job their best efforts. An even bigger problem is that unhappy sailors will probably leave the Navy as soon as they can.

The Navy considers retaining the training and skills of experienced sailors a priority.

The Navy could increase the salary of sailors assigned to unpleasant duty stations, but its budget is limited. Consequently, minimizing the cost of the solution was a constraint the officers faced when tackling this problem.

What actions could Navy officers take to staff the unpleasant duty stations at minimum cost while making the assigned sailors as happy as possible? How could applying auction theory help them address this challenge? At the end of this chapter, you will learn how the Navy answered these questions.

Sources: "Navy Offers Assignment Incentive Pay for Billets in Guam and Sasebo," *America's Navy*, March 3, 2004; http://www.navy.mil/submit/display.asp?story_id = 12187 http://www.military.com/benefits/military-pay/special-pay.

Introduction

Information plays a critical role in numerous decisions. This chapter examines the effect of information on managerial decision making in four important areas:

- **Intellectual property.** Profit-seeking managers must prevent competitors from using certain information. For example, Merck's managers want to prevent other pharmaceutical companies from using the formula to produce Keytruda, its cancer-fighting immunotherapy drug. Google's managers know that protecting the coding of their search algorithms from competitors is vital to their company's success.

- **Forecasting.** Managers rarely have all of the information they would like when they make decisions. As you learned in Chapter 14, uncertainty about the demand for products makes managers unsure of the quantity to produce. Forecasting demand helps managers make better decisions. Gathering the required information for a forecast is costly, so managers must decide when these forecasts are most valuable.
- **Auctions.** Auctions reflect incomplete information about price. Organizations hold auctions to determine the price to charge (or pay) because it can be cheaper to conduct an auction than to collect and process information about the price on their own. Understanding different types of auctions, how to approach the bidding process, and the expected revenue from the different types of auctions can increase profitability and help you in your career as a manager.
- **Asymmetric information.** Some information is simply too costly for managers to acquire. For example, your auto insurance company would like to know how risky you are as a driver. You know, but credibly conveying that information to them is simply too expensive. Managers need to know what actions they should take when facing a situation with asymmetric information—that is, a situation in which one party to a transaction has relevant information not available to the other party.

    To cover this wide range of information-related issues, this chapter includes five sections:

- **Section 15.1** examines how patents, trade secrets, copyrights, and trademarks protect intellectual property.
- **Section 15.2** focuses on fluctuations in demand and the factors that affect the value of demand forecasts.
- **Section 15.3** explores auctions and the strategies to pursue in different types of auctions.
- **Section 15.4** explains how asymmetric information can affect a business and the actions managers can take to limit negative impacts.
- **Section 15.5** discusses how you can apply what you have learned about information to make better decisions about forecasting demand, holding or participating in an auction, and coping with asymmetric information.

15.1 Intellectual Property

Learning Objective 15.1 Describe the reasons and methods for protecting intellectual property.

The subject of this chapter is information, so let's start by answering a basic question: What exactly is information? An economist's pragmatic answer is that information is just another product, though one with two peculiar characteristics that make it different from other goods or services:

1. Information can be expensive to produce but is cheap to copy and communicate.
2. One firm's use of a particular piece of information does not prevent other firms from simultaneously using the exact same information.

These differences affect how firms deal with the information they create as well as government policy toward information.

For some firms, producing information is their most important activity. Take Celgene Corporation, one of the nation's largest biotech companies. Each year Celgene's managers approve the expenditure of billions of dollars to discover and research the effects of potential new drugs. The type of information that Celgene obtains from its research is part of its intellectual property. **Intellectual property** refers to the intangible creations of human intelligence, such as information about future plans or production processes as well as inventions, artistic works, literary works, and trademarks.

Intellectual property The intangible creations of human intelligence, such as information about future plans or production processes as well as inventions, artistic works, literary works, and trademarks.

Because the information contained in intellectual property is valuable to competitors, firms must protect it. At this point, the two unique characteristics of information emerge. Suppose that Celgene Corporation has spent $1.3 billion to discover and develop a new biotech drug to fight multiple myeloma (a blood cancer). Once Celgene has discovered that information, it is cheap to copy and transmit, perhaps to other pharmaceutical companies. Even as Celgene is using the information, its competitors could also use it to produce a competing drug, thereby drastically decreasing Celgene's profit. Of course, the managers at Celgene realize this potential outcome and will spend the $1.3 billion only if they can protect their intellectual property. Recognizing this situation, governments have established laws that give firms and individuals the incentive to continue creating intellectual property through patents and trade secrets, copyrights, and trademarks.

Patents and Trade Secrets

Firms can protect information in the form of inventions and other industrial know-how under two types of laws: patent law and trade secret law. Patents and trade secrets both establish ownership rights to inventions and other technical improvements. Because patents usually confer more robust protection, managers faced with a choice between the two often opt for a patent.

Patents

A **patent** is a legal grant to the patent holder of exclusive rights to an invention for a specified period, which in the United States is usually 20 years from the date of application.[1] To qualify for patent protection, an invention must meet three statutory criteria: novelty, usefulness, and nonobviousness. An invention normally meets the novelty requirement if the patent applicant is the first to invent the claimed innovation. The usefulness requirement is satisfied if the invention works as intended and serves some minimal human need. The nonobviousness condition is met if the invention is not obvious to a person with ordinary skill working in the area. For example, suppose that someone copies DJI's Phantom 4 Pro drone, adds a flashing red LED light to the top, and tries to patent it as a new drone. The U.S. Patent and Trademark Office (USPTO) will deny the "new" drone a patent because the LED-equipped drone is an obvious modification of an existing product.

Patent A legal grant to the patent holder of exclusive rights to an invention for a specified period.

The principal economic justification for patent rights is to give individuals and firms the financial incentive to create new goods and services. In the absence of patent rights, society will fail to achieve the optimal amount of innovation because inventors, such as Celgene Corporation, have less incentive to invest in innovations and to disclose how to make and use them. Patents overcome these potential market

---

1 If the U.S. Patent and Trademark Office fails to meet deadlines for processing a patent, the life of the patent is extended past 20 years. Pharmaceutical drugs can receive an extension of up to 5 years depending on how long the legally required testing took and how long the U.S. Food and Drug Administration took to approve the drug. Design patents—which are granted for the ornamental design of a functional product, such as a Coca-Cola bottle—have a 15-year life.

failures by permitting inventors to obtain a monopoly and the accompanying potential for an economic profit while at the same time requiring patent holders to disclose relevant information about their innovations that will allow others to develop still newer inventions.

Patent protection is not permanent. This fact reflects the social trade-off created by a patent: Before the product is invented, the economic profit from the patent-created monopoly gives inventors the incentive to research the potential invention, thereby benefiting society by creating a new, valuable product. But once the product exists, the patent-created monopoly harms society by leading to a deadweight loss (see Section 6.2). The temporary nature of patents attempts to balance the social gain from inventing the product against that social harm from the monopoly.

To file for a patent, the inventor must submit a written document to the USPTO that includes a description of the invention and an explanation of its functions. If the USPTO grants the application, the patent holder may exclude anyone else from making, using, or selling the invention in the United States for a specified period. A patent holder who believes someone else is making, using, or selling the patented product without permission may file suit for patent infringement. If the patent holder prevails, the court may issue an injunction requiring the offender to cease the infringing activity and may award damages to compensate the patent holder for the infringement, that is, compensate the patent holder for the lost profits. Apple has vigorously defended its iPhone patents by taking alleged infringers, such as Samsung, to court. Although the courts overturned some of the judgments on appeal, eventually Samsung paid Apple over $500 million to settle a patent infringement suit.

Enforcing patent rights is the main line of business for some companies, called patent holding companies, nonpracticing entities, or, somewhat more colorfully (and definitely more negatively), "patent trolls." Such companies buy a portfolio of patents, search for firms they believe are infringing, and then demand fees and threaten lawsuits to enforce the patents. Advocates of such companies claim that they protect the rights of patent holders against companies that would use the information in the patent and offer nothing in return. Detractors view them as white-collar pirates, demanding ransom for what the critics sometimes characterize as overly broad, nebulous patents. The outcomes of the infringement lawsuits are mixed. In some cases, the patent holding company prevails and collects substantial damages from the infringing firm. In others, the alleged infringer wins, and the court rules the patent invalid.

Trade Secrets

Trade secret Any information used to conduct the business that the firm has taken steps to keep private.

Trade secret law provides another way for firms to protect their intellectual property. A **trade secret** is any information used to conduct the business that the firm has taken steps to keep private. Trade secrets include customer lists, product recipes, and plans for future expansion.

Trade secret law differs from patent law in four crucial respects:

1. **Government approval.** Unlike a patent, businesses do not need to obtain government approval of the secret to protect it. Common law and state statutory law are the primary sources of trade secret protection.
2. **Disclosure.** Unlike patent law, trade secret law discourages the owner from making any public disclosure because that would result in the information losing its protected status.
3. **Duration.** Unlike patent protection, which lasts for a definite time frame, trade secret protection has an indefinite duration. Some trade secrets may last

indefinitely, such as the still-secret formula for Coca-Cola, which was created in 1888. On the other hand, because car companies constantly disassemble competitors' products to uncover unpatented innovations, the life of trade secrets in the automotive industry is short.

4. **Security.** Trade secret protection is more easily lost than patent protection. Unlike a patent holder, the owner of a trade secret cannot prevent a competitor from independently inventing the same product or reverse engineering it.

If a trade secret's owner can prove that an infringer is illegally using that trade secret, the court may issue an injunction preventing its use and award monetary damages. A winning plaintiff is entitled to the larger of two amounts: the plaintiff's own lost profits or the defendant's profits attributable to the infringement. The judicial goal of the financial penalty is to make infringement and unlawful use of trade secrets unprofitable. For example, Kolon Industries paid DuPont $275 million in restitution for using DuPont's stolen trade secrets for Kevlar bulletproof vests.

Socially, an important difference between patents and trade secrets lies in the disclosure requirement. A patent holder *must* disclose the workings of the patent to the public. The fact of disclosure allows others to build on the patent—for example, by developing a better drug based on prior, patented research. The developer will need to pay a fee to the patent holder, but society gets a more effective product. Trade secrets are kept secret, however, so no one can build on them. For example, no one can try to develop a more tasty cola using Coca-Cola's recipe as the starting point because no one knows Coca-Cola's formulation. Of course, from the perspective of managers at The Coca-Cola Company, the indefinite lifespan of a trade secret is a definite advantage over a patent.

Copyrights

A **copyright** is a legal grant to the holder of exclusive rights for a specified period of time for a work of authorship that is original and fixed in a tangible medium of expression. Copyrights are granted for literary, musical, dramatic, and choreographic works; pictorial, graphic, and sculptural works; motion pictures and other audiovisual works; sound recordings; and architectural works. A copyright exists from the moment of creation and initially belongs to the creator, but the creator can sell the copyright. In the case of works created by individuals, the copyright is in effect for the life of the creator plus 70 years; for works created by corporations, the copyright runs for 95 years from the first publication or 120 years from the creation, whichever period is shorter.

A copyright gives the owner five exclusive rights over the copyrighted work:

Copyright A legal grant to the holder of exclusive rights for a specified period of time for a work of authorship that is original and fixed in a tangible medium of expression.

1. **Reproduction right.** Entitles copyright owners to make copies of their own work and to authorize others to do so. A high school band director who photocopies sheet music is infringing on the owner's copyright. Of the five rights, this is usually the most important.
2. **Adaptation right.** Gives copyright owners the exclusive right to prepare derivative works based on the copyrighted work and to approve derivative works, such as different arrangements of a song.
3. **Distribution right.** Gives copyright owners the exclusive right to distribute copies of the work to the public. Once the copyright owners have distributed a particular copy, however, the *first sale doctrine* allows the person who purchased the copy to redistribute it as desired. For example, you can resell a DVD you purchase to whomever you wish once you are done with it.

4. **Public performance right.** Entitles copyright owners to authorize (or reject) the public performance of a work. For example, when planning a theatrical production, the producer must apply for the right to use the work.
5. **Public display right.** Entitles copyright owners to authorize (or reject) the public display of a work. For example, owners must approve the duplication of books as a pdf files before someone else can make them available on the Internet.

The courts protect copyrights and allow a copyright holder to file suit against an infringer. If the plaintiff prevails, the court may issue an injunction preventing further infringement and may award damages. Similar to judgments in trade secret cases, plaintiffs in copyright law cases are usually entitled to the larger of two amounts: their own lost profits or the defendant's profits attributable to the infringement.

The economic effects of copyright are similar to those of patents. In the absence of copyright protection, a suboptimal number of works will be created and published because of the ability of others to use (and profit from) these works without compensation. Copyrights give the holders a monopoly and the potential to make an economic profit, increasing the incentive to create new works of authorship. However, economists generally believe that the length of copyright protection is unjustifiably long. Instead of merely increasing the incentive to create new works, the length of a copyright increases the owner's incentive to protect the monopoly profit. For example, at the urging of copyright holders, the government increased the length of protection in 1976 and again in 1998. In opposing increases in the length of copyright protection, economists point out that increasing the time span of protection gives the owners a longer-lived monopoly but creates no incentive effects for those works because they *already* exist, so there is no added benefit to society.

Trademarks

Trademark Any word, name, device, or other symbol that identifies a unique source of a good or service.

Another type of intellectual property law deals with trademarks. A **trademark** is any word, name, device, or other symbol that identifies a unique source of a good or service. Trademark law establishes property rights for distinctive commercial marks or symbols. The first firm to make a lawful, commercial use of a mark to identify its product or service generally acquires the right to exclude others from using the same or a confusingly similar mark for a related product or service. The more famous the mark, the greater the likelihood a court will enjoin others from using a similar designation, even on unrelated products or services. For example, the courts prevented the owners of a motel from using the name "McSleep" for their motel because McDonald's Corporation claimed that consumers would assume that McDonald's owned the motel. Trademark rights persist for as long as consumers continue to identify the mark with the unique source.

A trademark holder who believes that another company or person is infringing can file a lawsuit. If the plaintiff prevails, the court may issue an injunction prohibiting the infringing activity. The trademark holder may also be entitled to a financial award equal to the defendant's profit attributable to the infringement plus any damages sustained by the plaintiff. Of course, going to court to prevent infringement of a trademark (or any other method used to protect intellectual property) is not a decision for a manager to make lightly. Legal action can be very expensive, take a long time to resolve, and have an uncertain outcome.

Intellectual property is just one way in which information affects managerial decision making. Another is the fact that managers almost always have, at best, only incomplete information about the demand for their product, which makes it difficult to determine the profit-maximizing quantity to produce. The next section examines factors that affect the value of demand forecasts.

Patent Infringement

Owners protect their patents because successful patents create a monopoly that can be profitable. Suppose that a company holds a patent for a product with demand given by

$$Q^d = 1{,}000 - 10P$$

and marginal revenue given by

$$MR = 100 - 0.2Q$$

The marginal cost (MC) and average total cost (ATC) are both constant and equal to $40.

a. What quantity will the monopoly patent holder produce? What price will the monopoly patent holder charge? What will be the patent holder's economic profit?

Now a counterfeiter enters the market by producing counterfeit products that infringe on the patent. After the patent holder has maximized profit, the demand remaining for the counterfeiter is

$$Q^d = 700 - 10P$$

with marginal revenue of

$$MR = 70 - 0.2Q$$

Suppose that the counterfeiter is as efficient as the legitimate patent holder, so its average total cost and marginal cost also equal $40 per unit.

b. If the patent holder does not change its production, what quantity will the counterfeiter produce? What will be the total quantity produced by the two firms?

c. Based on the total quantity produced, what will be the market price? What will be the patent holder's economic profit? What amount of damages does the patent holder suffer from the counterfeiter's production?

Answer

a. The patent holder is a monopoly and maximizes profit by producing the quantity that sets $MR = MC$, or $100 - 0.2Q = 40$. Accordingly, the profit-maximizing quantity is 300 units. The demand equation can be solved for P: $P = 100 - 0.1Q$. Using the quantity of 300 in this equation gives the profit-maximizing price of $70 per unit. The firm's economic profit equals $(P - ATC) \times Q$, or $(\$70 - \$40) \times 300 = \$9{,}000$.

b. The counterfeiter also maximizes profit by producing the quantity that sets $MR = MC$, or $70 - 0.2Q = 40$. So the profit-maximizing quantity is 150 units. There will be a total of $300 + 150 = 450$ units produced.

c. Using the price equation from the market demand, with 450 units produced the price is $P = 100 - (0.1 \times 450) = \$55$. The patent holder's economic profit falls to $(\$55 - \$40) \times 300 = \$4{,}500$, so the patent holder has suffered damages of $\$9{,}000 - \$4{,}500 = \$4{,}500$.

15.2 Value of Forecasts

Learning Objective 15.2 Discuss factors that affect the value of forecasting fluctuations in demand.

To use the profit-maximization rule (produce the quantity that sets $MR = MC$), you must know both the marginal revenue and the marginal cost. If your demand is subject to random fluctuations, then the marginal revenue will also be random.[2] Forecasts help match your production to the projected demand so that you produce where your marginal revenue equals your marginal cost, thereby maximizing your profit. Demand forecasts are not free, however. You could purchase a forecast from a firm specializing in forecasting, or you could hire a statistician to create one. Both options are costly. As a manager, you may need to determine the value of a new forecast or of refinements to an existing forecast to determine how much you are willing to pay for this information.

Random Demand Model

Suppose that you are a manager at a firm like Estrella River Ranch, one of more than 200 California vineyards growing cabernet sauvignon grapes. (For ease of comparison, this example continues from the one introduced in Chapter 14.) Assume that your firm is perfectly competitive. At the start of each growing season, you must make a decision about the quantity of grapes you will grow. The demand for these grapes fluctuates unpredictably, so when you make your production decision, you do not know the price you will receive. Figure 15.1 shows your firm's marginal cost

Figure 15.1 Variable Demand

Your firm's marginal cost curve (MC) is linear and upward sloping. The demand for grapes might be high, shown by demand and marginal revenue curve $d_H = MR_H$, or low, shown by demand and marginal revenue curve $d_L = MR_L$.

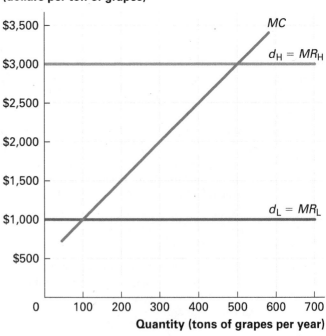

Price and cost
(dollars per ton of grapes)

---

2 If it is the cost that fluctuates rather than the demand, then the marginal cost is unknown. The same principles that we discuss for the value of demand forecasts apply to the value of cost forecasts.

curve (*MC*) and potential demand curves. For simplicity, assume that the *MC* curve is linear and that demand changes randomly, so that it is high 50 percent of the time (shown in the figure by $d_H = MR_H$) and low 50 percent of the time (shown in the figure as $d_L = MR_L$).

Loss from Uncertainty

You must make your production decision at the start of the growing season, before you know the demand and price. If you knew demand would be high, you would produce 500 tons of grapes. If you knew demand would be low, you would produce 100 tons of grapes. You cannot store wine grapes, so if you make the wrong choice, you lose profit. If you produce 500 tons of grapes and demand is low, all of the tons between 100 and 500 tons create a loss because their marginal cost exceeds their marginal revenue (Figure 15.2). You incur a total loss of $400,000, equal to the area of the dark red triangle in Figure 15.2. If you produce 100 tons of grapes and demand is high, then you forego the profit on all of the tons between 100 and 500 tons. These tons would be profitable because their marginal revenue exceeds their marginal cost. The unfortunately low production reduces your profit by an amount equal to the area of the light red triangle in Figure 15.2, which coincidentally is also $400,000.

Expected Value

As you learned in Section 14.2, when faced with unpredictable random changes in demand, a reasonable decision for profit-maximizing managers is to set the expected marginal revenue equal to the marginal cost. Recall that an *expected value* is a weighted average of the possible outcomes, where the weights are the probabilities of the outcomes (see Section 14.1). In the example at hand, with a

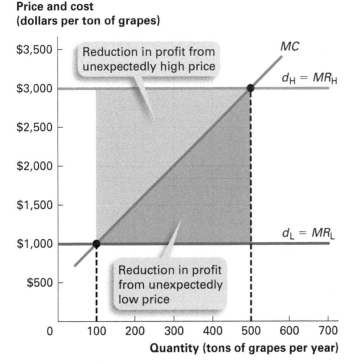

Price and cost
(dollars per ton of grapes)

Figure 15.2 Loss of Profit from Unexpected Changes in Demand

When demand is low, producing 100 tons of grapes maximizes profit. If your firm produces 500 tons of grapes, it loses a total of $400,000 (the area of the dark red triangle) on all tons of grapes between 100 and 500 tons because the marginal cost of all of these tons exceeds their marginal revenue. When demand is high, producing 500 tons of grapes maximizes profit. If your firm produces 100 tons of grapes, it has a total foregone profit of $400,000 (the area of the light red triangle) on all tons of grapes between 100 and 500 tons because the marginal revenue of all of these tons exceeds their marginal cost.

Figure 15.3 Maximizing Expected Profit

When demand is unpredictable, producing 300 tons of grapes, the quantity that sets the expected marginal revenue equal to the marginal cost, $E[MR] = MC$, maximizes your firm's expected profit by minimizing the average reduction in profit.

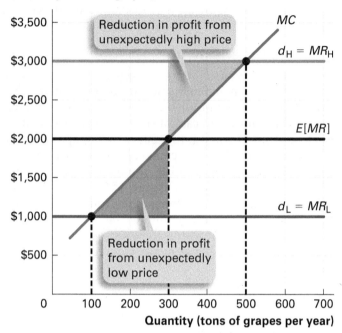

50 percent probability of the high marginal revenue of $3,000 and a 50 percent probability of the low marginal revenue of $1,000, the expected marginal revenue, $E[MR]$, is

$$E[MR] = (\$3,000 \times 0.50) + (\$1,000 \times 0.50) = \$2,000$$

If you produce so that $E[MR] = MC$, you never produce the quantity that sets the *actual* marginal revenue ($3,000 if demand is high or $1,000 if demand is low) equal to the marginal cost. Nonetheless, Figure 15.3 shows that producing the quantity of grapes that sets $E[MR] = MC$ maximizes your expected profit. Compared to the profit you would make if you knew the demand, the average reduction in profit from underproducing (if demand is high) or overproducing (if demand is low) is smallest when 300 tons are produced.

Factors Affecting the Value of Forecasts

Can you do better than produce so that $E[MR] = MC$ by forecasting the correct demand? In other words, can forecasting your demand increase your profit? The answer depends on whether the cost of the forecast outweighs its benefit. The cost of a forecast varies widely depending on the method of acquisition, so we can provide no general insight there. The elements that help determine the value of the prediction—that is, the increase in the expected profit from the forecast—are more general, so they are worthy of discussion. Three general factors determine the value of a forecast: the accuracy of the forecast, the variability of the demand, and how much marginal cost changes when output changes. The value of the forecast is higher when it is more accurate, when demand is more variable, and when changes in production result in smaller changes in the marginal cost. It is sometimes possible to develop precise formulas for the value of a demand forecast based on these three factors.[3] However, a thorough understanding of how these factors influence a forecast's value is more useful for managers than the precise formulas or their derivations, which apply to specific, highly abstract models.

Accuracy of the Forecast

The greater the accuracy of a forecast, the higher its value because the larger the increase in expected profit. That seemingly obvious observation raises another question: How do you measure accuracy? Many forecasts use regression, a procedure explained in Chapter 3 (see Sections 3.1, 3.2, and 3.3). The easiest way to measure the accuracy of a regression is with its R^2 statistic (or, more simply and more commonly, R^2), a concept you learned about in Section 3.2. Recall that R^2 is a measure of how much of the variation in the actual values of the dependent variable is captured by the predicted values from the regression. More intuitively, the R^2 measures how closely the predicted (forecasted) values match the actual values. R^2 ranges from 1.00 (100 percent) to 0.00 (0 percent). The closer the R^2 is to 1.00, the more closely the forecasted (predicted) values fit the actual data. As a result, the higher the R^2, the more valuable the forecast.

Although impossible to create in reality, a forecast with an R^2 of 1.00 would match all fluctuations in demand perfectly, eliminating all uncertainty. In this happy case, you would have all of the information necessary to maximize your profit in every period because you would know in advance the actual demand and actual marginal revenue. With this unlikely degree of accuracy, the value of the forecast is the amount of the profit you would otherwise lose due to a lack of information.

Variability of the Demand

The variability of demand and the resulting variability of marginal revenue also influence the value of a forecast. The greater the variability of demand, the larger the loss from uncertainty, which means the greater the gain from forecasting the changes. Of course, the greater the gain, the more valuable the forecast.

Figure 15.4 illustrates how variability in demand affects the value of a forecast. Figure 15.4(a) illustrates a larger variability in demand. The demand and hence price for grapes varies between $3,000 per ton and $1,000 per ton. If the managers know that demand is high, they know that the marginal revenue is $3,000 per ton, so the profit-maximizing output of grapes is 500 tons. Alternatively, if the managers know that demand is low, they know that the marginal revenue is $1,000 per ton and the optimal production is only 100 tons. The large variability in demand leads to a large range for the profit-maximizing quantity, between 500 and 100 tons. Figure 15.4(b) illustrates a situation in which the demand and price for grapes varies only between $2,500 and $1,500 per ton, so that the profit-maximizing quantity ranges only between 400 tons (when demand is high) and 200 tons (when demand is low).

The larger the variability in demand, the larger the difference between the quantity produced with no information about demand (the quantity where the *expected*

---

3 The model we have been using, perfect competition with a linear marginal cost curve and random demand, has a very precise formula for the value of a demand forecast. In this case, the value equals $\frac{R^2 \times \sigma_P^2}{2m}$, where R^2 is the percentage fit of the regression predicting the price, σ_P^2 is the variance of the price, and m is the slope of the marginal cost curve. See Section 3.2 for a more detailed discussion of R^2.

Figure 15.4 Effect of Variability in Demand

(a) Larger Variability in Demand
The variability in demand is large, so the gain in profit from correctly forecasting the demand (the two green triangles) is large.

(b) Smaller Variability in Demand
The variability in demand is small, so the gain in profit from correctly forecasting the demand (the two green triangles) is small.

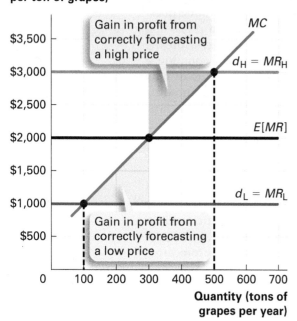

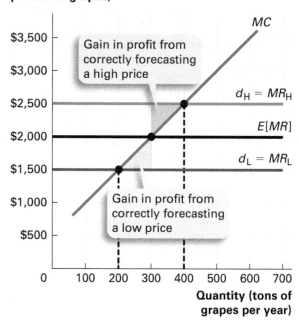

marginal revenue equals the marginal cost) and the quantity produced with a perfect forecast of demand (the quantity where the *actual* marginal revenue equals the marginal cost). The greater the difference, the greater the gain in profit from a correct forecast, and, accordingly, the greater the value of the forecast. In each part of Figure 15.4, the green triangles are the gain in profit from correctly forecasting the price. Without forecasting, your firm produces 300 tons of grapes, the quantity that sets $E[MR] = MC$. The area of each dark green triangle equals the gain in profit when the forecast correctly predicts the price will be high ($100,000 in Figure 15.4(a) with the large variability and $25,000 in Figure 15.4(b) with the small variability). In this case, the firm gains profit because it produces additional profitable units. The light green triangles show the gain in profit when the forecast correctly predicts the price will be low. (Coincidentally, these amounts of gain are also $100,000 with the large variability and $25,000 with the small variability.) In this case, the firm gains profit because it does not produce unprofitable units.

Because high and low demand each occur 50 percent of the time, with the larger variability in demand, the average increase in profit from a perfect forecast is equal to ($100,000 × 0.50) + ($100,000 × 0.50) = $100,000, and with the smaller variability in demand is equal to ($25,000 × 0.50) + ($25,000 × 0.50) = $25,000. If the variability of the demand is larger, the gain in profit is larger. Intuitively, the gain from an accurate forecast in Figure 15.4(a) is much larger simply because there is more potential profit.

Change in Marginal Cost When Production Changes

The third factor that affects the value of a forecast is the change in marginal cost when production changes. The smaller the change in marginal cost, the flatter the marginal cost curve. With a flatter marginal cost curve, the quantity produced is more sensitive to changes in demand. In this case, an accurate demand forecast is quite valuable because it can create a large change in output, resulting in a large increase in profit. Conversely, if the change in the marginal cost is larger when output changes, the marginal cost curve is steeper. The quantity produced does not change much with changes in demand. In this case, even if a manager makes no adjustments in production in response to changes in demand, the loss of profit is small, making a demand forecast less valuable.

The slope of the marginal cost curve measures how much the marginal cost changes when output changes. In Figure 15.5(a), the marginal cost changes by a smaller amount as output changes: For every 100-ton increase in the production of grapes, the marginal cost changes by only $500 per ton, making the marginal cost curve in this figure relatively flat. In Figure 15.5(b), the marginal cost changes by a larger amount as production changes: For every 100-ton increase in the production of grapes, the marginal cost changes by $1,000 per ton, making the marginal cost curve in this figure steeper.

Figure 15.5 **The Size of the Change in Marginal Cost When Production Changes**

(a) **Small Change in Marginal Cost with Changes in Production**
The change in the marginal cost is small when the quantity changes, making the marginal cost curve flatter. The gain of profit from correctly forecasting the demand (the two green triangles) is large.

(b) **Large Change in Marginal Cost with Changes in Production**
The change in the marginal cost is large when the quantity changes, making the marginal cost curve steeper. The gain of profit from correctly forecasting the demand (the two green triangles) is small.

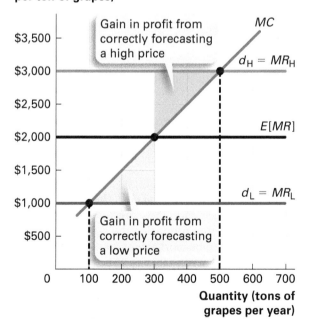

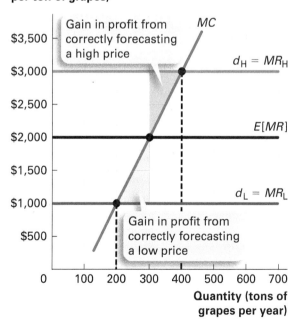

With the marginal cost curve shown in Figure 15.5(a), a manager who can forecast changes in demand will respond by making large changes in production. Compared to producing where $E[MR] = MC$ (300 tons), if you forecast that demand will be high, you respond by increasing production by 200 tons to 500 tons, thereby increasing your profit by $100,000, the area of the large dark green triangle. Similarly, if you forecast that demand will be low, you decrease production by 200 tons to 100 tons, thereby increasing your profit by (coincidentally) $100,000, the area of the large light green triangle.

Figure 15.5(b) shows that if your marginal cost changes by a larger amount, you will not make the same dramatic swings in production when faced with changes in demand. In this figure, now if you forecast that demand will be high, you increase production by only 100 tons to 400 tons, increasing your profit by only $50,000, the area of the small dark green triangle. Similarly, if you forecast that demand will be low, you decrease production by only 100 tons to 200 tons, and increase your profit by (again, coincidentally) only $50,000, the area of the small light green triangle.

Comparing the areas of the similarly colored triangles in Figures 15.5(a) and 15.5(b) shows that the profit from forecasting changes in demand is smaller in 15.5(b), where the marginal cost changes by a lot when production changes. In this case, even a large change in demand causes only a small change in production and a small change in profit, which means a forecast is not too valuable. On the other hand, in a situation such as that in 15.5(a), where the marginal cost does not change much when production changes, a forecast of demand can lead to a large increase in profit, which makes a forecast valuable.

Trying to forecast the appropriate price is sometimes too costly. In some cases, auctions can provide information about the value of an item if the seller (or buyer) is willing to accept the price set by the bidders. Although providing information about the appropriate price and efficiently allocating the product being sold are important economic functions of auctions, it is more significant for managers to know bidding strategies for different types of auctions and the expected revenue each of these auctions will raise. These topics are included in the next section.

SOLVED PROBLEM

Value of a Forecast

You work for a firm like Dyno Nobel, one of many perfectly competitive producers of dynamite. Your staff economists have estimated that the marginal cost (MC) of production of a pound of dynamite is given by

$$MC = 10 + (0.000000667 \times Q)$$

Each year the price is either $50 per pound or $30 per pound, with a 50/50 chance of either price. You must make your production decision before you know the price.

a. What is the expected price of a pound of dynamite?

b. Draw a diagram similar to Figure 15.3, showing the marginal cost; the two demand and marginal revenue curves, $d_H = MR_H$ and $d_L = MR_L$; the expected marginal revenue curve, $E[MR]$; and the reduction in profit from producing the quantity that sets the expected marginal revenue equal to the marginal cost rather than the quantity that you would produce if you knew what the price actually would be. What quantity sets the expected marginal revenue equal to the marginal cost, or $E[MR] = MC$?

c. If you had the information necessary to perfectly predict the demand, what would be the increase in profit? What is the value of a forecast that perfectly predicts the price?

Answer

a. The expected price equals = ($50 per pound × 0.50) + ($30 per pound × 0.50) = $40 per pound.

b. The figure shows the reduction in profit from the price turning out to be high (the area of the light red triangle) and the reduction in profit from the price turning out to be low (the area of the dark red triangle). It also shows that the quantity that sets $E[MR] = MC$ is 45 million pounds per year.

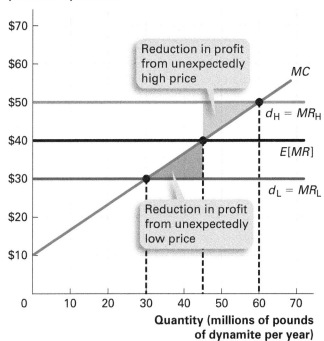

c. The increase in profit from a perfect forecast equals the profit that otherwise would be lost by producing the quantity that sets $E[MR] = MC$. If the price is high, the reduction in profit from not forecasting the price is equal to the area of the light red triangle: $\frac{1}{2}$ × 15 million pounds × $10 per pound = $75 million. If you can forecast that the price will be high, your profit will increase by $75 million. Similarly, if you can forecast that the price will be low, your profit will increase by the area of the dark red triangle, coincidentally also $75 million. Because a high price occurs 50 percent of the time and a low price occurs the other 50 percent of the time, the total increase in profit equals ($75 million × 0.50) + ($75 million × 0.50) = $75 million. The increase in profit equals the value of the forecast, so in this situation the value of the forecast is $75 million.

15.3 Auctions

Learning Objective 15.3 Explain the optimal bidding strategy for and expected revenue from different types of auctions.

In some instances, managers want to sell (or buy) goods or services that are unique, so markets for their specific products do not exist. For example:

- Mexico plans to auction one oil field per year through at least 2018. The oil companies are the buyers of these oil fields, and Mexican government officials are the sellers.
- Managers of U.S. defense firms know that the U.S. government will solicit bids to produce the next generation of long-range bombers. The defense companies will be the sellers in this auction, and U.S. government officials will be the buyers.

In these instances and others, there is no established market. Mexican officials and managers of oil producers cannot sell and buy in a market for oil fields, and managers of defense firms and U.S. government officials cannot meet in a market for long-range bombers. So buyers and sellers of these types of unique products often use auctions to buy and sell them.

In other instances, managers want to sell (or buy) goods or services with prices that vary in unpredictable ways. For example, Feeding America is the largest U.S. food bank. Its managers must distribute donated food among its 200 affiliates. An affiliate's valuation of any particular donated food item will vary according to its inventory, the expected demand for the item, and a variety of unique characteristics. So in order to distribute the food to the location where it is most highly valued, the managers of Feeding America use auctions in which the affiliates bid for the different items.

Auctions are also commonplace for managers whose jobs deal with spectrum frequencies, real estate, government contracts, and construction contracts. Some of the managers in these markets are concerned with bidding in auctions, while others conduct them. You never know whether your career will take you to a position in which you need to participate in an auction. So this section reviews the different auction types as well as optimal bidding strategies and the expected price (or revenue) for each one.

Types of Auctions

Thanks to television and movies, the most familiar type of auction is the open-outcry auction, in which bidders compete by raising one another's bid. There are, however, actually four different types of auctions: English auction (ascending bid); Dutch auction (descending bid); sealed-bid first-price auction; and sealed-bid second-price auction. Each type has different characteristics and gives bidders different amounts of information.

English Auction

English auction An ascending-bid auction in which each participant observes the other participants' bids and can raise the currently high bid until no one is willing to submit a higher bid; the highest bidder wins the auction and pays the amount of the bid.

The open-outcry auction just described is an **English auction**, an ascending-bid auction in which each participant observes the other participants' bids and can raise the currently high bid until no one is willing to submit a higher bid. At the start of an English auction, the auctioneer suggests an opening bid. In some cases, bidders are able to place a lower opening bid, but in others, the suggested opening bid is the lowest price for which the auctioneer will sell the item. Once a bidder makes an acceptable opening bid, the auctioneer raises the opening bid by a prespecified bid increment and asks if anyone is willing to pay the higher price. As long as a participant is willing to pay the higher price, the bidding process continues. The auction stops when participants stop submitting bids, at which time the highest bidder wins the auction and pays the amount of the bid. The bidders in an English auction may have substantial information: (1) They often know who is bidding, and (2) they usually know the price that causes each participant to drop out of the auction.

Dutch Auction

A **Dutch auction** is a descending-bid auction in which the auctioneer starts with a high price and then lowers it until one participant bids. That bidder wins the lot and pays the amount of the bid. In a Dutch auction, the bidders have very little information about the maximum price the other participants are willing to pay because they observe only a single bid.

Dutch auction A descending-bid auction in which the auctioneer starts with a high price and then lowers it until one participant bids; that bidder wins the lot and pays the amount of the bid.

Sealed-Bid First-Price Auction

Sealed-bid first-price auctions are the most common type of auction in business settings. In a **sealed-bid first-price auction**, the participants submit sealed bids. The participants have no knowledge of one another's bids when determining their bids. Once the deadline for submitting bids has passed, the auctioneer opens the sealed bids, and if the auction is selling a product, the participant with the highest bid wins the item and pays the amount of the bid. (If the auction is for buying a product—as when the U.S. Navy solicits bids to upgrade its Ship Self-Defense Systems—the participant with the *lowest* bid wins, and the Navy pays the amount of the bid.)

Sealed-bid first-price auction An auction in which the participants submit sealed bids; at the end of the auction, the auctioneer opens the sealed bids, and if the auction is for selling a product, the participant with the highest bid wins the item and pays the amount of the bid.

Sealed-Bid Second-Price Auction

Sealed-bid second-price auctions are uncommon, but they can help you understand strategies for the other auction types. Similar to a sealed-bid first-price auction, in a **sealed-bid second-price auction**, the participants submit sealed bids. At the end of the auction, the auctioneer opens the bids, and when the auction is for selling a product, the participant with the highest bid wins but pays the amount of the *second-highest* bid. As with a sealed-bid first-price auction, the participants determine their bids with no information about competitors' bids.

Sealed-bid second-price auction: An auction in which the participants submit sealed bids; at the end, the auctioneer opens the bids, and the participant with the highest bid wins the item but pays the amount of the *second-highest* bid.

Google AdWords auctions are sealed-bid second-price auctions. In these auctions, participants bid on the order in which their advertisements will be displayed whenever someone uses Google to search for a specified word or phrase. The bidder with the highest bid wins the first placement in the list of advertisers, the second-highest bid wins the second place in the list, and so on. But the highest bidder pays only the second-highest bid, the second-highest bidder pays only the third-highest bid, and so on.

Bidding Strategy

A participant in any type of auction must develop a bidding strategy. The optimal strategies are based, in part, on how the product is valued. There are three general valuation scenarios:

- **Independent private value.** A participant's value of an auction item does not depend on the other participants' values of that item because the valuations are independent of each other. For example, you are bidding on a vacant office building, and your company has secured a tenant who will pay $10,000 a month in rent. The value to you is the profit you will make from winning the auction and then renting it to your tenant. This value is private to you and is independent of the other participants' values. The fact that another bidder has secured a tenant who will pay $6,000 per month has no effect on your value of the building.
- **Correlated value.** Each participant assigns a unique estimated value to the item but the valuations are not independent. Each participant's estimated value is correlated

with the other participants' estimated values, so if one bidder's valuation is high, it is likely that the other bidders' values are also high. For example, when Nortel, a bankrupt data-networking-equipment manufacturer, auctioned its patents, each of the bidders—Intel, Apple, Microsoft, Sony, and others—assigned its own estimated value to the patents depending on how the company intended to use them. If Intel estimated that the patents were highly valuable, then it is likely that the other participants such as Apple, Microsoft, and Sony also found the patents highly valuable.

- **Common value.** The value of the item is the same for all bidders, but this common value is unknown to any participant. Each of the bidders estimates the value of the item using its own information. For example, in 2014, when the U.S. government auctioned oil rights to the (infamous) Teapot Dome oil field in Wyoming, the true value of the field was unknown to the participating oil producers, but the unknown value (the quantity of oil and hence the profit the field might produce) was the same for all bidders.[4]

There is a key difference between correlated values and common values. In a correlated-value auction, the (unknown) true value of the auction item varies among bidders, but in a common-value auction, the (unknown) true value is the same for all bidders. For example, Nortel's patents might be worth more to Intel than to Apple because of Intel's stronger desire to enter the markets protected by the patents. In contrast, the value of the Teapot Dome oil field is the same for all oil producers because the (unknown) quantity of oil is fixed.

Bidding Strategy with Independent Private Values

The bidding strategy in auctions with independent private values is the most straightforward. For example, as a manager working for a firm like Clark Freight Line, you and the managers of competing truckers—including Andragon Logistics and Speedy-Bee Delivery Services—will attend Cannon Sales' annual summer truck auction. Say that you are all looking for a new Peterbilt 367 to add to your fleets. Your strategy for bidding will depend on the value of the truck to your company, which you base on the expected profit from owning the truck. Clearly, there is some risk of earning less as well as the possibility of earning more, but if you are indifferent about the uncertainty surrounding the expected profit (so that you are risk neutral), the value of the truck is equal to its expected profit. If you do not like the uncertainty (so that you are risk averse), the value of the truck is less than its expected profit, and the more you dislike risk, the more you discount your valuation. (See Section 14.6 for more on the topic of risk aversion.) Suppose that you calculate the truck's value to be $145,000, Andragon Logistics values it at $100,000, and Speedy-Bee Delivery calculates their value to be $120,000. Each of the three firms' values is independent and private. Given these values, let's explore the bidding strategy to use in each type of auction.

English Auction In an English auction, the strategy is clear: Keep bidding up to your value, and stop once bidding exceeds that amount. In the Peterbilt example, all three firms bid to $100,000, and then Andragon Logistics drops out. You and Speedy-Bee Delivery bid up to $120,000, and then Speedy-Bee stops bidding. So you, as the bidder for Clark Freight, win the auction for $120,000.[5]

---

4 In reality, different producers with different technologies might be able to make different profits from the oil field, but these differences are small compared to the overall total profit. To simplify the analysis, we make the common assumption that the profit (or value) is the same for all bidders.

5 If Speedy-Bee bids $120,000, you might actually win the truck for one bid increment above $120,000. Because bid increments are small, for simplicity we ignore them.

Sealed-Bid Second-Price Auction   Perhaps surprisingly, the strategy in a sealed-bid second-price auction is not complicated: Submit a bid equal to your valuation of the product. Why is this strategy optimal? Keep in mind that you pay the amount of the second-highest bid, not the amount of your own bid. Let's explore the various possibilities. You certainly do not want to submit a bid higher than your valuation. Although a higher bid increases your chance of winning, if you bid high and the second-highest bid also exceeds your valuation, you have actually lost: You will end up paying more than you think the item is worth! If you bid high and the second-highest bid is less than your valuation, bidding more does not increase your chances of winning the auction or the amount you pay. Accordingly, bidding more than your valuation is an inferior strategy because it cannot help you—it can only not affect you or hurt you. You definitely do not want to submit a bid lower than your valuation because a lower bid decreases your chances of winning and does not affect the price you pay if you win. Therefore, the optimal strategy is to submit a bid equal to your valuation of the item.

In the Peterbilt example, if all three bidders follow this optimal strategy, Andragon Logistics will bid $100,000, Speedy-Bee Delivery will bid $120,000, and you will bid $145,000. You will win the auction and pay $120,000, the second-highest valuation of the product. The price you pay, the valuation of the second-highest bidder, is the same as in an English auction!

Dutch Auction   You might think the optimal strategy in a Dutch auction is to signal your bid the instant the countdown reaches your valuation of the product. Actually, however, that strategy is *not* optimal. Generally, you want to reduce your bid below your valuation because the lower the price you pay, the greater the worth (the profit) to you. Suppose that you have somehow discovered that Speedy-Bee Delivery has the second-highest valuation of $120,000. Rather than bid at $145,000, you will signal your bid at $120,000.01, increasing your profit from the truck by nearly $25,000.

In reality, however, it is unlikely you will ever know the precise value of the second-highest bidder, so you need to estimate the difference between your valuation and the next-highest valuation and then bid below your valuation by slightly less than that amount. Saying that it is difficult to estimate the next-highest valuation is an understatement. The difference between valuations depends on so many factors specific to the particular auction that it is hard to offer many general principles aside from one: The more participants in the auction, the closer the next-highest valuation to your valuation. So the more bidders in the auction, the less you should reduce your bid below *your* valuation.

Of course, even if you are the bidder with the highest valuation, your estimate of the difference may be too high, and you will lose the auction if you don't bid in time. On the other hand, if your estimate is too low you may bid too quickly, allowing you to win the auction but pay more than necessary, decreasing your profit. On average, in a Dutch auction, if you have the highest valuation, expect to pay a bid approximately equal to the second-highest valuation.

Sealed-Bid First-Price Auction   You may be surprised to learn that the strategy in a sealed-bid first-price auction is exactly the same as in a Dutch auction. The reason the strategies are identical becomes clear when you consider that the bidders have precisely the same information in both auction types. Specifically, during both types of auctions, bidders gather no new information about the other participants' valuations. So in both types of auctions, your optimal strategy is to assume that your valuation is the highest, reduce it by an amount slightly less than the difference you estimate between your valuation and the second-highest valuation, and bid this amount. If you have the highest valuation, you again expect to pay a bid approximately equal to the second-highest valuation.

Bidding Strategy with Correlated Values or Common Values

The bidding strategy in auctions with correlated values or common values is more complicated because if you win the auction, you have just received some potentially bad news: No one else valued the item as highly as you did. You may have fallen victim to the **winner's curse**, the result in an auction in which the winner pays more than the true value of the item and is likely to incur a loss. Avoiding the winner's curse is important because no one wants to incur a loss (much less a curse). As a manager bidding in the auction of an item with a correlated value or common value, how can you dodge the winner's curse? Unfortunately, there is no precise formula. Instead, there are general observations that can help you escape the winner's curse.

Winner's curse The result in an auction in which the winner pays more than the true value of the item and is likely to incur a loss.

The likelihood of suffering the winner's curse increases as the number of bidders increases because the more bidders in an auction, the greater the probability that at least one buyer will overestimate the true value of the item and wind up the victim of the winner's curse. The prospect of suffering the winner's curse also increases if a firm has less information than its competitors and/or if there is significant uncertainty about the true value of the item being auctioned. The managerial lessons from these results are clear: Try to participate in auctions with only a few other bidders, ensure that you are not at an informational handicap, and be less aggressive in your bidding strategy if the true value of the item is highly uncertain.

If you knew the true value of the item, you would never fall prey to the winner's curse, so one other obvious piece of advice is to research the item's true value. Even so, unless you are 100 percent certain of the true value, you must reduce your maximum bid below your estimated valuation to avoid the winner's curse. For example, as a manager working for a firm like Canadian Natural Resources, a large oil producer, you are considering your bid for the right to drill in Teapot Dome, the oil field in Wyoming. Your petroleum geologists estimate that there are 310 million of barrels of oil in the field. You calculate that you will make an economic profit of $40 on each barrel, for an estimated total of $1.24 billion of economic profit. To avoid the winner's curse, you should decrease your maximum bid to a figure below your estimated expected profit.

Two other factors also can affect your bid adjustment: uncertainty and type of auction. First, the less certain you are of your estimates, the more you should adjust your maximum bid downward. Second, you should decrease your maximum bid the most in a Dutch auction and in a sealed-bid first-price auction because you pay the full amount of your winning bid. In these auctions, keeping in mind that all participants will lower their maximum bids, try to set your bid just above the second-highest bid. You should decrease your maximum bid by less in an English auction and in a sealed-bid second-price auction. In an English auction, if you win, you are automatically just above the second-highest bid, so there is no need to make any further downward adjustment to get to the second-highest valuation. If you prevail in a sealed-bid second-price auction, you pay the next-lowest bid, which again offsets some of the potential loss from the winner's curse.

In addition, your maximum bid can change during an English auction as you observe your competitors' bids. This new information might cause you to reevaluate your maximum bid. For example, if the Department of Energy uses an English auction to sell the production rights to the Teapot Dome oil field, hearing your competitors' bids can provide you with some additional information about the value of the oil field. When the bidding starts, say that you establish a maximum bid of $1.20 billion. You bid $1.19 billion, World Oil enters a bid of $1.21 billion, and Unlimited Energy follows with a bid of $1.23 billion. Next, Sioux Corporation outbids all of you at $1.24 billion. These bids should cause you to ask yourself, What do these companies know that I do not? Maybe your geologists randomly sampled lower-yielding

Strategy in an English Auction of a U.S. Silver Dollar

In 2014, Stacks Bowers auctioned the highest-grade 1794 U.S. silver dollar known. Using an English auction, the bidding opened at $2.2 million and rose quickly to $6 million by increments of $250,000. Suppose that your maximum bid is $10 million. Once the bid reaches $6 million, there are still several other bidders. You can either increase the bid by the next increment to $6.25 million or jump the bid to $10 million. What might you do?

Answer

The coin has some elements of a common value: The higher different bidders value it, the higher each bidder values it, if for no other reason than the bidder's confidence in its resale value. If you take a deep breath and jump the bid to $10 million, you deprive your competition of the information about other bidders' valuations and prevent them from revising their valuations upward. You hope no one else bids and the auctioneer's hammer falls, so you walk away with the coin for $10 million. This strategy is risky, of course. If the other bidders would have dropped out at bids below $10 million, you risk paying more than necessary. (By the way, the bidder did jump the bid and won the coin for $10 million!)

areas and there is more oil than your estimated 310 million barrels. Perhaps the other participants estimated a higher profit because they forecast a higher price for each barrel. Based on the bids you observe, you might adjust your valuation and maximum bid higher—say to $1.30 billion. If you do, you can outbid Sioux Corporation with a bid of $1.25 billion.

The bidding strategy just outlined for an English auction is easier to describe than to implement. You must use the new information you gain from the other participants' bidding to adjust your maximum bid. The challenge, of course, is to determine how much you should adjust. Two qualitative results provide some guidance:

- **Confidence in your valuation.** The less confident you are that your original valuation is correct, the more you should adjust it in the light of the new information. The converse is also true: The more confident you are that your original valuation is correct, the less you should adjust it based on the new information.
- **Accuracy of others' past valuations.** The more accurate the valuations of other bidders have been in the past, the more you should adjust your valuation based on their bids.

Keep in mind that you can adjust your valuation downward as well as upward. For example, say that you anticipate a maximum bid of $1.20 billion when the bidding for the oil field starts. If you see other bidders begin to drop out at around $800 million, you might want to adjust your valuation and maximum bid downward.

Winner's Curse When Selling a Product

The auction examples presented to this point all deal with *buying* a product. Managers must often submit bids to *sell* products, as when Boeing and other aircraft manufacturers submit bids to build and sell new long-range bombers to the Defense Department. In this case, the valuation of the product is the estimated cost, including the profit the bidder expects to make. When selling, the winner's curse occurs if a winning bid is too *low*, so that the bidder makes less profit than expected or perhaps even incurs an economic loss. Bidders who are selling products must *increase* their bids to avoid the winner's curse, but otherwise the same general strategies apply. For example, the less confidence you have in your cost estimate, the more you should increase your bid to avoid a loss, and in a sealed-bid first-price auction, you should increase your bid by more than in an English auction.

Expected Revenue

Managers in charge of holding auctions must decide what type to conduct. When planning their annual summer truck auction and the sale of the Teapot Dome field, the managers at Cannon Sales and the Department of Energy, respectively, select the type of auction that will generate the most revenue and maximize profit. The type of auction can depend on whether the items being auctioned have independent private values, correlated values, or common values.

If the products being auctioned have independent private values, such as a Peterbilt 367, the expected revenue is the same for all auction types and for each item equals the second-highest valuation. The conclusion that different types of auctions have the same expected revenue is called **revenue equivalence**. In this case, the manager can select any auction type.

Revenue equivalence The conclusion that different types of auctions have the same expected revenue.

Consider each type of auction in turn to see why they show revenue equivalence:

- **English auction.** The participant with the highest valuation wins with a bid equal to the second-highest valuation.
- **Sealed-bid second-price auction.** Participants' optimal strategy is to place bids equal to their own valuations, so the bidder with the highest valuation wins and pays a price equal to the second-highest valuation.
- **Dutch auction and sealed-bid first-price auction.** Participants' optimal strategy is to place bids lower than their own valuations. On average, the winning bid from the participant with the highest valuation equals the second-highest valuation.

The bidders' valuations do not change during an auction of an item with independent private value, since the value of the item does not depend on the other participants' valuations. Because the valuations are fixed and (on average) the winning bid equals the second-highest valuation, the expected revenue from each type of auction is the same.

The bidders' valuations of a product with correlated or common value *can* change during an English auction, so revenue equivalence does not hold. That result creates a question: Which kind of auction should the auctioneer use? The smaller the bidders' reduction from their valuations, the higher their bids, so the greater the amount of revenue the seller collects. When bidders use their optimal strategies, an English auction has the highest expected revenue because it has the smallest reduction in valuation. English auctions have more risk, however. If participants notice other bidders dropping out at low bids, they may immediately revise their maximum bids downward. The risk associated with the English auction might lead risk-averse managers to use a different type auction. A Dutch auction and a sealed-bid first-price auction have larger reductions in their valuations, so they have lower expected revenues. Bidders in sealed-bid second-price auctions reduce their bids less than in Dutch auctions or sealed-bid first-price auctions and more than in English auctions. In addition, because they pay only the second- highest bid, the expected revenue for this type of auction is also less than that for an English auction. In short, there is no one-size-fits-all optimal type of auction for selling correlated value or common value products.

Table 15.1 compares the different types of auctions, the information they provide bidders, the optimal bidding strategies, and the expected revenue.

Information presents another challenge to managerial decision making when one party to a transaction has some relevant information and the other party does not. This situation occurs often enough that it creates issues that almost all managers face in one form or another. Because these issues are wide ranging and can affect managers' decisions in so many areas, the next section describes this scenario, called asymmetric information.

Table 15.1 Comparison of Different Types of Auctions

Type of Auction	Mode of Operation and Information	Bidding Strategy		Expected Revenue	
		Independent Private Value	Common or Correlated Value	Independent Private Value	Common or Correlated Value
English auction	Ascending bid; the highest bidder wins. Bidders observe competitors' bids during auction.	Bid up to the valuation.	Bid less than the valuation, but adjust the amount during the auction based on competitors' bids.	Equals second-highest valuation	Highest
Dutch auction	Descending bid; the first bidder wins. Bidders observe prices at which no one bids. At the end of the auction, bidders observe only the winning bid.	Bid less than the valuation. The bid is the same as in a sealed-bid first-price auction.	Bid less than the valuation.	Equals second-highest valuation	Lower than an English auction
Sealed-bid first-price auction	Sealed bids are submitted; the highest bidder wins and pays the amount of the bid. At the end of the auction, bidders observe only the winning bid.	Bid less than the valuation. The bid is the same as in a Dutch auction.	Bid less than the valuation.	Equals second-highest valuation	Lower than an English auction
Sealed-bid second-price auction	Sealed bids are submitted; the highest bidder wins and pays the amount of the second-highest bid. At the end of the auction, bidders observe only the winning bid.	Bid the valuation.	Bid less than the valuation but more than in a sealed-bid first-price auction.	Equals second-highest valuation	Lower than an English auction

SOLVED PROBLEM

The San Francisco Giants Strike Out

In 2007, Barry Zito was one of the best pitchers in Major League Baseball. In his first seven years with the Oakland Athletics, he won 102 games and lost only 63. In 2002, he won the Cy Young Award for being the best pitcher of the year. In 2007, Mr. Zito became a free agent and was able to sell his services to any team. A bidding war broke out. The Texas Rangers offered a six-year contract for $84 million, and the New York Mets offered a five-year contract for $75 million. The San Francisco Giants ultimately won, signing Mr. Zito to a seven-year contract worth $126 million. Suppose that the San Francisco Giants management valued Mr. Zito's services at $126 million. What suggestion would you have given them about their decision to offer him $126 million?

Answer

You should point out the potential for a winner's curse. No other team was willing to pay $126 million, so if that was the value the Giants' managers assigned to Mr. Zito's services, they needed to offer a lower salary. In this case, the Giants probably overpaid by not offering a contract with a salary below their valuation. In fact, the Giants did end up suffering the winner's curse. During his seven years with the Giants, Mr. Zito's record was 63 wins and 80 losses. After never having a losing season with the Oakland Athletics, he had only one winning season with the Giants.

15.4 Asymmetric Information

Learning Objective 15.4 Describe strategies managers can use to overcome the challenges of asymmetric information.

Information is not always shared equally. Frequently, some parties to a transaction have relevant private information that is unknown to the other parties, a situation that economists call **asymmetric information**.

Asymmetric information A situation in which some parties to a transaction have relevant private information that is unknown to the other parties.

Two important types of asymmetric information are hidden characteristics and hidden actions. A *hidden characteristic* is a fact or tendency about a person or object in a transaction known to some of the parties but not the others. For example:

1. Consumers looking to buy health insurance using the marketplaces provided by the Affordable Care Act have private information about the general state of their health that the potential insurers do not.
2. The salespeople at an auto dealership trying to sell a used car have private information about the quality of the used car unknown to potential buyers.

A *hidden action* is an action taken by one party in a transaction that the other parties cannot observe. An example of a hidden action is the old adage "The mice will play when the cat is away." An example less relevant to cats but more relevant to managers is salespeople taking advantage of an off-site supervisor meeting to huddle in the back room, updating their Facebook status or tweeting and retweeting on Twitter rather than walking the floor to make sales.

Asymmetric information can lead the better-informed parties to try to take advantage of the less-well-informed parties. Two problems result from this tendency: adverse selection and moral hazard. Adverse selection is the result of hidden characteristics, and moral hazard is the result of hidden actions.

Adverse Selection

Adverse selection is a situation in which some of the parties to a transaction know of a hidden characteristic that will increase their benefit at the expense of the other parties. As a manager, anytime you change the conditions of a sale, you must first ask yourself if you will fall prey to adverse selection. The executives at Amazon.com created Amazon Prime, a program in which customers who pay $99 per year get "free" two-day shipping for all of their purchases. It is likely that customers who join Amazon Prime order more shipments (and create significantly higher shipping costs) than customers who do not join the program. In 2015, Consumer Intelligence Research Partners estimated that, on average, Prime members spent about $1,100 per year on Amazon and non-Prime members spent about $600. If Amazon.com's managers had not taken the hidden characteristic of those customers (higher-than-normal shipping costs) into account when pricing the program, they could have set the price so low that Amazon.com would have suffered substantial losses.

> **Adverse selection** A situation in which some of the parties to a transaction know of a hidden characteristic that will increase their benefit at the expense of the other parties.

Managers of insurance companies must be especially concerned with adverse selection. GEICO is a large automobile insurance company. For simplicity, let's say that drivers come in two types: safe drivers, who slow down and stop when a traffic light turns yellow, and risky drivers, who see yellow lights as a sign to speed up so they can beat the red light. Safe drivers will be in fewer accidents and are therefore cheaper for GEICO to insure than risky drivers. Competition in the market for automobile insurance forces GEICO to charge a lower price to drivers it believes are safer and a higher price to drivers it believes are riskier, but the firm cannot tell for certain whether a particular customer is safe or risky. That private information is a hidden characteristic, known to the customer but not to GEICO. If GEICO's managers design low-price policies that they believe will appeal to safe drivers but that instead appeal to risky drivers, this adverse selection can wind up inflicting a severe economic loss on GEICO.

More generally, managers of any type of insurance company must be very careful to avoid the adverse selection that results from selling more policies than expected to risky, high-cost customers. In one of the first years that the marketplaces established under the Affordable Care Act were in operation, Highmark Health, a nonprofit health insurance company, lost $318 million because it offered a policy that attracted many more than the expected number of consumers with chronic health conditions that required extensive—and expensive—care. Because Highmark underestimated this number, Highmark's managers set a price for the insurance that was too low and did not cover the costs.

Lemons Problem

In extreme cases, adverse selection can result in a market absolutely failing to function. The classic example, first introduced by the Nobel Prize–winning economist George Akerlof in 1970, examines the used car market. The insights from this example apply to *any* used equipment market, however. Akerlof's model is based on the fact that used cars vary in quality. For simplicity, suppose that there are only two levels of quality: *lemons*, which comprise 50 percent of the market and are worth $8,000 to their current owners, and *cream puffs*, which comprise the other 50 percent of the market and are worth $14,000 to their current owners. The owners are selling the cars, and from experience, they know the quality of the cars. Buyers value a lemon at $9,000 and a cream puff at $15,000. If the buyers also knew the quality of every car they inspected, the market would function efficiently: Lemons would sell for a price between $8,000 and $9,000 (say, $8,500), and cream puffs would sell for a price between $14,000 and $15,000 (say, $14,500).

Now make the more realistic assumption that buyers do *not* know the quality of any specific car. The current owners have private information that results in a hidden characteristic: The quality of the car. How well does the market function in the presence of this private information? Is it still possible to buy a high-quality used car? Buyers cannot rely on sellers to tell them the truth about the cars: Every seller wants to get a high price, so all will claim that their cars are cream puffs and worth the high price of $14,500. Clearly, at this price, the sellers of low-quality cars will continue to offer their cars for sale. Suppose that the sellers of high-quality cars also continue to offer their cars for sale. In this case, a buyer has a 50/50 chance of buying a lemon or of buying a cream puff. Because the buyers value a lemon at $9,000 and a cream puff at $15,000, given the random 50/50 chance, on average buyers expect to get a car valued at $12,000. So buyers are willing to pay up to $12,000 for a used car but no more. The owners of high-quality cars will not offer cars for sale at $12,000 because their cars are worth $14,000 to them. Realizing this result, buyers correctly conclude that the only cars offered for sale will be lemons, so they lower their offer to pay to $8,500, the price of a lemon. Lemon owners will sell their cars for this price, so in this extreme case the market for lemons functions. Adverse selection, however, makes the market for high-quality used cars nonexistent.

Overcoming the Adverse Selection Problem

At its core, adverse selection is the result of asymmetric information. If both parties to the transaction shared information equally, then adverse selection problems would disappear. Screening, signaling, and certification are three ways that market participants can share information, thereby overcoming the adverse selection problem.

Screening   Managers of insurance companies, such as GEICO, would like to know their customers' private information about driving tendencies, but they cannot simply ask. No customer will admit to being in the high-risk class because GEICO will then assign them to the high-priced policies. So GEICO managers must screen their customers in some way. **Screening** refers to methods used by the uninformed parties to gather at least some of the private information they do not possess.

Screening Methods used by the uninformed parties to gather at least some of the private information they do not possess.

Some screening methods are straightforward. Before GEICO sells automobile insurance to a driver, the firm collects information on the customer's past driving record, which correlates with a driver's riskiness: Drivers with violations on their records tend to be riskier drivers. If a driver has accumulated a record of past accidents or tickets, GEICO concludes that the driver is riskier and is likely to cost more to insure, so the firm charges a higher price.

Of course, this screening method is imperfect, so GEICO's managers combine it with another screen: self-revelation. **Self-revelation** is a mechanism that causes the parties with private information to reveal at least part of this information to the uninformed parties.

Self-revelation A mechanism that causes the parties with private information to reveal at least part of this information to the uninformed parties.

GEICO's managers use combinations of the deductible and premium to induce self-revelation. The deductible is the amount of a loss that the insured must pay. For example, in the case of an accident, the owner of a policy with a $1,000 deductible must pay the first $1,000 of the loss before the insurance company pays anything. The higher the deductible is, the more an accident costs the policy holder, and the less it costs the company. The premium is the price the customer pays for the insurance. Consider two types of policies: one with a low premium and a high deductible and the other with a high premium and a low deductible.

- **Low premium/high deductible.** This policy appeals to people who know they are safe drivers. They are willing to accept a high deductible for two reasons: (1) They expect they will not be in accidents and will not have to pay the deductible, and (2) they benefit by paying a low premium. Risky drivers will not like this policy because they know that an accident—and then their payment of the high deductible—is likely.
- **High premium/low deductible.** This policy appeals to people who know they are risky drivers. They are willing to pay a high premium because they know that they may well be in an accident and will benefit from the low deductible. Safe drivers will not accept this policy because they know they will be paying more for a low deductible that will be of little use to them, since they expect no accidents.

The goal of these two different insurance policies is to create a separating equilibrium that separates drivers into the appropriate risk pools and thereby maximizes profit. GEICO's profit will be less if their managers cannot separate the drivers into the correct risk pools and must offer a single premium/deductible combination. The firm's profit will also be less if the managers create a low-price policy that is expected to appeal to safer drivers (and therefore expected to be low cost) but that instead attracts risky drivers (and therefore winds up being high cost). This is the misfortune that befell Highmark Health.

Signaling   Signaling is another way to address the challenge of adverse selection. **Signaling** is a mechanism that enables informed parties to share their private information about a hidden characteristic with uninformed parties. In the case of the used car market, sellers of high-quality cars have private information that they would like to signal to the uninformed parties (the buyers). In particular, an owner of a cream puff wants to inform buyers that the car is high quality so it can command a high price. The owner might be able to signal the high quality of the car by offering a warranty that promises to repair any problem experienced during the first year of ownership. Warranties are costly to lemon owners, whose cars are more likely to break down within the first year, but are less costly to cream puff owners because the high quality of their cars makes a breakdown less likely. For example, using the numbers above, if the owner of a lemon can convince a buyer that the car is actually a cream puff, the owner stands to make $6,000 more profit: the price of a cream puff, $14,500, minus the price of a lemon, $8,500. If the anticipated cost of repairs during the first year exceeds $6,000, offering the warranty to convince the buyer that the car is high quality is not profitable for the lemon's owner. So offering a warranty can be a credible signal that the car for sale is a high-quality cream puff.

> **Signaling** A mechanism that enables informed parties to share their private information about a hidden characteristic with uninformed parties.

In reality, it is difficult to find an automobile manufacturer that does not offer some sort of warrantied "certified, pre-owned" used cars. John Deere even offers certified, pre-owned tractors, combines, sprayers, and harvesters. In all of these cases, the sellers are signaling buyers that they are selling high-quality vehicles.

A warranty is one example of signaling. As noted in the previous example, for a signal to be credible, it must be more costly to send the signal for the parties who do not have the desirable hidden characteristic (the lemon owners) than for those who actually have it (the cream puff owners). More specifically, for a signal to be credible, the cost of falsely sending it must outweigh the profit.

When a firm uses an initial public offering (IPO) of stock to go public—to become a publicly owned company—signaling can play a key role in the stock's valuation. In an IPO, the owners sell some of their ownership by offering shares in the company to the public. The company's owners set both the price at which the shares are offered and the number of shares for sale. The price depends on the *perceived* value of the company. The original owners have private information about the company's *true* value. If they believe the stock market is undervaluing the company in the IPO, they will sell only a small number of shares and retain the rest to wait for the price to rise. Retaining shares sends a credible signal that the owners believe the company is undervalued. The owners of an overvalued company will sell most of their shares because retaining them will be costly when other investors catch on and the price of the stock falls. The sale of a large number of shares sends the signal that the owners think the company is overvalued.

Your degree is also a signal. If you earn a master of business administration (MBA) degree, it will signal that you have attained a great deal of important, valuable skills and knowledge, referred to as *human capital*. In addition, your MBA signals some hidden characteristics: an intense interest in your career and the drive to succeed. The higher salary that MBAs receive reflects *both* their increased human capital from that level of education *and* the positive signal the degree sends to employers. It is very costly for someone without an MBA degree to send this same signal.

Trademarks—specifically, brand names—also serve as signals. While driving down the interstate, if you see a set of golden arches and a McDonald's sign, you have virtually complete and highly credible information about the type and quality of food you can buy there. If you see a sign advertising a local restaurant, the type and quality of food remain hidden characteristics. The executives at McDonald's make immense efforts to maintain the credibility of the signal they are sending. They require the independently owned, franchised restaurants to maintain strict quality controls, and (as noted in Section 15.1), they pursue anyone they believe is infringing on their trademark to ensure that they are signaling a consistent message.

Certification   A third solution to the challenges created by adverse selection is certification. **Certification** is publication of information by an independent third party. *Consumer Reports* and Yelp are examples of independent third parties. For third-party certification to overcome the problem of adverse selection, consumers must believe that it is unbiased. For this reason, the managers at Consumers Union, the company that publishes *Consumer Reports*, have set a policy of accepting no advertising. Yelp accepts advertising, so its managers must work diligently to maintain consumers' belief that its crowd-sourced reviews are unbiased.

Independent accounting companies audit companies of all sizes. The audit report is an independent certification of a company's financial status. Sometimes audits are required. For example, the New York Stock Exchange requires that an independent auditor evaluate each of its listed companies at least once a year. This requirement eliminates the hidden characteristic of a company's financial status.

Independent third parties certify more than just companies, products, and services. To become a certified public accountant (CPA) in the United States, accountants must pass an exam created and graded by the American Institute of Certified Public Accountants. By passing this test, CPAs make public their skill, which otherwise would remain a hidden characteristic.

Economists, however, point out that certification may have potential drawbacks for society. For example, to practice cosmetology in California, hair stylists and other cosmetology professionals must pass an exam administered by the California Board of Barbering and Cosmetology. Before taking the exam, the applicant must complete 1,600 hours of training at an approved college for cosmetology. A cosmetologist's skill is a hidden characteristic, and passing the exam signals possession of that skill, but 1,600 hours of training at an approved college may seem excessive and unattainable to many potential cosmetologists. Instead of serving as an independent certifier of quality, the California Board of Barbering and Cosmetology may be using its requirements to decrease the supply of cosmetologists. In 2016, five of the nine members of the board worked in and represented the industry—and possibly stood to

Certification Publication of information by an independent third party.

benefit from a decrease in supply and the resulting increase in price of cosmetology services. If certification decreases supply and serves as a barrier to entry, it increases the price and market power of the suppliers already in the market, harming society by creating a deadweight loss (see Section 6.2).

Moral Hazard

Moral hazard is a situation in which some of the parties to a transaction take hidden actions that increase their benefit at the expense of the other parties. It frequently occurs after participants have already entered into a contract or an agreement. Moral hazard problems arise when the parties to the transaction have conflicting objectives, and the supervising parties cannot monitor the other parties.

Moral hazard problems are commonplace. For example, in a cost-plus-fixed-fee contract, a contractor agrees to pay the other firm all of the costs involved in executing the contract plus a fixed fee as profit. This type of arrangement has an obvious moral hazard problem: The firm with the contract has no incentive to minimize the cost of executing the contract. Although a cost-plus-fixed-fee contract might be optimal when the quality of the finished product is paramount, such as in the U.S. manned space program, in many instances such arrangements simply lead to higher costs.

Slight contractual variations, however, can alter the incentives of the firm with the contract. The managers of many government agencies have moved to cost-plus-incentive-fee contracts or cost-plus-award-fee contracts. A *cost-plus-incentive-fee contract* establishes certain explicit criteria that the firm must meet to gain an incentive fee. For example, if the contract specifies a certain cost or a certain delivery date and the firm meets the requirements, the firm receives an additional fee (the incentive). Under a *cost-plus-award-fee contract*, the firm receives a fixed fee plus the potential to win an additional financial award depending on the evaluation of the agency granting the contract. The incentives in this type of contract, however, are less concrete than those in cost-plus-incentive-fee contracts because the agency alone determines whether the firm is entitled to the award.

The cost-plus-incentive-fee contract exemplifies one general solution to moral hazard: The less-informed participants need to change the other parties' incentives to focus on achieving the less-informed participants' goal.

Principal–Agent Problem

One moral hazard problem occurs so frequently economists have given it a name: the principal–agent problem. The **principal–agent problem** occurs when a principal hires an agent to perform duties that align with the principal's objectives but not with the agent's objectives. Let's return to the example of salespeople hanging out in a back room. When the managers at a car dealership hire salespeople, their objective is for them to work the floor making sales. The salespeople would probably rather relax, perhaps by Facebooking in the back room or taking an extended lunch. The objective of the managers differs from those of the salespeople. If the managers cannot observe the salespeople's actions, there is a risk that the salespeople will advance their agenda—shirking—instead of the managers' objective—selling. The issue faced by the principals (the managers in our example) is how to shape the incentives of the agents (the salespeople) so that they advance the principals' objectives rather than their own.

A scandal at Wells Fargo & Company illustrates how principal–agent problems can lead to very significant costs. Wells Fargo is an immense bank. Its top executives, the principals, wanted the banks' employees, the agents, to sell customers different Wells Fargo products. The CEO even had a slogan, "Eight is great," suggesting that each customer should use eight of Wells Fargo's products. The employees realized that their salaries and even their jobs depended on these sales. Because the company was

Moral hazard A situation in which some of the parties to a transaction take hidden actions that increase their benefit at the expense of the other parties.

Principal–agent problem A problem that occurs when a principal hires an agent to perform duties that align with the principal's objectives but not with the agent's objectives.

so large, the employees were able to actively pursue their own self-interest of retaining their jobs and being awarded raises by opening accounts and credit cards for customers without telling the customer. Eventually, employees opened 1.5 million deposit accounts and issued 500,000 credit cards without the customers' knowledge, leading to $2.6 million in revenue for Wells Fargo. The information flowing up the hierarchy to the top managers, of course, reflected only the good news of increased sales. Regulators finally caught on, however, and fined Wells Fargo approximately $175 million. The company also faces more potential costs because lawyers have filed numerous cases alleging harm to Wells Fargo customers. So the principal–agent problem may wind up costing Wells Fargo hundreds of millions of dollars.

One solution to the principal–agent problem is immediate: Monitor the agents. However, monitoring will be unprofitable if the marginal cost of monitoring exceeds its marginal benefit. In such cases, principals must find other solutions. Returning to the general solution of creating incentives for the agents to advance the principals' agenda rather than their own, let's examine two possible approaches for motivating employees: sales commissions and profit sharing.

Sales Commission Linking the agent's compensation to the principal's objective is one way to overcome a principal–agent problem. The managers at the car dealership have many other important tasks to perform and cannot closely observe each and every salesperson, so the marginal cost of additional monitoring probably exceeds the marginal benefit. In attempting to solve this principal–agent problem, consider two types of wage contracts: a contract specifying a straight salary and a contract with a sales commission:

- **Salary.** If the manager pays a salesperson a straight salary—say, $45,000 per year— the salesperson has no incentive to work the floor and increase the company's sales. A hidden action—such as taking a long lunch—costs the salesperson nothing, so there's nothing to prevent the principal–agent problem from rearing its ugly head.
- **Sales commission.** By compensating the salesperson using a commission structure based on the price of the cars sold, the number of sales made, or the total revenue of the cars sold, the manager changes the salesperson's incentives. In this case, shirking costs the salesperson because it decreases income. The extra hour at lunch is no longer free—it might cost the salesperson a sale! Tying income to sales is a common way sales managers try to overcome the principal–agent problem. Of course, as the Wells Fargo case illustrates, managers must still do some monitoring to prevent the salespeople from subverting the program to advance their own agendas.

Profit Sharing In the salesperson example, the contract links the agent's income to the firm's revenue. This link makes sense when the worker is directly involved in helping generate the revenue. It makes less sense if the worker has no direct impact on the revenue. Consider a programmer working for Alphabet's subsidiary, Google. Tying the programmer's salary to Google's revenue is nonsensical because the programmer has little impact on revenues. Tying the programmer's compensation to Google's *profit* is better because efficient programming can increase profit. That is just what Google does by giving many of its workers shares of stock in Alphabet. If Google's profit increases, the value of the stock rises, which boosts the workers' incomes. Contracts with profit-sharing clauses also help reduce the principal–agent problem.

In large corporations, the principal–agent problem between shareholders (the company's owners) and the top executives who manage the company on a day-to-day basis can be severe. The shareholders' objective is to maximize the firm's profit. The executives, however, may be more interested in the perquisites ("perks") of the job, such as travel by private corporate jet or company-paid memberships in exclusive golf clubs. Boards of directors (which represent the owners) often include stock options as part of the top executives' compensation contracts to align the executives' and owners' objectives more closely. Stock options allow the executives to purchase company-held shares of the company's stock at prespecified prices. The executives are the owners of the options and control when they exercise them—that is, the timing of their stock purchases and sales. For example, an option might allow the executives to purchase 100,000 shares of the company's stock at $50 per share. If the stock rises above $50, the executives can exercise the option, buy the stock at $50 per share, and sell it immediately for more, locking in a profit. Executives who work diligently to increase profit cause the price of the company's stock to rise. The hard work will result in increased income when the executives exercise the options *and* will benefit the shareholders, the company's owners. Effectively, stock options help align the agents' objective with the principals' objective, reducing the principal–agent problem.

Stock options do not eliminate the principal–agent problem entirely for two reasons:

1. The company's profit depends on the actions of all of its employees, not just those of a particular high-ranking executive.
2. Stock prices fluctuate for reasons not directly related to a company's profit. If the economy plunges into a recession, stock prices generally fall, depriving even the hardest-working executives of the additional income. When the economy enters a strong expansion, stock prices generally rise, rewarding even the laziest executives with additional income. These types of fluctuations lessen the incentive effects of stock options.

The approaches to overcoming principal–agent problems attempt to align the incentives of the agents and principals, but none of them causes the agents to *replace* their objective with the principals' objective. All such policies mitigate the problem, rather than totally eliminating it. Using a commission structure to link salespeople's salaries to their sales helps limit the principal–agent problem, but if a salesperson thinks the odds of making a sale at 4 P.M. on the day before Thanksgiving are slim, he or she might slide out the door early, rather than staying to the bitter end just in case a customer shows up.

Adverse Selection and Insurance Companies

SOLVED PROBLEM

As a manager at Driver's Insurance Company, you know that out of every 100 drivers, there are 20 risky drivers and 80 safe drivers. A risky driver costs your company $3,000 per year to insure, and a safe driver costs only $500. You design a policy that you think will appeal to safe drivers and expect that out of every 100 drivers insured by this policy, 10 will be risky drivers and 90 will be safe drivers. The price (premium) Driver's charges for this policy is $1,000 per year. The policy ends up appealing more strongly to risky drivers than expected, so that out of every 100 drivers insured, 30 are risky drivers and only 70 are safe drivers.

a. For every 100 drivers insured, what economic profit do you expect to make?
b. For every 100 drivers insured, what economic profit do you actually make?
c. Why is there a difference between the expected profit and actual profit? What changes to the insurance policy could you make to restore the policy to profitability?

(Continues)

SOLVED PROBLEM (*continued*)

Answer

a. The revenue per 100 drivers is $1,000 per driver × 100 drivers, or $100,000. The cost you expect per 100 drivers is the cost of the risky drivers, $3,000 per driver × 10 drivers = $30,000, plus the cost of the safe drivers, $500 per driver × 90 drivers = $45,000, for a total cost of $30,000 + $45,000 = $75,000. You expect to make an economic profit of $100,000 − $75,000, or $25,000.

b. The revenue remains the same at $100,000. The actual cost per 100 drivers is the cost of the risky drivers, $3,000 per driver × 30 drivers = $90,000, and the cost of the safe drivers, $500 per driver × 70 drivers = $35,000, for an actual total cost of $90,000 + $35,000 = $125,000. You incur an economic loss of $100,000 − $125,000, or −$25,000.

c. The expected profit swings to an actual loss due to adverse selection: The policy has attracted more risky drivers than expected. To make the policy profitable, you could raise the price. You could also change the terms of the policy to make it less attractive to risky drivers by increasing the deductible. Because a driver who has an accident must now pay a higher amount than before, the policy becomes less attractive to risky drivers. This change will reduce the number of risky drivers who buy the policy, which will reduce your cost and help move the policy toward profitability.

15.5 Decisions about Information

Learning Objective 15.5 Apply what you have learned about information to make better managerial decisions.

As you have seen throughout the chapter, information is crucial to managers. This section applies and extends the economic models presented in this chapter to help you to make better business decisions.

Value of Forecasts for Different Time Periods

One of the lessons from Section 15.2 is that forecasting demand is likely to be *less* profitable if (1) the forecasts of demand are inaccurate, (2) you experience small fluctuations in demand, and (3) changes in output cause large changes in your marginal cost. Producing where expected marginal revenue equals marginal cost is difficult enough. In the face of the three conditions just mentioned, there is little need to incur the expense of a demand forecast because its value is small.

 Use these observations to determine the value of forecasting demand over different time periods. Suppose that you work for a copper producer and are thinking of forecasting demand for your copper on a week-by-week basis. While your forecasts of demand may be quite accurate, there will probably be only small fluctuations in demand for copper from one week to another. In addition, your marginal cost curve is likely to be quite steep because it is very costly to make drastic changes in the quantity of copper produced in the short run. Consequently, it may not make sense to incur the cost of a weekly forecast of demand.

Suppose instead that you are considering forecasting demand for copper on a quarterly or half-year basis. Your demand forecast is probably less accurate than a weekly forecast, but on the other hand, the demand fluctuations are probably larger, and the marginal cost of changing the quantity is probably smaller. As a manager, you might decide it is worthwhile to obtain forecasts of longer-term changes in demand for copper but not short-term changes. In other words, you might forego attempts to match very short-term fluctuations in demand for copper because the payoff is simply not there and focus instead on changing production in response to long-term changes in demand. In addition, if you can maintain inventories of copper, letting changes in inventory smooth short-term unpredicted fluctuations in demand and changing production only to meet longer-term forecasted changes might be profit maximizing.

Managing the Winner's Curse When Selling a Product

As a manager holding an auction, you know that bidders for items with correlated or common values hedge their bids to avoid the winner's curse: Buyers will lower their bids, and sellers will raise them. This hedging can cost you profit. You want buyers to place bids that are close to their estimated valuations and sellers to place bids that are close to their estimated costs because such bidding increases your profit.

Managers can increase an auction's payoff by revealing more information about the auctioned item. For example, state departments of transportation (DOTs) frequently conduct auctions in which construction companies submit bids to build or repair highways. Such work is a common value item. If the construction costs are high for the highway construction company you manage—say, a firm like the large highway construction company, the Knife River Corporation—they will be high for all bidders. Because you are submitting a bid to sell your services, you boost your bid upward from your cost estimate to avoid the winner's curse.

A state DOT typically awards each contract to the lowest bidder, so its managers want to create conditions that lead participants such as your firm to decrease the amount of the upward boost and instead submit lower bids. DOT managers understand that the more confidence bidders have in their cost estimates, the lower the bids they submit will be, so the policy in some states—such as Ohio—is for the DOT to provide its own cost estimates to potential bidders. Providing this information increases the bidders' confidence in their own cost estimates, leading to lower bids.

Regardless of whether an auction's purpose is to sell a product or buy one, providing information can benefit the auction's managers because it gives the bidders more confidence in their valuations. However, the benefit occurs only if providing the information is a *policy* and not just a random occurrence. For example, if a DOT provides cost estimates only for some projects, bidders will worry that a project without a cost estimate has some hidden costs that the DOT does not want to reveal. On such projects, the bidders will substantially increase their bids to avoid submitting a bid that is too low to cover their costs, which will force the DOT to pay a high price for these projects.

Incentives and the Principal–Agent Problem

The principal–agent problem is ubiquitous. As you learned in Section 15.4, basing salespeople's pay on commissions is one technique that helps overcome it. The custom of tipping at restaurants is another: Many servers would rather take it easy instead of doing the hard work necessary to provide excellent service. While managers cannot easily observe the quality of a server's work, it is easy for the customers to observe whether a server's performance is poor, adequate, or excellent. So most U.S. restaurants typically pay their servers a low minimum wage, with the rest of their earnings relying on customers' tips. This arrangement gives servers the incentive to work hard and take excellent care of their customers. If they shirk by taking a load off their tired feet, rather than returning frequently to the table to check on the diners, the low tips they receive reduce their income. By providing the top-notch service the managers want, the servers benefit themselves by increasing their income.

Some managers modify the scheme that pays servers based on *their* tips by combining all the servers' tips and then giving each server the same share of the total tips. This procedure appeals to servers who are risk averse because it helps eliminate the risk of a shift that randomly turns out to have nothing but small tippers, thereby causing the server's income to be extremely low for that day. (See Section 14.6 for a discussion of risk aversion.) Making the job more appealing to servers helps managers if for no other reason than it reduces labor turnover. The policy of combining tips, however, has a drawback because it reduces servers' incentives to take care of their customers. All of the servers realize that if they provide poor service, *their* tips will be smaller, so the total tips collected by all the servers will be lower, but the shortfall will be spread among *all* the servers and not fall only on them. Consequently, this policy modification diminishes each server's incentive to be diligent about providing good service.[6]

Even if the tips are not commingled, there is another principal–agent problem with basing servers' pay primarily on tips. The servers have an incentive to give diners more than they paid for, such as free drinks or desserts, to get larger tips. These free items, which add to the restaurant's cost, don't cost the servers a penny and increase their likelihood of receiving a large tip. Restaurant owners and managers may be able to monitor this aspect of servers' behavior using security cameras. Because the cost of security cameras is decreasing, more managers are deciding that the marginal benefit of this sort of monitoring exceeds its marginal cost, especially at bars, where the bartender's ability to give a customer a free drink is maximized. Although the cameras do not allow an observer to determine if the servers are treating the diners well on a personal level, they do allow managers to observe whether the servers are treating diners to free food or drinks.

The persistence of the principal–agent problem illustrates another managerial lesson: No matter the context, your policy is unlikely to solve the principal–agent problem completely. Accordingly, as a profit-maximizing manager, you must continually remain alert for new techniques and technology that will allow you to further reduce its impact. The security cameras installed in restaurants are one example, but these types of advances can occur in many fields. Trucking companies now use GPS trackers to ensure that their drivers do not take unauthorized side excursions, and more managers use software to monitor employees' computer use to limit their natural tendency to explore the Internet, rather than work.

---

6 Some managers also pay the kitchen staff a fixed amount out of the total tips. This policy further reduces the servers' incentives to provide the level of service the managers desire though it does increase the kitchen staff's incentives to work more diligently.

Revisiting How Auctions Float the Navy's Boat

At the beginning of this chapter, you learned that high-ranking U.S. Navy officers faced the challenge of motivating sailors to accept undesirable duty stations voluntarily while minimizing the cost of staffing the stations. To achieve these goals, the officers created the Assignment Incentive Pay (AIP) Program. This program allows sailors to bid for the disagreeable duty stations by indicating how much extra pay they would need to accept the position. It caps the maximum that sailors can bid, but eligible sailors can bid up to the maximum in increments of $50 per month. The officers in charge of the program start with the lowest bids and work their way up until they have filled the duty roster. A winning sailor receives the amount of his or her bid for as long as the Navy keeps the sailor on that undesirable station.

The Navy's AIP Program is effectively a sealed-bid first-price auction because (1) no sailor sees the bids from the other sailors and (2) winning sailors receive the amount of their bids. The item, the undesirable duty station, is an independent private value item because each sailor's perception of the undesirability of the assignment is unique. For example, a duty station at sea for an extended period of time is perhaps more disagreeable for a married sailor with small children than for a single sailor with no dependents.

In a sealed-bid first-price auction in which the bidders are buying a product, the high bid wins, and the optimal strategy is for bidders to lower their bids below the highest price they are willing to pay. Because the sailors are *selling* their services, the winning bid will be the *lowest* one, and the optimal strategy is to raise their

bids *above* the least they will accept. Ideally, a sailor will estimate the bid that is right at the cutoff between the accepted bids and the rejected bids. This cutoff bid will be the highest bid the Navy accepts. If the cutoff bid is less than the amount the sailor wants, the sailor may as well not bid at all. If the cutoff bid is more than the amount the sailor wants, however, the optimal bid for the sailor to make is the cutoff bid.

Since one of the Navy's goals in designing the AIP Program was to minimize its cost of staffing the undesirable duty stations, Navy officers could have selected an auction format that made the bids immediately public. However, the officers realized that this might encourage collusion on the part of the sailors to boost the bids. Unlike most auctions, the bidders—the sailors—will interact for an extended period of time after the auction, so anyone not participating in the collusion and submitting a bid deemed too low could face prolonged negative peer pressure from the rest of the group. So a sealed-bid auction seems a better approach. Constructing the AIP Program as a sealed-bid second-price auction, in which all winners receive the same bonus, the highest acceptable bid, would increase the Navy's cost because the Navy would have to pay *every* sailor the maximum acceptable bid. As long as some bidders do not raise their bids enough, the cost of the sealed-bid first-price auction will be less than that of the sealed-bid second-price auction. Unless the sailors have a great deal of experience with AIP auctions, there is a fair chance that some will not boost their bids enough, so the result of a sealed-bid first-price auction is likely to be lowest cost to the Navy.

Summary: The Bottom Line

15.1 Intellectual Property
- Intellectual property refers to the intangible creations of human intelligence and includes information about future plans or production processes as well as inventions, artistic works, literary works, and trademarks.
- Depending on the type of intellectual property, the owner can legally protect it with a patent, trade secret, copyright, or trademark. Anyone infringing on intellectual property is subject to legal penalties.

15.2 Value of Forecasts
- When demand fluctuates randomly, managers can use demand forecasts to better match production with demand.
- Forecasts can increase a firm's profit. The value of the forecast depends on its accuracy, the variability of demand, and the amount by which marginal cost changes when the quantity produced changes.

15.3 Auctions

- In an English auction, the price starts low and works its way higher until no one is willing to top the winning bid. A Dutch auction begins with a high price, which the auctioneer lowers until someone bids and wins. In a sealed-bid first-price auction, the bidders submit secret bids, and the bidder with the highest bid wins and pays the amount of that bid. In a sealed-bid second-price auction, the winning bidder pays the amount of the second-highest bid.
- For items with independent private values, the optimal bidding strategy in an English auction and in a sealed-bid second-price auction is to bid up to the valuation of the product. The optimal bidding strategy in a Dutch auction and in a sealed-bid first-price auction is to decrease the bid below the valuation of the product.
- For items with correlated values or common values, the optimal bidding strategy is to bid below the valuation of the product. During an English auction, the valuation can be adjusted—upward or downward—based on competitors' bids.
- For items with independent private values, all of the auction types have the same expected revenue (revenue equivalence). For items with correlated or common values, the expected revenue differs depending on the type of auction.

15.4 Asymmetric Information

- Asymmetric information occurs when some parties to a transaction have relevant private information (hidden characteristics or hidden actions) that is unknown to the other parties. In such situations, the informed parties may try to take advantage of the uninformed parties.

- Adverse selection occurs when some parties to a transaction know of a hidden characteristic that will increase their benefit at the expense of the other parties. Screening, signaling, and certification by third parties can overcome problems created by adverse selection.
- Moral hazard is a situation in which some of the parties to a transaction take hidden actions that increase their benefit at the expense of the other parties.
- A common moral hazard is the principal–agent problem, which occurs when a principal hires an agent to perform duties that align with the principal's objective but not with the agent's objective. Commissions, profit sharing, cost-plus-incentive-fee contracts, and cost-plus-award-fee contracts help overcome the principal–agent problem by giving the agent the incentive to work toward the principal's objective.

15.5 Managerial Application: Decisions About Information

- Demand forecasts for short time periods are likely to be less profitable than demand forecasts for longer time periods.
- When you are auctioning correlated or common value items, you can increase your profit by establishing a policy to reveal more information about the items being auctioned. The additional information increases bidders' certainty about their valuations (if the bidders are buying) or their costs (if the bidders are selling).
- Because any policy you formulate to deal with a principal–agent problem is unlikely to completely eliminate it, you need to keep watch for technological changes that can better address it.

Key Terms and Concepts

Adverse selection	Moral hazard	Self-revelation
Asymmetric information	Patent	Signaling
Certification	Principal–agent problem	Trademark
Copyright	Revenue equivalence	Trade secret
Dutch auction	Screening	Winner's curse
English auction	Sealed-bid first-price auction	
Intellectual property	Sealed-bid second-price auction	

Questions and Problems

15.1 Intellectual Property

Learning Objective 15.1 Describe the reasons and methods for protecting intellectual property.

1.1 Your company discovers a new way to make improved ceramic ball bearings. Discuss the pros and cons of patenting the procedure versus keeping it a trade secret.

1.2 You are an executive at a company that manufactures DRAM memory modules. You have a patented procedure for producing your modules that a start-up company begins to use. You instantly file suit and win the case. In the year before the start-up used your production method, your firm's profit was $100 million; in the year the other company infringed, your profit was $40 million.

    a. In the year the rival infringed, its profit was $30 million. What amount of damages are you entitled to recover from the infringing company?

    b. Now suppose that in the year that the other company infringed, its profit was $80 million. What amount of damages are you entitled to recover from the infringing company?

1.3 You are still an executive at the company that manufactures DRAM memory modules. You keep your procedure for producing your modules a trade secret. One year a start-up company begins to use the same procedure. You instantly file suit and win the case. In the year before the other company illegally gained access to your production method, your firm's profit was $100 million; in the year the other company used your trade secret, your profit was $40 million.

    a. In the year that the other company used your trade secret, its profit was $30 million. What amount of damages are you entitled to recover from the infringing company?

    b. Now suppose that in the year the competitor used your trade secret, its profit was $80 million. What amount of damages are you entitled to recover from the infringing company?

1.4 Still an executive at the company that manufactures DRAM memory modules, you have trademarked the name of a line of high-performance modules, HyperactX. One year a start-up company begins to produce modules and sell them using a name eerily similar to your trademarked name, HiperactX. You instantly file suit and win the case. In the year before the other company infringed on your trademark, your firm's profit was $100 million; in the year the other company infringed, your profit was $40 million.

    a. In the year that the rival infringed on your trademark, its profit was $30 million. What amount of damages are you entitled to recover from the infringing company?

    b. Now suppose that in the year the company infringed on your trademark, it profit was $80 million. What amount of damages are you entitled to recover from the infringing company?

1.5 Lebbeus Woods is the author of several copyrighted books of fantasy architecture. One of Mr. Woods' drawings is of a room containing a high-backed chair attached to a wall, a sphere hanging from the ceiling, and other paraphernalia. Director Terry Gilliam saw a copy of this drawing and used it as his inspiration for a handful of scenes in the movie *12 Monkeys*. After Universal Studios released the movie, Mr. Woods sued for copyright infringement. He won a preliminary injunction against the public performance or distribution of the film because the defendants had copied his drawing, albeit into a different medium and only for a few brief scenes in a two-hour movie.

    a. How would you measure the damages, if any, suffered by Mr. Woods? (Hint: There is no totally correct answer to this question.)

    b. How much of Universal Studios' profit was attributable to the infringement? (Hint: Again there is no totally correct answer.)

15.2 Value of Forecasts

Learning Objective 15.2 Discuss factors that affect the value of forecasting fluctuations in demand.

2.1 Suppose that you are a manager at Tyson Foods, a processor of pork and beef. Pork has large demand fluctuations, and beef has smaller demand fluctuations. The marginal cost curve is the same for both products.

    a. Your research department has time to gather the information necessary to produce a perfect demand forecast for only one of the two products. Which demand do you ask them to forecast? Explain your answer.

b. The research department says it can provide a forecast of either demand with an R^2 of 0.50. Which demand do you ask them to forecast? Explain your answer.

2.2 You are a manager at a firm like Stanford Chemicals, one of many perfectly competitive producers of hyaluronic acid (used in eye cream). The marginal cost of producing a pound of hyaluronic acid is given by $MC = 5.0 + 0.5Q$. The equilibrium price of hyaluronic acid is $25 per pound 50 percent of the time and $15 per pound the other 50 percent. Suppose that with no forecast of demand, you produce the quantity where $E[MR] = MC$. What is the maximum price that you are willing to pay for a perfect forecast?

2.3 The demand for farmed salmon from your firm is random. Assume that the market is perfectly competitive and that on any given day the price of a pound is either $4.40 or $4.80, with a probability of 0.50 for either possibility. The marginal cost of producing a pound of salmon is $MC = 0.02Q$.
   a. What is your firm's expected price and expected marginal revenue?
   b. If you produce so that your expected marginal revenue equals your marginal cost, $E[MR] = MC$, how much profit is lost if the price turns out to be $4.80? How much is lost if the price turns out to be $4.40?
   c. Presuming that each day you can change the price of your salmon, what is the value of a perfect forecast of the demand?

2.4 The price in a perfectly competitive market for copper bracelets is unknown before the managers must decide on how much output to produce, so the managers produce the quantity of bracelets that sets the expected marginal revenue equal to marginal cost, of $E[MR] = MC$. There is an equal probability that the price will be $12 or $8. If the firm's marginal cost function is $MC = 5 + 0.01Q$, what is the value of a perfect forecast of the demand?

15.3 Auctions

Learning Objective 15.3 Explain the optimal bidding strategy for and expected revenue from different types of auctions.

3.1 You are bidding in an auction for a certified, used tractor. You determine that the economic profit you can make from the tractor is $80,000. You do not care about any risk or uncertainty in your estimate of the economic profit. Other bidders have their own valuations of the tractor, which depend on their unique uses for it.

a. If the auction is an English auction, is your maximum bid more than, less than, or equal to $80,000? Explain your answer.
b. If the auction is a Dutch auction, is your maximum bid more than, less than, or equal to $80,000? Explain your answer.
c. If the auction is a sealed-bid first-price auction, is your bid more than, less than, or equal to $80,000? Explain your answer.
d. If the auction is a sealed-bid second-price auction, is your bid more than, less than, or equal to $80,000? Explain your answer.

3.2 You are bidding in an auction for a small natural gas field in Mexico. There are 12 other bidders. You estimate that the economic profit available from the field is $20 million. Other bidders have their own projections of the economic profit from the field.
a. If the field is sold using an English auction, as the auction starts is your maximum bid more than, less than, or equal to $20 million? Might you change this maximum as the auction proceeds? Explain your answers.
b. If the field is sold using a Dutch auction, as the auction starts is your maximum bid more than, less than, or equal to $20 million? Might you change this maximum as the auction proceeds? Explain your answers.
c. If the field is sold using a sealed-bid first-price auction, as the auction starts is your bid more than, less than, or equal to $20 million? Might you change your bid as the auction proceeds? Explain your answers.
d. If the field is sold using a sealed-bid second-price auction, as the auction starts is your bid more than, less than, or equal to $20 million? Might you change this bid as the auction proceeds? Explain your answers.

3.3 Why is a winner's curse less likely in auctions for independent private value items than in auctions for common value or correlated value items?

3.4 Explain how managers can try to avoid the winner's curse.

3.5 You are a manager for a firm like Mecum Auctions, a company that auctions collector automobiles.
a. Even though you are working for the auctioneer, you must be concerned about the winner's curse. Explain why.
b. Why did your company make the decision to allow the bidders to closely examine the automobiles?
c. What type of auction do you want to hold? Explain your answer.

15.4 Asymmetric Information

Learning Objective 15.4 Describe strategies managers can use to overcome the challenges of asymmetric information.

4.1 Health insurance plans can be characterized by their premium (their price) and their deductible (the amount the patient must pay before the insurance starts to pay). You are in the HR department of a business that provides a self-insured health insurance plan for its employees; that is, the firm itself collects the premiums its employees pay and then pays the health claims above the deductible. Your company offers a conventional plan with a relatively high premium and a low deductible. Younger people are generally healthier and so require less health care than do older people. For simplicity, suppose that 50 percent of your employees are young and 50 percent older.

  a. How does having the young workers buy health insurance benefit the older workers?

  A relatively new health plan is the high-deductible health plan (HDHP). This type of plan has a low premium and a high deductible. Suppose that your company introduces an HDHP that is maintained by an independent company; that is, another company collects the premiums and pays the claims. Your company continues to offer its self-insured conventional plan.

  b. Which workers are more likely to buy the HDHP and which are more likely to buy the conventional plan?

  c. Suppose that after your company introduces the HDHP option, you expect 50 percent of the employees to enroll in it. How will you adjust the premium of your conventional plan?

  d. Suppose that with the adjustment you describe in part c, the HDHP appeals to more employees than expected, so that 80 percent of the employees select it. Does this response pose a problem for your company? Explain your answer.

4.2 The Progressive Corporation offers its automobile insurance customers the opportunity to participate in its Snapshot program. Snapshot is a small box that is plugged into the car and records the number of miles driven, the number of miles driven between midnight and 4 A.M., and whether the driver uses hard or soft braking. The program is voluntary; customers do not have to participate. Suppose that 80 percent of Progressive's customers are safe drivers and 20 percent are risky drivers.

  a. Initially, the program offered discounts to drivers determined to be safe. The program did not penalize risky drivers. What do you think were the approximate percentages of safe drivers and risky drivers that participated in the Snapshot program? Explain your answer.

  b. Recently, Progressive changed the details of the Snapshot program so that Progressive gives drivers determined to be safe a discount and hits drivers determined to be risky with a surcharge. How do you think this change affected the percentages of safe drivers and risky drivers participating in the Snapshot program?

4.3 Many television advertisements for exercise equipment, pain relievers, and food supplements offer 100 percent money-back guarantees. Do those guarantees provide any information to consumers? Explain your answer.

4.4 Brand names provide information to the consumer, including the identity of the manufacturer. Why is this good for the manufacturer?

4.5 You are currently studying to earn a degree. Explain in your own words how your degree can signal relevant hidden characteristics to potential employers.

4.6 Corporations sometimes buy back shares of their stock, which they then cancel, so that the number of outstanding shares is smaller. For example, in 2017, American Airlines Group announced that it would buy back $2 billion of its shares. What signal are managers sending when they announce a share buyback?

4.7 Explain the difference between moral hazard and adverse selection.

4.8 The bonuses of midlevel bank loan managers are often based on the profits but not the losses of the loans they approve. Suppose that an executive can make two types of loans: risky loans, which yield a large profit if they are successful and incur a large loss if they fail, and safe loans, which return a small profit if they are successful and incur a small loss if they fail. If a bank incurs a sufficiently large loss, the government takes it over and usually merges it with another, stronger bank. Some of the midlevel executives will lose their jobs, but most will retain them.

  a. After a loan manager is hired, what moral hazard problem do the bank's top executives face?

b. If you were a bank executive, what actions could you take to mitigate the moral hazard?

c. If you were a government regulator, what regulations could you suggest to mitigate the moral hazard?

15.5 Managerial Application: Decisions about Information

Learning Objective 15.5 Apply what you have learned about information to make better managerial decisions.

5.1 Suppose that you are an executive with the North Dakota Department of Trust Lands, the state government agency that manages the lands given to the state by the federal government when North Dakota achieved statehood. One of your tasks is managing the auctions for mineral rights, such as natural gas, on these lands. You could either allow the potential bidders the opportunity to completely examine the land up for auction or require them to bid without a thorough examination. You goal is to maximize the state's revenue. What decision do you make? Does it matter if you allow bidders to examine some but not all of the land that is for sale? Explain your answers.

5.2 When Nortel Networks, a bankrupt data-networking equipment manufacturer auctioned its patents, it allowed all the potential bidders to thoroughly examine the patents. Why did Nortel's managers make the decision to allow bidders to do this?

5.3 Professional athletes are incredibly competitive, even outside their own sports. Many professional baseball players, for example, would eagerly play pickup basketball games.

a. Because he fears injury, a baseball player does not play pickup basketball games before he signs a long-term contract. After he signs the contract, he starts to play pickup games. What economic phenomenon does the baseball team face?

b. How might a team prevent its players from participating in such games?

5.4 The Federal Motor Carrier Safety Administration (FMCSA) regulates the hours a truck driver may drive. One regulation limits the time a driver may drive to a maximum of 11 hours and then only after taking 10 consecutive hours off. The FMCSA can fine a company up to $16,000 for violating this regulation. Clearly, trucking companies do not want to pay fines because they cut into the companies' profit. Companies usually pay drivers for the miles driven, at rates up to $0.60 per mile.

a. In the relationship between the firms' managers and drivers, who are the principals and who are the agents? Carefully explain the principal–agent problem faced by managers of trucking firms.

b. Suppose that you are a manager for a large trucking firm. What actions might you take to overcome the principal–agent problem?

5.5 Suppose that you are in charge of security at the Museum of Modern Art in New York. You have hired guards to protect the art overnight while the museum is closed.

a. Carefully explain the principal–agent problem you face.

b. What actions might you take to overcome the principal–agent problem?

 # MyLab Economics Auto-Graded Excel Projects

15.1. Alorica is a customer relationship management firm that provides customized customer support via phone, Internet, and social media for companies in a variety of industries. It has many locations in North America, Latin America, Asia Pacific, and Europe. It also allows some employees to work at home. Alorica's employees provide customer support for many firms in many different industries, including retail, health care, media, financial services, technology, and travel. Providing quality customer support and maintaining its reputation are among the most important focuses of Alorica's business practices.

In an effort to mitigate the effects of the principal–agent problem, suppose that a firm similar to Alorica is trying to determine the level of quality control it should use for one of its call centers. The firm can hire quality control managers for $17 an hour to listen to the calls of its customer service representatives. Quality control managers can listen to and score an average of eight calls per hour.

Accompanies problem 15.1.

	A	B
1	Quality Control Manager Information	
2	Hourly Cost per Manager per Hour	
3	Number of Managers Hired	
4	Calls Monitored per Manager	
5	Total Calls Monitored per Hour	
6	Total Manager Cost per Hour	
7		
8	Customer Service Rep Information	
9	Number of Representatives	
10	Calls per Hour per Rep	
11	Total Calls per Hour	
12	Error Rate	
13	Errors per Hour	
14	Error Cost per Hour	
15		
16	Combined Cost Information	
17	Manager Costs per Hour	
18	Error Costs per Hour	
19	Difference	
20		

a. Using the information and template provided, fill in the Quality Control Manager Information template. Start with 0 managers hired.

b. This company employs 100 customer service representatives who answer 15 calls per hour. Suppose that the error rate for calls is 15 percent with no quality checks but decreases by 0.5 percent (.005) for every five calls monitored. Each error costs the company $1.50 on average. Use this information to fill in the Customer Service Rep Information template. Use a formula to automatically calculate the error rate as the number of calls monitored increases.

c. Use formulas to complete the Combined Cost Information template. The final cell in this section should be Manager Costs - Error Costs. Your goal is to find the number of quality control managers needed to equate the cost of monitoring with the cost of errors.

d. Using Solver, set Difference as your objective to a value of 0 by changing Number of Managers Hired (cell B3). Once Solver finds an answer, round the number of managers up to the nearest whole number by changing cell B3. How many managers should you hire? What is the error rate with this many managers? What is the cost of errors and monitoring per hour? Explain why this change is a good idea.

e. Suppose that this firm can allow its quality control managers to work from home and pay them $15 an hour instead of $17. Change the Quality Control Manager Information template to reflect this change. Use Solver to resolve this problem, and round the number of managers up to the nearest whole number. How many managers should you hire? What is the error rate with this many managers? What is the cost of errors and monitoring per hour? Should you make this change? Why or why not?

15.2. The Weinandt Family Farm in Wynot, NE, raises livestock and grows crops. Commonly grown crops in Nebraska are corn and soybeans. Suppose that you are helping a farm similar to the Weinandt Family Farm make decisions about how much corn to grow this year. The market for corn, an agricultural product, is perfectly competitive.

The price for corn over the last 10 years has ranged from a low of $2.72 per bushel in 2008 to a record high of $8.40 per bushel in 2012. The cost of producing corn also varies, as some years involve a drought or flooding, which greatly increases the cost of production.

Suppose that the farm you are advising is in a situation similar to that of the Weinandt Family Farm. Your research provided you with the information on corn prices and the probability of those corn prices in the table provided. In addition, you compiled data on the costs of producing corn for various years and various amounts. You noticed that the cost of producing corn fell into three main categories: a high cost which coincides with years of high drought or flooding; a moderate cost which coincides with typical years; and a low cost which coincides with years of ideal conditions. High costs occur 30 percent of the time, moderate costs occur 50 percent of the time, and low costs occur 20 percent of the time.

a. Using the price information to find the mid-range prices ($2.50, $3.50, etc.), find the expected marginal revenue the farm can expect to receive for a bushel of corn.

b. Using the cost information and probabilities given, create an expected marginal cost schedule.

c. What is the expected price per bushel of corn? How many bushels of corn do you recommend that the farm produce at this price?

676 **CHAPTER 15** Managerial Decisions About Information

Accompanies problem 15.2.

	A	B	C	D	E
1	Price per Bushel Range	Mid-Range Price	Probability of Price Range		
2	$2.00-2.99		0.02		
3	$3.00-3.99		0.39		
4	$4.00-4.99		0.25		
5	$5.00-$5.99		0.16		
6	$6.00-$6.99		0.11		
7	$7.00-7.99		0.06		
8	$8.00-8.99		0.01		
9	Expected Marginal Revenue				
10					
11	Number of Bushels (1000s)	High Cost	Moderate Cost	Low Cost	Expected Marginal Cost
12	30	$4.80	$3.95	$3.25	
13	35	$4.90	$4.00	$3.35	
14	40	$5.00	$4.05	$3.45	
15	45	$5.10	$4.10	$3.55	
16	50	$5.20	$4.15	$3.65	
17	55	$5.30	$4.20	$3.75	
18	60	$5.40	$4.25	$3.85	
19	65	$5.50	$4.30	$3.95	
20	70	$5.60	$4.35	$4.05	
21	75	$5.70	$4.40	$4.15	
22	80	$5.80	$4.45	$4.25	
23	PROBABILITIES				
24					

d. Suppose the Farmer's Almanac predicts increases in weather variability in the coming years and states that conditions coinciding with high costs have a 60 percent probability of occurrence, conditions coinciding with moderate costs have a 35 percent probability of occurrence, and conditions coinciding with low costs have a 5 percent probability of occurrence. Use the information to update the cost probabilities. What level of corn production would you recommend to the farm under these conditions?

CHAPTER 16

Using Present Value to Make Multiperiod Managerial Decisions

Learning Objectives

After studying Chapter 16, you will be able to:

16.1 Explain the importance of present value calculations to managerial decision making.

16.2 Describe how salvage values, taxation, debt financing, depreciation, and risk affect capital budgeting.

16.3 Use present value calculations to answer the make-or-buy questions that managers face.

16.4 Apply the concepts of present value and the net present value rule to make profit-maximizing managerial decisions.

Why Did Ziosk's Managers Give Their Tablets to Chili's for Free?

Have you ever gone to a restaurant and waited a long time to order or to get the check from your server? Technology and innovation are gradually changing that dining experience. Ziosk, a Dallas-based technology company, produces small, wireless tabletop tablets that allow diners to order drinks and desserts, pay their bills by swiping a credit card, and—for a fee—play games. In 2013, the managers at Ziosk announced a major new contract: They would provide wireless tabletop tablets for all of Brinker International's 823 company-owned Chili's Grill and Bar restaurants as well as many of the 400 franchised locations. Although Ziosk provides the tablets for free, it collects a fraction of restaurants' sales.

If providing the tablets at each Chili's location costs $15,000, Ziosk's managers must make an expenditure of well over $12 million before they see a single penny of revenue. Suppose that Ziosk tests the tablets in several Chili's restaurants and data indicate that Ziosk will collect $7,000 in operating profits per restaurant each year. Will the contract be profitable for Ziosk? How much profit will it make? This chapter provides the tools you need to answer these questions, which involve the comparison of expenditures made in the present to profits collected in the future. By the end of the chapter, you will understand how to approach such problems and make profit-maximizing decisions with the same confidence as Ziosk's managers.

Sources: Mohana Ravindranath, "At Chili's, Tablets Help Wait Staff Turn Over Tables," *Washington Post,* June 29, 2014; Alex Konrad, "Chili's to Install Tablets at Every Table: More Tips but a Cloudier Future for Servers," *Forbes,* September 17, 2013; Venessa Wong, "That Tablet on the Restaurant Table Will Make You Spend More," *Bloomberg Businessweek,* September 18, 2013.

Introduction

When a firm incurs costs and receives revenues in the same time frame, economic models and analysis proceed as though the firm pays the costs and receives the revenues simultaneously. For example, when Tropicana's managers hire manufacturing associates to produce orange juice at their Bradenton plant, they analyze the decision assuming simultaneous payment of wages and receipt of revenue from selling the orange juice. Firms, however, often make decisions anticipated to return profits throughout many periods in the future. When Tropicana's managers were planning the purchase of a new blow-molding machine and assembly line to produce an

Capital budgeting The process of evaluating investments that will generate profits and losses in the future.

innovative orange juice carafe, they expected the equipment and assembly line to yield profits for many years. This decision involves **capital budgeting**, the process of evaluating investments that will generate profits and losses in the future.

Capital budgeting requires managers to decide whether to spend money now to earn profit in future periods. Managers face many such investment decisions, which may include the following:

- **Construction of production facilities.** When a firm decides to produce a good—chemicals, furniture, shoes, or orange juice—it needs to build production facilities before production and sales can begin. Once built, the company will use the facilities for years.
- **Construction of a sports facility.** Building baseball parks, golf courses, and tennis courts requires substantial initial expenditures that are expected to generate future profits for many years.
- **Purchase of a franchise.** A franchise is the legal right for someone to use a company's logo and sell its goods or services in a specific location. If you purchase a franchise from Burger King, you must pay that company a substantial franchise fee in advance of opening the outlet, which you might then operate for as long as 15 or 20 years.

In all of these examples (and more), managers must compare cash flows in different periods. When considering capital budgeting, typically the cash outflows are the cost, and the cash inflows are the profit. The basic question is whether the anticipated profit in future periods will cover the cost incurred in the current period.

To analyze the profitability of an investment, you need to understand the connection between present values and future values. To help you analyze costs and benefits spread over time in an economically sound way, this chapter includes four sections:

- **Section 16.1** presents the fundamentals of present value.
- **Section 16.2** explains how to use the net present value rule to make profitable decisions about capital budgeting.
- **Section 16.3** demonstrates how managers can use present value in decisions about whether to make or purchase inputs (make-or-buy decisions).
- **Section 16.4** shows how you can apply present value and the net present value rule to make better managerial decisions.

16.1 Fundamentals of Present Value

Learning Objective 16.1 Explain the importance of present value calculations to managerial decision making.

In many business contexts, firms incur the cost of an investment now and reap the profit from it in the future. For example, in the orange juice example, Tropicana's executives purchased new blow-molding equipment and a high-speed assembly line that rinses the containers, fills them with orange juice, labels them, packs them on pallets, wraps the pallets, and conveys the pallets to the loading docks. The company paid for the equipment when it was installed, anticipating that its investment would return additional profit in the future.

In order to analyze costs and benefits that are paid and received at different times, you must value them at a single point in time. Why? As you will learn shortly, funds you will receive or pay in the future are worth less than the same amount received or paid in the present. This section shows how to convert the future sums (called future values) into their worth in the present, or present values. These calculations can be complex in real-world business situations, but the basic concepts and fundamentals are straightforward.

Calculating Future Values

The **future value (FV)** is the amount that a sum of money in the present grows to be worth at a point in the future. For a concrete example of a future value, consider Lynn, a lender who can earn 10 percent interest annually on her loans. If she lends $1.00, at the end of the year she has $1.10—the dollar she loaned plus $0.10 in interest. In terms of a formula, at the end of a year she has

$$\$1.00 \times 1.10 = \$1.10$$

The $1.10 is the future value of the $1.00 after one year at an interest rate of 10 percent per year; that is, $1.00 now is equivalent to $1.10 one year in the future. As a result, Lynn is indifferent between receiving $1.00 today and receiving $1.10 in a year because she can invest the $1.00 today so that it grows to $1.10 in a year.

Now suppose that Lynn does not collect her $1.10 at the end of the year but instead continues to lend it for a second year at the same 10 percent interest rate.[1] Lynn does not receive just an additional $0.10 in interest in the second year. Instead, she earns 10 percent interest on the original $1.00 loan (another $0.10 in interest) *and* 10 percent interest on the $0.10 she earned in the first year ($0.01), for a combined—or compounded—amount of $0.11 in interest for the second year. At the end of two years, Lynn will have $1.21. Interest compounds because in future years it is earned on both the principal and the interest received in earlier years. In terms of a formula, at the end of the second year Lynn has

$$(\$1.00 \times 1.10) \times 1.10 = \$1.00 \times (1.10)^2 = \$1.21$$

where $1.21 is the future value of $1.00 invested at 10 percent for two years.

This expression generalizes to cover any time frame and any interest rate. The future value of $1.00 at an annual interest rate of i percent in n years equals

$$\$1.00 \times (1 + i)^n = FV$$

Figure 16.1 shows the effect of compounding by illustrating how the future value of $1.00 grows over time when the interest rate is 10 percent.

The future value of any specific dollar amount of money in n years equals the future value of $1.00 multiplied by that particular amount. So, the future value of any current amount of money is that amount's current value, that is, its present value (PV), multiplied by $\$1.00 \times (1 + i)^n$, or

$$PV \times (1 + i)^n = FV \qquad\qquad \textbf{16.1}$$

Future value (FV) The amount that a sum of money in the present grows to be worth at a point in the future.

---

1 If the interest rate changes from one year to the next or interest payments are made at different frequencies than annually, the analysis is somewhat more complicated, but the general qualitative results do not change. For ease of presentation, we assume throughout the chapter that the interest rate does not change and that interest payments are made once, at the end of the year. We leave the more complicated analysis for a finance course.

Figure 16.1 Growth of Future Value

When the interest rate is 10 percent, the future value of $1.00 grows as illustrated, so that at the end of 20 years the future value is $6.73.

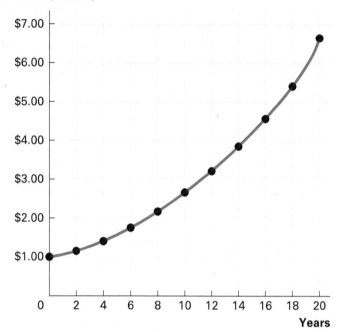

Future value of one dollar (dollars)

For example, if Lynn lends $930,000 for 12 years at 8 percent interest, she can use Equation 16.1 with $PV = \$930,000$, $i = 0.08$, and $n = 12$ to show that at the end of 12 years she has

$$\$930,000 \times (1.08)^{12} = \$2,341,898$$

Calculating Present Values

You have just learned how to change present values of money into future values. The reverse of this procedure, changing future values of money into present values, is even more important. The **present value (PV)** is the worth today of an amount of money to be paid or received in the future.

The most basic present-value result is that $1.00 to be received at some point in the future is worth less than $1.00 received today because the $1.00 received today can be saved and earn compound interest over time. Suppose that you will receive $1.00 in one year, during which time the interest rate is 10 percent. To determine how much that future dollar is worth in the present, ask the following question: What amount of money received today and earning a 10 percent return will be worth $1.00 in a year? You can use Equation 16.1 to answer this question. PV is the amount of money received today, and FV is the money received in a year, $1.00. Making these substitutions, Equation 16.1 shows that

$$PV \times (1.10)^1 = \$1.00$$

Rearranging to solve for PV gives

$$PV = \frac{\$1.00}{1.10} = \$0.91$$

Present value (PV) The worth today of an amount of money to be paid or received in the future.

So \$1.00 that you will receive in a year is worth only \$0.91 today if the interest rate is 10 percent. The \$0.09 difference between the present value, \$0.91, and future value, \$1.00, is the interest paid on the \$0.91 for one year. You are indifferent between receiving \$1.00 in a year and receiving \$0.91 today because you can save the \$0.91 and it will grow to equal \$1.00 in a year.

If instead of getting the \$1.00 in one year, suppose you will receive the \$1.00 at the end of two years. The calculation is now a bit more complicated, but the principle is the same. Suppose that the interest rate is 10 percent in the second year as well. Let PV be the amount that, if received today, grows with compounded interest to equal the future amount. Because you will receive the future dollar in two years, the present amount earns interest for two years, which modifies Equation 16.1 to

$$PV \times (1.10)^2 = \$1.00$$

Rearranging to solve for PV gives

$$PV = \frac{\$1.00}{(1.10)^2} = \$0.83$$

The present value of the \$1.00 you will receive two years from now is only 83 cents if the interest rate is 10 percent. In other words, \$1.00 two years in the future is the same as \$0.83 in the present when the interest rate is 10 percent. Again, the difference between the present value of \$0.83 and the future value of \$1.00—\$0.17—is the (compound) interest paid for two years on the \$0.83. And once again, you are indifferent between receiving \$1.00 in two years and receiving \$0.83 today because you can save the \$0.83 and it will grow to equal \$1.00 in two years.

This calculation generalizes. The present value of \$1.00 to be received in n years when the interest rate is i percent per year is

$$PV = \frac{\$1.00}{(1 + i)^n} = \frac{1}{(1 + i)^n} \times \$1.00$$

Once you compute the present value of \$1.00, the present value of any other amount of money in n years equals that amount multiplied by the present value of \$1.00. Accordingly, if FV is the amount of money in the future, its present value equals $[\frac{1}{(1 + i)^n} \times \$1.00] \times FV$, or

$$PV = \frac{1}{(1 + i)^n} \times FV \qquad \text{16.2}$$

For example, using Equation 16.2 to determine the present value of \$300,000 in four years at an interest rate of 3 percent gives

$$\frac{1}{(1.03)^4} \times \$300,000 = \$266,550$$

In other words, \$300,000 in four years is the same as \$266,550 today when the interest rate is 3 percent.

Equation 16.2 allows you to directly calculate the present value of any sum you will receive or pay in the future at any interest rate. Suppose that Sears Holdings

Corporation wants to close one of its Sears stores in a shopping mall owned by Simon Property Group (Simon Group), a commercial real estate company. Say that as compensation for the foregone rent, Sears' managers propose paying $4.5 million to Simon Group after three years. To decide whether this payment is adequate, Simon Group's managers want to know the present value (today's value) of this hypothetical payment. If the interest rate is 6 percent for the three years, the present value of the payment is $\frac{1}{(1.06)^3} \times \$4,500,000 = \$3,778,287$. If Simon Group invests $3,778,287 at 6 percent per year for three years, the investment will grow to be worth $4,500,000 at the end of the three-year period. Simon Group's managers realize that Sears Holdings' managers are offering them the equivalent of an immediate payment of $3,778,287 as compensation for closing the store. With this information, they can make a more informed decision about whether or not to accept the proposed payout.

Discount Factor and Discount Rate

Discount factor The term used to convert future funds into their value in the present: $\frac{1}{(1+i)^n}$.

Discount rate The interest rate used to calculate the discount factor.

The **discount factor,** the term used to convert future funds into their value in the present, is the term to the right of the equal sign in Equation 16.2: $\frac{1}{(1+i)^n}$. The name *discount factor* comes from the fact that it discounts (reduces) the future value to convert it to the present value. Indeed, analysts often describe converting the future value to the present value as *discounting* the future payment. The interest rate used to calculate the discount factor is the **discount rate.**

Table 16.1 contains discount factors for periods from 1 to 10 years and discount rates from 1 percent to 9 percent, which you can use to calculate the present value of future money.[2] For example, the present value of $100.00 to be received six years in the future with a discount rate of 4 percent is equal to $100.00 multiplied by the discount factor from the table, 0.7903 (highlighted in red), or $100.00 \times 0.7903 = \$79.03$.

Table 16.1 Discount Factors

The discount factor multiplied by a future sum of money shows the present value of that sum received in the specified number of years at the specified discount rate.

		Discount Rate (percent per year)								
		1%	2%	3%	4%	5%	6%	7%	8%	9%
Number of years	1	0.9901	0.9804	0.9709	0.9615	0.9524	0.9434	0.9346	0.9259	0.9174
	2	0.9803	0.9612	0.9426	0.9246	0.9070	0.8900	0.8734	0.8573	0.8417
	3	0.9706	0.9423	0.9151	0.8890	0.8638	0.8396	0.8163	0.7938	0.7722
	4	0.9610	0.9238	0.8885	0.8548	0.8227	0.7921	0.7629	0.7350	0.7084
	5	0.9515	0.9057	0.8626	0.8219	0.7835	0.7473	0.7130	0.6806	0.6499
	6	0.9420	0.8880	0.8375	0.7903	0.7462	0.7050	0.6663	0.6302	0.5963
	7	0.9327	0.8706	0.8131	0.7599	0.7107	0.6651	0.6227	0.5835	0.5470
	8	0.9235	0.8535	0.7894	0.7307	0.6768	0.6274	0.5820	0.5403	0.5019
	9	0.9143	0.8368	0.7664	0.7026	0.6446	0.5919	0.5439	0.5002	0.4604
	10	0.9053	0.8203	0.7441	0.6756	0.6139	0.5584	0.5083	0.4632	0.4224

---

2 The discount factors in the table are rounded to 4 decimal places. Using more decimal places will make a small difference in the calculated results.

You can use this calculation to explain how the discount rate influences the discount factor and present value. You know that $79.03 saved at an interest rate of 4 percent grows to equal $100.00 in six years. The difference between the future value of $100.00 and the present value of $79.03, $20.97, is the interest that accrues over the six years. The more interest that can be earned, the smaller the present value, and the smaller the discount factor. This insight explains two patterns shown in Table 16.1:

- **The larger the discount rate, the smaller the discount factor.** If you read across a row in Table 16.1 from left to right, the discount factors become smaller as the discount rate rises. The higher the discount rate, the more interest that money in the present can earn, so the smaller the discount factor.
- **The longer the period of time until the future sum of money is received, the smaller the discount factor.** If you read down a column in Table 16.1, the discount factors become smaller as the number of years increases. The longer the period of time until receiving the future amount, the more interest that can be earned, so the smaller the discount factor.

Managers who are aware of these patterns know immediately that the higher the interest rate used as the discount rate and/or the longer the period until they receive or pay a sum of money, the smaller that sum's present value. Understanding these two important patterns can help guide you to good decisions about long-term financial planning.

Clearly, the choice of the discount rate used in the discount factor has an important effect on the present value of future amounts of money. A detailed discussion of the influences on the choice of the discount rate appears in Section 16.2.

Valuing a Stream of Future Payments

To this point, the discounting has involved a single future payment. In reality, however, businesses often receive (or pay) a series or stream of future amounts of money. Thankfully, discounting a stream of future payments to the present value is straightforward: Using the basic present value equation, Equation 16.2, you discount each payment and then add the discounted values. The sum of the discounted values is the present value of the stream of payments. In terms of an equation, when there are T periods and future payments of FV_t, one payment received in each period, and the interest rate for each period equal to i, the present value is equal to

$$PV = \left[\frac{1}{(1+i)} \times FV_1\right] + \left[\frac{1}{(1+i)^2} \times FV_2\right] + \left[\frac{1}{(1+i)^3} \times FV_3\right] + \cdots$$
$$+ \left[\frac{1}{(1+i)^T} \times FV_T\right] = \sum_{j=1}^{T}\left[\frac{1}{(1+i)^j} \times FV_j\right]$$

In the equation, the Σ symbol means *summation*.

Let's apply this equation to a hypothetical Sears Holdings example. Suppose that a contract for a Sears store in another mall owned by Simon Group calls for Sears Holdings to make a lease payment of $1 million at the end of each of the next three years, with a balloon payment of $4 million at the end of the fourth year.

Table 16.2 Present Value of a Stream of Payments

The present value of the stream of payments is the sum of the present values of each of the payments.

Year	Payment	Present Value of Payment
1	$1,000,000	$925,900
2	1,000,000	857,300
3	1,000,000	793,800
4	4,000,000	2,940,000
Sum	$7,000,000	$5,517,000

The interest rate is 8 percent. The following equation shows how the present value of these payments is calculated:

$$PV = \left[\frac{1}{(1.08)} \times \$1,000,000\right] + \left[\frac{1}{(1.08)^2} \times \$1,000,000\right] + \left[\frac{1}{(1.08)^3} \times \$1,000,000\right]$$
$$+ \left[\frac{1}{(1.08)^4} \times \$4,000,000\right]$$

The third column of Table 16.2 shows the present value of each of the individual payments, assuming an interest rate of 8 percent. The sum of these present values—$5,517,000—is the present value of the stream of payments that Simon Group will receive from Sears Holdings over four years.

Even though Sears Holdings makes payments totaling $7,000,000 over the four years, the present value of the stream of payments is only $5,517,000. If Sears Holdings makes an immediate payment of $5,517,000 to Simon Group, the latter can invest it at 8 percent and take out $1,000,000 at the end of each of the first three years, $4,000,000 at the end of the fourth year, and have nothing left over. Alternatively, if Sears Holdings deposits $5,517,000 today in an account that pays 8 percent interest, it can use the $5,517,000 plus the interest earnings to make the series of payments it owes Simon Group. This amount of money will just cover the three $1,000,000 payments at the end of each of the first three years and the $4,000,000 payment at the end of the fourth year. After making the last $4,000,000 payment in four years, the account balance will be zero. Consequently, the $5,517,000 is the present value of the contract to *both* Sears Holdings and Simon Group.

Using Excel to Calculate the Present Value of a Stream of Unequal Payments

Excel is a powerful tool that you can use to calculate the present value of a stream of payments. Excel has a formula (NPV, found in the "Financial" section of the "Formulas" tab) that directly calculates the net present value of *future* payments. Be careful when using the formula because it does not automatically include current-period values. Even though Excel has the NPV function, let's set it aside and instead use Excel to demonstrate the calculations in detail to help reinforce your understanding of present value. Say that you want to calculate the present value of 10 payments you will receive in the future. Instead of waiting for someone in the research department to provide this information, you can calculate the present value yourself using Excel. Figure 16.2 shows how to set up this problem in Excel.

Figure 16.2 Entering the Data and the Present Value Formula in Microsoft Excel

The period in which the money is received is entered in column A under the heading Period, and the amount of each period's payment is entered in column B under the heading Payment. The discount rate used to discount the money is in column E, under the heading Discount Rate. Column C, where the present value of each payment will be calculated, is labeled Present value, and row 12, where the total present value will be calculated, is labeled Sums. The formula used to calculate the present value for C2 is illustrated in the fx box. This general formula is used for each of the payments.

C2 fx =B2*(1/(1+E2))^A2

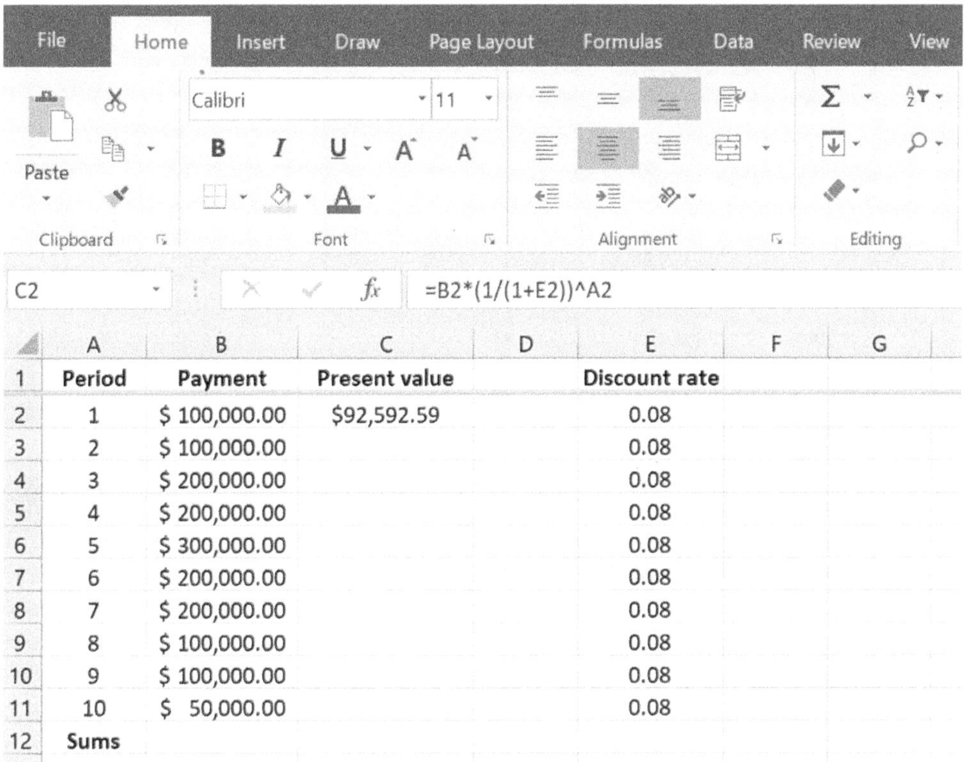

	A	B	C	D	E	F	G
1	Period	Payment	Present value		Discount rate		
2	1	$ 100,000.00	$92,592.59		0.08		
3	2	$ 100,000.00			0.08		
4	3	$ 200,000.00			0.08		
5	4	$ 200,000.00			0.08		
6	5	$ 300,000.00			0.08		
7	6	$ 200,000.00			0.08		
8	7	$ 200,000.00			0.08		
9	8	$ 100,000.00			0.08		
10	9	$ 100,000.00			0.08		
11	10	$ 50,000.00			0.08		
12	Sums						

Start by entering the future payments. Once you have entered them, the next step is to discount the payments to the present. Figure 16.2 shows the formula for the present value of the first payment in cell C2 as well as in the fx box. In the present value formula, cell B2 is the future payment, cell E2 is the discount rate, and cell A2 is the period. This formula is used to discount all future payments, but, of course, the particular cells used in the formula change.

After calculating the present value for each of the payments, your last step is to click on the "Σ" function (see the black arrow in Figure 16.3) to sum all of the individual present values. Figure 16.3 shows the present values, their sum, and the sum of the 10 payments. The present value of the stream of payments is $1,058,217.32. The total amount of the payments is $1,550,000.00. The present value is less than the sum of the payments because each of the payments is discounted—reduced—when converted to its present value.

As you can see, using Excel makes it easy to calculate the present value of a stream of payments. Perhaps more importantly, Excel makes it easy to determine how changes in the payment stream and/or the discount rate affect the present value. Determining the sensitivity of the results to changes in the payment stream or the discount rate is imperative because it can affect your confidence about decisions based on the present value calculations.

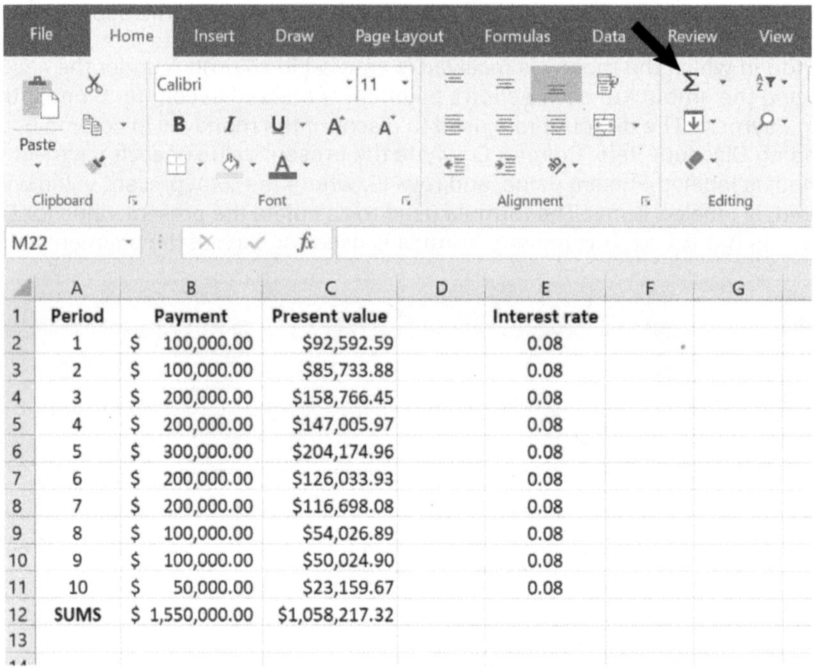

Figure 16.3 Calculating the Present Value in Microsoft Excel

The "Σ" function, indicated by the black arrow, sums the column of present values and the column of payments.

	A	B	C	D	E	F	G
1	Period	Payment	Present value		Interest rate		
2	1	$ 100,000.00	$92,592.59		0.08		
3	2	$ 100,000.00	$85,733.88		0.08		
4	3	$ 200,000.00	$158,766.45		0.08		
5	4	$ 200,000.00	$147,005.97		0.08		
6	5	$ 300,000.00	$204,174.96		0.08		
7	6	$ 200,000.00	$126,033.93		0.08		
8	7	$ 200,000.00	$116,698.08		0.08		
9	8	$ 100,000.00	$54,026.89		0.08		
10	9	$ 100,000.00	$50,024.90		0.08		
11	10	$ 50,000.00	$23,159.67		0.08		
12	SUMS	$ 1,550,000.00	$1,058,217.32				
13							

Calculating the Present Value of a Stream of Equal Payments

The preceding example included different payment amounts over time, but often businesses receive (or pay) a stream of *equal* payments over time. Determining the present value of a stream of equal future payments is straightforward. Let's return once more to a Sears Holdings example. Suppose that Sears Holdings and Simon Group sign another contract that calls for a payment of $1,700,000 from Sears Holdings to Simon Group at the end of each year for four years. At a discount rate of 8 percent for each year, the present value of this stream of payments is equal to

$$PV = \left[\frac{1}{(1.08)} \times \$1{,}700{,}000\right] + \left[\frac{1}{(1.08)^2} \times \$1{,}700{,}000\right] + \left[\frac{1}{(1.08)^3} \times \$1{,}700{,}000\right]$$

$$+ \left[\frac{1}{(1.08)^4} \times \$1{,}700{,}000\right]$$

$$= \$1{,}700{,}000 \times \left(\left[\frac{1}{(1.08)}\right] + \left[\frac{1}{(1.08)^2}\right] + \left[\frac{1}{(1.08)^3}\right] + \left[\frac{1}{(1.08)^4}\right]\right)$$

$$= \$1{,}700{,}000 \times \sum_{j=1}^{4} \frac{1}{(1.08)^j}$$

In the last equation, the term $\sum_{j=1}^{4} \frac{1}{(1.08)^j}$ is called the *annuity factor*. It applies when there is a stream of equal payments. The general equation for the present value of a stream of n equal payments is

$$PV = FV \times \left[\sum_{j=1}^{n} \frac{1}{(1+i)^j}\right] \qquad\qquad 16.3$$

where FV is the annual payment, i is the discount rate, and the term in brackets is the annuity factor.

Table 16.3 presents annuity factors for various discount rates and payment periods up to 10 years. The annuity factor for a stream of four equal payments with a discount rate of 8 percent is 3.3121 (shown in red in the table). So the stream of four hypothetical payments of $1,700,000 from Sears Holdings to Simon Group has a present value of $1,700,000 × 3.3121 = $5,630,570. The interpretation of this present value remains the same: If Sears Holdings deposits $5,630,570 today in an account paying 8 percent interest, it can use the $5,630,570 plus the interest earnings to make the required four annual payments of $1,700,000. There will be nothing left in the account after the last payment.

Comparing Contracts

Recall that the first hypothetical contract analyzed in this section has Sears Holdings making three annual payments of $1,000,000 each, followed by a balloon payment of $4,000,000 in year four. The total payment Sears makes to Simon Group is $7,000,000, with a present value of $5,517,000. Compare this contract with the second hypothetical contract above that has Sears Holdings making four equal annual payments of $1,700,000. The total payment Sears makes to Simon Group under this contract is $6,800,000, with a present value of $5,630,570. Although the total amount paid is greater under the first contract than the second one, the managers at Sears Holdings prefer the first contract because the present value is less. Effectively, Sears Holdings needs to set aside less money at the present time to fund the first contract than the second one. The managers at Simon Group prefer the second contract for the same reason. If Simon Group receives payments according to the second contract, it can invest the payments and ultimately have a larger amount than under the first contract.

The present value of the first contract is less than the present value of the second, even though the total payment is greater under the first one. Why is this the case? The first contract includes a large payment—$4,000,000—that will be made well into the future. Because Sears Holdings makes the balloon payment

Table 16.3 Annuity Factors

The annuity factor multiplied by the amount of the annual payment equals the present value of payments for the specified number of years at the specified discount rate.

		Discount Rate (percent per year)								
		1%	2%	3%	4%	5%	6%	7%	8%	9%
	1	0.9901	0.9804	0.9709	0.9615	0.9524	0.9434	0.9346	0.9259	0.9174
	2	1.9704	1.9416	1.9135	1.8861	1.8594	1.8334	1.8080	1.7833	1.7591
	3	2.9410	2.8839	2.8286	2.7751	2.7232	2.6730	2.6243	2.5771	2.5313
	4	3.9020	3.8077	3.7171	3.6299	3.5460	3.4651	3.3872	3.3121	3.2397
Number of years	5	4.8534	4.7135	4.5797	4.4518	4.3295	4.2124	4.1002	3.9927	3.8897
	6	5.7955	5.6014	5.4172	5.2421	5.0757	4.9173	4.7665	4.6229	4.4859
	7	6.7282	6.4720	6.2302	6.0021	5.7864	5.5824	5.3893	5.2064	5.0330
	8	7.6517	7.3255	7.0197	6.7327	6.4632	6.2098	5.9713	5.7466	5.5348
	9	8.5660	8.1622	7.7861	7.4353	7.1078	6.8017	6.5152	6.2469	5.9952
	10	9.4713	8.9826	8.5302	8.1109	7.2717	7.3601	7.0236	6.7101	6.4177

four years from now, its present value is relatively small ($2.94 million, as shown in Table 16.2). The present value of the first contract is smaller than that of the second one because Sears Holdings pays more of the first one in the more distant future.

Future and Present Value Formulas

The key formulas for calculating future and present values are presented in the box below.

FORMULAS FOR FUTURE AND PRESENT VALUES

Future Value

Equation 16.1: $PV \times (1 + i)^n = FV$

Present Value

Equation 16.2: $PV = \dfrac{1}{(1 + i)^n} \times FV$

Annuity Value

Equation 16.3: $PV = FV \times \sum_{j=1}^{n} \dfrac{1}{(1 + i)^j}$

PV is the present value, FV is the future value, i is the discount rate, and n is the number of years.

Managers use present value calculations to determine the profitability of decisions such as capital budgeting, in which the inflows and outflows occur at different times. In the next section, you will learn how to use these calculations to determine the profitability of an investment.

SOLVED PROBLEM

Choosing a Loan Repayment Schedule

You are negotiating a $1 million loan for your employer. The lender offers you a choice:

- Payment schedule A requires you to pay $100,000 at the end of the year for the first five years, with a final payment of $1,000,000 at the end of the sixth year, for a total of $1.5 million in payments.
- Payment schedule B requires you to make one payment of $300,000 at the end of the fifth year and a second payment of $1,300,000 at the end of the sixth year, for a total of $1.6 million in payments.

If your discount rate is 8 percent, which payment schedule would you prefer and why?

Answer

You want the payment schedule that has the lowest present value. Using the annuity and discount factors in the table, the present value of payment schedule A equals

$$\left[\frac{1}{(1+0.08)} \times \$100,000\right] + \left[\frac{1}{(1+0.08)^2} \times \$100,000\right] + \left[\frac{1}{(1+0.08)^3} \times \$100,000\right] + \left[\frac{1}{(1+0.08)^4} \times \$100,000\right]$$

$$+ \left[\frac{1}{(1+0.08)^5} \times \$100,000\right] + \left[\frac{1}{(1+0.08)^6} \times \$1,000,000\right] = \$1,029,470$$

The present value of the payment schedule B is

$$\left[\frac{1}{(1+0.08)^5} \times \$300,000\right] + \left[\frac{1}{(1+0.08)^6} \times \$1,300,000\right] = \$1,023,440$$

You prefer payment schedule B because its present value is smaller, which means the present cost to you of schedule B is less than that of schedule A.

16.2 Evaluating Investment Options

Learning Objective 16.2 Describe how salvage values, taxation, debt financing, depreciation, and risk affect capital budgeting.

Capital budgeting involves evaluating current-period investments that will generate profits and losses in the future. Generally, firms incur an investment's costs, the outflows, before they reap the profits, the inflows. Accordingly, managers must compare the present value of a firm's costs to the present value of its stream of profits.

Net Present Value and the Net Present Value Rule

Managers make investments in order to earn profits. When the firm incurs the costs in the present and receives the profits during future periods, profit-maximizing managers must compare the *present* cost of the investment to its stream of *future* profits. Because the profits arrive in the future, the managers must discount them back to the present. By discounting the profits, they can compare the *present* cost of the investment to the *present* worth of the profits and use the net present value rule.

Net Present Value Rule

The **net present value (*NPV*)** of an investment is the difference between the present value of future operating profits from an investment and the present value of the cost of the investment:

NPV = Present value of future operating profits − Present value of the cost   **16.4**

Net present value (*NPV*) The difference between the present value of future operating profits from an investment and the present value of the cost of the investment.

Equation 16.4 subtracts (or "nets out") the present value of the cost of the investment from the present value of the investment's stream of future operating profits. The *operating profit* is the additional revenue generated by the investment minus the additional operating costs. The operating costs include all costs of operating or running the investment but do *not* include any interest payments made to finance it. Operating profits omit the interest payments because, as you will learn, these payments are captured in the cost of the investment.

If the net present value is positive, the present value of the investment's stream of future operating profits exceeds the present value of its cost. Put a bit differently, today's value of the future operating profits from the investment exceeds today's value of the cost of the investment. In this case, a successful manager makes the investment because the profits it generates are more than enough to pay back all of its costs. If the net present value is negative, however, the present value of the investment's stream of future operating profits is less than the present value of its cost. In other words, today's value of the future operating profits from the investment is less than today's value of the cost of the investment, so a profit-maximizing manager should reject the investment. The following box summarizes this very straightforward and very important *net present value rule*.

NET PRESENT VALUE RULE

NPV = Present value of future operating profits − Present value of the cost

- If *NPV* is positive, the manager should make the investment.
- If *NPV* is negative, the manager should reject the investment.

To demonstrate use of the net present value rule, let's start by examining how to measure the present value of the cost of an investment. Assume that the investment takes only one period to make. Also assume that the interest rate the firm must pay on its debt is the same as its discount rate. Later discussion focuses on the factors that determine managers' choice of discount rate.

Present Value of the Cost of an Investment

Measuring the cost of an investment might seem complicated because the firm can finance it either by using internally generated funds or by borrowing funds from a lender. But the present value of the cost is the same in either case:

- **Internally generated funds.** If the cost of the investment is C, the firm pays all of it in the present period, and there are no future-period interest costs. The cost paid in the present period, C, is equal to the present value of the cost of the investment.
- **Funds borrowed from a lender.** If the firm borrows from an outside lender, it must make interest payments in future periods. Continue to assume that the cost of the investment is C. In the most extreme case, the firm pays the maximum amount of interest, borrows the *entire* amount, C, and makes *no* interest payments until the last period, when it pays back the principal as well as *all* of the accrued interest. If the loan is for n periods and the interest rate is i, Equation 16.1 shows that in period n (when the loan is due) the firm owes $C \times (1 + i)^n = FV$, where FV is the future value, or future cost, of the debt. Now you must determine the present value of the future cost of the debt—that is, the present value of FV. The firm's discount rate is i, the same as the interest rate on the loan, so Equation 16.2 shows that the present value of the future cost equals $\frac{1}{(1+i)^n} \times FV$. Substitute the future cost of the debt in period n when the loan comes due, $FV = C \times (1 + i)^n$, into the present value calculation to show that the present value of the investment's cost equals

$$\frac{1}{(1+i)^n} \times FV = \frac{1}{(1+i)^n} \times [C \times (1+i)^n] = \frac{(1+i)^n}{(1+i)^n} \times C = C$$

When the maximum amount of interest is paid, the present value of the cost of the investment is C, the same as the initial cost of the investment.

As these calculations show, the present value of the cost of the investment is the same whether the firm finances the investment using its own internally generated funds and pays no interest or borrows from and pays the maximum amount of interest to an outside lender. The result is the same for intermediate cases, as when the firm borrows part of the cost of the investment and/or makes interest payments in multiple periods: The present value of the cost of the investment equals the initial cost of the investment, C, as long as the discount rate equals the interest rate on the loan.

Using Net Present Value

Let's use Equation 16.4, which defines net present value, to calculate the net present value of an investment. If the cost of the investment is C_0 and the operating profit in future period t is π_t, the net present value of the investment is the discounted flow of operating profits minus the initial cost of the investment:

$$NPV = \left[\frac{1}{(1+i)} \times \pi_1\right] + \left[\frac{1}{(1+i)^2} \times \pi_2\right] + \left[\frac{1}{(1+i)^3} \times \pi_3\right] + \ldots$$
$$+ \left[\frac{1}{(1+i)^{Tn}} \times \pi_T\right] - C_0 = \sum_{j=1}^{T}\left[\frac{1}{(1+i)^j} \times \pi_j\right] - C_0 \qquad 16.5$$

where i is the firm's discount rate and T is the number of years the project generates profits. This calculation does not require the operating profit to be the same from year to year. Indeed, you would not expect your profits to be the same every year.

As a manager, how can you use this equation? Consider a capital budgeting problem facing your firm, which may be a company like the Heartland Food Corporation, the second-largest franchisee of Burger King restaurants in the United States with 137 restaurants. Burger King offers your firm a contract to open and operate another restaurant for 20 years for a franchise fee of $50,000. You and the firm's other executives must calculate the net present value of opening and operating this restaurant. You begin by calculating the cost of opening the restaurant. In addition to the $50,000 franchise fee, these costs include acquiring the land, constructing the restaurant, and training the workforce. The total cost of opening a new Burger King restaurant typically approaches $2 million, so you can use that as the cost of your firm's investment. The potential investment makes sense for your firm only if the present value of the operating profits earned over the life of the franchise contract exceeds $2,000,000. Using Equation 16.5, the net present value of this investment opportunity is

$$NPV = \left[\frac{1}{(1+i)} \times \pi_1\right] + \left[\frac{1}{(1+i)^2} \times \pi_2\right] + \left[\frac{1}{(1+i)^3} \times \pi_3\right] + \ldots$$
$$+ \left[\frac{1}{(1+i)^{20}} \times \pi_{20}\right] - \$2,000,000 \qquad 16.6$$

To use this expression in deciding whether to undertake the investment, you must estimate the future operating profits of the new restaurant (π_t) and select a discount rate (i). You and the other managers can use your experiences with the Burger King restaurants you already operate to help estimate the profits. If you did not have this experience, you might use regression analysis (see Chapter 3) to estimate the profits. Suppose that your company has already determined the discount rate it uses. After inserting these data into the net present value formula, if the net present value is positive (so the present value of the future profits exceeds the present value of the cost of opening the new restaurant), you will open the restaurant. If the net present value is negative, you will not open the restaurant.

Extensions to the Net Present Value Rule

Now that you understand the basic net present value equation, let's explore how to modify it to account for situations you may encounter as a manager, including salvage values, taxation, and depreciation allowances.

Salvage Values

To simplify the discussion of present value, we have assumed that the project or physical facility disappears after the stream of payments concludes. That assumption is unrealistic. For example, once The Mosaic Company exhausts one of its phosphate mines, it must clean and restore the site, so it will incur costs for the reclamation of the land after the stream of profits from the mine has ended. Alternatively, a facility might have some value after the stream of profits has concluded. After the Dallas Cowboys built a new football stadium in 2008, they dismantled the old Texas Stadium and sold pieces of it as souvenirs and memorabilia, so the team received some additional profit from the old stadium even after the profits from the games played there had ended.

Salvage values can be positive (as with the additional profit from the Cowboys' old stadium) or negative (as with the costs of restoring The Mosaic Company's mined land). Denoting the salvage value as S and presuming it occurs in year n, adjust the net present value expression in Equation 16.5 to

$$NPV = \sum_{j=1}^{T}\left[\frac{1}{(1 + i)^j} \times \pi_j\right] - C_0 + \left[\frac{1}{(1 + i)^n} \times S\right]$$

The new term, $\frac{1}{(1 + i)^n} \times S$, takes the salvage value into account. The managers must discount the salvage value as shown in the equation because the firm receives or pays the salvage value in year n. If the salvage value is negative, it reduces the net present value, making the investment less likely. If the salvage value is positive, the net present value increases, which raises the likelihood that managers will undertake the project.

For a specific example of how to incorporate salvage value, let's return to the fast-food example. Suppose that when the contract ends, your firm expects to level the Burger King restaurant at a cost of $1.5 million and sell the land for $4.0 million, thereby netting an additional $2.5 million in positive salvage value at the end of the 20-year contract. Including the present value of the positive salvage value affects the net present value of the investment in the new Burger King restaurant. In other words, an additional term must be included in Equation 16.6: $\frac{1}{(1 + i)^{20}} \times \$2,500,000$. In this case, the salvage value adds another positive sum to the net present value and makes your firm more likely to proceed with the project.

Taxation

Taxes also affect net present value. Like salvage values, their impact has been omitted until this point in the discussion because they complicate the calculation. Taxes play such a pervasive role, however, that ultimately they must be incorporated to make the analysis more realistic.

DECISION
SNAPSHOT   Salvage Value at a Car Rental Firm

You are a manager at a car rental company similar to Avis Car Rental. You can buy a Ford Focus for $21,000, rent it for two years, and make an operating profit of $4,500 per year, which you receive at the end of each year. After two years, you can sell the car for $15,000. If your discount rate is 9 percent, should you purchase the car?

Answer
To determine whether to purchase the car, you must determine its net present value:

$$NPV = \left[\frac{1}{(1+0.09)} \times \$4,500\right] + \left[\frac{1}{(1+0.09)^2} \times \$4,500\right]$$
$$+ \left[\frac{1}{(1+0.09)^2} \times \$15,000\right] - \$21,000 = -\$458.55$$

Because the net present value is negative, you should not purchase this car.

Taxation takes a variety of forms in the United States. A firm might be subject to a *unit tax* (a tax per unit sold, such as the federal excise tax of $0.184 per gallon of gasoline), an *ad valorem tax* (a percentage of the price of the product, such as a sales tax of 6 percent), and/or a tax on profits or income (such as the corporate income tax). The following discussion focuses on the effect of taxes on profits or income. Once you understand how to incorporate an income tax in the determination of net present value, including other types of taxes will become straightforward.

Business income taxes are imposed on the firm's *taxable profit*, an amount that equals the firm's total revenue minus its total costs. This section initially examines how taxation alone affects the net present values of different methods of financing an investment (self-financed and debt-financed). Then it extends the analysis to include the effect of depreciation allowances.

Effect of Taxation on Self-Financed Investments In the most straightforward case—when a firm uses its own funds to self-finance an investment—the operating profit (π) is the same as the taxable profit on which taxes are levied. Let τ be the income tax rate. If τ is 10 percent, the firm retains $(1-\tau)$ or 90 percent as its after-tax profit, so that out of every $100 of profit, the firm pays $10 in taxes and retains $90 as after-tax profit. In the absence of a profits tax, Equation 16.5 gives the net present value of a project. Considering taxes changes the formula to

$$NPV = \sum_{j=1}^{T}\left[\frac{1}{(1+i)^j} \times (1-\tau) \times \pi_j\right] - C_0$$

where $1-\tau$ is the percentage of the pretax operating profit retained by the firm. Because the tax reduces the profits received by the firm but has no effect on the initial sum that must be invested, some projects that would be green-lighted on a pretax basis (because they are profitable) are rejected on a posttax basis because they become unprofitable.

To clarify the effect of taxation on net present value, consider American Tower Corporation, a company that owns or operates over 20,000 cellular towers in the United States. Suppose that as a manager of a similar company, you have the opportunity to build an additional cellular tower at a cost of $200,000. Say that the tower generates $40,000 of operating profit each year for eight years, your discount rate is 9 percent, the salvage value at the end of the eight years is zero, and your firm finances the tower using its own funds. Start by calculating the net present value with no taxes. In this case, use Equation 16.5 to determine the net present value of the tower:

$$NPV = \sum_{j=1}^{8}\left[\frac{1}{(1.09)^j} \times \$40{,}000\right] - \$200{,}000 = \$221{,}392 - \$200{,}000 = \$21{,}392$$

The net present value is positive, so in the absence of taxes you make the investment in the new tower.

Now consider the same scenario with the addition of a profits tax. Suppose that the tax rate (τ) on your company's profit is 10 percent each period. At this tax rate, you keep 90 percent of the profit and pay 10 percent in taxes. When you are deciding whether to make the investment, you now calculate the net present value of the tower as

$$NPV = \sum_{j=1}^{8}\left[\frac{1}{(1.09)^j} \times (1 - 0.10) \times \$40{,}000\right] - \$200{,}000 = \$199{,}253 - \$200{,}000$$

$$= -\$747 \tag{16.7}$$

Once the firm must pay taxes, the after-tax net present value is negative, so the investment in the new tower is no longer profitable. You should reject the investment. This result generalizes: The higher the tax rate, the lower the after-tax profits and the lower the after-tax net present value of the investment, so the firm is less likely to make the investment.

Effect of Taxation on Debt-Financed Investments   Now suppose that your firm finances the investment by borrowing the funds rather than using its own. Because the fraction financed, the length of the loan, and the timing of interest payments all vary from loan to loan, there is no general case. Instead, you can see the effect of taxation on the net present value of debt-financed investments with an extension of the cellular tower example. To make the analysis straightforward, we make three assumptions: (1) Your company finances the entire cost of the new tower with a loan, (2) the loan is for eight years at an interest rate of 9 percent, and (3) in the eighth year, your firm repays the entire principal of the loan year plus that year's annual interest, after making interest-only payments for the first seven years.[3] The debt financing alters the calculation of net present value in three ways:

1. Currently (2017) tax laws levy income taxes on the firm's operating profit minus its interest payments. In other words, tax laws consider interest payments as another cost. Consequently, for years one through eight, the additional cost of the interest payment is subtracted from your firm's operating profit to determine its taxable profit. Each year's interest payment is $200,000 × 0.09, or $18,000. This additional cost reduces the taxable profit in each of these eight years

---

3 Managers can analyze more complicated (and more realistic) loans by modifying the analysis that follows and using Excel for the calculations.

from $40,000 to $22,000. Therefore, the profit on which the tax is levied is $22,000 for each of the first eight years.

2. The initial cost of the investment (C_0) can no longer be included in the calculation of net present value because the deductibility of interest changes the effective cost of the investment. Instead, you must use the present value of each period's after-tax profit to calculate the net present value.

3. In year eight, your firm repays the $200,000 loan, which is another cost in that year.

Considering items 1–3, at a tax rate of 10 percent the calculation of net present value becomes

$$NPV = \sum_{j=1}^{8} \left[\frac{1}{(1.09)^j} \times (1 - 0.10) \times \$22,000 \right] + \left[\frac{1}{(1.09)^8} \times -\$200,000 \right] = \$9,209$$

Financing the investment with debt *increases* the net present value. Indeed, financing using internally generated funds—as shown in Equation 16.7—makes the investment unprofitable, but financing with debt now makes that same investment profitable. The idea that incurring an additional cost (borrowing the funds) can swing a previously unprofitable investment to profitability might be difficult to grasp. It hinges on two facts:

1. The interest payments are tax deductible. The government effectively helps pay part of the investment's cost because the interest payments decrease the amount of tax the firm must pay.

2. Borrowing pushes off paying for the investment until the loan comes due (period eight in this example). Because the $200,000 cost of the investment does not need to be paid until year eight, its present value, $\left[\frac{1}{(1.09)^8} \right] \times -\$200,000 = -\$100,380$, is significantly less than the present value when the firm finances the investment using its own funds ($200,000).

In the example at hand, these effects are enough to nudge the investment to profitability, but that is not always the case. For example, if the tax rate in the example was 20 percent rather than 10 percent, the investment would remain unprofitable.

Depreciation Allowance

Using the firm's capital equipment is not free—it entails a cost, called depreciation, because usage inflicts wear and tear. Economists measure *economic depreciation* as the decrease in the market value of the capital (see Section 1.4). Economic depreciation measures the opportunity cost of using the capital. Accountants, however, cannot use economic depreciation. Instead, they must use one of several accounting depreciation methods approved by the Internal Revenue Service (IRS) to calculate a *depreciation allowance*. Currently (2017) tax laws treat the depreciation allowance as another cost, so accountants subtract it from the firm's operating profit before calculating the tax. All of the IRS-approved methods depend in one way or another on the cost of the equipment and the equipment's usable life. They differ according to how much depreciation allowance is calculated for each year of the equipment's life. The least complicated method is *straight-line depreciation*, which assumes the capital equipment wears out by the same fraction for each year of its life. For example, if the life span of a $200,000 cellular tower built by American Tower is eight years, then straight-line depreciation gives an allowance of $\frac{\$200,000}{8\ \text{years}}$, or $25,000 per year. More generally, if the cost of an investment is C_0 and the investment lasts for n years, the straight-line depreciation allowance is $\frac{C_0}{n}$ per year.

Effect of the Depreciation Allowance on Investment Decisions To study the effect of the depreciation allowance on investment decisions, assume that a firm's managers are deciding whether to make an investment of C_0. To simplify the analysis and focus entirely on the depreciation allowance, assume that the firm is financing the investment using its own funds, so there is no interest expense. Call δ_t the depreciation allowance in period t. To calculate its taxable profit, the firm subtracts this amount from its operating profit, so the firm's taxable profit equals $\pi_t - \delta_t$. Because the depreciation allowance is strictly arbitrary—essentially a random amount determined by tax code regulations—it does not reflect a cost, so the firm's operating profit remains π_t while the taxable profit becomes $\pi_t - \delta_t$. Given the taxable income and the tax rate of τ, the firm's tax payment is $(\pi_t - \delta_t) \times \tau$. So the total after-tax profit in period t is the operating profit minus the tax payment:

$$\pi_t - [(\pi_t - \delta_t) \times \tau] = \pi_t - (\pi_t \times \tau) + (\delta_t \times \tau) = [(1 - \tau) \times \pi_t] + (\delta_t \times \tau)$$

Recall that when depreciation was ignored, the after-tax profit was $(1 - \tau) \times \pi_t$. Comparing the after-tax profits shows that the depreciation allowance increases the after-tax profit by $\pi_t \times \tau$. It might seem odd that *subtracting* something from the operating profit *boosts* the after-tax profit. This apparent paradox is resolved when you consider that the depreciation allowance reduces the profit subject to taxation, thereby decreasing the amount of tax the firm pays.

Discounting each period's after-tax profit gives the NPV equation:

$$NPV = \sum_{j=1}^{T}\left(\frac{1}{(1+i)^j} \times \{[(1-\tau) \times \pi_j] + (\delta_j \times \tau)\}\right) - C_0$$

Including the effect of the depreciation allowance increases each period's after-tax profit, increasing the net present value of the project.

The effects of the depreciation allowance and interest expense are similar. Both act as *tax shields*, deductions that decrease the taxes due. With this comparison in mind, it makes sense that adding the depreciation allowance raises the new present value of an investment.

Let's return to the cellular tower example to see how the depreciation allowance affects the decision about the additional cellular tower. Say that you decide to use straight-line depreciation in calculating the new present value, your firm pays the cost of the tower using its own funds, and the tax rate is 10 percent. From the calculation in Equation 16.7, you know that without taking depreciation into account you will not build the tower because the net present value of the tower is negative, −$747. Once you incorporate the depreciation allowance into the picture, you need to recompute the after-tax profits for the eight years of the tower's life. The operating profit is $40,000 per year, so the after-tax profit, $(1 - \tau) \times \pi$, is $36,000. To this after-tax profit you must add the impact of the depreciation tax shield, $\delta \times \tau$. With straight-line depreciation, the tower's depreciation allowance is $25,000 per year, so $\delta \times \tau$. equals $2,500. By bringing the depreciation allowance into the picture, your company saves $2,500 on each year's tax bill, thereby increasing the total annual after-tax profit: $[(1 - \tau) \times \pi] + (\delta \times \tau) = \$36,000 + \$2,500 = \$38,500$. Accordingly, the NPV equation becomes

$$NPV = \sum_{j=1}^{8}\left[\frac{1}{(1.09)^j} \times \$38,500\right] - \$200,000 = \$213,090 - \$200,000 = \$13,090$$

Including the depreciation allowance nudges the net present value of the proposed investment from −$747 to $13,090, an increase large enough to flip the manager's decision from rejecting the investment to accepting it. Of course, consideration of depreciation will not always change the managerial decision, but its role as a tax shield means that it will always increase the net present value.

DECISION
SNAPSHOT

Depreciation Allowance: Should a Tax Firm Take It Now or Later?

Say that you are the owner of a firm like the local H&R Block and you are deciding the timing of an expenditure of $75,000 on new computers. You will buy the computers with your own internally generated funds. The computers will increase your before-tax operating profit by $32,000 per year for three years, after which they are valueless. Each year's profit accrues at the end of the year. Suppose that your tax rate is 40 percent. In 2014, Section 179 of the IRS code allowed you to claim a special depreciation allowance of up to $500,000 of an investment in the first year of operation. However, the law specified that in 2015 and thereafter you could take the special depreciation allowance only up to $25,000 but you could take it in the first, second, and third years. Your discount rate is 9 percent per year. Should you purchase the computers on December 31, 2014, or on January 1, 2015? Explain your answer.

Answer

If you purchase the computers on December 31, 2014, you can take the special depreciation allowance on the entire $75,000, so the tax shield from the depreciation allowance is $0.40 \times \$75,000$. You receive this reduction in taxes in the first period. Accordingly, the net present value equals

$$NPV = \left(\frac{1}{(1 + 0.09)} \times \{[(1 - 0.40) \times \$32,000] + (0.40 \times \$75,000)\} \right)$$

$$+ \left\{ \frac{1}{(1 + 0.09)^2} \times [(1 - 0.40) \times \$32,000] \right\} + \left\{ \frac{1}{(1 + 0.09)^3} \times [(1 - 0.40) \times \$32,000] \right\}$$

$$- \$75,000 = \$1,122.96$$

If you purchase the computers on January 1, 2015, the tax shield from the depreciation allowance is only $0.40 \times \$25,000$, but you receive it in all three years. So the net present value equals

$$NPV = \left(\frac{1}{(1 + 0.09)} \times \{[(1 - 0.40) \times \$32,000] + (0.40 \times \$25,000)\} \right)$$

$$+ \left(\frac{1}{(1 + 0.09)^2} \times \{[(1 - 0.40) \times \$32,000] + (0.40 \times \$25,000)\} \right)$$

$$+ \left(\frac{1}{(1 + 0.09)^3} \times \{[(1 - 0.40) \times \$32,000] + (0.40 \times \$25,000)\} \right)$$

$$- \$75,000 = -\$1,086.04$$

The net present value is positive if you make the investment in 2014 but negative if you make it in 2015. To maximize profit, you should make the investment in 2014 rather than 2015.

Selection of the Discount Rate

The net present value rule compares the present value of the profits from an investment to the present value of its cost. Because the present value of a future amount is equal to that future value multiplied by the discount factor, $PV = \left[\frac{1}{(1 + i)^n}\right] \times FV$, it is clear that the discount rate influences the present value. Examining some numerical examples demonstrates the magnitude of the impact of a change in the discount rate. Consider the present value of $100,000 to be received in five years at alternative discount rates of 3 percent, 6 percent, and 9 percent:

- At a 3 percent discount rate, the present value is $86,260.
- At 6 percent, the present value falls by more than $10,000 to $74,730.
- At 9 percent, it falls still lower to $64,990.

Increasing the discount rate from 3 percent to 9 percent lowers the present value by over $20,000. Selecting the discount rate is important because of its large effect on the present value. This observation raises the following question: How do managers determine the discount rate used in the present value calculations?

Many large firms have finance departments tasked with selecting the appropriate interest rate to use as the discount rate. For example, your financial analysts might determine that your company's shareholders want at least a 15 percent return on each investment, so they set the discount rate at 15 percent. In such firms, managers generally have little discretion about the discount rate they can use.

In other firms, however, selecting the discount rate requires serious managerial attention. At the most fundamental level, the discount rate should reflect the opportunity cost of the funds used to finance the project. If the firm borrows the funds, the managers should use the interest rate on the loan as the discount rate because that interest rate is the opportunity cost to the company. If the firm uses internally generated funds to finance the investment, the funds still have an opportunity cost because the managers could loan the funds to other firms or deposit them in a financial institution and, in both cases, receive interest income. In these cases, the managers should use the interest rate on the loan or the deposit as the discount rate. In many cases, however, it is difficult to determine the opportunity cost, so managers often use the *weighted average cost of capital* as the discount rate. To find the weighted average cost of capital, they take the interest rate for each component of the firm's financial capital—such as loans, bonds, and stock—and weight it according to its fraction of the firm's total financial capital. For example, if bonds have an interest rate of 5 percent and account for 60 percent (0.60) of your firm's financial capital and stocks have a rate of return of 10 percent and account for the remaining 40 percent (0.40), then your firm's weighted average cost of capital is $(5.0 \text{ percent} \times 0.60) + (10.0 \text{ percent} \times 0.40) = 7.0$ percent.

Risk and the Net Present Value Rule

To this point, the discussion has not considered risk, such as the possibility that future profits will be less than expected. In the extreme, a competitor may develop a vastly superior product, so that the investment yields zero profits. For example, new drugs completely supplanted Merck's 2011 drug for hepatitis C, Victrelis, so that even though it cost Merck hundreds of millions of dollars to develop the drug, within four years of its introduction to the market, Merck stopped selling it, and its profit plunged to zero.

More generally, you have learned about the effects of future profits, future salvage values, future tax policies, and future discount rates as if they are known quantities, but in reality, they are subject to unpredictable changes. As a manager, you must use research, experience, and your best business judgment to determine estimates or expectations of these variables. Even so, you face the risk that actual values are unlikely to materialize exactly as planned. You can account for risk by adjusting the discount rate or by adjusting the profit flows.

Risk-Adjusted Discount Rate

If a project involves risk, often managers account for the risk by raising the discount rate they use. Raising the discount rate decreases the present value of future profits, implicitly recognizing the risk that the future profits will be less than expected. Unfortunately, for capital budgeting problems, there is no precise formula that managers can use to determine the exact amount of the upward adjustment. Qualitatively, however, the greater the risk is, the larger the upward adjustment should be.

Risk-Adjusted Profit Flows

If an investment project faces a risk that is insurable, the managers should adjust the flows of costs and profits rather than the discount rate. For example, Barrick Gold, a Canadian mining company, operates its Lagunes Norte Mine in Peru. Suppose that you are a manager of another Canadian mining company and you invest $100 million in your Peruvian mine. You worry that the government may expropriate the mine; that is, the government may take over your mine and give you nothing in exchange. You can buy political risk insurance from a government agency, Export Development Canada, or from private insurers. This insurance will compensate your firm if expropriation occurs. Suppose that before buying insurance your firm expects the investment will increase its profit by $18 million per year for the next 10 years. If the political insurance costs $3 million per year and you buy the insurance, the company's profits increase by only $15 million per year, so you would use this profit in the net present value calculation. If you do not buy the insurance, the company still incurs an opportunity cost for the risk, and therefore you should reduce the expected stream of profits by $3 million per year and again use $15 million for the profit in the net present value calculation. In both cases, you have adjusted the profit flows for the risk, so you do not need to further adjust the discount rate.

Sensitivity Analysis

Regardless of how managers adjust for risk, they should check the sensitivity of their results by calculating multiple net present values using a range of expected values for the different variables. Change each variable one at a time, and determine how sensitive the results are to changes in the factor. For example, you might calculate the net present value of your Peruvian mine several ways. You could

- Change the cost of the expansion to $110 million but not change the profit stream or the discount rate.
- Change the profit stream from 10 years to 8 years but not change the cost or the discount rate.
- Increase the discount rate by 2 percentage points but not change the cost or the profit stream.

Of course, there are a variety of other changes to explore. The goals of the sensitivity analysis are twofold: First, it may give you a better idea of which aspects are most important for the project's net present value. Second, if you discover that changes in a particular factor lead to large changes in the net present value, it might be worthwhile for you to spend more time and resources to fine-tune your estimate of that factor.

To this point, the discussion has used the net present value rule to determine the profitability of capital budgeting investments. The rule, however, applies in many more situations than just capital budgeting. For example, managers often face the decision of whether to buy an input or manufacture it themselves. To make this decision, the managers must compare the immediate costs they incur to set up the production of the input to the flow of future cost savings from producing the input. The next section uses the net present value rule to study these make-or-buy decisions.

| SOLVED PROBLEM | # Investment Decision for an Electric Car Maker |

Suppose that you and the other managers of an electric car maker like Tesla, Inc., have announced your plan to build a huge, 10-million-square-foot battery factory at a cost of $5 to $6 billion. The factory is so big that it will take three years to construct. Your firm will share the cost of building the factory with partners, and your share of the cost will be $2 billion. Your firm has accumulated a series of past losses. The tax laws allow you to deduct these losses from any future profits and thereby eliminate any tax liability, so you can ignore the effect of taxes in your calculations.

a. To build the factory, your firm will pay $800 million at the end of the first year, $800 million at the end of the second year, and $400 million at the end of the third year. If the discount rate is 9 percent per year, what is the present value of the cost of the investment?

b. You and the other managers believe that your share of the operating profit from the factory will be $500 million per year for 10 years after the factory is completed. After 10 years, technology will have changed, so the factory will have no value. What is the present value of the profit from your firm's investment?

c. Should you make the $2 billion investment? Why or why not?

ANSWER

a. The present value of the cost of the investment equals

$$\left[\frac{1}{(1+0.09)} \times \$800 \text{ million}\right] + \left[\frac{1}{(1+0.09)^2} \times \$800 \text{ million}\right] + \left[\frac{1}{(1+0.09)^3} \times \$400 \text{ million}\right]$$

$$= \$1.716 \text{ billion}$$

b. The present value of the operating profit from the investment equals

$$\left[\frac{1}{(1+0.09)^4} \times \$500 \text{ million}\right] + \left[\frac{1}{(1+0.09)^5} \times \$500 \text{ million}\right] + \dots$$

$$+ \left[\frac{1}{(1+0.09)^{13}} \times \$500 \text{ million}\right] = \$2.478 \text{ billion}$$

c. The net present value of the investment is $2.478 billion − $1.716 billion = $0.762 billion. You should make the investment because the net present value is positive.

16.3 Make-or-Buy Decisions

Learning Objective 16.3 Use present value calculations to answer the make or buy questions that managers face.

In addition to deciding what outputs to produce, managers must decide whether to produce in-house any of the required inputs. You initially studied aspects of this question in Chapter 11 when you explored issues surrounding vertical integration. That chapter ignored the timing of cost expenditures and receipts of profit (or cost savings). Let's now return to the question to investigate the role played by timing. To simplify the analysis, ignore the issues described in Chapter 11 and instead examine whether a manager should incur *present*-period costs in order to produce the inputs in *future* periods. Once you understand this aspect of the decision, combining it with the issues explained in Chapter 11 is straightforward.

The decision whether to produce (make) or purchase (buy) an input is fundamentally the same as any other investment decision because it comes down to comparing the present value of the profit (or cost savings) of the project to the present value of the costs of the project. So managers making these decisions again need to use the net present value rule.

Make-or-Buy Basics

Let's return to the example presented in the introduction to this chapter, in which Tropicana purchased equipment to manufacture a carafe container for its orange juice. Prior to the purchase of the equipment, Tropicana's managers faced a seemingly simple question: Should they make the plastic carafe containers or buy them from another company? Why do you think that the managers decided to make the containers themselves? A superficial answer is that the decision maximized Tropicana's profit, but a deeper analysis reveals the importance of present value considerations in the firm's decision.

Cost always plays a key role in make-or-buy decisions. Production of a small quantity of an input is often unprofitable. For example, it would be very costly to keep a carpenter on the payroll of a small interior design firm if he or she makes only one table and one bookshelf each year. It would obviously be cheaper for the interior design firm to order the table and bookshelf from a separate woodworking firm.

For a firm like Tropicana, on the other hand, there might be considerable economies of scale in making carafes. Recall from Chapter 4 that *economies of scale* are achieved if the long-run average cost falls when output increases. Suppose another juice firm is considering whether to make or buy carafes. Figure 16.4 shows that its hypothetical long-run average cost curve has significant economies of scale in the production of containers: Producing 13 million containers per year results in a much lower average cost than producing only 3 million. These economies of scale affect the firm's managerial decision:

- If this firm plans to use 13 million containers per year, with these numbers it could make sense for the firm to make the containers itself because it is able to gain the economies of scale and produce at a low cost.
- If the firm plans to use only 3 million containers per year, making the containers probably would be more expensive than buying them from a specialty firm. A specialty firm might be able to sell 3 million containers to the firm at a price lower than the juice firm's production cost because of the specialty firm's expertise in this endeavor. If the juice firm's managers try to gain the economies of scale by producing 13 million containers and selling the excess 10 million to other companies, this effort involved costs of its own, especially because the firm specializes in producing orange juice but has no particular skill in making plastic containers.

Figure 16.4 Economies of Scale

The long-run average cost, *LAC*, of producing 13 million containers per year is much lower than that of producing 3 million containers per year.

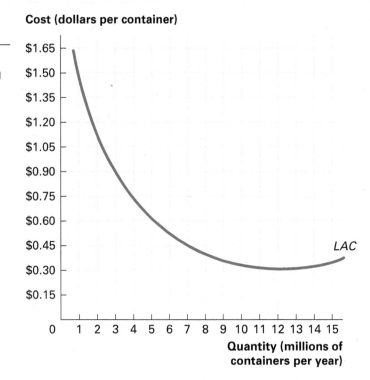

Cost (dollars per container)

In addition to economies of scale, other cost savings can result from producing an input rather than purchasing it:

- **Transportation costs.** If the juice firm itself produces the carafes, it may not need to pay the cost of transporting 13 million of them from the manufacturer to the firm's plant. Instead, depending on the machine's location, employees might be able to merely wheel the containers from the blow-molding machine to the assembly line.

- **Communication costs.** Communication about input specifications and needs is cheaper within a firm than across firms. If managers of the juice firm find that they need more containers in a particular week, they can approve overtime for the workers who operate the blow-molding machine more quickly than they can negotiate the delivery of additional units from another firm.

- **Contract compliance costs.** If the juice firm makes the input rather than purchasing it, there is no need for (costly) monitoring of the selling firm's compliance with the contract. In particular, the firm does not need to worry about a potential hold-up problem. Recall from Chapter 11 that the *hold-up problem* occurs when one party to an agreement has the incentive to increase its profit by unilaterally changing the terms of an agreement or insisting on renegotiation once the other party has invested in a transaction-specific asset (see Section 11.2). For example, if the juice firm outsources the production of the carafe to another firm, that firm can demand contract renegotiation and a higher price for the carafes *after* the juice firm has installed its new assembly line, which is useless without those specific carafe containers.

- **Quality control costs.** A firm is likely to be more efficient in monitoring and controlling the quality of inputs it produces than in monitoring and controlling the quality of inputs it purchases. In 2013, food safety officials discovered that Taco Bell's supplier had mixed horse meat with the beef that Taco Bell outlets served across Europe. Taco Bell's sales took a hit. Managers could have avoided the scandal if the firm had ground its own beef, rather than purchasing it from outside suppliers.

Another consideration that affects make-or-buy decisions is the need for secrecy. A firm has more control over its own employees than those of suppliers. Managers trying to protect their trade secrets may find it worthwhile to produce an input even when other considerations favor purchase.

Make-or-Buy Net Present Value Calculations

An example can help clarify the analysis of the make-or-buy problem and illustrate how a manager can use the net present value equation in making this important decision. Suppose that the juice company looking to acquire carafes can buy them for $0.50 per container or produce them at a cost of $0.30 if it buys a $15 million blow-molding machine.[4] For simplicity, ignore any tax issues, assume that the cost of $0.30 includes the cost of depreciation and all other costs, and also assume that the company pays for the machine out of its internally generated cash.

To determine whether to make or buy the containers, the managers need to know four things: (1) the company's discount rate, (2) the life span of the blow-molding equipment, (3) the value of the equipment at the end of its life span, and (4) the number of containers they need each year. Suppose that the appropriate discount rate is 8 percent and the equipment's life span is seven years, after which it has no salvage value. Whether the hypothetical $15 million investment is worthwhile depends on the anticipated quantity.

Producing rather than buying the containers saves $0.20 ($0.50 − $0.30) per container. Consequently the total annual cost savings are $0.20 × Q, where Q is the annual quantity produced. Because these savings accrue over the life of the equipment, the managers need to compare the present value of the cost savings to the cost of purchasing the machine. If the company produces the same number of containers each year, the net present value of purchasing the blow-molding machine is[5]

$$NPV = \sum_{j=1}^{7} \left[\frac{1}{(1.08)^j} \times (\$0.20 \times Q) \right] - \$15,000,000$$

$$= \sum_{j=1}^{7} \left[\frac{1}{(1.08)^j} \times \$0.20 \right] \times Q - \$15,000,000$$

$$= (\$1.041 \times Q) - \$15,000,000$$

The managers should buy the blow-molding machine if the net present value of the purchase is positive, that is, if ($1.041 × Q) − $15,000,000 > 0. They can solve the inequality as

($1.041 × Q) − $15,000,000 > 0 → $1.041 × Q > $15,000,000 → Q > 14,409,222

In other words, the net present value is positive for any quantity of containers that is greater than 14,409,222 per year. If the managers anticipate using more than 14,409,222 carafe containers per year, it is cheaper to make the containers. Of course, if they expect to use fewer than 14,409,222 per year, it is less expensive to purchase the containers from an outside firm.

---

4 Assume that the marginal cost does not depend on the quantity produced. In other words, ignore any economies or diseconomies of scale so that the marginal cost curve is constant at $0.30 per carafe.

5 In the net present value equation, the present value of the cost saving is calculated as follows:
$\sum_{j=1}^{7} \frac{1}{(1.08)^j} \times (\$0.20 \times Q) = \left[\sum_{j=1}^{7} \frac{1}{(1.08)^j} \times \$0.20 \right] \times Q = [5.2064 \times \$0.20] \times Q = \$1.041 \times Q$. The 5.2064 term is equal to $\sum_{j=1}^{7} \frac{1}{(1.08)^j}$.

A Make-or-Buy Decision with Learning by Doing

You have seen how managers can decide whether to make or buy the containers they need. Let's modify the example by supposing that the more carafes the company produces, the more the workers learn how to operate the machine efficiently. If the company buys the blow-molding machine, say that these learning-by-doing economies (see Section 4.3) lower the cost of producing a carafe by 1¢ to $0.29 in the second year and by another 1¢ to $0.28 in the third year. As the machine ages, the cost of servicing it increases, so that in the fourth and fifth years the cost of a carafe remains $0.28 per carafe but then rises to $0.29 in the sixth year and to $0.30 in the seventh year. The company produces the same number of carafes in each of the seven years. With these changes, should the managers buy the machine? Why or why not?

Answer

The cost saving for a carafe from buying the blow-molding machine is $0.50 per carafe minus the cost of the carafe, which means the cost saving per carafe is $0.20 the first year; $0.21 the second year; $0.22 the third, fourth, and fifth years; $0.21 the sixth year; and $0.20 the seventh year. Let Q be the number of carafes produced per year. Accordingly, the net present value from buying the machine is now

$$NPV = \left[\frac{1}{(1.08)} \times (\$0.20 \times Q)\right] + \left[\frac{1}{(1.08)^2} \times (\$0.21 \times Q)\right] + \left[\frac{1}{(1.08)^3} \times (\$0.22 \times Q)\right]$$

$$+ \left[\frac{1}{(1.08)^4} \times (\$0.22 \times Q)\right] + \left[\frac{1}{(1.08)^5} \times (\$0.22 \times Q)\right] + \left[\frac{1}{(1.08)^6} \times (\$0.21 \times Q)\right]$$

$$+ \left[\frac{1}{(1.08)^7} \times (\$0.20 \times Q)\right] - \$15,000,000 = (1.100 \times Q) - \$15,000,000$$

The managers will buy the blow-molding machine if $(1.100 \times Q) - \$15,000,000 > 0$, which means the managers will buy the machine if they plan to produce more than 13,636,363 containers per year.

16.4 Present Value and Net Present Value

Learning Objective 16.4 Apply the concepts of present value and the net present value rule to make profit-maximizing managerial decisions.

Managers must use the concepts of present value and net present value whenever they make decisions that will lead to profits or costs that flow into or out of the business during future periods. This section includes three applications to increase your familiarity with these important concepts.

Valuing Financial Assets

You can apply present value to managerial decisions other than investment projects. Financial assets are also valued in this way. For example, a bond is essentially a promise to pay money at specified future dates. The issuer of the bond promises to make interest payments at specified times and then to repay the principal amount of the bond at some point in the future. Once issued, a bond's price in the bond market can fluctuate. The bond's price equals the present value of the stream of payments because sellers will accept no less than the present value and buyers will pay no more than the present value. So the present value is the only acceptable price. For example, in 1994, The Boeing Company sold bonds for $10,000 each. Each bond promised to pay $750 in interest per year through 2042 and then to pay $750 in interest as well as the principal amount in 2043. You can determine the price of the bond in the bond market on January 1, 2019, by calculating the present value of the stream of future payments. At that time, the bond had 25 annual interest payments left and, of course, the one principal payment. Suppose that the discount rate is 5 percent. The present value of these payments equals

$$PV = \left[\frac{1}{(1.05)} \times \$750\right] + \left[\frac{1}{(1.05)^2} \times \$750\right] + \left[\frac{1}{(1.05)^3} \times \$750\right] + \ldots$$

$$+ \left[\frac{1}{(1.05)^{25}} \times \$750\right] + \left[\frac{1}{(1.05)^{25}} \times \$10,000\right] = \$13,523.49$$

This calculation means that the price of the bond on January 1, 2019, was $13,523.49.

The present value calculations demonstrate how a change in the interest rate affects the price of the bond. Suppose that the interest rate used as the basis for the discount rate rises. The increase in the discount rate reduces the present value of the stream of future payments and thereby decreases the price of the bond. In other words, an increase in the interest rate lowers the price of bonds in the bond market. For example, if the interest rate rises, increasing the discount rate to 8 percent, the present value and price of Boeing's bond would be

$$PV = \left[\frac{1}{(1.08)} \times \$750\right] + \left[\frac{1}{(1.08)^2} \times \$750\right] + \left[\frac{1}{(1.08)^3} \times \$750\right] + \ldots$$

$$+ \left[\frac{1}{(1.08)^{25}} \times \$750\right] + \left[\frac{1}{(1.08)^{25}} \times \$10,000\right] = \$9,466.34$$

When the discount rate rises from 5 percent to 8 percent, the price of the bond falls from $13,523.49 to $9,466.34. Of course, the reverse is also true: If the discount rate falls, then the price of bonds rises.

Riskier bonds will have a higher discount rate than safer ones. So if the risk that the issuing company will not be able to make the future interest or principal payments increases, the discount rate rises, and the price of the bond falls. This effect is particularly visible to anyone who follows the prices of so-called *junk bonds*, bonds with a substantial risk that the issuer will not make the promised interest or principal payments. When this risk rises, the price of a junk bond immediately falls.

Using the Net Present Value Rule in the Real World

This chapter has used simplified economic models to show how managers should approach capital budgeting decisions using the net present value rule. Although the models are vastly simpler than actual projects that you will encounter in your career, you should calculate the net present value and use the net present value rule to evaluate *any* business decision that involves the payment and/or receipt of money at different times in the future. For example, firms must pay for advertising campaigns in the present in exchange for (hopefully!) increased profits in the future. Because this decision involves costs and profits in different periods, you should use the net present value rule to decide if the proposed campaign should be undertaken.

Similarly, when a firm enters a new market, it must often pay substantial costs before any profits begin to flow. Once again, you should use the net present value rule to determine if entering the new market will be profitable.

The most straightforward calculation of net present value compares the present value of profits received in the future to the costs incurred in the present, but the equation applies equally well if the costs are also incurred in the future. In this case, the present value of the costs is calculated, and the net present value equation compares the present value of profits to the present value of costs. Once you acknowledge that costs as well as profits can occur in the future, two general principles emerge:

- The sooner a profit occurs, the better. Why? The sooner the profit occurs, the less it is discounted, and the larger the positive effect it has on the net present value.
- The later a cost occurs, the better. Why? The later the cost occurs, the more it is discounted, and the smaller the negative effect it has on the net present value.

As a manager, these two general principles show you that your goal should be to accelerate profits and delay costs.

For an example of how costs can occur in more than one year, suppose that the trustees of a nonprofit medical center, such as the Mary Greeley Medical Center in Ames, Iowa, are considering whether to mount a two-year advertising campaign by spending $2 million this year and $1 million in the next year. They determine that the campaign will lead to an additional surplus (what a nonprofit calls its profit) of $800,000 for five years, starting this year and continuing for four more years. The trustees believe that the appropriate discount rate is 7 percent. Presuming the expenditures on advertising and flows of surplus occur at the end of the year, they calculate the net present value of the advertising campaign as follows:

$$NPV = \left\{ \left[\frac{1}{(1.07)^1} \times \$800,000 \right] + \left[\frac{1}{(1.07)^2} \times \$800,000 \right] + \ldots + \left[\frac{1}{(1.07)^5} \times \$800,000 \right] \right\}$$

$$- \left\{ \left[\frac{1}{(1.07)} \times \$2,000,000 \right] + \left[\frac{1}{(1.07)^2} \times \$1,000,000 \right] \right\}$$

The first set of curly brackets contains the present value of the inflows of additional surplus, and the second set contains the present value of the advertising cost outflows. Notice that the cost of the second year of advertising must be discounted because it occurs in the future. Calculating these present values gives

$$NPV = \$3,280,160 - \$2,742,598 = \$537,562$$

This calculation shows that the trustees should go ahead with the advertising campaign because its net present value is positive. It also shows the general conclusion that regardless of when the costs are incurred and the profits reaped, the net present value rule remains the same: A project that involves profits and costs in the present and future should be undertaken only if the present value of the profits exceeds the present value of the costs.

The Effect of Tax Shields on Net Present Value

Interest paid on debt-financed investments serves as a tax shield. The cellular tower example in Section 16.2 made several simplifying assumptions to clarify important points about net present value. For example, the assumption of a 10 percent tax rate on profits simplified the analysis. The tax structure will surely be more complicated in reality, but, at least under the current tax laws, the interest paid on any debt-financed investment will still be tax deductible. As long as interest expense is deductible, it serves as a tax shield that raises the net present value of potential projects.

The depreciation allowance is another tax shield. The government imposes taxes on the profit from an investment after subtracting the depreciation allowance. By decreasing the taxes that the firm must pay, the depreciation allowance boosts the investment's profit, increasing its net present value. Just like interest, the depreciation allowance acts as a tax shield that raises the net present value of potential projects.

Accounting depreciation is an arbitrary amount that depends on IRS regulations, and there are different IRS-approved methods of calculating the depreciation allowance. As a manager, you generally want to select the method that produces a larger depreciation allowance in periods closer to the present because that decision will maximize the net present value of the asset. For a small business, tax laws currently allow the entire amount of the investment up to a fixed limit ($500,000 in 2016 and thereafter indexed to inflation) to be deducted immediately from the firm's profit. This immediate depreciation allowance is called *expensing the investment* because it allows the business to treat the amount spent on investment like any other expense. Expensing the investment is generally optimal because it immediately boosts the tax shield.

Although it is generally best to take the depreciation allowance as early as possible, effective managers must think carefully about expected changes in the tax rate. If you believe that the tax rate will be substantially higher in the future, delaying the depreciation allowance might make sense because it will shield more of your firm's profit later on. Such a delay subjects the profit to more discounting, however, so it is not universally optimal. Fortunately, working through different scenarios is relatively easy using a spreadsheet. Exploring how different changes in tax laws might affect the profitability of a proposal should be part of the sensitivity analysis you undertake before accepting or rejecting a project.

Revisiting Why Ziosk's Managers Give Their Tablets to Chili's for Free

Before signing their contract with Chili's, Ziosk's managers needed to ensure that the terms of the contract would allow them to make a profit. They therefore first calculated the net present value of placing their tablets in the restaurants to be certain that it was positive.

The actual contract between Ziosk and Chili's is, of course, confidential. By making a few assumptions, we can demonstrate the type of calculations Ziosk's managers used to determine profitability. For simplicity, let's concentrate on the 823 company-owned restaurants. So suppose the following:

- Providing the tablets at each Chili's costs $15,000, for a total cost of 823 × $15,000 = $12,345,000.

- Ziosk finances the tablets using its own internally generated funds, and the tablets and the contract last for three years, after which time the tablets are valueless (the salvage value is zero).
- The accounting depreciation is straight-line depreciation, so the depreciation allowance is one-third of the tablets' cost each year.
- At the end of each year, Ziosk collects $7,000 in operating profit per restaurant as its share of the purchases made on the tablet, and Ziosk's discount rate is 12 percent.
- Ziosk's tax rate is 20 percent.

Ziosk's managers must determine the after-tax profit in each period. The analysis is similar to the derivation of American Tower's after-tax profit: Ziosk's after-tax profit equals its operating profit minus the tax it pays. Ziosk's annual operating profit is equal to

$7,000 per restaurant × 823 restaurants = $5,761,000

Ziosk's tax is based on its operating profit minus its depreciation allowance. The annual allowance is one-third of the total expenditure on tablets, or

1/3 × $12,345,000 = $4,115,000

Ziosk's taxable profit is $5,761,000 − $4,115,000 = $1,646,000. At a tax rate of 20 percent, Ziosk's tax is

0.20 × $1,646,000 = $329,200

Ziosk's after-tax profit each period is its operating profit minus its tax, or

$5,761,000 − $329,200 = $5,431,800

With this (hypothetical) information, Ziosk's managers can now calculate the net present value of its investment in tablets:

$$NPV = \left[\frac{1}{(1.12)} \times \$5,431,800 \right] + \left[\frac{1}{(1.12)^2} \times \$5,431,800 \right]$$
$$+ \left[\frac{1}{(1.12)^3} \times \$5,431,800 \right] - \$12,345,000$$
$$= \$701,267$$

where the discount factor, $\left[\frac{1}{(1.12)} \right]$, reflects the assumed discount rate of 12 percent.

Because the net present value in this example is positive, Ziosk's managers believe they will make a profit from the contract, so they will enter into an agreement with Chili's. The hypothetical present value of the profit, $701,267, is the value of the profit at the present time.

Summary: The Bottom Line

16.1 Fundamentals of Present Value

- Present value is the worth *today* of a sum of money to be paid or received in the *future*.
- The present value of $1.00 to be received or paid n years in the future when the interest rate is i is equal to $PV = \frac{1}{(1 + i)^n} \times \$1.00$. The term used to calculate the current value of the future funds, $\frac{1}{(1 + i)^n}$, is the discount factor. The interest rate used in calculating the discount factor is the discount rate.
- The present value of a stream of payments is the sum of the present values of the individual payments. The higher the discount rate and the longer the time until the money is paid or received, the smaller its present value.

16.2 Evaluating Investment Options

- Investments in capital equipment typically involve the expenditure of money in the present in exchange for anticipated future profits.
- The net present value of an investment is the difference between the present value of its future operating profits and the present value of its cost:

$$NPV = \sum_{j=1}^{n} \left[\frac{1}{(1 + i)^j} \times \pi_j \right] - C_0$$

where i is the discount rate, π_j is the operating profit in period j, C_0 is the cost incurred in the present period, and the profits extend over n periods.

- The net present value rule is to make an investment if the net present value of the investment is positive because in this case the investment is profitable. Do not make the investment if the net present value of the investment is negative because then it is not profitable.
- Calculations of net present value can include positive or negative salvage values. Taxation, depreciation allowances, and risk make the present value calculations more complicated, but the net present value rule remains unchanged.
- The net present value of the investment depends on the discount rate used in the present value calculations, so careful consideration of the appropriate discount rate is essential.

16.3 Make-or-Buy Decisions

- Make-or-buy decisions for a firm's input hinge on the present value of the savings from making the input versus the present value of the necessary investment. The net present value is the basis for decisions about whether to make or buy an input.

- If the net present value of making an input is positive, the firm should manufacture the input. If the net present value is negative, the firm should purchase the input.

16.4 Managerial Application: Present Value and Net Present Value

- The price of a bond equals the present value of the interest payments plus the present value of the principal payment.

- When making a capital budgeting decision, your goal is to accelerate the profits you will receive and delay the costs you will incur. These actions increase the net present value of a project.
- Whenever profits are received and/or costs are incurred at different times, you should use the net present value rule to maximize profit.
- Because the depreciation allowance acts as a tax shield, generally you should select the accounting depreciation method that provides the maximum depreciation allowance as early as possible.

Key Terms and Concepts

Capital budgeting

Discount factor

Discount rate

Future value (FV)

Net present value (NPV)

Present value (PV)

Questions and Problems

16.1 Fundamentals of Present Value

Learning Objective 16.1 Explain the importance of present value calculations to managerial decision making.

1.1 What is the present value of $500,000 received at the end of 20 years at a discount rate of 6 percent?

1.2 What is the present value of $80,000 per year for 10 years at a discount rate of 9 percent? Explain your answer.

1.3 What is the impact of an increase in the discount rate on the discount factor? Explain your answer.

1.4 When the discount rate rises, what happens to the present value of an amount of money you will receive in the future? Why?

1.5 The longer the time until an amount of money will be received, the larger the discount factor. Why?

1.6 Use the discount factors presented in Table 16.1 to answer the following questions:
  a. What is the present value of $1,000 received at the end of four years if the discount rate is 6 percent?
  b. What is the present value of $1,000 received at the end of eight years if the discount rate is 6 percent?
  c. What is the present value of $1,000 received at the end of eight years if the discount rate is 9 percent?

1.7 What is the present value of $10,000 received at the end of the year for the next seven years at a discount rate of 6 percent? Now suppose that the payments are delayed for a year, so that the seven payments will be made at the end of the second year, the third year, and so on until the end of the eighth year. What is the present value of the payments now? Why are your answers different?

1.8 The New York Yankees signed pitcher Masahiro Tanaka to a seven-year contract. Because Mr. Tanaka was under contract in Japan with the Golden Eagles, the Yankees paid them $20 million to release him. Mr. Tanaka's contract calls for payments of $22 million per year for six years and $23 million in year seven. Assuming an 8 percent discount rate and that Mr. Tanaka's salary is paid annually, starting 12 months after the fee paid the Golden Eagles, what is the present value of the Yankees' commitment, including the fee paid to the Golden Eagles, on the signing day of the contract?

1.9 In your role as a manager, you are negotiating a contract with a construction company to build part of a new plant. The construction will take three years and will cost $9 million. Would you prefer a contract that calls for equal payments of $3 million over three years or one that specifies payments of $1 million the first year, $2 million the second year, and $6 million the third year? Do you need to know the interest rate used as your discount rate to answer this question? Why or why not?

16.2 Evaluating Investment Options

Learning Objective 16.2 Describe how salvage values, taxation, debt financing, depreciation, and risk affect capital budgeting.

2.1 You can make an investment that will immediately cost $52,000. If you make the investment, your after-tax operating profit will be $13,000 per year for five years. After the five years, the profit will be zero, and the scrap value also will be zero. You will finance the investment with internally generated funds and receive the profit at the end of each year.

  a. What is the net present value equation for this investment?

  b. If your discount rate is 6 percent, will you make the investment?

  c. If your discount rate is 9 percent, will you make the investment?

  d. Are your answers to parts b and c the same or different? Why?

2.2 Why does including the depreciation allowance as another cost *increase* the net present value of an investment?

2.3 Your company owns a minor league baseball team and is considering building a new stadium. The local governments refuse to help build the stadium, so you must fund it yourself. The stadium will cost $10 million and will have a 20-year life span, after which it will be valueless. It will take a year to build, so you cannot use the stadium until the second year. You are planning to finance it with a loan. The loan will require that you make interest payments of $500,000 at the end of years one through five. At the end of year five, you will also have to make a balloon payment of the $10 million principal. You expect that the operating profit from the new stadium will be $3 million per year from the 2nd year (when the stadium will open) through the 21st year (when it will close). The accounting depreciation allowance will be $1 million per year for the first 10 years, after which it will be zero. Your tax rate is 20 percent of your taxable profit. Your discount rate is 9 percent. What is the net present value of building the stadium?

16.3 Make-or-Buy Decisions

Learning Objective 16.3 Use present value calculations to answer the make-or-buy questions that managers face.

3.1 You are a manager at a firm like Terrapin Ridge Farms, a company that produces dressings, dips, sauces, and jams. One of the jams is strawberry and fig. Currently, your company buys 20,000 pounds of strawberries from local farmers at a price of $1.00 per pound. One local farmer has offered you the chance to buy a strawberry farm for an immediate payment of $25,000. This farm will produce the 20,000 pounds you need. You calculate that if you buy the farm, a pound of strawberries will cost you $0.80. Suppose that your discount rate is 8 percent per year and you plan to retain ownership of the farm for 20 years, at the end of which time you will sell it at a price of $60,000. Assume that whether or not you buy the strawberries or grow them, you pay the costs at the end of the year. Should you recommend that the owners of your firm buy the farm? Why or why not?

3.2 As a manager at AbbVie, a major pharmaceutical company, you work in the division responsible for the best-selling drug Humira. Humira is administered in preloaded syringes. To investigate the sort of calculation you might make, let's explore a hypothetical case. Suppose that AbbVie buys 3 million syringes from other companies each year and pays $2.05 per syringe. Your division is considering producing the syringes internally. Suppose that for an *immediate* expenditure of $2 million to purchase capital equipment, you can produce syringes at a cost of $1.90 per syringe. AbbVie's lawyers and analysts have determined that AbbVie will be able to sell Humira for 12 more years, after which generic drug companies will take over the market and AbbVie's sales will fall to zero. The capital equipment will still be worth $2 million after 12 years. Assume that for each of the 12 years, AbbVie will need 3 million syringes. Also assume that if you buy the syringes, you will pay for them at the end of the year and if you produce them, you will also pay the costs of production at the end of the year. If the discount rate is 9 percent, should you decide to buy the capital equipment and produce the syringes? Why or why not?

3.3 Say that you are manager at a firm like LGI Technology, a lighting company that produces LED lights. Currently, your firm manufactures the LEDs it uses in-house. Technological advances have led to a new type of LED. Your firm can continue to produce the more advanced LEDs by buying new machinery for an immediate payment of $80 million. You determine that this machinery will enable your firm to produce 1 billion LEDs for this year and each of the next four years. After that, a still newer technology will necessitate another type LED and will make the machinery valueless. The machinery will enable your firm to produce LEDs at a cost of $0.10 each. Alternatively, your firm can contract with suppliers to buy the LEDs for $0.12 each. Suppose that if your firm continues to manufacture its LEDs, it will pay the cost at the end of the year and if your firm buys LEDs from outside suppliers, it will pay the suppliers at the end of the year. If you use a discount rate of 6 percent, should your firm continue to produce its own LEDs? Why or why not?

3.4 As a manager at BMW, you are considering leasing a plant to build batteries for your electric-powered BMW i3 vehicle. Suppose that BMW's current cost of batteries is $8,000 per car. You predict sales of 10,000 cars per year for this year and each of the following six years. If BMW leases the plant, you expect that the cost of batteries will be $7,800 per car. Suppose also that leasing the plant requires an immediate up-front lease payment of $10 million but no further payments. At the end of the lease, BMW will turn the plant back to its owners. Assume that BMW will pay the cost of buying the batteries or of manufacturing them at the end of each year.
   a. If you use a discount rate of 6 percent, should BMW lease the plant? Why or why not?
   b. If you use a discount rate of 10 percent, should BMW lease the plant? Why or why not?

16.4 Managerial Application: Present Value and Net Present Value

Learning Objective 16.4 Apply the concepts of present value and the net present value rule to make profit-maximizing managerial decisions.

4.1 Say that you work for a bank that has purchased a bond issued by Verizon. The bond promises to make interest payments of $500 at the end of each year for the next six years. At the end of the sixth year, the bond also pays the $10,000 principal. If the discount rate is 7 percent, what is the present value of this stream of payments?

4.2 You have sold bonds that promise to pay $400 in interest at the end of each year until the end of the year in which the bond matures. At that time you will also pay the $10,000 in principal.
   a. If the bond has 10 more years until it matures and the discount rate is 5 percent, what is the price of the bond? Suppose that the discount rate rises to 9 percent. Now what is the price of the bond? (Hint: You can use Tables 16.1 and 16.3 for the discount factors and annuity factors.) How has the rise in the discount rate affected the price of the bond?
   b. Suppose that the bond has only 5 more years until it matures. If the discount rate is 5 percent, what is the price of the bond? Suppose that the discount rate rises to 9 percent. Now what is the price of the bond? How has the rise in the discount rate affected the price of the bond?
   c. Which bond price reacted more to the rise in the discount rate: the bond with the 10-year life span or the bond with the 5-year life span? Explain the difference in the responses to the change in the discount rate.

4.3 Noting the success of Energizer's long-running advertising campaign featuring a robotic rabbit and AFLAC's campaign showcasing a duck, you decide to combine the two ideas and run a two-year advertising campaign for your company featuring a robotic duck. You forecast that at the end of the first year, you will incur an advertising cost of $100,000 but make no profit. At the end of the second year, you will incur another cost of $100,000, and your advertising will lead to an additional after-tax operating profit of $120,000. At the end of the third year, you will have no further costs, but the lingering effects of your advertising will lead to another after-tax profit of $120,000. There are no further costs or profits, and you are financing the campaign with internally generated funds. If your discount rate is 8 percent, should you undertake the advertising campaign? Why or why not?

4.4 You are the manager of a large printing shop. You have the opportunity to buy a used six-color offset press for $1,000,000. Transporting and installing the press costs another

$1,500,000 and will take a year to accomplish. Once installed, the press will create additional operating profit of $400,000 per year for eight years after taxes and after the depreciation allowance. At the end of eight years, the press will be worth $500,000. You pay the $1,000,000 cost of the press immediately and the $1,500,000 for transportation and installation at the end of year one. The $400,000 in profit is received at the end of year two, year three, and so on until the end of year nine, when the last payment is received and the press's value is $500,000.

a. If the discount rate is 6 percent, should you buy the press? Why or why not?

b. If the discount rate is 10 percent, should you buy the press? Why or why not?

c. If the discount rate is 4 percent, should you buy the press? Why or why not?

4.5 A competitor has infringed your patent, so you are entitled to recover lost profits. You have calculated lost profits of $10 million. The jury, in a burst of common sense, has awarded your company the entire $10 million. The defendant threatens to appeal. The appellate process will take five years. During the appeal, your company will earn post-judgment interest of 6 percent per year. Your firm's discount rate is 9 percent per year. Assume that the probability of winning the appeal is 100 percent, that the costs of the appellate process are zero, and that the annual interest and the eventual payment will be paid at the end of the year. What is the lowest sum that you will take in exchange for the defendant's promise not to appeal? Explain your answer.

4.6 You are deciding whether to send several of your employees to a training session. The cost of the session is $20,000. You estimate that if they receive this training, your firm's after-tax operating profit will increase by $5,000 per year for five years. If your firm's discount rate is 8 percent, should you send the employees to the training session? Why or why not?

4.7 Employee Paul was injured at your plant. Last year Paul had $100,000 in medical expenses (which your firm has already paid). This year and every other year in the future those expenses will increase by 10 percent per year. The medical expenses are all paid at the end of the year. The average salary in Paul's profession last year was $50,000. Because of the accident, Paul earns only 80 percent of that average, so last year he earned only $40,000 (and your firm has already paid his lost 20 percent, or $10,000). Labor economists expect workers in Paul's occupation to experience a 3 percent annual increase in earnings. Paul's lost wages are paid at the end of each year. Assume that Paul has a 10-year work life and a 20-year expected life remaining. Also assume that the appropriate discount rate is 5 percent. Ignoring any tax considerations, what must your company pay Paul to make him whole financially? Explain your answer.

MyLab Economics Auto-Graded Excel Projects

16.1. Riverside Technologies Incorporated (RTI) is a small firm in North Sioux City, SD, that provides IT solutions for other companies. In addition to providing IT services and computer hardware (i.e., laptops, desktops, and tablets), RTI has decided to add customized computer bags for companies as well. Companies can have RTI create computer bags and other accessories with a custom logo.

Suppose that a firm like RTI wants to add embroidery service for their customers. The firm would need to invest in five high-end embroidery machines, which can embroider high-quality graphics that can handle repeated use on backpacks, laptop cases, and tablet covers. These machines will cost $15,000 each and have an expected life of five years. The firm will also need to hire someone to operate the machines at a salary of $40,000 per year plus benefits equal to 25 percent of salary. The firm provides a cost-of-living increase to salary (including benefits) of 3 percent annually.

Suppose that the firm has enough in cash reserves to finance this expansion into a new product line itself; however, the firm could also take out a loan to finance the expansion. If financing the expansion itself, the firm will be giving up 2 percent interest on a CD account. If using a loan to finance the expansion, the firm will pay an interest rate equal to 5.75 percent; assume this interest rate is paid annually on the full amount needed to finance the machines.

Accompanies problem 16.1.

	A	B	C	D	E	F	G	H
23	SELF-FINANCING							
24	CD Interest Rate							
25								
26	Year	Operating Profit	Interest Payment	Depreciation	Taxable Profit	Taxes Paid	Profit After Taxes	Present Value
27	1							
28	2							
29	3							
30	4							
31	5							
32							Present Value of Future Profits	
33							Present Cost of Investment	
34							Net Present Value	
35								
36								
37	DEBT-FINANCING							
38	Loan Interest Rate							
39								
40	Year	Operating Profit	Interest Payment	Depreciation	Taxable Profit	Taxes Paid	Profit After Taxes	Present Value
41	1							
42	2							
43	3							
44	4							
45	5							
46							Present Value of Future Profits	
47							Present Cost of Investment	
48							Net Present Value	
49								

The firm's sales department has assured management it will be able to sell laptop bags, backpacks, or tablet cases to a minimum of 2,500 customers. Each customized item will sell for $50 and will cost $15 to purchase and customize.

a. Using the template, calculate operating profit for both the self-financing scenario and the debt-financing scenario. This analysis should include revenue and costs associated with producing the product, annual salary and benefits of the employee hired to operate the machines, and loan payments where relevant.

b. Next, find costs that can be deducted from profit to lower the tax bill. Assuming a straight-line depreciation, find the annual depreciation allowance for both financing options. For the case where interest is paid, find the amount of interest that can be deducted.

c. Calculate the taxable profit; taxes paid, assuming a 10 percent tax rate; and profit after taxes. Remember that the depreciation allowance is only a cost for the purposes of taxes.

d. Find the present value of profit after taxes for each year using either the CD interest rate or the loan rate as appropriate; add the yearly present values to find the present value of future profits. Subtract from this the cost of the investment; remember you've already included the costs of the loan in your operating profit for the case of debt financing.

e. How should the firm finance this expansion? Explain your reasoning.

16.2. Suppose that you are a consultant for a firm like Yoo, a company building apartments and condominiums worldwide. You are charged with determining the number of floors to include in a proposed structure in Quito, Ecuador. Each floor will have 10 separate living spaces. They will be rented as apartments for the first 10 years, after which they will be sold as condominiums, so that the firm loses ownership of them. Higher floors are more expensive to build but also bring higher rents and higher prices when sold. Each floor costs 10 percent more to build than the floor beneath it, and each floor adds 3 percent to the rent and price of the living space directly beneath it.

The ground floor costs $1,000,000 to construct. A living space on the ground floor will yield $1,000 per month in rent, with operating costs and taxes costing $200 per month for each month it is rented. Assume that a housing shortage in Quito will ensure these living spaces remain full with a waiting list.

	A	B	C	D	E	F	G	H	I	J	K
19											
20	Discount Rate										
21			Floor 1		Floor 2		Floor 3		Floor 4		Floor 5
22	Year	After-Tax Profit	Present Value	After-Tax Profit	Present Value	After-Tax Profit	Present Value	After-Tax Profit	Present Value	After-Tax Profit	Present Value
23	1										
24	2										
25	3										
26	4										
27	5										
28	6										
29	7										
30	8										
31	9										
32	10										
33	Present Value of Future Profits										
34	Present Cost of Investment										
35	Net Present Value										
36											

Suppose that the firm rents the spaces for 10 years, with the profit being received at the end of each year. After the 10 years, the firm can sell each living space on the ground floor for $100,000. The discount rate is 6 percent.

a. Using the template, find the net present value of the first floor. Calculate the after-tax profit of floor 1 for each of the 10 years (remember that the firm will sell the living spaces at the end of the 10th year), and then find the present value of the after-tax profit using the discount rate (see Figure 16.2 for this calculation). Compare the present value of future profits with the cost of the investment in the first floor. What is the net present value of floor 1?

b. Repeat this process for additional floors. Keep in mind that higher floors are more expensive to build but also command higher rents and sale prices at the end of 10 years. What are the net present values of floors 2–5?

c. How many floors should the firm build?

CASE STUDY
Analyzing Predatory Pricing as an Investment

Introduction

In 1911, the U.S. Justice Department charged Standard Oil of New Jersey (now ExxonMobil) with unlawfully monopolizing the petroleum industry. More specifically, Standard Oil allegedly used profits made in its noncompetitive geographic markets to fund below-cost pricing in its competitive markets. After forcing its competitors into bankruptcy, Standard Oil allegedly then raised its price to the monopoly level and earned an economic profit. Standard Oil lost the antitrust case brought against it, and the U.S. Supreme Court's judgment forced the company to break into 34 independent companies.

Standard Oil allegedly was engaged in *predatory pricing*, the use of below-cost pricing to drive competitors out of business in order to boost the price and make an economic profit. Predatory pricing is illegal under Section 2 of the Sherman Act. (See Section 9.2 for a more complete discussion of illegality of predatory pricing.) But even if predatory pricing were legal, it might not be a sensible business strategy because it might not be profitable. This case analyzes the profitability of predatory pricing—*not* because we suggest its use but because it is possible to mount a successful defense against an accusation of predatory pricing by demonstrating that it would not be profitable.

Net Present Value of Predatory Pricing

Managers employing predatory pricing know they will incur losses from their below-cost pricing until they can drive the competitors out of business. Only then are managers able to boost their prices and make an economic profit. The fact that costs are incurred first and profits are gained later makes the business strategy of predatory pricing similar to an investment: The firm incurs costs in one or more periods and makes profits in one or more future periods. So, you can analyze the profitability of predatory pricing using the present value concepts that you learned in this chapter.

To calculate the profitability of predatory pricing, start by calculating the present value of the losses incurred by the predator firm using predatory pricing. Suppose that it takes T periods for the managers to drive the competitors out of business. Each period the managers incur a loss of L_j from their below-cost pricing. The cost of predatory pricing is the present value of the losses.

If the discount rate is i, then the cost of the investment in predatory pricing is equal to

$$PV_{\text{LOSS}} = \sum_{j=1}^{T}\left(\left[\frac{1}{(1+i)^j}\right] \times [L_j]\right)$$

After the T periods it takes the predator to drive the competitors from the market, in period T + 1 the firm successfully monopolizes the market. Economic profits (say, π_j) begin to flow in period T + 1 and continue for some period of time (say, until period N), after which new competitors might enter the market. The present value of these economic profits is

$$PV_{\text{PROFIT}} = \sum_{j=T+1}^{N}\left[\frac{1}{(1+i)^j} \times \pi_j\right]$$

The net present value of predatory pricing equals the present value of the profits (PV_{PROFIT}) minus the present value of the cost of engaging in predatory pricing (PV_{LOSS}):

$$NPV = PV_{\text{PROFIT}} - PV_{\text{LOSS}}$$

For predatory pricing to be profitable, the net present value must be positive; that is, $PV_{\text{PROFIT}} > PV_{\text{LOSS}}$. Indeed, in its 1993 decision in *Brooke Group Ltd. v. Brown & Williamson Tobacco Corp.*, the Supreme Court recognized this logic and introduced the concept of recoupment: The present value of the profits the predatory firm makes must exceed the present value of the losses it incurs. In this decision, the Court said that the plaintiff in a predatory pricing case must demonstrate that the defendant had a reasonable expectation of subsequently recouping its "investment" in the below-cost prices. Such recoupment can occur only if today's low prices lead to a significant increase in future prices as a result of a substantial lessening of competition.

For an example of how these present value formulas can be used, let's examine a case that is famous (at least among economists and lawyers). In the 1986 antitrust case of *Matsushita Electric Industrial Company, Ltd. v. Zenith Radio Corp.*, U.S. television producer Zenith alleged that Japanese television producer Matsushita (producer of Panasonic televisions) engaged in predatory pricing by setting low prices in the United States in an attempt to drive U.S. competitors out of business. Zenith claimed that Matsushita had charged below-cost prices for its televisions for 20 years.

Because you do not know how much Matsushita's managers expected to lose in their initial years, or what they anticipated their economic profits afterward would be, or even how long they thought their losses or profits would last, you cannot directly calculate the net present value from Matsushita's alleged predatory pricing. But you can gain insight into the profitability of the alleged scheme by asking another question: How much economic profit does Matsushita need to make for each annual dollar of economic loss it incurs because of its below-cost pricing? To judge the profitability and hence the likelihood of Matsushita engaging in predatory pricing for 20 years, suppose that

- The discount rate is 7 percent.
- Matsushita's managers believe that after 20 years their scheme will be successful in driving all U.S. producers from the market.
- Matsushita's managers also believe that once the U.S. producers are gone, they will make economic profits for the next 20 years.

With these assumptions, the present value of each dollar of economic loss equals

$$PV_{LOSS} = \sum_{j=1}^{20}\left[\frac{1}{(1.07)^j} \times \$1\right]$$

which, using Excel, gives $PV_{LOSS} = \$10.59$.

For Matsushita's alleged predatory pricing to make economic sense, the net present value must be positive; that is, $PV_{PROFIT} - PV_{LOSS} > 0$. Using this value for PV_{LOSS} shows that PV_{PROFIT} must be greater than \$10.59 for the net present value to be positive. In other words, for each annual dollar of loss, the present value of the profit realized once the competitors are gone must be at least \$10.59. Suppose that Matsushita's economic profit is the same each year. Call the annual economic profit per annual dollar of loss π, so that the present value of the 20-year profit stream starting in year 21 and extending to year 40 is

$$PV_{PROFIT} = \sum_{j=21}^{40}\left[\frac{1}{(1.07)^j} \times \pi\right]$$

For this present value to equal \$10.59, another Excel calculation shows that the annual economic profit, π, must equal \$3.87. So if Matsushita's managers believed it would take 20 years to force their competitors out of the market, to make back the initial loss they must have expected to make at least \$3.87 of economic profit per year for every yearly dollar of economic loss the company incurred.

The *Matsushita* case was decided before the 1983 *Brooke Group* decision, so Zenith Radio Corp. did not need to demonstrate recoupment. Even so, recouping \$3.87 for every dollar of loss seems highly unlikely, so it is also unlikely that Matsushita was actually engaged in predatory pricing. In addition, U.S. producers remained in the market even after 20 years. Essentially, if Matsushita had engaged in predatory pricing, its efforts had failed. Eventually, U.S. producers did leave the market, but a short time later Korean producers entered the market, which gave Matsushita an even shorter period in which to recoup its losses. The brief period of profitability makes predatory pricing even less likely. The courts agreed and found Matsushita not guilty.

Your Decisions

Suppose that the managers of a video game manufacturer (the predator) are considering predatory pricing to drive its competitors from the market even though they know such pricing is illegal. Setting aside for a moment the illegality of predatory pricing (which brings with it the possibility of litigation and the chance of sanctions), suppose that the managers estimate it will take four years for them to drive their competitors out of business and for each of these years the firm will incur an economic loss of \$1 million at the end of the year. Suppose that the predator's managers think that once the competitors are gone, they will make an economic profit of \$1.13 million per year as long as new firms do not enter the market. The managers believe they will make this economic profit at the end of each year for six years but after 6 years new firms will enter the market and the predator's economic profit will then be zero. The firm's discount rate is 8 percent.

1. What is the present value of the firm's economic loss?
2. Ignoring the illegality of the act and possible prosecution, for how many years must the predator earn the economic profit of \$1.13 million to make the predatory pricing profitable?
3. Based on the managers' estimate that they will make the economic profit of \$1.13 million for six years, is the predatory pricing profitable?
4. Suppose that the Department of Justice catches wind of the predator's actions and files suit against the predator. Present several examples of false assertions the predator's managers might make in order to defend themselves against the charge of predatory pricing.

Source: Roger Blair and David Kaserman, *Antitrust Economics*, 2nd ed. (Oxford, UK: Oxford University Press, 2008), https://supreme.justia.com/cases/federal/us/475/574/case.html.

CHAPTER 1
Managerial Economics and Decision Making

1.1 Managerial Economics and Your Career

1.2 **False.** Economic models are simple and abstract in order to clarify the key factors most relevant to the issue at hand. Eliminating the confusing clutter of relatively insignificant details will allow the manager to make better decisions.

1.2 Firms and Their Organizational Structure

2.2 Corporations have a perpetual life. Large firms need a perpetual life so that they will continue operating beyond the death of any one shareholder and instill confidence in lenders. They also need limited liability to attract investors.

1.3 Profit, Accounting Cost, and Opportunity Cost

3.2 The New York Jets are a profit-maximizing firm. It was not profitable for the Jets to "do the right thing," so the Jets' managers did not adjust Mr. Kendall's contract higher. To the extent that "doing the right thing" is inconsistent with profit maximization, Mr. Kendall should not have been surprised.

3.4 Opportunity cost is a better indicator than accounting cost because it considers the return from alternative uses of the firm's resources. Consequently opportunity cost measures the *actual* cost of using resources.

3.6 Explicit costs are costs incurred for which there is a cash outflow from the company. Implicit costs do not involve a cash outflow.
   a. Explicit cost
   b. Explicit cost
   c. Implicit cost
   d. Explicit cost
   e. Explicit cost

3.8 The owners are not taking the opportunity cost of owning their building into account. For instance, it may be more profitable for them to simply rent out their building to their competitor (Kohl's).

3.10 By allocating more shelf space to Post cereals, Safeway loses space to allocate to other products (and the associated profit). The foregone profit that could have been earned on those products is Safeway's opportunity cost.

3.12 The opportunity cost is the next best alternative to farming the land. So we need to determine which alternative is more profitable: renting the farm to another farmer or selling it and investing the proceeds at 6 percent. The money gained from selling the land is $100 \times \$40,000 = \$4,000,000$. Investing this at 6 percent gives an annual return of $0.06 \times \$4,000,000 = \$240,000$. Renting to another farmer gives $100 \times \$2,000 = \$200,000$ per year. Therefore, the opportunity cost of farming the land yourself is the foregone $240,000/year return from selling the land and investing the proceeds at 6 percent.

3.14 a. At $300 per ton, the opportunity cost per day of feeding all the cattle is $\$300 \times 200 = \$60,000$.

   b. The price of barley is $200 per ton, so the total opportunity cost is now $\$200 \times 200 = \$40,000$.

   c. The amount initially paid for the stockpile of barley is a sunk cost. Whether the feed is bought at the current market price or drawn from the stockpile, the opportunity cost is the same because the next best alternative to using the stored barley to feed the cattle is selling it at the market price. Consequently, when the price of barley changes, so, too, does the opportunity cost of feeding the cattle.

1.4 Marginal Analysis

4.2 The marginal benefit is now higher than the marginal cost of advertisement. The marginal analysis rule tells us it is optimal to do an action if the marginal benefit exceeds the marginal cost. With the increase in marginal benefit, more advertisements are optimal, so we should increase the marketing budget until the marginal benefit equals the marginal cost.

CHAPTER 2
Demand and Supply

2.1 Demand

1.2 The description of iceberg lettuce as an inferior good is incorrect in economic terms. In economic terms, an inferior good is not necessarily a low-quality good. Rather, it is a good for which demand decreases as consumer income increases.

1.4 a. The demand for jeans decreases so the demand curve shifts to the left.

b. There will be a downward movement along the demand curve for jeans, resulting in an increase in the quantity demanded.

c. The demand for jeans increases so the demand curve shifts to the right.

d. The demand for jeans decreases so the demand curve shifts to the left.

2.2 Supply

2.2 An increase in the price of cheese is an increase in the cost of producing pizza. This change decreases the supply of pizza and shifts the supply curve to the left.

2.4 a. The supply of jeans decreases so the supply curve shifts to the left.

b. The supply of jeans increases so the supply curve shifts to the right.

c. There will be an upward movement along the supply curve, resulting in an increase in the quantity supplied.

d. The supply of jeans increases so the supply curve shifts to the right.

2.3 Market Equilibrium

3.2 If the price is less than the equilibrium price, there will be a shortage of the product. Whenever the product is offered for sale, it rapidly sells out. Managers find it hard to keep the product in inventory, so they respond by raising the price. As the price rises, the quantity demanded decreases and the quantity supplied increases, both of which help reduce the amount of the shortage. The price continues to rise until it reaches the equilibrium price, at which point the shortage is eliminated and the price stops rising.

3.4 In equilibrium, the quantity supplied is equal to the quantity demanded ($Q^s = Q^d$). Substituting the equations for Q^s and Q^d gives $100 + 2P = 1,000 - 10P$. Solving this equation for price gives

$$100 + 2P = 1,000 - 10P$$
$$12P = 900$$
$$P = \$75$$

Substitute the equilibrium price of $75 into either the demand or the supply function to get the equilibrium quantity. Using the supply function gives

$$Q = 100 + (2 \times 75) = 250$$

The figure shows the demand and supply curves that result from the demand and supply functions in the problem. In the figure, the equilibrium price is $75, and the equilibrium quantity is 250, exactly as calculated using the algebraic functions.

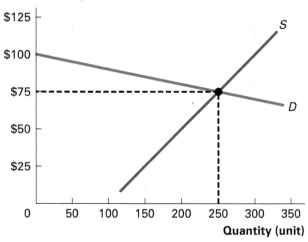

Price (dollars per unit)

2.4 Competition and Society

4.2 By producing the efficient quantity, competitive markets maximize social gains. When a competitive market produces the equilibrium quantity, each of the units up to the equilibrium quantity has a marginal social benefit that exceeds its marginal social cost. Consequently, producing and consuming each of these units results in a gain for society or, phrased differently, results in increasing society's surplus of benefit over cost. By producing the equilibrium quantity, all of the units for which the marginal social benefit exceeds the marginal social cost are produced and consumed so a competitive market maximizes the social gains or, again phrased differently, maximizes society's total surplus of benefit over cost.

2.5 Changes in Market Equilibrium

5.2 If more people favor wearing jeans, the demand curve for jeans shifts to the right. The supply curve does not shift. If the number of jean producers decreases, the supply curve for jeans shifts to the left. The demand curve does not shift.

5.4 A bountiful peanut harvest lowers the price of peanuts. Because peanuts are an input used to produce

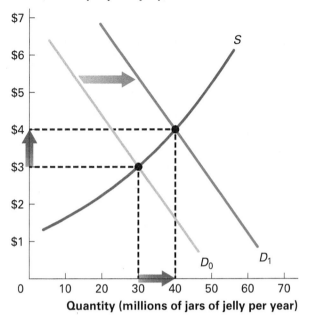

Price (dollars per jar of jelly)

Quantity (millions of jars of jelly per year)

Cowhide and beef are complements in production, so the supply of cowhide decreases and the supply curve of cowhide shifts to the left. This change increases the equilibrium price and decreases the equilibrium quantity of cowhide. Cowhide is used to produce baseball gloves, so the increase in price is an increase in cost for producers of baseball gloves. The increase in cost decreases the supply of baseball gloves, and the supply curve for baseball gloves shifts to the left. Therefore, as the figure illustrates, the equilibrium price of a baseball glove rises, and the equilibrium quantity of baseball gloves falls.

5.8   The increase in income increases the demand for new homes, and the demand curve shifts to the right. The higher price of plywood increases the cost of building new homes, so the supply decreases and the supply curve shifts to the left. These changes are illustrated in the figures. In the first figure, the increase in demand exceeds the decrease in supply;

peanut butter, the lower price reduces the cost of producing peanut butter. The fall in cost increases the supply of peanut butter, resulting in a lower price for peanut butter. The fall in the price of the complement good, peanut butter, increases the demand for jelly, so the demand curve for jelly shifts to the right. The figure shows that the result is a higher equilibrium price and equilibrium quantity of jelly.

5.6   Because mad cow disease decreases the demand for beef, the equilibrium price and quantity of beef fall.

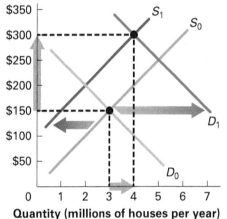

Price (thousands of dollars per house)

Quantity (millions of houses per year)

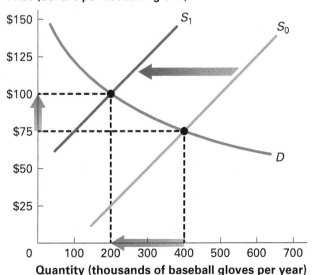

Price (dollars per baseball glove)

Quantity (thousands of baseball gloves per year)

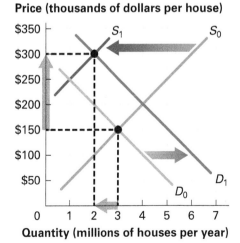

Price (thousands of dollars per house)

Quantity (millions of houses per year)

in the second figure, the sizes of the shifts are reversed. The figures show that the equilibrium price unambiguously rises, to $300,000 per house in both figures. But the effect on the equilibrium quantity is ambiguous. In the first figure, the quantity increases to 4 million houses, but in the second figure, the quantity decreases to 2 million homes.

5.10 a. The higher minimum wage increases firms' costs. Consequently the supply decreases and the supply curve shifts to the left. The equilibrium price rises and the equilibrium quantity decreases.

b. Consumer surplus will decrease. The price rises, which decreases the consumer surplus. Additionally, consumers respond to the higher price by decreasing the quantity they demand, so they consume less of the product, which also decreases the consumer surplus. Diagrammatically, the size of the consumer surplus triangle before the increase in cost is larger than the size after the increase in cost.

2.6 Price Controls

6.2 The minimum wage affects lower-skilled labor more than any other group. Teenagers are generally lower skilled, in part because they have the least work experience. Consequently, they are the age group with the highest proportion of workers earning minimum wage. An increase in the minimum wage causes firms to decrease the quantity of lower-skilled labor they demand. Because teenagers have the least work experience and so are generally the least skilled, they experience the majority of the layoffs and have the hardest time finding new jobs.

2.7 Managerial Application: Using The Demand and Supply Model

7.2 Cereal producers use corn in the production of cereal. An increase in the price of corn increases the costs of cereal producers (including Kellogg's), shifting the supply curve for cereal leftward. At the same time, increasing consumer incomes increase the demand for name-brand cereal and shift the demand curve for name-brand cereal to the right. The figures below show how these changes affect the market for name-brand cereal. They differ because in the first figure the shift in the demand curve exceeds that in the supply curve, while in the second figure the magnitudes of the shifts are reversed. The price rises in both figures, so it is unambiguous that the price of name-brand cereal rises. The effect on the quantity, however, is ambiguous. The first figure shows that it increases if the change in demand is larger, but the second figure shows that it decreases if the change in supply is larger.

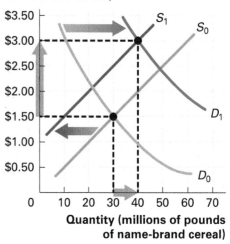

Price (dollars per pound of name-brand cereal)

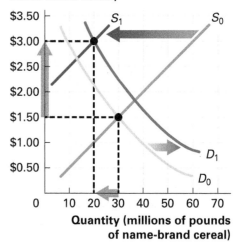

Price (dollars per pound of name-brand cereal)

7.4 Demographic information helps breweries forecast demand for their product. For example, the demand for beer will be higher in a region with a larger number of young adult males. Using supply and demand analysis, the brewery executives should expect higher-than-average quantity and price in these areas.

7.6 The demand for scientific cat food decreases, so the demand curve shifts to the left. The result is a fall in both the equilibrium quantity and the equilibrium price. Top management could shift production toward natural cat foods and use marketing that emphasizes the natural aspects of their products. They might also consider rebranding their cat food with a name that emphasizes its natural attributes.

CHAPTER **3**
Measuring and Using Demand

3.1 Regression: Estimating Demand

1.2 The random error term is included to capture any residual variation that is not explained by the independent variable(s).

3.2 Intrepreting the Results of Regression Analysis

2.2 The R^2 statistic measures how much variation in the observed dependent variable is explained by the predicted values of the regression. It is important because it is a measure of the goodness-of-fit, since it shows how close the predicted values are to the actual data.

3.3 Limitations of Regression Analysis

3.2 This procedure is not correct. The analyst should try other functional forms and compare them to the results of the log-linear regression.

3.4 Elasticity

4.2

	Elasticity	Percentage Change in Price	Percentage Change in Quantity Demanded
a.	1.5	8 percent	12 percent
b.	1.4	6 percent	8.4 percent
c.	0.6	6 percent	3.6 percent
d.	1.2	5 percent	6 percent
e.	0.4	15 percent	6 percent

4.4 The quantity demanded is $Q^d = 2{,}000 - (20 \times \$60) = 800$. So the price elasticity equals $\varepsilon = |b \times (P/Q^d)| = |{-}20 \times (\$60/800)| = 1.50$.

4.6 The demand function is log-linear, so the price elasticity of demand is 2.0, the coefficient of price.

4.8 a. Raise the price.
  b. Lower the price.
  c. Total revenue does not change for a price hike or a price cut.

4.10 Broiler chicken is a broader category than your brand of chicken. Although the demand for broiler chicken is inelastic at 0.5, so that an in crease in price for all broiler chickens will raise the total revenue of all firms taken together, the demand for your brand of chicken will be higher—perhaps greater than 1.0. In that case, a price increase would actually *decrease* your revenue.

4.12 The income elasticity is positive and a little less than 1.0. This means the quantity demanded will increase, but it will increase a little less than income. Therefore, the fraction of income spent on clothing and footwear will get a little smaller.

3.5 Managerial Application: Use of Regression Analysis and Elasticity

5.2 The income elasticity of demand is defined as ε_{INC} = (Percentage change in Q^d)/(Percentage change in INCOME). Rearranging this equation shows that $\varepsilon_{INC} \times$ (Percentage change in INCOME) = (Percentage change in Q^d). Consequently, (Percentage change in Q^d) = 1.9×3.8 percent = 7.22 percent. In other words, the demand for General Motors' cars will increase by 7.22 percent.

5.4 The price elasticity of demand is $\varepsilon = |$(Percentage change in Q^d)/(Percentage change in P)$|$, so rearranging the definition shows that (Percentage change in Q^d)/ε = (Percentage change in P). In the equilibrium, the quantity demanded equals the equilibrium quantity, so (Percentage change in P) = 10 percent/0.4 = 25 percent. The price of natural gas will fall by 25 percent.

5.6 a. The estimated demand function is

$$Q^d = 200.18 - 5.02P$$
$$(4.68) \quad (0.26)$$

where the standard errors are in parentheses below the estimated coefficients. As expected, the coefficient for price is negative and statistically significant. The R^2 value is 0.90, indicating a very good fit.

  b. The quantities demanded and the price elasticities calculated using the estimated demand function from part a are in the table below. The price elasticity of demand is calculated using the equation $\varepsilon = |b \times (P/Q^d)|$. The price elasticity increases as price increases. Demand is elastic for prices above $20, inelastic for prices below $20, and unit elastic at approximately $20.

Price (dollars)	Quantity Demanded	Price Elasticity of Demand
$10	150.0	0.33
15	124.9	0.60
20	99.8	1.01
25	74.7	1.68
30	49.6	3.04

CHAPTER 4
Production and Costs

4.1 Production

1.2 You should expect the marginal product of labor to initially be increasing, then decreasing, and then negative.

1.4 Technological improvement increases the productivity of all inputs. It will affect the marginal product of capital in the same way as it does the marginal product of labor—for any quantity of capital, the marginal product of capital curve shifts upward.

4.2 Cost Minimization

2.2 Let MP_{HS} be the marginal product of high-skilled labor, W_{HS} be the wage rate for high-skilled labor, MP_{LS} be the marginal product of low-skilled labor, and W_{LS} be the wage rate of low-skilled labor. Then the cost-minimization rule for these inputs is $\frac{MP_{HS}}{W_{HS}} = \frac{MP_{LS}}{W_{LS}}$. Now see if this is true for this firm under current conditions.

$$\frac{MP_{HS}}{W_{HS}} = \frac{60}{40} = 1.5 \text{ units per hour}$$

$$\frac{MP_{LS}}{W_{LS}} = \frac{15}{15} = 1 \text{ unit per hour}$$

$$\text{So} \frac{MP_{HS}}{W_{HS}} > \frac{MP_{LS}}{W_{LS}}$$

Therefore, the firm is not minimizing its cost. It can lower cost by using more high-skilled labor and less low skilled labor. For example, spending $2 more on high-skilled labor increases production by $2 × 1.5 = 3.0 units while spending $3 less on low-skilled labor decreases production by $3 × 1 = 3.0 units, thereby leaving the output the same but lowering the cost.

2.4 The ratio of marginal product to price for veterinarians is $\frac{20}{300} = \frac{1}{15}$ so that changing spending on veterinarians by $1 changes the number of cases seen per day by $\frac{1}{15}$ of a case. For assistants, it is $\frac{10}{100} = \frac{1}{10}$, and for technicians, it is $\frac{15}{150} = \frac{1}{10}$ so that changing spending on veterinary assistants or technicians by $1 changes the number of cases seen per day by $\frac{1}{10}$. Your hospitals are not minimizing cost because $\frac{1}{10} = \frac{1}{10} > \frac{1}{15}$. You should spend more on assistants and technicians by hiring more but spend less on veterinarians by letting some go.

2.6 You should ignore X_3 because the quantity of that input is fixed. Instead, use the cost-minimization rule for inputs X_1 and X_2 only. Call MP_{X1} the marginal product of X_1, P_{X1} the cost of X_1, MP_{X2} the marginal product of X_2, and P_{X2} the cost of X_2. Then minimizing cost requires you to employ enough X_1 and X_2 to produce your desired amount of output and such that $\frac{MP_{X1}}{P_{X1}} = \frac{MP_{X2}}{P_{X2}}$.

4.3 Short-Run Cost

3.2 The short-run average total cost curve is U-shaped because of the relationship between marginal cost and average cost. When marginal cost is below average total cost, the average decreases. When marginal cost is above average total cost, the average increases. For the first units produced, marginal cost is typically less than average total cost, so the average total cost initially falls. As more units are produced and marginal cost starts to increase, average total cost *still* falls until it reaches its minimum when it intersects the marginal cost curve. Thereafter, the average total cost rises because the marginal cost exceeds average total cost. This results in a U-shaped average total cost curve.

3.4 If the marginal product of a variable input decreases as more of the input is used, each additional unit of output requires more of this input. Because more of the input must be purchased, the cost of an additional unit of output increases. Therefore, the marginal cost curve slopes upward, showing that the marginal cost of additional units of output increases.

3.6 Wages are a variable cost and so part of the firm's total cost. An increase in the minimum wage increases the variable and total cost of quick-service restaurants. Consequently, the average variable cost curve and average total cost curve both shift upward. The marginal cost curve also shifts upward because with the higher wage rate, the additional cost of producing another burger by hiring an additional worker increases. The restaurant's average fixed cost curve, however, does not change because the fixed costs have not changed.

3.8 The executives of Energizer Holdings must have concluded that there are diseconomies of scope when producing such different products. The total cost of producing these two categories of goods would then be higher if they are all produced by the same firm. Splitting into two firms eliminates this problem and reduces costs.

Labor, L	Capital, K	Output, Q	Average Total Cost, ATC	Capital, K	Output, Q	Average Total Cost, ATC	Capital, K	Output, Q	Average Total Cost, ATC
0	2	0	X	3	0	X	4	0	X
1	2	100	$22.00	3	160	$20.00	4	210	$20.00
2	2	800	3.00	3	1,200	2.83	4	1,350	3.26
3	2	1,300	2.00	3	1,800	2.00	4	2,200	2.09
4	2	1,475	1.90	3	2,100	1.81	4	2,600	1.85
5	2	1,500	2.00	3	2,200	1.82	4	2,700	1.85
6	2	1,510	2.12	3	2,220	1.89	4	2,710	1.92

4.4 Long-Run Cost

4.2 a. See the table.

b. You should use 2 units of capital. This amount of capital minimizes your average total cost according to the table ($2.00 at 1,300 units of output).

c. You should use 3 units of capital. This amount of capital minimizes your average total cost according to the table ($1.81 at 2,100 units of output).

d. For 0 to approximately 1,500 units of production, you should use 2 units of capital. This minimizes your average total cost according to the table.

4.4 Because your company is producing in the range with constant returns to scale, no matter how you increase your output—by using more labor, using more capital, or using more labor and more capital—your average cost is constant. You are already producing at the minimum long-run average cost, so you cannot further lower it.

4.5 Managerial Application: Using Production and Cost Theory

5.2 a. First, calculate how many additional architect-hours are needed. Currently, the firm has $8 \times 40 = 320$ architect-hours available per week. This amount leaves a gap of 80 hours per week. Next, compute the overtime wages. The architects currently earn $= \$12.50$ per hour. Their overtime wage rate is $\$12.50 \times 1.5 = \$18.75$. Finally, compute the total overtime wages paid for the project: $\$18.75 \times 80$ hours $\times 20$ weeks $= \$30,000$.

b. The firm needs two architects working 40-hour weeks to fill the gap for this project.

c. The manager of the firm should hire the new architects. The fixed cost to hire the additional architects is $2 \times \$2,000 = \$4,000$. Their wages over the course of the project are $\$500 \times 20$ weeks $\times 2$ architects $= \$20,000$. The total cost of hiring additional architects is $24,000, a $6,000 savings over paying overtime to the existing workforce.

5.4 The cost-minimization rule is satisfied by hiring two more Assistant Public Defenders, one more Senior Assistant Public Defender, and one more Special Assistant Public Defender:

$$\frac{120}{\$6,000} = \frac{200}{\$10,000} = \frac{240}{\$12,000}$$

This combination of new employees covers exactly an additional 700 cases per month.

CHAPTER 5
Perfect Competition

5.1 Characteristics of Competitive Markets

1.2 In perfectly competitive markets, buyers have perfect information about the price and the product. Advertising will not provide any new information to consumers or change their behavior. Furthermore, the firms all produce identical products, so there is no value in claiming your product is superior to those produced by your competitors.

1.4 There are many correct answers. Common examples include utilities and telecoms (legal barriers and cost advantage after entry) and firms that derive a cost advantage from patent-protected technology, copyrights, or trade secrets.

5.2 Short-Run Profit Maximization in Competitive Markets

2.2 The market demand curve is downward sloping, while the demand curve faced by a perfectly competitive firm is horizontal at the equilibrium market price. The firm's demand curve is horizontal at the market price because a perfectly competitive firm is a price taker—it is too small to have any effect on price.

2.4 Marginal cost is the change in total cost from a change in output. In terms of an equation, the marginal cost is $MC = \frac{\Delta TC}{\Delta q}$.

2.6 To maximize profit, marginal analysis demonstrates that you need to produce the quantity where $MR = MC$. The marginal cost of tending one more yard is $25, and the marginal revenue is the price ($40). $MR > MC$, so increasing output will increase your profit.

2.8 The price is $50, which means the marginal revenue is $50. The profit-maximizing quantity of sugar beets is the quantity that sets $MR = MC$. From the table, total cost increases by $50 when producing the 5,002nd ton, so the marginal cost for this ton is $50. Consequently, the profit-maximizing quantity is 5,002 tons. Sproule Farms' economic profit is

$$\text{Economic profit} = (P - ATC) \times q = (P \times q) - TC$$
$$= (\$50 \times 5,002) - \$235,600 = \$14,500$$

2.10 The profit-maximizing price is $60 because a perfectly competitive firm is a price taker. The profit-maximizing quantity is found where $MR = MC$. Because $P = MR$ for a perfectly competitive firm, profit is maximized at the quantity where $MR = MC = \$60$. Using the formula for MC, the profit-maximizing quantity is

$$\$60 = 10 + 0.25q$$
$$q = 200$$

2.12 It is not possible for the firm's economic profit to decrease as long as the firm produces the profit-maximizing quantity (where $MR = MC$). The firm will always produce a quantity that lies on the marginal cost curve. For any point on the marginal cost curve above average total cost, the firm earns an economic profit that increases as price increases. If the firm initially has an economic loss, it is producing at a point on its marginal cost curve but below the average total cost. So, in this case, as the price rises, the firm moves up along its marginal cost curve, and its economic loss decreases.

2.14 The decision to remain open or close hinges on a comparison between the total revenue and the total variable cost or, equivalently, between the price (P) and the average variable cost (AVC). So the dairy farm should remain open if $P > AVC$ and should close if $P < AVC$. All costs become variable in the long run. As more costs become variable, the total variable cost and hence the average variable cost increase. So if you are open in the short run, eventually the price will become less than the average variable cost, $P < AVC$. At this moment, you should shut down.

2.16 The marginal revenue is the market price ($6) for a perfectly competitive firm ($MR = \$6$). Now we need the marginal cost. From the table, producing the 100,005th bushel adds $6 to the total cost, so the marginal cost of this bushel is $6 ($MC = \$6$). Consequently, 100,005 bushels is the profit-maximizing quantity because this is the quantity where marginal revenue and marginal cost are equal. Therefore, it is profit maximizing to produce 100,005 bushels of wheat.

5.3 Long-Run Profit Maximization in Competitive Markets

3.2 Perfectly competitive firms earn a competitive return (zero economic profit) in the long run. This result occurs because firms will exit when incurring an economic loss (thereby raising the price and eventually eliminating the economic loss) and will enter when other firms are making an economic profit (thereby lowering the price and eventually eliminating the economic profit).

3.4 In the figure, the initial market demand curve is D_0, so the firm's initial demand and marginal revenue curve is $d_0 = MR_0$. An increase in the market demand raises the market price, shifting the demand curve facing an individual firm upward. In the short run, a typical firm will make an economic profit. In the figure, the increase in market demand shifts the market demand curve from D_0 to D_1 and raises the price from $400 per ton of paper to $600. The firm's demand curve shifts from $d_0 = MR_0$ to $d_1 = MR_1$. Before the increase in market demand, the firm was producing 6 tons of paper per month and making only a competitive return (zero economic profit). After the increase in demand, the firm produces 8 tons of paper and makes an economic profit because $P > ATC$. In the long run, entry by new firms increases the market supply and shifts the market supply curve to the right. This lowers the market price back to the minimum of the long-run average cost curve, $400 per ton in the figure, and a typical firm will once again make only a competitive return.

3.6 a. The fall in the price of flour shifts your marginal cost curve downward. You should increase your production until $MR = MC$ to maximize your profits.

b. Economic profits in the bagel industry will entice new firms to enter the market. The market supply curve will shift rightward until the equilibrium price is the minimum of the firms' new long-run average cost.

c. You should plan for the price to fall as new firms enter the market. Be cautious about increasing the scale of your production because the price eventually will fall due to entry by new firms.

Accompanies problem 3.4.

**Price (dollars per
ton of paper)**

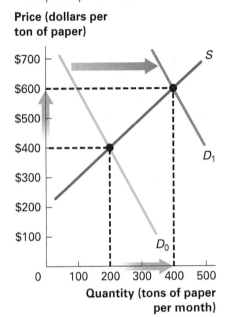

**Price and cost (dollars
per ton of paper)**

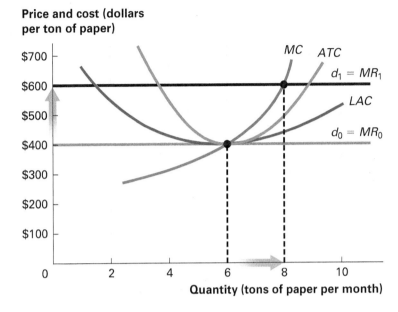

5.4 Managerial Application: Perfect Competition

4.2 If the market price of your product increases, it is tempting to believe this good fortune will last forever. However, this price change will be only temporary. Increasing your scale of production in the face of a temporary price increase may result in economic losses. Even if the price increase is the result of a permanent increase in demand, other firms will enter the market, which will reduce the market price. As a manager of a perfectly competitive firm, you must be careful not to overexpand in response to a price increase. If you do, once the price falls you may find yourself incurring an economic loss.

CHAPTER 6
Monopoly and Monopolistic Competition

6.1 A Monopoly Market

1.2 No, Kellogg's is not a monopolist because there are many close substitutes for Kellogg's Corn Flakes. The barriers to entry into the market for cereal are not insurmountable either. Kellogg's meets only one requirement to be a monopolist: It is the only seller of Kellogg's Corn Flakes.

1.4 The completed table is shown. The demand curve and marginal revenue curve, in the figure, share a vertical intercept at $42. The demand curve's slope is −1, while the marginal revenue curve's slope is twice that at −2.

Price, P	Quantity, Q	Marginal revenue, MR
$30	12	
		$17
29	13	
		15
28	14	
		13
27	15	
		11
26	16	
		9
25	17	
		7
24	18	
		5
23	19	
		3
22	20	
		1
21	21	
		−1
20	22	
		−3
19	23	

Accompanies problem 1.4.

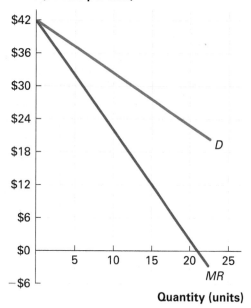

Price (dollars per unit)

b. From the table in the text, the marginal revenue curve has a slope of −1. This slope is double the demand curve's slope, which must therefore be $-\frac{1}{2}$. Extending the *MR* curve to the vertical axis shows that the vertical intercept is $21. Because the demand curve will be linear with the same vertical intercept as the *MR* curve, the demand equation is $P = 21 - \frac{1}{2}Q$. Using the profit-maximizing quantity, 14, in this equation (or using the figure) shows that the profit-maximizing price is $14.

Price (dollars per unit)

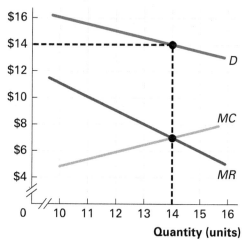

Quantity (units)

1.6 Marginal revenue is defined as the change in total revenue for a given change in output. This term becomes negative when the gain in revenue from increased output is smaller than the loss in revenue from lowering the price on all the initial units of output.

6.2 Monopoly Profit Maximization

2.2 The statement is correct. We can see this by examining the equation for marginal revenue as a function of the firm's price elasticity of demand:

$$MR = P \times \left(1 - \frac{1}{\varepsilon}\right)$$

When demand is inelastic ($\varepsilon < 1$), $\frac{1}{\varepsilon}$ is greater than 1.0, so the marginal revenue is negative. Producing units of output on the inelastic portion of the demand curve always yields a net loss because these units increase the total cost while reducing the total revenue. Therefore, the monopolist will produce on the elastic portion of the demand curve for its product. However, there is a special case: If the monopolist has zero marginal cost, the profit-maximizing quantity will be on the unit-elastic ($\varepsilon = 1$) portion of the demand curve.

2.4 a. The profit-maximizing quantity is found by setting marginal revenue equal to marginal cost. This occurs when the firm produces 14 units.

2.6 a. Profit is maximized when marginal revenue equals marginal cost. From the diagram, $MR = MC$ when output is 60 million chips per month. At this quantity of output, the demand curve shows that the profit-maximizing price is $6.

b. At 60 million chips per month, the average total cost is $2. Then the firm's economic profit is

$$(P - ATC) \times Q = (6 - 2) \times 60 \text{ million} = \$240 \text{ million}$$

c. The current economic profit will continue as long as the memory chip is protected by patent. If the patent expires, an insurmountable barrier to entry would no longer protect the firm. Entry by competitors would eliminate the firm's profits in the long run.

2.8 See the figure. The marginal revenue curve has the same vertical intercept as the demand curve and a slope that is twice that of the demand curve. The *MR* and *MC* curves intersect at 12 units, the profit-maximizing quantity. The associated price found on the demand curve is $26. Your firm's profit is $(P - ATC) \times Q = (26 - 2) \times 12 = \$288$.

Accompanies problem 2.8.

Price (dollars per unit)

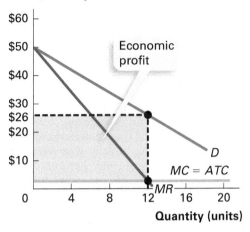

2.10 a.   The new lower wage rate means the firm's costs are lower at every level of output. This means the firm's marginal cost curve shifts downward. The marginal revenue curve does not change.

b.   After the marginal cost curve shifts downward, the new intersection of the marginal revenue and marginal cost curves is farther to the right. So the profit-maximizing quantity is larger after the wage rate falls. The price associated with this quantity is lower.

2.12 The assertion is true. Monopolies maximize their profit by producing where $MR = MC$. For a monopoly, $P > MR$. Combining these two points shows that $P > MC$.

2.14 a.   The firm's economic profit is: $(P - ATC) \times Q = (10 - 7.50) \times 300 = \$750$.

b.   If the firm's managers change its price and output, profits will fall. We know this because the profit found in part (a) used the profit-maximizing price and output. Any other choices of price and output will result in lower economic profits.

2.16 If a new drug is not patented and the discoverer attempts to keep its formula trade secret, a rival company could discover the formula. Maintaining an economic profit with a trade secret in this industry is not possible because rival firms can simply create their own close substitutes or identical drugs. A trade secret then is not an insurmountable barrier to entry. Pharmaceutical companies are better off using patents.

2.18 a.   The minimum efficient scale is 35 billion kilowatt hours per year.

b.   The profit-maximizing quantity occurs where the MR and LMC curves intersect. The figure in the text shows this quantity is 20 billion kilowatt hours. The price associated with this quantity is 12¢. The average cost at this quantity is 8¢. Therefore, the economic profit is $(P - ATC) \times Q = (0.12 - 0.08) \times 20$ billion $= \$800$ million.

c.   The new entrant produces 0.25×20 billion $= 5$ billion kilowatt hours. The entrant's average cost is 14¢ at this quantity. The entrant will incur an economic loss because your firm's price is lower than the entrant's average cost.

6.3 Dominant Firm

3.2 a.   First, subtract the imports from the market demand curve to derive the residual demand facing Alcoa. Next, derive the residual marginal revenue curve from the residual demand curve. Then find the profit-maximizing quantity from the intersection of the marginal cost and residual marginal revenue curves. Finally, find the profit-maximizing price from the point on the residual demand curve associated with the profit-maximizing quantity.

b.   A government ban on imports would give Alcoa a monopoly. Now the demand curve facing Alcoa is the entire market demand curve. Alcoa's managers use the market marginal revenue curve, MR, and produce the quantity that sets $MR = MC$. They find the profit-maximizing price from the market demand curve associated with this quantity.

3.4 a.   To calculate the price elasticities of demand, use Equation 3.4 from Chapter 3, $\varepsilon = |b \times (P/Q^d)|$ in which b is the change in the quantity demanded resulting from a change in the price, $b = (\Delta Q^d / \Delta P)$. For the market demand, $b = -2$ and for the residual demand, $b = -6$. Using these values for b, the table shows the price elasticities of demand.

Price (dollars per unit)	Market Demand (units)	Price Elasticity of Demand for Market Demand	Competitive Supply (units)	Residual Demand (units)	Price Elasticity of Demand for Residual Demand
50	70	1.43	50	20	15.0
45	80	1.13	30	50	5.4
40	90	0.89	10	80	3.0

b.   The price elasticity of demand is much higher for the residual demand than for the market demand.

3.6 The competitive fringe reduces the profit of the dominant firm because the competitive fringe limits the dominant firm's ability to control total output. As the dominant firm restricts its output in an effort to increase price, the competitive fringe expands its output in order to increase its own profit. In addition, the dominant firm's markup becomes smaller as the competitive fringe becomes larger, which also reduces the dominant firm's economic profit.

6.4 Monopolistic Competition

4.2 The marginal cost of producing a washing machine is less than its marginal revenue. A monopolistically competitive firm maximizes profits by producing the quantity where marginal revenue is equal to marginal cost. Whirlpool's managers should increase its output of washing machines until marginal revenue is equal to marginal cost. They then should lower the price to the highest possible level at which the profit-maximizing quantity is sold.

4.4 The profit-maximizing quantity is the amount that sets $MR = MC$. To determine this quantity, first rearrange the terms of the demand equation to obtain the inverse demand function, which gives P as a function of Q:

$$Q = 300 - 10P$$
$$10P = 300 - Q$$
$$P = 30 - \frac{Q}{10}.$$

Now, because the demand curve is linear, double the slope to get the marginal revenue equation: $MR = 30 - \frac{Q}{5}$. Next, set marginal revenue equal to marginal cost, and solve for the profit-maximizing quantity:

$$30 - \frac{Q}{5} = 10$$
$$Q = 100$$

Finally, substitute this quantity into the demand equation to obtain the profit-maximizing price:

$$P = 30 - \frac{(100)}{10}$$
$$P = \$20$$

6.5 Managerial Application: The Monopoly, Dominant Firm, and Monopolistic Competition Models

5.2 Use the markup equation to find the profit-maximizing price from the marginal cost and the price elasticity of demand:

$$P = MC \times \left(\frac{\varepsilon}{\varepsilon - 1}\right)$$
$$P = \$30 \times \frac{2}{2 - 1} = \$60$$

When the price elasticity of demand is lowered to 1.8 through advertising, then

$$P = MC \times \left(\frac{\varepsilon}{\varepsilon - 1}\right)$$
$$P = \$30 \times \frac{1.8}{1.8 - 1} = \$67.50$$

5.4 Your company's advertising allows you to increase the price you charge and the quantity you produce. In the figure, the advertising shifts the demand curve from D_0 to D_1 and the marginal revenue curve from MR_0 to MR_1. Initially, your company produces 150 million cups of coffee per week and sells them for $2.50 per cup. After the advertising, your company increases its production to 200 million cups per week and raises its price to $4.00 per cup.

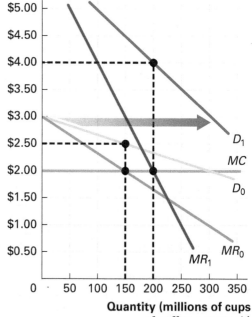

Price and cost (dollars per cup of coffee)

CHAPTER 7
Cartels and Oligopoly

7.1 Cartels

1.2 a. Each firm maximize its profits by producing the quantity that sets $MR = MC$. When the market is competitive, each firm faces a horizontal demand curve at the equilibrium price, so $P = MR$. Combining these two conditions shows that the price of the product is given by

$P = MC = \$40$. Substitute this price into the demand equation, and solve for the quantity:

$$800 - 2Q = 40$$
$$-2Q = -760$$
$$Q = 380$$

Each firm makes zero economic profit because $P = ATC = \$40$, so the combined economic profit of all the firms is also zero.

b. When the firms form a price-fixing cartel that maximizes the cartel's profit, they produce the quantity that sets $MR = MC$:

$$800 - 4Q = 40$$
$$-4Q = -760$$
$$Q = 190$$

Substitute this quantity into the demand equation, and solve for the price:

$$P = 800 - (2 \times 190) = \$420$$

The cartel's total economic profit equals $(P - ATC) \times Q$, or

Economic profit $= (P - ATC) \times Q = (\$420 - \$40) \times 190$
$$= \$72,200$$

c. The firm makes $420 of additional revenue from selling one additional unit. The cost of producing this additional unit is $40. The cheater makes an additional $380 in economic profit.

1.4 The trade association might be helping to sustain an illegal cartel by reporting its members' prices. Reporting prices would facilitate collusion by reassuring all cartel members that no one is cheating on their agreement.

7.2 Tacit Collusion

2.2 By preannouncing their prices, these firms are able to signal other managers about any price changes in advance. This action promotes collusion by reducing uncertainty among managers about the tacitly agreed-on price. Making prices public also helps to detect cheating on any tacit (or, illegal explicit) agreement about what price to charge.

2.4 A firm is more likely to be the price leader if it can use either its size or its cost advantage to credibly threaten a price war. Saudi Arabia is both one of the largest and the lowest-cost producers in OPEC, so it is very likely to be the price leader.

7.3 Four Types of Oligopolies

3.2 a. As a monopoly, Gamer Great will produce the quantity at which $MR = MC$. The figure in the problem shows that this quantity is 6 million

game consoles per year. The demand curve shows that the highest price that enables this quantity to be sold is $500. Consequently, Gamer Great's economic profit is $(P - ATC) \times Q = (\$500 - \$300) \times 6,000,000 = \$1,200,000,000$.

b. You can construct the best-response curves similarly to the procedure used in the chapter. Start by supposing that Gamer Great is the only firm in the market so that Player produces 0. Determine Gamer Great's production. (As you saw above, it is 6 million consoles.) Next suppose that Player enters and produces 6 million consoles. Gamer Great's new demand curve shifts to the left by 6 million so that its profit-maximizing production becomes 3 million consoles. You now have two points on Gamer Great's best response curve: The best response when Player produces 0 and when Player produces 6 million. Gamer Great's best-response curve will be linear, so use these two points to determine the best-response curve for Gamer Great. Follow a similar procedure for Player. The figure shows the two best-response curves. The equations for these best response curves are

- Gamer Great best response: $Q_{GG} = 6 - (Q_P/2)$ and
- Player best response: $Q_P = 6 - (Q_{GG}/2)$.

c. When Player enters the market, Gamer Great is producing the monopoly output of 6 million consoles per year. From Player's best-response

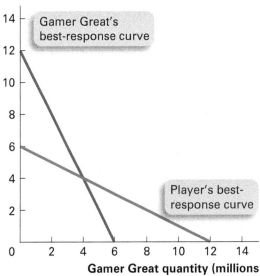

Player quantity (millions of game consoles per year)

Gamer Great's best-response curve

Player's best-response curve

Gamer Great quantity (millions of game consoles per year)

curve, we can see that its best response is to produce 3 million consoles per year.

d. Now Player is producing 3 million consoles per year. Gamer Great will react by lowering its output to 4.5 million consoles per year, found using Gamer Great's best-response curve.

e. In the Cournot equilibrium, the intersection of the best-response curves gives both firms' quantity. These curves intersect where $Q_{GG} = Q_P = 4$ million, so both firms produce 4 million consoles.

The total industry output is $Q_{GG} + Q_P = 8$ million per year. Using the demand curve from the problem to solve for price as a function of the quantity shows that $P = 700 - 0.000033Q$. Consequently the price of 8 million consoles per year is $436 per console. With this price, each firm's economic profit is

$$\text{Economic profit} = (P - ATC) \times Q$$
$$= (\$436 - \$300) \times 4,000,000$$
$$= \$544,000,000$$

Both firms are identical, produce the same quantity, and face the same price, so both firms make the same economic profit.

3.4 a. If your products are identical to your rival's, you will sell zero units if you raise the price above the equilibrium price. All the demand for the product will shift to your rival. Your economic profit is zero, or if you have fixed costs, you will incur an economic loss equal to your fixed costs.

b. The quantity demanded of your product will fall but not to zero because the products are not perfect substitutes.

3.6 a. The firm will produce the quantity that sets $MR = MC$:

$$100 - 0.2Q = 40$$
$$-0.2Q = -60$$
$$Q = 300$$

Find the profit-maximizing price by substituting the quantity produced into the market demand equation:

$$P = 100 - 0.1Q$$
$$= 100 - (0.1 \times 300)$$
$$= \$70$$

The economic profit equals $(P - ATC) \times Q$, or $(\$70 - \$40) \times 300 = \$9,000$.

b. First, construct the best-response curves for the two firms (call them Firm 1 and Firm 2).

You can calculate these curves similarly to the method used in the chapter: First, suppose that Firm 1 is the only firm in the market so that Firm 2 produces 0. Determine Firm 1's production. (As you saw above, it is 300.) Next suppose that Firm 2 enters and produces 100 dinners. Firm 1's new demand is $Q = 900 - 10P$ so its new marginal revenue is $MR = 90 - 0.2Q$. The marginal cost remains $40, so setting $MR = MC$ shows that the new profit-maximizing quantity is 250 dinners. You now have two points on Firm 1's best response curve: The best response when Firm 2 produces 0 and when Firm 2 produces 100. Firm 1's best-response curve will be linear, so use these two points to determine the best-response curve for Firm 1. Follow a similar procedure for Firm 2. The equations for these curves are

$$Q_1 = 300 - Q_2/2$$
$$Q_2 = 300 - Q_1/2$$

These curves intersect at $Q_1 = Q_2 = 200$. Consequently, the total industry output is equal to $Q_1 + Q_2 = 400$. Substitute this quantity into the market demand function to get the equilibrium price:

$$P = 100 - 0.1Q$$
$$= 100 - (0.1 \times 400)$$
$$= \$60$$

Next, find each firm's economic profit:

$$\text{Economic profit} = (P - ATC) \times Q$$
$$= (\$60 - \$40) \times 200$$
$$= \$4,000$$

Both firms are identical, produce the same quantity, and face the same price, so both firms earn the same economic profit.

c. In the Bertrand model, the rival firms undercut each other on price until the prices equal their marginal cost, $40. The total market demand at this price is

$$P = 100 - 0.1Q$$
$$40 = 100 - 0.1Q$$
$$-60 = -0.1Q$$
$$Q = 600$$

Both firms sell an identical product, so they will split the market demand evenly. Each firm sells 300 steak dinners and makes zero economic profit because $P = ATC$.

7.4 Managerial Application: Cartels and Oligopolies

4.2 By matching your price, the new company may be signaling its willingness to tacitly collude with you as the price leader. The company is producing half of the monopoly profit-maximizing quantity. You could signal your tacit agreement to cooperate by cutting your output to 30,000. In this way, you and the new company will share the monopoly economic profit, which is larger than any other profit available. Alternatively you could lower your price in an attempt to drive your rival out of the market. In this case, however, you must be careful not to become mired in Bertrand competition because that would eventually lead to you making zero economic profit.

CHAPTER 8

Game Theory and Oligopoly

8.1 Basic Game Theory and Games

1.2 a.

Microsoft

b. The payoff matrix shows that spending a lot is Sony's best response to either strategy chosen by Microsoft. The same is true for Microsoft's response to Sony. Therefore, spending a lot on advertising is the dominant strategy for both Sony and Microsoft.

c. The Nash equilibrium occurs where both Sony and Microsoft play their dominant strategies: spend a lot on advertising. Neither firm can increase its profits by unilaterally deviating from this outcome.

1.4 a. For both UPS and FedEx, choosing a high price is the dominant strategy. Neither firm can increase its profit by switching to a low-price strategy. Therefore, the Nash equilibrium occurs where both firms set a high price.

b. This is not a prisoners' dilemma game because these firms cannot increase both their profits through cooperation.

c. Although each firm has the possibility of making a higher profit, each set of managers realizes that its rival won't cooperate. Accordingly, the managers are likely to be satisfied with the Nash equilibrium. Neither firm can be made better off without another firm losing profits. This outcome is what we expect if these firms cooperated.

1.6 In a prisoners' dilemma game, the cooperative equilibrium yields higher profits for both players, but, compared to the cooperative equilibrium, defecting yields a still-higher profit to the defector in the period in which it alone cheats. Both the grim trigger and tit-for-tat strategies punish your rival for choosing to defect. The more forgiving tit-for-tat strategy allows the punishment to end when your rival demonstrates a willingness to cooperate. This might sustain cooperation (and the associated higher profits) for more periods than the grim trigger. The grim trigger strategy, however, means that a one-time defection yields a persistent punishment. This fact mans that a (potential) defector must compare the one-period gain against lower profits during the entire future, which might be enough to sustain cooperation for more periods than the tit-for-tat strategy.

1.8 A dominated strategy earns less profit than an alternative strategy regardless of the opponent's choice of strategy. It is never profit maximizing to choose a dominated strategy because, by definition, there is a different strategy that yields higher profit.

8.2 Advanced Games

2.2 a. There are two Nash equilibria: (1) Woolworths expands and Coles does not expand and (2) Woolworths does not expand and Coles expands. In both cases, neither firm can increase its profit by unilaterally deviating from the equilibrium.

b. Even with the announcement Woolworths' and Coles' incentives still diverge. The announcement is cheap talk. For example, if Woolworths started to expand by building new stores before Coles, Coles would immediately abandon its announcement and not expand since, with Woolworths' expansion, Coles' profit by not expanding is larger than its profit by expanding. Because Woolworths knows the announcement is merely cheap talk, it does not change the equilibrium.

2.4 a. No, there is no pure-strategy Nash equilibrium. For any outcome in the payoff matrix, at least one firm can increase its profits by unilaterally changing its strategy.

b. Yes, there is a mixed-strategy Nash equilibrium. Suppose that Express Scripts (ES) chooses a high-bid strategy with probability r. Then CVS's expected profit from choosing a high bid is

$$\text{Profit}_{\text{High}}^{\text{CVS}} = (r \times \$2\,\text{billion}) + [(1 - r) \times \$0\,\text{billion}]$$

and CVS's expected profit from choosing a low price is

$$\text{Profit}_{\text{Low}}^{\text{CVS}} = (r \times \$1\,\text{billion}) + [(1 - r) \times \$2\,\text{billion}]$$

Express Scripts will choose r such that CVS's expected profit from choosing a high price equals CVS's expected profit from choosing a low price:

$$\text{Profit}_{\text{High}}^{\text{CVS}} = \text{Profit}_{\text{Low}}^{\text{CVS}}$$

$$(r \times \$2\,\text{billion}) + [(1 - r) \times \$0\,\text{billion}]$$
$$= (r \times \$1\,\text{billion}) + [(1 - r) \times \$2\,\text{billion}]$$

Solve this equation for r:

$$r = \frac{2}{3} = 0.67$$

So, Express Scripts submits a high bid 67 percent of the time and a low bid 33 percent of the time.

Now suppose that CVS chooses a high price with probability p. Then Express Scripts' expected profit from choosing a high price is

$$\text{Profit}_{\text{High}}^{\text{ES}} = (p \times \$4\,\text{billion}) + [(1 - p) \times \$3\,\text{billion}]$$

and Express Scripts' expected profit from choosing a low price is

$$\text{Profit}_{\text{Low}}^{\text{ES}} = (p \times \$5\,\text{billion}) + [(1 - p) \times \$2\,\text{billion}]$$

CVS will choose p such that Express Scripts' expected profit from choosing a high price equals Express Scripts' expected profit from choosing a low price:

$$\text{Profit}_{\text{High}}^{\text{ES}} = \text{Profit}_{\text{Low}}^{\text{ES}},$$

$$(p \times \$4\,\text{billion}) + [(1 - p) \times \$3\,\text{billion}]$$
$$= (p \times \$5\,\text{billion}) + [(1 - p) \times \$2\,\text{billion}]$$

Solve this equation for p:

$$p = \frac{1}{2} = 0.50$$

So, CVS submits a high bid 50 percent of the time and a low bid 50 percent of the time.

Thus, the mixed-strategy Nash equilibrium occurs when CVS submits a high price bid with a probability of 0.50 (50 percent) a low-price with a probability also of 50 percent, while Express Scripts a high-price bid with a probability of 0.67 (67 percent) and, accordingly, a bid with a low price the other 33 percent of the time.

8.3 Sequential Games

3.2 Threats are credible when they are preceded by a costly or irreversible commitment or when they are in the player's best interest. If it is possible for a player to renege on a threat without cost, rivals will not take the threat seriously.

3.4 a. Use backward induction to determine Microsoft's optimal amount of investment. When Microsoft chooses high investment, Electronic Arts responds with medium investment. When Microsoft chooses medium investment, Electronic Arts also chooses medium investment. When Microsoft chooses low investment, Electronic Arts also chooses low investment. Of the corresponding terminal nodes, Microsoft earns the highest profit at the node where both firms choose medium investment.

b. Yes, the outcome differs. Both firms agree to a contract where both firms choose high investment because this outcome increases both firms' profits over the solution in part a. The contract is necessary for this outcome to occur because otherwise Electronic Arts could increase its profits further by choosing medium investment.

8.4 Managerial Application: Game Theory

4.2 You are facing an end-period problem. With the expiration of the contract, the tuna supplier has no incentive to behave cooperatively. The supplier foresees the end of your business relationship and may decrease the quality of tuna supplied to you, make late deliveries, or otherwise make noncooperative decisions to maximize its profits at your restaurant's expense. You can address this by either negotiating or starting negotiation of a new contract with your tuna supplier.

4.4 a.

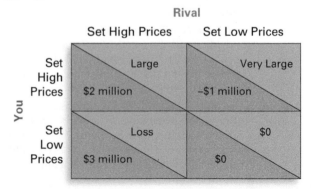

Accompanies problem 4.6.

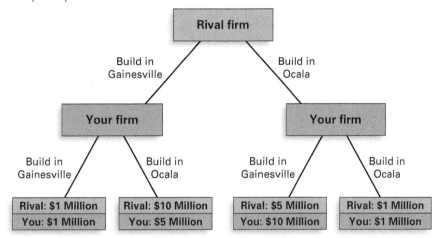

b. Your dominant strategy is to set low prices. The same is true for your rival. In the Nash equilibrium, both you and your rival set low prices and earn zero economic profit.

c. In the cooperative equilibrium, you and your rival both set high prices. You could adopt a trigger strategy such as tit-for-tat to give your rival an incentive to cooperate.

4.6 a. See the accompanying game tree. Backward induction shows that the Nash equilibrium has your rival developing in Gainesville and you developing in Ocala. In particular, your rival reasons as follows: If your rival builds in Gainesville, you will build in Ocala because that gives you the larger profit. With this outcome, your rival makes a profit of $10 million. On the other hand, if your rival builds in Ocala, you will build in Gainesville because that gives you the larger profit. In this case, your rival makes a profit of $5 million. Your rival realizes that building in Gainesville offers the larger profit, so your rival builds in Gainesville and you build in Ocala.

b. This announcement is not credible. Your rival still gets to submit the first building plan, so it is still optimal for you to respond by selecting the opposite town. Your announcement doesn't change your profit-maximizing decision.

c. Assuming your rival is able to verify the sale, this announcement is a credible threat. You have irreversibly committed to develop in Gainesville because this is the only lot you have left. No matter what your rival chooses, you will always develop the Gainesville lot. Now your rival faces two choices: develop in Gainesville and make a profit of $1 million, or develop in Ocala and make a profit of $5 million. In the Nash equilibrium, your rival will build in Ocala, and you will build in Gainesville.

d. The answers in parts b and c are different because you made a credible commitment in part c. Selling the Ocala lot irreversibly altered the game tree, removing the terminal node reached in the Nash equilibrium in parts a and b.

CHAPTER 9

A Manager's Guide to Antitrust Policy

9.1 Overview of U.S. Antitrust Policy

1.2 As manager of the Lightning Bolt train, you should use the profit-maximization rule, which means you will charge the monopoly price. To maximize profit, first set marginal revenue equal to marginal cost to find the profit-maximizing quantity; then find the market price for this quantity on the demand curve. This rate is "all that the traffic will bear" in the sense that it is the highest price consumers are willing to pay at this level of output. However, the phrase itself is vague, so it is unclear what the farmers meant to say.

9.2 The Sherman Act

2.2 The competing managers in the Chinese Restaurant Association have agreed to raise their prices. This is a price-fixing agreement, which is a per se violation of Section 1 of the Sherman Act. Illegal per se means the offending firms have no legal defense no matter how praiseworthy their stated intention. The Department of Justice will file suit and find that price fixing occurred, after which the participating firms will face fines.

2.4 This agreement is a price-fixing agreement. Although it does not specify a price, it does eliminate what is essentially a discount (interest-free credit). Consequently, even though it is not a direct agreement to raise prices, these firms are agreeing to indirectly raise prices. You can expect these beer wholesalers were found guilty of violating Section 1 of the Sherman Act because price fixing is illegal per se.

2.6 This assertion is incorrect. The agreement is an example of market division, which is a per se violation of Section 1 of the Sherman Act.

2.8 The *Brooke Group* ruling laid out two requirements to convict a firm of predatory pricing: (1) price below cost and (2) recoupment. Free samples are clearly priced below cost. However, the recoupment requirement is unlikely to be met. A plaintiff bringing suit against your firm would need to demonstrate that your free samples substantially lessened competition in the shampoo market and thereby allowed you to raise your price enough to recoup the losses you incurred by giving away your 3-ounce bottles. It is highly unlikely your samples will push any competitors out of the market—and there are no significant barriers to entry—so this is not predatory conduct.

2.10 Recoupment implies that predatory pricing has reduced competition, enabling the firm to raise prices. If there is no expectation of recoupment, then pricing below cost must not have been effective as an anticompetitive practice. Additionally, if a profit-maximizing firm cannot recoup its losses, then it will not engage in predatory pricing.

9.3 The Clayton Act

3.2 This offer is not a tying arrangement because sale of the car wash is not conditioned on sale of gas; that is, the car wash does not require the purchase of gasoline. The free car wash with every fill-up does not prevent customers from buying a car wash without buying gas.

3.4 This is an exclusive dealing contract. Such deals are legal because they have procompetitive effects. Both Ford Motor Company and the dealerships now have an incentive to advertise and promote Ford cars. Ford's advertisements draw business to the dealerships, and the dealerships' promotional activities bring business to Ford in kind. All this advertising informs consumers and makes the market for cars more efficient.

3.6 The phrase "substantially lessen competition or tend to create a monopoly" is important because it means none of the business practices covered by the Clayton Act are considered illegal per se. Unlike in price-fixing cases, businesses prosecuted under the Clayton Act can defend themselves by arguing their practices are not anticompetitive, that is, they do substantially lessen competition and do not tend to create a monopoly.

9.4 U.S. Merger Policy

4.2 The antitrust authorities determine the relevant market with a number of different tools: the SSNIP test, the cross-elasticity of demand, the similarity of products, and geographic proximity. The SSNIP test, for example, takes all the firms producing the same product as do the two merging firms and supposes that all these firms join together. The analysts then determine if this hypothetical large firm is able to raise the price and sustain it. If yes, then according to the SSNIP test the market consists of these firms. If not, then the analysts add to the hypothetical firm other firms producing a similar product, and ask if this larger firm can raise the price and sustain it. Once again, if yes the market consists of these firms and if not still more firms are added to the hypothetical firm until the answer becomes yes, at which time the market is determined. Or, a large cross-elasticity of demand between products produced by the different firms indicates that the products are close substitutes, which means the firms compete in the same market. Similarly, a close degree of similarity among the firms' products suggests that firms are competing in the same market. Finally, if the products are close geographically, then the two firms may be in the same market.

9.5 International Competition Laws

5.2 In the United States, resale price maintenance is subject to the rule of reason. The EU takes a much harsher stance, requiring firms using resale price maintenance to prove substantial gains in efficiency. Furthermore, resale price maintenance is generally illegal if it is undertaken by a dominant firm. If the selling firm has more than a 30 percent market share in the product being sold or the buying firm has more than a 30 percent market share of purchases, resale price maintenance is illegal.

5.4 Yes, this is possible because Chinese antitrust law takes into account the combined market share of multiple firms. A firm with a 10 percent market share is a dominant firm if there is another firm in the same market with a 56.6 percent (or more) market share. It could also be grouped with two other firms that together have a market share greater than 65 percent.

9.6 Managerial Application: Antitrust Policy

6.2 a. Under EU law, Google is clearly a dominant firm. In Europe, it is illegal for dominant firms to charge an unfair price, so Google should take care not to charge too high a price in the EU market. If Google is convicted of charging a price that is illegally too high in the EU, it can face significant fines. In the United States, there is no equivalent provision, so Google is free to charge as high a price as it chooses.

b. This strategy is a form of price discrimination. Google definitely should avoid using this strategy in the EU because Article 102 prohibits dominant firms from engaging in price discrimination if it places a trading partner at a competitive disadvantage. In this case, Italian restaurants are at a disadvantage to their German counterparts. In addition, the EU competition authorities treat price discrimination that occurs along national boundaries especially harshly. In the United States, price discrimination is illegal only if it is anticompetitive.

6.4 In China, a firm can be classified as a dominant firm if it is one of three firms with total market share greater than 75 percent. Chinese antitrust officials can classify Sogou as a dominant firm because together with Baidu and Qihoo, it has total market share of 96 percent. Sogou can be prosecuted for charging "unfairly high" prices even if its larger competitors are not, so Sogou's managers face a legal issue.

CHAPTER **10**

Advanced Pricing Decisions

10.1 Price Discrimination

1.2 The marginal cost of additional passengers is at least partially based on the weight they add to the plane, as more weight increases fuel consumption. It is not price discrimination to charge customers different prices based on the difference in the marginal costs of serving them, so to the extent the difference in ticket prices reflects the difference in marginal costs, this is not an example of price discrimination.

1.4 The managers at Cherished Cat are charging different prices for different quantities of cat litter; the first 18 pounds have a price of $8.24 while the next 22 pounds (40 pounds minus 18 pounds) have a price of only $7.75 ($15.99 minus $8.24). This pricing is an example of second-degree price discrimination.

1.6 The meat producers are using third-degree price discrimination by selling at different prices to two groups of "consumers" (people and dog-owning people). Charcoal is added to prevent arbitrage. If meat producers did not add charcoal to the ground beef intended for dogs, customers could buy that meat and then consume it themselves or resell to it other humans.

1.8 MasterCuts should change its prices. If the marginal revenue of an adult haircut is higher than the marginal revenue of a child's haircut, MasterCuts can increase its profit by selling more adult haircuts and fewer child haircuts until both marginal revenues are equal. Consequently, MasterCuts should reduce the price of adult haircuts to sell more adult haircuts and increase the price of child haircuts to sell fewer child haircuts.

1.10 a. Think of each customer type as a separate market. Then, we need to derive the marginal revenue from each customer type's demand function. First, for students,

$$Q_S = 400,000 - 1,000P_S$$

We can solve this demand function to give P as a function of Q_S, which is the inverse demand function:

$$P_S = 400 - (Q_S/1,000)$$

Finally, because the demand is linear, the marginal revenue curve has the same vertical intercept as the demand curve and a slope equal to twice that of the demand curve. So, double the slope of the inverse demand function to yield the marginal revenue function:

$$MR_S = 400 - (Q_S/500)$$

Next, do the same three steps for businesspeople:

$$Q_B = 900,000 - 1,000P_B$$
$$P_B = 900 - (Q_B/1,000)$$
$$MR_B = 900 - (Q_B/500)$$

Maximizing profit when selling the output in the two markets requires that $MR_S = MR_B$. Because the marginal cost is equal to $0, that means that $MR_S = MR_B = $0. Consequently, to determine the profit-maximizing quantities in the two markets, start with students:

$$MR_S = 400 - (Q_S/500) = 0$$
$$Q_S = 200,000$$

The corresponding rental price for students is

$$P_S = 400 - (Q_S/1,000)$$
$$= 400 - (200,000/1,000]$$
$$= $200$$

For businesspeople, the profit-maximizing quantity is

$$MR_B = 900 - (Q_B/500) = 0$$
$$Q_B = 450,000$$

The corresponding rental price for businesspeople is

$$P_B = 900 - (Q_B/1,000)$$
$$= 900 - (450,000/1,000)$$
$$= $450$$

Adobe's economic profit is its total revenue minus its total cost. The total revenue equals the sum of the price multiplied by the quantity for each customer. Adobe's only cost is its $5 million of fixed cost. So the economic profit is

$$(P_S \times Q_S) + (P_B \times Q_B) - \$5 \text{ million}$$
$$= (\$200 \times 200{,}000) + (\$450 \times 450{,}000) - \$5{,}000{,}000$$
$$= \$237.5 \text{ million}$$

b. First, construct the overall demand curve. This demand curve is the horizontal sum of the two demand curves. The students demand zero units when the rental price is $400 or greater. For these prices, the overall demand is just the demand function for businesspeople. Below $400, the combined demand function is the sum of both demands:

P ≥ $400

$$Q = 900{,}000 - 1{,}000P$$

P < $400

$$Q = (900{,}000 - 1{,}000P) + (400{,}000 - 1{,}000P)$$
$$= 1{,}300{,}000 - 2{,}000P$$

Note that when $P \geq 400$, then $Q \leq 500{,}000$ and when $P < 400$, then $Q > 500{,}000$. Then the inverse overall demand function—that is, P as a function of Q—is

$$P = 900 - (Q/1{,}000), \text{ if } Q \leq 500{,}000$$
$$P = 650 - (Q/2{,}000), \text{ if } Q > 500{,}000$$

For both inverse demand functions, double the slope to derive the marginal revenue curve:

$$MR = 900 - (Q/500), \text{ if } Q \leq 500{,}000$$
$$MR = 650 - (Q/1{,}000), \text{ if } Q > 500{,}000$$

The profit-maximizing quantity is found where $MR = MC$. The marginal cost equals 0. Because of the jump in the MR curve at $Q = 500{,}000$ the MC curve intersects the MR curve at two quantities. One point of intersection results if only businesspeople are served:

$$0 = 900 - (Q/500)$$
$$Q = 450{,}000$$

In this case, the corresponding rental price from the demand function for businesspeople is

$$P = 900 - (450{,}000/1{,}000)$$
$$= \$450$$

The other point of intersection results if both students and businesspeople are served:

$$0 = 650 - (Q/1{,}000)$$
$$Q = 650{,}000$$

The corresponding rental price from the overall demand curve is

$$P = 650 - (650{,}000/2{,}000)$$
$$= \$325$$

Adobe's managers will pick whichever of these two solutions yields the highest economic profit. The profit from just serving businesspeople is

$$\text{Profit} = (\$450 \times 450{,}000) - \$5 \text{ million}$$
$$= \$197.5 \text{ million}$$

The profit from serving both types of customer is

$$\text{Profit} = (\$325 \times 650{,}000) - \$5 \text{ million}$$
$$= \$206.25 \text{ million}$$

The profit from serving both students and businesspeople is higher, so Adobe will sell 650,000 programs and charge $325 per program.

c. Adobe's profit is larger when it price discriminates, $206.25 million versus $197.5 million. This gain in profit occurs because Adobe is able to convert more consumer surplus into profit with two different rental prices (one for students and one for businesspeople) than it can with one rental price.

d. There are four conditions for successful third-degree price discrimination: market power, different groups of customers, distinct groups, and no arbitrage. Adobe clearly has the first three, but it must take action to prevent arbitrage. For example, Adobe could require students to verify active enrollment to purchase at the student price to reduce or prevent arbitrage.

10.2 Peak-Load Pricing

2.2 Wednesday from 9:30 P.M. to 11:30 P.M. is a slow time for a sports bar. So, this is a period of off-peak demand for the sports bar. It is profit maximizing to offer lower prices in the off-peak period, so this pricing strategy is an example of peak-load pricing.

2.4 Yes, market power is required to practice peak-load pricing. Otherwise, the firm cannot raise its price above its marginal cost.

2.6 First, find the profit-maximizing level of capacity (which is also the profit-maximizing quantity during the peak period). The profit-maximizing quantity sets the peak-period marginal revenue equal to the long-run marginal cost, which is the sum of the marginal operating cost and the marginal cost of capacity. To determine the marginal revenue function, solve the peak demand function for price to obtain the inverse demand function—that is, the price as a function of the quantity:

$$Q_{\text{PEAK}} = 4{,}200 - 40P_{\text{PEAK}} \Rightarrow P_{\text{PEAK}} = 105 - (Q_{\text{PEAK}}/40)$$

Double the slope to derive the peak-period marginal revenue function:

$$MR_{\text{PEAK}} = 105 - (Q_{\text{PEAK}}/20)$$

The long-run marginal cost (MC_{LR}) equals the sum of the marginal capacity cost ($15 per diner) and the marginal cost of a meal ($20 per diner), so the long-run marginal cost is $35 per diner. Set the peak-period marginal revenue equal to the long-run marginal cost, and solve for the profit-maximizing quantity:

$$MR_{\text{PEAK}} = MC_{\text{LR}}$$

so

$$105 - (Q_{\text{PEAK}}/20) = 35 \Rightarrow Q_{\text{PEAK}} = 1{,}400$$

The restaurant will serve 1,400 diners per week in the peak period. Substitute this quantity into the peak inverse demand function to obtain the profit-maximizing price of a meal during the peak period:

$$P_{\text{PEAK}} = 105 - (1{,}400/40)$$
$$P_{\text{PEAK}} = \$70$$

Next, calculate the profit-maximizing price and quantity during the off-peak period. Following the same procedure as for the peak period, invert the off-peak demand function, and then double its slope to obtain the off-peak marginal revenue function:

$$Q_{\text{OFF-PEAK}} = 1{,}800 - 20P_{\text{OFF-PEAK}}$$

or

$$P_{\text{OFF-PEAK}} = 90 - (Q_{\text{OFF-PEAK}}/20)$$

so that

$$MR_{\text{OFF-PEAK}} = 90 - (Q_{\text{OFF-PEAK}}/10)$$

The short-run marginal cost (MC_{SR}) is equal to the marginal cost of a meal ($20 per diner). Set the off-peak marginal revenue equal to short-run marginal cost and solve for the profit-maximizing quantity:

$$MR_{\text{OFF-PEAK}} = MC_{\text{SR}}$$
$$90 - (Q_{\text{OFF-PEAK}}/10) = 20 \Rightarrow Q_{\text{OFF-PEAK}} = 700$$

The restaurant will serve 700 diners per week in the off-peak period. Substitute this quantity into the off-peak inverse demand function to obtain the profit-maximizing price during the off-peak period:

$$P_{\text{OFF-PEAK}} = 90 - (700/20)$$
$$P_{\text{OFF-PEAK}} = \$55$$

During the peak period, the restaurant will serve 1,400 diners per week at a price of $70 per meal, and during the off-peak period, the restaurant will serve 700 diners per week at a price of $55 per meal.

10.3 Nonlinear Pricing

3.2 Two-part pricing is characterized by a fixed fee and a per-unit price. In this case, the $50 bus pass is the fixed fee, and the price per unit (the price per ride) is $0.

3.4 a. When the managers set a single price, the profit-maximizing number of rounds of golf is the quantity that sets the marginal revenue equal to the marginal cost:

$$100 - 2Q = 20$$
$$Q = 40$$

The profit-maximizing price per round of golf is found using the demand function at $Q = 40$:

$$40 = 100 - P$$
$$P = \$60$$

So with a single price, the managers set a price of $60 per round and each golfer plays 40 rounds.

b. Using two-part pricing, because the players are identical the price per round is the marginal cost ($20). The demand function shows that each golfer will play $Q = 100 - 20 = 80$ rounds at this price. The optimal fixed membership fee is the individual's consumer surplus from consuming these 80 rounds. To find the area of the consumer surplus triangle, we need the base and height. The base of the consumer surplus triangle is the quantity consumed (80 rounds), and the height is the difference between the vertical intercept of the demand curve ($100) and the price per round ($20). Using the formula for computing the area of a triangle, the consumer surplus (CS) is

$$CS = \tfrac{1}{2} \times \text{Base} \times \text{Height}$$
$$= \tfrac{1}{2} \times 80 \times (\$100 - \$20) = \$3{,}200$$

c. For a linear demand curve and horizontal marginal cost curve, the profit-maximizing all-or-nothing package offers the quantity demanded when price is equal to marginal cost and charges the monopoly price per unit. The problem has exactly these characteristics, so use that result to determine the quantity and price. The marginal cost is $20 per round, so when the price is $20 per round, part b showed that the quantity is 80 rounds. From part a, the monopoly price is $60 per round. Thus, the all-or-nothing offer is 80 rounds priced at $60 per round, for a total $4,800 for the package.

d. For parts a and c, calculate the economic profit using the formula $(P - ATC) \times Q$. Because there is no fixed cost, since the marginal cost is constant MC equals ATC.

The economic profit in part a with the conventional single price is

$$\text{Profit} = (\$60 - \$20) \times 40 = \$1,600$$

The economic profit in part c with the all-or-nothing offer is

$$\text{Profit} = (\$60 - \$20) \times 80 = \$3,200$$

For part b, the economic profit is the sum of the fixed access fee plus the profit per round of golf played. The access fee is $3,200. The profit per round is the price minus the marginal cost or $20 - $20 = $0. So the economic profit for the two-part pricing in part b is $3,200.

3.6 The club should use two-part pricing, with the price per round equal to the marginal cost of a round ($10) and a membership fee equal to the consumer surplus. To find the amount of the consumer surplus, we need to find the area of the consumer surplus triangle. First, use the demand function to find the quantity demanded at $10 (this is the base of the consumer surplus triangle):

$$Q = 100 - 10 = 90$$

Second, the height of the consumer surplus triangle is the difference between the vertical intercept of the demand curve ($100) and the price per round ($10). Using the formula for computing the area of a triangle, the consumer surplus (CS) is

$$CS = \frac{1}{2} \times \text{Base} \times \text{Height}$$
$$= \frac{1}{2} \times 90 \times (\$100 - \$10) = \$4,050$$

The individual's consumer surplus is also the profit-maximizing membership fee because this amount is the maximum the customer is willing to pay for 90 rounds of golf. The club's economic profit per member is the membership fee plus the profit per round of golf. Because the price of a round equals the marginal cost of a round, there is no profit from the rounds of golf. Consequently, the profit per member is the membership fee of $4,050. Because there are 400 members, the club's total economic profit is 400 × $4,050, or $1,620,000.

We can check these calculations by using the figure, which shows that when the price of a round of golf is $10 per round, a golfer plays 90 rounds per year. With this price and quantity, the golfer's consumer surplus is equal to the area of the green triangle, $\frac{1}{2} \times 90$ rounds $\times$ ($100 - $10) = $4,050. Just as before, the club should set its annual fixed membership fee equal to this amount. Because the price of a round of golf exactly covers the cost of a round, the club's economic profit per golfer is equal to the membership fee, $4,050. Because there are 400 members, the club's total economic profit is 400 × $8,100 = $1,620,000, exactly the amount calculated before.

Price and cost (dollars per round of golf)

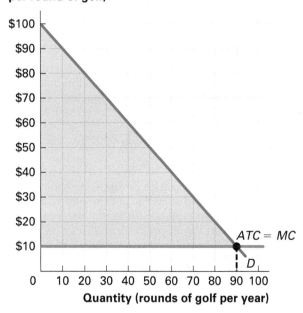

3.8 a. If you set a price of $0.75 for the nature channel, you sell the channel to both customers, and you make a total profit of $1.50. If you set a price of $2.00 for the nature channel, you sell the channel only to customer B, and you make a total profit of $2.00. The profit-maximizing price of the travel channel is $2.00.

If you set a price of $2.00 for the travel channel, you sell the channel to both customers, and you make a total profit of $4.00. If you set a price of $3.00 for the travel channel, you sell the channel only to customer B, and you make a total profit of $3.00. The profit-maximizing price of the travel channel is $2.00.

Your total profit is maximized by setting a price of $2.00 for the nature channel, which gives you a profit of $2.00 from the nature channel, and by setting a price of $2.00 for the travel channel, which gives you a profit of $4.00 from the travel channel, for a total profit of $6.00.

b. If you bundle both channels, customer A is willing to pay $2.75 for the bundle, and customer B is willing to pay $5.00 for the bundle. If you set a price of $2.75, both customers will buy the bundle, for a total profit of $5.50. If you set a price of $5.00, only customer B will buy the bundle, so your total profit is $5.00. The profit-maximizing price is $2.75 for the bundle, which gives you a total profit of $5.50.

c. Your profit is higher ($6.00 versus $5.50) if you do not bundle the two channels.

d. If you set a price of $0.75 for the nature channel, you sell the channel to both customers, and you make a total profit of $1.50. If you set a price of $2.00 for the nature channel, you sell the channel only to customer B, and you make a total profit of $2.00. The profit-maximizing price of the travel channel is $2.00.

If you set a price of $2.00 for the travel channel, you sell the channel to both customers, and you make a total profit of $4.00. If you set a price of $3.00 for the travel channel, you sell the channel only to customer B, and you make a total profit of $3.00. The profit-maximizing price of the travel channel is $2.00.

Your total profit is maximized by setting a price of $2.00 for the nature channel, which gives you a profit of $2.00 from the nature channel, and by setting a price of $2.00 for the travel channel, which gives you a profit of $4.00 from the travel channel, for a total profit of $6.00.

e. If you bundle both channels, customer A is willing to pay $3.75 for the bundle, and customer B is willing to pay $4.00 for the bundle. If you set a price of $3.75, both customers will buy the bundle, for a total profit of $7.50. If you set a price of $4.00, only customer B will buy the bundle, so your total profit is $4.00. The profit-maximizing price is $3.75 for the bundle, for a total profit of $7.50.

f. Your profit is higher ($7.50 versus $6.00) if you bundle the two channels.

10.4 Managerial Application: Use of Advanced Pricing Decisions

4.2 The restaurant managers are engaging in peak-load pricing with lunch as the off-peak period. The demand for lunch is lower than the demand for dinner. It follows that the profit-maximizing price is

also lower, as lunch customers have a lower willingness to pay.

4.4 The club can set separate annual dues for each type of golfer because it is able to engage in price discrimination. The greens fee will be set at the marginal cost ($10) to maximize the consumer surplus of both types of golfers, and then the annual dues will be set to the consumer surplus for each type. First, find the rounds of golf played by adult golfers:

$$10 = 120 - Q$$
$$Q = 110$$

Now we need to find the annual dues for adult golfers. The consumer surplus is a triangle with the base equal to the rounds of golf played by adult golfers, 110. The height is the difference between the vertical intercept of the demand curve ($120) and the greens fee ($10). Using the formula for computing the area of a triangle, the consumer surplus (CS) is

$$CS = \frac{1}{2} \times \text{Base} \times \text{Height}$$
$$= \frac{1}{2} \times 110 \times (\$120 - \$10) = \$6{,}050$$

Consequently, the annual dues for adult golfers are $6,050.

Make similar calculations for the junior golfers. Again, find the rounds of golf played:

$$10 = 80 - Q$$
$$Q = 70$$

Then find the annual dues for junior golfers. The base of the consumer surplus triangle for the juniors is the rounds of golf played by junior golfers, 70. The height is the difference between the vertical intercept of the demand curve ($80) and the greens fee ($10). Using the formula for computing the area of a triangle, the consumer surplus (CS) is

$$CS = \frac{1}{2} \times 70 \times (\$80 - \$10) = \$2{,}450$$

So junior golfers pay annual dues of $2,450.

CHAPTER 11
Decisions About Vertical Integration and Distribution

11.1 The Basics of Vertical Integration

1.2 Managers use the transfer price to divide the accounting profit among divisions within the firm. For example, if the transfer price charged by the manufacturing division to the retail division is equal to the marginal cost of the product, then the retail division of the firm will be allocated the entire profit. When the transfer price is above the marginal cost, the manufacturing division records the difference as profit. The economic profit of the firm remains the same regardless. Managers can set transfer prices such that they allocate more of the firm's profit to the division with the lowest tax rate, which will reduce the firm's total tax liability and increase its after-tax profit. Clearly, managers would prefer to allocate all the profit to the division facing the lowest tax rate. However, many countries have laws requiring that transfer prices into or out of the country equal the price that would be charged to an independent customer.

11.2 The Economics of Vertical Integration

2.2 As the inputs became more standardized, the information costs of producing computers by using markets declined. The potential for a holdup problem declined as well because standardized parts mean that fewer or no transaction-specific assets are required. The incentive for firms to vertically integrate was reduced as a result.

2.4 Independent can producers who invest in the transaction-specific assets necessary to produce these special cans expose themselves to the holdup problem. Once the investment is made, the independent producer can sell these special cans only to Anheuser-Busch. This fact gives Anheuser-Busch an incentive to renege on the initial agreement and offer to buy the cans at a lower price. The independent producers then have to take the lower offer because no other buyer will purchase the special cans.

2.6 Starbuck's managers probably expect the Middle Eastern market to require managers with different kinds of expertise. The cultures, languages, and hiring processes are quite different from those in the United States. Leaving these issues to local owners rather than U.S.-based managers reduces managerial diseconomies.

11.3 Vertical Integration and Market Structure

3.2 a. If you both produce and distribute the product, your profit-maximizing price and output are the monopoly price and output. Start by constructing the marginal revenue. The marginal revenue curve has the same vertical intercept as the inverse demand curve and a slope that is twice that of the inverse demand curve:

$$MR = 100 - 2Q$$

Set the marginal revenue equal to the total marginal cost ($MC_P + MC_D$), and solve for the profit-maximizing quantity:

$$MR = MC_P + MC_D$$

or

$$100 - 2Q = 10 + 50 \Rightarrow Q = 20$$

Now use this quantity in the inverse demand to determine the profit-maximizing (retail) price for the profit-maximizing output:

$$P = 100 - 20 = \$80$$

b. The average total cost of production is $50 and the average total cost of distribution is $10. Accordingly, the average total cost (ATC) of both production and distribution is $60. So, the total economic profit equals $(P - ATC) \times Q$, or

$$[\$80 - (10 + 50)] \times 20 = \$400$$

c. For any retail price, the wholesale price equals the retail price minus the marginal cost of distribution, or:

$$P_W = P - MC_D$$

The inverse demand function shows that $P = 100 - Q$ and the marginal cost of distribution is $10. So, the wholesale price equals:

$$P_W = 90 - Q$$

This expression is the wholesale demand function. The wholesale marginal revenue has the same vertical intercept (90) and a slope that is twice that of the demand curve, so the wholesale marginal revenue is given by:

$$MR_W = 90 - 2Q$$

The profit-maximizing quantity for your firm to produce is the quantity that sets the wholesale marginal revenue (MR_W) equal to the marginal cost of production (MC_P):

$$MR_W = MC_P$$

or

$$90 - 2Q = 50 \Rightarrow Q = 20$$

Use the profit-maximizing quantity in the wholesale demand function to get the profit-maximizing wholesale price:

$$P_W = 90 - 20 = \$70$$

Using the wholesale price and output and the average total cost of production (ATC_P), your economic profit equals:

$$\begin{aligned} \text{Profit} &= (P_W - ATC_P) \times Q = (70 - 50) \times 20 \\ &= \$400 \end{aligned}$$

Price and cost (dollars per printer)

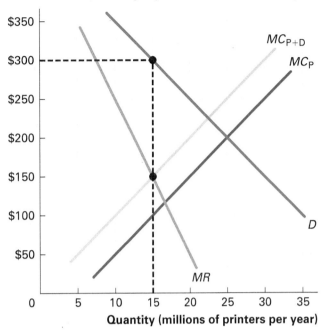

The retail distribution sector is competitive, so the retail price is equal to the distributors' marginal cost, $P_W + MC_D$, or:

$$P = P_W + MC_D = \$70 + \$10 = \$80$$

3.4 a. To determine the profit-maximizing quantity and price you need the wholesale demand and wholesale marginal revenue functions. The wholesale demand is equal to the retail demand (D) minus the marginal cost of distribution (MC_D), so for any quantity, the wholesale demand curve lies $50 below the retail demand curve. In the first figure, the wholesale demand curve is labeled D_W. The marginal revenue for this demand has the same vertical intercept as the demand curve and a slope that is twice that of the demand curve. In the figure, the wholesale marginal revenue curve is labeled MR_W. The profit-maximizing quantity of printers is the quantity that sets the wholesale marginal revenue equal to the marginal cost of production (MC_P), which, from the figure, is 15 million printers. The wholesale price is determined using the wholesale demand and is $250 per printer, the highest price that enables your company to sell the 15 million printers it produces. The retail price of the printers is equal to the wholesale price plus the marginal cost of distribution ($50), which is $300. Alternatively, the retail price can be determined directly from the retail demand curve as $300 per printer.

b. Now your firm is a monopolist facing the retail demand curve (labelled D in the second figure)

Price and cost (dollars per printer)

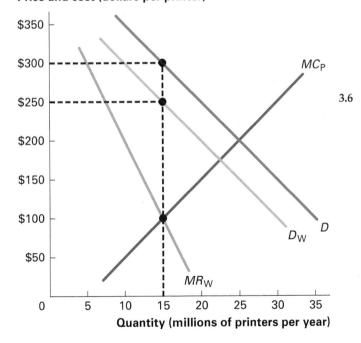

with its marginal revenue curve (labelled MR). The marginal revenue curve has the same vertical intercept as the demand curve and has a slope twice that of the demand curve. As the monopoly producer and distributor, your marginal cost includes both the marginal cost of production *and* distribution, so it is equal to $MC_P + MC_D$. This marginal cost curve is shown in the figure and is labeled MC_{P+D}. It is constructed by adding $50 (which equals MC_D) to MC_P at every quantity. You maximize your profit by producing the quantity that sets $MR = MC_P + MC_D$, which is 15 million printers. The retail price is determined using the retail demand and is $300, the highest price that enables your firm to sell the 15 million printers it produces.

3.6 a. i. The wholesale demand, wholesale marginal revenue, and marginal cost of production are needed to determine the wholesale price and quantity. The wholesale demand is based on the retailer's marginal revenue, which, in turn, is based on the retail demand. So to start, the monopoly retailer's marginal revenue function has the same vertical intercept as the inverse demand function and a slope that is twice that of the inverse demand function:

$$MR = 100 - 2Q$$

The monopoly retailer's wholesale demand function equals the retail marginal revenue minus the marginal cost of distribution:

$$P_W = MR - MC_D$$

or,

$$P_W = 100 - 2Q - 10 \Rightarrow P_W = 90 - 2Q$$

This demand function is the inverse wholesale demand function facing the producer. To maximize profit, the producer must produce the quantity that sets the wholesale marginal revenue (MR_W) equal to the marginal cost of production (MC_P). The wholesale marginal revenue function has the same vertical intercept as the inverse wholesale demand function and a slope twice that of the inverse wholesale demand function, so

$$MR_W = 90 - 4Q$$

The marginal cost of production (MC_P) is equal to 50. To maximize profit, the firm produces so that

$$MR_W = MC_P$$

or

$$90 - 4Q = 50 \Rightarrow Q = 10$$

Use the profit-maximizing quantity, 10, in the inverse wholesale demand function to get the profit-maximizing wholesale price:

$$P_W = 90 - (2 \times 10) = \$70$$

ii. Using the wholesale profit-maximizing price and output and the average total cost of production (ATC_P), the producer's economic profit is

$$\begin{aligned} \text{Profit} &= (P_W - ATC_P) \times Q \\ &= (70 - 50) \times 10 = \$200 \end{aligned}$$

iii. Now turn to the retail distributor's profit-maximization decision. The retail distributor will purchase the quantity that sets the distributor's marginal revenue equal to the distributor's marginal cost. The marginal revenue is from the retail demand, and is $MR = 100 - 2Q$. The marginal cost is the sum of the wholesale price for a unit plus the marginal cost of distribution. Since the wholesale price is $70 per unit and the marginal cost of distribution is $10, the retailer's marginal cost is $80. So the retail distributor's profit-maximizing quantity is determined by

$$100 - 2Q = 80 \Rightarrow Q = 10$$

The retail distributor buys all of the wholesaler's output, which is as expected. To calculate the profit-maximizing retail price, use the profit-maximizing quantity, 10, in the retail inverse demand function:

$$P = 100 - Q = 100 - 10 = \$90$$

iv. To calculate the retail distributor's economic profit, use the result that the retailer's $ATC = P_W + MC_D$ so the retailer's average total cost equals $70 + $10 = $80. Then the economic profit equals

$$\begin{aligned} \text{Profit} &= (P - ATC) \times Q \\ &= [90 - (70 + 10)] \times 10 = \$100 \end{aligned}$$

b. Yes, you should vertically integrate to avoid the double marginalization problem and thereby earn a higher economic profit. We can show this result by finding the total profit for the vertically integrated firm. The vertically integrated firm produces the quantity that sets the retail marginal revenue (MR) equal to the marginal cost (MC). The retail marginal revenue function was derived before and is $MR = 100 - 2Q$.

The marginal cost has two components, the marginal cost of production and the marginal cost of distribution, or $MC = MC_P + MC_D$. So the profit-maximizing quantity is given by

$$MR = MC_P + MC_D$$

or

$$100 - 2Q = 50 + 10 \Rightarrow Q = 20$$

To determine the profit-maximizing retail price, substitute this quantity into the inverse retail demand function:

$$P = 100 - Q \Rightarrow 100 - 20 = \$80$$

For an integrated firm, the profit-maximizing quantity is 20 units and the profit-maximizing price is $80. The average total cost is equal to the average total cost of production ($50) plus the average total cost of distribution ($10), or $60. Consequently, the vertically integrated firm's economic profit equals:

$$\text{Profit} = (P - ATC) \times Q = (80 - 60) \times 20 = \$400$$

In part a, the combined economic profit of the distributor and retailer was only $300. Once they merge, the (combined) economic profit is $400. Vertical integration has increased the total economic profit.

3.8   Backward integration into a competitive production sector will not increase PVH's profits because PVH is already collecting all the economic profit in the market as the monopoly distributor.

3.10 This statement is false. After integrating forward, the upstream firm is the owner of the downstream subsidiaries. Raising the price charged to these subsidiaries is an increase in the transfer price, so the fall in the profits at the downstream division of the firm is precisely offset by the increase in profits at the upstream division of the firm. There is no net change in the total profit. (However, if the transfer price moves the taxable profit from a high-tax to a low-tax domicile, the company's after-tax profit increases.)

11.4 Managerial Application: Vertical Integration and Distribution

4.2 When the analyst calls these dealers "efficient," let's assume that this means vertical integration will not result in cost savings related to transaction costs, managerial diseconomies, or similar areas. Even so, if these dealers have some market power and make an economic profit (perhaps because they have a local monopoly in their geographic area), then the manufacturer can increase its profit with vertical integration because this integration eliminates double marginalization.

CHAPTER 12

Decisions About Production, Products, and Location

12.1 Joint Production

1.2 a. Beef and cowhides are produced from steers, so the demand for steers is the sum of the demand for beef and the demand for cowhides. Accordingly, if the demand for beef decreases, so will the demand for steers. Graphically, the demand curves for beef and steers both shift leftward. The new equilibrium price and quantity of steers are lower as a result.

b. Beef and cowhides are produced in fixed proportions from steers. The decrease in the demand for steers causes a decrease in the equilibrium quantity of steers, which results in fewer cowhides being produced. The reduced production of cowhides raises their price.

1.4 When the price of jet fuel falls, one reaction of Tesoro's managers is to refine less oil. This reaction lowers their total production of all refined oil products. Their second reaction is to refine oil into proportionally less jet fuel and more of the other oil products.

1.6 Raising the production of one good raises your company's total profit from that particular good but lowers the total profit from the other good. Marginal analysis helps you find the proportions of boards and sawdust that maximize the total overall profit. The profit-maximizing combination is the combination where the increase in profit from increased production of one good is equal to the loss in profit from decreased production of the other good.

12.2 The Multi-Plant Firm

2.2 Newmont Mining Company's managers are not maximizing their firm's profits. They should produce the quantity that sets their overall marginal cost equal to their marginal revenue and then allocate production between the two mines so that the marginal cost at each mine is equal to the firm's marginal revenue. This necessarily means that the marginal costs of the mines are equal if they are maximizing their profits. Because the marginal cost at the Twin Creeks Mine is less than the marginal cost at the Carlin Mine, if the managers rearranged production by producing one more ton at the Twin Creeks Mine and one less at the Carlin Mine, their total production would remain the same, but their total costs would be lower.

2.4 Producing where marginal revenue is equal to each plant's marginal cost will result in too many units produced because the marginal revenue curve is for *total* production, not the *individual* production at an individual plant. If the firm produced where each *factory's* marginal cost equaled the *market* marginal revenue, it would have produced more than the profit-maximizing quantity because the overall marginal cost of the total quantity produced would exceed the marginal revenue. This situation is not profit maximizing because the firm would be producing units that are unprofitable.

2.6 In general for a firm with multiple plants, it is profit maximizing to produce the quantity that sets the overall marginal cost equal to the marginal revenue and then allocate production among the plants so that the marginal cost at each one is equal to the firm's marginal revenue. In a perfectly competitive industry, the market price is the marginal revenue, so the marginal revenue is constant at $50 at any quantity. This result makes the analysis easier. Because the marginal revenue is constant, you can set the marginal cost at each of your plants equal to $50 and solve for the quantity produced at each plant. For plant 1, we have

$$MR = mc_1$$
$$50 = 10 + q_1$$
$$q_1 = 40$$

For plant 2, we have

$$MR = mc_2$$
$$50 = 10 + 0.5q_2$$
$$q_2 = 80$$

Finally, for plant 3, we have

$$MR = mc_3$$
$$50 = 10 + 0.1q_3$$
$$q_3 = 400$$

12.3 Location Decisions

3.2 Doubling the number of warehouses increased the complexity of Amazon.com's operations and possibly introduced significant managerial diseconomies. The additional profit from expanding the number of warehouses may have been less than the increase in cost from these managerial diseconomies, so Amazon.com's total profit fell.

3.4 In part, Bridgestone's managers do not centralize production because having multiple plants in different areas reduces the cost of transporting tires to customers and retailers. In addition, by having multiple plants, managers can react to factors that change the cost at one plant—say, an increase in transportation costs into or out of one plant or an increase in the cost of electricity—by switching more production to another plant or plants.

3.6 Risky jobs have higher wages because of the compensating wage differential that is paid to reflect the danger to workers. The riskier the job, the higher the wage rate. Expenditures incurred to reduce these risks lower the compensating wage differential and reduce the firm's cost. If the cost reduction from lower wages is more than the expenditure to reduce the risk, the firm's profit increases by making the expenditure.

12.4 Decisions about Product Quality

4.2 The slogan "Quality Is Job 1" suggests Ford is improving the quality of its products as much as possible. At this point, the marginal cost of such quality improvements is surely larger than the marginal revenue due to higher-quality products. Ford could increase its profit by lowering product quality, so if the slogan was strictly true, the amount of Ford's quality improvement was not profit maximizing.

4.4 American Italian Pasta Company can lower its cost by blending more low-quality wheat into its pasta products. Consumers, however, are willing to pay only a lower price for a lower-quality product. American Italian Pasta Company's managers must compare the marginal revenue they will lose from their customers to the lower marginal cost of producing lower-quality pasta.

12.5 Optimal Inventories

5.2 a. The equation for the cost-minimizing order quantity is

$$Q_{ORDER} = \sqrt{\frac{2 \times C_{FC} \times Q}{C}}$$

Using the values given in the problem, the cost-minimizing quantity to order is

$$Q_{ORDER} = \sqrt{\frac{2 \times \$10 \times 800}{\$40}} = 20$$

The number of orders is $Q/Q_{ORDER} = 800/20 = 40$. The total cost is

$$\frac{(C \times Q_{ORDER})}{2} + \left[C_{FC} \times \left(\frac{Q}{Q_{ORDER}} \right) \right] + (C_{VAR} \times Q)$$

Using the values given in the problem, the total cost is

$$(\$40 \times 20)/2 + (\$10 \times 40) + (\$200 \times 800) = \$160,800$$

b. If 80 smartphones are ordered each time, the number of orders is $800/80 = 10$. The total cost becomes

$$(\$40 \times 80)/2 + (\$10 \times 10) + (\$200 \times 800) = \$161,700$$

c. If 10 smartphones are ordered each time, the number of orders is $800/10 = 80$. The total cost becomes

$$(\$40 \times 10)/2 + (\$10 \times 80) + (\$200 \times 800) = \$161,000$$

d. Ordering 80 or 10 smartphones results in higher total costs than ordering the quantity from the economic order quantity model, 20 smartphones. Ordering 20 smartphones minimizes the total cost of ordering and carrying smartphones in inventory.

5.4 An increase in the fixed cost of placing an order, C_{FC}, increases the size of the order. We can see this result from the equation for the optimal order quantity:

$$Q_{ORDER} = \sqrt{\frac{2 \times C_{FC} \times Q}{C}}$$

This equation shows that the optimal order quantity increases as the fixed cost of ordering increases.

Marginal analysis gives the same result. As the fixed cost of ordering increases, the marginal benefit of increasing the quantity ordered increases because then fewer orders must be placed, thereby avoiding the higher fixed cost. The marginal cost of increasing the order size is unchanged, so $MB > MC$. Marginal analysis tells us the optimal quantity per order sets $MB = MC$, so the quantity ordered is too low when $MB > MC$. Accordingly, as the fixed cost of ordering increases, the optimal quantity per order increases.

5.6 The marginal benefit of increasing the order quantity is the reduction in the fixed cost of ordering. The marginal cost is the increase in the carrying cost associated with larger orders. As usual, managers maximize profit by choosing the quantity that sets the marginal benefit equal to the marginal cost.

12.6 Managerial Application: Production, Products, and Location

6.2   Higher gasoline prices lead to higher transportation costs for your customers. Consequently, customers in Europe are willing to pay a higher price at a closer pharmacy than are customers in the United States located near an equally close pharmacy. Your marginal revenue from locating closer to consumers is therefore higher in Europe. All else equal, the profit-maximizing location for stores in Europe will be closer to customers than in the United States. So you will locate more small, local pharmacies in Europe than the United States.

CHAPTER **13**

Marketing Decisions: Advertising and Promotion

13.1 Profit-Maximizing Advertising by a Firm

1.2   a.   See the figure. The curves with the subscript 0 apply when there is zero advertising, with subscript 1 when there is one campaign, and with subscript 2 when there is two campaigns. With no advertising, the profit-maximizing quantity is found where $MR_0 = MC$. This quantity is 300 pizzas per day. The profit-maximizing price is the

Price and cost (dollars per pizza)

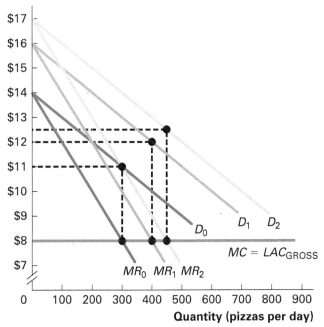

highest price consumers will pay for this quantity. From the demand curve, this price is $11. The pizzeria's economic profit is $(P - LAC_{GROSS}) \times Q = (\$11 - \$8) \times 300 = \$900$.

b.   The marginal benefit from the first advertising campaign is the amount by which it increases the pizzeria's gross profit. As shown in the figure, the profit-maximizing quantity and price with one campaign are 400 pizzas per day (the quantity at which $MR_1 = MC$) and $12 (from demand curve D_1), respectively. This price and quantity yield an economic profit of $(\$12 - \$8) \times 400 = \$1,600$. This economic profit is $700 more than without a campaign, so the marginal benefit is $700.

c.   As shown in the figure, the profit-maximizing quantity and price with two campaigns are 450 pizzas per day (the quantity at which $MR_2 = MC$) and $12.50 (from demand curve D_2), respectively. This price and quantity yield an economic profit of $(\$12.50 - \$8) \times 450 = \$2,025$. Therefore, the marginal benefit from a second campaign is $425, the increase in economic profit from running the second campaign.

d.   Each campaign costs $600. The first campaign has a marginal benefit of $700. This is greater than the marginal cost of the campaign, so it is profitable. The second campaign is not profitable because the marginal benefit is $425, which is less than the marginal cost.

1.4   The marginal cost of advertising is $500 per week. The marginal benefit is how much each additional campaign increases your restaurant's gross profit. The profit-maximizing number of campaigns sets this marginal benefit equal to marginal cost, which occurs at three campaigns.

1.6   a.   Your marginal benefit schedule is the amount by which each campaign increases your gross profit: $12 million for the first campaign, $8 million for the second, and so on.

b.   The marginal cost of an advertising campaign is its price: $4 million.

c.   The profit-maximizing number of campaigns sets your marginal benefit equal to marginal cost, which occurs at three campaigns.

13.2 Optimal Advertising by an Industry

2.2   The amount of the CBB's advertising is not the profit-maximizing amount because the marginal benefit ($5) is greater than the marginal cost ($1). The CBB could increase the industry's profit by raising more funds and purchasing more advertising.

2.4 **a.** The industry-wide marginal benefit schedule is the sum of the marginal benefits to the individual firms at every quantity. This sum is shown in the table below:

Quantity of Advertisements (units)	Industry-Wide Marginal Benefit
1	$700
2	560
3	420
4	280
5	140

b. The profit-maximizing quantity of advertisements sets the industry-wide marginal benefit equal to the marginal cost of an additional advertisement (the price), which occurs at four advertisements.

c. An advertisement costs $280, and four are purchased, so the total cost is 4 × $280 = $1,120.

d. Fairness is ambiguous; different people can have different beliefs about what is fair. One method that might be considered fair is for each firm to pay in proportion to its marginal benefit. Firm A should pay 4 × $40 = $160, Firm B should pay 4 × $60 = $240, and so on. This allocation can be considered fair because firms pay an amount proportional to the benefit they receive. Another method that might be considered fair is for each firm to pay one-fourth of the cost, or $280 each.

e. If you allocate the costs according to the marginal benefits, firms with a greater marginal benefit from advertising will pay a larger percentage of the total cost of advertising. These firms will complain that the other firms are not paying enough. If you allocate costs so each firm pays one-fourth of the cost, the firms that receive less benefit from the advertising will complain that they are paying too much.

13.3 False Advertising

3.2 **a.** This is an experience good. The consumer cannot determine the durability of a tire before it is purchased but can after using it for a period of time.

b. This is an inspection good. A consumer can easily observe when a flight is scheduled to take off. Whether the flight actually takes off at the scheduled time is another matter.

c. This is a credence good. It is impossible for the consumer to determine the organic nature of prepackaged chicken.

d. This is an inspection good. A consumer can weigh the smartphone without making a purchase.

e. This is an experience good. The consumer cannot determine battery life before purchase, but after using the smartphone for some time, the consumer will learn how long the battery lasts.

f. This is a credence good. Although physical characteristics of the fender such as color and appearance are inspection goods, the inherent quality of the fender cannot be determined by the consumer.

3.4 You can make a complaint to the FTC about the firm engaging in false advertising and file a civil suit under the Lanham Act. If you win the civil suit, you may collect as damages any profits lost due to your competitor's false advertising.

13.4 Resale Price Maintenance and Product Promotion

4.2 Retailers that do not provide product-specific services are free riding on those that do because they benefit from the increased demand created by the product-specific services. Free riders can sell for a lower price because they do not incur the costs of these services. In this case, customers can receive the services from retailers that offer them but then buy the product at a lower price from the free-riding retailers. The retailers providing the services may well decide to stop, which can decrease overall sales of the product, thereby harming the manufacturer.

4.4 **a.** As the figure shows, both services increase demand by more than they decrease supply, so you want your retailers to both display and demonstrate your cameras.

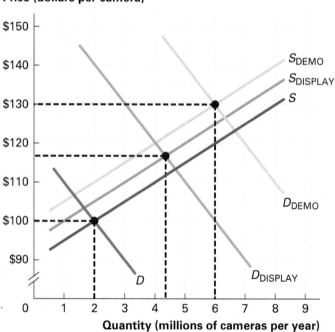

Price (dollars per camera)

b. You should set the minimum price that covers retailers' costs of providing both services, which the figure shows is $130.

13.5 International Marketing: Entry and Corruption Laws

5.2 You should be concerned about possible bribery by the foreign firm; if bribery has indeed occurred, your firm will be in violation of the FCPA after you purchase the foreign firm.

5.4
a. This is clearly a bribe offered and paid to a government official, which is an FCPA violation.
b. Bribery is an FCPA violation even if the bribe is offered but not paid. The promise of a bribe is enough for your firm to be liable under the FCPA.
c. Even if the bribe is ineffective, it is a violation of the FCPA. Your firm is still liable even though the government official did not follow through on the promise to award the contract to your firm.

13.6 Managerial Appliction: Marketing and Promotional Decisions

6.2
a. The equilibrium price is $59 because that price sets the quantity supplied equal to the quantity demanded. The equilibrium quantity is 11,000 units per week.
b. The following table summarizes the changes to quantity supplied and quantity demanded at each price when product-specific services are offered:

Price (dollars per unit)	Quantity Supplied (units per week)	Quantity Demanded (units per week)
62	12,000	12,000
63	13,000	11,000
64	14,000	10,000
65	15,000	9,000

Now the equilibrium price is $62, and the equilibrium quantity is 12,000 units per week. These services have increased your profit. Because the equilibrium quantity has increased, your company is selling 1,000 more units per week to retailers, thereby increasing your profit.
c. You should set the minimum price of $62. This price covers your retailers' initial costs ($60 at the profit-maximizing level of output, 12,000 units per week) plus the additional cost of demonstrating the product ($2) per unit.

CHAPTER 14
Business Decisions Under Uncertainty

14.1 Basics of Probability

1.2 Use the expected value formula to solve this problem. The probability that his salary will be $4.0 million (when the team exercises the option) is 0.60. That means the probability the team doesn't exercise the option is 0.40. His salary in this case is $500,000. The expected payment to Larry is ($4.0 million $\times$ 0.60) + ($500,000 $\times$ 0.40) = $2.6 million.

1.4 Use the expected value formula to solve this problem. You will receive $80,000 with a probability of 0.30; you will receive $90,000 with a probability of 0.50; and, you will receive $105,000 with a probability of 0.20. Consequently your expected income, $E[\text{INCOME}]$, is equal to

($80,000 $\times$ 0.30) + ($90,000 $\times$ 0.50) + ($105,000 $\times$ 0.20) = $90,000

1.6 Using the information provided in the table, the expected price of diesel fuel, $E[\text{PRICE}]$, is equal to

($2.50 $\times$ 0.10) + ($2.60 $\times$ 0.20) + ($2.70 $\times$ 0.20) + ($2.80 $\times$ 0.40) + ($2.90 $\times$ 0.10) = $2.72

14.2 Profit Maximization with Random Demand and Random Cost

2.2
a. The quantity of corn that maximizes expected profit is the amount that sets the expected marginal revenue equal to the marginal cost. Because the corn farm is perfectly competitive, the expected marginal revenue is the expected price. The expected price equals the two prices, $12 and $6, each weighted by its probability of occurrence: 2/3 and 1/3, respectively. So the expected price and expected marginal revenue is

$$E[P] = E[MR] = (\$12 \times 2/3) + (\$6 \times 1/3) = \$10$$

Using this expected marginal revenue, the figure in the problem shows that 40,000 bushels of corn is the quantity that sets the expected marginal revenue equal to the marginal cost. So 40,000 bushels of corn maximize the farm's expected profit.
b. If you knew the actual price, you would produce wherever $MR = MC$. So you would produce either 50,000 bushels when the price is $12 or 20,000 bushels when the price is $6.

Price and cost (dollars per bushel of corn)

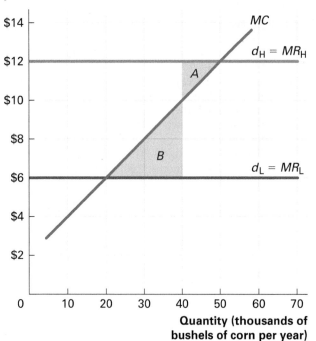

c. We can see how much profit is lost graphically using the figure. The quantity of corn that maximizes the expected profit is 40,000 bushels. If the actual price is $12 and you knew this would be the price, you would produce 50,000 bushels. So the loss of profit from producing 40,000 bushels rather than 50,000 is equal to the area of triangle A in the figure, which equals

$$1/2 \times (50{,}000 - 40{,}000) \times (\$12 - \$10) = \$10{,}000$$

Accordingly, you lose $10,000 of profit because you do not know that the price will be $12 per bushel.

If the actual price is $6 and you knew this would be the price, you would produce 20,000 bushels. So the loss from producing 40,000 bushels rather than 20,000 is equal to the area of triangle B in the figure, which is

$$1/2 \times (40{,}000 - 20{,}000) \times (\$10 - \$6) = \$40{,}000$$

Consequently, you lose $40,000 of profit because you do not know that the price will be $9 per bushel.

2.4 a. To maximize expected profit, requires producing where $E(MR) = MC$. The expected marginal revenue is equal to the expected price because this firm is in a perfectly competitive market. Equal probability means the probability

of either price is 0.50, so the expected price and marginal revenue is

$$E[P] = E[MR] = (\$4.40 \times 0.50) + (\$4.80 \times 0.50) = \$4.60$$

The quantity that maximizes expected profit is the amount that equates the expected marginal revenue to the marginal cost, so using the marginal cost function gives the profit-maximizing quantity

$$0.02Q = 4.60$$
$$Q = 230$$

b. If the actual price is $4.80 and the managers know this, because $P = MR$, the profit-maximizing quantity is

$$0.02Q = 4.80$$
$$Q = 240$$

The lost profit is the area of a triangle with its base equal to the difference between the actual profit-maximizing quantity and the expected profit-maximizing quantity $(240 - 230)$ and its height equal to the difference between the actual price and the expected price $(\$4.80 - \$4.60)$. Using the area of a triangle formula, this lost profit is

$$1/2 \times (240 - 230) \times (\$4.80 - \$4.60) = \$1$$

If the actual price is $4.40 and the managers know this, the profit-maximizing quantity is

$$0.02Q = 4.40$$
$$Q = 220$$

The amount of lost profit is the area of a triangle with its base equal to the difference between the expected profit-maximizing quantity and the actual profit-maximizing quantity $(230 - 220)$ and its height equal to the difference between the expected price and the actual price $(\$4.60 - \$4.40)$. In this case, the lost profit is

$$1/2 \times (230 - 220) \times (\$4.60 - \$4.40) = \$1$$

2.6 a. Start by using the demand function to solve for the price (P) as a function of the quantity demanded (Q):

$$P = 100 - 0.1Q$$

This equation is called the inverse demand function. The marginal revenue has the same vertical intercept as the inverse demand function (100) and a slope twice that of the inverse demand function (0.2):

$$MR = 100 - 0.2Q$$

Next, find the expected marginal cost facing the monopolist. The probabilities of the high price and the low price both equal 0.50, so the expected marginal cost is

$$E[MC] = (\$50 \times 0.50) + (\$30 \times 0.50) = \$40$$

Equate the expected marginal cost with the marginal revenue function to find the expected profit-maximizing quantity:

$$40 = 100 - 0.2Q$$
$$Q = 300$$

Substitute this quantity into the inverse demand function to find the expected profit-maximizing price:

$$P = 100 - 0.1Q$$
$$= \$70$$

b.   The expected marginal cost is now

$$E[MC] = (\$60 \times 0.50) + (\$20 \times 0.50) = \$40$$

This expected marginal cost is the same as in part a. Consequently, the quantity and price that maximize the monopolist's expected profit are the same as before: The quantity is 300, and the price is $70.

c.   The answers to parts a and b are identical because the expected marginal cost did not change.

14.3 Optimal Inventories with Random Demand

3.2   a.   The completed table has the answers.

b.   The optimal quantity of cars to keep in inventory is the quantity that sets the expected marginal benefit equal to the expected marginal cost—in other words, where

$$\text{Profit per car} \times \text{Prob}(Q^D \geq Q) = \text{Loss per car} \times \text{Prob}(Q^D < Q)$$

Using the values in the table, the quantity that solves this equation is 97 cars.

3.4   A fall in the price in the secondary market decreases the profit (or increases the loss) from selling on the secondary market. The expected marginal benefit from holding inventory does not change, but the expected marginal cost of holding inventory increases. The optimal inventory decreases.

14.4 Minimizing the Cost of Random Adverse Events

4.2   The fall in the cost of patent searches as a result of computerization shifts the marginal cost of avoiding an accident curve downward, as more patents can be searched at a lower cost. The cost-minimizing quantity of patent searches is higher than before. As a result, the profit-maximizing rate of patent infringement is lower.

14.5 The Business Decision to Settle Litigation

5.2   You should consider settling the suit even if you are innocent. You should be concerned with minimizing your expected loss due to the suit. Litigating carries the risk that you will lose despite your innocence as well as the certainty of legal fees. You can avoid both of these by settling.

5.4   a.   The plaintiffs will receive a total of $320 million if they win, which they expect to occur with a probability of 0.75. If they lose, which occurs

Accompanies problem 3.2.

Quantity of Cars Demanded	Probability This Quantity Is Demanded	Probability of Selling This Quantity or More, Prob($Q^D \geq Q$)	Probability of Selling Less Than This Quantity, Prob($Q^D < Q$)
90	0.05	1.00	0
91	0.05	0.95	0.05
92	0.10	0.90	0.10
93	0.10	0.80	0.20
94	0.20	0.70	0.30
95	0.20	0.50	0.50
96	0.10	0.30	0.70
97	0.10	0.20	0.80
98	0.05	0.10	0.90
99	0.05	0.05	0.95
100	0	0	1.00

with a probability of 0.25, they will receive nothing. The plaintiffs' expected gain is

$$E[GAIN] = (\$320 \text{ million} \times 0.75) + (\$0 \times 0.25) - \$20 \text{ million}$$
$$= \$220 \text{ million}$$

Your firm pays $320 million if the plaintiffs win and $0 otherwise. Your expected loss is

$$E[LOSS] = (\$320 \text{ million} \times 0.60) + (\$0 \times 0.40) + \$20 \text{ million}$$
$$= \$212 \text{ million}$$

Your expected loss, $212 million, is smaller than the plaintiffs' expected gain, $220 million, so you would not be willing to pay the plaintiffs' expected gain in order to settle. Therefore, settlement is unlikely in this case.

b. Now the plaintiffs' expected gain is

$$E[GAIN] = (\$100 \text{ million} \times 0.75) + (\$0 \times 0.25) - \$20 \text{ million}$$
$$= \$55 \text{ million}$$

Your expected loss is now

$$E[LOSS] = (\$100 \text{ million} \times 0.60) + (\$0 \times 0.40) + \$20 \text{ million}$$
$$= \$80 \text{ million}$$

Your expected loss, $80 million, is larger than the plaintiffs' expected gain, $55 million, so you would be willing to pay the plaintiffs' expected gain in order to settle. Therefore, settlement is now likely.

14.6 Risk Aversion

6.2 a. A settlement is unlikely because the plaintiff's expected gain exceeds your expected loss.

b. If you become risk averse, you become willing to pay more than your expected loss to avoid the possibility of paying $40 million if you lose the case. A settlement of $4 million, although greater than your expected loss, becomes more appealing due to your risk aversion, thereby making a settlement more likely.

14.7 Managerial Application: Making Business Decisions Under Uncertainty

7.2 The marginal benefit of trimming your lead time is $200,000, the amount of reduction in your expected loss. The marginal cost is the cost of trimming an additional day of lead time. The profit-maximizing number of days to trim is the quantity where the marginal benefit equals the marginal cost, which is two days of lead time.

7.4 a. Using the values in the text table, the expected damages are

$$(\$40,000 \times 0.30) + (\$50,000 \times 0.20) + (\$70,000 \times 0.20)$$
$$+ (\$80,000 \times 0.10) + (\$100,000 \times 0.10) + (\$120,000 \times 0.10)$$
$$= \$66,000$$

b. The expected loss is equal to:

$$E[LOSS] = (\$66,000 \times 0.50) + (\$0 \times 0.50) + \$100,000 = \$133,000$$

c. With these changes, the expected damages are

$$(\$40,000 \times 0.30) + (\$50,000 \times 0.20) + (\$70,000 \times 0.20)$$
$$+ (\$80,000 \times 0.10) + (\$100,000 \times 0.10) + (\$120,000 \times 0.09)$$
$$+ (\$4 \text{ million} \times 0.01) = \$104,800$$

Your expected loss from litigation is now

$$E[LOSS] = (\$104,800 \times 0.50) + (\$0 \times 0.50) + \$100,000$$
$$= \$152,400$$

You are now more likely to settle because the expected loss has increased. In addition, if you are risk averse, the likelihood that you will settle has increased due to the risk of a potentially very large ($4 million) payment.

CHAPTER 15
Managerial Decisions About Information

15.1 Intellectual Property

1.2 a. Your firm is entitled to collect damages adequate to compensate for the infringement. Assuming the reduction in profit after the start-up used your procedure is entirely due to the infringement, you would have earned $100 million but for the infringing company, so you may collect $100 million − $40 million = $60 million in damages.

b. Once again, assuming the reduction in profit after the start-up used your procedure is entirely due to the infringement, you would have earned $100 million but for the infringing company, so you may again collect $100 million − $40 million = $60 million in damages.

1.4 a. You are entitled to the other company's profit attributable to the infringement as well as any damages sustained by your firm. Your lost profit is $100 million − $40 million = $60 million. The other company's profit is $30 million, so you may collect a total of $60 million + $30 million = $90 million.

b. Again, assuming the other company's entire profit and your entire reduction in profit are attributable to the infringement, your company may now collect $60 million (your lost profit) + $80 million (the other company's profit), or $140 million.

15.2 Value of Forecasts

2.2 To determine what you would pay for a perfect forecast, you must calculate your profit with a perfect forecast and compare it to the expected profit when you have no information about the price beyond its expected value.

Because your firm is a perfectly competitive producer, the equilibrium price is also its marginal revenue. The expected marginal revenue is then

$$E[MR] = (\$25 \times 0.50) + (\$15 \times 0.50) = \$20$$

If you have no information about the marginal revenue beyond its expected value, you maximize expected profit by producing the quantity that sets $E[MR] = MC$. In the case at hand, that means

$$\$20 = \$5 + \$0.50Q \Rightarrow Q = 30$$

Now suppose that the price turns out to be $25 (the high price) and you correctly forecast this price. Then the profit-maximizing output is

$$\$25 = \$5 + \$0.50Q \Rightarrow Q = 40$$

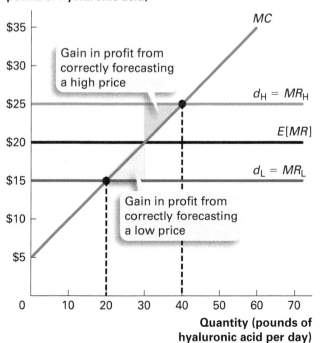

Price and cost (dollars per pound of hyaluronic acid)

Next, suppose that the price turns out to be $15 (the low price) and you correctly forecast this price. Then the profit-maximizing output is

$$\$15 = \$5 + \$0.50Q \Rightarrow Q = 20$$

To determine the amount you would be willing to pay for a perfect forecast, you need to find the increase in profit from correctly forecasting the price. The figure illustrates this gain. The area of the upper dark green triangle is the gain in profit from correctly forecasting a high price. Its area is $\frac{1}{2} \times (40 - 30) \times (\$25 - \$20) = \$25$. The area of the lower light green triangle is the gain in profit from correctly forecasting a low price. Its area is $\frac{1}{2} \times (30 - 20) \times (\$20 - \$15) = \$25$. The high price occurs half the time, and the low price occurs half the time. Therefore, the gain in profit from correctly forecasting the price is equal to $(0.5 \times \$25) + (0.5 \times \$25) = \$25$, so you should pay $25 at most for a perfect forecast.

2.4 The value of a perfect forecast is equal to the difference between the profit when the firm accurately forecasts the price and the profit when the firm produces the quantity that sets $E[MR] = MC$.

Because the firm is a perfectly competitive producer, the price is also its marginal revenue. So as the first step the expected price equals the expected marginal revenue:

$$E[P] = E[MR] = (\$12 \times 0.50) + (\$8 \times 0.50) = \$10$$

Next, using the expected marginal revenue, solve for the quantity that sets $E[MR] = MC$:

$$\$10 = \$5 + \$0.01Q \Rightarrow Q = 500$$

Now, suppose that the price turns out to be $12 (the high price). If this price is forecast, the profit-maximizing quantity is the amount that sets $MR = MC$:

$$\$12 = \$5 + \$0.01Q \Rightarrow Q = 700$$

When the price is high, the gain in profit from the forecast equals the difference between the price and the marginal cost for all the copper bracelets between 500 and 700. Using the figure, the increase in profit equals the area of the dark green triangle:

$$\frac{1}{2} \times (700 - 500) \times (\$12 - \$10) = \$200$$

So the profit gained from forecasting the high price is $200.

Now suppose that the price turns out to be $8 (the low price). If this price is forecast, the profit-maximizing quantity is the amount that sets $MR = MC$:

$$\$8 = \$5 + \$0.01Q \Rightarrow Q = 300$$

Price and cost (dollars per bracelet)

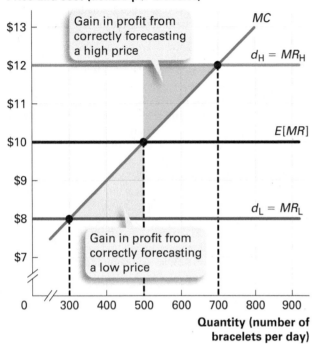

When the price is low, the increase in profit from the forecast is the difference between the marginal cost and the price for all the copper bracelets between 300 and 500. Using the figure, the gained profit equals the area of the light green triangle:

$$\tfrac{1}{2} \times (500 - 300) \times (\$10 - \$8) = \$200$$

So when the price is low, the increase in profit is (also) $200.

When the price is higher than average, a perfect forecast gives the firm an additional $200 in profit, and when the price is lower than average, a perfect forecast also gives an additional $200 in profit. One-half the time the price is higher than average, and one-half the time the price is lower. So the firm gains $(0.50 \times \$200) + (0.50 \times \$200) = \$200$ in additional profit from a perfect forecast. This amount is the value of a perfect forecast.

15.3 Auctions

3.2 a. You should bid less than $20 million because you are uncertain about your valuation, but you might change this maximum bid during the auction. If the other bidders are placing much higher bids than you expected, you should increase your maximum bid because they probably have additional information you lack. Conversely, you should decrease your maximum bid if the other bidders are placing lower bids than you expected.

b. You should bid less than $20 million. You pay whatever you bid, so you should decrease your bid below your valuation depending on how uncertain you are about the valuation of the field. You do not receive any information from competing bidders because the first to bid wins, so you will not change your maximum bid as the auction proceeds.

c. You should bid less than $20 million. Your strategy is the same as for the Dutch auction. You do not receive any information from competing bidders because bids are sealed, so you will not change your maximum bid as the auction proceeds.

d. You should bid less than $20 million but more than your bids in parts b and c because if you win, you will pay only the second-highest bid, rather than your own. Even if you have vastly overestimated the value of the field, you may avoid the winner's curse if the second-highest bid is more reasonable. You do not receive any information from competing bidders because bids are sealed, so you will not change your maximum bid as the auction proceeds.

3.4 Aside from knowing the true value of the auctioned item, there is no certain way to avoid the winner's curse. However, managers can mitigate the risk of the winner's curse by bidding below their valuations, avoiding auctions with many bidders, and trying to obtain as much information about the item as possible (or at least more than their competitors have).

15.4 Asymmetric Information

4.2 a. You should expect approximately the same breakdown of safe versus risky drivers (80 percent versus 20 percent) because there seems to be no reason not to join. All drivers would like the chance for discounts, even if the risky drivers must be very lucky to get them.

b. Risky drivers likely left the program to avoid surcharges, leaving only safe drivers. With this change, it is probable that more than 80 percent of the Snapshot program drivers are safe and less than 20 percent are risky.

4.4 Brand names act as signals. Manufacturers with a good brand reputation are signaling to consumers that their products are high quality, rather than "lemons." Consumers are therefore more likely to buy products from these manufacturers.

4.6 A share buyback indicates the managers of the firm believe their company's stock is undervalued; that is, its price is less than it should be. If American Airlines' stock price was higher than the managers' valuation, it would not make sense for them to initiate a share buyback. Because the managers probably have some private information about the company's true valuation, the buyback signals that the managers believe the company's stock is underpriced relative to what they think it's true value is.

4.8   a.   This situation is a principal–agent problem. The top executives are the principals, and the loan managers are the agents. This principal–agent problem reflects moral hazard because the loan managers know the risk of the loans they make, but the executives that oversee them have less information about the risk. The executives might prefer a less risky portfolio of loans, but the loan managers have the incentive to make only risky loans because they substantially gain if the loan pays off but lose little to nothing if the loan fails.

    b.   As a bank executive, you could make the loan managers' bonuses depend on profits *net* of losses to give the loan managers the incentive to be more averse to the risk of losses.

    c.   You could use regulations to limit the number of loans of the type that often turn out to be risky. You could also require that the bank tie its executives' compensation to the number of defaulted loans, which gives the executives the incentive to discover ways to limit the moral hazard.

15.5 Managerial Application: Decisions about Information

5.2   When Nortel's managers allowed bidders to examine the patents, the managers reduced bidders' uncertainty about their value. That gave bidders more confidence in their valuations, and they placed bids closer to these valuations because they had less concern about the winner's curse. So by allowing the bidders to examine the patents, Nortel's managers increased their auction revenue.

5.4   a.   The managers are the principals, and the drivers are the agents. Managers want to avoid paying fines, so they want drivers to obey FMCSA regulations. On the other hand, the drivers want to maximize the number of miles they drive in order to earn more money. Driving more than the maximum allowable hours enables drivers to increase their mileage, but this violates FMCSA regulations. So the managers face the principal–agent problem of motivating drivers to obey the regulations.

    b.   You could pay drivers on an hourly basis with a cap of 11 hours to avoid violating FMCSA regulations. However, this would likely create an additional principal–agent problem: Now drivers want to maximize their time on the road, not their distance driven, so they will likely get to their destination more slowly. Another option is to place a monitoring system, such as GPS, in the drivers' trucks. Such a system could prevent the truck from starting if the driver has already driven 11 hours and/or hasn't taken 10 consecutive hours off.

CHAPTER 16

Using Present Value to Make Multiperiod Managerial Decisions

16.1 Fundamentals of Present Value

1.2   Using the annuity factor from Table 16.3 for discounting a sum of money received for 10 years at an interest rate of 9 percent (6.1446), the present value is equal to $PV = 6.1446 \times \$80,000 = \$491,568$. This sum, \$491,568, invested at 9 percent interest for 10 years, will grow to equal the same amount as the \$80,000 received every year for 10 years and invested at 9 percent interest.

1.4   When the discount rate rises, the present value of a future payment decreases. This change occurs because the higher the discount rate, the more interest that can be earned on money in the present. Consequently, less money is necessary in the present to grow to equal the amount of the future payment.

1.6   a.   The discount factor from Table 16.1 is 0.7921. Therefore, the present value is $\$1,000 \times 0.7921 = \$792.10$.

    b.   The discount factor from Table 16.1 is 0.6274. Therefore, the present value is $\$1,000 \times 0.6274 = \$627.40$.

    c.   The discount factor from Table 16.1 is 0.5019. Therefore, the present value is $\$1,000 \times 0.5019 = \$501.90$.

1.8   The fee paid to the Golden Eagles, \$20 million, was received in the present so it is not discounted. The present value of Tanaka's contract is then

$$PV = \$20 \text{ million} + \sum_{j=1}^{6}\left[\frac{1}{(1.08)^j} \times \$22 \text{ million}\right] + \left[\frac{1}{(1.08)^7} \times \$23 \text{ million}\right] = \$135.12 \text{ million}$$

16.2 Evaluating Investment Options

2.2   The depreciation allowance decreases the firm's taxable profit, which lowers the amount the firm must pay in taxes and thereby increases the firm's after-tax profit. The increase in the after-tax profit increases the net present value of the firm's investment. In other words, because depreciation is tax deductible, the net present value of the investment increases.

16.3 Make-or-Buy Decisions

3.2 Making syringes internally yields a cost saving of $2.05 − $1.90 = $0.15 per syringe. You will sell 3,000,000 syringes per year, so if you buy the equipment, the annual cost savings are $0.15 × 3,000,000 = $450,000. You can also sell the capital equipment for the same price you initially paid for it, $2,000,000. However, because this sale will occur in 12 years, this amount must be discounted. Thus, the net present value of producing syringes internally is

$$NPV = \sum_{j=1}^{12} \left[\frac{1}{(1.09)^j} \times \$450,000 \right]$$
$$+ \left[\frac{1}{(1.09)^{12}} \times \$2,000,000 \right] - \$2,000,000$$
$$= \$1,933,395.82$$

The net present value is positive, so you should make your own syringes.

3.4 **a.** BMW will save $8,000 − $7,800 = $200 per car if it produces the batteries internally. The managers expect to sell 10,000 cars per year, so the annual cost savings from leasing the factory are $200 × 10,000 = $2,000,000. The factory is leased, not bought, so there is no salvage value though there is the $10 million lease payment that must be immediately paid. The net present value of producing these batteries internally is

$$NPV = \sum_{j=1}^{7} \left[\frac{1}{(1+.06)^j} \times \$2,000,000 \right] - \$10,000,000$$
$$= \$1,164,762.88$$

The net present value is positive, so you should lease the plant to produce batteries internally.

b. With a discount rate of 10 percent (0.10), the net present value is now

$$NPV = \sum_{j=1}^{7} \left[\frac{1}{(1.10)^j} \times \$2,000,000 \right] - \$10,000,000$$
$$= -\$263,162.36$$

Now the net present value is negative, so you should not lease the plant.

16.4 Managerial Application: Present Value and Net Present Value

4.2 **a.** The price of a bond is its present value for a given discount rate. At a discount rate of 5 percent and using the annuity factor from Table 16.2 (7.2717) for the annual payments and the discount factor from Table 16.1 (0.6139) for the principal repayment, the present value of this bond is

$$PV = \sum_{j=1}^{10} \left[\frac{1}{(1.05)^j} \times \$400 \right] + \left[\frac{1}{(1.05)^{10}} \times \$10,000 \right]$$
$$= \$9,047.68$$

If the discount rate rises to 9 percent, then using the annuity factor from Table 16.2 (6.4177) for the annual payments and the discount factor from Table 16.1 (0.4224) for the principal repayment, the present value of the bond falls to

$$PV = \sum_{j=1}^{10} \left[\frac{1}{(1.09)^j} \times \$400 \right] + \left[\frac{1}{(1.09)^{10}} \times \$10,000 \right]$$
$$= \$6,791.08$$

This result shows the price of the bond falls as the discount rate rises.

b. Using the annuity factor (4.3295) and discount factor (0.7835) from the tables, the price of the bond at a 5 percent discount rate is

$$PV = \sum_{j=1}^{5} \left[\frac{1}{(1.05)^j} \times \$400 \right] + \left[\frac{1}{(1.05)^5} \times \$10,000 \right]$$
$$= \$9,566.80$$

Now at a 9 percent discount rate, and using the annuity factor (3.8897) and discount factor (0.6499) from the tables, the price is

$$PV = \sum_{j=1}^{5} \left[\frac{1}{(1.09)^j} \times \$400 \right] + \left[\frac{1}{(1.09)^5} \times \$10,000 \right]$$
$$= \$8,054.88$$

Once again, the price of the bond falls as the discount rate rises.

c. The bond with more years until maturity fell the most when the discount rate increased. This difference occurs because the longer the maturity is, the further in the future the principal is received, and therefore the more heavily it is discounted. Consequently, the bond with the longer time until maturity reacts more strongly to the rise in the interest rate.

4.4 **a.** Because you immediately pay the $1 million for the press, you do not discount this amount. However, since you pay the $1.5 million for transportation and installation after a year, that amount must be discounted. Consequently, the net present value of your investment in the press is

$$NPV = \sum_{j=2}^{9}\left[\frac{1}{(1.06)^{j}} \times \$400,000\right] + \left[\frac{1}{(1.06)^{9}} \times \$500,000\right]$$
$$- \left\{\$1,000,000 + \left[\frac{1}{(1.06)} \times \$1,500,000\right]\right\} = \$224,173.31$$

The net present value is positive, so you should buy the press.

b. When the discount rate rises to 10 percent, the new net present value is

$$NPV = \sum_{j=2}^{9}\left[\frac{1}{(1.10)^{j}} \times \$400,000\right] + \left[\frac{1}{(1.10)^{9}} \times \$500,000\right]$$
$$- \left\{\$1,000,000 + \left[\frac{1}{(1.10)} \times \$1,500,000\right]\right\} = -\$211,614.39$$

With the higher discount rate, the net present value is negatives so you should not buy the press.

c. When the discount rate falls to 4 percent, the net present value is

$$NPV = \sum_{j=2}^{9}\left[\frac{1}{(1.04)^{j}} \times \$400,000\right] + \left[\frac{1}{(1.04)^{9}} \times \$500,000\right]$$
$$- \left\{\$1,000,000 + \left[\frac{1}{(1.04)} \times \$1,500,000\right]\right\} = \$498,502.94$$

The net present value is positive, so you should buy the press.

4.6   You should send your employees to training if the net present value is positive.

$$NPV = \sum_{j=1}^{5}\left[\frac{1}{(1.08)^{j}} \times \$5,000\right] - \$20,000$$
$$= -\$36.45$$

The net present value is negative so you should not send your employees to training.

ANSWER KEY TO CALCULUS APPENDICES

CHAPTER 1 APPENDIX
The Calculus of Marginal Analysis

A1.2 a. The total benefit is equal to Moose's total revenue: $TR = P \times Q$, or $TR = \$5Q$. The marginal benefit of producing and selling each additional hamburger is $MB = (dTR)/(dQ)$, or $MB = \$5$.

b. The marginal cost of producing and selling each additional hamburger is $MC = (dTC)/(dQ)$, or

$$MC = \frac{d(0.01Q^2 - 25)}{dQ} = 0.02Q$$

c. Set $MB = MC$, or $5 = 0.02Q$. Solving for Q shows that Q^* equals 250 hamburgers.

A1.4 a. Determine the surplus-maximizing number of security personnel, x^*, by using the power rule and quotient rule to take the derivative of the surplus function with respect to x:

$$\frac{dSurplus}{dx} = \frac{(x^2 + 4) \times (2 \times 100 \times x) - (100x^2 - 20) \times (2x)}{(x^2 + 4)^2} - 8.4$$

$$= \frac{840x}{x^4 + 8x^2 + 16} - 8.4$$

Setting dSurplus/dx equal to zero, and solving for the surplus-maximizing quantity of security personnel gives $x^* = 4$ security personnel.

b. The total surplus equals $\frac{100x^2 - 20}{x^2 + 4} - 8.40x$, where x is the number of security personnel. Scott's surplus-maximizing number, x^*, is 4 security personnel, which then achieves a surplus of $\frac{(100 \times 4^2) - 20}{4^2 + 4} - (8.40 \times 4)$, or surplus of 45.4.

CHAPTER 3 APPENDIX
The Calculus of Elasticity

A3.2 The weekly demand for sandwiches at a local sandwich shop is given by:

$$Q^d = 2{,}000 - 5P + 2P_j - 0.01INCOME,$$

where Q^d is the number of sandwiches demanded per week, P is the price, of a sandwich P_j is the price of a related product, and INCOME is the average monthly income of consumers.

a. Suppose that $P = \$10, P_j = \$50$, and INCOME $= \$5{,}000$. What is the value of the cross-price elasticity of demand? Is the related product a substitute good or a complement?

Start with the partial derivative of the quantity demanded with respect to the price of the related product: $\partial Q^d/\partial P_j = 2$. Next calculate the quantity demanded:

$$Q^d = 2{,}000 - (5 \times 10) + (2 \times 50) - (0.01 \times 5{,}000)$$
$$= 2{,}000$$

Now use these in the definition of the cross-price elasticity of demand,

$$\varepsilon_{CROSS} = \left(\frac{\partial Q^d}{\partial P_j}\right) \times \left(\frac{P_j}{Q^d}\right) = (2) \times \left(\frac{50}{2{,}000}\right) = 0.05$$

Because the cross-price elasticity of demand is positive, the related product is a substitute good.

b. Suppose that $P = \$10, P_j = \$50$, and INCOME $= \$5{,}000$. What is the value of the income elasticity of demand? Are sandwiches a normal or an inferior good?

Start with the partial derivative of the quantity demanded with respect to income: $\partial Q^d/\partial INCOME = -0.01$. Next calculate the quantity demanded:

$$Q^d = 2{,}000 - (5 \times 10) + (2 \times 50) - (0.01 \times 5{,}000)$$
$$= 2{,}000$$

Now use these in the definition of the income elasticity,

$$\varepsilon_{INC} = \left(\frac{\partial Q^d}{\partial INCOME}\right) \times \left(\frac{INCOME}{Q^d}\right)$$

$$= (-0.01) \times \left(\frac{5{,}000}{2{,}000}\right) = -0.025$$

Because the income elasticity of demand is negative, sandwiches are an inferior good.

A3.4 The monthly demand for bus rides in Miami, Florida depends on the price of a train ride, the price of a bus ride, and the average monthly income of riders. Some consumers might choose to ride the train instead of the bus, while other riders might use both forms of transportation to get to their final destination. The demand function for bus rides is:

$$Q^d = 9{,}750 - 500P + 250P_j + 5\text{INCOME},$$

where Q^d is the number of train rides demanded per month, P is the price of a ride, P_j is the price of a train ticket, and INCOME is the average monthly income of riders.

a. Suppose that $P = \$1.50$, $P_j = \$4.00$, and INCOME = \$3,000. What is the monthly quantity of bus rides demanded?

    Using the prices and income in the demand function shows that the quantity demanded equals:

$$Q^d = 9{,}750 - (500 \times \$1.50) + (250 \times \$4.00)$$
$$+ (5 \times 3{,}000) = 25{,}000 \text{ rides}$$

b. Suppose that $P = \$1.50$, $P_j = \$4.00$, and INCOME = \$3,000. What is the value of the cross-price elasticity of demand? Based on your answer, are train rides and bus rides substitutes or complements?

    The cross-price elasticity of demand equals $\varepsilon_{CROSS} = \left(\dfrac{\partial Q^d}{\partial P_j}\right) \times \left(\dfrac{P_j}{Q^d}\right)$. The partial derivative of the demand function with respect to the price of a train ticket, $(\partial Q^d / \partial P_j)$, is equal to 250. From part a, the quantity demanded, Q^d, is equal to 25,000. Consequently the cross-price elasticity of demand equals:

$$\varepsilon_{CROSS} = \left(\dfrac{\partial Q^d}{\partial P_j}\right) \times \left(\dfrac{P_j}{Q^d}\right) = (250) \times \left(\dfrac{4}{25{,}000}\right)$$

$$= 0.04.$$

    Because the cross-price elasticity of demand is positive, train rides and bus rides are substitutes.

c. Suppose that $P = \$1.50$, $P_j = \$4.00$, and INCOME = \$3,000. What is the value of the income elasticity of demand? Based on your answer, are train rides an inferior or a normal good?

    The income elasticity of demand equals $\varepsilon_{INC} = \left(\dfrac{\partial Q^d}{\partial \text{INCOME}}\right) \times \left(\dfrac{\text{INCOME}}{Q^d}\right).$ The partial derivative of the demand function with respect to income, $(\partial Q^d / \partial \text{INCOME})$, is 5. From part a, the quantity demanded, Q^d, is

equal to 25,000. Consequently the income elasticity of demand equals:

$$\varepsilon_{INC} = \left(\dfrac{\partial Q^d}{\partial \text{INCOME}}\right) \times \left(\dfrac{\text{INCOME}}{Q^d}\right)$$
$$= (5) \times \left(\dfrac{3{,}000}{25{,}000}\right) = 0.6.$$

Because the income elasticity of demand is positive, train rides are a normal good.

CHAPTER **4** APPENDIX
The Calculus of Cost

A4.2 Suppose that the total cost of producing a business law handbook is:

$$TC(Q) = 10{,}000 + 25Q^2 - 10Q,$$

where Q is the total number of handbooks produced.

a. What is the equation for the average total cost of producing handbooks, as a function of the quantity of handbooks produced?

    The average total cost, ATC, equals the total cost, $TC(Q) = 10{,}000 + 25Q^2 - 10Q$, divided by the quantity, Q. Consequently the average total cost equals:

$$ATC(Q) = \dfrac{10{,}000}{Q} + 25Q - 10.$$

b. At what quantity, Q^*, is the average total cost of producing a handbook minimized? What is the value of the average total cost at Q^*?

    The average total cost is minimized when $\frac{dATC}{dQ} = 0$. Using the quotient rule to take the derivative derivative of the average total cost function in part a with respect to Q gives:

$$\dfrac{dATC}{dQ} = -\dfrac{10{,}000}{Q^2} + 25 = 0.$$

    Solving this equation for the cost-minimizing quantity, the average total cost is minimized when $Q^* = 20$ handbooks. Using this quantity in the equation for the ATC from part a, the average total cost equals:

$$ATC(20) = \dfrac{10{,}000}{20} + (25 \times 20) - 10 = \$990.$$

c. At the quantity Q^* that you identified in part b, what is the marginal cost of an additional handbook?

To start, determine the marginal cost:

$$MC = \frac{dTC}{dQ} = 50Q - 10$$

Substituting $Q^* = 20$ into the equation for the marginal cost gives $MC(20) = \$990$. Of course, this result shows that when the average total cost is at its minimum, $\$990$, it equals the marginal cost, also $\$990$.

A4.4 Rose's Roses is a local flower shop specializing in rose bouquets for weddings. Rose can produce her magnificent bouquets using roses imported from Colombia or roses imported from Ecuador. Due to altitude and Ecuador's location on the equator, the Ecuadorean roses are slightly larger, meaning Rose needs fewer of them to produce each bouquet. Rose produces her bouquets according to the following production function:

$$Q = (0.1R_C) + (0.125R_E),$$

where Q is the quantity of bouquets produced, and R_C and R_E are the quantities of Colombian roses and Ecuadorian roses used, respectively. The price of a Colombian rose is $P_C = \$0.45$, and the price of an Ecuadorian rose is $P_E = \$0.45$.

a. Referring to the production function given above, what is the slope of the isoquant line, dR_E/dR_C?

The slope of the isoquant line is equal to the (negative of the) ratio of the marginal products, $-\frac{MP_C}{MP_E}$. The MP_C equals $\frac{\partial Q}{\partial R_C}$, which is 0.1. And the MP_E equals $\frac{\partial Q}{\partial R_E}$, which is 0.125. Therefore, the slope of the isoquant equals:

$$-\frac{MP_C}{MP_E} = -\frac{0.1}{0.125} = -0.8$$

b. What is the slope of the isocost line, dR_E/dR_C?

The slope of the isocost line is equal to the (negative of the) ratio of the input prices, $-\left(\frac{P_C}{P_E}\right)$. Therefore, the slope of the isocost line equals:

$$-\frac{P_C}{P_E} = -\frac{0.45}{0.45} = -1$$

c. Based on your answers to part a and part b, how many Colombian roses and how many Ecuadorian roses will Rose use in each of her magnificent bouquets?

Due to her production function, the slopes of the isoquant and the isocost line will never be equal: The isocost line will always be steeper than the isoquant. This result means that Rose will only use Ecuadorian roses when producing her bouquet. When Rose uses zero Colombian roses, her production function becomes $Q = (0.125R_E)$. Then to produce $Q = 1$ bouquets, the production function shows that:

$$1 = (0.125R_E),$$

so that the number of Ecuadorian roses is $R_E = 8$.

This result, while mathematically odd, is very intuitive from a managerial perspective: If two inputs have the same price, and one of them is *always* more productive, firms should only employ the more productive input. In this question, Colombian roses and Ecuadorian roses have the same price but the marginal product of an Ecuadorian rose is 0.125 while the marginal product of a Colombian rose is only 0.1.

CHAPTER 5 APPENDIX
The Calculus of Profit Maximization for Perfectly Competitive Firms

A5.2 a. The average total cost equals the total cost divided by the quantity. So the average total cost function is

$$ATC(q) = \frac{40}{q} + 0.1q - 0.2$$

b. The average total cost is minimized when $\frac{dATC}{dq} = 0$. Taking the derivative of the average total cost function from part a with respect to quantity gives

$$\frac{dATC}{dq} = -\frac{40}{q^2} + 0.1 = 0$$

Solving this equation shows that the average total cost is minimized when $q^* = 20$ empanadas. When 20 empanadas are produced, the average total cost equals

$$ATC(20) = \frac{40}{20} + (0.1 \times 20) - 0.2 = \$3.80$$

c. The profit-maximizing quantity is the amount that sets marginal revenue equal to marginal cost. So, to begin, take the derivative of the total cost function with respect to quantity to obtain the marginal cost function:

$$MC(q) = 0.2q - 0.2$$

Setting this marginal cost function equal to the marginal revenue of $\$4.20$—that is,

0.2q − 0.2 = 4.20—shows that the profit-maximizing quantity is 22 empanadas.

When q = 22, the average total cost is $ATC(22) = \frac{40}{22} + (0.1 \times 22) − 0.2 = \$3.82$. Use this value to calculate the economic profit:

Economic profit = $(P − ATC) \times q = (4.2 − 3.82) \times 22$
$$= 0.38 \times 22 = \$8.36$$

d. Setting the marginal cost function, $MC(q) = 0.2q − 0.2$, equal to the marginal revenue of $3—that is, $0.2q − 0.2 = 3$—shows that the profit-maximizing quantity is 16 empanadas.

When q = 16, the average total cost is $ATC(16) = \frac{40}{16} + (0.1 \times 16) − 0.2 = \$3.90$. Use this value to calculate the economic profit, which is actually an economic loss:

Economic profit = $(P − ATC) \times q = (3 − 3.90) \times 16$
$$= −0.9 \times 16 = −\$14.40$$

A5.4 a. Marginal cost equals the derivative of total cost with respect to quantity. Take the derivative of the total cost function in the problem:

$$MC = \frac{dTC}{dq} = \frac{d(10 + 0.025q^2)}{dq} = \$0.05q$$

b. The marginal revenue equals the price, $2.00.

c. The profit maximizing quantity of lemonade is the quantity that sets MR equal to MC, or

$$2.00 = 0.05q \Rightarrow q = 40 \text{ cups of lemonade}$$

Jessica's profit-maximizing quantity is 40 cups of lemonade. Her economic profit equals her total revenue minus her total cost at the profit-maximizing quantity, or:

$$(2.00 \times 40) − (10 + 0.025 \times 40^2) = 80 − 50 = \$30$$

Jessica is making an economic profit of $30.

CHAPTER **6** APPENDIX
The Calculus of Profit Maximization for Firms with Market Power

A6.2 a. Begin by determining the marginal revenue (MR) and marginal cost (MC). MR is equal to $\frac{dTR}{dQ}$, and TR = P × Q. Use the demand function, and solve for $P: P = 100 − (\frac{Q}{100})$. This expression is the inverse demand function. Use it in the equation for total revenue to get

$$TR = \left(100 − \frac{Q}{100}\right) \times Q = 100Q − \frac{Q^2}{100}$$

Now, taking the derivative of TR with respect to Q gives

$$MR = 100 − \left(\frac{Q}{50}\right)$$

Next, we need the marginal cost. Take the derivative of TC with respect to Q to calculate the marginal cost:

$$MC = 4$$

To determine the profit-maximizing quantity, (Q^*), set MR = MC, and solve for the quantity:

$$100 − \left(\frac{Q}{50}\right) = 4$$
$$Q^* = 4,800$$

Finally, determine the profit-maximizing price that consumers will pay for 4,800 pet carriers by substituting $Q^* = 4,800$ into the inverse demand function:

$$P^* = 100 − \left(\frac{4,800}{100}\right)$$
$$P^* = \$52$$

b. The amount of economic profit (or loss) equals total revenue (TR) minus total cost (TC). Use the profit-maximizing quantity, $Q^* = 4,800$, and the profit-maximizing price, $P^* = \$52$, to get

Profit = $TR − TC = (\$4,800 \times 52) − ([30,400 + ([4 \times 4,800])$
$$= \$200,000$$

PetCarry has an economic profit of $200,000.

A6.4 a. MR is equal to $\frac{dTR}{dQ}$, and TR = P × Q. To calculate the total revenue, start by using the demand function, and solve for $P: P = 3.85 − 0.1Q$. This expression is the inverse demand function. To calculate the total revenue, use the inverse demand function in the equation for total revenue to get

$$TR = (3.85 − 0.1Q) \times Q = 3.85Q − 0.1Q^2$$

Finally, taking the derivative of TR with respect to Q gives

$$MR = 3.85 − 0.2Q$$

b. MC is equal to $\frac{dTC}{dQ}$. Take the derivative of TC, $TC(Q) = 30 + 0.25Q$, with respect to Q to calculate the marginal cost:

$$MC = 0.25$$

c. To determine Jessica's profit-maximizing quantity of lemonade, set Jessica's marginal revenue equal to her marginal cost:

$$3.85 - 0.2Q = 0.25$$

Solving for Q, the profit-maximizing quantity is $Q^* = 18$ cups of lemonade.

d. To determine Jessica's profit-maximizing price, substitute the profit-maximizing quantity, $Q^* = 18$, into the inverse demand function:

$$P = 3.85 - (0.1 \times 18) = \$2.05$$

CHAPTER 7 APPENDIX
The Calculus of Oligopoly

A7.2 a. We begin by determining the best-response function for The Beaulieu Group. We do this by constructing the firm's profit, then maximizing the profit by taking the derivative of it with respect to The Beaulieu Group's quantity and setting it equal to zero, and finally solving for q_B. The first step is the profit function:

$$\text{Profit}(q_B) = [(100 - 4q_A - 4q_B) \times q_B] - 36q_B$$

where $(100 - 4q_A - 4q_B) \times q_B$ is the total revenue and $36q_B$ is the total cost. Next, taking the derivative with respect to q_B, we obtain

$$64 - 4q_A - 8q_B = 0$$

Thus, The Beaulieu Group's best-response function is given by

$$q_B = 8 - 0.5q_A$$

Next, determine Alvarez Inc.'s profit function:

$$\text{Profit}(q_A) = (100 - 4q_A - 4q_B) \times q_A - 36q_A$$

Because Alvarez Inc. is a Stackelberg leader, Alvarez's managers take account of The Beaulieu Group's best-response function. So use The Beaulieu Group's best-response function in Alvarez Inc.'s profit function:

$$(100 - 4q_A - 4 \times [8 - 0.5q_A]) \times q_A - 36q_A$$
$$= 32q_A - 2q_A^2$$

Now, to maximize Alvarez's profit, take the derivative with respect to q_A, and set it equal to zero:

$$32 - 4q_A = 0 \Rightarrow q_A = 8$$

Thus, Alvarez Inc. will produce 8 hours of consulting services daily. Using this result in The Beaulieu Group's best-response function shows that The Beaulieu Group will produce 4 hours of consulting services daily.

b. The total quantity of consulting services is $q_A + q_B = 4 + 8 = 12$. Then, using this quantity in the inverse demand function, $P = 100 - [4 \times (q_A + q_B)]$, gives the price of an hour of consulting services as

$$P = 100 - (4 \times 12) = \$52$$

Alvarez Inc. makes an economic profit of

$$\text{Profit} = (\$52 - \$36) \times 8 = 16 \times 8 = \$128 \text{ daily}$$

and The Beaulieu Group makes an economic profit of

$$\text{Profit} = (\$52 - \$36) \times 4 = 16 \times 4 = \$64 \text{ daily}$$

A7.4 a. To begin, the total quantity of tutoring services is $Q = q_A + q_B$. Use this result in the inverse market demand function to yield

$$P = 80 - [0.5 \times (q_A + q_B)] = 80 - 0.5q_A - 0.5q_B$$

Next use this expression for P to construct your profit function:

$$\text{Profit} = [(80 - 0.5q_A - 0.5q_B) \times q_A] - (240 + 0.25q_A^2)$$

where $(80 - 0.5q_A - 0.5q_B) \times q_A$ is your total revenue and $(240 + 0.25q_A^2)$ is your total cost. Take the derivative of the profit function with respect to the quantity q_A:

$$\frac{d\text{Profit}}{dq_A} = (80 - 0.5q_A - 0.5q_B) - 0.5q_A - 0.5q_A$$
$$= 80 - 1.5q_A - 0.5q_B$$

Set this derivative equal to zero to give your first-order condition for profit maximization:

$$80 - 1.5q_A - 0.5q_B = 0$$

Because you and Bernardo have the same costs and face the same demand, each of you will have the same quantity of tutoring services. That means that $q_A = q_B$. Substitute q_A for q_B in the first-order condition and then solve for q_A:

$$80 - 1.5q_A - 0.5q_A = 0 \Rightarrow 80 - 2.0q_A = 0$$
$$\Rightarrow q_A = 40 \text{ hours}$$

Because you and Bernardo both offer the same quantity of tutoring services, $q_A = 40$ hours means that Bernardo also offers 40 hours of tutoring services, so $q_B = 40$ hours.

b. Because each of you provides 40 hours of tutoring services, the total market quantity is 80 hours. Use this quantity in the inverse market demand function, $P = 80 - 0.5Q$, to determine that the price of an hour of tutoring service:

$$P = 80 - (0.5 \times 80) = \$40 \text{ per hour}$$

CHAPTER **10** APPENDIX
The Calculus of Advanced Pricing Decisions

A10.2 Because there are equal numbers of business and vacation travelers, base the calculations on one of each type of traveler. Begin by determining ThomasAir's profit function. ThomasAir earns two types of revenue: revenue from the membership fee and revenue from the ticket sales.

The membership fee equals the amount of consumer surplus that vacation travelers, who are the low-demand travelers, enjoy at the chosen per-flight ticket price. Because the demand curve is linear, the amount of consumer surplus equals the area of a triangle computed using the formula $\frac{1}{2} \times$ Base $\times$ Height. The base equals the quantity demanded at the per-flight ticket price of P, which, using the demand function for vacation travelers, is $q_V = 400 - 2.5P$. The height of the triangle equals the distance between the vertical intercept of the demand curve and the per-flight price of a ticket. To determine the vertical intercept, use the demand function for vacation travelers, and solve it for P as a function of q_V:

$$P = 160 - 0.4q_V$$

When $q_V = 0$, the vertical intercept is $P = 160$, so the height of the consumer surplus triangle equals $(160 - P)$. Consequently, the membership fee (FEE) for a traveler equals

$$\text{FEE} = \frac{1}{2} \times (400 - 2.5P) \times (160 - P)$$
$$= \frac{1}{2} \times (64{,}000 - 800P + 2.5P^2)$$

The membership fee above is for one traveler, so the total fee for the two travelers under consideration is twice that, or

$$\text{TOTAL FEE} = 64{,}000 - 800P + 2.5P^2$$

ThomasAir also earns revenue from its ticket sales. With a per-ticket price of P, from a business traveler the revenue is $P \times q_B$, or, using the demand function for business travelers, $q_B = 800 - 5P$

$$P \times (800 - 5P) = 800P - 5P^2$$

Similarly, ThomasAir receives revenue from a vacation traveler of $P \times q_V$, or, using the demand function for vacation travelers, $q_V = 400 - 2.5P$

$$P \times (400 - 2.5P) = 400P - 2.5P^2$$

Therefore, ThomasAir's revenue from the tickets sold is

$$(800P - 5P^2) + (400P - 2.5P^2) = 1{,}200P - 7.5P^2$$

where the equality comes from collecting like terms.

ThomasAir's total cost for a flight is $40 \times (q_B + q_V)$. Using the demand functions for the quantity of trips demanded by business travelers (q_B) and vacation travelers (q_V) gives

$$\text{Total cost} = 40 \times [(800 - 5P) + (400 - 2.5P)]$$
$$= 40 \times [1{,}200 - 7.5P]$$
$$= 48{,}000 - 300P$$

Adding the two sources of revenue, the membership fee and the ticket sales, and subtracting the total cost, ThomasAir's profit function is

$$\text{Profit} = (64{,}000 - 800P + 2.5P^2) + (1{,}200P - 7.5P^2)$$
$$- (48{,}000 - 300P)$$

Collecting like terms, the profit function simplifies to

$$\text{Profit} = -5.0P^2 + 700P + 16{,}000$$

To determine the profit-maximizing price per flight (P^*), take the derivative of the profit function with respect to P, and set it equal to zero. This gives the first-order condition for profit maximization:

$$-10P + 700 = 0$$

which means that $P^* = \$70$ per ticket.

The membership fee per person is $\text{FEE} = \frac{1}{2} \times (64{,}000 - 800P + 2.5P^2)$. Substituting the profit-maximizing price of a flight gives the membership fee of \$10,125.

A10.4 a. Start by determining the expressions for MR_P, MR_G, and MC. MR_P is equal to $\frac{\partial TR}{\partial q_P}$, and MR_G is equal to $\frac{\partial TR}{\partial q_G}$, where TR is total revenue. Total revenue equals the sum of the revenue from sales to private companies ($P_P \times q_P$) and the revenue from sales to the federal government ($P_G \times q_G$). Use the inverse demand functions for the prices and multiply them by the quantities to obtain the total revenue function:

$$TR = [(400 - 0.2q_P) \times q_P] + [(250 - 0.25q_G) \times q_G]$$
$$= (400q_P - 0.2q_P^2) + (250q_G - 0.25q_G^2)$$

Using the total revenue function to calculate the marginal revenues gives

$$MR_P = \frac{\partial TR}{\partial q_P} = 400 - 0.4q_P$$

and

$$MR_G = \frac{\partial TR}{\partial q_G} = 250 - 0.5q_G$$

Finally, $MC = \frac{dTC}{dQ}$, so taking this derivative gives

$$MC = 50$$

Next, to solve for the profit-maximizing q_P and q_G, set MR_P equal to MC and MR_G equal to MC:

$$400 - 0.4q_P = 50 \Rightarrow q_P = 875$$
$$250 - 0.5q_G = 50 \Rightarrow q_G = 400$$

Use these profit-maximizing values for q_P and q_G in the inverse demand functions to solve for the profit-maximizing prices for the two classes of customers:

$$P_P = 400 - (0.2 \times 875) \Rightarrow P_P = \$225$$
$$P_G = 250 - (0.25 \times 400) \Rightarrow P_G = \$150$$

So Arnold and Associates sells 875 hours of consulting services to private firms at a price of $225 per hour and 400 hours of consulting services to the federal government at a price of $150 per hour.

b. The amount of economic profit (or loss) is equal to total revenue minus total cost. The total revenue function was derived in the answer to part a and the total cost function is given in the problem, so the profit equals:

$$\text{Profit} = (400q_P - 0.2q_P^2) + (250q_G - 0.25q_G^2)$$
$$- [50(q_P + q_G) + 150{,}000]$$

Consequently, when $q_P = 875$ and $q_G = 400$, the firm makes an economic profit of $43,125.

CHAPTER 12 APPENDIX
The Calculus of Multi-Plant Profit-Maximization and Inventory Decisions

A12.2 a. Because the total sales are 500,000 packs per year, increasing the order size means that fewer orders are necessary, so increasing the order size decreases the ordering cost. Consequently, the marginal benefit of increasing the order size is the marginal decrease in the ordering cost. The equation for the total ordering cost is

$$\frac{C_{FC} \times Q}{Q_{ORDER}} + (C_{VAR} \times Q)$$

where C_{FC} is the fixed cost of the order ($1.50), C_{VAR} is the variable cost of ordering ($3 per pack), Q is the total annual quantity sold (500,000 packs), and Q_{ORDER} is the quantity ordered. So the total ordering cost is

$$\frac{\$1.50 \times 500{,}000}{Q_{ORDER}} + (\$3 \times 500{,}000)$$
$$= \frac{\$750{,}000}{Q_{ORDER}} + \$1{,}500{,}000$$

The marginal benefit of changing the size of the order is the reduction in total ordering cost. It is equal to the derivative of the total ordering cost with respect to the quantity ordered or, using the quotient rule,

$$MB_{ORDER} = \frac{\$750{,}000}{Q_{ORDER}^2}$$

b. Because sales occur at a constant rate, increasing the order size means Penny Shaving Club holds more units in inventory, so increasing the order size increases the carrying cost. Consequently, the marginal cost of increasing the order size, Q_{ORDER}, is the increase in the carrying cost. The quantity held in inventory starts at Q_{ORDER} and ends, just before the next order, at 0. Consequently, the average amount held in inventory is $\frac{Q_{ORDER}}{2}$, so the equation for the carrying cost is

$$C \times \frac{Q_{ORDER}}{2}$$

where C is the annual carrying cost of holding a pack in inventory, $6. Thus, the annual carrying cost is

$$\$6 \times \frac{Q_{ORDER}}{2} = \$3Q_{ORDER}$$

The marginal cost of changing the order size is the derivative of the total annual carrying cost with respect to the quantity ordered, or

$$MC_{ORDER} = \$3$$

c. The profit-maximizing order size sets the marginal benefit of increasing the order size equal to the marginal cost of increasing the order size:

$$MB_{ORDER} = MC_{ORDER}$$
$$\frac{\$750{,}000}{Q_{ORDER}^2} = \$3$$
$$Q_{ORDER} = 500 \text{ packs of razors}$$

A12.4 a. Jessica's profit equals her total revenue (TR) minus her total cost (TC). Total revenue equals the price multiplied by the quantity. The price comes from the inverse demand function, so the total revenue function is

$$TR(q_1) = (900 - 25q_1) \times q_1 = 900q_1 - 25q_1^2$$

The total cost is $TC(Q) = 50q_1^2$. So Jessica's profit function is

$$\begin{aligned}\text{PROFIT}(q_1) &= TR(q_1) - TC(q_1)\\ &= (900q_1 - 25q_1^2) - 50q_1^2\end{aligned}$$

Taking the derivative of the profit function with respect to q_1 and setting it equal to zero gives the first-order condition for profit maximization:

$$900 - 50q_1 - 100q_1 = 0$$

Solving this first-order condition shows that the profit-maximizing number of cases of limoncello is 6 per day. Using this quantity in the inverse demand function gives the profit-maximizing price of a case of limoncello:

$$P = 900 - (25 \times 6) = \$750$$

b. The amount of economic profit (or loss) is equal to total revenue minus total cost. Total revenue equals the price multiplied by the quantity: $TR = \$750 \times 6 = \$4,500$. The total cost is from the total cost function: $TC = 50q_1^2 = \$1,800$. Consequently, the total economic profit equals $\$4,500 - \$1,800 = \$2,700$.

c. Jessica's profit equals her total revenue (TR) minus her total cost (TC). Total revenue equals the price multiplied by the quantity. The price comes from the inverse demand function: $P = 900 - 25Q = 900 - 25(q_1 + q_2) = 900 - 25q_1 - 25q_2$. So the total revenue is

$$\begin{aligned}TR &= (900 - 25q_1 - 25q_2) \times (q_1 + q_2)\\ &= 900q_1 + 900q_2 - 25q_1^2 - 25q_2^2 - 50q_1q_2\end{aligned}$$

The total cost is $TC = 50q_1^2 + 50q_2^2$. Consequently, Jessica's profit function, $TR - TC$, is

$$\begin{aligned}\text{PROFIT} = &(900q_1 + 900q_2 - 25q_1^2 - 25q_2^2 - 50q_1q_2)\\ &- (50q_1^2 + 50q_2^2)\end{aligned}$$

Taking the partial derivatives of this profit function with respect to q_1 and q_2 and setting them equal to zero gives the first-order conditions for profit maximization:

$$\frac{\partial \text{PROFIT}}{\partial q_1} = 900 - 50q_1 - 50q_2 - 100q_1 = 0$$

and

$$\frac{\partial \text{PROFIT}}{\partial q_2} = 900 - 50q_1 - 50q_2 - 100q_2 = 0$$

Solving these first-order conditions shows that the profit-maximizing number of cases of limoncello is $q_1 = 4.5$ per day at plant 1 and $q_2 = 4.5$ per day at plant 2. Thus, the total number of cases produced each day is 9. Using these quantities in the inverse demand function shows that the price is:

$$900 - (25 \times 4.5) - (25 \times 4.5) = \$675 \text{ per case.}$$

d. The amount of economic profit (or loss) is equal to total revenue minus total cost. The total revenue equals the price multiplied by the quantity: $TR = \$675 \times 9 = \$6,075$. The total cost is from the total cost function: $TC = 50q_1^2 + 50q_2^2 = (50 \times 4.5^2) + (50 \times 4.5^2) = \$2,025$. Consequently, the total profit equals $\$6,075 - \$2,025 = \$4,050$.

CHAPTER **13** APPENDIX
The Calculus of Advertising

A13.2 a. Start by determining the profit function. Profit equals total revenue (TR) minus total cost (TC). Total revenue equals $P \times Q$, so multiply the price from the inverse demand function by the quantity:

$$(280 + 2A - 1.2Q) \times Q = 280Q + 2AQ - 1.2Q^2$$

Next, calculate the profit function, $TR - TC$:

$$\begin{aligned}\text{Profit} = &(280Q + 2AQ - 1.2Q^2) - (0.8Q^2\\ &+ 25.5A^2 - 10A)\end{aligned}$$

Taking the partial derivatives of this profit function with respect to Q and A and setting them equal to zero gives the first-order conditions for profit maximization:

$$\frac{\partial \text{PROFIT}}{\partial Q} = 280 + 2A - 4Q = 0$$

$$\frac{\partial \text{PROFIT}}{\partial A} = 2Q - 51A + 10 = 0$$

Solve this system of equations for the profit-maximizing quantity (Q^*) and the profit-maximizing number of advertisements (A^*). The profit-maximizing quantity is $Q^* = 71.5$ hours of consulting, and the profit-maximizing number of advertisements is $A^* = 3$ advertisements per week.

b. Substitute the profit-maximizing quantity, $Q^* = 71.5$, and profit-maximizing number of advertisements, $A^* = 3$, into the inverse demand function to find the profit-maximizing price, P^*, of Walter's consulting services:

$$P^* = 280 + (2 \times 3) - (1.2 \times 71.5) = \$200.20$$

c. The amount of economic profit (or loss) equals total revenue minus total cost. Total revenue equals the price multiplied by the quantity ($P^* \times Q^*$), and the cost function gives the total cost. So the economic profit (or loss) is

$$(\$200.20 \times 71.5) - [(0.8 \times 71.5^2) + (25.5 \times 3^2) - (10 \times 3)]$$
$$= \$10,025.00$$

A13.4 a. Start by determining the profit function. Profit equals total revenue (TR) minus total cost (TC). Total revenue equals $P \times Q$, so multiply the price from the inverse demand function by the quantity:

$$(20,000 + 100A - 25Q) \times Q = 20,000Q + 100AQ - 25Q^2$$

Next, calculate the profit function, $TR - TC$:

$$\text{Profit} = (20,000Q + 100AQ - 25Q^2) - (5,000Q + 200A^2)$$

Taking the partial derivatives of this profit function with respect to Q and A and setting them equal to zero gives the first-order conditions for profit maximization:

$$\frac{\partial \text{PROFIT}}{\partial Q} = 15,000 + 100A - 50Q = 0$$

$$\frac{\partial \text{PROFIT}}{\partial A} = 100Q - 400A = 0$$

Solve this system of equations for the profit-maximizing quantity, Q^*, and the profit-maximizing number of advertisements, A^*. The profit-maximizing quantity is $Q^* = 600$ students, and the profit-maximizing number of advertisements is $A^* = 150$ billboards.

b. Substitute the profit-maximizing quantity, $Q^* = 600$, and the profit-maximizing number of billboards, $A^* = 150$, into the inverse demand function to find the profit-maximizing tuition:

$$P^* = 20,000 + (100 \times 150) - (25 \times 600) = \$20,000$$

c. The amount of economic profit (or loss) equals total revenue minus total cost. Total revenue equals the price multiplied by the quantity ($P^* \times Q^*$), and the total cost function gives the total cost. So the economic profit is

$$\text{Profit} = (\$20,000 \times 600) - [(5,000 \times 600) + (200 \times 150^2)]$$
$$= \$4,500,000$$

INDEX